Children

A Chronological Approach

Fifth Canadian Edition

Robert V. Kail
Purdue University

Theresa Zolner
Athabasca University

 **Pearson**

EDITORIAL DIRECTOR: Claudine O'Donnell
ACQUISITIONS EDITOR: Darcey Pepper
MARKETING MANAGER: Leigh-Anne Graham
PROGRAM MANAGER: Madhu Ranadive
SENIOR PROJECT MANAGER: Jessica Hellen
DEVELOPMENTAL EDITOR: Patti Sayle
MEDIA DEVELOPER: Kelli Cadet
PRODUCTION SERVICES: Cenveo® Publisher Services
PERMISSIONS PROJECT MANAGER: Kathryn O'Handley

PHOTO PERMISSIONS RESEARCH: Integra Publishing Services, Inc.
TEXT PERMISSIONS RESEARCH: Integra Publishing Services, Inc.
COVER DESIGNER: Cenveo Publisher Services
COVER IMAGE: Monkey Business Images/Shutterstock
VICE-PRESIDENT, CROSS MEDIA AND PUBLISHING SERVICES: Gary Bennett

Pearson Canada Inc., 26 Prince Andrew Place, Don Mills, Ontario M3C 2T8.

978-0-13-443130-7

1   17

Library and Archives Canada Cataloguing in Publication

Kail, Robert V., author
      Children : a chronological approach / Robert V. Kail, Theresa Zolner.
—Fifth Canadian edition.

Includes bibliographical references and index.
ISBN 978-0-13-443130-7 (softcover)

      1. Child psychology—Textbooks. 2. Child development—Textbooks.
3. Infant psychology—Textbooks. 4. Infants—Development—Textbooks.
5. Adolescent psychology—Textbooks. 6. Adolescence—Textbooks.
I. Zolner, Theresa, 1963-, author II. Title.

BF721.K33 2017   305.231   C2017-900281-3

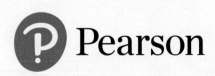

Brief Contents

1 Child Development: Theories and Themes   1

2 Research in Child Development   21

3 Genetic Bases of Child Development   45

4 Prenatal Development and Birth   67

5 Physical Development in Infants and Toddlers   100

6 Cognition in Infants and Toddlers   138

7 Social and Emotional Development in Infants and Toddlers   164

8 Physical Growth in Preschool Children   193

9 Cognitive Development in Preschool Children   216

10 Social and Emotional Development in Preschool Children   249

11 Physical Development in Middle Childhood   285

12 Cognitive Development in Middle Childhood   302

13 Social and Emotional Development in Middle Childhood   341

14 Physical Growth in Adolescents   377

15 Cognitive Processes in Adolescents   405

16 Social and Emotional Development in Adolescents   434

Contents

Preface   xii
About the Authors   xvi

1 Child Development: Theories and Themes   1

1.1   Theories of Child Development   2
      Canada's Unique Contribution   3
      The Biological Perspective   3
      The Psychodynamic Perspective   5
          Theory of Personality 5 • Theory of Psychosexual
          Development 5 • Erikson's Psychosocial Theory 7
      The Learning Perspective   7
          Early Learning Theories 7 • Social Cognitive Theory 8
      The Cognitive-Developmental Perspective   9
      The Contextual Perspective   10
      Newer Approaches to Child Development   12
          Information-Processing Theory 12 • Evolutionary
          Theory 12 • Developmental Psychopathology 13
      The Big Picture   13
1.2   Themes in Child-Development Research   15
      Early Development Is Related to Later
      Development but Not Perfectly   16
      Development Is Always Jointly Influenced
      by Heredity and Environment   16
      Children Help Determine Their Own Development   17
      Development in Different Domains Is Connected   17
Summary   19

2 Research in Child Development   21

2.1   Doing Child-Development Research   22
      Measurement in Child-Development Research   22
          Systematic Observation 22 • Sampling Behaviour
          with Tasks 23 • Self-Reports 24 • Representative
          Sampling 26
      General Designs for Research   26
          Correlational Studies 27 • Experimental Studies 30
      Methods for Studying Development   31
          Longitudinal Studies 31 • Cross-Sectional Studies 33
      Ethical Responsibilities   35
      Communicating Research Results   37
2.2   Child-Development Research
      and Family Policy   38
      Background   38
      Ways to Influence Social Policy   39
          Build Understanding of Children and Their Development 39
          • Serve as an Advocate for Children 39 • Evaluate Policies
          and Programs 40 • Develop a Model Program 40

          An Emphasis on Policy Implications
          Improves Research   41
Summary   42

3 Genetic Bases of Child Development   45

3.1   Mechanisms of Heredity   46
      The Biology of Heredity   46
      Single Gene Inheritance   49
      Behavioural Genetics   52
          Methods of Behavioural Genetics 53
      Nonshared Environmental Influences   55
3.2   Genetic Disorders   57
      Inherited Disorders   57
      Abnormal Chromosomes   58
3.3   Heredity Is Not Destiny   60
      Genes, the Environment, and Behaviour   61
      Reaction Range   61
      Changing Relations between Nature and Nurture   62
Summary   64

4 Prenatal Development and Birth   67

4.1   From Conception to Birth   68
      Period of the Zygote (Weeks 1–2)   69
      Period of the Embryo (Weeks 3–8)   70
      Period of the Fetus (Weeks 9–38)   71
4.2   Influences on Prenatal Development   75
      General Risk Factors   75
          Nutrition 75 • Stress 76 • Mother's Age 76
      Teratogens: Diseases, Drugs, and
      Environmental Hazards   77
          Diseases 78 • Drugs 78 • Environmental Hazards 79
      How Teratogens Influence Prenatal Development   81
          The Real World of Prenatal Risk 83
      Prenatal Diagnosis and Treatment   83
4.3   Happy Birthday!   86
      Labour and Delivery   86
      Approaches to Childbirth   88
      Birth Complications   90
          Lack of Oxygen 90 • Prematurity and
          Low Birth Weight 91
      The Newborn   92
          Newborn States 93 • Crying 93 • Sleeping 94
          • Sudden Infant Death Syndrome 95
      Postpartum Depression   95
Summary   97

5   Physical Development in Infants and Toddlers   100

5.1   Healthy Growth   101
Features of Human Growth   101
Variations on the Average Profile   103
Mechanisms of Physical Growth   103
Heredity 103 • Hormones 104 • Nutrition 104
Challenges to Healthy Growth   106
Malnutrition 107 • Diseases 107 • Accidents 108
5.2   The Developing Nervous System   109
A Basic Nerve Cell   109
Organization of the Mature Brain   110
The Developing Brain   111
Emerging Brain Structures 111 • Structure and Function 112
• The Frontal Cortex 114 • Brain Plasticity 115
5.3   Motor Development   116
The Infant's Reflexes   116
Locomotion   117
Posture and Balance 119 • Stepping 120 • Perceptual
Factors 120 • Coordinating Skills 120 • Beyond Walking 120
Fine-Motor Skills   120
Reaching and Grasping 121 • Handedness 122
Maturation, Experience, and Motor Skill   122
5.4   Sensory and Perceptual Processes   124
Smell, Taste, and Touch   124
Hearing   125
Seeing   126
Perceptual Constancies 128 • Depth 129
• Perceiving Objects 130
Integrating Sensory Information   133
Summary   135

6   Cognition in Infants and Toddlers   138

6.1   Piaget's Theory   139
Basic Principles of Piaget's Theory   140
Assimilation and Accommodation 140 • Equilibration
and Stages of Cognitive Development 141
Piaget's Sensorimotor Stage   142
Substage 1: Exercising Reflexes (Roughly Birth to 1 Month) 142
• Substage 2: Learning to Adapt (Roughly 1 to 4 Months) 142
• Substage 3: Making Interesting Events (Roughly 4 to
8 Months) 142 • Substage 4: Using Means to Achieve Ends
(Roughly 8 to 12 Months) 143 • Substage 5: Experimenting
(Roughly 12 to 18 Months) 143 • Substage 6: Mental
Representation (Roughly 18 to 24 Months) 143
Evaluating Piaget's Account of Sensorimotor Thought   144
The Child as Theorist   145
Naive Physics 145 • Naive Biology 147
6.2   Information Processing   147
Basic Features of the Information-Processing Approach   148
Learning   150
Habituation 150 • Classical Conditioning 151 • Operant
Conditioning 151 • Imitation 151
Memory   151
Understanding the World   153
Understanding Numbers 153 • Exploring
the Environment 153
Individual Differences in Ability   154
6.3   Language   155
Perceiving Speech   155
First Steps to Speaking   157
First Words   158
Fast Mapping Meanings to Words   158
Joint Attention 159 • Constraints on Word Names 159
• Sentence Cues 160 • Naming Errors 160
Styles of Learning Language   161
Summary   162

7   Social and Emotional Development in Infants and Toddlers   164

7.1   Emotions   165
Basic Emotions   166
Happiness 167 • Negative Emotions 167
Complex Emotions   168
Recognizing and Using Others' Emotions   168
Regulating Emotions   169
7.2   Relationships with Others   170
The Growth of Attachment   171
Quality of Attachment   173
Consequences of Quality of Attachment 175
• Factors Determining Quality of Attachment 176
• Parenting Skill, Work, and Child Care 179
Onset of Peer Interactions   181
7.3   Self-Concept   182
Origins of Self-Recognition   182
Moving beyond Self-Recognition   183
7.4   Temperament   184
What Is Temperament?   185
Hereditary and Environmental Contributions to Temperament   186
Stability of Temperament   187
Temperament and Other Aspects of Development   188
Summary   190

8   Physical Growth in Preschool Children   193

8.1   Physical Growth   194
Body Growth   194
Brain Development   196
Sleep   197
8.2   Motor Development   199
Gross-Motor Skills   199
Fine-Motor Skills   201
Handedness   202
Gender Differences in Motor Skills   203

8.3   Health and Wellness   204
Nutrition   205
Encouraging Healthy Eating   207
Threats to Children's Development   207
Minor Illnesses 208 • Chronic Illnesses 208
• Accidents 209 • Environmental Contributions to Illness
and Injury 210 • Impact of Hospitalization 210
Jurisdictional Authority and
Children's Health   211
Summary   213

9   Cognitive Development in Preschool Children   216

9.1   Cognitive Processes   217
Piaget's Account   217
Characteristics of Preoperational Thinking 218
• Extending Piaget's Account: Children's Naive
Theories 221
Information-Processing Perspectives on
Preschool Thinking   223
Attention 224 • Memory 225 • Counting 226
Vygotsky's Theory of Cognitive Development   227
The Zone of Proximal Development 228
• Scaffolding 228 • Private Speech 228
9.2   Language   230
Encouraging Word Learning   230
From Two-Word Speech
to Complex Sentences   231
How Children Acquire Grammar   234
9.3   Communicating with Others   237
Taking Turns   237
Speaking Effectively   238
Listening Well   239
9.4   Early Childhood Education   240
Varieties of Early Childhood Education   241
Preschool Programs for Economically
Disadvantaged Children   243
Using TV to Educate Preschool Children   244
Summary   246

10   Social and Emotional Development in Preschool Children   249

10.1   Self   250
Gender Roles   250
Gender Identity   252
The Socializing Influences of People and the Media 252
• Cognitive Theories of Gender Identity 255
• Biological Influences 256
Self-Esteem   257
10.2   Relationships with Parents   258
The Family as a System   259
Dimensions and Styles   260
Cultural Differences in Warmth and Control 261
• Parenting Styles 261

Parental Behaviour   263
Direct Instruction 263 • Learning by Observing 263
• Feedback 264
Children's Contributions   265
Family Configuration   266
The Role of Grandparents 266 • Children of
Gay and Lesbian Parents 267
10.3   Relationships with Siblings and Peers   268
Sibling Relationships   269
First-Born, Later-Born, and Only Children 269
• Qualities of Sibling Relationships 269
Peer Relationships and Preschoolers' Play   272
Make-Believe 273 • Solitary Play 274
• Parental Influence 274
10.4   Moral Development: Learning
to Control One's Behaviour   275
Beginnings of Self-Control   276
Parental Influences   278
Temperamental Influences on Self-Control   279
Improving Self-Control   280
Learning about Moral Rules   281
Summary   282

11   Physical Development in Middle Childhood   285

11.1   Growth of the Body   286
Physical Growth   286
Nutrition   288
Obesity 289
Tooth Development   291
Vision and Hearing   292
11.2   Motor Development   293
Development of Motor Skills   294
Gender Differences in Motor Skill 294
Physical Fitness   295
Participating in Sports   296
Accidents   297
Summary   300

12   Cognitive Development in Middle Childhood   302

12.1   Cognitive Processes   303
Concrete Operational Thinking   303
Memory Skills   304
Strategies for Remembering 304 • Knowledge
and Memory 306
12.2   The Nature of Intelligence   309
Psychometric Theories   309
Gardner's Theory of Multiple Intelligences   310
Sternberg's Triarchic Theory of
Successful Intelligence   312
12.3   Individual Differences in Intellectual Skills   315
Binet and the Development of Intelligence Testing   315
Do Intelligence Tests Work?   316

Hereditary and Environmental Factors   318

Impact of Culture and Social Class   320

Gender Differences in Intellectual Abilities
and Achievement   323

Verbal Ability 323 • Spatial Ability 323
• Mathematics 324

12.4 Academic Skills   326

Reading Skills   326

Prereading Skills 327 • Recognizing Words 327
• Comprehension 329

Writing Skills   330

Greater Knowledge and Access to Knowledge
about Topics 330 • Greater Understanding of How
to Organize Writing 330 • Greater Ease in Dealing
with the Mechanical Requirements of Writing 331
• Greater Skill in Revising 331

Math Skills   332

International Studies of Mathematics Achievement 333

12.5 Effective Schools   335

School-Based Influences on Student
Achievement   335

Teacher-Based Influences on Student
Achievement   336

The Role of Computers 337

Summary   338

13 Social and Emotional Development in Middle Childhood   341

13.1 Self-Esteem   342

Measuring Self-Esteem   342

Developmental Change in Self-Esteem   343

Sources of Self-Esteem   344

Consequences of Low Self-Esteem   346

13.2 Relationships with Peers   347

An Overview of Peer Interactions
in Middle Childhood   347

Friendship   349

Quality and Consequences of Friendship 349

Popularity and Rejection   350

Consequences of Rejection 351
• Causes of Rejection 351

Prejudice   352

13.3 Helping Others   354

Skills Underlying Prosocial Behaviour   355

Situational Influences   355

Socializing Prosocial Behaviour   356

13.4 Aggression   357

The Nature of Children's Aggressive
Behaviour   358

The Impact of Aggression on Children   359

Aggression in Families 359 • Abuse of
Children 361 • Impact of Television 364
• Cognitive Processes 365

Victims of Peer Aggression   366

13.5 Families in the Early Twenty-First Century   368

After-School Care   368

Divorce   370

Family Life after Divorce 370 • Impact of
Divorce on Children 371 • Adjusting to Divorce 372
• Blended Families 373 • Skip-Generation Families 374
• Foster Families 374

Summary   374

14 Physical Growth in Adolescents   377

14.1 Pubertal Changes   378

Signs of Physical Maturation   378

Physical Growth 379 • Sexual Maturation 380

Mechanisms of Maturation   381

Psychological Impact of Puberty   383

Body Image 383 • Response to Menarche and
Spermarche 383 • Cognitive Control and
the Developing Brain 383 • Rate of Maturation 386

14.2 Sexuality   387

Sexual Behaviour   387

Sexually Transmitted Infections (STIs) 390
• Teenage Pregnancy and Contraception 391

Sexual Orientation   393

Sexual Coercion   395

A Final Remark 396

14.3 Health   397

Nutrition   398

Anorexia and Bulimia 398

Physical Fitness   399

Threats to Adolescent Well-Being   401

Summary   402

15 Cognitive Processes in Adolescents   405

15.1 Cognition   406

Piaget's Stage of Formal Operational Reasoning   406

Theory of Actual Thinking or Possible Thinking 408

Information Processing during Adolescence   408

Basic Processes of Working Memory and
Processing Speed 409 • Content Knowledge 409
• Strategies and Metacognitive Skill 410

15.2 Reasoning about Moral Issues   411

Kohlberg's Theory   411

Support for Kohlberg's Theory 413

Gilligan's Ethic of Caring   414

Promoting Moral Reasoning   417

15.3 The World of Work   419

Career Development   419

Personality-Type Theory 420

Part-Time Employment   423

15.4 Special Challenges   425

Learning Disabilities   425

Attention Deficit Hyperactivity Disorder   427

Intellectual Delay   429

Summary   431

16 Social and Emotional
     Development in Adolescents   434

16.1 Identity and Self-Esteem   435
  The Search for Identity   435
  Ethnic Identity   439
  Self-Esteem in Adolescence   441
16.2 Relationships with Parents
     and Peers   442
  Parent–Child Relationships
  in Adolescence   442
  Relationships with Peers   444
    Groups 444 • Group Structure 446
    • Peer Pressure 446 • Friendship 448
    • Romantic Relationships 448

16.3 The Dark Side   450
  Alcohol and Drug Use   450
  Depression   452
    Treating Depression 454
  Delinquency   455
    Causes of Delinquency 456
    • Treatment and Prevention 457
Summary   458

Glossary   461

References   469

Name Index   529

Subject Index   546

Boxes

MAKING CHILDREN'S LIVES BETTER

Longitudinal Research Conducted on Young People in Canada 34

PKU Resources for Parents through the Montreal Children's Hospital 59

Five Steps toward a Healthy Baby 74

text4baby 81

What's the Best Food for Babies? 106

Jordan's Principle 212

Tim Horton Children's Foundation 298

How Can We Help Children Who Have Experienced Abuse? 363

Preventing Date Rape 397

Mental Health Services for Children 429

Understanding the Combined Effect of Historical Events on Children's Lives in the Present 452

CHILDREN AND FAMILIES AROUND THE WORLD

Why Do Persons of African Heritage Inherit Sickle-Cell Disease? 51

Healthy Eating in Brazil 105

Learning to Walk in Hopi Culture 123

Do Babies from Different Cultures Cry the Same? 187

Growing Up Bilingual 232

Grandmothers in African American Families 267

New Ideas in Family Nutrition . . . or Are These Old Ideas? 289

How Culture Defines What Is Intelligent 313

Keys to Popularity 351

Aid to Children and Adolescents at Risk 362

How the Apache Celebrate Menarche 384

Moral Reasoning in India 415

The Impact of War on Children 453

RESEARCH TO PRACTICE

The Effects of Prenatal Maternal Stress on Children's Cognitive Development: Project Ice Storm 56

Infants' Knowledge of Their Bodies 146

Temperament, Parental Influence, and Self-Control 279

The Carolina Abecedarian Project 320

How Parents Influence Adolescents' Sexual Behaviour 390

Promoting Strong Development through Strong Ethnic Identity 441

CHILD DEVELOPMENT AND FAMILY POLICY

Screening for PKU 63

Back to Sleep! Dodo sur le dos! 95

Determining Guidelines for Infant and Toddler Child Care 180

Providing Children with a Head Start for School 244

Assessing the Consequences of China's One-Child Policy 270

Preventing Osteoporosis 381

Promoting More Advanced Moral Reasoning 418

LOOKING AHEAD

Fetal Activity Predicts Infant Fussiness *74*

Self-Control during the Preschool Years Predicts Later Behaviour, Personality, and Achievement *277*

Predicting Reading Skill *327*

Adolescent Friendships Predict Quality of Relationships in the Midthirties *449*

REAL CHILDREN

Calming Bradley *94*

A Father's Attachment *177*

Very Cute 177

Christine, Egocentrism, and Animism 218

Preface

I am especially pleased to present to you the fifth Canadian edition of *Children: A Chronological Approach*, written for those engaged in introductory learning and teaching of child development from a psychological perspective. The authentic Canadian context of the book, as well as the chronological unfolding of developmental events in childhood, will help your students to grasp child development concepts in a way that is culturally meaningful and conceptually accessible to them.

I sincerely hope that you enjoy this new edition of *Children: A Chronological Approach.* The book retains and updates useful features from the previous edition and introduces several new ones, designed to enhance the learning experience. I use this text in my own classes and have found these added features to be helpful to students; they also help me to better advise students on ways to improve their performance in the course.

Recent Advances in Research

- Updated content on comparing variables—Chapter 2
- Updated content on how genetics affect behaviour—Chapter 3
- Updated content on nutrition for babies and toddlers in Canada and internationally—Chapter 5
- Updated content on habituation—Chapter 6
- Updated content on bilingualism in Canada—Chapter 9
- Updated content on the benefits of full-day kindergarten—Chapter 9
- Updated content on the effects of violence on children—Chapter 13
- Updated content on cultural response to menarche and spermarche—Chapter 14
- Updated content on sexual behaviour, and sexual behaviour online in older children—Chapter 14
- Updated content on STIs—Chapter 14
- Updated content on LGBTQ teens—Chapter 14

Retained Features

As with previous editions of the text, research findings are situated and understood within Canada's unique cultural and socio-political context, which is especially relevant to students at Canadian colleges and universities. Additional key features we retained are listed below:

- Our vignette star, Sophie, returns in **chapter-opening mini vignettes** that highlight a major developmental focus for each chapter.
- Prominently displayed on the inside front cover of the text is a developmental milestones review chart that provides an at-a-glance look at the major developmental changes that occur for each major period from prenatal through adolescence.
- Each chapter features numbered learning objectives that are reiterated in the body of the text to correlate objectives with content.
- **Marginal key terms** retained for students' quick review while studying.
- **Modular structure** maintained.
- *Ask Yourself* reflection questions added at critical junctures within each module.
- *Chapter Critical Review* is streamlined into point form that makes for easier scanning and overview of summarized information.
- *See for Yourself* pointers continue to suggest activities that allow students to observe topics in child development first-hand.
- This new edition continues to highlight the most important information in child development research for students new to the study of developmental psychology. The recurring feature presents different scenarios and asks the question "What would a ____ do?," offering insights to students studying in a variety of disciplines, including early childhood development, social work, education, psychology, nursing, and medicine.

Canadian Cultural Context

Information on Canadian cultural context, previously contained in Chapter 1, now appears throughout the entire text. Therefore, consider asking your students to read the section below, titled *Culture and Terminology: A Word about This Book*, so that they understand how cultural groups in Canada tend to be labelled and the impact that Canadian social realities have on understanding research conducted both inside and outside of Canada.

Culture and Terminology: A Word about This Book

As you begin to study child development, you should become familiar with the basic terms we use to describe infancy, childhood, and adolescence. Note that each term provided below refers to a specific range of ages.

- newborn: birth to 1 month
- infant: 1 month to 1 year
- toddler: 1 to 2 years
- preschooler: 2 to 6 years
- middle childhood: 6 to 12 years
- adolescent: 12 to 18 years
- adult: 18 years and older

For variety, we sometimes use other terms—*babies*, *youngsters*, *youth*, and *elementary school children*—that are less frequently tied to specific age ranges. When we do use these other terms, you will be able to tell from the chapter content which group of people is being discussed.

We also will use very specific terminology to describe research findings from different cultural and ethnic groups. The appropriate terms to describe different cultural, racial, and ethnic groups tend to change over time and to vary from country to country. For example, the terms Indian, Aboriginal, Indigenous, North American Indian, and First Nations all have been used to describe the First Peoples of Canada. In this book, we will use the terms First Nations, Inuit, and Métis because they are, broadly speaking, the terms used by the people from those cultural groups themselves. Part of the problem with cultural and ethnic terminology in child-development research is that, in Canada, we do not necessarily use the same terms as our American counterparts, particularly in research studies. Canada has a very different population settlement history than the United States, although some similarities exist. For example, both countries started out populated with persons of First Nations heritage, and both countries experienced major waves of immigration from Britain. Later waves of immigration came from other parts of Western and Eastern Europe and from other countries around the world. However, Canadian and American experiences of treaties, governance, immigrant settlement, the geographical patterns of settlement, and the proportions of the various cultural groups in the nation differ greatly.

Psychological researchers in the United States tend to identify five primary groups as culturally distinct: Native Americans, Hispanic Americans, Asian Americans, European Americans, and African Americans. However, the labelling of these groups for research is not wholly satisfactory, because the labels refer more to race than to culture. For example, within the Native American group, many

different cultures are represented. In Canada, we might think of Anishinabe, Lakhota, Blackfoot, Assiniboine, and others, but these groups can be broken down into still smaller cultural groups. Cree, for example, includes Swampy Cree, Plains Cree, and Moose Cree. Each group tends to come from a different geographical area, and each speaks its own dialect of Cree. The same is true for all other racial groups—they can be broken down into smaller cultural groups that are quite distinct from each other.

For example, some writers use the term "European American" and others use "White." Unfortunately, both terms are extremely broad and superficial. Included in the "European American" group, for example, are British, German, and Bulgarian immigrants to Canada, all of whom are radically different from each other in terms of their history, language, and culture. Of course, not all European Americans are "White" in terms of skin colour either. Therefore, broad labels for cultural groups might not be very effective and might account for why sometimes in research as much variability emerges within a cultural group as between cultural groups. Canadian researchers sometimes create similar problems with the terms "Anglophone" and "Francophone." Francophones are frequently identified as people who are ethnically French and who speak French, whereas Anglophones speak English but might come from any number of non-French cultures. Therefore, the culture or characteristics that are represented by "Anglophone" are often unclear, except that these people speak English and are not French. Furthermore, as many Francophones also speak English, the distinction between the groups is blurred even further.

Over the past decade, an explosion of discussion has occurred within psychology about what researchers are really measuring when they classify research participants by race (Ota Wang & Sue, 2005; Shields et al., 2005; Sternberg, Grigorenko, & Kidd, 2005). Arguments abound about what race, as a variable, measures, given that sociocultural groupings within races can be very distinct and that some cultures may contain people from more than one race. Nevertheless, race is important because people tend to classify each other naturally according to racial groupings (Smedley & Smedley, 2005; Wing Sue et al., 2007). However, with advances in research on human neurology and the human genome, scientists have recognized that social classifications by race are not always supported by genetic markers, which makes race a social construct (Cooper, 2005; Eberhardt, 2005; Ota Wang & Sue, 2005; Smedley & Smedley, 2005) with a complicated connection to biology (Hartigan, 2009).

Also, some researchers have objected to the use of "race" as a substitute, or "proxy variable," for other social and environmental variables that negatively affect racial minorities, such as poverty, oppression, and racism

(Ota Wang & Sue, 2005; Shields et al., 2005). On the other hand, researchers in pharmacology and medicine have demonstrated race-based differences in disease prevalence as well as physiological processing of various medications. Therefore, discussion and research should continue to determine how the concept of race might be discussed and studied within psychology (Bonham, Warshauer-Baker, & Collins, 2005; Helms, Jernigan, & Mascher, 2005; Whitfield & McClearn, 2005).

Given the recent controversy about the merits and demerits of classifying research participants by race, reporting on research in an introductory text like this one becomes difficult when so much of the research is based on racial variables and classifications. When we report on research results in this text, we are obliged to use the terms the researchers, themselves, have used, even if those terms might be problematic. When researchers have identified subgroups in their research sample, we will use the more specific terms in describing results. When you see more general terms, such as "White" or "European," remember that conclusions might not apply equally to all subgroups within the larger group. In future, psychological researchers will need to rise to the challenge of defining and measuring human social categories more meaningfully and accurately.

Support Materials

Children: A Chronological Approach, Fifth Canadian Edition, is accompanied by a superb set of ancillary materials.

Student Supplements

REVEL™

Designed for the way today's students read, think, and learn, REVEL is a ground-breaking immersive learning experience. It's based on a simple premise: When students are engaged deeply, they learn more and get better results.

Built in collaboration with educators and students, REVEL brings course content to life with rich media and assessments—integrated directly within the authors' narrative—that provide opportunities for students to read, learn and practice in one environment.

Learn more about REVEL
http://www.pearsonhighered.com/revel/

My Virtual Child

What kinds of theories do you have about children? What ideas inform your thoughts and beliefs about the lives of children, how they are raised, and the nature of the human person? Use your access card and follow this link www.myvirtualchild.com to learn more about the world of the child. You can even virtually try to raise your own child.

peerScholar

Firmly grounded in published research, peerScholar is a powerful online pedagogical tool that helps develop your students' critical and creative thinking skills. peerScholar facilitates this through the process of creation, evaluation, and reflection. Working in stages, students begin by submitting a written assignment. peerScholar then circulates their work for others to review, a process that can be anonymous or not depending on your preference. Students receive peer feedback and evaluations immediately, reinforcing their learning and driving the development of higher-order thinking skills. Students can then resubmit revised work, again depending on your preference. Contact your Pearson Representative to learn more about peerScholar and the research behind it.

Instructor Supplements

The following supplements can be downloaded by instructors from a password-protected location on Pearson Canada's online catalogue (vig.pearsoned.ca). Apply for your instructor access code online or ask your sales rep.

- **Instructor's Manual** Designed to make your lectures more effective and to save you preparation time, this resource gathers together the most effective activities and strategies for teaching your developmental psychology course.

- **PowerPoint Presentations** Each chapter's Power-Point presentation highlights the key points covered in the text.

- **Test Item File** This test bank in Microsoft Word format contains over 2000 multiple-choice, true/false, and short-answer essay questions, and many enhancements.

- **Computerized Test Bank.** Pearson's computerized test banks allow instructors to filter and select questions to create quizzes, tests, or homework. Instructors can revise questions or add their own and may be able to choose print or online options. These questions are also available in Microsoft Word format.

- **Image Library** This set of images is designed to be used in large lecture settings and includes illustrations and figures from the text.

Learning Solutions Managers

Pearson's Learning Solutions Managers work with faculty and campus course designers to ensure that Pearson technology products, assessment tools, and online course materials are tailored to meet your specific needs. This highly qualified team is dedicated to helping schools take full advantage of a wide range of educational resources by assisting in the integration of a variety of instructional materials and media formats. Your local Pearson Canada sales representative can provide you with more details about this service program.

Acknowledgments

I would sincerely like to acknowledge and thank Mallory Skrip, designer and illustrator, for her art and photography contributions for this text. In addition, I would like to thank all the editorial and technical staff who worked to make this fifth Canadian edition a worthy and beautiful educational resource in the field of child and adolescent development. I especially would like to acknowledge and thank my team at Pearson, in particular Darcey Pepper, Madhu Ranadive, Patti Sayle, Jessica Hellen, and Kathy O'Handley for their professionalism, encouragement, and support on this project, as well as the team at Cenveo for their vigilance and talents provided during the text's time in production. Generating a new edition of a text is a challenging task, and having a supportive editorial and production team makes all the difference. I also would like to thank all of the people who gave of their valuable time to review the text and offer their thoughts and suggestions for its improvement.

Finally, a word of gratitude for all of our supplement authors. The instructor's manual, PowerPoint slides, and test bank are great resources that help increase the value of this book to many instructors. We especially wish to thank Michelle Edey from the Sheridan Institute of Technology and Advanced Learning for her excellent work in creating the interactive component for our REVEL edition. It is our hope that these quizzes and interactive learning widgets will help bring the concepts to life.

Dr. Theresa Zolner, R. Psych.

About the Authors

Robert V. Kail is Professor of Psychological Sciences at Purdue University. His undergraduate degree is from Ohio Wesleyan University and his Ph.D. is from the University of Michigan. Kail is editor of the *Journal of Experimental Child Psychology* and of *Advances in Child Development and Behavior*. He received the McCandless Young Scientist Award from the American Psychological Association, was named the Distinguished Sesquicentennial Alumnus in Psychology by Ohio Wesleyan University, and is a fellow of the Association for Psychological Science. His research focuses on cognitive development during childhood and adolescence. Away from the office, he enjoys photography and working out.

Theresa Zolner is a child and family clinician, researcher, and author with a primary interest in community and cultural psychology. Dr. Zolner has retained a life-long interest in working with people who have been affected by discrimination, oppression, or objectification in various forms. In particular, she has dedicated much of her professional career to working with persons of First Nations heritage, particularly youth living in high-risk circumstances, as well as homeless, street, and foster children in Canada. Dr. Zolner also does scholarly work on Eastern European cultural settlement in Canada and has a special interest in Christian psychology, family spirituality, and rural psychology.

Dedication

To Chauncy
—Robert V. Kail

To Jack
—Theresa Zolner

Chapter 1
Child Development: Theories and Themes

Evasilieva/Fotolia

 ## MODULE

1.1 Theories of Child Development

1.2 Themes in Child-Development Research

Connect to My Virtual Child

What kinds of theories do you have about children? What ideas inform your thoughts and beliefs about the lives of children, how they are raised, and the nature of the human person? Use your access card and follow this link www.myvirtualchild.com to learn more about the world of the child. You can even virtually try to raise your own child.

Terry and Mabel have been together for a while, and, lately, they have been thinking about starting a family. Every time they see a couple with a baby walk by, they wonder about having a child. As they discuss the beliefs their own parents taught them about children, they wonder . . . what are the most important aspects of and ideas about child development?

1.1 Theories of Child Development

 ## Learning Objectives

After reading the module, you should be able to do the following:

LO1 Describe Canada's unique contribution to developmental research.

LO2 State the major tenets of the biological perspective.

LO3 Explain how psychodynamic theories account for development.

LO4 Identify the focus of learning theories.

LO5 Describe how cognitive-developmental theories explain changes in children's thinking.

LO6 Name the main points of the contextual approach.

LO7 Explain recent approaches to the study of child development.

LO8 Identify where you can read more about the history of psychology.

Questions about child development have occupied the minds of some of the greatest writers and philosophers in history. For example, nearly 400 years ago, English philosopher John Locke (1632–1704) claimed that the human infant is born *tabula rasa*—as a "blank slate." Locke believed that experience moulds the infant, child, adolescent, and adult into a unique individual. Locke's view was challenged by French philosopher Jean-Jacques Rousseau (1712–1778), who believed that newborns were endowed with an innate sense of justice and morality that unfolds naturally as children grow.

By the middle of the nineteenth century, progress in Western science had merged with growing concerns about children's welfare to bring about the first Western scientific theories of child development. In child development, a **theory** is an organized set of ideas designed to explain and make predictions about development. For example, suppose your friends have a baby daughter who cries often. You could imagine several explanations for her crying. Maybe the baby cries because she's hungry; maybe she cries to get her parents to hold her; maybe she cries because she's simply a cranky baby. Each of these explanations is a very simple theory to explain why the baby cries so much. Formal developmental theories are much more complicated than these, but their purpose is the same—to explain behaviour and make predictions about development.

In addition to proposing explanations for behaviour and development, theories are a source of predictions that can be tested through research. Think about the different explanations for the crying baby. Each one leads to unique predictions. If, for example, the baby is crying because she's hungry, we predict that feeding her should stop the crying. When results of research match a prediction based on a theory, the

Theory:

an organized set of ideas designed to explain and make predictions about development; also, any organized set of ideas designed to explain and make predictions about natural phenomena.

theory gains support. When results differ from a prediction, the theory is revised and more research done.

Many theories have guided research and thought about children's development for the past 100 years. Researchers have embraced some theories for a period and then abandoned them when those theories were disproved or generated few testable predictions. Nevertheless, understanding historical theories is critical because they set the stage for current theories of child development.

Some theories share common assumptions and ideas about children and development, so they can be grouped together. In the next few pages, we sketch five major theoretical perspectives in child-development research: biological, psychodynamic, learning, cognitive-developmental, and contextual. As you read about each theory, think about how it differs from the others in its explanation of development.

Canada's Unique Contribution

LO1 Describe Canada's unique contribution to developmental research.

Canada's contributions to the field of psychology extend back over 100 years to James Mark Baldwin, who came to Canada from Princeton University and was the first psychologist appointed at the University of Toronto. Baldwin's appointment was controversial largely because he was a "materialist" interested in studying the mind empirically (experientially) and not philosophically (Hoff, 1992). Baldwin set up the very first psychological laboratory in Canada. His initial budget at the University of Toronto was $1550 for set-up, with an annual maintenance allowance of $300—probably a lot of money at that time (Baldwin, 1892). In fact, this was the first psychological laboratory anywhere in the British Empire (1892).

Baldwin's theoretical influence on the field of child development was as important as his experimental lab. He strongly believed that theory must guide experimentation—that theory should come first (Baldwin, 1906). Coming from what we would now call a social psychological perspective, Baldwin insisted that children's development occurs in stages, an idea that would later be advanced by Jean Piaget. Baldwin believed that development proceeded from simple behavioural movements gradually coordinated into more complex behaviours and leading to adult forms of abstract thought (1906). He theorized about many concepts that child-development researchers continue to investigate today, including research methodology, colour perception, handedness, movements, suggestion, imitation, adaptation, volition, attitudes and expressions, memory, consciousness, thought, and more.

Canada has a strong history of research in child development. While much of this research is conducted at Canadian universities, the Government of Canada (primarily through Statistics Canada and Health Canada) also produces a wealth of researched information about Canadian children's development and the difficulties they face. Another of Canada's contributions to psychology involves access to historical information about the field. In 1997, Dr. Christopher Green, at York University, set up an invaluable website that contains a large number of early works in the history of psychology (http://psychclassics.yorku.ca). Using this resource, you can read many of the original works written by theorists in child development whom we will be discussing next.

The Biological Perspective

LO2 State the major tenets of the biological perspective.

According to the biological perspective, cognitive, personality, physical, and motor development proceed according to a biological plan. The earliest researcher to

Herbert Gehr/The LIFE Picture Collection/Getty Images

Arnold Gesell

empirically study and describe children's development was G. Stanley Hall (1846–1924). Hall studied about 100 000 children and interviewed hundreds of school personnel in an effort to describe the "normal" child (Brooks-Gunn & Johnson, 2006). His goal was to reconstruct the study of psychology to include the study of children, and he based his work on evolutionary biology rather than the physical sciences, as was more common with other researchers (2006).

Approaches to research in evolutionary biology derived, in Hall's time, primarily from the work of Charles Darwin (1809–1882), who published a theory of evolution that promoted important concepts that have had wide-ranging impact on all areas of scientific study. Most important was Darwin's concept that organisms whose individual traits are best suited, or adapted, for survival in a particular environment are the organisms most likely to survive. As a result, the strongest and fastest organisms are not necessarily the ones that survive, as survival depends on a fit between the characteristics of the organism and the environment in which it lives. If the organism survives, it can reproduce some of its genetic traits in offspring. The best-adapted offspring then reproduce in an ongoing process of environmental adaptation that Darwin termed **natural selection**. Through this theory, Darwin proposed that current traits of animals and people can have an evolutionary history that extends back over generations of reproduction spanning eons of time. Darwin's ideas had a dramatic impact on scientists, particularly those who took a biological approach to understanding development.

One of the first biological theories, **maturational theory**, was proposed by Arnold Gesell (1880–1961). According to Gesell, child development reflects a specific and prearranged scheme or plan within the body. For Gesell, development is a natural unfolding of a biological plan; experience matters little. Like Rousseau, Gesell encouraged parents to let their children develop naturally. He claimed that, without interference from adults, behaviours like speech, play, and reasoning would emerge spontaneously according to a predetermined developmental timetable.

Other biological theorists give greater weight to experience. Ethological theorists view development from an evolutionary perspective. In **ethological theory**, many behaviours are adaptive—that is, they have survival value. For example, crying is adaptive for infants because it elicits caregiving from others. Ethological theorists assume that people inherit many of these adaptive behaviours, but they also believe that experience is important for development. However, ethologists propose that animals are biologically programmed so that some kinds of learning occur only at critical times in development. A **critical period** is the time in development when a specific type of learning can take place; before or after the critical period, the same learning is difficult or impossible.

One of the best-known examples of the concept of a critical period comes from Konrad Lorenz (1903–1989), a Nobel Prize–winning Austrian zoologist (Brigandt, 2005). Lorenz noticed that newly hatched chicks follow their mother and theorized that chicks are biologically programmed to follow the first moving object they see after hatching. Usually this was the mother, so following her was the first step in **imprinting**, creating an emotional bond with the mother. Lorenz tested his theory by showing that, if he removed the mother immediately after the chicks hatched and replaced her with another moving object, the chicks would follow that object and treat it as "mother." In humans, this emotional bond is called **attachment**, and theories about attachment grew out of biologists' observations of animals' behaviour.

Natural selection:

an ongoing process in nature that results in survival of those organisms that are best adapted to their environments.

Maturational theory:

a theory that views development as unfolding according to a specific and prearranged scheme or plan within the body.

Ethological theory:

a theory that views development from an evolutionary perspective, such that human behaviours can be adaptive and have survival value.

Critical period:

the time in development when a specific type of learning best takes place.

Imprinting:

the instinctive creation of an emotional bond between a newborn animal and the animal's mother.

Attachment:

the emotional bond that forms between people, particularly children and their parents.

Lorenz also discovered that, for imprinting to occur, the chick had to see the moving object within about a day of hatching. In other words, the critical period for imprinting lasts about a day. When chicks experience the moving object outside of the critical period, imprinting does not take place. Therefore, even though the underlying mechanism is biological, experience is essential for triggering programmed, adaptive behaviours.

Ethological theory and maturational theory both highlight the biological bases of development. Biological theorists remind us that children's genes, which are the product of a long evolutionary history, influence virtually every aspect of children's development.

Konrad Lorenz

The Psychodynamic Perspective

LO3 Explain how psychodynamic theories account for development.

The psychodynamic perspective has its roots in Sigmund Freud's (1856–1939) late nineteenth and early twentieth century work. Freud was a physician specializing in diseases of the nervous system. Many of his patients were adults suffering from conditions that had no obvious biological cause. As Freud listened to his patients describe their problems, he theorized that early experiences establish enduring, lifelong patterns. Using his patients' case histories, Freud created **psychoanalysis**, a psychological theory proposing that development is largely determined by how well people resolve unconscious conflicts that arise during development. Freud's original theory has been highly criticized for its limited base of initial research and its controversial claims about women. However, his ideas about personality and psychosexual development have been influential in developmental research.

Sigmund Freud

THEORY OF PERSONALITY.   Freud proposed that personality includes three primary theoretical components that emerge at distinct periods of development: the id, ego, and superego.

The **id** is a reservoir of primitive instincts and drives. It is present at birth and presses for immediate gratification of bodily needs and wants. A hungry baby crying illustrates the id in action. The **ego** is the practical, rational component of personality. The ego begins to emerge during the first year of life, as infants learn that they cannot always have what they want. The ego tries to resolve conflicts that occur when the instinctive demands of the id encounter the obstacles of the real world. The ego tries to meet the id's desires with realistic and socially acceptable objects and actions. Suppose, for example, a child, Billy, sees a friend playing with an attractive toy. Billy's id would urge him to grab the toy, but his ego would encourage him to play with the friend and the toy co-operatively.

The third component of personality, the **superego**, is the "moral agent" in the child's personality, a conscience. It emerges during the preschool years as children begin to internalize adult standards of right and wrong. If the friend in the previous example left the attractive toy unattended, Billy's id might urge him to grab it and run; his superego might remind him that taking another child's toy is wrong.

THEORY OF PSYCHOSEXUAL DEVELOPMENT.   A second aspect of psychoanalysis was Freud's account of psychosexual development. Freud believed that humans, through a force called **libido**, are instinctively motivated from birth to experience physical pleasure. As children grow, libido shifts to different parts of the body, termed "erogenous zones." For example, in their first year, infants seek pleasure orally,

Psychoanalysis:

Freud's psychological theory and method of treatment for unresolved unconscious conflict.

Id:

one of three Freudian components of personality; a reservoir of primitive instincts and drives.

Ego:

one of three Freudian components of personality; tries to realistically meet the demands of the id.

Superego:

one of three Freudian components of personality; acts as the moral agent of personality.

Libido:

an instinctive energy or force that motivates humans to experience pleasure.

"Today: The collective unconscious..."

usually by sucking, so Freud called this the oral stage. Freud proposed several developmental stages, each characterized by gratification of needs associated with an erogenous zone (see Table 1–1 A Comparison of Freudian and Eriksonian Stage Theories).

Freud believed that development proceeds best when children's needs at each stage are met but not exceeded. If children's needs are not met adequately, children become frustrated and find moving on to more mature forms of pleasure difficult, and they become developmentally fixated at a certain stage. For example, an adult whose needs for oral stimulation were not met in infancy might try to satisfy those needs by smoking. However, if children are overindulged at one stage, they see little need to progress to more advanced stages. In Freud's view, parents have the difficult task of satisfying children's needs without spoiling them.

Modern psychoanalytic theorists understand that heredity and environment both influence children, but they also recognize that a family's responses, or **environmental reactions**, to hereditary conditions shape children's adjustment and development (Diem-Wille, 2011). An interesting concept is that of **body ego**, which develops in the early years during the process of closeness and separation between child and parent and contributes to the development of a sense of individual self (2011). Nurturing the child through physical and emotional care also helps to create a **psychic skin**, which holds this sense of self together (Diem-Wille, 2011; Feldman, 2011; Netzer-Stein, 2012). Other developments in this area include the merging of psychoanalytic theory with biological approaches in psychology to produce a new theory called **neuropsychoanalysis** (Bernstein, 2011).

Environmental reactions:
a family's responses to hereditary conditions.

Body ego:
a person's sense of the self as an individual.

Psychic skin:
a person's capacity for protecting and containing his or her internal emotional states.

Neuropsychoanalysis:
the study of the relationship between psychoanalytic theory and biological approaches in psychology.

Table 1–1 A Comparison of Freudian and Eriksonian Stage Theories

	Freud: Psychosexual Stages		Erikson: Psychosocial Stages	
Age	Stage	Task	Stage	Task
Birth to 1 year	Oral	Erogenous zone: mouth; gratify oral sucking urges	Basic trust vs. mistrust	To develop a sense that the world is safe, a "good place"
1 to 3 years	Anal	Erogenous zone: anus; release and withhold feces	Autonomy vs. shame and doubt	To realize that one is an independent person who can make decisions
3 to 6 years	Phallic	Erogenous zone: genitalia; learn to suppress attraction to the parent of the opposite sex and identify with the parent of the same sex	Initiative vs. guilt	To develop a willingness to try new things and to handle failure
6 years to adolescence	Latency	Erogenous zone: none; libido is repressed as children go about daily business	Industry vs. inferiority	To learn basic skills and to work with others
Adolescence	Genital	Erogenous zone: genitalia; attraction to the opposite sex (not the parent)	Identity vs. identity confusion	To develop a lasting and integrated sense of self
Young adulthood			Intimacy vs. isolation	To commit to another in a loving relationship
Middle adulthood			Generativity vs. stagnation	To contribute to younger people through child-rearing, child care, or other productive work
Later life		Integrity vs. despair	To view one's life as satisfactory and worth living	

ERIKSON'S PSYCHOSOCIAL THEORY. Erik Erikson (1902–1994) believed that the psychological and social aspects of development are as important as the biological and sexual aspects that Freud emphasized. Erikson worked with Anna Freud, Sigmund Freud's daughter, at the Vienna Psychoanalytic Institute. Erikson's theory is an offshoot of Freudian theory; therefore, it is a **psychodynamic theory**. Although psychoanalytically trained, Erikson's ideas about lifespan development were rooted in knowledge gained from First Nations peoples in the United States, including the Lakhota and Yurok (Erikson, 2000). In Erikson's **psychosocial theory**, development consists of a sequence of eight stages, each defined by a unique crisis or social challenge (see Table 1–1 A Comparison of Freudian and Eriksonian Stage Theories). The name of each stage reflects the challenge that individuals face at a particular period. For example, the challenge for young adults is to become involved in a loving relationship. Adults who establish this relationship experience intimacy; those who don't experience isolation. George Vaillant has extended and elaborated upon Erikson's original theory and added six adult developmental stages extending from early adulthood to old age: identity, intimacy, career consolidation, generativity, keeper of the meaning, and integrity (Vaillant, 2003).

Like Freud, Erikson argued that earlier stages of development provide the foundation for later stages. For example, according to Erikson, adolescents who do not meet the challenge of developing an identity will have difficulty establishing truly intimate relationships and risk becoming overly dependent on their partners as a source of identity.

Whether we use the terms "unconscious conflicts," "challenges," or "crises," psychodynamic theorists emphasize that the journey to adulthood is fraught with obstacles. Outcomes of development reflect the manner and ease with which children navigate life's tasks. When children overcome early obstacles easily, they are better able to handle later ones.

The Learning Perspective

LO4 Identify the focus of learning theories.

Learning theorists endorse John Locke's view that the infant's mind is a blank slate on which experience writes. John Watson (1878–1958) was the first theorist to apply this approach to child development. Watson extended the work of Russian researcher Ivan Pavlov on **classical conditioning**, which is a theory of associative learning. These theorists demonstrated that animals and people can learn to respond in a particular manner to a stimulus that normally would not elicit that type of response. For example, dogs normally salivate in response to food but not to the sound of a bell. Pavlov demonstrated that, if a tone were sounded each time a dog smelled food, the dog would begin to salivate in response to the tone without any food being present: The dog would learn to associate the tone with food and respond to it by salivating.

Watson argued that learning is the crucial factor in determining the course of a child's development and behaviour. He assumed that, with correct techniques, anything could be learned by almost anyone. Watson demonstrated his ideas by training 11-month-old "Little Albert" to fear a rat. Each time Albert reached for the animal, the experimenters struck a steel bar with a hammer, producing a loud and frightening sound. Eventually, Albert associated the sound with the rat and began to demonstrate signs of fear with the rat (Watson & Rayner, 1920).

EARLY LEARNING THEORIES. Following Watson, B. F. Skinner (1904–1990) studied learning through **operant conditioning**, in which the consequences of a behaviour affect whether that behaviour is repeated in the future. Skinner showed that two kinds of consequences were especially influential. A **reinforcement** is a consequence that increases the future likelihood of the behaviour it follows.

Psychodynamic theories: theories that are offshoots of Freudian psychoanalysis.

Psychosocial theory: Erik Erikson's psychoanalytic theory that development occurs in a sequence of stages defined by a unique crisis or social challenge.

Erik Erikson

Classical conditioning: a theory of associative learning that later gave rise to behaviourism.

Operant conditioning: a behavioural theory about how the consequences of a behaviour can affect future occurrences of that behaviour.

Reinforcement: a consequence that increases the future likelihood of the behaviour it follows.

B. F. Skinner

Punishment:

an aversive consequence that decreases the future likelihood of the behaviour it follows primarily when the child is in the presence of an authority figure.

Imitation:

behaving in the manner one sees others behaving.

Vicarious (observational) learning:

a method of learning in which one acquires knowledge by watching others' behaviours and the consequences or outcomes of those behaviours.

Positive reinforcement means giving a reward, such as gold stars, praise, or pay-cheques, to increase the likelihood that a behaviour will recur. Parents can use positive reinforcement to encourage particular behaviours in children by saying, for example, that doing a half hour of reading will be rewarded with a half hour of video game time afterward. Negative reinforcement means rewarding by taking away something unpleasant. For example, a half hour of reading before supper is rewarded with getting out of washing the dishes.

A **punishment** is an aversive consequence that decreases the future likelihood of the behaviour it follows. Punishment suppresses a behaviour either by causing something unpleasant to occur or by withholding a pleasant event. For example, if their daughter failed to clean her room, parents could punish her by making her do extra chores (adding something unpleasant) or by not allowing her to watch television (withholding a pleasant event).

Skinner's research was done primarily with animals, but developmental researchers soon showed that the principles of operant conditioning could be used to modify children's behaviour (Baer & Wolf, 1968). Applied properly, reinforcement and punishment have a powerful effect on children, but notice that thinking or cognition does not play a role in early behavioural theory.

In behavioural theory, generating an aversive event and withholding a pleasant event are both forms of punishment for inappropriate behaviour.

SOCIAL COGNITIVE THEORY. In a groundbreaking article, Alberta-born Albert Bandura (1925–) published a critique of learning theory, saying that learning theorists were ignoring the importance of social relationships and the role of imitation in learning. He proposed that people can learn without personal reinforcement simply by watching those around them, through **imitation** or **vicarious (observational) learning** (Bandura, 1962). For example, imitation occurs when a toddler throws a toy after seeing a friend do so, or when a child offers to help an elderly person carry groceries because she's seen her parents do the same.

Children are more likely to imitate a person whom they admire in some way, such as a popular, smart, or talented person, or when they want to fit into a particular group (Over & Carpenter, 2013). Children are also more likely to imitate when they see a behaviour rewarded rather than punished. Children do not automatically mimic what they see and hear; instead, they look to others for information about what behaviours are appropriate. When admired people are rewarded for their behaviour, imitation makes sense.

Bandura based his **social cognitive theory** of personality on this complex view of reward, punishment, and imitation. Bandura called his theory "cognitive" because he believed that children are actively trying to understand their world; the theory is "social" because other people are important sources of information about the world.

Bandura (1997) also argued that experience gives children a sense of **self-efficacy**, beliefs about their own levels of ability, skill, and talent to affect events having an impact on them personally. Self-efficacy beliefs help determine when children will imitate others. A child who sees herself as musically untalented, for example, will not try to imitate Celine Dion singing on stage, despite the fact that Celine is gifted and internationally famous. Thus, whether a child imitates another person depends on who the other person is, whether that person's behaviour is rewarded, and whether the child has beliefs about self-efficacy. For Bandura, the social-cognitive child actively interprets experience using cognition.

Social cognitive theory:

a theory of personality that views the environment, behaviour, and cognitions as important in shaping development.

Self-efficacy:

beliefs about one's own levels of ability, skill, and talent.

Albert Bandura

The Cognitive-Developmental Perspective

LO5 Describe how cognitive-developmental theories explain changes in children's thinking.

The cognitive-developmental perspective focuses on how children think and how their thinking changes over time. Jean Piaget (1896–1980) proposed one of the best known of these theories. He believed that youngsters are naturally motivated to make sense of the physical and social world. For example, infants want to know about objects (What happens when I poke this toy?) and people (Who is this person who feeds me?).

Jean Piaget

Piaget argued that children act like scientists in creating theories about the physical and social worlds they are trying to understand. They try to weave all they know about objects and people into a theory that explains how their world works. When the world works the way the child expects, the child's belief in that theory grows stronger. When events do not go as expected, the child must revise the theory, just as a scientist would. For example, a baby's theory of objects might include the idea that, "If I let go of this rattle, it will fly up in the air." When the baby lets go of the rattle, it falls to the floor, and the baby learns something about rattles. Eventually, babies learn that dropped objects fall to the floor—but they will have to revise that theory when they come into contact with helium balloons!

According to Piaget, at a few points in development, children realize that a theory cannot be revised. When this happens, radical changes take place, the theory must be discarded, and a completely new theory about the world develops. Piaget claimed that radical revisions occur three times in development: once at about age 2, a second time at about age 7, and a third time just before adolescence. Piaget theorized that children go through four distinct stages in cognitive development. Each stage represents a fundamental change in how children understand and organize their experiences, and each stage is characterized by more sophisticated types of reasoning. The first of these is the sensorimotor stage. As the name implies, sensorimotor thinking is closely linked to the infant's basic sensory and motor skills (see Table 1–2 Piaget's Four Stages of Cognitive Development).

Piagetian concepts have been debated widely in psychology, with some researchers rejecting them outright in favour of newer, information-processing approaches, which we will discuss later in this chapter. Canadian psychologist Robbie Case created what might be thought of as a theoretical hybrid, blending features of Piagetian theory with information-processing theory into what is termed neo-Piagetian theory.

According to Piaget, children go through four stages of cognitive development, the first of which is the sensorimotor stage.

Table 1–2 Piaget's Four Stages of Cognitive Development

Stage	Approximate Age	Characteristics
Sensorimotor	Birth to 2 years	Infant's knowledge of the world is based on senses and motor skills. By the end of the period, infant uses mental representations.
Preoperational thought	2 to 6 years	Child learns how to use symbols such as words and numbers to represent aspects of the world but relates to the world only through his or her perspective.
Concrete operational thought	7 to 11 years	Child understands and applies logical operations to experiences, provided the experiences are focused on the here and now.
Formal operational thought	Adolescence and beyond	Adolescent or adult thinks abstractly, speculates on hypothetical situations, and reasons deductively about what may be possible.

The Contextual Perspective

LO6 Name the main points of the contextual approach.

Most theorists agree that the environment is important to development. Traditionally, most child development theorists have emphasized environmental forces that affect children directly. Examples of direct environmental influences are a parent praising a child or a preschool teacher discouraging boys from playing with dolls. These direct influences are important in children's lives, but, in the contextual perspective, they are one part of a much larger system, with each element of the system influencing all other elements. This larger system includes parents and siblings as well as individuals outside the immediate family, such as extended family, friends, and teachers. The system also includes organizations that influence development, such as schools, television stations, tribal councils, workplaces, and churches or temples.

All these people and institutions fit together to form a person's **culture**—the knowledge, attitudes, beliefs, symbols, and behaviours associated with a group of people. A culture provides the context in which a child develops, and it influences development from infancy through adulthood. The word "culture" can be used in a variety of ways, but it generally refers to the way that a group of people organize their families, parent and socialize their children, make laws or rules, cook food, create art, work, celebrate, worship, learn, define their values, and help each other. Often, people who share a culture come from a particular geographical area or share a common history.

One of the first theorists to emphasize cultural context in children's development was Lev Vygotsky (1896–1934). A Russian psychologist, Vygotsky focused on ways that adults convey to children the beliefs, customs, and skills of their culture. Vygotsky believed that, because a fundamental aim of society is to enable children to acquire essential cultural values and skills, every aspect of a child's development must be considered in cultural context. For example, many parents in North America want their children to work hard in school and be accepted into postsecondary study because, in Western nations, this can be the key to good employment. However, most parents want their children to acquire important skills for good living, whether those skills involve hunting, house-building, spelling, or running a space station.

Urie Bronfenbrenner (1917–2005) also promoted a contextual view of development. Bronfenbrenner portrayed the developing child as embedded in a series of complex and interactive systems, sometimes referred to as an **ecological theory**. As Figure 1–1 shows, Bronfenbrenner (1979, 1995; Bronfenbrenner & Morris, 1998) divided the environment into five levels: the microsystem, the mesosystem, the exosystem, the macrosystem, and the chronosystem. At any point in life, the microsystem consists of the people and objects in an individual's immediate environment. These are the people closest to a child, such as parents or siblings. Some children have more than one microsystem; for example, a young child might have family and daycare in his or her microsystem, while some children's microsystems might include extended family. As you can imagine, microsystems strongly influence development.

Microsystems themselves connect to create the mesosystem, which represents the fact that what happens in one microsystem can influence other microsystems. Perhaps you've found that if you have a stressful day at work or school, you're grouchy at home. This indicates that your mesosystem is alive and well; your microsystems of home and work are emotionally interconnected for you.

The exosystem includes social settings that a person might not experience first-hand but that still influence development. For example, a mother's work environment

Culture:

the knowledge, attitudes, beliefs, symbolic representations, and behaviours associated with a group of people.

Ecological theory:

a theory of development that views the child as embedded in a series of complex and interactive systems.

Culture involves the knowledge, attitudes, beliefs, symbols, and behaviours of a group of people.

Wong Sze Fei/Fotolia

Lev Vygotsky

SPUTNIK/Alamy Stock Photo

Urie Bronfenbrenner

AP Images

Figure 1–1 In Bronfenbrenner's theory, the microsystem, the mesosystem, and the exosystem are different environmental systems embedded in the macrosystem, which is the broader cultural context. The chronosystem refers to the time and era in which development occurs.

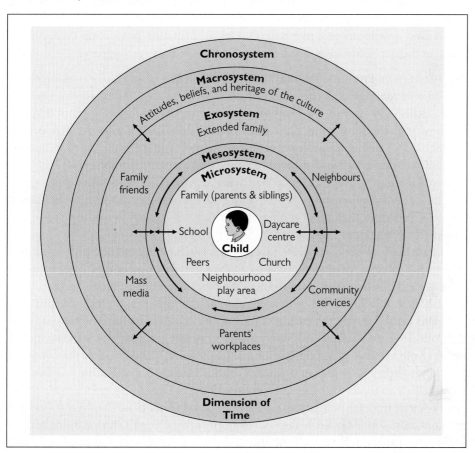

is part of her child's exosystem because she might pay more attention to her child when her work is going well and less attention when she's under work-related stress. Although the influence of the exosystem is second-hand, its effects on the developing child can be strong.

The broadest environmental context is the macrosystem, which includes the subcultures and cultures in which the microsystem, mesosystem, and exosystem are embedded. A mother, her workplace, her child, and the child's school are part of a larger cultural setting, such as Acadian families living in the Maritimes or Jamaican immigrants living in Toronto. Members of these cultural groups share a common identity, a common heritage, and common values. The macrosystem constantly changes because cultures are dynamic and constantly changing. Thus, every generation develops in its own macrosystem. The chronosystem emphasizes that development takes place over time and during certain eras. Changes in children or their environments during development can alter the child's experiences as well as how development progresses over time.

Bronfenbrenner and other contextual theorists would agree with learning theorists that the environment shapes children's development. However, the contextual theorist would insist that "environment" means much more than reinforcements and observations central to learning theory. The contextual theorist would emphasize the different levels of environmental influence on the child beyond the more immediate context of family relationships.

Newer Approaches to Child Development

LO7 **Explain recent approaches to the study of child development.**

In addition to the theories just discussed, some newer approaches in developmental psychology have arisen: in particular, information-processing theory, evolutionary theory, and developmental psychopathology. Information-processing theory is the oldest of these in terms of its research development within the discipline.

INFORMATION-PROCESSING THEORY.   Unlike Piaget, not all theorists interested in children's cognition view development as a series of stages. Information-processing theorists draw heavily on the example of how computers work to explain thinking and how it changes over time. Just as computers consist of hardware (disk drives, random-access memory, and a central processing unit) and software (the programs we use), information-processing theorists propose that human cognition consists of mental hardware and software. **Mental hardware** refers to cognitive structures, including memories and where they are stored. **Mental software** includes organized sets of cognitive processes that allow children to perform tasks, such as reading a sentence, playing the piano, or hitting a softball.

Using the example of computers, we can explain how information-processing psychologists explain developmental change in thinking. Today's personal computers can accomplish much more than those built in the 1950s due to better hardware (e.g., more memory and a faster central processing unit) and more sophisticated software (e.g., spell checkers). Like more advanced computers, adolescents have better hardware and software than younger children, who are more like last year's out-of-date model. For example, older children can often solve math word problems better than younger ones because they have greater memory capacity to store the facts of the problem and because their methods for performing arithmetic operations are more efficient.

For both information-processing and Piagetian theorists, children's thinking becomes more sophisticated as they develop. However, Piaget's work is a single, comprehensive theory, whereas information processing represents a general approach based on various research findings about specific components of cognitive development. The advantage of Piaget's work is that it is comprehensive and offers a theoretically consistent understanding of how development occurs. The advantage of the information-processing approach is that specific components of cognition are described with great precision. Whereas Piaget emphasized the "whole" of cognitive development, information-processing theorists emphasize the "parts." Both views are important for complete understanding of cognitive development.

Another difference between the two approaches is that Piaget emphasized qualitative change in cognition, believing that children's thinking remained at one stage for years and then changed abruptly as it moved into the next stage. In contrast, changes in information-processing ability typically produce a steady increase in cognitive skill. Information-processing approaches focus on cognitive change as continuous and gradual, implying a focus on quantitative change rather than qualitative change. Qualitative change refers to change in type or essence (quality), whereas quantitative change refers to change in amount or value (quantity). As both types of change occur in development, Piagetian and information-processing theory complement each other. In fact, some researchers have attempted to combine the two theories in an effort to come up with stronger cognitive-developmental theories.

EVOLUTIONARY THEORY.   As you read earlier, attachment theory grew out of biologists' attempts to understand how animal behaviour promoted survival from an evolutionary perspective. Evolutionary theory itself is not new; however, its use is relatively new in psychology (Bjorklund & Pellegrini, 2000). The central idea in evolutionary theory in terms of child development is that evolution shapes which behaviours and characteristics contribute most to the survival of infants and children and,

Mental hardware:

cognitive structures, including memories and where they are stored.

Mental software:

organized sets of cognitive processes, such as reading.

consequently, the survival of humanity (Bjorklund & Pellegrini, 2000). For example, Martin Smith (1991), developmental researcher at the University of Victoria, has been studying the evolutionary value of grandchild–grandparent relationships as a kind of investment in the survival of one's own kin. This new approach to understanding child development has been called **evolutionary developmental psychology**. Bjorklund and Pellegrini (2000) emphasized the importance of having a unified perspective in psychology, and they described evolutionary theory as one possible overarching approach, or metatheory, to unite the various subfields within developmental psychology and psychology in general.

Bjorklund and Pellegrini pointed out that evolutionary theory has become the organizing theory for study in the biological sciences, and some areas of developmental psychology include the study of the relationship between genetics and behaviour. Evolutionary psychologists argue that it is adaptive for caregivers to look after their children and help them survive, and they study how children's behaviour helps them adapt on a daily basis.

DEVELOPMENTAL PSYCHOPATHOLOGY.   All of the approaches discussed so far in this chapter have focused on normal aspects of child development. However, an area of psychology concerned with children's atypical development has arisen. Like evolutionary theory, **developmental psychopathology** attempts to present a broad, unified understanding of how abnormal development can occur. Eric Mash, from the University of Calgary, and David Wolfe, from the University of Western Ontario, are proponents of developmental psychopathology. They view development as a dynamic process that involves continual reorganization and transformation during a person's lifespan (Mash & Wolfe, 2002). As children age, their development becomes increasingly differentiated and integrated into complex and hierarchical networks that are influenced by a multitude of factors. From a developmental psychopathology perspective, many different variables have a role in shaping outcomes of development, including both biological-genetic and environmental variables.

Although developmental psychopathology focuses on how abnormalities in development can occur, abnormal development cannot be understood without also understanding what is normal. Developmental psychopathology researchers try to differentiate between what is normal and abnormal from biological, social, emotional, and intellectual perspectives. However, developmental psychopathology is not just a child-development theory; it also includes a focus on diagnosis and treatment of psychological disorders. Therefore, a psychologist would require clinical training before becoming fully competent in this area.

Evolutionary developmental psychology: an approach to developmental psychology using evolutionary theory as a metatheory of human development in an attempt to have psychologists agree on a unified perspective of humanity.

Developmental psychopathology: a theory of child development that tries to explain how abnormal development occurs within a view of development as a dynamic process involving continual transformation during the lifespan.

The Big Picture

LO8 Identify where you can read more about the history of psychology.

Comparing so many major perspectives in these few pages is like trying to see all the major sights of a large city in one day. If you dwell too much or too little in any one area, you could end up with an incomplete or biased impression of how psychology has developed historically. The summary in Table 1–3, Characteristics of Developmental Perspectives, gives you a capsule account of all eight perspectives.

Some of the best work in the theory and history of psychology has been done by Canadian psychologists. If you want to read more broadly in this area, you might consider perusing the journal *Theory and Psychology*, which is produced out of the University of Calgary and publishes articles from scholars all over the world. Psychologists in Canada particularly noted for their writings include Charles Tolman (Victoria), John Mills (British Columbia), Leendert Mos (Alberta), Christopher Green (York), and Henderikus Stam (Calgary). Other Canadian psychologists have made significant contributions to our understanding of theory and history in psychology, contributing to

Table 1–3 Summary Table

Characteristics of Developmental Perspectives		
Biological	Development is determined primarily by biological forces.	Maturational theory: emphasizes development as a natural unfolding of a biological plan. Ethological: emphasizes the adaptive nature of behaviour and the importance of experience during critical periods of development.
Psychodynamic	Development is determined primarily by how a child resolves conflicts at different ages.	Freud: emphasizes the conflict between primitive biological forces and societal standards for right and wrong. Erikson: emphasizes the challenges posed by the formation of trust, autonomy, initiative, industry, and identity.
Learning	Development is determined primarily by a child's environment.	Skinner: emphasizes the role of reinforcement and punishment in response to behaviour. Bandura: emphasizes children's efforts to understand their world, using reinforcement, punishment, and others' behaviour.
Cognitive-Developmental	Development reflects children's efforts to understand the world.	Piaget: emphasizes the different stages of thinking that result from children's changing theories of the world.
Contextual	Development is influenced by immediate and more distant environments, which typically influence each other.	Vygotsky: emphasizes the role of parents (and other adults) in conveying culture to the next generation. Bronfenbrenner: emphasizes the influences of the microsystem, mesosystem, exosystem, macrosystem, and chronosystem.
Information-Processing	Development is understood by analogy to the workings of a computer, with mental hardware and software as well as input and output processes.	Information-processing theory: emphasizes changes in thinking that reflect changes in mental hardware and mental software. No unified theory exists, but a variety of individual models have been proposed by a number of researchers.
Evolutionary Theory	Development is influenced by the process of evolution, which favours characteristics of children that have value to the survival of the species.	Bjorklund and Pellegrini: emphasize evolutionary theory as a possible unifying metatheory uniting various subfields within developmental psychology as well as psychology in general. Martin Smith: emphasizes the survival value of relationships between grandparents and grandchildren.
Developmental Psychopathology	Developmental outcome is shaped by many different variables, including both biological-genetic and environmental factors.	Mash and Wolfe: emphasize dynamic transformation throughout the lifespan and focus on how abnormal development can occur.

an important base of learning in the discipline. In addition, several noted Canadian psychologists sit on the editorial board for the American Psychological Association's journal *History of Psychology*, which is also an important resource.

As we mentioned at the beginning of this module, some of these theories are no longer considered valid as comprehensive theories of development. Nevertheless, they have all been invaluable in fostering research that led psychologists to formulate modern theories. For example, few psychologists today believe that Piaget's theory provides the definitive account of changes in children's thinking. Even so, this theory forms the foundation for a number of modern theories, including theories about infants' understanding of objects and preschoolers' theory of mind, and it has spawned neo-Piagetian research on development. Similarly, Erikson's theory has become less prominent in research but has contributed to work on mother–infant attachment and formation of identity during adolescence.

These examples reflect a common trend in theories of child development. Classic developmental theories were very broad, attempting to account for development across a wide age range and a variety of different phenomena. For the most part, this approach has given way to theories that account for much more restricted phenomena, usually across a narrower age range (e.g., understanding of objects in infancy and identity formation in adolescence). In general, this shift produces theories that are more precise in the sense that they are more likely to produce specific, testable hypotheses. What's lost in the change, of course, is breadth: Modern theories are less likely to make connections between different phenomena.

Throughout this text, we describe modern theories that are derived from the various perspectives listed in Table 1–3, Characteristics of Developmental Perspectives, because no single perspective provides a truly complete explanation of all aspects of children's development. Theories from the cognitive-developmental perspective are useful for understanding how children's cognition changes as they grow older. Theories from the contextual and learning perspectives are particularly valuable in explaining how environmental forces such as parents, peers, schools, and culture influence children's development. By drawing upon all the perspectives, we'll be better able to understand the different forces that contribute to children's development. Just as you can better appreciate a beautiful painting by examining it from different viewpoints, developmental researchers often rely upon multiple perspectives to understand why children develop as they do.

Ask Yourself

Freud and Piaget both proposed stage theories of children's development. Although the theories differed in emphasis— Freud was concerned with psychosexual growth and Piaget was concerned with cognitive growth—can you see similarities in their approaches to development?

1.2 Themes in Child-Development Research

 Learning Objectives

After reading the module, you should be able to do the following:

LO9 Demonstrate how well developmental outcomes can be predicted from early life.

LO10 Understand how heredity and environment influence development.

LO11 Specify what role children have in their own development.

LO12 State how development in different domains is connected.

Several fundamental themes occur in child-development research and form the focus of this module. These themes provide a foundation you can use to organize the many specific facts about child development that fill this text. Four themes will help you unify your own understanding of child development. Also, every chapter ends with Critical Review questions that will help you link topics, themes, and theories across age ranges.

Here are the four unifying themes.

Early Development Is Related to Later Development but Not Perfectly

LO9 Demonstrate how well developmental outcomes can be predicted from early life.

This theme has to do with the "predictability" of development. Do you believe that happy, cheerful 5-year-olds remain outgoing and friendly throughout their lives? If you do, this shows that you believe development is a continuous process. According to this view, once a child begins going down a particular developmental pathway, he or she stays on that path throughout life. In other words, if a child is friendly and smart at age 5, that child should be friendly and smart at ages 15 and 25. The other view, however, is that development is not continuous. According to this view, a child might be friendly and smart at age 5, obnoxious and foolish at 15, and quiet but wise at 25! Thus, the continuity versus discontinuity issue is really about the "connectedness" of development: Are early aspects of development consistently related to later aspects?

In reality, neither of these views is accurate. Development is not perfectly predictable. A friendly, smart child does not guarantee a friendly, smart adolescent or adult, but the chances of a friendly, smart adult are greater than if the child were obnoxious and foolish. There are many ways to become a friendly and smart 15-year-old; being a friendly and smart 5-year-old is not a required step, but it is probably the most direct route!

Development Is Always Jointly Influenced by Heredity and Environment

LO10 Understand how heredity and environment influence development.

We'll introduce this theme with a story about Robert Kail's sons. Ben, Robert's first son, was a delightful baby and toddler. He awoke each morning with a smile on his face, eager to start another fun-filled day. When Ben was upset, which occurred infrequently, he was quickly consoled by being held or rocked. Robert presumed that his son's cheerful disposition must reflect fabulous parenting. Consequently, he was stunned when his second son, Matt, spent much of his first year being fussy and cranky. He was easily irritated and hard to soothe. Why wasn't the all-star parenting that had been so effective with Ben working with Matt? The answer, of course, is that parenting wasn't the sole cause of Ben's happiness. Robert thought environmental influences (i.e., parenting) accounted for Ben's amiable disposition, but in fact, biological influences (i.e., genetics) also played an important role.

This anecdote illustrates the nature–nurture issue: What roles do biology (nature) and environment (nurture) play in child development? If a child is outgoing and friendly, is it due to heredity or experiences in the world? Scientists once hoped to answer questions like this by identifying either heredity or environment as the cause. Their goal was to be able to say, for example, that intelligence was due to heredity or that personality was due to experience. In his years at the University of Toronto around the turn of the twentieth century, Baldwin advanced the idea that development is jointly influenced by nature and nurture. Today we know that Baldwin was correct in that virtually no aspects of child development are due exclusively to either heredity or environment. Instead, development is always shaped by both—nature and nurture interact. In fact, a major aim of developmental research is to understand how heredity and environment jointly determine children's development. Biology will be more influential in some areas and environment in others.

Children Help Determine Their Own Development

LO11   Specify what role children have in their own development.

When teaching child development, we sometimes ask students about their ideas for child-rearing. It's interesting to hear students' responses. Many have big plans for their future children. It's just as interesting, though, to watch students who already have children roll their eyes in a "You don't have a clue" way at what the others are saying. The students in class who are parents admit that they too once had grand designs about child-rearing. What they quickly learned, however, was that their children help shape the way in which they parent.

These two points of view illustrate the active–passive child issue: Are children simply at the mercy of the environment (passive child) or do children actively influence their own development through their unique individual characteristics (active child)? The passive view corresponds to Locke's description of the child as a blank slate on which experience writes, whereas the active view corresponds to Rousseau's view of development as a natural unfolding that takes place within the child. Today we know that experiences are indeed crucial, but not always in the way Locke envisioned. Often it's a child's interpretation of experience that has an important impact on shaping development. From birth, children try to make sense of their world; in the process, they help shape their own futures.

In addition, the unique characteristics of children contribute to the experiences they have with others. The parent–child relationship is a complex interplay of dynamics that are continually affected by the personalities and experiences of the people within the relationship. On the one hand, a highly defiant child might encourage a parent to become more authoritarian. On the other hand, a highly authoritarian parent might encourage defiance in a child. People are also able to affect each other in positive ways, creating warm, supportive, and loving relationships that nurture growth.

How would defiance affect parental behaviour in the future?

Jupiterimages/Pixland/Thinkstock/Getty Images

Development in Different Domains Is Connected

LO12   State how development in different domains is connected.

Developmental researchers usually examine different domains or areas of development, such as physical growth, cognition, language, personality, and social relationships. One researcher might study how children learn to speak grammatically; another might explore children's reasoning about moral issues. Of course, each aspect of development is not an independent entity completely separate from the others. On the contrary, development in different domains is always interconnected. For example, advances in cognitive development can affect social development. As children grow cognitively (e.g., advance in knowledge and learning strategies), their social development also changes (e.g., they make friends with children who share common interests with them).

Now that you've read about the four major themes in child development research, let's review them before we move on.

- Continuity: Early development is related to later development but not perfectly.
- Nature and nurture: Development is always jointly influenced by heredity and environment.
- Active child: Children help determine their own development.
- Connections: Development in different domains is connected.

Most child psychologists would agree that these are important general themes in children's development. However, in the same way that lumber, bricks, pipe, and wiring can be used to assemble an incredible variety of homes, these themes show up in many ways in the major theories of child development.

Think, for example, about the nature–nurture issue. Of the many perspectives presented here, the biological perspective is at one extreme, emphasizing the impact of nature; at the other extreme are the learning and contextual perspectives emphasizing nurture.

The perspectives also take into account different degrees of connectedness across different domains of development. Piaget's cognitive-developmental theory takes the hardest line: Because children strive to have a single integrated theory to explain the world, cognitive and social growth are closely interconnected. The learning perspective, in contrast, holds that the degree of connectedness depends entirely on the nature of environmental influences. Similar environmental influences in different domains of children's lives produce many connections; dissimilar environmental influences would produce few connections. The developmental psychopathology perspective maintains that everything is interconnected and affects everything else.

Ask Yourself

How might parents respond differently to a very active child compared to a very quiet child?

What might cause parents and children to develop negative interactions with each other?

not want to co-operate with your research procedures. What would you do in this circumstance? To whom are you most responsible in the study, and what are your ethical duties with regard to child assent?

What Would a Researcher Do?

Imagine you are studying children's attitudes toward sports. You have the consent of a child's parents, but the child does

Summary

1.1 Theories of Child Development

- Theories are important because they provide the explanations for development and hypotheses for research.

Canada's Unique Contribution

- James Mark Baldwin started the first psychological lab in Canada and developed important theoretical ideas about children's development.

- Traditionally, five broad theoretical perspectives have guided researchers: biological, psychodynamic, learning, cognitive-developmental, and contextual.

The Biological Perspective

- Biological factors are critical in shaping development.

- In maturational theory, child development reflects a natural unfolding of a prearranged biological plan.

- In ethological theory, children's behaviour often has survival value (is adaptive).

The Psychodynamic Perspective

- Developed by Freud, the psychodynamic perspective emphasized the role of unconscious conflict in development.

- The id, ego, and superego form the structure of personality.

- The different psychosexual stages of development focus on physical pleasure through different erogenous zones of the body.

- Erikson proposed an offshoot psychodynamic theory of psychosocial development consisting of eight stages, each characterized by a particular psychosocial struggle.

The Learning Perspective

- Learning theory focuses on observable behaviour rather than cognition or the unconscious.

- Operant conditioning is based on the idea that behaviours are shaped by events that occur after them.

- Social cognitive theorists focus on behaviour and cognition, proposing that people learn by interacting with and observing others as well as actively interpreting the events they observe.

The Cognitive-Developmental Perspective

- In Piagetian theory, children cognitively create their own theories to explain how the world works.

- Development occurs via maturation and a combination of both qualitative and quantitative change.

The Contextual Perspective

- Vygotsky emphasized the role of culture and social learning in children's development.

- Bronfenbrenner proposed that development occurs in the context of interconnected systems: the microsystem, mesosystem, exosystem, macrosystem, and chronosystem.

Newer Approaches to Child Development

- Three new approaches to the study of child development are information-processing theory, evolutionary theory, and developmental psychopathology.

- Information-processing theory is based on a computer model of human cognition in which memory is like "mental hardware" and cognitive processes are like "mental software."

- Evolutionary theorists believe that, through the process of evolution, behaviours and characteristics of infants and children have been developed because of their value to the survival of the child and the entire species.

- Developmental psychopathology theorists see development as a dynamic and hierarchical process that involves continual reorganization and transformation across a person's lifespan, with all variables affecting all other variables.

1.2 Themes in Child-Development Research

- Four themes help unify the findings from developmental research that are presented throughout this text.

- Theme 1: Early development is related to later development but not perfectly; research supports the view that development is not completely rigid as in the continuous pathway view, nor is it completely flexible as in the discontinuous/changing pathways view.

- Theme 2: Development is always jointly influenced by heredity and environment; scientists view heredity and environment as interactive forces that both influence development.

- Theme 3: Children help determine their own development; modern scientists believe that children constantly interpret their own experiences and, through their individual characteristics, also influence the experiences they have.

- Theme 4: Development in different domains is connected; cognitive, physical, social, and emotional development affect each other.

Chapter Critical Review

1. Discuss the advantages and disadvantages of grand theories versus smaller-scale theories of development. Give an example of a research question for which each type of theory might be most useful.

2. Discuss the two psychodynamic theories presented in Module 1.1 in terms of the continuity–discontinuity theme.

3. Discuss the various learning theories presented in Module 1.1 in terms of the active–passive theme.

4. Compare and contrast Piaget's cognitive theory with information-processing theory. Explain how each theory would explain a specific activity, such as a 1-year-old who repeatedly drops a spoon over the side of a high chair.

5. Describe three new approaches in developmental psychology.

See for Yourself

One good way to see how children influence their own development is to interview parents who have more than one child. Ask them whether they used the same child-rearing methods with each child or different techniques with each. If they used different techniques, find out why. You should see that, although parents try to be consistent in a general philosophy for rearing their children, many of the specific parenting techniques will vary from one child to the next, reflecting the children's influence on the parents. See for yourself!

Chapter 2
Research in Child Development

 MODULE

2.1 Doing Child-Development Research

2.2 Child-Development Research and Family Policy

Connect to My Virtual Child

How much of your child's personality is inherited through genetics, and how much comes from the environment? How will your parenting decisions affect your child's development? What decisions would you make when it comes to raising a newborn? Use your access card and follow this link www.myvirtualchild.com to learn more about the world of the child. You can even virtually try to raise your own child.

Mabel and Terry started taking the idea of having a baby more seriously. They began reading about best ways to plan for starting a family. As they read through various books and magazines and watched endless shows about having a baby, they came across more perspectives and "expert advice" than they could have imagined. They found themselves starting to feel overwhelmed by the amount of information available and began to question what kinds of information about babies and child development were reliable.

2.1 Doing Child-Development Research

 ## Learning Objectives

After reading the module, you should be able to do the following:

LO1 Discuss how scientists measure topics of interest in children's development.

LO2 List what general research designs are used in child-development research and note which designs are unique to child-development research.

LO3 Describe common methods for studying development.

LO4 Detail what ethical procedures researchers must follow.

LO5 Understand how researchers communicate results to other scientists.

Child-development researchers must make several important decisions as they prepare to study a topic. They decide how to measure the topic of interest; they design their study; they ensure their proposed research respects the rights of participants; and, once the study is complete, they share their results with others. These steps are not done in one order: Researchers often must consider all aspects of research at once or move back and forth between these steps until they have met all necessary criteria. For simplicity, however, we will discuss each step in sequence.

Measurement in Child-Development Research

LO1 **Discuss how scientists measure topics of interest in children's development.**

Like other sciences, child-development research depends upon important tools. Researchers must decide how to measure the relationship or behaviour they want to study. Questions about relationships between people are one of the most important types of questions psychologists can ask (Perlman, 2007). Child-development researchers typically use one of three approaches: observing systematically, using tasks to sample behaviour, and directly asking children or others (e.g., parents, teachers) for information.

SYSTEMATIC OBSERVATION. As the name implies, **systematic observation** involves watching children and carefully recording what they do or say. Two forms of systematic observation are common. In **naturalistic observation**, children are observed as they behave spontaneously in some real-life situation. Of course,

Systematic observation:

a research technique that involves watching and carefully recording what people do or say.

Naturalistic observation:

a research technique that involves observing people in real-life situations and recording data about their behaviour based on certain predetermined variables of interest for study.

researchers can't keep track of everything that a child does. They must decide ahead of time which **variables**—factors subject to change—to record. They also must decide how often during an observation session a record of behaviour should be made. In her writings about the education of young children, Maria Montessori emphasized the importance of systematic observation of young children's behaviour. She proposed that early childhood educators use principles of systematic observation in the classroom in order to come to understand the children well and to be able to then

Variables:

factors of interest that researchers study that are subject to change under various research conditions.

offer the kinds of experiences and activities that would most benefit them (Fell, 2000). In a recent publication regarding early childhood education, the Government of New Zealand recognized systematic observation of children as a best practice (Farquhar, 2003).

In **structured observation**, the researcher creates a setting that is likely to elicit the behaviour of interest. Structured observations are particularly useful for studying behaviours that are difficult to observe naturally. Some phenomena occur rarely, such as emergencies. An investigator using natural observations to study children's responses to emergencies wouldn't make much progress because emergencies usually happen unpredictably. However, using structured observation, an investigator could set up a situation and watch how children respond to it, as long as that situation is ethical and does not endanger the children in any way.

Naturalistic observation occurs in a child's regular environment.

Structured observation:

a research technique that involves creating a setting or circumstances designed to bring about certain behaviours of interest for study.

Other behaviours are difficult for researchers to observe because they occur in private settings, such as the behaviour between siblings in a family home. However, siblings could be asked to come to the researcher's lab, where they would be asked to perform some activity typical of siblings, such as playing a game or deciding what movie to see. By observing siblings' interactions, perhaps through one-way glass, researchers could learn more about how siblings interact. Although structured observations allow researchers to observe behaviours that would otherwise be difficult to study, investigators must be careful that the settings they create do not alter the behaviour of interest or expose participants to undue risk.

In her classic work on the study of mother–child attachment, Mary Ainsworth (Ainsworth & Wittig, 1969) used a structured observation technique called the Strange Situation. Using this technique, researchers would document children's reactions to being left alternately with mother, a stranger, alone, and then with mother again. At each step in the procedure, researchers would document the child's response to change. This research led to a classification system for children's attachment behaviours.

SAMPLING BEHAVIOUR WITH TASKS. When investigators can't observe a behaviour directly, an alternative is to create tasks that are thought to sample the behaviour of interest. For example, to measure children's ability to differentiate emotions, investigators sometimes use the task shown in Figure 2–1. The child has been asked to look at the photographs and point to the person who is happy. To measure working memory, investigators sometimes use a digit-span task. Children listen as a sequence of numbers is spoken aloud, about one per second. After the last digit is presented, children are asked to repeat the digits in order. Sometimes

In a structured observation of play, the adult observer usually records play behaviours on a form according to certain objectives or time periods.

Figure 2–1

children are asked to repeat the digits in reverse order. This task is thought to demonstrate a child's capacity for short-term memory and attention.

Sampling behaviour with tasks is popular in child-development research because of its convenience. A major problem, however, is the extent to which the task samples the actual behaviour of interest. **Ecological validity** is the degree to which conclusions from research can inform us about behaviour in real-life situations. For example, asking children to judge emotions from photographs might not be valid because photos do not contain all of the same types of emotional cues that real-life circumstances contain. In real life, facial features are usually moving, and movement might be one of the clues children use to judge emotions. Also, facial expressions often are accompanied by sounds, which can be clues to emotion. Finally, children often judge expressions of people they know (e.g., parents). Knowing the "usual" appearance of a face can help children judge emotions more accurately.

SELF-REPORTS. The third common approach to measurement—asking directly—is actually a special case of using tasks to measure children's behaviour. **Self-reports** are simply people's thoughts or ideas about questions related to a topic of interest. Questions also can be posed to other people who know the child, such as parents, teachers, or daycare providers. When questions are posed in written form, the format is a questionnaire; when questions are posed orally, the format is an interview. In either format, questions are created that probe different aspects of the topic of interest. For example, if you believe that children more often become friends when they have interests in common, then research participants might be told the following:

> Ted and Dave just met each other at school. Ted likes reading science fiction, playing clarinet, and practising for the rodeo with his palomino horse. Dave likes watching MuchMusic, playing video games, and getting out on the field with his soccer team. Do you think Ted and Dave will become friends?

Children would be asked to decide, perhaps using a rating scale, if the boys are likely to become friends.

Self-reports are useful because they can lead directly to information on the topic of interest. They are also relatively convenient and often can be administered to groups. However, self-reports are not always valid measures of children's behaviour because people's answers are sometimes inaccurate. For example, an adolescent asked about childhood friends might not remember those friendships well. Also, people sometimes answer incorrectly due to a response bias; that is, some responses might be more socially acceptable than others, and people are more likely to select those than socially unacceptable answers. For example, children might be reluctant to admit that they have no friends at all. Caregivers can provide biased responses as well, perhaps exaggerating children's accomplishments or problems. In addition, research participants

Ecological validity:

the degree to which conclusions from research can provide information about behaviour in real-life situations.

Self-reports:

questionnaires that elicit people's thoughts or ideas about a topic of interest for study.

Table 2–1 Ways of Measuring Behaviour in Child-Development Research

Method	Strength	Weakness
Systematic Observation		
Naturalistic Observation	Captures children's behaviour in its natural setting	Difficult to use with behaviours that are rare or private
Structured Observation	Can be used to study behaviours that are rare or private	May be invalid if the structured setting distorts the behaviour
Sampling Behaviour with Tasks	Convenient: can be used to study most behaviours	May be invalid if the task does not sample behaviour as it occurs naturally
Self-Reports (Written Questionnaires or Interviews)	Convenient: can be used to study most behaviours	May be invalid because respondents answer incorrectly due to forgetting, demand characteristics, or bias

sometimes try to read situational cues in order to determine how the researcher wants them to respond. These situational cues are referred to as **demand characteristics**, and they sometimes lead research participants to provide the "correct" answer or response to a research question or situation (Orne, 1962). As long as investigators keep these weaknesses in mind and sample information from more than one type of source, self-reports can be a valuable tool for child-development research.

The three approaches to measurement are summarized in Table 2–1.

After researchers choose a method of measurement, they must show that it is both reliable and valid (DeVellis, 1991). A measure is **reliable** if the results are consistent over time. A measure of friendship, for example, would be reliable to the extent that it yields the same results about friendship each time it is administered. All measures used in child-development research must be shown to be reliable or they cannot be used. A measure is **valid** if conclusions based on the measure actually mean what the researcher hypothesized they would mean. For example, conclusions based on a measure of friendship are valid only if it can be shown that the researcher measured friendship and not, for example, popularity (e.g., Brodeur, Mercier, Dussault, Deaudelin, & Richer, 2006).

Many different kinds of statistical validity exist. However, **convergent validity** is often established by showing that the measure in question is closely related to another measure known to be valid. Researchers sometimes also look for **divergent validity**, in which the validity of a measure is compared with that of one measuring the exact opposite of a variable. For example, if the researcher is using a test of anxiety in a study, the researcher might be satisfied if (1) a positive correlation existed between the study's measure and scores on another valid measure of anxiety, and (2) a negative correlation existed between scores on the study's measure and another valid measure of emotional stability or wellness. Because it is possible to have a measure that is reliable but not valid, researchers must ensure that their measures are both reliable and valid. For example, a tape measure might be a reasonably reliable measure of a child's physical height, but as a measure of friendship, it would not be valid. Friendship can't be measured in centimetres, but it could be measured by observation of play or through a self-report questionnaire.

Throughout this text, you'll come across many studies using these different methods. You'll also see that studies of the same topic or behaviour often use different methods. Many topics can be studied in different ways. Because the approaches to measurement have different strengths and weaknesses, finding the same results regardless of the approach leads to particularly strong conclusions. Suppose, for example, that a researcher using self-reports claimed that arguments are more common in boys' friendships than in girls' friendships. It would be reassuring if other investigators found the same result from systematic observation and from sampling behaviour with tasks.

Demand characteristics:
situational cues that suggest to a research participant how a researcher wants the participant to respond.

Reliability:
statistical information about the degree to which a measure yields consistent results over time.

Validity:
statistical information about the degree to which conclusions based on a measure actually mean what a researcher hypothesized they would mean.

Convergent validity:
statistical information about the degree to which a measure yields results that are theoretically similar to and positively correlated with another well-established measure of the same variable.

Divergent validity:
statistical information about the degree to which a measure yields results that are theoretically different from and negatively correlated with another well-established measure of an opposite variable.

Population:

the set or group of all people from which a sample is drawn in a research study.

Sample:

a subgroup of a population who participates in a study. Results based on the sample are generalized to the entire population if the sample is representative of that population.

North American samples may not adequately represent children from developing nations.

REPRESENTATIVE SAMPLING. Valid measures depend not only upon the method of measurement but also upon the children who are tested. Researchers are usually interested in broad groups of children called **populations**. Examples of populations would be all British Columbia 7-year-olds or all Korean adolescents. However, it would be extremely difficult for researchers to study every member of such large groups. Virtually all studies include only a **sample** of children, which is a subset of the population. Researchers must take care that their sample actually is representative of the population of interest. An unrepresentative sample can lead to invalid research. For example, what would you think about a study of Grade 3 friendships if you learned that the sample consisted of only 8-year-olds who had no friends? You would, quite correctly, decide that this sample is not representative of the population of 8-year-olds, and you would question its results. In addition, Sharp, Pelletier, and Lévesque (2006) found that, in some cases, offering a reward to study participants can increase both the size and the representativeness of a study's sample.

The issue of population sampling is very important in Canadian psychological research because Canada is a very socially diverse and geographically large country. What seems to be true for a sample of children from Ontario or Quebec might not be true, or might be only partially true, for a sample of children from Manitoba or Yukon. Each region in Canada has different population characteristics and a different settlement history. Available services, as well as provincial regulations and laws, vary greatly from province to province, particularly for important issues such as daycare, education, and health care. We cannot assume that the living circumstances of children across Canada are the same. Great differences also exist in terms of access to services and standard of living from province to province, making some research studies applicable only to the region in which the study occurred (Williams, Zolner, Bertrand, & Davis, 2004). In addition, significant differences exist for children living in First Nations and Inuit communities. Therefore, in order to achieve research findings that truly have national implications, the sample should be drawn from a national pool of participants. In some cases, attention must be paid to how local circumstances differ, and special studies of unique populations might be necessary. Finally, clinicians and researchers both need to consider the appropriate use of psychological measures in terms of culture, as the usefulness and validity of an instrument can vary depending on cultural and other characteristics of the groups with which a measure is being used (Burns, Walsh, Gomez, & Hafetz, 2006).

As you read on, you'll discover that much of the research we describe was conducted with samples of middle-class youngsters of Western European heritage, and many of the studies were performed in the United States. Are these samples representative of children in Canada? Of children in developing countries? Of Aboriginal children? Not always. In general, you should be careful not to assume that findings from one group necessarily apply to other groups.

General Designs for Research

LO2 List what general research designs are used in child-development research and note which designs are unique to child-development research.

Having selected a way to measure the topic or behaviour of interest, researchers must then put this measure into a research design. Child-development researchers usually use one of two study designs: correlational or experimental.

CORRELATIONAL STUDIES.   In a **correlational study**, investigators look at relations between variables as they exist naturally in the world. In the simplest possible correlational study, a researcher measures two variables to see how they are related. For example, Williams and colleagues (2004) wanted to know the relationship between the frequency of substance use and mental health in adolescents from Alberta. They used a large enough sample of youth to study how developmental period and type of substance used might affect the youths' mental health. They also used certain statistical procedures to determine whether youth who self-reported higher drug and alcohol use also had higher scores on a questionnaire about emotional problems. They found different relationships (correlations) between the level of emotional disorder and the frequency of substance use for the various age groups in the study.

"The research proves tall rats are more confident than short rats. At least I think it does. I've never been good at this."

For example, using data from the 12- to 14-year-old group, the researchers found that adolescents using tobacco, alcohol, or marijuana at least once per week in the previous year had significantly higher scores on the emotional disorder questionnaire than adolescents who never used these substances. For use of cocaine/crack, stimulants, glue/solvents, tranquilizers, and opiates, adolescents using one of these substances at least three times in the previous year had significantly higher scores on the emotional disorder questionnaire than abstainers.

In looking at the correlations between age, substance use, and emotional disorder, these researchers also were able to derive some other interesting findings. For example, they noted that adolescents using marijuana five or fewer times in total or who used alcohol only once or twice on special occasions during the previous year had scores on the emotional disorder questionnaire that did not significantly differ from the scores of abstainers. They also found that adolescents using tobacco less than once per week also had scores that did not differ significantly from those of abstainers.

In addition, when the researchers compared data across age groupings, they were able to see that, unlike the 12- to 14-year-old group, youths 18 and older using tobacco six to seven times per week or alcohol up to three times per week had equivalent scores on the emotional disorders questionnaire to those of abstainers. All of these results were obtained by comparing the statistical correlation between scores on the variables under study, which were emotional problems and age, as well as the type and frequency of substances used.

The results of a correlational study are usually expressed as a **correlation coefficient**, commonly abbreviated r, which stands for the direction and strength of a relationship between two variables. Correlations can range from −1.0 to 0 to +1.0. For example,

Correlational study:
the study of the relationship between variables that naturally coexist in the world.

Correlation coefficient (r):
a numerical, statistical value representing both the direction and the strength of relationship between variables.

- When r equals 0, two variables are completely unrelated: Youth drug use is unrelated to youth's level of emotional disorder.

- When r is greater than 0, scores are positively related: Youth who have higher drug use tend to have higher emotional disorder levels than youth who use drugs less.

- When r is less than 0, scores are inversely related: The higher the drug use, the lower the incidence of emotional health problems for the youth.

When interpreting a correlation coefficient, pay attention to both the sign and the size of the correlation. The sign indicates the direction of the relation between variables: A positive sign means that larger values on one variable are associated with larger values on the second variable. A negative sign means that larger values on one variable are associated with smaller values on a second variable.

The strength of a relation is measured by how much the correlation differs from 0, in either a positive or a negative direction. To determine the strength of a relationship, look at the absolute value of r. Absolute value is the number (r) without the

+ or − sign. If the correlation between drug use and emotional disorder were 9, this would indicate a very strong relation between these variables. Knowing a youth's age and drug use, you might predict reasonably accurately how emotionally disordered the youth might be. A correlation of 3 would indicate a relatively weak link between the variables. Sometimes it is difficult to determine the strength of a correlation. For example, in the substance-use study discussed earlier, the researchers were unable to determine the relationship between the use of hallucinogens and emotional disorder in 12- to 14-year-olds for the simple reason that not enough youth in this age range reported using hallucinogenic substances. If researchers do not have adequate data to make a comparison, then the correlation cannot be computed.

The results of a correlational study reveal whether variables are related, but this research design doesn't address the question of cause and effect between the variables. For example, in discussing limitations of the Alberta substance-use study, the researchers pointed out, "This is a correlational study that says nothing about causal direction. It is only plausible speculation that the relationship between frequent substance use and poor mental health is causally related, or that the association between abstinence and good mental health is due to a common third factor" (Williams et al., 2004).

In other words, the question might be asked whether substance use causes poor mental health or whether poor mental health causes substance use. Alternatively, perhaps another variable affects substance use altogether. The Canadian Centre for Addiction and Mental Health (CAMH) has been tracking substance use by Canadian adolescents for a number of decades. CAMH reported that the greatest amount of substance use by Canadian adolescents, prior to the late 1990s, was in 1979, when one in three Canadian adolescents were estimated to be abusing some kind of substance (Paglia-Boak, Mann, Adlaf, & Rehm, 2009). Perhaps the "drug culture" of the era affected this usage. CAMH research on substance abuse by Canadian adolescents has also shown a decline in the attitude that drug use is harmful, which could have an effect on usage and/or mental health. Also, as Williams and colleagues (2004) pointed out, regional information about substance use might be relevant only to that particular region of the country.

The important point to remember here is that correlation in no way implies causation, as illustrated in Figure 2–2. When investigators want to track down causes, they

Figure 2–2

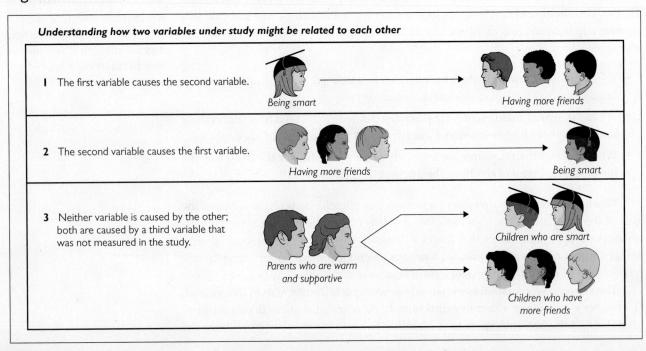

Understanding how two variables under study might be related to each other

1   The first variable causes the second variable.

Being smart   *Having more friends*

2   The second variable causes the first variable.

Having more friends   *Being smart*

3   Neither variable is caused by the other; both are caused by a third variable that was not measured in the study.

Parents who are warm and supportive

Children who are smart

Children who have more friends

must use an experimental study. True experiments in developmental psychology are difficult to conduct because researchers rarely are able to control all variables contributing to a situation. Remember what developmental psychopathology theory says about how all aspects of development are interrelated? Developmental researchers could not possibly control everything. However, random assignment of participants to groups can increase control over some variables and minimize the possibility of bias in research.

Finally, we have to consider what methods are used to compare variables to each other to determine whether significant findings exist. When researchers compare variables to each other, they often use statistical calculations to determine whether measurements of one variable are significantly different from measurements of another variable. For example, if an average of 10 inches of rain falls in June one year and an average of 12 inches of rain falls in June the next year, researchers might compare whether these two averages are significantly different, from a statistical perspective, or whether the two-inch difference actually is within the normally expected parameters for rainfall in that area.

One way that researchers often judge whether a difference is statistically significant is by use of a statistical value called a "p-value." A **p-value** shows the probability of obtaining a particular measurement if, in fact, no real difference existed between the conditions being observed. In more plain language, if we assume that there really is no difference between rainfall averages observed in June, then what is the likelihood that we would have observed these results? If the likelihood is high that we would have observed these results, then p-values will be high. If the likelihood is low that we would have observed these results, then p-values will be low. Researchers looking for significant differences between observations determine that the differences are significant if statistically calculated p-values are low. By low, we usually say that there must be less than a 5 percent chance of obtaining the results that were observed. Some researchers use an even higher standard, declaring that there must be less than a 1 percent chance of obtaining the results that were observed.

Despite their common use in social science research, p-values and similar statistics were banned from publication in the journal *Basic and Applied Social Psychology*. Instead, the editors required researchers to use alternate methods of reporting research findings (Trafimow & Marks, 2015) in articles published in that journal, such as descriptive statistics and effect sizes, rather than inferential statistics, such as p-values. **Descriptive statistics** are basic numerical summaries of data, such as averages or ranges of scores. **Inferential statistics** go beyond a particular set of data in order to *infer* how closely the data in a sample might represent all possible data that could have been collected about the variable being observed. For example, if you take rainfall estimates for a few years, descriptive statistics tells you about the particular data you gathered for the years that you gathered it. Inferential statistics would tell you whether that data is a good sample of all possible years that rainfall could be measured. Inferential statistics uses methods of predication and probability, whereas descriptive statistics merely summarize the actual data gathered. However, not everyone agrees that inferential statistics are the best choice for researchers.

In 2016, the American Statistical Association published a statement on the use of p-values in research (Wasserstein & Lazar, 2016) in which they commented on researchers' overreliance on p-values in drawing conclusions from research findings:

> Cherry-picking promising findings ... leads to spurious excess of statistically significant results in the published literature and should be vigorously avoided. One need not formally carry out multiple statistical tests for this problem to arise: Whenever a researcher chooses what to present based on statistical results, valid interpretation of those results is severely compromised if the reader is not informed of the choice and its basis. Researchers should disclose the number of hypotheses explored during the study, all data collection decisions, all statistical analyses conducted and all p-values computed. Valid

P-value:

the probability of obtaining a particular measurement if, in fact, no real difference existed between the conditions being compared.

Descriptive statistics:

basic numerical summaries of research data.

Inferential statistics:

statistical calculations that go beyond basic description of research data to infer or predict how well the data represents the total population of observations from which data might be gathered.

scientific conclusions based on p-values and related statistics cannot be drawn without at least knowing how many and which analyses were conducted, and how those analyses (including p-values) were selected for reporting. (p. 129–133)

This statement has great implications for psychological research, as many researchers rely on the size of p-values to interpret their findings. When you read articles in the psychological literature, you might note how many of those researchers have relied solely on p-values for interpretation of their results. In future, psychological researchers will need to revise their research methods and focus on other ways to judge the quality of data, not the least of which will be to determine whether their findings can be replicated in other studies and by other researchers. This points us to the higher value of extended programs of research over the publication of any one individual study. Data that is replicated across several studies, methods, and researchers is likely to be much more significant than data that has been observed only once and thought to be significant based on a single inferential statistic such as a p-value.

EXPERIMENTAL STUDIES. An **experiment** is a systematic way of manipulating the key factor(s) that an investigator thinks causes a particular behaviour. The factor that is manipulated is called the **independent variable**; the behaviour that is measured is called the **dependent variable**. In an experiment, the investigator begins with one or more treatments, circumstances, or events (independent variables) that are thought to affect a particular behaviour. Children are then assigned randomly to different experimental conditions. Next, the dependent variable is measured in the group of children experiencing each experimental condition. In experiments, children are randomly assigned to treatment groups, giving each child an equal chance of being assigned to any group. Any differences between the groups can then be attributed to the differential treatment the children received in the experiment rather than to other factors, such as how children were selected for placement in treatment groups. Unlike independent and dependent variables, variables that explain or account for any relationship between independent and dependent variables are called **mediator variables** (Ota Wang & Sue, 2005). For example, parental income might mediate the relationship between geographic location and type of daycare provided to children.

For example, Bigler, Averhart, and Liben (2003) found that children's vocational interests, as well as their perceptions of occupational status, were affected by the racial makeup of the workforce. These researchers sampled African American children in Grades 1 and 6 from a racially diverse school in the American Midwest, half of whom were from upper-middle socio-economic backgrounds and half of whom were from lower socio-economic backgrounds.

First, the researchers interviewed the children about their perceptions of the status of various occupations (some real and some made up by the researchers) as well as their own vocational aspirations. Then the children were randomly assigned to three groups, and each group was shown one of three drawings of workers. In the first drawing, the workers were four African Americans. In the second drawing, the workers were four European Americans. In the third drawing, the workers were two European Americans and two African Americans. Children rated the status of known and invented jobs differently depending on the race of the people portrayed doing the job.

Use of random assignment in this study was a powerful way to demonstrate that children tend to describe jobs predominantly done by European Americans as having higher status than jobs predominately done by African Americans, suggesting that race affects children's judgments about occupational status independently of the effect of the job qualities being portrayed in the drawings. The researchers further concluded that this was not an effect solely based on stereotyping because, when asked who "should" be performing familiar jobs, children tended to say that either African Americans or European Americans should perform any job.

Experiment:

a research method in which variables are systematically manipulated in order to discover the causal effect of one variable on another.

Independent variable:

the variable that is manipulated in a study.

Dependent variable:

the variable in a study that is measured and that changes as a result of the action of the independent variable.

Mediator variable:

a variable that explains or accounts for any relationship observed between an independent and a dependent variable.

Child-development researchers usually conduct their experiments in laboratory-like settings to control all the variables that might influence the outcome of the research. A shortcoming of laboratory work is that the behaviour of interest is not studied in its natural setting. Consequently, the potential problem always exists that the results could be invalid because they are artificial—specific to the laboratory setting and not representative of the behaviour in the "real world."

To avoid this limitation, researchers sometimes rely upon a special type of experiment. In a **field experiment**, the researcher manipulates independent variables in a natural setting so that the results are more likely to be representative of behaviour in real-world settings. To illustrate a field experiment, let's consider the hypothesis that children share more with friends. We might conduct the research in a classroom where students must complete a group assignment. In collaboration with teachers, children are placed in groups of three—in some groups, all three children are good friends; in others, the three children are acquaintances but not friends. When the assignment is complete, the teacher gives each group leader many stickers and tells the leader to distribute them to group members based on how much each child contributed. We predict that leaders will share more (i.e., distribute the stickers more evenly) when group members are friends than when they are not.

Field experiments allow investigators to draw strong conclusions about cause and effect because they embed manipulation of an independent variable in a natural setting. However, field experiments are often impractical to conduct because of logistical problems. In most natural settings, children are supervised by adults (e.g., parents and teachers) who must be willing to become allies in the proposed research. Adults might not want to change their routines to fit a researcher's needs. In addition, researchers usually sacrifice some control in field experiments. In the example of distributing stickers to group members, some children no doubt actually worked harder than others, which means that children's sharing will not be based simply on whether the other children are friends.

Both correlational and experimental research designs have strengths and weaknesses. Consequently, no single investigation can definitely answer a question, and researchers rarely rely on one study or even one method to reach conclusions. Instead, they prefer to find converging evidence from as many different kinds of studies as possible.

Methods for Studying Development

LO3   **Describe common methods for studying development.**

Sometimes child-development research is directed at a single age group, such as Grade 5 children in the experiment on sharing between friends and nonfriends. However, child-development researchers often want to know about how children change as they develop over time. In these cases, investigators must make one further decision: Will the study be longitudinal or cross-sectional?

LONGITUDINAL STUDIES.   In a **longitudinal study**, the same individuals are observed or tested repeatedly at different points in their lives. As the name implies, the longitudinal approach takes a lengthwise view of development and is the most direct way to watch growth occur. As Figure 2–3 shows, in a longitudinal study, children might be tested first at age 6 and then again at ages 9 and 12. The longitudinal approach is well suited to studying almost any aspect of development and is the only way to answer certain questions about the continuity or discontinuity of behaviour. For example, in the Alberta substance-use study discussed earlier, the researchers noted that, based on findings from longitudinal research, substance use tends to be highest in the late teen years, extending somewhat into the early twenties. These researchers also noted that youth who fail to curb their substance use

Field experiment:
a type of experiment in which the independent variable is manipulated in a naturalistic setting.

Longitudinal study:
a type of research study in which the variables of interest are measured in the same research participants repeatedly over time.

Figure 2–3

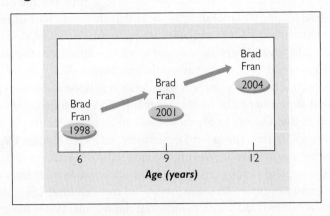

after their early twenties appear to be at higher risk for problems with their mental health. Such research findings can come only as the result of studying a phenomenon over time.

Usually longitudinal studies extend over years, but not always. In a **microgenetic study**, children are tested repeatedly over a span of days or weeks, typically with the aim of observing change directly as it occurs. For example, researchers might test children every week, starting when they are 12 months old and continuing until 18 months. Microgenetic studies are particularly useful when investigators have hypotheses about a specific age when developmental change should occur.

Another longitudinal alternative is the **sequential design**, in which groups of children born in different time periods are studied over time. For example, we might follow a group of 5-year-olds, a group of 10-year-olds, and a group of 15-year-olds over a five-year period, measuring all children in each group on the same variables. This method, in effect, combines the cross-sectional and longitudinal approaches and has important advantages over other methods. First of all, we can learn about something called a **cohort effect**, which is the effect of a particular event, culture, or historical experience on a particular group of children. The reason the sequential design is so powerful is that it enables researchers to compare data across age but also over time.

For example, we might expect that youth growing up in Canada who were 15 in 1995 would react differently if we asked them about their feelings regarding war than would people who were over 75 in 1995. The 15-year-olds would not have had an experience of war during their lives, so they likely would not react the same as the 75-year-olds, who lived through World War II. On the other hand, we might see quite a different result if we were to measure people's attitudes to war and terrorism since the World Trade Center attack in 2001. An event of that magnitude can affect an entire generation—even multiple generations—in terms of the "in" views about international conflict. For example, in recent years, more young people in Canada have been attending Remembrance Day ceremonies, perhaps in recognition that war, international conflict, and the contribution of Canada's veterans are significant to everyone's lives. A sequential design enables researchers to make comparisons between groups across periods of time so that they can tease out these kinds of differences between groups due to the era in which the groups grew up.

Longitudinal approaches, however, have disadvantages that frequently offset their strengths (Block & Block, 2006). If children are given the same test many times, they may become "test-wise." Therefore, improvement observed over time might be due to **practice effects**, or becoming good at doing a test, rather than because of some particular change in development. Changing the test from one session to the next solves the practice problem but raises the question of how to compare responses to different tests. Another problem is the constancy of the sample over the course of

Microgenetic study:

a type of research study in which the variables of interest are measured in the same research participants repeatedly over a short period of time, such as days or weeks, in order to capture an aspect of rapid developmental change.

Sequential design:

a type of research study in which the variables of interest are measured repeatedly over time in the same groups of research participants, with each group having been born in a different time period.

Cohort effect:

the impact of a particular event, culture, or historical experience on a particular group of people.

Practice effect:

becoming "test-wise" and achieving better scores on a test than on previous occasions because of repeated exposure to the test.

Figure 2–4

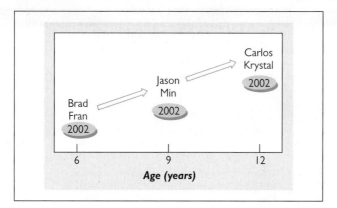

research. It is difficult to maintain contact with children over time in a highly mobile society. Even among those who do not move away, some lose interest and choose not to continue. Loss of participants in a study is called **attrition**. These "dropouts" often differ in significant ways from participants who stay in the study, and this fact alone could distort the outcome. For example, a group of children might seem to show intellectual growth between ages 4 and 7. What might actually have happened, however, is that those who found earlier testing most difficult are the very ones who have quit the study, causing the group average to increase in the next round. Because of these and other problems with the longitudinal method, child-development researchers often use cross-sectional studies instead.

CROSS-SECTIONAL STUDIES.   In a **cross-sectional study**, developmental changes are identified by testing children of different ages at one point in their development. In other words, as shown in Figure 2–4, a researcher might chart the differences in some attribute between, for example, 6-, 9-, and 12-year-olds. The cross-sectional approach avoids almost all the problems associated with repeated testing, including practice effects and attrition (loss of participants over time), but cross-sectional research has its own weaknesses. Because children are tested at only one point in their development, we learn nothing about the continuity of development. Consequently, we cannot tell if an aggressive 4-year-old remains aggressive at age 10, because an individual child would be tested at age 4 or age 10 but not at both ages. You might think that the Alberta substance-use study discussed earlier was a sequential design because it compared multiple groups on a number of variables. However, that study was only cross-sectional in nature, as the samples were taken at one point in time. Because these groups were not studied repeatedly over a series of years, the study was not longitudinal. Measuring a variable in a sample of research participants at one point in time is a cross-sectional study, no matter how many variables or groups are studied at that one point in time.

   Unlike sequential studies, cross-sectional studies are limited by cohort effects, meaning that differences between age groups (cohorts) might result as much from environmental events as from developmental processes. In a simple cross-sectional study, we compare children from two age groups. If we find differences, we attribute them to differences in age because cross-sectional researchers assume that when the older children were younger, they were like children in the younger age group. However, this isn't always true. Suppose, for example, that a researcher measures creativity in 8- and 14-year-olds. If the 8-year-olds are found to be more imaginative than the 14-year-olds, should we conclude that imagination declines between these ages? Not necessarily. Perhaps a new curriculum to nourish creativity was introduced in kindergarten and Grade 1 before the 8-year-olds entered these grades but after the older children had completed them. Because only the younger children experienced the curriculum, the difference between the two groups is difficult to interpret. Even

Attrition:

loss of participants in a study.

Cross-sectional study:

a research study in which a variable of interest is measured at one point in time across persons of different ages or characteristics.

Table 2–2 Designs Used in Child-Development Research

Type of Design	Definition	Strengths	Weaknesses
General Designs Correlational	Observe variables as they exist in the world and determine their relations	Behaviour is measured as it occurs naturally	Cannot determine cause and effect
Experimental	Manipulate independent and dependent variables	Control of variables allows conclusions about cause and effect	Work is often laboratory-based, which can be artificial
Developmental Methods Longitudinal	One group of children is tested repeatedly as they develop	Only way to chart an individual's development and look at the continuity of behaviour over time	Participants drop out, and repeated testing can distort performance
Cross-sectional	Children of different ages are tested at the same time	Convenient, avoids problems associated with longitudinal studies	Cannot study continuity of behaviour; cohort effects complicate interpretation of differences between groups

longitudinal studies can be limited by cohort effects if only one cohort is being studied over a period of time. In this case, because only one cohort is studied, researchers might never realize that their findings are simply the result of a particular cohort's experiences and attitudes rather than a true finding about child development.

Each of the two general research designs can be used with either of the two methods that are unique to studying development. When combined, four prototypical designs result: cross-sectional correlational studies, cross-sectional experimental studies, longitudinal correlational studies, and longitudinal experimental studies. One example of an important longitudinal research study conducted in Canada and with which you should become familiar is the National Longitudinal Survey of Children and Youth (NLSCY), which you can read more about in the following feature, Making Children's Lives Better.

The different designs are summarized in Table 2–2. In this text, you'll read about studies using these various designs, although cross-sectional tends to be used more frequently than longitudinal. Why? For most development researchers, the ease and reduced cost of cross-sectional studies, compared to longitudinal studies, more than compensates for the limitations of the cross-sectional design.

Making Children's Lives Better
Longitudinal Research Conducted on Young People in Canada

A major Canadian research initiative, called the National Longitudinal Survey of Children and Youth (NLSCY, 2008), was undertaken in 1994. The study was initiated jointly by Statistics Canada and Human Resources Development Canada, and it focused on the development and well-being of Canadian children from birth to early adulthood. The NLSCY researchers tracked variables affecting children's emotional, social, and behavioural development over a period of time, including physical development, health, learning, social environment (friends, schools, family, community), and behaviour. Whenever you see the initials NLSCY in this text, remember that the data being discussed are from this particular study.

In this national survey, families from all 10 Canadian provinces as well as the territories were included, with the exception of those living on First Nations reserves, on Crown lands, in institutions, in very remote regions of the country, or who were full-time members of the Canadian Armed Forces. The design of the study is complex, with both longitudinal and cross-sectional sampling occurring. To give a sense of the size of the samples, in the fourth cycle of surveying, the longitudinal sample included approximately 27 000 children, and the cross-sectional sample included approximately 9500 households.

Data collection for this study occurred by computer-assisted telephone interviewing as well as computer-assisted personal interviewing. In both cases, the person having the greatest familiarity with the child was interviewed. Older children completed some aptitude and self-administered questionnaires, and the child's teacher and school principal were also asked to complete questionnaires. More information, as well as survey examples, is available on the project's webpage (www23.statcan.gc.ca/imdb/p2SV.pl?Function=get Survey&SDDS=4450&Item_Id=25609&lang=en).

The NLSCY stands as a unique effort in Canadian history and has already begun to produce a wealth of important information about child and adolescent health and well-being in Canada. While the survey project includes information from the major areas in Canada, it will not be able to provide much information about conditions for youth belonging to groups not sampled (e.g., people living in First Nations communities, military families, families in very remote areas). In addition, because the survey sampling is random, the survey provides a "national average" perspective on the lives of children and youth but not necessarily information about particular cultural groups within the nation. Given that culture is an important aspect of socialization and well-being, national averages are not the best method by which to capture the health and well-being of a particular cultural grouping of people (Zolner, 2003a).

Ethical Responsibilities

LO4 Detail what ethical procedures researchers must follow.

When selecting a way of measuring a behaviour of interest and choosing an appropriate research design, one very important step remains. Researchers must keep an important issue in mind: whether their research plans are ethical and do not violate the rights of the participating children. Under the guidance and direction of Jean Pettifor and Carole Sinclair, the Canadian Psychological Association (CPA) has published the Canadian Code of Ethics for Psychologists, which is available online (www.cpa. ca/aboutcpa/committees/ethics/codeofethics). The code identifies four ethical principles that Canadian psychologists must consider in research and clinical work.

While all of the four principles are important, sometimes they can conflict with each other. A unique feature of CPA's code is that it indicates not just the ethical principles but also the order in which they should be prioritized when a psychologist considers an ethical dilemma. Volume 39, issue number 3 of the CPA journal *Canadian Psychology* is a special issue devoted to the historical development of the CPA code, as well as some of its unique features, and is worth having a look at in some detail. Table 2–3 summarizes the CPA code's four principles.

Most professional organizations and government agencies have codes of conduct that specify the rights of research participants and procedures to protect those participants. The following guidelines typically are included in all those codes:

- Minimize risks to research participants: Use methods that have the least potential for harm or stress for research participants. During the research, monitor the procedures as well as the participants' reactions to be sure of avoiding any unforeseen stress or harm. A cost–benefit analysis should be undertaken in order to

Table 2–3 Principles of the Canadian Code of Ethics for Psychologists

Priority Level	Principle	Description
I	Respect for the dignity of persons	Given greatest weight except in circumstances of a true emergency, when the physical safety of a person is imminently threatened.
II	Responsible caring	Responsible caring can be carried out only if the psychologist is competent in the area of practice or research being done, with the highest respect for the dignity of persons.
III	Integrity in relationships	Values such as openness and straightforwardness are reflected in this category, which, at times, might be overridden by the need to respect the dignity and responsible caring for a person.
IV	Responsibility to society	If a person's needs conflict with what is of greatest benefit to society, a solution might be difficult to reach. According to this code of ethics, the dignity and well-being of a person should not be violated in favour of what a society wants or values.

ensure that risks assumed are reasonable and ethical in relation to the anticipated benefits from research findings.

- Describe the research to potential participants so they can determine if they wish to participate: Prospective research participants should be told all details of the research and intended use of their data in a way that allows them to understand the information and then provide informed consent about participating. A signed form is not adequate: It is the duty of the researcher to make certain that the person understands the nature of that consent, hence the importance of obtaining informed consent. As minors, children are not legally able to give informed consent. Therefore, researchers must describe the study to parents or guardians and ask them for consent regarding their children's participation. All participants should have the right to withdraw from the study if they wish, and the assent of children should also be obtained.

- Avoid deception; if participants must be deceived, provide a thorough explanation of the true nature of the research as soon as possible: Providing complete information about a study in advance can sometimes bias or distort participants' responses. Consequently, investigators sometimes provide only partial information or even mislead participants about the true purpose of the study. As soon as it is feasible—typically just after the data-gathering session—any false information must be corrected and the reasons for the deception provided.

- Keep results anonymous or confidential: Research results should be anonymous, which means that participants' data cannot be linked to their names. When anonymity is not possible, research results should be confidential, which means that only the investigator conducting the study knows the identities of the individuals.

Researchers must convince ethics review boards consisting of researchers from many disciplines that they have carefully addressed each of these ethical points. Only then may they begin their study. If the review board objects to some aspects of the proposed study, the researcher must revise those aspects and present them anew for the review board's approval. In Canada, university-based ethics review boards and granting agencies adhere to the Tri-Council Policy Statement 2: Ethical Conduct for Research Involving Humans (2014; TCPS 2 is the first comprehensive revision since its adoption in 1998). This new second edition of the tri-council document is available online at the website of the Government of Canada's Interagency Advisory Panel on Research Ethics (www.pre.ethics.gc.ca). This document sets out protection for both human and animal research participants and contributes greatly to national research standards across disciplines in Canada (Adair, 2001).

Although researchers must have legal, caregiver-provided informed consent in order to perform research with a particular child, obtaining the child's own assent is equally important. Children should never be forced to participate in a study just because a parent has given consent for that participation. In order to respect the dignity of children, they should be free to not participate at any point before or during testing, if they feel that they do not want to participate.

Because children are immature, they do not always use the most sophisticated means to indicate that they do not want to participate. Theresa Zolner remembers one research participant in particular who did not want to participate in a study of children's knowledge of print functions, which was being conducted in an Edmonton elementary school. During the testing session, Theresa and a fellow researcher were interviewing elementary-school children using a hand puppet named Xeno. Most of the children responded enthusiastically to the study; however, one girl, who was about 7 years of age, was a little reluctant. She responded to a few questions and then asked to get a drink of water. They let her go to the fountain. After she came back, she sat for a minute or two and then asked to go to the washroom. They let her go to the washroom. When she came back, she asked to go to the washroom again. They asked her if she wanted to stop and go back to her classroom, and, with great enthusiasm, she nodded her head and then scooted out of her chair and back to class.

The researcher has the duty to pay attention to signs that a child is not assenting to the research, which might be indicated in a variety of ways, both verbal and nonverbal. Theresa's daughter witnessed a research-related incident once when children were being asked to participate in a medical research study involving the drawing of some blood. The study took place on the same day that the children were receiving a vaccination at school. All of the children were lined up in the school gymnasium in order to receive their shot. Then, some children moved on to the blood-drawing line, while others were allowed to go back to their classroom, depending on whether parents had consented to the research participation. Theresa and her husband had not consented to their daughter's participation, but as she stood in line waiting to receive the vaccination, she became horrified by watching other children have their blood drawn. She said that some of them were crying, and one tried to run away, only to be physically brought back to the blood-drawing chair in order to "voluntarily participate." Clearly, if a child must be dragged into the research setting, the child is not assenting to the research. Forcing children to participate or forcing other children to watch this kind of situation violates the first ethical principal in the CPA code of ethics. What other ethical concerns, according to the CPA code of ethics, might be raised in relation to this study?

Communicating Research Results

LO5 **Understand how researchers communicate results to other scientists.**

When the study is complete and the data analyzed, researchers write a report of their work. This report describes, in great detail, what the researchers did and why, the results, and the implications of those results. The researchers submit the report to one of several academic journals specializing in child development. Some of these are *Child Development, Developmental Psychology, Journal of Experimental Child Psychology, Infant Behavior and Development, Cognitive Development, Canadian Children, Early Childhood Research and Practice, Social Development,* and the *Journal of Abnormal Child Psychology.*

The editor of the journal then asks several researchers in child development to read and critique the report. This process is called "peer review." Sometimes these reviewers suggest changes to the report, and sometimes they might reject the report altogether, although the editor usually has final say. If, after peer review, the editor of the journal accepts the report, it appears in the journal and other researchers can read it. Unpublished research reports sometimes form a valuable basis for professional conversation about a research phenomenon, but published research reports continue to set the standard for peer acceptance in the discipline.

Peer review is a difficult process. If you're aspiring to a career in academia, you might well be advised early on to develop a thick skin: Academics can be relentlessly unforgiving. In fact, Hadjistavropoulos and Bieling (2000) published an article in *Canadian Psychology* discussing the nature of peer review in North America. They pointed out that reviewer comments on research manuscripts could be inappropriate, in part because the comments are typically anonymous. While not all reviewer comments are inappropriate, some are so negative that they actually violate Principle I of the CPA code of ethics, which is to respect the dignity of the person. Hadjistavropoulos and Bieling cited examples in which the character of the researcher was attacked. In one instance, a reviewer said that a researcher should start revising a report first by "burning the entire manuscript" (p. 152–159). Other reviewer comments were described as "mean-spirited," "an avenue for professional nastiness," or "overly caustic" (p. 152–159). Hadjistavropoulos and Bieling recommended not that the peer review process be scrapped but that psychologists be held accountable using the CPA code of ethics as the accepted standard for how to treat colleagues and write about their work.

Ask Yourself

Suppose you wanted to determine the impact of divorce on children's academic achievement. What would be the merits of correlational versus experimental research on this topic?

How would a longitudinal study differ from a cross-sectional study in the above study?

If you were an early childhood educator, and a researcher wanted to conduct a study in your daycare centre without parental consent, what would you do? Considering the ethical principles of the Canadian Psychological Association mentioned in Table 2–3, what would you tell this researcher about why this type of research would be inappropriate?

2.2 Child-Development Research and Family Policy

 Learning Objectives

After reading the module, you should be able to do the following:

LO6 Describe why child-development researchers recently have become more involved in designing social policy.

LO7 State how child-development researchers influence family policy.

LO8 Discuss how concern for family policy has improved child-development research.

Family policy:

laws and regulations that directly or indirectly affect families with children.

Family policy refers to laws and regulations that directly or indirectly affect families with children. Unfortunately, experts do not always use child-development research to create policies for child-care facilities or certify that neighbourhood facilities meet those standards. In the rest of this module, we'll explore how research is used to foster children's development through sound family policies.

Background

LO6 **Describe why child-development researchers recently have become more involved in designing social policy.**

Many child-development researchers are interested in applying their work to improving children's lives. After all, when a researcher discovers that one set of conditions enhances children's growth but a second set does not, using that knowledge to form standards and policies seems natural.

Links between child development and family policy have become much stronger in recent years, mostly because families in Canada are changing. The "traditional" family in which children are cared for by a stay-at-home mom and a working dad has given way to families with a single parent, families in which both parents are employed outside the home, and blended families that include stepparents and step- or half-siblings.

According to Vezina (2012), based on data from the NLSCY, about 80 percent of Canadian children live with both parents. About 10 percent of children live with parents in stepfamilies, and about 10 percent of children live with a single parent. These findings are similar to the earlier findings of Ross, Scott, and Kelly (1999). According to Vezina, the parents in 86 percent of intact families are married and in 14 percent are living common-law. In stepfamilies, the parents in 52 percent are married and in 42 percent are living common-law. Vezina noted that 48 percent of parents living in stepfamilies want to get married.

Changes in a child's family life raise questions that trouble child-development professionals, parents, and policy makers alike. For example, when a parental relationship breaks up, who should gain custody of the children? When children spend most days at a child-care facility, what are the effects? Child-development researchers now work to provide empirically studied answers to questions like these in the hopes of developing better policies as well as guidelines for evidence-based practice in clinical care of children and their families. **Evidence-based practice** is an approach to practice in health services using those methods of intervention and assessment that have been demonstrated, through the best available research evidence, to be effective (APA Presidential Task Force on Evidence-Based Practice, 2006). Recommendations also have been proposed for training Canadian psychologists to practise using evidence-based interventions (Hunsley, 2007).

Researchers have been studying the effects of daycare on children.

Evidence-based practice:
an approach to working with people in health services using methods of intervention and assessment that have been demonstrated through empirical research to be effective.

Because of societal changes affecting Canada's children, many Canadian child-development researchers now participate actively in designing and implementing social policy concerning children and their families. In the next section, we'll look at the many different roles that child-development researchers play in formulating social policy.

Ways to Influence Social Policy

LO7 **State how child-development researchers influence family policy.**

Child-development researchers contribute to sound family policy through a number of distinct pathways (White, 1996).

BUILD UNDERSTANDING OF CHILDREN AND THEIR DEVELOPMENT. Sound policies should be based on an accurate understanding of the key factors affecting children's development, not on stereotypes or assumptions about children and youth (Gilliam & Bales, 2001). For example, although for years Canada accepted as policy that First Nations, Métis, and Inuit children should be placed in residential schools, many people in Canada have begun to address questions about the impact of residential school policies on First Nations, Métis, and Inuit children and their families. Developing an understanding of the impact of residential schools on children can help Aboriginal people and others understand not only the impact of this kind of schooling on children and families but also how to help people who were affected directly or intergenerationally by residential schools. More importantly, understanding the impact of residential schools also can help communities understand how to help themselves. Finally, this kind of information will assist Canadian governments in setting proper ground rules for social policy in education and child welfare so that initiatives created for children and families can help, not hurt, them.

SERVE AS AN ADVOCATE FOR CHILDREN. Children are ill-prepared to represent their own interests. They cannot vote and do not have the financial resources to hire lobbyists or prepare media campaigns. Often parents like to serve as advocates for their

Goodluz/ShutterStock

One research finding that might have social policy implications is that non-custodial parents who pay child support tend to stay more involved with their children.

children, but individual parents usually lack the expertise and resources to represent children adequately. However, child-development researchers—typically in conjunction with a child advocacy group—can alert policy makers to children's needs and can argue for family policy that addresses those needs.

Child-development researchers can influence policy by providing needed knowledge, acting as advocates for children, evaluating programs, and devising model programs.

One well-known advocacy group for children in Canada is Child Find. Based in Winnipeg, Manitoba, with provincial offices across Canada, Child Find's mandate is to (1) assist in the location of children who are missing, (2) provide preventative safety education, and (3) generally advocate for the rights of children against, for example, sexual exploitation and abuse, child pornography, and the sale and trafficking of children (www.childfind.ca). Child Find has launched new initiatives, as well, to prevent child exploitation via the internet. It also promotes online education regarding safety, runaway prevention, location of missing children, prevention of child exploitation and abuse, and safe babysitting practices.

EVALUATE POLICIES AND PROGRAMS. Sometimes policies and programs affect families and children even though they are not the primary targets of the policy. In this case, child-development experts might be called to evaluate aspects of policy that affect families and children, often using two important tools. One is existing theory and research in child development, which can indicate how policy features are likely to affect families and children. The second important tool is a rather large catalogue of methods to assess family functioning and child development. By using existing findings to predict the likely impact of policies and by providing proven methods to measure impact, child-development researchers can help judge how families and children will be affected by policies.

DEVELOP A MODEL PROGRAM. Elected officials usually like results, so one of the best ways to sway policy makers is to create a program with measurable and demonstrable outcomes.

The School of the 21st Century (21C) illustrates this approach (Zigler & Gilman, 1996). Devised by Edward Zigler at Yale University, this voluntary program uses a community-based school model that integrates preschool and school-age child care as well as family support services. The Government of Saskatchewan recently proposed a similar kind of community-based, integrative model for its schools (see http://edadm821.files.wordpress.com/2013/01/schoolplus-final-report.pdf).

Monkey Business/ShutterStock

A parent educator makes a home visit.

The 21C program includes home visits by parent educators as well as information about other community services available to families. Special attention also has been paid to early literacy as well as the experience of immigrant children (School of the 21st Century, 2002).

Since 1988, the 21C program has spread to more than 500 rural and urban schools across the United States. Children attending 21C schools tend to learn more and have fewer behavioural problems; in addition, their parents are more involved in school and report less stress associated with arranging adequate child care (e.g., Finn-Stevenson, Desimone, & Chung, 1998). 21C is a textbook example of first showing that a program effectively addresses a problem, then letting that success convince policy makers on a wider scale.

An Emphasis on Policy Implications Improves Research

LO8 Discuss how concern for family policy has improved child-development research.

Child-development research undoubtedly can lead to more informed policies toward children and their families as well as improved theory and research. When doing basic research, a common tactic is for researchers to simplify the problem or research question, often by examining certain very limited or narrow aspects of children's development. In contrast, when formulating programs for children, policy makers cannot use the basic researcher's "slice and dice" approach, because in real children, all variables are interconnected. Change in one variable usually leads to change in another. Consequently, focusing on family policy forces researchers to take a much broader perspective on child development than they might otherwise take.

A concern for family policy has improved the methods researchers use. As we described in Module 2.1, the strongest claims about cause and effect come from genuine experiments in which participants are assigned randomly to various experimental conditions. Unfortunately, random assignment is often impossible in policy-oriented research, for pragmatic or ethical reasons. For example, we cannot randomly assign children to high-school-educated versus college-educated parents or to single- versus dual-parent families. Consequently, child-development researchers and statisticians have devised more powerful correlational methods that permit some statements about causality (West, Biesanz, & Pitts, 2000). A **quasi-experimental design** includes multiple groups that are not formed by random assignment. For example, researchers might want to compare children's reading level at the end of a school year in two schools, whereby one school uses a traditional reading curriculum and another uses an innovative curriculum. Because children were not assigned randomly to the two schools, this is a quasi-experiment. Children in the two schools might differ in reading or reading-related skills at the beginning of the year, prior to the onset of reading instruction. New methods allow researchers to account for such possible differences— using statistics to equate the groups of children at the beginning of the year—thereby making it easier to compare them at the end of the year and make conclusions about causality.

Quasi-experimental design: an approach to research involving comparison of groups whose members are not randomly selected.

The message here should be clear: Closer links between child-development research and family policy produce better policy and better research. To emphasize this connection, many of the other chapters in this text have a feature called Child Development and Family Policy. These features provide concrete examples of the close ties between research and social policy.

Ask Yourself

Suppose a child-development researcher was interested in the impact of nutrition on children's physical and cognitive development. Describe several different ways in which the researcher might help to form public policy concerning children's nutrition.

Imagine you are a nurse working on a pediatric unit in a hospital. One of the children in your care does not want to eat, and you want to document the situation so that nutritional and medical staff can help the child. What kinds of observations might assist you in communicating effective information to the child's health-care team?

What Would a Community Health Nurse Do?

Mabel and Terry didn't have very much information, even though they were considering starting a family. As a community health nurse, you would be in a unique position to help Mabel and Terry learn more about becoming parents. What approach would you take in helping them become more confident in their decision to become parents? How might research help you help them? In what ways might you share this information, and what would you share?

Summary

2.1 Doing Child-Development Research

Measurement in Child-Development Research

- Researchers need to decide at the outset of their research how to measure the topic of interest.

- Systematic observation involves recording children's behaviour as it takes place, either in a natural environment (naturalistic observation) or in a structured setting (structured observation).

- Researchers sometimes create tasks to obtain samples of children's behaviour.

- In self-reports, children answer questions about their thoughts, feelings, or experiences that are posed by the experimenter.

- In most research designs, researchers must obtain a sample that is representative of some larger population.

General Designs for Research

- In correlational studies, investigators examine relations between variables as they occur naturally.

- A correlation coefficient, r, represents the strength and direction of relationship between variables.

- A correlation coefficient can vary from -1 (strong negative relation) to 0 (no relation) to $+1$ (strong positive relation).

- Correlational studies cannot determine cause and effect.

- Researchers do experimental studies in which they manipulate an independent variable to determine the impact on a dependent variable.

- Experimental studies allow conclusions about cause and effect.

- Strict control of all possible variables often makes the experimental situation artificial.

- Field studies involve manipulation of independent variables in a natural setting.

- The best approach is to use both experimental and correlational studies or sequential designs to provide converging and diverging evidence and control for cohort effects.

Methods for Studying Development

- Some researchers use a longitudinal design in which the same children are observed repeatedly as they grow.

- The longitudinal design provides evidence of actual patterns of individual growth, but the design does have shortcomings.

- In longitudinal designs, repeated testing can affect performance, and some children may drop out of the project.

- Cross-sectional designs involve testing children in different age groups.

- The cross-sectional design avoids the problems of the longitudinal design but provides no information about individual growth.

- In the cross-sectional design, what appear to be differences due to age might be cohort effects.
- The sequential design combines both cross-sectional and longitudinal data, limiting the impact of cohort effects on the study's findings.
- The National Longitudinal Survey of Children and Youth is an example of a major Canadian research study that is both longitudinal and cross-sectional in design.

Ethical Responsibilities

- Planning research involves selecting methods that preserve the rights of research participants.
- Informed parental consent and child assent are important to obtain before proceeding with data collection.
- Experimenters must minimize the risks to potential research participants, describe the research so that potential participants can decide if they want to participate or withdraw, avoid deception, and keep results anonymous or confidential.
- The Canadian Psychological Association has produced a Canadian Code of Ethics for Psychologists, which focuses on four key ethical principles and suggests a hierarchy of importance by which to consider the four principles in order to find solutions to ethical dilemmas.

Communicating Research Results

- Once research data are collected and analyzed, investigators publish the results in scientific journals where they can be read and criticized by others.
- Peer-reviewed and published studies form the main foundation of scientific knowledge about child development.

2.2 Child-Development Research and Family Policy

Background

- Child-development researchers have become increasingly interested in applying the results of their work to family policy.
- Interest in family policy is related to changes in the Canadian family, infant mortality, child abuse, and other variables suggesting that Canadian children and youth face many challenges to healthy development.

Ways to Influence Social Policy

- Child-development researchers help to shape family policy by providing useful knowledge about children and their development.
- Child-development research provides a source of accurate information upon which good social policies can be based.
- Child-development researchers contribute to social policy development by serving as advocates for children, by evaluating the impact of programs on families and children, and by developing effective programs that can be implemented elsewhere.

An Emphasis on Policy Implications Improves Research

- Focusing on public policy implications improves research because researchers must take a broader perspective on children's development than they otherwise would.
- Policy-related research has produced more sophisticated research methods, such as the quasi-experimental design.

Chapter Critical Review

1. Choose a topic in child development that interests you (e.g., the effects of daycare on infants and toddlers, or the relation between parenting style and a child's popularity with peers—the possibilities are endless). Working through the steps described in Module 2.1, design a research project that could be used to study the topic you have chosen.

2. Go to your library and find an issue of a child-development journal such as *Child Development*, *Developmental Psychology*, or *Journal of Experimental Child Psychology*. Go through the issue and classify each study into one of the four principal categories (e.g., cross-sectional experimental or

longitudinal correlational). What type of study is most common?

3. Explain in your own words why investigators can make judgments about causation when they use experimental research designs but not when they use correlational designs.

4. Find a newspaper report about child-development research. Determine what the investigators were trying to discover, and summarize their results. Do the results have public policy implications? If so, what impact are the investigators having on legislation or public policy?

See for Yourself

A good first step toward learning about child-development research is to read the reports of research that scientists publish in journals. Visit your library and locate some child-development journals. Look at the contents of an issue to get an idea of the many different topics that child-development researchers study. When you find an article on a topic that interests you, skim the contents and try to determine what design the investigator(s) used. See for yourself!

Chapter 3
Genetic Bases of Child Development

Kieren Welch/Fotolia

 ## MODULE

3.1 Mechanisms of Heredity

3.2 Genetic Disorders

3.3 Heredity Is Not Destiny

Connect to My Virtual Child

What kinds of theories do you have about children? What ideas inform your thoughts and beliefs about the lives of children, how they are raised, and the nature of the human person? Use your access card and follow this link www.myvirtualchild.com to learn more about the world of the child. You can even virtually try to raise your own child.

Mabel and Terry didn't really anticipate that having a baby could be so complicated. As they began planning their family, they selected an obstetrician and went for some initial counselling. Both had a history of genetic disorders in their families, and their physician talked to them about different types of tests that might need to be done to ensure the health of a future baby. In addition, Mabel, who would be carrying the baby, had to make adjustments to her lifestyle in order to get ready to carry a child. With all the preparations they were going through, Mabel and Terry wondered: Wasn't having a baby supposed to be the most natural process in the world?

3.1 Mechanisms of Heredity

 ## Learning Objectives

After reading the module, you should be able to do the following:

LO1 Define chromosomes and genes.

LO2 Explain the mechanism of heredity for dominant and recessive traits.

LO3 Understand how heredity influences behavioural and psychological development.

LO4 Describe the importance of nonshared environmental influences.

When parents are expecting a child, they can experience a mix of emotions—anticipation, hope, excitement, anxiety, and concern. Parents looking forward to the birth of a child sometimes are worried about the health of their baby, and even more so if the family has a history of inherited disease. For example, sickle-cell disease is an inherited condition that affects many people, particularly people of African heritage, who appear to be more prone to this painful disease than other groups. It is especially worrisome because people with sickle-cell disease often die from infections before age 20.

Before we can help parents address concerns about their developing baby's health, we need to know more about sickle-cell disease. Red blood cells carry oxygen and carbon dioxide to and from the body. When a person has sickle-cell disease, the red blood cells look long and curved like a sickle. These stiff, misshapen cells cannot pass through small blood vessels, called capillaries, so oxygen cannot reach all parts of the body. The trapped sickle cells also block the way of white blood cells, the body's natural defence against bacteria. In order to understand how an inherited condition like sickle-cell disease is transmitted, we need to examine how heredity works.

The Biology of Heredity

LO1 Define chromosomes and genes.

When a man ejaculates, the teaspoon of semen that is produced contains from 200 million to 500 million sperm. Only a few hundred of these sperm actually complete the 15- to 18-centimetre journey to a woman's fallopian tubes during unprotected, heterosexual intercourse. If an egg is present, many sperm simultaneously begin to burrow their way through the cluster of nurturing cells surrounding the egg. When a sperm finally breaks through the egg's cellular wall, conception occurs, and chemical changes immediately prevent all other sperm from penetrating the egg.

Each egg or sperm, also called a **gamete**, contains 23 individual **chromosomes**, organic structures in the cell's nucleus that contain genetic material. When a sperm penetrates an egg, their chromosomes combine to produce 23 pairs of chromosomes, and the development of a new human being begins. Gametes are created through a process called **meiosis**. During meiosis, egg and sperm cells are produced that contain half the amount of genetic material normally contained in all other bodily cells, so that, when an egg and sperm combine, they each contribute half the necessary genetic material (23 chromosomes) for development of a person. If egg and sperm each had a full complement of genetic material (46 chromosomes), then the resulting person would have 92 chromosomes, twice what human development requires. Their children would have 184, and so on. Meiosis prevents this from happening, making sure that each gamete has only 23 chromosomes to contribute. For boys, the process of meiosis (sperm production) begins in puberty and continues throughout the lifespan. For girls, meiosis occurs during the baby girl's gestation, with all gametes (eggs) being present in her at birth. Each meiotic division in girls results in the production of one viable egg and three that die off immediately. Each meiotic division in boys produces four sperm. Bodily cells other than gametes are produced through **mitosis**, a process in which cells divide and create exact copies of themselves. Natural conception only occurs through the joining of gametes—sperm and egg—not through any other bodily cell fusion.

Before the invention of new reproductive technologies, natural conception took place only after heterosexual intercourse. In 1978, Louise Brown became the first person born after being conceived in a lab dish instead of her mother's body. The world referred to her as a "test-tube baby." This reproductive technology has become a multibillion-dollar industry (Beck, 1994).

Many new techniques are available to couples who are unable to conceive a child together. The fertilization of an egg outside the uterus is known as **ectogenesis** (Murphy, 2012). The best-known technique, **in vitro fertilization**, involves mixing sperm and egg together in a lab dish and then placing several fertilized eggs in the mother about 24 hours later, with the hope that one will become implanted in the wall of her uterus.

The sperm and egg usually come from a child's biological parents but sometimes are provided by donors. Occasionally, parents allow their sperm and eggs to be implanted in another woman—a surrogate mother—who carries the baby throughout pregnancy. Technically, a baby could have as many as five "parents": the sperm and egg donors; the surrogate mother who carries the baby; and the parent(s) who raise the child. The 2004 Canadian Assisted Human Reproduction Act specifies, however, that people may not pay for gametes or surrogacy services, and surrogate mothers cannot be under the age of 21.

New reproductive techniques offer hope for couples who cannot conceive. About 20 percent of attempts at in vitro fertilization succeed, but, when fertilization does succeed, couples are more likely to have twins or triplets. When multiple eggs are transferred to the uterus, the odds that at least one or more fertilized egg will implant in the mother's uterus increase. Although technology has improved options for couples wanting children, pregnancy-on-demand is still science fiction, and the procedures are rife with moral and ethical concerns for many people. In particular, some researchers

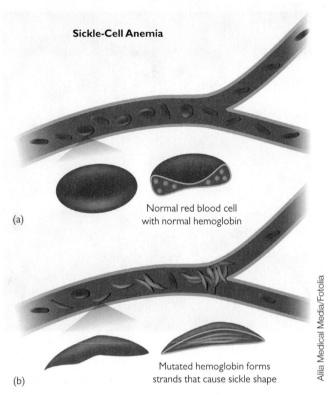

Sickle-Cell Anemia

(a) Normal red blood cell with normal hemoglobin

(b) Mutated hemoglobin forms strands that cause sickle shape

(a) Normal red blood cells
(b) Misshapen red blood cells characteristic of sickle-cell disease

Alila Medical Media/Fotolia

Gamete:

an egg or sperm cell.

Chromosomes:

organic structures in the cell's nucleus that contain genetic material.

Meiosis:

the biological process of cell division resulting in gametes that have 23 chromosomes, which is half the amount of genetic material normally seen in a human cell.

Mitosis:

the biological process of cell division resulting in bodily cells that are exact copies of their parent cells and have a full set of 46 chromosomes.

Ectogenesis:

fertilizing an egg outside the uterus.

In vitro fertilization:

an artificial form of egg fertilization in which egg and sperm are united in a laboratory dish.

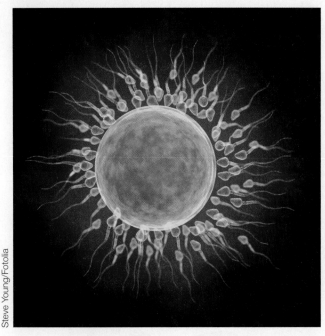

Sperm and egg before conception.

have begun to study concerns about what happens to fertilized eggs that are not implanted in the mother, including their commodification, use in research, exploitation, and disposal (Fadel, 2012; Grubb, Muramoto, & Matson, 2011; Haimes, Taylor, & Turkmendag, 2012; Richie, 2012; Sharp et al., 2010).

Reproductive techniques are offered in Canada at many mainstream health facilities; however, prospective parents must pay for these procedures themselves. Sometimes the initial consultation appointment is covered by provincial health insurance, but not always. Some employer-sponsored, private insurance plans cover a portion of the costs. Unfortunately, many people who would like to try a procedure such as in vitro fertilization cannot afford to do so because the procedures cost thousands of dollars each time they are performed.

Whatever the source of the egg and sperm, and wherever they meet, their merger is a momentous event: The resulting 23 pairs of chromosomes define a child's genotype, which is his or her complete inherited biological makeup.

Autosomes:

the first 22 pairs of chromosomes that are not sex chromosomes.

Sex chromosomes:

the twenty-third pair of chromosomes, which determines the gender of a person—XX for female and XY for male.

Deoxyribonucleic acid (DNA):

a molecule made up of chemical components, called nucleotide bases, which form the code for specific genes.

The nucleus of every normal human cell contains 46 chromosomes, organized into pairs ranging from the largest to the smallest. The first 22 pairs of chromosomes are called **autosomes**, and the chromosomes in each autosome pair are about the same size. The twenty-third pair of chromosomes, however, is different because it defines the sex of the child. For boys, one chromosome in the pair is much larger than the other. Researchers call the larger chromosome X, and the smaller chromosome Y.

The X and Y chromosomes are known as the **sex chromosomes**. An egg always contains an X (larger) twenty-third chromosome, but a sperm can contain either an X or a Y chromosome. When an X-carrying sperm fertilizes the egg, the child's twenty-third chromosome pair will be XX and the resulting child will be a girl. When a Y-carrying sperm fertilizes the egg, the twenty-third pair is XY and the resulting child will be a boy. Therefore, the sex of a child is determined not by the egg but by the sperm.

Each chromosome in a cell's nucleus consists of one molecule of **deoxyribonucleic acid**—DNA for short. The DNA molecule, called a double helix, resembles a spiral staircase. The "rungs" of the staircase carry the genetic code and are made up of

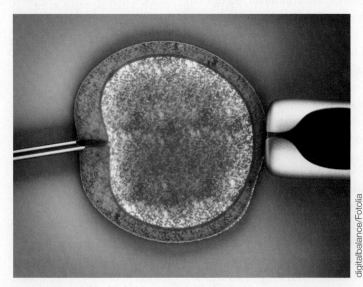

In vitro fertilization.

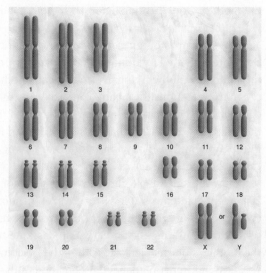

People have 23 sets of chromosomes.

specifically paired chemical components, called nucleotide bases: Adenine is paired with thymine; guanine is paired with cytosine (see Figure 3-1). The order of the nucleotide pairs forms the instructions, or "code," for the cell to create certain amino acids, proteins, and enzymes, which are important biological building blocks. Each group of nucleotide bases that provides a specific set of biochemical instructions is a **gene**. For example, three consecutive thymine nucleotides form the instruction to create the amino acid phenylalanine.

Although the DNA molecule is known to be a double helix, researchers have discovered the possibility that nucleotide bases (primarily guanine) form four-sided "quadruplex" structures, which is hypothesized to happen during DNA replication (Biffi, Tannahill, McCafferty, & Balasubramanian, 2013). As Biffi and colleagues have indicated, more research needs to occur to map the location of these structures and the nature of their roles in the genome, including whether they are stabilizing, helpful, or harmful to cells.

All together, a child's 46 chromosomes include roughly 30 000 to 50 000 genes. Through biochemical instructions that are coded in the DNA, genes regulate the development of a person's inherited characteristics and abilities, called *traits*. The complete set of genes that makes up a person's heredity is known as the person's **genotype**.

The genotype, along with environmental influences, makes up a person's **phenotype**, which includes an individual's physical, behavioural, and psychological features. For example, eye colour is determined by genotype; in fact, a person's total facial appearance is part of that person's phenotype—for example, eye colour, eyebrow appearance, scars, or perhaps the person is missing a toenail. All of these characteristics, whether caused by genetics or some environmental event, form the phenotype of the person.

A person's phenotype results from genetic and environmental factors. Genes can affect genes, environmental factors can affect other environmental factors, environmental factors can affect genes, and genes can also affect environmental factors. In essence, all factors within this complex network affect each other, providing feedback and adjustment that bring about ongoing change within any organism and environment (Whitfield & McClearn, 2005). In other words, nature and nurture affect each other on an ongoing basis, and change resulting from a dynamic and complex interplay of factors is a reality of all life.

Figure 3-1

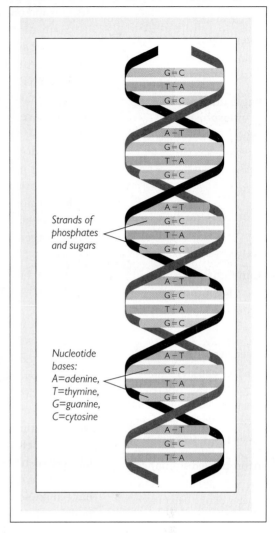

Strands of phosphates and sugars

Nucleotide bases:
A=adenine,
T=thymine,
G=guanine,
C=cytosine

Gene:

a group of chemical compounds, called nucleotide bases, which generate the production of a protein or other important biological building blocks in the body.

Genotype:

the complete set of genes that makes up a person's heredity.

Phenotype:

a person's genotype plus all other environmental influences that make up that person's physical, behavioural, and psychological characteristics.

Alleles:

a specific form of a gene.

Single Gene Inheritance

LO2 Explain the mechanism of heredity for dominant and recessive traits.

How do genetic instructions produce the misshapen red blood cells of sickle-cell disease? Genes come in different forms, called **alleles**. Just as a child inherits 23 chromosomes from mother and 23 from father, the child also inherits one version of each gene (one allele) from each parent. Sometimes the alleles in the pair of chromosomes are the same, making them **homozygous**. Sometimes the alleles are different from each other, making them **heterozygous**. In the case of sickle cells, for example, two alleles are present on chromosome 11. One allele has instructions for normal red blood cells, while the other has instructions for sickle-shaped red blood cells. If a baby is homozygous for a trait—in this case, red blood cell production—he or she would have two

Homozygosity:

having alleles of a gene that are identical to each other.

Heterozygosity:

having alleles of a gene that are different from each other.

Single nucleotide polymorphisms:

a change in the expected nucleotide base at a particular location within a strand of DNA.

Dominant:

an allele whose chemical instructions are always followed and expressed.

Recessive:

an allele whose chemical instructions are ignored in the presence of a dominant allele or expressed in the presence of another recessive allele.

Incomplete dominance:

a genetic situation in which aspects of two heterozygous alleles are both expressed.

alleles for normal cells or two alleles for sickle-shaped cells. On the other hand, if the baby is heterozygous for the trait, he or she would have one allele for normal cell production and one for sickle-shaped cells.

Some disease states, such as sickle-cell anemia, are associated with gene mutations called **single nucleotide polymorphisms** (SNP) that result in faulty instructions for protein production (Sternberg, Grigorenko, & Kidd, 2005; Whitfield & McClearn, 2005). In SNPs, the normal nucleotide base expected in a particular position is altered. SNPs may also be found in segments of DNA not responsible for coding proteins and can have an impact on other aspects of genetic expression in these circumstances (Whitfield & McClearn, 2005).

How does a genotype influence a phenotype? If a person is homozygous for a trait, then the answer is simple: When both alleles are the same, and therefore have chemical instructions for the same phenotype, that phenotype results. If a baby had alleles for normal red blood cells on both chromosomes in the eleventh pair, he or she would be almost guaranteed to have normal cells. If the baby had two alleles for sickle-shaped cells instead, he or she would almost certainly suffer from sickle-cell disease.

When a person is heterozygous for a trait, the situation is more complex. Often one allele is **dominant**, which means that its chemical instructions are always followed, whereas instructions from the **recessive** allele are ignored. In the case of sickle-cell disease, the allele for normal cells is dominant and the allele for sickle-shaped cells is recessive. If a mother and father each contribute an allele for normal red blood cells, their baby will not develop sickle-cell disease. On the other hand, if their baby inherits two recessive alleles, he or she almost certainly will develop sickle-cell disease.

However, this is not the end of the story, as their baby might be affected in another way. Sometimes one allele does not dominate another completely, a situation known as **incomplete dominance**. In incomplete dominance, the phenotype that results often falls between the phenotype associated with either allele. This is the case for the genes that control red blood cells. Individuals with one dominant and one recessive allele have **sickle-cell trait** (as distinct from sickle-cell disease): In most situations these individuals have no problems, but when they are seriously short of oxygen, they suffer a temporary, relatively mild form of the disease. Thus, sickle-cell trait is likely to appear when the person exercises vigorously or is at high altitudes (Sullivan, 1987).

Figure 3-2 summarizes what we've learned about sickle-cell disease. The letter *A* denotes the allele for normal blood cells, and *a* denotes the allele for sickle-shaped cells. In the diagram, the father's genotype is homozygous dominant. From the mother's family history, we see that she could be homozygous dominant or heterozygous; in the diagram, we've assumed the latter. You can see that this mother and father cannot have a baby with sickle-cell disease, but it is possible for them to have a baby with sickle-cell trait. One reason that groups of people might share physical and other genetic traits results from **endogamy**, which is a tendency to preferentially mate with people of the same social or cultural group. However, no one population of people is perfectly distinct from all others. Rather, gradual differences between groups living in nearby geographical areas can be seen. Continuous genetic variation observed between geographic regions is called **clinal variation**.

One aspect of sickle-cell disease that we haven't considered so far is why this disorder primarily affects people of African heritage. The feature Children and Families around the World addresses this point and, in the process, tells more about how heredity operates.

Figure 3-2

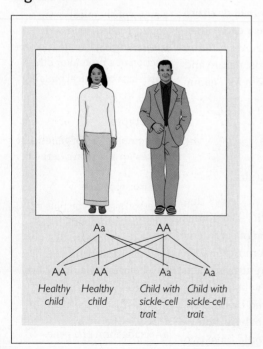

Aa	AA

AA	AA	Aa	Aa
Healthy child	Healthy child	Child with sickle-cell trait	Child with sickle-cell trait

Children and Families around the World

Why Do Persons of African Heritage Inherit Sickle-Cell Disease?

Sickle-cell disease affects about 1 in 400 children of African heritage. In contrast, virtually no children of Western or Eastern European heritage have the disorder. You might be surprised to find out that the sickle-cell allele has a unique benefit: Individuals with this allele are more resistant to malaria, an infectious disease and a leading cause of childhood death worldwide. Transmitted by mosquitoes, malaria is most common in warm climates, including many parts of Africa. Compared to Africans who have alleles for normal blood cells, Africans with the sickle-cell allele are less likely to die from malaria, which means that the sickle-cell allele has a higher likelihood of being passed on to the next generation.

This explanation of sickle-cell disease has two implications. First, sickle-cell disease should be common in any group of people living where malaria is common. In fact, sickle-cell disease also affects persons of Hispanic heritage who can trace their roots to malaria-prone regions of the Caribbean, Central America, and South America. Second, malaria is rare in Canada and the United States, suggesting that the sickle-cell allele has no survival value

to people of African heritage in these countries. Therefore, the sickle-cell allele should become less common in successive generations of African descendants, and evidence exists that this is happening.

You can see that the impact of heredity is influenced by the environment. An allele with survival value in one environment might not have any survival value in another. According to the Canadian Task Force on Preventive Health Care (n.d.), the carrier rate in Canada for the sickle-cell trait might be higher than in the United States, with approximately 67 Black infants being born annually with this disease (see also Canadian Haemoglobinopathy Association, 2015). In Canada, death from sickle-cell anemia peaks between the ages of 1 and 3, primarily as the result of complications from infection by the bacterium *Streptococcus pneumoniae*. People who survive past the age of 3 might suffer from a variety of problems, including strokes, spleen and kidney dysfunction, bone and joint pain, ulcers, cholecystitis, and liver dysfunction.

In each of these instances, individuals with a recessive trait have two recessive alleles, one from each parent. Individuals with a dominant trait have at least one dominant allele.

The simple genetic mechanism responsible for sickle-cell disease, involving a single gene pair with one dominant allele and one recessive allele, is also responsible for numerous other common traits, as shown in Table 3-1.

You'll notice that Table 3-1 includes many biological traits but lacks behavioural and psychological traits. Behavioural and psychological characteristics can be inherited, but the genetic mechanism behind them is more complex, with very few one gene–one effect relationships. In addition, Whitfield and McClearn (2005) have pointed out that, although one major gene might be primarily associated with a

Sickle-cell trait:

a characteristic of individuals who have one dominant and one recessive allele for the genetic production of red blood cells, resulting in partial expression of sickle-cell anemia.

Endogamy:

a preference for mating with people from one's own social or cultural group.

Clinal variation:

continuous genetic variation observed between geographic regions.

Table 3-1 Some Common Phenotypes Associated with Single Pairs of Genes

Dominant Phenotype	Recessive Phenotype
Curly hair	Straight hair
Normal hair	Pattern baldness (men)
Dark hair	Blond hair
Thick lips	Thin lips
Cheek dimples	No dimples
Normal hearing	Some types of deafness
Normal vision	Nearsightedness
Farsightedness	Normal vision
Normal colour vision	Red-green colour blindness
Type A blood	Type O blood
Type B blood	Type O blood
Rh-positive blood	Rh-negative blood

SOURCE: McKusick, 1995.

disease state, that gene might not be the only one associated with a particular pattern of symptoms, as certain kinds of allele configurations at a variety of locations along the genome can be associated with similar kinds of symptoms.

Behavioural Genetics

LO3 Understand how heredity influences behavioural and psychological development.

Behavioural genetics:

the study of the inheritance of behavioural and psychological traits.

Behavioural genetics is the branch of genetics that deals with inheritance of behavioural and psychological traits. Behavioural genetics is complex, in part because behavioural and psychological traits are complex. The traits controlled by single genes usually represent "either–or" characteristics. For example, a person either has normal colour vision or has red-green colour blindness; a person has blood that clots normally, has sickle-cell trait, or has sickle-cell disease. A person either has dimples or doesn't.

Most important behavioural and psychological characteristics are not either–or traits but represent a broad range of outcomes along a continuum of possibilities. Take extroversion as an example. You probably know a few extremely outgoing individuals and a few intensely shy ones, but most of your friends and acquaintances are somewhere in between. Classifying your friends would produce a distribution of individuals across a continuum, from extreme extroversion at one end to extreme introversion at the other.

Polygenic inheritance:

the contribution of many genes to a person's phenotypic expression.

Many behavioural and psychological characteristics are distributed in this fashion, including intelligence and many aspects of personality. When phenotypes reflect the combined activity of many separate genes, the pattern is known as **polygenic inheritance**. Because so many genes are involved in polygenic inheritance, we usually cannot trace the contribution of each gene directly. For example, let's suppose that four gene pairs contribute to extroversion, that the allele for extroversion is dominant, and that the total level of extroversion is simply the sum of the dominant alleles' contribution. If we continue to use uppercase letters to represent dominant alleles and lowercase letters to represent the recessive allele, the four gene pairs would be Aa, Bb, Cc, and Dd.

These four pairs of genes produce 81 possible genotypes and 9 distinct phenotypes. For example, a person with the genotype AABBCCDD has 8 alleles for extroversion (a real party-goer). A person with the genotype aabbccdd has no alleles for extroversion (and might rather read than party). All other genotypes involve some combinations of dominant and recessive alleles, so these are associated with phenotypes representing intermediate levels of extroversion. In fact, the diagram shows that the most common outcome is for people to inherit exactly 4 dominant and 4 recessive alleles: 19 of the 81 genotypes produce this pattern (e.g., AABbccDd, AaBbcCDd). A few extreme cases (very outgoing or very shy), when coupled with many intermediate cases, produce the familiar bell-shaped distribution that characterizes many behavioural and psychological traits (see Figure 3-3).

This example is completely hypothetical. Extroversion is not based on the combined influence of eight pairs of genes. We merely want to show how several genes working together could produce a continuum of genetic possibilities. It is also important to remember that a person's phenotype—their characteristics and behaviour in real life—will be affected by more than just their genetic makeup. However, a mechanism akin to our example is probably involved in the inheritance of many psychological traits (Plomin, Fulker, Corley, & DeFries, 1997).

Max really likes those genetic markers.

Figure 3-3

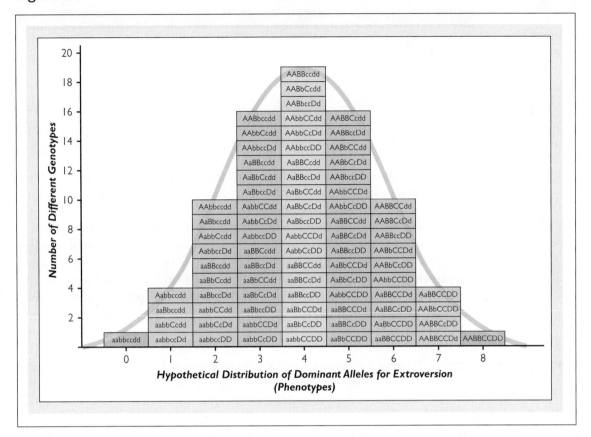

Hypothetical Distribution of Dominant Alleles for Extroversion (Phenotypes)

METHODS OF BEHAVIOURAL GENETICS. If many psychological traits involve countless genes, how can we hope to unravel the influence of heredity? Twins provide some important clues. Identical twins, called **monozygotic twins**, come from a single fertilized egg that splits into two separate clusters, each of which develops into a baby. Therefore, monozygotic twins have the same genotype, which explains why they look identical. In contrast, fraternal, or **dizygotic twins**, come from two separate eggs fertilized by two separate sperm during the same incidence of fertilization. On average, fraternal twins are just like any other siblings; about half their genes are the same. In twin studies, researchers compare identical and fraternal twins on a variable such as intelligence to measure the influence of heredity. If identical twins are more alike than fraternal twins, this suggests a greater role for heredity.

An example will help illustrate the logic underlying comparisons of identical and fraternal twins. Suppose we want to determine whether extroversion is inherited. We would first measure extroversion in a large number of identical and fraternal twins. We might use a questionnaire with scores ranging from 0 to 100 (100 indicating maximal extroversion). Some of the results are shown in Table 3-2.

Look first at the results for the fraternal twins. Most have similar scores: The Aikman twins both have high scores, but the Hampton twins have low scores. Looking at the identical twins, their scores are even more alike, typically differing by no more than five points. This

Monozygotic (identical) twins:

biological siblings who both developed from the same fertilized egg, which split into two separate clusters, each of which formed into separate but identical babies.

Monozygotic twins have the same genotype.

Dizygotic (fraternal) twins: biological siblings who developed from two separate eggs fertilized by two separate sperm during the same incidence of fertilization.

Table 3-2 Twins' Scores on a Measure of Extroversion

Fraternal Twins			Identical Twins		
Family	One Twin	Other Twin	Family	One Twin	Other Twin
Aikman	80	95	Mayer	100	95
Bird	70	50	Harbaugh	32	30
Hampton	10	35	Levesque	18	15
Stewart	25	5	Bettis	55	60
Kozak	40	65	Chan	70	62

greater similarity among identical twins than fraternal twins provides evidence that extroversion is inherited, just as the fact that identical twins look more alike than fraternal twins is evidence that facial appearance is inherited.

Adopted children are another important source of information about heredity. In this case, adopted children are compared with their biological parents and their adoptive parents. The idea is that biological parents provide the child's genes, but adoptive parents provide the child's environment. Consequently, if a behaviour has genetic roots, then adopted children should resemble their biological parents more than their adoptive parents. If we wanted to use an adoption study to determine whether extroversion is inherited, we would measure extroversion in a large sample of adopted children, their biological mothers, and their adoptive mothers. (Mothers are studied because obtaining data from biological fathers of adopted children is often difficult.) The results of this hypothetical study are shown in Table 3-3.

First, compare the children's scores with their biological mothers' scores. Overall, they are related: Extroverted children like Ricky tend to have extroverted biological mothers. Introverted children like Troy tend to have introverted biological mothers. In contrast, children's scores don't show any clear relation to their adoptive mothers' scores. For example, although Ricky has the highest score and Troy has the lowest, their adoptive mothers have very similar scores. Children's greater similarity to biological than to adoptive parents would be evidence that extroversion is inherited.

Twin studies and adoption studies are not foolproof. Maybe you thought of a potential flaw of twin studies: Parents and other people might treat identical twins more similarly than they treat fraternal twins. This would make identical twins more similar than fraternal twins in their experiences as well as in their genes.

However, adoption studies have their own Achilles heel. Adoption agencies sometimes try to place youngsters with adoptive parents who are like their biological parents in terms of intelligence, ethnicity, income status, or other important variables. This can bias adoption studies because biological and adoptive parents end up being similar.

However, because twin and adoption studies have different faults, we can be confident of research findings if the two kinds of studies nevertheless produce similar results about the influence of heredity. In addition, behaviour geneticists are moving beyond traditional methods such as twin and adoption studies (Plomin et al., 1997;

Table 3-3 Scores from an Adoption Study on a Measure of Extroversion

Child	Child's Score	Biological Mother's Score	Adoptive Mother's Score
Anita	60	70	35
Jerome	45	50	25
Kerri	40	30	80
Ricky	90	80	50
Troy	25	5	55

Plomin & Rutter, 1998). Today, particular segments of DNA can be isolated in human chromosomes. These segments then serve as genetic markers for specific alleles (Plomin & Asbury, 2001). The procedure is complicated, but the basic approach often begins by identifying people who differ in the behavioural or psychological trait of interest. For example, researchers might identify children who are outgoing and children who are shy, or they might identify children who read well and children who read poorly. DNA is sampled from the children by swabbing their mouths with cotton. The cells are analyzed in a lab, and the DNA markers for the two groups are compared. If the markers differ significantly and consistently, then the alleles near the marker probably contributed to the differences between the groups.

Techniques like these have the potential to identify the many different genes that contribute to complex behavioural and psychological traits (Plomin, 2002). Of course, these new methods have limitations. Some require very large samples of children, which can be hard to obtain for rare disorders. Also, some require that an investigator have an idea, before even beginning the study, about which chromosomes to search for and where. These can be major hurdles, but when used with traditional methods of behaviour genetics (e.g., adoption studies), the new methods promise a much greater understanding of how genes influence behaviour and development.

Research to date indicates that genetic influence is strongest in three major areas: intelligence, psychopathology, and personality (Goldsmith, Lemery, Buss, & Campos, 1999; Neiderhiser, Reiss, Hetherington, & Plomin, 1999). In the case of intelligence, identical twins' scores on IQ tests are consistently more alike than fraternal twins' scores (Plomin et al., 1997). Researchers have also found that heredity is an important component of two major psychological disorders: depression and schizophrenia (Bock & Goode, 1996; Cardno, Sham, Farmer, Murray, & McGuffin, 2002). In **depression**, individuals have pervasive feelings of sadness or irritability, difficulties with concentration, and a variety of other symptoms, including problems with sleep, weight, and fatigue for at least two weeks. In **schizophrenia**, individuals usually hallucinate, have confused or sparse language, have unusual ideas, and often engage in bizarre behaviour. Twin studies show remarkable similarity in monozygotic twins for these disorders. In depression, for example, if one identical twin is depressed, the other twin has roughly a 70 percent chance of becoming depressed. For fraternal twins, the odds are much lower—only 25 percent (Gottesman, 1993; Rowe, 1994). Some new research with mice has taken an interesting turn away from studies about genetic mechanisms in schizophrenia to studying the possible impact of maternal viral infections on children's in utero brain development (Fatemi, Cuadra, El-Fakahany, Sidwell, & Thuras, 2000; Patterson, 2002).

Nonshared Environmental Influences

LO4 **Describe the importance of nonshared environmental influences.**

As evidenced by studies of twins, psychologists traditionally have regarded family environment as an important variable in understanding children's development. Sometimes people presume that children within a family should be similar because they all receive the same type of parenting and live in the same household. However, dozens of behavioural genetic studies show that, in reality, siblings are not very much alike in their cognitive and social development (Dunn & Plomin, 1990).

Does this mean that family environment is not important? No. These findings point to the importance of **nonshared environmental influences**, the experiences and circumstances within a family that make siblings different from one another (Deater-Deckard, 2000; Plomin, Asbury, Dip, & Dunn, 2001). The family environment is important, but it usually affects each child in a unique way. Each child in a family is likely to have different experiences in daily family life. For example, parents might be more affectionate with one child than another; they might use more physical punishment

Depression:

a psychological disorder in which a person has pervasive feelings of sadness or irritability, as well as other symptoms, for a period of at least two weeks.

Schizophrenia:

a psychological disorder in which individuals have unusual perceptual experiences, difficulties with thought and language, and bizarre behaviour.

Nonshared environmental influences:

experiences and circumstances within a family that contribute to siblings being different from each other.

imageegami/Fotolia

The family environment affects each child in a unique way.

with one child than another; or they may have higher expectations for school achievement for one child than another. All these contrasting parental influences tend to make siblings different, not alike. Family environments are important, but as we describe their influence throughout this text, you should remember that families create multiple, unique environments for each child in the household.

We will look at intelligence in some detail later. For now, keep in mind two conclusions from twin and adoption studies. On the one hand, the impact of heredity on behavioural development is substantial and widespread. Heredity has a sizable influence on such different aspects of development as intelligence and personality. In understanding children and their development, we must always think about how heredity might contribute. On the other hand, heredity is never the sole determinant of behavioural development. For example, 50 percent of the differences among children's scores on intelligence tests is due to heredity, but the remaining 50 percent is due to environment. Throughout this text, we'll see that the course of development is controlled by both heredity and environment and that each can have a varying influence over development. For example, in the Research to Practice feature, you'll read about how environmental factors can affect even prenatal development, which many people think of as being tightly controlled by genetic factors.

Genetic and environmental influences on various aspects of behaviour have been studied, such as aggression (Brendgen

Research to Practice

The Effects of Prenatal Maternal Stress on Children's Cognitive Development: Project Ice Storm

Two Quebec researchers, Suzanne King and David Laplante (2005), studied the impact of pregnant women's experience of stress on their infant's later development. They noted that researchers have had difficulty sorting out the objective effects of prenatal maternal stress on infant development for two reasons: (1) People's subjective reactions to stress vary, and (2) mothers may genetically transmit characteristics of temperament to their developing children. As a result, researchers have been unable to isolate the unique, objective effect of stressors on prenatal development. To help sort these issues out, King and Laplante designed a longitudinal study to determine the effect of the Quebec ice storm of January 1998 on the cognitive, language, and play development of children who were developing in utero during that time and whose mothers were exposed to the storm.

King and Laplante found that the mothers experienced a number of stressors as a result of the ice storm,

including loss of electricity and telephone service as well as having to find a place to stay for, on average, 9.2 days. Many who remained in their homes had to look after guests for an average of 30 days. Half experienced damage to their homes and a loss of income as a result of the storm. Some were physically injured, and one-third were worried about the safety of their loved ones. Approximately 16.6 percent of the mothers potentially would have met criteria for posttraumatic stress disorder. King and Laplante found moderate to high prenatal maternal stress to be associated with poorer cognitive, language, and play development at age 2.

They concluded that, independent of maternal personality, a major stressful event, such as the ice storm, can negatively affect the language and cognitive development of an unborn child. They also found that the severity and timing of the stressor can affect infant temperament, physical development, behavioural and emotional functioning, as well as perinatal outcomes, which are outcomes around the time of the child's birth. Therefore, management of stress during pregnancy is important to a developing child, although, as with the ice storm, not all stressors can be avoided.

Ask Yourself

The goal of twin and adoption studies is to reveal the contributions of genetics and environment to development. However, a problem with twin studies is that identical twins might be treated more similarly than fraternal twins, and a problem with adoption studies is that children's biological parents might resemble their adoptive parents. How could investigators determine whether these problems were present in their research?

et al., 2005), parenting (Boivin, Vitaro, & Pouli, 2005), psychological disorders like autism (Connors et al., 2005; Rasalam et al., 2005) and attentional disorders (Cornish et al., 2005; Khan & Faraone, 2006; Voeller, 2004), learning disabilities (Voeller, 2004), and fear responses (Fox et al., 2005), as well as many other topics in child development.

3.2 Genetic Disorders

 ## Learning Objectives

After reading the module, you should be able to do the following:

LO5 List a number of disorders that are inherited.

LO6 State what disorders are caused by too many or too few chromosomes.

Some children are affected by heredity in a special way: They have genetic disorders that disrupt the usual pattern of development. Genetics can derail development in two ways. First, some disorders are inherited. Sickle-cell disease is one example of an inherited disorder. Second, sometimes eggs or sperm do not have 23 chromosomes. In this module, we'll see how inherited disorders and abnormal numbers of chromosomes can alter a child's development.

Inherited Disorders

LO5 List a number of disorders that are inherited.

In Module 3.1, we saw that sickle-cell disease affects people who inherit two recessive alleles. In fact, sickle-cell disease is one of many disorders that are homozygous-recessive—triggered when a child inherits recessive alleles from both parents. Table 3-4 lists four of the more common disorders that are inherited in this manner. Quebec researchers have been studying a particular area of that province, Saguenay-Lac-St-Jean, where a high incidence of autosomal recessive disorders has been observed (De Braekeleer & Gauthier, 1996). In that community, 45.5 percent of people affected by recessive disorders were third cousins, as compared with 32.9 percent of people in the comparison group. De Braekeleer and Gauthier attributed the high incidence of recessive disorders in that community to inbreeding.

Relatively few serious disorders are caused by dominant alleles. Why? If the allele for the disorder were dominant, every person with at least one of these alleles would have the disorder. Individuals affected with serious genetic disorders might not live

Table 3-4 Common Disorders Associated with Recessive Alleles

Disorder	Frequency	Characteristics
Albinism	1 in 10 000 to 1 in 20 000 births	Skin lacks melanin, which causes visual problems and extreme sensitivity to light.
Cystic fibrosis	1 in 2500 births among European North Americans; less common in African and Asian North Americans	Excess mucus clogs digestive and respiratory tracts. Lung infections common.
Phenylketonuria (PKU)	1 in 10 000 births	Phenylalanine, an amino acid, accumulates in the body and damages the nervous system, causing cognitive delay.
Tay-Sachs disease	1 in 3000 births among Jews of European descent	The nervous system degenerates in infancy, causing deafness, blindness, cognitive delay, and, during the preschool years, death.

SOURCE: Based on Committee on Genetics, 1996; McKusick, 1995.

Huntington's disease:
a fatal disease characterized by progressive degeneration of the nervous system.

long enough to reproduce, so dominant alleles that produce fatal disorders soon vanish from the species. An exception is **Huntington's disease**, a fatal disease characterized by progressive degeneration of the nervous system. Huntington's disease is caused by a dominant allele found on chromosome 4. Individuals who inherit this disorder develop normally through childhood, adolescence, and young adulthood. However, during middle age, nerve cells begin to deteriorate, causing muscle spasms, depression, and significant changes in personality (Shiwach, 1994). The symptoms of Huntington's disease often appear after affected adults have produced children, many of whom go on to develop the disease themselves.

Fortunately, most inherited disorders are rare. Phenylketonuria (PKU), for example, occurs once in every 10 000 births, and Huntington's disease occurs even less frequently. Nevertheless, adults who think a disorder runs in their family might want to know if their children might inherit it. The Making Children's Lives Better feature shows one way to help families with the genetic disorder PKU.

More common than inherited diseases are disorders caused by the wrong number of chromosomes, as we'll see in the next section.

Abnormal Chromosomes

LO6 State what disorders are caused by too many or too few chromosomes.

Sometimes individuals do not receive the normal complement of 46 chromosomes. If they are born with extra, missing, or damaged chromosomes, development is always disrupted. A good example of this disrupted development is **Down syndrome**, a genetic disorder caused by an extra twenty-first chromosome. Down syndrome results in cognitive delay, almond-shaped eyes, a fold over the eyelid, and other developmental challenges. In addition, for children with Down syndrome, the head, neck, and nose are usually smaller than normal. During the first several months, babies with Down syndrome seem to develop normally. Thereafter, their mental and behavioural development begins to lag behind that of the average child. For example, a child with Down syndrome might not sit up without help until about 1 year, not walk until 2, or not talk until 3, which might be months or even years behind children without Down syndrome.

Parenting a child with Down syndrome presents special challenges. During the preschool years, children

Down syndrome:
a genetic disorder caused by an extra twenty-first chromosome.

denys_kuvaiev/Fotolia

Children with Down syndrome show signs of developmental delay.

Making Children's Lives Better

PKU Resources for Parents through the Montreal Children's Hospital

One way to help make children's lives better is to educate parents about children's particular needs. Children who are born with genetic conditions, such as PKU, require special care to ensure their unique developmental challenges are recognized, accepted, and attended to by their parents. When parents first learn that they are expecting a child, it is not unusual for them to have hopes for what that child will be like, how they will care for the child, and the kinds of opportunities their child will have. However, many parents do not include in their dreams the idea that they might have a child with a particular illness or disease that will alter the parents' views of their child's expected development. The effect of this information on parents can be devastating and requires a restructuring of their worldview to accommodate a new understanding about parenting (Read, 2004). One important aspect of adjustment is the parents' struggle to understand all the vocabulary associated with a genetic condition, which, itself, can be confusing and threatening for a family (Schnell, 2000).

In order to facilitate acceptance by and education of parents who have children diagnosed with PKU, the Biochemical Genetics Unit of Montreal Children's Hospital prepared an excellent parent resource booklet (www.pahdb.mcgill.ca/?Topic=Information&Section=Clinical&Page=1). The booklet includes extensive information about PKU, such as the nature of PKU, how it is treated, and problems that could arise during development. It also contains photos and stories about young people living with PKU in order to show that, despite the special dietary care involved in parenting a child with the condition, that child can still live a normal life. Of special note is that the information in the booklet is presented in a manner that is easy for most parents to understand.

An important feature of the booklet is its glossary. As Schnell (2000) pointed out, the language of genetics is unfamiliar for most parents. All those new medical terms can be very scary. The Montreal Children's Hospital PKU resource booklet describes concepts that parents will hear from medical professionals on a regular basis.

In addition, the booklet lists important online links and provides a contact for the National Food Distribution Centre in Montreal, a nonprofit food bank that distributes foods helpful in the management of metabolic conditions like PKU. The National Food Distribution Centre was organized in 1974 by the Biochemical Genetics Unit at the Montreal Children's Hospital, in co-operation with other Canadian physicians and genetic counsellors. The products that the centre distributes are imported from all over the world and distributed nationally to Canadian clinics and hospitals as well as internationally.

One goal of booklets like this one is to help parents develop a sense of competent control for managing their child's health. They also provide parents with a sense of confidence, optimism, and hope that their children will be able to grow up satisfactorily.

---

with Down syndrome need to participate in programs to prepare them for school. In elementary and secondary school, children with Down syndrome (and other children with disabilities) are typically placed in regular classes, a practice known as **mainstreaming**. The academic achievements of children with Down syndrome are likely limited. Nevertheless, many people with Down syndrome lead happy and fulfilling lives.

The extra twenty-first chromosome in individuals with Down syndrome is usually provided by the egg (Antonarakis & the Down Syndrome Collaborative Group, 1991). Why the egg provides an extra autosome is unknown. However, the odds that a woman will bear a child with Down syndrome increase markedly as she gets older. For a woman in her late twenties, the risk of giving birth to a baby with Down syndrome is about 1 in 1000; for a woman in her early forties, the risk is about 1 in 50. The increased risk might be because a woman's eggs have been in her ovaries since her own prenatal development. Eggs might deteriorate over time as part of aging or because an older woman has a longer history of exposure to hazards in the environment, such as X-rays, that can damage her eggs.

An extra, missing, or damaged autosome has far-reaching consequences for development because the autosomes contain huge amounts of genetic material. In fact, nearly half of all fertilized eggs abort spontaneously within two weeks, primarily due to abnormal autosomes. Thus, most eggs that cannot develop normally are naturally destroyed (Moore & Persaud, 1993).

Mainstreaming:

an educational practice in which children with serious developmental disabilities are placed in classrooms with children who do not have these types of disabilities.

Table 3-5 Common Disorders Associated with the Sex Chromosomes

Disorder	Sex Chromosomes	Frequency	Characteristics
Klinefelter's syndrome	XXY	1 in 500 male births	Tall, small testicles, sterile, below-normal intelligence, passive
XYY complement	XYY	1 in 1000 male births	Tall, some cases apparently have below-normal intelligence
Turner's syndrome	X	1 in 2500–5000 female births	Short, limited development of secondary sex characteristics, problems perceiving spatial relations
XXX syndrome	XXX	1 in 500-1200 female births	Normal stature but female births delayed motor and language development

SOURCE: Based on Bancroft, Axworthy, & Ratcliffe, 1982; Bender, Linden, & Robinson, 1991; Downey et al., 1991; Bender, Linden, & Robinson, 1987; Plomin, Nitz, & Rowe, 1990.

Abnormal sex chromosomes also can disrupt development. Table 3-5 lists four of the more frequent disorders associated with atypical numbers of X and Y chromosomes. Keep in mind that "frequent" is a relative term; although these disorders are more frequent than PKU or Huntington's disease, the chart shows that most still are rare. Notice that no disorders consist solely of Y chromosomes. The presence of an X chromosome appears to be necessary for life.

These genetic disorders demonstrate the remarkable power of heredity. Nevertheless, to fully understand how heredity influences development, we need to consider the environment, which we'll do in Module 3.3.

Ask Yourself

How might delayed cognitive development in children with Down syndrome affect their social relationships with parents, siblings, and peers?

3.3 Heredity Is Not Destiny

 ## Learning Objectives

After reading the module, you should be able to do the following:

LO7 Describe how genes affect behaviour.

LO8 Understand how heredity and environment are related to genotype and phenotype as children develop.

LO9 Trace how family environments influence children's development.

Many people mistakenly view heredity as a set of phenotypes that unfold automatically from the genotypes that are set at conception. Nothing could be further from the truth. Although genotypes are fixed when the sperm fertilizes the egg, phenotypes are not fixed. Instead, heredity and environment combine to direct a child's behavioural and psychological development.

Genes, the Environment, and Behaviour

LO7 **Describe how genes affect behaviour.**

You know from Module 3.1 that no single intelligence gene and no one shyness gene exist; instead, many genes work together to influence these and other aspects of behavioural development. Still, how do genes work together to make some children brighter than others and some children more outgoing than others? That is, how does the information in strands of DNA end up influencing a child's behavioural and psychological development?

The specific paths from genes to behaviour are largely uncharted, but some of their general properties are known. The most important point is that genes never cause behaviour directly; instead, they influence behaviour indirectly by making behaviours more or less likely. For example, no gene exists for dunking a basketball, but genes do regulate bone length. As a consequence, some people grow taller than others and are therefore more capable of dunking. Similarly, no gene exists for alcoholism, but genes do regulate how the body breaks down alcohol that is consumed. Consequently, some people become nauseated because their bodies cannot break down alcohol and are therefore less likely to become alcoholics. These examples show that genes for height and breaking down alcohol affect behaviour indirectly by changing the odds that a person can dunk a basketball or become an alcoholic.

Another important property of gene behaviour paths is that the behavioural consequences of genetic instructions depend on environments. To understand how heredity affects behaviour, we must consider the environment in which genetic instructions are carried out. New research highlights our understanding that genes are as much a product of behavioural and environmental influences as a cause of them (Lerner, 2015). To argue that genes produce environments or directly cause particular behaviours is to engage in **genetic reductionism** (Lerner, 2015). Instead, plenty of evidence now points to the fact that genetic change over time is more the product of complex evolutionary processes and not the direct cause of evolutionary change over generations (Lerner, 2015).

Genetic reductionism: reducing the cause of environmental conditions and behaviours exclusively to genes.

In the remaining sections of this module, we'll look at other aspects of links between heredity and environment.

Reaction Range

LO8 **Understand how heredity and environment are related to genotype and phenotype as children develop.**

If you read the fine print on a can of diet pop made with aspartame (and some other food products), you'll usually see a warning that the product contains phenylalanine. Children with PKU are missing an enzyme needed to break down phenylalanine. When phenylalanine accumulates, it damages the nervous system and leads to cognitive delay. Why the warning on diet pop? Researchers have found that a child who has the genotype for PKU but who is not exposed to phenylalanine will have normal intelligence. As diet pop made with aspartame contains high levels of phenylalanine, producers post a notice to warn people who cannot break down this chemical. In Canada, producers of products containing aspartame are subject to strict controls under the Food and Drugs Act and Regulations due to the effect phenylalanine can have on development in children with PKU (Health Canada, 2005). The disorder PKU illustrates that development depends upon both hereditary and environmental factors—in this case, diet. And as you'll see in the Child Development and Family Policy feature, PKU represents an exciting example of how research has influenced family policy.

Reaction range: the extent to which full genetic expression can occur, based on the limits imposed by the environment.

Through interaction of the environment with a person's heredity, a range of phenotypes become possible. **Reaction range** refers to the range of phenotypic expression

Figure 3-4

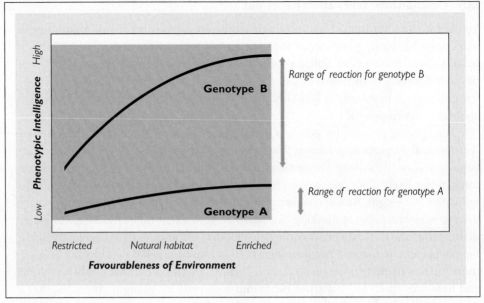

SOURCE: Gottesman, 1963.

possible for a genotype, considering environmental factors. Within the concept of reaction range is the understanding that a genotype is manifested in reaction to the specific environment where development takes place. Figure 3-4 illustrates this fact by showing how phenotypic intelligence might vary, depending on the environment. Look first at genotypic intelligence A, which has a small reaction range. This genotype leads to much the same phenotypic intelligence, no matter whether development takes place in an enriched environment filled with stimulation from parents, siblings, and books, or in an impoverished environment that lacks all such stimulation. In contrast, genotype B has a larger reaction range: The enriched environment leads to a much greater phenotypic intelligence than the impoverished environment. Thus, a single genotype can lead to a range of phenotypes, depending on the quality of the rearing environment.

The conclusion to be drawn from the example is obvious: One genotype can be associated with quite different phenotypes, depending upon the level of intellectual stimulation in the environment. Of course, what makes a "good" or "rich" environment is not the same for all facets of behavioural or psychological development. Throughout this text, you will see how specific kinds of environments influence very particular aspects of development. You will also see how genetic makeup can, in turn, influence the kind of environments to which people end up being exposed (Gottlieb, 2000).

Changing Relations between Nature and Nurture

LO9 **Trace how family environments influence children's development.**

How nature (genetics) and nurture (environment) work together partly depends on a child's age. Sandra Scarr (1992, 1993; Scarr & McCartney, 1983) described three types of relations between heredity and environment. In the first, a **passive gene–environment relation**, parents pass on genotypes to their children and provide much of the early environment for their young children. For example, bright parents are likely to transmit genes that make for bright children. Bright parents are also likely to provide books, museum visits, and discussions that are intellectually stimulating. In this case, heredity and environment are positively related: Both foster brighter children. In both respects, children are passive recipients of heredity and environment. This passive type of relation is most common with infants and young children.

Passive gene–environment relation:

a relationship between heredity and environment in which the parents pass on genotypes to children and also provide much of the early environment supporting expression of those genes.

Child Development and Family Policy

Screening for PKU

PKU was first discovered in 1934 when a Norwegian mother asked a physician, Dr. Asbjørn Følling, to help her two children, both of whom had an intellectual delay. Dr. Følling discovered that the children had large amounts of phenylpyruvic acid in their urine and phenylalanine in their blood. By the 1950s, other scientists had determined that the build-up of phenylalanine damaged the nervous system and that a low-protein diet would leave the nervous system unharmed. The missing link was an effective way to diagnose PKU in newborns, before phenylalanine had a chance to accumulate and cause damage.

In 1959, Dr. Robert Guthrie devised a quick, inexpensive, and effective way to determine levels of phenylalanine in a newborn's blood. Dr. Guthrie and the U.S. National Association for Retarded Children lobbied for laws requiring newborns to be screened for PKU. In 1965, New York became the first state to require mandatory screening; by the end of the 1960s, most U.S. states required screening. Today, PKU screening is conducted at birth throughout North America. PKU screening is done in newborn babies and has been conducted in Canada since the 1960s (CANPKU, 2016; Vockley et al., 2014).

In the second type of relation, an **evocative gene–environment relation**, different genotypes evoke different responses from the environment. For example, children who are bright (due in part to their genes) might pay greater attention to their teachers, ask more questions, and in turn receive greater positive attention in school than children who are not as bright. Children who are friendly and outgoing (again, due in part to their genes) might elicit more interactions with others (in particular, more satisfying interactions) than children who are not as friendly and outgoing. In the evocative relation, which is common in young children, a child's genotype evokes or prompts people to respond differently to the child.

In the third type of relation, **active gene–environment relation**, individuals actively seek environments related to their genetic makeup. Children who are bright (due in part to heredity) might actively seek peers, adults, and activities that strengthen their intellectual development. Similarly, youths who are outgoing (due in part to heredity) seek the company of other people, particularly extroverts like themselves. This process of deliberately seeking environments that fit one's heredity is called **niche-picking**. Niche-picking is first seen in childhood and becomes more common as children get older and can control their environments.

Genes and environment rarely influence development on their own. Instead, nature and nurture interact. Experiences determine which phenotypes emerge, and genotypes influence the nature of children's experiences. To understand how genes influence development, we need to look carefully at how environments work.

Much of what we have said about genes, environment, and development is summarized in Figure 3-5 (Lytton, 2000). Parents are the source of children's genes and, at least for young children, the primary source of children's experiences. Children's genes also influence the experiences that they have and the impact of those experiences on them. However, to capture the idea of nonshared environmental influences, we would need a separate diagram for each child, reflecting the fact that parents provide unique genes and a unique family environment for each of their children.

Evocative gene–environment relation:
a relationship between heredity and environment in which different genotypes evoke different responses from the environment.

Active gene–environment relation:
a relationship between heredity and environment in which individuals actively seek environments suitable to their genotype.

Niche-picking:
the process of deliberately selecting an environment suitable to one's genotype.

Luis Louro/Fotolia

Extroverted youth often like to spend time with other extroverted youth.

Figure 3-5

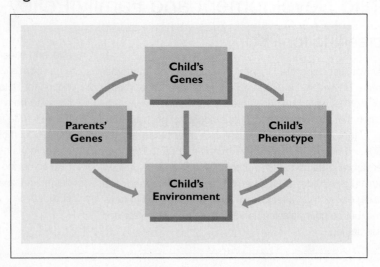

Most of this text explains the links among nature, nurture, and development. We can first see the interaction of nature and nurture during prenatal development.

Ask Yourself

What Would a Geneticist Do?

If you were a geneticist and you found out that expectant parents were going to have a child with a genetic abnormality, how would you advise them? What issues might become important in your discussion?

Summary

3.1 Mechanisms of Heredity

The Biology of Heredity

- Gametes (sperm or egg) are produced through meiosis; other bodily cells reproduce through mitosis.

- At conception, the 23 chromosomes in the sperm merge with the 23 chromosomes in the egg.

- The 46 chromosomes that result include 22 pairs of autosomes plus 2 sex chromosomes.

- Each individual chromosome is one molecule of DNA.

- DNA is made up of nucleotide pairs organized in a structure that resembles a spiral staircase.

- The nucleotide pairs in DNA are adenine–thymine and guanine–cytosine.

- A section of DNA that provides specific biochemical instructions is called a gene.

- All of a person's genes make up a genotype.

- Phenotype refers to the physical, behavioural, and psychological characteristics that develop when the genotype is exposed to a specific environment.

Single Gene Inheritance

- Different forms of the same gene are called alleles.

- A person who inherits the same allele on a pair of chromosomes is homozygous for that gene.

- The biochemical instructions on homozygous alleles are followed.

- A person who inherits different alleles is heterozygous for that gene.

- In the case of heterozygous alleles, the instructions of the dominant allele are followed and those of the recessive allele are ignored.

- In incomplete dominance, the person is heterozygous but the phenotype is midway between the dominant and recessive phenotypes.

Behavioural Genetics

- Behavioural and psychological phenotypes that reflect an underlying continuum (such as intelligence) often involve polygenic inheritance.

- In polygenic inheritance, the phenotype reflects the combined activity of many distinct genes.

- Polygenic inheritance has been examined traditionally by studying twins and adopted children and more recently by identifying DNA markers.

- Substantial influence of heredity has been identified through studies of polygenic inheritance in three areas: intelligence, psychological disorders, and personality.

Nonshared Environmental Influences

- Family environments affect each child in the family differently, which refers to the concept of nonshared environmental influences.

- Each child's experience in the family and relationship with other family members will be different, even for monozygotic twins.

3.2 Genetic Disorders

Inherited Disorders

- Most inherited disorders are carried by recessive alleles: sickle-cell disease, albinism, cystic fibrosis, PKU, and Tay-Sachs disease.

- Inherited disorders are rarely carried by dominant alleles because individuals with such a disorder usually don't live long enough to have children, except in the case of Huntington's disease, which doesn't become symptomatic until middle age.

Abnormal Chromosomes

- Most fertilized eggs that do not have 46 chromosomes are aborted spontaneously soon after conception, except in the case of Down syndrome, which is caused by an extra twenty-first chromosome.

- Individuals with Down syndrome have a distinctive appearance and are cognitively delayed.

- Disorders of the sex chromosomes are more common because these chromosomes contain less genetic material than autosomes.

- Sex chromosome disorders include Klinefelter's syndrome, XYY complement, Turner's syndrome, and XXX syndrome.

3.3 Heredity Is Not Destiny

Genes, the Environment, and Behaviour

- Genes never influence behaviour directly but affect behaviour indirectly by increasing the odds that a child will behave in a particular way.

- The impact of a gene on behaviour depends on the environment in which the genetic instructions are carried out.

Reaction Range

- One genotype can lead to different phenotypes, due to reaction range, because the outcome of heredity depends upon the environment in which development occurs.

- An example of the effect of reaction range is PKU, which does not lead to cognitive delay when individuals with the disorder maintain a diet low in phenylalanine.

Changing Relations between Nature and Nurture

- In infants and young children, the gene–environment relation is passive: Parents pass on genotypes to their children and provide much of the early environment for their young children.

- An evocative gene–environment relation increasingly occurs during development as the child's genotype evokes responses from the environment.

- In older children and adolescents, an active gene–environment relationship is common because older individuals actively seek environments related to their genetic makeup.

Chapter Critical Review

1. Discuss the benefits and drawbacks of assisted reproduction methods such as in vitro fertilization, surrogate parenting, and egg donation. Are these techniques changing our definitions of "parent" and "environment"?

2. A woman with curly dark hair and a man with straight blond hair have two children, one with straight blond hair and one with straight dark hair. Explain how this is possible (hint: Refer back to Table 3-1, Some Common Phenotypes Associated with Single Pairs of Genes).

3. Explain why psychologists use twin studies and adoption studies for research in behavioural genetics. What general insights have such studies provided to the nature–nurture question?

4. How do genes influence behaviour? Describe the general process and give a specific example.

5. How does the concept of nonshared environment help explain some of the links among nature, nurture, and development?

See for Yourself

The Human Genome Project, launched in the late 1980s by U.S. scientists, aims to identify the exact location of all human genes. It is a vast undertaking that first requires determining the sequence of roughly 3 billion pairs of nucleotides and 21 000 to 25 000 genes like those shown in Figure 3-1 (Ota Wang & Sue, 2005). About 99.9 percent of any one person's genetic code is identical to the genetic code of any other unrelated person (Ota Wang & Sue, 2005). According to Genome Canada, the human genome, written out, would be as long as 800 dictionaries. It would take a person about 50 years to type out the human genome, working at a speed of 60 words per minute for 8 hours per day. To store the human genome on your computer, you would need three gigs of space (or the nucleus of a tiny cell) (Genome Canada, 2010). The project has produced maps of each chromosome showing the location of known genes. You can see these maps at a website maintained by the Human Genome Project (www.ncbi.nlm.nih.gov/projects/genome/genemap99). At this site, you can also select a "favourite" chromosome and explore which genes have been located on it. See for yourself!

Chapter 4
Prenatal Development and Birth

ZouZou/Shutterstock

∨ MODULE

4.1 From Conception to Birth

4.2 Influences on Prenatal Development

4.3 Happy Birthday!

Connect to My Virtual Child

What kinds of theories do you have about children? What ideas inform your thoughts and beliefs about the lives of children, how they are raised, and the nature of the human person? Use your access card and follow this link www.myvirtualchild.com to learn more about the world of the child. You can even virtually try to raise your own child.

It was official: Terry and Mabel were expecting their first baby! They alternated between feeling excited and feeling worried, but most of all they couldn't wait to meet the unique person who was forming inside of Mabel. As the baby grew, Mabel felt little flutters of movement inside her, almost like little tickles, but toward the time of delivery, Terry kept saying that the baby was going to be great at football because he or she was such a great kicker. They wondered: Will the baby be a boy or girl?

4.1 From Conception to Birth

 ## Learning Objectives

After reading the module, you should be able to do the following:

LO1 Recount what happens to a fertilized egg in the first two weeks after conception.

LO2 Describe when body structures and internal organs emerge in prenatal development.

LO3 Note when body systems begin to function well enough to support life.

Prenatal development:

the changes that transform the fertilized egg into a newborn human.

Prenatal development begins when a sperm fertilizes an egg. The changes that transform the fertilized egg into a newborn human make up **prenatal development**. Health professionals usually measure pregnancy duration from the start of the last menstrual period, which is usually two weeks before conception; as a result, many people talk about pregnancy lasting 40 weeks. However, prenatal gestation, itself, takes an average of 38 weeks and can vary by as much as 37 days (5 weeks) in individual cases (Jukic, Baird, Weinberg, McConnaughey, & Wilcox, 2013).

The 38 weeks of prenatal development are divided into three stages: the period of the zygote, the period of the embryo, and the period of the fetus. Each period gets its name from the term used to describe the baby-to-be at that point in prenatal development. In this module, we'll trace the major developments during each period and find out what happens during pregnancy.

Period of the Zygote (Weeks 1–2)

LO1 Recount what happens to a fertilized egg in the first two weeks after conception.

Figure 4–1 traces the major events of the first period of prenatal development, which begins with fertilization and lasts about two weeks. It ends when the fertilized egg, called a **zygote**, implants itself in the wall of the uterus. During these two weeks, the zygote grows rapidly through cell division. It travels down the fallopian tube toward the uterus, and, within hours, the zygote undergoes its first cell division. Further cell division then occurs every 12 hours. After about four days, the zygote consists of approximately 100 cells and resembles a hollow, fluid-filled ball.

By the end of the first week, the zygote reaches the uterus. The next step is **implantation**: The zygote burrows into the uterine wall and connects to the mother's blood vessels. Implantation takes about a week to complete and triggers hormonal changes that prevent menstruation. Some women have difficulty becoming pregnant not because they can't conceive but because the zygote fails to implant.

An implanted zygote is less than 1 millimetre in diameter, but its cells have already begun to differentiate. In Figure 4–2, which shows a cross-section of the zygote and the wall of the uterus, you can see different layers of cells. A small cluster of cells near the center of the zygote, the **germ disc**, eventually develops into the baby. The other cells become structures that support, nourish, and protect the developing child. The layer of cells closest

Zygote:

a fertilized egg.

Implantation:

the burrowing of the zygote into the uterine wall.

Germ disc:

a small cluster of cells near the zygote's center that develops into the baby.

An implanted zygote.

Mopic/Fotolia

Figure 4–1

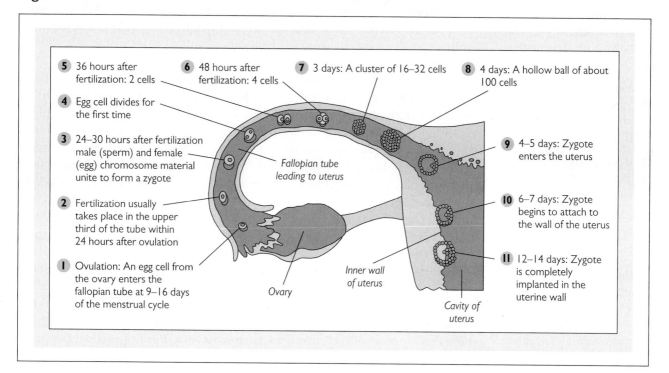

5 36 hours after fertilization: 2 cells

6 48 hours after fertilization: 4 cells

7 3 days: A cluster of 16–32 cells

8 4 days: A hollow ball of about 100 cells

4 Egg cell divides for the first time

3 24–30 hours after fertilization male (sperm) and female (egg) chromosome material unite to form a zygote

Fallopian tube leading to uterus

9 4–5 days: Zygote enters the uterus

2 Fertilization usually takes place in the upper third of the tube within 24 hours after ovulation

10 6–7 days: Zygote begins to attach to the wall of the uterus

1 Ovulation: An egg cell from the ovary enters the fallopian tube at 9–16 days of the menstrual cycle

Ovary

Inner wall of uterus

Cavity of uterus

11 12–14 days: Zygote is completely implanted in the uterine wall

Figure 4–2

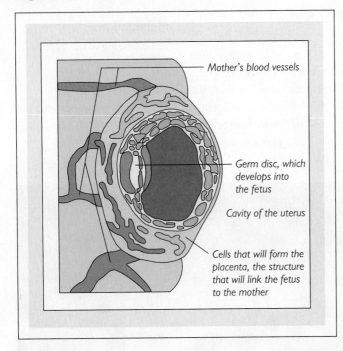

Mother's blood vessels

Germ disc, which develops into the fetus

Cavity of the uterus

Cells that will form the placenta, the structure that will link the fetus to the mother

Placenta:
a uterine structure for exchanging nutrients and wastes between mother and baby.

Embryo:
an embedded zygote.

Ectoderm:
the outer layer of the embryo, which becomes the hair, outer skin, and nervous system.

Mesoderm:
the middle layer of the embryo, which becomes the muscles, bones, and circulatory system.

Endoderm:
the inner layer of the embryo, which becomes the digestive system and lungs.

Amnion or amniotic sac:
the sac in which the baby develops.

Amniotic fluid:
the liquid that fills the amnion and cushions the baby.

Umbilical cord:
a cord-like structure containing blood vessels that joins the developing baby through the baby's abdomen to the mother's placenta.

to the uterus becomes the **placenta**, a structure for exchanging nutrients and wastes between the mother and her baby.

Implantation and differentiation of cells mark the end of the period of the zygote. Comfortably sheltered in the uterus, the zygote is well prepared for the remaining 36 weeks of the marvellous journey to birth.

Period of the Embryo (Weeks 3–8)

LO2 Describe when body structures and internal organs emerge in prenatal development.

Once the zygote completely embeds itself in the uterine wall, it becomes an **embryo**. This new period typically begins the third week after conception and lasts until the end of the eighth week. During the period of the embryo, body structures and internal organs develop. At the beginning of the period, three layers form in the embryo. The outer layer, or **ectoderm**, will become hair, the outer layer of skin, and the nervous system; the middle layer, or **mesoderm**, will form muscles, bones, and the circulatory system; the inner layer, or **endoderm**, will form the digestive system and the lungs.

One way to see the dramatic changes that occur during the embryonic period is to compare a 3-week-old embryo with an 8-week-old embryo. The 3-week-old embryo is about 2 millimetres long. Cell specialization is underway, but the embryo looks more like a salamander than a human being. However, growth and specialization proceed so rapidly that an 8-week-old embryo looks very different. You can see eyes, jaw, arms, and legs.

The brain and the nervous system are also developing rapidly, and the heart has been beating for nearly a month. Most of the organs found in a mature human are in place in some form, except the sex organs. Despite all this sophisticated development, the embryo is only about 2 centimetres long and weighs less than 30 grams, making it much too small for the mother to feel physically.

The embryo's environment is shown in Figure 4–3. The embryo rests in a sac called the **amnion or amniotic sac**, which is filled with **amniotic fluid** to cushion the embryo and maintain a constant temperature. The embryo is linked to the mother by the umbilical cord and the placenta. The **umbilical cord** houses blood vessels that join the embryo to the placenta. In the placenta, the blood vessels from the umbilical cord run close to the mother's blood vessels but aren't actually connected to them. Instead, the blood flows through villi, finger-like projections from the umbilical blood vessels that are shown in the enlarged view in Figure 4–3. As you can see, villi lie in close proximity to the mother's blood vessels, which allows nutrients, oxygen, vitamins, and waste products to be exchanged between mother and embryo.

Growth in the period of the embryo follows two important principles, which can be characterized as "from the top down" and "from the center out." First, the head develops before the rest of the body. Such growth from the head to the base of the spine illustrates the **cephalocaudal** principle (from the top down). Second, arms and legs develop before hands and feet. Growth of parts near the center of the body before those that are more distant illustrates the **proximodistal** principle (from the center out). Growth after birth also follows these principles.

Figure 4–3

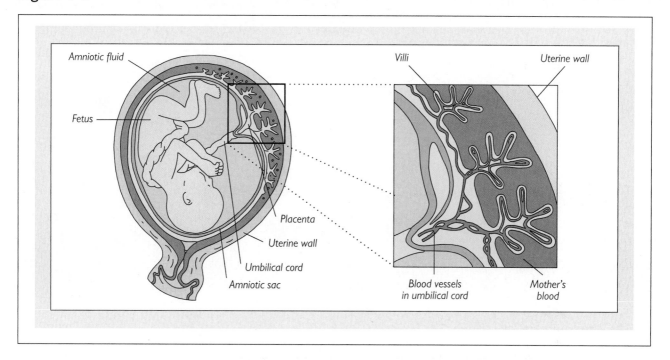

With body structures and internal organs in place, another major milestone passes in prenatal development. What's left is for these structures and organs to begin working properly. This is accomplished in the final period of prenatal development, as we'll see in the next section.

Period of the Fetus (Weeks 9–38)

LO3 Note when body systems begin to function well enough to support life.

The final and longest phase of prenatal development, the period of the **fetus**, extends from the ninth week after conception until birth. During this period, the baby-to-be becomes much larger, and its bodily systems begin to work. The increase in size is remarkable. At the beginning of this period, the fetus weighs less than 30 grams. At

Cephalocaudal:
growth from the top and extending downward.

Proximodistal:
growth from the center and extending outward.

Fetus:
after the eighth week of gestation until birth, the developing baby is called a fetus.

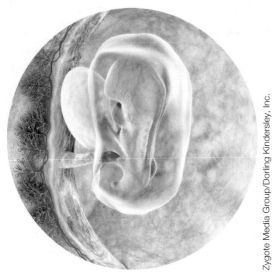

An embryo at three weeks.

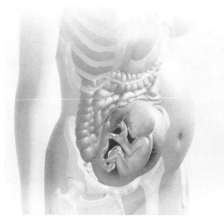

An embryo at eight weeks.

Figure 4–4

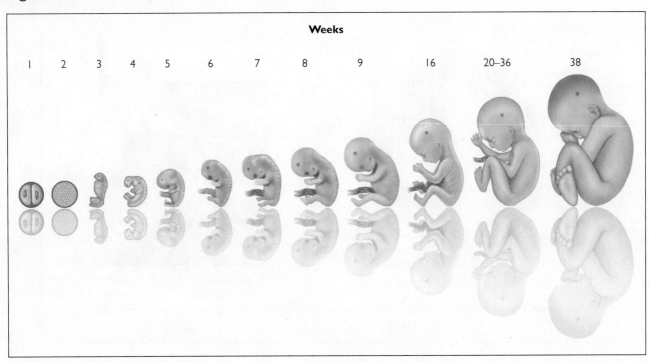

Cerebral cortex:
the folded surface of the brain that regulates many human behaviours.

Vernix:
a thick, greasy coating on the skin that protects the baby during gestation.

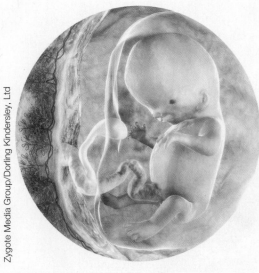

By 5.5 to 7 months, a fetus can often survive.

about four months, the fetus weighs roughly 100 to 225 grams, enough for most mothers to feel movement. In the last five months of pregnancy, the fetus gains an additional 3 to 3.6 kilograms before birth. Figure 4–4, which depicts the fetus at one-eighth of its actual size, illustrates these incredible increases in size.

During the fetal period, the finishing touches are put on the body systems essential to human life, such as the nervous, respiratory, and digestive systems. Some highlights of this period include the following:

- At four weeks after conception, a flat set of cells curls to form a tube. One end of the tube swells to form the brain; the rest forms the spinal cord. By the start of the fetal period, the brain has distinct structures and has begun to regulate body functions. During the period of the fetus, all regions of the brain grow, particularly the **cerebral cortex**, the folded surface of the brain that regulates many important human behaviours.

- Near the end of the embryonic period, male embryos develop testes and female embryos develop ovaries. In the third month, a female fetus develops a vagina and labia. In a male fetus, the testes secrete a hormone that causes cells to develop into a penis and scrotum. If this hormone is not secreted, the developing fetus will have female genitalia.

- In the fifth and sixth months after conception, eyebrows, eyelashes, and scalp hair emerge. The skin thickens and is covered with a thick, greasy substance, **vernix**, which protects the fetus during its long bath in amniotic fluid.

With these and other rapid changes, by 22 to 28 weeks most systems function well enough to support the fetus if it is born at this time, making this age range the **age of viability**. By this age, the fetus has a distinctly baby-like look. However, babies born this early have trouble breathing because their lungs are not yet mature. Also, they cannot regulate their body temperature very well because they lack the insulating layer of fat that appears in the eighth month of gestation. With modern neonatal intensive care, infants born this early can survive, but they face other challenges, as we'll describe in Module 4.3.

The changes of the fetal period also mean that the fetus actually emits behaviours (Joseph, 2000) and responds to stimulation (Birnholz & Benacerraf, 1983; Kisilevsky & Low, 1998). For example, although we can't observe it directly, external sounds, such as music, probably cause the fetal heart rate to increase and might cause the fetus to move. Also, the fetus develops regular cycles of activity: Most mothers report times when the fetus is moving and other times when the fetus is still (DiPietro, Hodgson, Costigan, & Hilton, 1996). Some fetuses are more active than others, and these differences predict infants' behaviour at 6 months of age.

A developing fetus might respond to external stimulation with an increased heart rate and movement.

Age of viability:
the age at which most bodily systems function well enough to support life once the baby is born.

Remarkably, newborns apparently can recognize some of the sounds they hear during prenatal development. DeCasper and Spence (1986) had pregnant women read aloud the famous Dr. Seuss story *The Cat in the Hat* twice a day for the last two months of pregnancy. As newborns, then, these babies had heard *The Cat in the Hat* for more than three hours. The newborns were then allowed to suck on a mechanical nipple connected to a tape recorder so that the baby's sucking could turn the tape on or off. The investigators discovered that babies would suck to hear a tape of their mother reading *The Cat in the Hat* but not to hear her reading other stories. Evidently, newborns recognized the familiar, rhythmic quality of *The Cat in the Hat* from their prenatal story-time. These and other important prenatal changes are summarized in Table 4–1.

The milestones listed in the table make it clear that prenatal development prepares the fetus with skills for living as a newborn baby, but these astonishing prenatal changes can take place only when a family provides a healthy environment for the baby-to-be. We also know that characteristics of the infant are related to how the baby adjusts after being born. The Looking Ahead feature that follows describes how activity level of the baby before being born can be related to level of infant fussiness later on.

Table 4–1 Summary Table

Changes during Prenatal Development		
Stage	**Duration (after conception)**	**Principal Changes**
1. Period of the zygote	0–2 weeks	Egg is fertilized, zygote becomes implanted in wall of uterus
2. Period of the embryo	3–8 weeks	Period of rapid growth, most body structures begin to form
3. Period of the fetus	9–38 weeks	Huge increase in size, most body systems begin to function

Looking Ahead

Fetal Activity Predicts Infant Fussiness

Some pregnant women say that the fetus is active constantly, almost as if it's exercising to prepare for birth! Other women report little movement; the fetus seems to be perpetually quiet. Are these differences in the activity level of a fetus related to later aspects of an infant's development? Janet DiPietro and her colleagues (DiPietro, Hodgson, Costigan, & Johnson, 1996) addressed this question by measuring fetal activity level approximately one month before birth. Pregnant women lay quietly for about an hour with a device attached to their abdomen that recorded motor activity (e.g., moving an arm or leg) but not breathing or hiccupping. When babies were 6 months old, mothers completed a questionnaire that assessed many aspects of infants' behaviour. DiPietro and her colleagues found a correlation of 0.6 between fetal activity level and fussiness at 6 months. That is, a more active fetus tends to be fussier at 6 months, which means that the infant cries more often and more intensely, is more difficult to soothe when upset, and is moodier overall. In other words, an active fetus is more likely than an inactive fetus to become an unhappy, difficult baby. This finding suggests that infant fussiness might reflect nature more than nurture. If fussiness were due primarily to an infant's experiences after birth, then measures taken before birth should not predict fussiness. Because fussiness relates to fetal activity, biology rather than experiences after birth would seem to be the key factor in the onset of fussy behaviour in babies. Later research by DiPietro and colleagues (DiPietro, Hilton, Hawkins, Costigan, & Pressman, 2002) has also linked infant prenatal activity with maternal stress levels.

Making Children's Lives Better

Five Steps toward a Healthy Baby

The steps listed below are common ones to follow during pregnancy, but the most important one is to follow the advice of your physician. Also, as critically important as these steps are, they unfortunately do not guarantee a healthy baby. In Module 4.2, we'll see how prenatal development can sometimes go awry.

1. Visit a health-care professional for regular prenatal checkups. You should have monthly visits until you get close to your due date, when you will have a checkup every other week or maybe even weekly.

2. Eat healthy foods. Be sure your diet includes foods from each of the five major food groups (cereals, fruits, vegetables, dairy products, and meats and beans). Your health-care professional might recommend that you supplement your diet with vitamins, minerals, and iron to be sure you are providing your baby with all the nutrients he or she needs.

3. Stop drinking alcohol, stop smoking cigarettes, and limit caffeinated beverages. Consult your health-care professional before taking any over-the-counter medications or prescription drugs.

4. Exercise throughout pregnancy. If you are physically fit, your body is better equipped to handle the needs of the baby.

5. Get enough rest, especially during the last two months of pregnancy. Also, attend childbirth education classes so that you'll be prepared for labour, delivery, and your new baby.

Ask Yourself

How might the mother–fetus relationship affect fetal prenatal development? Could the mother–father relationship have an effect on fetal prenatal development?

4.2 Influences on Prenatal Development

Learning Objectives

After reading the module, you should be able to do the following:

LO4 Explain how prenatal development is influenced by a pregnant woman's nutrition, the stress she experiences while pregnant, and her age.

LO5 Define what a teratogen is, and state what specific diseases, drugs, and environmental hazards can be teratogens.

LO6 Detail exactly how teratogens affect prenatal development.

LO7 Summarize how prenatal development can be monitored and how abnormal prenatal development can be corrected.

Parents have many concerns when they are expecting a child. For example, they might worry about things like, "Is radiation from the monitor harmful to my baby?" or "Can we have a glass of wine to help unwind from the stress of the day?" or "Will my baby have a genetic problem?" All of these concerns are well founded. Beginning with conception, environmental factors influence the course of prenatal development, and they are the focus of this module, which covers problems that sometimes arise in pregnancy.

General Risk Factors

LO4 **Explain how prenatal development is influenced by a pregnant woman's nutrition, the stress she experiences while pregnant, and her age.**

As the name implies, general risk factors can have widespread effects on prenatal development. Scientists have identified three general risk factors: nutrition, stress, and a mother's age.

NUTRITION. The mother is the developing child's sole source of nutrition, so a balanced diet that includes foods from each of the five major food groups is vital. Most pregnant women need to increase their intake of calories by about 10 to 20 percent to meet the needs of prenatal development. A woman should expect to gain between 11 and 16 kilograms during pregnancy, assuming that her weight was normal before pregnancy. A woman who was underweight before becoming pregnant may gain as much as 18 kilograms; a woman who was overweight should gain at least 7 kilograms (Institute of Medicine, 1990). Of this gain, about one-third reflects the weight of the baby, the placenta, and the fluid in the amniotic sac; another third comes from increases in a woman's fat stores; yet another third comes from the increased volume of blood and increases in the size of her breasts and uterus (Whitney & Hamilton, 1987).

Sheer amount of food is only part of the equation for a healthy pregnancy. What a pregnant woman eats is also very important. Proteins, vitamins, and minerals are essential for normal prenatal development. For example, folic acid, one of the B vitamins, is important for the baby's nervous system to develop properly (Shaw, Schaffer, Velie, Morland, & Harris, 1995). When mothers do not consume adequate amounts of folic acid, their babies are at risk for **spina bifida**, a disorder in which the

Spina bifida:
a disorder in which an embryo's neural tube does not close properly during development.

embryo's neural tube does not close properly during the first month of pregnancy. Since the neural tube develops into the brain and spinal cord, when it does not close properly the result is permanent damage to the spinal cord and the nervous system. Many children with spina bifida need crutches, braces, or wheelchairs. Other prenatal problems have also been traced to inadequate proteins, vitamins, or minerals, so health-care professionals typically recommend that pregnant women supplement their diet with additional proteins, vitamins, and minerals.

When a pregnant woman does not provide adequate nourishment, the infant is likely to be born prematurely and to be underweight. Inadequate nourishment during the last few months of pregnancy can particularly affect the nervous system, because this is a time of rapid brain growth. Finally, babies who do not receive adequate nourishment are vulnerable to illness (Guttmacher & Kaiser, 1986).

STRESS. Does a pregnant woman's mood affect the zygote, embryo, or fetus in her uterus? Is a woman who is happy during pregnancy more likely to give birth to a happy baby? Is a pregnant woman who works in a stressful environment more likely to give birth to an irritable baby? These questions address the impact on prenatal development of *chronic stress*, which refers to a person's physical and psychological responses to threatening or challenging situations. We can answer these questions with some certainty for nonhumans. When pregnant female animals experience constant stress—such as repeated electric shock or intense overcrowding—their offspring are often smaller than average and prone to other physical and behavioural problems (Schneider, 1992). In addition, stress seems to cause greater harm when experienced early in pregnancy (Schneider, Roughton, Koehler, & Lubach, 1999).

Determining the impact of stress on human pregnancy is more difficult because it would be unethical to expose pregnant women to conditions of extreme stress. Therefore, we must rely solely on correlational studies. These typically show that women who report greater anxiety during pregnancy more often give birth early or have babies who weigh less than average (Copper et al., 1996; Paarlberg et al., 1995). Increased stress can harm prenatal development in several ways. First, when a pregnant woman experiences stress, her body secretes hormones that reduce the flow of oxygen to the fetus while increasing its heart rate and activity level (Monk et al., 2000). Second, stress can weaken a pregnant woman's immune system, making her more susceptible to illness (Cohen & Williamson, 1991), which can, in turn, damage fetal development. Third, pregnant women under stress are more likely to smoke cigarettes or drink alcohol and less likely to rest, exercise, and eat properly. All of these behaviours endanger prenatal development.

The results described here apply to women who experience prolonged, extreme stress. Virtually all women become anxious or upset sometime during pregnancy. Occasional, relatively mild anxiety is not thought to have any harmful consequences for prenatal development.

MOTHER'S AGE. Traditionally, a woman's twenties were thought to be her prime childbearing years. Teenage women, as well as women who were 30 or older, were considered less fit for the challenge of pregnancy. Is being 20-something really important for a successful pregnancy? Let's answer this question separately for teenage and older women. Compared to women in their twenties, teenage women are more

Violetstar/Fotolia

The workplace is a major source of stress for many people.

likely to have problems during pregnancy, labour, and delivery largely because pregnant teenagers often do not get good prenatal care. Teenagers often are unaware of the need for prenatal checkups and do not seek them out. However, Goldenberg and Klerman (1995) found that, when differences in prenatal care are taken into account, African-American teenagers were just as likely as women in their twenties to have problem-free pregnancies and give birth to healthy babies.

Nevertheless, children of teenage mothers generally tend to do less well in school and have behavioural problems more often (Dryfoos, 1990). The problems of teenage motherhood—incomplete education, poverty, and marital difficulties—affect the child's later development (Furstenberg, Brooks-Gunn, & Morgan, 1987).

Of course, not all teenage mothers and their infants follow this dismal life course. Some teenage mothers finish school, find good jobs, and have happy marriages; their children do well in school, both academically and socially. However, teenage pregnancies with happy endings are definitely the exception; for most teenage mothers and their children, life is a struggle. Educating teenagers about the true consequences of teen pregnancy is crucial.

More women are having babies after the age of 30.

Are older women better suited for pregnancy? This is an important question because today's women are waiting longer than ever to have children. Completing an education and beginning a career often delay childbearing. Many women in Canada are waiting until they are older to have children, which increases the incidence of high-risk births (Bushnik & Garner, 2008; Public Health Agency of Canada, 2008). In addition, the overall birth rate in Canada has been steadily dropping since 1990.

Traditionally, older women were thought to have more difficult pregnancies and more complicated labour and delivery. Today, we know that women in their thirties who are in good health are no more risk-prone during pregnancy, labour, and delivery than women in their twenties (Ales, Druzin, & Santini, 1990). Women in their forties, however, are more likely to give birth to babies with Down syndrome.

Prenatal development is most likely to proceed normally when women are healthy and eat right, receive proper health care, and lead lives that are free from extreme or chronic stress. But even in these optimal cases, prenatal development can be disrupted, as we'll see in the next section.

Teratogens: Diseases, Drugs, and Environmental Hazards

LO5 **Define what a teratogen is, and state what specific diseases, drugs, and environmental hazards can be teratogens.**

In the late 1950s, pregnant women in West Germany and elsewhere were introduced to the drug thalidomide to help them sleep and control symptoms of nausea. Many of these women later gave birth to babies with deformed or missing arms, legs, hands, or fingers (Jensen, Benson, & Bobak, 1981). Thalidomide was a powerful **teratogen**, an agent that disrupts normal prenatal development. Ultimately, more than 7000 babies worldwide were harmed before thalidomide was withdrawn from the market (Moore & Persaud, 1993).

Canadian women also were prescribed thalidomide, which led to birth defects in some Canadian children. Currently, the Thalidomide Victims Association of Canada represents 125 people living with birth defects caused by thalidomide. Its website (www.thalidomide.ca) documents people's experiences living with the effects of thalidomide as well as current issues around use of the drug. This group advocates

Teratogen:

any agent that disrupts normal prenatal development.

Kirill Linnik/Shutterstock

Table 4–2 Summary Table

Teratogenic Diseases and Their Consequences	
Disease	**Potential Consequences**
AIDS	Frequent infections, neurological disorders, death
Cytomegalovirus	Deafness, blindness, abnormally small head, cognitive delay
Genital herpes	Encephalitis, enlarged spleen, improper blood clotting
Rubella (German measles)	Cognitive delay; damage to eyes, ears, and heart
Syphilis	Damage to the central nervous system, teeth, and bones

caution regarding the use of thalidomide, which has been reintroduced as a drug in Canada for the management of conditions associated with some cancers.

Prompted by the thalidomide disaster, researchers began to study teratogens extensively. Today, we know a great deal about many teratogens, including diseases, drugs, and environmental hazards.

DISEASES. Sometimes women become ill while pregnant. Most diseases, such as colds or strains of flu, do not affect the developing baby. However, bacterial and viral infections can be very harmful and, in some cases, fatal to the embryo or fetus; five of the most common are listed in Table 4–2.

Some of these diseases pass from the mother through the placenta to attack the embryo or fetus directly. They include cytomegalovirus (a type of herpes), rubella, and syphilis. Other diseases attack at birth: The virus is present in the lining of the birth canal, and the baby is infected as it passes through to be born. Genital herpes is transmitted this way. AIDS may be transmitted both ways—through the placenta and during passage through the birth canal.

The only way to guarantee that these diseases do not disrupt prenatal development is for a woman not to contract the disease before or during her pregnancy. Medication might help the woman but might not prevent the disease from damaging the developing baby. New research, however, has resulted in the possibility of a vaccine to decrease cytomegalovirus infection in women of childbearing age (Pass et al., 2009). Also, new insights into antibodies that neutralize many forms of HIV, with the possibility of a new vaccine being developed, are promising (Zhou et al., 2010).

DRUGS. Thalidomide illustrates the harm that drugs can cause during prenatal development. Table 4–3 lists other drugs that are known teratogens. Most of the drugs in the list are substances that are used routinely by many—alcohol, aspirin, caffeine, nicotine. Nevertheless, when consumed by pregnant women, these and other drugs present specific dangers (Behnke & Eyler, 1993; Guerrini, Thomson, & Gurling, 2007; Martin, Dombrowski, Mullis, Wisenbaker, & Huttunen, 2006; Till, Koren, & Rovet, 2001).

Table 4–3 Summary Table

Teratogenic Drugs and Their Consequences	
Drug	**Potential Consequences**
Alcohol	Fetal alcohol spectrum disorder, cognitive deficits, heart damage, retarded growth
Aspirin	Deficits in intelligence, attention, and motor skill
Caffeine	Lower birth weight, decreased muscle tone
Cocaine and heroin	Retarded growth, irritability in newborns
Marijuana	Lower birth weight, less motor control
Nicotine	Retarded growth, possible cognitive impairments
Solvents	Cognitive delays, neuromotor functioning deficits

Cigarette smoking demonstrates the potential harm from these drugs (Cornelius, Taylor, Geva, & Day, 1995; Day, Richardson, Goldschmidt, & Cornelius, 2000; Fried, O'Connell, & Watkinson, 1992). The nicotine in cigarette smoke constricts blood vessels, which reduces the oxygen and nutrients that can reach the fetus via the placenta. Therefore, pregnant women who smoke are more likely to miscarry (abort the fetus spontaneously) and to bear children who are smaller than average at birth. Birth complications are also more frequent, and researchers have started to make connections between prenatal exposure to cigarette smoke and long-term, adverse effects on behaviour and attention (Fried & Watkinson, 1990; Gusella & Fried, 1984; Wakschlag, 2002; Wakschlag & Hans, 2002). Finally, even second-hand smoke harms the fetus. In Canada, some researchers have demonstrated that Aboriginal women tend to smoke at a much higher rate during pregnancy than do non-Aboriginal women (Heaman & Chalmers, 2005). When pregnant women don't smoke but fathers do, babies tend to be smaller at birth (Friedman & Polifka, 1996). The message is clear and simple: Pregnant women shouldn't smoke, and they should avoid others who do.

One difficulty with sorting out the effects of smoking on child development is that sometimes when mothers smoke, they also consume alcohol. Alcohol is a known teratogen, and researchers sometimes have difficulty sorting out the effects of smoking on babies from the very harmful effects that alcohol has. Pregnant women who consume alcohol can give birth to babies with **fetal alcohol spectrum disorder (FASD)**. Children with FASD usually grow more slowly than normal and have heart problems. Youngsters born with FASD often have a small head, a thin upper lip, a short nose, and widely spaced eyes. Many of these children experience cognitive delay, poor social judgment, and limited motor skills (Niebyl, 1991). Preschoolers with FASD tend to have particular difficulty with language, cognitive tasks, and visual-motor coordination (Janzen, Nanson, & Block, 1995). When women drink moderately throughout pregnancy, their children often have lower scores on tests of attention, memory, and intelligence (Streissguth, Barr, Sampson, & Bookstein, 1994). No amount of alcohol during pregnancy is known to be safe; therefore, women should completely abstain from alcohol consumption while pregnant. Avoiding alcohol consumption during pregnancy and at times when one is at risk of becoming pregnant makes FASD 100 percent preventable (Paton & Croom, 2010).

Fetal alcohol spectrum disorder (FASD): a developmental disorder caused by maternal consumption of alcohol during pregnancy.

The Government of Canada has developed a drug strategy to work, in part, on the impact of FASD in this country, and new methods are being developed for the diagnosis of FASD (Caprara, Nash, Greenbaum, Rovet, & Koren, 2007; Chudley et al., 2005). In an attempt to prevent, monitor, and treat FASD, the government has released a Best Practices document discussing these issues (Roberts & Nanson, 2000). At the present time, FASD is a medical diagnosis, not a psychological diagnosis. Of every 1000 babies born in Canada, 9 have FASD, which is the main cause of developmental disability for Canadian children (Public Health Agency of Canada, 2005a).

A child with typical signs of FASD.

ENVIRONMENTAL HAZARDS.   Because Canada is an industrialized nation, Canadians are often exposed to toxins through food, water, and air. Chemicals associated with industrial waste are the most common environmental teratogens, and the quantities involved are usually minute. However, as is true for drugs, amounts that go unnoticed by an adult can cause serious damage to prenatal development (Dietrich, 2000). Several environmental hazards that are known teratogens are listed in Table 4–4.

Although X-rays are included in this table, radiation associated with computer monitors and video display terminals (VDTs) is not. Several major studies have examined the impact of exposure to the electromagnetic fields that are generated by VDTs and found no negative results. For example, Schnorr and her colleagues (1991) compared the pregnancies in telephone operators who worked at VDTs at least

Table 4–4 Summary Table

Environmental Teratogens and Their Consequences	
Hazard	Potential Consequences
Lead	Cognitive delay
Mercury	Retarded growth, cognitive delay, cerebral palsy
PCBs	Impaired memory and verbal skills
X-rays	Retarded growth, leukemia, cognitive delay

25 hours weekly with operators who never used VDTs. For both groups of women, about 15 percent of the pregnancies ended in miscarriage. Other studies have not found a connection between exposure to VDTs and birth defects (Parazzini, Luchini, La Vecchia, & Crosignani, 1993). Evidently, VDTs can be used safely by pregnant women.

Another serious environmental hazard for Canadian women are polychlorinated biphenyls (PCBs), which were used for many years in paints and electrical transformers but were subsequently banned due to their toxic effects on people and the environment. PCBs can seep into groundwater, contaminating both animals and fish. Stewart, Reihman, Lonky, Darvill, and Pagano (2000) looked at the relationship between neonatal behaviour and exposure to PCBs in infants whose mothers had consumed contaminated fish from Lake Ontario. These researchers tested babies' cognitive-behavioural capabilities twice, once at between 12 and 24 hours and once again at between 25 and 48 hours after birth using the Neonatal Behavioral Assessment Scale (NBAS). Scores on each part of the NBAS were correlated with PCB levels found in samples of blood taken from each infant's umbilical cord after birth. The investigators also recorded measurements of other contaminants, such as lead and mercury, in the infants' cord blood for comparison.

A significant relationship was detected between exposure to heavily chlorinated PCBs and performance on two scales of the NBAS related to attention and physiological response to stress 24 to 48 hours after birth. Babies with the highest levels of PCB exposure did more poorly overall on the NBAS, performing significantly below children who had lower or no exposure to PCBs. Performance on the NBAS generally was unrelated to other measured contaminants, such as lead or mercury. The research team concluded that the most heavily chlorinated PCBs have a teratogenic effect on cognitive and behavioural functioning of newborns, while little effect was found for other contaminants.

Environmental teratogens are treacherous because people often are unaware of their presence and impact. For example, we now know that air pollution can affect lung development even in 10- to 18-year-olds (Gauderman et al., 2004). The invisibility of environmental teratogens makes it more difficult for a pregnant woman to protect herself. For example, bisphenol A, which often has been used in plastics such as baby bottles and water bottles, can affect hormonal functioning and is linked to aggression and other behavioural problems in girls exposed during gestation (Braun et al., 2009). In addition, methylmercury in fish is also teratogenic, and restrictions have been placed on consumption of freshwater fish in Canada as a result (see, for example, Alberta Health and Wellness, 2009).

Pregnant women need to be particularly careful of the foods they eat and the air they breathe. They should try to do the following: (1) Clean foods thoroughly to rid them of insecticides; (2) avoid convenience foods that contain chemical additives; (3) stay away from air contaminated by household products such as cleansers, paint strippers, and fertilizers; and (4) try not to handle cats and kitty-litter boxes, as cats can spread toxoplasmosis, a disease harmful to developing babies.

Women in jobs that require contact with potential teratogens (e.g., housecleaners, hairdressers) should switch to less potent chemicals, such as baking soda, and wear protective gloves, aprons, and masks to reduce contact with potential teratogens. Finally, because new environmental teratogens may be discovered, pregnant women should check with a health-care professional to learn if other materials should be avoided. Another way that mothers are getting some digital support to help optimize their babies' development is discussed in the Making Children's Lives Better feature that follows.

How Teratogens Influence Prenatal Development

LO6 **Detail exactly how teratogens affect prenatal development.**

By assembling all the evidence of harm caused by diseases, drugs, and environmental hazards, scientists have identified four important general principles about how teratogens usually work (Hogge, 1990; Vorhees & Mollnow, 1987).

1. The impact of a teratogen depends upon the genotype of the child. A substance might be harmful to one species but not to another. To determine its safety, thalidomide had been tested on pregnant rats and rabbits, and their offspring had normal limbs, yet when pregnant women took the same drug in comparable doses, many gave birth to children with deformed limbs. Thalidomide was harmless to rats and rabbits but not to people. Moreover, some women who took thalidomide gave birth to babies with normal limbs while others taking comparable doses at the same time in their pregnancies gave birth to babies with deformities. Apparently, a person's genotype can buffer some teratogenic effects; however, it is nearly impossible to tell in advance how susceptible a person will be to a teratogen.

Making Children's Lives Better

text4baby

The National Healthy Mothers, Healthy Babies Coalition (HMHB) in the United States has begun a new, funded service for pregnant women and new moms called text4baby. The service is free and provides information about maternal and child health through texts delivered to the mother's cell phone. The program is offered in English or Spanish—all moms have to do is text BABY (BEBE in Spanish) to 511411 from somewhere in the United States, and they will begin to receive free text messages each week that are timed to their baby's due date or birth date. The texts continue to come during the mother's pregnancy and throughout the baby's first year. They also can download a free app to access information about prenatal and infant health and safety.

General information texts come once per day in the first six days and then three times per week after that. Information covered in the text messages include topics critical to the mother and child's health, including immunization and diseases, nutrition and breastfeeding, prenatal care, emotional well-being, substance use, labour and delivery, mental health/family violence, birth defect prevention, oral health, car seat safety, exercise and fitness, developmental milestones, safe sleep, and others.

SOURCE: National Healthy Mothers, Healthy Babies Coalition, 2010. Reprinted with permission.

2. The impact of teratogens changes over the course of prenatal development. The timing of exposure to a teratogen is very important. Figure 4–5 shows how the consequences of teratogens differ for the periods of the zygote, embryo, and fetus. During the period of the zygote, exposure to teratogens usually results in spontaneous abortion of the fertilized egg. Sometimes the zygote can overcome the teratogenic effect and continue to develop normally. During the embryonic period, exposure can produce major defects in body structure. For example, some women who took thalidomide during the embryonic period had babies with ill-formed or missing limbs. Women who contract rubella during the embryonic period can have babies with heart defects. During the fetal period, exposure to teratogens can either produce minor defects in body structure or cause body systems to function improperly. For example, when women drink alcohol during the fetal period, the fetus develops fewer brain cells.

Evidence also exists that cocaine has a teratogenic effect on the developing baby. Cocaine binds to human sperm, which then acts as a transmitter of that cocaine to the human ovum during fertilization (Cone, Kato, & Hillsgrove, 1996; Yazigi, Odem, & Polakoski, 1991). Studies of children exposed to cocaine in utero have had varied results, but most show some effect for cocaine exposure on head circumference, language performance, distractibility, and higher levels of motor activity (Koren, 1993; Loebstein & Koren, 1997; Nulman et al., 2001). Other researchers have found structural impairments and physical defects to the heart, optical system, genito-urinary system, and bones (Espy, Kaufmann, & Glisky, 1999; Plessinger & Woods, 1998). Furthermore, children can be born addicted to the drug, which results in symptoms of withdrawal and significant physiological challenges to the child (Delaney-Black et al., 1996). Finally, children born to mothers who abuse cocaine tend to be affected by other factors, such as poor nutrition and prenatal care, putting newborns at risk for perhaps one of the most challenging conditions, low birth weight.

Figure 4–5

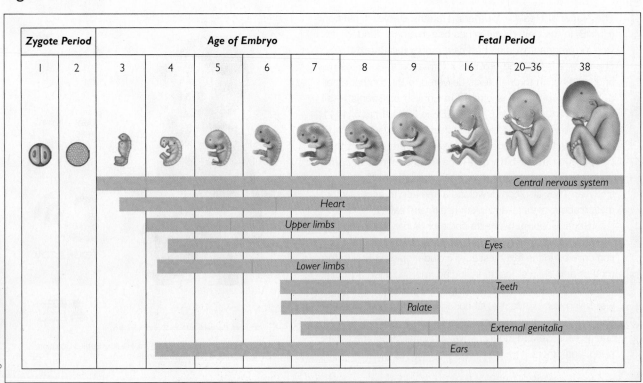

Dragana Gerasimoski/Shutterstock

Even within the different periods of prenatal development, developing body parts and systems are more vulnerable at some times than at others. The mauve shading in Figure 4–5 indicates a time of maximum vulnerability; tan shading indicates a time when the developing child is less vulnerable. The heart, for example, is most sensitive to teratogens during the first two-thirds of the embryonic period. Exposure to teratogens before this time rarely produces heart damage; exposure after this time usually results in milder damage.

3. Each teratogen affects a specific aspect (or specific aspects) of prenatal development. Said another way, teratogens do not harm all body systems; instead, damage is selective. If a woman contracts rubella, her baby could have problems with its eyes, ears, and heart, but have normal limbs. If a mother consumes PCB-contaminated fish, her baby typically has normal body parts and normal motor skills, though cognitive skills will be affected (Jacobson, Jacobson, & Humphrey, 1990). Many different teratogens can affect the same bodily systems.

4. Damage from teratogens is not always evident at birth but can appear later in life. In the case of malformed limbs or babies born addicted to cocaine, the effects of a teratogen are obvious immediately. A cocaine-addicted baby goes through withdrawal—shaking, crying, and being unable to sleep. Sometimes, however, the damage from a teratogen becomes evident only as the child develops. For example, between 1947 and 1971, many pregnant women in North America and Europe took the drug diethylstilbestrol (DES) to prevent miscarriages. Their babies appeared normal at birth, but, as adults, their daughters are more likely to have a rare cancer of the vagina and to have difficulty becoming pregnant themselves (Friedman & Polifka, 1996). Sons of women who took DES can be less fertile and at risk for cancer of the testes (Sharpe & Skakkebaek, 1993). These are cases in which the impact of the teratogen is not evident until decades after birth.

THE REAL WORLD OF PRENATAL RISK.   We have discussed risk factors individually, as if each were the only potential threat to prenatal development. In reality, many infants are exposed to multiple general risks and multiple teratogens (Giberson & Weinberg, 1992; Richardson, 1998). For example, pregnant women under extreme stress might drink alcohol and take aspirin and other legal or illegal drugs. Many of these same women live in poverty, which means they might receive inadequate nutrition and minimal medical care during pregnancy. When all these risks are combined, prenatal development rarely is optimal.

From what we've said so far in this module, you might think that the developing child has little chance of escaping harm, but most babies are born in good health. Of course, a good policy for pregnant women is to avoid diseases, drugs, and environmental hazards that are known teratogens. This, coupled with thorough prenatal medical care and adequate nutrition, is the best foundation for normal prenatal development.

Prenatal Diagnosis and Treatment

LO7 **Summarize how prenatal development can be monitored and how abnormal prenatal development can be corrected.**

"I really don't care whether I have a boy or girl, just as long as the baby's healthy." Legions of parents worldwide have felt this way, but, until recently, all they could do was hope for the best. However, advances in technology have given parents a window into whether their baby is developing normally.

Even before a woman becomes pregnant, a couple can meet with a genetic counsellor, who constructs a family tree for each prospective parent to check for inheritable

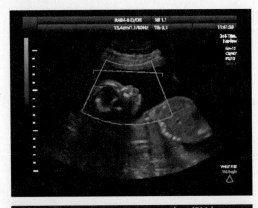

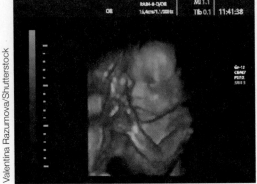

Valentina Razumova/Shutterstock

Diagnostic imaging has become highly sophisticated.

Ultrasound:

a medical procedure that involves imaging a developing baby using sound waves.

Amniocentesis:

a medical procedure in which a sample of amniotic fluid is taken and tested for genetic disorders.

Hagen/www.Cartoonstock.com

Jungle Ultrasound

No, there's only one baby Mrs Kong, but it looks like a very big one!

disorders. If it turns out that one (or both) carries a disorder, further tests can determine the person's genotype. With this detailed information, a genetic counsellor can discuss choices with the prospective parents. They may choose to go ahead and conceive, taking their chances that the child will be healthy, or they could decide to use donated sperm or eggs. Other choices would be to adopt a child or choose not to parent at all.

After a woman is pregnant, how can we know if prenatal development is progressing normally? Traditionally, obstetricians gauged development by feeling the size and position of the fetus through a woman's abdomen. This technique was not very precise and, of course, couldn't be done at all until the fetus was large enough to feel. Today, however, new techniques have revolutionized our ability to monitor prenatal growth and development. A standard part of prenatal care in North America is **ultrasound**, a procedure using sound waves to generate a picture of the fetus. During an ultrasound, an instrument about the size of a small hair dryer is rubbed over the woman's abdomen and an image of the fetus appears on a nearby monitor. The pictures generated are grainy, and it takes an expert's eye to distinguish what's what. Nevertheless, this painless procedure often thrills parents, who are able to see their baby breathe and move.

Ultrasound can be used as early as four or five weeks after conception; before this time, the fetus is not large enough to generate an interpretable image. Ultrasound pictures are useful for determining the position of the fetus in the uterus and, at 16 to 20 weeks after conception, its gender. Ultrasound can also help in detecting multiple pregnancies. Finally, ultrasound can be used to identify gross physical deformities, such as abnormal growth of the head.

More advanced forms of ultrasound have been developed that offer high-quality, detailed visualization of a fetus. The first three-dimensional (3-D) ultrasound system was developed in 1984 by Kazunori Baba from the Institute of Medical Electronics at the University of Tokyo (Woo, 2004). Now, using 3-D and 4-D ultrasound techniques, health-care professionals can learn much more about a fetus than was possible with older 2-D techniques. Nowadays, when parents have a high-level 3-D or 4-D scan done, they can take home a CD of their baby in utero, unlike in previous years, when parents were given only a grainy black-and-white printout.

Using this kind of advanced technology, physicians can evaluate the health and developmental status of a fetus. When a genetic disorder is suspected, two other techniques are particularly valuable because they provide a sample of fetal cells that can be analyzed. In **amniocentesis**, a needle is inserted through the mother's abdomen to obtain a sample of the amniotic fluid that surrounds the fetus. Amniocentesis is typically performed approximately 16 weeks after conception. As you can see in Figure 4–6, ultrasound is used to guide the needle into the uterus. The amniotic fluid contains skin cells that can be grown in a laboratory dish and then analyzed to determine the genotype of the fetus.

In **chorionic villus sampling (CVS)**, a sample of tissue is obtained from the chorion, which is part of the placenta, and analyzed. Figure 4–7 shows that a small tube, inserted through the vagina and into the uterus, is used to collect a small plug of cells from the placenta. CVS is often preferred over amniocentesis because CVS can be done about eight weeks after conception, nearly two months earlier than amniocentesis. In both cases, results are returned from the lab within several days.

Figure 4–6

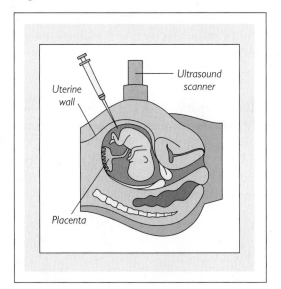

Figure 4–7

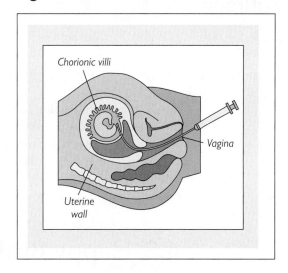

With samples obtained from either amniocentesis or CVS, about 200 different genetic disorders can be detected. These procedures are virtually error-free, but at a price: Miscarriages are slightly more likely—1 or 2 percent more—after amniocentesis or CVS (Cunningham, MacDonald, & Gant, 1989). A woman must decide if the information gained from amniocentesis or CVS justifies the slight risk of a miscarriage.

Ultrasound, amniocentesis, and CVS have made it much easier to determine whether prenatal development is progressing normally. What happens when it is not? Options for treating fetuses in utero have arisen as a result of a whole new field called **fetal medicine**. One approach in fetal medicine is to treat disorders medically, by administering drugs or hormones to the fetus directly. In one case, when ultrasound pictures showed a fetus with an enlarged thyroid gland that would have made delivery difficult, a hormone was injected into the amniotic fluid to shrink the thyroid gland and allow normal delivery (Davidson, Richards, Schatz, & Fisher, 1991). In another case, amniocentesis revealed that a fetus had inherited an immune system disorder that would leave the baby highly vulnerable to infections, so healthy immune cells were injected into the umbilical cord (Elmer-DeWitt, 1994).

Another way to correct prenatal problems is via fetal surgery. Doctors partially remove the fetus from the uterus, perform corrective surgery, and return the fetus to the uterus. Some cases of spina bifida have been corrected with fetal surgery in the seventh or eighth month of pregnancy. Surgeons cut through the mother's abdominal wall to expose the fetus, then cut through the fetal abdominal wall; the spinal cord is repaired and the fetus is returned to the uterus (Grovak, 1999).

When fetal surgery first came into use, it was applied to correct some heart defects and urinary tract blockages (Ohlendorf-Moffat, 1991). However, surgery now is used for a number of congenital defects in fetuses, including hernias, giant neck masses that obstruct fetal airways, lung tumours, and fetal wounds. Not all mothers and their fetuses are strong candidates for fetal surgery, so careful evaluation of both must occur prior to the surgery. At the present time, only two centres in the world perform open fetal surgery procedures, which are done only for rare, life-threatening conditions (Center for Fetal Diagnosis and Treatment, n.d.).

Yet another approach to treating prenatal problems is genetic engineering, the process of replacing defective genes with synthetic normal genes. Take phenylketonuria (PKU) as an example. In theory, it should be possible to take a sample of cells from the fetus, remove the recessive genes from the twelfth pair of chromosomes, and

Chorionic villus sampling (CVS):
a medical procedure in which a sample of placental cells is taken and tested for genetic disorders.

Fetal medicine:
a medical practice specialty focusing on treating fetal health problems in utero.

Ask Yourself

How does the impact of teratogens on the fetus demonstrate nature and nurture in action during prenatal development?

What might influence the decision of people over the age of 40 to have a child?

replace them with the dominant genes. These "repaired" cells could then be injected into the fetus, where they would multiply and cause enough enzyme to be produced to break down phenylalanine, thereby avoiding PKU (Verma, 1990).

As with fetal surgery, however, translating idea into practice has been difficult (Marshall, 1995). Nevertheless, gene therapy has proven successful, and research continues to be done, typically with animals, toward advancing practice in this area.

4.3 Happy Birthday!

 ## Learning Objectives

After reading the module, you should be able to do the following:

LO8 List the stages of labour and delivery.

LO9 Describe "natural" ways of coping with the pain of childbirth, and state under what circumstances childbirth at home might be safe.

LO10 Identify some complications that can occur during birth.

LO11 Summarize how we determine whether a baby is healthy and what behavioural states are common in newborns.

LO12 Understand the characteristics of postpartum depression and its effects.

Pregnant women look forward to birth, to see their babies and, of course, to relieve the discomfort that tends to increase in the later weeks of pregnancy. As women near the end of pregnancy, they find that sleeping and breathing become more difficult, they tire more rapidly, they become constipated, and their legs and feet swell.

In this module, we'll see the different stages and possible problems involved in birth, review various approaches to childbirth, and look at the value of participating in childbirth classes.

Labour and Delivery

LO8 List the stages of labour and delivery.

In a typical pregnancy, a woman goes into labour about 38 weeks after conception. Scientists don't know all the events that initiate labour, but one key element seems to be a "ready" signal from an area of the fetal brain that tracks the progress of developing body organs and systems (Palca, 1991).

"Labour" is named appropriately, as it is the most intense, prolonged physical effort of any human experience. Labour is usually divided into three stages

Figure 4–8

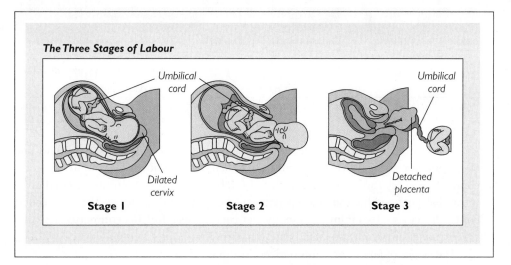

The Three Stages of Labour

Umbilical cord

Umbilical cord

Dilated cervix

Detached placenta

Stage 1 **Stage 2** **Stage 3**

(see Figure 4–8). The first stage of labour begins when the muscles of the uterus start to contract, forcing amniotic fluid against the opening at the bottom of the uterus. The opening is called the **cervix**, and it is the entryway to the birth canal. The wave-like motion of the amniotic fluid with each contraction causes the cervix to enlarge gradually.

In the early phase of Stage 1, the contractions are weak and spaced irregularly. By the end of the early phase, the cervix is about 5 centimetres in diameter. In the late phase of Stage 1, contractions are stronger and occur at regular intervals. By the end of the late phase, the cervix is about 7 to 8 centimetres in diameter. In the transition phase of Stage 1, contractions are intense and sometimes occur without interruption. Women report that the transition phase is the most painful part of labour. At the end of transition, the cervix is about 10 centimetres in diameter.

Stage 1 typically lasts from 12 to 24 hours for the birth of a first child, and most of the time is spent in the early phase of cervical dilation. Stage 1 is usually shorter for subsequent births, with 3 to 8 hours being common. However, these times are only rough approximations; the actual times vary greatly among women and are virtually impossible to predict.

When the cervix is fully dilated, the second stage of labour begins. Most women feel a strong urge to push the baby out with their abdominal muscles. This pushing, along with uterine contractions, propels the baby down the birth canal. Soon the top of the baby's head appears, an event known as **crowning**. In about an hour for first births and less for later births, the baby passes through the birth canal and emerges from the mother's body. Most babies arrive head-first, but a small percentage come out feet-first or bottom-first, which is known as a **breech presentation**. Some researchers have found that babies who have developed in a breech position have normal neuromotor development and may actually experience a roomier environment in utero than fetuses developing head-down (Fong, Buis, Savelsbergh, & de Vries, 2005). The baby's birth marks the end of the second stage of labour.

After the baby is born, the placenta (afterbirth) is expelled from the uterus in the third stage of labour, which usually lasts about 10 or 15 minutes. You can see the growing intensity of labour in the following typical account. For Tatiana, a 27-year-old who was pregnant for the first time, the early phase of Stage 1 labour lasted 18 hours. For the first four hours, Tatiana averaged one contraction every 20 minutes. Each contraction lasted approximately 30 seconds. Then the contractions became longer, lasting 45 seconds. They came about every 15 minutes for 3 hours, and then every 8 to 10 minutes for another 11 hours. At this point, Tatiana's cervix was 5 centimetres in diameter—the early phase was over.

Cervix:
the opening at the end of the uterus (top of the vagina) that forms the entryway to the birth canal.

Crowning:
the appearance of the top of the baby's head outside the birth canal.

Breech presentation:
a physical position in utero in which the developing baby's feet, rather than the head, are closest to the birth canal.

Table 4–5 Summary Table

Stages of Labour		
Stage	Duration	Primary Event
1	12–24 hours	Cervix enlarges to 10 cm
2	1 hour	Baby moves down the birth canal
3	10–15 minutes	Placenta is expelled

The late phase of Stage 1 lasted three hours. For two hours, Tatiana had one 60-second contraction every five minutes. Then, for one hour, she had a 75-second contraction every three minutes. At this point, her cervix was 8 centimetres in diameter, and she entered the transition phase. For the next 30 minutes, she had a 90-second contraction every two minutes. Finally, her cervix was a full 10 centimetres, and she could push. Thirty minutes later, Basil was born.

The stages of labour are summarized in Table 4–5.

Approaches to Childbirth

LO9 Describe "natural" ways of coping with the pain of childbirth, and state under what circumstances childbirth at home might be safe.

In the early and mid-twentieth century, when Canadian women went into labour, they typically were admitted to a nearby hospital, where they were administered an anaesthetic to minimize their pain. Fathers went to a waiting room, where they had to wait for news of their spouses and babies. After recovering from anaesthesia, a mother would be allowed to see her baby. Fathers were allowed limited visiting privileges, and children under 12 years of age usually were not allowed in the hospital for visits at all.

Since the 1960s, many Canadian women have used more "natural" or prepared approaches to childbirth, viewing labour and delivery as life events to be celebrated, not a medical procedure to be endured. Hospitals tend to have birthing rooms, which are designed to be more comfortable and "homey," rather than sterile and institutional. Fathers or birth-coaches and doulas are encouraged to stay with the mother and be part of the child's birth. A **doula** is a person who provides professional support and education about birth but does not provide medical intervention. In Canada, 97 percent of mothers receive prenatal health care, and 88 percent of mothers receive that care from physicians or **obstetricians**, as compared with other health-care professionals such as midwives or nurses (Canadian Institute for Health Information, 2004a). However, the number of physicians who provide maternity care has been decreasing, while the rate of Caesarean sections has been increasing (Harris et al., 2012).

In a **Caesarean section (C-section)**, an incision is made in the mother's abdomen to remove the baby from the uterus. In a report on Canadian birthing practices, the Canadian Institute for Health Information (2004a) indicated that 22.5 percent of in-hospital births during 2001–2002 were by Caesarean section, with an increase in use of obstetricians for delivery over family physicians. However, family-physician–attended births continue to be more prevalent in rural Canada due to lower availability of obstetricians and anaesthesia services in rural areas (Canadian Institute for Health Information, 2004a).

Midwives can assist mothers in the delivery of their babies by normal, spontaneous vaginal delivery. Midwifery includes the assessment and monitoring of women and their babies as well as the provision of care during pregnancy, labour, and the postpartum period (Ryerson University, 2003). Approximately 3 percent of families in Canada choose to use a midwife for delivery rather than have their baby delivered

Doula:
a nonmedically trained person who provides coaching, personal support, and education about birth but does not provide medical care or intervention during the birth process.

Obstetrician:
a physician who specializes in women's health and reproduction.

Caesarean section (C-section):
delivery of a baby through a surgical incision in the mother's abdomen.

Midwife:
a person who is not a physician but who is trained to assist mothers in the physical delivery of their babies by normal, spontaneous vaginal delivery.

by a physician (Canadian Institute for Health Information, 2004a). In Canada, provincial governments regulate the practice of midwifery; in other parts of the world, midwifery is not necessarily regulated by governments. An ancient practice, midwifery is practised more commonly in other parts of the world. The Canadian Association for Midwives provides education and advocacy regarding birthplace choices and methods. Postsecondary educational programs are now offered in midwifery, and a few four-year undergraduate degree programs are available.

The South Community Birth Program in Vancouver, B.C., is an interdisciplinary program of care that includes family physicians, midwives, doulas, and community health nurses serving a multiethnic, low-income population. Researchers ran a six-year study that compared more than 1200 women in the program to women receiving standard medical care for pregnancy and birth (Harris et al., 2012). The researchers found that, in an area affected by lower-than-average availability of maternity care, women attending this collaborative program were less likely to have a C-section, were more likely to breastfeed their babies, had shorter hospital stays, and were more likely to be delivered by a midwife than an obstetrician (Harris et al., 2012).

One fundamental belief of all prepared approaches to birthing practice is that birth is more likely to be problem-free and rewarding when mothers and fathers understand what typically will occur during pregnancy, labour, and delivery. Consequently, prepared childbirth means going to classes to learn basic facts about pregnancy and childbirth as well as how to manage the pain of childbirth. Natural methods of dealing with pain are emphasized over medication because, when a woman is locally or generally anaesthetized, she can't use her abdominal muscles to help push the baby through the birth canal. Without this pushing, the obstetrician may have to use mechanical devices to pull the baby through the birth canal, which involves some risk of injury to the baby (Johanson et al., 1993). Also, drugs that reduce the pain of childbirth might cross the placenta and affect the baby. In large doses, these drugs may cause a newborn to be withdrawn or irritable for days or weeks (Brazelton, Nugent, & Lester, 1987). These effects are temporary, but they could give the parents the impression that theirs is a difficult baby. Therefore, minimizing the use of pain-relieving drugs during birth is best.

Childbirth classes emphasize three strategies to counteract labour pain without drugs. First, because pain often feels greater when a person is tense, pregnant women learn ways to relax during labour. One technique is deep breathing. Second, women are taught visual imagery—picturing in detail a reassuring, pleasant scene or experience. Whenever they begin to experience pain during labour, they focus intensely on this image instead of on the pain. A third strategy is to involve a supportive coach. The father-to-be, a relative, or a close friend attends childbirth classes with the mother-to-be and acts as a birthing coach to help the mother through her baby's delivery. A professional labour coach, or doula, also can be hired. The coach learns the techniques for coping with pain and practices them with the pregnant woman. During labour and delivery, the coach is present to help the woman use the techniques she has learned and to offer support and encouragement.

Researchers have found that childbirth classes are useful (Hetherington, 1990). Although most mothers who attend childbirth classes use some medication to reduce the pain of labour, they typically use less than mothers who do not attend childbirth classes. Also, mothers and fathers who attend childbirth classes feel more positive about labour and birth compared to mothers and fathers who do not attend classes.

Kati Molin/Shutterstock

Some women choose to have the births of their babies attended by a midwife.

Childbirth classes help prepare parents for their baby's birth.

Sometimes, however, cultural differences have an effect on women's birth experiences. Chalmers and Hashi (2000) interviewed 432 women from Somalia who had experienced genital mutilation (female circumcision) and who had given birth to children in Ontario. Somali women expressed their dissatisfaction with physicians' knowledge about how to care for them during and after childbirth as well as with the quality of care provided. Chalmers and Hashi made recommendations for more culturally informed treatment of these women when entering the Ontario health care system.

For many North Americans accustomed to hospital delivery, home delivery can seem like a risky proposition, but it can be safe. Birth problems are no more common in babies delivered at home than in babies delivered in a hospital, if the woman is healthy, her pregnancy has been problem-free, the labour and delivery are expected to be problem-free, and a trained health-care professional, such as a midwife, is present to assist (Rooks et al., 1989). If there is any reason to believe problems requiring medical assistance might occur, labour and delivery should take place in the hospital.

Another alternative to home or hospital birth is the birthing centre, which typically is a small, independent clinic. A woman, her coach, and other supportive people, such as family members, are assigned a birthing room, which usually has a homey atmosphere. A doctor, nurse, or midwife attends the labour and delivery in the birthing room, where the birth can be observed by all. Like home deliveries, birthing centres are best for deliveries that are expected to be trouble-free.

Birth Complications

LO10 Identify some complications that can occur during birth.

Women who are healthy when they become pregnant usually have a normal pregnancy, labour, and delivery. When women are not healthy or don't receive adequate prenatal care, problems can surface during labour and delivery. (Of course, even healthy women face these problems, but not as often.) In this section, we'll look at problems associated with lack of oxygen, being born too early, and being born underweight.

Anoxia:
complete oxygen deprivation (lack of oxygen).

Placental abruption:
detachment of the placenta from the uterine wall.

Hypoxia:
a reduced supply of oxygen.

LACK OF OXYGEN.   Until birth, the fetus obtains oxygen from the mother's blood that flows through the placenta and umbilical cord. If this flow of blood is disrupted, infants do not receive oxygen, a condition known as **anoxia**. Anoxia sometimes occurs during labour and delivery because the umbilical cord is pinched or squeezed shut, cutting off the flow of blood. Anoxia could also reflect **placental abruption**, which occurs when the placenta becomes detached from the wall of the uterus, severing the connection to the mother's blood supply. Anoxia is very serious because it can lead to cognitive delay or death (Petrie, 1991). Reduced oxygen supply is called **hypoxia** and also has serious consequences for infant development, particularly cognitive development (Hogan, de Haan, Datta, & Kirkham, 2006).

To guard against anoxia and hypoxia, fetal heart rate can be monitored during labour, either by ultrasound or with a tiny electrode that is passed through the vagina and attached to the scalp of the fetus. An abrupt change in heart rate can be a sign that the fetus is not receiving enough oxygen. If heart rate does change suddenly, a health-care professional will try to confirm whether or not the fetus is in distress, perhaps by measuring the fetal heart rate with a stethoscope on the mother's abdomen.

When a fetus is in distress, a doctor might want to remove it from the mother's uterus surgically by performing a C-section (Guillemin, 1993). A C-section is riskier for mothers than a vaginal delivery because of increased bleeding and greater danger of infection. A C-section poses little risk for babies, although they are often briefly depressed from the anaesthesia that the mother receives before the operation. Mother–infant interactions are much the same for babies delivered vaginally or by either planned or unplanned C-sections (Durik, Hyde, & Clark, 2000).

PREMATURITY AND LOW BIRTH WEIGHT.   Normally, gestation takes 38 weeks from conception to birth. **Premature infants** are born less than 38 weeks after conception. **Small-for-date infants** are substantially smaller than would be expected based on the length of time since conception. Sometimes these two complications coincide, but not necessarily. Some, but not all, small-for-date infants are premature, and some, but not all, premature infants are small-for-date. In other words, an infant can go the full nine-month term and be under the average 3- to 3.6-kilogram birth weight of newborns; the child would be small-for-date but not premature. Similarly, an infant born at seven months that weighs 1300 grams, the average weight of a seven-month fetus, is only premature. However, if the baby born after seven months weighs less than the average, it is both premature and small-for-date.

> **Prematurity:**
> when a baby is born less than 38 weeks after conception.
>
> **Small-for-date infants:**
> babies who are substantially smaller at birth than expected based on length of time since conception.

Of the two complications, prematurity is the less serious. In the first year or so, premature infants often lag behind full-term infants in many facets of development, but by age 2 or 3 years, differences vanish and most premature babies develop normally thereafter (Greenberg & Crnic, 1988). One of the greatest challenges for premature infants is damage to or underdevelopment of the cerebellum in the brain, which can result in later deficits in aspects of cognition, behaviour, attention, and socialization (Volpe, 2009).

Prospects are usually not so optimistic for small-for-date babies. These infants most often are born to women who smoke cigarettes or drink alcohol frequently during pregnancy or who do not eat enough nutritious food (Chomitz, Cheung, & Lieberman, 1995). Babies who weigh less than 1500 grams at birth often do not survive; when they do, they are usually delayed in their cognitive and motor development (Ventura, Martin, Curtin, & Mathews, 1997). Babies considered specifically to be low birth weight are typically under 2500 grams (Kershaw, Irwin, Trafford, & Hertzman, 2005).

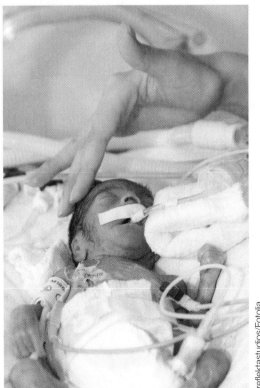

Small-for-date babies who weigh more than 1500 grams have better prospects, though some do not reach as high a developmental level as others (Zubrick et al., 2000). This is also true, but to a lesser extent, for babies who weigh less than 1500 grams. Environmental factors turn out to be critical in these cases. Development of small-for-date infants depends upon the quality of care they receive in the hospital and at home. These babies can thrive if they receive excellent medical care and their home environment is supportive and stimulating. Unfortunately, not all at-risk babies have these optimal experiences. Many receive inadequate medical care because their families are living in poverty and can't afford such care. Others experience stress or disorder in their family life. In these cases, development is usually delayed, and a variety of developmental deficits may be observed, particularly in motion processing (Jakobson, Frisk, & Downie, 2006; Losch & Dammann, 2004; MacKay et al., 2005).

The importance of a supportive environment for at-risk babies was demonstrated dramatically in a classic longitudinal study of all children born in 1955 on the Hawaiian island of Kauai (Werner, 1995). At-risk newborns in stable homes with two

Low birth weight babies face many developmental challenges.

Figure 4–9

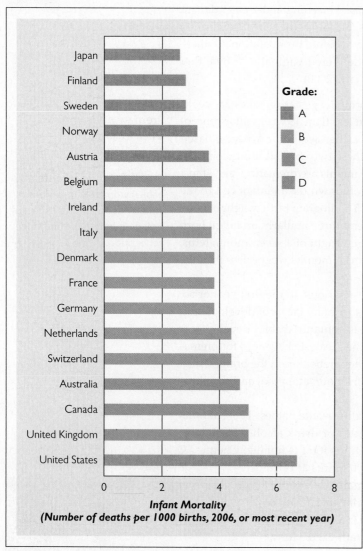

SOURCE: The Conference Board of Canada, 2010.

Infant mortality:
the number of infants out of 1000 births who die before their first birthday.

supportive, mentally healthy parents present throughout childhood were ultimately indistinguishable from children born without birth complications. When at-risk newborns had an unstable family environment—because of divorce, parental alcoholism, or mental illness, for example—they lagged behind their peers in intellectual and social development.

The Hawaiian study underscores a point we have made several times in this chapter: Development proceeds best when pregnant women receive good prenatal care and children live in a supportive environment. Unfortunately, some babies do not fare well. The term **infant mortality** refers to the number of infants out of 1000 births who die before their first birthday. In Canada, about five babies out of 1000 live less than a year (see Figure 4–9). Canada's infant mortality rate has declined at least 60 percent from the mortality rate in previous generations (Federal, Provincial, and Territorial Advisory Committee on Population Health, 1999). However, according to the Conference Board of Canada, in comparison with 17 peer countries, Canada is second last in its level of infant mortality, only one step above the infant mortality rate for the United States (Conference Board of Canada, 2016).

Low birth weight leading to infant death usually can be prevented if a pregnant woman receives regular prenatal care. In the United States, many pregnant women receive inadequate or no prenatal care. Virtually every country that ranks ahead of the United States, including Canada, provides complete prenatal care at little or no cost as well as paid leaves of absence for pregnant women (Kamerman, 1993).

Prenatal development is the foundation of all development, and only with regular prenatal checkups can we know if this foundation is being laid properly. Pregnant women and the children they carry need this care, and countries need to ensure that these women and children receive it.

The Newborn

LO11 Summarize how we determine whether a baby is healthy and what behavioural states are common in newborns.

Newborn babies are actually rather homely looking. They are covered with blood and vernix, the white-coloured "grease" that protects their skin during the many months of prenatal development. If they are delivered vaginally, newborns' heads are usually temporarily distorted, a result of coming through the birth canal. Their bellies stick out, and they are bow-legged. Still, to their parents, a newborn often seems to be the most beautiful being on the planet!

How can we tell if a newborn baby is healthy? The **Apgar score**, a measure devised by Virginia Apgar, is used to evaluate the newborn baby's condition. Health

Apgar score:
a numerical scale used to rate a newborn baby's vital signs.

professionals look for five vital signs: breathing, heartbeat, muscle tone, presence of reflexes such as coughing, and skin tone. As you can see in Table 4–6, each of the five vital signs receives a score of 0, 1, or 2, with 2 being optimal.

The five scores are added together, and a score of 7 or more indicates a baby in good physical condition. A score of 4 to 6 means the newborn will need special attention and care. A score of 3 or less signals a life-threatening situation that requires emergency medical care (Apgar, 1953).

The Apgar score provides a quick, approximate assessment of the newborn's status by focusing on the body systems needed to sustain life. For a comprehensive evaluation of the newborn's well-being, pediatricians and child-development specialists use the Neonatal Behavioral Assessment Scale, or NBAS for short (Brazelton, 1984). As you read earlier in this chapter, the NBAS evaluates a broad range of newborn abilities and behaviours that the infant needs to adjust to life outside the uterus, including reflexes, hearing, vision, alertness, irritability, and consolability (how easily the infant is soothed). The NBAS, along with a thorough physical examination, is particularly helpful in diagnosing disorders of the central nervous system (Brazelton et al., 1987).

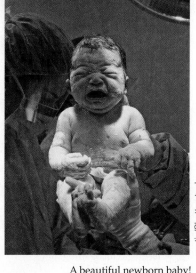
A beautiful newborn baby!

NEWBORN STATES.   Newborns spend most of their day alternating between four states (St. James-Roberts & Plewis, 1996; Wolff, 1987):

- *Alert inactivity.* The baby is calm with eyes open and attentive; the baby looks to be deliberately inspecting the environment.
- *Waking activity.* The baby's eyes are open, but they seem unfocused; the baby moves arms or legs in bursts of uncoordinated motion.
- *Crying.* The baby cries vigorously and usually makes agitated but uncoordinated motions.
- *Sleeping.* The baby's eyes are closed and the baby drifts back and forth from periods of regular breathing and stillness to periods of irregular breathing and gentle arm and leg motion.

CRYING.   Of these states, crying captures the attention of parents and researchers alike. Newborns spend two to three hours each day crying or on the verge of crying. If you've not spent much time around newborns, you might think that all crying is pretty much alike. In fact, scientists and parents can identify three distinctive types of cries (Snow, 1998). A basic cry starts softly, then gradually becomes more intense and usually occurs when a baby is hungry or tired; a mad cry is a more intense version of a basic cry; and a pain cry begins with a sudden, long burst of crying, followed by a long pause, and gasping.

Crying is actually the newborn's first attempt to communicate with others. When a baby cries, it tells its parents that it's hungry, tired, angry, or hurt. By responding, parents encourage their newborn's efforts to communicate.

Parents are naturally concerned when their baby cries, and, if they can't quiet a crying baby, their concern mounts and can easily give way to frustration and

Newborns cry—a lot.

Table 4–6 Five Signs Evaluated in the Apgar Score

Points	Activity (Muscle Tone)	Pulse	Grimace (Response to Irritating Stimulus)	Appearance (Skin Colour)	Respiration
2	Baby moves limbs actively	100 beats per minute or more	Baby cries intensely	Normal colour all over	Strong breathing and crying
1	Baby moves limbs slightly	Fewer than 100 beats per minute	Baby grimaces or cries	Normal colour except for extremities	Slow, irregular breathing
0	No movement; muscles flaccid	Not detectable	Baby does not respond	Baby is blue-grey, pale all over	No breathing

Justin Paget/Corbis

Night feedings can be tiring for parents.

annoyance. It's no surprise, then, that parents develop little tricks for soothing their babies. The Real Children feature shows what one mother did when her baby cried.

SLEEPING. Crying gets parents' attention, but sleep is what newborns do more than anything else. They sleep 16 to 18 hours daily. The problem for tired parents is that newborns sleep in naps taken around the clock. Newborns typically go through a cycle of wakefulness and sleep about every four hours. That is, they will be awake for about an hour, sleep for three hours, then start the cycle anew. During the hour when newborns are awake, they regularly move between the different waking states several times. Cycles of alert inactivity, waking activity, and crying are common.

As babies grow older, the sleep-wake cycle gradually begins to correspond to the day-night cycle (St. James-Roberts & Plewis, 1996). Most babies will begin sleeping through the night at about 3 or 4 months of age, which is regarded as a major milestone by bleary-eyed parents.

Rapid-eye-movement (REM) sleep:

a period during sleep involving small physical movements or twitches of the eyes, mouth, arms, and legs (irregular sleep).

Non-REM sleep:

a period during sleep that is motorically quiet and involves steady breathing, heart rate, and brain activity.

Roughly half of newborns' sleep is irregular or **rapid-eye-movement (REM) sleep**, a time when the body is quite active. During REM sleep, newborns move their arms and legs slightly, they might grimace, and their eyes might dart beneath their eyelids. Brain waves register fast activity, the heart beats more rapidly, and breathing is more rapid. In regular or **non-REM sleep**, breathing, heart rate, and brain activity are steady, and newborns lie quietly without the twitching associated with REM sleep. REM sleep becomes less frequent as infants grow. By 4 months, only 40 percent of sleep is REM sleep. By the first birthday, REM sleep drops to 25 percent, not far from the adult average of 20 percent (Halpern, MacLean, & Baumeister, 1995).

The function of REM sleep is still debated. Older children and adults dream during REM sleep, and brain waves during REM sleep resemble those of an alert, awake person. Consequently, many scientists believe that REM sleep stimulates the brain in some way that helps foster growth in the nervous system (Halpern et al., 1995; Roffwarg, Muzio, & Dement, 1966). We know that REM sleep is associated with the increased production of proteins as well as the stimulation of learning and memory in the brain (Diekelmann, 2010; Rodríguez-Vázquez, Camacho-Arroyo, & Velázquez-Moctezuma, 2012).

Real Children

Calming Bradley

Whenever 4-week-old Bradley cried, Rae's first reaction was to try to figure out why he was crying. Was he hungry? Was his diaper wet? Simply addressing the needs that caused Bradley to cry in the first place usually worked. If he continued to cry, she found that the best way to quiet Bradley was to lift him to her shoulder and rock him or walk with him. The combination of being upright, restrained, in physical contact with her, and moving all helped to calm him. Sometimes Rae would swaddle Bradley—wrap him tightly in a blanket—and then rock him in a cradle or take him for a ride in a stroller. Another

method Rae used sometimes was to give Bradley a pacifier to suck; sucking seemed to allow Bradley to calm himself. Sometimes, as a last resort, she'd strap Bradley in his car seat and go on a drive. The motion of the car seemed to soothe him.

Rae's techniques weren't foolproof. Some would work one day but not another. Sometimes Rae combined these techniques, for example, taking a swaddled Bradley to her shoulder. Sometimes nothing seemed to work, so she'd just put Bradley in his crib. And sometimes, as if he were teasing Rae, Bradley would stop crying spontaneously and go right to sleep!

We also know that sleep, in general, may be particularly important for learning in infancy due to its ability to facilitate neural maturation, consolidate memory for events that happened during periods of wakefulness, and help infants process sensory stimuli and relationships in the environment (Rodríguez-Vázquez, Camacho-Arroyo, & Velázquez-Moctezuma, 2012; Tarullo, Balsam, & Fifer, 2011). Sleep also has been connected to immune function (DeKeyser Ganz, 2012) as well as to other regulatory systems in the body.

SUDDEN INFANT DEATH SYNDROME.   For many parents of young babies, sleep is sometimes a cause of concern. In **sudden infant death syndrome (SIDS)**, also called "crib death," a healthy baby dies suddenly and unexpectedly, for no apparent reason. In Canada, three babies die every week from SIDS, usually while sleeping (Sloan & Cotroneo, 2002), and SIDS is the most common cause of postneonatal death (Hunt & Hauck, 2006).

Scientists don't know the exact causes of SIDS, but they do know several contributing factors. Babies are more vulnerable to SIDS if they were born prematurely or with low birth weight. They are also more vulnerable if their parents smoke cigarettes. SIDS is more likely when a baby sleeps on its stomach (face-down) than when it sleeps on its back (face-up). Finally, SIDS is more likely during winter, when babies sometimes become overheated from too many blankets and too-heavy sleepwear (Carroll & Loughlin, 1994; Hunt & Hauck, 2006). Evidently, SIDS infants, many of whom were born prematurely or with low birth weight, are less able to withstand physiological stresses and imbalances that are brought on by cigarette smoke, breathing that is temporarily interrupted, or overheating. British researchers have found that sleeping with a pacifier may reduce infants' risk for SIDS (Li et al., 2006), but other researchers continue to study and debate the underlying factors in this tragic and frustrating cause of postneonatal death (Goldwater, 2011).

As evidence about causes of SIDS accumulated, child advocates called for action. The result is described in the Child Development and Family Policy feature.

SIDS:
sudden infant death syndrome in which a healthy baby dies suddenly, usually during sleep, for no apparent reason (crib death).

Postpartum Depression

LO12 **Understand the characteristics of postpartum depression and its effects.**

For parents, the time immediately after a trouble-free birth is full of excitement, pride, and joy—the much-anticipated baby is finally here! Yet roughly half of all new mothers find that their initial excitement gives way to irritation, resentment, and crying

Child Development and Family Policy
Back to Sleep! Dodo sur le dos!

Health Canada has released guidelines to help Canadian parents reduce the incidence of SIDS in our country. The Health Canada guidelines focus, first of all, on the importance of putting babies to sleep on their backs on a firm and flat surface, unless a specific medical condition makes this impossible. In that case, Health Canada advises parents to follow the advice of their physician regarding management of the child's particular health problem. The main difficulty with putting younger babies to sleep on their tummies is that, if they do not have the motor control to turn over, they can become suffocated by cushiony surfaces, clothing, pillows, stuffed toys, blankets, or other items that do not allow proper circulation of air around a baby's face. Once babies are old enough to turn from front to back on their own, they do not need to be forced to sleep on their backs. To prevent development of temporary flat spots on the back of babies' heads from lying on their backs all the time, Health Canada recommends some "tummy time" when the baby is awake and under close supervision.

Other factors that Health Canada identified as increasing an infant's risk for SIDS include bed-sharing, cigarette smoking around the baby, and inattentive parenting, especially due to substance abuse. Finally, Health Canada advises parents not to over-dress babies so that they become overheated and, whenever possible, to breastfeed (Sloan & Cotroneo, 2002).

spells. These feelings usually last a week or two and probably reflect both the stress of caring for a new baby and physiological changes as a woman's body returns to a nonpregnant state (Brockington, 1996).

Postpartum depression: feelings of low self-worth, disturbed sleep, poor appetite, and apathy in the months after delivering a baby.

For 10 to 15 percent of new mothers, however, irritability continues for months and is often accompanied by feelings of low self-worth, disturbed sleep, poor appetite, and apathy—a condition known as **postpartum depression**. Postpartum depression does not strike randomly. Biology contributes: Particularly high levels of hormones during the later phases of pregnancy place women at risk for postpartum depression (Harris et al., 1994). Experience also contributes: Women are more likely to experience postpartum depression when they were depressed before pregnancy, are coping with other life stresses (e.g., the death of a loved one, moving), did not plan to become pregnant, experience general adversity, have a poor relationship with their parenting partner, and lack other adults (e.g., the father) to support their adjustment to motherhood (Bernazzani et al., 2004; Brockington, 1996; Campbell, Cohn, Flanagan, Popper, & Meyers, 1992).

Women who are lethargic, depressed, or apathetic might not mother warmly and enthusiastically. They also might not touch and cuddle their new babies much or talk to them. If the depression lasts only a few weeks, babies are unaffected. However, if postpartum depression lasts for months and months, children of depressed mothers are more likely to become depressed themselves and are also at risk for other behavioural problems (Murray, Fiori-Cowley, Hooper, & Cooper, 1996).

Ask Yourself

What might influence a mother's choice to have pain medication administered during childbirth?

Do studies on the long-term effects of prematurity and low birth weight provide evidence for continuity in development or discontinuity in development? Why?

What might be some consequences of inadequate sleep for both parents and newborns?

What Would a Social Worker Do?

Imagine you're a social worker and you receive a report from the hospital that a teenage girl just delivered a baby and doesn't seem to have any family support. What do you think you would have to do in order to help both the baby and the mother? Should the mother keep her baby? Why or why not? What might help keep this family intact?

Summary

4.1 From Conception to Birth

Period of the Zygote (Weeks 1–2)

- The period of the zygote lasts two weeks and begins when the egg is fertilized by the sperm in the fallopian tube.

- The period of the zygote ends when the fertilized egg has implanted in the wall of the uterus.

- By the end of this period, cells have begun to differentiate.

Period of the Embryo (Weeks 3–8)

- The period of the embryo begins two weeks after conception and ends eight weeks after conception.

- This is a period of rapid growth, when most major body structures are formed.

Period of the Fetus (Weeks 9–38)

- The period of the fetus begins eight weeks after conception and lasts until birth.

- This period is marked by an increase in the size of the fetus and changes in the body systems necessary for life.

4.2 Influences on Prenatal Development

General Risk Factors

- Prenatal development can be adversely affected if a pregnant mother does not provide adequate nutrition for the developing baby or when she experiences considerable stress during pregnancy.

- Teenagers often have problem pregnancies because they rarely receive adequate prenatal care.

- Women in their thirties are likely to have problem-free pregnancies if they are in good health before becoming pregnant.

Teratogens: Diseases, Drugs, and Environmental Hazards

- Teratogens are agents that can cause abnormal prenatal development.

- Several diseases and many drugs that adults take are teratogens.

- Environmental teratogens are particularly dangerous because a pregnant woman might not know when these substances are present.

How Teratogens Influence Prenatal Development

- The effect of teratogens depends upon the genotype of the developing child, when during prenatal development the exposure occurs, and the amount of exposure.

- The impact of a teratogen might not be evident until later in life.

Prenatal Diagnosis and Treatment

- Many techniques are used to track prenatal development, including ultrasound, amniocentesis, and chorionic villus sampling.

- The new field of fetal medicine seeks to correct problems of prenatal development medically, surgically, or through genetic engineering.

4.3 Happy Birthday!

Labour and Delivery

- Labour consists of three stages: enlargement of the cervix, movement of the baby through the birth canal, and expulsion of the placenta.

Approaches to Childbirth

- Prepared childbirth assumes that parents should understand what takes place during pregnancy and birth.

- In natural childbirth, pain-relieving medications are avoided because they prevent women from pushing during labour and because they affect the fetus.

- In natural childbirth, women learn to cope with pain through relaxation, visual imagery, and the help of a supportive coach.

- Home birth can be safe when the mother is healthy, labour and birth are expected to be trouble-free, and a health-care professional is present to deliver the baby.

Birth Complications

- During labour and delivery, the flow of blood to the fetus can be disrupted, either because the umbilical cord is squeezed shut or because the placenta becomes detached from the wall of the uterus.

- Interrupted blood flow causes anoxia, a lack of oxygen to the fetus.

- If the fetus is in danger, the obstetrician might do a Caesarean section and surgically remove the baby from the uterus.

- Premature babies develop more slowly at first but catch up by 2 or 3 years of age.

- One of the greatest risks for premature babies is a damaged or underdeveloped cerebellum.

- Small-for-date babies often do not fare well, particularly if they weigh less than 1500 grams at birth and if their environment is stressful.

- Infant mortality is on the decline in Canada but is relatively high in the United States, primarily because of low birth weight and inadequate prenatal care.

The Newborn

- The Apgar score measures five vital signs to determine a newborn baby's physical well-being.

- The Neonatal Behavioral Assessment Scale (NBAS) provides a comprehensive evaluation of a baby's behavioural and physical status.

- Newborns spend their day in one of four states: alert inactivity, waking activity, crying, and sleeping.

- Newborns spend two-thirds of every day asleep and go through a sleep–wake cycle every four hours.

- By 3 or 4 months, most babies sleep through the night.

- Newborns spend about half their time in REM sleep.

- Some healthy babies die from sudden infant death syndrome (SIDS).

- Prematurity and low birth weight increase the risk of SIDS.

- Babies are also vulnerable to SIDS when they sleep on their tummies, are overheated, or are exposed to cigarette smoke.

- Use of a pacifier may reduce risk for SIDS.

Postpartum Depression

- After giving birth, many women briefly experience irritation and crying spells.

- Some mothers experience postpartum depression, during which they experience irritability, poor appetite, disturbed sleep, and emotional apathy.

Chapter Critical Review

1. Consider two research studies discussed in Module 4.1—the DiPietro study of fetal activity and infant fussiness and the DeCasper and Spence study of reading aloud during pregnancy. What do these studies suggest about connections between prenatal and postnatal development?

2. Design a public health program to alert women that lifestyle can affect the development of a fetus even before a woman knows she is pregnant. What groups of women might find special benefit from your program?

3. Review the four principles of how teratogens affect development that were discussed earlier in this chapter. Explain how these principles are related to the principles of reaction range and gene–environment relations.

See for Yourself

Words can hardly capture the miracle of a newborn baby. If you have never seen a newborn, you need to see one, or even better, a roomful. Arrange to visit the maternity ward of a local hospital, which may include a nursery for newborns. Through a viewing window, you will be able to observe a few newborns. These babies will no longer be covered with blood or vernix, but you will be able to see how the newborn's head is often distorted by its journey through the birth canal.

As you watch the babies, look for reflexive behaviour and changes in states. Watch while a baby sucks its fingers. Find a baby who seems to be awake and alert, and note how long the baby stays this way. When alertness wanes, watch for the behaviours that replace it. Finally, observe how different the newborns look and act from each other. The wonderful variety and diversity found among human beings is already evident in humans who are only hours or days old. See for yourself!

Chapter 5
Physical Development in Infants and Toddlers

Gyula Gyukli/Fotolia

⋁ MODULE

5.1 Healthy Growth

5.2 The Developing Nervous System

5.3 Motor Development

5.4 Sensory and Perceptual Processes

Connect to My Virtual Child

What kinds of theories do you have about children? What ideas inform your thoughts and beliefs about the lives of children, how they are raised, and the nature of the human person? Use your access card and follow this link www.myvirtualchild.com to learn more about the world of the child. You can even virtually try to raise your own child.

Sophie looked so precious in the little baby outfits she received as presents when she was born. However, Terry and Mabel were dismayed when they realized that, after wearing the outfits just a couple of times, Sophie had already outgrown them. With her knack for math, Mabel figured out that Sophie had doubled her birth weight by 3 months of age. If she continued growing at that rate, she'd weigh nearly as much as a jet airliner! Thankfully, Sophie's pediatrician told Mabel and Terry that Sophie's growth was normal and that infants typically triple their weight by their first birthday (McCall, 1979).

5.1 Healthy Growth

 ## Learning Objectives

After reading the module, you should be able to do the following:

LO1 Create a table outlining the important features of physical growth in infants and toddlers and how they vary from child to child.

LO2 Recognize the difference between average and normal in secular growth trends.

LO3 Describe how heredity, hormones, and nutrition contribute to physical growth.

LO4 Summarize how malnutrition, disease, and accidents affect infants' and toddlers' physical growth.

For parents and children alike, physical growth and safety are topics of great interest. Parents marvel at how quickly babies grow in length and weight; 2-year-olds proudly proclaim, "I big!" and parents worry about the potential harm to their children from accidents.

In this module, we'll examine some of the basic features of physical growth and variations in growth patterns. We'll also consider the mechanisms responsible for growth. Finally, we'll end the module by seeing how malnutrition, disease, and accidents are, for some children, significant obstacles to healthy growth.

Features of Human Growth

LO1 **Create a table outlining the important features of physical growth in infants and toddlers and how they vary from child to child.**

Probably the most obvious way to measure physical growth is in terms of height and weight. The growth charts in Table 5–1 show cut-off points for healthy growth and development for Canadian children. Recently, the Dietitians of Canada and the Canadian Pediatric Society (2010) changed their growth chart guidelines and adopted use of the growth charts developed by the World Health Organization (de Onis & Yip, 1996; World Health Organization Multicentre Study Group, 2006). An interesting rule of thumb regarding children's growth is that boys achieve half their adult height by 2 years and girls by 18 months.

Human growth follows the cephalocaudal principle. As a result, toddlers have a disproportionately large head and trunk, making them top-heavy compared with

Table 5–1 Cut-Off Points for Healthy Growth and Development

Growth Status	Indicator	Percentile	
Birth to 2 years			
Underweight	Weight for age	<3rd	
Severe underweight	Weight for age	<0.1st	
Stunting	Length for age	<3rd	
Severe stunting	Length for age	<0.1st	
Wasting	Weight for length	<3rd	
Severe wasting	Weight for length	<0.1st	
Risk of overweight	Weight for length	>85th	
Overweight	Weight for length	>97th	
Obesity	Weight for length	>99.9th	
Growth Status	**Indicator**	**Percentile**	
		2–5 years	5–19 years[†]
Underweight	Weight for age	<3rd	<3rd*
Severe underweight	Weight for age	<0.1st	<0.1st*
Stunting	Height for age	<3rd	<3rd
Severe stunting	Height for age	<0.1st	<0.1st
Wasting	BMI for age	<3rd	<3rd
Severe wasting	BMI for age	<0.1st	<0.1st
Risk of overweight	BMI for age	>85th	N/A
Overweight	BMI for age	>97th	>85th
Obesity	BMI for age	>99.9th	>97th
Severe obesity	BMI for age	N/A	>99.9th

*Weight for age not recommended after 10 years of age—use body mass index (BMI) for age instead.
[†]More conservative cut-off criteria are used for young children because of growth and lack of data on functional significance of upper cut-offs and to avoid the risks of putting young children on diets.
N/A: Not applicable
SOURCE: Based on data from the World Health Organization Multicentre Study Group, 2006.

older children. As growth of the hips, legs, and feet catches up, children's bodies take on more adult proportions.

Another important feature of physical growth takes place inside the body, with the development of muscle, fat, and bones. Virtually all the body's muscle fibres are present at birth. During childhood, muscles become longer and thicker as individual fibres fuse together. This process accelerates during adolescence, particularly for boys.

A layer of fat first appears under the skin near the end of the fetal period. Fat continues to accumulate rapidly during the first year after birth, producing the familiar appearance we call "baby fat." During the preschool years, children actually become leaner, but in the early elementary school years they begin to acquire more fat again. This happens gradually at first, then more rapidly during adolescence. The increase in fat during adolescence is more pronounced in girls than in boys. Up to the age of 2, children at high risk for adult obesity, based on family factors, tend not to differ in terms of body mass from children at low risk for adult obesity; however, increases in weight become more noticeable by age 4, with fat masses being higher by age 6 in children at high risk for adult obesity (Berkowitz, Stallings, Maislin, & Stunkard, 2005; Stunkard, Berkowitz, Schoeller, Maislin, & Stallings, 2004).

Bone begins to form during prenatal development. What will become bone starts as cartilage, a soft, flexible tissue. During the embryonic period, the middle of the tissue turns

mitgirl/Fotolia

Body proportions change as children grow.

to bone. Then, shortly before birth, the ends of the cartilage structures, known as **epiphyses**, turn to bone. Now the structure is hard at each end and in the middle. Working from the middle, cartilage turns to bone until finally the enlarging middle section reaches the epiphyses, ending skeletal growth.

Epiphyses:
the ends of the cartilage structures that turn into bone.

If you combine the changes in muscle, fat, and bone with changes in body size and shape, you have a fairly complete picture of physical growth during childhood. Of course, the picture of children's physical growth that we have described in these pages is a typical profile; important variations on this prototype exist, as you'll see in the next section.

Variations on the Average Profile

LO2 **Recognize the difference between average and normal in secular growth trends.**

Today, adults and children are taller and heavier than people of previous generations. Changes in physical development from one generation to the next that are related to environmental factors are known as **secular growth trends**. Secular trends in industrialized nations like Canada, Australia, the United States, and Western Europe have been quite large. Trends in secular growth can be seen in the sizes of knights' armour from the fifteenth and sixteenth centuries at the Metropolitan Museum of Art (www. metmuseum.org)—people have indeed increased in height over time.

Secular growth trends:
changes in physical development from one generation to the next that are related to environmental factors.

We also need to remember that "average" and "normal" are not the same. Many children are much taller or shorter than average and are perfectly normal, of course. For example, for North American 18-month-old girls, normal weights range from approximately 9 to 13 kilograms. In other words, an extremely light but normal 18-month-old girl would weigh only about two-thirds as much as her extremely heavy but normal peer. What is normal can vary greatly, and this applies not only to weight and other aspects of physical growth but also to all aspects of development. Whenever a typical or average age is given for a developmental milestone, you should remember that the normal range for passing the milestone is much wider. Some children pass the milestone sooner than the stated age and some later, but all might be within normal limits.

Mechanisms of Physical Growth

LO3 **Describe how heredity, hormones, and nutrition contribute to physical growth.**

It's easy to take physical growth for granted. Compared to other milestones of child development, such as learning to read, physical growth seems to come easily. Children, like weeds, seem to sprout without any effort at all. In reality, of course, physical growth is complicated; to understand it, we need to consider three factors: heredity, hormones, and nutrition.

HEREDITY.   Donny and Dean are identical twins. Throughout childhood, they never differed in height by more than 8 centimetres. In contrast, fraternal twins Sam and Max usually differed by at least 5 centimetres and sometimes by as much as 30 centimetres. These variations are typical for identical and fraternal twins: The correlation between heights of identical twins is usually larger than 0.9, whereas the correlation for fraternal twins is approximately 0.5 (Wilson, 1986). This finding indicates that heredity plays a role in determining both a person's adult height and the rate at which the person achieves adult height.

Both parents contribute equally to their children's height. The correlation between the average of the two parents' heights and their child's is about 0.7 (Plomin, 1990). Obviously, as a general rule, two tall parents will have tall children; two short parents will have short children; and one tall parent and one short parent will have average-height offspring.

HORMONES. How are genetic instructions translated into actual growth? Part of the answer involves **hormones**, chemicals that are released by glands and travel in the bloodstream to act on other areas of the body. One of these glands, the pituitary, is located deep in the brain. A few times each day, the pituitary secretes growth hormone (GH). This usually happens during sleep but sometimes after exercise. From the pituitary, GH travels to the liver, where it triggers the release of another hormone, somatomedin, which causes muscles and bones to grow (Tanner, 1990).

Without adequate amounts of GH, a child develops dwarfism. Most dwarf adults have normal proportions, but they are quite short, measuring about 120 to 135 centimetres tall. Dwarfism can be treated with injections of GH so children grow to normal height.

Another hormone, **thyroxine**, released by the thyroid gland in the neck, is essential for the proper development of nerve cells. Without thyroxine, nerve cells do not develop properly and cognitive delay results (Kasatkina et al., 2006). Thyroxine also seems to be essential for most cells in the body to function properly, so deficiencies in thyroxine can retard physical growth by making the pituitary gland itself ineffective. On the other hand, too much thyroxine, or imbalances in thyroid hormone excretion, can cause other kinds of pathologies and have been linked to anxiety-related problems (McCracken & Hanna, 2005). Some researchers also have hypothesized that decreased maternal thyroid function as a result of alcohol consumption during pregnancy may be what predisposes offspring to cognitive delays, although research at this stage is preliminary and only modelled in rats (Wilcoxon, Kuo, Disterhoft, & Redei, 2005).

NUTRITION. The third factor affecting physical growth is nutrition, which is particularly important during infancy, when physical growth is so rapid. In a 2-month-old, roughly 40 percent of the body's energy is devoted to growth. Most of the remaining energy fuels basic bodily functions, such as digestion and respiration.

Because growth requires so much energy, young babies must consume an enormous number of calories in relation to their body weight. While an adult needs to consume only 33 to 44 calories per kilogram, depending upon level of activity (National Research Council, 1989), a 5.5-kilogram 3-month-old should eat about 110 calories per kilogram of body weight, or about 600 calories. What's the best way for babies to receive the calories they need? The Making Children's Lives Better feature has some answers.

Introduction of only one food at a time is a good rule. A 7-month-old having cheese for the first time, for instance, should have no other new foods for a few days. In this way, allergies that might develop—skin rash or diarrhea—can be linked to a particular food, making it easier to prevent recurrences. Of note for parents is that a Calgary researcher (Elliott, 2010) found that commercial baby food may have an excessive proportion of calories (more than 20 percent) coming from sugar. Excess intake of simple carbohydrates can contribute to obesity and other health-related problems.

The many benefits of breastfeeding do not mean that bottle-feeding is harmful. Commercial formula, when prepared in sanitary conditions, does not contain protective maternal antibodies, but it provides generally the same nutrients as human milk. Although infants may develop allergies from formula, bottle-feeding has advantages of its own. For example, fathers can enjoy the intimacy of feeding the baby too. Long-term longitudinal studies typically find that breastfed and bottle-fed babies are similar in physical and psychological development (Fergusson, Horwood, & Shannon, 1987), so women in industrialized countries can choose either method and know that their babies' dietary needs will be met.

In developing nations, bottle-feeding is potentially disastrous. Often, the only water available to prepare formula is contaminated, causing chronic infant diarrhea, which can lead to dehydration and death. Also, in an effort to conserve valuable

Hormones:
chemicals that are released by glands and travel in the bloodstream to act on other areas of the body.

Thyroxine:
a hormone released by the thyroid gland that is essential for nerve-cell development.

formula, parents might use less formula than indicated, which can lead to malnutrition. For these reasons, the World Health Organization strongly advocates breast-feeding as the primary source of nutrition for infants and toddlers in developing nations.

By 2 years, growth slows, so children need less to eat. This is also a time when many children become picky eaters. Toddlers and preschool children often find foods "yucky" that they once ate willingly. Although finickiness can be annoying, it can actually be adaptive for increasingly independent preschoolers. Because toddlers don't know what is safe to eat and what isn't, eating only familiar foods protects them from potential harm (Birch & Fisher, 1995).

Toddlers can be picky eaters.

An important point to bear in mind, though, is that children eat what their parents give them. In Canada, the diet of the typical family has been changing over time (Statistics Canada, 2010) with a reduction in consumption of red meat, dairy, fats, and processed juices and an increase in consumption of chicken, fish, nuts, grains, beans, and coffee. Despite ubiquitous warnings about the dangers of over-consuming sugar and simple carbohydrates, Canadian consumption of sugar has been on the rise. Canada's Food Guide provides recommendations for the types of foods to eat; however, it is based on a biomedical understanding of nutrition and does not do a very good job of reflecting foods that are culturally meaningful or that encompass non-biomedical understandings of food and health (Anderson, Mah, & Sellen, 2015). As a result, Canada's Food Guide tends to reflect food categories but does not relate well to the many cultures of people in Canada and the variety of foods that they tend to consume on a daily basis or for other purposes, such as celebrations. In addition, Canada's Food Guide likely recommends higher consumption of carbohydrates than what might be optimal for maintenance of low blood sugar and health.

Instead of focusing on what to eat, the Government of Brazil has set an example for healthy nutrition by helping its citizens understand how to eat, as you can see in Children and Families around the World.

Children and Families around the World

Healthy Eating in Brazil

Rather than using a food guide, Brazil has published 10 dietary guidelines that focus on healthy eating practices:

1. Focus on eating a great variety of natural and minimally processed foods that are primarily of plant origin. Eat all food types (e.g., natural cereals, legumes, roots/tubers, vegetables, fruits, nuts, milk, eggs, and meat).
2. Use fats, sugar, and salt in small amounts.
3. Limit processed foods, particularly manufactured foods, including breads, cheeses, foods in brines, and fruits in syrup.
4. Avoid highly processed foods, such as packaged snacks, soft drinks, instant noodles, and sweetened cereals. They have an unbalanced nutritional composition, and the way that they are produced, distributed, marketed, and consumed can have a negative impact on our social life, culture, and environment.
5. Eat regularly, slowly, and carefully in an appropriate environment (clean, comfortable, quiet) and with pleasant company. Try not to snack between meals, and avoid eating in places that pressure you to eat unlimited amounts of food. Share food-related household activities with others.
6. Shop from suppliers that offer natural and minimally processed foods, such as farmers markets, supermarkets, or directly from producers. Try to buy organic, locally grown foods in season.

(continued)

7. Cook your own food. Work on your cooking skills with others who are knowledgeable, and share those skills with others, particularly with children.

8. Make food and eating a priority in your life, and plan your time well so that you have the time to shop and cook properly. Make mealtime special and pleasurable. Revisit how you live your life so that you are giving proper priority to food and eating.

9. When you eat out, go to places that serve freshly made meals at good prices. Buffets and places that charge by weight of food consumed are good choices. Avoid fast-food chains.

10. Do not trust food advertising and marketing, as its purpose is to increase sales, not to inform and educate. Teach children to be critical of all forms of food marketing and advertising (Ministry of Health of Brazil, 2014).

Making Children's Lives Better

What's the Best Food for Babies?

Breastfeeding is the best way to ensure that babies get the nourishment they need. Human milk contains the proper amounts of carbohydrates, fat, protein, vitamins, and minerals for babies. Statistics Canada recently found that mothers who use breast pumps, have flexible work schedules, and nurse their babies part-time often breastfeed their babies longer; however, receiving leave from work, itself, does not seem to contribute much to a woman's decision to breastfeed (Health Canada, 2004c). Many factors contribute to whether or how long a mother decides to breastfeed. In Canada, although breastfeeding is recommended as the only food for babies until the age of 6 months, only about 16 percent of mothers feed their babies breast milk exclusively until 6 months of age (Chalmers, Dzakpasu, Heaman, & Kaczorowski, 2008). About 60 percent of Canadian mothers still feed their 6-month-olds breast milk at least part of the time.

Breastfeeding also has several other advantages compared to bottle-feeding (Shelov, 1993; Sullivan & Birch, 1990).

Breastfed babies are ill less often because breast milk contains the mother's antibodies. Breastfed babies also are less prone to diarrhea and constipation. Breastfed babies typically make the transition to solid foods more easily, apparently because they are accustomed to changes in the taste of breast milk that reflect the mother's diet. Also, breast milk cannot be contaminated like formula can, which is a significant problem in developing countries when formula is used to bottle-feed babies. Therefore, children benefit from being breastfed for the first year, or longer, with iron-enriched solid foods introduced gradually at about 6 months of age. As children cannot get all of their nutritional needs met after 6 months of age from breast milk alone, solid foods should be introduced. In addition, Health Canada recommends supplementation of vitamin D in children who are breastfed due to challenges with vitamin D deficiencies in Canada (Health Canada, 2004d). One possible "menu" for a North American infant during the first year is shown in Table 5–2.

Table 5–2 Ages When Solid Foods Can Be Introduced in an Infant's Diet

Age (months)	Food
6–9	Rice cereal, then other cereals
6–9	Strained vegetables, then strained fruits
7–9	Protein foods (cheese, yogurt, cooked beans, pureed meats)
9–10	Finely chopped meat, toast, crackers
10–12	Egg yolk

SOURCE: Adapted from Whitney, Cataldo, & Rolfes, 1987, and CPS Nutrition Committee, 2006.

Challenges to Healthy Growth

LO4 Summarize how malnutrition, disease, and accidents affect infants' and toddlers' physical growth.

Sadly, an adequate diet is only a dream for many of the world's children, including children right here in Canada. In addition, many children worldwide are affected by diseases and accidental injuries. We'll look at these many challenges to healthy growth in this last section of Module 5.1.

ut one in three children under age 5 is **malnour-** for their age (World Health Organization, 1995). es, but malnutrition is common in industrialized Walsh, and Connor (2001) reported findings from f Children and Youth (NLSCY) that 1.6 percent of iencing hunger. They also reported that 37.5 per- ery few months. Many North American children y are malnourished. For example, approximately l States receive inadequate amounts of iron, and en's Defense Fund, 1996; Pollitt, 1994).

damaging during infancy because growth is so al study conducted in Barbados in the West Indies isey, & Forde, 1986) followed a group of children infants and another adequately nourished group s older children, the two groups were indis- alnourished as infants were just as tall and rs. However, the children with a history of r scores on intelligence tests. They also had school, being easily distracted. Malnutrition arently damages the brain, affecting a child's ion (Morgane et al., 1993).

ave a simple cure, but the solution is more od. Malnourished children are often listless ng them to conserve energy. However, when rgic, their parents might provide fewer expe- riences to foster the children's development. For example, parents who start out reading to a child might give up if the child seems uninterested or inattentive. The result is a self-perpetuating cycle in which malnourished children lack both the physical nutrients and the cognitive stimulation for strong growth.

To break this negative cycle, children need more than a better diet. Their parents also must be taught how to foster development. Programs that combine dietary supplements with parent training offer promise in treating malnutrition (Valenzuela, 1997). Children in these programs often catch up with their peers in physical and intellectual growth, showing that the best way to treat malnutri- tion is by addressing both biological and socio-cultural factors (Super, Herrera, & Mora, 1990). Nutrition education for children and families also is possible; how- ever, while nutrition education might result in improved knowledge about nutri- tion, it won't necessarily improve attitudes or behaviours (Wagner, Meusel, & Kirch, 2005). A combination of food availability, nutrition education, and behavioural change is necessary to prevent malnutrition; parents' nurturing engagement with the child also remains one of the most crucial aspects for promoting early brain development (Knitzer, 2007).

DISEASES. Using the most recent data available, the World Health Organization (WHO; World Health Organization, 2016) reported that, in 2015, 5.9 million children under the age of 5 died. More than half of these deaths could be prevented through basic, affordable interventions. For example, children can be saved from diarrhea and dehydration by consuming clean and safe water containing salt and potassium. The leading causes for mortality in young children are preterm birth complications, pneumonia, birth asphyxia, diarrhea, and malaria, with about 45 percent of all child deaths being related to malnutrition (World Health Organization, 2016). Children in sub-Saharan Africa are more than 14 times more likely to die before the age of 5 in comparison with children in more developed regions of the world (World Health Organization, 2016).

Malnourished:
a lack of adequate nutrition indicated, in part, by children being small for their age.

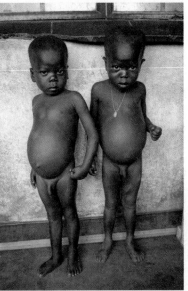

Malnourished children need more than just dietary change.

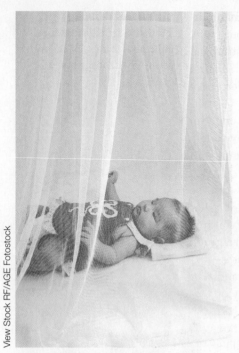

Netting can protect children from insect-borne diseases.

Certain disorders are increasing in prevalence for children. For example, diagnosis of asthma in children under the age of 15 increased approximately 9 percent in Canada between 1994 (2.5 percent) and 2001 (11.1 percent), with a rate of 15.5 percent in Atlantic Canada (Garner & Kohen, 2008). A few reasons for the higher rate in Atlantic Canada might include differences in health-care delivery, genetic predisposition, and levels of exposure to environmental pollutants, such as automotive exhaust. West Nile virus also has become a known concern in North America over the past few years, although it seems to affect middle-aged and elderly people more severely than children.

Some disorders can be prevented or their impact contained through a program of immunization and by educating parents about the importance of vaccination and possible risks (O'Dell & Brownlow, 2005; Petts & Niemeyer, 2004). Although much has been made in the media of the possible association of the measles-mumps-rubella vaccination with autism, to date no definitive evidence exists that that vaccination causes autism (Doja & Roberts, 2006; Lancet, 2010).

As part of a vigorous effort to prevent childhood illness, for the past two decades WHO has worked to vaccinate children worldwide. Due to these efforts, vaccination rates have skyrocketed in many developing countries. More recently, WHO joined with the United Nations Children's Fund (UNICEF) to create Integrated Management of Childhood Illness (IMCI), a program to combat the five conditions that account for the vast majority of childhood deaths: pneumonia, diarrhea, measles, malaria, and malnutrition (World Health Organization, 1997). Because many children who are ill have symptoms related to two or more of these five conditions, IMCI uses an integrated strategy that focuses on the overall health of the child.

Training health-care professionals to become more skilled in dealing with childhood illnesses is one component of IMCI. A second component is improving health-care systems so that they are better able to respond to childhood illness (e.g., ensuring that required medicines are available). A third component involves changing family and community practices to make them more conducive to healthy growth. For example, children are encouraged to sleep in netting that protects them from mosquitoes that carry malaria. IMCI has been adopted in more than 60 countries and is playing a pivotal role in improving children's health worldwide.

ACCIDENTS. Although infant mortality tends to be related more to birth defects and low birth weight, after the first year of life children are more likely to die from accidents than from any other single cause (Centers for Disease Control and Prevention, 2000). Motor vehicle accidents are the most common cause of accidental death in infants and toddlers. Regrettably, many of these deaths could be prevented if the youngsters were restrained properly in an approved infant car seat. In addition, new Canadian recommendations include the use of booster seats for youth up to age 9 or even older, depending on the height and weight of the child; most children ages 4 to 9 do not have the proper bodily proportions to benefit from the use of a seat belt without a booster seat that ensures safe seat-belt positioning (Safe Kids Canada, 2004).

Many infants and toddlers also drown, die from burns, or suffocate, often as a result of inadequate adult supervision or inadequate protective fencing around pools. Young children are often eager to explore their environments yet are unable to recognize many hazards, so they require constant supervision.

Safety-approved car and booster seats can protect children from serious injury.

Ask Yourself

What contributes to malnutrition in industrialized nations?

What difficulties might a parent face in getting a 9-year-old to use a booster seat? What should the parent do in response?

5.2 The Developing Nervous System

 ## Learning Objectives

After reading the module, you should be able to do the following:

LO5 Draw a nerve cell and identify its major parts.

LO6 Discuss how the brain is organized.

LO7 Identify when the brain is formed during prenatal development and when different regions of the brain begin to function.

The physical changes we see in the first years of children's lives are impressive, but even more awe-inspiring are the changes we cannot see, those involving the brain and the nervous system. An infant's feelings of hunger and a toddler's laugh both reflect the functioning brain and the rest of the nervous system. All the information that children learn—including language and other cognitive skills—is stored in the brain.

A Basic Nerve Cell

LO5 Draw a nerve cell and identify its major parts.

The basic unit of the brain and the rest of the nervous system is the **neuron**, a cell that specializes in receiving and transmitting information. Neurons come in many different shapes. Figure 5–1 makes it easier to understand the basic parts found in all neurons.

Neuron:
a cell in the nervous system that specializes in transmitting information.

Figure 5–1

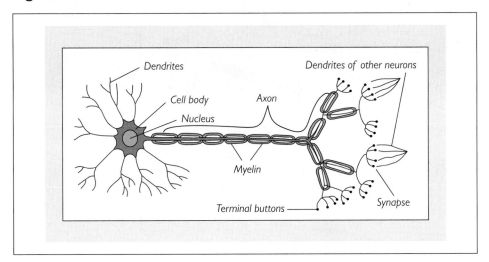

Neuronal cell body:

a structure at the center of the neuron containing biological mechanisms for maintaining cellular life.

Dendrites:

branch-like extensions off the neuron that allow for intercellular communication.

Axon:

the tube-shaped structure attached to the cell body that transmits electrical messages received through the dendrites to other neurons.

Myelin:

a fatty sheath that insulates the axon and speeds information transfer.

Terminal buttons:

structures at the ends of an axon that release neurotransmitters.

Neurotransmitters:

chemicals that affect the firing of surrounding neurons.

Synapse:

a gap or space between neurons.

Cerebral hemispheres:

the right and left halves of the cerebral cortex.

Corpus callosum:

a thick bundle of axons that join the left and right hemispheres of the cerebral cortex.

Frontal cortex:

an area at the front of the brain that is responsible for planful activities and personality.

The **cell body** at the center of the neuron contains the basic biological machinery that keeps the neuron alive. The receiving end of the neuron, the **dendrite**, looks like a tree with many branches.

The many-branched dendrite allows one neuron to receive input from many thousands of other neurons (Morgan & Gibson, 1991). The tube-shaped structure at the other end of the cell body is the **axon**, which sends information to other neurons. The axon is wrapped in **myelin**, a fatty sheath that allows it to transmit information more rapidly. The boost in neural speed from myelin is like the difference between driving and flying: from about 1.8 metres per second to 15 metres per second. At the end of the axon are small knobs called **terminal buttons**, which release **neurotransmitters**, chemicals that carry information to nearby neurons. Finally, you'll see that the terminal buttons of one axon don't actually touch the dendrites of other neurons. The gap between one neuron and the next is a **synapse**. Neurotransmitters cross synapses to carry information between neurons.

Organization of the Mature Brain

LO6 Discuss how the brain is organized.

Take 50 to 100 billion neurons and you have the beginnings of a human brain. An adult's brain weighs a little less than 1.3 kilograms and could easily fit into two hands. The wrinkled surface of the brain is the cerebral cortex. Made up of about 10 billion neurons, the cortex regulates many of the functions that we think of as distinctly human. The cortex consists of left and right halves, called **cerebral hemispheres**, which are linked by millions of axons in a thick bundle called the **corpus callosum**. The characteristics that you value most—your engaging personality, your way with words, your uncanny knack for reading others—are all controlled by specific regions of the cortex, many of which are shown in Figure 5–2.

Personality and your ability to make and carry out plans are largely functions of an area at the front of the brain called the **frontal cortex**. For most people, the abilities to produce and understand language, to reason, and to compute are largely due to neurons in the cortex of the left hemisphere. Also for most people, artistic and musical abilities, perception of spatial relationships, and ability to recognize faces and emotions come from neurons in the right hemisphere.

Figure 5–2

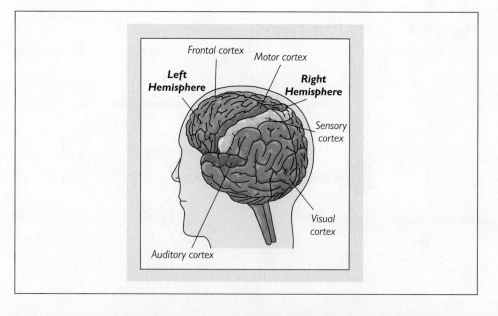

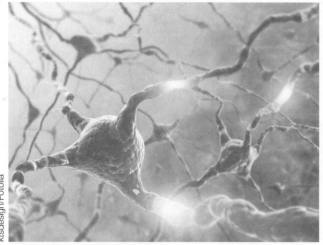

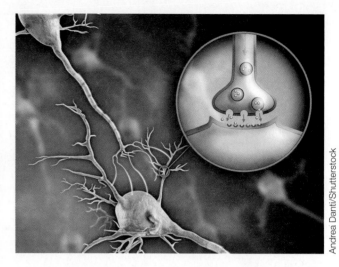

Neurons and neural connections.

Now that you know a bit about the organization of the mature brain, let's look at how the brain develops and begins to function.

The Developing Brain

LO7 Identify when the brain is formed during prenatal development and when different regions of the brain begin to function.

Scientists who study the brain's development are guided by key questions about how and when brain structures develop, when brain regions begin to function, and why brain regions take on different functions.

EMERGING BRAIN STRUCTURES.   The beginnings of brain development can be traced to the period of the zygote. At roughly three weeks after conception, a group of cells form a flat structure known as the **neural plate**.

At four weeks, the neural plate folds to form the neural tube, which ultimately becomes the brain and spinal cord. When the ends of the tube fuse shut, neurons are produced in one small region of the neural tube. Production of neurons begins about 10 weeks after conception, and, by 28 weeks, the developing brain has virtually all the neurons it will ever have. During these weeks, neurons form at the incredible rate of more than 4000 per second (Kolb, 1989).

From the neuron-manufacturing site in the neural tube, neurons migrate to their final positions in the brain. The brain is built in stages, beginning with the innermost layers. Neurons in the deepest layer are positioned first, followed by neurons in the second layer, and so on. This layering process continues until all six layers of the mature brain are in place, which occurs about seven months after conception (Rakic, 1995).

In the fourth month of prenatal development, axons begin to acquire myelin, the fatty sheath that speeds neural transmission. This process continues through infancy and into childhood and adolescence (Casaer, 1993). Neurons that carry sensory information are the first to acquire myelin; neurons in the cortex are among the last. You can see the effect of more myelin in improved coordination and reaction times. The older the infant—and, later, the child—the more rapid and coordinated his or her reactions, which we will discuss further in Module 5.3.

In the months after birth, the brain grows rapidly. Axons and dendrites grow longer, and, like a maturing tree, dendrites quickly sprout new limbs. As the number of dendrites increases, so does the number of synapses; this rapid neural growth is shown in Figure 5–3. Soon after the baby's first birthday, synapses begin

Neural plate:

a group of cells forming about three weeks after conception that develops into the neural tube, the brain, and the spinal cord.

Figure 5–3

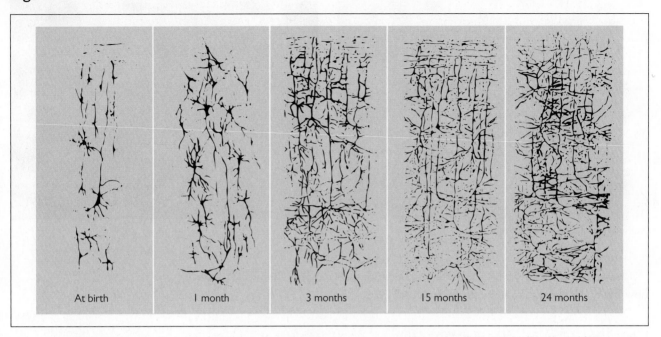

At birth | 1 month | 3 months | 15 months | 24 months

to disappear gradually, a phenomenon known as **synaptic pruning**. Thus, beginning in infancy and continuing into early adolescence, the brain goes through its own version of "downsizing," weeding out unnecessary connections between neurons (Johnson, 1998).

STRUCTURE AND FUNCTION. Because the mature brain is largely specialized, with many psychological functions localized in particular regions, a natural question for developmental researchers is how early in development brain functioning becomes localized. To answer this question, scientists have used many different

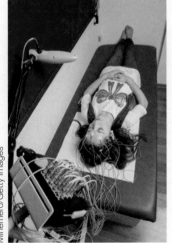

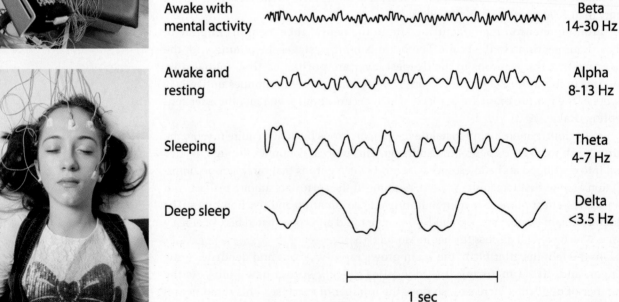

Normal Adult Brain Waves

Awake with mental activity	Beta 14-30 Hz
Awake and resting	Alpha 8-13 Hz
Sleeping	Theta 4-7 Hz
Deep sleep	Delta <3.5 Hz

1 sec

An EEG shows a person's brain wave pattern.

methods to map functions onto particular brain regions in both healthy infants and children who have experienced brain damage. Children who suffer brain injuries provide valuable insights into brain structure and function. If a region of the brain regulates a particular function (e.g., understanding speech), then damage to that region should impair the function. While studies are conducted of children's abilities and disabilities after injury, many studies of infant brain functioning involve some form of neuroimaging technique. The main forms of neuroimaging are as follows:

- *Measurement of electrical activity:* Metal electrodes placed on an infant's scalp produce an **electroencephalogram (EEG)**, a pattern of brain waves. If a region of the brain regulates a function, then the region should show distinctive EEG patterns while a child is using that function.

- *Measurement of activation in the brain:* One method, **functional magnetic resonance imaging (fMRI)**, uses magnetic fields to track the flow of blood in the brain. Another method, **positron emission tomography (PET scan)**, traces use of glucose in the brain. If a region of the brain helps to regulate a function, then blood flow and use of glucose (a sugar that is a source of energy) should be higher in that region when a child performs that function.

A new area of neuroimaging that appears to be more promising for study of infant brains is the use of **functional near infrared spectroscopy (fNIRS;** Lloyd-Fox, Blasi, & Elwell, 2010). In fNIRS, infants are fitted with a kind of helmet that contains electrodes that are attached to the child's skull. Infrared light travels through the device and penetrates a few centimetres into the child's brain to measure blood flow in areas of the brain as different stimuli are presented to the infant (e.g., a checkerboard pattern to look at). Unlike fMRI, the fNIRS method is silent, so auditory stimuli also can be presented. The fNIRS technique has been used to study a variety of behaviours, including eye gaze, biological motion processing, maternal face and emotion recognition, action observation, and object permanence (Lloyd-Fox, Blasi, & Elwell, 2010).

None of these neuroimaging methods is perfect. When studying children with brain injuries, for example, multiple areas of the brain might be damaged, making it hard to link impaired functioning to a particular brain region. Also, most imaging techniques can have potential hazards. A PET scan, for example, requires injecting children with a radioactive form of glucose. In addition, many of these methods require the infant to sit very still, which typically requires the infant to be sleeping or sedated and makes studying awake infants very difficult (Lloyd-Fox, Blasi, & Elwell, 2010). The fNIRS is easier to use with infants, but it doesn't give as clear a spatial image, particularly in deep-brain areas, as the fMRI, and the EEG still seems to give a clearer tracking over time of brain activity (Lloyd-Fox, Blasi, & Elwell, 2010).

Despite these limitations, the combined outcome of research using these different approaches indicates that many areas of the cortex begin to function early in life. EEG studies, for example, show that a newborn infant's left hemisphere generates more electrical activity in response to speech than the right hemisphere (Molfese & Burger-Judisch, 1991), suggesting that, by birth, the cortex of the left hemisphere is already specialized for language processing. This specialization allows for language to develop rapidly during infancy.

The right hemisphere influences many nonlinguistic functions. Music elicits greater electrical activity in the infant's right hemisphere than in the left. Furthermore, children who suffer brain damage to the right hemisphere often have difficulty connecting parts to form an integrated whole (Stiles, 2000), implicating the right hemisphere in understanding spatial relations. Other functions, such as recognizing faces, come more gradually but are under the right hemisphere's control by the preschool years (Hahn, 1987).

Synaptic pruning:

a period in infancy (and then later in adolescence) during which synapses begin to disappear as the brain weeds out unnecessary or underutilized connections between neurons.

Electroencephalogram (EEG):

an electrical measurement of brain waves.

Functional magnetic resonance imaging (fMRI):

a medical test that measures the flow of blood in the brain using magnetic fields.

Positron emission tomography (PET scan):

a medical test that traces glucose uptake in the brain.

Functional near infrared spectroscopy (fNIRS):

a neuroimaging technique that measures blood flow in the brain and is less invasive than fMRI and easier to use with infants.

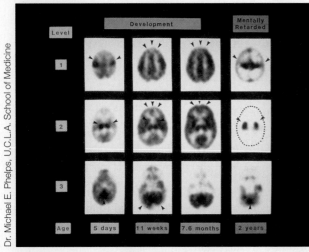

PET scan results for children of various ages.

THE FRONTAL CORTEX. Like the left and right hemispheres, the frontal cortex begins to function early. PET scans show that little activity exists in the frontal cortex of 5-day-old babies. Activity increases considerably by 11 weeks and approaches adult levels seven or eight months after birth (Chugani & Phelps, 1986). Obviously, 8-month-olds cannot plan and function as adults do, but their frontal cortex has become very active.

The frontal cortex regulates primarily deliberate, goal-oriented behaviour. To understand research that leads to this conclusion, think back to a time when you had to change your regular routine. At the start of a new school year, perhaps you were assigned a new locker. For the first few days, you might have turned down the old hallway, reflecting last year's habit, instead of walking on to your new locker. To override your old response, maybe you deliberately reminded yourself to walk past the old hallway and turn at the new one.

Overriding responses that have become incorrect or inappropriate is an important part of deliberate, goal-directed behaviour. Children and adults with damage to the frontal cortex often have difficulty inhibiting responses that are no longer appropriate (Diamond, Prevor, Callender, & Druin, 1997). The frontal cortex begins to regulate inappropriate responding at about 1 year of age and gradually achieves greater control throughout the preschool and school-age years (Welsh, Pennington, & Groisser, 1991). Thus, children gradually become better able to regulate their behaviour to achieve cognitive and social goals.

Not only does the frontal cortex regulate responses, it also regulates feelings such as happiness, sadness, and fear. Nathan Fox (1991) believes that "emotional experience arises from two opposing innate action tendencies in the organism: approach and exploration of the novel versus freezing, fleeing, or withdrawal from harmful or dangerous stimuli" (p. 865). That is, emotions like happiness and curiosity stem from an organism's desire to approach a stimulus, and emotions like distress, disgust, or fear come from the desire to avoid a stimulus. The study of infant emotional experience and regulation is the focus of a new area of clinical research and treatment in psychology called infant mental health (Mares, Newman, & Warren, 2005).

Fox and his co-investigators have shown that the left frontal cortex tends to regulate emotions stemming from the tendency to approach, while the right frontal cortex regulates emotions stemming from avoidance. For example, when babies display joy, the EEG reveals more activity in the left frontal area, and when babies display stress or disgust, the right frontal area is more electrically active. We also know that the left frontal cortex regulates infants' tendency to approach or explore stimuli, and the right frontal cortex regulates infants' tendency to avoid or escape stimuli (Calkins, Fox, & Marshall, 1996). Hane and Fox (2006) found that mothers providing low-quality caregiving had infants with greater right frontal asymmetry on an EEG. These infants also expressed more negative emotion during caregiving activities, were more fearful, and had lower "joint attention" in comparison to infants receiving high-quality care. Joint attention refers to an infant's ability to share or coordinate attention with another person (Charman, 2003).

The brain begins to specialize early in life. Language processing is associated primarily with the left hemisphere; recognizing nonspeech sounds, emotions, and faces is associated with the right hemisphere; and regulating emotions and intentional behaviour is a function of

Babies can show emotion.

the frontal cortex. Of course, this early specialization does not mean that the brain is functionally mature. Over the remainder of development, these and other regions of the brain continue to become more specialized.

We have described the typical pattern of brain localization, but it is not the only pattern. In some left-handed individuals, for example, the assignment of function to left and right hemispheres is reversed from the usual pattern (Springer & Deutsch, 1998). When individuals suffer brain injury, some cognitive functions usually are impaired, but, over months and years, some functioning—and, less often, all functioning—is restored (Kolb & Whishaw, 1998). These examples raise the issue of how certain functions come to be localized in brain regions and how readily they are transferred to other regions.

BRAIN PLASTICITY.   **Neuroplasticity** refers to the extent to which brain organization is flexible. How "plastic" is the human brain? Answers to this question reflect the familiar views on the nature–nurture issue (Nelson, 1999; Stiles, 1998). Some theorists believe that organization of brain function is predetermined genetically; it's simply in most children's genes that, for example, the left hemisphere will specialize in language processing. According to this view, the brain is like a house—a structure that's specialized from the very beginning, with some rooms designed for cooking, others for sleeping, and others for bathing. Other theorists believe that few functions are rigidly assigned to specific brain sites at conception. Instead, experience helps determine the functional organization of the brain. According to this view, the brain is more like an office building—an all-purpose structure with rooms designed to be used flexibly to meet the different business needs of the companies with offices in the building.

Neuroplasticity:
the extent to which brain organization is flexible.

Research designed to test these views shows that the brain has some plasticity. Children who experience a head injury might experience a developmental problem, such as impaired language skills, after the injury, depending on the area of the brain that sustained the most impact and how that area interacts with other areas of the brain. Due to the brain's plasticity, though, children can heal and recover at least some loss of function over time as other neurons take over processing from the damaged neurons. This recovery of function is not uncommon, particularly for young children, and shows that the brain is plastic (Witelson, 1987).

However, the brain is not completely plastic—all brains have a similar structure and similar mapping of functions on those structures. The visual cortex, for example, is almost always located near the back of the brain. The sensory cortex and motor cortex always run across the middle of the brain. However, if a neuron's function is not specified at conception, how do different neurons take on different functions and in much the same pattern for most people? Researchers are trying to answer this question, and many details still need to be worked out. The answer probably lies in complex biochemical processes (Barinaga, 1997; Kunzig, 1998).

As neurons are created and begin migrating through the layers of cortex, cellular biochemistry makes some paths more attractive than others. An individual neuron can end up in many different locations because genetic instructions do not assign specific brain regions. Thus, the human brain is plastic—its organization and function can be affected by experience—but its development follows some general biochemical instructions that ensure most people end up with brains organized along similar lines.

Ask Yourself

How does the pattern of development of the brain, described in this module, compare to the general pattern of physical growth described in Module 5.1?

What do you think is the purpose of synaptic pruning?

5.3 Motor Development

 Learning Objectives

After reading the module, you should be able to do the following:

LO8 State how reflexes help infants interact with the world.

LO9 Detail the component skills involved in learning to walk and at what age infants typically master them.

LO10 Describe how infants learn to coordinate the use of their hands and why most children begin to prefer to use one hand.

LO11 Discuss how maturation and experience influence children's acquisition of motor skills.

Motor skills:

coordinated movements of the muscles and limbs.

Children learn locomotion at different rates, but they tend to learn to crawl before they learn to walk. Crawling is an activity involving **motor skills**—coordinated movements of the muscles and limbs. In crawling, as with other activities, success demands that each movement be done in a precise way and in a specific sequence. For example, to use a stick shift properly, you need to move the clutch pedal, the gas pedal, and the stick shift in specific ways and in exactly the right sequence in order to drive a car.

If new activities are demanding for adults, think about the challenges infants face. Infants must learn **locomotion**—that is, to move about in the world. Newborns are relatively immobile, but infants soon learn to crawl, stand, and walk. Learning to move upright through the environment leaves the arms and hands free. Taking full advantage of this arrangement, the human hand has fully independent fingers (instead of a paw), with the thumb opposing the remaining four fingers. An opposable thumb enables humans to grasp and manipulate objects. Infants must learn the **fine-motor skills** associated with grasping, holding, and manipulating objects. In the case of feeding, for example, infants progress from being fed by others to holding a bottle, to feeding themselves with their fingers, to eating with a spoon. Each new skill requires incredibly complex physical movements. Later, infants learn **gross-motor skills**, which involve coordination of large-muscle groups for activities like crawling and walking.

Locomotion:

moving about in the world.

Fine-motor skills:

activities, such as grasping, holding, and manipulating objects, that involve small-muscle groups.

Gross-motor skills:

activities, such as running, throwing, and jumping, requiring large-muscle groups.

The Infant's Reflexes

LO8 State how reflexes help infants interact with the world.

Most newborns are well prepared to begin interacting with their world. The newborn is endowed with a rich set of **reflexes**, unlearned responses triggered by a specific form of stimulation. Table 5–3 shows the many reflexes commonly found in newborn babies.

Some reflexes pave the way for newborns to get the nutrients they need to grow: Rooting and sucking ensure that the newborn is well prepared to begin a new diet of life-sustaining milk. Other reflexes protect the newborn from danger in the environment. The blink and withdrawal reflexes, for example, help newborns avoid unpleasant stimulation. Other reflexes serve as the foundation for larger, voluntary patterns of motor activity. For example, the stepping reflex looks like a precursor to walking, and babies who practise the stepping reflex learn to walk earlier (Zelazo, 1983).

Reflexes:

unlearned responses that are triggered by a specific form of stimulation.

Table 5–3 Summary Table

Some Major Reflexes Found in Newborns		
Name	Response	Significance
Babinski	A baby's toes fan out when the sole of the foot is stroked from heel to toe.	Unknown
Blink	A baby's eyes close in response to bright light or loud noise.	Protects the eyes
Moro	A baby throws its arms out and then inward (as if embracing) in response to loud noise or when its head falls.	May help a baby cling to its mother
Palmar	A baby grasps an object placed in the palm of its hand.	Precursor to voluntary walking
Rooting	When a baby's cheek is stroked, it turns its head toward the stroking and opens its mouth.	Helps a baby find the nipple
Stepping	A baby who is held upright by an adult and is then moved forward begins to step rhythmically.	Precursor to voluntary walking
Sucking	A baby sucks when an object is placed in its mouth.	Permits feeding
Withdrawal	A baby withdraws its foot when the sole is pricked with a pin.	Protects a baby from unpleasant stimulation

Reflexes indicate whether the newborn's nervous system is working properly. For example, infants with damage to their sciatic nerve, which is found in the spinal cord, do not show the withdrawal reflex, and infants who have problems with the lower part of the spine do not show the Babinski reflex. If these or other reflexes are weak or missing altogether, a thorough physical and behavioural assessment of the baby is required.

Locomotion

LO9 Detail the component skills involved in learning to walk and at what age infants typically master them.

In little more than a year, advances in posture and locomotion change the newborn from a person with limited movement into an upright, standing individual who walks through the environment. Figure 5–4 shows some of the important milestones in motor development. The chart reflects the age by which most infants achieve various motor skills; however, some individual variability in achievement exists for all children. With that in mind, we can say that by about 4 months, most babies can sit upright with support. By 7 months, they can sit without support, and by 9 months, they can stand if they hold on to an object for support. A typical 14-month-old can stand alone briefly and walk with assistance. By 24 months, most children can climb steps, walk backward, and kick a ball.

Researchers once thought these developmental milestones reflected maturation (e.g., McGraw, 1935). Walking, for example, emerged naturally when the necessary muscles and neural circuits matured. However, researchers have discovered that other variables can and do have an impact on motor development. For example, Inal and Yidiz (2012) found that 15 minutes of massage per day resulted in improvements in both cognitive and motor development of healthy, full-term babies. Medical complications and surgery can affect gross-motor development, as a team of researchers found to be the case in babies undergoing cardiac surgery (Long, Harris, Eldrige, & Galea, 2012). On the other hand, Doreen Bartlett (1998) found that, for children who live in moderate climates, the seasons can have an effect on infant motor development. However, when she studied a group of 7-month-old infants in Edmonton, where the climate conditions are more extreme, she found no effect for seasonality. More research in this area will help to identify how seasonality interacts with infants' developing motor skills.

Figure 5–4

0 month: Fetal posture	1 month: Chin up	2 months: Chest up	3 months: Reach and miss
4 months: Sit with support	5 months: Sit on lap, grasp object	6 months: Sit on high chair, grasp dangling object	7 months: Sit alone
8 months: Stand with help	9 months: Stand holding furniture	10 months: Creep	11 months: Walk when led
12 months: Pull to stand by furniture	13 months: Climb stair steps	14 months: Stand alone	15 months: Walk alone

SOURCE: Based on Shirley, 1931, and Bayley, 1969.

Dynamic systems theory:
upholds that motor development involves many distinct skills, organized and reorganized over time to meet demands of specific tasks.

As a result, researchers have begun to see motor development as comprising much more than just skills based on simple maturation. Instead, locomotion—and, in fact, all of motor development—is viewed from a new perspective. According to **dynamic systems theory**, motor development involves many distinct skills organized and reorganized over time to meet demands of specific tasks. For example, walking requires maintaining balance, moving limbs, perceiving the environment, and having a reason to move. Only by understanding each of these skills and how they are combined to allow movement in a specific situation can we understand walking (Thelen & Smith, 1998).

In the past, many Canadian parents used infant walkers to support children's locomotion before they were able to walk. Infant walkers (or "baby walkers") were designed for children able to sit up but not yet able to walk. While sitting in the walker, the baby could use leg movements to make the walker, which was on wheels, move around a room. Unfortunately, while babies could move around a room in a walker, they had no real control over where they went, given their limited cognitive and motor skills. As a result, many babies sustained serious injuries from falling down staircases or moving within reach of dangerous objects. In 1989, a voluntary industry ban was placed on infant walkers; however, because Canadian parents kept using them, Health Canada enacted a nationwide ban on infant walkers, which includes a ban on the sale of both new and used walkers in stores, flea markets, garage sales, or any other venue (Health Canada, 2004b). Canada is the first country in the world to enact such a ban.

As you will see in the remainder of this section, learning to walk actually requires the maturity and coalescence of many component skills in order to help the child gain control over this important gross-motor skill.

Crawling soon turns into first steps.

POSTURE AND BALANCE. The ability to maintain an upright posture is fundamental to walking, but upright posture is virtually impossible for newborns and young infants because of the shape of their body. Cephalocaudal growth means that an infant is top-heavy. Consequently, as soon as an infant starts to lose balance, the infant tumbles over. Only with growth of the legs and muscles can infants maintain an upright posture (Thelen, Ulrich, & Jensen, 1989). Also, as Canadian researchers have discovered, a certain amount of practice is necessary for locomotion actually to occur (Zelazo, Zelazo, Cohen, & Zelazo, 1993), and behavioural control requires involvement of the child's visual system as well as large-muscle groups to aid locomotion (Proteau & Elliott, 1992).

A study of preterm infants in Brazil showed a lag in development of basic postural and locomotive skills between the ages of 1 and 12 months in comparison with normal-term infants (Formiga & Linhares, 2012). A few months after birth, preterm infants go through a period of growth called "catching up," in which they put on weight rapidly. Once preterm infants have gained body weight, they can distribute gravity better within their bodies and gain better muscle control. With increased muscle control comes increased postural control and mastery over the important skill of sitting upright independently, which, in Brazilian preterm infants, tended to happen between 6 and 8 months of age (Formiga & Linhares, 2012). However, after 8 months of age, when full-term infants tend to show increasing mobility through crawling and climbing to stand, Brazilian preterm infants again demonstrated lags in development. Researchers hypothesized that the preterm infants likely did not have adequate practice moving around in a prone position, attributed to parental fear of placing preterm infants prone due to risk of SIDS. The researchers, therefore, recommended monitoring of preterm infants' motor skills after 12 months of age due to the particular challenges they faced in gross-motor skill development.

Once infants can stand upright, they must continuously adjust their posture to avoid falling down. By a few months after birth, infants begin to use visual cues and an inner-ear mechanism to adjust their posture (Schmuckler, 1997). To show use of visual cues for balance, researchers had babies sit in a room with striped walls that move. When adults sit in such a room, they perceive themselves as moving (not the walls) and adjust their posture accordingly; so do infants, which shows that they use vision to maintain upright posture (Bertenthal & Clifton, 1998; see also Schmuckler, 1996a, 1996b, 1997). In addition, when 4-month-olds who are propped in a sitting position lose their balance, they try to keep their head upright. They do this even when blindfolded, which means they are using cues from their inner ear to maintain balance (Woollacott, Shumway-Cook, & Williams, 1989).

Testing a baby's stepping response.

STEPPING.   Another essential element of walking is moving the legs alternately, repeatedly transferring the weight of the body from one foot to the other. Children don't step spontaneously until approximately 10 months because they must be able to stand to step. Thelen and Ulrich (1991) devised a clever procedure to see if babies can step if they are held upright. Infants were placed on a treadmill and held upright by an adult. When the belt on the treadmill started to move, infants could respond in one of several ways. They might simply let both legs be dragged backward by the belt, or they might let their legs be dragged briefly, then move them forward together in a hopping motion. Many 6- and 7-month-olds demonstrated the mature pattern of alternating steps on each leg. Even more amazing is that when the treadmill was equipped with separate belts for each leg that moved at different speeds, babies adjusted, stepping more rapidly on the faster belt.

Apparently, the alternate stepping motion that is essential for walking is evident long before infants walk alone. Walking unassisted is not possible, though, until other component skills are mastered.

PERCEPTUAL FACTORS.   Many infants learn to walk in the relative security of flat, uncluttered floors at home. However, they soon discover that the environment offers a variety of surfaces, some more conducive to walking than others. Infants use perceptual information to judge whether a surface is suitable for walking. When placed on a surface that gives way underfoot (e.g., a waterbed), they quickly judge it unsuitable for walking and resort to crawling (Gibson et al., 1987). When toddlers encounter a surface that slopes down steeply, few try to walk down, as doing so would result in a fall. Instead, they slide or scoot backward (Adolph, 1997; Adolph, Eppler, & Gibson, 1993). Results like these show that infants use perceptual cues to decide whether a surface is safe for walking.

COORDINATING SKILLS.   Dynamic systems theory emphasizes that learning to walk demands orchestration of many individual skills. Each component skill must first be mastered alone and then integrated with the other skills (Clark & Phillips, 1993; Werner, 1948). That is, mastery of intricate motions requires both **differentiation** (mastery of component skills) and **integration** (combining those component skills in proper sequence into a coherent, working whole). In the case of walking, not until 12 to 15 months of age has the child mastered the component skills so that they can be integrated to allow independent, unsupported walking. Researchers at the University of Manitoba (Campbell, Eaton, & McKeen, 2002) have found that, over time, children's ability to integrate behaviours into appropriate motor movements depends, in part, on knowing when to inhibit movements that are not appropriate as well.

Differentiation:

mastery of component skills.

Integration:

combining component skills in proper sequence into a coherent, working whole.

BEYOND WALKING.   If you can recall the feeling of freedom that accompanied receipt of your first driver's licence, you can imagine how the world expands for infants and toddlers as they learn to move independently. The first tentative steps soon are followed by others that are more skilled. Most children learn to run a few months after they walk alone. Like walking, running requires moving the legs alternately, but running is more complicated because a runner actually becomes airborne briefly. To progress beyond walking to running, children must learn to propel themselves into the air and to maintain their balance as they land (Bertenthal & Clifton, 1998).

Fine-Motor Skills

LO10 Describe how infants learn to coordinate the use of their hands and why most children begin to prefer to use one hand.

A major accomplishment of infancy is skilled use of the hands (Bertenthal & Clifton, 1998). Newborns have little apparent control of their hands, but 1-year-olds are extraordinarily talented.

REACHING AND GRASPING. At about 4 months, infants can successfully reach for objects (Bertenthal & Clifton, 1998). These early reaches often look clumsy and for a good reason. When infants reach, they don't move their arm and hand directly and smoothly to the desired object, as older children and adults do. Instead, the infant's hand moves like a ship under the direction of an unskilled navigator—it moves a short distance, slows, then moves again in a slightly different direction, a process that's repeated until the hand finally contacts the object (McCarty & Ashmead, 1999). As infants grow, their reaches have fewer movements, though they are still not as continuous and smooth as older children's and adults' reaches (Berthier, 1996).

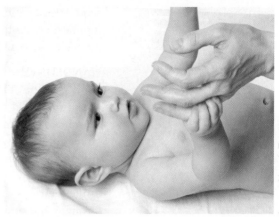

Grasping at 4 months.

Grasping, too, becomes more efficient during infancy. Most 4-month-olds just use their fingers to hold objects. They wrap an object tightly with their fingers alone. Not until 7 or 8 months do most infants use their thumbs to hold objects (Siddiqui, 1995). At about this same age, infants begin to position their hands to make it easier to grasp an object. If trying to grasp a long thin rod, for example, infants place their fingers perpendicular to the rod, which is the best position for grasping (Bertenthal & Clifton, 1998).

Infants' growing control of each hand is accompanied by greater coordination of the two hands. Although 4-month-olds use both hands, their motions are not coordinated; rather, each hand seems to have a mind of its own. Infants might hold a toy motionless in one hand while shaking a rattle in the other. At roughly 5 to 6 months of age, infants can coordinate the motions of their hands so that each hand performs different actions that serve a common goal. A child might, for example, hold a toy animal in one hand and pet it with the other (Karniol, 1989).

At 13 months, babies use their hands for different functions.

These many changes in reaching and grasping are well illustrated as infants learn to feed themselves. At about 6 months, they are often given finger foods such as sliced bananas and green beans. Infants can easily pick up such foods, but getting them into their mouths is another story. The hand grasping the food might be raised to the cheek, then moved to the edge of the lips, and, finally, shoved into the mouth. Mission accomplished, but only with many detours along the way! Eye–hand coordination improves rapidly, so, before long, foods varying in size, shape, and texture reach the mouth directly.

At about the first birthday, youngsters usually are ready to try eating with a spoon. At first, they play with the spoon, dipping it into a dish filled with food or sucking on an empty spoon. With a little help, they learn to fill the spoon with food and eat from it, although the motion is awkward, as babies don't rotate their wrists. Instead, most 1-year-olds fill a spoon by placing it directly over a dish and lowering it until the spoon is full. Then the baby will raise the spoon up, all the while keeping the wrist rigid. In contrast, 2-year-olds rotate the hand at the wrist while scooping food from a dish and placing the spoon in the mouth—the same motion that adults use.

In each of these actions, the same principles of dynamic systems theory apply, as with locomotion. Complex acts involve many component movements. Each must be performed correctly and in the proper sequence. Development involves first mastering the separate elements and then assembling them in sequence to form a smoothly functioning whole. Eating finger

Babies learn to use utensils and make demands!

food, for example, requires grasping food, moving the hand to the mouth, and releasing the food. As the demands of tasks change and as children develop, the same skills are often reassembled to form different sequences of movements.

HANDEDNESS. When young babies reach for objects, they don't seem to prefer one hand over the other; they use their left and right hands interchangeably. They might shake a rattle in the left hand and, moments later, pick up blocks with the right. In one study, infants and toddlers were videotaped as they played with toys that could be manipulated with two hands, such as a pinwheel (Cornwell, Harris, & Fitzgerald, 1991). The 9-month-olds used left and right hands equally, but by 13 months, most grasped the toy with their right hand. Then they used their left hand to steady the toy while their right hand manipulated it. This early preference for one hand becomes stronger and more consistent during the preschool years. By the time children are ready to enter kindergarten, handedness is well established and very difficult to reverse (McManus et al., 1988).

Heredity plays a role in handedness (Corballis, 1997). Two parents who are right-handed tend to have right-handed children. Children who are left-handed generally have a parent or grandparent who also is left-handed. However, experience also contributes to handedness. Modern industrial cultures favour right-handedness. School desks, scissors, and can openers, for example, are designed for right-handed people and can be used by left-handers only with difficulty. Some cultures and religions also have particular rules or beliefs about handedness, which can affect how or when people use their right or left hands (Harris, 1983; Levy, 1976).

Igor Yaruta/Fotolia

Handedness is affected by heredity and environmental influences.

Maturation, Experience, and Motor Skill

LO11 **Discuss how maturation and experience influence children's acquisition of motor skills.**

For locomotion and fine-motor skills, the big picture is much the same: Progress is rapid during the first year of a baby's life as fundamental skills are mastered and combined to generate even more complex behaviours. The progress we observe in gross-motor (large-muscle) or fine-motor skills is due to a combination of maturation (genetics) and experience. While you might wonder whether parental reports of their children's gross-motor development are accurate, researchers in Winnipeg found in one study that, in fact, they can be very reliable (Bodnarchuk & Eaton, 2004).

The maturational sequence of motor development that we have described for locomotion and fine-motor skill holds for most cultures. Despite enormous variation across cultures in child-rearing practices, motor development proceeds in much the same way and at roughly the same rate worldwide. This general point is well illustrated in the feature on Children and Families around the World.

Of course, maturation and experience are not mutually exclusive. Just because maturation figures importantly in the development of one gross-motor skill, walking, it does not imply that experience plays no role. In fact, practice and training do affect children's mastery of many motor skills. Here, too, studies of other cultures are revealing. In some African countries, young infants are given daily practice walking under the tutelage of a parent or sibling. In addition, infants are commonly carried by their parents in a piggyback style, which helps develop muscles in the infants' trunk and legs. These infants walk months earlier than North American infants (Super, 1981).

Experience can improve the rate of motor development, but the improvement is limited to the specific muscle groups that are involved. Just as daily practice kicking a soccer ball won't improve your golf game, infants who receive much practice in one

Mike Greenlar/The Image Works

This style of carrying children develops their trunk and leg muscles.

motor skill usually don't improve in others. Zelazo and her colleagues (1993) had parents make their 6-week-old infants practise stepping. Other parents had their infants practise sitting. After seven weeks of practice, the two groups of infants, as well as a control group of 6-week-olds who had no practice of any kind, were tested in their ability to step and sit. For both stepping and sitting, infants showed improvement in the skill they had practised. When infants were tested on the skill they had not practised, they did no better than infants in the control group. Thus, the impact of practice was specific, not widespread.

Experience becomes even more important in complex actions. Mastering discrete skills, connecting them in the correct sequence, and then timing them properly requires more than a few simple repetitions. Observing others, repeated practice, and receiving feedback regarding errors is required. Of course, learning a complex behaviour must build upon maturational changes, but with biological readiness and practice, youngsters learn a gamut of complex motor behaviours, from hitting a tennis ball, to playing a violin, to signing with people who do not hear.

Children and Families around the World

Learning to Walk in Hopi Culture

Traditionally, infants in Hopi culture are secured to cradleboards, which prevent them from moving hands or legs, rolling over, or raising their bodies. Infants feed and sleep while secured to the board; they are removed from the cradleboard only for a change of clothes. This practice begins the day the infant is born and continues for the first three months. Thereafter, infants are allowed time off the boards so they can move around. Time off the cradleboard increases gradually, but, for most of the first year, infants sleep on the boards and spend some part of their waking time on them as well.

Obviously, the cradleboard strictly limits the infant's ability to locomote during much of the first year, a time when most infants are learning to sit, creep, and crawl. Nevertheless, Dennis and Dennis (1940) discovered that infants reared with cradleboards learn to walk at approximately 15 months—about the same age as Hopi children reared by parents who had adopted Western practices and no longer used cradleboards.

When the Dennis and Dennis (1940) study was repeated more than 40 years later, the story remained the same. Chisholm (1983) studied Navajo infants who spent much of their infancy secured to cradleboards. They, too, began to walk at about the same age as infants whose parents did not use cradleboards, confirming the importance of maturation in learning to walk.

The security of a cradleboard.

Therefore, a restrictive environment that massively reduces opportunities for practice has no apparent effect on the age of onset for walking. This suggests that the timing of an infant's first steps is determined more by an underlying genetic timetable than by specific experiences or practice. Similarly, when infants practise crawling on their bellies, this helps them crawl on hands and feet because many of the motions are the same (Adolph, Vereijken, & Denny, 1998). However, when infants practise crawling on steep slopes, there is no transfer to walking on steep slopes because the motions differ (Adolph, 1997).

Ask Yourself

Are you right-handed or left-handed? Should society make more accommodation for people who are left-handed?

What kinds of activities might enhance fine-motor skill development in children? What activities might enhance gross-motor skill development?

5.4 Sensory and Perceptual Processes

⌄ Learning Objectives

After reading the module, you should be able to do the following:

LO12 Describe the sensory abilities of the newborn.

LO13 State how well infants hear and how they use sounds to understand the world.

LO14 State how accurate infants' vision is and whether they perceive colour and depth.

LO15 Summarize how infants integrate information from different senses.

Parents often wonder about their newborn's sensory and perceptual skills. To help you understand these skills, you need to remember that people have different kinds of sense organs, each receptive to a unique kind of physical energy. The retina at the back of the eye, for example, is sensitive to some types of electromagnetic energy, and sight is the result. The eardrum detects changes in air pressure, and hearing is the result. Cells at the top of the nasal passage detect airborne molecules, and olfaction (smell) is the result. In each case, the sense organ translates the physical stimulation into nerve impulses that are sent to the brain.

Since infants can't tell us what they smell, hear, or see, researchers have had to devise other ways to find out. In many studies, an investigator presents two stimuli to a baby, such as a high-pitched tone and a low-pitched tone or a sweet-tasting substance and a sour-tasting substance. Then the investigator records the baby's physiological responses, such as heart rate or facial expression or head movement. If the baby consistently responds differently to the two stimuli, the conclusion is that baby must be able to distinguish between them.

Another approach is based on the fact that infants usually prefer novel stimuli over familiar stimuli. Researchers use this fact to study perception by repeatedly presenting one stimulus (e.g., a low-pitched tone) until an infant barely responds. Then they present a second stimulus (e.g., a higher-pitched tone). If the infant responds strongly, then it can distinguish the two stimuli.

Smell, Taste, and Touch

LO12 Describe the sensory abilities of the newborn.

Newborns have a keen sense of smell. Infants respond positively to pleasant smells and negatively to unpleasant odours (Mennella & Beauchamp, 1997). They have a relaxed and content facial expression when they smell honey or chocolate but frown, grimace, or turn away when they smell rotten eggs or ammonia. Young babies also can recognize familiar odours. Newborns will look in the direction of a pad saturated with their own amniotic fluid (Schaal, Marlier, & Soussignan, 1998). They also will turn toward a pad saturated with the odour of their mother's breast or perfume (Porter, Makin, Davis, & Christensen, 1991). Preterm infants who are exposed to the smell of their mother's milk for two minutes prior to breastfeeding were found to feed longer and tended to have shorter hospital stays in comparison with those who are not exposed to the smell of their mother's milk prior to feeding (Raimbault, Saliba, & Porter, 2007).

In addition, newborns have a highly developed sense of taste. They readily differentiate salty, sour, bitter, and sweet tastes (Rostenstein & Oster, 1997). Most infants seem to have a "sweet tooth." They react to sweet substances by smiling, sucking, and licking their lips. In contrast, infants grimace when fed bitter- or sour-tasting substances (Kaijura, Cowart, & Beauchamp, 1992). Infants are also sensitive to changes in the taste of breast milk that reflect a mother's diet. Infants will nurse more after their mother has consumed a sweet-tasting substance, such as vanilla (Mennella & Beauchamp, 1996).

Newborns are sensitive to touch. As we described in Module 5.3, many areas of the newborn's body respond reflexively when touched. Touching an infant's cheek, mouth, hand, or foot produces reflexive movements, demonstrating that infants perceive touch.

Babies can feel pain.

If babies react to touch, does this mean they experience pain? This was once difficult to answer because pain has such a subjective element to it, and methods for studying pain were not well established. Since infants cannot express their pain to us directly, we must use indirect evidence, in part by observing infants' reactions to painful stimuli. However, sometimes it is difficult for researchers to distinguish true pain from stress in infants by observing their behaviours (Whitfield & Grunau, 2000).

The infant's nervous system definitely is capable of transmitting pain: Receptors for pain in the skin are just as plentiful in infants as they are in adults (Anand & Hickey, 1987). Furthermore, babies' behaviour in response to apparent pain-provoking stimuli also suggests that they experience pain (Buchholz, Karl, Pomietto, & Lynn, 1998). Consider, for example, a baby receiving an inoculation. She lowers her eyebrows, purses her lips, and opens her mouth to cry. The pain cry begins suddenly, is high-pitched, and is not easily soothed. The baby also becomes agitated, moving her hands, arms, and legs (Craig, Whitfield, Grunau, Linton, & Hadjistavropoulos, 1993). All together, these signs strongly suggest that babies experience pain (Chamberlain, 1998).

Whitfield and Grunau (2000) have been considering the impact of pain on babies' neurological and developmental outcomes. They also have been interested in the short-term and long-term effects of analgesic medications (painkillers) in babies. Whitfield and Grunau have been studying extremely low-birth-weight babies, who typically experience repeated pain as they mature in early infancy or as a result of intensive and lifesaving medical procedures. These researchers concluded that pain causes stress in babies, which can have an adverse effect on long-term neurological and developmental outcomes as well as their subsequent reactivity to pain. In preterm infants, facial expressions and heart rate tend to be the most sensitive indicators of pain perception (Holst et al., 2005). We also know that level of parental anxiety can predict how distressed an infant may become during a medical procedure, such as an immunization (Bernard & Cohen, 2006).

Perceptual skills such as smell, taste, and sensitivity to pain are extraordinarily useful to newborns and young babies. Smell and touch help them recognize their mothers. Smell and taste make learning to eat much easier. Early development of smell, taste, and touch prepare newborns and young babies to learn about the world. On the other hand, responsivity to pain enables babies to signal caregivers for assistance.

Hearing

LO13 State how well infants hear and how they use sounds to understand the world.

A fetus can hear at about seven or eight months' gestation (Fulford et al., 2004; Holst et al., 2005; Kisilevsky, Hains, Jacquet, Granier-Deferre, & Lecanuet, 2004; Krueger, Holditch-Davis, Quint, & DeCasper, 2004). Therefore, as you might expect, newborns typically respond to sounds in their surroundings. If a parent is quiet but then coughs, an infant might startle, blink, and move its arms or legs. These responses might seem natural, but they do indeed indicate that infants are sensitive to sound.

Auditory threshold:

the quietest sound that a person can hear.

Not surprisingly, infants do not hear as well as adults. **Auditory threshold** refers to the quietest sound that a person can hear. An adult's auditory threshold is fairly easy to measure: A tone is presented, and the adult signals when it is heard. To test auditory thresholds in infants, who cannot report what they hear, researchers have devised a number of clever techniques (Aslin, Jusczyk, & Pisoni, 1998). For example, in one method, the infant is seated on a parent's lap. Both parent and baby wear head-phones, as does an observer seated in another room who watches the baby through an observation window. The observer signals the experimenter when the baby is atten-tive, and the experimenter either presents a tone over the baby's headphones or does nothing. Neither the observer nor the parent knows when tones are going to be pre-sented, and they can't hear the tones through their headphones. On each trial, the observer simply judges whether the baby responds in any fashion, such as turning its head or changing its facial expression or activity level. Afterward, the experimenter determines how well the observer's judgments match the trials: If a baby can hear the tone, the observer should have noted a response only when a tone was presented.

Working with newborns is not easy because they tend to fall asleep during research trials! However, alternating silence with "white noise," Morrongiello and Trehub (1987) found that 6-month-old infants are able to discriminate a change in the duration of silence as small as 20 milliseconds and that this auditory discrimination ability becomes even better in the preschool (15 msec) and adult (10 msec) years.

This type of testing reveals that, overall, adults can hear better than infants and adults can hear some very quiet sounds that infants can't (Aslin, Jusczyk, & Pisoni, 1998). More importantly, this testing shows that infants best hear sounds that have pitches in the range of human speech—neither very high nor very low. Infants can dif-ferentiate vowels from consonant sounds, and by 4½ months they can recognize their own names (Jusczyk, 1995; Mandel, Jusczyk, & Pisoni, 1995).

Infants also use sound to locate objects, determining whether they originate from the left or right and near or far. In one study (Clifton, Perris, & Bullinger, 1991), 7-month-olds were shown a rattle. Then the experimenters darkened the room and shook the rattle, either 15 centimetres away from the infant or about 60 centimetres away. Infants often reached for the rattle in the dark when it was 15 centimetres away but seldom when it was 60 centimetres away. These 7-month-olds were quite capable of using sound to estimate distance, in this case distinguishing a toy they could reach from one they could not. Canadian researchers have determined that newborns can detect the general location and distance of a sound, an ability called **auditory (sound) localization** (Hillier, Hewitt, & Morrongiello, 1992; Morrongiello, Fenwick, Hillier, & Chance, 1994).

Auditory (sound) localization:

the ability to detect from where a sound is coming.

As you can see, by the middle of the first year, most infants respond to much of the information provided by sound. However, their full auditory capacity likely is not reached until about 30 months of age (Hulecki & Small, 2011).

Seeing

LO14 **State how accurate infants' vision is and whether they perceive colour and depth.**

If you've watched infants you've probably noticed that, while awake, they spend a lot of time looking around. Sometimes they seem to be scanning their environment broadly, and sometimes they seem to be focusing on nearby objects. Infants have vision similar to that of adults, but not entirely.

Visual acuity:

the smallest pattern that can be dependably distinguished.

From birth, babies respond to light and can track moving objects with their eyes, but how clear is their vision, and how can we measure its clarity? **Visual acuity** is defined as the smallest pattern that can be distinguished dependably. You've undoubt-edly had your visual acuity measured by trying to read rows of progressively smaller letters or numbers from a chart. The same basic logic is used in tests of infants' acuity,

Figure 5–5

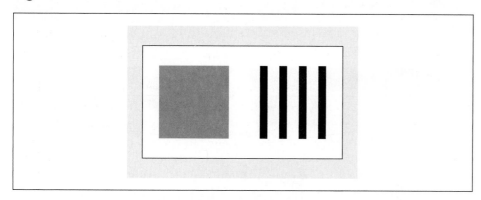

which are based on two premises. First, most infants will look at patterned stimuli instead of plain, nonpatterned stimuli. For example, if we were to show the two stimuli in Figure 5–5 to infants, most would look longer at the striped pattern than at the grey pattern. Second, as we make the lines narrower (along with the spaces between them), eventually the black and white stripes become so fine that they simply blend together and appear grey, just like the all-grey pattern.

To estimate an infant's acuity, then, we pair the grey square with squares that differ in the width of their stripes, like those in Figure 5–6: When infants look at the two stimuli equally, it indicates that they are no longer able to distinguish the stripes of the patterned stimulus. By measuring the width of the stripes and their distance from an infant's eye, we can estimate acuity (detecting thinner stripes indicates better acuity).

Measurements of this sort indicate that newborns and 1-month-olds see at 6 metres what normal adults see at 60 to 120 metres. Infants' acuity improves rapidly and by their first birthday is essentially the same as a normal adult's (Kellman & Banks, 1998).

Not only do infants begin to see the world with greater acuity during the first year, they also begin to see it in colour! Adams and Courage (1998) demonstrated that infants are not lacking in particular colour perception but tend to respond to colour of higher saturation levels than an adult would be able to perceive. These researchers concluded that newborns have a generally more immature and inefficient optical system for detection of colour.

The wavelength of light is the source of colour perception. Figure 5–7 shows that lights we see as red have a relatively long wavelength, whereas violet, at the other end of the colour spectrum, has a much shorter wavelength. We detect wavelength—and therefore colour—with specialized neurons called **cones** that are in the retina of the eye. Some cones are particularly sensitive to short-wavelength light (blues and violets), others are sensitive to medium-wavelength light (greens and yellows), and still

Cones:

specialized neurons located in the retina of the eye.

Figure 5–6

Figure 5–7

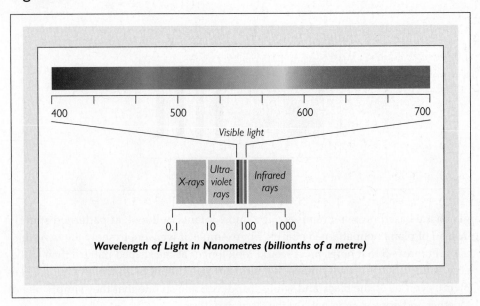

others to long-wavelength light (reds and oranges). These different kinds of cones are linked in complex circuits of neurons in the eye and in the brain, and this neural circuitry allows us to see the world in colour.

These circuits gradually begin to function in the first few months after birth, so that, by 3 months, the three kinds of cones and their associated circuits are working, allowing infants to see the full range of colours (Kellman & Banks, 1998).

In fact, by 3 to 4 months, infants' colour perception seems similar to adults' (Adams & Courage, 1995). In particular, infants, like adults, tend to see categories of colour. For example, if a yellow light's wavelength is gradually increased, the infant will suddenly perceive it as a shade of red rather than a shade of yellow.

To study infants' perception of colour categories, researchers use the same technique used to test visual acuity. First, infants are repeatedly shown the same coloured light; it might be a light with a wavelength of 600 nanometres (billionths of a metre), which adults call yellow. Infants look intently at first, then look less. When this happens, a new light is shown. The wavelength of the new light always differs from the original by the same amount—20 nanometres, for example. For some babies, the wavelength is decreased 20 nanometres; adults still consider this a yellow light. For other babies, the wavelength is increased 20 nanometres; adults judge this as a green light. Infants look longer at a new light from a new colour category than a new light from the same, familiar colour category. This result indicates that infants view the stimuli as adults do—in categories of colour (Dannemiller, 1998; Teller & Bornstein, 1987). In addition, by 6 months of age, a five-fold improvement in visual ability is observed primarily due to having more visual experience (Maurer & Lewis, 2001). Visual experience in infancy can have an impact on visual acuity throughout child development and into adulthood (LeGrand, Mondloch, Maurer, & Brent, 2003).

Infants not only perceive colour and depth, they also achieve many perceptual constancies.

Size constancy:

the realization that an object's actual size remains the same despite changes in the size of its retinal image.

PERCEPTUAL CONSTANCIES.   Early on, infants master **size constancy**, the realization that an object's actual size remains the same despite changes in the size of its retinal image. How do we know that infants have a rudimentary sense of size constancy? Suppose we let an infant look at an unfamiliar teddy bear. Then we show the infant the same bear, at a different distance, paired with a larger replica of the bear. If infants lack size constancy, the two bears will be equally novel, and babies should

Figure 5–8

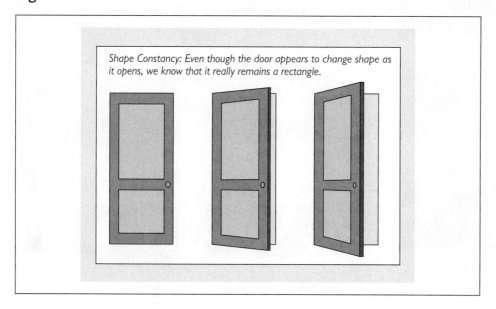

Shape Constancy: Even though the door appears to change shape as it opens, we know that it really remains a rectangle.

respond to each similarly. If, instead, babies have size constancy, they will recognize the first bear as familiar, the larger bear as novel, and be more likely to respond to the novel bear. In fact, by 4 or 5 months, babies treat the bear that they've seen twice at different distances—and, therefore, with different retinal images—as familiar (Granrud, 1986). This outcome is possible only if infants have size constancy. Thus, infants do not believe that mothers (and other people or objects) constantly change size as they move closer or farther away.

Size is just one of several perceptual constancies. Others are brightness and colour constancy as well as shape constancy, shown in Figure 5–8. All these constancies are achieved, at least in rudimentary form, by 4 months (Aslin, 1987; Dannemiller, 1998).

If you think about it, the message from the perceptual constancies is that "seeing is not believing"—at least not always. A good part of perception, therefore, is knowing how to make sense out of what we see. Another important part of making sense out of what we see is deciding how near or far away an object is.

DEPTH.   People see objects as having three dimensions: height, width, and depth. The retina of the eye is flat, so height and width can be represented directly on its two-dimensional surface. But the third dimension, depth, cannot be represented directly on a surface, so how do we perceive depth? How do we decide if objects are nearby or far away? We use perceptual processing to infer depth.

Eleanor Gibson and Richard Walk (1960) used a special apparatus to address the question of whether infants perceive depth. The **visual cliff** is a glass-covered platform; on one side, a pattern appears directly under the glass, but, on the other, it appears several feet below the glass. Consequently, one side looks shallow, but the other appears to have a steep drop-off, like a cliff.

In the experiment, the baby is placed on the platform, and the mother coaxes the infant to come to her. Most babies willingly crawl to their mother when she stands on the shallow side, but virtually all babies refuse to cross the deep side, even when the mother calls the infant by name and tries to lure him or her with an attractive toy. Clearly, infants can perceive depth by the time they are old enough to crawl.

When babies as young as 1½ months (who can't crawl) are simply placed on the deep side of the platform, their heartbeat slows down. Heart rate often decelerates when people notice something interesting, so this would suggest that 1½-month-olds notice that the deep side is different. At 7 months, infants' heart rate accelerates, a sign of fear. Therefore, although young babies can detect a difference between the shallow

Visual cliff:
a glass-covered platform used for measuring infant depth perception.

Crawling facilitates depth perception.

Texture provides a clue to distance perception. We understand the blurred flowers to be farther away from us than the more distinct flowers.

Interposition provides a clue to distance perception.

Retinal disparity:

differences in position on the left and right retinas for objects perceived to be nearby.

Texture gradient:

cues for depth perception arising from an object's surface texture, with nearer objects having finer details and farther ones having coarser details.

Relative size provides a clue to distance perception. We understand that the runners who look smaller are farther away than the runners who look larger.

Perceptual processes interpret sensory information.

and deep sides of the visual cliff, only older, crawling babies are actually afraid of the deep side (Campos, Hiatt, Ramsay, Henderson, & Svejda, 1978).

Infants use several kinds of cues to infer depth. One, **retinal disparity**, is based on the fact that the left and right eyes often see slightly different versions of the same scene. When objects are distant, the images appear in very similar positions on the retina; when objects are near, the images appear in much different positions. Thus, greater disparity in positions of the image on the retina signals that an object is close. By 4 to 6 months, infants use retinal disparity as a depth cue, correctly inferring that objects are nearby when disparity is great (Kellman & Banks, 1998; Yonas & Owsley, 1987).

Other cues for depth that depend on the arrangement of objects in the environment include texture gradient, relative size, and interposition. With **texture gradient**, the texture of objects changes from coarse but distinct for nearby objects to finer and less distinct for distant objects.

With **relative size**, nearby objects look substantially larger than objects in the distance. Therefore, we judge smaller objects to be farther away from us than larger objects.

With **interposition**, nearby objects partially obscure more distant objects. Therefore, we judge obscured objects to be more distant than non-obscured objects.

By 7 months, infants use most of these cues to judge distance (Kellman & Banks, 1998). In one study (Arterberry, Yonas, & Bensen, 1989), babies saw what appeared to be two toys resting on a checkered surface that gave linear perspective and texture gradients as depth cues. In fact, the checkered surface was a flat photograph.

Infants were tested with one eye covered so that retinal disparity would not provide a cue to depth. Most 7-month-olds reached for the toy that looked closer, but 5-month-olds reached for the two toys equally often. Evidently, 7-month-olds use linear perspective and texture gradient to infer depth, but 5-month-olds do not.

PERCEIVING OBJECTS. When you look at the photo on the left, what do you see? You probably recognize it as part of a human eye even though the photograph really is just a composite of many differently coloured dots. In this case, perception actually creates an object from sensory stimulation.

Figure 5–9

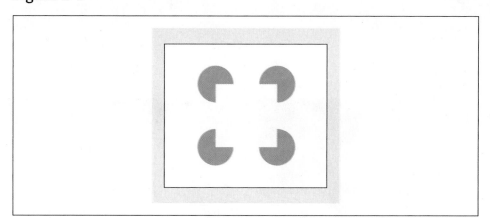

Relative size:

cues for depth perception arising from an object's size, with larger objects being nearer and smaller objects being farther away.

Interposition:

cues for depth perception arising from the degree to which an object is blocked from view by other objects, with nearer objects being in full view and farther objects being partially obstructed from view.

Edges:

lines that mark the boundaries of objects.

Edges play an important role in defining objects (Kellman & Banks, 1998). **Edges** are lines that mark the boundaries of objects. We use edges to distinguish one object from another and from background. In the photo of the eyeball, for example, two circles of blue dots define the inner and outer edges of the iris; these edges cause us to see all the other blue dots as part of the same "thing"—the iris.

Early in their first year, infants use edges to identify objects. Infants' perception of edges is shown in some fascinating research involving patterns like the one in Figure 5–9. When you see this pattern, it's almost impossible not to see a square. Of course, there's no actual physical stimulus that corresponds to the square. Instead, the cut-out portions of each circle are corners that define lines, creating an edge. It's this created edge that allows our perceptual system to "see" a square.

When infants view these circles, they also "see" a square. In one study (Ghim, 1990), 3-month-olds were shown a real square. After six presentations of the square, infants were shown four patterns similar to the one in Figure 5–9; all consisted of four circles, but only one of them portrayed the subjective experience of "seeing" a square. The rest portrayed "imperfect" squares that were missing one of the corners. Having seen squares repeatedly, 3-month-olds looked much longer at the "imperfect" squares than at the pattern portraying a full square. Evidently, the full square looked familiar to them, so they spent less time looking at it. Of course, the only way that the pattern with the full square could be familiar to them is if the infants "saw" a square created by the four circles, as in Figure 5–9, and interpreted this as yet another presentation of the actual square they had seen previously.

Edges are most useful in distinguishing stationary objects. When motion is present, we use it to help define objects by following a simple rule: Elements that move together are usually part of the same object (Kellman & Banks, 1998). For example, at the left of Figure 5–10, a pencil appears to be moving back and forth behind a coloured square. If the square were removed, you would be surprised to see a pair of pencil stubs, as shown on the right side of the diagram. The common movement of the pencil's eraser and point led us to believe that they were part of the same pencil. New research findings suggest that, like adults, infants have two anatomically separate visual systems, one for determining perception of objects and another for interpreting visual information from objects that are moving (Wermeskerken, Kamp, & Hofsten, 2013).

By 2 to 4 months of age, infants, too, are surprised by demonstrations like this. If they see the moving pencils display, they will then look very briefly at a whole pencil, apparently because they expected it. In contrast, if after seeing the moving pencil they're shown the two pencil stubs, they look much longer, as if trying to figure out what happened (Eizenman & Bertenthal, 1998; Johnson & Aslin, 1995).

Figure 5–10

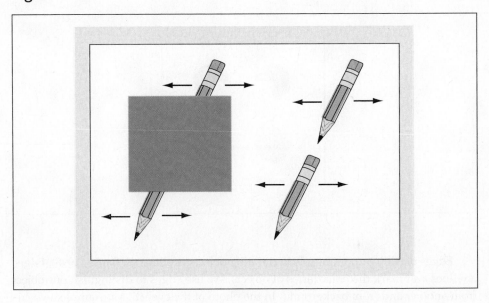

Evidently, even very young babies use common motion to create objects from different parts.

One object that's particularly important for infants is the human face. Young babies readily look at faces. From Figure 5–11, which shows a pattern of eye fixations, you can see that 1-month-olds look mostly at the outer edges of the face. Three-month-olds, however, focus almost entirely on the interior of the face, particularly the eyes and lips.

Some researchers believe that general principles of perception explain how infants perceive faces (Aslin, 1987). They argue that infants are attracted to faces because faces have stimuli that move (the eyes and mouth) and stimuli with dark and light contrast (the eyes, lips, and teeth). Dannemiller and Stephens (1988) found that when face and nonface stimuli are matched for a number of important variables (such as the amount of black/white contrast or the size and number of elements), 1-month-olds typically look at face and nonface stimuli equally. In other words, until at least 6 weeks of age, infants look at faces because of general perceptual principles (for example, babies like contrasting stimuli), not because faces are intrinsically attractive to infants.

Figure 5–11

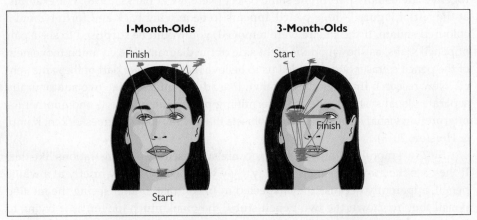

Figure 5–12

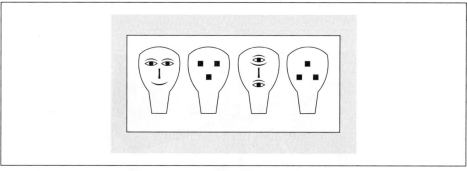

SOURCE: Morton & Johnson, 1991.

Canadian researchers have found similar results: Newborns will look more readily at a stimulus that looks like a face than they will at a stimulus that is blank (Easterbrook, Kisilevsky, Hains, & Muir, 1999; Easterbrook, Kisilevsky, Muir, & Laplante, 1999); however, they do not show a preference for a typical human face over a "scrambled" human face (see Figure 5–12), even though they can demonstrate an ability to discriminate between the two stimuli (Easterbrook, Kisilevsky, Muir, et al., 1999). These researchers also found that infants prefer tracking a face-like stimulus as compared with tracking just two eyes or other singular features of a human face, such as just the mouth (Easterbrook, Kisilevsky, Hains, et al., 1999).

More research is needed to decide whether face perception follows general perceptual principles or represents a special case. What is clear, though, is that, by 2 or 3 months of age, babies have the perceptual skills that allow them to begin to distinguish individual faces (Carey, 1992). This ability is essential because it provides the basis for social relationships that infants form during the rest of the first year.

Integrating Sensory Information

LO15 Summarize how infants integrate information from different senses.

Although babies have separate sensory systems, like adults, most infant experiences are better described as "multimedia events." A nursing mother provides visual and taste cues to her baby. A rattle stimulates vision, hearing, and touch. From experiences like these, infants learn to integrate information from different senses.

By 1 month—and possibly at birth—infants can integrate sensory information (Bahrick, 1992). For example, 1-month-olds can recognize an object visually that they had only touched previously (Gibson & Walker, 1984). By 4 months, infants are quite skilled at integrating sights and sounds: They can connect the characteristic sounds of male and female voices with the characteristic appearances of male and female faces (Poulin-Dubois, Serbin, Kenyon, & Derbyshire, 1994).

In addition, Bahrick, Netto, and Hernandez-Reif (1998) used video images paired with speakers of different ages to determine whether infants understand speakers' ages (e.g., video of a young boy with an audiotape of a man's voice, as portrayed in Figure 5–13). If infants had no preference for the videotape matching the audiotape, they should look at the two videos equally. The bars in Figure 5–14 show the percentage of time that infants actually spent watching the video image that matched the audiotaped voice. The 4-month-olds had no preference on the first six videos but looked longer at the matching videos

**Darling,
you were supposed to "blow out" the candles...**

Hagen/www.Cartoonstock.com

Figure 5–13

on the second six videos. For 7-month-olds, the pattern was reversed: They looked longer at the matching video during the first six videos but not on the second six.

According to these researchers, both 4- and 7-month-olds are able to integrate the typical appearances of face and typical sounds of voices. That is, infants know that childish faces tend to have childish voices and adult faces tend to have adult voices. The fact that these outcomes were found in different sets of videos also highlights the obstacles associated with doing experimentation with young infants: Apparently the 4-month-olds took longer to figure out what was involved in the study, and the 7-month-olds lost interest more quickly.

Integrating sight and sound is yet another variation on the theme that has dominated this module: Infants' sensory and perceptual skills are impressive. Infants can distinguish sounds, and, at about 7 months, can use sound to locate objects. Their vision is a little blurry at first but will improve rapidly, and, in a few months, they can see colours fully. Within only a month, they can make connections between sights, sounds, and other senses. In short, babies are well prepared to make sense out of the environment.

Figure 5–14

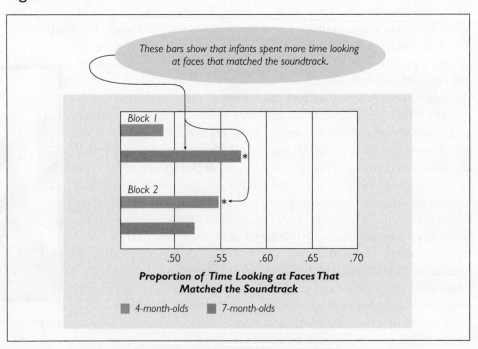

Ask Yourself

How are infants' sensory and perceptual skills affected by both nature and nurture? Why might parental anxiety predict how distressed an infant might become during an immunization?

What Would a Grandparent Do?

Imagine you were a grandparent and you noticed that your infant grandchild was slightly overweight. When mentioned to your daughter and son-in-law, neither of them considered it to be a problem. What would you do in this situation? How much should a grandparent get involved in his or her grandchild's parenting?

Summary

5.1   Healthy Growth

Features of Human Growth

- Infant and toddler physical growth is rapid and involves height and weight as well as development of muscles, fat, and bones.

- Growth is cephalocaudal (top-down) and proximodistal (from the center toward the outside) in nature.

Variations on the Average Profile

- Children born today tend to be larger than previous generations.

- Age peers vary considerably in height and weight.

Mechanisms of Physical Growth

- Height and weight are influenced by heredity.

- Growth hormone (GH) affects bone and muscle growth, and thyroxine affects nerve cells.

- Nutrition is especially important during infancy because it is a period of rapid growth.

- Breastfeeding provides babies with all the nutrients they need and has other health advantages as well.

Challenges to Healthy Growth

- Healthy development is a challenge for many children.

- Malnutrition is a worldwide threat to infant development and requires improving children's diet as well as parental knowledge.

- Infectious disease is another serious threat.

- In North America, toddlers are more likely to die from accidents than any other single cause.

5.2   The Developing Nervous System

A Basic Nerve Cell

- Nerve cells are composed of a cell body, a dendrite, and an axon.

- The neuronal cell body contains the biological mechanisms for maintenance of cellular life

Organization of the Mature Brain

- The mature brain consists of billions of neurons organized into nearly identical left and right hemispheres connected by the corpus callosum.

- The frontal cortex is associated with personality and goal-directed behaviour.

- The left cortex is associated with language, and the right cortex is associated with nonverbal processes.

The Developing Brain

- Brain structure begins to be formed during prenatal development, when neurons form at an incredible rate.

- After birth, neurons in the central nervous system become wrapped in myelin, allowing them to transmit information more rapidly.

- Throughout childhood, unused synapses disappear gradually through a process of synaptic pruning.

- Methods used to investigate brain functioning in children include (a) studying children with brain damage, (b) recording electrical activity in the brain, and (c) using imaging techniques.

- Major imaging techniques used with infants include EEG, PET, fMRI, and fNIRS.

- An infant's brain begins to function early in life.

- Left cortex language processing occurs around the time of birth.

- The right cortex controls some nonverbal functions, such as perception of music, very early in infancy.

- Control of other right-hemisphere functions, such as understanding spatial relations, is achieved by the preschool years.

- The frontal cortex regulates goal-directed behaviour and emotions by the baby's first birthday.

5.3 Motor Development

The Infant's Reflexes

- Babies are born with many reflexes to help them adjust to life outside the uterus, protect them, and form the basis for later motor behaviour.

Locomotion

- Infants progress through a sequence of motor milestones during the first year, culminating in walking by around the first birthday.

- The dynamic systems theory of motor development suggests that learning to walk involves differentiation of individual skills in sequence, such as maintaining balance and stepping on alternate legs, and then integrating these skills into a coherent whole.

Fine-Motor Skills

- Reaching and grasping become more precise in the first year, reflecting the principles of dynamic systems theory.

- Most people are right-handed, a preference that emerges after the first birthday.

- Handedness is determined by heredity but can be influenced by experience and cultural values.

Maturation, Experience, and Motor Skill

- Biology and experience both shape the mastery of motor skills.

- The basic timetable for motor milestones is similar around the world, which indicates underlying biological causes.

- Specific experience can accelerate motor development, particularly for complex motor skills.

5.4 Sensory and Perceptual Processes

Smell, Taste, and Touch

- Newborns can smell and taste, preferring sweet substances over bitter and sour tastes.

- Infants respond to touch, and they experience pain.

Hearing

- Babies can hear but are less sensitive to higher- and lower-pitched sounds than adults.

- Babies can distinguish different sounds and use sound to locate objects in space.

Seeing

- A newborn's visual acuity is relatively poor, but 1-year-olds can see as well as an adult with normal vision.

- By 3 or 4 months, children see colour as well as adults do.

- Infants use edges and motion to distinguish objects.

- Infants perceive faces early in the first year, but it is not clear whether this ability is based on specific perceptual mechanisms or on the same processes used to see other objects.

Integrating Sensory Information

- Soon after birth, infants coordinate information from different senses.

- Infants recognize by sight an object that they've felt previously.

- Infants learn to integrate what they see with what they hear.

Chapter Critical Review

1. Explain how the example of malnutrition (Module 5.1) illustrates at least two of the four themes of child development.

2. Based on the research described in Module 5.2, explain the relation between emotional experience and response to stimuli. Why are both located in the frontal cortex?

3. Given the information presented in Module 5.3, summarize what parents can do to enhance their child's motor development.

4. Speculate on the survival benefits to infants of the perceptual abilities described in Module 5.4. Why should infants be able to distinguish between tastes and odour, react to sounds, and process visual information?

5. How would a psychologist who adopts the learning perspective explain the research on sensory integration? How would the explanation of psychologists who adopt the information-processing perspective differ?

See for Yourself

How can you decide if a toddler is left- or right-handed? Adults can tell us which hand they use for writing or throwing, but we need a more concrete approach with toddlers, who don't even know left from right. Ask some toddlers to do the following tasks (derived from McManus et al., 1988):

1. Colour a square.

2. Throw a ball.

3. Thread a bead onto a string.

4. Turn over cards placed on a table.

5. Brush their teeth.

6. Blow their nose with a tissue.

7. Pick a piece of candy from a bag.

8. Comb their hair.

You should see that most toddlers use their right hand on many tasks but not on others. Few will show a strong preference for one hand over the other. See for yourself!

Chapter 6
Cognition in Infants and Toddlers

oksun70/Fotolia

∨ MODULE

6.1 Piaget's Theory

6.2 Information Processing

6.3 Language

After Sophie was born, Terry and Mabel found that they could spend hours just gazing at their newborn daughter. She was so beautiful! Terry and Mabel were very careful as they picked up Sophie and carried her around. They knew her small body contained a developing brain that was so important to her learning and ability to reason about the world. As they looked deeply into Sophie's deep, bright eyes, they wondered . . . "What is she thinking?"

Connect to My Virtual Child

What kinds of theories do you have about children? What ideas inform your thoughts and beliefs about the lives of children, how they are raised, and the nature of the human person? Use your access card and follow this link www.myvirtualchild.com to learn more about the world of the child. You can even virtually try to raise your own child.

6.1 Piaget's Theory

 ## Learning Objectives

After reading the module, you should be able to do the following:

LO1 Describe how assimilation, accommodation, and equilibration explain the ways that children's thinking changes with age.

LO2 Explain how thinking becomes more advanced as infants progress through the six substages of the sensorimotor stage.

LO3 State some criticisms of Piaget's account of cognitive processes in infants and toddlers.

LO4 Explain the nature of young children's naive theories of physics and biology.

We know that the first years of a child's life, up to age 6, form the most foundational time in terms of brain development (Early Years Study Reference Group, 1999). We also know that a child's brain develops primarily as a result of repeated stimulation to sensory pathways and synaptic connections in the brain and that early levels of stimulation can affect children's later levels of capacity in terms of both cognitive ability and biological functioning (Early Years Study Reference Group, 1999; Ghazi & Ullah, 2015; Walker, Chang, Powell, & Grantham-McGregor, 2005). Research in developmental psychology has been highly influenced by the work of Jean Piaget, who decided to investigate the origins of knowledge not as philosophers had—through discussion and debate—but by doing experiments with children. Piaget was different from other psychological theorists of his day primarily in that he thought of intelligent behaviour as resulting from a child's attempts to adapt to the environment (Goncu & Abel, 2010). As a result, for Piaget, children's cognitive development arose out of constant interaction between their level of maturation and their experiences in the world. This differed significantly from other behaviourists of the time, who saw intelligence as arising solely out of children's experience with the world. Piaget's thoughts about children's development of cognitive abilities continue to be relevant to our understanding of child development today.

Basic Principles of Piaget's Theory

LO1 Describe how assimilation, accommodation, and equilibration explain the ways that children's thinking changes with age.

Piaget believed that children are naturally curious. They constantly want to make sense of their experiences and, in the process, construct their understanding of the world. For Piaget, children at all ages are like scientists: They create theories about how the world works. Of course, children's theories are often incomplete, but their theories are valuable because they make the world seem more predictable. Piaget believed children's development results from their active engagement with their experiences in the world, which enables them to reach more advanced levels of maturation. As a result, both experiences and maturation are important in Piagetian theory, with children seen as active contributors toward their own development.

According to Piaget, children's engagement with the world helps them to develop **schemas**, psychological structures that organize experience. Schemas are mental categories or conceptual models of interrelated events, objects, and knowledge that children build as they gain experience with situations, people, and objects around them. During infancy, most schemas are based on an infant's own actions. Initially, infants need to learn that they can move their bodies and control how those movements occur. Eventually, though, infants come to learn how to use their bodies, especially their hands, to interact with objects external to them.

As children develop, they eventually become able to create schemas based on abstract concepts. For example, the typical Canadian teen learns the meaning of the formula $C^2 = A^2 + B^2$, which is a highly abstract way of representing spatial relationships using mathematical symbols. In history class, an adolescent might learn about political ideologies, including the abstract concepts of fascism, capitalism, and socialism.

Throughout development, children learn how aspects of their world relate to each other. They collect this knowledge together in schemas, which then help them to navigate events and relationships in their world. Children find out about these events and relationships first by understanding how parts of their bodies relate to each other, how they can use their bodies to manipulate objects in the world, and how aspects of the world can be represented by words, gestures, objects, and concepts. As children develop, their basis for creating schemas shifts from physical movements to the functional, conceptual, and abstract properties of objects, events, and ideas. However, according to Piaget, children's knowledge about the world always arises out of experience with the world, which helps a child to develop more knowledge and then move, through a process of maturation, to a higher level of cognitive development.

ASSIMILATION AND ACCOMMODATION. Children's schemas change with increasing experience and as a result of two processes working together: assimilation and accommodation. **Assimilation** occurs when new experiences are incorporated into existing schemas. In other words, the child has an understanding about the world that the child then applies to other, new situations. Imagine a baby who has learned to grasp a favourite toy. The baby will soon discover that this grasping schema will work not only on that favourite toy but also on other small objects. **Accommodation** occurs when schemas are modified based on experience. In other words, as a result of an experience, the child changes a previously held understanding about the world. For example, by trying out the grasping schema with various objects, the baby learns that some objects must be lifted with two hands and some can't be lifted at all.

Assimilation and accommodation are easy to understand if you remember Piaget's belief that infants, children, and adolescents create theories to understand the world around them. Discovering that a small block can be picked up with one hand or that an Alaskan husky can't be picked up at all forces the infant, like a good scientist, to revise the theory to include this new information.

Schemas:
psychological structures that organize experience through mental categories and conceptual models of knowledge.

Assimilation:
cognitively incorporating new experiences into existing schemas.

Accommodation:
cognitive modification of schemas as a result of experience.

For example, let's say a child sees a butterfly and says "bug." Now let's say the child's parent corrects the child by saying "butterfly." Piaget would say that, when the parent named the butterfly, the child formed a schema something like "butterflies are bugs with big wings." Let's say that, on another occasion, the child saw a moth and said "butterfly" and then was corrected: "moth." The second "butterfly" differed in colour but was still a bug with big wings, so the child readily assimilated into a cognitive schema for butterflies. However, when the child was told the second one was a moth, the child was then forced to accommodate this new experience; the result was a change to the schema for butterflies to make it more precise. The new schema might be something like "butterflies are bugs with thin bodies and big, colourful wings." The child might also create a new schema, something like "a moth is a bug like a butterfly but with a bigger body and plain-coloured wings."

EQUILIBRATION AND STAGES OF COGNITIVE DEVELOPMENT.   Assimilation and accommodation are usually in balance or equilibrium. Children find they can readily assimilate most experiences into their existing schemas, but occasionally they need to accommodate their schemas to adjust to new experiences. When children spend much more time accommodating than assimilating, the balance becomes upset, and a state of disequilibrium results. When disequilibrium occurs, children reorganize their schemas to return to a state of equilibrium, a process that Piaget called **equilibration**. To restore the balance, outmoded ways of thinking are replaced by qualitatively different, more advanced schemas.

Equilibration:
the process of reorganizing schemas to incorporate new information or experience.

One way to understand equilibration is to return to the metaphor of the child as scientist. Good scientific theories will explain some phenomena nicely but require revision to explain others. Children's theories allow them to understand many experiences by predicting, for example, what will happen ("It's morning, so it's time for breakfast") or who will do what ("Mom's gone to work, so Dad will take me to school"). However, these theories must be modified when predictions go awry ("Dad thinks I'm old enough to walk to school by myself, so he won't take me").

This baby is developing a schema involving grasping.

Sometimes scientists discover critical flaws in their theories, causing them to create a new theory that is fundamentally different. For example, when Copernicus realized that the earth-centred theory of the solar system was wrong, he retained the concept of a central object but proposed that it was the sun, which represented a fundamental change in the theory. In much the same way, children discover the critical flaws in their theories that prevent them from making good predictions about the world, and they alter their theories so they can develop more accurate schemas.

According to Piaget, these revolutionary changes in thought occur three times over the lifespan, at approximately 2, 7, and 11 years of age, dividing cognitive development into four stages (see Table 6–1).

Table 6–1 Piaget's Four Stages of Cognitive Development

Stage	Approximate Age	Characteristics
Sensorimotor	Birth to 2 years	Infant's knowledge of the world is based on senses and motor skills.
Preoperational thought	2 to 6 years	Child learns how to use symbols, such as words and numbers, to represent aspects of the world.
Concrete operational thought	7 to 11 years	Child understands and applies logical operations to experiences.
Formal operational thought	Adolescence and beyond	Adolescent or adult thinks abstractly.

Each of these stages is marked by a distinct way of understanding the world. The ages listed are only approximate, with some youngsters developing more rapidly than others. However, Piaget held that all children go through all four stages in sequence: Sensorimotor thought gives rise to preoperational thought, followed by concrete operations and then formal operations.

In the rest of this module, we will look at the first cognitive developmental stage in detail.

Piaget's Sensorimotor Stage

LO2 Explain how thinking becomes more advanced as infants progress through the six substages of the sensorimotor stage.

We know that infants' perceptual and motor skills improve quickly throughout the first year. Piaget proposed that these rapidly changing skills in the first two years of life form a distinct phase in child development, the **sensorimotor stage**, because they primarily involve infants' cognitive understanding of the world through simple and, later, complex motor schemas. Consisting of six substages, the sensorimotor stage extends from birth to approximately 2 years. During this time, the infant progresses from developing schemas based on simple, reflex actions to symbolic processing in an orderly sequence.

Sensorimotor stage:
a Piagetian stage of early development characterized by rapidly changing perceptual and motor skills.

After infancy, schemas become based primarily on functional or conceptual relationships, not sensorimotor actions. Children's advancing awareness of speech sounds, coupled with their increased locomotion, enable them to access more parts of their world and then label those parts with particular words. These words and their associated meanings help children develop categories of information based on the appearance and function of objects. As they develop, children come to understand that words, numbers, and actions can symbolize aspects of their world. However, while still in infancy, they cannot rely on language, so they must use the basic sensorimotor skills they have to explore their surroundings.

SUBSTAGE 1: EXERCISING REFLEXES (ROUGHLY BIRTH TO 1 MONTH). Newborns initially rely on reflex responses to stimuli, some of which become more coordinated behavioural schemas. Just as major-league hockey players can release a slapshot with greater power and control than minor leaguers, 1-month-olds suck more vigorously and steadily than newborns.

SUBSTAGE 2: LEARNING TO ADAPT (ROUGHLY 1 TO 4 MONTHS). During these early months, reflexes are modified by experience. The chief mechanism for change is the **primary circular reaction**, which occurs when infants use their own bodies to accidentally produce a pleasing event and then try to recreate the event. For example, a baby girl might happen to touch her lips with her thumb, initiating pleasing sensations associated with sucking. Later, the infant tries to recreate these sensations by guiding her thumb to her mouth. Sucking no longer occurs only reflexively when a mother places a nipple at the infant's mouth; instead, the infant has found a way to self-initiate sucking.

Primary circular reaction:
recreating a pleasing event with the body.

SUBSTAGE 3: MAKING INTERESTING EVENTS (ROUGHLY 4 TO 8 MONTHS). Primary circular reactions involve the infant's own body and no other objects. However, beginning in Substage 3, as the infant shows greater interest in the world, objects become incorporated into circular reactions. For example, an infant might accidentally shake a rattle. Hearing the interesting noise, the infant shakes the rattle again and again, expressing great pleasure at the noise.

Secondary circular reaction:
learning about the sensations and actions associated with objects.

Novel actions that are repeated with objects are called **secondary circular reactions**. Secondary circular reactions represent an infant's first efforts to explore properties and actions of objects in the environment. No longer are infants grasping objects reflexively simply because something came in contact with their hands. Instead, they are learning about the sensations and actions associated with objects.

SUBSTAGE 4: USING MEANS TO ACHIEVE ENDS (ROUGHLY 8 TO 12 MONTHS). This substage marks the onset of deliberate, intentional behaviour because the "means" (action/method) and "end" (purpose/goal) of activities become distinct. If, for example, a father places his hand in front of a toy, an infant will move the hand to be able to play with the toy. The "moving dad's hand" schema is the means to achieve the goal of "grasping the toy." Using one action as a means to achieve a particular end is the first indication of purposeful behaviour during infancy.

SUBSTAGE 5: EXPERIMENTING (ROUGHLY 12 TO 18 MONTHS). The infant at this stage is an active experimenter with new objects. An infant will repeat old schemas with objects, in what Piaget called a **tertiary circular reaction**, as if trying to understand why different objects yield different outcomes. An infant in Substage 5 might deliberately shake a number of different objects trying to discover which produce sounds and which do not. Alternatively, an infant might drop different objects out of the crib to see what happens, discovering that stuffed animals land quietly, but bigger toys make a more satisfying clunk.

As babies develop, they interact more with objects external to themselves.

Tertiary circular reactions represent a significant extension of the intentional behaviour that emerged in Substage 4. In this substage, babies repeat actions with different objects solely for the purpose of seeing what will happen.

SUBSTAGE 6: MENTAL REPRESENTATION (ROUGHLY 18 TO 24 MONTHS). By 18 months, most infants are able to think about what is happening around them without having to physically explore a situation. In addition, they become more able to mentally work through simple problems that present themselves to the child. At this stage we see children form early capabilities at make-believe play. Early attempts at make-believe play often result from **deferred imitation**, which is children's ability to imitate actions that they have observed at an earlier time. At this stage in development, children are beginning to work with symbols, such as words and gestures, to form an internal, mental representation of their world. They eventually become capable of just thinking about that mental representation without having to physically act it out.

Tertiary circular reaction: repetition of old schemas with objects of different kinds.

Deferred imitation: acting out events or behaviours seen at an earlier time.

The ability to mentally represent the world internally marks the end of sensorimotor thought and the beginning of preoperational thought. A summary of changes that occur during the sensorimotor stage is shown in Table 6–2.

Table 6–2 Summary Table

Six Substages of Sensorimotor Development			
Substage	Age (months)	Accomplishment	Examples
1	0–1	Reflexes become coordinated	Sucking a nipple
2	1–4	Primary circular reactions appear, first learned adaptations to the world	Thumb sucking
3	4–8	Secondary circular reactions emerge, allowing infants to learn about objects	Shaking a toy to hear it rattle
4	8–12	Means–end sequencing develops, the onset of intentional behaviour	Moving an obstacle to reach a toy
5	12–18	Tertiary circular reactions appear, allowing children to experiment with new behaviours	Shaking different toys to hear the sounds they make
6	18–24	Mental representation of the world	Deferred imitation, the start of make-believe play

Evaluating Piaget's Account of Sensorimotor Thought

LO3 State some criticisms of Piaget's account of cognitive processes in infants and toddlers.

Despite Piaget's considerable success, some aspects of his cognitive developmental theory have held up better than others. For example, Piaget explained cognitive development with constructs like accommodation, assimilation, and equilibration.

Subsequent researchers have found other ways to explain children's performance on Piagetian tasks. For example, Piaget thought that a fundamental task of infancy was mastering **object permanence**—understanding that objects exist independently of oneself and one's actions. He claimed that 1- to 4-month-olds believe that objects no longer exist when they disappear from view—out of sight means out of mind. If you take a favourite toy from a 3-month-old and, in plain view of the infant, hide it under a cloth, the infant will not look for it, even though the shape of the toy is clearly visible under the cloth and within reach!

Object permanence: understanding that objects continue to exist independently of one's own actions.

At 8 months, infants search for objects, but their understanding of object permanence remains incomplete. If 8- to 10-month-olds see an object hidden under one container and then see it hidden under a second container, they routinely look for the toy under the first container. Piaget claimed that this behaviour showed only a fragmentary understanding of objects because infants did not distinguish the object from the actions they used to locate it, such as lifting a particular container. At about 12 months, rather than accepting that the object has just disappeared, infants will look for a missing object in several different locations. According to Piaget, not until approximately 18 months do infants apparently have full understanding of object permanence, such that if an object is moved without the infant's knowledge, the infant knows it is still in existence somewhere. For example, if a parent cleans up toys while a child is sleeping, then the child can engage in a self-directed search for a particular toy upon awakening, knowing that it still exists somewhere in the house.

However, investigators have questioned Piaget's conclusions (Baillargeon, 1994; Case, 1999; Smith, Thelen, Titzer, & McLin, 1999), noting that some fairly minor changes in procedures can affect 8- to 10-month-olds' success on the hidden object task. An infant is more likely to look under the correct container if, for example, the interval between hiding and looking is brief and if the containers are easily distinguished from each other. Therefore, infants who are unsuccessful on this task might be showing poor memory rather than inadequate understanding of the nature of objects (Marcovitch & Zelazo, 1999; Wellman, Cross, & Bartsch, 1986).

In addition, by devising some clever procedures, other investigators have shown that babies understand objects much earlier than Piaget claimed. Renée Baillargeon (1987, 1994), for example, assessed object permanence using the procedure shown in Figure 6–1. Infants first saw a silver screen that appeared to be rotating back and forth. When they were familiar with this display, one of two new displays was shown. In the possible event, an orange box appeared in a position behind the screen, making it impossible for the screen to rotate as far back as it had previously. Instead, the screen rotated until it made contact with the box, then rotated forward. In the impossible event, shown in the diagram, the orange box appeared, but the screen continued to rotate as before. The screen rotated back until it was flat, then rotated forward, again revealing the orange box. The illusion was possible because the box was mounted on a moveable platform that allowed it to drop out of the way of the moving screen. However, from the infant's perspective, it appeared as if the box vanished behind the screen, only to reappear.

The disappearance and reappearance of the box violates the idea that objects exist permanently. Consequently, an infant who understands the permanence of objects should find the impossible event a truly novel stimulus and look at it longer than

Figure 6–1

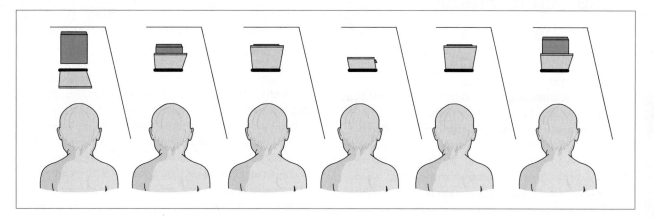

the possible event. Baillargeon found that 4½-month-olds consistently looked longer at the impossible event than the possible event, apparently thinking the impossible event was novel, just as we are surprised when an object vanishes from a magician's scarf. Evidently, then, infants have some understanding of object permanence early in the first year of life.

Alternative explanations for infants' performance on object permanence tasks do not mean that Piaget's theory is fundamentally wrong. They merely mean that the theory needs some revision to include important constructs that Piaget overlooked.

The Child as Theorist

LO4 Explain the nature of young children's naive theories of physics and biology.

Children's theories are usually called "naive theories" because, unlike real scientific theories, they are not created by specialists, and they are rarely evaluated by formal experimentation. Naive theories are, nevertheless, valuable in allowing children (and adults) to understand new experiences and predict future events.

In Piaget's view, children formulate a grand, comprehensive theory that attempts to explain an enormous variety of phenomena—including reasoning about objects, people, and morals—within a common framework. More recent views maintain the idea of children as theorists but propose that children, like scientists, develop specialized theories about much narrower areas. Some of the theories that young children first develop concern physics and biology. That is, based on their experiences, young children rapidly develop theories that organize their knowledge about properties of objects and living things (Wellman & Gelman, 1998), as you will see in the Research to Practice feature.

NAIVE PHYSICS.   We know that young babies are able to distinguish objects. From their perceptions, infants learn a lot about the properties of objects. By 3 or 4 months, for instance, normally developing infants know that objects move along connected, continuous paths and that objects cannot move "through" other objects (Spelke, 1994; von Hofsten, Vishton, Spelke, Feng, & Rosander, 1998). Infants look longer at moving objects that violate these properties (e.g., a ball that somehow rolls "through" a solid wall), suggesting that infants are surprised when objects move in ways not predicted by their naive theory of physics. Also, by approximately 6 months of age, infants expect a stationary object to move following a collision, and they understand that the distance travelled by that object depends on the size of the colliding object (Kotovsky & Baillargeon, 1998; Spelke, 1994).

These three types of knowledge together form a schema of the body that develops in the first two years of life. Sensorimotor knowledge develops first, during infancy.

Research to Practice

Infants' Knowledge of Their Bodies

Sensorimotor knowledge in infants provides a critical first understanding of something very basic about people: We have bodies. Current researchers in child development often describe conscious cognition as "embodied," which is a fancy term meaning that people's cognitive knowledge is both informed and limited by the sensory and motor abilities of the human body (Slaughter et al., 2004a, 2004b, 2004c, 2004d). Everything we experience within the human world comes to us through our senses and our physical capabilities. Interestingly, though, infants are not born with a completely innate knowledge of their bodies. Instead, they have to learn through experience that they have bodies, what body parts they have, and what these parts can do.

Virginia Slaughter and her research team (2004a, 2004b, 2004c, 2004d) studied infants' knowledge of the human body and discovered some interesting findings. Considering what we know from neuropsychological research and the developing nervous system, Slaughter and her team found that infants understand their bodies in three ways: (1) through short-term mental representations of the body based on sensorimotor experiences; (2) through long-term knowledge of the physical location and interrelationships of body parts, which is a kind of visuospatial knowledge; and (3) through semantic understanding that comes by learning the names of body parts, which is called lexical-semantic knowledge.

Then, visuospatial knowledge develops by about 18 months. Finally, lexical-semantic knowledge develops along with the acquisition of language and becomes more detailed as children grow.

Slaughter and her team (2004c, p. 22) found that visuospatial knowledge occurs at varying developmental levels of complexity in infants. Babies first learn to discriminate people from animals, then learn to distinguish proper bodies from "scrambled" images of bodies (see Figure 6–2), then learn to localize body parts, and then learn to understand human figure drawings. Another important finding from the research conducted by Slaughter and her team is that children tend to learn about the parts and proper arrangement of faces before they learn about how the rest of the body's parts fit together, which usually occurs after age 1 (Slaughter et al., 2004c).

Figure 6–2

SOURCE: Republished with permission of John Wiley & Sons, Inc., from V. Slaughter, in Slaughter, V., Heron, M., Tilse, E., Jenkins, L., Müller, U., & Liebermann, D. (2004c), *Origins and early development of human body knowledge, Monographs of the Society for Research In Child Development*, 2004, 69(2):vii, 1-102, Figure 3, pg. 40, "Scrambled images of bodies" permission conveyed through Copyright Clearance Center, Inc.

Later in the first year, infants come to understand the importance of gravity. At this time, but not before, infants will look intently at an object that appears to float in midair with no obvious means of support because it violates their understanding of gravity (Baillargeon, 1998).

These amazing demonstrations attest to the fact that the infant is an accomplished naive physicist. Of course, the infant's theories are far from complete; naive understanding of physics takes place throughout the preschool years and later (e.g., Au, 1994). However, infants rapidly create a reasonably accurate theory of some basic properties of objects, a theory that helps them understand why objects in their world, such as toys, act as they do.

Children start to learn the difference between animate and inanimate objects early.

NAIVE BIOLOGY.   When your computer crashes, do you think to yourself, "Oh, it must be feeling ill"? When you accidentally break your coffee mug, do you say, "Gosh, its parents will be terribly upset"? Of course not. Computers and coffee cups are inanimate, but illness and parenthood are properties of animate objects. In fact, the difference between animate and inanimate objects is so fundamental that, by knowing an object is animate, our naive theory of biology allows us to infer many properties of the object.

Even toddlers have some basic understanding about different properties of animate and inanimate objects. Toddlers usually understand, for example, that animate objects drink but inanimate objects do not. Plus, they understand from a fairly early age that keys are used to open inanimate objects but not animate objects (Mandler & McDonough, 1998). However, although toddlers and preschoolers might know some basic properties of animate and inanimate objects, they are a long way from being able to cognitively grasp other, major differences between these groups of objects. While an adult might understand that a computer doesn't become "sick" with a virus, a young child, on the other hand, might think exactly that. Nevertheless, young children's naive theories of biology and physics provide them with powerful tools for making sense of their world and for understanding new experiences.

Ask Yourself

People continue to learn throughout their lives. What new schemas have you developed over the past year or so?

What is the benefit of object permanence, and what would life be like if we didn't develop it?

6.2 Information Processing

∨ Learning Objectives

After reading the module, you should be able to do the following:

LO5 Describe the basic characteristics of the information-processing approach.

LO6 Explain how infants learn.

LO7 Explain how infants remember.

LO8 Identify what infants and toddlers understand about numbers and about their environments.

LO9 Summarize how intelligence is measured in infants and toddlers.

When a newborn baby is first brought home, everything can seem surprising or startling to the child—the family dog, the TV, the doorbell—everything is new. However, after a few days, the baby might seem to hardly notice these same stimuli or might sleep right through them. Even in these few days, babies' information processing can change so much that they quickly learn to ignore sounds that once had startled them. In this module, we'll learn about information processing as a general framework and more about information processing in infants and toddlers. As you read, you will learn how babies "tune out" distracting noise.

Basic Features of the Information-Processing Approach

LO5 Describe the basic characteristics of the information-processing approach.

Information processing:
a theory proposing that human cognition is like computer hardware and software.

The simple distinction between computer hardware and computer software is the basis of an approach to human cognition known as **information processing**. The information-processing approach arose in the 1960s and is now a principal and useful approach to cognitive development (Kail & Bisanz, 1992; Klahr & MacWhinney, 1998; Vigneau, Lavergne, & Brault, 1998). Information-processing theorists believe human thinking is based on both mental hardware and mental software. Mental hardware refers to mental and neural structures that are built in and that allow the mind to operate. If the hardware in a personal computer refers to random-access memory, the central processor, and the other structural components, what is mental hardware? Information-processing theorists generally agree that mental hardware has three components: sensory memory, working memory, and long-term memory. Figure 6–3 shows how they are related.

Sensory memory:
raw, unanalyzed information held for only a few seconds.

Sensory memory is where information is held in raw, unanalyzed form very briefly (no longer than a few seconds). For example, clench your fist and then look at your palms as you open and close your hand. If you watch your palm, you'll see an image of your fingers that lasts momentarily as you extend your fingers. What you're seeing is an image stored in sensory memory.

Working memory:
the active, cognitive manipulation of information.

Working memory is the site of ongoing cognitive activity. Some theorists compare working memory to a carpenter's workbench that includes space for storing project materials as well as space to work with them by sawing, nailing, and painting (Klatzky, 1980). In much the same way, working memory includes both ongoing cognitive processes and the information that they require (Baddeley, 1996). For example,

Figure 6–3

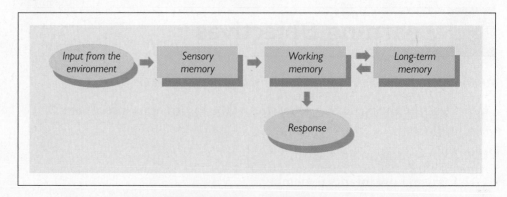

as you read these sentences, part of working memory is allocated to the cognitive processes responsible for determining the meanings of individual words; working memory also stores the results of these analyses briefly while they are used by other cognitive processes to give meaning to sequences of words.

If you're familiar with personal computers, you'll recognize that working memory resembles random-access memory (RAM) because that's where we load programs we want to run and temporarily store the data those programs are using.

Unlike working memory, which is short term, **long-term memory** is a limitless, permanent storehouse of knowledge of the world. Long-term memory is like a computer's hard drive, a fairly permanent storehouse of programs and data. Long-term memory includes facts (Nunavut is a new Canadian territory), personal events (Jenny just celebrated her first birthday), and skills (how to float and swim in water).

Long-term memory:
limitless, permanent storage of acquired information.

Information rarely is forgotten from long-term memory, but it can be hard to access. For example, do you remember the name of the famous Canadian researcher who, along with his assistant, discovered insulin? If his name doesn't come to mind, look at this list: Marconi, Bell, Banting, Bombardier. Now do you know the answer? (If not, it appears at the end of this paragraph.) Just as books are sometimes misplaced in a library, you sometimes cannot find a fact in long-term memory. Given a list of names, though, you can go directly to the location in long-term memory associated with each name and determine which is the famed Canadian chemist (Frederick G. Banting)!

In addition to sensory, working (short-term), and long-term memory, some researchers have noted other forms of memory, including **procedural memory**, which is memory for how to do things, and **semantic memory**, which is memory for particular facts. Another type is **autobiographical or episodic memory**, which is memory for specific events that have occurred for a person. Impairments in episodic memory have been noted in children born very prematurely and who have experienced low levels of oxygen, an event called hypoxia (Briscoe, Gathercole, & Marlow, 2001; Isaacs et al., 2000; Vargha-Khadem et al., 1997).

Procedural memory:
memory for how to do things.

Semantic memory:
memory for particular facts.

Autobiographical or episodic memory:
people's memory of the significant events and experiences of their own lives.

Continuing with the computer model of information-processing theory, these various kinds of memory, or mental hardware, enable children to "run" mental software. Computers have software programs, which allow you to perform tasks such as word processing or calculations. In much the same way, mental software refers to mental programs that are the basis for performing particular mental tasks, such as reading, doing arithmetic, or finding your way to and from school.

Let's look at a simple example to see how information-processing psychologists analyze cognitive processes. Suppose a mother asks her son to make his bed, brush his teeth, and take out the trash. A bit later, the mother wonders if she asked her son about the trash, so she says, "Did I ask you to take out the trash?" Almost immediately, he says, "Yes." Despite the speed of the boy's reply, information-processing theorists believe that his mental software has gone through a number of steps to answer the question, as shown in Figure 6–4. First, the mental software must take in and allocate resources to the mother's question. That is, the software must perceive and decode the sounds of the mother's speech to give them meaning. Next, the software searches working memory and long-term memory for the mother's requested tasks. When that list is located and retrieved, the software compares "take out the trash" with each of the items on the list. Finding a match, the software selects "yes" as the appropriate answer to the question. Thus, the processes of perceiving, paying attention to, understanding, searching, comparing, and responding create a mental program that allows the boy to answer his mother.

Figure 6–4

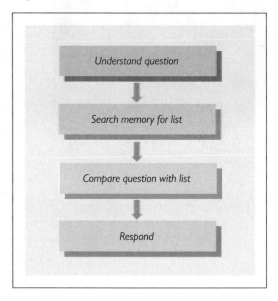

Children can improve their performance of certain tasks by altering the attention and memory strategies they use. For example, University of Alberta researchers Donald Heth, Ed Cornell, and Tonya Flood (2002) studied way-finding in both children and adults. They noted that people tend to believe way-finding is a natural ability or gift that some people have. In order to study cognitive processes in way-finding, they asked 72 children (age 6) and 72 adults (ages 18–44) to learn an outdoor route from point A to point B. Then they had the participants rate their own sense of direction ability before being asked to walk the route in reverse, from point B to point A. These researchers found that self-rating prior to an experience of route reversal was a weak predictor of actual performance. They also found that both children and adults could improve their route reversal performance by telling them to take a look back while learning the route, in anticipation of their return on route reversal. They concluded from these findings that beliefs about sense of direction are based on a person's recollecting the effectiveness of the attention and memory strategies they used during past way-finding situations.

Another important contribution to child development theory came from Robbie Case. Case was a noted Canadian developmental psychologist who combined aspects of information-processing theory with Piagetian theory into a novel approach referred to as "neo-Piagetian." In the **neo-Piagetian approach** to understanding children's cognitive development, Case retained Piaget's stage theory but revised it, saying that movement from one stage to the next was due to advances in information processing–related skills and abilities, not simply to maturation. Case essentially argued that, as children's memory capacity and ability to mentally manipulate information improved, so too did children's overall cognitive ability and understanding of the world (Case, 1999, 1998).

Learning

LO6 Explain how infants learn.

Infants are born with many abilities that allow them to learn from experience. This learning can take many forms, including habituation, classical conditioning, operant conditioning, and imitation. One thing we know for sure, though, is that learning means a change in cognition.

HABITUATION.   When babies, children, and adults are presented with a strong or unfamiliar stimulus, an **orienting response** usually occurs: A person physically reacts (starts), looks at the stimulus, and experiences changes in heart rate and brain wave activity. Collectively, these responses indicate that the person has noticed the stimulus. However, after repeated presentations of the same stimulus, people usually become familiar with it, and the orienting response disappears. **Habituation** is a state of diminished responding to a stimulus as it becomes more familiar. **Dishabituation** occurs when a person becomes actively aware of the stimulus again.

The orienting response and habituation are both useful to infants. Orienting makes the infant aware of potentially important or dangerous events in the environment. However, as constantly responding to insignificant stimuli is unnecessary, habituation keeps infants from wasting energy on biologically insignificant events (Rovee-Collier, 1987).

Habituation is an infant processing measure that is related to developing cognitive abilities, including memory, intelligence, and language (Cuevas & Bell, 2014). An infant's habituation and visual recognition abilities are part of a broad executive attention network in the brain involving the anterior cingulated gyrus, prefrontal cortex, and basal ganglia, which begins to emerge in the second half of an infant's first year (Cuevas &

Neo-Piagetian approach:
a theory of cognitive development that retains Piagetian stage theory but takes an information-processing approach to skill development.

Orienting response:
a physical reaction to a strong or unfamiliar stimulus.

Habituation:
a state of diminished responding to a stimulus as it becomes more familiar.

Dishabituation:
a state of reorientation, when a person becomes aware of a stimulus to which the person previously had habituated.

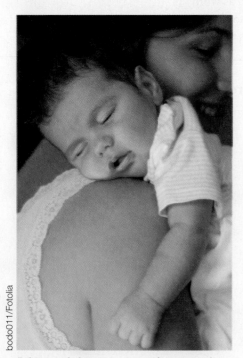

bodo011/Fotolia

Babies can habituate to insignificant stimuli in the environment.

Bell, 2014). The co-development of the orienting and executive attention abilities of an infant can predict a child's executive function abilities later in childhood (Cuevas & Bell, 2014). Infants who are more efficient at processing information tend to have higher executive function throughout early childhood (Cuevas & Bell, 2014).

CLASSICAL CONDITIONING. Some of the most famous experiments in psychology were conducted with dogs by Russian physiologist Ivan Pavlov, who discovered that, if something always happened just before feeding (e.g., if a bell sounded), dogs would learn to salivate in response to that event. In **classical conditioning**, a previously neutral stimulus elicits a response that was originally produced by another natural stimulus. In Pavlov's experiments, the bell was a neutral stimulus that did not naturally cause dogs to salivate. However, by repeatedly pairing the bell with food, the sound of the bell began to elicit salivation. Similarly, infants will suck reflexively when sugar water is placed in the mouth with a dropper; if a tone precedes the drops of sugar water, infants will learn to suck when they hear the tone (Lipsitt, 1990).

Classical conditioning: a form of learning in which a previously neutral stimulus elicits a response that was originally produced by another natural stimulus.

Classical conditioning gives infants a sense of order in their worlds. Through classical conditioning, infants learn that a stimulus is a signal for what will happen next. An infant might smile when she hears the family dog's collar because she knows the dog is coming to play with her. A toddler might smile when he hears water running in the bathroom because he looks forward to having a bath.

OPERANT CONDITIONING. In classical conditioning, infants learn to associate events in their environment. **Operant conditioning** involves the relation between the consequences of behaviour and the likelihood that the behaviour will reoccur. When a child's behaviour leads to pleasant consequences, the child probably will behave similarly in the future; when the child's behaviour leads to unpleasant consequences, the child probably will not repeat the behaviour. When a baby smiles, an adult might hug the baby in return, making the baby more likely to smile in the future. When a baby grabs a family heirloom, an adult might say "No!" sharply and take the object away, making the baby less likely to grab the heirloom in the future.

Operant conditioning: a form of learning in which the observed consequences of a behaviour affect the likelihood that the behaviour will reoccur.

IMITATION. People can learn simply by watching others behave. For example, children might learn new snowboarding moves by watching peers; they might develop ideas about romantic relationships by watching TV; and they might learn new words by talking with a friend. Infants, too, are capable of imitation (Barr & Hayne, 1999): A 10-month-old might imitate an adult waving a finger back and forth or copy another infant who knocks down a tower of blocks.

More startling is the claim that even newborns imitate. Meltzoff and Moore (1989, 1994) claimed that 2- to 3-week-olds would stick out their tongues or open and close their mouths to match an adult's acts; however, other researchers have not consistently obtained these results. In addition, some researchers do not consider this to be a true form of imitation because newborns can already open and close their mouths and stick out their tongues, so the behaviour is not new for them (Anisfeld, 1991, 1996).

Babies learn to associate stimuli, such as a family pet, with play and fun.

oksun70/Fotolia

Memory

LO7 Explain how infants remember.

Young babies remember events for days or even weeks at a time. We know this largely due to Carolyn Rovee-Collier's (1997, 1999) innovative research design. Rovee-Collier attached a ribbon from a mobile to a 2- or 3-month-old's foot. Once this was done, babies very quickly began to realize that they could make the mobile turn by kicking their leg. Within a few minutes, babies would begin to kick actively in order to make the mobile move.

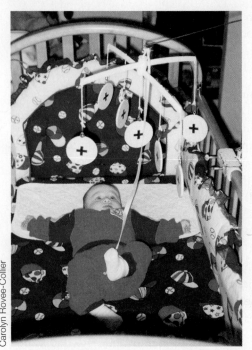

Carolyn Rovee-Collier

Rovee-Collier's ribbon-mobile research procedure.

While the initially rapid learning is an impressive research finding in itself, Rovee-Collier found something even more interesting with this methodology. Once an infant had learned to move the mobile by kicking, Rovee-Collier would wait several days and then bring the mobile back to the infant's home. She found that babies would still kick to make the mobile move. If she waited a few more weeks before returning, babies would again kick; however, if Rovee-Collier waited several weeks to return, most babies forgot that kicking moved the mobile. When that happened, Rovee-Collier gave them a reminder—she moved the mobile herself without attaching the ribbon to their foot. Then she would return the next day, hook up the apparatus, and the babies would kick to move the mobile. Finally, Rovee-Collier used the same methodology but changed the form of the mobile itself, from blocks with the letter A on them to blocks with 2s on them. Once the form of the mobile had been changed, the babies no longer kicked (Bhatt, Rovee-Collier, & Weiner, 1994). This latter finding demonstrated that the babies associated kicking to move the mobile with certain features of the mobile. Once those features changed, the babies no longer kicked strongly in order to make the mobile move. Through her research, Rovee-Collier was able to demonstrate that three important features of memory exist as early as 2 and 3 months of age: (1) an event from the past is remembered; (2) over time, the event can no longer be recalled; and (3) a cue can serve to recall a memory that seems to have been forgotten.

Although memory begins in infancy, children, adolescents, and adults remember little from these years (Kail, 1990). **Infantile amnesia** refers to the inability to remember events from early in one's life. Adults recall nothing from infancy, but they remember an ever-increasing number of events from about age 3 or 4 years (Eacott, 1999; Schneider & Bjorklund, 1998; see also Peterson & Rideout, 1998; Quas et al., 1999). Very early memory for events typically arises from listening to others tell us about our early experiences and from viewing photos or videos of those events, not from actual memories of those experiences.

Infantile amnesia:
the inability to remember events from early in one's life.

Infantile amnesia has several possible explanations. One emphasizes language: Once children learn to talk, they tend to rely on language to represent their past (Nelson, 1993). Consequently, their earlier, prelingual experiences might be difficult to retrieve from memory. Another explanation for infantile amnesia is based on a child's sense of self. The key idea is that 1- and 2-year-olds rapidly acquire a sense that they exist independently and are someone. Some theorists (Harley & Reese, 1999; Howe & Courage, 1997) argue that a child's sense of self provides an organizing framework for children's memories of events from their own lives. Infants and toddlers lack an organized sense of self, so they can't organize memories of life events, which prevents their recall later in life.

Wang, Conway, and Hou (2007) found cultural differences in the experience of infantile amnesia. They found that, in cultures that have a relational sense of self, such as in Chinese cultures that emphasize collective identities, people tend to have a longer period of infantile amnesia and fewer early childhood memories. Cultures that promote more of an autonomous or individualized sense of self tend to have people with shorter periods of infantile amnesia and more early childhood memories. Wang, Conway, and Hou (2007) also found that cultures that emphasized more elaborative memory talk also had shorter periods of infantile amnesia and more early childhood memories. Elaborative memory talk involves a way of engaging in conversation that encourages extended discussion and idea exchange through turn-taking and open-ended questions (Peterson & Warren, 2009).

AS/Fotolia

Children's earliest memories often are based on photos or stories told to them by others.

Understanding the World

LO8 Identify what infants and toddlers understand about numbers and about their environments.

Powerful learning and memory skills allow infants and toddlers to learn much about their worlds. This rapid growth is well illustrated by research on their understanding of numbers and the environment.

UNDERSTANDING NUMBERS.   Basic number skills originate in infancy long before babies learn the names of numbers. Many babies experience daily variation in quantity. They play with two blocks and see that another baby has three; they watch as a father sorts laundry and finds two black socks but only one blue sock; and they eat one half of a sandwich for lunch while an older brother eats two.

From these experiences, babies apparently come to appreciate that quantity or amount is one of the ways in which objects in the world can differ. This conclusion is based on research in which babies are shown pictures like those in Figure 6–5. The actual objects in the pictures differ, as do their size, colour, and position. The only common element is that, at first, each picture always depicts two of something.

When the first of these pictures is shown, an infant will look at it for several seconds. After several pictures have been shown, an infant habituates, glancing briefly at the picture, then looking away, as if saying, "Enough of these pictures of two things." Once habituation has occurred, if a picture of a single object or of three objects is shown, infants dishabituate and look for several seconds with renewed interest. Typically, 5-month-olds can distinguish two objects from three and, less often, three objects from four (Canfield & Smith, 1996; Wynn, 1996) based on shape and colour (Bornstein, 1981). Quantity might be another characteristic to which infants are sensitive. That is, just as colours and shapes are basic perceptual properties, small quantities ("twoness" and "three-ness") also might be perceptually obvious (Strauss & Curtis, 1984).

EXPLORING THE ENVIRONMENT.   Before infants can walk, they travel through environments in parents' arms, in strollers, and in various types of vehicles. Even when they are sitting still, infants see people and objects move in their environments. As soon as infants can crawl, they begin to explore their environments directly. According to Piaget (Piaget & Inhelder, 1967), an infant's early understanding of the environment is quite limited. Infants first think of the positions of objects in space exclusively in terms of the objects' positions relative to the child's own body—what Piaget called an **egocentric frame of reference**. Only later do children acquire an **objective frame of reference** in which an object's location is thought of relative to the positions of other objects in space. These are key trends in child development: moving

Egocentric frame of reference:
thinking of objects in space exclusively in terms of their relationship to the child's own body position.

Objective frame of reference:
thinking of objects in space relative to the position of objects or persons other than oneself.

Figure 6–5

from internal to external points of reference in the world and moving from concrete to abstract understandings about the world.

The shift from egocentric to objective frames of reference is shown by research in which youngsters are seated in a room with two identical windows, one to the child's left and one to the child's right. When the child is looking straight ahead, an experimenter sounds a buzzer. Shortly thereafter, a person appears in the left window, saying the infant's name and showing toys (Acredolo, 1978, 1979). Infants and toddlers quickly learn to anticipate the appearance of the person in this window when they hear the buzzer.

After infants have learned to anticipate the person, they are turned 180 degrees, so that they are facing the window from the opposite direction. Once again the buzzer sounds. Up to about 12 months, infants consistently look left—as they had before (but now incorrectly)—showing an egocentric frame of reference. After 12 months, toddlers increasingly look to the right—a different direction but toward the correct window. By 12 months, infants realize that, even though they have moved, the object has not, so they look to the same window as before, even though this means turning in a different direction (Acredolo, 1978; Wishart & Bower, 1982).

Individual Differences in Ability

LO9 Summarize how intelligence is measured in infants and toddlers.

So far in this chapter, we have emphasized patterns of cognitive development that apply to most infants and toddlers; we have ignored the fact that individual infants and toddlers often differ considerably in the ease and skill with which their cognitive processes function. These individual differences are, however, measured in psychological tests devised for infants and toddlers. For example, the *Bayley Scales of Infant Development* (Bayley, 1970, 1993), designed for 2- to 42-month-olds, consists of mental and motor tasks or "scales." The mental scale assesses an infant's adaptive behaviour, such as attending to visual and auditory stimuli, following directions, looking for a fallen toy, and imitating relative to other infants of the same age. The motor scale assesses an infant's motor control, coordination, and ability to manipulate objects relative to other infants of the same age. For example, most 6-month-olds turn their head toward an object that the examiner drops on the floor, most 12-month-olds imitate the examiner's actions, and most 16-month-olds build a tower from three blocks. The scales also assess habituation, memory, and problem solving.

In general, scores from infant intelligence tests are not related to intelligence scores obtained later in childhood, adolescence, or adulthood (McCall, 1989). However, they are important tools for assessing whether an infant is meeting expected milestones in development within appropriate age ranges. Infant intelligence tests tend to focus on sensorimotor skills and abilities, whereas tests of older children and adults focus more on cognitive processes such as language, arithmetic, and tasks of nonverbal problem solving. However, a baby's ability to habituate and dishabituate is moderately predictive of later IQ (Bornstein, 1997).

Other factors also can affect learning. For example, the steroid hormone cortisol, produced by the adrenal gland on the kidney, has an impact on learning and memory (Haley, Weinberg, & Grunau, 2006). Infants with higher cortisol levels had better memory than those with lower levels, regardless of whether the infants were premature or full-term.

Ask Yourself

To what sounds have you habituated as you read this chapter? How long do you think it will take you to habituate to them again?

What elements of the information-processing approach seem to emphasize nature? What elements emphasize nurture? How does information processing's emphasis on nature and nurture compare with Piaget's emphasis?

6.3 Language

 ## Learning Objectives

After reading the module, you should be able to do the following:

LO10 List when infants can hear and produce basic speech sounds.

LO11 Describe what babbling is and how children make the transition from babbling to talking.

LO12 Understand how infants begin to form their first words.

LO13 Explain how children learn new words.

LO14 Identify the different styles of language learning that young children use.

From birth, infants make sounds: They laugh, cry, and make some sounds that resemble speech. Around their first birthday, most youngsters say their first words, and, by age 2, most children have a vocabulary of a few hundred words. Most children achieve these milestones with extraordinary ease and speed. Learning theorists emphasize imitation and reward in language acquisition. However, modern theories view language acquisition from a cognitive perspective and describe language acquisition in terms of mastering many distinct skills.

Perceiving Speech

LO10 List when infants can hear and produce basic speech sounds.

To be able to learn a language, infants need to be able to distinguish the basic speech sounds. The basic building blocks of language are **phonemes**, unique sounds that are joined to create words. Phonemes include consonant sounds, such as the sound of *t* in toe and tap, along with vowel sounds, such as the sound of *e* in get and bed. Infants can distinguish many of these sounds, some of them by as early as one month after birth (Aslin, Jusczyk, & Pisoni, 1998).

Phonemes:

unique sounds joined to create words.

Researchers have devised a number of clever techniques to determine whether babies respond differently to distinct sounds. One approach is illustrated in Figure 6–6. A rubber nipple is connected to a tape recorder so that sucking turns on the tape and sound comes out of a loudspeaker. In just a few minutes, 1-month-olds learn the relation between their sucking and the sound: They suck rapidly to hear a tape that consists of nothing more than the sound of *p* as in pin, pet, and pat (pronounced "puh").

Figure 6–6

After a few more minutes, infants seemingly tire of this repetitive sound, and they suck less often, which represents the habituation phenomenon described in Module 6.2. If the tape is changed to a different sound, such as the sound of *b* in bed, bat, or bird (pronounced "buh"), babies begin sucking rapidly again. Evidently, they recognize that the sound of *b* is different from *p* because they suck more often to hear the new sound (Jusczyk, 1995).

Not all languages use the same set of phonemes; a sound that is important in one language might be ignored in another. Unlike

English, for example, French and Polish differentiate between nasal and non-nasal vowels. To hear the difference, say the word *rod*. Now repeat it, while holding your nose. The subtle difference between the two sounds illustrates a non-nasal vowel (the first version of rod) and a nasal one (the second).

Babies growing up in homes where only English is spoken have no regular experience with nasal versus non-nasal vowels, but they can still hear the difference between them, unlike their parents, who cannot. Interestingly, toward their first birthday, infants become primarily "tuned" to the sounds of the language(s) to which they are exposed on a daily basis. In addition, they seem to lose the ability to recognize sounds not part of their native language environment (Werker & Lalonde, 1988; Werker & Tees, 1999). Findings like these suggest that newborns are biologically capable of hearing the entire range of phonemes in all languages. However, as they grow older, they focus on linguistic distinctions that are most meaningful in their immediate linguistic environment (Best, 1995; Kuhl, 1993; Werker et al., 2007).

Children become "tuned" to the language to which they are exposed in infancy.

Of course, hearing individual phonemes is only the first step in understanding speech. One of the biggest challenges for infants is understanding recurring patterns of sounds—words. When 7- to 8-month-olds hear a word repeatedly in different sentences, they later pay more attention to this word than to words they haven't heard previously. Evidently, 7- and 8-month-olds can listen to sentences and recognize the sound patterns that they hear repeatedly (Jusczyk & Aslin, 1995; Saffran, Aslin, & Newport, 1996). By 6 months, infants can look at the correct parent when they hear "mommy" or "daddy" (Tincoff & Jusczyk, 1999).

In order to pick out where individual words begin and end in a flow of conversation, infants pay attention to linguistic stress, which is important in all languages. English contains many one-syllable words that are stressed and many two-syllable words that have a stressed syllable followed by an unstressed syllable (e.g., pup´py, tooth´-paste, bas´-ket). Infants pay more attention to stressed syllables than unstressed syllables, which is a good strategy for identifying the beginnings of words (Aslin et al., 1998; Mattys, Jusczyk, Luce, & Morgan, 1999).

Linguistic stress is not a foolproof sign because many two-syllable words have stress on the second syllable (e.g., gui-tar´, sur-prise´), so infants need other methods to identify words in speech. In fact, infants also notice syllables that go together frequently and pay particular attention to new combinations of sounds. For example, Aslin, Saffran, and Newport (1998) presented 8-month-olds with the following sounds, consisting of four, three-syllable artificial words repeated in a random order:

pa bi ku go la tu da ro pi ti bu do da ro pi go la tu pa bi ku da ro pi . . .

We've inserted gaps between the syllables and words so that you can see them more easily, but, in the study, there were no breaks at all—just a steady flow of syllables for three minutes. Later, infants listened to these words less than to new words that were novel combinations of the same syllables. They detected *pa bi ku*, *go la tu*, *da ro pi*, and *ti bu do* as familiar patterns and listened to them less than words like *tu da ro*, a new word made up from syllables they'd already heard.

Detecting stressed syllables and syllables that occur together provides infants with two powerful tools for identifying words in speech. Of course, they don't yet understand the meanings of these words; they just recognize a word as a distinct configuration of sounds. However, early acquisition of speech sounds provides the foundation for learning vocabulary, which will support later discoveries relating to grammar (Swingley, 2008) and early literacy (Hemphill & Tivnan, 2008).

People often use infant-directed speech with babies.

Parents, other adults, and even other children often help infants master language sounds by talking in a distinctive style. In **infant-directed speech** (formerly known as "motherese"), people speak slowly and with exaggerated changes in pitch and loudness. Caregivers alternate between speaking softly and loudly and between high and low pitches. Infant-directed speech can attract infants' attention more than adult-directed speech (Kaplan, Goldstein, Huckeby, & Cooper, 1995) because its slower pace and accentuated changes provide infants with more—and more obvious—language clues.

Infant-directed speech helps infants perceive the sounds that are fundamental to their language. But how do infants accomplish the next step, producing speech? We answer this question in the next section of this module.

Infant-directed speech: speaking slowly in exaggerated changes of pitch and loudness when communicating with babies; formerly called "motherese."

First Steps to Speaking

LO11 Describe what babbling is and how children make the transition from babbling to talking.

As any new parent can testify, newborns and young babies use sound to communicate: They cry to indicate discomfort or distress. By 2 months, babies begin to make sounds that are language-based. They begin to produce vowel-like sounds, such as "ooooooo" or "ahhhhhh," known as **cooing**. Sometimes infants become quite excited as they coo, perhaps reflecting the joy of simply playing with sounds.

After cooing comes **babbling**, speech-like sound that has no meaning. A typical 5- or 6-month-old might say "dah" or "bah," utterances that sound like a single syllable consisting of a consonant and a vowel. Over the next few months, babbling becomes more elaborate as babies experiment with more complex speech sounds. Older infants sometimes repeat a sound, as in "bah-bah-bah," and begin to combine different sounds, "dah-mah-bah" (Oller & Lynch, 1992).

At roughly 7 months, infants' babbling includes **intonation**, a pattern of rising or falling pitch similar to the rising and falling pattern of speech in normal conversation. For example, in an English statement, pitch first rises and then falls toward the end of the sentence. In questions, however, the pitch is level and then rises toward the end of the question. Older babies' babbling reflects these patterns: Babies who are brought up by English-speaking parents have both the declarative and the interrogative patterns of intonation in their babbling. Babies exposed to languages with other patterns of intonation, such as Japanese or French, reflect their language's intonation in their babbling (Levitt & Utman, 1992).

The appearance of intonation in babbling indicates a strong link between perception and production of speech: Infants' babbling is influenced by the characteristics of the speech they hear. Deaf children make simple sounds consisting of a consonant and a vowel, such as "bah," but this kind of babbling can remain simple for several months before developing into longer, repetitive sequences of syllables. However, they can show evidence of a kind of babbling when learning sign language early, as they will try sequences of signs that are meaningless but that match the tempo and duration of meaningful signing (Oller & Eilers, 1988; Pettito & Marentette, 1991).

As Pettito and colleagues (2000) have noted, sign language actually works to activate the auditory cortex in people who are profoundly deaf, suggesting that neural mechanisms exist in the human brain for processing language specifically, not just speech.

Children with cerebral palsy also have difficulty with babbling, but for a different reason. As Levin (1999) found, normal control over breathing is essential to being able to produce speech-related sounds. Children with cerebral palsy might have more difficulty than other children with controlling air expiration, resulting in monosyllabic and delayed babbling as compared with babies of the same age without cerebral palsy (Levin, 1999).

Cooing: long strings of vowel sounds produced by babies around 2 months of age.

Babbling: speech-like sound that has no meaning.

Intonation: a pattern of rising or falling pitch similar to the pattern in normal conversation.

However, most children learn by the middle of the first year to reproduce the language around them by using their lips, tongue, and teeth to gradually begin making sounds that approximate real words (Poulson, Kymissis, Reeve, Andreatos, & Reeve, 1991).

First Words

LO12 Understand how infants begin to form their first words.

When the ability to produce sound is coupled with the 1-year-old's advanced ability to perceive speech sounds, the stage is set for the infant's first true words. Soon after their first birthday, most infants begin to talk. Typically, their first words are an extension of advanced babbling, consisting of a consonant-vowel pair that is repeated. Mama and dada are probably the most common first words that stem from advanced babbling. Other North American early vocabulary often includes the words for animals, food, and toys (Nelson, 1973).

An infant's first words represent an important insight: Speech is more than just entertaining sound; instead, sounds form words that refer to objects, actions, and properties. That is, infants come to understand that words are symbols, concepts, and sounds that stand for entities, objects, and ideas in their world. Words open up a whole new world for infants. For example, with the onset of language, infants have a much more direct and sophisticated way of signalling that they are experiencing pain rather than just by crying (Craig, Stanford, Fairbairn, & Chambers, 2006). Words are more precise and communicate much faster when something is wrong.

One of the foremost developmental psychologists researching infant speech perception is Janet Werker at the University of British Columbia. Werker, along with colleague Athena Vouloumanos (Vouloumanos & Werker, 2004), studied whether infants at ages 2½ months, 4½ months, and 6½ months could tell the difference between normal speech and nonsense speech that has the same pitch and timing properties as regular speech. Using a habituation–dishabituation methodology, they found that infants listened longer to real speech sounds, as compared with nonspeech, and concluded that bias toward actual human speech encourages rapid development of speech in infancy.

Based on their experiences listening to actual human speech, infants begin to form cognitive concepts such as "round, bouncy things" and "furry things that bark." With the insight that speech sounds can denote these concepts, they begin to match words and concepts (Reich, 1986). They also begin to use symbols in other areas. Gestures are symbols, and infants begin to gesture shortly before their first birthday (Goodwyn & Acredolo, 1993; Rodrigo et al., 2006). Young children might smack their lips to indicate hunger or wave "bye-bye" when leaving. Both words and gestures reflect the child's developing ability to use symbols to represent actions and objects, one of humanity's greatest abilities.

Gesturing usually begins around a child's first birthday.

Fast Mapping Meanings to Words

LO13 Explain how children learn new words.

Naming explosion: a period of language learning around 18 months of age when children rapidly acquire new words.

Once children have the insight that a word can symbolize an object or action, their vocabularies grow slowly at first. A typical 15-month-old, for example, might learn two to three new words each week. However, at about 18 months, many children experience a **naming explosion**, during which they learn new words, particularly names of objects, much more rapidly than before. Children at 18 months learn 10 or more new words each week (Fenson et al., 1994).

This rapid rate of word learning is astonishing when we realize that most words have many plausible but incorrect referents. To illustrate, for example, a mother might point to a vase of flowers and say, "Flowers. These are flowers. See the flowers." To the mother, this all seems crystal clear and incredibly straightforward. But what might a child learn from this experience? Perhaps the child learns the correct referent for "flowers," but a youngster could, just as reasonably, conclude that the word "flowers" refers to the petals, to the colour of the flowers, or to the mother's actions in pointing to the flowers.

Surprisingly, most youngsters learn the proper meanings of simple words in just a few presentations. Children's ability to connect new words to referents so rapidly that they cannot be considering all possible meanings for the new word is termed **fast mapping**. Fast mapping meaning onto new words suggests that children must use rules or strategies to link words with their meanings (Carey, 1978; Yu, 2008). Researchers found that young children use fast-mapping strategies to help them learn word meanings (Deak, 2000; Woodward & Markman, 1998).

Fast mapping:
the ability of children to rapidly connect new words to their referents.

JOINT ATTENTION.   Parents encourage word learning by carefully watching what interests their children. When toddlers touch or look at an object, parents often label it for them. When a youngster points to a banana, a parent might say, "Banana, that's a banana." Of course, to take advantage of this help, infants must be able to tell when parents are labelling instead of just conversing. In fact, when adults label an unfamiliar object, 18- to 20-month-olds assume that the label is the object's name only when adults show signs that they are referring to the object. For example, toddlers are more likely to learn an object's name when adults look at the object while saying its name than when adults look elsewhere while labelling (Baldwin, Markman, Bill, Desjardins, & Irwin, 1996; Moore, Angelopoulos, & Bennett, 1999). Therefore, beginning in the toddler years, parents and children work together to create conditions that foster word learning: Parents label objects, and youngsters rely on adults' behaviour to interpret the words they hear.

CONSTRAINTS ON WORD NAMES.   Joint attention simplifies word learning for children, but the problem still remains: How does a toddler know that "banana" refers to the object she's touching, as opposed to her activity (touching) or to the object's colour? Many researchers believe that young children follow several simple rules that limit their conclusions about what labels mean.

Au and Glusman (1990) identified one of the rules that young children use: If an unfamiliar word is heard in the presence of objects that already have names and objects that don't, the word refers to one of the objects that doesn't have a name. Au and Glusman showed preschoolers a stuffed animal with pink horns that otherwise resembled a monkey and called it a mido. The word mido was then repeated several times, always referring to the stuffed animal with pink horns. Later, these youngsters were asked to find a theri in a set of stuffed animals that included several mido. Never having heard of a theri, they

Fast mapping helps children rapidly learn new words for objects.

selected other stuffed animals. Knowing that mido referred to monkey-like animals with pink horns, they decided that theri must refer to one of the other stuffed animals.

Researchers have discovered several other simple rules that help children match words with the correct referent (Bélanger & Hall, 2006; Hall & Graham, 1999; Waxman & Markow, 1995; Woodward & Markman, 1998):

- A name refers to a whole object, not its parts or its relation to other objects, and refers not just to this particular object but to all objects of the same type. For example, when a grandparent points to a stuffed animal on a shelf and says, "Dinosaur," children conclude that dinosaur refers to the entire dinosaur, not just its ears or nose, not to the fact that the dinosaur is on a shelf, and not to this specific dinosaur but to all dinosaur-like objects.

- If an object already has a name and another name is presented, the new name denotes a subcategory of the original name. If the child who knows the meaning of dinosaur sees a brother point to another dinosaur and hears the brother say "T-Rex," the child will conclude that T-Rex is a special type of dinosaur.

- Given many similar category members, a word applied consistently to only one of them is a proper noun. If a child who knows the term *dinosaur* sees that one of a group of dinosaurs is always called "Dino," the child will conclude that Dino is the name of that dinosaur. This kind of learning tends to occur between 16 and 20 months.

Rules like these make it possible for children to learn words rapidly because they reduce the number of possible referents.

SENTENCE CUES. Children hear many unfamiliar words embedded in sentences containing words they already know. The other words and the overall sentence structure can be helpful clues to a word's meaning.

Children tend to attribute new words to unfamiliar rather than familiar objects or actions.

For example, when a parent describes an event using familiar words but an unfamiliar verb, children often infer that the verb refers to the action performed by the subject of the sentence (Fisher, 1996; Woodward & Markman, 1998). For example, when youngsters hear, "The man is juggling," they will infer that juggling refers to the man's actions with the balls, because they already know the concept *man*.

As another example of how sentence context aids word learning, look at the blocks in Figure 6–7 and point to the *boz* block. We imagine you pointed to the middle block because in English, adjectives usually precede the nouns they modify, so you inferred that *boz* is an adjective describing block. Since *the* before *boz* implies that only one block is *boz*, you picked the middle one, having decided that *boz* means "winged." Preschool children, too, use sentence cues like these to judge word meanings (Gelman & Markman, 1985; Hall, Waxman, & Hurwitz, 1993).

NAMING ERRORS. Of course, these rules for learning new words are not perfect. A common mistake is **underextension**, defining a word too narrowly. Using car to refer only to the family car and ball only to refer to a favourite toy ball are examples of underextension. Between 1 and 3 years, children sometimes make the opposite error, **overextension**, defining a word too broadly. Children

Underextension:
when a word is defined too narrowly.

Overextension:
when a word is defined too broadly.

Figure 6–7

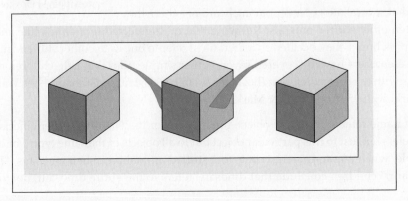

might use toque to refer to ball-caps and helmets or doggie to refer to all four-legged animals.

The overextension error occurs more frequently when children are producing words than when they are comprehending words. Two-year-old Jason might say "doggie" to refer to a goat but, nevertheless, will correctly point to a picture of a goat when asked. Because overextension is more common in word production, it might actually reflect another fast-mapping rule that children follow: "If you can't remember the name for an object, say the name of a related object" (Naigles & Gelman, 1995). Both underextension and overextension disappear gradually as youngsters refine meanings for words based on the feedback they receive from parents and others.

Styles of Learning Language

LO14 Identify the different styles of language learning that young children use.

As youngsters expand their vocabularies, they often adopt a distinctive style of learning language (Bates, Bretherton, & Snyder, 1988). Some children have a **referential style**: Their vocabularies mainly consist of words that name objects, persons, or actions. For example, Rachel, with a referential style, had 41 name words in her 50-word vocabulary but only two words for social interaction or questions. Other children have an **expressive style**: Their vocabularies include some names but also many social phrases that are used like a single word, such as "go away," "what's that?" and "I want it." Elizabeth, a child with an expressive style, had a more balanced vocabulary than Rachel, with 24 name words and 14 for social interactions and questions.

Children with the referential style primarily use language as an intellectual tool—a means of learning and talking about objects (Masur, 1995). In contrast, children with an expressive style use language as more of a social tool—a way of enhancing interactions with others. Of course, both of these functions—intellectual and social—are important functions of language, and, as you might expect, most children blend the referential and expressive styles of learning language.

Referential style: a child's initial tendency to learn primarily words that name objects, persons, or actions instead of social phrases.

Expressive style: a child's initial tendency to learn primarily social phrases in language rather than naming objects.

Ask Yourself

You learned earlier about the relationship between maternal caregiving and infant expressions of negative emotion. Once infants learn language, how do you think maternal caregiving might affect a baby's expression of pain through words?

What are the main differences between information-processing theory and Piagetian theory?

What Would an Early-Childhood Educator Do?

Say you're an early-childhood educator working in a daycare for infants and toddlers and you notice that one 18-month-old girl isn't speaking any sentences yet. She says words and points to things but doesn't make longer utterances. Should you be concerned? What should you do?

Summary

6.1 Piaget's Theory

Basic Principles of Piaget's Theory

- Children construct their understanding of the world by creating schemas: mental categories of related events, objects, and knowledge that change constantly.

- Infants' schemas are based on actions, but older children's and adolescents' schemas are based on functional, conceptual, and abstract properties.

- In assimilation, experiences are readily incorporated into existing schemas.

- In accommodation, experiences cause schemas to be modified.

- When accommodation becomes much more frequent than assimilation, children reorganize their schemas, which produces four different stages of mental development from infancy through adulthood.

Piaget's Sensorimotor Stage

- Piaget's sensorimotor stage occurs in the first two years of life and is divided into six substages.

- By 8 to 12 months, one sensorimotor schema is used in the service of another; by 12 to 18 months, infants experiment with sensorimotor schemas; and by 18 to 24 months, infants begin to engage in symbolic processing.

Evaluating Piaget's Account of Sensorimotor Thought

- Children's performance on tasks, such as object permanence, is sometimes better explained by ideas that are not part of Piaget's theory.

The Child as Theorist

- The current view of child cognition is that children are specialists who generate naive theories in particular domains, such as physics and biology.

6.2 Information Processing

Basic Features of the Information-Processing Approach

- Cognitive development involves changes in mental hardware and mental software.

- Mental hardware includes sensory, working, and long-term memories.

- Mental software refers to mental programs that allow people to perform specific tasks.

Learning

- As a stimulus becomes more familiar, infants habituate or respond less to it.

- Infants are capable of learning through classical conditioning, operant conditioning, and imitation.

Memory

- Studies of kicking show that infants can remember, forget, and be reminded of events that occurred in the past.

- Infantile amnesia refers to children's and adults' inability to remember events from early in life.

- Infantile amnesia might reflect the acquisition of language, infants' lack of an organized sense of self, or cultural differences relating to sense of self and elaborative memory talk.

Understanding the World

- Infants can distinguish quantities probably by means of basic perceptual processes.

- By 12 months, infants are more likely to know positions of objects relative to other objects, which is called an objective frame of reference.

Individual Differences in Ability

- Infant intelligence tests include mental and motor scales.

- Scores on infant intelligence tests are not highly correlated with adult IQ.

- Infant intelligence tests are useful for determining whether development is progressing normally.

- Habituation predicts later IQ more accurately than infant intelligence tests.

6.3 Language

Perceiving Speech

- Phonemes are the basic units of sound that make up words.

- Infants can hear phonemes from foreign languages, but this ability is lost by their first birthday.
- Before they speak, infants can recognize words by noticing stress and syllables that go together.
- Early speech sound detection leads to development of a vocabulary, which supports later literacy.
- Infants prefer infant-directed speech because it provides them with important language clues.

First Steps to Speaking

- Babies coo at about 3 months, followed by babbling of a single syllable.
- Babbling turns into longer syllables and develops intonation over several months.
- Deaf children babble later than children with normal hearing, but they make partial signs that are thought to be analogous to babbling.

First Words

- Children's first words represent a cognitive accomplishment that is not specific to language but extends to other areas, including gestures.

- The onset of language is due to a child's ability to interpret and use symbols.

Fast Mapping Meanings to Words

- Children use several fast-mapping rules to determine probable meanings of new words: joint attention, constraints, and sentence cues.
- Fast-mapping rules do not always lead to correct word meanings.
- Underextension occurs when a child's meaning of a word is narrower than an adult's meaning (e.g., only Snoopy is a dog).
- Overextension occurs when a child's meaning of a word is broader than an adult's meaning (e.g., all four-legged animals are dogs).

Styles of Learning Language

- A referential style in learning words emphasizes words as names and uses language as an intellectual tool (e.g., cat, tree, book).
- An expressive style emphasizes phrases and uses language as a social tool (e.g., "What's that?").

Chapter Critical Review

1. Explain what Piaget meant when he referred to children as scientists.

2. Compare and contrast the Piagetian and information-processing views of cognition, as described in Modules 6.1 and 6.2.

3. If Piaget created an intelligence test, how would it differ from the tests described in Module 6.2?

4. In some cultures, parents encourage children's speech development by such means as talking to them constantly and consciously naming objects. In other cultures, children's natural language development is taken for granted. Based on what you learned in Module 6.3, which approach makes more sense?

See for Yourself

It's eye-opening to observe infants performing simple versions of the learning tasks. For example, in the presence of a baby, ring a bell every 15 seconds. The baby should orient to the first few rings but then habituate. If the infant has a mobile, tie a ribbon from the infant's leg to the mobile. In a few minutes, the infant should be kicking frequently, demonstrating operant conditioning (kicking recurs because it produces pleasant consequences). From watching infants perform these and other learning tasks, you will appreciate that even very young infants are surprisingly capable learners! See for yourself!

Chapter 7
Social and Emotional Development in Infants and Toddlers

WONG SZE FEI/Fotolia

∨ MODULE

7.1 Emotions

7.2 Relationships with Others

7.3 Self-Concept

7.4 Temperament

Connect to My Virtual Child

What kinds of theories do you have about children? What ideas inform your thoughts and beliefs about the lives of children, how they are raised, and the nature of the human person? Use your access card and follow this link www.myvirtualchild.com to learn more about the world of the child. You can even virtually try to raise your own child.

As Sophie grew, Mabel and Terry noticed that she spent a lot of time watching other people. While other babies would run right into a group, Sophie liked to take her time, hovering around the edges and looking at what all the children were doing before cautiously approaching and picking up one of the toys. Mabel was a little surprised, because she, herself, was such a go-getter, but she and Terry laughed when they realized that Terry, too, kind of liked to hang around the edges of groups before jumping into the action. They wondered . . . maybe Sophie had a personality similar to Terry's.

7.1 Emotions

 ## Learning Objectives

After reading the module, you should be able to do the following:

LO1 Identify when infants begin to express basic emotions.

LO2 Define what complex emotions are, and state when they develop.

LO3 Describe when infants begin to understand other people's emotions and how they use this information to guide their own behaviour.

LO4 State when infants and toddlers begin to regulate their own emotions.

Happiness, anger, and surprise, along with fear, disgust, and sadness, are considered basic emotions. People worldwide experience these emotions, and each basic emotion consists of three elements: a subjective feeling, a physiological change, and an overt behaviour (Izard, 1991). For example, suppose you awaken to a thunderstorm and then discover that your roommate has left for class with your umbrella. Subjectively, you might experience negative thoughts and anger; physiologically, your heart would beat faster and your muscles would tighten up; and behaviourally, you probably would scowl.

In addition to basic emotions, people feel complex emotions such as pride, guilt, and embarrassment. Unlike basic emotions, complex emotions have an evaluative component to them. For example, a 2-year-old who has spilled juice all over the floor might hang his head in shame; another 2-year-old who has, for the first time, finished a difficult puzzle alone will smile in a way that radiates pride. In contrast to basic emotions, complex emotions are not expressed the same way in all cultures.

In this module, we look at when children first express basic and complex emotions, how children come to understand emotions in others, and, finally, how children regulate their emotions.

Basic Emotions

LO1 Identify when infants begin to express basic emotions.

If you're a fan of that classic show *Star Trek*, you know that Mr. Spock feels little emotion because he's half Vulcan, and people from the planet Vulcan don't have emotions. Human infants are never relatively free of emotion like Mr. Spock. Emotions are with us from very early in life. In fact, the facial expressions of babies can be so revealing that it's often not difficult to tell when they are sad, happy, and angry. However, babies' distinctive facial expressions do not necessarily mean the infants are actually experiencing these emotions. Facial expressions are only one component of emotion—the behavioural manifestation. Emotion also involves physiological responses and subjective feelings. Of course, infants can't describe their feelings to us verbally, so we don't know much about their personal experiences. We're on firmer ground with the physiological element. At least some of the physiological responses that accompany facial expressions are the same in infants and adults. For example, when infants and adults smile—which suggests they're happy—the left frontal cortex of the brain tends to have more electrical activity than the right frontal cortex (Fox, Kimmerly, & Schafer, 1991).

Some psychologists use this and similar findings to argue that facial expressions are reliable clues to an infant's emotional state (Hess, Philippot, & Blairy, 1998; Strayer & Roberts, 1997). Izard (1991) demonstrated that infants and adults worldwide express basic emotions in much the same way. For example, when afraid, people tend to open their eyes wide, raise their eyebrows, and have a relaxed but slightly open mouth. The universality of emotional expression suggests that humans are biologically programmed to express basic emotions in specific ways.

Another finding that links infants' facial expressions to emotions is that, by 5 to 6 months, infants' facial expressions change predictably and meaningfully in response to events. When a happy mother greets her baby, the baby usually smiles in return; when a tired, distracted mother picks up her baby too quickly, the baby usually frowns at her. These kinds of findings suggest that, by the middle of the first year (and maybe earlier), facial expressions are fairly reliable indicators of an infant's emotional state (Izard et al., 1995; Weinberg & Tronick, 1994).

Facial expressions can provide clues to an infant's emotional state.

If facial expressions provide a window into a baby's emotions, what do they tell us about the early phases of emotional development? Let's start with happiness.

HAPPINESS.   During the first few weeks after birth, infants begin to smile, but this kind of smiling seems to be related to internal physiological states. An infant might smile after feeding or while asleep, for example. At about 2 months, infants start to make **social smiles** when they see another human face. Sometimes social smiling is accompanied by cooing (Sroufe & Waters, 1976). Smiling and cooing seem to be the infant's way of expressing pleasure at seeing another person.

At about 4 months, smiling is joined by laughter, which usually occurs when a baby experiences vigorous physical stimulation (Sroufe & Wunsch, 1972). Gently tickling 4-month-olds is a good way to prompt a laugh. Toward the end of the first year, infants often laugh when familiar events take a novel turn. For example, a 1-year-old will laugh when mom pretends to drink from a baby bottle or dad drapes a diaper around his waist. Laughter is now a response to psychological as well as physical stimulation.

The early development of positive feelings, like happiness, are linked primarily to physical states, such as feeling full after a meal or being tickled. Later, feelings of happiness reflect psychological states, such as the pleasure of seeing another person or an unusual event.

Fear: eyes wide open, eyebrows raised, mouth open and relaxed.

NEGATIVE EMOTIONS.   We know much less about the development of negative emotions such as fear, anger, and sadness. Certainly, newborns express distress, but specific negative emotions are hard to verify. Anger emerges gradually, with distinct displays appearing between 4 and 6 months of age. Infants will become angry, for example, if a favourite food or toy is taken away (Sternberg & Campos, 1990). Reflecting their growing understanding of goal-directed behaviour, infants also become angry when their attempts to achieve a goal are not met. For example, if a parent restrains an infant who is trying to pick up a desired object, the guaranteed result is an angry baby.

Like anger, fear seems to be rare in newborns and young infants. The first distinct signs of fear emerge at about 6 months when infants become wary in the presence of an unfamiliar adult, a reaction known as **stranger wariness**. When a stranger approaches, a 6-month-old typically looks away and begins to fuss (Mangelsdorf, Shapiro, & Marzolf, 1995). If the stranger picks up the baby without giving that baby a chance to become more familiar with the person, the outcome is fairly predictable: The baby will cry, look frightened, and reach with outstretched arms in the direction of someone familiar.

How wary an infant feels around strangers depends on a number of factors (Thompson & Limber, 1991). First, infants tend to be less fearful of strangers when the environment is familiar and more fearful when it is not. Second, the amount of anxiety depends on the stranger's behaviour. Instead of rushing to greet or pick up the baby, a stranger should talk with other adults and, after a while, perhaps offer the baby a toy (Mangelsdorf, 1992). When approached this way, many infants will soon be curious about the stranger instead of afraid. Finally, stranger wariness relates to a very important concept in child development called attachment, which you will read about more extensively later in this chapter.

Wariness of strangers is adaptive because it emerges at the same time that children begin to master creeping and crawling. Babies are inquisitive and want to use their new locomotor skills to explore the environment. Being wary of strangers provides a natural restraint against the tendency to wander away

Social smiles:
smiling in response to seeing another human face.

Stranger wariness:
signs of fear in an infant in response to an unfamiliar adult.

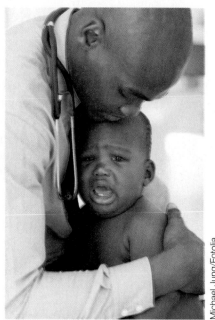

This baby is showing distress relating to stranger wariness.

glenda/Shutterstock

Toddlers can feel pride in their achievements.

from familiar caregivers. During the second year, wariness of strangers gradually declines as toddlers learn to interpret facial expressions and become better at recognizing when a stranger is friendly.

Although children worldwide express basic emotions, cultural differences do exist regarding the frequency of emotional expression. In one study (Camras et al., 1998), European American 11-month-olds cried and smiled more often than Chinese 11-month-olds. In another study (Zahn-Waxler, Friedman, Cole, Mizuta, & Hiruma, 1996), U.S. preschoolers were more likely than Japanese preschoolers to express anger in interpersonal conflicts. Therefore, even though basic emotions are rooted in biology, how and when they are expressed is influenced by culture.

Complex Emotions

LO2 Define what complex emotions are, and state when they develop.

Basic emotions appear early in infancy, but complex emotions, such as feelings of guilt, embarrassment, or pride, don't emerge until 18 to 24 months of age (Lewis, 1992). Complex emotions depend on the child's reflexive understanding of the self, which typically occurs between 15 and 18 months (as we'll see in Module 7.3). Children feel guilty or embarrassed, for example, when they've done something that they know they shouldn't have done: A child who breaks a toy is often thinking, "You told me to be careful, but I wasn't!" Similarly, children feel pride when they've done something that was challenging, thinking, "This was hard, but I did it all by myself!" For children to experience complex emotions, they need to be more cognitively advanced, which explains why complex emotions don't appear until the very end of infancy (Lewis, Alessandri, & Sullivan, 1992).

In sum, complex emotions like guilt and pride require more sophisticated understanding than basic emotions like happiness and fear, which are more biologically based. By age 2, children can express both basic and complex emotions. Of course, expressing emotions is only part of the developmental story. Children must also learn to recognize others' emotions, which is our next topic.

Recognizing and Using Others' Emotions

LO3 Describe when infants begin to understand other people's emotions and how they use this information to guide their own behaviour.

By 6 or 7 months, infants begin to distinguish facial expressions associated with different emotions. A 6-month-old can, for example, distinguish a happy, smiling face from a sad, frowning face (Ludemann, 1991; Ludemann & Nelson, 1988). Typically, baby girls are more accurate than baby boys at recognizing adults' facial expressions of emotion (McClure, 2000).

Strictly speaking, these studies tell us only that infants can discriminate facial expressions, not necessarily the actual emotions being portrayed. Other researchers, however, found that some 6-month-olds can recognize the actual emotions. The best evidence is that infants often match their own emotions to other people's emotions. When happy mothers smile and talk in a pleasant voice, infants express happiness too. If mothers are angry or sad, infants become distressed too (Haviland & Lelwica, 1987). In addition, infants look longer at happy faces when they hear happy-sounding talk and longer at angry faces when they hear angry-sounding talk (Soken & Pick, 1999).

Also, like adults, infants use others' emotions to direct their behaviour. Infants in an unfamiliar or ambiguous situation will look at a trusted caregiver, such as mother or father, as if searching for clues to help them know how to react, a phenomenon known as **social referencing**. For example, in a study by Hirshberg and Svejda (1990), 12-month-olds were shown novel toys that made sounds, such as a stuffed alligator that hissed. For some toys, parents were told to look happy; for others, parents were told to look afraid. When parents looked afraid, their infants, too, appeared distressed and moved away from the toys.

Social referencing: looking at a trusted caregiver for clues about how to react to a situation.

In other studies of social referencing, infants watched an adult express happiness when looking inside one box but disgust when looking inside another. Infants were more likely to explore the box that elicited happiness (Repacholi, 1998). Furthermore, facial expressions or vocal expressions alone provide infants with enough information to decide whether they want to explore an unfamiliar object (Mumme, Fernald, & Herrera, 1996).

As you can see, social referencing shows that infants rely on their parents' emotions and behaviour to help them regulate their own emotions and behaviour. However, social referencing does not necessarily decline as children become more familiar with aspects of their world. In fact, as Canadian research demonstrated, the more infants understand about causal relations between events in the world, the more they will socially reference adults' reactions to those events (Desrochers, Ricard, Decarie, & Allard, 1994). Through social references, children rely on their parents for basic information about how to interpret objects and events in the world, even as they come to learn more about those events, which forms an important building block in learning how to regulate behavioural responses and emotional reactions. Children who grow up with poor caregiver models of emotion and behaviour regulation could be at risk, themselves, for developing poor strategies for emotion and behaviour regulation.

Regulating Emotions

LO4 **State when infants and toddlers begin to regulate their own emotions.**

Think back to a time when you were really angry at a good friend. Did you shout at the friend? Did you try to discuss matters calmly? Or did you simply ignore the situation altogether? Shouting is a direct expression of anger, but calm conversation and overlooking a situation are also purposeful attempts at regulating emotion. People often regulate emotions; for example, we might routinely try to suppress fear (because we know there's no real need to be afraid of the dark), anger (because we don't want to let a friend know just how upset we are), and joy (because we don't want to seem like we're gloating over good fortune).

Child-development researchers have discovered that emotion regulation clearly begins in infancy. By 4 to 6 months, infants use simple strategies to regulate their emotions (Buss & Goldsmith, 1998; Mangelsdorf et al., 1995). When something frightens or confuses an infant—for example, a stranger or a mother who suddenly stops responding—they often look away, just as older children and even adults often turn away or close their eyes to block out disturbing stimuli. Frightened infants also move closer to a parent, another effective way of helping to control their fear (Parritz, 1996). As children become older, they devise even more effective strategies for dealing with emotions, such as reassuring themselves that there's no reason to be afraid of the dark. However, the initial effort to control emotions, instead of being overwhelmed by them, emerges in infancy.

Although many people talk about emotions in terms of intangible "feelings," Marc Lewis, from the University of Toronto, and his colleague Jim Steiben (2004) found that emotion regulation cannot be separated from the activation of emotion centres in the brain. Lewis and Steiben argued that emotion regulation appears to be mediated by areas of the prefrontal cortex in the frontal lobe, which exert control over other areas of the brain. They also pointed out that areas of the frontal lobe in children who tend to internalize (suppress) emotion typically are more sensitive to anxiety than the brains of children who externalize (act out) emotion. They concluded, therefore, that effortful regulation of negative emotion differs, in part, according to children's varying frontal lobe mediation of those emotional states (Lewis & Steiben, 2004).

In addition, both genetics and parenting also have their impact on children's emotion regulation. Based on a review of research, Propper and Moore (2006) concluded that infant emotionality is regulated, in part, by a particular gene, which also is linked to the experience later in life with depression, externalizing behaviour, and impulse control problems. However, the impact of this genetic predisposition appears greater when it occurs in a context of insensitive parenting, abusive or neglectful environments, or other negative family contexts. Other research points to evidence of a relationship between marital conflict and infant emotional withdrawal (Crockenberg, Leerkes, & Lekka, 2007). In summarizing the development of infant emotion regulation, we can say that babies have the basis for emotion regulation in their neural and physiological systems, but they develop further skills for emotion regulation by interacting with the environment (Zeman, Cassano, Perry-Parrish, & Stegall, 2006).

Ask Yourself

Most theories of cognitive development, such as Piaget's and the information-processing approach, don't explicitly consider emotion. How might emotions affect thinking? How could these theories incorporate emotion?

7.2 Relationships with Others

Learning Objectives

After reading the module, you should be able to do the following:

LO5 Detail how an attachment relationship develops between an infant and a primary caregiver.

LO6 Describe the different types of attachment relationships, the consequences of different types of relationships, and how child care affects attachment relations.

LO7 Summarize how infants and toddlers first interact with peers.

Should parents protect their babies from all experience of fear, or can fear be adaptive?

The social-emotional relationship that develops between an infant and a parent is special. This is a baby's first social-emotional relationship, so psychologists and parents alike believe it should be satisfying and trouble-free to set the stage well for later relationships. In this module, we'll look at the steps involved in creating the baby's first emotional relationship. Along the way, we'll see why babies sometimes cry when left with a sitter, and we'll also discuss children's first interactions with peers.

The Growth of Attachment

LO5 **Detail how an attachment relationship develops between an infant and a primary caregiver.**

Sigmund Freud was the first modern scientific theorist to emphasize the importance of emotional ties to the mother for psychological development. Today, the dominant view of early human relationships comes from John Bowlby (1969, 1991). His work originated in ethology, a branch of biology concerned with adaptive behaviours in different species. According to Bowlby, children who form an **attachment** to an adult—that is, an enduring social-emotional relationship—are more likely to survive. This adult is usually the mother but need not be; the key is a strong emotional relationship with a responsive, caring person who is consistently available to the child, so attachments can form with fathers, grandparents, or other caregivers as well. Attachment is a key developmental concept, and clinical assessment of children's attachment can be an important clue to the child's well-being and emotional adjustment (Zeanah, Berlin, & Boris, 2011).

Attachment:
an enduring social-emotional relationship.

Bowlby (1969) argued that evolution favours behaviours likely to elicit caregiving from an adult, such as clinging, sucking, crying, and smiling. He maintained that, over the course of human evolution, these behaviours have become a standard part of the human infant's biological heritage. The responses they evoke in adults create an interactive system that leads to the formation of attachment relationships.

The attachment relationship develops gradually over the first several months after birth, reflecting the baby's growing perceptual and cognitive skills. First, the infant must learn the difference between people and other objects. Typically, in the first few months, babies begin to respond differently to people and to objects—for example, smiling more and vocalizing more to people—suggesting that they have begun to identify members of the social world.

During these months, mother and infant begin to synchronize their interactions. Remember that young babies' behaviours go through cycles. Infants move between states of alertness and attentiveness to states of distress and inattentiveness. Caregivers begin to recognize these states of behaviour and adjust their own behaviour accordingly. A mother who notices that her baby is awake and alert will begin to smile at and talk to her baby. These interactions often continue until the baby's state changes, which prompts the mother to stop. In fact, by 3 months of age, if a mother does not interact with her alert baby (but, instead, stares silently), the baby becomes at least moderately distressed, looking away from her and sometimes crying (Toda & Fogel, 1993).

Therefore, mothers and infants gradually synchronize their behaviours so that they are both "on" at the same time (Gable & Isabella, 1992). In their Canadian studies, Pederson, Moran, and colleagues found similar results with both average and developmentally delayed children (Moran, Pederson, Pettit, & Krupka, 1992; Pederson, Gleason, Moran, & Bento, 1998; Pederson & Moran, 1996). These interactions provide the foundation for more sophisticated communication and foster the infant's trust that the mother will respond predictably and reassuringly.

However, other factors can disrupt the development of a strong mother–infant bond (Grossman, Grossman, & Waters, 2005; Klier, 2006; Madigan et al., 2006; Madigan, Moran, & Pederson, 2006; Maybery, Ling, Szakacs, & Reupert, 2005). Maternal experience of depression is one such factor that has

Caregivers and babies learn to synchronize their behaviours.

drubig-photo/Fotolia

Monkey Business/Fotolia

Babies explore the environment using an attachment figure as a secure base.

Internal working model: a set of expectations about parents' availability and responsivity generally and in times of stress.

a great impact on attachment development in the first 14 months of life, and particularly in the first 4 months (Moehler, Brunner, Wiebel, Reck, & Resch, 2006). Also, in the years after World War II, many European infants and toddlers lived in orphanages. They were well fed and clothed but typically were cared for by a constantly changing cast of adults, sometimes having as many as 50 caregivers by age 4. Lacking a strong emotional bond with any one adult during their formative years, the development of these children was disrupted, sometimes severely (Tizard & Hodges, 1978).

By approximately 6 or 7 months, most infants have singled out the primary attachment figure—usually the mother—as a special individual. An infant will smile at the mother and cling to her more than to other people. The infant's primary attachment figure becomes that infant's stable social-emotional base. For example, a 7-month-old will explore a novel environment but periodically look toward mother, as if seeking reassurance that all is well. The behaviour suggests the infant trusts mother and indicates the attachment relationship has been established. In addition, this behaviour reflects important cognitive growth: It means that the infant has a mental representation of the mother, an understanding that she will be there to meet the infant's needs (Lewis, Koroshegyi, Douglas, & Kampe, 1997). The child's initial representation of a primary caregiver, coupled with the quality of attachment that develops early in life, forms the child's internal working model of attachment relationships as the child matures. An **internal working model** is a set of expectations about parents' availability and responsivity generally and in times of stress.

The formation of the attachment bond also explains why older babies often cry when left with a sitter. Babies become emotionally attached to their parents and expect them to be nearby. So, when separated from one or both parents and left with a sitter, a baby can become upset as a result of the expectation that the parents remain nearby.

In Canada, attachment typically first develops between infants and their mothers because mothers are usually the primary caregivers of Canadian infants. Most babies soon become attached to their fathers too, but they interact differently with fathers. Fathers typically spend much more time playing with their babies than taking care of them. In many countries around the world—Australia, India, Israel, Italy, Japan, and the United States—"playmate" is the common role for fathers (Roopnarine, 1992). Fathers even tend to play with infants differently than mothers. Physical play is the norm for fathers, particularly with sons, whereas mothers spend more time reading and talking to babies, showing them toys, and playing games like patty-cake (Parke, 1990).

Given the opportunity to play with mothers or fathers, infants more often choose their fathers. However, when infants are distressed, mothers are preferred (Field, 1990). Thus, although most infants become attached to both parents, according to psychological research findings to date, mothers and fathers often have distinct roles in their children's early social development. While fathers are an important source of love and caregiving for infants, depression in fathers tends to be associated with low engagement in activities with the child, higher levels of aggravation and parenting stress, and lower quality of relationship and supportiveness between the child's mother and the child's father (Bronte-Tinkew, Moore, & Matthews, 2007).

Another important finding about attachment is the potential relationship between emotional bonds and physiological perception. According to researchers, a relationship exists between olfaction—the sense of smell—and attachment (Dubas, Dubas, Heijkoop, & Aken, 2009). In a study of parental attachment to children, fathers who could identify the smell of their child showed more attachment and affection toward their children, as well as fewer ignoring behaviours, in comparison with fathers who could not identify their children's smell (Dubas et al., 2009). Mothers' recognition of their children's smell was related to tendency to use physical punishment—they tended to use less physical punishment if they could identify the smell of their own child (Dubas et al., 2009). The researchers postulated that, in the case of fathers, olfaction is a way for fathers to tell whether they are genetically related to particular offspring. They further postulated that olfaction is related to overall allocations of care-related behaviour toward children (Dubas et al., 2009).

Quality of Attachment

LO6 **Describe the different types of attachment relationships, the consequences of different types of relationships, and how child care affects attachment relations.**

Attachment between infant and mother usually occurs by 8 or 9 months of age, but the attachment can take different forms. While the emotional bond we call attachment occurs universally between children and their caregivers, we now know that the manner in which that attachment relationship is developed and expressed varies from culture to culture (St. Joseph Women's Health Centre, n.d.). This is a particularly important finding for psychologists in Canada, as this nation includes people from many different cultures. Researchers from the St. Joseph Women's Health Centre (n.d.) in Toronto interviewed people across Canada, representing 50 different nations, and, based on these interviews as well as focus groups, the researchers concluded that both similarities and differences exist in attachment beliefs, practices, and values among caregivers—in this case, mothers from differing countries of origin.

While attachment in childhood has been a topic of interest in psychological research, so too has the concept of attachment as an emotional connection that is important across the lifespan. Over the past decade, researchers have begun to extend their understanding of attachment to relationships beyond the primary caregiver, including, for example, extended family relationships, dating relationships, and sexual relationships in adulthood. A child's internal working model of attachment, developed early in life, can have a strong impact on the development of attachments with other people as the child matures. At the same time, however, some researchers (Waters, Merrick, Treboux, Crowell, & Albersheim, 2000) have suggested that a child's internal working model of attachment can change over the lifespan as a result of life experiences and changes in relationships (Waters et al., 2000).

Our current understanding of attachment derives primarily from Mary Ainsworth's (1978, 1993) landmark research. Ainsworth did her original research and teaching in psychology at the University of Toronto, where she investigated attachment relationships using a procedure that has come to be known as the Strange Situation. As shown in Figure 7–1, the Strange Situation involves a series of episodes, each about three minutes long. The mother and infant enter an unfamiliar room filled with interesting toys. The mother leaves briefly, then mother and baby are reunited. Meanwhile, the experimenter observes the baby, recording the baby's responses to both events.

Based on how the infant reacts to separation from the mother and then to reunion, Ainsworth (1993) and other researchers (Main & Cassidy, 1988) have identified four primary types of attachment relationships. One is a secure attachment and three are forms of insecure attachments.

Figure 7–1

1. Observer shows the experimental room to mother and infant then leaves the room.

2. Infant is allowed to explore the playroom for 3 minutes; mother watches but does not participate.

3. A stranger enters the room and remains silent for 1 minute, then talks to the baby for a minute, and then approaches the baby. Mother leaves unobtrusively.

4. The stranger does not play with the baby but attempts to comfort the baby if necessary.

5. After 3 minutes, the mother returns and greets and consoles the baby.

6. When the baby has returned to play, the mother leaves again, this time saying "bye-bye" as she leaves.

7. The stranger attempts to calm and play with the baby.

8. After 3 minutes, the mother returns and the stranger leaves.

SOURCE: Mallory Skrip Designs

Attachment researchers rely on babies' reactions to research scenarios in order to make judgments about quality of attachment.

- *Secure attachment:* The baby might or might not cry when the mother leaves, but when she returns, the baby wants to be with her, and, if the baby is crying, it stops. Babies in this group seem to be saying, "I missed you terribly, but now that you're back, I'm okay." Approximately 60 to 65 percent of American babies have secure attachment relationships.

- *Avoidant attachment:* The baby is not upset when the mother leaves and, when she returns, might ignore her by looking or turning away. Infants with an avoidant attachment look as if they're saying, "You're not here when I want you. I always have to take care of myself!" About 20 percent of American infants have avoidant attachment, which is one of the three forms of insecure attachment.

- *Resistant attachment:* The baby is upset when the mother leaves, remains upset or even angry when she returns, and is difficult to console. These babies seem to be telling the mother, "Why do you do this? I need you desperately, yet you just leave me without warning. I get so angry when you're like this!" About 10 to 15 percent of American babies have resistant attachment, which is another form of insecure attachment.

- *Disorganized (disoriented) attachment:* The baby seems confused when the mother leaves and, when she returns, not to really understand what's happening. The baby often has a dazed look on his or her face, as if wondering, "What's going on here? I want you to be here, but you left and now you're back. I don't know whether to laugh or cry!" About 5 to 10 percent of American babies have disorganized attachment, the last of the three kinds of insecure attachment.

Secure attachments and the different forms of insecure attachments are observed worldwide. As you can see in Figure 7–2, secure attachments are the most common throughout the world (Sagi, van IJzendoorn, Aviezer, Donnell, & Mayseless, 1994; van IJzendoorn & Kroonenberg, 1988). This is fortunate because, as we'll see, a secure attachment provides a solid base for later social development. For example, Barry Schneider, from the University of Ottawa, and his colleagues performed an analysis of studies done on maternal–child attachment. Schneider, Atkinson, and Tardiff (2001) found evidence that early maternal–child attachment was related to later peer relationships, particularly in terms of close peer relationships in middle childhood. These researchers also looked at studies of infant–father attachments, but their findings were inconclusive. Other researchers, however, have found that infants typically form the same type of attachment relationships with both parents (Fox et al., 1991). An infant who is securely attached to mother usually is securely attached to father too. Siblings usually have the same type of attachment relationships with their parents (Rosen & Burke, 1999). In addition, Canadian research shows that children coming from families where the parents have a stable marital relationship tend to be more likely to have secure attachment (Doyle, Markiewicz, Brendgen, Lieberman, & Voss, 2000).

CONSEQUENCES OF QUALITY OF ATTACHMENT. Erikson, Bowlby, and other theorists (Madigan et al., 2006; Sroufe & Fleeson, 1986) believe that attachment, as the first social relationship, lays the basic foundation for later social relationships in life (Lyons-Ruth, Dutra, Schuder, & Bianchi, 2006; Möller, Hwang, & Wickberg, 2006). In this view, infants who experience the trust and compassion of a secure attachment should develop into preschool children who interact confidently and successfully with their peers. In contrast, infants who do not experience a successful, satisfying first relationship should be more prone to problems in their social interactions as preschoolers.

Both of these predictions are supported by research, as the following findings demonstrate:

- Children with secure attachment relationships have higher-quality friendships and fewer conflicts in their friendships than children with insecure attachment relationships (Lieberman, Doyle, & Markiewicz, 1999).

- School-age children are less likely to have behaviour problems if they have secure attachment relationships and more likely if they have insecure attachment relationships (Carlson, 1998; Wakschlag & Hans, 1999).

- At a summer camp, 11-year-olds who had secure attachment relationships as infants interacted more skillfully with their peers and had more close friends than

Figure 7–2

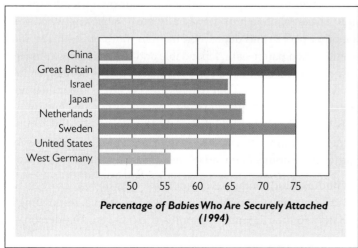

Percentage of Babies Who Are Securely Attached (1994)

Attachment supports growth and development of the infant.

11-year-olds who had insecure attachment relationships (Elicker, Englund, & Sroufe, 1992).

- Canadian researcher Elaine Scharfe (2000) noted that securely attached children tend to have superior understanding of emotions, better ability to regulate emotions, and more emotional expressiveness than insecurely attached children, suggesting a relationship between secure attachment and emotional intelligence.

The conclusion seems inescapable: As infants who have secure attachment relationships develop, their social interactions tend to be more satisfying and their emotional health seems to be more stable. Secure attachment evidently promotes trust and confidence in other people, which leads to more skilled and confident social interactions later in childhood. Attachment quality is also posited to affect basic neural systems and brain development, making the intergenerational transmission of attachment an important area of research (Fonagy & Target, 2005).

Of course, attachment is only one step on the long road of social development. Infants who are not able to develop a secure emotional bond with a caregiver early in life are not doomed; however, interference with their social development can occur if they consistently are not able to form this kind of important bond with another person early in life. The inability to form an attachment relationship might occur for a variety of reasons (Minde, 2003), including being raised in an abusive or neglectful environment, never having a consistent caregiver (as in an orphanage), or having an extremely depressed or mentally ill caregiver. In addition, some health conditions, such as autism or profound brain injury, can interfere with attachment development.

FACTORS DETERMINING QUALITY OF ATTACHMENT. Because secure attachment is so important to a child's later development, researchers have tried to identify the factors involved. Undoubtedly the most important is the interaction between parents and their babies (DeWolff & van IJzendoorn, 1997). A secure attachment is most likely when parents respond to infants predictably and appropriately. Consistent and appropriate responses to a child's needs convey that social interactions are predictable and satisfying, and this behaviour apparently instills in infants the trust and confidence that are the hallmark of secure attachment.

Why does predictable and responsive parenting promote secure attachment relationships? To answer this question, think about your own friendships and romantic relationships. These relationships are usually most satisfying when we believe we can trust the other people and depend on them in times of need. The same seems to hold for infants. When parents are dependable and caring, babies come to trust them, knowing they can be relied upon for comfort. That is, babies develop an internal working model in which they believe their parents are concerned about their needs and will try to meet them (Bretherton, 1992). As you can see in the Real Children feature, the interactions between Talia, Max, and their father are warm, sensitive, and caring.

Many research findings attest to the importance of a caregiver's sensitivity to a child's needs for developing secure attachment:

- In a longitudinal study, infants were more likely to have a secure attachment relationship at 12 months when their parents were sensitive, responding quickly and appropriately to their infant at 3 months (Cox, Owen, Henderson, & Margand, 1992).

Jack.Q/Fotolia

Real Children

A Father's Attachment

Much psychological research about attachment has focused on mothers. However, fathers can play an equally important role in the development of their children. Quebec father Bruce Gottfred parents twins Max and Talia full-time in their family's home. The following is a post from Bruce's blog, in which he makes observations of his 1-year-old twins' behaviour. Notice the warmth with which he writes about his children and the kinds of behaviours that he, as a parent, finds interesting, amusing, and a source of justifiable pride. In terms of attachment, you might also notice the sensitivity and responsiveness with which he behaves toward his young children.

Very Cute

Yes they are. I can't seem to find the camera right now so I can't show you how cute they are, but I'll mention a few things they've done in the last few days.

Talia has begun to tell us her name. She taps her chest with two fingers and with a very serious expression says, "Ta-ya!"

Since weaning them, we've replaced the bedtime nursing session with a cuddle, a story, and a cup of warm milk. Talia's favourite story is Goodnight Gorilla, which involves a naughty Gorilla letting all the animals out of the zoo to follow the zookeeper to bed. We must have run through it at least a hundred times in the past few weeks. In the story, there's a mouse that follows all the animals around while carrying a banana—which the gorilla eats on the last page. On every page she sticks her finger out and pins the mouse, exclaiming, "Nana!"

Today Max was sitting on my lap and started to pretend to eat something. He picked up whatever it was between his thumb and forefinger and put it in his mouth. He did this a few times then looked at me with a tight-lipped smile and offered me some. I opened my mouth and he put his fingers in. Yum!

Talia is walking pretty well now. She has a sort of Charlie Chaplin gait. Yesterday Opa was over and had to see her new trick. With everyone making a big fuss over Talia, Max decided he wanted to walk too. He climbed to his feet and threw his arms up and fell forward, big smile on his face.

Brooks, Rosie/www.Cartoonstock.com

Who's the daddy!

Up again and down again. He was too excited. Finally he calmed down enough to get his balance before he tried to move forward and walked a few steps! Good job, Max!

Yesterday out in the driveway Max decided he wanted to eat some gravel. I used the pinky-hook to take it out of his mouth and throw it away. He crawled to where I threw it and picked up the exact same piece of grey stone, indistinguishable from all the other pieces of grey stone. Hook, throw—and he sees where it lands and gets it again! He didn't find it the next time.

Max was playing with a ball. Talia crawled over and took it away from him. Max cried. I told Talia to give the ball back to Max, knowing that it would never happen. But to my surprise, she understood me and offered the ball to Max. What a smart girl! I thought. And not just smart but also capable of empathy! She's amazing! And then, while looking at me with an evil grin, she yanked the ball away just as Max was reaching for it. She's normal.

UPDATE: I found the camera. It was outside in the pocket of the stroller. Luckily all the rain we've had in the last few days didn't damage it. Now I can add a couple of pictures to this post.

Source: Gottfred, 2004.

Here's Talia destroying Mama's crocuses:

And here's Max ready to go on an adventure. He's loaded his cart with gravel to eat on the journey . . .

- In a study conducted in Israel, infants were less likely to develop secure attachment when they slept in dormitories with other children under 12, where they received inconsistent (if any) attention when they became upset overnight (Sagi et al., 1994).
- In a study conducted in the Netherlands, infants were more likely to form a secure attachment when their mother had three months of training that emphasized monitoring an infant's signals and responding appropriately and promptly (van den Boom, 1994, 1995).

Therefore, secure attachment is most likely when parents are sensitive and responsive. Of course, not all caregivers react to babies in a reliable and reassuring manner. Some respond intermittently or only after the infant has cried long and hard. When these caregivers finally respond, they sometimes are annoyed by the infant's demands and might misinterpret the infant's intent. Over time, these babies tend to see social relationships as inconsistent and frustrating, conditions that do little to foster trust and confidence.

Why are some parents more responsive and, thus, more likely to foster secure attachment than others? In modern attachment theory (e.g., Cassidy, 1994), parents have internal working models of the attachment relationship with their own parents, and these working models guide interactions with their own infants. When questioned about attachment relationships with the Adult Attachment Interview (George, Kaplan, & Main, 1985), adults can be classified into one of three groups:

- Autonomous adults describe childhood experiences objectively and mention both positive and negative aspects of their parents.
- Dismissive adults describe childhood experiences in very general terms and often idealize their parents.
- Preoccupied adults describe childhood experiences emotionally and often express anger or confusion regarding their relationships with their parents.

Similar findings have been achieved from the Parental Bonding Instrument (Manassis, Owens, Adam, West, & Sheldon-Keller, 1999), except in cases where people showed particular idealization or anger toward their mothers.

According to attachment theory, only parents with autonomous attachment representations are likely to provide the sensitive caregiving that promotes secure attachment. In fact, many studies show that parents' autonomous attachment representations are associated with sensitive caregiving and, in turn, with secure attachment in their infants (Aviezer, Sagi, Joels, & Ziv, 1999; Pederson et al., 1998; van IJzendoorn, 1995). Furthermore, longitudinal research (Beckwith, Cohen, & Hamilton, 1999) shows that infants with secure attachment tend to become adults with autonomous attachment representations, completing the circle.

The sensitive and responsive caregiving that is essential for secure attachment is often taxing, particularly for parents of babies with difficult temperaments. Babies who fuss often and are difficult to console are more prone to developing insecure attachment (Goldsmith & Harman, 1994; Seifer, Schiller, Sameroff, Resnick, & Riordan, 1996). Insecure attachment might also be more likely when a difficult, emotional infant has a mother whose personality is rigid and inflexible than when the mother is accepting and flexible (Mangelsdorf, Gunnar, Kestenbaum, Lang, & Andreas, 1990). Rigid mothers do not adjust well to the often erratic demands of their difficult babies; instead, they want the baby to adjust to them. This means that rigid mothers less often provide the responsive, sensitive care necessary for secure attachment.

Fortunately, education and even brief training for mothers of infants can help them respond to their babies more effectively (Gauthier, 2003; Kern et al., 2004; Wendland-Carro, Piccinini, & Millar, 1999). Mothers can be taught how to interact more sensitively, affectionately, and responsively, paving the way for secure attachment and the lifelong benefits associated with a positive internal working model of interpersonal relationships.

Despite our knowledge that attachment relationships are essential to children's development and well-being, some children still fail to develop strong attachment relationships with any caregiver early in life. This can happen if caregivers are neglectful or abusive toward a child. It can also happen if no one primary caregiver is regularly available for a child, as in the case of children who are moved around from an early age to multiple foster home placements (Jones & Kruk, 2005; Millward, Kennedy, Towlson, & Minnis, 2006; Minnis, Everett, Pelosi, Dunn, & Knapp, 2006; Palmer, 1996).

As we saw earlier in the chapter, children at a very young age can demonstrate stranger wariness, in part due to their attachment to a primary caregiver and their subsequent unwillingness to be separated for very long, or at all, from that person, who is so very important to them. On the other hand, we also see children who will go from person to person without any objection at all, or who, at later ages, will readily approach unfamiliar adults and immediately become inappropriately friendly or affectionate with them. These children might approach people whom they barely know and tell them they love them or give hugs seemingly indiscriminately. This kind of behaviour can occur for a number of reasons, but one of those reasons is due to their failure to develop an attachment relationship with a primary caregiver. Conversely, children who have not had the opportunity to develop a strong attachment relationship sometimes respond with resistance, confusion, or inhibited behaviour toward caregivers. In either case, children who have disordered patterns of attachment in infancy or early childhood could be exhibiting signs of **reactive attachment disorder**, which is a pattern of inappropriate interpersonal behaviours in children thought to develop primarily from disruptions in formation of attachment to a primary caregiver early in life (Minde, 2003). Considerable controversy exists regarding the clinical treatment of attachment-related conditions, which is a relatively new area of clinical research (Chaffin et al., 2006).

Attachment behaviours also have been studied in children who have experienced profound privation as a result of living in an institutional setting such as an orphanage. **Privation** is a condition in which the basic necessities and comforts of life are not adequately provided. After political changes in Romanian society occurred in the late 1980s, hundreds of thousands of children were placed in orphanages, where they were extremely deprived of physical and emotional nurturance. Just over 1000 Romanian children were adopted by Canadian families shortly thereafter. Canadian researcher Chisholm, and colleagues, began to study the indiscriminate friendliness these children appeared to show toward others (Ames, 1997; Chisholm, 1998; Chisholm, Carter, Ames, & Morison, 1995). These researchers found that, although children respond with variability to situations of prolonged early institutional privation, they generally show disordered attachment behaviours and cognitive deficits. These challenges continue to be studied and are the focus of much ongoing research (Rutter, 1997; Zeanah & Gleason, 2015).

PARENTING SKILL, WORK, AND CHILD CARE.   Since the 1970s, the existence of more single-parent households and families with two working parents has made child care a fact of life for many North American families. Parents and policy makers alike have been concerned about the impact, in general, of such care on children and, more specifically, its impact on attachment. Is there, for example, a maximum amount of time per week that infants should spend in care outside the home or a minimum age below which infants should not be placed in care outside the home? The Child Development and Family Policy feature describes work that has attempted to answer these and other questions about the impact of early child care on children's development.

Reactive attachment disorder:
a mental disorder involving disturbances in emotional functioning and a pattern of inappropriate interpersonal behaviours in children, thought to result from disrupted early attachments.

Privation:
a condition in which the basic necessities and comforts of life are not adequately provided.

Child Development and Family Policy
Determining Guidelines for Infant and Toddler Child Care

The American National Institute of Child Health and Human Development conducted a longitudinal study on the impact of child care on American infants and toddlers. The researchers found no overall negative effect of child care on mother–infant attachment (NICHD Early Child Care Research Network, 1997). A secure mother–infant attachment was just as likely, regardless of child care quality, time spent in care, age entering care, frequency in care provider changeover, or type of child care (e.g., daycare, babysitter in the home).

However, when the effects of child care were considered along with characteristics of mothers, an important pattern was detected: When less sensitive and less responsive mothers placed their infants in low-quality child care, insecure attachments were more common. Poor-quality care added to the risks already present from poor parenting. Therefore, high-quality care does not disrupt attachment, but quality of parenting is essential to the development of secure attachment.

Gagne (2003) investigated the influence that parental employment and use of child care had on children's cognitive development. Gagne found that having parents who work and spending hours in child care had little effect on school readiness for most preschoolers. In addition, children from higher-income families who were in substitute care had better cognitive outcomes than children who came from lower-income families.

Gagne's findings might result from children of higher-income families having greater overall access to resources, including a higher quality of child care. However, Gagne also found that children with mothers who had higher levels of education and above-average parenting skills had higher cognitive outcomes when their mothers did not take jobs outside the family home. Similarly, children whose fathers had above-average levels of education had higher cognitive outcomes when their fathers worked part-time. In fact, Canadian parents who worked part-time spent considerably more time with their children than parents employed in full-time jobs (Applied Research Branch, 2003).

Researchers who conducted the Canadian Transition to Care study found that use of child care can buffer the otherwise negative effect of difficult infant temperament on mother–infant relationships (McKim, Cramer, Stuart, & O'Connor, 1999). Early entry into child care was linked to lower levels of maternal depression. On the other hand, employed mothers choosing to stay home tended to provide more unstable care for their children and to be more depressed than those who continued working and who wanted to work (McKim et al., 1999).

Commercial zoning now often includes a focus on children's needs, too.

Steve Rosset/Fotolia

While some benefits can be realized in child care, the care should be of high quality. In general, high-quality child care has the following features (Burchinal et al., 2000; Lamb, 1999; Rosenthal & Vandell, 1996):

- a low ratio of children to caregivers
- well-trained, experienced staff
- low staff turnover
- ample opportunities for educational and social stimulation
- effective communication between parents and daycare workers concerning the general aims and routine functioning of the daycare program

Collectively, these variables do not guarantee that a child will receive high-quality care. Sensitive, responsive caregiving—the same behaviour that promotes secure attachment relationships—is the real key to high-quality child care. Centres that have well-trained, experienced staff caring for a relatively small number of children are more likely to provide good care, but the only way to know the quality of care with certainty is to observe that care for yourself (Lamb, 1998).

Fortunately, employers have begun to realize that convenient, high-quality child care makes for a better employee. In Flint, Michigan, child care was part of the contract negotiated between the United Auto Workers and General Motors. Many cities have modified their zoning codes so that new shopping complexes and office buildings must include child-care facilities. Businesses are realizing that the availability of excellent child care helps attract and retain skilled employees. With effort, organization, and help from the community and businesses, full-time employment and high-quality caregiving can be compatible. In Canada, each province is responsible for setting standards for child care, and attention to issues pertaining to child-care delivery is coordinated by the National Association for the Education of Young Children (see www.naeyc.org).

Onset of Peer Interactions

LO7 **Summarize how infants and toddlers first interact with peers.**

First social relationships are usually with parents, but infants rapidly expand their social horizons. Peer interactions begin surprisingly early in infancy. Two 6-month-olds together will look, smile, and point at one another. Over the next few months, infants laugh and babble when with other infants (Hartup, 1983; Rubin, Bukowski, & Parker, 1998).

In parallel play, children play with toys on their own but often also watch each other.

Researchers at the Yale Center for Infant Cognition found that, between the ages of 6 and 10 months, infants begin to engage in social evaluation of people based on those people's behaviour toward others (Hamlin, Wynn, & Bloom, 2007). These researchers found that preverbal infants tend to prefer people who help others rather than harm or hinder others. In addition, they prefer a "neutral" individual to one who hinders others and prefer a helpful person to one who behaves neutrally toward others (Hamlin et al., 2007). Budding research from this Yale research suggests that infants may have a rudimentary sense of morality hard-wired from birth (Bloom, 2010), which would make sense, as the psychological processes involved in social cognition have a neural basis (Adolphs, 2009).

Beginning at about the first birthday and continuing through the preschool years, youngsters' peer relations rapidly become more complex. In a classic early study, Parten (1932) identified a developmental sequence that began with **nonsocial play**—children playing alone or watching others play but not playing themselves. Later, children progressed to more elaborate forms of play, with each child having a well-defined role. Today, researchers no longer share Parten's view that children move through each stage of play in a rigid sequence, but the different forms of play that she distinguished are useful nonetheless.

Nonsocial play: playing alone or watching others play.

The first type of social play to appear—soon after the first birthday—is **parallel play**: Youngsters play alone but maintain a keen interest in what other children are doing. During parallel play, exchanges between youngsters begin to occur. When one talks or smiles, the other usually responds (Howes, Unger, & Seidner, 1990).

Parallel play: playing alone but near others while maintaining an interest in what the others are doing.

Beginning around 15 to 18 months, toddlers no longer just watch one another at play. In **simple social play**, youngsters engage in similar activities, talk to or smile at one another, and offer each other toys. Play becomes truly interactive (Howes & Matheson, 1992). An example of simple social play would be two 20-month-olds pushing toy cars along the floor, making "car sounds," and periodically trading cars. Canadian research on social pretend play with children who have language impairments showed that social pretend play supports greater conversational richness between age peers than do other forms of play (DeKroon, Kyte, & Johnson, 2002). These researchers further noted that the quality of social play varied with the characteristics of the child's play partner in terms of such factors as interpersonal responsiveness, verbal skill, adaptability, and play theme knowledge.

Simple social play: youngsters interacting socially during play activities.

Toward the second birthday, youngsters begin to engage in **co-operative play**: Now children organize their play around a distinct theme and take on special roles based on that theme. For example, children might play hide-and-seek and alternate roles of hider and finder, or they might have a tea party and alternate being the host and guest.

Co-operative play: play that is organized around a distinct theme and involves children taking on special roles based on that theme.

This rapid progression toward more complex play continues during the preschool years.

Ask Yourself

How do an infant's behaviours contribute to the formation of attachment? How do the caregiver's behaviours contribute?

What responsibility might a government social service agency have to help ensure that infants in foster care develop good attachment relationships?

7.3 Self-Concept

Learning Objectives

After reading the module, you should be able to do the following:

LO8 Identify when infants first recognize themselves.

LO9 Describe how, following self-recognition, infants acquire a self-concept.

Self-concept:
attitudes, behaviours, and values that a person believes make the self unique.

A person's **self-concept** refers to the attitudes, behaviours, and values that a person believes make him or her a unique individual. Part of one teenage girl's self-concept is evident in her answer to the question "Who are you?"

> I'm sensitive, friendly, outgoing, popular, and tolerant, though I can also be shy, self-conscious, and even obnoxious! I'd like to be friendly and tolerant all of the time. That's the kind of person I want to be, and I'm disappointed when I'm not. I'm responsible, even studious now and then, but on the other hand, I'm a goof-off, too, because if you're too studious, you won't be popular. (Harter, 1990, p. 352)

As an adult, your answer to the "Who are you?" question is probably even more complex because, after all, most people are complex beings. But how did you acquire this complex self-concept? How do young children learn to recognize themselves and understand who they are? We'll answer these questions in this module, beginning with the origins of an infant's sense of self.

Origins of Self-Recognition

LO8 Identify when infants first recognize themselves.

What is the starting point for children's development of self-concept? Following the lead of the nineteenth-century philosopher and psychologist William James, modern researchers believe that the foundation of self-concept is the child's awareness that he or she exists. At some point early in life, children must realize that they exist independently of other people and objects in the environment and that their existence continues over time (Frye & Zelazo, 2003).

Measuring the onset of this awareness is not easy. Obviously, we can't simply ask a 3-year-old, "So, tell me, when did you first realize that you existed and that you weren't simply part of the furniture?" A less direct approach is needed. One interesting way that investigators have tried to measure self-awareness is through the use of a mirror. In the latter part of their first year, babies sometimes touch the face in the mirror or wave at it, but none of their behaviours indicates that they recognize themselves in the mirror. Instead, babies act as if the face in the mirror is simply a very interesting stimulus.

This baby needs to learn that the reflection in the mirror is of herself.

How would we know that infants recognize themselves in a mirror? One clever approach is to have the parent surreptitiously place a red mark on the infant's nose while wiping the baby's face. Then, the infant is returned to the mirror. Many 1-year-olds touch the red mark on the mirror, showing that they notice the mark on the face in the mirror. By 15 months, however, an important change occurs: Babies see the red mark in the mirror, then reach up and touch their own noses. By age 2, virtually all children do this (Bullock & Lütkenhaus, 1990; Lewis & Brooks-Gunn, 1979). When older toddlers notice the red mark in the mirror, they understand that the funny-looking nose in the mirror is their own.

Do you doubt that the mirror task shows an infant's emerging sense of self? Perhaps you think it tells more about an infant's growing understanding of mirrors than the baby's self-awareness. One way to examine this possibility would be to test infants who have never seen mirrors previously. Priel and deSchonen (1986) took this approach, testing infants from Israeli desert communities. These babies had never seen mirrors or, for that matter, virtually any reflective surfaces because they lived in tents. Nevertheless, the same developmental trend appeared in the desert infants as in a comparison group of infants living in a nearby city. No 6- to 12-month-olds in either group touched their noses after they saw the mark, some 13- to 19-month-olds did, and nearly all the 20- to 26-month-olds did.

We don't need to rely solely on the mirror task to know that self-awareness emerges between 18 and 24 months. During this same period, toddlers look more at photographs of themselves than at photos of other children. Also, toddlers tend to refer to themselves by name or with a personal pronoun, such as "I" or "me," and sometimes they know their age and their gender. These changes suggest that self-awareness is well established in most children by age 2 (Lewis, 1987).

As you might imagine, toddlers' self-awareness is quite fragile initially. To illustrate, in one study (Povinelli & Simon, 1998), 3-year-olds were videotaped playing a game, during which an experimenter surreptitiously placed a sticker on the child's head. A few minutes later, children watched a videotape of themselves playing the game. Although almost all children recognized themselves in the videotape, fewer than half reached up to take the sticker off their head. (In contrast, virtually all 4-year-olds reached.) The results suggested that toddlers' self-awareness is not strongly linked across time but is, instead, focused largely on the present. Young children seemingly don't make the connection between the current self ("I am watching a videotape") and the previous self ("Just a few minutes ago, there was a sticker on my head").

Youngsters' growing self-recognition probably reflects their cognitive development. For example, when children with Down syndrome achieve a mental age of about 18 months, they typically recognize themselves in the mirror task (Loveland, 1987a, 1987b). Apparently, self-recognition requires cognitive skills that usually emerge sometime in the middle of the second year, and it emerges after the establishment of deferred imitation skills (Nielsen & Dissanayake, 2004).

Moving beyond Self-Recognition

LO9 **Describe how, following self-recognition, infants acquire a self-concept.**

Once self-awareness is established, children begin to acquire a self-concept. That is, once children fully understand that they exist and that they have a unique mental life,

Self-awareness changes children's interactions with peers.

they begin to wonder who they are. They want to define themselves. How do children develop a self-concept?

Some important insights into the early phases of this process came from work by Laura Levine (1983), who studied 20- to 28-month-olds. This is the period when children are just beginning to become self-aware. Children were tested on several measures of self-awareness, including the mirror recognition task. They were also observed as they interacted with an unfamiliar peer in a playroom filled with toys. The key finding was that children who were self-aware were much more likely to say "Mine!" while playing with toys than children who were not yet self-aware.

Maybe you think these self-aware children were being confrontational in saying "Mine," as in, "This car is mine, and don't even think about taking it," but they weren't. Actually, self-aware children were more likely to make positive comments during peer interactions. Levine argued that claiming toys from other children was an important way of defining the self within the social world and was not simply an aggressive or negative act.

As toddlers grow, their self-concepts rapidly move beyond claiming possessions and become much more elaborate.

Ask Yourself

According to Piaget's theory and the information-processing perspective, what specific cognitive changes might be crucial in order for children to become self-aware?

What are the key times that crucial developmental skills emerge in infants and toddlers? Make a chart for yourself of the typical times language, motor, social, and cognitive skills emerge in the first two years of life.

7.4 Temperament

∨ Learning Objectives

After reading the module, you should be able to do the following:

LO10 List the different features of temperament.

LO11 Discuss how heredity and environment influence temperament.

LO12 Identify how stable a child's temperament is across childhood.

LO13 Describe the consequences of different temperaments.

Temperament:
an infant's consistent mood and style of behaviour.

When you've observed young babies, were some babies quiet most of the time while others cried often and impatiently? Maybe you saw some infants who responded warmly to strangers and others who seemed very shy. An infant's consistent mood and style of behaviour is referred to as **temperament**. Temperament does not refer so much to what babies do as to how they do what they do. For example, all babies become upset occasionally and cry. However, some recover quickly, while others are very hard to console. These differences in emotion and style of behaviour are evident in the first few weeks after birth and remain important throughout life.

Let's start this module by looking at different ways that psychologists define temperament.

What Is Temperament?

LO10 **List the different features of temperament.**

Alexander Thomas and Stella Chess (Chess & Thomas, 1986; Thomas, Chess, & Birch, 1968) pioneered the study of temperament. In 1956, they began the New York Longitudinal Study, tracing the lives of 141 individuals from infancy through adulthood. Thomas and Chess gathered their initial data by interviewing the babies' parents and asking individuals unfamiliar with the children to observe them at home. Based on these interviews and observations, Thomas and Chess evaluated the behaviour of the 141 infants along the nine temperamental dimensions listed in Table 7–1.

Using these nine dimensions, Thomas and Chess could place most infants into one of three groups. About 40 percent of the babies were categorized as "easy" babies. These infants were usually happy and cheerful, tended to adjust well to new situations, and followed regular routines for eating, sleeping, and toileting. About 10 percent of the babies were categorized as "difficult." As you might imagine, in many respects they were the opposite of the easy babies: Difficult babies were often unhappy, did not adjust well to new situations, and followed irregular routines for eating and sleeping. Difficult babies tended to withdraw from novel experiences, and they responded intensely to novel stimulation.

In addition, about 15 percent of the babies were categorized as "slow-to-warm-up." Like difficult babies, slow-to-warm-up babies tended to be unhappy and did not adjust well when placed in new situations. Unlike difficult babies, slow-to-warm-up babies did not respond intensely, and they tended to be relatively inactive. The remaining babies—roughly one-third—did not fit into any of the groups; in general, they rated as average on most of the nine dimensions.

Although the New York Longitudinal Study launched the modern study of infant temperament, not all investigators agree with Thomas and Chess's nine dimensions and three groups. For example, Arnold Buss and Robert Plomin (1975, 1984) proposed that temperament involves three primary dimensions—emotionality, activity, and sociability. **Emotionality** refers to the strength of the infant's emotional response to a situation, the ease with which that response is triggered, and the ease with which

Emotionality:
the strength of an emotional response to a situation, the ease with which that response is triggered, and the ease of return to a nonemotional state.

Table 7–1 Dimensions of Temperament in the New York Longitudinal Study

Dimension	Description
Activity level	Amount of physical and motor activity in daily situations
Rhythmicity	Regularity in eating, sleeping, toileting
Approach/withdrawal	Response to a novel object (accepting vs. rejecting)
Distractibility	Ease with which ongoing activity is disrupted by competing stimuli
Adaptability	Ease with which the child adjusts to changes in the environment
Intensity of reaction	Energy level of the child's responses
Mood	Balance between happy and unhappy behaviour
Threshold	Level of stimulation needed for the child to respond
Attention span and persistence	Amount of time devoted to an activity, particularly with obstacles or distractions present

Activity:
the tempo and vigour of a child's movements.

Sociability:
the extent to which a person prefers to be with other people.

the infant can be returned to a nonemotional state. At one extreme are infants whose emotional responses are strong, easily triggered, and not easily calmed; at the other extreme are infants whose responses are subdued, relatively difficult to elicit, and readily soothed. **Activity** refers to the tempo and vigour of a child's movements. Active infants are always busy, like to explore their environment, and enjoy vigorous play. Inactive infants have a more controlled behavioural tempo and are more likely to enjoy quiet play. **Sociability** is the extent to which a person prefers to be with other people. Some infants relish contact with others, seek their attention, and prefer play that involves other people. Other infants enjoy solitude and are quite content to play alone with toys.

Solitary play can be enjoyable.

If you compare these three dimensions with the nine listed in Table 7–1, you'll see a great deal of overlap. For example, Buss and Plomin's emotionality dimension combines the intensity and threshold dimensions of Thomas and Chess's study. In fact, the major theories of temperament include many of the same elements (Shiner, 1998). Schmidt, from McMaster University, and Fox, from the University of Maryland, teamed up to perform a longitudinal study (2002) of individual differences in behaviour and temperament in children. They followed children from the first few months of life into their preschool years and found two main types of child temperament: bold/exuberant and shy/socially withdrawn. After observing children into the preschool years, Schmidt and Fox (2002) concluded that these temperament types remain relatively stable for the first four years of a child's life and that certain genetically linked characteristics of behaviour and physiology are associated with the two temperaments.

Hereditary and Environmental Contributions to Temperament

LO11 Discuss how heredity and environment influence temperament.

While researchers like Schmidt and Fox look for the genetic underpinnings of children's temperament, most theorists agree that temperament reflects both heredity and experience. The influence of heredity is shown in twin studies: Identical twins are more alike in most aspects of temperament than fraternal twins. For example, Goldsmith, Buss, and Lemery (1997) found that the correlation for identical twins' activity level was 0.72, but the correlation for fraternal twins was only 0.38. In other words, if one identical twin is temperamentally active, the other usually is too. Goldsmith et al. (1997) also found that identical twins were more alike than fraternal twins with respect to social fearfulness (shyness), persistence, and proneness to anger.

Recently, scientists looking for links between genes and temperament came up with a surprising finding: Infants and toddlers who are upset by novel stimulation (and who often become shy preschoolers) have narrower faces than youngsters who respond calmly to novel stimulation (Arcus & Kagan, 1995). This observation is interesting because the brain and the facial skeleton originate from the same set of cells during prenatal development. Thus, one fascinating hypothesis is that genes influence levels of hormones that affect both facial growth and temperament.

The environment, including parenting, also contributes to children's temperament, perhaps even more than researchers previously acknowledged (Roisman & Fraley, 2006). Positive emotionality—youngsters who laugh often, seem to be generally happy, and often express pleasure—seems to reflect environmental influences (Goldsmith et al., 1997). Conversely, infants more often develop intense, difficult temperaments when mothers are abrupt in dealing with them and lack confidence (Belsky, Fish, & Isabella, 1991).

Heredity and experience both play a part in children's development. The Children and Families around the World feature tells us more about this story.

There's no question that heredity and experience cause babies' temperaments to differ, but how stable is temperament across infancy and the toddler years? We'll find out in the next section.

Identical twins are usually more temperamentally alike than fraternal twins.

Felix Mizioznikov/Fotolia

Stability of Temperament

LO12 **Identify how stable a child's temperament is across childhood.**

Do calm, easygoing babies grow up to be calm, easygoing children, adolescents, and adults? Are difficult, irritable infants destined to grow up to be cranky, whiny children? The first answers to these questions came from the Fels Longitudinal Project, a study of many aspects of physical and psychological development from infancy. Although not a study of temperament per se, Jerome Kagan and his collaborators (Kagan, 1989; Kagan & Moss, 1962) found that fearful preschoolers in the Fels project tended to be inhibited as older children and adolescents.

Spurred by findings like this one, later investigators attempted to learn more about the stability of temperament. Their research shows that temperament is somewhat stable during the infant and toddler years. An active fetus is more likely to be an

Children and Families around the World

Do Babies from Different Cultures Cry the Same?

If you've ever watched an infant receiving a vaccination, you know the inevitable response. After the syringe is removed, the infant's eyes open wide, and the baby begins to cry. Infants differ in how intensely they cry and in how readily they are soothed, reflecting differences in the emotionality dimension of temperament. Virtually all North American babies cry, making it easy to suppose that crying is a universal response to the pain from the inoculation—but it's not.

In stressful situations like getting a shot, Japanese and Chinese infants are less likely to cry (Kagan et al., 1994). Lewis, Ramsay, and Kawakami (1993) found that most European American 4-month-olds cried loudly within five seconds of an injection, but only half the Japanese

babies in their study cried. Furthermore, when Japanese and Chinese babies become upset, they are soothed more readily than European American babies. Lewis and his colleagues found that about three-fourths of the Japanese babies were no longer crying 90 seconds after the injection compared to fewer than half of the European American babies.

Why are Asian infants less visibly emotional than their North American counterparts? Heredity might be involved. Perhaps the genes that contribute to emotionality are less common among Asians than among European Americans, but we can't overlook experience. Compared to European American mothers, Japanese mothers spend more time in close physical contact with their babies, constantly and gently soothing them; this might reduce the tendency to respond emotionally.

Gina Smith/Fotolia

Infant temperament can affect how parents interact with babies.

active infant and is also more likely to be a difficult, unadaptive infant (DiPietro et al., 1996). Newborns who cry under moderate stress tend, as 5-month-olds, to cry when they are placed in stressful situations (Stifter & Fox, 1990). Also, as we mentioned before, infants who are frightened or upset by novel stimulation tend to be inhibited and less sociable as preschoolers (Kagan, Snidman, & Arcus, 1998).

Therefore, evidence suggests that temperament is at least somewhat stable throughout infancy and the toddler years (Lemery, Goldsmith, Klinnert, & Mrazek, 1999). Of course, the links are not perfect. For example, some fearful infants became sociable preschoolers, and some infants who responded calmly to novel stimulation became inhibited as preschoolers.

Though temperament is only moderately stable during infancy and toddlerhood, it can still shape development in important ways. For example, an infant's temperament might determine the experiences that parents provide. Parents might read more to quiet babies but play more physical games with their active babies. These different experiences, driven by the infants' temperaments, contribute to each infant's development, despite the fact that the infants' temperaments could change over the years. In the next section, we'll see some of the connections between temperament and other aspects of development.

Temperament and Other Aspects of Development

LO13 Describe the consequences of different temperaments.

One of the goals of Thomas and Chess's study was to discover temperamental features of infants that would predict later psychological adjustment. In fact, Thomas and Chess discovered that about two-thirds of the preschoolers with difficult temperaments had developed behavioural problems by the time they entered school. In contrast, fewer than one-fifth of the children with easy temperaments had behavioural problems (Thomas et al., 1968).

Other scientists have followed Thomas and Chess's lead in looking for links between temperament and outcomes of development, and they found that temperament is an important influence on development. Here are some illustrative examples:

- Persistent children are likely to succeed in school, whereas active and distractible children are less likely to succeed (Martin, Olejnik, & Gaddis, 1994).

- Shy, inhibited children often have difficulty interacting with their peers and often do not cope effectively with problems (Eisenberg, Shepard, Fabes, Murphy, & Guthrie, 1998; Kochanska & Radke-Yarrow, 1992).

- Anxious, fearful children are more likely to comply with a parent's rules and requests, even when the parent is not present (Kochanska, 1995).

- Extroverted, uninhibited toddlers are more likely to have accidents that cause injury (Schwebel & Plumert, 1999).

Temperament also influences children's behaviour toward other people. When people are in obvious distress, some children readily step forward to help, but others seem reluctant to help. Young, Fox, and Zahn-Waxler (1999) argued that temperament might be part of the answer. Specifically, inhibited, shy youngsters might find it difficult to overcome their reticence to help another, particularly when they do not know the person and when the other person does not specifically request help. Young and her colleagues examined this hypothesis by studying inhibition and helping in 2-year-olds.

These researchers videotaped children interacting with their mother and a stranger during free play. During the session, the experimenter pretended that she had caught her fingers in the clipboard and was injured. Later in the session, the mother also feigned an injury by bumping into a chair. While pretending to be injured, the experimenter and the mother did not solicit the child's help in any way, either directly (e.g., by saying, "Help me, help me") or indirectly (e.g., by calling the child's name). Later, observers scored children's behaviours on several dimensions, including avoiding the experimenter (inhibition), expressing concern for the injured person (concerned expression), or offering ways of reducing distress (helpful behaviour).

Figure 7–3 shows some correlations between inhibition and the two variables expressing concern and helping behaviour in the study. With regard to the mothers, neither correlation is significant, which indicates that, when interacting with their moms, shy and outgoing children were equally likely to express concern and to provide help. The results differ for helping the experimenter. The correlation between inhibition and expressing concern is, again, small, indicating that shy and outgoing youngsters were equally likely to express concern when the experimenter feigned injury. However, the correlation between inhibition and helping was negative: Shy, inhibited 2-year-olds were less likely than outgoing 2-year-olds to help an experimenter who appeared to be hurt.

As a result, the researchers concluded that a young child's temperament helps to predict whether that child will help. When mothers and experimenters feigned injury, both shy and outgoing children noticed and were disturbed by their mothers' distress. Outgoing children typically translated this concern into action, helping both mothers and experimenters. In contrast, shy youngsters helped mothers but could not overcome their reluctance to help an unfamiliar adult who was not asking for help. Even though shy children see that a person is suffering, their apprehensiveness in unfamiliar social settings may prevent them from helping.

Even more impressive are the findings from longitudinal studies showing that children's temperament predicts important aspects of adults' lives. In a study conducted in Sweden (Kerr, Lambert, & Bem, 1996), shy boys and girls married later than non-shy children. In addition, shy boys became fathers later than non-shy boys, and shy girls were less educated than non-shy girls.

Figure 7–3

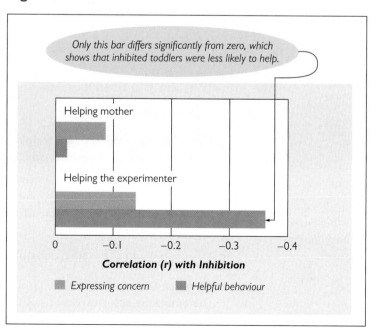

Only this bar differs significantly from zero, which shows that inhibited toddlers were less likely to help.

Helping mother

Helping the experimenter

0   −0.1   −0.2   −0.3   −0.4

Correlation (r) with Inhibition

■ *Expressing concern*   ■ *Helpful behaviour*

Although these findings underscore that temperament is an important force in infants' and toddlers' development, temperament rarely acts alone. Instead, the influence of temperament often depends on the environment in which children develop. To illustrate, let's consider the link between temperament and behaviour problems. Infants and toddlers who temperamentally resist control—they are difficult to manage, often unresponsive, and sometimes impulsive—tend to be prone to behaviour problems, particularly aggression, when they are older. However, more careful analysis shows that resistant temperament leads to behaviour problems primarily when mothers do not exert much control over their children. Among mothers who do exert control—they prohibit, warn, and scold their children when necessary—resistant temperament is not linked to behaviour problems (Bates et al., 1998).

Similarly, young children who are anxious and fearful tend to be more compliant. But, again, careful analysis shows this is true only when parents encourage compliance with discipline that elicits mild distress (Kochanska, 1997). When a parent asks a child to pick up toys promptly or be punished, fearful, anxious children are more likely to comply than fearless children because fearful children worry about the possibility of punishment. However, when parents seek compliance by encouraging their children to co-operate, anxious temperament is no longer linked to compliance: If a parent asks a child to pick up toys because it will be helpful to the parent, fearful and fearless children are equally likely to comply.

Thus, the relation between temperament and compliance to a parent's request depends very much on how that request is framed. Only by considering these other factors can we understand links between temperament and development.

Ask Yourself

What are the biological bases of temperament? How do nature and nurture interact to influence temperament?

What Would a Babysitter Do?

Mabel and Terry are beginning to notice aspects of Sophie's personality even though she is still very young. As the family's babysitter, you can see that Sophie is starting to assert herself more when around others and that she doesn't always listen when spoken to. As a babysitter who is with Sophie four hours an evening, twice per week, what could you do to help Sophie listen when you ask her to pick up her toys or get ready for bed? What would help, and what would not help for a child of Sophie's age?

Summary

7.1 Emotions

Basic Emotions

- Psychologists often use infants' facial expressions to judge when different emotional states emerge in development.

- The earliest indicator of happiness is the social smile, which emerges at about 2 months; laughter appears at about 4 months.

- Anger and fear are both evident by about 6 months of age.

- Fear first appears in infancy as stranger wariness.

Complex Emotions

- Complex emotions have an evaluative component and include guilt, embarrassment, and pride.

- Complex emotions appear between 18 and 24 months and require more sophisticated cognitive skills than basic emotions like happiness and fear.

Recognizing and Using Others' Emotions

- By 6 months, infants have begun to recognize the emotions associated with different facial expressions.

- Infants use information about emotion to help them evaluate unfamiliar people and situations.

Regulating Emotions

- Infants use simple strategies (e.g., looking away) to regulate emotions such as fear.

7.2 Relationships with Others

The Growth of Attachment

- Attachment is an enduring social-emotional relationship between infant and parent or primary caregiver.

- Many behaviours that contribute to the formation of attachment are biologically programmed.

- By about 6 or 7 months, infants have identified a primary attachment figure, typically the mother, but later become attached to other family members, including fathers, siblings, and extended family members.

Quality of Attachment

- The research procedure known as the Strange Situation, in which infant and mother are separated briefly, reveals four primary forms of attachment: secure, avoidant, resistant, and disorganized.

- Secure attachment is most common and involves infants having complete trust in the mother.

- In avoidant attachment, infants deal with lack of trust by ignoring the mother.

- In resistant attachment, infants seem angry with the mother.

- In disorganized (disoriented) attachment, infants seem to not understand the mother's absence.

- Children with secure attachment relationships during infancy often interact with their peers more skillfully.

- Secure attachment is most likely to occur when mothers respond sensitively and consistently to their infants.

- Adults who have autonomous representations of attachment to their own parents are most likely to use the sensitive caregiving that promotes secure attachments in their own children.

- Child care in Canada is common and may involve being cared for by a relative or sitter in the family's home, in a daycare provider's home, or in a daycare centre.

- Attachment relationships in infants and toddlers are not harmed by high-quality child care.

- Responsive parenting is important to the development of secure attachment.

Onset of Peer Interactions

- Children have a developing sense of morality from about 6 months of age.

- Children's first real peer interactions, at about 12 to 15 months, take the form of parallel play, in which infants play alone while watching each other.

- Simple social play emerges later, in which toddlers engage in similar activities and interact with one another.

- At about 2 years, co-operative play organized around a theme becomes common.

7.3 Self-Concept

Origins of Self-Recognition

- At about 15 months, infants begin to recognize themselves in the mirror, one of the first signs of self-awareness.

- At about 15 months, infants also begin to prefer to look at pictures of themselves, to refer to themselves by name and with personal pronouns, and sometimes to know their age and gender.

- By 2 years most children have the rudiments of self-awareness, but this early understanding is fragile.

Moving beyond Self-Recognition

- After toddlers become self-aware, they begin to acquire a self-concept.

- Material possessions are one of the first elements involved in young children's developing self-concepts.

7.4 Temperament

What Is Temperament?

- Temperament refers to stable patterns of behaviour that are evident soon after birth.

- The New York Longitudinal Study researchers have suggested three temperamental patterns: easy, difficult, and slow-to-warm-up.

- Other research suggests that the dimensions of temperament are emotionality, activity, and sociability.

- The major theories of temperament include many of the same elements organized differently.

Hereditary and Environmental Contributions to Temperament

- Major theorists agree that both heredity and environment contribute to temperament.

- For many dimensions of temperament, identical twins are more alike than fraternal twins.

- Positive emotionality reflects environmental influences, and difficult temperament is linked to abrupt parenting.

Stability of Temperament

- Temperament is somewhat stable during infancy and the toddler years and moderately stable into childhood and adolescence.

- For many children, temperament does change as they develop.

Temperament and Other Aspects of Development

- Many investigators have shown that temperament is related to other aspects of development.

- Difficult babies are more likely to have behavioural problems by the time they are old enough to attend school.

- Persistent children are more successful in school.

- Shy children sometimes have problems with peers.

- Anxious children are more compliant with parents.

- Inhibited children are less likely to help a stranger in distress.

- The impact of temperament always depends on the environment in which children develop.

Chapter Critical Review

1. Explain why stranger wariness (Module 7.1) and attachment (Module 7.2) are adaptive responses.

2. How does an infant's or child's temperament (Module 7.4) affect the development of attachments (Module 7.2) and the development of social behaviour (Module 7.2)? Give several examples of your own to demonstrate the interactions between the various factors discussed in the text.

3. Imagine that your best friend is the mother of a 3-month-old. Your friend is about to return to her job as an architect, but she's afraid that she'll harm her baby by going back to work. What could you say to reassure her?

4. How might sensory and perceptual skills contribute to the formation of attachment between infants and caregivers?

See for Yourself

Arrange to visit a local daycare centre where you can unobtrusively observe toddlers for several days. In Canadian colleges and universities, ethical approval is required from an Ethics Review Board in order to perform a project or observation of this nature, so make sure you have proper ethics approval in place before observing children in a daycare setting. Your child development instructor would be able to assist you with this kind of approval application. Once you're at the daycare centre, and you are observing the children, see if you can detect temperamental differences. Can you identify an emotional child, an active child, and a social child? Also, notice how adults respond to the youngsters. Confirm whether or not the same behaviours lead to different responses from adults, depending on the child's temperament. See for yourself!

Chapter 8
Physical Growth in Preschool Children

Kimberly Reinick/Fotolia

 MODULE

8.1 Physical Growth

8.2 Motor Development

8.3 Health and Wellness

Connect to My Virtual Child

What kinds of theories do you have about children? What ideas inform your thoughts and beliefs about the lives of children, how they are raised, and the nature of the human person? Use your access card and follow this link www.myvirtualchild.com to learn more about the world of the child. You can even virtually try to raise your own child.

One sunny Saturday morning, while Terry and Mabel were having morning coffee, Sophie came out of her bedroom and turned slowly in a circle with a big grin on her face. She was wearing a pair of blue pants and a bright pink shirt. The buttons on the shirt were done up unevenly, and she had shoes on, but they were on the wrong feet. Sophie smiled at her parents and exclaimed, "I dressed myself!" Terry and Mabel wondered . . . how did little Sophie grow up so fast?

8.1 Physical Growth

 ## Learning Objectives

After reading the module, you should be able to do the following:

LO1 Describe the changes that take place in preschool children's growing bodies.

LO2 Explain how the brain becomes more powerful during the preschool years.

LO3 Discuss how much preschool children sleep and the problems that sometimes disrupt their sleep.

The preschool years are a time of continued physical growth, and individual differences in growth become obvious. We'll begin this module by examining these physical changes and then look at changes in brain functioning. We'll end the module with a discussion of sleep, an important contributor to children's growth.

Body Growth

LO1 Describe the changes that take place in preschool children's growing bodies.

Growth during the preschool years is not nearly as rapid as during the infant and toddler years. The average 2-year-old boy or girl is about 85 centimetres tall and weighs about 13 kilograms; over the next four years, both gain about 5 to 8 centimetres and 1.8 kilograms a year, so that, as 6-year-olds, they're about 112 centimetres tall and weigh 20.5 kilograms.

As was true for infants and toddlers, the range of individual normal growth for preschoolers is amazing. The graphs in Figure 8–1 show height and weight for children at the 5th and 95th percentiles, which represent the limits of normal growth; they also show height and weight for average children. The averages are combined

Figure 8–1

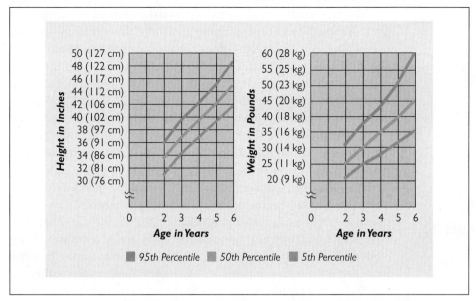

SOURCE: Based on data from World Health Organization Multicentre Study Group. (2006). WHO child growth standards based on length/height, weight and age. Acta Paediatrica, Suppl. 450, 76–85.

for boys and girls because gender differences in physical development are negligible during the preschool years. A 4-year-old child in the 95th percentile for weight is half again heavier (6.4 kilograms) than a child in the 5th percentile. Both are normal, but the difference is huge, particularly when you see the difference in actual 4-year-olds rather than as abstract points on a chart.

Because growth is stable during the preschool years, at this age we can more accurately predict a child's height as an adult. Weight isn't nearly as easy to predict because it's based on more factors than height and is more variable through adulthood.

The Canadian Paediatric Society (2004) publishes guidelines for the stunting/shortness and underweight/wasting categories. In these categories, children scoring below the 3rd percentile for height and weight on the growth charts are considered to be below recommended height and weight guidelines compared with age peers. Canadian-established guidelines also exist for overweight, obese, and head-circumference classifications (Canadian Paediatric Society, 2004). Weight-related guidelines for overweight and obese children tend to use the body mass index as a measure, with children being at or over the 85th percentile considered overweight and children at or over the 97th percentile considered obese relative to age peers (Canadian Paediatric Society, 2004). In terms of head circumference, children up to 3 years of age are considered at risk for health, nutritional, or developmental problems if their head circumference is at or under the 3rd percentile or at or over the 97th percentile relative to other children their age (Canadian Paediatric Society, 2004).

During childhood, increases in height and weight are accompanied by changes in body shape and appearance that make the preschool child's body appear more mature. The leg growth begins to catch up to that of the trunk. As you can see in Figure 8–2, older preschoolers have the body proportions of older children instead of the infant's top-heavy look. Also, preschoolers lose baby fat, which makes their bodies appear more slender and less like the chubby look of an infant.

Over the preschool years, muscles develop, and more cartilage turns to bone. These changes help to make children stronger. However, as bone becomes harder, it becomes more likely to break, not bend. Consequently, a

Figure 8–2

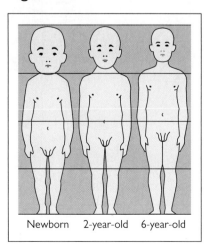

Newborn   2-year-old   6-year-old

Figure 8–3

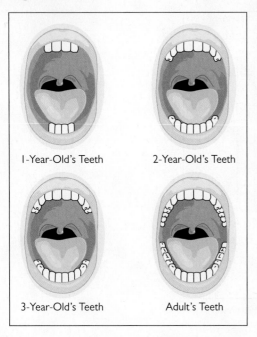

1-Year-Old's Teeth   2-Year-Old's Teeth

3-Year-Old's Teeth   Adult's Teeth

hard fall that would have only bruised a toddler is more likely to fracture an older child's bone.

The preschool years also produce remarkable changes in children's teeth. Although teeth begin forming prenatally, the first tooth—usually one of the lower front teeth—does not appear until 6 to 10 months of age. By 1 year, many infants have 4 teeth, and by age 3, children typically have all 20 primary (baby) teeth, shown in Figure 8–3. From 3 to 6 years, tooth development remains stable, but at about 5 or 6 years, children begin to lose primary teeth and permanent teeth begin to erupt.

Proper dental care should begin as soon as the first tooth appears. The Canadian Dental Association recommends that children visit a dentist within six months of the first tooth emerging or by the child's first birthday, and every six months after that, unless the child's dentist recommends another treatment schedule based on that child's particular dental needs (Canadian Dental Association, 2003). The Canadian Dental Association (2003) also recommends that parents use a soft, damp cloth to clean children's gums prior to the first tooth coming in. After teeth begin to emerge, parents are instructed to use a soft toothbrush regularly, offer healthy foods, and limit the number of treats children eat that contain sugar. (Care of children's primary teeth is particularly important, as disease in primary teeth can affect development of the permanent teeth that are forming and emerging from below them.)

Brain Development

LO2 Explain how the brain becomes more powerful during the preschool years.

Figure 8–4

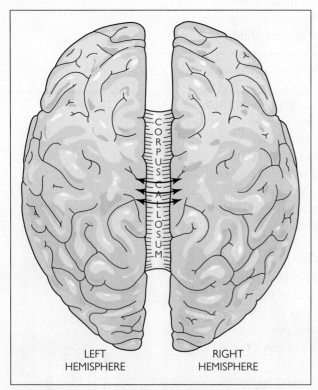

LEFT
HEMISPHERE

RIGHT
HEMISPHERE

SOURCE: From Martini, Frederic H.; Nath, Judi L., *Anatomy & Physiology*, 2nd Ed., (c) 2010, p. 413. Reprinted and Electronically reproduced by permission of Pearson Education, Inc., Upper Saddle River, New Jersey.

The preschool years are a time of rapid growth in the brain. In a normally developing child, the brain has reached 80 percent of its mature weight by age 3 and more than 90 percent by age 5. To put these numbers in perspective, typical 5-year-old children have achieved only 30 percent of their overall body weight. Therefore, the brain grows much more quickly than the body overall.

The preschool brain also changes in several ways that help it to operate more efficiently. The connective tissues on neurons that are understimulated are "pruned" back, and the pruning continues through the preschool years and again in adolescence (Woo & Crowell, 2005). Another process, myelinization, also progresses during the preschool years. One region that becomes myelinated during the preschool years is the corpus callosum. As you can see in Figure 8–4, the corpus callosum consists of bundles of neurons that link the left and right hemispheres. Myelinization of the corpus callosum is important because it allows the hemispheres to communicate more effectively with each other. Myelinization of other areas of the brain, such as those involved in perception, motor skills, and memory, could lead to better capacity in terms of memory and perceptual-motor coordination (Kail & Salthouse, 1994; Miller & Vernon, 1992; Todd, Swarzenski, Rossi, & Visconti, 1995; Witelson & Kigar, 1988). Stronger connectivity between synapses has also been implicated in better working-memory-related brain activity in childhood (Edin, Macoveanu, Olesen, Tegner, & Klingberg, 2007).

As the child matures, the brain also continues to become more specialized. Language-related skills, such as speaking and comprehending speech, become more localized in the brain's left hemisphere; skills associated with understanding emotions and comprehending spatial relations become more localized in the right hemisphere (Hellige, 1994). Such specialization allows the brain to operate more efficiently but at a price—the more specialized the brain is, the less plasticity it has. A highly plastic brain is one that has more area available for reorganization; therefore, it is more readily able to recover from injury or adapt to functional loss, especially since other areas of the brain sometimes are able to take over functions lost through injury or disease (Johnston, 2004).

Sleep

LO3 Discuss how much preschool children sleep and the problems that sometimes disrupt their sleep.

Sleep is an important element in children's growth because most growth hormone (GH) is secreted when children are sleeping. In fact, sleep routines should be well established by the preschool years. In Figure 8–5, you can see that 2-year-olds spend about 13 hours sleeping, compared to just under 11 hours for 6-year-olds. The chart also shows an important transition that typically occurs at about age 4, when most youngsters give up their afternoon nap and sleep longer at night to compensate. This can be a challenging time for caregivers who like to use naptime as an opportunity to complete some work or to relax.

Following an active day, preschool children often drift off to sleep easily. However, most children will have an occasional night when bedtime is a struggle. Furthermore, for approximately 20 to 30 percent of preschool children, bedtime struggles occur nightly (Lozoff, Wolf, & Davis, 1985). More often than not, these bedtime problems reflect the absence of a regular bedtime routine that's followed consistently. Getting children ready for bed can be a wonderful end to the day—a private, quiet time that's enjoyed by parent and child. However, bedtime can also be frustrating and trying when children resist going to bed. The key to a pleasant bedtime is to establish a bedtime routine that helps children wind down from busy daytime activities. This routine should start and end at about the same times every night and should be followed as closely as possible. The younger the child, the more a parent will be required to help directly with and supervise aspects of this routine, such as bathing and brushing teeth.

A good bedtime routine usually takes from 15 to 45 minutes to complete, depending on the child. As children go through the steps in the routine, parents can ask them, "What's next?" (followed by enthusiastic praise when they give the right answer!). This kind of prompting helps children be aware of and remember the routine until they have mastered it themselves. It's best not to rush through the bedtime routine. Most children know when their parents aren't really paying attention to them. A rushed bedtime routine will make a child more uptight than relaxed and likely will result in the child having a hard time settling down to sleep easily.

Sometimes, just when children get settled into bed, they want to talk. This is normal. As children relax, they do what adults often do—think about their day. This can be a good time to converse or reflect quietly with your child about people and events; however, it isn't a good

Figure 8–5

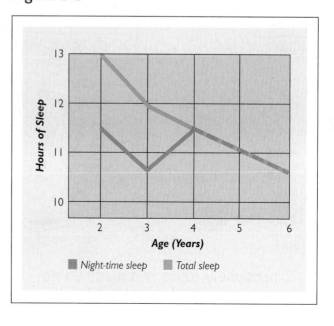

Hours of Sleep vs. Age (Years)

Night-time sleep   Total sleep

Good routines reinforce healthy bedtimes.

Nightmares:

dreaming that occurs toward morning that is vivid, frightening, and usually wakes the child.

Night terrors:

waking in a panicked state, breathing rapidly and perspiring heavily.

"I purposely keep it a mess so no monsters move in."

time for boisterous jokes and excited talk or for bringing up issues that are upsetting. If your child mentions something during this time that is a bigger topic of conversation than bedtime permits, reassure your child about the concern and then remember to talk about the problem the next day at a better time—unless, of course, it's an emergency that should be dealt with right away!

After children are in bed, they sometimes cry or call out for parents—"I need a glass of water." "I'm scared." "It's too dark!" What should parents do? If they believe the child's request is legitimate—it concerns something that truly makes it hard for them to fall asleep—then parents should respond promptly. If, however, the child's request is a delay tactic to avoid falling asleep, it's better to tell the child firmly something like "No more games; now go to sleep" and then not return for unnecessary requests. When parents respond to unnecessary bedtime requests, they're reinforcing the child's behaviour, making it more likely that children will call out after bedtime on subsequent nights.

Sometimes children are fearful when left alone in the dark. Genuine fearfulness should be attended to properly. For example, if a child is afraid of noises in the night, helping the child to recognize those same noises during the day will reassure them when they hear the sounds in the dark. Sometimes, however, children have more specific fears about more realistic events, such as robbers breaking in or a fire. Children need to know that their parents are in charge and will protect them from harm. Parents also might consider consulting with a clinical child psychologist to help them deal with intense or persistent fearfulness in their child.

After preschool children are asleep, they will sleep peacefully through most nights. Many children have **nightmares**—vivid, frightening dreams occurring toward morning that usually wake the child. Occasional nightmares are normal and need nothing more than on-the-spot parental comfort and reassurance. Sometimes a parent can pinpoint the cause of nightmares, such as watching scary movies, and fix the problem. Persistent, repeated, or troubling nightmares might require professional intervention (Mindell & Cashman, 1995).

Two other sleep disturbances are much rarer than nightmares but are quick to capture a parent's attention. In **night terrors**, children wake in a panicked state, breathing rapidly and perspiring heavily. Because they are not fully awake, children in this state will often not respond to the parent and typically go back to sleep quickly. They usually don't remember the episode the following morning. Night terrors usually occur early in the night and seem to be a by-product of waking too rapidly from a deep sleep. Although often very frightening to parents, night terrors rarely indicate any underlying problem in children (Adair & Bauchner, 1993).

A second sleep disturbance is sleepwalking, in which children get out of bed during deep sleep and walk. The only real danger in sleepwalking is that children can injure themselves. Consequently, parents should wake sleepwalking children and get them back to bed. If children sleepwalk regularly, parents should be sure that the child's environment has no special hazards, such as unguarded stairways.

A final bedtime concern is wetting, often more of a problem for boys than for girls. Most North American children are toilet trained by 2 or 3 years of age. Once trained, they are usually quite successful at staying dry during the day. At night, however, about 25 percent of 4-year-olds wet the bed occasionally (Wille, 1994), which is perfectly normal; almost all preschool children grow out of the problem by age 6. If the problem persists, a number of simple methods to help children stay dry at night are available with help from a pediatrician and clinical child psychologist (American Psychiatric Association, 1994; Rappaport, 1993). The Canadian Paediatric Society (www.caringforkids.cps.ca) has an excellent online resource for helping parents with children who wet the bed as well as with a number of other child-related concerns.

Ask Yourself

Does change in height and weight during the preschool years provide evidence for continuity of development or discontinuity of development?

Think about what you learned about operant conditioning and consider how best to encourage children to follow a good bedtime routine.

8.2 Motor Development

 ## Learning Objectives

After reading the module, you should be able to do the following:

LO4 Explain how children's gross-motor skills improve during the preschool years.

LO5 Explain how children's fine-motor skills improve during the preschool years.

LO6 Identify how similar left- and right-handed children are.

LO7 Discover how preschool boys and girls differ in their motor skills.

Because preschool children get bigger, develop stronger muscles, and have more powerful brains, their motor skills show some amazing improvements during these years. We'll trace these improvements in this module. First, we'll see how gross- and fine-motor skills improve; then we'll look at handedness. We'll end by examining gender differences in motor development, and we'll learn about typical growth trends for young boys and girls.

Gross-Motor Skills

LO4 Explain how children's gross-motor skills improve during the preschool years.

Most infants learn to walk by 18 months of age. Through the preschool years, children move beyond simple walking to running and jumping and other complex motor skills that require greater coordination and precise timing of movements, such as swinging.

miolanasvetlana/Fotolia

Unstructured gross-motor play.

Children's improved skill is evident in their running and hopping. Most 2-year-olds have a hurried walk instead of a true run; they move their legs stiffly (rather than bending them at the knees) and are not airborne, as is the case when running. By 5 or 6 years, children run easily, quickly changing directions or speed. Similarly, an average 2- or 3-year-old will hop a few times on one foot, typically keeping the upper body very stiff; by 5 or 6, children can hop long distances on one foot or alternate hopping first on one foot a few times and then on the other.

In addition, preschool children become much more proficient at coordinating the motions of their arms and legs. This is particularly apparent when youngsters try to throw or catch a ball. In Figure 8–6, you can see that 2- and 3-year-olds throw using the forearm almost exclusively; in contrast, 6-year-olds step into a throw, rotating their upper body to help propel the ball. Similarly,

Figure 8–6

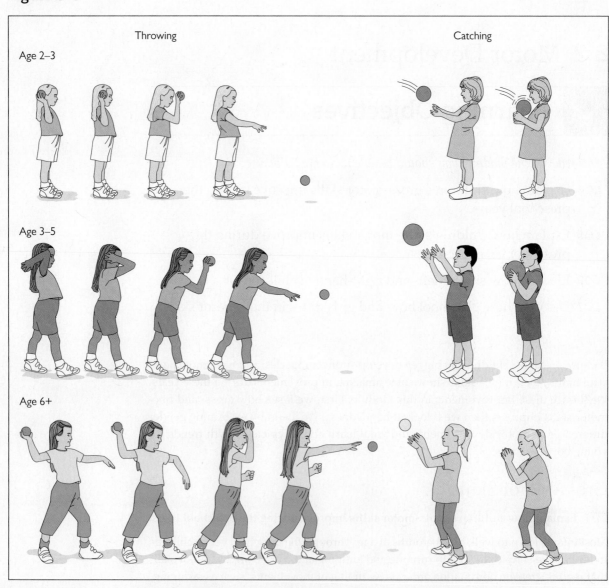

a 2-year-old can catch a ball only if it happens to land squarely on the extended forearms; by age 6, children use their legs to move to the ball and then adjust their upper body and forearms to absorb the force of the ball.

With their advanced motor skills, older preschoolers delight in unstructured play. They enjoy activities like swinging, climbing over jungle gyms, and balancing on a beam. Some learn to ride a tricycle or ski downhill. Others begin to participate in organized sports: Many communities have soccer and baseball or softball programs in which the game is simplified to require only age-appropriate skills.

Fine-Motor Skills

LO5 **Explain how children's fine-motor skills improve during the preschool years.**

Changes in fine-motor skill occur along with the changes in gross-motor skills just described. Preschool children become much more dexterous, able to make many precise and delicate movements with their hands and fingers. Improved fine-motor skill means that preschool children can begin to care for themselves. No longer must they rely primarily on parents to feed and clothe them; instead, they become increasingly skilled at feeding and dressing themselves. A 2- or 3-year-old, for example, can put on some simple clothing and use zippers but not buttons; by 3 or 4 years, children can fasten buttons and take off their clothes when going to the bathroom; most 5-year-olds can dress and undress themselves, except for tying shoes, which children typically master at about age 6.

Preschoolers become capable of complex, coordinated gross-motor skills.

Greater fine-motor coordination also leads to improvements in preschool children's printing. Part of this improvement comes because young children hold pens and pencils more efficiently as they develop. When adults hold a pen or pencil, they usually rest it on the middle finger, then keep it there with the thumb and the index finger. In contrast, when they mix batter or paint, they are more likely to wrap the spoon tightly with the thumb and all four fingers. Each grip is well suited for its task

A typical grip for stirring and painting, which require strength.

A typical grip for writing and drawing, which require precision.

because writing or drawing requires precise motions with relatively little strength, but mixing requires more strength and less precision. By age 5, children are well on their way to gripping pens in the effective manner that adults use. In contrast, 3-year-olds, who are trying to discover forms of writing that work best for them, are still experimenting with different ways to hold a pen.

A better grip also improves preschoolers' drawing. Given a crayon or marker, most preschool children love to draw. Over more than 30 years, Rhoda Kellogg (1970) collected and analyzed several million drawings by preschool children and found that they follow a common developmental pattern as the drawings become progressively more complex.

Progression in drawing ability reflects more than improvements in fine-motor skill; it also reflects cognitive growth that allows children to understand more of what they see about them. Compared to younger preschool children, older preschool children often have a plan before they start to draw; they want to draw Mom or a car. Older children are more concerned that their art be realistic, depicting objects accurately. Ironically, many accomplished artists strive to create styles that do not represent reality (Winner, 1989).

Handedness

LO6 Identify how similar left- and right-handed children are.

By age 2, a child's hand preference is clear; most children—about 90 percent—use their right hand for fine-motor activities, such as colouring, brushing teeth, or zipping a jacket. At this age, youngsters occasionally use their nonpreferred hand for tasks, but, between the ages of 6 and 10, children typically use their nonpreferred hand only when the preferred hand is busy doing something else (Pryde, Bryden, & Roy, 2000). After the age of 10, children (and also adults) will use their nonpreferred hands particularly if they are performing a task on that side of the body (Pryde et al., 2000).

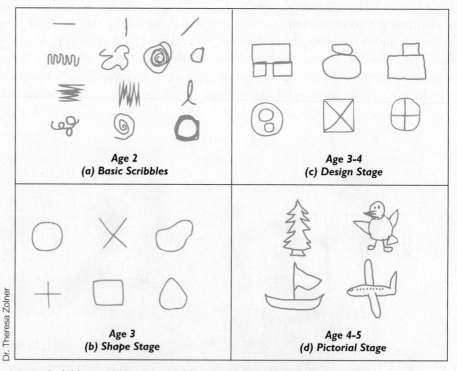

Dr. Theresa Zolner

Age 2
(a) Basic Scribbles

Age 3-4
(c) Design Stage

Age 3
(b) Shape Stage

Age 4-5
(d) Pictorial Stage

At age 2, children scribble; about 20 different scribbles are common, including vertical, horizontal, zigzag, and circular lines. At this age, children are delighted by the simple lines that are created just by moving a crayon or marker across paper.

At age 3, most children are in the **shape stage**, in which they draw six basic shapes: circles, rectangles, triangles, crosses, Xs, and odd-shaped forms.

At age 3 or 4, most children move into the **design stage**, in which they combine the six basic shapes to create more complex patterns.

At age 4 or 5, children typically enter the **pictorial stage**, in which they begin to depict recognizable objects, such as people, animals, plants, or vehicles.

Movements of the right hand (as well as the right arm and right leg) are controlled by regions in the brain's left hemisphere; movements of the left hand, arm, and leg are controlled by regions in the brain's right hemisphere. In right-handed people, the left hemisphere is often called the dominant hemisphere because the left hemisphere and right hand are associated with greater dexterity than the right hemisphere and left hand. Brain **lateralization** means that each half of the brain has functional specialization, making the two halves different from each other. Interestingly, although language functions (e.g., speaking and comprehension) are almost always lateralized in the left (dominant) hemisphere of right-handers, the pattern is more varied in left-handers. Most show the same pattern as right-handers, but language is lateralized in the right (dominant) hemisphere in some left-handed people and more evenly distributed between the two hemispheres in others (Bryden & Saxby, 1986; Coren, 1992; Hiscock & Kinsbourne, 1987).

Many adults view being left-handed as a disadvantage. In fact, gauche, which means awkward, and sinister, which means evil, are derived from foreign words that mean left. The industrialized world does seem to favour right-handed people: Desks, can-openers, scissors, and guitars tend to be designed for right-handers, not left-handers. Moreover, left-handed children and adults are more likely to have migraine headaches and allergies and suffer from language-based problems, such as stuttering and reading disability (Coren & Halpern, 1991). Yet left-handed individuals are often artistically and spatially talented, perhaps due to right-brain dominance, where musical and spatial abilities usually are lateralized (Smith, Meyers, & Kline, 1989). Michelangelo, Leonardo da Vinci, and Pablo Picasso, for example, were all left-handed. Overall, left-handed children also tend to have greater mathematical talent. In one study of mathematically gifted children, 20 percent were left-handed, which is about twice the number that would have been expected based on the number of left-handed children in the population (Bower, 1985).

Gender Differences in Motor Skills

LO7 Discover how preschool boys and girls differ in their motor skills.

Although preschool boys and girls don't differ much in height and weight, preschool boys tend to be a bit more muscular. Consequently, earlier studies showed boys to have the advantage on motor tasks that rely on strength, such as running or throwing (Garai & Scheinfield, 1968), a difference that becomes more prevalent during puberty. More recent studies of hand strength in preschool boys and girls showed no differences; however, activities such as throwing and catching are related to hand length, such that children with larger hands tend also to have greater ability to grip and pinch (Bear-Lehman, Kafko, Mah, Mosquera, & Reilly, 2002; Loovis & Butterfield, 2003). In addition, boys tend to be more active than girls (Eaton & Yu, 1986). During quiet activities such as story time, preschool boys are more often the ones who are squirming around or tickling each other, while girls are most likely to listen attentively.

Shape stage:
the period during which children draw six basic shapes.

Design stage:
the period during which children combine the six basic shapes into more complex patterns.

Pictorial stage:
the period during which children depict recognizable objects in drawings.

Lateralization:
the functional specialization of each half of the brain, which makes each half different from the other.

Left-handedness has been linked to artistic and mathematical talents.

Social encouragement can reinforce gender-stereotyped activities.

When activities require that children coordinate the movements of their limbs—balancing on one foot, hopping, or skipping—young girls tend to be more skilled than boys (Haines, 2003). Similarly, in activities that require fine-motor coordination—fastening buttons, stringing beads on a thread, printing legibly—girls are usually more skilled than boys (Cratty, 1979). However, as Haines (2003) pointed out, these strengths might be attributable to socialized play differences between boys and girls. Thus, typical gender differences in motor skills might be due more to socialization and how others in their world encourage children to play than they are to musculature or other male–female physical differences (Golombok & Fivush, 1994).

Ask Yourself

How might an ethologist explain gender differences in motor skills? How might a social cognitive theorist explain these differences?

Why do you think society places so much emphasis on right- versus left-handedness?

8.3 Health and Wellness

⌄ Learning Objectives

After reading the module, you should be able to do the following:

LO8 List the kinds of foods preschool children should eat.

LO9 Relate what parents can do if their preschool children become picky eaters.

LO10 Name the threats to children's development in the preschool years.

LO11 Understand the complications around health service delivery for children in Canada.

Compared with many childhood tasks, physical growth seems easy: "If you feed them, they will grow." Of course, parenting is no *Field of Dreams*. As we'll see in the first part of this module, what children are fed matters a great deal. We'll also learn that children can be picky eaters and don't necessarily want to eat what they are fed. In the second part of this module, we'll look at some of the factors that can threaten healthy development in preschool children.

Nutrition

LO8 List the kinds of foods preschool children should eat.

The foods that children eat and the liquids they drink fuel the growth we described in Module 8.1. Because preschoolers grow more slowly than infants and toddlers, they need to eat less per kilogram than before. Preschoolers should consume about 90 calories per kilogram of body weight, which works out to be roughly 1500 to 1700 calories daily for many preschool children.

However, number of calories alone is not the determining factor for a healthy diet. Children and adults need variety so that they achieve a balance of foods from all major food groups. Serving sizes for children are not the same as for adults. Also, the quantity of food a child requires depends on a variety of factors, including the child's body size, activity level, appetite, age, and growth rate. Table 8–1 shows Health Canada's guidelines for child-size servings. Younger children, say age 2 or 3, likely would consume servings on the lower end of these suggested sizes. Older children,

Table 8–1 Meeting Preschoolers' Nutritional Needs: What Are Child-Sized Servings?

| Foods | Amount | Number of Food Guide Servings | | | | |
		Vegetables and fruit	Grain products	Milk and alternatives	Meat and alternatives	Oils and fats
Breakfast						
Smoothie made with						
2% milk and	125 mL (1/2 cup)			1/2		
frozen berries	60 mL (1/4 cup)	1/2				
Whole grain cereal with	15 g		1/2			
2% milk	125 mL (1/2 cup)			1/2		
Snack						
Sliced banana	1/2	1/2				
Lunch						
Butternut squash soup	125 mL (1/2 cup)	1				
Tuna wrap made with						
half of a whole-wheat tortilla,	1/2		1			
tuna,	38 g (1 1/4 oz)				1/2	
green peppers and	60 mL (1/4 cup)	1/2				
mayonnaise	5 mL (1 tsp)					✓
2% milk	125 mL (1/2 cup)			1/2		
Snack						
Cucumber slices with	60 mL (1/4 cup)	1/2				
dip	15 mL (1 Tbsp)					✓
2% milk	125 mL (1/2 cup)			1/2		
Dinner						
Stir fry made with						
broccoli, carrots and cauliflower [frozen medley] and	125 mL (1/2 cup)	1				
chicken on	38 g (1 1/4 oz)				1/2	
cooked brown rice	125 mL (1/2 cup)		1			
Oil to cook stir fry	5 mL (1 tsp)					✓
Roll with	1/2 (18 g)		1/2			
non-hydrogenated margarine	5 mL (1 tsp)					✓
Total Food Guide Servings for the day		**4**	**3**	**2**	**1**	**30 mL**

Fast food is usually a nutritionally poor choice.

say age 4 and up, likely would consume servings on the upper end of these suggested sizes. The servings listed in the table are definitely not a complete list of the foods appropriate for young children; they simply are examples of healthy choices and quantities for preschoolers. (For more interesting information about Canada's Food Guide and preschoolers, check out www.hc-sc.gc.ca/fn-an/food-guide-aliment/choose-choix/advice-conseil/child-enfant-eng.php.)

A healthy diet not only draws upon all major food groups but also limits sugar and fat. For preschool children, no more than approximately 30 percent of the daily caloric intake should come from fat, which works out to be roughly 500 calories from fat. Unfortunately, too many parents feed their preschool children fast-food meals, which can have nearly 600 calories from fat alone, 100 more calories from fat than young children should consume all day! Excessive fat intake contributes to obesity, so parents need to limit their preschool children's unnecessary fat intake (Whitaker, Wright, Pepe, Seidel, & Dietz, 1997).

Health Canada has taken an active interest in rates of childhood obesity in Canadian children. Obese babies have a very low probability of growing into obese adults (Feldman & Beagan, 1994); however, an established pattern of poor eating and low levels of exercise can contribute to an increased risk for obesity in childhood. Children who are obese have a greater likelihood of social and emotional problems resulting from poor self-image and social rejection relating in part to the strong cultural bias against obesity that exists in North America (Feldman & Beagan, 1994).

Prevalence rates for childhood obesity in Canada vary depending on the definition of obesity used as well as the assessment measures (Feldman & Beagan, 1994). Katzmarzyk, Perusse, Rao, and Bouchard (1999) found that a significant risk for familial obesity exists in Canada and concluded that genetic factors contribute to obesity rates for Canadian families. Furthermore, regional differences exist in obesity rates, with children in Atlantic Canada being more than twice as likely to be obese as those on the Prairies (Canadian Institute for Health Information, 2003). Obesity rates also tend to be linked to social class, with rates as high as 25 percent in lower-income families and 5 percent in higher-income families (Feldman & Beagan, 1994). According to Feldman and Beagan (1994), approximately 5 percent of children have an underlying disease process that produces the obesity, but researchers concluded that most obese children simply take in more calories than they expend, making control of exercise and diet very important during the childhood years. At the time of writing, approximately one in three children in Canada are obese (Roberts, Shields, de Groh, Aziz, & Gilbert, 2012). Within this third, 15.1 percent are boys and 8 percent are girls. By middle childhood, this difference grows even more to 19 percent of boys and only 6 percent of girls.

However, environmental and genetic factors can interact, affecting two conditions that have been increasingly escalating: obesity and asthma. Hilary Sandig and her colleagues (Sandig et al., 2007) conducted research into the relationship between obesity and asthma. In asthmatic people, Th2 immune cells in the lungs overreact to environmental stimuli and cause inflammation, bringing about asthmatic reactions. However, in addition to their role in asthma, Th2 cells also have been observed to cause the release of "melanin-concentrating hormone" (MCH), which causes an increase in appetite and could result in overeating. In addition, obesity itself is hypothesized to produce low levels of inflammation in the body, placing a person at higher risk for allergic reactions and asthma and additional release of MCH. Despite the important results of this study, the action of Th2 cells is not perfectly understood, especially since not all asthmatic persons are obese.

Encouraging Healthy Eating

LO9 **Relate what parents can do if their preschool children become picky eaters.**

Encouraging preschool children to eat healthy foods is difficult for parents because some preschoolers become notoriously picky eaters and seem to refuse virtually everything, especially nutritious foods that health-conscious parents want them to eat. Parents should not be overly concerned about this finicky period. Although some children do eat less than before in terms of calories per kilogram, virtually all picky eaters take in adequate food for growth. Even older children can be picky or overly tempted by junk food. Theresa Zolner remembers when her own child came home from elementary school one day, complaining miserably, "I'm the only one at school who has to eat a healthy lunch!" Ensuring that children follow healthy diets is not the easiest parental task.

Nevertheless, picky children can make mealtime miserable for all. What's a parent to do? It's best for parents to understand what normal eating is like for most preschoolers. Health Canada (2002) provides some examples of normal preschool eating habits:

- being curious about new foods and ways of eating them
- examining the chicken sandwich before they eat it
- accepting toast only if it is cut in triangles
- trying only a bite of squash today—maybe more tomorrow
- drinking milk only if they can pour it into their own glass
- loving carrots on Tuesday, refusing them on Wednesday
- insisting the apple be whole—not in slices
- wanting a peanut butter sandwich for lunch every day for a week
- gobbling up the cookies they helped to prepare when they are fresh from the oven
- preferring simple foods they can recognize
- drinking soup out of a coffee mug just like Mom's

To encourage children to be more open-minded about food, experts (American Academy of Pediatrics, 2010; Leach, 1991) have recommended several guidelines for parents:

- When possible, allow children to select from among different healthy foods (e.g., milk versus yogurt).
- Allow children to eat foods in any order they want.
- Offer children new foods one at a time and in small amounts; encourage but don't force children to eat new foods.
- Don't force children to eat all the food on their plates.
- Don't spend mealtimes talking about what the child is or is not eating; instead, talk about other topics that interest the child.
- Never use food to reward or punish children.

By following these guidelines, mealtimes can be pleasant, and children can receive the nutrition they need to grow.

Threats to Children's Development

LO10 **Name the threats to children's development in the preschool years.**

If you ask a group of parents about their preschool children's health-related problems, you're likely to get a long list. Some items on the list, like colds and coughs,

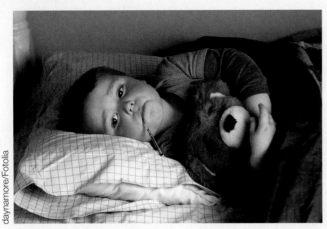

Minor illnesses build up immunity and teach children how their bodies work.

are mainly annoying. Many parents would claim that a runny nose is a permanent state in their preschool children! Other problems on the list are much more serious, sometimes requiring hospitalization. In the next few pages, we'll look at the gamut of illness and injuries that affect preschool children's health. In addition to the developmental threats mentioned in this section, child abuse is a serious threat.

MINOR ILLNESSES. Most preschoolers are all too familiar with coughs and sniffles. The average preschool child has seven or eight colds a year. Preschool children are particularly vulnerable to respiratory illnesses because their lungs are still developing. Fortunately, most children are ill for only a few days. While nobody likes to be sick, minor illness helps a child's body develop immunity to more serious diseases. Also, by being ill and recovering, young children begin to learn about the way that their bodies work and can become prepared to deal with future, more serious illness (Parmalee, 1986).

CHRONIC ILLNESSES. Many children suffer from chronic health conditions, such as asthma, juvenile diabetes, or cancer. With chronic conditions, children must contend with their illness on a daily basis rather than getting over it like the flu. Children with leukemia must receive periodic treatments of chemotherapy over two to three years. Children with asthma must learn to use inhalers and keep to a regular dosage schedule.

Fortunately, most chronic illnesses are uncommon. An exception is asthma, the most common chronic disease of childhood. According to Health Canada (1999), asthma is on the increase in Canada and affects 8.25 percent of Canadian children under 4 years of age (12.25 percent of young people under the age of 20). For people who have asthma, passages in their lungs that carry air become temporarily inflamed and narrow and interfere with air transport. Allergies, smoke, respiratory viruses, pet dander, mould spores, and dust mites all can trigger asthma attacks, which can last from a few minutes to several days. An attack can be fatal if oxygen flow becomes blocked completely. While asthma attacks can require emergency medical intervention and be life threatening, when asthma is managed properly, there are virtually no limits to what children with asthma can do.

One way that researchers are attempting to understand chronic illness in children and adults is to better understand the makeup of the human body (Institute of Infections and Immunity, 2009). Every person carries around trillions of microorganisms on their skin and inside the body—microbes, such as viruses, bacteria, and protozoa, which make up what scientists call the "human microbiome" (Institute of Infections and Immunity, 2009). The human body contains about 10 times as many microbes as cells, and these microbes carry more genetic information within them than is contained in the human genome. The genetic information in microbes also interacts with the genetic information in human cells and has an impact on the occurrence or prevention of a variety of health conditions, such as gastrointestinal illnesses, asthma, obesity, and arthritis. Disruptions within the normal human microbiome are associated with both behavioural and neurological changes in the person. Understanding the human microbiome could lead to a better understanding of human health and psychology.

The researchers involved in the Human Microbiome Project are attempting to sequence and understand the genetic structure and functioning of the human microbiome across a variety of sites on the human body to see whether all people share a core set of microbes and how those microbes affect human health and well-being. Through the Canadian Institute of Health Research and the Institute of Infections and

Immunity, Canada has launched the Canadian Microbiome Initiative and is participating in the Human Microbiome Project, as are other nations, such as the EU, Japan, and Australia (Institute of Infections and Immunity, 2009).

For example, Emma Allen-Vercoe from the University of Guelph is studying the impact of human stress hormones on microbes in the human gut, which could better show how stress affects human health. At the University of Alberta, Anita Kozyrsky and her research team (Azad et al., 2013) found that gut microbiomes for babies can differ depending on how babies are born—by C-section or by vaginal birth—as well as whether they are fed with infant formula or breast milk. According to these researchers, infants born by elective C-section have an especially low richness and diversity of gut bacteria. Infants fed formula have a higher richness of bacteria but also an overrepresentation of bacteria such as *Clostridium difficile*, which can lead to health problems like diarrhea. These researchers are continuing to study whether any microbes are critical to infant health and how birth and feeding affect the health of the infant biome.

ACCIDENTS. Preschool children are frequently eager to explore the unknown but often lack the cognitive skills to determine whether they are endangering themselves. As a consequence, many preschoolers are hurt in accidents. Many childhood accidents are falls that result in bruising, some bleeding, and a few tears but no lasting harm. However, some are more serious. In fact, accidents are the leading cause of death in preschool children. Thousands of young children die every year in auto accidents, drownings, and fires (Health Canada, 1998). Farm-related accidents are one cause of childhood injury and death that persists across the age range from birth to age 19 (Health Canada, 1998), with head trauma and being run over by tractors (whether riding or standing by) being the greatest sources of machinery-related injury for young people (Health Canada, 1998; Pickett, Berg, & Murphy, 2004).

The term "accident" implies that the event happened by chance and no one was to blame. In reality, many of the accidents that hurt or kill young children can be foreseen and prevented. Table 8–2 lists some of the common accidents that hurt young

Every year, thousands of young children are hurt in accidents.

the24studio/Fotolia

Table 8–2 Ways to Reduce Accident Risk for Young Children

Type of Accident	Ways to Reduce Risk
Vehicle accidents	Children should always ride in a properly installed, approved car seat and should stay clear of large or dangerous farm equipment.
Drowning	Children should never be left unattended near sources of water, particularly swimming areas but also bathtubs or buckets filled with water.
Poisoning	Keep all medications in child-resistant containers; keep them and all other harmful substances (e.g., animal poisons, cleansers) out of children's way (out of reach, locked up, or both).
Cycling	When a child rides in a seat on a bicycle, be sure that the seat is installed properly, that the child is strapped in securely, and that the child wears a helmet. When riding a tricycle or bicycle, the child should stay off streets, be supervised by a parent, and wear a helmet.
Firearms	All firearms should be locked in a safe place, with ammunition stored in a separate, locked location. Children should not have access to the keys.
Fires	Install smoke detectors, and check them regularly. Keep fire extinguishers handy. Tell children how to leave the house in case of a fire, practise leaving the house, and have a safety plan.

children along with some effective methods of prevention. Following these prevention strategies is easy and substantially reduces the chance that a child will be harmed in an accident.

ENVIRONMENTAL CONTRIBUTIONS TO ILLNESS AND INJURY.   Not all children are equally prone to illness and injury. Instead, some are more likely to be ill, and others are more injury-prone. Why? Stress is one factor. Many children experience serious stress at some point in their lives—coping with a move to an unfamiliar neighbourhood, with their parents' marital conflicts, or with the death of a pet or close person. In these circumstances, children are more likely to become ill, perhaps because stress reduces their resistance to disease (Beautrais, Fergusson, & Shannon, 1982). When parents are under stress, their children are at greater risk for illness and injury. Caught up in their own stress, parents might be less cautious in dealing with hazardous situations, or they might pay less attention to the symptoms of their children with chronic illness (Craft, Montgomery, & Peters, 1992).

Poverty also contributes to illness. For children living in poverty, health-related problems often begin before birth, when their mothers receive inadequate prenatal care and follow an inadequate diet. After birth, many youngsters living in poverty do not eat adequately, and, of course, poverty is stressful for children and parents alike, accentuating the impact it has on children's health.

In Canada, as in many European countries, health care is universally available to all children (Lie, 1990; Verbrugge, 1990), although some children continue to have less access than others, depending on their location and, in some provinces, the ability of families to pay health premiums. In these countries, healthy, disease-free growth is seen in the same light as an education—a fundamental right of all children, regardless of income or race. Regrettably, until recently, most U.S. children had no such guarantee when it came to health care, and the country continues to bear a substantial medical, psychological, and economic burden as a consequence (Children's Defense Fund, 1996).

IMPACT OF HOSPITALIZATION.   Sometimes children with asthma and other chronic illnesses must be hospitalized to receive the care they need. Few adults enjoy being hospitalized, so it's no surprise that young children often find the experience difficult. Preschool children are usually upset at being separated from parents (sometimes for the first time). Children are often afraid of what's going to happen to them in this unfamiliar setting, and they dislike the lack of control that people commonly feel in a hospital environment (Whaley & Wong, 1991).

Working together, parents and health-care professionals can make a hospital stay more predictable and less traumatic for children. Parents can be encouraged to spend as much time as possible with their hospitalized child. Some hospitals even allow rooming in—parents can sleep in the same room with their child. For times when a parent can't be present, a warm and caring nurse can be assigned to the child to act as a parental substitute. Clinical psychologists and social workers sometimes are involved in preparing children for hospital stays. They show children what's going to happen by giving them tours ahead of time and allowing the children to see and touch items they will come into contact with while in the hospital. For example, children might be allowed to handle and play with sample IV tubes, needles (without the sharps), or other hospital paraphernalia so that they are not frightened when they see these items later. Of course, this kind of psychoeducational preparation should only be done with supervision from a qualified clinician. Also, health-care professionals can allow children some choices while in hospital, such as what to eat and what toys to play with, so they don't feel completely powerless (Whaley & Wong, 1991). By addressing preschool children's concerns ahead of time, the hospital stay can become much less stressful for the child.

Jurisdictional Authority and Children's Health

LO11 Understand the complications around health service delivery for children in Canada.

In Canada, jurisdictional authority for certain kinds of service delivery is divided between federal, provincial, and territorial governments. For example, national defence is a federal responsibility, and education is a provincial one. Sometimes, assistance or service delivery to children can be affected by intergovernmental disputes or failure to acknowledge responsibility for a particular area. McKechnie (2000) noted, as a case in point, that services to children with fetal alcohol spectrum disorder (FASD) cross a number of jurisdictional authorities, including education, justice, social services, employment, health, and housing. As a result, in order for people with FASD to have their needs met, co-operation is required of several levels or departments of government in Canada, including provincial, federal, territorial, and tribal. Unfortunately, government policies, as well as communication mishaps and barriers, often prevent children from qualifying for necessary services or obtaining services from any source at all (McKechnie, 2000).

On February 23, 2007, the Assembly of First Nations (AFN) and the First Nations Child and Family Caring Society of Canada (FNCFCSC) jointly filed a rights complaint with the Canadian Human Rights Commission against the Government of Canada (First Nations Child and Family Caring Society of Canada, 2010). These agencies have claimed that the Government of Canada has systematically underfunded child welfare services for First Nations children and families in Canada, which has resulted in 27 000 Aboriginal children being placed in foster homes (see Assembly of First Nations, 2007a, 2007b; Assembly of First Nations Health and Social Secretariat, 2009; Clark, 2007). According to the AFN, this number represents 1 in 10 Aboriginal children in care, compared with 1 in 200 non-Aboriginal children.

Neglect is the main reason First Nations children end up in foster care in Canada (Earle Fox, 2004; Trocmé et al., 2001). However, according to FNCFCSC, neglect in Aboriginal communities really is an umbrella category for problems stemming from poverty, poor housing, and substance abuse (First Nations Child and Family Caring Society of Canada, 2005a, 2005b; MacDonald, 2006; see also Lafrance & Bastien, 2007). Despite the numbers of First Nations children in foster care, these children often are denied or delayed services as a result of jurisdictional disputes, typically between federal and provincial governments (FNCFCSC, 2005a, 2005b). For example, during 2006–2007, 12 First Nations' Child and Family Service (FNCFS) agencies in Canada experienced a total of 393 jurisdictional disputes over services to children in their care (FNCFCSC, 2005a, 2005b).

In the famous case of "Jordan," a Manitoba First Nations child, jurisdictional disputes dragged on for two years after physicians wanted to discharge Jordan from the hospital to live in a family-home setting. Unfortunately, Jordan's serious health problems required that he receive special kinds of in-home services, which resulted in a protracted dispute between Health Canada, Indian Affairs, and the provincial government. Consequently, Jordan spent the remaining two years of his life in the hospital, when he could have been living in a family-home setting, and he died before these governments were able to resolve their jurisdictional turf war. As you will see in the Making Children's Lives Better feature, Jordan's story has resulted in a movement within Canada to require governments to adopt a "child-first" approach to service delivery for children.

Ask Yourself

Why do environmental factors, such as family stress and poverty, place some children at greater risk for injury?

How difficult is it for you to understand, relate to, or agree with the struggles that First Nations children and families have experienced with health and social service delivery in Canada?

Check out this article on misconceptions about Aboriginal peoples at http://tricitiesecd.ca/files/4013/3599/2965/FACTSandMisconceptions.pdf to see if any of your questions are addressed there.

Making Children's Lives Better

Jordan's Principle

First Nations children, like all children in Canada, are entitled to receive equal treatment and benefit under Canadian law. However, poor coordination among federal, territorial, and provincial governments has left many children without timely—or any—access to necessary health or other services. As a result, the FNCFCS has recommended that a "child-first" principle, called "Jordan's Principle," be adopted by all levels of government involved in providing services to children (First Nations Child and Family Caring Society of Canada, n.d., p. 17). The recommendation of the FNCFCS appears as follows:

> We recommend that a child first principle be adopted whereby the government (provincial or federal) who first receives a request for payment of services for a First Nations child will pay without disruption or delay when these services are otherwise available to non Aboriginal children in similar [sic] circumstances. The government then has the option of referring the matter to a jurisdictional dispute resolution process.

Adoption of Jordan's Principle would not detract from children's rights; instead, it might ensure that children receive the services they need instead of waiting for governments to settle bureaucratic disputes that inflict further trauma on children and families.

Jurisdictional disputes over services for First Nations children arise because social-service delivery for First Nations children in Canada is an extremely complex matter. Because of the way Canadian federal and provincial laws are written, children living off reserve have to access services through federal and provincial agencies only and may not access services from their home First Nations; however, on reserve, FNCFS (First Nations Child and Family Services) agencies often have authority to deliver services to First Nations youth belonging to a particular band or tribal agency. If a child moves between that child's First Nation and a town or city, then complicated case-transfer arrangements or protocols must be followed in order to transfer care for the child from one type of service

agency to another. These case-transfer protocols do not always work and have resulted in serious gaps in services to children, some of which have directly resulted in children's deaths. In addition, these matters are not dealt with in the same manner from province to province, increasing the possibility of unequal treatment for children in different jurisdictions within Canada.

To obtain the legal authority for service delivery to First Nations children, a particular First Nation must seek out an agreement with the provincial government delegating authority to that First Nation for child welfare services, which, according to Canadian law, is a provincial responsibility. However, in order to actually run its FNCFS agency, the First Nation must also enter into an agreement with the federal department of Indian Affairs for funding. Therefore, the authority of the FNCFS agency is affected by both federal and provincial legislative authorities as well as First Nations legislation. In addition, considerable disagreement has occurred between Indian Affairs and FNCFS agencies regarding funding formulas for child welfare services. Even when FNCFS agencies hold a legal mandate to provide necessary services on reserve, they are always forced to answer to two different levels of government in the delivery of those services in addition to their own First Nations legislative authorities.

Unfortunately, federal and provincial governments do not always effectively communicate with each other, and they also do not always (perhaps rarely) understand the cultures, perspectives, and needs of particular First Nations. Sometimes, even federal and provincial legislation conflict. For example, First Nations fall under federal labour and privacy legislation; however, provincial governments may require First Nations to conform to provincial labour and privacy legislation and standards, regardless of federal laws. Therefore, First Nations might be required to meet nearly impossible demands for federal funders on the one hand and for provincial powers on the other. Communication efforts between these three levels of governments also are affected by historically negative relationships as well as federal and provincial governmental policies designed to assimilate or annihilate, rather than respect, the unique cultures of First Nations peoples. Many more issues could be mentioned, such as the complete and historical lack of a national Indian Affairs policy and funding strategy for special education for First Nations children, despite extraordinarily high need in this area.

As a result, First Nations children and families typically are caught within a tangled web of jurisdictional disputes, funding shortages, low levels of infrastructure development, poor coordination of communication and service delivery, a lack of culturally appropriate bureaucrats and service providers, as well as general disrespect for their cultural values and ways. Many First Nations peoples complain that governments offer "Band-Aid solutions" to serious health, social, and wellness problems that First Nations face. The AFN and the FNCFCS have placed some hope in the ability of the Canadian Human Rights Commission to address social inequities in service delivery to Aboriginal children. For now, we will have to wait to see how their claim is adjudicated.

Ask Yourself

What Would a Teacher in a Northern School Do?

Every child's family is different, and people come from a variety of cultural backgrounds and experiences. A more common experience for some professionals in Canada, such as teachers, nurses, and law-enforcement officers, is the experience of being placed in a northern community, particularly early on in one's career. Many of these professionals have had little or no contact with Canada's north and are not very familiar with the social and geographic aspects of living in the north. If you were placed as a teacher in a northern school, how would you adjust? What do you think you could do to make your experience positive? What might make it more difficult for you to fit in and do your job well?

Summary

8.1 Physical Growth

Body Growth

- Preschool children grow steadily, adding about 5 to 8 centimetres and 1.8 kilograms each year.

- Preschool children begin to look more mature because their bodies have more adult-like proportions and less fat.

- During the preschool years, much cartilage turns to bone, and children acquire, typically by age 3, all 20 primary teeth.

Brain Development

- Between 2 and 5 years, unnecessary synaptic connections are pruned, and neurons in the corpus callosum, sensory, and motor regions of the brain become wrapped in myelin.

- The brain becomes more specialized, with specific functions (e.g., comprehending speech) becoming lateralized in particular brain regions.

Sleep

- Preschool children typically sleep about 12 hours each night.

- Many children occasionally have problems falling asleep, which can be helped by following a consistent bedtime routine.

- Many children experience occasional nightmares; less common are night terrors and sleepwalking.

- Many preschool children wet their beds during the night; this, too, is not a major problem unless it persists past the preschool years.

8.2 Motor Development

Gross-Motor Skills

- Children's gross-motor skills improve steadily throughout the preschool years.

- Children become more skilled at running and hopping as well as at throwing and catching a ball.

- Most 2- or 3-year-olds throw a ball using only their forearms, but 6-year-olds use their arm, upper body, and legs.

Fine-Motor Skills

- Preschool children become much more dexterous, which makes it possible for them to feed and clothe themselves.
- Greater fine-motor coordination also means that drawings become much more complex.
- Children's first drawings—at about age 2—consist of scribbles; youngsters rapidly progress to drawing shapes and combining shapes.
- At about age 4 or 5, children begin to draw recognizable objects, such as people and animals.

Handedness

- Most preschool children use their right hand most of the time.
- For most children, language functioning is typically localized in the left hemisphere.
- For some left-handed children language is localized in the right hemisphere, and for other left-handed children it is localized in both hemispheres.
- Left-handed children and adults are more prone to some health problems and language disorders but tend to be more talented artistically, spatially, and mathematically.

Gender Differences in Motor Skills

- Young boys tend to be more active than girls and have an advantage on tasks that rely on strength.
- Girls usually perform better than boys on tasks that require coordinated movements of the limbs or fine-motor coordination.

8.3 Health and Wellness

Nutrition

- Most preschool children need a diet of roughly 1500 to 1700 calories, from each of the five food groups, that is low in sugar and fat.

Encouraging Healthy Eating

- To discourage "picky eating," parents should allow children to make some choice in food, to eat in any sequence, and to finish without having to eat everything on the plate.

Threats to Children's Development

- Preschool children frequently have minor illnesses, such as colds.
- Having a minor illness benefits children by helping them develop immunities and by teaching them about the nature of illness and recovery.
- Most chronic illnesses are rare, but an increasing number of children are asthmatic and have difficulty breathing because air passages in their lungs are inflamed.
- Children with asthma can lead normal lives as long as they follow their physician's guidelines, such as taking proper medications.
- More preschool children die from accidents than from any other cause.
- Parents can either avoid most accidents entirely (e.g., by ensuring that children cannot get to poisons) or reduce the chance for injury from an accident (e.g., by having children always ride in a car seat).
- Children are more prone to illness and injury when they are living in stress and when they live in poverty.
- Hospitalization often upsets children because of the separation from parents, the fear of the unknown, and the loss of control.

Jurisdictional Authority and Children's Health

- Governmental disputes and inaction, often arising out of jurisdictional turf wars, have a serious impact on service delivery to children, especially those of Aboriginal heritage in Canada.

Chapter Critical Review

1. Your sister is very upset because her 4-year-old son is the smallest boy in his preschool class. Most of the other boys weigh 3.5 to 4.5 kilograms more than he does. Should she be concerned about his weight? What would you say to her?

2. According to the material in Module 8.2, are young children's early efforts to draw limited primarily by their perceptual skills or by their motor skills?

3. You saw in Module 8.1 that children's brains reach their adult size and weight much sooner than their bodies do. What are the implications of this fact for social policy? In what way is the rapid growth of brain tissue adaptive for human infants and preschoolers?

See for Yourself

Arrange to visit a preschool program—one that enrols children between the ages of 2 and 6. Ask if you may watch the children as they colour or if you may simply observe the drawings that are probably displayed around the classroom. Take the descriptions of the different types of children's drawings and find examples of each. You should be struck by the rapid progress that children make in their drawings. See for yourself!

Chapter 9
Cognitive Development in Preschool Children

Anna Karwowska/Fotolia

MODULE

9.1 Cognitive Processes

9.2 Language

9.3 Communicating with Others

9.4 Early Childhood Education

Connect to My Virtual Child

What kinds of theories do you have about children? What ideas inform your thoughts and beliefs about the lives of children, how they are raised, and the nature of the human person? Use your access card and following this link www.myvirtualchild.com to learn more about the world of the child. You can even virtually try to raise your own child.

Sophie was such a joy for Terry and Mabel! Every day she learned new words and shared interesting, sweet, and sometimes hilarious ideas with them. Terry and Mabel started to see how Sophie's mini-experiments with things led to her learning more about the world around her. They also recognized that they had a big impact on Sophie's learning and how she reacted to objects and events. They wondered . . . who was more responsible for gains in Sophie's learning, Sophie or themselves?

9.1 Cognitive Processes

 ## Learning Objectives

After reading the module, you should be able to do the following:

LO1 Name the distinguishing features of thought during the preoperational stage.

LO2 Discuss how children's information-processing ability improves during the preschool years.

LO3 Explain why Vygotsky viewed development as an apprenticeship.

By the time children enter the preschool years, an extraordinary amount of cognitive development has taken place. However, preschoolers have a long way to travel on the road to cognitive maturity. In this module, we'll look at preschoolers' thinking from three perspectives: Piagetian, information processing, and that of Lev Vygotsky.

Piaget's Account

LO1 Name the distinguishing features of thought during the preoperational stage.

According to Jean Piaget's theory, most preschoolers have made the transition from sensorimotor thinking to preoperational thinking. The **preoperational stage**, which spans ages 2 to 7, is marked by the child's use of symbols to represent objects and events. Throughout this period, preschool children gradually become proficient at using common symbols, such as words, gestures, graphs, maps, and models. In the first part of this section, we'll describe Piaget's original account of preoperational thinking. Then we'll describe newer research that complements Piaget's account.

Preoperational stage:
in Piagetian theory, the stage of cognitive development during which children use symbols to represent objects and events.

Figure 9–1

Egocentrism:
seeing the world primarily from the perspective of self rather than of other people.

Centration:
in Piagetian theory, the term for narrowly focused thought, typically during the preoperational stage.

Animism:
crediting inanimate objects with life and lifelike properties.

CHARACTERISTICS OF PREOPERATIONAL THINKING. Although preschool children's ability to use symbols represents a huge advance over sensorimotor thinking, preschool children's thinking is quite limited compared to that of school-age children due to three important characteristics of preoperational thought: egocentrism, centration, and appearance as reality.

Preoperational children typically believe that others see and understand the world exactly as they do. **Egocentrism** refers to young children's difficulty in seeing the world from another's perspective. When youngsters stubbornly cling to their own way, they are not simply being contrary. Instead, preoperational children do not comprehend that other people have different ideas and feelings.

In the drawing in Figure 9–1, the man is asking the preschooler to select the photograph that shows how the objects on the table look to the man. Most preschoolers will select photo 3, which shows how the objects look to the child, not photo 1, the correct choice. Preoperational youngsters evidently suppose that the mountains are seen the same way by all; they presume that theirs is the only view, not one of many possible views (Piaget & Inhelder, 1956).

Egocentrism also explains why babies do unusual things sometimes, like nodding instead of verbally responding while talking on the phone. A baby talking on the phone is aware that he or she is nodding, and the baby assumes that the person on the other end of the phone conversation knows that too. This is part of infant egocentrism, and it takes a while before babies realize that others do not see the world the way they do. In the Real Children feature, we'll see yet another manifestation of this egocentrism.

A second characteristic of preoperational thinking is that children seem to have the psychological equivalent of tunnel vision: They often concentrate on one aspect of a problem but totally ignore other equally relevant aspects. **Centration** is Piaget's term for this narrowly focused thought that characterizes preoperational youngsters.

Piaget demonstrated centration in his experiments involving conservation. In the conservation experiments, Piaget wanted to determine when children realize that important characteristics of objects stay the same despite changes in their physical appearance. Some tasks that Piaget used to study conservation are shown in Figure 9–2. Each begins with identical objects. Then one of the objects or object sets is transformed, and children are asked if the objects are the same in terms of some important feature.

Real Children
Christine, Egocentrism, and Animism

Because of their egocentrism, preschool children sometimes attribute their own thoughts and feelings to others. Preoperational children sometimes credit inanimate objects with life and lifelike properties, a phenomenon known as **animism** (Piaget, 1929). A 3½-year-old, Christine, illustrated preoperational animism in the following conversation she had with Robert Kail on a rainy day:

RK: Is the sun happy today?
Christine: No. It's sad today.

RK: Why?
Christine: Because it's cloudy. He can't shine, and he can't see me!
RK: What about your trike? Is it happy?
Christine: No, he's very sad too.
RK: Why is that?
Christine: Because I can't ride him, and because he's all alone in the garage.

Caught up in her egocentrism, Christine believes that objects like the sun and her tricycle think and feel as she does.

A typical conservation problem involves conservation of liquid quantity. Children are shown identical beakers filled with the same amount of juice. After children agree that the two beakers have the same amount of juice, the juice is poured from one beaker into a taller, thinner beaker. The juice looks different in the tall, thin beaker—it rises higher. Of course, the amount is unchanged, but preoperational children claim that the tall, thin beaker has more juice than the original beaker. Similarly, if the juice is poured into a wider beaker, they believe it has less.

According to Piaget, preoperational children focus on the level of the juice in the beaker and ignore other factors, such as the width of the beaker. If the juice is higher after it is poured, preoperational children believe that there must be more juice now

Piagetian conservation task.

Maya Barnes Johansen/The Image Works

Figure 9–2

Type of Conservation	Starting Configuration	Transformation	Final Configuration
Liquid quantity	*Is there the same amount of water in each glass?*	Pour water from one glass into a shorter, wider glass.	*Now is there the same amount of water in each glass, or does one have more?*
Number	*Are there the same number of pennies in each row?*	Stretch out the top row of pennies, push together the bottom row.	*Now are there the same number of pennies in each row, or does one row have more?*
Length	*Are these sticks the same length?*	Move one stick to the left and the other to the right.	*Now are the sticks the same length, or is one longer?*
Mass	*Does each ball have the same amount of clay?*	Roll one ball so that it looks like a sausage.	*Now does each piece have the same amount of clay, or does one have more?*
Area	*Does each cow have the same amount of grass to eat?*	Spread out the squares in one field.	*Now does each cow have the same amount to eat, or does one cow have more?*

Nomad_Soul/Shutterstock

Children at the preoperational stage are easily fooled by appearances.

than before. Because preoperational thinking over-focuses on one aspect of a situation, these youngsters ignore the fact that the change in the level of the juice is always accompanied by a change in the diameter of the beaker. Due to centration, they are overlooking other parts of the problem that would tell them the quantity is unchanged.

In other conservation problems, preoperational children also tend to focus on only one aspect of the problem. In conservation of number, for example, preoperational children concentrate on the fact that, after the transformation, one row of objects appears longer than the other. In conservation of length, preoperational children concentrate on the fact that, after the transformation, the end of one stick is farther to the right than the end of the other.

A final feature of preoperational thinking is that preschool children believe an object's appearance tells what the object is really like. For instance, many a 3-year-old has watched with quiet fascination as an older brother or sister puts on a ghoulish costume only to erupt in frightened tears when the makeup or mask goes on. For preschoolers, the scary face is reality, not just "my sibling in a mask."

Confusion between appearance and reality is a general characteristic of preoperational thinking not limited to costumes and masks. Consider the following cases where appearances and reality conflict:

- a boy is angry because a friend is being mean but smiles because he's afraid the friend will leave if he reveals his anger
- a glass of milk looks brown when seen through sunglasses
- a piece of hard rubber looks like real food (e.g., like a piece of pizza)

Older children and adults know that appearances can be deceiving: The boy looks happy (but is really angry), the milk looks brown (but is really white), and the object looks like food (but is really rubber). Preoperational children confuse appearance and reality, thinking the boy is happy, the milk is brown, and the food is edible.

Distinguishing appearance from reality is particularly difficult for children in the early years of preoperational thinking. This difficulty is evident in research on children's use of models. A model of a house, for example, can be an interesting object in its own right as well as a representation of an actual house. The ability to use scale models develops early in the preoperational period. If young children watch an adult hide a toy in a full-size room and then try to find the toy in an exact model of the room, 3-year-olds find the hidden toy readily, but 2½-year-olds do not (DeLoache, Miller, & Rosengren, 1997). The 2½-year-olds tend to see the model as an attractive object but not as a model, or symbol, of the room. Confusion about appearance and reality is a deep-seated characteristic of preoperational thinking (especially in the early years of this stage), as are egocentrism and centration. The defining characteristics of preoperational thought are summarized in Table 9–1.

Callaghan and Rankin (2002) tried to see if 28-month-old Nova Scotia children's comprehension of graphic symbols, in this case drawings, could be accelerated by early training in how drawings represented actual objects as compared with children who received less of the same training at 32 months. Callaghan and Rankin found that the 28-month-olds showed accelerated understanding of graphic symbols; however, 32-month-olds caught up with them after only one month of training. Callaghan and Rankin also found links between children's graphic symbol comprehension and their play and language abilities. These findings illustrate an important developmental

Table 9–1 Summary Table

Characteristics of Preoperational Thinking		
Characteristic	**Definition**	**Example**
Egocentrism	Child believes that all people see the world as he or she does.	A child gestures during a telephone conversation, not realizing that the listener cannot see the gestures.
Centration	Child focuses on one aspect of a problem or situation but ignores other relevant aspects.	In conservation of quantity, the child pays attention to the height of the liquid in the beaker but ignores the diameter of the beaker.
Appearance as reality	Child assumes that an object really is what it appears to be.	Child mistakes a person wearing a Halloween mask for a "real" monster.

principle: Earlier training does not always mean better performance later, since more mature children can often catch on to a task or activity quickly due to their more advanced developmental capabilities.

EXTENDING PIAGET'S ACCOUNT: CHILDREN'S NAIVE THEORIES. Researchers have expanded Piaget's account to show that infants create naive theories of physics and biology. These theories become more elaborate in the preschool years. For example, preschool children's naive theories of biology come to include many of the specific properties associated with animate objects (Wellman & Gelman, 1998). Many 4-year-olds' theories of biology include the following elements:

- *Movement:* Children understand that animals can move themselves but inanimate objects can be moved only by other objects or by people. Shown an animal and a toy hopping across a table in exactly the same manner, preschoolers claim that only the animal can move itself (Gelman & Gottfried, 1996).

- *Growth:* Children understand that, from their first appearance, animals get bigger and physically more complex but that inanimate objects do not change in this way. They believe, for example, that sea otters and termites become larger as time goes by but that tea kettles and teddy bears do not (Rosengren, Gelman, Kalish, & McCormick, 1991).

- *Internal parts:* Children know that the insides of animate objects contain different materials than the insides of inanimate objects. Preschool children judge that blood and bones are more likely to be inside an animate object but that cotton and metal are more likely to be inside an inanimate object (Simons & Keil, 1995).

- *Inheritance:* Children realize that only living things have offspring that resemble their parents. Asked to explain why a dog is pink, preschoolers believe that some biological characteristic of the parents probably made the dog pink; asked to explain why a can is pink, preschoolers rely on mechanical causes (e.g., a worker used a machine) not biological ones (Springer & Keil, 1991; Weissman & Kalish, 1999).

- *Healing:* Children understand that, when injured, animate things heal by regrowth whereas inanimate things must be fixed by humans. Preschoolers know that hair will grow back when cut from a child's head but must be repaired by a person when cut from a doll's head (Backscheider, Shatz, & Gelman, 1993).

Findings like these clarify that older preschoolers' naive theories of biology are complex. Of course, their theories aren't complete; they don't know, for instance, that genes are the biological basis for inheritance (Springer & Keil, 1991), and preschoolers' theories include some misconceptions: They believe, for example, that adopted children will physically resemble their adoptive parents (Solomon, Johnson, Zaitchik, & Carey, 1996).

As toddlers and preschoolers, children form a naive theory in another area—psychology! In many situations, adults try to explain to children why people act as they do, and these explanations often emphasize that desires or goals cause people's behaviour. Just as naive physics allows us to predict how objects act, naive psychology allows us to predict how people act (Lillard, 1999).

Collectively, a person's ideas about connections between thoughts, beliefs, and behaviour form a **theory of mind**, a naive understanding of the relations between mind and behaviour. Children's theory of mind moves through three phases during the preschool years (Wellman, 1991, 1992). In the earliest phase, common in 2-year-olds, children are aware of desires, and they often speak of their wants and likes, as in "Lemme see" or "I wanna sit." They also link their desires to their behaviour, such as "I happy there's more cookies" (Wellman, 1991). Therefore, by age 2, children understand that they and other people have desires and that desires are related to behaviour.

By about age 3, children clearly distinguish the mental world from the physical world. For example, if told about one girl who has a cookie and another girl who is thinking about a cookie, 3-year-olds know that only the first girl's cookie can be seen, touched, and eaten (Harris, Brown, Marriot, Whithall, & Harmer, 1991). Also, most 3-year-olds use "mental verbs" like think, believe, remember, and forget, suggesting that they have a new understanding of different mental states (Bartsch & Wellman, 1995). Although 3-year-olds talk about thoughts and beliefs, they usually emphasize desires when trying to explain why people act as they do.

In addition, they also become capable of lying to cover up bad behaviour (Evans & Lee, 2013). Starting around age 3, evidence suggests that children are able to recognize when they have not done what they were supposed to do but then deny the misbehaviour. For example, Evans and Lee (2013) instructed children between the ages of 2 and 4 not to peek at a toy that was hidden. Although 80 percent of children peeked at the toy, most 2-year-olds told the truth when asked if they peeked. However, with increasing age, more children denied having peeked. Nevertheless, they did not later cover up the fact that they knew what the toy was. Therefore, although at this young age children might be capable of lying, they are not very sophisticated at it and easily give themselves away when disclosing knowledge obtained by disobedience (i.e., from peeking at the toy). By age 7, children become capable of detecting complex forms of deceit in others and are quite sophisticated in understanding when someone might be lying or trying to deceive them (Adenzato & Bucciarelli, 2008).

Not until age 4 do mental states really take centre stage in children's understanding of their own and others' actions. By age 4, children understand that their own and others' behaviour is based on their beliefs about events and situations, even when those beliefs are wrong. Rutherford and Rogers (2003) suggested that theory of mind is necessary to a child's ability to engage in pretend play with other children. They proposed that deficits in pretend play for children diagnosed with autism may be linked to deficits in theory of mind. Pellicano (2007) proposed that theory of mind deficits may be due to difficulties in **executive functioning** present early in life. Executive functioning refers to a child's ability to engage in intentional, self-regulated behaviour. Cognitive abilities involved in executive functioning include attention, concentration, planning, organizing, and reflecting on one's own thoughts and behaviour. Some researchers also have noted white matter abnormalities in the brains of children with autism, which could disrupt information processing, particularly across the corpus callosum (Vogan et al., 2016). You'll learn more about executive functioning in the information-processing section of this chapter.

In children who are not autistic, the developmental transformation from egocentrism to a theory of mind is particularly evident when the children are tested on false-belief tasks like the one in Figure 9–3. In all false-belief tasks, a situation is set up so that the child being tested has accurate information but someone else does not. For example, in the story in Figure 9–3, the child being tested knows that the marble is really in the box, but Sally, the girl in the story, believes that the marble is still in the basket. Remarkably, although 4-year-olds correctly say that Sally will look for the

Theory of mind:
a person's understanding of the relations between mind and behaviour.

Executive functioning:
a set of cognitive abilities that enable intentional, self-regulated behaviour.

marble in the basket (acting on her false belief), most 3-year-olds say she will look in the box. The 4-year-olds understand that Sally's behaviour is based on her beliefs, despite the fact that her beliefs are incorrect (Frye, 1993). As Bartsch and Wellman (1995) phrased it, 4-year-olds "realize that people not only have thoughts and beliefs, but also that thoughts and beliefs are crucial to explaining why people do things; that is, actors' pursuits of their desires are inevitably shaped by their beliefs about the world" (p. 144).

New research in theory of mind has demonstrated that counterfactual thinking also plays an important role in developing theory of mind (Guajardo & Turley-Ames, 2003; Riggs, Peterson, Robinson, & Mitchell, 1998). **Counterfactual thinking** refers to a person's understanding that a situation or fact is counter or opposite to reality. Counterfactual thought is first demonstrated through a child's engagement with pretend play, perhaps as early as age 2, and involves the child making mental comparisons between real life and an imagined alternative situation (Guajardo & Turley-Ames, 2003). Once children become better able to make judgments about the veracity of information and engage in activities that are counter to reality (e.g., "you be the mom and I'll be the dad"), they begin to develop a theory of mind. Therefore, naive psychology flourishes in the preschool years with children beginning to reason about how events are related in the world.

Information-Processing Perspectives on Preschool Thinking

LO2 Discuss how children's information-processing ability improves during the preschool years.

Unlike the theory advanced by Piaget, the preschool years are not regarded as a separate stage according to the information-processing approach. Instead, these years are thought to include continued growth of many cognitive skills. Robert Kail remembers playing the card game "war" with his preschool son Ben. In this game, each player turns a card over from the top of his or her deck. The player with the high card wins the hand; the game is over when one player has all the cards. For an adult, the game is boring because there is no room for strategy—the outcome is based purely on luck, and it seems to go on forever! Nevertheless, Robert remembers being impressed by the many skills necessary for 4-year-old Ben to play. He had to know the numbers 2 to 10, plus the non-numerical cards, to determine the high card in each round. He had to know the special rules that applied when the cards played had the same value, and he had to know the rule for deciding when the game was over—all of which are simple for an adult, yet Ben clearly could not have played the game when he was 2 years old.

Kail (2007) noted that age-related improvements in reasoning and problem-solving abilities can be linked to children's continuous improvements specifically in

Figure 9–3

This is Sally. Sally has a basket.

This is Anne. Anne has a box.

Sally has a marble. She puts the marble into her basket.

Sally goes out for a walk.

Anne takes the marble out of the basket and puts it into the box.

Now Sally comes back. She wants to play with her marble. Where will she look for her marble?

SOURCE: Based on Frith, 1989.

Counterfactual thinking: understanding that a situation or fact is opposite to reality.

speed of information processing as well as increased retention of information in working memory. In the next few pages, we'll look at preschool children's improving skills in attention, memory, and counting.

ATTENTION. Our perceptual systems are marvellously powerful, providing us with far more information than we could consciously interpret at any one point in time. **Attention** is the process by which we select information to be processed further. In a class, for example, where the task is to direct your attention to the lecture, it is easy to ignore other stimuli—such as the buzzing of fluorescent lights in the classroom—if the lecture is interesting. If the lecture is boring, other stimuli, such as those lights, might intrude and capture your attention. You might have to actively remind yourself to refocus on the lecture. We are always negotiating the balance between perceptual input and directed attention in our everyday activities.

The roots of attention can be seen in infancy, when children first learn what to pay attention to and what can be ignored. However, regulation of attention improves during the preschool years. Ruff, Capozzoli, and Weissberg (1998) observed and videotaped preschoolers (aged 2½ and 4½) in several settings. In one, children sat at a table watching hand puppets and dolls enact brief skits. In another, children were told they could play with an assortment of toys on a tabletop. Ruff and her colleagues found that children who were actively engaged in the puppet show or free play—as inferred by their posture, facial expressions, spontaneous comments, and the like—exhibited focused attention. Children who left the table exhibited active inattention.

The results, shown in Figure 9–4, illustrate two important characteristics of attention during the preschool years. First, attention improved markedly during this period. In both settings, the 4½-year-olds spent much more time than the 2½-year-olds in focused attention and much less time in active inattention. Second, the 4½-year-olds, though more attentive than the younger children, still spent less than half the time in a state of focused attention. Maintaining focused attention is a demanding skill that emerges gradually during normal development (Enns, 1990).

While attention typically improves with age from birth through adolescence, researchers at the Hospital for Sick Children in Toronto found that biological factors, such as closed head injuries or diseases, can have a direct impact on children's ability to attend (Dennis, Guger, Roncadin, Barnes, & Schachar, 2001; Rovet & Hepworth, 2001). For most children, attention usually improves with age, in part because older

Attention:

the process by which information is selected to be processed further.

Figure 9–4

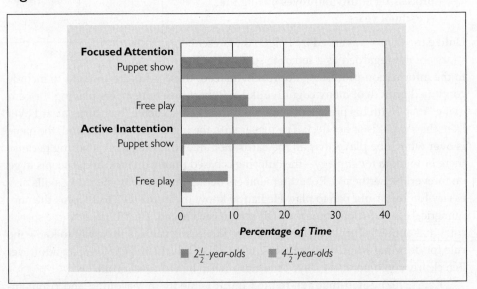

SOURCE: Based on data from Ruff, H. A., Capozzoli, M., & Weissberg, R. (1998). Age, individuality, and context as factors in sustained visual attention during the preschool years. Developmental Psychology, 34, 454–464.

Figure 9–5

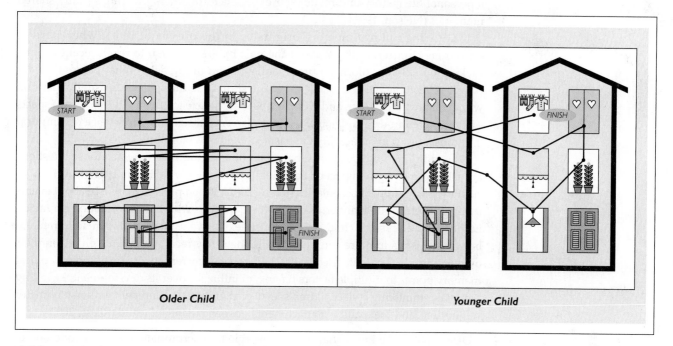

Older Child   **Younger Child**

children and adolescents are more likely to remind themselves to pay attention. They also are more likely to have picked up on some strategies for improving their attention. For example, if asked whether the two houses in Figure 9–5 are the same, older children typically will compare the top windows and work down in a fairly systematic manner until they have compared all six pairs of windows. In contrast, younger children direct their attention haphazardly, so they often don't find the differing windows. As they become older, children learn that systematic comparison is a strategy that improves accuracy and efficiency in making comparisons.

Poulin-Dubois and Forbes (2002) demonstrated that, by the middle of their second year, toddlers can infer the meaning of new words from people's "action intentions." In other words, when children are able to observe the gestures and eye-gaze of an adult along with hearing a new word, they can figure out what that word might mean.

Another approach to helping youngsters focus their attention is to make relevant information more obvious than irrelevant information by minimizing distractions. For example, closing a classroom door can reduce the salience of competing stimuli. Similarly, when preschoolers are working on a task, removing objects not necessary for the task will help them stay focused on it.

MEMORY. We know that infants are able to remember. However, a special feature of memory, autobiographical memory, emerges in the preschool years. **Autobiographical memory** refers to people's memory of the significant events and experiences of their own lives. You can experience your own autobiographical memory by answering these questions:

> Who was your teacher in first grade?
>
> What was your first paying job?
>
> Name a famous person you once saw or met.

In answering these questions, you searched memory, just as you would search memory to answer questions such as "What is the capital of Alberta?" and "Who invented the snowmobile?" However, answers to questions about Alberta (Edmonton) and snowmobiles (Joseph Armand Bombardier) are based on general knowledge you might not have experienced personally; answers to questions about your first teacher, your first job, and your encounter with a famous person are based on

Autobiographical memory: people's memory of the significant events and experiences of their own lives.

knowledge unique to your own life. Autobiographical memory helps people construct a personal life history and relate their experiences to others, creating socially shared memories (Nelson, 1993).

Autobiographical memory originates in the preschool years, when parents encourage children to think about the past by asking them to recall recent events. Picking up a 3-year-old from preschool, a parent might ask, "What games did you play?" or "Who gave you a snack?" In questions like these, parents usually focus on who, what, where, when, and why. In this way, they teach their children what aspects of events are important. Their questions also emphasize the importance of temporal and causal order in organizing the past (Schneider & Bjorklund, 1998).

In addition to the questions that a parent asks, the style in which those questions are asked can have an impact on autobiographical memory (Haden, 1998) as well as the richness of children's vocabularies (Reese, 2002). When parents reminisce about events in a highly elaborate manner, asking many questions with new information contained in them and discussing children's responses extensively, their children tend to remember those events in more complex detail when they recall them later, either on their own or with their parents (Reese, 2002). In general, current theory on autobiographical memory points to multiple factors having an influence over its development, including parental reminiscing style, children's level of cognitive development, understanding of self-in-time, and the quality of attachment between parent and child (Reese, 2002).

COUNTING.   We know that infants are able to discriminate quantities long before they can count. However, by 2 years, most youngsters know some number words and have begun to count. Usually, their counting is full of mistakes. They might count—"1, 2, 6, 7"—skipping 3, 4, and 5. Gelman and Meck (1986) charted preschoolers' understanding of counting. The researchers simply placed several objects in front of a child and asked, "How many?" By analyzing children's answers to many of these questions, Gelman and Meck discovered that, by age 3, most children have mastered three basic principles of counting, at least when it comes to counting up to five objects.

- *One-to-one principle:* There must be one and only one number name for each object that is counted. A child who counts three objects as "1, 2, a" understands this principle because the number of number words matches the number of objects to be counted.

- *Stable-order principle:* Number names must be counted in the same order. A child who counts in the same sequence—for example, consistently counting four objects as "1, 2, 4, 5"—shows understanding of this principle.

- *Cardinality principle:* The last number name differs from the previous ones in a counting sequence by denoting the number of objects in a set. Typically, 3-year-olds reveal their understanding of this principle by repeating the last number name, often with emphasis: "1, 2, 4, 8 . . . EIGHT!"

During the preschool years, children master these basic principles and apply them to ever larger sets of objects. By age 5, most youngsters apply these counting principles to as many as nine objects. Of course, children's understanding of these principles does not mean that they always count accurately. On the contrary, children can apply all these principles consistently while counting incorrectly. They must master the conventional sequence of the number names and the counting principles to count accurately.

Learning the number names beyond nine is easier because the counting words can be generated based on rules for combining decade number names (20, 30, 40) with unit names (1, 2, 3, 4). Later, similar rules are used for hundreds, thousands, and so on. By age 4, most youngsters know the numbers to 20, and some can count to 99. Usually, they stop counting at a number ending in 9 (29, 59), apparently because they don't know the next decade name (Siegler & Robinson, 1982).

Learning to count beyond 10 is more complicated in English than in other languages. For example, eleven and twelve are completely irregular names, following no rules. Also, the remaining "teen" number names differ from the 20s, 30s, and so on because the decade number name comes after the unit number (thir-TEEN, four-TEEN) rather than before it (TWENTY-three, THIRTY-four). Also, some decade names only loosely correspond to the unit names on which they are based: Twenty, thirty, and fifty resemble two, three, and five but are not the same.

In contrast, the Chinese, Japanese, and Korean number systems are almost perfectly regular. Eleven and twelve are expressed as ten-one and ten-two. Two-ten and two-ten-one are names for 20 and 21. The direct correspondence between number names and the base-10 system makes it easier for Asian youngsters to learn base-10 concepts (Miura, Kim, Chang, & Okamoto, 1988).

Chinese, Korean, and Japanese number systems enable easier learning of base-10 concepts.

While system of number can have an effect on the acquisition of numeracy skills, Canadian researchers have found other, new information about children's counting. For example, Klein and Bisanz (2000) showed that preschoolers' ability to perform simple arithmetic operations is affected by the amount of information they are able to hold in working memory. Coplan, Barber, and Lagace-Seguin (1999) demonstrated that a child's temperament can also affect a child's learning in terms of counting and early reading skills. As you can see, acquisition of a skill such as counting is normally associated with cognitive development but is affected by the child's socio-emotional reality as well. Finally, Kail (2007) found that increases in a child's processing speed supports greater ability in working memory, which may have a direct impact on children's ability to engage in inductive reasoning.

Vygotsky's Theory of Cognitive Development

LO3 **Explain why Vygotsky viewed development as an apprenticeship.**

Piaget and neo-Piagetian theorists have tended to describe children's developmental journey as one they make alone. Recognizing this tendency in developmental theory and research, Kessen (1979) objected to psychologists' describing children as if they live in a vacuum. Kessen pointed out that the practice of seeing the child as a "unit" of analysis separate from other people and culture is a cultural invention that should be avoided in theory and research.

Lev Vygotsky (1896–1934), a Russian psychologist, proposed a very different account of child development. Influenced by the structure and beliefs of an Eastern European culture, Vygotsky saw development as a social relationship through which children collaborate with others who are more experienced. According to Vygotsky (1978), children rarely make much headway on the developmental path when they walk alone; they progress when they walk hand in hand with a skilled caregiver, and learning arises out of their interactions with each other. Rather than seeing the child as an individual explorer in the world, Vygotsky focused on the important role that socio-cultural support played in children's physical and intellectual growth in a cultural world.

Vygotsky died of tuberculosis at age 37 and did not complete his theory of cognitive development. Nevertheless, his ideas are influential because they fill some gaps in the Piagetian and neo-Piagetian accounts. Vygotsky made two primary contributions to the field of psychology: his socio-cultural theory of cognitive development and his support for a theory of disability (Das, 1995). In terms of his socio-cultural theory of development, three of his most important contributions are the zone of proximal development, scaffolding, and private speech.

THE ZONE OF PROXIMAL DEVELOPMENT.   Four-year-old Ian and his dad often work on puzzles together. Ian does most of the work, but his dad sometimes correctly orients a piece or finds one Ian needs. When Ian tries to do the same puzzles alone, he rarely can complete them. The difference between what Ian can do with assistance and what he can do alone defines the **zone of proximal development**, the difference between a child's performance with a little help from a person with more skill and the child's performance without that help (Wertsch & Tulviste, 1992).

Think, for example, about a preschooler who is asked to clean her bedroom. She doesn't know where to begin. By structuring the task for the child—"start by putting away your books, then your toys, then your dirty clothes"—an adult can help the child accomplish what she cannot do by herself. Just as training wheels help children learn to ride a bike by allowing them to concentrate on aspects of bicycling other than balance, adults help children perform effectively by providing structure, hints, and reminders.

The idea of a zone of proximal development follows naturally from Vygotsky's basic premise that cognition develops first in a social setting and only gradually comes under the child's independent control. Understanding how the shift from social to individual learning occurs brings us to the second of Vygotsky's key contributions, scaffolding.

Vygotsky viewed cognitive development as a collaboration between a novice child and more skilled teachers who scaffold the child's learning.

SCAFFOLDING.   Have you ever had the good fortune to work with a master teacher, one who seemed to know exactly when to say something to help you over an obstacle but otherwise let you work uninterrupted? **Scaffolding** is a teaching style that matches the amount of necessary assistance to the learner's needs. Early in learning a new task, such as cleaning the bedroom, an adult provides a lot of direct instruction. However, as the child begins to catch on to the task, the teacher provides less instruction and only occasional reminders (McNaughton & Leyland, 1990).

The defining characteristic of scaffolding—giving help but not more than is needed—clearly promotes learning (Plumert & Nichols-Whitehead, 1996). Youngsters do not learn readily when they are constantly told what to do or when they are simply left to struggle through a problem unaided. However, when teachers collaborate with them—allowing children to take on more of a task as they master its different elements—children learn more effectively (Pacifici & Bearison, 1991). Scaffolding is an important technique for transferring cognitive skills from others to the child.

PRIVATE SPEECH.   Children sometimes talk to themselves while playing, a behaviour called **private speech**. Vygotsky (1934/1986) viewed private speech as an intermediate step toward self-regulation of cognitive skills. At first, children's behaviour is regulated by speech from other people that is directed toward them. When youngsters first try to control their own behaviour and thoughts without others present, they instruct themselves by speaking aloud. In this circumstance, their comments are not directed to others but instead help children regulate their own behaviour. Finally, as children gain greater skill, private speech becomes **inner speech**, Vygotsky's term for thought.

If children use private speech to help control their behaviour, then we should see children using it more often on difficult tasks than on easy tasks, and more often after a mistake than after a correct response. These predictions are generally supported in research (Berk, 1992) documenting the power of language in helping children learn to control their own behaviour and cognition.

Jamieson (1995) studied private speech with deaf children in British Columbia as they used sign language that was not directed at any particular listener. She found definite use of private speech in deaf children's sign language. Of the deaf children she studied, the ones who also had deaf mothers tended to use a more sophisticated

Zone of proximal development:
in Vygotskian theory, the difference between what a child can do without the support of a more experienced caregiver and what the child can do with that support.

Scaffolding:
in Vygotskian theory, a teaching style that matches the amount of assistance to the learner's needs.

Private speech:
in Vygotskian theory, comments not directed to others but that help children regulate their own behaviour.

Inner speech:
in Vygotskian theory, inner speech is thought.

Scaffolding matches amount of instruction to a child's need for it.

Children learn to regulate their own behaviour using private speech.

and mature form of signed private speech than those who did not have deaf mothers. Jamieson concluded that her findings support Vygotsky's proposition that private speech derives from a child's experience with early forms of social communication.

The key components of Vygotsky's theory are summarized in Table 9–2. His view of cognitive development as an apprenticeship, a collaboration between expert and novice, complements the other views described in this module. Each perspective—Piaget's theory, the information-processing approach, and Vygotsky's work—provides a unique lens for understanding cognition during the preschool years.

Table 9–2 Summary Table

Key Concepts in Vygotsky's Theory		
Concept	**Defined**	**Example**
Zone of proximal development	The difference between what children can do alone and what they can do with assistance	A child makes little progress cleaning his room alone but accomplishes the task readily when a parent provides structure (e.g., "Start by getting stuff off the floor").
Scaffolding	Providing instruction that matches the learner's needs exactly—neither too much instruction nor too little	A teacher provides much help when a child is first learning to distinguish "b" from "d" but provides less help as the child learns the difference.
Private speech	Speech that is not directed at others but instead guides the child's own behaviour	A child working on a puzzle says to herself, "Start by looking for pieces with straight edges."

Ask Yourself

Compare the role of cultural influences on cognitive development according to Piaget's theory, information-processing approaches, and Vygotsky's theory.

How might the cultural backgrounds of Piaget and Vygotsky have affected the major content or approach of each psychologist's theory of cognitive development?

9.2 Language

Learning Objectives

After reading the module, you should be able to do the following:

LO4 Describe the conditions that help preschoolers expand their vocabularies.

LO5 Understand how children progress from speaking single words to complicated sentences.

LO6 Discuss how a child acquires the grammar of the child's native language.

Not long after children begin to talk, they start combining words to form simple sentences. A typical 2-year-old has a vocabulary of a few hundred words and speaks in sentences that are two or three words long. At the end of the preschool years, a typical 5-year-old has a vocabulary of several thousand words and speaks in sentences that are five or more words long. These impressive changes in language are the focus of this module. We'll begin with word learning and then look at how children master rules for combining words to create longer sentences.

Encouraging Word Learning

LO4 Describe the conditions that help preschoolers expand their vocabularies.

Children's vocabularies increase steadily during the preschool years. For children to expand their vocabularies, they need to hear others speak. Not surprisingly, children learn words more rapidly if their parents speak to them frequently (Roberts, Burchinal, & Durham, 1999). Of course, sheer quantity of parental speech is not all that matters. Parents can foster word learning by naming objects that are the focus of a child's attention (Dunham, Dunham, & Curwin, 1993). Parents can name different items on store shelves as they point to them. During a walk, parents can label the objects—birds, plants, vehicles—that the child sees.

Parents can also help children learn words by reading books with them. However, the way parents read makes a difference. When parents carefully describe pictures as they read, preschoolers' vocabularies increase (Reese & Cox, 1999). Asking children questions also helps. In a study of 4-year-olds (Sénéchal, Thomas, & Monker, 1995), some parents simply read the story while children listened. Other parents read the story but stopped periodically to ask a "what" or "where" question that the child could answer with the target word. Later, the researchers tested children's abilities to recognize the target words and produce them. Figure 9–6 shows that children who answered questions recognized more target words than children who only listened. Children who answered questions were also much more likely to produce the target words.

Why is questioning effective? When an adult reads a sentence (e.g., Arthur is angling.) then asks a question (e.g., What is Arthur doing?), a child must match the new word (angling) with the pictured activity (fishing) and say the word aloud. When parents read without questioning, children can ignore words they don't understand. Questioning forces children to identify meanings of new words and practise saying them.

Figure 9–6

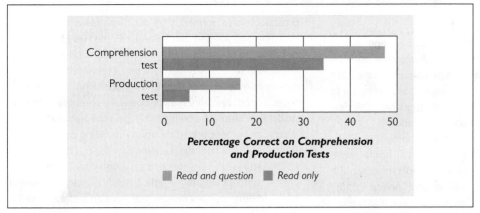

Percentage Correct on Comprehension and Production Tests

■ *Read and question*   ■ *Read only*

SOURCE: Based on data from Sénéchal, M., Thomas, E., & Monker, J. (1995). Individual differences in 4-year-old children's acquisition of vocabulary during storybook reading. Journal of Educational Psychology, 87, 218–229.

Research on reading to children points to a simple but powerful conclusion: Children are most likely to learn new words when they participate in activities that force them to understand the meanings of new words and then use those new words. Can learning new words be affected by culture? The Children and Families around the World feature has the answer.

From Two-Word Speech to Complex Sentences

LO5 Understand how children progress from speaking single words to complicated sentences.

At about 1½ years, children begin to combine individual words to create two-word sentences, like more juice, gimme cookie, truck go, my truck, Mommy go, Daddy eat. Researchers call this kind of talk **telegraphic speech** because, like telegrams of days gone by, it consists only of words directly relevant to meaning, such as important verbs and nouns.

In their two-word speech, children follow rules to express different meanings. For example, the sentences *truck go* and *Daddy eat* are both about agents—people or objects that do something and the actions they perform. Here the rule is "agent + action." In contrast, my truck is about a possessor and a possession; the rule for creating these sentences is "possessor + possession."

When children are in the two-word stage, they use several basic rules to express meaning (Brown, 1973). These rules are listed in Table 9–3.

Telegraphic speech: talk consisting only of words directly relevant to meaning, such as important verbs and nouns.

Table 9–3 Rules Used to Express Meaning during the Two-Word Stage

Rule	Example
agent + action	"Daddy eat"
possessor + possession	"my pencil"
action + object	"gimme cookie"
agent + object	"girl car" (meaning the girl is pushing the car)
action + location	"put chair" (meaning put the object on the chair)
entity + location	"truck chair" (meaning the truck is on the chair)
attribute + entity	"big drum"
demonstrative + entity	"that cup"

SOURCE: Based on Brown, R. (1973). A first language: The early stages. Cambridge, MA: Harvard University Press.

Children and Families around the World

Growing Up Bilingual

Canada is truly a multicultural country, and language-related statistics in Canada are quite complex. Across the country, almost 67 percent of Canadians who participated in the 2011 census identified their primary language spoken at home to be English. For Canada's other official language, 20.6 percent regularly speak French at home—and about 11 percent regularly speak a nonofficial language at home. Less than 1 percent speak both English and French at home, while about 3 percent speak either English or French plus another nonofficial language in the home (Statistics Canada, 2013).

Based on Canadian statistics, you can see that many of the people in this country speak a language other than English on a regular basis. However, day-to-day business in Canada tends to occur in either English or French, so children must learn one of those languages if they are not reared into one or the other from birth. An interesting psychological question can be posed regarding whether learning two languages is easier or harder than learning just one language. For much of the twentieth century, the general view was that bilingualism harmed children's development (Thompson, 1952).

Psychological studies lead to quite a different picture. When 1- and 2-year-olds learn two languages simultaneously, they tend to progress somewhat slowly at first because they mix words from the two languages. However, as Baker (1993) and Lanza (1992) found, by age 3 or 4, children can separate the languages; by the time they begin elementary school, most are as proficient as monolingual children in both languages (Baker, 1993; Lanza, 1992). Bialystok (1997) found that bilingual preschoolers are more likely to understand that the printed form of a word is unrelated to the meaning of the word. For example, bilingual preschoolers are less likely to believe that words denoting large objects (e.g., car) are longer than words denoting small objects (e.g., spider). Bilingual children have also been found to better understand that words are simply arbitrary symbols. Bilingual youngsters, for instance, are more likely than monolingual children to understand that, as long as all English-speakers agreed, dog could refer to cats and cat could refer to dogs (Bialystok, 1988, 1991; Campbell & Sais, 1995). In addition, they appear to do better on tasks of selective attention than do monolingual children (Bialystok, 1992) and on a task requiring complex information processing along with fast reaction time (Bialystok, 2006).

In addition, researchers have been studying the relationship between math performance and language. In a study of Canadian French- and English-speaking preschoolers between the ages of 36 and 67 months, Lefevre, Clarke, and Stringer (2002) found that children's counting ability was affected both by their knowledge of the counting string and by cultural differences in parenting practices. According to these researchers, French-speaking preschoolers performed more poorly on tasks of rote counting and number recognition, but the two groups did not differ on counting of objects. They concluded that French-speaking children might find it more difficult to master number names than English-speaking peers, perhaps, in part, because French-speaking parents tended to report less emphasis on teaching their children numbers, letters, and words than did English-speaking parents. Based on these findings, Lefevre, Clarke, and Stringer cautioned researchers that groups who appear to differ only in terms of language might actually be very different in terms of other cultural factors that have an impact on task performance.

Ellen Bialystok (2001) also discussed the implications of comparing different cultural groups in studies of bilingualism and pointed to potential problems in making assertions about bilingualism by comparing groups across cultures. While some advantages of bilingual education have been demonstrated, the research findings taken as a whole are somewhat contradictory, and problems have been noted with children's development of adequate vocabulary when learning two languages at an early age. Nevertheless, Bialystok concluded that high-level proficiency in two languages seems to contribute to strong achievement overall and is not detrimental either to children's first-language performance or their cognitive development, which appears to benefit from greater flexibility in mental processing from the learning of two languages. Despite children's general ability to acquire a second language more easily than adults, Bialystok noted that second-language learning for children is difficult and requires extended support from their families and educational communities (Bialystok, 2001). More recent research points to differences in ability to recall words or exert cognitive control between monolingual and bilingual individuals, with monolingual children being better at word recall and bilingual children being better at cognitive control (Bialystok, Craik, & Luk, 2008; Bialystok & Feng, 2009).

Bialystok's research findings are particularly important in Canada, given the great number of cultural groups here, including new immigrants. In Canada, many children do not speak English fluently, or at all, when they first come into the Canadian education system. Bialystok pointed out that nobody is truly monolingual, as exposure to other languages in life is inevitable. Perhaps Bialystok (2001) described bilingualism best as the ability to function well, not with perfect fluency, in both languages. New immigrants must be able to function adequately in order to survive in Canadian society, and this kind of pragmatic understanding can only help educational policy development in Canada.

Much of the debate over language of instruction is ethno-political in nature. Some people believe that Canada should have one official language, and some believe it should have two. Others feel that use of multiple official languages should be possible, just as in Switzerland, which has four. However, looking at the research, we can see that the best method of instruction tends to use the child's native language as well as the primary language(s) of the nation (Padilla et al., 1991; Wong-Fillmore, Ammon, McLaughlin, & Ammon, 1985), facilitating both cultural consistency and skill in acquiring the dominant language(s) used by people in that society. Realistically, the success of bilingual programs might depend, to a large degree, on the positive multicultural orientation of parents and teachers supporting those programs (Taylor, 1987).

Of course, not all children use all eight rules, but most do, and this is true of children around the world (Tager-Flusberg, 1993). Regardless of the language they learn, children's two-word sentences follow a common set of rules that are very useful in describing ideas concerning people and objects, their actions, and their properties.

Beginning at about the second birthday, children move to three-word and even longer sentences. Their longer sentences are filled with **grammatical morphemes**, words or endings of words (such as -ing, -ed, or -s) that make a sentence grammatical. To illustrate, a child of 18 months might say, "kick ball," but a 3-year-old would be more likely to say, "I am kicking the ball." Compared to the 18-month-old's telegraphic speech, the 3-year-old has added several elements, including a pronoun, I, to serve as the subject of the sentence; the auxiliary verb am; -ing to the verb kick; and an article, the, before ball. Each of these grammatical morphemes makes the older child's sentence slightly more meaningful and much more grammatically correct.

Grammatical morphemes: words or endings of words that make a sentence grammatical.

How do children learn all of these subtle nuances of grammar? Conceivably, a child might learn that kicking describes an action that is ongoing and that kicked describes an action that occurred in the past. Later, the child might learn that raining describes current weather and rained describes past weather. Learning different tenses for individual verbs—one by one—would be remarkably slow going. More effective would be to learn the general rules that "verb + -ing" denotes an ongoing activity and "verb + -ed" denotes a past activity. In fact, this is what children do: They learn general rules about grammatical morphemes.

Jean Berko (1958) conducted one of the very first studies of children's grammatical morphemes. Berko showed that children's use of grammatical morphemes is based on their growing knowledge of grammatical rules, not simply memory for individual words. She showed preschoolers pictures of nonsense objects like the one in Figure 9–7. The experimenter labelled it saying, "This is a wug." Then youngsters were shown pictures of two of the objects while the experimenter said, "Now there is another one. There are two of them. There are two . . ." Most children spontaneously said, "Wugs." Because wug is a novel word, children could answer correctly only by applying the rule of adding -s to indicate plural.

Overregularization: applying rules to words that are exceptions to the rule.

Sometimes, of course, applying the general rule can lead to very creative communication. As a 3-year-old, Robert Kail's daughter would say, "unvelcro it," meaning detach the Velcro. She had never heard unvelcro, but she created this word from the rule that "un- + verb" means to reverse or stop the action of a verb. Creating such novel words is, in fact, evidence that children learn grammar by applying rules, not by learning individual words.

Additional evidence that children master grammar by learning rules comes from preschoolers' **overregularization**—applying rules to words that are exceptions to the rule. Youngsters learning English might incorrectly add -s instead of using an irregular plural—two

Figure 9–7

This is a wug.

Now there is another one. There are two of them. There are two _____ .

mans instead of two men or two foots instead of two feet. With the past tense, children might add -ed instead of using an irregular past tense—I goed instead of I went or she runned instead of she ran (Marcus et al., 1992). Children apparently know the general rule but not all the words that are exceptions to that rule.

The rules governing grammatical morphemes range from fairly simple to very complex. The rule for plurals—add -s—is simple to apply, and, as you might expect, it's one of the first grammatical morphemes that children master. Adding -ing to denote ongoing action is also simple and it too is mastered early. More complex forms, such as the various forms of the verb "to be" are mastered later; but, remarkably, by the end of the preschool years, children typically have mastered most of the rules that govern grammatical morphemes.

At the same time that preschoolers are mastering grammatical morphemes, they extend their speech beyond the subject-verb-object construction that is basic to English. You can see these changes in the way children ask questions. Children's questions during two-word speech are marked by intonation alone. Soon after children can declare "My ball," they can also ask "My ball?" Children quickly discover wh- words (who, what, when, where, why), but they don't use them correctly. Many youngsters merely attach the wh- word to the beginning of a sentence without changing the rest of the sentence: "What he eating?" "What we see?" By 3 or 3½ years, youngsters insert the required auxiliary verb before the subject, creating "What is he eating?" or "What did we see?" (deVilliers & deVilliers, 1985).

Between ages 3 and 6 years, children also learn to use negation ("That isn't a butterfly") and embedded sentences ("Jennifer thinks that Bill took the ball"). They begin to comprehend passive voice ("The ball was kicked by the girl") as opposed to the active voice ("The girl kicked the ball"), although full understanding of this form continues to develop into the elementary school years (Tager-Flusberg, 1993). In short, by the time most children enter kindergarten, they use most of the grammatical forms of their native language with great skill. As children approach adolescence, they master more complex sentence structures, using words such as "which" and "that" to form subordinate clauses: "Jessie has a copy of the book that we talked about in school today."

How Children Acquire Grammar

LO6 Discuss how a child acquires the grammar of the child's native language.

If you were asked to explain how children master grammar, where would you begin? You might propose that children learn to speak grammatically by listening to and then copying adult sentences. In fact, B. F. Skinner (1957) and other learning theorists once claimed that all aspects of language—sounds, words, grammar, and communication—were learned through imitation and reinforcement (Whitehurst & Vasta, 1975).

Critics were quick to point out some flaws in the learning explanation of grammar. One problem is that children produce many more sentences than they have ever heard. In fact, most of children's sentences are novel, which is difficult to explain in terms of simple imitation of adult speech. Also troublesome for learning theory is that, even when children imitate adult sentences, they do not imitate adult grammar. In simply trying to repeat, "I am drawing a picture," young children will say, "I draw picture." Linguist Noam Chomsky (1957, 1995) argued that grammatical rules are far too complex for toddlers and preschoolers to infer them solely on the basis of speech that they have heard. In addition, children not only have to learn how to apply grammar but also when not to use a particular grammatical structure or rule (Slobin, 1985). If grammatical rules are not acquired solely through imitation and reinforcement, perhaps children are born with mechanisms that simplify the task of learning grammar (Slobin, 1985). According to this view, children are born with neural circuits in the brain that allow them to infer the grammar of the language they hear. That is, grammar itself is not built into the child's nervous system, but processes that guide the learning of grammar are.

The idea that inborn mechanisms help children learn grammar might not be as intuitively appealing as imitation, but many findings indirectly support this view:

Figure 9–8

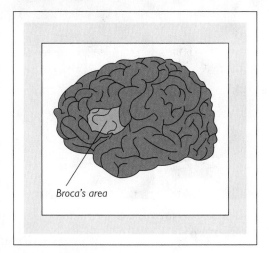

Broca's area

1. Specific regions of the brain are known to be involved in language processing. If children are born with a "grammar-learning processor," it should be possible to locate a specific region or regions of the brain involved in learning grammar. For most people, the left hemisphere of the brain plays a critical role in understanding language. Some functions of language have been located even more precisely. For example, the shaded area in Figure 9–8 is Broca's area, a region in the left frontal cortex necessary for combining words into meaningful sentences. The fact that specific areas in the brain have well-defined functions for language make it plausible that children have specialized neural circuits to help them learn grammar.

2. Only humans learn grammar readily. If grammar is learned solely through imitation and reinforcement, then it should be possible to teach rudimentary grammar to nonhumans. If, instead, learning grammar depends upon specialized neural mechanisms that are unique to humans, then efforts to teach grammar to nonhumans should fail. This prediction has been tested many times by trying to teach grammar to chimpanzees, the species closest to humans on the evolutionary ladder. Chimpanzees have been taught to communicate using gestures taken from sign language or with plastic chips to stand for words. The result? Chimps master only simple grammatical rules governing two-word speech, but only with intensive and sustained effort that is completely unlike the preschool child's seemingly automatic learning of grammar (Savage-Rumbaugh et al., 1993; Seyfarth & Cheney, 1996).

3. A critical period for learning language exists. A critical period refers to a time in development when children master skills or behaviours readily. Apparently, the period from birth to about 12 years is critical to acquiring language generally and mastering grammar particularly. If children do not acquire language in this period, they will never truly master language later. Evidence of a critical period for language comes from studies of isolated children. In one tragic instance, a baby girl named Genie was abused by being continually restrained. No one was permitted to talk to Genie, and she was beaten when she made any noise. When Genie was discovered at age 13, her language was extremely basic. After several years of language training, her language use resembled the telegraphic speech of a 2-year-old (Curtiss, 1989; Rymer, 1993), and she was unable to master any higher grammatical forms.

Further evidence of a critical period for language comes from studies of individuals learning second languages. According to Newport (1991), individuals master the grammar of a foreign language at the level of a native speaker only if they are exposed to the language prior to adolescence.

While the evidence in favour of an inborn grammar-learning device is impressive, it is only indirect. As yet, no definitive finding makes an airtight case for the existence of a grammar-learning device (Maratsos, 1998), so psychologists must look for other explanations.

Chimps can learn to communicate using gestures.

Semantic bootstrapping hypothesis:

children rely upon their knowledge of word meanings to discover grammatical rules.

Some theorists (e.g., Braine, 1992) believe that children learn grammar using the same cognitive skills that allow them to learn other rules and regularities in their environments. According to the **semantic bootstrapping hypothesis**, children rely upon their knowledge of word meanings to discover grammatical rules (Bates & MacWhinney, 1987). That is, children notice that some words (nouns) typically refer to objects and others (verbs) to actions. They also notice that nouns and verbs have distinct functions in sentences. By detecting such regularities in speech, children gradually infer the grammatical rules that provide structure for their language.

Some researchers believe that built-in neural circuits help children infer the grammar of their native language; other researchers believe children use cognitive skills to find regular patterns in the speech they hear.

Both the grammar-learning device and the bootstrapping hypothesis could be correct: Children might learn grammar using some mechanisms that are specific to language as well as some that are not (Maratsos, 1998). Those who adopt the grammar-learning perspective and those who adopt the semantic bootstrapping view both agree that language experience is important because it provides the information from which grammatical rules are inferred. After all, children growing up in a home where Japanese is spoken master Japanese grammar, not Russian or English grammar.

For many children, parents' speech is the prime source of information about language. Parents fine-tune their speech so that it includes examples of the speech that their children are attempting to master (Hoff-Ginsberg, 1990). For example, when 2- and 3-year-olds begin to experiment with pronouns like you, I, she, and he, their parents provide many examples of how to use these pronouns correctly. Similarly, as these children begin to use auxiliary verbs such as have, has, was, and did, parents use speech that is especially rich in these verbs (Sokolov, 1993). By providing extra instances of the parts of speech that children are learning, parents make it easier for children to master new grammatical rules.

Parents also provide feedback to help children evaluate their tentative grammatical rules. Most of the feedback is indirect. When a child's speech is incorrect or incomplete, parents shouldn't say, "That's wrong!" or "How ungrammatical!" Instead, they should rephrase or elaborate on the child's remark. For example, if a child were to say, "Doggie go," the parent could say, "Yes, the doggie went home." A good reply captures the meaning of the child's remark while demonstrating correct grammatical forms (Bohannon, MacWhinney, & Snow, 1990). Parents don't provide feedback for all utterances; in fact, a majority of children's errors go uncorrected. However, the amount of feedback given is sufficient for children to reject incorrect hypotheses about grammatical rules and adjust their speaking, or retain correct ones (Bohannon, Padgett, Nelson, & Mark, 1996).

As yet, no single, comprehensive theory exists of how children master grammar, but general agreement exists that such a theory will include the importance of a language-rich environment, some mechanisms to explain learning grammar, and the idea that children actively seek out regularities in their language environments. All three factors keep children on the trail that leads to mastering grammar (MacWhinney, 1998). New approaches to understanding language acquisition take an interactionist perspective, which values information about genetic, environmental, and neurologically based learning theories to understand how children learn to master language across a variety of learning domains (Chapman, 2007).

Ask Yourself

Children master grammar during the preschool years. How well does this feat match Piaget's view of the preschool child's thinking?

What might Chomsky say to Vygotsky about children's language acquisition?

How might an interactionist perspective to language development address the various debates about the contributions of nature and nurture to children's language acquisition?

9.3 Communicating with Others

 ## Learning Objectives

After reading the module, you should be able to do the following:

LO7 Explain when and how children learn conversational turn-taking.

LO8 List the skills required to be an effective speaker.

LO9 Describe what is involved in becoming a good listener.

Miscommunication between people occurs easily and can lead to arguments. Two people might talk at the same time, make rambling or incoherent remarks, or not really listen to each other during a conversation. In contrast, effective oral communication relies upon several simple guidelines:

- People should take turns, alternating as speaker and listener.
- A speaker's remarks should relate to the topic and be understandable to the listener.
- A listener should pay attention and let the speaker know if his or her remarks don't make sense.

Complete mastery of these pragmatic skills is a lifelong pursuit; after all, even adults miscommunicate with one another because they don't observe one or more of these rules. However, youngsters grasp many of the basics of communication early in life. Let's see.

Taking Turns

LO7 Explain when and how children learn conversational turn-taking.

Many parents begin to encourage turn-taking long before infants say their first words (Field & Widmayer, 1982):

Parent:	Can you see the bird?
Infant (cooing):	Oooo
Parent:	It is a pretty little bird.
Infant:	Oooo
Parent:	Yes! It's a chickadee.

Soon after 1-year-olds begin to speak, their parents normally encourage them to participate in conversational turn-taking. To help children along, parents often carry

"What happened in school today? Read my blog."

Marty Bucella/CartoonStock Ltd.

both sides of a conversation to demonstrate how the roles of speaker and listener alternate (Shatz, 1983):

| Parent (to infant): | What's Amy doing? |
| Parent (illustrating reply): | She's dancing. |

Parents and other caregivers seem to do whatever is necessary to allow infants and toddlers to fit into a conversation. That is, caregivers scaffold youngsters' attempts to converse, making it more likely that children will succeed.

By age 2, spontaneous turn-taking is common in conversations between youngsters and adults (Barton & Tomasello, 1991). By age 3, children have progressed to the point that, if a listener fails to reply promptly, the child will repeat the comment in order to elicit a response (Garvey & Berninger, 1981). A 3-year-old might say, "Hi, Paul" to an older sibling who's busy reading. If Paul doesn't answer in a few seconds, the 3-year-old might say, "Hi, Paul," again. When Paul remains unresponsive, the 3-year-old is likely to shout, "PAUL!"—showing that, by this age, children understand the conversational convention that a comment deserves a response. Preschool children seem to interpret the lack of a response as "I guess you didn't hear me, so I'll say it again, louder!"

Speaking Effectively

LO8 List the skills required to be an effective speaker.

When do children first try to initiate communications with others? Wanting to tell something to someone else is a deliberate act, and, based on Piaget's description of sensorimotor thinking, we wouldn't expect much communication until near the first birthday. In fact, what appears to be the first deliberate attempt to communicate typically emerges at around 10 months (Bates, Benigni, Bretherton, Camaioni, & Volterra, 1979; Golinkoff, 1993). Infants at this age might point to or touch an object. They continue this behaviour until their caregiver acknowledges them.

After the first birthday, children begin to use speech to communicate and often initiate conversations with adults (Bloom, Margulis, Tinker, & Fujita, 1996). Toddlers' first conversations are about themselves, but their conversational scope expands rapidly to include objects in the environment (e.g., toys, food). Later, conversations begin to include more abstract ideas, such as hypothetical objects and past or future events (Foster, 1986).

Of course, young children are not always skilled conversational partners. At times their communications are confusing, leaving a listener to wonder, "What was that all about?" Every message—whether an informal conversation or a formal lecture—should have a clear meaning, but saying something clearly is often difficult because clarity can be judged only by considering the listener's age, experience, and knowledge of the topic as well as the context of the conversation. For example, think about the simple request, "Please hand me the ladle." This

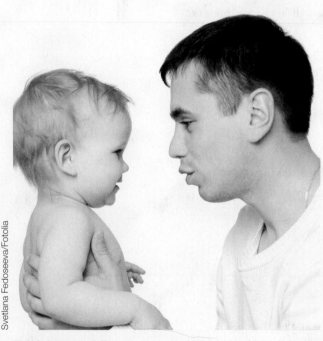

This father is modelling conversational turn-taking for his baby.

Svetlana Fedoseeva/Fotolia

message might be clear to older listeners familiar with different types of utensils, but it won't mean much to younger listeners who think all cooking spoons are alike. If the utensil drawer has several ladles of assorted sizes, the message won't be clear even to a knowledgeable listener.

Constructing clear messages is a fine art, but, amazingly, by the preschool years, youngsters begin to adjust their messages to match the listener and the context. In a classic study, Marilyn Shatz and Rochel Gelman (1973) asked 4-year-olds to explain how a toy worked, once to a 2-year-old and once to an adult. Shatz and Gelman found that 4-year-olds talked more overall to adults than to 2-year-olds and used longer sentences with adult listeners than with 2-year-old listeners. Also, children used simpler grammar and more attention-getting words, such as see, look, watch, and hey, when speaking with 2-year-olds. Here, for example, is how one 4-year-old child explained the toy to her two different listeners. (By the way, the toy is a garage with drivers and trucks that carry marbles to a dumping station):

> To adult listener: You're supposed to put one of these persons in, see? Then one goes with the other little girl, and then the little boy. He's the little boy, and he drives. And then they back up . . . And then the little girl falls out, and then it goes backward.

> To two-year-old listener: Watch, Perry. Watch this. He's back in here. Now he drives up. Look, Perry. Look here, Perry. Those are marbles, Perry. Put the men in here. Now I'll do it. (Shatz & Gelman, 1973, p. 13)

Shatz and Gelman's findings show that, in formulating a clear message, preschoolers are sensitive to the importance of the audience. In addition, preschool children give more elaborate messages to listeners who are unfamiliar with a topic than to listeners who are familiar with it (O'Neill, 1996). For example, a child describing where to find a toy will give more detailed directions to a listener whose eyes were covered when the toy was hidden.

Preschoolers clearly have begun to understand the factors that must be considered in creating clear messages. Even so, sometimes messages are not clear to listeners. Speakers must pay attention to listeners; if listeners don't seem to understand the message, speakers must try again. And, in fact, preschool children seem to understand that when listeners misunderstand, speakers should do something, such as repeating what they said (Shwe & Markman, 1997). In the grander scheme of things, repeating what you've just said is not a very good strategy, but it is a first step in trying to make oneself better understood.

Thus, preschool children express themselves to others and adjust their conversations to fit listeners. Are they equally adept at listening? We'll find out in the next section.

Listening Well

LO9 Describe what is involved in becoming a good listener.

Listening well might seem easy, but it's not—a skilled listener must continuously decide whether a speaker's remarks make sense. If they do, then a listener needs to make an appropriate reply, typically by extending the conversation with another remark that's on the topic.

Few toddlers master this fundamental conversation skill. Their replies are more likely to be unrelated to the topic than related to it (Bloom, Rocissano, & Hood, 1976). Asked, "Where's the sock?" a 1½-year-old might say something like, "I'm hungry!" By 3 years, children are more adept at continuing conversations by making remarks that relate to the topic being discussed.

If a message is vague or confusing, a listener should ask the speaker to clarify the message. This seems obvious enough, but young children do not always realize when a message is ambiguous. Told to find "the red toy," they might promptly select the red ball from a pile that includes a red toy car, a red block, and a red toy hammer. Instead of asking the speaker which specific red toy, young listeners often assume that they know which toy the speaker had in mind (Beal & Belgrad, 1990). Only when messages almost defy comprehension—they are too soft to be heard or give obviously ambiguous or even conflicting information—do youngsters detect a problem. How do you think good listening relates to the idea of a youngster's theory of mind?

Because young children's remarks often contain ambiguities and because, as listeners, they often do not detect ambiguities, young children often miscommunicate. Throughout the preschool and elementary school years, youngsters gradually master the many skills involved in determining whether a message is consistent and clear (Ackerman, 1993).

Sometimes messages are confusing because they conflict with what a listener thinks is true. For example, suppose a child is told that the family cat, who always stays indoors, has run away. Even preschoolers are more likely to believe such a message when told by a parent than by a classmate because they know the parent is better informed about this particular topic (Robinson, Champion, & Mitchell, 1999).

Ask Yourself

Preschool children are often poor communicators: Their comments often do not relate to a topic or may be incomprehensible to a listener. How might these limits in communication skill affect a parent's way of disciplining a preschool child?

9.4 Early Childhood Education

 ## Learning Objectives

After reading the module, you should be able to do the following:

LO10 Identify how the aims of preschool programs are best achieved.

LO11 Explain how effective Head Start programs are.

LO12 Discuss whether television can be used to educate preschool children.

More than 150 years ago, German educator Friedrich Froebel argued that young children are like flowers: When cared for properly, they blossom and become beautiful. Based on this philosophy, Froebel created the first kindergarten—literally, a garden of children. Froebel believed that, through play, children learn what they can do and what they can become.

In the twentieth century, these same ideas were extended to even younger children and resulted in early childhood education. In this module, we'll look at the many different forms of early childhood education, and, as we do, we'll see how education affects children's learning and development.

Varieties of Early Childhood Education

LO10 **Identify how the aims of preschool programs are best achieved.**

When Theresa Zolner was a child, she attended a neighbourhood program called a "play school," which was a kind of early childhood education program. Her play school was held at a local church and operated every weekday morning. On a regular basis, the children in the program made crafts, played games, sang songs, and socialized with each other in a structured, educational setting supervised by adults.

North American communities typically have a huge number and variety of programs for preschool children, some of which are publicly operated, some privately, and some by tribal, religious, or other organizations.

Let's begin by distinguishing daycare centres from preschools. The aim of daycare is to care for children while their parents are at work; the aim of a preschool is to nurture children's intellectual, social, and emotional growth while socializing them into a group educational setting. The distinction between daycare and preschool is no longer clear-cut because many daycare centres provide the same kinds of enriched, growth-promoting activities that were once the province of preschools. As preschool programs have become more extensive—growing from two or three hours a few days each week to all morning or all afternoon five days each week—they have become a form of child care.

In recognition of the important role that early education and good child care play in Canadian society, which contains so many dual-income families, the Government of Ontario has moved to full-day kindergarten for 4- and 5-year-olds who are enrolled in publicly funded elementary schools (www.edu.gov.on.ca/kindergarten). The program is organized around play-based learning and includes learning by both exploration and guided instruction. Built into the program are many opportunities for formal and informal assessment of children's abilities so that early intervention plans can be made for children at risk for developmental and learning challenges as they enter Grade 1. These methods of assessment require ongoing teamwork and collaboration among educators as they reflect upon their interactions with children in the program. Researchers conducting longitudinal studies on full-day kindergarten in Canada have found that full-day kindergarten may not have the long-term academic benefit for as many children as anticipated, with positive outcomes so far being limited to better numeracy skills in girls who come from low-income areas (Brownell et al., 2015). However, it may benefit the economics of the family, as some have pointed out that full-day kindergarten amounts to a large cost savings for families who otherwise would have to pay for full-day childcare. This has led to a controversy in Canada over whether parents who can afford to pay for childcare should be paying for full-day kindergarten instead of having it funded through budget allocations for public education (Taylor, 2014).

Programs of early childhood education vary not just in terms of program length but also in terms of the extent to which the teacher provides a structured curriculum that has explicit instructional goals. In child-focused programs, the goal is to educate the whole child—physically, cognitively, socially, and emotionally. Children learn through play, typically in the context of activities that teachers have prepared for them. In more academically oriented programs, teachers follow an explicit curriculum to help preschool children achieve explicit goals for linguistic, cognitive, social, and emotional growth.

Both daycare centres and preschools can promote children's development.

Becoming a good group member is a primary focus of Japanese preschool.

These approaches are alike in using play to anchor teaching and learning. They differ primarily in the explicitness of instructional goals and their emphasis on achieving them.

Most North American parents agree with an emphasis on using preschool programs to educate the whole child. That is, they want preschools to help their youngsters get a good start academically, to socialize the child in a group setting, and to encourage children to become self-reliant. These goals are not shared worldwide, however. In China, parents emphasize academic preparation. In contrast, when Japanese parents send youngsters to preschool, they want them to learn the value of being a good group member (Tobin, Wu, & Davidson, 1989).

In creating preschool programs, many early childhood educators have found Piaget's theory a rich source of ideas (Siegler, 1998). Piaget's view of cognitive development has some straightforward implications for teaching practices that promote children's growth:

- Cognitive growth occurs as children construct their own understanding of the world, so the teacher's role is to create environments where children can discover for themselves how the world works. A teacher shouldn't simply try to tell children how the letters a and b differ but, instead, should provide children with materials that allow them to discover the differences for themselves.

- Children benefit from experience only when they can interpret this experience with their current cognitive structures. It follows, then, that the best teaching experiences are slightly ahead of the children's current skills. As a youngster begins to recognize letters, instead of jumping right to letter-sound skills, a teacher should go to slightly more difficult letter-discrimination problems.

- Cognitive growth can be particularly rapid when children discover inconsistencies and errors in their own thinking. Teachers should, therefore, encourage children to look at the consistency of their thinking but then let children take the lead in sorting out the inconsistencies. If a child is making mistakes in distinguishing letters, a teacher shouldn't correct the error directly but should encourage the child to look at a large number of these errors to discover what he or she is doing wrong.

Drawing upon these and other guidelines, the National Association for the Education of Young Children (NAEYC), the foremost association in North America for early childhood educators, has proposed a set of guidelines for developmentally appropriate practices in early childhood education. These practices are shown in Table 9–4. For more about NAEYC, check out their website (www.naeyc.org).

In Canada, the Canadian Association for Young Children (CAYC) supports goals similar to those of the NAEYC and has issued a position statement on play: "Children learn through play. Through their play, children develop sensory motor control, eye-hand coordination and problem solving skills. Physical, social, intellectual and emotional development are all enhanced through play" (CAYC, n.d.). In addition, the CAYC offers the following key points on their website (www.cayc.ca) in support of the idea that play promotes cognitive development:

- Children need essential time to play.
- Children need to direct their play.
- Children need the decision-making practice that play provides.

Table 9–4 NAEYC Recommendations for Developmentally Appropriate Practices in Early Childhood Education

Practice	Description
Create a caring community of learners	The early childhood setting functions as a community of learners in which all participants—children, families, teachers—contribute to each other's well-being and learning.
Teach to enhance development and learning	Teachers use their knowledge of child development to provide appropriate learning experiences that allow children to acquire important knowledge and skills.
Assess children's learning and development	Age-appropriate assessment of young children's progress is used to benefit children—in adapting teaching to meet children's needs, for communicating with the child's family, and for evaluating the program's effectiveness.
Establish reciprocal relationships with families	Early childhood teachers work in collaborative partnerships with families. Teachers acknowledge parents' goals for children and respond with respect to parents' preferences and concerns without abdicating professional responsibility to children.

SOURCE: Based on NAEYC, 1997. NAEYC/Nat'l Assoc for the Education of Young Children.

- Children need an appropriate space in which to play.
- Children need certain materials for play.
- Children need adults to support and enable their play.

Preschool programs that embrace most of the NAEYC or CAYC guidelines tend to be more effective: Children who "graduate" from such programs tend to be better prepared for kindergarten and Grade 1. Their behaviour in the classroom is more appropriate and they tend to work harder and do better in school (Hart, Charlesworth, Burts, & DeWolf, 1993). Consequently, parents should spend the extra time to find preschool programs that follow these guidelines.

Preschool Programs for Economically Disadvantaged Children

LO11 Explain how effective Head Start programs are.

Effective preschool education is particularly important for children who are economically disadvantaged. Without preschool, children from low-income families often enter kindergarten or Grade 1 lacking key readiness skills for academic success, which means they rapidly fall behind their peers who have these skills. Consequently, providing preschool experiences for children from poor families has long been a part of North American government policies to eliminate poverty. The Child Development and Family Policy feature traces the beginnings of these programs.

How effectively do programs such as Head Start meet the needs of preschool youngsters? The very nature of Head Start makes this question hard to answer. First of all, no two Head Start programs are exactly alike, so blanket statements about the effectiveness of Head Start programming cannot, in general, be made. However, high-quality Head Start programs are effective overall. That is, Head Start programs that adhere to guidelines like those suggested by Health Canada, the NAEYC, and the CAYC are successful in many respects. Children in Head Start programs are healthier and do better in school (Lazar & Darlington, 1982; Zigler & Styfco, 1994) than children who begin school without having participated in such a program. For example, Head Start graduates are less likely to repeat a grade level or to be placed in special education classes, and they are more likely to graduate from high school. Thus, investing in Head Start pays real dividends in dollars not spent on special education or welfare and, more importantly, in improved quality of life for the children who participate.

Child Development and Family Policy

Providing Children with a Head Start for School

For more than 35 years, Head Start has been a strong force in helping to foster the development of preschool children from low-income families. In the early 1960s, child-development researchers argued that environmental influences on children's development were much stronger than had been estimated previously.

The second force was a political twist of fate. When U.S. President Lyndon Johnson launched the War on Poverty in 1964, the Office of Economic Opportunity (OEO) was the command centre. Sargent Shriver, OEO's first director, found himself with a huge budget surplus. Realizing that no programs were aimed at children per se and that such programs would be much less politically controversial, Shriver envisioned a program that would better prepare poor children for Grade 1. In December 1964, he convened a 14-member planning committee that included professionals from medicine, social work, education, and psychology. Over a six-week period, the planning committee devised a comprehensive program that would, by involving professionals and parents, meet the health and educational needs of young children. In May 1965, President Johnson announced the opening of Head Start, and by that summer, a half-million American youngsters were enrolled. The program continues today and has now served the needs of millions of North American children living in poverty.

Closer to home, Health Canada (2001b) developed a national early intervention strategy for children of Métis, Inuit, and First Nations heritage, called the Aboriginal Head Start program (Public Health Agency of Canada, 1998). The mandate of Aboriginal Head Start (Public Health Agency of Canada, 2005b) is as follows:

- Foster the spiritual, emotional, intellectual, and physical growth of the child.
- Foster a desire in the child for lifelong learning.
- Support parents and guardians as the prime teachers and caregivers of their children, making sure parents and caregivers play a key role in the planning, development, operation, and evaluation of the program.
- Recognize and support extended families in teaching and caring for children.
- Involve the local Aboriginal community in the planning, development, operation, and evaluation of the program.
- Ensure that the program works with and is supported by other community programs and services.
- Ensure that human and financial resources are used in the best way possible to produce positive outcomes and experiences for Aboriginal children, parents, families, and communities.

Aboriginal Head Start programs are delivered differently from community to community, but they all include particular emphasis on education, health promotion, nutrition, culture and language, social support, and parental involvement. This kind of early intervention program offers support for Aboriginal families and also promotes culturally based education and learning. While many of the concepts and programs focused on psychology are based on mainstream Western learning, some efforts are now being made to determine how a better understanding of cultural foundations for a people can enhance programming and services from both an educational and a clinical perspective (Zolner, 2003a, 2003b).

Using TV to Educate Preschool Children

LO12 Discuss whether television can be used to educate preschool children.

The year 1969 was a watershed in the history of children's television. That year marked the appearance of a program designed to use the power of video and animation to foster preschool skills, including recognizing letters and numbers, counting, and building vocabulary. The program achieved its goals. Preschoolers who watched the show regularly were more proficient at the targeted academic skills than preschoolers who watched infrequently. Regular viewers also adjusted to school more readily, according to teachers' ratings (Bogatz & Ball, 1972).

You've likely realized that we're talking about *Sesame Street*, home of Big Bird, Bert, Ernie, and other memorable characters. Since 1969, the Children's Television Workshop has helped educate generations of preschoolers through its television production of *Sesame Street*.

More recent studies confirm that *Sesame Street* remains effective. Rice, Huston, Truglio, and Wright (1990), for example, found that children who had watched *Sesame Street* frequently at age 3 had larger vocabularies as 5-year-olds than children who watched infrequently.

Research with other TV programs leads to the same conclusion. Youngsters who watch TV shows that emphasize prosocial behaviour, such as *Mr. Dress-Up*, are more likely to behave prosocially (Huston & Wright, 1998). In fact, a comprehensive analysis revealed that the impact of viewing prosocial TV programs is much greater than the impact of viewing televised violence (Hearold, 1986).

Although research indicates that prosocial behaviour can be influenced by TV watching, two important factors restrict the actual prosocial impact of TV viewing. First, prosocial behaviours are portrayed far less frequently than aggressive behaviours, so opportunities to learn prosocial behaviours from television are limited. Second, the rela-

Sesame Street characters.

tively small number of prosocial programs compete with other kinds of television programs and other non-TV activities for children's time, so children simply might not watch the few prosocial programs that are televised. Consequently, we are far from harnessing the power of television for prosocial uses.

Television has its critics. Although they concede that some TV programs help children learn, they also argue that the medium itself—independent of the contents of programs—has several harmful effects on viewers, particularly young children (Huston & Wright, 1998). One common criticism is that, because TV programs consist of many brief segments presented in rapid succession, children who watch a lot of TV develop short attention spans and have difficulty concentrating in school. Another concern heard frequently is that, because TV provides ready-made, simple-to-interpret images, children who watch a lot of TV become passive, lazy thinkers who are less creative. Finally, some recent findings point to the ability of 1-year-olds to perceive and react to negative emotion presented in televised form (Mumme & Fernald, 2003); therefore, you might reconsider allowing your baby to view emotionally intense shows.

Neither of these first two criticisms is consistently supported by research (Huston & Wright, 1998). The first criticism—TV watching reduces attention—is the easiest to dismiss. Research repeatedly shows that TV viewing does not lead to reduced attention, greater impulsivity, reduced task persistence, or increased activity levels (Foster & Watkins, 2010). However, one longitudinal study from New Zealand reported a connection between watching three or more hours of television per day and attention problems in adolescence (Landhuis, Poulton, Welch, & Hancox, 2007). Three hours of television per day is a lot of television for a youngster! Think of all the time a child is not spending engaged in play, learning to read, or participating in family activities if the child is watching three hours of TV every night.

One way that parents might consider limiting children's television is to have a "no movies on a school night" rule. Movies are usually 1½ to 2 hours long, which is too much TV watching on a school night, given play, personal hygiene, homework, and family duties that need to be done. Try to leave the movies for a weekend and keep school nights for brief one-half- to one-hour shows only.

As for the criticism that TV viewing fosters lazy thinking and stifles creativity, the evidence is mixed. Many studies find no link between amount of TV viewing and creativity. Some find a negative relationship in which, as children watch more TV, they tend to get lower scores on tests of creativity (Valkenburg & van der Voort, 1994, 1995). Child-development researchers don't know why the negative effects aren't found more consistently, although one idea is that the effects depend on what programs children watch, not simply on the amount of TV watched.

In general, then, although the contents of TV programs can clearly influence children (positively or negatively, depending on what children watch), no strong evidence exists that TV watching per se has harmful effects on children's cognition. On the other hand, extended television watching promotes obesity, detracts from time spent doing physical activities, and reduces face-to-face time spent with other children and adults. Therefore, extensive television watching is not recommended (Canadian Paediatric Society, 2003). The American Academy of Pediatrics Committee on Public Education (2001) suggests that television watching should be discouraged in children under the age of 2. Happily, some evidence shows that, when in the presence of a parent, a video, and a novel toy, infants will direct more attention to a new toy than to a video—but least to the parent (Courage, Murphy, Goulding, & Setliff, 2010)!

Ask Yourself

How do successful Head Start programs demonstrate connections among different domains of development?

What Would a Responsible Parent Do?

We know that an infant can perceive negative emotion in films and TV shows. If you were the parent of a 1-year-old, what would you do if other people wanted to watch intensely scary or violent shows in the presence of your child? What if friends invited you to a scary movie and said, "Bring baby along!" How would you handle these kinds of situations, and what might be challenging about them?

Summary

9.1 Cognitive Processes

Piaget's Account

- From 2 to 7 years, children are in Piaget's preoperational stage.
- In the preoperational stage, children's thinking is limited by egocentrism and centration, and they confuse appearance with reality.
- Older preschoolers' theories about biology distinguish properties of animate and inanimate objects.
- Older preschoolers' theories of psychology gradually include the idea that behaviour is based on people's beliefs about events and situations.
- In early childhood, the ability to distinguish reality from fantasy begins with pretend play and involves counterfactual thinking.

Information-Processing Perspectives on Preschool Thinking

- Compared to older children, preschool children are less able to pay attention, primarily because they lack well-developed strategies for paying attention.
- Autobiographical memory emerges in the preschool years, often prompted by parents questioning children about past events.
- Young children's memory of the past is inaccurate because they cannot distinguish what actually happened from what adults suggest might have happened.
- Preschoolers begin to count at age 2.
- By age 3, most preschoolers have mastered the one-to-one, stable-order, and cardinality principles when counting small sets of objects.

Vygotsky's Theory of Cognitive Development

- Vygotsky believed that cognition develops first in a social setting and only gradually comes under the child's independent control.

- The zone of proximal development is the difference between what children can do with assistance and what they can do alone.

- Scaffolding is a teaching style that allows children to take on more and more of a task as they master its different components.

- Control of cognitive skills is most readily transferred from others to the child through scaffolding.

- Children often talk to themselves using private speech when they are performing a difficult task or after they have made a mistake.

9.2 Language

Encouraging Word Learning

- Children's word learning is fostered by being read to and by watching television.

- Fostering word learning depends on making children think about the meanings of new words.

From Two-Word Speech to Complex Sentences

- Not long after their first birthday, children produce two-word sentences based on simple rules for expressing ideas or needs.

- Moving from two-word to more complex sentences involves adding grammatical morphemes.

- Children first master grammatical morphemes that express simple relations and then those that denote complex relations.

- As children acquire grammatical morphemes, they also extend their speech to other sentence forms, such as questions, and more complex constructions, such as passive sentences.

How Children Acquire Grammar

- Some researchers claim that the brain is prewired to help children learn grammar.

- Findings consistent with the argument that the brain is prewired to acquire grammar include specialized regions in the brain for processing language, the inability of chimpanzees to master grammar, and critical periods in language acquisition.

- Other researchers believe that children use general cognitive skills to infer grammatical rules from regularities in the speech that they hear.

- Language experience is important for learning grammar.

- Parents provide examples of the rules of speech that their children are trying to master and feedback concerning grammatical rules.

9.3 Communicating with Others

Taking Turns

- Parents encourage turn-taking even before infants talk and, later, demonstrate both speaker and listener roles.

- By age 3, children spontaneously take turns and prompt one another to speak.

Speaking Effectively

- Before they can speak, infants use gestures and noises to communicate.

- During the preschool years, children gradually become more skilled at constructing clear messages, in part by adjusting their speech to fit the listener's needs.

- During the preschool years, children begin to monitor their listeners' comprehension, repeating messages if necessary.

Listening Well

- Toddlers are not good conversationalists because their remarks often don't relate to the topic.

- Preschoolers are unlikely to identify ambiguities in another's speech.

9.4 Early Childhood Education

Varieties of Early Childhood Education

- Most early childhood education programs emphasize play.

- Academically oriented programs embed play in explicit instructional goals.

- According to Piaget's theory, early childhood education is most effective when it emphasizes children's discovery, provides experiences that are just ahead of the child's current skills, and allows children to discover inconsistencies in their thinking.

- Guidelines by the NAEYC and CAYC for developmentally appropriate teaching practices call for creating a caring community of learners, teaching that enhances development, assessing children's learning, and establishing relationships with families.

Preschool Programs for Economically Disadvantaged Children

- Head Start was created in the United States during the 1960s.

- Children from low-income families who participate in high-quality Head Start programs are healthier and do better in school.

- In Canada, many children attend Aboriginal Head Start programs.

Using TV to Educate Preschool Children

- Children who watch *Sesame Street* regularly improve their academic skills and adjust to school more readily.

- When children watch programs that emphasize prosocial skills, they are more likely to behave prosocially.

- Although critics have suggested that frequent TV viewing leads to reduced attention and reduced creativity, research does not consistently support these criticisms.

Chapter Critical Review

1. What, in your opinion, is the most important cognitive change that takes place during the preschool years? Support your opinion by explaining the adaptive importance of that change.

2. Compare three major explanations for how children acquire grammar: learning, inborn neural circuits, and semantic bootstrapping (Module 9.2). Which best fits each of the cognitive theories described in Module 9.1?

3. Piaget's theory provides some useful guidelines for effective preschool programs. What guidelines for such programs can you derive from the information-processing approach? From Vygotsky's theory?

4. Some policy makers have argued that TV programs like *Sesame Street* could be used to achieve the goals of Head Start programs but much less expensively. What would be the strengths and weaknesses of such a policy?

See for Yourself

Berko's (1958) "wugs" test is fun to try with preschool children. Photocopy the drawing in Figure 9–7 and show it to a preschooler, repeating the instructions that appear on that page. You should find that the child quite predictably answers, "two wugs." Create some pictures of your own to examine other grammatical morphemes, such as adding -ing to denote ongoing activity or adding -ed to indicate past tense. See for yourself!

Chapter 10
Social and Emotional Development in Preschool Children

Anna Omelchenko/Shutterstock

 MODULE

10.1 Self

10.2 Relationships with Parents

10.3 Relationships with Siblings and Peers

10.4 Moral Development: Learning to Control One's Behaviour

Mabel and Terry enrolled Sophie at play school. One day, when they came to pick her up, they saw her playing "mom and dad" with her friend Sui Lan. The two playmates were trying to convince their friend, Jill, to be their "baby." Next to Sophie were two other children, Luke and Aurelio, who were crawling under a table and pretending it was a cave. Another child, Kerry, was drawing a picture of her house, complete with her pet gerbil. Two other girls, Elaine and Keisha, were arguing about which puzzle to do. Terry and Mabel marvelled at the busyness of the children and wondered . . . how did they learn to play so imaginatively?

Connect to My Virtual Child

What kinds of theories do you have about children? What ideas inform your thoughts and beliefs about the lives of children, how they are raised, and the nature of the human person? Use your access card and follow this link www.myvirtualchild.com to learn more about the world of the child. You can even virtually try to raise your own child.

10.1 Self

Learning Objectives

After reading the module, you should be able to do the following:

LO1 Understand gender stereotyping and how it may differ for boys and girls.

LO2 Explain how adults, children, and biology contribute to children's learning of gender roles.

LO3 Recognize whether preschool children have high self-esteem.

By 15 to 18 months, toddlers begin to acquire a concept of self. They begin to define themselves, a process that accelerates in the preschool years. Youngsters now are likely to define themselves in terms of physical characteristics ("I have blue eyes"), their preferences ("I like spaghetti"), and their competencies ("I can count to 50"). What these features have in common is a focus on a child's characteristics that are observable and concrete (Damon & Hart, 1988).

A particularly important element in the child's search for the self is self-identifying as a boy or girl and learning behaviours commonly associated with each role. We'll examine this process, and, as we do, we'll learn how children develop a sense of self and come to value themselves as people.

Gender Roles

LO1 **Understand gender stereotyping and how it may differ for boys and girls.**

Social role:

a set of cultural guidelines for how a person should behave.

Gender roles:

the culturally prescribed roles considered appropriate for males and females.

Gender stereotypes:

beliefs about how males and females differ in personality traits, interests, and behaviours.

Like a role in a play, a **social role** is a set of cultural guidelines for how a person should behave. The social roles associated with gender are among the first that children learn. During the preschool years, children learn about **gender roles**—the culturally prescribed roles considered appropriate for males and females. All cultures have **gender stereotypes**—beliefs about how males and females differ in personality traits, interests, and behaviours. Of course, because stereotypes are beliefs, they may or may not be true. For example, read the following sentence:

Terry is active, independent, competitive, and aggressive.

As you were reading this sentence, you probably assumed that Terry was a male. Why? Although Terry is a common name for both males and females, the adjectives used to describe Terry are more commonly associated with men than women. Table 10–1 lists traits that college students typically associate with males and females.

Table 10–1 Features Judged by College Students to Be Characteristically Male or Female

Male	Female
Independent	Emotional
Aggressive	Home-oriented
Not excitable	Kind
Skilled in business	Cries easily
Mechanical aptitude	Creative
Outspoken	Considerate
Acts as a leader	Devotes self to others
Self-confident	Needs approval
Ambitious	Gentle
Not easily influenced	Aware of others' feelings
Dominant	Excitable

SOURCE: Based on Williams, J. E., & Best, D. L. (1990). Measuring sex stereotypes: A thirty-nation study (rev. ed.). Newbury Park, CA: Sage Publications.

The traits stereotypically associated with men are called **instrumental** because they describe individuals who act on the environment and influence it. In contrast, the traits stereotypically associated with women are called **expressive** because they describe emotional functioning and individuals who value interpersonal relations.

North American men and women tend to believe that instrumental traits typify men, whereas expressive traits typify women (Lutz & Ruble, 1995; T. L. Ruble, 1983; Williams & Best, 1990). However, these views are not shared by adults worldwide. Williams and Best (1990) studied 300 different traits in participants across 30 countries. Figure 10–1 contains results for just four traits and seven countries. You can see that each trait shows considerable cultural variation. For example, most Canadian and virtually all American participants considered men aggressive, but only a slight majority of Nigerian participants did. As you can see, North American views of men and women are not shared worldwide (Neto & Furnham, 2005). In fact, Americans' gender stereotypes are more extreme than those of any other country listed. Keep this in mind as you think about what men and women can and cannot do and what they should and should not do. Your ideas about gender are shaped by your culture's beliefs, which are not held universally.

By the time North American children are ready to enter elementary school, they have learned much about gender stereotypes. Canadian researchers (Poulin-Dubois, Serbin, Eichstedt, Sen, & Beissel, 2002) examined toddlers' knowledge of gender stereotypes, focusing on traditionally feminine and masculine household activities. They asked 63 toddlers to choose a male or female doll to imitate nine stereotypically masculine, feminine, or neutral activities (e.g., shaving, vacuuming, sleeping). They found that gender stereotyping of activities familiar to the child occurs in girls as young as 24 months and in boys by 31 months.

Preschool children's views of gender tend to be rigid too. They do not yet understand that gender stereotypes sometimes do not apply. In one study (Martin, 1989), 4-year-olds were told about hypothetical children, some of whom had friends of the same gender and gender-role typical interests. Others had friends of the opposite gender and gender-role atypical interests: "Tommy is a 5-year-old boy whose best friend is a girl. Tommy likes to iron with an ironing board." When children were asked how much the hypothetical child would like to play with masculine and feminine toys, they based their judgments solely on the hypothetical

Instrumental traits:

personality characteristics that reflect active involvement with and influence over the environment and that are stereotypically associated with men.

Expressive traits:

personality characteristics that reflect emotional functioning and a focus on interpersonal relations and that are stereotypically associated with women.

Dan Reynolds/CartoonStock Ltd.

Figure 10-1

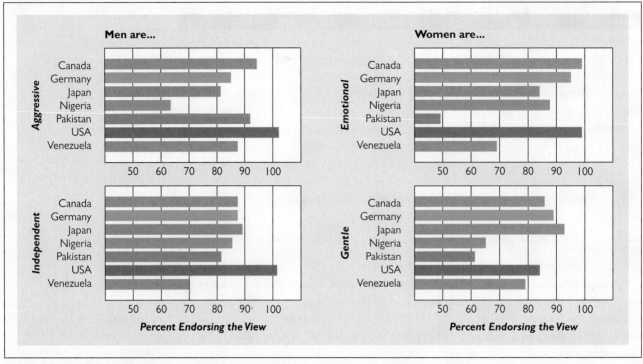

SOURCE: Based on Williams, J. E., & Best, D. L. (1990). Measuring sex stereotypes: A thirty-nation study (rev. ed.). Newbury Park, CA: Sage Publications.

Stereotyped assumptions can lead to unwarranted inferences about a person.

Gender identity:

the perception of oneself as either male or female.

child's sex: The hypothetical boys would like masculine toys, the hypothetical girls, the feminine ones. Even though Tommy likes to play with a girl and pretend to iron, 4-year-olds thought he would want to play with masculine toys.

Thus, preschool children tend to see gender stereotypes as guidelines for behaviour that are binding for all boys and girls (Signorella, Bigler, & Liben, 1993; Taylor, 1996). Unfortunately, stereotypes are limiting. If we have stereotyped views, we respond to boys and girls on the basis of gender, not as individuals. Making stereotyped assumptions about gender leads to a whole host of inferences about behaviour and personality that might not be true (Stern & Karraker, 1989). However, children are exposed to gender-based expectations from infancy onward (Pomerleau, Bolduc, Malcuit, & Cossette, 1990), which send them not-so-subtle messages about how they should play and behave as girls and boys.

Gender Identity

LO2 **Explain how adults, children, and biology contribute to children's learning of gender roles.**

As youngsters learn the behaviours culturally expected of boys and girls, they begin to identify with one of these groups. Children forge a **gender identity**, the perception of oneself as either male or female. In the next section, we'll look at how children develop a sense of being either male or female.

THE SOCIALIZING INFLUENCES OF PEOPLE AND THE MEDIA. According to social learning theorists like Albert Bandura (1977, 1986), children learn gender roles in much the same way that they learn other social behaviours: through reinforcement and observational learning. Parents and others shape appropriate gender roles in children, and children learn what their culture considers appropriate behaviour for boys and girls by watching how adults and peers interact and respond to each other.

Research findings have supported the social-learning perspective. For example, Lytton and Romney (1991) conducted an extensive analysis of 172 studies involving 27 836 children and found that parents tend to interact equally with sons and daughters, in the sense that mothers and fathers are equally warm to their sons and daughters, encouraging both sons and daughters to achieve and become independent. However, parents tended to differ slightly in terms of their choice of toys in play, such that daughters were encouraged to play with dolls, dress up, or help adults, whereas sons were encouraged to engage in rough-and-tumble play or block-building. In addition, children's literature tends to portray more male title and main characters overall than female characters (Clark, Guilmain, Saucier, & Tavarez, 2003; Gooden & Gooden, 2001; Hamilton, Anderson, Broaddus, & Young, 2006).

Snow, Jacklin, and Maccoby (1983) found that fathers are more likely than mothers to treat sons and daughters differently and to encourage gender-based play. Fathers also pushed their sons toward independence but tended to accept dependence in their daughters (Snow, Jacklin, & Maccoby, 1983). For example, a father might urge his son to jump off a diving board ("Be a man!") but not be so insistent with his daughter ("That's okay, honey"). Apparently mothers are more likely to respond based on their knowledge of the individual child's needs, but fathers tend to respond based on gender stereotypes. A mother responds to her son knowing that he's smart but unsure of himself; a father might respond based on how he thinks boys should behave.

Peers are also influential. Preschoolers are critical of peers who engage in cross-gender play (Langlois & Downs, 1980), particularly of boys who like feminine toys or who play at feminine activities. Both a boy who plays with dolls and a girl who plays with trucks will be ignored, teased, or ridiculed by their peers, but the boy more harshly than the girl (Levy, Taylor, & Gelman, 1995). Once children learn rules about gender-typical play, they often harshly punish peers who violate those rules.

Peers influence gender roles in another way too. Between 2 and 3 years of age, children begin to prefer playing with peers of the same gender. Little boys play together with cars, and little girls play together with dolls. This preference increases during childhood, reaching a peak in preadolescence. Then the tide begins to turn, but even in adulthood, time spent at work and at leisure is, quite commonly, segregated by gender (Hartup, 1983). Men might play sports or cards together more often than women, whereas women might like to shop or have lunch together. This tendency for boys to play with boys and girls with girls has several distinctive features (Maccoby, 1990):

Children enjoy a variety of activities, not just gender-related play.

- In some cultures, adults select playmates for children. However, in cultures where children choose playmates, boys select boys as playmates and girls select girls.

- Children spontaneously select playmates of the same gender. Adult pressure ("James, why don't you play with John, not Amy") is not necessary.

- Children resist parents' efforts to get them to play with members of the opposite sex. Girls are often unhappy when parents encourage them to play with boys, and boys are often unhappy when parents urge them to play with girls.

- Children's reluctance to play with members of the opposite sex is not restricted to gender-typed games, such as playing house or playing with cars. Boys and girls prefer playmates of the same gender even in gender-neutral activities such as playing tag or doing puzzles.

Enabling:

interactions that tend to support others and sustain the interaction.

Constricting:
interactions that result in one partner threatening, contradicting, or dominating the other.

Why do boys and girls seem to spend the most time playing with children of the same gender? Eleanor Maccoby (1988, 1990) believes that two factors are critical. First, boys specifically prefer rough-and-tumble play and generally are more competitive and dominating in their interactions. Girls' play is not as rough and is less competitive, so Maccoby argues that boys' style of play may be aversive to girls.

Second, when girls and boys play together, girls do not readily influence boys. Girls' interactions with one another are typically **enabling**—their actions and remarks tend to support others and sustain the interaction. In contrast, boys' interactions are often **constricting**—one partner tries to emerge as the victor by threatening, contradicting, or dominating the other. Girls may find that an enabling style is ineffective with boys. Boys tend to ignore girls' suggestions about what to do and their efforts to resolve conflicts with discussion.

Regardless of the exact cause, early segregation of playmates by style of play means that boys learn primarily from boys and girls from girls. Gender-based play, therefore, helps solidify a child's emerging sense of gender identity and sharpens the contrast between their own and the other gender.

Television also influences children's gender-role learning. Women on television tend to be cast in romantic, marital, or family roles; they are depicted as emotional, passive, and weak. Men are more often cast in leadership or professional roles and are depicted as rational, active, and strong (Huston et al., 1992). Even Sunday newspaper comics put forth particular perspectives on gender roles and the family (Brabant & Mooney, 1999). Consequently, children who watch a lot of TV end up with more stereotyped views of males and females. For example, Kimball (1986) studied gender-role stereotypes in a small Canadian town that was located in a valley and could not receive TV programs until a transmitter was installed in 1974. Children's views of personality traits, behaviours, occupations, and peer relations were measured before and after TV was introduced.

Figure 10–2 shows changes in boys' and girls' views; positive numbers indicate a change toward more stereotyped views. Boys' views were more stereotyped on all four dimensions. For example, after TV was introduced, boys believed that girls could be teachers and cooks, whereas boys could be physicians and judges. Girls' views were more stereotyped only for traits and peer relations. After TV was introduced, girls believed that boasting and swearing were characteristic of boys and that sharing and helping were characteristic of girls. Findings like these indicate that TV viewing causes children to adopt many of the stereotypes that dominate television programming (Signorielli & Lears, 1992). Gender stereotyping in the media has more of an impact on children than on adults because, as people age, they are exposed to a greater range of experiences that lessen the overall impact of messages from media (Oppliger, 2007). This is not to say that adults engage in less gender stereotyping than

Figure 10–2

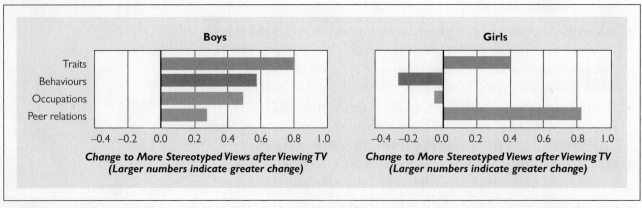

SOURCE: Based on data from Kimball, M. M. (1986). Television and sex-role attitudes. In T. M. Williams (Ed.), The impact of television (pp. 265–301). New York: Academic Press.

children though. As Powlishta (2000) found, adults tended to be more gender stereo-typed than children in their views of others and also tended to view female characteristics as more childlike than traits ordinarily associated with masculinity.

As you can see, studies of parents, peers, and media show that children learn much about gender roles simply by observation. However, observation cannot be the entire explanation; otherwise, boys growing up in very traditional families, where women do most of the child-rearing, would tend to behave more like their mothers than their fathers. In fact, an important element of gender is not just observing but also learning to identify with one gender. This aspect of gender-role learning is the focus of cognitive theories, which we'll examine next.

COGNITIVE THEORIES OF GENDER IDENTITY.   According to Lawrence Kohlberg (1966; Kohlberg & Ullian, 1974), full understanding of gender develops gradually and involves three elements:

- **Gender labelling**: By age 2 or 3, children understand that they are either boys or girls and label themselves accordingly.

- **Gender stability**: During the preschool years, children begin to understand that gender is stable: Boys become men and girls become women. However, children in this stage believe that a girl who wears her hair like a boy will become a boy and that a boy who plays with dolls will become a girl (Fagot, 1985).

- **Gender consistency**: Between 4 and 7 years, most children understand that maleness and femaleness do not change over situations or according to personal wishes. They understand that a child's gender is unaffected by the clothing that a child wears or the toys that a child likes.

A 4-year-old knows that he or she is a boy or a girl. However, he or she has yet to develop a sense of gender stability or gender consistency. When children understand labels, stability, and consistency, they have mastered **gender constancy**.

According to Kohlberg's theory, only children who understand gender constancy should have extensive knowledge of gender-stereotyped activities (Newman, Cooper, & Ruble, 1995). That is, not until children understand that gender is constant do they begin to learn what is appropriate and possible for their gender and what is not.

Children's interest in gender-typical behaviour usually emerges only after they understand gender constancy (Szkrybalo & Ruble, 1999). For example, Martin and Little (1990) measured preschool children's understanding of gender and their knowledge of gender-typed activities (for example, that girls play with dolls and that boys play with airplanes). The youngest children in their study—3½- to 4-year-olds—did not understand gender constancy, and they knew little of gender-stereotyped activities. By age 4, children understood gender constancy but still knew little of gender-stereotyped activities. By 4½ years, many children understood gender constancy and knew gender-typical and gender-atypical activities. Importantly, no children lacked gender constancy but knew about gender-stereotyped activities, a combination that is impossible according to Kohlberg's theory.

Kohlberg's theory specifies when children begin learning about gender-appropriate behaviour and activities (once they understand gender constancy) but does not explain how such learning takes place. A theory proposed by Martin and Halverson (1987), illustrated in Figure 10–3, addresses how children learn about gender. In **gender-schema theory**, children first decide if an object, activity, or behaviour is female or male then use this information to decide whether they should learn more about the object, activity, or behaviour. That is, once children know their gender, they pay attention primarily to experiences and events that are gender appropriate (Martin & Ruble, 2004; Martin & Halverson, 1987). According to gender-schema theory, a preschool boy who is watching a group of girls playing in the sand will decide that playing in the sand is for girls and that, because he is a boy, playing in the sand is not for him. Seeing a group of older boys playing football, he

Gender labelling:
learning to name who is a boy and who is a girl.

Gender stability:
understanding that a person's natural gender does not change.

Gender consistency:
understanding that maleness and femaleness do not change based on situations or personal wishes.

Gender constancy:
the knowledge that gender can be identified, is stable, and remains consistent over time.

Gender-schema theory:
using gender-based information to decide whether an activity or object is worth learning more about.

Figure 10–3

Doll — Who for? — For boys — I am a girl — For girls

Not for me → Avoid

For me → Approach and learn

SOURCE: Based on Martin, C. L., & Halverson, C. F. (1987). The roles of cognition in sex roles and sex typing. In D. B. Carter (Ed.), Current conceptions of sex roles and sex typing: Theory and research. New York: Praeger.

will decide that football is for boys, and because he is a boy, football is acceptable and he should learn more about it.

According to gender-schema theory, after children understand gender, it's as if they see the world through special glasses that allow only gender-typical activities to be in focus (Liben & Signorella, 1993; Serbin, Poulin-Dubois, Colburne, Sen, & Eichstedt, 2001). After children understand gender, their choices in TV program selection begin to shift along gender-specific lines (Luecke-Aleksa, Anderson, Collins, & Schmitt, 1995). In addition, they begin to use gender labels to evaluate toys and activities. Shown an unfamiliar toy and told that children of a specific gender really like this toy, children like the toy much more if others of their gender do too (Martin, Eisenbud, & Rose, 1995).

This selective viewing of the world explains a great deal about children's learning of gender roles, but, as we'll see in the next section, one final, important element needs to be considered.

BIOLOGICAL INFLUENCES. A fertilized human egg has 23 pairs of chromosomes. If the twenty-third pair includes an X and a Y chromosome, then testes will develop about six weeks after conception; if the twenty-third pair includes two X chromosomes, then ovaries will appear about 10 weeks after conception. During prenatal development, the testes and ovaries secrete hormones that regulate the formation of male and female genitals and some features of the central nervous system. This raises an obvious question: Do these hormones also contribute to gender differences in behaviour and, in turn, social roles? As you can imagine, this question is not easy to answer because psychologists cannot experiment directly with hormones as they are secreted during prenatal development. We do know that hormones are a factor in gender differences associated with aggressive behaviour; however, their role in other gender-based differences in behaviour is less clear.

Let's look at some evidence that supports a role for biological influence:

- On questionnaires that measure instrumental traits associated with males (such as being independent, self-confident, aggressive) and expressive traits associated with females

Based on gender-schema theory, children make decisions about gender-based activities by watching other children play.

(such as being emotional, creative, considerate), identical twins' answers are more similar than fraternal twins' answers (Mitchell, Baker, & Jacklin, 1989). This result suggests that how expressive or instrumental a child might be depends, in part, on heredity.

- During prenatal development, the adrenal glands sometimes malfunction and, as a result, some females are inadvertently exposed to unusually large amounts of male hormones, such as androgen. Growing up, some of these girls prefer masculine activities (such as playing with cars instead of dolls) and male playmates to a much greater extent than girls not exposed to these amounts of androgen (Berenbaum & Snyder, 1995; Collaer & Hines, 1995), which suggests that androgen influences the development of masculine traits.

Neither of these findings provides ironclad evidence that biology promotes children's learning of gender roles. The studies of twins suggest, at best, possible hereditary influence but don't tell how biology might promote learning of gender roles. The studies of prenatal exposure to androgen are not completely convincing because the levels of hormones are so much greater than normal that it's risky to make judgments about the effect of normal hormone levels.

Perhaps the most accurate conclusion to draw is that biology, the socializing influence of people and media, and the child's own efforts to understand gender-typical behaviour all help children to learn gender roles and acquire a gender identity. In the next section, we'll see that as children's identities become better developed, they start to like some aspects of themselves more than others.

Self-Esteem

LO3 **Recognize whether preschool children have high self-esteem.**

During the preschool years, children begin to take more responsibility for themselves. For example, they dress themselves. They also begin to identify with adults and begin to understand the opportunities that are available in their culture. Play begins to have purpose as children explore adult roles, such as mother, father, teacher, athlete, or musician. Youngsters start to explore the environment on their own, asking innumerable questions about the world and imagining possibilities for themselves.

Erik Erikson, in the theory of psychosocial development, argued that young children soon realize their initiative can place them in conflict with others. According to Erikson, purpose is achieved with a balance between individual initiative and a willingness to co-operate with others.

Erikson claimed that achieving purpose was a normal developmental milestone, just as most infants become attached to caregivers. One of the by-products of this psychosocial growth is that preschool children acquire **self-esteem**, the first feelings of their own worth. Children with high self-esteem judge themselves favourably and feel positively about themselves. Children with low self-esteem judge themselves negatively, are unhappy with themselves, and often would rather be someone else. In addition, findings from a study in Japan suggest that children who see themselves as prosocial tended to help their friends more and engage more in prosocial behaviour during free play (Ito, 2006).

During the preschool years, self-esteem is often measured with an approach pioneered by Harter and Pike (1984). The sample pictures in Figure 10–4 show a girl either solving a puzzle easily or having difficulty. During testing, children are first asked to point to the pictured child who is most like them. Then they point to the larger circle if they believe that they are "a lot" like the child in that picture or the smaller one if they believe they are "a little" like the child in that picture. Harter and Pike used 24 pairs of pictures like these to measure children's self-worth in four areas: cognitive competence, physical competence, acceptance by peers, and acceptance by mother.

Self-esteem:

feelings about personal worth.

Figure 10–4

SOURCE: Based on Harter, S., & Pike, R. (1984). The pictorial scale of perceived competence and social acceptance for young children. Child Development, 55, 1969–1982.

When psychologists use methods like these, they typically find preschool children have very positive views of themselves across many different domains. For example, when Harter and Pike (1984) used the pictures shown in Figure 10–4 to estimate kindergarten children's cognitive competence (e.g., the child solves puzzles easily), the average score was 3.6 out of a possible 4. In other words, virtually all the children said they were either a little or a lot like the competent child. Most preschool children have extraordinarily high self-esteem; they are full of self-confidence and eager to take on new tasks. In fact, self-esteem is at its peak at this age and drops when children enter school.

Ask Yourself

What evidence supports the role of the environment in the development of children's gender identities? What evidence shows the influence of biology?

List your favourite television shows and movies. How many of them have leading male characters? How many have leading female characters?

10.2 Relationships with Parents

 ## Learning Objectives

After reading the module, you should be able to do the following:

LO4 Describe a systems view of family dynamics.

LO5 Name the primary dimensions of parenting.

LO6 Identify what parental behaviours affect children's development.

LO7 Explain the ways children help determine how parents rear them.

LO8 Recognize the role that family configuration plays in children's development.

Parents go about child-rearing in many different ways. In this module, you'll learn about different approaches that parents take to raising children. Let's begin by thinking about parents as an important element in the family system.

The Family as a System

LO4 Describe a systems view of family dynamics.

A simple-minded view of child-rearing is that parents' actions are all that really matter. That is, through their behaviour, parents directly and indirectly determine their children's development. This view of parents as all-powerful was part of early psychological theories (e.g., Watson, 1925) and may be naively held by some first-time parents. Most current theorists now view families from a broader, ecological perspective, with families seen as a system of interacting elements: parents and children influencing one another (Parke & Buriel, 1998) and, in turn, interacting with other, larger systems.

According to the systems view, parents influence their children, both directly (e.g., by encouraging them to study hard) and indirectly (e.g., by being generous and kind to others). However, the influence is mutual, as children influence their parents too. By their behaviours, attitudes, and interests, children affect how their parents behave toward them. When, for example, children resist discipline, parents might use verbal reasoning less and be more inclined to use physical methods (Ritchie, 1999) or become authoritarian.

Even more subtle influences become apparent when families are viewed as systems of interacting elements. For example, fathers' behaviours can affect mother–child relationships—a demanding husband can leave his wife with little time, energy, or interest in helping their daughter with homework. Or, when siblings argue constantly, parents can become preoccupied with managing conflict rather than providing a richly stimulating home environment.

These examples show that narrowly focusing on parents' impact on children misses the complexities of family life. But there is even more to the systems view. The family itself is embedded in other social systems, such as neighbourhoods and religious institutions (Parke & Buriel, 1998), which affect family dynamics, sometimes positively and sometimes negatively, depending on the values and wishes of the family as compared with those various institutions. At times, the impact of the larger systems is indirect, as when work schedules cause a parent to be away from home or when schools must eliminate programs that benefit children. Although these kinds of changes are not targeted to affect a particular family (which is why they are considered indirect influences), the impact of work schedules or community programming can have a very great effect on any one family. For example, late afternoon and evening shift work (e.g., 3 p.m. to 11 p.m.) has a pronounced effect on child-rearing for preschoolers, school-age children, and adolescents, particularly in single-parent homes. Also, a family's particular culture has an impact on how children are raised and how the family interacts with the larger social system in which they live.

Figure 10–5 summarizes the numerous interactive influences that exist in a systems view of families. In the remainder of this module, we'll describe parents' influences on children and then how children affect their parents' behaviour. Finally, we'll consider how parent–child influences vary with culture and family configuration.

Figure 10–5

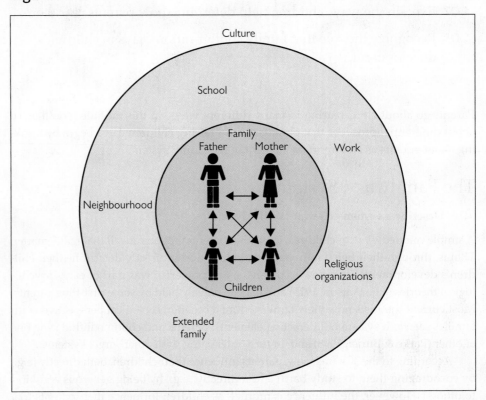

Dimensions and Styles

LO5 Name the primary dimensions of parenting.

Parenting can be described in terms of general dimensions that are like personality traits in that they represent stable aspects of parental behaviour—aspects that hold across different situations (Holden & Miller, 1999).

Research consistently reveals two general dimensions of parental behaviour. One is the degree of warmth and responsiveness that parents show their children. Another is the amount of control parents exert over their children. Other aspects of a parent's life have an effect on parenting ability, including mental and physical health of the parent, the particular needs of a child, and the degree to which parents live a healthy lifestyle within a prosocial network of supportive relationships.

In terms of parenting traits, let's look first at warmth and responsiveness. At one end of the spectrum are parents who are openly warm and affectionate with their children. They are involved with them, respond to their emotional needs, and spend considerable time with them. At the other end of the spectrum are parents who are relatively uninvolved with their children and sometimes even hostile toward them. These parents often seem more focused on their own needs and interests than their children's. Warm parents enjoy hearing their children describe the day's activities; uninvolved or hostile parents aren't interested, considering it a waste of their time. Warm parents see when their children are upset and try to comfort them; uninvolved or hostile parents pay little attention to their children's emotional states and invest little effort comforting them when they're upset.

As you might expect, children benefit from warm and responsive parenting (Pettit, Bates, & Dodge, 1997). When

Helping and praising are important aspects of parenting that can increase children's compliance.

parents are warm toward them, children typically feel secure and are better behaved. In contrast, when parents are uninvolved or hostile, their children are often anxious and behaviourally challenging. When their parents are uninvolved with them, children can develop low self-esteem (Rothbaum & Weisz, 1994).

A second general dimension of parental behaviour concerns the control that parents exercise over their children's behaviour. At one end of this spectrum are controlling, demanding parents who virtually run their children's lives. Over-control is shown by parents who never let their children explore the world around them or interact with other people. At the other end of the spectrum are parents who make few demands and rarely exert any control. Their children are allowed to do almost anything without fear of parental reproach.

Neither extreme is desirable. Over-control deprives children of the opportunity to meet behavioural standards on their own, which is the ultimate goal of socialization. When parents direct every aspect of preschoolers' lives, their children never learn to make decisions for themselves. Under-control fails children because it doesn't teach them cultural standards for behaviour. When parents allow preschoolers to do whatever they want, their children don't learn they are in fact accountable for their behaviour.

Parents need to achieve a balance, maintaining adequate control while still allowing children freedom to make some decisions for themselves. This is often easier said than done, but a good starting point is setting expectations appropriate for the child's age (e.g., a toddler putting away toys), showing the child how to meet them, and then rewarding the child for compliance (Powers & Roberts, 1995; Rotto & Kratochwill, 1994). Once expectations are set, they should be enforced consistently. When parents enforce rules erratically, children come to see rules as optional instead of obligatory, and they will avoid complying with them (Conger, Patterson, & Ge, 1995).

Effective control is also based on good communication. Parents should explain their expectations and the consequences for noncompliance. If a mother wants her son to clean his room, she should explain that a messy room is unsafe, makes it difficult to find toys he wants, and becomes a health hazard. Parents can also encourage children to ask questions if they don't understand or disagree with standards. If the son feels that his mother's expectations for orderliness are so high that it's impossible to play in his room, he should be able to raise the issue without fear of making her angry.

A balanced approach to control—based on age-appropriate expectations, consistency, and communication—protects against over- and under-control because it is developmentally appropriate for children and open to change as the child matures.

CULTURAL DIFFERENCES IN WARMTH AND CONTROL. Control and warmth are universal aspects of parents' behaviour, but views about the "proper" amounts of each vary with particular cultures. Parents of European heritage often want their children to be happy and self-reliant individuals, and they believe these goals can best be achieved when parents are warm and exert moderate control (Goodnow, 1992; Spence, 1985). In many Asian and Latin American countries, however, individualism is less important than co-operation and collaboration (Okagaki & Sternberg, 1993). In China, for example, Confucian principles dictate that parents are always right and that emotional restraint is the key to family harmony (Chao, 1994). In fact, consistent with their cultural values, mothers and fathers in China are more likely to emphasize parental control and less likely to express affection than are mothers and fathers in the United States (Lin & Fu, 1990).

PARENTING STYLES. Combining the dimensions of warmth and control produces four prototypical styles of parenting, as shown in Figure 10–6 (Baumrind, 1975, 1991).

- **Authoritarian parenting** combines high control with little warmth. These parents lay down the rules and expect them to be followed without discussion.

Authoritarian parenting: high control with low levels of warmth.

Figure 10–6

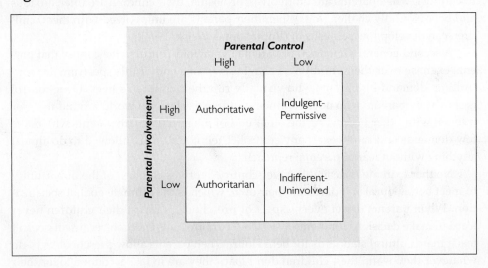

Hard work, respect, and obedience are what authoritarian parents wish to cultivate in their children. There is little give-and-take between parent and child because authoritarian parents do not value children's needs or wishes.

Authoritative parenting:

reasonable control with a lot of warmth and responsiveness to children.

Indulgent-permissive parenting:

a lot of warmth and caring but little control.

Indifferent-uninvolved parenting:

uninterested, uninvolved parenting.

- **Authoritative parenting** combines a fair degree of parental control with being warm and responsive to children. Authoritative parents explain rules and encourage discussion. They tend to explain their decision and try to find compromises that enable children's requests to be allowed but in healthy ways. For example, a child who asks for a cookie might be permitted to have a cookie after supper.

- **Indulgent-permissive parenting** offers warmth and caring but little parental control. These parents generally accept their children's behaviour and rarely provide consequences for misbehaviour. An indulgent-permissive parent would readily agree to a child's request to have a snack, for example, simply because it is something the child wants to do.

- **Indifferent-uninvolved parenting** provides neither warmth nor control. Indifferent-uninvolved parents provide for their children's basic physical needs but little else. They try to minimize the amount of time spent with their children and avoid becoming emotionally involved with them. Children who have parents with this style tend to try to do things without asking, knowing that their parents wouldn't care and would rather not be bothered.

Of these four styles, children are usually best served by the combination of warmth and control that is the hallmark of authoritative parenting (Baumrind, 1991; Maccoby & Martin, 1983). Children with authoritative parents tend to be responsible, self-reliant, and friendly. In contrast, children with authoritarian parents typically have lower self-esteem and are less skilled socially. Children with indulgent-permissive parents are often impulsive and easily frustrated. Children with indifferent-uninvolved parents tend to have low self-esteem and be impulsive, aggressive, and moody.

The benefits of authoritative parenting are not restricted to children of Western European heritage. They also apply to children and parents from several different ethnic groups, including people of African, Asian, and Hispanic descent (Brody & Flor, 1998; Steinberg, Lamborn, Dornbusch, & Darling, 1992). However, some researchers found that authoritarian parenting can benefit children growing up in poverty (Furstenberg, 1993). Why? When youngsters grow up in neighbourhoods with a lot of violence and crime, strict obedience to parents can protect children (Kelley, Power, & Wimbush, 1992).

As important as these different dimensions and styles are for understanding parenting, there is more to effective child-rearing, as we'll see in the next section.

Parental Behaviour

LO6 **Identify what parental behaviours affect children's development.**

A combination of both control and warmth works best in parenting.

Dimensions and styles are general characterizations of how parents typically behave. If, for example, we describe a parent as warm or controlling, you immediately have a sense of that parent's usual style in dealing with his or her children. Nevertheless, the price for such a broad description is that it tells us little about how parents behave in specific situations and how these parental behaviours influence children's development. Put another way, what specific behavioural techniques can parents use to influence their children? Researchers who study parents name three: direct instruction, modelling, and feedback.

DIRECT INSTRUCTION. Parents often tell their children what to do. But simply playing the role of drill sergeant in ordering children around—"Clean your room!" "Turn off the TV!"—is not very effective in obtaining compliance. A better approach is direct instruction, telling a child what to do, when to do it, and why. Instead of just shouting, "Share your candy with your brother!" a parent should explain when and why it's important to share with a sibling. A parent might also ask a child what the child thinks should be done and then discuss possible choices and their implications.

In addition, just as coaches help athletes master sports skills, parents can help their youngsters master social and emotional skills. Parents can explain links between emotions and behaviour—"Caitlin is sad because you broke her crayon" (Gottman, Katz, & Hooven, 1996). They can also teach how to deal with difficult social situations—"When you ask Lindsey if she can sleep over, do it privately so you won't hurt Kaycee's or Hannah's feelings" (Mize & Pettit, 1997). In general, children who get this sort of parental "coaching" tend to be more socially skilled and, not surprisingly, get along better with their peers.

Direct instruction and coaching are particularly powerful when paired with modelling. Urging children to act in a particular way, such as sharing with others, is more compelling when children also see others sharing. In the next section, we'll see how children learn by observing others.

LEARNING BY OBSERVING. Children learn a great deal from parents simply by watching them. The parents' modelling and the youngsters' observational learning thus lead to imitation, so children's behaviour resembles the behaviour they observe. Observational learning can also produce **counterimitation**, learning what should not be done. If an older sibling kicks a friend, and parents punish the older sibling, the younger child may learn not to kick others.

Sometimes observational learning leads to **disinhibition**, an increase in all behaviours like those observed. Children who watch their parents shouting angrily, for example, are more likely to yell at or push a younger sibling. In other words, observation of aggression can lead to a general increase in aggression. Put still another way, aggressive responses became disinhibited. The opposite effect, in which an entire class of behaviours is made less likely, is known as **inhibition**. When a child sees parents punish a sibling, the child is less likely to behave in the ways that led the sibling to be punished.

So far, we've seen that parents influence their children's development by direct instruction and by acting as models that children can observe. In the next section, we'll see how parents use feedback to affect children's behaviour.

Counterimitation:

learning by observation what should not be done.

Disinhibition:

an increase in all behaviours like those observed, particularly aggression.

Inhibition:

a decrease in one or more types of behaviour.

Reinforcement:

any action that increases the likelihood of the response that it follows.

Punishment:

any action that decreases the likelihood of the response that it follows.

Negative reinforcement trap:

reinforcing the very behaviours that are being targeted for elimination.

FEEDBACK. By giving feedback to their children, parents indicate whether a behaviour is appropriate and should continue or is inappropriate and should stop. Feedback comes in two general forms. **Reinforcement** is any action that increases the likelihood of the response that it follows. Parents may use praise to reinforce a child's studying or give a reward for completing household chores. **Punishment** is any action that decreases the likelihood of the response that it follows. Parents could forbid children to watch television when they get poor grades in school or make children go to bed early for neglecting household chores.

Psychologists have made some surprising discoveries concerning the nature of reward and punishment. For example, parents often unwittingly reinforce the very behaviours they want to discourage, a situation called the **negative reinforcement trap** (Patterson, 1980). The negative reinforcement trap occurs in three steps. In the first step, the mother tells her son to do something he doesn't want to do. In the next step, the son responds with some behaviour that most parents find intolerable: He argues, complains, or whines—not just briefly, but for an extended period of time. In the last step, the mother gives in, saying that the son needn't do as she told him initially—simply to get the son to stop the behaviour that is so intolerable.

What children soon learn from these kinds of situations is that arguing (or complaining or whining) works; the parent has rewarded that behaviour by withdrawing the request the son did not like. Although we usually think a behaviour is strengthened when it is followed by the presentation of something that is valued, behaviour is also strengthened when it is followed by the removal of something that is disliked, which is called negative reinforcement, hence the "negative reinforcement trap."

As for punishment, research (Parke, 1977) shows that punishment works best when

- administered directly after the undesirable behaviour occurs, not hours later.

- an undesirable behaviour always leads to punishment, not usually or occasionally.

- accompanied by an explanation of why the child was punished and how punishment can be avoided in the future.

- the child has a warm, affectionate relationship with the person administering the punishment.

dacasdo/Fotolia

Parental feedback should never be cruel.

At the same time, punishment has serious drawbacks. One is that punishment is primarily suppressive: Punished responses are stopped, but only temporarily if children do not learn new behaviours to replace undesirable ones. For example, denying TV to brothers who are fighting stops the undesirable behaviour, but fighting is likely to recur unless the boys learn new ways of solving their disputes.

A second drawback is that punishment can have undesirable side effects. Children become upset as they are being punished, which makes it unlikely that they will understand the feedback punishment is meant to convey. A child denied TV for misbehaving may become angry over the punishment itself and ignore why he's being punished. Furthermore, when children are punished physically, they often imitate this behaviour with peers and younger siblings (Whitehurst & Vasta, 1977). Children who are spanked often use aggression to resolve their disputes with others.

HaywireMedia/Fotolia

Parents can find children's extended arguing or whining difficult to endure.

One method combines the best features of punishment while avoiding its short-comings. In **time-out**, a child who misbehaves briefly sits alone in a quiet, unstimulating location or is excluded for a short period of time from a desirable activity. Time-out can occur nearly anywhere, as long as the child remains properly supervised and is sitting in a safe place. For example, a child might be asked to sit on a particular chair for a time or sit in a bedroom alone. Parents can become quite creative with time-out consequences too, like when a parent turns off favourite music while driving if a child is being belligerent or noncompliant. What is most important for caregivers to remember is that time-out should only take place in a child-safe environment under continued supervision by an adult. Possibly the worst places for a parent to put a child in time-out would be the bathroom or the kitchen, where serious hazards would be within easy reach of the child. Time-out is a form of punishment because it interrupts the child's ongoing activity and isolates the child from other family members, toys, books, and, generally, all forms of rewarding stimulation.

Time-away is another technique for managing children's behaviour. In **time-away**, children are diverted from an activity that was generating conflict to some other, usually quieter, activity. For example, if a child becomes aggressive while playing with blocks, that child might be diverted to looking at books or doing a table activity, such as drawing, until the child has had an opportunity to cool off and regain self-control.

Sometimes, you might see the terms "time-out" and "time-away" used interchangeably. However, time-out is more of a consequence, and time-away is more of a diversion.

In time-out, the period is sufficiently brief—usually no more than one minute per year of the child's age. During time-out, both parent and child typically calm down. Then, when time-out is over, a parent can talk with the child and explain why the particular behaviour was objectionable and what the child should have done instead. Reasoning like this—even with preschool children—is effective because it emphasizes why the consequence occurred and how it can be avoided in the future. Some children's behaviour can become very challenging during time-out. If a parent is finding that a child's behaviour seems impossible to control, intervention from a clinical child psychologist would be advisable in order to determine ways in which the parent and child can interact more effectively together and the parent can regain behavioural control over the child.

Thus, parents can positively influence children's behaviour by direct instruction, by modelling behaviour that they value and not modelling behaviours they don't want their children to learn, by giving feedback, and by using an effective parenting style. In the next section, we'll switch perspectives and see how children affect their parents' behaviour.

Time-out:

being required to sit alone in a quiet, unstimulating location or being excluded for a short period of time from a desirable activity.

Time-away:

being diverted from an activity that was generating conflict to some other, usually quieter, activity.

Children's Contributions

LO7 Explain the ways children help determine how parents rear them.

We emphasized earlier that the family is a dynamic, interactive system in which parents and children influence each other. In fact, children begin at birth to influence the way their parents treat them. That is, parents behave differently depending upon a child's specific behaviour (Kochanska, 1993).

To illustrate the reciprocal influence of parents and children, imagine two children with different temperaments as they respond to a parent's authoritative style. The first child has an easy temperament, readily complies with parental requests, and responds well to family discussions about parental expectations. These types of parent–child relations are a textbook example of successful authoritative parenting. However, suppose the second child has a difficult temperament and complies reluctantly and sometimes not at all. Over time, the parent becomes more controlling and less affectionate. The child in turn complies even less in the future, leading the parent to adopt an authoritarian parenting style (Bates, Pettit, Dodge, & Ridge, 1998).

Time-out should always be supervised and occur in a safe environment.

As this example illustrates, parenting behaviours and styles often evolve as a consequence of the child's behaviour. With a young child who is eager to please adults and less active, a parent might discover that a modest amount of control is adequate. For an active child who is not as eager to please, a parent might need to be more controlling and directive (Dumas, LaFreniere, & Serketich, 1995; Hastings & Rubin, 1999). Influence is reciprocal and iterative: Children's behaviour helps determine how parents treat them, and the resulting parental behaviour influences children's behaviour, which, in turn, causes parents to again change their behaviour (Stice & Barrera, 1995).

As time goes by, these reciprocal influences lead many families to adopt routine ways of interacting with each other. Some families end up functioning smoothly: Parents and children co-operate, anticipate each other's needs, and are generally happy. Unfortunately, other families end up troubled: Disagreements are common, parents spend much time trying unsuccessfully to control their defiant children, and everyone is often angry and upset (Belsky, Woodworth, & Crnic, 1996; Kochanska, 1997).

Over the long term, such troubled families do not fare well, so it's important that these negative reciprocal influences be nipped in the bud (Carrere & Gottman, 1999; Christensen & Heavey, 1999). When parents recognize the problem early on, they can modify their own behaviour. For example, they can try to be less controlling, which sometimes causes children to be less defiant. We are not suggesting that parents allow children to do as they please. Instead, parents should decide aspects of children's lives where they need to exert less control and relinquish it.

Parents should also discuss expectations for appropriate behaviour with their preschoolers. Such discussions may seem odd for children so young, but, phrased properly, these conversations can help parents and children to better understand one another. And, just as important, they help to establish a style for dealing with family issues that will serve everyone well as the children grow.

Of course, many parents find it hard to view family functioning objectively because they are, after all, an integral part of that family. And parents often lack the expertise needed to change their children's behaviour. In these circumstances, a clinical child psychologist can provide invaluable assistance, identifying the obstacles to successful family functioning and suggesting ways to eliminate them.

Family Configuration

LO8 Recognize the role that family configuration plays in children's development.

Families have primary responsibility for helping children become integrated members of their cultures—this aim is much the same worldwide (Whiting & Child, 1953). However, what constitutes a family differs widely around the world and even within Canada. Beyond the traditional Western arrangement of a mother, father, and their children, many configurations are possible. We'll look at two of these in this section.

THE ROLE OF GRANDPARENTS. In Canada, only 2 percent of families have three generations (children, parents, grandparents) living together (Statistics Canada, 2004a). In many cultures around the world, grandparents play crucial roles in children's lives. One influential analysis suggested five specific styles of grandparenting (Neugarten & Weinstein, 1964):

- Formal grandparents express strong interest in the grandchild but maintain a hands-off attitude toward child-rearing.

- Fun-seeking grandparents see themselves as a primary source of fun for their grandchildren but avoid more serious interactions.

- Distant grandparents have little contact with grandchildren, except as part of holidays or other family celebrations.

Defiance encourages authoritarian parenting.

- Dispensing-family-wisdom grandparents provide information and advice to parents and grandchildren alike.
- Surrogate-parent grandparents assume many of the normal roles and responsibilities of a parent.

Christensen (2000) noted that grandparents also play a very important role in reinforcing the confidence and strength of family identity in lesbian stepfamilies. Of these different styles, we know the most about the surrogate-parent style because it is particularly common in African American families. The Children and Families around the World feature describes the important role of grandmothers in African American family life.

CHILDREN OF GAY AND LESBIAN PARENTS. In Canada, 0.8 percent of couples self-identified on the 2011 Census as being gay, in comparison with 99.2 percent who identified themselves as heterosexual (Statistics Canada, 2012). These data are consistent with prevalence data for same-sex couples in Australia, the United Kingdom, and Ireland. In the United States, as of 2010, about 0.6 percent of couples self-identified as gay.

Children and Families around the World

Grandmothers in African American Families

Approximately one in eight African American children live with their grandmothers, compared to only one in 25 European American children (US Bureau of the Census, 1994). Why is this? A quarter of all African American children grow up in chronic poverty, and living with relatives is one way of sharing—and thereby reducing—the costs associated with housing and child care.

African American grandmothers who live with their daughters and their children frequently become involved in rearing their grandchildren, adopting the surrogate-parent style (Pearson, Hunter, Ensminger, & Kellam, 1990). When the daughter is a teenage mother, the grandmother might be the child's primary caregiver, an arrangement that benefits both the adolescent mother and the child. Freed from the obligations of child-rearing, the adolescent mother is able to improve her situation by, for example, finishing school. The child benefits because grandmothers are often more effective mothers than teenage mothers: Grandmothers tend to be less punitive and very responsive to their grandchildren (Chase-Lansdale, Brooks-Gunn, & Zamsky, 1994; Wilson, 1989).

This family arrangement works well for children. In terms of achievement and adjustment, children living with their mothers and grandmothers resemble children living in two-parent families, and they tend to be better off than children in single-parent families (Wilson, 1989). Even when grandmothers are not living in the house, children benefit when their mothers receive social and emotional support from grandmothers and other relatives: Children are more self-reliant and less likely to become involved in delinquent activities such as drug use and vandalism (Taylor & Roberts, 1995).

Grandmothers tend to be very responsive to their grandchildren.

Thus, grandmothers and other relatives can ease the burden of child-rearing in African American families living in poverty, and, not surprisingly, children benefit from the added warmth, support, and guidance of an extended family.

The majority of same-sex couples in Canada are male (54.5 percent). Of gay couples in Canada, about two-thirds live common-law, and close to one-third are legally married (Statistics Canada, 2012). About 9 percent of same-sex couples have children living with them, and of that 9 percent, the greater majority are female. In terms of geographic distribution, 45.6 percent of same-sex couples in Canada live in Toronto, Montreal, or Vancouver (Statistics Canada, 2012).

Research on gay and lesbian parents and their children is scarce, and most has involved children who were born to a heterosexual marriage that ended in divorce when the mother came out as a lesbian. Most of these lesbian mothers to date in research have been of European heritage and are well educated.

As parents, gay and lesbian couples are more similar to heterosexual couples than different. There is no indication that people who are gay and lesbian are less effective in their parenting than people who are heterosexual. Children reared by gay and lesbian parents seem to develop much like children reared by heterosexual couples (Chan, Raboy, & Patterson, 1998; Golombok et al., 2003; Patterson, 1992, 2006). Preschool boys and girls apparently identify with their own gender and acquire the usual accompaniment of gender-based preferences, interests, activities, and friends. In other respects—such as self-concept, social skill, moral reasoning, and intelligence—children of lesbian mothers resemble children of heterosexual parents. As Patterson (2006) noted, quality of family relationships appears to be a more important factor in children's development than parental sexual orientation.

Research on children raised in families other than a two-parent family with mother and father demonstrates that children's development can be effectively nurtured in other family styles and settings too.

Ask Yourself

Most descriptions of parenting focus on the impact of parents on their children's development. Think about the alternative: How do children's actions and characteristics affect a parent's behaviour?

How might the use of time-out versus time-away affect children, depending on their temperament?

10.3 Relationships with Siblings and Peers

 ## Learning Objectives

After reading the module, you should be able to do the following:

LO9 Understand what factors affect sibling relationships.

LO10 Describe the types of children's play and their importance in development.

Children's first social relationships are usually with parents, but their social horizons expand rapidly. In many families, children form relationships with siblings. We'll study these relationships in the first part of this module, including the circumstance of the only child. During the preschool years, most children's social relationships move beyond the family to include peers; we'll study those relationships in the second part of this module.

Sibling Relationships

LO9 **Understand what factors affect sibling relationships.**

For most of a year, all first-born children are only children. Some children remain "onlies" forever, but most are surrounded by brothers and sisters. Some first-borns are joined by many siblings in rapid succession; others are simply joined by a single brother or sister. In Saskatchewan, many more families have just one child living at home than have two or three children (Statistics Canada, 2004a). If a family acquires new members, parent–child relationships become more complex. Parents can no longer focus on a single child but must adjust to the needs of multiple children. Just as important, siblings influence each other's development not just during childhood but throughout life. To understand sibling influence, let's look at differences among first-born, later-born, and only children.

Only children are more likely to succeed academically.

FIRST-BORN, LATER-BORN, AND ONLY CHILDREN.   First-born children are often "guinea pigs" for most parents, who have a lot of enthusiasm but little practical experience rearing children. Parents typically have high expectations for their first-borns and are both more affectionate and more punitive with them. As more children arrive, parents become more adept at their roles, having learned "the tricks of the parent trade" with earlier children. With later-born children, parents have more realistic expectations and are more relaxed in their discipline (e.g., Baskett, 1985).

The different approaches that parents take with their first-borns and later-borns help explain differences that are commonly observed between these children. First-born children generally have higher scores on intelligence tests and are more likely to go to college or university. They are also more willing to conform to parents' and adults' requests. Later-born children, perhaps because they are less concerned about pleasing parents and adults but need to get along with older siblings, are more popular with their peers and more innovative (Eaton, Chipperfield, & Singbeil, 1989).

And what about only children? Conventional wisdom says that parents dote on "onlies," with the result that only children are selfish and egotistical. Is the folklore correct? From a comprehensive analysis of more than 100 studies, the answer is no. In fact, only children were found more likely to succeed in school than other children and to have higher levels of intelligence, leadership, autonomy, and maturity (Falbo & Polit, 1986). Thus, contrary to the popular stereotype, only children are not "spoiled brats" who boss around parents, peers, and teachers. Instead, only children are, for the most part, much like children who grow up with siblings.

Research on only children has important implications for China, where only children are the norm due to government efforts to limit family size. The Child Development and Family Policy feature tells the story.

In discussing first-born, later-born, and only children, we have not yet described relationships that exist between siblings. These can be powerful forces on development, as we'll see next.

QUALITIES OF SIBLING RELATIONSHIPS.   From the very beginning, sibling relationships are complicated. On the one hand, most expectant parents are excited by

Child Development and Family Policy

Assessing the Consequences of China's One-Child Policy

With more than a billion citizens, the People's Republic of China has the largest population of any country in the world, making up roughly 20 percent of the world's population. Chinese leaders have maintained that a large, rapidly growing population was an obstacle to economic growth and improved standard of living. Consequently, in 1979 the Chinese government implemented a policy to limit family size to one child per family. The policy was promoted with billboards that advertised the benefits of having only one child.

Parents were encouraged to use contraceptives to reduce the birth rate and, notably, one-child families received many economic benefits: cash bonuses, better health and child care, and more desirable housing. This policy resulted in families who primarily have only one child. Many studies have compared only and non-only children in China; most comparisons find no differences between them in terms of prosocial co-operation and personality. When differences are found, the advantage often goes to the only child (Jiao, Ji, & Jing, 1996; Yang, Ollendick, Dong, Xia, & Lin, 1995). In 2015, the Chinese government revised the policy to allow for families to have up to two children rather than just one.

As Chinese only children enter adulthood, one concern is for care of their elderly parents. Traditionally, children have

A Chinese billboard promoting a one-child-per-family government policy.

been responsible for their aging parents. This task becomes more financially and psychologically demanding when not shared with other siblings. Research will be needed to determine whether older people receive adequate care and to determine the impact on only children of providing such care. This sort of research will play an important role in helping to determine the long-term consequences of China's decision to limit family size.

the prospect of another child, and their enthusiasm is contagious: Their children, too, eagerly await the arrival of the newest family member. On the other hand, the birth of a sibling is often distressing for older children, who may become withdrawn or return to more childish behaviour because of the changes that occur in their lives, particularly the need to share parental attention and affection (Gottlieb & Mendelson, 1990). However, distress can be avoided if parents remain responsive to their older children's needs (Howe & Ross, 1990). In fact, one of the benefits of a sibling's birth is that fathers often become more involved with their older children (Stewart, Mobley, Van Tuyl, & Salvador, 1987).

Many older siblings enjoy helping their parents take care of newborns (Wagner, Schubert, & Schubert, 1985). Older children often will play with the baby, console it, feed it, or change its diapers. As the infant grows, interactions between siblings become more frequent and more complicated. For example, toddlers tend to talk more to parents than to older siblings. By the time the younger sibling is 4 years old, the situation is reversed: 4-year-olds talk more to older siblings than to their mothers (Brown & Dunn, 1992). Older siblings become a source of care and comfort for younger siblings when they are distressed or upset (Garner, Jones, & Palmer, 1994).

As time goes by, some siblings grow close, becoming best friends in ways that nonsiblings can never be. Other siblings constantly argue, compete, and simply do not get along with each other. The basic pattern of sibling interaction seems to be established early in development and remains fairly stable. Dunn, Slomkowski, and Beardsall (1994), for example, interviewed mothers twice about their children's interaction, first when the children were 3- and 5-year-olds and again seven years later, when the children were 10- and 12-year-olds. Dunn and her colleagues found that siblings who got along as preschoolers often continued to get along as young adolescents, whereas siblings who quarrelled as preschoolers often quarrelled as young adolescents.

Why are some sibling relationships so filled with love and respect, whereas others are dominated by jealousy and resentment? Put more simply, what factors contribute to the quality of sibling relationships? First, children's gender and temperament matter. Sibling relations are more likely to be warm and harmonious between siblings of the same gender than between siblings of opposite gender (Dunn & Kendrick, 1981) and when neither sibling is temperamentally emotional (Brody, Stoneman, & McCoy, 1994). Age is also important: Sibling relationships generally improve as the younger child approaches adolescence because siblings begin to perceive one another as equals (Buhrmester & Furman, 1990).

Parents also contribute to the quality of sibling relationships, both directly and indirectly (Brody, 1998). The direct influence stems from parents' treatment of their children. Siblings more often get along when they believe that parents have no "favourites" but treat all siblings fairly (Kowal & Kramer, 1997). When parents lavishly praise one child's accomplishments while ignoring another's, children notice the difference and their sibling relationship suffers.

Older children often like to interact with infant siblings.

This doesn't mean that parents must treat all of their children the same. Children understand that parents should treat their kids differently—based on their age or personal needs. Only when differential treatment is not justified do sibling relationships tend to deteriorate (Kowal & Kramer, 1997). The indirect influence of parents on sibling relationships stems from the quality of the parents' relationship with each other: A warm, harmonious relationship between parents fosters positive sibling relationships; conflict between parents is associated with conflict between siblings (Erel, Margolin, & John, 1998; Volling & Belsky, 1992). When parents don't get along, their relationship with the children can change, leading to conflict among siblings (Brody et al., 1994).

One practical implication of these findings is that in their pursuit of family harmony (otherwise known as peace and quiet), parents can influence some of the factors affecting sibling relationships but not others. Parents can help reduce friction between siblings by being fair, equally affectionate, responsive, and caring with all of their children and by modelling caring for one another. At the same time, some dissension is natural in families, especially those with preschool boys and girls: Children's different interests often lead to arguments.

Faced with common simple conflicts—Who decides which TV show to watch? Who gets to eat the last cookie? Who gets to hold the new puppy?—a 3-year-old brother and a 5-year-old sister will argue because they lack the social and cognitive skills that allow them to find mutually satisfying compromises.

When siblings, particularly young children, do fight, parents should intervene. Siblings often fight because they're competing for limited resources: They want to play with the same toy or they want to watch different programs on TV. In other words, they get into situations in which they have a conflict of interests. Here parents can arrange for some form of co-operation. Siblings also fight

Harmonious parental relationships foster positive sibling relationships.

because one child is bored and, for lack of anything else to do, begins to interfere with a sibling's activities. Parents can solve this problem by helping the first child become engaged in some activity of his or her own. And sometimes the best strategy simply is to separate feuding siblings.

By intervening in these ways, not only can parents resolve a dispute, they can also show children more sophisticated ways to negotiate; later, children often try to use these techniques themselves instead of fighting (Kramer, Perozynski, & Chung, 1999; Pearlman & Ross, 1997). Starting in the preschool years and extending into adolescence, young people are able to contribute to the resolution of their own conflicts. Between siblings, however, a number of factors can have an impact on whether or how that kind of resolution takes place. For example, researchers at the University of Waterloo (Ram & Ross, 2001) found that the quality of the relationship between siblings, as well as the degree to which they are in a conflict of interest situation with each other, affects how creatively and effectively they solve problems that arise. If two siblings have a high conflict of interest but a positive relationship, they can engage in constructive negotiations more easily and come up with effective, even creative, solutions to their problems; however, high conflict and destructive forms of negotiation can result if a sibling relationship is negative (Ram & Ross, 2001). So, although children can work through conflicts, their ability to do so depends on a number of different factors.

Peer Relationships and Preschoolers' Play

LO10 Describe the types of children's play and their importance in development.

Peer interactions begin in infancy with the emergence of parallel play at about the first birthday. Co-operative play, in which children organize their play around a theme and take on special roles, appears toward the second birthday but is not very common. However, by the time children are 3½ to 4 years old, parallel play is much less common, and co-operative play is the norm (Howes & Matheson, 1992). Co-operative play typically involves peers of the same gender, a preference that increases until, by the end of the preschool years, youngsters choose playmates of the same gender about two-thirds of the time (LaFreniere, Strayer, & Gauthier, 1984).

Conflicts occur often in preschoolers' play, and youngsters often use aggression to resolve their conflicts (Hay, Castle, & Davies, 2000). Among preschoolers, common aggressive behaviours include hitting, kicking, pushing, or biting others as well as grabbing toys from other children. By the end of the preschool years, some preschoolers resort to **bullying**, in which the aggression is unprovoked and has, as its sole goal, gaining power over another child through social, verbal, or physical harassment (Crick, Casas, & Ku, 1999; Garrity, Baris, & Porter, 2000). Some researchers have found that children as young as 9 months old can recognize whether others are different from them and show favouritism to those most similar to themselves (Hamlin, Mahajan, Liberman, & Wynn, 2013). These researchers have pointed out that this may be a very basic aspect of human socialization from early development onward.

Bullying:
unprovoked aggression, which has, as its sole goal, gaining power over another through social, verbal, or physical harassment.

Of course, preschoolers' interactions are not always aggressive; sometimes they act prosocially. When preschool children see other people who are obviously hurt or upset, they often appear concerned. They might try to comfort the person by hugging them or patting them or try to determine why the person is upset (Zahn-Waxler, Radke-Yarrow, Wagner, & Chapman, 1992). Apparently, at this early age, children recognize signs of distress, but their attempts to be helpful are limited because their knowledge of what they can do to help is limited. As youngsters acquire more strategies to help others, their preferred strategies become more adult-like (Strayer & Schroeder, 1989). For example, if a sister was upset because her favourite toy became broken, a 3-year-old brother might comfort her by patting her on the back.

In contrast, a 9-year-old brother might reassure his sister that the toy can be fixed.

MAKE-BELIEVE. During the preschool years, co-operative play often takes the form of make-believe. Preschoolers have telephone conversations with imaginary partners or pretend to drink imaginary juice. In early phases of make-believe, children rely on realistic props to support their play. While pretending to drink, younger preschoolers use a real cup; while pretending to drive a car, they use a toy steering wheel.

In later phases of make-believe, children no longer need realistic props; instead, they can imagine that a block is the cup or that a paper plate is the steering wheel. Of course, this gradual movement toward more abstract make-believe is possible because of cognitive growth that occurs during the preschool years (Harris & Kavanaugh, 1993).

As you might suspect, make-believe reflects the values important in a child's culture (Bornstein, Haynes, Pascual, Painter, & Galperin, 1999). For example, Farver and Shin (1997) studied the make-believe play of European American preschoolers and Korean American preschoolers. The Korean American children came from recently immigrated families, so they still held traditional Korean values, such as an emphasis on the family and on harmony over conflict. The two groups of children differed in the themes of their make-believe play. Adventure and fantasy were favourite themes for European American youngsters, but family roles and everyday activities were favourites of the Korean American children.

In addition, the groups differed in their style of play during make-believe. European American children were more assertive in their make-believe and more likely to disagree with their play partner's ideas about pretending ("I want to be the king; you be the mom!"). Korean American children were more polite and more likely to strive for harmony ("Could I please be king?"). Thus, cultural values influence both the content and the form of make-believe.

Make-believe play not only is entertaining for children, but it also seems to promote cognitive development (Berk, 1994). Children who spend much time in make-believe play tend to be more advanced in language, memory, and reasoning. They also tend to have a more sophisticated understanding of other people's thoughts, beliefs, and feelings (Howe, Petrakos, & Rinaldi, 1998; Youngblade & Dunn, 1995). Children with more advanced ability to sustain attention also seem to be more socially competent and to engage in more complex forms of play (Murphy, Bennett, Brinkman, & McNamara, 2007).

Yet another benefit of make-believe is that it allows children to explore topics that frighten them. Children who are afraid of the dark may reassure a doll that is also afraid of the dark. By explaining to the doll why she shouldn't be afraid, children come to understand and regulate their own fear of darkness. Or children may pretend that a doll has misbehaved and must be punished, which allows them to experience the parent's anger and the doll's guilt. Make-believe allows children to explore other emotions too, including joy and affection (Gottman, 1986).

By the end of the preschool years, some children learn how to bully others.

Preschool children sometimes comfort each other.

Make-believe play promotes cognitive development.

For many preschool children, make-believe play involves imaginary companions. Children can usually describe their imaginary playmates in some detail, mentioning gender and age as well as the colour of their hair and eyes. Imaginary companions were once thought to be fairly rare and a sign of possible developmental problems. But more recent research shows that nearly two-thirds of all preschoolers report imaginary companions (Taylor, Cartwright, & Carlson, 1993).

Moreover, an imaginary companion is associated with many positive social characteristics: Preschoolers with imaginary friends tend to be more sociable and have more real friends than other preschoolers. Furthermore, vivid fantasy play with imaginary companions does not mean that the distinction between fantasy and reality is blurred: Children with imaginary companions can distinguish fantasy from reality just as accurately as youngsters without imaginary companions (Taylor et al., 1993).

SOLITARY PLAY.   At times throughout the preschool years, many children prefer to play alone. Should parents be worried? Usually, no. Solitary play comes in many forms and most is normal—even healthy (Lloyd & Howe, 2003). Spending free-play time alone colouring, solving puzzles, or assembling blocks is not a sign of maladjustment. Many youngsters enjoy solitary activities and at other times choose very social play. Furthermore, sometimes the physical set-up of a play area, such as a play centre like you might see at many preschools and daycares, actually encourages solitary play in children (Petrakos & Howe, 1996). Playing alone in a setting designed for solitary play, of course, would be perfectly normal.

Nevertheless, some forms of solitary play are signs that children are uneasy or reticent to interact with others (Coplan, Rubin, Fox, Calkins, & Stewart, 1994; Harrist, Zaia, Bates, Dodge, & Pettit, 1997; Lloyd & Howe, 2003). One type of unhealthy solitary play is aimless wandering. Sometimes children go from one preschool activity centre to the next, as if trying to decide what to do, but really they just keep wandering. They never settle into play with others or engage in constructive, solitary play. Hovering is another unhealthy type of solitary play: A child stands near peers who are playing, watching them play but not participating. Over time, these behaviours can suggest the presence of high social anxiety and might require intervention from a professional (Ladd, 1998).

PARENTAL INFLUENCE.   Parents get involved in their preschool children's play in several ways (Isley, O'Neil, Clatfelter, & Parke, 1999). Sometimes they take the role of playmate (and many parents deserve an Oscar for their performances). They use the opportunity to scaffold their children's play, often raising it to more sophisticated levels (Tamis-LeMonda & Bornstein, 1996). For example, if a toddler is stacking toy plates, a parent might help the child stack the plates (play at the same level) or might pretend to wash each plate (play at a more advanced level). When parents demonstrate more advanced forms of play, their children often play at the more advanced levels later (Bornstein, Haynes, O'Reilly, & Painter, 1996).

Another parental role during preschoolers' play is that of mediator. Preschoolers often disagree, argue, and fight. Children play more co-operatively and longer when parents are present to help iron out conflicts (Mize, Pettit, & Brown, 1995; Parke & Bhavnagri, 1989). When young children can't agree on what to play, a parent can negotiate a mutually acceptable activity. When both youngsters want to play with the same toy, a parent can arrange for them to share. Here, too, parents scaffold their preschoolers' play, smoothing the interaction by providing some of the social skills that preschoolers lack.

Yet another parental role is that of coach. Preschool children often encounter social problems that, although minor from an adult's perspective, seem overwhelming to the child. For example, a child might be colouring when another child approaches and demands the crayon the child is using. Parents can help their preschoolers understand

and handle such problems. When parents coach—and when their advice is constructive—their children tend to be skilled socially and less aggressive (Mize & Pettit, 1997).

Parents also influence the success of their children's peer interactions in a much less direct manner. Children's relationships with peers are most successful when, as infants, they had a secure attachment relationship (Ladd & Le Sieur, 1995; Lieberman et al., 1999).

Why does quality of attachment predict the success of children's peer relationships? One view is that a child's relationship with his or her parents is the internal working model for all future social relationships. When the parent–child relationship is high quality and emotionally satisfying, children

Mediation is an important parental responsibility.

are encouraged to form relationships with other people. Another possibility is that a secure attachment relationship makes an infant feel more confident about exploring the environment, which, in turn, provides more opportunities to interact with peers. These two views are not mutually exclusive; both may contribute to the relative ease with which securely attached children interact with their peers (Hartup, 1992b).

Ask Yourself

How does preschool children's play illustrate connections between physical, cognitive, social, and emotional development?

Trace how play in the preschool years differs from what you learned about infant and toddler play.

10.4 Moral Development: Learning to Control One's Behaviour

 ## Learning Objectives

After reading the module, you should be able to do the following:

LO11 Identify when self-control begins and how it changes as children develop.

LO12 Describe how parents influence their children's ability to maintain self-control.

LO13 Understand how a child's temperament can influence self-control.

LO14 List the strategies children can use to improve self-control.

LO15 Recognize when preschoolers begin to understand that moral rules are different from other rules.

Self-control:

the ability to regulate thought, behaviour, and emotional reactions in a planful manner rather than giving in to impulse.

Parents often wish that young children had greater **self-control**, the ability to rise above immediate pressures and not give in to impulse. A child who saves her allowance to buy a much-desired object instead of spending it immediately on candy is showing self-control, as is an adolescent who studies for an exam instead of going to the mall with his friends, knowing that tomorrow he can enjoy the mall and a good grade on his exam.

Self-control is one of the first steps toward moral behaviour because children must learn that they cannot constantly do whatever tempts them at the moment. Instead, society has rules for behaviour, and children must learn to regulate their behaviours and emotions to get along well with others (Rawn & Vohs, 2006).

In this module, we'll first see how self-control emerges during the preschool years. Then we'll discuss some of the factors that determine how well children control themselves. Finally, we'll look at strategies that children use to improve their self-control and at children's understanding of the special nature of moral rules.

Beginnings of Self-Control

LO11 Identify when self-control begins and how it changes as children develop.

Self-control begins during infancy and the preschool years. Claire Kopp (1982, 1987) believes that, starting around the first birthday, self-control develops in three phases that initially arise out of infants' initial learning about the basics of self-soothing:

- Infancy: Babies initially learn about self-soothing through parental regulatory activities, such as distracting the infant from an upsetting stimulus (Rothbart, Posner, & Kieras, 2006).

- Phase 1: At approximately the first birthday, infants become aware that people impose demands on them and that they must react accordingly. They learn that they are not entirely free to behave as they wish; instead, others set limits on what they can do. These limits reflect both concern for their safety ("Don't touch! It's hot") as well as early socialization efforts ("Don't grab Ravisha's toy").

- Phase 2: At about 2 years, toddlers have internalized some of the controls imposed by others, and they are capable of some self-control in parents' absence. For example, although a child might want to play with a toy that another toddler has, the child might inhibit the desire to just grab the toy, perhaps because someone told him not to take things from others.

- Phase 3: At about 3 years, children become capable of greater self-regulation, which "involves flexible and adaptive control processes that can meet quickly changing situational demands" (Kopp, 1987, p. 38). Children can devise ways to regulate their own behaviour. To return to the example of a playmate's interesting toy, children might tell themselves that they really don't want to play with it, or they might turn to another activity that removes the temptation to grab it.

Of course, preschoolers have much to learn about regulating impulsive behaviour, and control is achieved only gradually throughout the elementary school years. Individual preschoolers differ tremendously in their degree of self-control. Some show greater restraint and control, while others show little.

Individual differences are evident in research that examines consistency in self-control. Vaughn, Kopp, and Krakow (1984), for example, examined preschoolers' self-control on three different tasks. On one task, the child was told to not touch a novel telephone while the experimenter left the room; on a second task, the child was asked to wait for a signal before beginning to search for hidden food; on a third, the experimenter said that an attractively wrapped package was a gift for the child, who was not to touch it until the experimenter and mother had finished some paperwork. These researchers found that, although children were far from perfectly consistent, in general a child who had good self-control on one task tended to have good control on other tasks too.

Perhaps you wonder about the validity of these tasks. Are these tasks really measuring important aspects of self-control in children's natural environments? Mothers' reports of their youngsters' self-control represent one source of evidence for the validity of these tasks. Children who are less likely to touch prohibited toys are, according to their mothers' reports, more likely to spontaneously confess to misdeeds at home and more likely to do as asked at home without parental supervision (Kochanska, DeVet, Goldman, Murray, & Putnam, 1994). The Looking Ahead feature provides some truly remarkable evidence that laboratory tasks measure important facets of children's self-control in their natural environments.

Preschoolers are capable of some self-control.

Obviously, individuals differ in their ability to resist temptation, and this characteristic is remarkably stable over time. But why are some preschoolers (and, later, adolescents) better able than others to exert self-control? As you'll see in the next section of this module, parents play an important role in determining children's self-control.

Looking Ahead

Self-Control during the Preschool Years Predicts Later Behaviour, Personality, and Achievement

Told not to touch a novel toy, some preschoolers patiently comply with the instruction for minutes on end; other preschoolers reach for the toy as soon as the experimenter leaves the room. These individual differences among children are striking and naturally make one wonder if the differences persist over the years. Results from longitudinal studies on the long-term consistency of self-control suggest that the differences are, in fact, remarkably stable. Rubin, Burgess, Dwyer, and Hastings (2003) studied 104 toddlers as they played with peers of the same gender and their mothers. They measured acting out, aggression, parenting, as well as emotional and behavioural regulation. They then observed behaviour in the same children two years later. These researchers found that conflict-aggressive behaviour at age 2 was related to acting out at age 4 for girls but not for boys. The relationship between problems with acting out at age 4 and initiation of aggressive actions at age 2 was strongest for those children who experienced high maternal negativity.

Temperament can also predict personality and achievement in adolescence. Shoda, Mischel, and Peake (1990) tracked down nearly 200 15- to 18-year-olds who had participated in self-control experiments as 4-year-olds. In the original experiments, 4-year-olds were told that if they waited alone in a room until the experimenter returned, they would receive a big prize. If they rang a bell to signal the experimenter to return, they would receive a much smaller prize. Then the researchers simply recorded the length of time children waited until the experimenter returned. You may be surprised to learn that the length of time that 4-year-olds waited was related to a host of characteristics measured some 11 to 14 years later. Table 10–2 shows some of the significant correlations between the 4-year-olds' ability to delay gratification and personality and scholastic aptitude scores as adolescents. Incredibly, the 4-year-olds who waited longer before calling the experimenter were still, as 15- to 18-year-olds, better able to exert self-control, more attentive and able to plan, and more inclined to have higher scholastic aptitude. We'll discuss self-control further later in the chapter.

Table 10–2 Correlations between Preschoolers' Delayed Gratification and Measures of Coping, Personality, and Academic Achievement in Adolescence

	Measure
Personality	
Likely to yield to temptation	−0.50
Easily distracted when trying to concentrate	−0.41
Planful, thinks ahead	0.36
Tends to go to pieces under stress, becomes rattled and disorganized	−0.34
SAT scores	
Verbal scale	0.42
Quantitative scale	0.57

SOURCE: From Shoda, Y., Mischel, W., & Peake, P. K. (1990). Predicting adolescent cognitive and self-regulatory competencies from preschool delay of gratification: Identifying diagnostic conditions. *Developmental Psychology*, 26, 978–986. American Psychological Association. Reprinted with permission. American Psychological Association (APA)

Parental Influences

LO12 Describe how parents influence their children's ability to maintain self-control.

When Robert Kail was growing up, he lived near two households in which both husbands had similar jobs with an engineering company and both wives worked full-time in the family home. Nevertheless, the lifestyles of these two families had little in common. One family always seemed to be the first on the block to own new toys: the first stereophonic record player, the first colour TV, the first Ford Mustang in 1964, and so on. The other family was as frugal as the first family was free-spending: Occasional trips to the repair shop kept the black-and-white TV working, children wore hand-me-down clothes, and the dad took a bus to work.

Obviously, the children growing up in these two families were exposed to very different models of self-control. Adults in the first family preferred immediate gratification, but those in the second family preferred to save their money for deferred goals. Children's self-control is influenced by their exposure to such models. Researchers who studied children imitating adults modelling high or low levels of self-control found that children can show self-restraint or be incredibly impulsive, depending upon how they observe others behave (Bandura & Mischel, 1965).

In addition, correlational studies show that parents' behaviour is related to their children's self-control, but not in a way that you may expect. Self-control is lower in children whose parents are very strict with them (Feldman & Wentzel, 1990). One interpretation of this finding is that strict parents over-control their children: By constantly directing them to do one thing but not another, parents impose external control and do not give their children either the opportunity or the incentive to internalize control for themselves. Consistent with this argument is the finding that children have greater self-control when parents encourage them to be independent and make their own decisions (Silverman & Ragusa, 1990).

So far, the story seems reasonably straightforward: For children to gain self-control, parents must relinquish some control. By gradually giving children developmentally appropriate opportunities to regulate their own behaviour and see the consequences of their choices, parents foster self-control in their children. For example, instead of insisting that preschool children follow a set after-dinner routine, parents can allow children to choose between colouring, reading, or playing a quiet game.

Nevertheless, more recent research shows that the story is not so simple after all. Temperament also affects children's responses to parents' efforts to promote self-control. We'll look at this research in the next section.

Temperamental Influences on Self-Control

LO13 Understand how a child's temperament can influence self-control.

Children's temperament helps determine their level of self-control. Highly emotional toddlers and preschoolers are less able to control themselves (Stifter, Spinrad, & Braungart-Rieker, 1999). That is, youngsters who have difficulty regulating their emotions usually have difficulty regulating their behaviour.

Temperament also influences how children respond to parents' efforts to teach self-control. The aspect of temperament that's most important for self-control is children's anxiety and fearfulness (Kochanska, 1991, 1993). Some anxious and fearful children become nervous at the prospect of potential wrongdoing. When told not to eat a cookie until after dinner, fearful children might leave the room because they're afraid that they might give in to temptation. With these children, a simple parental reminder usually guarantees compliance because they are so anxious about not following instructions, or getting caught, or having to confess to a misdeed. Their anxiety results in a kind of natural inhibition, although excessive anxiety and inhibition would not be healthy and could get in the way of normal interpersonal interactions.

For children who are not naturally fearful at the thought of misdeeds, other approaches are necessary. More effective with these children are positive appeals to the child to co-operate, appeals that build on the strong attachment relationship between parent and child. Fearless or bold children comply with parental requests out of positive feelings for a loved one, not out of distress caused by fear of misdeeds. As with anxiety, the interpersonal interactions of excessively bold children can suffer due to poor inhibition of behaviour. In addition, seemingly fearless children can be prone to accidents. Theresa Zolner remembers one little boy who was so fearless he had a habit of climbing up on his family's cupboards and refrigerator. Needless to say, this kind of behaviour can result in family conflict and risk for falls and injury.

The Research to Practice feature describes a study that links temperament to different methods for fostering self-control in children.

Research to Practice

Temperament, Parental Influence, and Self-Control

Grazyna Kochanska (1997) wanted to evaluate proposed links between children's temperament, parents' influence, and children's self-control. She believed temperamentally fearful children would have better self-control when parents used gentle discipline that elicited mild distress but that temperamentally bold children would have better self-control when parents appealed to their strong mutual attachment.

Kochanska's study included four variables: children's fearful temperament, parents' use of gentle discipline, strength of parent–child attachment, and children's self-control and compliance. Temperament was measured by having mothers complete questionnaires and by recording children's anxiety as they were asked to do different novel acts (e.g., put a hand inside a large box, jump on a trampoline). Use of gentle discipline was measured by observing mothers interacting with their children and coding for the presence of guiding, gentle requests

to comply. Parent–child attachment was measured by having mothers complete questionnaires that assessed attachment security. Children's self-control and compliance were tested (1) with games that posed a strong temptation to cheat (because the games were impossible to win by following the rules) and (2) with stories that allowed children to support (or condemn) a story character who took desirable toys from another story character.

Kochanska used the measures of temperament obtained from the 2½- to 3-year-olds to divide the sample into fearful and fearless toddlers. Next, she examined links between gentle discipline, attachment, and children's self-control (see Figure 10–7). For fearful children, self-control was associated more strongly with gentle discipline (and mild distress) than with attachment security. For fearless children, self-control was associated more strongly with attachment security than gentle discipline. The researchers concluded that parents influence their children's ability to maintain self-control, but the nature of that influence depends on children's temperament.

Figure 10–7

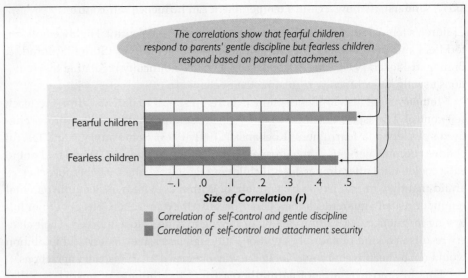

The correlations show that fearful children respond to parents' gentle discipline but fearless children respond based on parental attachment.

Fearful children

Fearless children

−.1   .0   .1   .2   .3   .4   .5

Size of Correlation (r)

■ *Correlation of self-control and gentle discipline*
■ *Correlation of self-control and attachment security*

SOURCE: Based on data from Kochanska, G. (1997). Multiple pathways to conscience for children with different temperaments: From toddlerhood to age 5. Developmental Psychology, 33, 228–240.

Of course, regardless of their temperament, children are not perfectly consistent in their self-control. Children who are able to resist temptation on one occasion may give in the next time. Why do children show self-control on some tasks but not others? As we'll see in the next section, the answer lies in children's plans for resisting temptation.

Improving Self-Control

LO14 List the strategies children can use to improve self-control.

Imagine it's one of the first nice days of spring. You have two major exams for which you should study, but it's so-o-o-o tempting to spend the entire day outside. What do you do to resist this temptation and stick to studying? You might remind yourself that these exams are very important. You might also move to a windowless room to keep your mind off the tempting weather. Stated more generally, effective ways to resist temptation include (a) reminding yourself of the importance of long-term goals over short-term temptations and (b) reducing the attraction of the tempting event.

During the preschool years, some youngsters begin to use both of these methods spontaneously to resist temptation. The ability to hold off immediate satisfaction in order to obtain a larger reward or a preferable outcome later is called **delay of gratification**. What attractive rewards have been used with children in delay-of-gratification research? Usually, it is an item that is attractive to the child (Silverman, 2003), such as a special toy, candy, or even a marshmallow. In a classic experiment by Mischel and Ebbesen (1970), 3- to 5-year-olds were asked to sit alone in a room for 15 minutes. If they waited the entire time, they would receive a desirable reward. Children could call the experimenter back to the room at any time by a prearranged signal; in this case, they would receive a much less desirable reward.

Some children, of course, were better able than others to wait the full 15 minutes. How did they do it? Some children talked to themselves: "I've gotta wait to get the best prize!" As Vygotsky described, these youngsters used private speech to control their own behaviour. Others sang, and still others invented games. All were effective techniques for enduring 15 boring minutes to receive a desired prize.

Later studies show that children who have a concrete way of handling the situation are far better able to resist temptation (Mischel, Shoda, & Rodriguez, 1989; Peake, Hebl, & Mischel, 2002) and that girls might be slightly better at this than boys

Delay of gratification:

the ability to hold off immediate satisfaction in order to obtain a larger reward or more preferable outcome later.

(Silverman, 2003). Effective plans include (a) reminders to avoid looking at the tempting object, (b) reminders of rules against touching a tempting object, and (c) activities designed to divert attention from the tempting object, such as playing with other objects. Parents can help children make a plan to resist temptation. For example, in the face of being tempted by cake, parents can instruct their children, "When you feel like you want to eat some cake, tell yourself, 'No cake until Mom gets home' and go play in your bedroom." These kinds of hints provide children with a plan for regulating their own behaviour.

In a new twist on the classic marshmallow study, researchers have found that the context in which children form experiences also affects their level of apparent self-control (Kidd, Palmeri, & Aslin, 2012). Kidd, Palmeri, and Aslin (2012) assigned children between the ages of 3 and 5 to two different groups. One group, in the "unreliable condition," was led to believe that the experimenters broke promises made to the children. They were given some used crayons to do a craft but told that, if they waited, they would be brought bigger and better art supplies. However, the new crayons never appeared. A similar experience then occurred, only with the promise of better stickers. Again, the children were disappointed. In the other group, the "reliable condition," the children were also promised better art supplies and stickers, and, in both cases, the children received what was promised.

After having experienced either the unreliable or the reliable condition, all of the participating children were put through the marshmallow task, being asked to wait 15 minutes to receive three additional marshmallows. The children who had been through the unreliable condition, except one, waited an average of 3 minutes, 2 seconds before tasting or eating the marshmallow in front of them. The children who had been through the reliable condition waited an average of 12 minutes, 2 seconds before tasting or eating the marshmallow. Nine of them waited the full 15 minutes. This strongly demonstrates that children's experiences about the reliability and stability of the world around them affect the appearance of self-control in a delay-of-gratification task like the marshmallow study.

Overall, then, how children think about—or, rather, avoid thinking about—tempting objects or outcomes in the context of their past experiences makes all the difference. Even preschoolers can achieve self-control by making plans that include appropriate self-instruction. As children learn to regulate their own behaviour, they also begin to learn about moral rules—cultural rights and wrongs—which are described in the last section of this module.

Learning about Moral Rules

LO15 **Recognize when preschoolers begin to understand that moral rules are different from other rules.**

The foundation of moral thinking is set in the preschool years. During these years children begin to understand that moral rules are special. Many rules are actually **social conventions**, arbitrary standards of behaviour agreed to by a cultural group to facilitate interactions within the group. Social convention says that we can eat french fries but not green beans with our fingers and that children can address peers but not teachers by their first names. In contrast, moral rules, such as prohibitions against murder and rape, are designed to protect people and are not arbitrary. By age 3, most children distinguish moral rules from social conventions. They judge that hurting other people and taking their possessions are more serious transgressions than eating ice cream with one's fingers or not paying attention to a story (Nucci & Weber, 1995; Smetana & Braeges, 1990).

Other research shows that preschoolers know the difference between lies and mistakes (Siegal & Peterson, 1998). When led to believe that they damaged an object, preschoolers often show traditional signs of guilt, such as distress, apologizing, and trying to right their wrong (Kochanska, Casey, & Fukumoto, 1995). Interesting

Social conventions:
arbitrary standards of behaviour agreed to by a cultural group to facilitate interactions within the group.

findings about children's involvement in tattling on each other came from research done at the University of Waterloo (Ross & den Bak-Lammers, 1998). These researchers studied families with children between the ages of 2 and 6. They found that older siblings tended to tattle more than younger ones and that this tattling increased with time. In addition, they found that, when tattling, the children tended to report on the behaviour of their siblings truthfully and in accordance with rules or standards for behaviour that their parents had emphasized as being important to the family. Aware of these standards, the older siblings tended to report on negative behaviour whether or not parents tended to respond positively or negatively to the tattling. However, Ross and den Bak-Lammers (1998) also noted that parents tended to respond attentively to the tattling rather than negatively.

Collectively, these findings tell us that preschoolers have begun to understand fundamental distinctions in the moral domain. This understanding provides the foundation for more sophisticated reasoning about moral issues.

Ask Yourself

Review the findings on delay of gratification in this chapter. Are these results more consistent with the view that development is a continuous or discontinuous process?

How might the various theories of cognitive development account for increasing development of self-control in childhood?

family brings their child to the program, but the child refuses to talk to the other children. This has been going on for three weeks, and the child pretty much just sits on the outskirts of the group watching everyone and playing with toys. What expectations would you have for a 4-year-old in this situation? What could be contributing to the child's response to your program?

What Would a Pastor Do?

You are the pastor of a community church in charge of a children's Sunday school program for 4-year-olds. Every week a

Summary

10.1 Self

Gender Roles

- Instrumental traits are usually associated with men and describe individuals who act on the world.

- Expressive traits are usually associated with women and describe individuals who value interpersonal relationships.

- By the end of the preschool years, children have learned many of the traits stereotypically associated with males and females.

Gender Identity

- Parents treat sons and daughters similarly, except in gender-related behaviour.

- Peers influence gender-role learning by discouraging cross-gender play.

- Children who watch television frequently tend to have stereotyped views of men and women.

- According to Kohlberg's theory, children learn that gender is constant over time.

- According to gender-schema theory, children learn about gender by paying attention to behaviours of people who have the same gender as them.

- Biological influence on gender roles is shown in twin studies and in the impact of male hormones on female prenatal development.

Self-Esteem

- Self-esteem is assessed by asking preschoolers to compare themselves to hypothetical children.

- Self-esteem tends to be very high during the preschool years.

10.2 Relationships with Parents

The Family as a System

- According to the systems approach, parents and children influence each other.

- The family itself is influenced by other social systems, such as neighbourhoods and religious organizations.

Dimensions and Styles

- One dimension of parenting is parental warmth: Children clearly benefit from warm, caring parents.

- Another dimension is control. Effective parenting involves setting appropriate standards and enforcing them consistently.

- Combining warmth and control yields four styles: (a) authoritarian parents are controlling but unresponsive; (b) authoritative parents are controlling but responsive; (c) indulgent-permissive parents are loving but exert little control; and (d) indifferent-uninvolved parents are neither warm nor controlling.

- Authoritative parenting is usually best for children.

Parental Behaviour

- Parents influence development by direct instruction, coaching, and serving as models for their children.

- Parents also use feedback to influence children's behaviour.

- Sometimes parents fall into the negative reinforcement trap, inadvertently reinforcing behaviours they want to discourage.

- Effective punishment is prompt, consistent, accompanied by an explanation, and delivered by a person with whom the child has a warm relationship.

- Punishment suppresses behaviours but does not eliminate them and often has side effects.

- Time-out is a useful form of punishment, and time-away is a form of behavioural diversion.

Children's Contributions

- Parenting is influenced by characteristics of children themselves (e.g., temperament).

- Families develop routine ways of interacting, which can be harmful if based on negative mutual influences.

Family Configuration

- Compared to North American parents, Chinese parents tend to be more controlling and less openly affectionate.

- African American grandmothers often live with their daughters, an arrangement that benefits children because grandmothers play an active role in child-rearing.

- Gay and lesbian parents are more similar to heterosexual parents than different; their children develop much like children reared by heterosexual couples.

10.3 Relationships with Siblings and Peers

Sibling Relationships

- First-born children are often more intelligent but less popular and innovative.

- Only children are generally comparable to children with siblings, but they often excel academically.

- The birth of a sibling is stressful for children when parents ignore older children's needs.

- Siblings get along better when they are of the same gender, parents treat them fairly, they enter adolescence, and they have parents who get along well.

Peer Relationships and Preschoolers' Play

- Co-operative play is common among preschoolers.

- Make-believe play promotes cognitive development and allows children to explore frightening topics in a nonthreatening way.

- Most, but not all, forms of solitary play are harmless.

- Parents foster children's play by acting as skilled playmates, mediating disputes, and coaching social skills.

10.4 Moral Development: Learning to Control One's Behaviour

Beginnings of Self-Control

- At 1 year, infants are first aware that others impose demands on them; by 3 years, youngsters can regulate their behaviour.

- Preschoolers with good self-control, who are learning to delay gratification, tend to become adolescents with good self-control.

Parental Influences

- When children observe adults who delay gratification, they more often delay gratification themselves.

- Children who have the best self-control tend to have parents who do not use harsh punishment and who encourage their children to make their own decisions.

Temperamental Influences on Self-Control

- With fearful children, reminders increase self-control and behavioural compliance.

- With fearless or bold children, appeals to the attachment relationship increase self-control.

Improving Self-Control

- Children can regulate their own behaviour when they have plans to help remember a goal and something to distract them from tempting objects.

Learning about Moral Rules

- Preschool children distinguish moral rules from social conventions, distinguish lies from mistakes, and show signs of guilt.

Chapter Critical Review

1. Refer back to Figure 10–1, which displays information about gender stereotypes in several cultures. Use the information in the graphs to hypothesize how the types of games that preschoolers in Nigeria or Venezuela play would differ from those children play in North America.

2. Consider the parenting style in your cultural group. How would you characterize it, using the classification in Module 10.2? What was the primary cultural influence on your parents' style when you were growing up: that of mainstream society (the macroculture) or that of a specific cultural group? Do you think that your parenting style will differ from that of your parents (or, if you are a parent, how does it differ)?

3. Suppose you heard the host of a radio talk show say, "What's wrong with Canadian youth today is that parents don't discipline the way they used to.

'Spare the rod and spoil the child' made sense before and still makes sense today." If you called in, what would you say in response to the host's remarks?

4. Most research on sibling relationships is based on families with two children because these families are easier to find than families with three or more children and because there's only one sibling relationship to consider. Think about how the conclusions about sibling relationships described in this module might need to be modified to apply to larger families.

5. Why does make-believe play become so important during the preschool years? In your answer, use what you have learned about cognitive development.

6. Compare and contrast the view of self-control presented in Module 10.4 with Vygotsky's ideas of self-control.

See for Yourself

Many students find it hard to believe that parents actually use the different styles described in Module 10.2. To convince yourself that parents really differ along these dimensions, visit a place where parents and young children interact together, such as a shopping mall, a fast-food restaurant, or a playground. Observe parents and their children, then judge their warmth and degree of control. For example, at the playground, see whether some parents eagerly play with children (warm parents) while others use this as an opportunity to read the newspaper (uninterested parents). See whether some parents allow children to choose their own activities or whether some parents make all the decisions. As you watch, decide whether some parents are using feedback and modelling constructively. You should observe an astonishing variety of parental behaviour, some effective and some not. See for yourself!

Chapter 11
Physical Development in Middle Childhood

Distinctive Images/Shutterstock

MODULE

11.1 Growth of the Body

11.2 Motor Development

Sophie liked school, but she especially loved recess time! Any kind of game was fun for Sophie, so Terry and Mabel started wondering about whether to sign her up for a team sport. Sophie was a little reluctant to join, though, because she didn't know many of the kids on the local ball team and found team sports different from just running around and playing with her friends. With a little help and encouragement from the community coach, Sophie tried on a helmet and picked up a bat, but she seemed a little timid. Terry and Mabel wondered . . . would Sophie be happier if they just did some physical activity together as a family?

Connect to My Virtual Child

What kinds of theories do you have about children? What ideas inform your thoughts and beliefs about the lives of children, how they are raised, and the nature of the human person? Use your access card and follow this link www.myvirtualchild.com to learn more about the world of the child. You can even virtually try to raise your own child.

11.1 Growth of the Body

 ## Learning Objectives

After reading the module, you should be able to do the following:

LO1 Recognize how much children grow in middle childhood.

LO2 Describe the nutritional needs of elementary school children and the best ways to approach malnutrition and obesity.

LO3 State when children's primary teeth begin to come in.

LO4 Identify the vision problems common in school-age children.

Middle childhood:
the period of development between the ages of 7 and 11.

The body grows steadily during **middle childhood**, which occurs between ages 7 and 11. We'll look at the nature of this growth in the first part of this module and then at the nutrition required to support this growth; we'll also learn about childhood obesity. We'll end the module by focusing on changes in children's teeth and vision.

Physical Growth

LO1 Recognize how much children grow in middle childhood.

Physical growth during the elementary school years continues at the steady pace established during the preschool years. From the graphs in Figure 11–1, you can see that a typical 6-year-old weighs about 20 kilograms and is 115 centimetres tall but grows to about 40 kilograms and 150 centimetres by age 12. In other words, most children gain about 3.5 kilograms and 5 to 7.5 centimetres per year. Many parents notice that their elementary school children outgrow shoes and pants more rapidly than they outgrow sweaters, shirts, or jackets; most of a child's increase in height comes from the legs, not the trunk.

Boys and girls are about the same size for most of these years (which is why they are combined in the graph), but girls are much more likely than boys to enter puberty toward the end of the elementary school years. Those who do grow rapidly, becoming much bigger than boys. Thus, at ages 11 and 12, the average girl is about 1.5 centimetres taller than the average boy.

As was true in the preschool years, individuals of the same age often differ markedly in their height and weight. Ethnic differences are also evident in children's growth: In these years, children of African heritage tend to be taller than children of European heritage, who are usually taller than children of Asian heritage (Webber, Wattigney, Srinivasan, & Berenson, 1995).

Figure 11–1

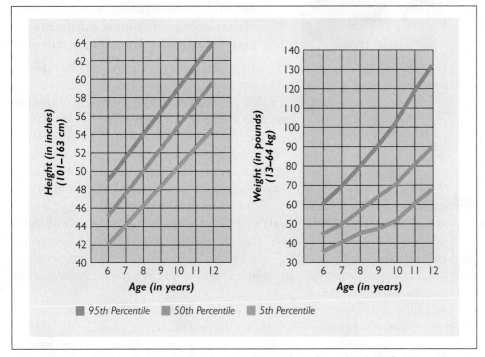

95th Percentile   50th Percentile   5th Percentile

SOURCE: Based on data from World Health Organization Multicentre Study Group. (2006). WHO child growth standards based on length/height, weight and age. Acta Paediatrica, Suppl. 450, 76–85.

Some children are unusually short because their bodies do not produce enough growth hormone. This condition, which affects about 1 child in 5000, is treated by injecting children daily with synthetic growth hormone, first made available in 1985. These injections begin in childhood and continue through adolescence, when growth would stop normally. When treated with growth hormone therapy, children often have a brief growth spurt, followed by more rapid growth than before they started therapy.

Use of growth hormone therapy has become widespread, but many health-care professionals remain skeptical about the necessity of its use with children of short stature. Being short, in itself, is not consistently related to adjustment problems (Sandberg, Brook, & Campos, 1994). From a Canadian perspective, Titus Chan's (2003) commentary in the Canadian Paediatric Society's official journal, *Paediatrics and Child Health*, is worth considering. Chan pointed out that growth hormone treatments are very expensive and do not necessarily make children taller as adults (they may just help them reach their natural adult height sooner). Chan (2003) further noted that physicians must weigh the costs and benefits of using public dollars to fund these treatments, which have little positive benefit overall, when they could be using those resources to pay for treatments that are more necessary.

After being treated with growth hormone, Chan reported, children initially of short stature still tend to be shorter, on average, than their peers once they reach their full adult height (Chan, 2003). In addition, the treatments could make children more prone to infections or result in unwanted side effects, such as an increase in serum insulin, which could lead to insulin resistance later (Chan, 2003). When blood insulin is too high, fat cells do not give up their energy, a situation that can prevent weight loss and lead to other problems, such as diabetes, high blood pressure, and high cholesterol levels. Given these many concerns, physicians now recommend growth hormone treatments only for children known to have deficiencies of this hormone, not simply for children with short stature (Brook, 2000; American Academy of Pediatrics Committee on Drugs and Committee on Bioethics, 1997).

Breakfast is still the most important meal of the day.

Nutrition

LO2 Describe the nutritional needs of elementary school children and the best ways to approach malnutrition and obesity.

As children enter elementary school, they need to eat more to support growth and to provide energy for their active lives. Although preschool children need to consume only about 1500 to 1700 calories per day, the average 7- to 10-year-old needs about 2400 calories each day. Of course, the exact figure depends on the child's age and size and can range anywhere from roughly 1700 to 3300 calories daily.

In their middle years, children need a well-balanced diet, just like when they were preschoolers. They should eat regularly from each of the five food groups identified in Canada's Food Guide. Too often children consume empty calories from foods that are high in sugar and fat but low in other nutrients, such as proteins, vitamins, and minerals.

In addition, school-age children need breakfast. In fact, breakfast should provide about one-quarter of a child's daily calories. During the school years, many children skip breakfast because they're too rushed in the morning. Consequently, parents should organize their mornings so that their children have enough time for breakfast. Eating a healthy breakfast wouldn't hurt the parents, either.

In fact, children and families who are rushed in the morning often develop bad eating habits that can lead to problems with nutrition and bowel health. Inadequate fibre and fluid intake can contribute to problems with regular functioning of the bowel. One significant problem that some children experience is "constipation and overflow," a condition in which the bowel becomes packed with hard fecal matter that is difficult to pass and results in irregular, painful movements as well as ongoing leakage of fluid that the child cannot hold in (Heins & Ritchie, 1985; Jennings, Davies, Costarelli, & Gettman, 2009; Mellon, Whiteside, & Friedrich, 2006).

Many school children skip breakfast because they live in poverty and their parents can't afford to feed them. For these youngsters, a missed breakfast is part of a much larger problem of malnutrition or subnutrition. Malnutrition is a worldwide problem—and is disturbingly common in North America. For school-age children, chronic malnutrition causes many problems, including slowed growth, irritability, sickness, and missed school. Even when they're in school, underfed children often have trouble remembering and concentrating on their schoolwork (Pollitt, 1995).

One solution is to provide free and reduced-price meals for children at school. Lunch programs are the most common, but breakfast and dinner are sometimes available too. These programs have a tremendously positive impact: Because children are better fed, they miss less school, and their achievement scores improve (Gleason, 1995; Meyers, Sampson, Weitzman, Rogers, & Kayne, 1989).

Although many children in Canada are undernourished, others have the opposite problem: excess calorie consumption leading to obesity. We'll look at this problem in the next section of this module. Plus, in the feature

"Both parents work. Neither likes to cook."

on Children and Families around the World, you will learn about how some cultures source protein by incorporating insects and worms into their diet.

OBESITY.   **Obesity** occurs when a child's body weight is at least 20 percent over the ideal body weight for the child's age and height. Overweight youngsters often are unpopular and have low self-esteem (Braet, Mervielde, & Vandereycken, 1997). Furthermore, they are at risk for many medical problems throughout life, including high blood pressure and diabetes, because the vast majority of overweight children and adolescents become overweight adults (Serdula et al., 1993).

Mendelson and White (1985) conducted a Canadian study of overweight children and noted interesting findings about weight and self-esteem. Mendelson and White studied children across three age groups: 8.5–11.4, 11.5–14.4, and 14.5–17.4 years. They found that the youngest children who were overweight did not differ in self-esteem from their normal-weight peers. In the middle group, self-esteem was affected for overweight boys but not girls, and in the oldest group, self-esteem was affected for overweight girls and not boys. They also found that children's body-esteem, how they felt about their bodies, was lower across all age groupings as compared with normal-weight peers.

Obesity:

the physical state of being 20 percent over ideal body weight, given a child's age and height.

Children and Families around the World

New Ideas in Family Nutrition . . . or Are These Old Ideas?

About 1900 edible insect species exist in the world, primarily in Asia, Africa, and South America, although other regions also boast some edible species. Few edible insect species thrive in Canada and Russia, partly owing to cold weather and small species size overall. The most popularly consumed insects include beetles, both in the larval and adult stages, followed by caterpillars and insects in the bee family. When children are raised in families that consume insects as part of their diet, they are socialized to have a positive attitude toward this source of protein.

The palm weevil, a pest found throughout South America, Africa, and Southern Asia, is the most popularly consumed beetle. Other popular beetles are the larvae of aquatic beetles, dung beetles, and wood-boring larvae. In the Netherlands, yellow mealworms are not uncommon. The mopane caterpillar, found in woodland areas of Africa, is the most frequently consumed worm (see Figure 11–2). The trade industry associated with insect harvest has been estimated at close to US$85 million per year. Bamboo caterpillars are harvested in Asia, and up to 27 species of caterpillar, such as red or white maguey worms, are thought to be consumed in the Chiapas region of Mexico. Regions of the world most associated with insect consumption are Africa, Southeast Asia, South Asia, and Latin America.

According a recent UN report (van Huis, Van Itterbeeck, Klunder, Mertens, Halloran, Juir, & Vantomme, 2013, p. 59), insect consumption has a number of advantages:

- They have high feed-conversion efficiency (an animal's capacity to convert feed mass into increased body mass, represented as kilogram of feed per kilogram of weight gain).
- They can be reared on organic side streams, reducing environmental contamination while adding value to waste.
- They emit relatively few greenhouse gases and relatively little ammonia.
- They require significantly less water than cattle rearing.
- They have few animal welfare issues, although the extent to which insects experience pain is largely unknown.
- They pose a low risk of transmitting zoonotic infections.

Although insects might seem to have advantages as a family nutrition staple, people in Western nations such as Canada rarely intentionally consume insects and are not willing to see them as a viable source of dietary protein.

Some insect products are quite commonly used in Western processed foods, such as carmine (red) dye from the cochineal beetle family. However, most Canadians see insects and insect-derived products, such as dyes and extracted proteins, as disgusting. A few think insects are an exciting novelty food, but by far, most people turn away from them. Sometimes attitudes can change. Wood and Looy (2000; Looy & Wood, 2006) found that "Bug Banquets" can change people's acceptance of eating insects by providing the opportunity to try them and by teaching people about insect nutrition. Although attitudes toward insect consumption tend to be culturally transmitted, education can increase people's awareness about insect-based nutrition.

Figure 11–2

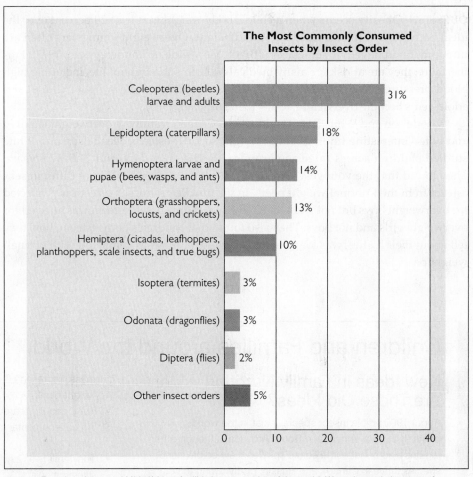

The Most Commonly Consumed Insects by Insect Order

- Coleoptera (beetles) larvae and adults — 31%
- Lepidoptera (caterpillars) — 18%
- Hymenoptera larvae and pupae (bees, wasps, and ants) — 14%
- Orthoptera (grasshoppers, locusts, and crickets) — 13%
- Hemiptera (cicadas, leafhoppers, planthoppers, scale insects, and true bugs) — 10%
- Isoptera (termites) — 3%
- Odonata (dragonflies) — 3%
- Diptera (flies) — 2%
- Other insect orders — 5%

SOURCE: Based on Jongema Y (2012) List of edible insect species of the world. Wageningen, Laboratory of Entomology, Wageningen University.

In later research, Mendelson, White, and Mendelson (1996) found that self-esteem was not so much related to actual weight but to a youngster's feelings about his or her appearance. Body-esteem continued to be related to weight in the sense that higher weights tended to be associated with lower levels of body-esteem. Some association also was demonstrated between body-esteem and overall levels of self-esteem, and these researchers found that levels of body-esteem (as well as self-esteem) tended to remain stable over a two-year period. Since that study, these researchers have developed a new measure of body-esteem for adolescents and adults (Mendelson, Mendelson, & White, 2001).

In Canada, rates of obesity vary and tend to be linked to social class. For example, in 1994, Feldman and Beagan suggested that children from less wealthy families had a higher risk of being obese than children from high-income families. This finding has been noted more recently, as well, in a Canadian study of children between the ages of 7 and 11 (Tremblay & Willms, 2003). Studying National Longitudinal Study of Children and Youth (NLSCY) data from 7216 children, Tremblay and Willms (2003) concluded that children who participate in physical activity, including organized and unorganized sports, have 10 to 24 percent less chance of being overweight and 23 to 43 percent less chance of being obese as compared with children who do not. In addition, they found TV watching and video-game playing increased children's risk for being overweight by 17 to 44 percent and increased their risk of being obese by 10 to 61 percent (Tremblay & Willms, 2003). Excess television watching and lower levels of physical activity have also been linked to obesity and higher risk for type 2 diabetes in Mohawk girls (Horn, Paradis, Potvin, Macaulay, & Desrosiers, 2001).

Health Canada has recognized childhood obesity as a serious problem of epidemic proportions and has been developing programs targeting nutrition and activity levels in school-age children. The Canadian Fitness and Lifestyle Research Institute (CFLRI) has been studying and promoting the importance of increased activity levels for Canadians, pointing to sedentary lifestyle as one of the major problems facing children and youth today. In 1998, the CFLRI issued a "Warning to Couch Potatoes" (CFLRI, 2005), and it has published a number of tips on its website for increasing activity level. Interestingly, although you might guess that children who are clinically hyperactive would have a lower risk for obesity, German researchers have shown this not to be true (Holtkamp et al., 2004).

In addition to lifestyle, heredity also can play an important role in childhood obesity. In adoption studies, children's and adolescents' weight tends to be related to the weight of their biological parents, not to the weight of their adoptive parents (Stunkard et al., 1986). Genes may influence obesity by influencing a person's activity level. In other words, being genetically more prone to inactivity makes burning off calories more difficult and gaining weight easier. Heredity may also help set **basal metabolic rate**, the speed at which the body consumes calories. Children and adolescents with a slower basal metabolic rate burn off calories less rapidly, which makes gaining weight easier (Epstein & Cluss, 1986).

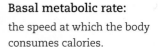

Basal metabolic rate: the speed at which the body consumes calories.

Environment is also influential. Television advertising, for example, encourages youth to eat tasty but fattening foods. Parents also can inadvertently encourage obesity by emphasizing external eating signals rather than internal one. Infants eat primarily because of internal signals: They eat when they experience hunger and stop eating when they feel full. Parents who urge children to "clean their plates" even when no longer hungry are teaching children to ignore internal cues to eating, making the children at risk for overeating (Birch, 1991). Overeating high-calorie foods and living a sedentary lifestyle together form what is perhaps the most challenging cause of childhood obesity today.

Most obese youth can lose weight. The most effective programs have several features in common (Epstein et al., 1995; Foreyt & Goodrick, 1995; Israel, Guile, Baker, & Silverman, 1994):

- The focus of the program is to change obese children's eating habits, encourage them to become more active, and discourage sedentary behaviour.

- As part of the treatment, children learn to monitor their eating, exercise, and sedentary behaviour. Goals are established in each area, and rewards are earned when the goals are met.

- Parents are trained to help children set realistic goals and to use behavioural principles to help children meet these goals. Parents also monitor their own lifestyles to be sure they aren't accidentally fostering their child's obesity.

When programs incorporate these features, obese children do lose weight. However, even after losing weight, many of these children remain overweight. Therefore, it is best to establish good eating and exercise habits in order to avoid obesity in the first place.

Tooth Development

LO3 State when children's primary teeth begin to come in.

Many 5- and 6-year-olds see the loss of a tooth as a sign of maturity. That's good, because after children's primary teeth begin to fall out, they lose teeth regularly—about four a year for the next five years! Primary teeth

Losing teeth is an important sign of increasing maturity for children.

are steadily replaced by permanent teeth. By age 12, most children will have approximately 24 teeth. The second molars (there are four) usually erupt between ages 11 and 13, and the third molars (wisdom teeth) appear in late adolescence or early adulthood, although not everyone gets these.

The health of baby teeth can affect the permanent teeth coming in after them. Severe tooth decay in baby teeth can work its way down far enough to affect the health of permanent teeth coming in afterward. Therefore, care is important for both baby and permanent teeth. Food that is not removed from the teeth combines with bacteria in the mouth to produce acid that eats through the tooth's enamel surface, creating a cavity. Regular brushing and flossing can prevent tooth decay. Unfortunately, children often do not have the fine-motor development or knowledge to brush their teeth properly. As a result, preschoolers and babies need to have parents look after their teeth for them until they are old enough to take over proper care of their own teeth.

Dental care is particularly important after eating foods high in starches and simple carbohydrates because these stimulate acid that leads to tooth decay. For decades, fluoride in toothpaste and drinking water was an integral part of the fight against tooth decay. The rationale has been that fluoride interferes with the formation of tooth-damaging acids and helps to repair tooth surfaces that have been damaged by acid.

However, researchers from the Department of Environmental Health at the Harvard School of Public Health found evidence of fluoride neurotoxicity in children as a result of high exposure through drinking water. This is a particular concern in communities where fluoride levels in drinking water can be high, such as in China. Because fluoride crosses the placenta, these researchers reported concerns over the possibility that prenatal exposure to fluoride could cause permanent brain damage, as they noted that the developing brain is particularly susceptible to teratogens. In discussing the studies of fluoride's effect on children's development, the researchers noted that "the consistency of their findings adds support to existing evidence of fluoride-associated cognitive deficits, and suggests that potential developmental neurotoxicity of fluoride should be a high research priority" (Choi, Guifan, Zhang, & Grandjean, 2012, p. 1367). Because many children's exposure to fluoride in drinking water is ongoing, parents should use only a pea-sized amount of toothpaste on their children's toothbrushes, and they must teach their children to rinse their mouths after brushing and spit out all the toothpaste, rather than swallow it. Finally, decay prevention also involves regular visits to the dentist and oral hygienist.

Malocclusion:

the dental condition whereby upper and lower permanent teeth do not meet properly.

When permanent teeth erupt, some children experience **malocclusion**—their upper and lower teeth don't meet properly. Malocclusion has many causes: heredity, early loss of primary teeth, an accident, or thumb-sucking after the permanent teeth erupt. Another problem for many children is that the permanent teeth are crooked or crowded or overlap. Malocclusion can make chewing difficult, and crowded teeth are prone to injury and decay. Orthodontists treat malocclusion, while dentists pull, fill, and heal teeth to help people maintain their overall dental health.

Removal of some permanent teeth to prevent crowding sometimes helps, as does wearing dental retainers or braces for six months to two years to correct malocclusion by moving teeth back into proper position.

Vision and Hearing

LO4 Identify the vision problems common in school-age children.

For the most part, children's sensory systems mature early in infancy and change little after the first two years. However, some physical changes continue to occur in children's sensory systems during the elementary school years, such as those we observe with the auditory system. The eustachian tube, which links the inner ear to the upper part of the throat, becomes longer and more curvy, helping to reduce the incidence of otitis media (ear infection), which causes temporary hearing loss and permanent loss if left uncorrected.

A common sensory disorder that can have psychosocial implications for children in these years involves vision (Rogow, 1999). In **myopia** (nearsightedness), the lens projects images of distant objects in front of the retina instead of on it, which means they look fuzzy instead of sharp. For example, Akilah, a Grade 4 student, often squinted when she tried to read the blackboard and complained that she didn't like being seated at a desk in the back of the room. A vision test revealed that Akilah suffered from myopia: Her near vision was clear, but her distant vision wasn't. Approximately 25 percent of school-age children are myopic, and the condition usually emerges between 8 and 12 years of age. Heredity clearly contributes, as myopia runs in families, and identical twins are more likely than fraternal twins to be myopic (Sperduto, Seigel, Roberts, & Rowland, 1983). However, experience is also a factor: Children who spend much time reading, working at a computer, or drawing—all activities that draw upon near vision—are more likely to become myopic. Happily, myopia is easily remedied with glasses; Akilah was fitted with glasses, and she no longer squinted or complained about sitting in the back of the room.

Braces can correct malocclusion.

Myopia:
nearsightedness.

Ask Yourself

Your friend Kim, who is overweight, is upset to find that her 10-year-old son is putting on weight. What can you tell Kim about the influence of genetics on childhood obesity? What would you suggest to help her son to avoid becoming obese?

11.2 Motor Development

 ## Learning Objectives

After reading the module, you should be able to do the following:

LO5 Describe how motor skills improve during the elementary school years and whether boys and girls differ in their motor skills.

LO6 Identify whether Canadian children are physically fit.

LO7 Discuss the benefits of participating in sports and the optimal circumstances for children to participate.

LO8 Understand the kinds of accidents common in school-age children and how they can be prevented.

Motor skills improve remarkably over the elementary school years. We'll trace these changes in the first part of this module; then, we'll see whether Canadian children are fit. Next, we'll examine children's participation in sports and see how coaches influence children in organized sports. Finally, we'll see how children's improved motor skills sometimes place them at risk for injury.

Figure 11–3

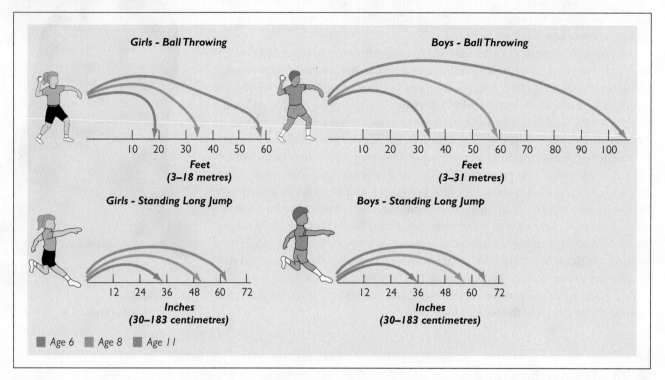

Girls - Ball Throwing

Boys - Ball Throwing

Feet
(3–18 metres)

Feet
(3–31 metres)

Girls - Standing Long Jump

Boys - Standing Long Jump

Inches
(30–183 centimetres)

Inches
(30–183 centimetres)

Age 6   Age 8   Age 11

Development of Motor Skills

LO5 **Describe how motor skills improve during the elementary school years and whether boys and girls differ in their motor skills.**

Elementary school children's greater size and strength contributes to improved motor skills. During these years, children steadily run faster and jump farther. For example, Figure 11–3 shows how far a typical boy and girl can throw a ball and how far they can jump (in the standing long jump). By the time children are 11 years old, they can throw a ball three times farther than they could at age 6, and they can jump nearly twice as far.

Fine-motor skills also improve as children move through the elementary school years. Children's greater dexterity is evident in a host of activities ranging from typing, writing, and drawing to working on puzzles, playing the piano, and building model cars. Children gain much greater control over their fingers and hands, making them much more nimble. This greater fine-motor coordination is obvious in children's handwriting.

Michael Salman (2002), at Toronto's Hospital for Sick Children, has been studying the development of perceptual and motor skills in children. He pointed to the important role of the cerebellum in the brain as mediating between children's motor movements, sensory perception, and the precise timing necessary to carry out an activity such as kicking a ball or picking up a glass of milk. Salman's work points to the importance of understanding that development occurs in multiple systems at the same time and requires careful coordination by the central nervous system.

GENDER DIFFERENCES IN MOTOR SKILL.   In both gross- and fine-motor skills, gender differences in performance exist. Girls tend to excel in fine-motor skills; for example, their handwriting tends to be better than boys', and girls tend to do better on a task in which pegs must be moved to

In middle childhood, children normally have greater size, strength, and motor skill.

Dr. Theresa Zolner

different positions on a board (Kail, 1991; Thomas & French, 1985). Girls also excel in gross-motor skills requiring flexibility and balance, such as tumbling. In gross-motor skills that emphasize strength, boys often have the advantage.

As children enter puberty, girls' bodies have proportionately more fat and less muscle than those of boys. This difference explains why, for example, boys can hang from a bar using their arms and hands much longer than girls can. However, for other gross-motor skills, such as running, throwing, and catching, body composition is not as important as experience (Smoll & Schutz, 1990). Girls in middle childhood are more often found on a swing set, jumping rope, or perhaps talking quietly in a group; in contrast, boys often play soccer or shoot baskets. Many girls and their parents believe that sports and physical fitness are less valuable for girls than boys (Eccles, Jacobs, & Harold, 1990). Consequently, girls spend less time in these sports and fitness-related activities than boys, depriving them of opportunities to practise, which is essential for developing motor skills (Eccles & Harold, 1991).

Physical Fitness

LO6 Identify whether Canadian children are physically fit.

Being active physically has many benefits for children: It helps promote growth of muscles and bone, promotes cardiovascular health (National High Blood Pressure Education Program Working Group, 1996), and can help establish a lifelong pattern of exercise. How fit are Canadian school-age children? An astonishing 51 percent of Canadian children are considered inactive, and this figure rises to 64 percent if we include adolescents (Cameron, Craig, Coles, & Cragg, 2001). Boys tend to be more active than girls, although researchers in this area acknowledge that it is difficult to measure children and youths' level of physical activity with complete reliability and validity (Cameron et al., 2001).

Many factors contribute to low levels of fitness. Many elementary schools do not include physical education class as a daily activity, offering it only once per week. Physical and Health Education Canada (PHE Canada) has been advocating for increased physical activity for Canadian children and youth, particularly through better physical education (www.phecanada.ca). In addition, the CFLRI (Cameron et al., 2001) has been encouraging increased physical activity through schools and implicates physical inactivity as a major cause for health problems among Canadians today.

Christine Seidel (1998), from the Summit School for Developmentally Disabled Children in Quebec, found that people with intellectual disabilities tend to exercise less frequently than their nondisabled peers. They tend to have lower levels of muscular strength, endurance, aerobic power, and flexibility. As a result, Seidel made the point that proper fitness assessments and regular fitness programming should be provided to people with intellectual disabilities to increase their level of fitness and quality of life overall (Seidel, 1998). Harvey and Reid (1997) came to a similar conclusion regarding needs in their study of the physical fitness and gross-motor skills of children with attentional problems.

Fine-motor skills improve as a result of greater dexterity.

Team sports are a good source of exercise, and they promote motor development.

Many experts believe that all children should have physical education more frequently each week. And many believe that physical education classes should offer a range of activities in which all children can participate and that can be the foundation for a lifelong program of fitness. Instead of emphasizing team sports such as touch football, physical education classes should emphasize activities like running, walking, racquet sports, and swimming; these can be done throughout adolescence and adulthood either alone or with another person (American Academy of Pediatrics Committee on Sports Medicine and Committee on School Health, 1989). Families can encourage fitness too. Instead of spending an afternoon watching TV and eating snacks, they could go walking or biking together.

Participating in Sports

LO7 Discuss the benefits of participating in sports and the optimal circumstances for children to participate.

In middle childhood, children's greater motor skill means they are able to participate in many team sports, including baseball, softball, basketball, and soccer. Obviously, when children play sports, they get exercise and improve their motor skills, but there are other hidden benefits as well. Sports can provide children a chance to learn important social skills, such as how to work effectively as part of a group, often in complementary roles. Playing sports also allows children to use their emerging cognitive skills as they devise new playing strategies or modify the rules of a game.

Across Canada, children have differing opportunities for participation in sport. Most children have access to some sporting activities through their schools, and sport researchers have come to see the school as having a primary role in laying a strong foundation for good exercise habits in Canadian children.

One organization, the Canadian Fitness and Lifestyle Research Institute (CFLRI), recently examined the role of the school in relation to children's participation in physical activity. CFLRI members were interested in the role of Canadian schools in supporting physical activity in youth through policies, facilities, programs, and other opportunities. They surveyed over 11 000 schools across Canada about the relation between a number of variables already existing in the Canadian educational system, such as physical education program location, availability, and evaluation.

The CFLRI found that, even in physical education classes, Canadian elementary school children spend nearly 20 percent of the time standing around being inactive, although activity levels increase somewhat during high school physical education. Only 16 percent of Canadian schools offer physical education classes on a daily basis, less often in the higher grades. CFLRI also found that only 40 percent of Canadian schools use physical education specialists to teach these classes.

The researchers at CFLRI also found that the majority of schools hold families responsible for transportation and entry costs to a sports activity. In addition, 43 percent of schools hold families responsible for providing the equipment necessary to participate in these activities. You might think that schools with lower-income families would be more likely to provide support for transportation, admission, and equipment. However, according to CFLRI, schools having a majority of low-income families were less likely to pay for these costs. Private versus public school differences were also noted, with students attending public schools in Canada being more likely to have to pay for the costs of their own equipment.

Finally, the CFLRI found that standards for evaluation of the quality of physical education varied considerably across all Canadian provinces, with schools in the Prairie provinces being more likely to use PHE Canada's national Quality Daily Physical Education standards than schools in the east. Based on their study findings, the CFLRI researchers made a number of recommendations, including (1) providing comprehensive physical activity programming in schools, (2) providing a supportive environment for participation in physical activity in schools, and (3) creating community partnerships to promote physical activity participation and education.

In days gone by, children gathered together informally—at a playground, a vacant lot, or someone's backyard—to play sports. However, when today's children participate, the setting is often an official league, organized and run by adults. This turns out to be a mixed blessing. Adults' involvement in children's sports has several advantages: Children receive knowledgeable feedback and learn how to improve their skills, and they can enjoy spending time with a positive role model. However, adults sometimes overemphasize competition instead of skill development. They can be so controlling that children have little opportunity to learn leadership skills, and they may emphasize drills, strategy, and winning to the point that the activity becomes more like work instead of play.

When adults encourage their players and emphasize skill development, children usually enjoy playing, often improve their skills, and increase their self-esteem (Smith & Smoll, 1997; Smoll, Smith, Barnett, & Everett, 1993). In contrast, when adults emphasize winning over skill development and criticize or punish players for bad plays, children often lose interest and tend to stop playing (Bailey & Rasmussen, 1996; Smith & Smoll, 1996). You may doubt that anyone coaching a young child could be cruel or critical, but Theresa Zolner's daughter once had a coach who consistently berated the children, argued with his own daughter on the bench, and told some children that they weren't making any contribution to the team despite the children's best efforts. Sometimes coaches scream at the players and threaten to remove them from the team if they don't do better. It's no wonder that some kids quit sports altogether when coaches act this way. Parents can also contribute to sports-related pressure. For example, across Canada, considerable public discussion has focused on parental behaviour at children's hockey games, where some parents scream at their children from the bleachers or get into physical altercations with other parents or coaches after becoming too worked up about the game.

In response to parental pressuring of children and inappropriate behaviour at games, Hockey Canada launched a public-awareness campaign to target "bad hockey parent" behaviour. The campaign consists of print and television advertisements designed to make parents more sensitive to the negative impact of parental pressure on children's well-being and motivation for participating in hockey. When children are given the opportunity to participate recreationally, without excessive pressure from adults, they will be more likely to want to continue, which can result in better health and emotional well-being for children in the long run. Sometimes, as a result of their life circumstances, children do not have access to these kinds of developmentally enriching activities and experiences. As you will see in the Making Children's Lives Better feature, one organization is trying to make a difference for some less fortunate Canadian children.

A poster from Hockey Canada's public awareness campaign.

Accidents

LO8 **Understand the kinds of accidents common in school-age children and how they can be prevented.**

While children often are eager to participate in physical activities, during middle childhood improved motor skills and greater independence place them at greater risk for injury. For example, children may walk to school unsupervised and need to cross busy streets or ride a bike on the road alongside much larger and faster vehicles.

In Canada, people under the age of 20 accounted for 16 percent of all injury hospitalizations in 2001–2002 (Canadian Institute for Health Information, 2004b). The most common causes for injury in young people under the age of 20 were unintentional

Making Children's Lives Better

Tim Horton Children's Foundation

In 1995, the Canadian Psychological Association awarded the Tim Horton Children's Foundation its Humanitarian Award, recognizing the foundation's important contributions to mental health promotion for children in Canada (CPA, n.d.). Originally founded in 1975, the Tim Horton Children's Foundation is a charitable, nonprofit organization with the primary goal of enabling access to enriched activities for children from low socio-economic status families. The foundation continues the humanitarian efforts of the late Tim Horton, who was a well-known Canadian hockey star with the National Hockey League.

Each year, the foundation sponsors thousands of children to attend one of its summer camps, where children are exposed to developmentally appropriate, challenging, and fun activities. Participation in these camps offers children an opportunity to have fun in a setting where they can experience positive peer relationships as well as improve their sense of self-confidence and pride in personal achievements. Funding for the camps is raised, in part, by Tim Hortons' "Camp Day," held in Canada and the United States. On Camp Day, Tim Hortons donates 100 percent of its proceeds from coffee sales to the foundation camp program. In 2012, Camp Day raised $11 million, which funded 15 000 children to attend these camps.

In addition to its summer camps, the Tim Horton Children's Foundation also sponsors a youth leadership program for kids between the ages of 13 and 18 who previously attended the camp. The youth leadership program involves more challenging kinds of activities, such as extended canoe trips and particular focus on personal and educational goals. Graduates of this program can become eligible for postsecondary scholarships to continue their education. The foundation also sponsors summer day camps, outdoor education and environmental programs, as well as the recreational, noncompetitive Timbits Hockey program. This latter program introduces approximately 50 000 4- to 9-year-old children per year in Canada to the fundamental skills of hockey in a positive and prosocial way.

The Tim Horton Children's Foundation is a wonderful example of how a large, international corporation can give so much good back to its local communities. For more information about the foundation, visit www.timhortons.com/ca/en/difference/childrens-foundation.html.

falls (40 percent), motor vehicle collisions (17 percent), being struck by a person or object (10 percent), and cycling (6 percent). In addition, 51 percent of near-drownings involve young people under the age of 20 in Canada (Canadian Institute for Health Information, 2004b).

Farley, Haddad, and Brown (1996) studied the effectiveness of a four-year bicycle helmet advocacy and promotion program designed to target approximately 8000 elementary school children from one region in Quebec. Activities in the program included promotional communications at the community level, educational activities, and projects designed to help families acquire helmets. As a result of the program, these researchers found an approximately 32 percent increase in helmet use, primarily in middle-class communities. The program was less effective in communities where families were of lower socio-economic status.

Clearly, parents need to be vigilant in requiring children to wear helmets on bicycles or similar equipment (e.g., skateboards, scooters) and to wear seat belts in cars. Although seat belts and helmets won't prevent accidents, they dramatically reduce the risk of injury (Peterson & Oliver, 1995). However, as Farley, Haddad, and Brown (1996) concluded, socio-economic status might have an impact on whether parents acquire this type of safety equipment.

In terms of water activities, nothing beats careful supervision by qualified lifeguards as well as proper swimming and water-safety education. Children should never be left alone around bathtubs, ponds, swimming pools, lakes, wells, troughs, or any other sources of water into which they might fall or wade.

Preventing accidents is not easy, in part because children often object to parents' efforts to ensure safety and in part because, in the process of taking advantage of their new skills and freedom, children often unknowingly endanger themselves. Parents can help by being good role models—by always fastening their own seat belts, wearing a helmet when biking, and insisting that children always wear seat belts and helmets, even when the trip is short or seems safe. By these actions, parents are not only protecting themselves and their children from injury but also helping their children to become much more safety conscious and less prone to take risks themselves (Tuchfarber, Zins, & Jason, 1997).

Parents can also prevent accidents by being realistic in assessing their own children's skills. Too often parents overestimate their children's abilities, particularly their cognitive and motor skills. Parents might allow a 7-year-old to cross a busy street, when, in fact, most children younger than 9 or 10 years will not look consistently before crossing and cannot accurately judge the amount of time they have to cross a street. Or parents may allow a child to ride to school in a bike lane adjacent to a street filled with traffic, even though children may not consistently pay attention while biking or may not have the motor control to manoeuvre their bikes around unexpected hazards, such as potholes.

Parents need to be aware that these situations are ripe for injury and should be avoided. In the first instance, the parent could accompany the child to the busy street, help the child cross, then let the child continue alone; in the second, the parent could insist that the child find a less busy route or use another form of transportation. Parents need to remember that school-age children's cognitive and motor skills are, in many respects, still quite limited; these limits can expose children to danger. Parents need to avoid these situations before accidents happen (Dunne, Asher, & Rivara, 1992).

Community- and school-based programs are important tools in efforts to reduce childhood accidents. Through such programs, children can learn safety-oriented behaviours that reduce their risk for injury. Successful programs often present material about safety to children but, more importantly, provide role-playing opportunities in which youngsters can practise safety skills. For example, children can be taught to "stop, drop, and roll" if their clothing is on fire, then be asked to practise this behaviour. Or children might be taught ways to cross a street safely (e.g., pick a safe spot to cross, then look left, right, and left again before crossing), then be allowed to practise this skill supervised by an adult. When programs like these are run in communities by schools or hospitals, children readily learn behaviours that promote safety (Zins, Garcia, Tuchfarber, Clark, & Laurence, 1994). However, although knowledge of safety rules is important, only actual compliance with those rules and good parental supervision will affect the number of accidents children experience (Morrongiello, Midgett, & Shields, 2001).

Ask Yourself

How does participation in sports illustrate connections between motor, cognitive, and social development in middle childhood?

Let's say you are a nurse working in a pediatric unit in a hospital. One of the children in your care does not want to eat, and you want to document the situation so that nutritional and medical staff can help the child. What kinds of observations might assist you in communicating effective information to the child's health-care team?

can start to put on weight if they are not physically active on a regular basis. If you were responsible for after-school programming for children between the ages of 8 and 11, what would you do to reduce the contribution of your program toward childhood obesity? How would you set up activities? What would you allow or not allow the children to eat? How would you keep them happy but also healthy when in your care?

What Would an After-School Care Supervisor Do?

Mabel and Terry's daughter, Sophie, wasn't sure about joining a sports team. However, in middle childhood, children

Summary

11.1 Growth of the Body

Physical Growth

- Elementary school children grow at a steady pace, more so in the legs than in the trunk.

- Boys and girls tend to be about the same size for many of these years, but large individual and cultural differences exist.

- Some children receive growth hormone because their bodies do not produce enough growth hormone naturally for normal growth.

- Children with adequate natural growth hormone might also receive synthetic growth hormone, but this practice is discouraged by scientists and health-care professionals.

Nutrition

- School-age children need approximately 2400 calories daily, preferably drawn from each of the five food groups.

- Children need to eat breakfast because this meal should provide approximately one-fourth of their calories and, without breakfast, they often have trouble concentrating in school.

- Many children living in poverty do not eat breakfast and do not receive adequate nutrition overall.

- Programs for free and reduced-price meals are often available for these children, but sometimes their parents do not realize that their children are eligible to participate.

- Many obese children are unpopular, have low self-esteem, and are at risk for medical disorders.

- Obesity reflects both heredity and acquired eating habits.

- The most effective programs for treating obesity in youth involve both children and parents setting eating and exercise goals and monitoring their daily progress.

Tooth Development

- Children start to lose primary teeth at 5 or 6 years of age.

- By age 12, children typically have 24 of their permanent teeth.

- Good dental hygiene includes frequent brushing, flossing, and regular checkups.

Vision and Hearing

- Most sensory systems change little in childhood, except hearing.

- The eustachian tube becomes longer and curvier, helping to reduce the incidence of ear infection.

- Many children have myopia, meaning they can see nearby objects clearly but not distant objects.

- Myopia reflects heredity and experience and is easily remedied with glasses.

11.2 Motor Development

Development of Motor Skills

- Fine- and gross-motor skills improve substantially over the middle childhood years, reflecting children's greater size and strength.

- Girls tend to excel in fine-motor skills that emphasize dexterity (e.g., handwriting) as well as gross-motor skills that require flexibility and balance (e.g., tumbling).

- Boys tend to excel in gross-motor skills that emphasize strength (e.g., throwing).

- Although some gender differences reflect differences in body makeup, they also reflect differing cultural expectations regarding motor skills for boys and girls.

Physical Fitness

- Although children report spending much time being physically active, fewer than half of school children meet all standards for physical fitness.

- Part of the explanation for the lack of fitness is the sad state of physical education programs in elementary schools.

- Elementary physical education classes are not taught often enough and involve too little actual physical activity.

- Television may also contribute to inactivity.

- Physical education in the schools needs to be more frequent and more oriented toward developing patterns of lifetime exercise.

- Families can become more active, thereby encouraging children's fitness.

Participating in Sports

- Many school-age children participate in team sports.

- Both boys and girls believe that sports participation enhances their self-esteem, helps them to master skills and learn about co-operation, and is a way to stay physically fit.

- Adult coaches often can help children improve their skills, but they sometimes overemphasize competition, are so controlling that children have little opportunity to experience leadership, and overemphasize drills, strategy, and performance, turning "play" into "work."

Accidents

- Because children in the middle years are more mobile and more independent, they're at greater risk for injury than preschool children.

- The most common cause of injury and death at this age is the automobile—children can be injured either as a passenger or as a pedestrian.

- Parents can help to prevent children's accidents by being good role models (e.g., always wearing their own seat belt in a car) and by insisting that their children wear seat belts in cars and helmets when biking.

- Parents also can help to prevent children's accidents by not overestimating their children's cognitive and motor skills.

- Another way to prevent children's accidents is through community- and school-based programs in which children learn safety behaviours and have the opportunity to practise them.

Chapter Critical Review

1. Growth hormones are used widely in North America. What cultural reasons account for their use?

2. Daniel, a 10-year-old whose favourite activities are reading, watching TV, playing computer and video games, and playing with his dog, is beginning to gain too much weight. Devise an exercise program and a healthy diet for Daniel.

3. Your local parks and recreation department has started a basketball program for Grade 2 children. Write a code of conduct for coaches and parents.

See for Yourself

To see some of the developmental differences in physical growth and motor skill we have described in this chapter, watch youth softball or soccer games. Most programs will have children grouped by age (e.g., Grades 3 and 4 together). Try to observe one game at each age level. As you watch, you should see obvious age differences in speed (how fast children run the bases), agility (children's control and grace as they swing a bat or field a ball), and strength (how hard and how far balls are hit). The age differences in physical growth and motor skill should be obvious, but also be sure to notice how much children of the same age differ in their size and ability. See for yourself!

Chapter 12
Cognitive Development in Middle Childhood

Eye Ubiquitous/SuperStock

∨ MODULE

12.1 Cognitive Processes

12.2 The Nature of Intelligence

12.3 Individual Differences in Intellectual Skills

12.4 Academic Skills

12.5 Effective Schools

Terry and Mabel just can't believe that Sophie is old enough to start kindergarten! They believe that she is a bright little girl, but they can't help but think about how formal schooling will affect their daughter and whether she has the ability and skills to achieve. They wonder . . . is she ready, and what will best help her learn to read, write, and do math, and how will she remember it all?

Connect to My Virtual Child

What kinds of theories do you have about children? What ideas inform your thoughts and beliefs about the lives of children, how they are raised, and the nature of the human person? Use your access card and follow this link www.myvirtualchild.com to learn more about the world of the child. You can even virtually try to raise your own child.

12.1 Cognitive Processes

∨ Learning Objectives

After reading the module, you should be able to do the following:

LO1 Describe the strengths and weaknesses of concrete operational thinking.

LO2 Discuss how strategies and knowledge help children to remember more effectively as they grow older.

Piaget and information-processing theorists agree that, by middle childhood, children's cognitive skills are remarkable, both in their own right and when compared to preschool children's skills. In this module, we'll look at both accounts, starting with Piaget's description of concrete operational thinking. Then, we'll look at information-processing accounts of memory skill, where we'll see how children learn to remember common information like telephone numbers.

Concrete Operational Thinking

LO1 **Describe the strengths and weaknesses of concrete operational thinking.**

According to Piaget, during middle childhood, children enter a new stage of cognitive development that is distinctly more like that of adults. In the **concrete operational stage**, which spans ages 7 to 11, children first use mental operations to solve problems and to reason. What are these mental operations that are so essential to concrete operational thinking? **Mental operations** are strategies and rules that make thinking more systematic and powerful. Some mental operations apply to numbers. For example, addition, subtraction, multiplication, and division are familiar arithmetic operations that children in the concrete operational stage use. Other mental operations apply to categories of objects. For example, classes can be added (mothers + fathers = parents) and subtracted (parents – mothers = fathers). Still other mental operations apply to spatial relations among objects. For example, if point A is near points B and C, then points B and C must be close to each other.

Concrete operational stage: a Piagetian cognitive stage of development during which children first use mental operations to solve problems and to reason.

Mental operations: strategies and rules that make thinking more systematic and powerful.

Mental operations give concrete operational thinking a rule-oriented, logical flavour that is missing in preoperational thought. Applied properly, mental operations yield consistent results. Taking the familiar case of arithmetic operations, 4 + 2 is always 6, not just usually or only on weekends.

Another important property of mental operations is that they can be reversed. Each operation has an inverse that can "undo" or reverse the effect of an operation. If you start with 5 and add 3, you get 8; by subtracting 3 from 8, you reverse your steps and return to 5. For Piaget, reversibility was an important aspect of cognitive maturity.

Concrete operational children are able to reverse their thinking in a way that preoperational youngsters cannot. In fact, being able to engage in mental reversal is part of why children in the concrete operational stage pass conservation tasks. Concrete operational thinkers understand that certain kinds of actions can be reversed, restoring objects to their original status.

Concrete operational thinking is much more powerful and flexible than preoperational thinking. Remember that preoperational children believe others see the world as they do (egocentric), are overly focused in their thinking (centration), and confuse appearances with reality. These limitations do not apply to children in the concrete operational stage.

Egocentrism wanes as youngsters gain more experience with friends and siblings who assert their own perspectives on the world (LeMare & Rubin, 1987). Learning from others that events can be interpreted in different ways shows children that problems can have different aspects that must be considered and that appearances can be deceiving. Aggressive children can have some difficulty in this area, as they have been noted to display poorer perspective-taking ability and higher levels of egocentrism than nonaggressive peers. On the other hand, some children who are intellectually gifted have been noted to have better perspective-taking skills and lower levels of egocentrism than age peers who are not thought to be intellectually gifted (Tarshis & Shore, 1991).

Although concrete operational thinking is a major cognitive advance, it has its limits. As the name implies, concrete operational thinking is limited to the tangible and concrete, to the here and now in very practical ways (Flavell, 1985). Thinking abstractly and hypothetically is beyond the ability of concrete operational thinkers and requires advances in development beyond what is normally seen in the middle childhood years.

Memory Skills

LO2 **Discuss how strategies and knowledge help children to remember more effectively as they grow older.**

Memory skills take center stage in information-processing approaches to child development. Children's memory improves rapidly during middle childhood, primarily due to two factors (Kail, 1990; Schneider & Bjorklund, 1998). First, as children grow, they use more effective strategies for remembering. Second, children's growing factual knowledge of the world allows them to organize information more completely and, therefore, remember better. We'll look at each of these factors in the next few pages.

STRATEGIES FOR REMEMBERING. Every day, children encounter new situations and information that they might or might not remember very well. One thing is for certain, however—use of strategies aid memory. Working memory is used for briefly storing a small amount of information, such as the words in these sentences. However, as you read additional sentences, they displace words read earlier from working memory. For you to learn what you are reading, the content must be transferred to long-term memory. Anything not transferred from working memory to long-term memory is lost.

Memory strategies are activities that improve remembering. Some strategies help maintain information in working memory. Others help transfer information to

Memory strategies:
activities that improve remembering.

long-term memory. Still others help retrieve information from long-term memory. Obviously, many memory strategies exist.

Children begin to use memory strategies early. Preschool children look at or touch objects that they've been told to remember (DeLoache, 1984; Marzolf & DeLoache, 1994). Looking and touching aren't very effective, but they tell us that preschoolers understand that they should be doing something to try to remember; remembering doesn't happen automatically!

During middle childhood, children begin to use more powerful strategies. For example, 7- and 8-year-olds use rehearsal, a strategy of repetitively naming information that is to be remembered. As children get older, they learn other memory strategies and when it is best to use them. Children in middle childhood begin to identify different kinds of memory problems and which memory strategies are most appropriate. For example, a child might write a friend's telephone number in a notebook, an effective method for recalling the number later that evening. As children go through middle childhood, they also tend to use strategies more effectively, although some evidence exists that children can be taught to use strategies better at younger ages. For example, Ackerman (1996) tested recall ability in 7- and 11-year-old children. He presented children with sets of three categorically related words (e.g., pig-horse-cow) and, after a few test trials, asked children to retrieve the third word in the triplet. While the 11-year-olds tended to recall more items than the 7-year-olds, the latter group was able to improve their performance with training (Ackerman, 1996).

Children learn to use other kinds of strategies in middle childhood as well, such as how to organize information so that it can be more easily recalled. For example, when reading a textbook or listening in class, the aim is to remember the main points, not the individual words or sentences. Rehearsal is ineffective for this task, but outlining and writing a summary are good strategies because they identify the main points and organize them (Kail, 1990). During middle childhood, children learn to use outlines to help them remember information in textbooks. Also, as children grow, they are more likely to write down information on calendars so they won't forget future events.

Successful learning and remembering involves identifying the goals of memory problems and choosing suitable strategies (Schneider & Bjorklund, 1998). Younger children sometimes misjudge the objectives of a memory task and choose an inappropriate strategy. For example, young children might believe they are supposed to remember a book passage verbatim when they only need to remember its gist, or they might understand a memory task but not pick the best strategy. For example, to remember the gist of a paragraph, a younger child might rehearse it (bad choice) while an older child would outline it (good choice) (Lovett & Pillow, 1996; Slate, Jones, & Dawson, 1993).

After children choose a memory strategy, they need to monitor its effectiveness. That is, they need to decide if the strategy is working. If it's not, they need to begin anew—reanalyzing the memory task to select a better approach. Through monitoring, children learn to accurately identify which material they have not learned and then focus their efforts on this material (Kail, 1990).

Children learn strategies for remembering as they mature.

Figure 12–1 summarizes the sequence of steps involved in monitoring the effectiveness of a memory strategy. Study goals might change from subject to subject in school, but the basic sequence still holds. Studying should always begin with a clear understanding of what goal you are trying to achieve, setting the stage for the events that follow. Too often, students read a text without any clear idea of what they should be getting out of the material. Having a well-defined goal at the outset of a study session—such as "learn Module 12.1"—will improve learning. With this goal, you develop

Figure 12–1

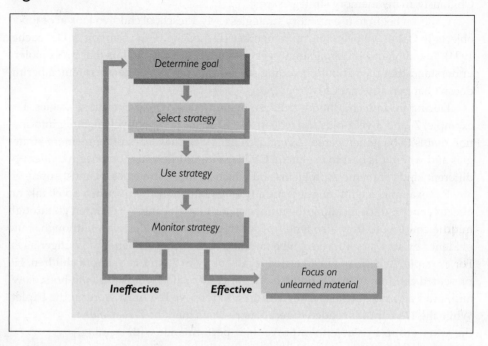

a plan, like (1) carefully reading the outline, learning objectives, and vignette that begin the module. Then, (2) skim the module, paying close attention to headings, sentences in the margins, boxes, and topic sentences of paragraphs. Now, before even reading the module, (3) write an outline of its main topics. If you can't, then you need to skim again and try again—you don't yet understand the overall structure of the module. If you can write an outline, then you know you are familiar with the basic contents of the chapter, and you're ready to go on to reading the module carefully to master its details.

Once people learn to keep the goal of a task in working memory, simple awareness of the goal can activate the "goal-plan structure" in long-term memory as well as elements in memory associated with the plan (Bower, 2008). Once a goal has been achieved (or abandoned), activation of the related plan for achieving the goal is rapidly inhibited (Bower, 2008).

Skilled use of strategies is one aspect of effective remembering; as you'll see in the next few pages, knowledge is also an aid to memory.

KNOWLEDGE AND MEMORY. Let's start our examination of how knowledge influences memory by looking at a study by Michelene Chi (1978). She asked 10-year-olds and adults to remember sequences of numbers. In Figure 12–2, you can see that adults remembered more numbers than children. Next, she asked participants to remember the positions of objects in a matrix. This time 10-year-olds' recall was much better than adults'.

What was responsible for this unexpected reversal of age and recall? Actually, the objects were chess pieces on a chessboard, and the children were skilled chess players, while the adults were novices. The positions of the pieces were taken from actual games and were familiar configurations for the child chess players. For the adults, who lacked knowledge of chess, the patterns seemed arbitrary. But the children had the knowledge to organize and give meaning to the patterns, so they could recognize and then recall the whole configuration instead of many isolated pieces. It was as if the adults were seeing this meaningless pattern

n n c c b a s b c c b n

while the children were seeing this

n b c c b s a b c c n n

When people have a highly elaborated system of knowledge about a particular topic, such as chess, they have an easier time recalling information about the topic in

Figure 12–2

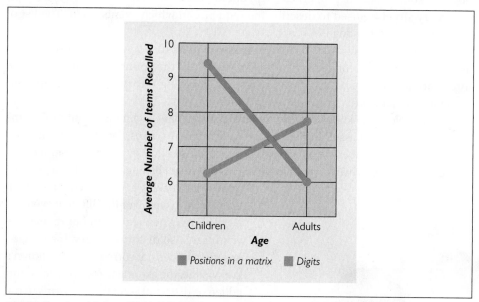

SOURCE: Based on data from Chi, M. T. H. (1978). Knowledge structures and memory development. In R. Siegler (Ed.), Children's thinking: What develops? Hillsdale, NJ: Erlbaum.

an organized manner. Learning new material is more difficult than learning material that can fit into an already organized system of knowledge that a person may have developed in memory. The lesson here is that elaborated knowledge also contributes to memory power.

The knowledge that allows a child to organize information and give it meaning usually increases with age (Schneider & Bjorklund, 1998). Researchers often depict knowledge as a network like the one in Figure 12–3, which shows part of a 10-year-old's knowledge of animals. The entries in the network are linked by different types

Figure 12–3

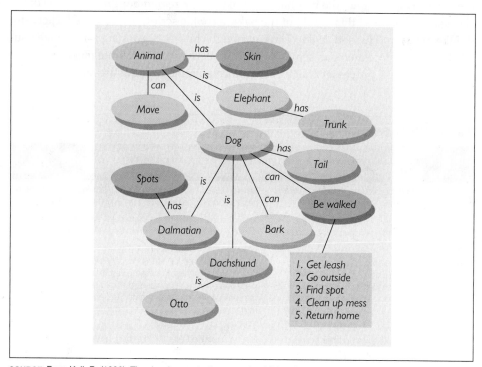

SOURCE: From Kail, R. (1990). The development of memory in children (3rd ed.). New York: W. H. Freeman. Reprinted by permission of Prof. Robert V. Kail, Ph. D.

Script:

a memory structure used to describe the sequence in which events occur.

of associations. Some of the links denote membership in categories (Dalmatian is a dog), and others denote properties (elephant has a trunk). Still others denote a **script**, a memory structure used to describe the sequence in which events occur. The list of events in walking the dog is a script.

A network diagram like this for a younger child would have fewer entries as well as fewer and weaker connecting links. Consequently, the youngster cannot organize information as extensively, which makes remembering information more difficult than for an older child.

Nevertheless, the knowledge that young children have is organized, and this turns out to be a powerful asset. In the case of events that fit scripts, for example, children needn't try to remember each individual activity; instead, they simply remember the script. For example, when a boy wants to tell his dad about baking cookies, he can simply retrieve the "baking cookies" script and use it to organize his recall of the different events.

Children develop cognitive scripts based on sequences of events, like those involved in baking cookies.

Though knowledge can improve memory, it can also distort memory. If a specific experience does not correspond to children's knowledge, the experience is likely to be forgotten or distorted so that it conforms to the child's knowledge. For example, when told a story about a female helicopter pilot, many youngsters will remember the pilot as a man because their network specifies that pilots are men (Levy & Boston, 1994). In addition, exposure to information that conflicts with a child's experience of an event can confuse the child and distort recollection of the source for the information the child remembers (Roberts & Powell, 2001).

Scripts, too, can distort memory because children cannot distinguish what they experienced from what is specified in the script. For example, the boy baking cookies may remember greasing the cookie sheet simply because this is part of the baking cookie script, not because he actually did the greasing (Hudson, 1988). Thus, although children's growing knowledge usually helps them to remember, sometimes it can interfere with accurate memory.

The different processes that affect children's remembering are summarized in Table 12–1.

Table 12–1 Summary Table

Information-Processing Elements That Aid Memory		
Element	**Definition**	**Example**
Strategies	Deliberate acts used to help a person remember	Before Melika had a chance to write her friend's number in her notebook, she rehearsed it: "743-1423 . . . 743-1423."
Monitoring	Assessing the effectiveness of a strategy and one's progress toward a learning goal	Monique tested herself on the weekly spelling list, then spent 20 minutes studying the words she had missed.
Knowledge	Understanding of relations between items that promotes remembering by organizing information to be remembered	When Sameer arrived at the grocery store, he realized he'd lost the list his mom had given him. Rather than walk home for it, he decided to think about different food groups—dairy products, meats, and so on—to help him remember what he was supposed to buy.
Scripts	Memory structure that allows people to remember events that occur in a specified order	Asked by his grandpa to describe a day at summer camp, Hector explained that the day began with breakfast, followed by two activity periods. Lunch came next, then a rest period, and two more activity periods . . . and so on.

wavebreakmedia/Shutterstock

Ask Yourself

How might nature and nurture contribute to improvements in memory skills during middle childhood?

12.2 The Nature of Intelligence

∨ Learning Objectives

After reading the module, you should be able to do the following:

LO3 Understand the psychometric view of the nature of intelligence.

LO4 Describe how Gardner's theory of multiple intelligences differs from the psychometric approach.

LO5 List the three components of Sternberg's triarchic theory of intelligence.

Before you read further, consider this: How would you define intelligence? Considerable debate exists over exactly how to define this concept (Miles, 2000). If you're typical of most North Americans, your definition probably includes the ability to reason logically, connect ideas, and solve real problems. You might mention verbal ability, meaning the ability to speak clearly and articulately. You might also mention social competence, referring, for example, to an interest in the world at large and the ability to admit when you make a mistake (Sternberg & Kaufman, 1998).

Many of these ideas about intelligence are included in psychological theories of intelligence. We'll begin by considering the oldest theories of intelligence, those associated with the psychometric tradition. Then we'll look at two newer approaches and, along the way, gain some insights into unique aspects of children's cognitive ability.

Psychometric Theories

LO3 Understand the psychometric view of the nature of intelligence.

In order to efficiently study psychological characteristics, such as intelligence and personality, psychologists usually begin by administering a large number of tests to many individuals. Then they look for patterns in performance across the different tests. The basic logic underlying this technique is similar to the logic a jungle hunter uses to decide whether some dark blobs in a river are three separate rotting logs or a single alligator (Cattell, 1965). If the blobs move together, the hunter decides they are part of the same structure, an alligator. If they do not move together, they are three different structures, three logs. Similarly, if changes in performance on one test are accompanied by changes in performance on a second test—that is, they move together on both—one might theorize that the tests are measuring the same attribute or factor. A **psychometric theory** is based on measurement of a psychological characteristic via a scorable questionnaire or other type of psychological test.

Suppose, for example, that you believe in the concept of general intelligence. That is, you believe that some people are smart regardless of the situation, task, or problem, whereas others are not so smart. According to this view, children's performance should be very consistent across tasks: Highly intelligent children should always attain high scores, and less intelligent children should always attain lower scores. As

Psychometric theory:

a theory based on measurement of a psychological characteristic, usually with a scorable questionnaire or other type of psychological test.

Psychometric g:

intelligence as defined and measured by mental tests.

early as 1904, Charles Spearman reported findings supporting the idea that a general factor for intelligence, or g, is responsible for performance on all mental tests. Some researchers have started referring to intelligence as defined and measured by mental tests as **psychometric g**, distinguishing it from broader, more inclusive concepts of intelligence (Sternberg et al., 2005).

Other researchers, however, have found that intelligence consists of distinct abilities. For example, Thurstone and Thurstone (1941) analyzed performance on a wide range of tasks and identified seven distinct patterns, each reflecting a unique ability: perceptual speed, word comprehension, word fluency, space, number, memory, and induction. Thurstone and Thurstone also acknowledged a general factor that operated in all tasks, but they emphasized that the specific factors were more useful in assessing and understanding intellectual ability.

These conflicting findings have led many psychometric theorists to propose hierarchical theories of intelligence that include both general and specific components. John Carroll (1993), for example, proposed the hierarchical theory with three levels shown in Figure 12–4. At the top of the hierarchy is g, general intelligence. In the level underneath g are eight broad categories of intellectual skill, ranging from fluid intelligence to processing speed. Each of the abilities in the second level is further divided into the skills listed in the third and most specific level. Crystallized intelligence, for example, includes understanding printed language, comprehending language, and knowing vocabulary.

Carroll's hierarchical theory is, in essence, a compromise between the two views of intelligence—general versus distinct abilities. Yet, some critics find it unsatisfactory because it ignores the research and theory on cognitive development described in Module 12.1. They believe we need to look beyond the psychometric approach to understanding intelligence. In the remainder of this module, we'll look at two newer theories that have gained a following.

Gardner's Theory of Multiple Intelligences

LO4 **Describe how Gardner's theory of multiple intelligences differs from the psychometric approach.**

Only recently have developmental psychologists viewed intelligence from the perspective of Piagetian theory and information-processing psychology. These new

Figure 12–4

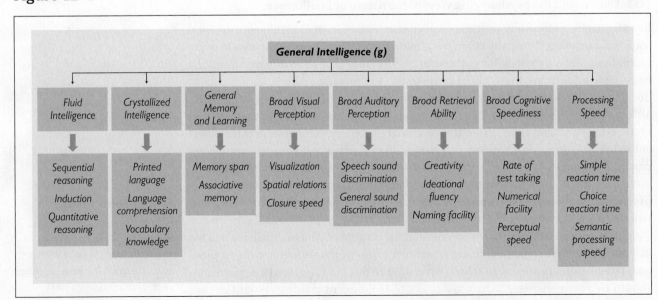

SOURCE: Based on Carroll, J. B. (1993). Human cognitive abilities: A survey of factor-analytic studies. New York: Cambridge University Press.

Table 12–2 Gardner's Seven Intelligences

Type of Intelligence	Definition
Linguistic	Knowing the meaning of words, having the ability to use words to understand new ideas, and using language to convey ideas to others
Logical-mathematical	Understanding relations that can exist among objects, actions, and ideas as well as the logical or mathematical relations that can be performed on them
Spatial	Perceiving objects accurately and imagining in the mind's eye the appearance of an object before and after it has been transformed
Musical	Comprehending and producing sounds varying in pitch, rhythm, and emotional tone
Bodily-kinesthetic	Using one's body in highly differentiated ways, as dancers, craftspeople, and athletes do
Interpersonal	Identifying different feelings, moods, motivations, and intentions in others
Intrapersonal	Understanding one's emotions and knowing one's strengths and weaknesses

SOURCE: From Copyright 1983, Gardner, H., *Frames of mind: The theory of multiple intelligences.* New York: Basic Books. Reprinted by permission of Perseus Books Group.

theories present a much broader theory of intelligence and how it develops. Among the most ambitious is Howard Gardner's (1983, 1993) theory of multiple intelligences. Rather than using test scores as the basis for his theory, Gardner drew on research in child development, studies of people with brain injuries, and studies of exceptionally talented people. He proposed seven distinct intelligences that are shown in Table 12–2. The first three intelligences in this list—linguistic intelligence, logical-mathematical intelligence, and spatial intelligence—are included in psychometric theories of intelligence. The last four intelligences are not: Musical, bodily-kinesthetic, interpersonal, and intrapersonal intelligences are unique to Gardner's theory. According to Gardner, a gifted athlete, a talented dancer, and a sensitive, caring child are demonstrating intellectual ability to the same extent as the child who does well in writing or arithmetic.

Each of Gardner's seven distinct intelligences has a unique developmental history. First of all, linguistic intelligence develops much earlier than the other six intelligences. Second, each intelligence is regulated by distinct regions of the brain, as shown in studies of persons who have sustained brain injuries. As you might recall from your reading about brain lateralization, different areas of the brain tend to become specialized for certain capacities. Spatial intelligence, for example, is regulated by particular regions in the brain's right hemisphere. Third, each ability is associated with special cases of exceptionally talented individuals. For example, unique musical intelligence is often demonstrated by **savants**, individuals who are cognitively delayed but also extremely talented in one particular domain (Miller, 1999). Child savants whose special talent is music can play a tune correctly after a single hearing and without ever having had formal musical training (Shuter-Dyson, 1982).

Prompted by Gardner's theory, researchers have begun to look at nontraditional aspects of intelligence. For example, one aspect of interpersonal intelligence is **social-cognitive flexibility**, which refers to a person's skill in solving social problems with relevant social knowledge. Jones and Day (1997) studied social-cognitive flexibility by presenting different social scenarios to adolescents. In one scenario, a man and a woman walk past each other; the woman says hello, but the man ignores her. Following each scenario, adolescents were asked a series of questions about what happened in the scenario. Some adolescents were much better at understanding that each scenario might have many different interpretations (e.g., "The man ignored the woman because he's very shy." "The man was lost in thought and didn't see her.") and that a person's interpretation of the scenario would cause them to act differently.

Adolescents who understood the different interpretations of the scenarios were not more skilled in solving verbal or logical reasoning problems, but they were more

Savant:

a person who is intellectually delayed but also extremely talented in one particular domain.

Social-cognitive flexibility:

a person's skill in solving social problems with relevant social knowledge.

Savants, such as 10-year-old Matt Savage, who can play a tune after hearing it only once, are gifted in one cognitive domain.

competent socially (e.g., could deal more effectively with peers) and were less likely to have social problems (e.g., be shy or anxious). As Gardner's theory predicts, acting skillfully in social situations is an element of intelligence that is distinct from the linguistic and logical-mathematical intelligences of psychometric theories.

The theory of multiple intelligences has important implications for education. Gardner (1993, 1995) believed that schools should foster all intelligences, not just the traditional linguistic and logical-mathematical intelligences. Teachers should capitalize on the strongest intelligences of individual children. Some students may best understand unfamiliar cultures, for example, by studying their dance, while other students may understand these cultures by studying their music.

Some American schools have enthusiastically embraced Gardner's ideas (Gardner, 1993); however, acceptable tests to evaluate progress in all the areas covered by Gardner's theory don't exist, so we also don't know if these schools are any better. Gardner's work has helped liberate researchers from narrow, psychometric-based views of intelligence. Plus, teachers know that you can engage a child in learning better if you let them draw on their strengths (e.g., using images or drawing) to help them with areas in which they are weaker. A cognitively engaged student tends to be more enthusiastic about learning and will be able to learn more than one who is disengaged. A comparably broad but different view of intelligence comes from another new theory that we'll look at in the next section.

Sternberg's Triarchic Theory of Successful Intelligence

Robert Sternberg's (1977) early work included a theory of how adults solve problems on intelligence tests. He developed this theory into what he called the **triarchic theory**, so called because it includes three parts or subtheories (Sternberg, 1985). He later revised it into a theory of "successful intelligence," proposing that the concept of intelligence refers to a person's skillful ability to obtain what that person wants in life within that person's own socio-cultural environment or context (Sternberg, 2003).

According to the **componential subtheory**, intelligence depends on basic cognitive processes called **components**. "Component" is simply Sternberg's term for the different information-processing skills described in Module 12.1, such as monitoring. Whether the task is solving an item on an intelligence test, reading a newspaper, or understanding a conversation, components must be selected and organized in the proper sequence to complete the task successfully. In this subtheory, intelligence reflects more efficient organization and use of components.

The triarchic theory includes two other subtheories. According to the **experiential subtheory**, intelligence is revealed in both novel and familiar tasks. For novel tasks, intelligence is associated with the ability to apply existing knowledge to a new situation. At the start of a new school year, for example, readily adjusting to new tasks is a sign of intelligence. Bright children learning multiplication readily draw upon relevant math knowledge to grasp what's involved in multiplication.

For familiar tasks, intelligence is associated with automatic processing. Completing a task automatically means using few mental resources (i.e., less working memory capacity). At the end of a school year, performing now-familiar school tasks automatically rather than with effort is a sign of intelligence. Bright children now solve multiplication problems automatically, without thinking about the intermediate steps.

According to the **contextual subtheory**, intelligent behaviour involves skillfully adapting to an environment. That is, intelligence is always partly defined by

Triarchic theory of successful intelligence:

Sternberg's theory about intelligence, as situated within a person's socio-cultural environment, based on three subtheories.

Componential subtheory:

the theory that intelligence depends on basic cognitive processes called components.

Components:

information-processing skills involved in basic cognitive processing.

Experiential subtheory:

the idea that intelligence is revealed in both novel and familiar tasks.

Contextual subtheory:

the idea that intelligent behaviour involves skillfully adapting to an environment.

Table 12–3 Summary Table

Subtheories in Sternberg's Triarchic Theory of Intelligence		
Subtheory	**Definition**	**Example**
Componential	Intelligence depends upon basic processes called components	Asked how a peach and a piece of cheese were alike and how they differed, Terrence retrieved from long-term memory the facts that both were food and that a peach was a fruit but cheese was a dairy product.
Experiential	Intelligent behaviour involves applying existing knowledge to novel tasks	Mickey has spent so many hours practising his multiplication tables that he doesn't even have to think about the problems anymore; the product simply pops into his mind effortlessly.
Contextual	Intelligent behaviour involves adapting to one's environment	When Deshawn couldn't get a ride to the mall, he looked up the bus schedule on the internet, and he found when the bus to the mall would go by his house.

the demands of an environment or cultural context. What is intelligent for children growing up in cities in North America may not be intelligent for children growing up in the Sahara desert, in the Australian outback, or on a remote island in the Pacific Ocean. Moreover, what is intelligent at home may not be intelligent in the neighbourhood, and expectations to that effect can be communicated in many ways to children (Huichang, Jing, Xinyin, & Lili, 2003). The Children and Families around the World feature illustrates how intelligent behaviour is always defined by the context.

The three subtheories are summarized in Table 12–3. In the table, you can see that, in contrast to the psychometric approach and to Gardner's theory, the triarchic theory

Children and Families around the World
How Culture Defines What Is Intelligent

In Brazil, some boys in middle childhood become involved in selling candy and fruit to bus passengers and pedestrians. These children often cannot identify the numbers on paper money, yet they know how to purchase their goods from wholesale stores, make change for customers, and keep track of their sales (Saxe, 1988).

Older children and adolescents who live on Pacific Ocean islands near New Guinea learn to sail boats hundreds of kilometres across open seas to get from one small island to the next. They have no formal training in mathematics, yet they are able to use a complex navigational system based on the positions of stars and estimates of the boat's speed (Hutchins, 1983).

If either the Brazilian street vendors or the island navigators were given the tests that measure intelligence in Canadian students, they would likely fare poorly, but they are not less intelligent than Canadian students. The skills that are important to Canadians assessed on intelligence tests may be less valued in other cultures and so are not cultivated in youngsters. Each culture defines what intelligent behaviour is and how it should be assessed. The specialized computing skills of street vendors and navigators are important measures of intelligence in their cultural settings, just as reading skills are in Canadian culture (Sternberg & Kaufman, 1998).

Brazilian street vendors develop complex knowledge of sales transactions.

Adolescents near New Guinea learn a complex form of navigation.

Table 12–4   Summary Table

Features of Major Perspectives on Intelligence	
Approach to Intelligence	**Distinguishing Features**
Psychometric	Intelligence as a hierarchy of general and specific skills
Gardner's theory of multiple intelligences	Seven distinct intelligences: linguistic, logical-mathematical, spatial, musical, bodily-kinesthetic, interpersonal, and intrapersonal intelligences
Sternberg's triarchic theory of successful intelligence	Intelligence is defined by socio-cultural context, experience, and information-processing components

does not identify specific contents of intelligence. Instead, Sternberg defined intelligence in terms of processes: the strategies people use to complete tasks (componential subtheory), the familiarity of those tasks (experiential subtheory), and the relevance of the tasks to personal and cultural goals (contextual subtheory).

In the triarchic theory, intelligence reflects strategies children use to complete tasks plus the familiarity and relevance of those tasks.

Sternberg also underscored the dangers of comparing test scores of different cultural, ethnic, or racial groups. Comparisons are usually invalid because the test items are not equally relevant in different cultures. In addition, most test items are not equally novel in different cultures. A vocabulary test, for example, is useful in assessing intelligence in cultures where formal education is essential to later employment outcomes. In cultures where schooling is not a key to success, a typical vocabulary test would not provide useful information because it would be irrelevant to cultural goals and much too novel. In short, intelligence is culturally defined (Sternberg, Grigorenko, & Bridglall, 2007).

As with Gardner's theory, researchers are still evaluating Sternberg's theory. For example, new studies of intelligence based on functional brain-imaging techniques have shed new light on the importance of a componential approach in understanding whether a general g factor for intelligence really exists. Hampshire, Highfield, Parkin, and Owen (2012) from the Brain and Mind Institute at the University of Western Ontario have provided some evidence that human intelligence arises from the interaction of a number of specialized networks within the brain that are anatomically distinct from each other. According to these researchers, when a person is presented with a cognitive task, relatively independent networks of the brain responsible for particular components of intelligence work together to address it. The main components of intelligence are identified as arising out of networks in the brain responsible for (1) short-term (working) memory, (2) reasoning/logical rules, and (3) verbal processing. Any task can require recruitment of multiple brain networks, but, according to this theory, the networks together result in what we call intelligence without the need for a high-order g factor beyond what can be accounted for by the networks themselves. More research in this area will help to better define this theory and confirm whether psychometric g is still a viable way to talk about the nature of intelligence.

As shown in Table 12–4, theorists are still debating the question of how to define intelligence, and even more debate exists about how it should validly be measured (Sternberg, Grigorenko, & Kidd, 2005). The construction, properties, and limitations of intelligence tests are the focus of the next module.

Ask Yourself

Compare and contrast the major perspectives on intelligence in terms of the extent to which they make connections between different aspects of development. That is, to what extent does each perspective emphasize cognitive processes versus integrating physical, cognitive, social, and emotional development?

12.3 Individual Differences in Intellectual Skills

Learning Objectives

After reading the module, you should be able to do the following:

LO6   Understand the origins of intelligence tests.

LO7   Describe ways to increase validity in testing for intelligence and achievement.

LO8   Understand the roles of heredity and environment in influencing intelligence.

LO9   Discuss how culture and social class influence intelligence test scores.

LO10 Identify known issues with regard to gender and intelligence.

At the beginning of the twentieth century, American schools faced a crisis. Between 1890 and 1915, school enrolment nearly doubled nationally as great numbers of immigrants arrived and reforms restricted child labour and emphasized education (Chapman, 1988). Increased enrolment meant that teachers had larger numbers of students who did not learn as readily as the "select few" students who had populated their classes previously. How to work with these seemingly less capable children was one of the pressing issues of the day. In this module, you'll see how intelligence tests were devised initially to assess individual differences in intellectual ability. Then we'll look at a simple question: How well do modern tests work? Finally, we'll examine how ethnicity, social class, gender, environment, and heredity influence intelligence as well as its measurement.

Binet and the Development of Intelligence Testing

LO6 **Understand the origins of intelligence tests.**

The problems facing educators at the beginning of the twentieth century were not unique to the United States. In 1904, the minister of public instruction in France asked two noted psychologists, Alfred Binet and Theophile Simon, to formulate a way to identify children who needed special instruction in school. Binet and Simon selected simple tasks that most French children of different ages could do, such as to name colours, count backwards, and remember numbers in order. Based on preliminary testing, Binet and Simon determined problems that normal 3-year-olds could solve, that normal 4-year-olds could solve, and so on. Children's **mental age**, or MA, referred to the difficulty of the problems they could solve correctly. A child who solved problems that the average 7-year-old could pass would have an MA of 7.

Mental age:
the difficulty level of problems that children could correctly solve at various ages.

Binet and Simon used mental age to distinguish children according to their measured intellectual ability. A child with greater ability would have the MA of an older child; for example, a 6-year-old with an MA of 9 was considered bright. A child with lower ability would have the MA of a younger child, such as a 6-year-old with an MA of 4. Using this formula, Binet and Simon demonstrated that children with higher measured ability did better in school than children with lower measured ability.

Figure 12–5

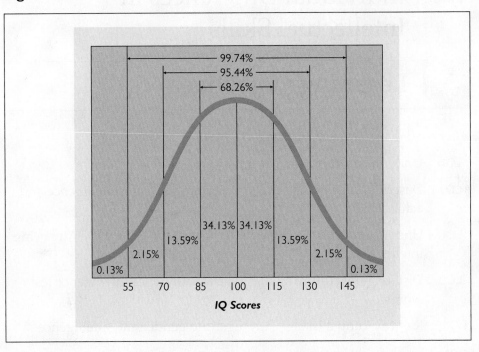

Lewis Terman, of Stanford University, revised Binet and Simon's test and published a version known as the Stanford-Binet in 1916. Terman described performance as an **intelligence quotient**, or IQ, which was the ratio of mental age to chronological age, multiplied by 100:

$$IQ = MA/CA \times 100$$

Using this formula, children who score in the average range will have an IQ of 100 because their mental age equals their chronological age. Figure 12–5 shows the typical distribution of test scores in the population. About two-thirds of children taking a test will have IQ scores between 85 and 115, and 95 percent will have scores between 70 and 130.

The IQ score can also be used to compare test performance in children of different ages. A 4-year-old with an MA of 5 has an IQ of 125 (5/4 × 100), the same as an 8-year-old with an MA of 10 (10/8 × 100).

IQ scores are no longer computed in this manner. Instead, children's IQ scores are calculated by comparing their test performance to others their age. When children perform at the average for their age, their IQ is 100. Children who perform above the average have IQs greater than 100; children who perform below the average have IQs below 100.

Intelligence quotient:

the mathematical ratio of mental age to chronological age.

Do Intelligence Tests Work?

LO7 Describe ways to increase validity in testing for intelligence and achievement.

Do IQ scores really reflect intelligence? This question raises the issue of validity, a statistical concept. One way that the validity of a test is determined is to compare test scores to scores from another test that you know is a good measure of a variable. This second test is called the "criterion." If scores on the first test correlate properly with scores on the criterion test, then chances are that your first test is valid. You also can compare test scores to other independent measures of what your test is thought to measure. For example, to measure the validity of a test of extroversion, children could take the test, and then they could be observed in a social setting. For example, the children could be observed during school recess to see who is outgoing and who is shy. The extroversion test would be valid if test scores correlated positively with observations of extroverted behaviour at recess time.

How would we extend this approach to intelligence tests? Ideally, we would administer the intelligence tests and then correlate the scores with other independent estimates of intelligence. Therein lies the problem. We must first consider how intelligence is being defined. If we are defining intelligence as psychometric g, then, within psychology, no other independent ways to estimate intelligence exist; the only way to measure psychometric g is with mental tests. Consequently, many follow Binet's lead and obtain measures of performance in school, using grades or teachers' ratings of their students. Correlations between these measures and scores on tests of psychometric g typically fall somewhere between 0.4 and 0.6 (Neisser et al., 1996). Obviously, some youngsters with high test scores do not excel in school, whereas others with low scores get good grades, suggesting that school performance is the result of more than just a person's level of psychometric g.

As a result, some psychologists make the case for dynamic testing instead of using traditional measures of IQ and psychometric g. **Dynamic testing** measures a child's learning potential by having the child learn something new in the presence of the examiner and with the examiner's help. The process is interactive and measures new achievement rather than past achievement. Dynamic testing is based on Vygotsky's ideas of the zone of proximal development and scaffolding. Learning potential can be estimated by the amount of material the child learns during interaction with the examiner and/or from the amount of help the child needs to learn the new material (Grigorenko & Sternberg, 1998).

Dynamic testing is a recent innovation and is still being evaluated. However, static and dynamic testing appear to provide useful and independent information. If the aim is to predict future levels of a child's skill, it is valuable to know a child's current level of skill (static testing) as well as the child's potential to acquire greater skill (dynamic testing). By combining both forms of testing, we achieve a more comprehensive view of a child's talents than we would by relying on either method alone (Day, Engelhardt, Maxwell, & Bolig, 1997).

The concept of dynamic testing fits well with the newly emphasized educational concepts of **differentiated instruction** and **response to intervention** (RTI; Fuchs, Compton, Fuchs, Bryant, & Davis, 2008; Fuchs, Mock, Morgan, & Young, 2003). Differentiated instruction involves making adaptations to the classroom environment and teaching methods to accommodate children's personal strengths, weaknesses, and preferred ways of learning. RTI requires educators to use evidence-based strategies for teaching children as well as to assess children's achievement regularly while being taught. RTI requires teachers to take baseline measurements of a child's achievement on a particular skill, then engage in an effective strategy for teaching the skill, and then measure the child's achievement level again. Children who do not respond well to the teaching intervention are then given opportunities to learn by other effective methods. Students who continue to struggle may then be referred for more specialized forms of assessment and intervention, which might or might not involve pulling them out of the regular classroom for help in order to bring their learning up to expected levels. RTI takes an early-intervention approach rather than a "wait to fail" approach to intervention; however, its effectiveness as an educational strategy has not been thoroughly determined, despite the fact that it is becoming increasingly required by law to be used in public educational systems (Shinn, 2007).

Dynamic testing:
measuring a child's learning potential by having the child learn something new in the presence of the examiner and with the examiner's help.

Differentiated instruction:
making adaptations to the classroom environment and teaching methods to accommodate children's personal strengths, weaknesses, and preferred ways of learning.

Response to intervention:
an educational model based on frequent progress monitoring and evidence-based, strategic responses to students' measured achievement levels.

Hereditary and Environmental Factors

LO8 Understand the roles of heredity and environment in influencing intelligence.

Considerable debate has occurred within psychology about whether cognitive ability is more determined by hereditary or environmental factors. Some of the evidence for hereditary factors is shown in Figure 12–6. If genes influence intelligence, then siblings' test scores should become more alike as siblings become more similar genetically (Plomin & Petrill, 1997). In other words, since identical twins are identical genetically, they should have virtually identical test scores, which would be a correlation of 1. Fraternal twins have about 50 percent of their genes in common, just like nontwins of the same biological parents. Consequently, their test scores should be (a) less similar than scores for identical twins, (b) as similar as other siblings who have the same biological parents, and (c) more similar than scores of children and their adopted siblings. You can see in Figure 12–6 that each of these predictions is supported.

Heredity also influences patterns of developmental change in IQ scores (Wilson, 1983). Patterns of developmental change in IQ are more alike for identical twins than for fraternal twins. If one identical twin gets higher IQ scores with age, the other twin almost certainly will too. In contrast, if one fraternal twin gets higher scores with age, the other twin may not necessarily show the same pattern.

Based on research with adopted children, the impact of heredity increases during childhood and adolescence: If heredity helps determine psychometric g and IQ, then children's IQs should be more like their biological parents' IQs than their adoptive parents' IQs. In fact, these correlations were computed in the Colorado Adoption Project (Plomin et al., 1997), which included adopted children as well as their biological and adoptive parents. Biological parents' IQ was measured before the child was born, adoptive parents' IQ was measured before the child's first birthday, and children's IQs were tested repeatedly in childhood and adolescence. The results, shown in Figure 12–7, are clear. At every age, the correlation between children's IQ and their biological parents' IQ (shown by the blue line) is greater than the correlation between children's IQ and their adoptive parents' IQ (shown by the red line). In fact, children's IQ scores are essentially unrelated to their adoptive parents' IQs.

Notice, too, that the relation between children's IQs and their biological parents' IQ actually gets stronger as children get older, and their test scores increasingly resemble their biological parents' scores. These results are evidence for the greater impact of heredity on IQ as a child grows.

Figure 12–6

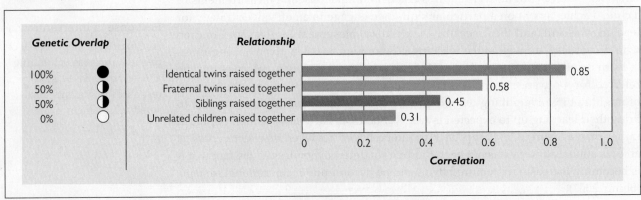

SOURCE: Based on data from Plomin, R., & Petrill, S. A. (1997). Genetics and intelligence: What's new? *Intelligence, 24,* 53–77.

Figure 12–7

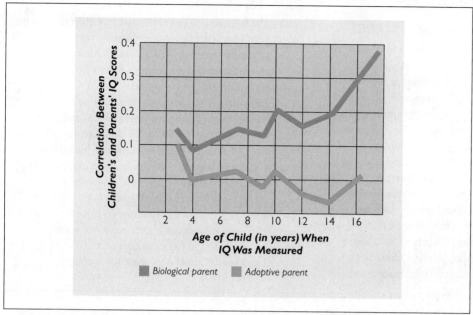

SOURCE: Based on data from Plomin, R., Fulker, D. W., Corley, R., & DeFries, J. C. (1997). Nature, nurture, and cognitive development from 1 to 16 years: A parentoffspring adoption study. Psychological Science, 8, 442–447.

However, these results do not mean that heredity is the sole determiner of IQ. In fact, two environmental factors that have a strong impact on IQ include families/ homes and preschool intervention or enrichment programs. For example, Bettye Caldwell and Robert Bradley (1994) developed the Home Observation for Measurement of the Environment (HOME), an inventory for assessing parents' behaviour as well as the quality and organization of the child's home environment.

HOME testing indicates that children with high test scores typically have parents who are stimulating, responsive, and involved (Bradley, Caldwell, & Rock, 1988). In addition, among children of European heritage, an environment that includes plenty of variety and appropriate play materials is linked to high test scores. For children of African heritage, a well-organized home environment is associated with higher scores (Bradley et al., 1989). That is, children tend to have higher IQs when their environments are well structured and predictable (e.g., meals are eaten at a regular time, homework is always done after dinner). Child-development researchers don't know why certain features of environments are particularly important for intelligence in different groups, but the more general point is that children's home environments clearly affect intelligence.

The importance of a stimulating environment for intelligence is also demonstrated by intervention programs that prepare economically disadvantaged children for school (Gorey, 2001). When children grow up in never-ending poverty, the cycle is predictable and tragic: Youngsters have few of the intellectual skills to succeed in school, so they fail; lacking an education, they find poor-paying jobs (if they can find any work at all), guaranteeing that their children, too, will grow up in poverty.

Since Project Head Start began in the United States, massive educational intervention has been an important tool in the effort to break this cycle of poverty. Head Start and other intervention programs teach preschool youngsters basic school readiness skills and social skills and offer guidance to parents (Ramey & Ramey, 1990). When children participate in these enrichment programs, their test scores go up and school achievement improves, particularly when intervention programs are extended beyond preschool into middle childhood (Reynolds & Temple, 1998). In the Research to Practice feature, we look at one of these success stories in detail.

Research to Practice
The Carolina Abecedarian Project

Since the 1960s, many intervention programs have demonstrated that young children's intelligence test scores can be raised with enrichment, but the improvement is often short-lived. That is, within a few years after completing the intervention program, test scores fall back to the same level as before the program. Frances Campbell and Craig Ramey (1994; Ramey & Campbell, 1991) designed the Carolina Abecedarian Project to see if massive and sustained intervention could produce more long-lasting changes.

The researchers worked with participants who were primarily African American preschool children between 4 months and 5 years of age born to mothers who were unemployed, had not completed high school, and had an average IQ of 85. Through their longitudinal study of early intervention programs in child care, writing, reading, and

math, the researchers demonstrated that children who had a full eight years of intervention generally had the highest intelligence and achievement scores; children with no intervention had the lowest scores (see Figure 12–8). The more intervention, the higher the scores.

Follow-up studies have found that these positive outcomes have continued into adolescence and young adulthood (Campbell & Ramey, 2008). Of course, massive intervention over eight years is expensive, but so are the economic consequences of poverty, unemployment, and their by-products. Programs like the Abecedarian Project show that the repetitive cycle of school failure and education can be broken and that intelligence is fostered by a stimulating and responsive environment in the early years. If you want your child to have the best chance of doing well in school and later in adulthood, start in the preschool years!

Impact of Culture and Social Class

LO9 Discuss how culture and social class influence intelligence test scores.

The results in Figure 12–9 have been the source of controversy for decades, particularly in the United States. They show that on many intelligence tests, Westerners of African heritage tend to score about 15 points lower than Westerners of European heritage (Brody, 1992). Some of the difference is due to socio-economic opportunities and under exposure at an early age to experiences necessary for academic learning. Consider the following facts about the impact poverty has in Canada and which children it might affect most.

- Approximately 3.5 million Canadians were living in poverty in 2004—more than 11 percent of the population.

Figure 12–8

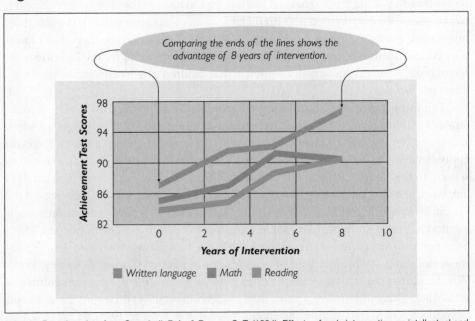

Comparing the ends of the lines shows the advantage of 8 years of intervention.

■ *Written language*   ■ *Math*   ■ *Reading*

(x-axis: *Years of Intervention*; y-axis: *Achievement Test Scores*)

SOURCE: Based on data from Campbell, F. A., & Ramey, C. T. (1994). Effects of early intervention on intellectual and academic achievement: A follow-up study of children from low-income families. Child Development, 65, 684–698.

Figure 12–9

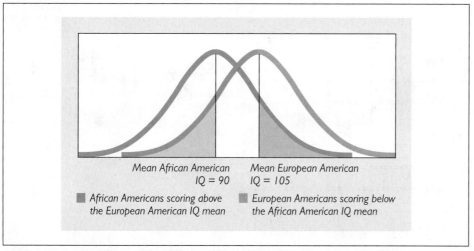

Mean African American
IQ = 90

Mean European American
IQ = 105

■ African Americans scoring above
  the European American IQ mean

■ European Americans scoring below
  the African American IQ mean

SOURCE: Based on data from Brody, N. (1992). Intelligence (2nd ed.). San Diego: Academic Press.

- The proportion of Canadian families living in poverty declined slightly, from 8.5 percent in 2003 to 7.8 percent (684 000) in 2004.

- Rates of poverty in 2004 were lowest among elderly families (2.1 percent) and highest among female lone-parent families (35.6 percent).

- 865 000 Canadian children under the age of 18 lived in poverty in 2004—one of every eight children.

- Families in British Columbia reported the highest poverty rates in 2004, with 10.3 percent living below the low-income cut-off level established by Statistics Canada.

- Family poverty rates were lowest in Prince Edward Island, at 3.2 percent (Canadian Council on Social Development, n.d.).

Typically, children from lower social classes have lower scores on intelligence tests, and African American children are more likely than European American children to live in lower socio-economic environments. When European American and African American children of comparable social class are compared, the difference in IQ test scores is reduced but not eliminated (Brooks-Gunn, Klebanov, & Duncan, 1996). Therefore, social class explains some, but not all, of the difference between European American and African American children's IQ scores. We'll caution you, however, that by focusing on groups of people rather than on individuals, it's easy to lose sight of the fact that individuals within these groups differ in intelligence. Look again at the graph; you'll see that the average difference in IQ scores between European Americans and African Americans is very small compared to the entire range of scores for these groups. Many African Americans achieve higher IQ scores than the average European American; many European Americans achieve lower IQ scores than the average African American. In fact, more variability usually occurs within groups than between groups on these types of measures (Sternberg et al., 2005).

Some critics contend that the difference in test scores between cultural groups reflects bias in the tests themselves. They argue that test items reflect the cultural heritage of the test creators, most of whom are middle-class European Americans, making tests biased against lower-class children of non-European heritage. This concern has existed in Canada with regard to the performance of Aboriginal children on tests of intelligence (Zolner, 2003a). For example, when testing verbal comprehension ability using intelligence tests with First Nations children, Theresa Zolner frequently finds that these children often provide interesting, elaborate answers to complex problems but from a cultural perspective that differs from the answers provided by the test

Figure 12–10

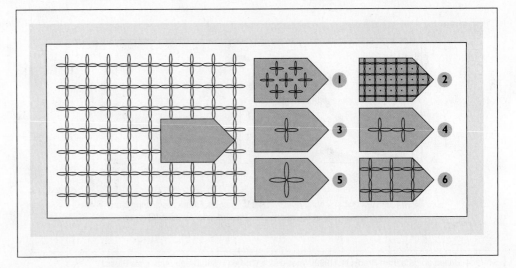

Culture-fair intelligence tests:

psychological tests designed to eliminate group differences due to culture.

developers. Therefore, rather than scoring points on the items, the youth receive zeros on those questions, which, ultimately, brings down their verbal comprehension scores. Nonverbal tests of intelligence, although also imperfect, avoid cultural biases in tests of verbal comprehension and social judgment but do not solve the problem of cultural bias entirely.

The problem of bias has led to the development of **culture-fair intelligence tests**, which include test items based on experiences common to many cultures. An example is Raven's Progressive Matrices, which consists solely of items like the one shown in Figure 12–10. Examinees are asked to select the piece that would complete the design correctly (6, in this case).

Culture-fair tests predict achievement in school but do not eliminate group differences in test scores, as the testing situation itself is a cultural phenomenon (Anastasi, 1988; Herrnstein & Murray, 1994). A culture-fair test will underestimate a child's intelligence if, for example, the child's culture encourages children to solve problems in collaboration with others and discourages them from excelling as individuals. For example, Theresa Zolner learned about the experiences of an American professor who went to teach at a Ukrainian university. Upon administering a test to his class, the professor became exasperated to find that the students were collaborating with each other on the examination. Despite the professor's best efforts to stop the students from collaborating, the students continued to do so in order to solve the examination problems. Then, to the professor's astonishment, some students left the examination, saying that they needed to study more before taking it. Focusing on collaboration and offering second chances were not key components of this professor's culture, but it was for the Ukrainian students. As a result of intercultural differences in abstract reasoning, Sternberg, Grigorenko, and Kidd (2005) pointed out that so-called "culture-fair" tests of intelligence are even more susceptible to cultural bias than other types of intelligence tests.

Moreover, because they are wary of questions posed by unfamiliar adults, economically disadvantaged children, typically from cultural minority groups, will answer test questions by saying, "I don't know." Foster children can have similar difficulties if they fear that the tester is really a child and family service worker who is there to take them away from their current home placement. Obviously, these reactions guarantee artificially low test scores. When these children are given extra time to feel at ease with the examiner, they respond less often with "I don't know," and their test scores improve considerably (Zigler & Finn-Stevenson, 1992).

In addition, children's experiences with authority figures in their culture can have a marked effect on their performance on a test or their behaviour in a classroom.

Theresa Zolner recalls one incident she observed in a preschool for refugee children. The preschool teachers thought they would introduce the children to a Canadian police officer as part of an ongoing effort to familiarize the children with Canadian society. When the officer entered the classroom, the children scattered and hid all over the room—under furniture, in closets, behind the teachers. Some children even tried to run out of the room. Most of the children in the classroom were refugees from South America who had gone through very traumatic experiences relating to people in military or police uniforms. As a result, they were not able to tolerate the classroom visit because their fear of authority overtook them. If children are very afraid of an authority figure, they will not perform up to their ability but can "shut down," flee, or be silent. If this were to happen in a testing situation, their test scores would not be valid.

If all tests reflect cultural influences, at least to some degree, how should we interpret test scores? Remember that tests assess successful adaptation to a particular cultural context. Most intelligence tests predict success in a school environment, which usually teaches middle-class values. Regardless of ethnic group, a child with a high test score has the intellectual skills needed for academic work based on middle-class values, including familiarity with the norms of the culture that set up the academic curriculum. A child with a low test score lacks those skills or might have a different complement of skills not valued by the cultural perspective reflected in the test. Does a low score mean a child is destined to fail in school? No. It simply means that, based on current skills and knowledge, the child may be unlikely to do well in that learning environment. Improving a child's skills (and cultural familiarity) without stripping her of her own cultural heritage and knowledge will improve her performance in a mainstream school.

Gender Differences in Intellectual Abilities and Achievement

LO10   Identify known issues with regard to gender and intelligence.

Boys and girls are similar in most cognitive skills. However, researchers have identified gender differences in three intellectual skills: Girls tend to have greater verbal skill, and boys tend to have greater mathematical and visual-spatial skill.

VERBAL ABILITY.   Janet Hyde and Marcia Linn (1988) summarized research on gender differences in verbal skill and found that females had greater verbal ability in 75 percent of the 165 studies that they analyzed. Usually the difference was small. But it was larger for general measures of verbal ability, unscrambling scrambled words, and quality of speech production. Girls also read, write, and spell better than boys (Feingold, 1993; Hedges & Nowell, 1995), and more boys have reading and other language-related problems, such as stuttering (Halpern, 1986).

These gender differences may result from biology. The left hemisphere of the brain, which is central to language, may mature more rapidly in girls than in boys (Diamond, Johnson, Young, & Singh, 1983), but experience also contributes. Reading, for instance, is often stereotyped as an activity for girls (Huston, 1983). Consequently, girls are more willing than boys to invest time and effort in mastering verbal skills like reading.

SPATIAL ABILITY.   In Module 12.2, you saw that spatial ability is a component of most models of intelligence. One aspect of spatial ability is **mental rotation**, the ability to imagine how an object will look after it has been moved in space. The items in Figure 12–11 test mental rotation: The task is to determine which of the figures labelled A through E are rotated versions of the figure in the box on the left. From childhood on, boys tend to have better mental rotation skill than girls (Vederhus & Krekling, 1996; Voyer, Voyer, & Bryden, 1995). However, throughout middle childhood, mental

Mental rotation:

the ability to imagine how an object will look after it has been moved in space.

Figure 12–11

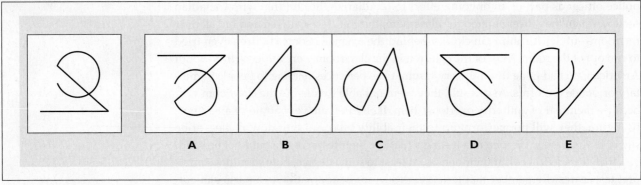

rotation remains difficult for both genders (Rigal, 1994, 1996) and requires children to cognitively manipulate different vantage points and perspectives in a fairly flexible manner. (The correct answers are C and D.)

Spatial ability also involves determining relations between objects in space while ignoring distracting information. For example, which of the tilted bottles of water in Figure 12–12 features the waterline drawn correctly? In an upright bottle, the waterline is at right angles to the sides of the bottle, but selecting the correct answer for the tilted bottle (A, in this case) requires that you ignore the conflicting perceptual information provided by the sides of the bottle. From adolescence on, boys are more accurate than girls on these kinds of spatial tasks (Voyer et al., 1995).

Both biological and experiential forces can contribute to gender differences in spatial ability, just as both contribute to gender differences in verbal ability (Casey, Nuttall, & Pezaris, 1999; Wang & Carr, 2014). For example, although, on average, boys tend to outperform girls in spatial ability, this does not hold true for boys from low socio-economic backgrounds (Levine, Vasilyeva, Lourenco, Newcombe, & Huttenlocher, 2005).

MATHEMATICS. Gender differences in math skill are complex. Standardized tests of math achievement tend to emphasize computational skills during middle childhood, and girls usually score higher than boys. Problem-solving and applying math concepts are emphasized in high school and university, and boys usually score higher than girls (Beller & Gafni, 1996). So, initially girls excel in math computation, but later boys excel in math problem-solving (Hyde, Fennema, & Lamon, 1990), despite the number of math courses taken (Kimball, 1989).

Figure 12–12

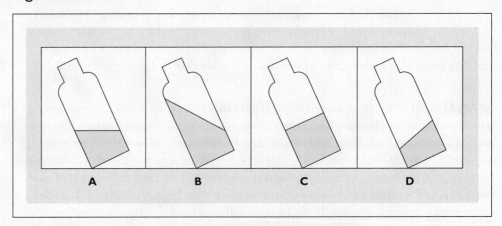

Paradoxically, the results are different for grades in math courses. Often no differences are detected in boys' and girls' grades, but, when a difference occurs, it invariably favours girls. This is even true for courses in high school and college or university—when males are getting higher scores on achievement tests (Kimball, 1989; Royer & Walles, 2007).

Why should girls get lower scores on tests of math achievement but higher grades in math courses? One idea is that girls and boys mght have different emotional experiences of math. Girls might have lower perceived competence in math, making them less confident when taking math achievement tests (Erturan & Jansen, 2015). Boys may be more confident in their math skills and may like the challenge of having to solve novel problems on standardized tests (Kimball, 1989). Because math is stereotyped as a masculine pursuit, girls tend to have less confidence in their own math abilities and be less likely to succeed in math (Casey, Nuttall, & Pezaris, 1997; Crawford, Chaffin, & Fitton, 1995).

This argument probably sounds familiar to you because the explanation is basically the same one used to explain gender differences in verbal skill: Boys succeed in math and girls succeed in language because children in each group are encouraged to pursue activities consistent with gender stereotypes. Lack of confidence about doing unfamiliar math makes the situation worse for girls, as does having an anxious female elementary math teacher (Beilock, Gunderson, Ramirez, & Levine, 2010).

Confidence can affect performance on standardized achievement tests.

Matt Antonino/Shutterstock

Because of findings like these, educators have worked hard to reduce gender stereotypes associated with math (Secada, Fennema, & Adajian, 1995). Also, encouraging girls with good self-esteem to identify with female social groups or models who do well in math, such as female college students in the sciences, can buffer or eliminate the impact of stereotypes on a girl's decision to stick with studies in math and science (Rydell & Boucher, 2010).

Unfortunately, gender differences in math continue. Hedges and Nowell (1995) evaluated data from the National Assessment of Educational Progress (NAEP) in the United States, which administers standardized tests in several areas to up to 100 000 students in Grades 3, 7, and 11. The researchers found that the gender difference in math achievement has been remarkably constant since the NAEP test was first administered in 1978.

What does it mean that gender differences are just as large at the start of the twenty-first century as they were in the last quarter of the twentieth century? Perhaps stereotypes for language and math have not changed. Maybe math is still communicated to youth as "a guy thing," despite decades of efforts to show girls that math is just as appropriate and interesting a subject for them and that girls can be just as successful in math as boys.

Another possibility is that biological factors contribute to gender differences in math. In particular, spatial ability, which we just discussed, may play a role. Some aspects of math are easier to understand if they can be visualized mentally. For example, being able to imagine a three-dimensional space where lines and planes intersect simplifies learning geometry. Boys may be more successful in some areas of math because they more often have the spatial skills that promote understanding (Casey et al., 1997).

One of the greatest proponents of the biological basis for differences in cognitive abilities between the genders is Doreen Kimura (1999). Arguing for the importance of biological and evolutionary influences, Kimura (1999) pointed to a series of studies in the research literature that she cited as demonstrating gender-based differences across a number of cognitive abilities, including mathematics, perception, language, spatial relationships, and motor skills. However, Kimura's stance on the definitiveness of these data remains controversial, with other researchers interpreting the same studies, and more, in radically different ways (e.g., Jaffee & Hyde, 2000). Most likely, gender difference in math is due to multiple factors: Some have roots in biology (e.g., spatial skill), but others have roots in experience (e.g., stereotypes concerning math).

Ask Yourself

Is psychometric g really that important?

Summarize gender differences in ability. How does nature contribute to these differences? How does nurture contribute?

12.4 Academic Skills

In this module, you'll learn about the academic skills that underlie children's mastery of the complex tasks of learning to read, write, and do arithmetic.

 Learning Objectives

After reading the module, you should be able to do the following:

LO11 Name the components of skilled reading.

LO12 Describe how children's writing improves with development.

LO13 State when children understand and use math skills.

Reading Skills

LO11   Name the components of skilled reading.

Try reading the following sentence:

Sumisu-san wa nawa o naifu de kirimashita.

You probably didn't make much headway, did you (unless you know Japanese)? Now try this one:

Snore secretary green plastic sleep trucks.

Word recognition:
the process of identifying a unique pattern of letters.

These are English words, and you probably read them quite easily, but did you get anything more out of this sentence than the one in Japanese? These examples show two important processes involved in skilled reading. **Word recognition** is the process of identifying a unique pattern of letters. Unless you know Japanese, your word recognition was not successful in the first sentence. You did not know that *nawa* means rope or that *kirimashita* is the past tense of the English verb *cut*. Furthermore, because you could not recognize individual words, you had no idea of the meaning of the sentence. **Comprehension** is the process of extracting meaning from a sequence of words.

Comprehension:
the process of extracting meaning from a sequence of words.

In the second sentence, your word recognition was fine, but comprehension was still impossible because the words were presented in a random sequence. These examples remind us just how difficult learning to read can be.

PREREADING SKILLS.   English words are made up of individual letters, so children need to know the letters of the alphabet before they can learn to read. Not surprising is the fact that kindergarten children who know most of their letters learn to read more easily than their peers who don't know their letters (Stevenson, Parker, Wilkinson, Hegion, & Fish, 1976). In addition, letters have distinctive sounds, and readers need to be able to hear these sounds, a skill known as **phonological awareness**. The Looking Ahead feature shows that children who can readily distinguish these sounds learn to read more readily than children who cannot.

Phonological awareness: the ability to distinguish the distinctive sounds of letters.

Much other research confirms the idea that sensitivity to the sounds of language is an essential step in learning to read (e.g., Hatcher & Hulme, 1999). Furthermore, phonological skills are not only important in learning to read in alphabet-based languages such as English but also in nonalphabet-based languages such as Chinese (Ho & Bryant, 1997).

RECOGNIZING WORDS.   The first step in actual reading is identifying individual words. One way to do this is to say the sounds associated with each letter, and then blend the sounds to produce a recognizable word. Such "sounding out" is a common technique among beginning readers. Older children sometimes sound out words but only when they are unfamiliar, which points to another common way of recognizing words (Coltheart, Curtis, Atkins, & Haller, 1993). Words are recognized through direct retrieval from long-term memory: As the individual letters in a word are identified, long-term memory is searched to see if there is a matching sequence of letters. Knowing that the letters are, in sequence, c-a-t, long-term memory is searched for a match, and the child recognizes the word as cat.

So far, word recognition may seem like a one-way street where readers first recognize letters and then recognize words. In reality, readers constantly use context to help them recognize letters and words. For example, readers typically recognize t faster in cast than in asct. That is, readers recognize letters faster when they appear in words than in nonwords. How do the nearby letters in cast help readers recognize the t? As children recognize the first letters in the word as c, a, and s, the possibilities for the last letter become more limited. Because English includes only four four-letter words that start with cas (well, five if you include Cass), the last letter can be only e, h, k,

Looking Ahead
Predicting Reading Skill

Reading well is an essential skill in modern society, yet many children never master it. Consequently, researchers have sought early indicators for children who will encounter difficulty learning to read. Phonological awareness is the best indicator available so far: Children who have trouble identifying different language sounds usually have problems learning to read.

For example, Wagner, Torgesen, and Rashotte (1997) measured kindergarten children's phonological awareness in a number of ways. In one task, the experimenter presented four words—fun, pin, bun, gun—and asked the child to pick the word that didn't rhyme with the others. In another task, children were asked to say the first,

last, or middle sound of a word: "What's the first sound in cat?"

After these children entered Grade 1, the experimenters measured the children's ability to read individual words. The investigators found that the correlation between children's performance on phonological awareness tasks in kindergarten and their reading score in Grade 1 was 0.82. That is, kindergarten children who were aware of letter sounds tended to be skilled readers in Grade 1, whereas kindergarten children who were unaware of letter sounds tended to be unskilled readers in Grade 1. As the children in this longitudinal study get older, phonological skills continue to be the best predictor of their reading ability (Wagner et al., 1997).

Reading with children in the preschool years is extremely important for later literacy.

or t. In contrast, there are no four-letter words (in English) that begin with acs, so all 26 letters must be checked, which takes more time than just checking four letters. In this way, a reader's knowledge of words simplifies the task of recognizing letters, which in turn makes it easier to recognize words (Seidenberg & McClelland, 1989).

Initially, researchers thought that using stories that had many rhymes would increase children's phonological awareness (Goswami & Bryant, 1990; Reese & Cox, 1999); however, new research has led scientists to conclude that this is not the case (Martin & Byrne, 2002). What continues to be important, however, is exposure to literacy in the preschool years (Foy & Mann, 2003). So, if rhyming stories, like *The Cat in the Hat* (Geisel, 1960), are fun and engaging, then children will be more interested in reading, will do it more frequently, and will learn more from it.

Readers also use the sentence context to speed up word recognition. Read these two sentences:

The last word in this sentence is cat.

The little girl's pet dog chased the cat.

Most readers recognize cat more rapidly in the second sentence. The reason is that the first seven words put severe limits on the last word: It must be something "chaseable," and, because the "chaser" is a dog, cat is a very likely candidate. In contrast, the first seven words in the first sentence put no limits on the last word; virtually any word could end the sentence. Both beginning and skilled readers use sentence context like this to help them recognize words (Kim & Goetz, 1994).

As you can imagine, most beginning readers rely more heavily on "sounding out" because they know fewer words. As they gain more reading experience, they are more likely to be able to retrieve a word directly from long-term memory. You might be tempted to summarize thus: "Beginning readers sound out, and more advanced readers retrieve directly." Don't! (Booth, Perfetti, & MacWhinney, 1999; Siegler, 1986). For example, when Robert Kail's daughter Laura was just beginning to read, she knew the, Laura, and several one-syllable words that ended in -at, such as bat, cat, and fat. Shown a sentence like

Most beginning readers rely on sounding out words.

Laura saw the fat cat run

she would say, "Laura s-s-s . . . ah-h . . . wuh . . . saw the fat cat er-r-r . . . uh-h-h . . . n-n-n . . . run." Familiar words were retrieved rapidly but the unfamiliar ones were slowly sounded out. With more experience, children sound out fewer words and retrieve more (Siegler, 1986), but even skilled readers sometimes fall back on sounding out when they confront unfamiliar words. Try reading this:

The clerk travelled downtown in a maglev.

You may well need to do some sounding out, then consult a dictionary (or look at the definition given before the Ask Yourself feature on page 335) for the correct meaning of "maglev." As children progress into middle childhood and adolescence, overreliance on sight words and a lack of knowledge in sounding out words (phonemic awareness) can result in low levels of literacy.

COMPREHENSION.   Once individual words are recognized, reading begins to have a lot in common with understanding speech. In other words, the means by which people understand a sequence of words is much the same whether the source of words is printed text or speech or, for that matter, Braille or sign language (Crowder & Wagner, 1992). In all of these cases, children derive meaning by combining words to form **propositions** or ideas and then combining propositions. For example, as you read

Propositions:

ideas developed by combining words.

The tall boy rode his bike

you spontaneously derive a number of propositions, including "There is a boy," "The boy is tall," and "The boy was riding." If this sentence was part of a larger body of text, you would derive propositions for each sentence, then link the propositions together to derive meaning for the passage as a whole (Perfetti & Curtis, 1986).

As children gain more reading experience, they better comprehend what they read. Several factors contribute to this improved comprehension (Siegler, 1998):

- Working memory capacity increases, which means that more experienced readers can store more of a sentence in memory as they try to identify the propositions it contains (Nation, Adams, Bowyer-Crane, & Snowling, 1999; Siegel, 1994): This extra capacity is handy when readers move from simple sentences, like "Kevin hit the ball," to more complex sentences, like "In the bottom of the ninth, with the bases loaded and the Blue Jays down 7–4, Joe put a line drive into the left-field bleachers, his second home run of the Series."

- Children acquire more general knowledge of their physical, social, and psychological worlds, which allows them to understand more of what they read (Bisanz, Das, Varnhagen, & Henderson, 1992; Graesser, Singer, & Trabasso, 1994): For example, even if a 6-year-old could recognize all of the words in the longer sentence about Joe's home run, the child would not fully comprehend the meaning of the passage because he or she lacks the necessary knowledge of baseball.

- With experience, children use more appropriate reading strategies: The goal of reading and the nature of the text dictate how you read. When reading a novel, for example, do you often skip sentences (or perhaps paragraphs or entire pages) to get to "the good parts"? This approach makes sense for pleasure reading but not for reading textbooks, recipes, or how-to manuals. Reading a textbook requires attention to both the overall organization and the relationship of details to that organization. Older, more experienced readers are better able to select a reading strategy that suits the material being read (Brown, Pressley, Van Meter, & Schuder, 1996).

- With experience, children better monitor their comprehension: When readers don't grasp the meaning of a passage because it is difficult or confusing, they read it again (Baker, 1994). Try this sentence (adapted from Carpenter & Daneman, 1981): "The fishing contest would draw fishermen from all around the region, including some of the best bass guitarists in the land." When you first encountered "bass guitarists" you probably interpreted "bass" as a fish. This didn't make much sense, so you reread the phrase to determine that "bass" refers to a type of guitar. More experienced readers are better able to realize that their understanding is not complete and take corrective action.

Thus, several factors contribute to improved comprehension as children get older. And greater comprehension, along with improved word recognition skills, explains

Table 12–5 Summary Table

Component Skills Involved in Reading	
Skill	**Definition**
Prereading skills	Knowing letter names
	Linking names of letters to the sounds they make
Recognizing words	Sounding out individual syllables
	Retrieving familiar word names from long-term memory
Comprehension	Understanding of word combinations based on interplay of working memory, understanding of the world, appropriate reading strategies, and effective monitoring of one's reading for sense

why most children are able to read ever more complex text as they grow. These factors are summarized in Table 12–5.

In the next part of this module, you'll see how information-processing psychologists use similar ideas to explain children's developing ability to write.

Writing Skills

LO12 Describe how children's writing improves with development.

Though few of us end up being a Mordecai Richler, a Margaret Atwood, or a Michael Crichton, most adults do write, both at home and at work. The basics of good writing are remarkably straightforward (Williams, 1997), but writing skill develops very gradually during childhood, adolescence, and young adulthood. Research indicates a number of factors that contribute to improved writing as children develop (Adams, Treiman, & Pressley, 1998; Siegler, 1998).

GREATER KNOWLEDGE AND ACCESS TO KNOWLEDGE ABOUT TOPICS. Writing is about telling something to others. With age, children have more to tell as they gain more knowledge about the world and incorporate this knowledge into their writing (Benton, Corkill, Sharp, Downey, & Khramtsova, 1995). For example, asked to write about a mayoral election, 8-year-olds are apt to describe it as being much like a popularity contest; 12-year-olds more often describe it in terms of political issues that are both subtle and complex. Of course, students are sometimes asked to write about topics quite unfamiliar to them. In this case, older children's and adolescents' writing is usually better because they are more adept at finding useful reference material and incorporating it into their writing.

GREATER UNDERSTANDING OF HOW TO ORGANIZE WRITING. One difficult aspect of writing is organization—arranging all the necessary information in a manner that readers find clear and interesting. In fact, children and young adolescents organize their writing differently than older adolescents and adults (Bereiter & Scardamalia, 1987). Young writers often use a **knowledge-telling strategy**, writing down information on the topic as they retrieve it from memory. For example, asked to write about the day's events at school, a Grade 2 student wrote:

> It is a rainy day. We hope the sun will shine. We got new spelling books. We had our pictures taken. We sang Happy Birthday to Barbara. (Waters, 1980, p. 155)

The story has no obvious structure. The first two sentences are about the weather, but the last three deal with completely independent topics. Apparently, the writer simply described each event as it came to mind.

Toward the end of middle childhood, children begin to use a **knowledge-transforming strategy**, deciding what information to include and how best to organize

Knowledge-telling strategy:
a writing strategy in which information on a topic is written down as it is retrieved from memory.

Knowledge-transforming strategy:
a writing strategy in which the writer decides what information to include and how to organize it before writing it down.

it for the point they wish to convey to their reader. This approach involves considering the purpose of writing (e.g., to inform, to persuade, to entertain) and the information needed to achieve this purpose. It also involves considering the needs, interests, and knowledge of the anticipated audience.

Asked to describe the day's events, older children's writing can take many forms, depending on the purpose and audience. An essay written to entertain peers about humorous events at school would differ from one written to convince parents about problems in schoolwork. And both of these essays would differ from one written to inform an exchange student about a typical day in a Canadian elementary school. In other words, although children's knowledge-telling strategy gets words on paper, the more mature, knowledge-transforming strategy produces a more cohesive text for the reader.

Older children's writing is better because these children know more about the world, organize their writing more effectively, and are better able to handle the mechanical requirements of writing.

GREATER EASE IN DEALING WITH THE MECHANICAL REQUIREMENTS OF WRITING. Soon after Robert Kail earned his pilot's licence, he took his son Matt for a flight. A few days later, Matt wrote the following story for his Grade 2 weekly writing assignment:

> This weekend I got to ride in a one propellered plane. But this time my dad was alone. He has his license now. It was a long ride. But I fell asleep after five minutes. But when we landed I woke up. My dad said, "You missed a good ride." My dad said, "You even missed the jets!" But I had fun.

Matt spent more than an hour writing this story, and the original is filled with erasures where he corrected misspelled words, ill-formed letters, and incorrect punctuation. Had Matt simply described the flight together aloud (instead of writing it), his task would have been much easier. In oral language, he could ignore capitalization, punctuation, spelling, and printing the individual letters. These many mechanical aspects of writing can be a burden for all writers but particularly for young writers.

In fact, research shows that when youngsters are absorbed by the task of printing letters correctly, the quality of their writing usually suffers (Jones & Christensen, 1999). As children master printed and cursive letters, they can pay more attention to other aspects of writing. Similarly, correct spelling and good sentence structure are particularly hard for younger writers, but, as they learn to spell and to generate clear sentences, they write more easily and more effectively (Graham, Berninger, Abbott, Abbott, & Whitaker, 1997; McCutchen, Covill, Hoyne, & Mildes, 1994).

GREATER SKILL IN REVISING. Few authors get it down right the first time. Instead, they revise and revise, then revise some more. In the words of one expert, "Experienced writers get something down on paper as fast as they can, just so they can revise it into something clearer" (Williams, 1997, p. 11).

Unfortunately, young writers often don't revise at all—the first draft is usually the final draft. To make matters worse, when young writers revise, the changes do not

Printing is a real challenge for beginning writers.

Lane V. Erickson/Shutterstock

Table 12–6 Summary Table

Factors Contributing to Improved Writing with Age	
Factor	**Defined**
Greater knowledge	Older children know more about the world and thus have more to write about.
Better organization	Older children organize information to convey a point to the reader, but younger children simply list topics as they come to mind.
Greater facility with mechanical requirements	Spelling, punctuation, and printing (or typing) are easier for older children, so they can concentrate on writing.
Greater skill in revising	Older children are better able to recognize and correct problems in their writing.

necessarily improve their writing (Fitzgerald, 1987). Effective revising requires being able to detect problems and to know how to correct them (Baker & Brown, 1984; Beal, 1996). As children develop, they're better able to find problems and to know how to correct them, particularly when the topic is familiar to them (McCutchen, Francis, & Kerr, 1997).

Table 12–6 lists the factors that contribute to better writing as children grow. Looking at the factors in Table 12–6, it's quite clear why good writing is so long in developing. Many different skills are involved, and each is complicated in its own right. Mastering them collectively is a huge challenge, one that spans all of childhood, adolescence, and adulthood. Much the same could be said for mastering quantitative skills, as we'll see in the next section.

Math Skills

LO13   State when children understand and use math skills.

Preschoolers understand many of the principles underlying counting, even if they sometimes stumble over the mechanics of counting. By kindergarten, children have mastered counting, and they use this skill as the starting point for learning to add.

Early addition skills frequently involve finger-counting.

For instance, suppose you ask a kindergartner to solve the following problem: "John had four oranges. Then Mary gave him two more oranges. How many oranges does John have now?" Many 6-year-old children solve the problem by counting. They first count out four fingers on one hand and then count out two more on the other. Finally, they count all six fingers on both hands. To subtract, they do the same procedure in reverse (Siegler & Jenkins, 1989; Siegler & Shrager, 1984).

Youngsters soon abandon this approach for a slightly more efficient method. Instead of counting the fingers on the first hand, they simultaneously extend the number of fingers on the first hand corresponding to the larger of the two numbers to be added. Next, they count out the smaller number with fingers on the second hand. Finally, they count all of the fingers to determine the sum (Groen & Resnick, 1977).

After children begin to receive formal arithmetic instruction in Grade 1, addition problems are less often solved by counting aloud or by counting fingers. Instead, children add and subtract by counting mentally. That is, children act as if they are counting silently, beginning with the larger number and adding on. By age 8 or 9, children have learned the addition tables so well that sums of the single-digit integers (from 0 to 9) are facts that are simply retrieved from memory (Ashcraft, 1982).

These counting strategies do not occur in a rigid developmental sequence. Individual children use many or all of these strategies, depending upon the problem. Children usually begin by trying to retrieve an answer from memory. If they are not reasonably confident that the retrieved answer is correct, then they resort to counting aloud or on fingers (Siegler, 1988). Retrieval is most likely for problems with small addends (e.g., 1 + 2, 2 + 4) because these problems are presented frequently in textbooks and by teachers. Consequently, the sum is highly associated with the problem, which makes the child confident that the retrieved answer is correct. In contrast, problems with larger addends, such as 9 + 8, are presented less often. The result is a weaker link between the addends and the sum and, consequently, a greater chance that children will need to determine an answer by counting.

Of course, arithmetic skills continue to improve as children move through elementary school. They become more proficient in addition and subtraction, learn multiplication and division, and move on to the more sophisticated mathematical concepts involved in algebra, geometry, trigonometry, and calculus.

"Hey, it's helped me get this video game generation interested in math..."

Dave Carpenter/CartoonStock Ltd.

INTERNATIONAL STUDIES OF MATHEMATICS ACHIEVEMENT. Figure 12–13 shows the results of the Third International Mathematics and Science Study (National Center for Education Statistics, 1997), which compares math and science achievement of students in 41 countries. Students in Canada scored substantially lower than students in other nations, such as Singapore and Korea, who scored the highest. Furthermore, the cultural differences in math achievement hold for both math operations and math problem-solving (Stevenson & Lee, 1990).

Figure 12–13

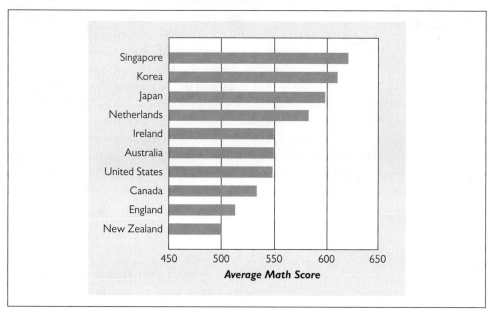

SOURCE: Based on data from National Center for Education Statistics. (1997). Pursuing excellence: A study of U.S. fourthgrade mathematics and science achievement in an international context. Washington, DC: US Government Printing Office.

Why do North American students rate so much lower than those in Singapore or other countries? Consider a typical Grade 5 student's day in Taipei, the largest city in Taiwan. Students attend school from 8 a.m. until 4 p.m. daily. Most evenings, students spend two to three hours doing homework. This academic routine is gruelling by North American standards, where Grade 5 students typically spend six to seven hours in school each day and less than an hour doing homework. As well, although many North American school children are unhappy when schoolwork intrudes on time for play and watching television, students in China tend to be enthusiastic about school and school-related activities, including homework.

Stevenson and Lee have conducted extensive inter-country comparisons of student performance in Japan, Taiwan, and the United States in an effort to determine what accounts for performance differences in school achievement. Although their work focuses on student performance in the United States, it is worth considering their findings here. In a comprehensive comparison of students in Japan, Taiwan, and the United States, Stevenson and Lee (1990) found many substantial differences:

- *Time in school and how it is used.* By Grade 5, students in Japan and Taiwan spend 50 percent more time in school than American students, and more of this time is devoted to academic activities than in the United States.

- *Time spent on homework and attitudes toward it.* Students in Taiwan and Japan spend more time on homework and value homework more than American students.

- *Parents' attitudes.* American parents are more often satisfied with their children's performance in school; in contrast, Japanese and Taiwanese parents set much higher standards for their children.

- *Parents' beliefs about effort and ability.* Japanese and Taiwanese parents believe more strongly than American parents that effort, not native ability, is the key factor in school success.

Asian children usually have their own study areas.

Thus, students in Japan and Taiwan excel because they spend more time both in and out of school on academic tasks. Furthermore, their parents (and teachers) set loftier scholastic goals and believe that students can attain these goals with hard work. Japanese classrooms even post a motto describing ideal students—*gambaru kodomo*—"they who strive the hardest."

Parents underscore the importance of schoolwork in many ways to their children. For example, even though homes and apartments in Japan and China are very small by Canadian standards, Asian youngsters typically have a desk in a quiet area where they can study undisturbed (Stevenson & Lee, 1990). For Japanese and Taiwanese teachers and parents, academic excellence is paramount, and it shows in their children's success.

What can North Americans learn from Japanese and Taiwanese educational systems? From their experiences with Asian students, teachers, and schools, Stevenson and Stigler (1992) suggest several ways North American schools could be improved:

- Give teachers more free time to prepare lessons and correct students' work.

- Improve teachers' training by allowing them to work closely with older, more experienced teachers.

- Organize instruction around sound principles of learning, such as providing multiple examples of concepts and giving students adequate opportunities to practise newly acquired skills.

- Set higher standards for children, who need to spend more time and effort in school-related activities in order to achieve those standards.

Changing teaching practices and attitudes toward achievement would begin to reduce the gap between North American students and students in other industrialized countries, particularly Asian countries. Ignoring the problem will mean an increasingly undereducated workforce and citizenry in a more complex world—an alarming prospect for the twenty-first century.

Definition of word on page 328: A *maglev* is a vehicle, such as a train, that moves above the ground by magnetic levitation. Due to reduced friction, these types of vehicles can usually move at high speeds.

Ask Yourself

Imagine two children just entering Grade 1. One has mastered prereading skills, can sound out many words, and recognizes a rapidly growing set of words. The second child knows most of the letters of the alphabet but only a handful of letter-sound correspondences. How are these differences in reading skills likely to lead to different experiences in Grade 1?

12.5 Effective Schools

 ## Learning Objectives

After reading the module, you should be able to do the following:

LO14 Identify the hallmarks of effective schools and effective teachers.

LO15 Describe how computers are used in school and their effects on instruction.

Education is largely under provincial jurisdiction in Canada. In addition, school boards often have local authority, which can result in notable differences between school districts despite the existence of provincial curriculum standards and criteria. Schools can differ on many dimensions, including their emphasis on academic goals and parental involvement. Teachers differ in how they run their classrooms, and different schools have different access to resources and funds for in-class and extracurricular programs. These and other variables affect how schools influence child development.

School-Based Influences on Student Achievement

LO14 **Identify the hallmarks of effective schools and effective teachers.**

Whether success is defined by the percentage of students who are literate, who graduate, or who go to university, some schools are successful and some are not. Researchers (Good & Brophy, 1994; Stevenson & Stigler, 1992; Walberg, 1995) have identified a number of factors associated with success in school:

- *Staff and students alike understand that academic excellence is the primary goal of the school and of every student in the school.* The school day emphasizes instruction (not simply filling time from 8:30 to 3:30 with nonacademic activities), and students are recognized publicly for their academic accomplishments.

- *The school climate is safe and nurturing.* Students know they can devote their energy to learning (instead of worrying about being harmed in school), and they know the staff truly wants to see them succeed.

- *Parents are involved.* In some cases, this involvement may be through formal arrangements such as parent–teacher organizations, or it may be informal. Parents may spend some time each week helping out or reading to a child. Such involvement signals to both teachers and students that parents are committed to students' success.

- *Progress of students, teachers, and programs is monitored.* The only way to know if schools are succeeding is by measuring performance. Students, teachers, and programs need to be evaluated regularly using objective measures that reflect academic goals.

Students in schools that follow these guidelines usually succeed. In schools where the guidelines are ignored, students more often fail.

Teacher-Based Influences on Student Achievement

LO15   **Describe how computers are used in school and their effects on instruction.**

Muellek Josef/Shutterstock

Individual teachers have a great impact on children's achievement.

On a daily basis, individual teachers have the most potential for impact on student learning. Take a moment to recall the teachers you had in Grades 1 through 8. Some you probably remember fondly because they were enthusiastic and innovative and made learning fun. You may remember others with bitterness. They might seem to have lost their love of teaching and children, making class very boring. Your experience tells you that some teachers do a better job of engaging students than do others, but personality and enthusiasm are not key elements. Although you may enjoy warm and eager teachers, researchers (Good & Brophy, 1994; Stevenson & Stigler, 1992; Walberg, 1995) have found that several other factors are critical for student achievement. Students tend to learn the most when teachers

- *manage the classroom effectively so they can devote most of their time to instruction.* When teachers spend a lot of time disciplining students, or when students do not move smoothly from one class activity to the next, instructional time is wasted, and students are apt to learn less.

- *believe they are responsible for their students' learning and that their students will learn when taught well.* When students don't understand a new topic, these teachers repeat the original instruction (in case the student missed something) or create new instruction (in case the student heard everything but just didn't "get it"). These teachers keep plugging away because they feel at fault if students don't learn.

- *emphasize mastery of topics.* Teachers should introduce a topic, then give students many opportunities to understand, practise, and apply the topic. Just as you'd find it hard to go directly from driver's ed to driving a race car, students more often achieve when they grasp a new topic thoroughly, then gradually move on to other, more advanced topics.

- *teach actively.* These teachers don't just talk or give students an endless stream of worksheets. Instead, they demonstrate topics concretely or have hands-on demonstrations for students. They also have students participate in class activities and encourage students to interact, to generate ideas, and to solve problems together.

- *pay careful attention to pacing.* Teachers should present material slowly enough that students can understand a new concept but not so slowly that students get bored.

- *value tutoring.* These teachers work with students individually or in small groups so they can gear their instruction to each student's level and check each student's understanding. They also encourage peer tutoring, in which more capable students tutor less capable students. Children who are tutored by peers do learn, and so do the tutors, evidently because teaching helps tutors organize their knowledge.

- *teach children techniques for monitoring and managing their own learning.* Students are more likely to achieve when they are taught how to recognize the aims of school tasks and know effective strategies for achieving those aims.

When teachers teach according to these guidelines, most of their students learn the material and enjoy school. When teachers don't observe these guidelines, their students often fail, or, at the very least, find learning difficult and school tedious (Good & Brophy, 1994; Stevenson & Stigler, 1992; Walberg, 1995).

THE ROLE OF COMPUTERS.   Some educational reformers argue that computers should be used to improve students' learning. Computers can be used in schools as tutors (Lepper & Gurtner, 1989) and enable instruction to be individualized and interactive. Students proceed at their own pace, receiving feedback and help when necessary. Computers are also a valuable medium for experiential learning (Lepper & Gurtner, 1989). Simulation programs allow students to explore the world in ways that would be impossible or dangerous otherwise. Students can change the law of gravity or see what happens to a city when no taxes are imposed. Finally, computers can help students achieve traditional academic goals more readily (Steelman, 1994). A graphics program can allow artistically untalented students to produce beautiful illustrations or students with handwriting disabilities to produce text more easily.

Many schools in Canada have equipped their classrooms with computers. While not every Canadian classroom has a computer, entire classrooms full of computers are not uncommon. Also, "cyber-schools" are not uncommon today in Canadian educational districts. Cyber-schools offer distance education to students online rather than in the traditional classroom setting and allow students to access a variety of courses online. Although the idea of distance education originally formed a part of efforts to develop cyber-schools, these schools are also appealing to students wanting to work more independently than is possible in a regular classroom and to students who cannot attend regular school as a result of, for example, health, mental health, or behavioural difficulties.

Not all researchers, educators, and policy makers are enthusiastic about computers taking on this kind of pivotal role in education. Some critics fear that computers eliminate an important human element in learning. Nevertheless, many students are becoming more interested in cyber-learning as their familiarity with computers increases.

Over-focusing on discipline wastes instructional time.

Fotokostic/Shutterstock

Ask Yourself

How do the factors associated with effective schools and effective teachers described in this module relate to the factors responsible for cultural differences in mathematics achievement described in Module 12.4?

What Would a Science Teacher Do?

When Theresa Zolner was young, she was interested in computers and science at school. She asked a teacher about participating in the computer club and was told, "That's for boys." If you were a science teacher, how would you respond to Theresa's question? What would you do to encourage science education in girls, and how would you manage gender expectations of children and their parents in a school for children in middle childhood?

Summary

12.1 Cognitive Processes

Concrete Operational Thinking

- Between ages 7 and 11, children use mental operations, but their thinking is focused on the concrete and real.

Memory Skills

- Preschool children use strategies to help them remember.

- Using memory strategies well depends upon analyzing the task's goal and monitoring the effectiveness of the strategy.

- Knowledge helps children organize information to be remembered.

- Knowledge can distort memory by causing children to forget information that does not conform to their knowledge or to "remember" events that did not actually take place.

12.2 The Nature of Intelligence

Psychometric Theories

- Describe intelligence as a general factor (g) or also as including specific factors.

- Hierarchical theories include both general and specific factors.

Gardner's Theory of Multiple Intelligences

- Includes linguistic, logical-mathematical, spatial, musical, bodily-kinesthetic, interpersonal, and intrapersonal intelligences.

- Has stimulated research on nontraditional forms of intelligence.

- Implies that schools should teach to each child's unique intellectual strengths.

Sternberg's Triarchic Theory of Successful Intelligence

- Includes three subtheories.

- The contextual subtheory specifies that intelligent behaviour is defined by the individual's culture.

- The experiential subtheory specifies that intelligence is associated with task familiarity.

- The componential subtheory specifies that intelligent behaviour involves organizing basic cognitive processes into an efficient strategy.

12.3 Individual Differences in Intellectual Skills

Binet and the Development of Intelligence Testing

- Binet created the first intelligence test, based on mental age, to identify students who would have difficulty in school.

- Terman created the Stanford-Binet, which introduced the concept of IQ.

Do Intelligence Tests Work?

- IQ tests are reasonably valid measures of achievement in school and performance in the workplace.

- Dynamic tests improve validity by measuring potential for future learning.

Hereditary and Environmental Factors

- Heredity has some impact on IQ.

- Siblings' IQ scores are more alike, as siblings are more similar genetically.

- Adopted children's IQ scores are more like their biological parents' test scores than their adoptive parents' scores.

- Well-organized home environments and early intervention programs demonstrate the impact of the environment on IQ.

Impact of Culture and Social Class

- Living in poverty often results in lower exposure to opportunities that boost early literacy.

- Cultural differences can affect IQ test outcomes, such that children who come from mainstream, middle-class backgrounds tend to do better on IQ tests.

- IQ scores remain valid predictors of school success because middle-class experience is often a prerequisite for school success in North American schools.

Gender Differences in Intellectual Abilities and Achievement

- On average, girls excel in verbal skills, and boys excel in spatial ability.

- Girls get better grades in math; boys get better scores on math achievement tests.

- Student and teacher anxiety can affect students' test performance and learning.

12.4 Academic Skills

Reading Skills

- Prereading skills include knowing letters and letter sounds.

- Beginning readers more often recognize words by sounding them out; advanced readers more often retrieve a word from long-term memory.

- Comprehension in children improves with age due to (1) an increase in working memory capacity, (2) an increase in world knowledge, and (3) improved skills in the ability to monitor what is read and to match reading strategies to the reading task.

Writing Skills

- As children develop, their writing improves because they (1) know more about the world, (2) organize their writing better, (3) master the mechanics of writing, and (4) revise better.

Math Skills

- Children first add and subtract by counting but later retrieve addition facts directly from memory.

- Canadian students lag behind students in other countries in mathematics due to differences in time spent on schoolwork and in parental attitudes.

12.5 Effective Schools

School-Based Influences on Student Achievement

- Successful schools emphasize academic excellence, are safe and nurturing, monitor progress, and urge parents to be involved.

Teacher-Based Influences on Student Achievement

- Students succeed when teachers manage classrooms effectively, take responsibility for students' learning, teach mastery of material, pace material well, value tutoring, and show children how to monitor learning.

- Computers are used in school as tutors, to provide experiential learning, and as a tool to achieve traditional academic goals.

Chapter Critical Review

1. If Jean Piaget were asked to define intelligence, how might his definition differ from a psychometrician's? How might it differ from Gardner's and Sternberg's definitions of intelligence?

2. Which perspective on intelligence best explains the abilities of musical savants, who are discussed in Module 12.2? Which best explains a person who is all-around gifted—good in all school subjects as well as socially skilled? Which best explains your personal intellectual gifts?

3. Explain why intelligence test scores do only a fair job of predicting school performance (see Module 12.3). What others factors might be involved in school success besides what intelligence tests measure?

4. A perennial debate in education is whether children should be taught to read with phonics (sounding out words) or with whole-word methods (recognizing entire words). Does the research described in Module 12.4 provide evidence that either method is more effective?

See for Yourself

The best way to understand the differences between good and bad teaching is to visit some actual school classrooms. Ask a few school principals if you can visit some classes in their schools. Take along the guidelines for good teaching listed in this chapter in the section Teacher-Based Influences on Student Achievement. Start by watching how the teachers and children interact and decide how much the teacher relies upon each of the principles. If possible, ask the teachers about teaching philosophies and practices, including their opinions about teaching principles. You'll probably see that, in today's classroom, consistently following all the principles is very challenging for a variety of reasons. See for yourself!

Chapter 13
Social and Emotional Development in Middle Childhood

Aman Ahmed Khan/Shutterstock

 ## MODULE

13.1 Self-Esteem

13.2 Relationships with Peers

13.3 Helping Others

13.4 Aggression

13.5 Families in the Early Twenty-First Century

Connect to My Virtual Child

What kinds of theories do you have about children? What ideas inform your thoughts and beliefs about the lives of children, how they are raised, and the nature of the human person? Use your access card and follow this link www.myvirtualchild.com to learn more about the world of the child. You can even virtually try to raise your own child.

Terry and Mabel picked up Sophie from school one day, only to find her in tears waiting by the front doors to the school. When they asked her why she was crying, Sophie threw her arms around Mabel's waist and said she never wanted to go to school again because the kids were so mean. Terry and Mabel knew Sophie was a kind and sensitive girl, and they wondered . . . what makes some children so kind while others can seem like such bullies?

13.1 Self-Esteem

 ## Learning Objectives

After reading the module, you should be able to do the following:

LO1 Describe how self-esteem is measured in school-age children.

LO2 Demonstrate how self-esteem changes in the elementary school years.

LO3 Identify the factors influencing the development of self-esteem.

LO4 Understand how children's development may be affected by low self-esteem.

In this module, we'll see how self-esteem is measured in elementary school children, how it changes as children develop, and what forces shape it.

Measuring Self-Esteem

LO1 Describe how self-esteem is measured in school-age children.

Preschool children's self-esteem is typically measured by showing pictures and asking youngsters to judge which of two hypothetical children they resemble (e.g., a child who makes friends easily or a child who does not make friends easily). With older children (and adolescents), self-esteem is often measured with questionnaires that require children to read statements like those in Figure 13–1. The most widely used self-esteem questionnaire of this sort is the Self-Perception Profile for Children (SPPC for short) devised by Susan Harter (1985, 1988), who made a pioneering effort in self-esteem research. The SPPC is designed to evaluate self-worth in children age 8 and older across the following five domains (Harter, 1988, p. 62):

- *Scholastic competence:* How competent or smart the child feels in doing school work.

- *Athletic competence:* How competent the child feels at sports and games requiring physical skill or athletic ability.

- *Social acceptance:* How popular or accepted the child feels in social interactions with peers.

- *Behavioural conduct:* How adequate the child feels about behaving the way one is supposed to.

- *Physical appearance:* How good-looking the child feels and how much the child likes his or her physical characteristics, such as height, weight, face, and hair.

The SPPC includes six statements for each domain. For example, Figure 13–1 lists two of the statements used to evaluate scholastic competence, shown as they actually

Figure 13–1

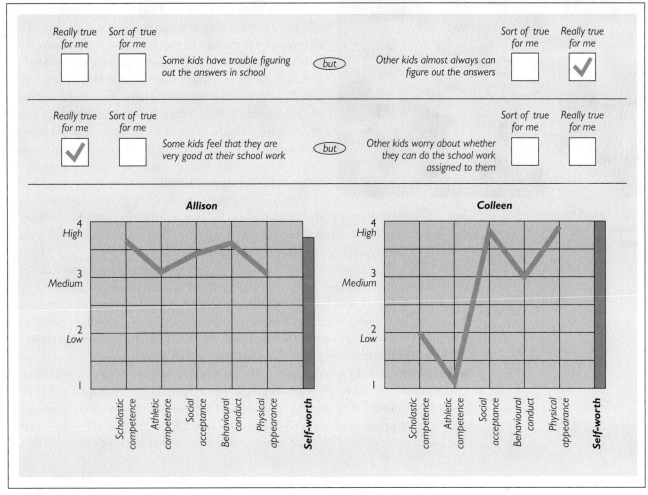

SOURCE: From Harter, S. (1985). Manual for the self-perception profile for children. Denver, CO: University of Denver. Used by permission.

appear on the SPPC. In both statements, the child has checked the response that indicates the highest level of self-esteem. A child's answers to all six statements are used to create an average level of self-esteem in that domain. The averages for each of the five domains are then used to generate a self-perception profile for each child. Two profiles are illustrated in the figure. Allison's self-esteem is high across all five domains; Colleen's self-esteem is much more varied. She feels positive about her social acceptance and physical appearance and, to a lesser extent, about her conduct. However, she feels negative about her scholastic and athletic competence.

Notice that each profile ends with a bar graph depicting the child's overall self-worth. Overall self-worth is measured on the SPPC with six more items, such as "Some kids like the way they are leading their life" and "Some kids like the kind of person they are." Children's responses to these statements are then averaged to create a measure of overall self-worth.

Developmental Change in Self-Esteem

LO2 Demonstrate how self-esteem changes in the elementary school years.

A drop in self-esteem as children move through the elementary school years in middle childhood is common because children begin to compare themselves with peers (Ruble, Boggiano, Feldman, & Loebl, 1980). Unlike at home, where parents might be their best fans, children attending school are exposed to more realistic feedback about their skills

Negative feedback about self-competence creates a drop in domain-specific self-esteem.

and performance. In school, a boy might discover that he is not necessarily the best reader or a girl might discover she is not the fastest runner. Instead, students might find out that they are only average readers or slow runners as compared with other students! These realizations often produce a modest drop in those dimensions of self-esteem in which the child compares less favourably to peers.

During middle childhood, self-esteem becomes more differentiated (Boivin, Vitaro, & Gagnon, 1992). Children are able to evaluate themselves in more domains as they develop, and their evaluations in each domain are increasingly independent. That is, younger children's ratings of self-esteem are often like Allison's (in Figure 13–1): The ratings are consistent across the different dimensions. In contrast, older children's (and adolescents') ratings more often resemble Colleen's, with self-esteem varying from one domain to another. That is, children develop multiple self-esteems, each linked to a specific content area.

In particular, children's academic self-concepts become especially well defined (Byrne & Gavin, 1996; Marsh & Yeung, 1997). As children accumulate success and failure experiences in school, they form beliefs about their ability in different content areas (e.g., English, math, science), and these beliefs contribute to students' overall academic self-concept. A child who believes that she is skilled at reading and math but not so skilled in science will probably have a positive academic self-concept overall. A child who believes he is untalented in most academic areas will likely have a negative academic self-concept.

Unfortunately, many individuals across the lifespan do not view themselves very positively. Some children are ambivalent about themselves; others actually feel negatively about themselves. Figure 13–2 shows that roughly 25 percent of 9- and 10-year-olds in one study (Cole, 1991) had negative self-esteem on three scales of the SPPC.

Sources of Self-Esteem

LO3 Identify the factors influencing the development of self-esteem.

Think back to Allison and Colleen, the two girls whose self-perceptions are graphed in Figure 13–1. Both girls evaluated their overall self-worth very positively. In general,

Figure 13–2

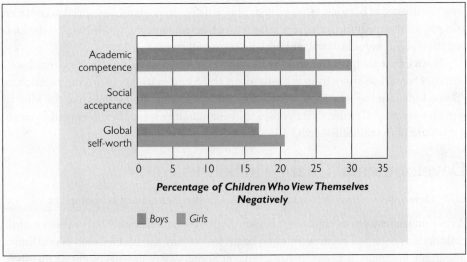

SOURCE: Based on data from Cole, D. A. (1991). Preliminary support for a competency-based model of depression in children. *Journal of Abnormal Psychology, 100,* 181–190.

they were happy with themselves and with their lives. Why do these girls feel so positively, while some children feel so negatively about themselves? You won't be surprised to learn that parenting plays a key role.

Children are more likely to view themselves positively when their parents are affectionate toward them and involved with them (Lord, Eccles, & McCarthy, 1994). Around the world, children have higher self-esteem when families live in harmony and parents nurture their children (Scott, Scott, & McCabe, 1991). A father who routinely hugs his daughter and gladly takes her to piano lessons is saying to her, "You are important to me." When children hear these kinds of validating messages regularly from parents, they are more apt to internalize the message and see themselves positively than if parents communicate negative or indifferent messages of worth to their children.

Extreme feedback fuels low academic self-esteem.

Parental discipline also is related to self-esteem. Children with high self-esteem generally have parents who aren't afraid to set rules and are open to discussing them with their children (Coopersmith, 1967). Parents who fail to set rules are, in effect, telling their children that they don't care—they don't value them enough to go to the trouble of creating rules and enforcing them. In much the same way, parents who refuse to discuss discipline with their children are saying, "Your opinions don't matter to me." Not surprisingly, when children internalize these messages, the result is lower overall self-worth (Andrews & Brown, 1993).

Allison's and Colleen's positive self-worth can be credited, at least in part, to their parents for being warm and involved, for establishing rules, and for discussing these rules with them. But how can we account for the fact that Allison views herself positively in all domains, whereas Colleen's self-perceptions are more varied? Social comparisons are important (Butler, 1992). Both girls have many opportunities during each day to compare themselves with peers. Allison is almost always the first to finish assignments, usually gets one of the highest grades in the class on exams, and is often asked by her teacher to help classmates on math and science problems.

Meanwhile, Colleen is usually among the last to finish assignments, typically gets low grades on tests, and is one of the students Allison helps with math and science. Daily classroom routines give every student ample opportunities to discover everyone's academic standing within the room. Soon, everyone knows that Allison is one of the most capable students and Colleen is one of the least capable. Allison understands that her classmates see her as academically gifted, so her academic self-esteem is quite high. Colleen knows that her classmates see her as not very talented academically, so her academic self-esteem is low.

However, children's self-esteem is not always linked to others' views. In order to investigate this, Dayan, Doyle, and Markiewicz (2000) studied self-esteem of idiocentric children and allocentric children. **Idiocentric** people tend to emphasize independence and personal needs and goals over those of others. **Allocentric** people tend to emphasize interdependence, affiliation, and co-operation with groups they belong to more than their own goals. Dayan and colleagues found that idiocentric children tended to report less social support from peers than allocentric children. The researchers also found that only allocentric children's self-esteem could be predicted by the level of social support these children experienced from their best friends. In other words, the self-esteem of allocentric children, who tended to focus on the importance of interdependence, was affected by the level of support they experienced from friends; however, this was not true for idiocentric children, who tended to focus more on the importance of independence and less on support from others.

Idiocentric:
emphasizing independence and personal needs and goals over those of others.

Allocentric:
interdependence, affiliation, and co-operation with groups an individual belongs to more than with personal goals.

Nevertheless, children's self-esteem largely is related to how they are viewed by those around them. Most children's self-esteem is high when others view them positively and low when others view them negatively (Hoge, Smit, & Hanson, 1990), although this is more applicable to allocentric than to idiocentric children. The relationship between self-esteem and perceptions by others has implications for academically talented youngsters placed in classes for children who are academically gifted. In a traditional classroom of students with a wide range of ability, talented youngsters compare themselves with other students and develop positive academic self-esteem. In classes for gifted students, many talented youngsters seem only average, and some seem below average. The resulting social comparisons can cause these children's academic self-esteem to drop (Marsh, Chessor, Craven, & Roche, 1995; Schneider, Clegg, Byrne, Leddingham, & Crombie, 1989). Students who value top-of-the-class status will be more affected by social comparisons in a gifted class than students who are more intent on mastering challenging material.

In examining sources of self-esteem—not just for children in gifted classes but for all children—several characteristics of teachers and schools should also be taken into account (Hoge et al., 1990). In general, self-esteem is greater when students work hard in school, get along with their peers, and avoid disciplinary problems. In addition, self-esteem is greater when students participate in extracurricular activities, such as music, student council, sports, and clubs. Finally, students' self-esteem is enhanced when the overall climate of the school is nurturing—when students believe that teachers care about them and listen to them. Grades matter too, but good grades affect students' self-esteem about specific disciplines—for example, in math or English—not their overall self-esteem (Hoge et al., 1990; Marsh & Yeung, 1997).

Consequences of Low Self-Esteem

LO4 Understand how children's development may be affected by low self-esteem.

Parents and teachers should make an effort to enhance children's self-esteem, because children with low self-esteem are at risk for many developmental problems. Children with low self-esteem are

- more likely to have problems with peers (Hymel, Rubin, Rowden, & LeMare, 1990).
- more prone to psychological disorders such as depression (Button, Sonuga-Burke, Davis, & Thompson, 1996; Garber, Robinson, & Valentiner, 1997).
- more likely to be involved in antisocial behaviour (Dubow, Edwards, & Ippolito, 1997).
- more likely to do poorly in school (Marsh & Yeung, 1997).

In looking at these outcomes, we need to be cautious about stating that each is caused by low self-esteem. In fact, in many cases, low self-esteem contributes to the outcome but is, itself, also caused by the outcome. Poor school performance is a case in point: Over time, children who are unskilled academically do not keep up in school, which causes a drop in their academic self-esteem, making them less confident and probably less successful in future school learning (Marsh & Yeung, 1997). The same kind of negative spiralling probably applies to the peer relationships in children with low self-esteem. Poor social skills lead to peer rejection, reducing self-esteem in the peer context and disrupting future peer interactions.

Understanding this complex pattern is important in deciding how to help children with low self-esteem. Some children could benefit from psychotherapy or other more social interventions meant to increase self-esteem. We need to remember that all children have some talents that can be nurtured. Taking the time to recognize each child creates the feeling of "being special" that promotes self-esteem in the child.

Ask Yourself

How do the long-term consequences of low self-esteem show connections between cognitive, social, and emotional development?

What kinds of activities or interventions might be helpful to prevent children from negatively spiralling in academic or social domains as a result of low self-esteem?

13.2 Relationships with Peers

∨ Learning Objectives

After reading the module, you should be able to do the following:

LO5 Understand how peer interactions change and grow during middle school.

LO6 Explain why children become friends and the value of friendship.

LO7 Identify why some children are more popular than others and the causes and consequences of being rejected.

LO8 Explain the origins of prejudice.

When children attend elementary school, the context of peer relations changes dramatically. Not only does the sheer number of peers increase dramatically, but children are often also exposed to a far more diverse set of peers than before. In addition, children find themselves interacting with peers in situations that range from reasonably structured with adult supervision (e.g., a classroom) to largely unstructured with minimal adult supervision (e.g., a playground during recess). Children's relationships change over time, usually becoming smoother as they get older and as they gain a greater understanding of other people's points of view. However, online relationships also become a factor for many students, as well as safety, especially since self-disclosure online tends to be greater at younger ages (Nosko, Wood, & Molema, 2010). In this module, we'll examine the changes in children's relationships with peers. Then we'll look at friendship and popularity.

An Overview of Peer Interactions in Middle Childhood

LO5 Understand how peer interactions change and grow during middle school.

An obvious change in children's peer relations during middle childhood is that children get along better than when they were younger. When conflicts arise, children in middle childhood are better able to resolve them because of their greater cognitive and social skills. Why? Perspective-taking is the key. As children move beyond the preschool years, they realize that others see the world differently, both literally and figuratively. Robert Selman (1980, 1981) drew upon Piaget's theory to explain how perspective-taking improves during childhood. According to Selman, preschool children sometimes know that two people can have different perspectives, but they may confuse the two perspectives. However, by the elementary school years, children know that perspectives differ because people have access to different information. Imagine two classmates: One is excited about a class field trip but the second is sad because she knows the trip has been cancelled. In the middle years, children understand that the children feel differently because only the second child knows that the trip has been cancelled.

Later in middle childhood, children take another step forward in their perspective-taking. Now they can see themselves as others do. Because older children are able to take another's perspective and to see themselves in others' eyes, social interactions are easier and conflicts can be resolved when they do arise.

One important finding, however, is that maltreatment and abuse can significantly impair children's development in this area, making it difficult for them to take another person's perspective (Burack et al., 2006). The more externalizing and internalizing problems maltreated youth demonstrated, the more difficulty they experienced in forming new relationships with others (Burack et al., 2006).

Because children in middle childhood are learning how to get along better and are becoming more mature, they tend to spend more and more time with peers without being under direct adult supervision. In one study (Zarbatany, Hartmann, & Rankin, 1990), investigators asked Canadian students in Grades 5 and 6 how they spent their time with peers. The students in the study indicated how often they participated with peers in each of 29 different activities. The results, shown in Figure 13–3, are not too surprising. The most common activities with peers are simple—just spending time together and talking to each other.

The figure also highlights another important feature of peer relations during middle childhood. Children reported that they played physical games a few times each week, which reflects, in part, the emergence of a special type of play at this point in development. In rough-and-tumble play, children playfully chase, punch, kick, shove, fight, and wrestle with peers. Notice "playfully" in this definition: Unlike aggression, where the intention is to do harm, rough-and-tumble play is for fun. When children are involved in rough-and-tumble play, they are usually smiling and sometimes laughing (Pellegrini & Smith, 1998). When parents or teachers intervene, the youngsters usually explain that there's no problem; they're just playing. Rough-and-tumble play is more common among boys than girls, and girls' rough-and-tumble play tends to emphasize running and chasing over wrestling and fighting.

Figure 13–3

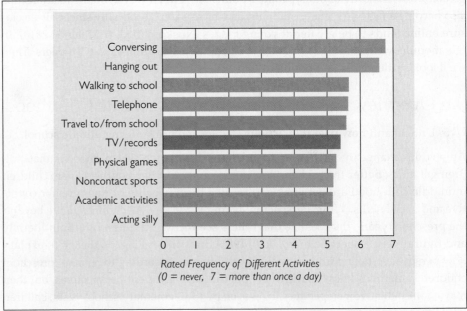

Rated Frequency of Different Activities
(0 = never, 7 = more than once a day)

SOURCE: Based on data from Zarbatany, L., Hartmann, D. P., & Rankin, D. B. (1990). The psychological functions of preadolescent peer activities. Child Development, 61, 1067–1080.

Friendship

LO6 Explain why children become friends and the value of friendship.

Over time, children develop special relationships with certain peers. **Friendship** is a voluntary relationship between two people who like each other. By the time children enter kindergarten, most claim to have a "best friend," which is typically a child they play with who is nice to them. At this point in development, friends tend to be alike in age, gender, and race (Hartup, 1992a), although some evidence points to increasing ethnic segregation with age (Hamm, 2000; Mouw & Entwisle, 2006).

Friendship:
a voluntary relationship based on mutual liking between two people.

Friendships are more common between children from the same race or ethnic group than between children from different groups. Friendships among children of different groups and ages are more common in schools where classes are smaller (Hallinan & Teixeira, 1987). Evidently, when classes are large, children select friends from the large number of available same-race peers. When fewer same-race peers are available in smaller classes, children more often become friends with other-race children. Interracial friendships are usually confined to school, unless children come from integrated neighbourhoods. That is, when children live in different, segregated neighbourhoods, their friendships do not usually extend to out-of-school settings (DuBois & Hirsch, 1990). Immigrant youth have the special challenge of overcoming cultural and language barriers in order to make friends in their new country. For immigrants to North America, increasing proficiency in English is associated with increased ability for youth to broaden social networks and choose friends (Hamm, Brown, & Heck, 2005; Tsai, 2006).

Of course, friends are usually alike not only in age, sex, and race. Children and adolescents are also drawn together because they have similar attitudes toward school, recreation, and the future (Haselager, Hartup, van Lieshout, & Riksen-Walraven, 1998; Newcomb & Bagwell, 1995). As time passes, friends become more similar in their attitudes and values (Hamm, 2000; Kandel, 1978).

Although children's friendships are overwhelmingly with members of their own gender, a few children have friendships with opposite-sex children. Boys and girls are equally likely to have opposite-sex friendships. The important factor in understanding these children is whether they have same- and opposite-sex friends or only opposite-sex friends. Children with same- and opposite-sex friendships tend to be very well adjusted and to have good social skills, whereas children with only opposite-sex friendships tend to be unpopular, less competent academically and socially, and have lower self-esteem. Children who have friends of the opposite gender not only might have difficulties with social skills and popularity; they also could have been rejected by peers and then form friendships with children of the opposite gender as a last resort (Kovacs, Parker, & Hoffman, 1996).

QUALITY AND CONSEQUENCES OF FRIENDSHIP.
The quality and longevity of friendships can vary in childhood. Sometimes friendships are brief because children have the skills to create friendships (they know funny stories, they kid around, they know good gossip) but lack the

Friends usually are alike in gender, age, and race.

SergiyN/Fotolia

skills to sustain them (they can't keep secrets, or they're too bossy) (Jiao, 1999; Parker & Seal, 1996). Sometimes friendships end because, when conflicts arise, children are more concerned about their own interests and are unwilling to compromise or negotiate (Fonzi, Schneider, Tani, & Tomada, 1997; Rose & Asher, 1999). At other times friendships end when children discover that their needs and interests aren't as similar as they thought initially (Gavin & Furman, 1996). Children in middle childhood also develop online friendships with age-peers, which tend to be similar in quality to in-person friendships (Buote, Wood, & Pratt, 2009).

Considering that friendships disintegrate for many reasons, you're probably reminded that truly good friends are to be treasured and valued, even good and safe online friends. Compared to children who lack friends, children with good friends have higher self-esteem, are less likely to be lonely and depressed, and more often act prosocially—sharing and co-operating with others (Hartup & Stevens, 1999; Ladd, 1998). Children with good friends tend to cope better with life stresses, such as the transition from elementary school to middle school or junior high (Berndt & Keefe, 1995), and they're less likely to be victimized by peers (Hodges, Boivin, Vitaro, & Bukowski, 1999). Also, children who have friends can have greater self-worth as young adults (Bagwell, Newcomb, & Bukowski, 1998).

Popularity and Rejection

LO7 **Identify why some children are more popular than others and the causes and consequences of being rejected.**

Good friends provide emotional support.

Popular and rejected children can be found in every classroom and neighbourhood. In fact, studies of popularity (Newcomb, Bukowski, & Pattee, 1993) reveal that most children can be placed in one of five categories:

* Popular children are liked by many classmates.
* Rejected children are disliked by many classmates.
* Controversial children are both liked and disliked by classmates.
* Average children are liked and disliked by some classmates but without the intensity found for popular, rejected, or controversial children.
* Neglected children are ignored by classmates.

Perhaps not surprisingly, smarter and physically attractive children are more often popular (Johnstone, Frame, & Bouman, 1992), but social skill remains key. Popular children are better at initiating social interactions with other children. They are more skillful at communicating and better at integrating themselves into an ongoing conversation or play session.

Popular children also seem skilled in assessing and monitoring their own social impact in various situations and in tailoring their responses to the requirements of new social situations (Ladd, 1998; Wentzel & Asher, 1995). In one study, popular children were more likely than unpopular ones to share, co-operate, and help, and they were less likely to start fights or break rules (Wentzel & Erdley, 1993). In another study, popular children were more likely to take turns and less likely to interrupt others (Black & Logan, 1995).

Unlike popular children, rejected children tend to be socially unskilled (Stormshak et al., 1999). Many rejected children are aggressive and attack peers without provocation (Dodge, Bates, & Pettit, 1990) or demonstrate poor self-control and disruptive behaviour in school (French, 1988, 1990). When conflicts arise, rejected children often become angry and retaliate (Bryant, 1992).

Being well liked as a result of sharing, helping, and being friendly seems straightforward but is not so easy for all children. Are popular behaviours specific to North American children or do they apply more internationally? The Children and Families around the World feature has the answer.

Parents' modelling of aggression hampers children's social skills development.

CONSEQUENCES OF REJECTION.   No one enjoys being rejected. In fact, repeated peer rejection in childhood can have serious long-term consequences (DeRosier, Kupersmidt, & Patterson, 1995; Downey, Lebolt, Rincon, & Freitas, 1998; Ladd, 1998). Rejected youngsters are more likely than youngsters in the other categories to drop out of school, commit juvenile offences, and suffer from psychopathology (Boivin, Hymel, & Bukowski, 1995; Vitaro, Tremblay, & Bukowski, 2001).

CAUSES OF REJECTION.   Peer rejection can be traced, at least in part, to parental influence (Ladd, 1998). Children see how their parents respond to different social situations and often imitate these responses later. Parents who are friendly and cooperative with others demonstrate effective social skills. Parents who are belligerent and combative demonstrate much less effective social skills. In particular, when parents typically respond to interpersonal conflict with intimidation or aggression, their

Children and Families around the World
Keys to Popularity

In Canada, popular children seem to know how to get along with others, and this finding holds for children in many cultures around the world (e.g., Casiglia, Coco, & Zappulla, 1998). Sometimes, however, popular children have other characteristics that are unique to their cultural setting. In Israel, for example, popular children are more likely to be direct and assertive than in other countries (Krispin, Sternberg, & Lamb, 1992). In China, popular children are more likely to be shy than in other countries (Chen, Rubin, & Li, 1995). Evidently, good social skills are at the core of popularity in most countries, but other features reflecting culturally specific values might also be important.

Other factors, such as socialization, can influence how children see themselves in relation to others. Many people in Sweden respect the Law of Jante, also called *jantelagen*. The idea of *jantelagen* is that the self should not be held in esteem above anybody else. Built into the idea of *jantelagen* is that everybody is equal and nobody is any better than anyone else. Swedish children are socialized to understand that,

even if you are skilled at something, you should not talk about yourself or see yourself as superior to others around you.

Jantelagen is related to the Swedish concept of *lagom*, a concept that doesn't really exist in English. In essence, *lagom* is a sign of polite acceptance, meaning something like "just good enough" or "however you serve it will be fine." Essentially, in keeping with the Law of Jante, Swedish people tend to avoid excessive praise or boasting and tend to take the middle path in describing or asking for things. Consequently, if you ask a Swedish man how he likes the tea you served him, he might say, "*Lagom*." If the tea was exceptionally good, the person might say, "*Lagom bra*," meaning "*lagom* good"—complimenting with humility and not wild exuberance, as you might hear in a North American conversation. However, if you asked a Swedish person if he wanted that tea very hot or cool, you might get the same response, "*Lagom*." In such a culture, children are taught not to make great interpersonal demands. A kind of interpersonal humility or self-effacement is built into the culture, and children become very aware of this expectation from an early age.

Table 13–1 Correlations between Children's Popularity and Rejection in Grades 3 to 6 and Academic Achievement, Social Skill, and Self-Worth

Outcome	Popularity in Grades 3 to 6	Rejection in Grades 3 to 6
Academic achievement	0.27	−0.25
Social skill	0.24	0.03
Self-worth	0.24	−0.22

SOURCE: Republished with permission of John Wiley & Sons, Inc., from Patricia Morison, Ann S. Masten, Peer Reputation in Middle Childhood as a Predictor of Adaptation in Adolescence: A Seven-Year Follow-up. *Child Development*, John Wiley and Sons, Oct 1, 1991, Copyright © 1991, John Wiley and Sons. Permission conveyed through Copyright Clearance Center, Inc.

children may imitate them, hampering their development of social skills and making them less popular in the long run (Keane, Brown, & Crenshaw, 1990).

Morison and Masten (1991) studied long-term consequences of children's level of popularity. Table 13–1 shows the correlations between popularity and rejection in Grades 3 to 6 and academic achievement, social skill, and self-worth measured seven years later. Children who were popular in Grades 3 to 6 were doing well in school, were socially skilled, and had high self-esteem seven years later.

In contrast, children who were rejected in Grades 3 to 6 were not doing well in school and had low self-esteem. Over time, popular children's prosocial skill pays long-term dividends; unfortunately, rejected children's lack of prosocial skill comes with a price as well.

Parents' disciplinary practices also affect their children's social skill and popularity. Inconsistent discipline—punishing a child for misbehaving one day and ignoring the same behaviour the next—is associated with antisocial and aggressive behaviour, paving the way to rejection (Dishion, 1990). Consistent punishment that is tied to parental love and affection is more likely to promote social skill and, in the process, popularity (Dekovic & Janssens, 1992).

In sum, parenting can lead to an aggressive interpersonal style in a child, which in turn leads to peer rejection. The implication, then, is that by teaching youngsters (and their parents) more effective ways of interacting with others, we can make rejection less likely. With improved social skills, rejected children might not resort to antisocial behaviours. Unpopular children can be taught how to initiate interaction, communicate clearly, and be friendly instead of whining and fighting. Learning skills that lead to peer acceptance can prevent long-term harm associated with being rejected (LaGreca, 1993; Mize & Ladd, 1990).

Prejudice

LO8 Explain the origins of prejudice.

By the preschool years, most children can distinguish males from females and can identify people from different ethnic groups (Aboud, 1993). Once children learn their membership in a specific group—"I'm a Vietnamese Canadian boy"—their view of children from other groups becomes more negative. **Prejudice** is a negative view of others based on their membership in a specific group.

Kindergarten children more often attribute positive traits (being friendly and smart) to their own group and negative traits (being mean and fighting a lot) to other groups (Bigler, Jones, & Lobliner, 1997; Black-Gutman & Hickson, 1996). During the elementary school years, prejudice usually declines somewhat (Powlishta, Serbin, Doyle, & White, 1994) due to changes in cognitive development. Preschoolers usually view people in social groups as more homogeneous (alike) than they really are and not as good as people from the child's own group. Older children understand that people in social groups are heterogeneous: They know that individual people—for example, Dene Canadians, girls, obese children—are not all alike. Plus, they have

Prejudice:
a negative view of others based on their membership in a specific group.

learned that people from different groups may be more alike than people from the same group. Gary, a boy of Saulteaux ancestry whose passion is computers, finds that he enjoys being with Victor, a second-generation Italian Canadian who shares his love of computers, but not Curtis, another Saulteaux boy whose passion is music. As children realize that social groups consist of all kinds of different people, prejudice lessens.

Prejudice may be less pronounced in older children, but it does not vanish. Older children remain biased positively toward their own group and negatively toward others (Powlishta et al., 1994). Of course, many adults have these same biases, and children frequently reflect the attitudes of those people who have the most influence on them, such as parents and grandparents.

One way to lessen prejudice is to encourage friendly and constructive contact between children from different groups (Ramsey, 1995). Adults can create situations in which children from different groups work together toward common goals in school, sports, or other activities. That being said, much of the research on prejudice occurs in laboratories and not in real-life scenarios (Paluck & Green, 2009). In their recent review of the psychological literature on prejudice, Paluck and Green (2009) noted that interventions designed to reduce prejudice are rarely evaluated using experimental methods. These researchers pointed out that the most promising types of interventions designed to reduce prejudice include reading about other cultures/people, co-operative learning activities, and the use of media to foster more positive attitudes between people of different cultures and lifestyles.

Increased interaction between children of different racial backgrounds was one of the consequences of the U.S. Supreme Court's decision in *Brown v. Board of Education*, a case that shows how child-development research influenced social policy. In 1950, African American children in most American states attended segregated schools, as had been the law for over 100 years. In the fall of 1950, the chapter of the National Association for the Advancement of Colored People (NAACP) in Topeka, Kansas, decided to test the constitutionality of the law. Thirteen African American parents, including Oliver Brown, attempted to enrol their children in White-only schools but were turned away.

The NAACP sued the Topeka Board of Education, arguing that segregation was harmful to African American children because it legitimized their second-class status. The NAACP pointed to Kenneth B. Clark's (1945; Clark & Clark, 1940) research finding that African American children, including those attending segregated schools in Topeka, typically thought White dolls were nice but Black dolls were bad. In May 1954, the U.S. Supreme Court rendered the landmark decision that segregated schools were unconstitutional. The impact of Clark's research and testimony was evident in the decision in *Brown v. Board of Education*.

In 1989, the Convention on the Rights of the Child became the first legally binding international instrument to address children's rights across civil, economic, cultural, political, and social areas. The Convention identifies the basic human rights to which children everywhere are entitled, including the right to survival; to develop to the fullest; to protection from harm, abuse, and exploitation; and to have full participation in family, cultural, and social life (see UNICEF, www.unicef.org/crc). These rights are rooted in four principles: (1) nondiscrimination, (2) the best interests of the child, (3) respect for the child's views, and (4) the right to life, survival, and development. The Convention defines types of rights but does not specify how those rights should be achieved in any one case.

In Canada, many groups, such as Free the Children, are dedicated to protecting the rights of children. In addition, child advocate positions have been created in many provinces. Children's advocates are involved in investigations of rights violations, public education, systemic policy and service reviews, and in other ways that enhance

AP Images

Dr. Kenneth B. Clark

the views and voice of children in Canadian society (Parker-Loewen, 2005). The actions of children's advocates may influence how services are delivered to children or what kinds of public policies are developed.

The primary goal of children's advocacy in Canada is to create an office with legislative authority to review children's rights issues with respect to children who receive services from agencies of a provincial government (Parker-Loewen, 2005). Not many people would argue with such a goal; however, how that goal is achieved is the source of much disagreement. Sometimes people's ideals clash, and people do not always agree about the relative rights of children versus that of parents or other organizations.

Unfortunately, children can be caught between warring government agencies or other parties and can be traumatized by decisions the children themselves are powerless to change. On the other hand, children also can learn to manipulate these very systems to their own advantage or detriment. The more children are exposed to official agencies and systems, the better they become at "working the system"—and the system, however seemingly beneficent, does not always actually work to their advantage.

Ask Yourself

What do the long-term consequences of being rejected tell us about continuity of development?

Around what issues might children's and parents' rights conflict? How might these issues be resolved?

What are the benefits and risks of promoting children's wants, needs, and interests above all else through official advocacy systems?

13.3 Helping Others

∨ Learning Objectives

After reading the module, you should be able to do the following:

LO9 List the skills children need to behave prosocially.

LO10 Describe the types of situations that influence children's prosocial behaviour.

LO11 Describe how parents can foster prosocial behaviour in their children.

Prosocial behaviour:
actions that promote harmony in a social group.

Altruism:
prosocial behaviour that helps another with no direct benefit to the individual performing the behaviour.

Most parents, teachers, and religions try to teach children to act co-operatively and generously in most situations. Actions that promote harmony in a social group are known as **prosocial behaviour**. Of course, co-operation often works because individuals gain more than they would by not co-operating. **Altruism** is a particular kind of prosocial behaviour whereby one person helps another with no direct benefit to the individual performing the behaviour. Altruism is driven by feelings of responsibility for other people. Two youngsters pooling their funds to buy a candy bar to share demonstrates co-operative behaviour. One youngster giving half her lunch to a friend who forgot his demonstrates altruism.

As a general rule, intentions to act prosocially increase with age, as do children's strategies for helping. Of course, children do not always respond to the needs of others. Some children attach greater priority to looking out for their own interests, while others are more likely to help out. In this module, you'll learn some of the factors that promote children's prosocial behaviour.

Skills Underlying Prosocial Behaviour

LO9 List the skills children need to behave prosocially.

Think back to an occasion when you helped someone. How did you know that the person needed help? Why did you decide to help? Although you didn't realize it at the time, your decision to help was probably based on some important skills:

"When my kids get out of line, I threaten to start a 'My Space' page and invite their friends."

Marty Bucella/CartoonStock Ltd.

- *Perspective-taking.* In Module 13.2, you learned about Selman's description of age-related improvements in perspective-taking. By the elementary-school years, children understand that people have different views, and they are able to see themselves as others do. In general, the better children understand the thoughts and feelings of other people, the more willing they are to share and help others (Eisenberg, 1988). For example, seeing an elderly adult trying to carry many packages, children in middle childhood might help because they can envision that carrying many things is a burden.

- *Empathy.* The ability to understand another person's emotions is **empathy**. Children who can appreciate another person's fear, disappointment, sorrow, or loneliness are more inclined to help than children who do not understand these emotions (Kochanska, Padavich, & Koenig, 1996; Roberts & Strayer, 1996). Parents who model positive, well-regulated emotional expression tend to have children with higher empathy and socio-emotional competence (Eisenberg et al., 2003; Michalik et al., 2007).

Empathy:
the ability to understand another person's emotions.

In sum, children who help others tend to be better able to take another's view and to appreciate another's emotions. Of course, perspective-taking and empathy do not guarantee that children always act altruistically. Even though children have the skills needed to act altruistically, they might not because of the particular situation, as we'll see in the next section.

Situational Influences

LO10 Describe the types of situations that influence children's prosocial behaviour.

Kind children occasionally disappoint us by being cruel, and children who are usually stingy sometimes surprise us by their generosity. Why? The setting helps determine whether children act altruistically. If children feel responsible to the person in need, such as a sibling or friend, they are more likely to help that person (Costin & Jones, 1992). Children

Connor Cottrell

Children can be very sensitive to the emotions and experiences of others.

also might act altruistically when they feel that they have the skills necessary to help the person in need (Peterson, 1983) and are feeling happy and successful (Moore, Underwood, & Rosenhan, 1973).

Suppose, for example, that a child is growing more and more upset because she can't figure out how to work a computer game. A nearby boy who knows little about computer games is not likely to help because he doesn't know what to do and could end up looking foolish (Peterson, 1983). He also is not likely to help if he had just made a mistake on the computer or failed at a task (Moore et al., 1973).

Finally, children act altruistically when their actions involve few or modest sacrifices: A child who has received an undesirable snack is more inclined to share it than one who has received a highly desirable snack (Eisenberg & Shell, 1986). Therefore, children are most likely to help when they feel responsible to the person in need, have the skills that are needed, are happy, and do not think they have to give up a lot by helping. They are least likely to help when they feel neither responsible nor capable of helping, are in a bad mood, or believe that helping will require a large personal sacrifice.

So far, we've seen that altruistic behaviour is determined by children's skills (such as perspective-taking) and by characteristics of situations (such as whether children feel competent to help in a particular situation). Whether children are altruistic is also determined by socialization, the topic of the next section.

Socializing Prosocial Behaviour

LO11 Describe how parents can foster prosocial behaviour in their children.

Dr. Martin Luther King Jr. said that his pursuit of civil rights for African Americans was particularly influenced by three people: Henry David Thoreau (a nineteenth-century American philosopher), Mohandas Gandhi (the leader of the Indian movement for independence from England), and his father, Dr. Martin Luther King Sr. Fostering prosocial behaviour in the child begins, first and foremost, in the child's home through reasoning, modelling, positive emotional expression, and praise. Parents whose favoured disciplinary strategy is reasoning tend to have children who behave prosocially (Hoffman, 1988, 1994). Repeated exposure to reasoning during discipline seems to promote children's ability to take the perspective of others (Hoffman, 1988).

Reasoning is one way that parents can influence prosocial behaviour; modelling is another. Children imitate others' behaviour, including prosocial behaviour. In laboratory studies, children imitate their peers' altruism (Wilson, Piazza, & Nagle, 1990). For example, children are more likely to donate toys to hospitalized children or to help older adults with household chores when they see other children doing so.

Of course, parents are the models to whom children are most continuously exposed, so they exert a powerful influence. For example, parents who report frequent feelings of warmth and concern for others tend to have children who experience stronger feelings of empathy (Eisenberg, Fabes, Schaller, Carlo, & Miller, 1991). When a mother is helpful and responsive, her children often imitate her by being co-operative, helpful, generous, and less critical of others (Bryant & Crockenberg, 1980). In addition, children's behaviour also has a reciprocal influence on how others, including parents, then behave toward them (Grusec, 1991).

Perhaps the most obvious way to foster sharing and other altruistic behaviour in children is to reward them directly for acts of generosity. Many parents reward prosocial acts with

Praise for behaviour and disposition can increase prosocial actions.

Table 13–2 Factors Contributing to Children's Prosocial Behaviour

General Category	Types of Influence	Children are more likely to help when . . .
Skills	Perspective-taking	they can take another person's point of view.
	Empathy	they feel another person's emotions.
Situational Influences	Feelings of responsibility	they feel responsible to the person in need.
	Feelings of competence	they feel competent to help.
	Mood	they're in the mood.
	Cost of altruism	the cost of prosocial behaviour is smaller.
Parents' Influence	Disciplinary strategy	parents use reasoning as their primary form of discipline.
	Emotional regulation	parents express emotion appropriately, especially positive emotion.
	Modelling	parents behave prosocially themselves.
	Reward	parents reward prosocial behaviour.

praise. Particularly effective is **dispositional praise**, linking the child's altruistic behaviour to an underlying altruistic disposition or characteristic of the person. For example, a parent might say, "Thanks for helping me make breakfast; I knew I could count on you because you are such a helpful person." When children repeatedly hear remarks like this, they are afforded an opportunity to see the value of these characteristics for themselves and so internalize them. When children begin to believe that they really are helpful (or nice or friendly), they are more likely to behave in a prosocial manner in situations where such behaviour would be expected or appropriate (Mills & Grusec, 1989).

Dispositional praise: linking the child's altruistic behaviour to an underlying altruistic characteristic of the person.

As you can see from Table 13–2, a variety of factors contribute to children's prosocial behaviour.

Ask Yourself

Despite parental influence, altruism also depends on characteristics of children themselves. Describe some of these characteristics.

What are some ways that parents can model good emotion regulation for their children?

13.4 Aggression

 ## Learning Objectives

After reading the module, you should be able to do the following:

LO12 Identify the forms of aggressive behaviour common during middle childhood.

LO13 Identify how families, television, and the child's own thoughts contribute to aggression.

LO14 Note why some children become victims of aggression.

If you think back to your years in elementary school, you can probably remember a class "bully," a child or, more often, a group of children who dominated other children

Aggression:
externalized behaviour meant
to harm others.

Assertiveness:
goal-directed behaviour that
respects the rights of others.

with threatening or demeaning acts. Such acts typify **aggression**, externalized behaviour meant to harm others. Aggressiveness is not the same as assertiveness, even though people often use these words interchangeably. You've probably heard praise for an "aggressive businessperson" or a ballplayer "aggressive at running the bases." Psychologists would call these behaviours assertive, not aggressive. **Assertiveness** is goal-directed behaviour to further the legitimate interests of individuals or the groups they represent while respecting the rights of others. Aggressive behaviour—physical, social, or verbal—is intended to harm, damage, dominate, or injure, and it violates the rights of others.

In this module, we will examine aggressive behaviour in children and, in the process, learn more about the impact of TV watching on behaviour.

The Nature of Children's Aggressive Behaviour

LO12 Identify the forms of aggressive behaviour common during middle childhood.

Instrumental aggression:
when a child uses aggression
to achieve an explicit goal.

Reactive aggression:
when one child's behaviour leads to another child's aggression.

Preschool children often use aggression to resolve their conflicts, and bullying (unprovoked aggression) emerges during the preschool years (Rubin et al., 2003). Two other forms of aggression are also seen in elementary school children. In **instrumental aggression**, a child uses aggression to achieve an explicit goal. Instrumental aggression would include shoving a child to get to the head of a lunch line or grabbing a toy away from another child. In **reactive aggression**, a child reacts aggressively to another child's behaviour. For example, a child who loses a game kicks the child who won.

Marini and colleagues from Brock University (2006) found that one factor really distinguished bullies from bullied youth or youth not involved in bullying: Bullies tended to believe that bullying and angry-aggressive coping behaviour were legitimate ways of acting toward others. In addition, the parents of bullies tended to have less knowledge of their children's behaviour around others than did parents of nonbullies.

Relational aggression:
hurting another person by
damaging that person's social
relationships.

Bullying and aggression are most likely to be expressed physically in younger children. As children grow older, they more often use language to express themselves. A particularly common form of verbal aggression is **relational aggression**, in which children, typically girls, hurt others by undermining their social relationships. For example, children might tell friends to avoid a child, gossip, or make hurtful remarks, such as "Everyone hates you!" (Crick & Werner, 1998; Galen & Underwood, 1997).

Verbal aggression definitely occurs more often as children grow, but physical aggression still occurs during middle childhood among both girls and boys. In one study, Grades 4 and 7 boys reported that nearly 50 percent of their conflicts with other boys involved physical aggression (Cairns, Cairns, Neckerman, Ferguson, & Gariépy, 1989). Mishna (2003) found that children with learning disabilities are particularly at risk for being bullied.

Although forms of aggression change with development, individual children's tendencies to behave aggressively are moderately stable, especially among boys. Kupersmidt and Coie (1990) measured aggressiveness in a group of 11-year-olds by having children list the names of classmates who frequently started fights. Seven years later, more than half the aggressive children had police records, compared to less than 10 percent of the nonaggressive children.

In another study, Stattin and Magnusson (1989) asked teachers to rate the aggression of over a thousand 10-year-olds. Their results, shown in Figure 13–4, indicate that teachers' ratings accurately predicted subsequent criminal activity. Boys in the least aggressive group committed relatively few criminal offences of any sort, while two-thirds of the most aggressive boys had committed offences, and nearly half

Figure 13-4

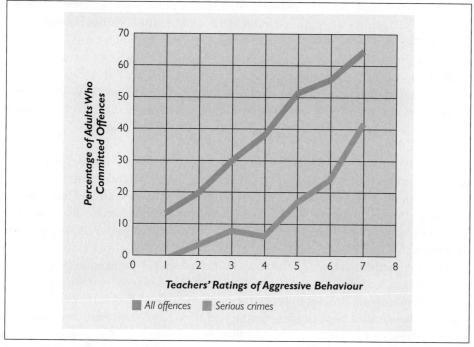

SOURCE: Based on data from Stattin, H., & Magnusson, D. (1989). The role of early aggressive behavior in the frequency, seriousness, and types of later crime. *Journal of Consulting and Clinical Psychology, 57,* 710–718.

had committed major offences, such as assault, theft, or robbery. Overall, girls committed far fewer offences, but teachers' ratings of aggressive behaviour still predicted which girls were more likely to have criminal records.

Findings from these and similar studies show that aggression is not simply a case of playful pushing and shoving that most children outgrow. On the contrary, a small minority of children who are highly aggressive develop into young adults who create havoc in society.

The Impact of Aggression on Children

LO13 Identify how families, television, and the child's own thoughts contribute to aggression.

For many years, psychologists believed that aggression was caused by frustration. The idea was that when children or adults were blocked from achieving a goal, they became frustrated and aggressed, often against the interfering person or object. Although frustration can lead to aggression (Berkowitz, 1989), researchers no longer believe that it's the sole cause of aggression; therefore, investigators have looked to other causes, including the family, television, and the child's own thoughts.

AGGRESSION IN FAMILIES. Early family experiences are a prime training ground for learning patterns of aggression. The pioneering research on family aggression was conducted by Gerald Patterson (1984), whose findings were based almost entirely on careful, systematic observation of aggressive children in their home environments. One fact that comes through clearly in Patterson's work is that parents and siblings play an enormous role in cultivating aggressive behaviour in children, and in ways that are subtle as well as obvious. Many parents and older siblings, for example, use physical punishment or threats to stop aggressive behaviour. Although the immediate effect might be to suppress aggression, physical punishment also serves as a model, vividly demonstrating that physical force "works" as a means of controlling others. The parent is saying, in effect, "You were right. The best way to get people to do what you want, or to stop them from doing what you don't want, is to hit them hard enough."

Not surprisingly, parents' use of harsh physical punishment is associated with aggressive behaviour in children. Dodge, Bates, and Pettit (1990) studied children who were so harshly punished physically that they were bruised or needed medical treatment. These children were rated twice as aggressive by both teachers and peers as children who had not experienced such harsh punishment. But strong or aggressive parental responses are not essential in making a child aggressive. When parents are coercive, unresponsive, and emotionally uninvested, their children are more likely to be aggressive as well (Hart, Nelson, Robinson, Olsen, & McNeilly-Choque, 1998; Rubin et al., 1998).

In many families with aggressive children, a vicious cycle seems to develop. Compared to families with nonaggressive children, both aggressive children and their parents are more likely to respond to neutral behaviour with aggression. Furthermore, once an aggressive exchange has begun, both parents and children are likely to escalate the exchange rather than break it off. Once a child has been labelled aggressive by parents and others, that child is more likely to be accused of aggression and singled out for punishment, even when the child has been behaving entirely appropriately (Patterson, 1984). The "aggressive child" will be accused of everything that goes wrong, from missing cookies to broken appliances, and other children's misbehaviours will be ignored. Nevertheless, Serbin and Karp (2003) demonstrated that children of parents who themselves have a history of aggression in childhood tend to have ongoing difficulties with social, behavioural, and health concerns. Serbin and Karp noted that children with parents who are involved with them, are nurturing and warm, and provide cognitive stimulation do not show the same pattern of problems often seen in aggressive children:

> In families with aggressive children, a vicious cycle often develops in which parents and children respond to neutral behaviour aggressively and escalate aggressive exchanges.

Also interested in the effects of parenting practices on children, Patterson (1984) emphasized that hitting a child for aggression does not usually inhibit aggression for very long. Instead, the best response to a child's aggression is to discourage it either by ignoring it or by giving a consequence for it while encouraging and rewarding other forms of nonaggressive social behaviour. An older brother who simply grabs the remote control from a younger sister should be given a consequence ("No TV for one day!") and then shown a better way to resolve the conflict ("Wait until your sister finishes her program, then ask if you can change the channel. If she says no, come see me."). Later, the child should be praised for co-operating rather than aggressing ("Thanks for asking your sister instead of just grabbing the remote control.").

Parents are not the only family members who influence children's aggression—siblings matter too. Among aggressive children, those who have good relationships with their siblings tend to be less aggressive and better adjusted than aggressive children who experience considerable sibling conflict (Stormshak et al., 1996). Good sibling relationships can provide aggressive children with opportunities to improve their social skills, or they can provide emotional support for aggressive youngsters.

Finally, children can elicit some of the very parental behaviours that foster their aggression. In evocative gene–environment interactions, children inherit characteristics that make some experiences more likely than others. With aggression, adoption and twin studies point to hereditary components in aggression (Deater-Deckard & Plomin, 1999; Rowe, Almeida, & Jacobson, 1999). Some children inherit a tendency to be impulsive, to have an angry temperament, or to regulate their own behaviour poorly. These characteristics can lead parents to react to these children more harshly, which then can provoke more aggression in the child (Ge, Conger, Cadoret, Neiderhiser, & Stewart, 1996). Thus, both parents and child contribute to a vicious circle of escalating aggression.

What is crucial to recognize, however, about parent–child aggression is that the parent, being a mature adult, is the responsible party. As angry or as hostile as a young child might become, it is the parent's responsibility to remain in control and to demonstrate appropriate emotional and behavioural self-regulation. There is no excuse for out-of-control aggression by a parent, as such abuse constitutes child maltreatment, which is illegal in Canada.

ABUSE OF CHILDREN. Child maltreatment comes in many forms (Goodman, Emery, & Haugaard, 1998). The two types of maltreatment are physical abuse, involving assault that leads to bodily injury, and sexual abuse, involving fondling, intercourse, other sexual behaviours, or exposure to sexual information that is not appropriate for a child's level of development. Another form of maltreatment is neglect, including lack of proper supervision and failure to give children adequate food, clothing, attention, nurturance, or medical care. Children can also be harmed by psychological abuse—ridicule, rejection, degradation, humiliation, and exposure to family violence. The frequency of these various forms of maltreatment is difficult to estimate because so many cases go unreported, and mandatory reporting requirements of suspected abuse differs markedly across countries and child-welfare jurisdictions (Rankin & Ornstein, 2009).

Abuse is wrong in any language.

The Canadian Incidence Study of Reported Child Abuse and Neglect was the first nationwide study of the incidence of child maltreatment in our country (Health Canada, 2001a). Of the cases in Canada that were reported and included in the most recent update of this study, 36 percent were substantiated through child and family service investigations, and 8 percent remained in "suspected" status. Approximately 30 percent of cases were determined to be unsubstantiated reports of abuse (Public Health Agency of Canada, 2010). The Public Health Agency of Canada (2010) found evidence of physical abuse in 20 percent of child maltreatment cases, sexual abuse in 3 percent, neglect in 34 percent, and emotional abuse in 9 percent.

Factors most likely to predict substantiation of a maltreatment allegation include the presence of emotional or physical harm to a child, police referral, and the existence of at least one prior substantiated maltreatment investigation (Trocmé, Knoke, Fallon, & MacLaurin, 2009; see also Fluke, 2009). Caregiver factors, such as lack of caregiver co-operation in the investigation, and housing risk factors, such as poor housing, increased the likelihood that an allegation of abuse would be investigated, but they were not helpful in distinguishing between cases that would end up being substantiated and those that would not (Trocmé et al., 2009; see also Fuller & Nieto, 2009).

Other researchers (Cross & Casanueva, 2009; Fakunmoju, 2009; Kohl, Johnson-Reid, & Drake, 2009) have suggested that child welfare agencies ought not to focus solely on the issue of substantiation of abuse but to focus instead on recording and addressing service needs of families as well as recommendations for possible further analysis of a situation in family court.

ESB Professional/Shutterstock

Poverty is associated with increased risk for maltreatment.

Children who experience abuse are faced with a number of developmental challenges. First of all, the abuse itself can cause lasting physical, emotional, social, and cognitive impairments. As a result of the emotional effects of abuse, children often have difficulty with peer relationships, in part because they can become too withdrawn or too aggressive (Bolger, Patterson, & Kupersmidt, 1998; Parker & Herrera, 1996). As you might suspect, emotional regulation can be difficult for children who have experienced abuse, as they often have not had good models for control of emotion and coping with negative emotions. Finally, children who experience abuse often live in a state of ongoing stress and anxiety, which can have a marked effect on their ability to concentrate at school. Maltreated children tend to have lower grades in school, score lower on standardized achievement tests, and be retained in a grade rather than promoted. Also, school-related behaviour problems, such as being disruptive in class, are common (Goodman et al., 1998; Trickett & McBride-Chang, 1995).

While abuse can have a broad and pervasive influence in a child's life, certain protective factors can improve the child's resiliency during development in the face of difficult life circumstances. As you will see in the Children and Families around the World feature, some organizations are trying to develop ways to help abused children access the assistance of adults who can help them. Knowing how to reach out for help is an important protective factor for children experiencing abuse. Another very important protective factor is for the child to have a strong, supportive relationship with a caring adult while growing up (Werner, 1992, 1993, 1996).

According to Pearce and Pezzot-Pearce (2005), child maltreatment, whether physical, sexual, emotional, or neglectful, constitutes a problem with serious legal, medical, and psychosocial implications for affected children and society in general. Maltreatment threatens the development of secure attachment relationships, particularly between 6 and 12 months of age—a critical time for attachment during infant development. As Pearce and Pezzot-Pearce (2005, p. 425) pointed out, abused infants and toddlers come to know the world as "a dangerous, malevolent place where the child's signals for help are ignored or met with angry or even aggressive outbursts from the

Children and Families around the World

Aid to Children and Adolescents at Risk

In Spain, the Aid to Children and Adolescents at Risk Foundation is trying to make a difference in how children experiencing abuse can help themselves. This organization has begun to install specialized billboard advertising that delivers one message to adults and a different message to children. The idea is based on the average heights of adults compared to the average heights of children. The system is not perfect, as adults who are under 4 feet

5 inches see the child-focused message; however, on average, the idea works.

The billboards are based on a lenticular top layer that shows one image to an adult and a bottom layer that shows a different image to a child. The adult sees an anti-child abuse ad with a photo of a child's face on it. The child sees the same ad, but the child's face has bruises on it. Text is included on the child's version, encouraging the child to call a child abuse hotline and providing the phone number. These ads are now being shown in other nations as well, such as in Mexico.

caregiver." Children with insecure attachments are at further risk for problems establishing stable relationships and regulating emotions.

Pearce and Pezzot-Pearce (2005) noted that maltreated children frequently exhibit both internalizing and externalizing behaviour. Internalizing problems might include suicidal ideation, depression, and anxiety, particularly in maltreated children who feel acutely ashamed or guilty about the abuse. Symptoms of externalizing behaviour might include physical aggression and sexualized behaviour. Neglect also has an impact on cognitive development, academic adjustment, and development of language. In addition, anxiety and neurological damage from physical attacks can affect attention, concentration, and learning (Pearce & Pezzot-Pearce, 2005).

No singular symptom or group of symptoms can accurately identify maltreated children (Pearce & Pezzot-Pearce, 2005). Some maltreated children demonstrate greater resiliency than others, with some showing few problems and others showing increasing problems over time. Maltreatment is a significant risk factor among the many that interact together to influence development, but the family's response to a disclosure of child maltreatment powerfully predicts how a child will cope. Supportive parents who protect their children and arrange for necessary services tend to have children with better outcomes than children whose parents blame them or disbelieve their disclosures of maltreatment (Pearce & Pezzot-Pearce, 2005). In the Making Children's Lives Better feature, prepared by Drs. Pearce and Pezzot-Pearce, you will learn more about lessening the effects of abuse on children.

Making Children's Lives Better

How Can We Help Children Who Have Experienced Abuse?

Maltreatment affects children's development in many ways. Psychologists must be prepared to address a variety of problematic behaviours, intervene in different settings and environments, and be mindful that therapy should never be conducted in isolation from the child's family or caregivers. How the family responds to the child is of critical importance. Psychologists must help caregivers manage their own reactions and develop adaptive parenting strategies that promote better functioning in their children. The following are key features of effective therapy with maltreated children:

- Therapy must be developmentally sensitive as well as sensitive to the child's and family's cultural traditions.
- A child and family require individualized intervention plans that identify specific goals and strategies.
- Therapy must help maltreated children reformulate the meaning of the abuse and develop healthier and more adaptive ways of coping with feelings and thoughts associated with it (e.g., self-blame).
- Children must be allowed to identify and express their thoughts, feelings, and anxiety, which can then be extinguished, as it is no longer associated with the traumatic experiences.
- Play therapy can elicit less anxiety in young children than talk therapy, which is more suited to older children.
- Play therapy—using drawings, puppet play, or small dolls—may afford the child a safe distance from traumatic events: It happened to the doll, not the child.

- Self-talk strategies can help children stop their maladaptive behaviours, generate prosocial behavioural strategies, and then implement those strategies.
- Development of empathy in school-age children may help them inhibit aggressive or sexual responses to others.
- Correcting the child's cognitive distortions about the abuse (e.g., self-blame) can be a first step in developing realistic self-protection strategies to reduce the probability of revictimization as well as feelings of powerlessness and inadequacy.
- The therapeutic relationship between the child and the psychologist can help change the child's understanding of relationships, especially for youngsters with insecure attachments who expect others to abuse or exploit them.
- A psychologist who is sensitive to the child's feelings, promotes a sense of safety and predictability in therapy sessions, and limits the child's aggressive behaviour in nonpunitive but firm ways is initiating a process to help the child to see others in a new way. However, caregivers close to the child also need to participate in this process so that the child's positive experiences are not limited to the therapy room but occur in the wider environment as well.

Source: Based on Pearce, J. W., & Pezzot-Pearce, T. D. (2005). How can we help children who have experienced abuse? In R. V. Kail, & T. Zolner (Eds.), *Children* (pp. 424–428). Toronto: Pearson Education Canada.

Mallory Skrip

Cartoons can be very violent.

IMPACT OF TELEVISION.   Most children watch television regularly by the time they're 3 years old, and, by the time they turn 15, most have spent more time watching television than going to school! In fact, throughout childhood they will have spent more time watching television than in any other activity except sleep (Liebert & Sprafkin, 1988).

Most North American children spend considerable time watching action-adventure programs that contain a heavy dose of modelled aggression. Heroes on these shows almost invariably end up in a fight with the villains, with the heroes usually winning and being rewarded with praise, admiration, and goodies for their aggressive behaviour. In fact, children's cartoons typically show one violent act every three minutes (with "violence" meaning use of physical force against another person), and the average North American youngster will see several thousand murders enacted on TV before adolescence (Waters, 1993).

According to Bandura's (1986) social cognitive theory, children learn by observing others, so if they observe violent behaviour (real or televised), some will act violently. Laboratory studies conducted in the 1960s by Bandura, Ross, and Ross (1963) made just this point. Children watched specially created TV programs showing an adult kicking and hitting a plastic "Bobo" doll. When children were given the opportunity to play with the doll, those who had seen the TV program were much more likely to behave aggressively toward the doll than children who had not seen the program.

Although critics doubted that viewing TV violence in more realistic settings (outside the lab) would have such pronounced effects on children (Klapper, 1968), subsequent research has confirmed some of what Bandura said. Indeed, broad consensus exists that violent media (TV programs, comic books, internet sites, literature, movies, music, music videos, sports, and video games) increase aggression in children, but disagreement still remains about whether violent media is a major factor in the development of real-world violence (Bushman, Gollwitzer, and Cruz, 2015). In addition, concerns continue to exist that many studies published on violence in the media have serious methodological flaws, which continues to fuel controversy in this field of study (Ferguson & Savage, 2012). Similar concerns have been raised with regard to research on violence in social media, including problems with defining online violence, overreliance on descriptive data, and the evolving landscape of social media (Patton et al., 2014).

Historically, researchers have found that viewing TV violence desensitizes children, making them more accepting of interpersonal violence (Donnerstein, Slaby, & Eron, 1994). Babysitters who are frequent viewers of TV violence are more inclined to let children "slug it out" because they see this as a normal, acceptable way of resolving conflicts (Drabman & Thomas, 1976). In addition, television programs can be like how-to manuals for the carrying out of violent acts (Comstock & Scharrer, 1999; Slaby, Roedell, Arezzo, & Hendrix, 1995). Huesmann (1986) found that 8-year-old boys who watched large doses of TV violence had the most extensive criminal records as 30-year-olds. The finding was true for girls as well, although girls had lower levels of criminal activity overall.

Clearly many Canadians are concerned about the amount of violence children are exposed to on television (Dubow & Miller, 1996), and they have good cause for concern. The answer from research is clear: Frequent exposure to TV violence makes all children more aggressive, with girls demonstrating more relational violence and boys more physical violence (Ostrov, Gentile, & Crick, 2006). Note that all children are affected by media violence, not just children who seem more prone to being aggressive (Huesmann., Moise-Titus, Podolski, & Eron, 2003).

The greatest concern, however, is not just with children who are exposed to violence in the media but also with those who have a "high and steady diet of violent TV shows in early childhood," who specifically identify with aggressive characters, and who perceive the violence to be realistic (Huesmann et al., 2003, p. 218). For these boys and girls, steady exposure to violence in early childhood predicted violent behaviour into adulthood, particularly when the perpetrator of violence (even if he's a "good guy") was glorified and rewarded for violent acts. Dirty Harry, a "cop" who is rewarded and gains glory through violence, is a worse model for children than a murderer who commits violent acts but is later brought to justice (Huesmann et al., 2003).

Despite TV's lasting impact on children, its effect becomes less pronounced in older children, adolescents, and adults (Browne & Hamilton-Giachritsis, 2005; Huesmann et al., 2003). Although TV violence can have an impact at any age, the impact of media violence tends to be short term, particularly in adults. In addition, TV can have a prosocial impact on social interactions, levels of aggression, altruism, and levels of stereotyping, particularly when children self-select prosocial content in the laboratory, as compared with those who watched antisocial content (Mares & Woodard, 2005). Encouraging children to think critically about what they are viewing may reduce the impact of modelled aggression in the media (Funk, 2005).

COGNITIVE PROCESSES.   Perceptual and cognitive skills also play a role in aggression. Dodge, Bates, and Pettit (1990) were the first to explore the cognitive aspects of aggression. They discovered that aggressive boys often respond aggressively because they are not skilled at interpreting other people's intentions and, without a clear interpretation in mind, they respond aggressively by default. That is, aggressive boys far too often think, "I don't know what you're up to, so, when in doubt, attack."

From findings like these, Crick and Dodge (1994; Dodge & Crick, 1990) formulated the information-processing model of children's thinking shown in Figure 13–5. According to the model, responding to a social stimulus involves several steps.

Figure 13–5

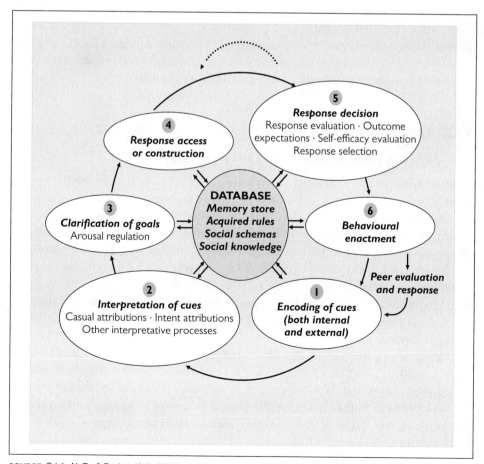

SOURCE: Crick, N. R., & Dodge, K. A. (1994). A review and reformulation of social information-processing mechanisms in children's social adjustment. Psychological Bulletin, 115, 74–101. American Psychological Association (APA).

First, children selectively attend to certain features of the social stimulus but not to others. Second, children try to interpret the features they have processed; that is, they try to give meaning to the social stimulus. Third, children evaluate their goals for the situation. Fourth, children retrieve from memory a behavioural response that is associated with the interpretation and goals of the situation. Fifth, children evaluate this response to determine if it is appropriate. Finally, they proceed with their behaviour.

Several investigators have shown that aggressive children's processing is biased and restricted in many of these steps and that this flawed information processing is associated with increased aggression (Crick & Werner, 1998; Egan, Monson, & Perry, 1998). Aggressive children are less likely to attend to features that signal nonhostile motives (Crick & Dodge, 1994). For example, suppose a child accidentally tears another child's homework. The first child is probably surprised and chagrined, both cues that the child did not tear the homework on purpose. Nevertheless, an aggressive child often does not process those cues and instead assumes that the first child's intent was hostile. As well, based on personal histories of being rejected and ridiculed by peers, many aggressive children believe that unfamiliar peers are unfriendly and uncaring (Burks, Dodge, Price, & Laird, 1999; MacKinnon-Lewis, Rabiner, & Starnes, 1999).

Aggressive children who are not skilled at interpreting and responding to others' actions could benefit from training in these skills to improve their social behaviour and peer interactions (Dodge & Crick, 1990). One approach is to teach aggressive children that aggression is painful and does not solve problems, that intentions can be understood by attending to relevant cues, and that there are more effective, prosocial ways to solve interpersonal disputes.

Of course, families are not the sole causes of aggression and violence. Poverty, racism, and terrorism also create a culture of aggression and violence (Coie & Dodge, 1998), but individual parents can be careful not to set the cycle of aggression in motion. Parents should respond to misbehaviour with reasoning instead of physical punishment. Also, children prone to aggression can be taught and rewarded for using equally effective but more prosocial ways to deal with conflict.

Victims of Peer Aggression

LO14 Note why some children become victims of aggression.

Every aggressive act is directed at someone. Most school children are the targets of an occasional aggressive act—a shove or kick to gain a desired toy, or a stinging insult by someone trying to save face. However, a small percentage of children are chronic targets of bullying. In both Europe and North America, about 10 percent of elementary school children and adolescents are chronic victims of aggression (Kochenderfer & Ladd, 1996; Olweus, 1994), and research on bullying is a rapidly expanding area in psychology (Stassen Berger, 2007). In addition to physical aggression, victimization can also occur by verbal abuse and social ostracism: Think of a child who is shunned by other children at recess time, who is called names, or who is gossiped about at school.

Using naturalistic observation in a study of Canadian schools, Craig, Pepler, and Atlas (2000) found that bullying was more common outdoors than indoors, taking place approximately 4.5 times per hour on the playground compared with 2.4 episodes per hour in the classroom. From early to late adolescence, youth reported that bullying complaints were highest around points of school transition and lowest at the end of high school (Pepler et al., 2006). Sexual harassment of peers within and across genders tended to increase during early adolescence and stabilize in later high school. Boys reported more sexual harassment and bullying than girls, overall, but no gender differences were noted for aggression when dating. Pepler and colleagues (2006) concluded that bullying should be understood as a problem in relationships, and prevention efforts should be targeted at reducing adolescents' use of aggression and power-and-control tactics in their relationships.

As you can well imagine, being tormented regularly by peers is hard on children and can lead to serious adjustment problems or even self-harm. One of the difficulties of dealing with peer bullying is that most instances of bullying occur in groups rather than one on one. Hawkins, Pepler, and Craig (2001) noted that in 88 percent of bullying incidents, peers were present, but in only 19 percent of those incidents did peers intervene. When they did intervene, peers were able to stop the bullying just over half of the time, although in many instances, peers intervened by behaving aggressively toward the bully.

Individual bullies usually have backup from age-peers who either actively participate in the bullying or are bystanders who do not intervene. This is part of what makes bullying situations so very intimidating for youngsters. It's much harder to stand up to a group than to stand up to an individual. As a consequence, feeling trapped by and powerless over repeated bullying incidents, children who are chronic victims of bullying are often lonely, anxious, and depressed; they often dislike school; and they have low self-esteem (Graham & Juvonen, 1998; Ladd & Ladd, 1998).

Bullies feel rewarded by a victim's signs of distress.

Children who are chronic targets of bullying can be divided into two groups: aggressive and passive victims. A small percentage of victims are actually aggressive themselves (Olweus, 1978; Schwartz, Dodge, Pettit, & Bates, 1997). These youngsters often overreact, are restless, and are easily irritated. Their aggressive peers soon learn that these children are easily baited. A group of children will, for example, insult or ridicule them, knowing that the aggressive victim will probably start a fight even though outnumbered.

However, the vast majority of bullied children are not overreactive, restless, or irritable. Instead, these children tend to be withdrawn, emotionally sensitive, and submissive—what we call passive victims. They are usually unwilling or unable to socially defend themselves from peers' aggression (Ladd & Ladd, 1998; Olweus, 1978). When attacked, these children tend to show obvious signs of distress, like crying, and give in to their attackers, thereby rewarding the bullies' aggressive behaviour. Management of emotional reactivity becomes an important goal for victims of bullies (Mahady-Wilton, Craig, & Pepler, 2000), as poor emotion regulation and emotional displays on the part of a victim just fuel bullies' aggressive behaviour.

Children who have been chronically bullied can be helped by being taught more effective and assertive interpersonal behaviours (e.g., don't lash out when you're insulted; don't show that you're afraid when you're threatened). In addition, increasing their self-esteem makes them less tolerant of personal attacks (Egan & Perry, 1998). Finally, one of the best ways to help victims is to foster their friendships with peers. When children have friends, they can be more protected by being in a group situation, and they're not as likely to be bullied (Hodges, Malone, & Perry, 1997).

Ask Yourself

Crick and Dodge's model of decision making draws upon the information-processing approach to cognitive development. Use that approach to suggest other possible causes of and remedies for children's aggressive behaviour.

Much research on modelled aggression has focused on television and video games. What kinds of violence might children be exposed to in other forms of media, and how can children's exposure be fairly monitored and limited without affecting the rights of adults?

What kinds of power and control tactics do some adolescents use inappropriately in their relationships?

13.5 Families in the Early Twenty-First Century

Learning Objectives

After reading the module, you should be able to do the following:

LO15 Describe how well children can care for themselves after school.

LO16 Summarize the effects of divorce and remarriage on children.

Canadian families face many new challenges in the twenty-first century. More families than ever before rely on two incomes for an adequate standard of living. When both parents work outside the home, they often can't watch their children after school. Formal after-school care is not always available, and many children are left to care for themselves. We'll see how children fare in self-care in the first part of the module.

Divorce is another challenge facing families. The number of divorces in Canada per year has been hovering around 70 000 nationally (Statistics Canada, 2004a). While this number tells us the number of couples going through divorce each year, summary statistics such as this do not tell us how many of those couples are going through their second or third divorce (or more). In fact, couples who go through multiple divorces may account for a good number of the divorces occurring annually. In the next section, we'll examine the effect of divorce on children in detail; as we do, we'll discover whether the effects of divorce are long-lasting or whether at least some of those effects are temporary.

After-School Care

LO15 Describe how well children can care for themselves after school.

When children enter elementary school, child care becomes easier for working parents. However, many children still need care before or after school, and in Canada, the quality of care varies greatly among after-school programs (Jacobs, White, Baillargeon, & Betsalel-Presser, 1995). Formal programs for before- and after-school care have been studied much less than daycare for infants and toddlers (Lamb, 1999). Nevertheless, the limited research that has been done suggests that many of the same variables associated with high-quality daycare for infants and toddlers are associated with high-quality before- and after-school care. Children benefit from well-trained, encouraging teachers; from low child-to-teacher ratios; and from a flexible, age-appropriate curriculum (Rosenthal & Vandell, 1996).

Many school-age children receive no formal care after school; they are left alone to care for themselves (Galambos & Maggs, 1991; Robinson, Rowland, & Coleman, 1986). Children who care for themselves are sometimes called **latchkey children**, a term that originated more than 200 years ago to describe children who are given a key to enter their own homes. Some latchkey children stay at home alone. Others may stay at friends' homes where adults are sometimes present; others still may go to unsupervised public places such as shopping malls, parks, or public libraries. Action for Children is a British organization that has recommended lengthening the school day so that at-risk children are not unsupervised between 3 and 7 p.m. (Action for Children, 2010).

The popular perception is that latchkey children are frightened and endangered, but research provides little support for this view. To the contrary, most older children who care for themselves at home after school fare as well as children in the care of parents or other adults (Lamb, 1999). In one study, Grade 3, 4 and 5 students who cared for themselves at home were no more anxious, headstrong, or dependent than children cared for by their mothers (Vandell & Ramanan, 1991).

Galambos and Maggs (1991) did find that children who spend much after-school time with peers were at higher risk for aggressive and delinquent behaviour than children who were not with peers after school. The combination of low parental monitoring, peer contact, and living in an unsafe neighbourhood can dramatically increase a child's risk for antisocial behaviour (Pettit, Bates, Dodge, & Meece, 1999).

To say, however, that most latchkey children are not at risk does not mean that parents should initiate children's self-care without careful planning. Robinson and colleagues (1986) suggested that parents contemplating self-care for their children should ask themselves the following basic questions:

A latchkey child.

Latchkey children: children who largely are under their own supervision after school.

- Is the child old enough and emotionally mature enough, regardless of age, to assume the responsibility of self-care? For example, does the child stay home alone for short time periods?

- Does the child live in a safe neighbourhood where crime is low and community cohesion is high and where neighbours and community facilities can be depended upon as support systems?

- Does the child's self-care arrangement provide for some type of adult supervision or monitoring, such as a telephone or pager?

If each of these questions can be answered yes, then self-care will probably work. The next step is to prepare the child for self-care. Children need to know after-school routines (e.g., acceptable ways of getting home from school and how to check in with a parent), rules for their own behaviour after school (e.g., acceptable and unacceptable activities), and how to handle emergencies (Peterson, 1989). Posting procedures and emergency phone numbers in a conspicuous location is often enough reassurance for children. With adequate preparation, children can care for themselves after school.

Lately, some parents have taken to "supervising" their children via electronic methods, such as email, text messaging, and instant messaging online. Supervision of children is important at every age, but the level of supervision needs to be tied to the maturity and ability of the child. Young children who are not mature enough to be alone must be supervised in person at all times. Staying in close contact with teens is also critical to their well-being as they mature.

Divorce

LO16 Summarize the effects of divorce and remarriage on children.

The parents of many Canadian youngsters divorce. In fact, divorce has become a common part of childhood in North America (Burns & Scott, 1994; Goodman et al., 1998; Hernandez, 1997; Stevenson & Black, 1995).

However, tracking true divorce rates across North America has been difficult for a couple of reasons. First, more couples are choosing to cohabit, and their separations are not tracked as divorces in the Canadian or U.S. courts. Second, some divorce rates have been inflated because of multiple marriages and divorces by the same people. In other words, the divorce rate might be lower than expected because some people are repeatedly marrying and divorcing, which makes divorce look like it is more prevalent than it actually is.

According to all theories of child development, divorce is distressing for children because it involves conflict between parents and, usually, separation from one of them. But what aspects of children's development are most affected by divorce? To begin to understand divorce, let's start with a profile of life after divorce.

FAMILY LIFE AFTER DIVORCE. After divorce, children often live with their mothers, though fathers are more likely to get custody today than in previous generations. About 15 percent of children live with their fathers after divorce (Meyer & Garasky, 1993). Little research has been done on family life in homes headed by single fathers, so most of the descriptions on the next few pages are based entirely on research done on children living with their mothers. However, Fabricius and Luecken (2007) found that more time spent living with fathers after divorce resulted in better relationships with fathers in the young adult years. Less time with fathers post divorce predicted poorer relationships with fathers, extended distress about the divorces, as well as poorer health outcomes in youth adulthood. In counselling both mothers and fathers regarding divorce, Lee and Hunsley (2001), from the University of Ottawa, recommended that both parents be advised of empirical findings on the effects of separation and divorce on children. Either way, some research findings exist to show that if the child's custodial parent functions well, the child's adjustment will be better (Spruijt & Iedema, 1998).

The best portrait of family life after divorce comes from the Virginia Longitudinal Study of Divorce and Remarriage conducted by Mavis Hetherington (1988, 1989, 1999; Hetherington, Cox, & Cox, 1982). The Virginia Study traced the lives of families for several years after divorce, along with a comparison sample of families with parents who did not divorce.

In the first few months after divorce, many mothers were less affectionate toward their children. They also accepted less mature behaviour from their children than they would have before the divorce and had a harder time controlling their children. The overall picture shows both mothers and children suffering the distress of a major change in life circumstances: Children regressed to less mature forms of behaviour, and mothers were less able to parent effectively. Fathers, too, were less able to control their children, but this was probably because most were extremely indulgent.

Two years after the divorce, mother–child relationships had improved, particularly for daughters. Mothers were more affectionate. They were more likely to expect age-appropriate behaviour from their children and to discipline their children effectively. Fathers also demanded more mature behaviour of their children, but many had become relatively uninvolved with their children.

Mothers and daughters can become very close in the years after a divorce.

Rob/Fotolia

Six years after divorce, the children in the study were entering adolescence. Family life continued to improve for mothers with daughters, and many grew extremely close over the years following divorce.

Unfortunately, family life was problematic for mothers with sons. These mothers often complained about their sons, who resisted discipline. Many mothers fell into the negative reinforcement trap. Mothers and sons were frequently in conflict, and overall, neither was very happy with the other or with the general quality of family life.

Results like these from the Virginia Study underscore that divorce changes family life for parents and children alike. In the next section, we'll look at the effects of these changes on children's development.

IMPACT OF DIVORCE ON CHILDREN. Some of the most convincing answers to how divorce affects development came from research by Amato and Keith (1991), who integrated the results of almost 100 studies involving more than 13 000 preschool through college-age children. In all areas they reviewed, including school achievement, conduct, adjustment, self-concept, and parent–child relations, children whose parents had divorced fared poorly compared to children from intact families. However, the effects of divorce were greater in the 1960s and 1970s than in later years when divorce became more frequent (and thus more familiar). School achievement, conduct, adjustment, and the like are still affected by divorce but not as much as before the 1980s.

When children of divorced parents become adults, the effects of divorce persist. As adults, children of divorce are more likely to become teenage parents and to become divorced themselves. Also, they report less satisfaction with life and are more likely to become depressed (Furstenberg & Teitler, 1994; Kiernan, 1992). For example, in one study (Chase-Lansdale, Cherlin, & Kiernan, 1995), 11 percent of children of divorce had serious emotional problems as adults compared to 8 percent of children from intact families. The difference is small—11 percent versus 8 percent—but divorce does increase the risk of emotional disorders in adulthood.

Some children are more affected by divorce than others. Amato and Keith's (1991) analysis, for example, showed that although the overall impact of divorce is the same for boys and girls, divorce is more harmful when it occurs during childhood and adolescence than during the preschool or college years. Also, children who are temperamentally more emotional tend to be more affected by divorce (Lengua, Sandler, West, Wolchik, & Curran, 1999).

Some children suffer more from divorce because of their tendency to interpret events negatively. Two children often have differing interpretations of exactly the same social event. Suppose, for example, that a father forgets to take a child on a promised outing. One child might believe that an emergency prevented the father from taking the child. A second child might believe that the father hadn't really wanted to spend time with the child in the first place and will never make similar plans again. Children who—like the second child—tend to interpret life events negatively are more likely to have behavioural problems following divorce (Mazur, Wolchik, Virdin, Sandler, & West, 1999).

How exactly does divorce influence development? Researchers have identified several aspects of a child's life that change (Amato & Keith, 1991). First, the absence of one parent means that children lose a role model, a source of parental help and emotional support, and a supervisor. For instance, a single parent might have to choose between helping one child complete an important paper or watching another child perform in a school play. The parent can't do both, and one child will miss out.

Second, single-parent families experience economic hardship, which creates stress and often means that activities once taken for granted are no longer available (Goodman et al., 1998). A family might no longer be able to afford purchasing books for pleasure reading, participating in music lessons, or taking part in other activities that promote child development. Moreover, when a single parent worries about having enough money for food and rent, the parent has less energy and effort to devote to parenting.

Table 13–3 Summary Table

Impact of Divorce on Children	
Aspect of Divorce	**Impact**
What is affected?	Children's school achievement, their conduct, psychological adjustment, self-concept, and relationships with their parents
Who is most affected?	School-age children and adolescents; children who are temperamentally emotional; children prone to interpret events negatively
Why is divorce harmful?	One parent is less accessible as a role model; single-parent families experience economic hardship; conflict between parents is distressing

Third, conflict between parents is extremely distressing to children and adolescents (Fincham, 1998), particularly for children who are emotionally insecure (Davies & Cummings, 1998). In fact, many of the problems ascribed to divorce are really caused by marital conflict occurring before the divorce (Erel & Burman, 1995; Shaw, Winslow, & Flanagan, 1999). Children whose parents are married but fight constantly often show many of the same effects associated with children of divorced parents.

The impact of divorce on children is summarized in Table 13–3.

ADJUSTING TO DIVORCE. Life for children after divorce is not all gloom and doom. Children adjust to their new circumstances (Chase-Lansdale & Hetherington, 1990). However, certain factors can ease the transition. Children adjust to divorce more readily if their divorced parents co-operate with each other, especially on disciplinary matters (Hetherington, 1989). In **joint custody**, both parents retain legal custody of their children. Children benefit from joint custody if their parents get along (Maccoby, Buchanon, Mnookin, & Dornbusch, 1993).

Joint custody:
a post divorce legal arrangement whereby both parents retain legal custody of their children.

Of course, many parents do not get along after a divorce, a circumstance that reduces the success of joint custody or eliminates it as an option. Traditionally, mothers have been awarded custody, but in recent years, fathers have been given custody more often, especially of sons. This practice coincides with findings that children often adjust better when they live with the parent of their same gender: Boys often fare better with fathers, and girls usually fare better with mothers (Goodman et al., 1998). One reason boys are often better off with their fathers is that boys are likely to become involved in negative reinforcement traps with their mothers. Another explanation is that both boys and girls tend to forge stronger emotional relationships with parents of their same gender (Zimiles & Lee, 1991). Nevertheless, for both boys and girls, effective parenting skills post divorce in both mothers and fathers can be a protective factor for children's well-being (Bastaits & Martelmans, 2016).

Lehr and MacMillan (2001) conducted research on the personal experiences of young, noncustodial fathers (ages 15–28) after separation and divorce in Canada. These fathers were involved to varying degrees with their children, and some were only just starting to become involved in their children's lives. Lehr and MacMillan reported that these fathers were difficult to engage and had difficulty reaching out for help. These fathers reported feeling lost and unsupported, which led the researchers to conclude that counselling services should become more proactive with this group, even suggesting that an advertising program be started to help engage fathers in accessing help. Maccoby and colleagues (1993) found that noncustodial mothers are more likely than noncustodial fathers to maintain close and frequent contact with their children (Maccoby et al., 1993).

Parents can reduce divorce-related stress and help children adjust to their new life circumstances. Parents should explain to children together, if possible, why they are divorcing and what their children can expect to happen. They should reassure children that they will always love them and always be their parents; parents must back up these words with actions by remaining involved in their children's lives, despite the increased difficulty of doing so. Finally, parents must expect that their children will sometimes be angry or sad about the divorce, and they should encourage children to discuss these feelings with them.

To help children deal with divorce, parents should not compete with each other for their children's love and attention; children adjust to divorce best when they maintain good relationships with both parents. Parents should neither take out their anger with each other on their children nor criticize their ex-spouse in front of the children. Finally, parents should not ask children to mediate disputes; parents should work out problems without putting the children in the middle.

Following all these rules all the time is not easy, and some parents' divorces are so volatile that the above recommendations become impossible. However, parents owe it to their children to try to follow most of these rules most of the time in order to minimize the disruptive effects of their divorce on their children's development.

Blended families face many challenges.

BLENDED FAMILIES. Following divorce, most children live in a single-parent household for about five years. However, more than two-thirds of men and women eventually remarry (Glick, 1989; Glick & Lin, 1986). The resulting unit, consisting of a biological parent, stepparent, and children, is known as a **blended family**. About 10 percent of Canadian children live in blended families (Statistics Canada, 2012). Because mothers are more often granted custody of children, the most common form of blended family in Canada is a mother, her children, and a stepfather (Cheal, 1996). Blended families have unique pressures associated with them, and approximately one-third of Canadian children who are living in blended families have reported feeling a lack of emotional support. Nevertheless, school-age boys typically benefit from the presence of a stepfather, particularly when he is warm and involved. School-age girls, however, tend not to adjust readily to their mother's remarriage, which can disrupt the intimate relationship often already established with her. As boys and girls leave the elementary school years and enter adolescence, both can benefit from the presence of a caring stepfather (Hetherington, 1993).

The best strategy for a stepfather is to be interested in new stepchildren but to avoid immediately encroaching on established relationships. A newly remarried mother must be careful that her enthusiasm for her new spouse does not come at the expense of time and affection for the children. Both parents and children need to have realistic expectations; bumps in the road can be navigated well if parents present a loving but united front in terms of equal application of age-appropriate rules to all children alike. However, this is easier said than done: Canadian children living in blended families reported problems with inconsistent discipline 43 percent of the time, as compared with 33 percent of children from intact families (Cheal, 1996). The blended family can be successful, but it takes effort because of the complicated relationships, conflicting loyalties, and jealousies that usually exist (Anderson, Greene, Hetherington, & Clingempeel, 1999).

In Canada, the presence of stepfathers in blended families outnumbers the presence of stepmothers approximately five to one (Cheal, 1996). In comparison with intact families or blended families with stepfathers, much less is known about blended families consisting of a father, his children, and a stepmother, although several factors can make a father's remarriage difficult for his children (Brand, Clingempeel, & Bowen-Woodward, 1988).

Over time, most children adjust to the blended family. If the marriage is stable, children can profit from the presence of two caring adults. Unfortunately, second

Blended family:
also called a stepfamily, this family consists of two adults living together either common-law or married who have biological children from one or both of those adults.

marriages are slightly more likely than first marriages to end in divorce, so many children relive the trauma. As you can imagine, another divorce—and possibly another remarriage—severely disrupts children's development, accentuating the problems that followed the initial divorce (Capaldi & Patterson, 1991).

SKIP-GENERATION FAMILIES.   Another type of family that is becoming more prevalent in Canada is the **skip-generation family**. This type of family consists of grandparents and grandchildren without the presence of the children's parents. About 30 000 children in Canada (0.5 percent of Canadian children) live in a skip-generation family, in comparison to 4.8 percent of children who live in a household with at least one parent and at least one grandparent. Within skip-generation families, about two-thirds of children (57.8 percent) live with a grandparent couple, and 42.2 percent of skip-generation families include grandchildren living with only one grandparent.

Although these families do not include the presence of the children's biological parents, their grandparents are in a parental role and provide both financial and emotional stability and resources for children who otherwise might have to enter the foster-care system. In Canada, Nunavut (2.2 percent), Northwest Territories (1.8 percent), and Saskatchewan (1.4 percent) have the highest number of skip-generation families (Statistics Canada, 2012).

FOSTER FAMILIES.   A **foster family** consists of at least one adult who is looking after a child who is not that person's biological child or relative. About 73 percent of foster families in Canada also include biological or adopted children in the home (Statistics Canada, 2012). Across Canada, 0.5 percent of children under the age of 14 live in foster care (Statistics Canada, 2012), which normally involves being placed with people other than biological family members. Of children who live in foster care, 52.5 percent are boys and 47.5 percent are girls. In terms of geographic location, the highest levels of children in foster care are in Manitoba (1.9 percent), Northwest Territories (1.7 percent), Nunavut (1.3 percent), and Yukon (1.3 percent).

Skip-generation family:
a family that consists of grandparents and grandchildren without the presence of the children's parents.

Foster family:
a family that consists of at least one adult and one child who is not the biological child or a relative of the foster parent.

Ask Yourself

The consequences of divorce are often widespread, yet not all children are affected equally. How do these phenomena show the connections of cognitive, social, and emotional development?

What would a developmental psychopathology perspective have to say about children's outcomes after parental divorce?

What Would a Coach Do?

You are the coach of a Little League softball team. One of the parents, whose child is on your team, keeps criticizing the child for making mistakes during practice. How can you deal with this parent without causing more anger or embarrassment for the child? What can you do to help the child feel better about his or her skills in the sport?

Summary

13.1 Self-Esteem

Measuring Self-Esteem

- Harter's Self-Perception Profile for Children (SPPC) enables psychologists to assess overall self-worth and self-esteem in five areas: scholastic competence, athletic competence, social

acceptance, behavioural conduct, and physical appearance.

Developmental Change in Self-Esteem

- Self-esteem usually declines somewhat during the elementary school years but becomes more differentiated as children evaluate themselves on more aspects of self-esteem, including different types of academic skills.

Sources of Self-Esteem

- Parental affection and involvement with children increases children's self-esteem.
- Setting rules and discussing disciplinary actions with children helps build their self-esteem.
- Self-esteem depends on peer comparisons and is usually greater when children know that others view them positively.

Consequences of Low Self-Esteem

- Low self-esteem in children is related to poor peer relations, psychological disorders, antisocial behaviour, and low school achievement.
- Therapy can enhance children's self-esteem.

13.2 Relationships with Peers

An Overview of Peer Interactions in Middle Childhood

- Peer relations improve during the elementary school years through talking, being together, and rough-and-tumble play.

Friendship

- Friendships are based on common interests and getting along well.
- Friends are usually similar in age, sex, race, and attitudes.
- Children with friends usually have better levels of adjustment and social skills.

Popularity and Rejection

- Popular children are socially skilled and generally share, co-operate, and help others.
- Aggressive children often are rejected by their peers, are unsuccessful in school, and demonstrate behavioural problems.
- Parents who are belligerent or who practise inconsistent discipline foster aggressive interpersonal styles in their children.

Prejudice

- Prejudice emerges in the preschool years but declines during the elementary school years as children's cognitive growth helps them understand that social groups are heterogeneous, not homogeneous.

- Older children and adolescents still show prejudice, which might be reduced by constructive exposure to individuals from other social groups.

13.3 Helping Others

Skills Underlying Prosocial Behaviour

- Children are more likely to behave prosocially when they are able to take others' perspectives and are empathic.

Situational Influences

- Children's prosocial behaviour is often influenced by situational characteristics.
- Children more often behave prosocially when they feel that they should and can help, when they are in a good mood, and when they believe that they have little to lose by helping.

Socializing Prosocial Behaviour

- Using reasoning in discipline, modelling prosocial behaviour, and praising children dispositionally for prosocial behaviour promotes prosocial behaviour in children.

13.4 Aggression

The Nature of Children's Aggressive Behaviour

- Physical aggression decreases but verbal aggression increases as children grow.
- Typical forms of aggression include bullying as well as instrumental and reactive aggression.
- Very aggressive children often become involved in criminal activities as adolescents and adults.

The Impact of Aggression on Children

- Abuse and use of harsh physical punishment foster aggressive behaviour in children.
- Excessive viewing of TV violence at an early age and lack of skill interpreting others' actions or intentions foster aggression in children.

Victims of Peer Aggression

- Children who are chronic targets of aggression are often lonely and anxious.
- Some victims of aggression tend to overreact when provoked; others tend to withdraw and submit.
- Victimization can be overcome and possibly prevented by increasing children's social skills, self-esteem, and number of friends.

13.5 Families in the Early Twenty-First Century

After-School Care

- Children can care for themselves after school if they are mature enough, live in a safe neighbourhood, and are monitored by an adult.

Divorce

- Directly after a divorce, a mother's parenting might be less effective and children might behave immaturely.

- Family life typically improves after divorce, except for mother–son relationships, which are often filled with conflict.

- Divorce harms children in many ways, ranging from school achievement to adjustment difficulties.

- The impact of divorce stems from less supervision of children, economic hardship, and conflict between parents.

- Children often benefit when parents get along, have joint custody, or when the children live with the parent of the same gender.

- When parents remarry, children sometimes have difficulty adjusting because stepparents may disturb existing parent–child relationships.

- Blended families tend to be associated with more stressors for children than intact families.

Chapter Critical Review

1. When gifted children are put in special classes, their intellectual development can be accelerated, sometimes at the expense of their self-esteem. Do you believe the intellectual gain is worth the potential drop in self-esteem? Why or why not?

2. Imagine that you and your child have just moved to a new town. What advice would you give your child about how to make new friends?

3. Suppose Grade 1 students wanted to raise money for a gift for one of their classmates who is in the hospital. Based on what you know about the factors that influence children to be altruistic, how would you help the students plan their fundraising?

4. Relate the description of the development of prosocial behaviour in Module 13.3 to cognitive development.

5. You have been asked to prepare a brochure for mothers who have recently divorced and will have custody of their children. What advice would you give them about what to expect as a single parent?

See for Yourself

Pick an evening when you can watch network television programming from 8:00 to 10:00 p.m. (prime time). Count each instance of (a) physical force by one person against another and (b) threats of harm to compel another to act against his or her will. Select one network randomly and watch the program for 10 minutes. Then turn to another network and watch that program for 10 minutes. Continue changing the channels every 10 minutes until the two hours are over. Of course, it won't be easy to follow the plots of all these programs, but you will end up with a wider sample of programming this way. Repeat this procedure on a Saturday morning when you can watch two hours of children's cartoons (i.e., not *South Park*!).

Now divide the total number of aggressive acts you counted by four to estimate the amount of aggression per hour. Multiply this figure by 6570 to estimate the number of aggressive acts seen by an average adolescent by age 12. (Why 6570? Two hours of daily TV viewing—a very conservative number—multiplied by 365 days times 9 years.) Then, ponder the possible results of that very large number. What do you think the consequences are of massive exposure to the televised message "Solve conflicts with aggression"? See for yourself!

Chapter 14
Physical Growth in Adolescents

Alexander Y/Fotolia

∨ MODULE

14.1 Pubertal Changes

14.2 Sexuality

14.3 Health

During the Olympics, Sophie just couldn't stop watching all of the events. When she saw Canadian after Canadian jump up on the podium to receive medals, Sophie was jumping up and down in the living room, waving a Canadian flag. She was so excited about the athletes, and she also kept talking about how attractive some of them were! Starry-eyed, Sophie announced that she wanted to compete for the Olympics one day too. Terry and Mabel were surprised at their daughter's teenage enthusiasm and marvelled at the changes she was undergoing as she matured both physically and (were they ready for it?) sexually!

Connect to My Virtual Child

What kinds of theories do you have about children? What ideas inform your thoughts and beliefs about the lives of children, how they are raised, and the nature of the human person? Use your access card and follow this link www.myvirtualchild.com to learn more about the world of the child. You can even virtually try to raise your own child.

14.1 Pubertal Changes

 ## Learning Objectives

After reading the module, you should be able to do the following:

LO1 Explain the physical changes that occur in adolescence and mark the transition to mature young adulthood.

LO2 List the factors that cause the physical changes associated with puberty.

LO3 Describe how physical changes affect adolescents' psychological development.

The appearance of body hair, the emergence of a girl's breasts, and the enlargement of a boy's penis and testicles are all signs that childhood is gone and adolescence is here. Many adolescents take great satisfaction in these signs of maturity. Others worry through their teenage years as they wait for the physical signs of adolescence to appear.

In this module, we'll begin by describing the normal pattern of physical changes that take place in adolescence and look at the mechanisms responsible for them. Then we'll discover the impact of these physical changes on adolescents' psychological functioning. As we do, we'll learn about the possible effects of physical maturation occurring earlier or later than that of age peers.

Signs of Physical Maturation

LO1 **Explain the physical changes that occur in adolescence and mark the transition to mature young adulthood.**

Puberty:

a time of physical transition to adulthood that involves both bodily growth and sexual maturation.

Puberty denotes two general types of physical changes that mark the transition from childhood to young adulthood. The first are bodily changes, including a dramatic increase in height and weight as well as changes in the body's fat and muscle contents. The second type of physical changes concern sexual maturation, including change in the reproductive organs and the appearance of secondary sexual characteristics, such as facial hair, body hair, and breasts on girls.

Figure 14–1

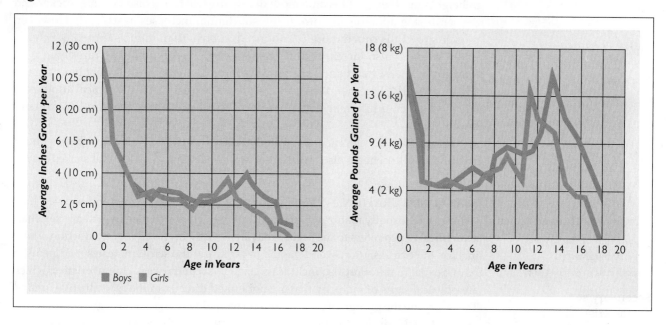

PHYSICAL GROWTH.   During middle childhood, a typical 6- to 10-year-old girl or boy steadily gains about 2 to 3 kilograms and grows 5 to 7.5 centimetres. In contrast, during the peak of the adolescent growth spurt, a girl can gain as much as 9 kilograms in a year and a boy, 11 kilograms (Marshall & Tanner, 1970).

Girls usually undergo their pubescent growth spurt before boys.

Figure 14–1 shows that girls typically begin their growth spurt about two years before boys do. Girls typically start the growth spurt at about age 11, reach their peak rate of growth at about 12, and achieve their mature stature around age 15. In contrast, boys start the growth spurt at 13, hit peak growth at 14, and reach mature stature around 17. This two-year difference in the growth spurt can lead to awkward social interactions between 11- and 12-year-old boys and girls because girls are often taller and much more mature-looking than boys.

Timing of growth spurts also accounts for why boys are, on average, taller than girls. Although girls begin to mature earlier than boys, their growth also levels off earlier. During the time that girls are having their growth spurt, boys are just continuing to grow steadily. This means that boys have about a two-year longer growth period than girls do before boys experience a growth spurt and then level off around age 17. Of course, not all girls and boys mature at the same time. Some girls and boys are "early bloomers," while others can be "later bloomers." The ages associated with growth and growth spurts given here are only averages.

In addition, body parts don't all mature at the same rate, making growth an asynchronous process. Instead, the head, hands, and feet usually begin to grow first, followed by growth in the arms and legs. The trunk and shoulders are the last to grow (Tanner, 1990). The result of these differing growth rates is that an adolescent's body sometimes seems to be out of proportion and awkward—like you see with older puppies, teenagers have a head, feet, and hands that are too big for the rest of the body. (Isn't that part of what makes them so cute?) Fortunately, these imbalances don't last long, as the later-developing parts catch up.

During the adolescent growth spurt, bones become longer, accounting for gains in height, and they also become more dense. Muscle fibres also become thicker and denser during adolescence, producing substantial increases in strength. However, muscle growth is much more pronounced in boys than in girls (Smoll & Schutz, 1990). Body fat also increases during adolescence, but much more rapidly in girls than boys. Finally, heart and lung capacity increase more in adolescent boys than in adolescent girls. Together, these changes help to explain why the typical adolescent boy is stronger, quicker, and has greater physical endurance than the typical adolescent girl.

In the Child Development and Family Policy feature, you'll see how healthy bone growth in adolescence is also an essential defence against a disease that strikes during middle age.

SEXUAL MATURATION.   Not only do adolescents become taller and heavier, they also become sexually mature. Sexual maturation includes change in **primary sex characteristics**, which refers to the organs that are directly involved in reproduction. These include the ovaries, uterus, and vagina in girls, and the scrotum, testes, and penis in boys. Sexual maturation also includes change in **secondary sex characteristics**, which are physical signs of maturity that are not linked directly to the reproductive organs. These include the growth of breasts and the widening of the pelvis in girls, the appearance of facial hair and the broadening of shoulders in boys, and the appearance of body hair and changes in voice and skin in both boys and girls.

Changes in primary and secondary sexual characteristics occur in a predictable sequence for boys and for girls. Figure 14–2 shows these changes and the ages when they typically occur for boys and girls. For girls, puberty begins with growth of the breasts and the growth spurt, followed by the appearance of pubic hair. **Menarche**,

Primary sex characteristics:

maturation of the organs directly involved in reproduction.

Secondary sex characteristics:

physical maturation, other than the reproductive organs, such as the development of breasts in girls and facial hair in boys.

Menarche:

the start of menstruation.

Figure 14–2

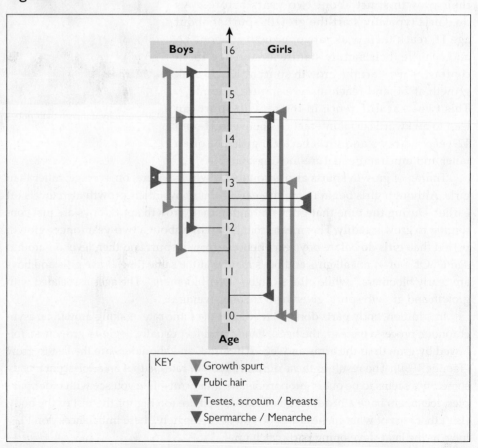

KEY
▼ Growth spurt
▼ Pubic hair
▼ Testes, scrotum / Breasts
▼ Spermarche / Menarche

Child Development and Family Policy

Preventing Osteoporosis

Osteoporosis is a disease that causes a person's bones to become thin and brittle and, as a consequence, to sometimes break. Although osteoporosis can strike at any age, people over 50 are at greatest risk because, at that age, bone tissue starts to break down more rapidly than new bone can be formed. Approximately 80 percent of people who have osteoporosis are women because, after menopause, the ovaries no longer produce estrogen, which guards against bone deterioration.

Osteoporosis often has its roots in childhood and adolescence, as this is when bones acquire nearly all of their mass. For bones to develop properly, children and adolescents need to consume approximately 1300 mg of calcium daily. This is the equivalent of about three cups of milk, half an ounce of cheese, and a cup of spinach. In addition, children and adolescents should engage in weight-bearing exercise for 30 minutes daily for at least five days a week. Weight-bearing exercises strengthen bones by causing them to carry the body weight. Walking, running, tennis, climbing stairs, aerobic dancing, and cross-country skiing are all good forms of weight-bearing exercise. Swimming, cycling, and rowing (machine or otherwise) do not require the bones to support body weight, so they are not good weight-bearing exercises (although, of course, they do benefit the heart, lungs, and muscles).

Communicating the importance of calcium intake and weight-bearing exercise might be one way we can help adolescents build strong bones and protect themselves against osteoporosis later in life.

---

the onset of menstruation, typically occurs at about age 13. Early menstrual cycles are usually irregular. During this time, young girls are especially at risk for pregnancy, as they cannot necessarily predict with any degree of certainty when they might be ovulating.

For boys, puberty usually commences with the growth of the testes and scrotum, followed by the appearance of pubic hair, the start of the growth spurt, and growth of the penis. By about age 13, most boys reach **spermarche**, the first spontaneous ejaculation of seminal fluid, or semen (Hirsch, Lunenfeld, Modan, Ovadia, & Shemesh, 1985). Initial ejaculations often contain relatively few sperm; only months or sometimes years later do sufficient sperm exist to fertilize an egg (Chilman, 1983).

Osteoporosis:
a disease of the bones, in which they become brittle and easily break.

Spermarche:
the first spontaneous ejaculation of seminal fluid.

Mechanisms of Maturation

LO2 List the factors that cause the physical changes associated with puberty.

The pituitary gland regulates many of the physical changes occurring during puberty and helps to regulate physical development by releasing growth hormone. In addition, the pituitary regulates pubertal changes by signalling other glands to secrete hormones. During the early elementary school years—long before any outward signs of puberty appear—the pituitary signals the adrenal glands to release androgens, initiating the biochemical changes that will produce body hair. A few years later in girls, the pituitary signals the ovaries to release estrogen, which causes the breasts to enlarge, the female genitals to mature, and fat to accumulate. In boys, the pituitary signals the testes to release the androgen testosterone, which causes the male genitals to mature and muscle mass to increase.

Although estrogen is often described as a female hormone and androgen as a male hormone, estrogen and androgen are present in both prepubescent boys and girls to the same degree. At the earliest onset of puberty, girls' adrenal glands secrete androgens. The amount is very small compared to that secreted by boys' testes but is enough to influence the emergence of body hair. In boys, the testes secrete very small amounts of estrogen, which explains why some boys' breasts enlarge, temporarily, early in adolescence.

The timing of pubertal events is regulated, in part, by genetics. For example, a mother's age at menarche is related to her daughter's age at menarche (Graber,

Amenorrhea:

the absence of a menstrual period in a girl who has achieved puberty.

Brooks-Gunn, & Warren, 1995). However, these genetic forces are strongly influenced by the environment, particularly an adolescent's nutrition and health. In general, puberty occurs earlier in adolescents who are well nourished and healthy than in adolescents who are not. For example, puberty occurs earlier in girls who are heavier and taller but later in girls who are afflicted with chronic illnesses or who receive inadequate nutrition (St. George, Williams, & Silva, 1994). On the other hand, girls involved in weight-restricting sports, such as gymnastics, tend to have a later menarche followed by more inconsistent periods (Iversen, 1990; Picard, 1999). Higher levels of competition were also associated with abnormal eating behaviour, psychiatric eating disorders, and **amenorrhea** (Picard, 1999).

Historical data point to the same conclusion concerning the importance of nutrition and health care for menarche. In many industrialized countries around the world, the average age of menarche has declined steadily over the past 150 years, at the beginning of which time menarche may have been as late as age 17 (Graham, Larsen, & Xu, 1999; Varea et al., 2000). More recent data show a continued decline. For example, in the United States, the average age of menarche was 13.3 in women born before 1920, compared to about 12.4 more recently (McDowell, Brody, & Hughes, 2007). This drop, in part, reflects improvements in health care over the past 100 years (Graham et al., 1999; Herman-Giddens, 2007; Varea et al., 2000); however, other less positive factors may play a role in earlier menarche, including obesity, decline of activity, and exposure to environmental toxins (Herman-Giddens, 2007; McDowell et al., 2007).

What may surprise you is that the social environment also influences pubertal onset, at least for girls. Menarche occurs at younger ages in girls who experience much family conflict (Belsky, Steinberg, & Draper, 1991; Moffit, Caspi, Belsky, & Silva, 1992). Furthermore, girls who are depressed begin to menstruate at a younger age than girls who are not depressed (Graber et al., 1995). Family conflict and depression may lead to early menarche by affecting levels of the hormones that trigger menarche (Graber et al., 1995).

Behavioural genetics researchers in the Netherlands have added to our understanding of the timing and onset of puberty by demonstrating that different factors in the environment affect different aspects of pubertal development, including menarche, breast development, and the appearance of pubic hair (van den Berg et al., 2006). Breast development usually is the first sign of puberty and has been observed as young as 7 years of age, sometimes due to normal processes and sometimes due to underlying pathologies. In addition, menarche onset is affected by geographical area, socio-cultural status, and ethnic factors (Ong, Ahmed, & Dunger, 2006). Early onset of puberty tends to be related to psychosocial problems, including international migration and adoption, homes with absent fathers, availability of particular nutrients in the diet, and malnutrition in the prenatal period and early years of development (van den Berg et al., 2006). Genes also express the timing of breast development and the appearance of pubic hair (Ong et al., 2006), although pubic hair appears to be affected by a different set of environmental factors than are breast development and menarche (van den Berg et al., 2006). In Canada, an 8.8-month decline in age at menarche has been observed, and links also have been made between body weight and menarche (Harris, Prior, & Koehoorn, 2008).

Considerable discussion has occurred in the research literature over the past decade about whether the onset of puberty actually has declined significantly, particularly in girls. While some declines have been noted (van den Berg et al., 2006), other researchers emphasized that declines in developed nations may not be as dramatic as initially thought (Whincup et al., 2001). In some areas, what might appear to be a dramatic decline in the onset of menarche could be due to a significant decline in the onset of menarche in disadvantaged populations, in which the average age of menarche was already higher than average (Ong et al., 2006).

Psychological Impact of Puberty

LO3 **Describe how physical changes affect adolescents' psychological development.**

Of course, teenagers are well aware of the changes taking place in their bodies. Not surprisingly, some of these changes affect adolescents' psychological development.

BODY IMAGE.   Compared to children and adults, adolescents are much more concerned about their overall appearance. Many Canadian teenagers look in the mirror regularly, checking for signs of additional physical change. Generally, girls tend to worry more about appearance and are more likely to be dissatisfied (Brooks-Gunn & Paikoff, 1993; Unger & Crawford, 1996), in part due to self-comparison with the young women unrealistically portrayed in online media. In contrast, boys are concerned about their appearance in early adolescence but become more pleased over the course of adolescence as pubertal change takes place (Gross, 1984).

RESPONSE TO MENARCHE AND SPERMARCHE.   Fortunately, many adolescent girls today know about menstruation before it happens—usually from discussions with their mothers or instruction at school. Being prepared, their responses are usually fairly mild. Most girls are moderately pleased at this new sign of maturity but moderately irritated by the inconvenience and messiness of menstruation (Brooks-Gunn & Ruble, 1982). Girls usually tell their moms about menarche right away and, after two or three menstrual periods, tell their friends too (Brooks-Gunn & Ruble, 1982). However, not all girls are prepared, and a lack of preparation can, indeed, make achieving menarche a difficult time for them. Cultural variation exists in terms of how menarche is experienced;

Checking for change in physical appearance.

however, the defining characteristic across a variety of cultures is secrecy, and few women report actual cultural rituals associated with their experience of menarche (Uskul, 2004), although some cultures do have specific rituals (see, for example, the Children and Families around the World feature to learn about how one culture celebrates menarche).

In general, less is known about boys' reaction to spermarche. Gaddis and Brooks-Gunn (1985) found that boys know about spontaneous ejaculations beforehand, and they often get their information by reading, not by asking parents. However, other researchers have found that boys often are actually surprised by the event, feel curious and more grown up after it, and keep it secret from others (Downs & Fuller, 1991; Stein & Reiser, 1994).

COGNITIVE CONTROL AND THE DEVELOPING BRAIN.   Adolescents are often thought to be extraordinarily moody—moving from joy to sadness to irritation to anger over the course of a day. And the source of teenage moodiness is often presumed to be the influx of hormones associated with puberty—hormones running wild. In fact, the evidence indicates that adolescents are moodier than children and adults but not primarily due to hormones (Steinberg & Morris, 2001), and this is more of a stereotype of adolescence (Gross & Hardin, 2007; Hines & Paulson, 2007). Researchers often find that rapid increases in hormone levels are associated with greater irritability and greater impulsivity, but the relations tend to be small and are found primarily in early adolescence (Buchanan, Eccles, & Becker, 1992).

If hormones are not responsible, what causes teenage mood changes? Some insights come from an elaborate study in which teenagers carried electronic pagers for a week (Csikszentmihalyi & Larson, 1984). When paged by researchers, the adolescents briefly described what they were doing and how they felt. The record of a

Children and Families around the World

How the Apache Celebrate Menarche

Many cultures have rituals—**rites of passage**—that mark the transition into adulthood. Rites of passage usually follow a script that changes little from year to year. During the ceremony, initiates usually wear apparel reserved for the occasion that denotes their special position. For example, generations of high school students have attended a graduation ceremony in which, wearing the traditional cap and gown, they march toward a stage (often accompanied by Edward Elgar's "Pomp and Circumstance") to receive their diplomas.

The Western Apache, who live in the southwest region of the United States, traditionally have a spectacular ceremony to celebrate a girl's menarche (Basso, 1970). After a girl's first period, a group of older adults decide when the ceremony will be held and select a sponsor—a woman of good character and wealth who is unrelated to the initiate. On the day before the ceremony, the sponsor serves a feast for the girl and her family; at the end of the ceremony, the family reciprocates, symbolizing that the sponsor is now a member of their family.

The ceremony itself begins at sunrise and lasts a few hours. The initiate dresses in ceremonial attire and goes through a number of phases with help from an older person, such as her sponsor, to mark her transition to maturity. The girl's rite of passage into adulthood is commemorated through the ceremony and understandings that are special to people of her cultural heritage.

The ceremony is a signal to all in the community that the initiate is now an adult, and it tells the initiate herself that her community now expects adult-like behaviour from her. Some evidence exists, however, that the use of puberty rituals may be in decline in some cultures, as women begin to see themselves in more modernized roles (Werbner, 2009).

Jeremy Woodhouse/Blend Images/Getty Images

Celebrating adolescent maturation.

Rites of passage:

rituals that mark transition to adulthood.

typical adolescent is shown in Figure 14–3. His mood shifts frequently from positive to negative, sometimes several times in a single day. For this boy, like most of the adolescents in the study, mood shifts were associated with changes in activities and social settings. Teens are more likely to report being in a good mood when with friends or during recreation; they tend to report being in a bad mood when in adult-regulated settings, such as school class-rooms or at a part-time job. Because adolescents often change activities and social settings many times in a single day, they appear to be moodier than adults.

Genuine moodiness in adolescence that is not related to social settings and activities is actually more rare and of concern. A primary cause of atypical moodiness is bipolar disorder, which is a serious mood disorder involving unstable swings in emotion (Koplewicz, 2002). In addition, a tendency to ruminate or brood extensively about things can be an early sign of risk for depression (Kuyken, Watkins, Holden, & Cook, 2006).

Ongoing problems with impulsivity also may not be what people think. Many young people seem to be impulsive during youth, and some hypothesizing about adolescent impulsivity being linked to issues of brain maturation has occurred. However, impulsive behaviour in adolescence can often be linked to problems with impulsivity in the early years and can be reduced through early interventions focused on goal-directed behaviour, such as educational achievement (Romer, 2010).

Nevertheless, sensation-seeking and risk-taking behaviour do increase during adolescence (Forbes & Dahl, 2010; Romer, 2010; Willoughby, Good, Adachi, Hamza, & Tavernier, 2014) and are related to increased rates of preventable injury and mortality. However, increases in risky behaviour does not tend to be linked

Figure 14–3

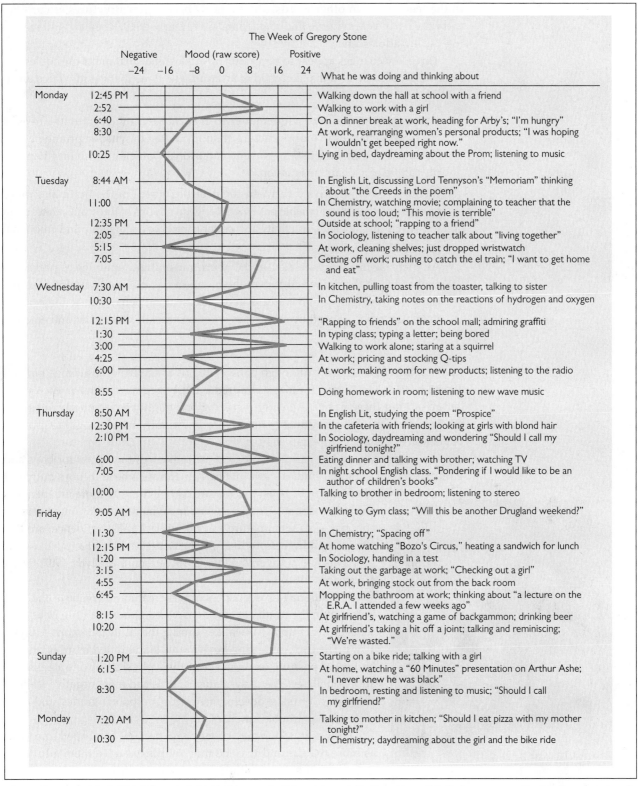

The Week of Gregory Stone

| | | Negative | Mood (raw score) | Positive | What he was doing and thinking about |

to structural deficits in the developing brain (Romer, 2010). Rather, Romer (2010) argued that adolescents have difficulty coping with new forms of adult behaviour (e.g., sexuality, romantic interests) that are driven, in part, by activation of hormones relating to puberty (Forbes & Dahl, 2010). In addition, asynchrony in maturational levels of development between the affective and cognitive control systems in the brain can lead to increased vulnerability for risk-taking behaviour in the teen years. In other words, although the basic brain structures are present from the early years (Luna, Padmanabhan, & O'Hearn, 2010), they are still maturing during adolescence.

Three key changes appear to occur during adolescence that make the adolescent brain very different from that of a child or an adult. The three changes identified are as follows (Steinberg, 2010):

- A change in the ratio of white matter to grey matter in the prefrontal areas of the brain—changes in brain structure are due not just to synaptic pruning but to changes in the characteristics of myelin and axonal diameter, which may improve the calibre of axonal transmission.

- Increases in connectivity between the prefrontal area of the brain and other areas—stronger, more reliable pathways between regions of the brain can result in improved functional connectivity and better control over cognitive and emotional processes.

- An increase in activity related to the neurotransmitter dopamine in pathways connecting to the prefrontal area of the brain—a rise in activity related to dopamine may bring about an increase in reward-seeking behaviour at a faster rate than maturation in cognitive control over reward-seeking behaviour and emotion regulation occurs.

RATE OF MATURATION.   Although puberty begins at age 10 in the average girl and age 12 in the average boy, for many children puberty begins months or even years before or after these norms. An early-maturing boy might begin puberty at age 11, whereas a late-maturing boy might start at 15 or 16. An early-maturing girl might start puberty at 9, a late-maturing girl at 14 or 15.

Maturing early or late has psychological consequences that differ for boys and girls. Several longitudinal studies show that early maturation benefits boys but, most often, not girls. Boys who mature early tend to be more independent and self-confident. They also tend to be more popular with peers. In contrast, girls who mature early often lack self-confidence, are less popular, and are more likely to be depressed and have behaviour problems (Ge, Conger, & Elder, 1996; Simmons & Blyth, 1987; Swarr & Richards, 1996).

The differing consequences of early maturation on boys and girls is shown in the results of an extensive longitudinal study of adolescents growing up in Milwaukee during the 1970s (Simmons & Blyth, 1987). The early-maturing boys in this study dated more often and had more positive feelings about their physical development and athletic abilities. The early-maturing girls had more negative feelings about their physical development, received poorer grades, and were more often in trouble in school.

Early maturation may benefit boys because others perceive them as more mature and may be more willing to give them adult-like responsibilities. Late-maturing boys often are frustrated because others treat them like little boys instead of like young men. Early maturation may hamper girls' development by leading them to associate with older adolescents who apparently encourage them to engage in age-inappropriate activities, such as drinking, smoking cigarettes, and sex, for which they are ill prepared (Ge et al., 1996).

Psychoneuroendocrinology is a new area in which researchers study the relationship between variables in psychology, neurology,

Rados; Brzozo/Fotolia

Which of these age-peer girls reached puberty first?

immunology, and endocrinology. For example, some researchers are examining the relationship between off-time (early or late) puberty onset and **cortisol reactivity**, which is the relationship of cortisol levels in the body to stress. Too high or too low a level of cortisol reactivity has been associated with antisocial behaviour in boys experiencing off-time onset of puberty (Susman et al., 2010).

Cortisol reactivity: the change in the body's cortisol levels in response to stress.

By young adulthood, many of the effects associated with rate of maturation vanish. When late-maturing boys finally mature, others will treat them like adults, and the few extra years of being treated like a child will not be harmful. For some adolescents, particularly early-maturing girls, rate of maturation can have long-lasting effects. A girl who matures early, who is pressured into sex, and who becomes pregnant ends up with a different life course than a girl who matures later and is better prepared to resist pressures for sex. Thus, sometimes rate of maturation can lead to events that influence the path that development follows through the rest of life.

Ask Yourself

At first blush, the onset of puberty would seem to be due entirely to biology. In fact, though, the child's environment influences the commencement of puberty. Summarize the ways in which biology and experience interact to trigger the beginning of puberty.

14.2 Sexuality

∨ Learning Objectives

After reading the module, you should be able to do the following:

LO4 Describe why some adolescents are sexually active and why so few use contraceptives.

LO5 Indicate what determines an adolescent's sexual orientation.

LO6 Discuss what circumstances make date rape especially likely.

Physical changes in adolescence make sexuality a central issue for teenagers. Teens are also preoccupied with sex because it is emphasized in the media and also seen as a way to establish adult status. In this module we'll explore the emergence of sexual behaviour during adolescence, and, as we do, we'll try to understand why many teenagers have sex without contraception.

Sexual Behaviour

LO4 Describe why some adolescents are sexually active and why so few use contraceptives.

Many adolescents first experience sexual behaviour as **masturbation**, self-stimulation of the genitals. Teenage boys are more likely than girls to report masturbation and to report beginning masturbating at a younger age (Oliver & Hyde, 1993). From masturbation, sexual experience usually progresses to kissing, petting above the waist, petting below the waist, and then to intercourse. For 12- and 13-year-old

Masturbation: self-stimulation of the genitals.

adolescents, sexual behaviour tends to include hugging, holding hands, and kissing, with heavy petting and intercourse occurring less often (Williams, Connolly, & Cribbie, 2008). For youth between the ages of 15 and 24 in Canada, the average age for first sexual intercourse is 16.5 (SIECCAN, 2009). By the end of adolescence, the majority of North American boys and girls acknowledge having had intercourse at least once (Jakobsen, 1997; Miller et al., 1997; Rodgers & Rowe, 1993), although participation rates have been declining among Canadian adolescents in recent years, according to the Sex Information and Education Council of Canada (SIECCAN, 2009).

While masturbation in youth is not uncommon, some research points to problems in psychosocial maturity that can arise in relation to a cultural acceptance of habitual masturbation, pornography, and recreational sex (Gisla, 2015), which has become much more common in popular culture (Garcia, Reiber, Massey, & Merriwether, 2012). Given the ubiquity of the internet for many societies, young people are exposed to explicit sexual information more frequently and easily than at any time in the past (Gunter, 2014; Shek, Xie, & Ma, 2015). Positive child development and family functioning are protective factors against adolescent use of pornography, but concern exists that childhood is becoming increasingly sexualized, resulting in both physical and psychological consequences (Olfman, 2008), including the objectification of girls and the reduction in social responsibility in boys. **Sexualization** of childhood is linked not just to early exposure to explicit sex in the media but also to the blurring of lines between adult and child fashion, music, and video games. In addition, exposure to pseudoestrogens can have an impact on pubertal development through increasing rates of obesity and the rising prevalence of these chemicals in foods and other products (Olfman, 2008).

For boys with more advanced pubertal development who are high in sensation seeking, internet pornography use tends to be higher and is associated with a decline in academic performance six months after use started (Beyens, Vandenbosch, & Eggermont, 2015). Boys, in general, report more online pornography and **sexting** behaviour than girls, and levels of online pornography use and sexting are affected by use of alcohol for boys (Morelli, Bianci, Baiocco, Pezzuti, & Chirumbolo., 2016). Use of online pornography in order to become aroused appears to increase with age for boys (Ševčikova & Daneback, 2014).

Ševčikova and Daneback (2014) found that about one-third of youth reported that they accessed pornography online to learn something about sex. On the other hand, many young people are exposed to explicit sexual content online without seeking it out. In one study, exposure to intrusive sexual content while online bothered most girls, although they did not tend to tell others about these experiences (Ševčikova, Simon, Daneback, & Kvapilik, 2015). Girls' likelihood of discussing online pornography in mixed-gender peer settings increased with age, particularly in the context of romantic relationships (Ševčikova & Daneback, 2014). However, both boys and girls were reluctant to discuss online pornography use with adults (Ševčikova & Daneback, 2014). High levels of online pornography use tend to be associated with youth who assume that people have sex early in life and that people generally favour a variety of sexual techniques (Weber, Quiring, & Daschmann, 2012). Parents who pay attention to these issues in their older children and are willing to discuss them might be able to correct mistaken assumptions in their youth. In addition, use of special software to filter and restrict child and youth access to the internet can protect against exposure to pornography.

Having said this, however, rates of sexual behaviour can be affected by problems with self-report. In other words, young people have to acknowledge that they are participating in sexual activity, and they have to report on that sexual involvement accurately and without exaggeration or bravado. Sexuality is a sensitive topic with young people, and they do not readily discuss the issue with adults, let

Sexualization:

putting sexual information into a context where it otherwise would not exist or does not normally occur.

Sexting:

sending a text message with sexual content.

alone with university researchers. As a result, efforts must be taken to improve the validity of results obtained through adolescent self-report of involvement in sexual behaviour. One way to improve reporting on sensitive topics, such as sexuality or substance abuse, is to increase the impersonal nature of the reporting by having adolescents fill out questionnaires without supervision or use computerized data entry to increase the privacy of self-report. These kinds of methods can improve the quality of data received from adolescents regarding sensitive issues (Williams et al., 2004).

In addition, the fact that most North American teenagers are sexually experienced by age 19 needs to be put in proper perspective. First, sexually "experienced" is a bit of a misnomer: Most teenagers have had intercourse with only one partner. Second, rates of sexual intercourse are intermittent during adolescence, and some adolescents do not have sex at all. Third, gender, regional, and ethnic differences abound in the prevalence of adolescent sexual activity. About 25 percent more boys have had sex than girls, African American adolescents begin sexual activity at a younger age than other groups, and teenagers living in rural areas and inner cities are more likely to be sexually active than teens living in the suburbs (Steinberg, 1999).

The Society of Obstetricians and Gynaecologists of Canada has produced a remarkable website (www.sexualityandu.ca) dedicated to providing adolescents with reliable information about sexuality and sexually transmitted infections. In addition, the Council of Ministers of Education, Canada (CMEC), in co-operation with Health Canada, released a study in 2002 of adolescent sexual health and AIDS infection. Both of these organizations emphasize the ongoing risk to Canadian youth of sexually transmitted infections, including AIDS, chlamydia, and the human papilloma virus.

CMEC (2002) found that, by Grade 9, 23 percent of boys and 19 percent of girls in Canada had experienced sexual intercourse; this rate rose to 40 percent of boys and 46 percent of girls by eleventh grade. Most youth reported familiarity with condom use, and approximately 25 percent of youth reported using both a condom and birth control pills at the time of their last intercourse, with condom use on the increase in recent years (SIECCAN, 2009). About 75 percent of Canadian youth surveyed report using condoms during intercourse (SIECCAN, 2009). Failure to use a condom can result from sexual intercourse being unplanned or unexpected (CMEC, 2002). In addition, use of condoms tends to decrease as adolescents become older, increasing risk for pregnancy and sexually transmitted infections (SIECCAN, 2009). Also available without parental consent in many areas is emergency contraception. The purpose of emergency contraception is to prevent implantation of a zygote after unprotected sex (SIECCAN, 2009). Although differing perspectives exist as to the morality and ethics of this contraceptive method, with many viewing the method as a form of abortion, the Adolescent Health Committee of the Canadian Pediatric Society issued a formal statement (which can be viewed at www.cps.ca/documents/position/emergency-contraception) indicating its position on adolescent use of this method to prevent unwanted pregnancies after unprotected or inadequately protected sexual intercourse.

CMEC (2002) also found that girls with low self-esteem and students with low attachment to school were more likely to engage in risky sexual behaviour. For both boys and girls, reasons for not having sex primarily were that they were "not ready" or "had not yet had the opportunity." Both boys and girls reported "love" and "curiosity/experimentation" as reasons for engaging in sexual activity. Brooks-Gunn and Paikoff (1993) noted that boys and girls can differ in their reasons for having sex, with most boys seeing sex as more recreational and girls often seeing sex as a form of romance and love.

Engaging in sexual behaviour can be affected by many factors, including culture, parenting style, and adolescent self-concept (Li, Connolly, Jiang, Pepler, & Craig, 2010;

Williams et al., 2008). In fact, a number of factors are involved (Capaldi, Crosby, & Stoolmiller, 1996; Windle & Windle, 1996). Parents' and peers' attitudes toward sex play a key role. In one study of high school students (Treboux & Busch-Rossnagel, 1995), positive attitudes toward sex by parents and friends were associated with students' positive attitudes, which, in turn, were associated with more frequent and more intense sexual behaviour. In another study of junior high and high school students (DiBlasio & Benda, 1990), sexually active adolescents believed that their friends were also sexually active. They also thought the rewards of sex (e.g., emotional and physical closeness) outweighed the costs (e.g., guilt and fear of pregnancy or infection). Thus, sexual activity reflects the influence of parents and peers as well as an individual's beliefs and values. Miller, Forehand, and Kotchick (1999) found that parents influence teens' sexual behaviour through a number of mechanisms, including the degree to which they monitor their teen's behaviour, the degree to which they communicate openly with their teens, and their own attitudes about sexual behaviour. They further found that active discouragement of sexual behaviour, knowledge of how their teens were spending their time, and open communication all contributed toward reducing adolescents' involvement in sexual behaviour.

The Research to Practice feature describes a study in which the investigators looked carefully at the nature of parents' influence on adolescents' sexual behaviour.

SEXUALLY TRANSMITTED INFECTIONS (STIs). Adolescent sexual activity is worrisome because a number of diseases are transmitted from one person to another through sexual intercourse. In addition, for people who have been diagnosed with a sexually transmitted infection, the re-infection rate after one year is 25 percent for women and about 14 percent for men (Peterman et al., 2006).

Sexually transmitted viral infections include genital herpes, hepatitis B, the human papilloma virus, genital warts, and the human immunodeficiency virus (HIV). Trichomoniasis is caused by a parasite, but sexually transmitted infections such as chlamydia, syphilis, and gonorrhea are caused by bacteria. According to the Canadian AIDS Treatment Information Exchange (CATIE, 2014), 80 percent of new cases of chlamydia were among youth as well as 67 percent of new cases of gonorrhea and 32 percent of new cases of syphilis. Although these infections can have serious complications if left untreated, they are usually cured readily with antibiotics if they are

Research to Practice

How Parents Influence Adolescents' Sexual Behaviour

Parents don't always feel that they have a lot of control over adolescent behaviour, particularly in the area of dating and sexual relationships. However, parents can and do have a greater degree of influence over adolescent sexual behaviour than they might realize. Miller, Forehand, and Kotchick (1999) studied parental influence over teen sexual behaviour, and they found that certain characteristics of parenting did, indeed, affect what teens did when they were not around their parents. In a study of 907 14- to 16-year-old African American and Hispanic high school students, these researchers found that certain kinds of relationship characteristics between parents and their

teens had important outcomes regarding teen sex. Both adolescent boys and girls tended to be less active sexually (less frequent sex and fewer partners) when parents monitored their behaviour carefully, communicated with them effectively, and did not endorse adolescent sex. Talking about sex-related issues per se was unrelated to adolescents' sexual behaviour. Parents definitely influence their teens' sexual behaviour in a number of distinct ways. To reduce teenage sex, parents should actively discourage it, know what adolescents do in their free time (and with whom), and have open, relaxed, and secure lines of communication with their youth. Teen sex is most likely to occur when parents approve of it, poorly supervise their teens, and rarely talk with them.

detected. For example, left untreated, chlamydia can cause infertility and other problems. Untreated syphilis can lead to serious cardiovascular problems, psychosis, and
other problems; as well, some STIs are fatal.

According to CATIE (2014, just over one-quarter of all new HIV diagnoses in
Canada occur in youth between the ages of 15 and 29. About 79 percent of youth HIV
diagnoses are in boys. Overall, boys make up 24 percent of HIV diagnoses in males,
while girls make up 20 percent of all HIV diagnoses in females. According to CATIE,
almost two-thirds of all HIV diagnoses in youth resulted from males having sex with
males. One-fifth were from heterosexual sex, 9 percent were from injection drug use,
and 3 percent were from a possible combination of males having sex with males and
using injection drugs at the same time. For youth in Canada, HIV is more prevalent
in youth who inject drugs, youth who live on the street, and males who have sex with
males (see also Siushansian, Nguyen, & Archibald, 2000).

The most common sexually transmitted infection in Canada is the human papilloma virus (HPV), according to the Society of Obstetricians and Gynaecologists of
Canada (SOGC, 2009). HPV is transferred by skin-to-skin contact during sex and
does not require penetration through intercourse to be transmitted. It affects the area
between the genitals and the anus. Although over 100 forms of HPV exist, most are
harmless and only about 30 are transmitted sexually. Some types of HPV cause warts
on the anus, vagina, vulva, penis, and thighs. Other HPV infections can be much more
serious, causing precancerous lesions, which can lead to cancers of the cervix, anus,
and other genital areas.

No tests currently are available to test for HPV infection, and most people will
not know that they have one. The more sexual partners a person has, the greater the
chance of contracting HPV. Also, although condoms work for many sexually transmitted infections, they do not cover all of the skin and, as a result, are not as effective in
controlling HPV infection. However, SOGC (2009) has made the following recommendations to control the incidence of HPV infection:

- Have absolutely no skin-to-skin sexual contact.
- Have one sexual/intimate partner forever.
- Women should have regular Pap tests to detect abnormal cervical cells.
- Women should consider the known pros and cons of having the vaccination now
  available to prevent certain types of HPV.

Unfortunately, SOGC estimates that about 75 percent of Canadians will experience one HPV infection during the course of their lifetime, although many Canadians
don't even know about the virus. Clearly, more public education and research will be
important to controlling the transmission of this type of virus.

TEENAGE PREGNANCY AND CONTRACEPTION.   Adolescents' sexual behaviour
also is a cause for concern because, in Canada, approximately 29 babies are born live
per 1000 girls between the ages of 15 and 19 and approximately 15 per 1000 for girls
between the ages of 15 and 17 (SIECCAN, 2009). This compares to a national rate
in the same age grouping of approximately 42 babies per 1000 in the United States
(Martin et al., 2009). Dryburgh (2000) noted varying teenage pregnancy rates among
the provinces. The Prairie provinces, Yukon, and Northwest Territories have had the
highest rates, while Quebec, the Maritimes, and Newfoundland and Labrador have
had the lowest rates.

In 2014, of 81 897 medically induced abortions performed in Canada, 31 940 were
performed for girls under the age of 25, with 11 percent of these for girls under the
age of 20 (Canadian Institute for Health Information (CIHI), 2014). Figure 14–4 shows
Canadian abortion rates across a number of age groups for the years 1997 to 2005.
According to Statistics Canada, the 2003 abortion rate among teenaged girls under the

Figure 14–4

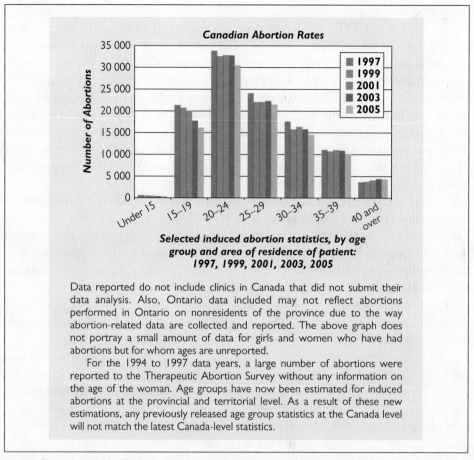

Selected induced abortion statistics, by age group and area of residence of patient: 1997, 1999, 2001, 2003, 2005

Data reported do not include clinics in Canada that did not submit their data analysis. Also, Ontario data included may not reflect abortions performed in Ontario on nonresidents of the province due to the way abortion-related data are collected and reported. The above graph does not portray a small amount of data for girls and women who have had abortions but for whom ages are unreported.

For the 1994 to 1997 data years, a large number of abortions were reported to the Therapeutic Abortion Survey without any information on the age of the woman. Age groups have now been estimated for induced abortions at the provincial and territorial level. As a result of these new estimations, any previously released age group statistics at the Canada level will not match the latest Canada-level statistics.

SOURCE: Based on data from Statistics Canada, 2008. Statistics Canada, Client Services Division.

age of 20 was 14.5 per 1000 girls, down from 15.7 the year before. The Canadian teenage abortion rate has declined gradually since 1997.

Use of contraceptives tends to decrease as adolescents become older, increasing risk for pregnancy and infection. Teenage mothers and their children usually face very difficult challenges. If this is the case, why do so many teens become pregnant? The answer is simple: Few sexually active teenagers use birth control. Those who do often use ineffective methods, such as withdrawal, or practise contraception inconsistently (Besharov & Gardiner, 1997; National Research Council, 1987).

Adolescents' infrequent use of contraceptives can be traced to the following factors (Adler, 1994; Gordon, 1996):

- *Ignorance:* Many adolescents are seriously misinformed about the facts of conception. For example, many do not know when conception is most likely to occur during the menstrual cycle, and some adolescents do not know how to use contraceptives.

- *Illusion of invulnerability:* Too many adolescents deny reality. They believe they are invincible—"It couldn't happen to me"—and that only others become pregnant.

- *Lack of motivation:* For some adolescent girls, becoming pregnant is appealing. They think having a child is a way to break away from parents, gain status as an independent-living adult, and have "someone to love them."

- *Lack of access:* Some teenagers do not know where to obtain contraceptives, and others are embarrassed to buy them.

One strategy to address teen pregnancy involves making contraceptives more readily available. In many high schools throughout the United States, students can obtain contraceptives, usually by visiting a health clinic located in the school. Many programs require parents' permission for students to obtain contraceptives, but some do not. For unmarried Canadian girls between the ages of 15 and 17 using contraception, the most frequent types used were oral contraception and condoms (Fisher & Black, 2007).

Providing contraceptives in schools is not the only solution to decreasing teenage pregnancy. Broader educational programs that present the truth about sex, teenage pregnancy, AIDS, and contraception can be effective for adolescents, who too often rely on peers for information about health and sexuality (Boyer & Hein, 1991; SIECCAN, 2009; Smylie, Maticka-Tyndale, & Boyd, 2008). Such programs not only teach the relevant biology but also include a focus on responsible sexual behaviour or abstention from premarital sex altogether (Dryfoos, 1990; SIECCAN, 2009). These programs might also have the added benefit of indirectly reducing the incidence of child abuse and neglect (Mersky & Reynolds, 2007).

One effective program in the United States is called Postponing Sexual Involvement (Howard & McCabe, 1990). Under the direction of trained, older adolescents, students discuss the pressures to become involved sexually, common "lines" that teens use to induce others to have sex, and strategies for responding to those lines. Accompanying the discussions are opportunities for students to practise the strategies in role-playing sessions. Students who participate in these programs are less likely to have intercourse; when they do have intercourse, they are more likely to use contraceptives (Howard & McCabe, 1990). What is clear, however, is that sexual education programs need to provide a full range of sexual health information, not only information on abstinence, so that students are fully educated about their sexual health (SIECCAN, 2009).

Sexual Orientation

LO5 Indicate what determines an adolescent's sexual orientation.

For most adolescents, dating and romance involve members of the opposite sex. However, as part of the search to establish an identity, many adolescents wonder, at least in passing, if they are homosexual. In fact, roughly 15 percent of adolescent boys and girls report emotional and sexual attractions to a member of their own sex (D'Augelli, 1996). For most adolescents, these experiences are simply a part of the larger process of role experimentation common to adolescence. However, the adolescent search for self-definition leads to roughly 5 percent of teenage boys and girls identifying themselves as gay in their sexual orientation. This identification usually occurs in mid-adolescence, but not until young adulthood do most gay individuals express their sexual orientation publicly (D'Augelli, 1996).

Why do gay and lesbian adolescents wait so long—three to five years—before declaring their sexual orientation? Many believe, correctly, that their peers are not likely to support them (Newman & Muzzonigro, 1993). For example, in one American survey, only 40 percent of 15- to 19-year-old boys agreed that they could befriend a gay person (Marsiglio, 1993). Adolescents who said that they could not befriend a gay peer were most often younger, identified themselves as religious fundamentalists, and had parents who were less educated.

The roots of sexual orientation are poorly understood and generate considerable controversy in both social and scientific circles (Bailey et al., 2016). Scientists have, however, discredited several theories of sexual orientation. Research (Bell, Weinberg,

About 5 percent of teens identify themselves as gay.

& Hammersmith, 1981; Golombok & Tasker, 1996; Patterson, 1992) shows that each of the following is false:

- Sons become gay when raised by a domineering mother and a weak father.
- Girls become lesbians when their father is their primary role model.
- Children raised by gay or lesbian parents usually adopt their parents' sexual orientation.
- Gay and lesbian adults were, as children, seduced by an older person of their sex.

If all these ideas are false, what determines a person's sexual orientation? Many have argued that biology plays an important role through heredity and hormones (Hamer, Hu, Magnuson, & Hu, 1993; Meyer-Bahlburg et al., 1995). Another idea (Bem, 1996) is that genes and hormones don't produce sexual orientation per se but lead to temperaments that affect children's preference for same- and opposite-sex activities. Children who do not enjoy gender-typical activities come to see themselves as different, ultimately leading to a different gender identity. In addition, the American Institute of Bisexuality has sponsored researchers who are proposing sexual orientation continuums rather than discrete categories for sexual orientation (Savin-Williams, 2016), making the description and study of sexual orientation much more complex than most researchers to date have examined.

In an effort to help people understand issues related to sexuality, the American Psychological Association (APA) has summarized research on sexual orientation in the following official statement:

> There is no consensus among scientists about the exact reasons that an individual develops a heterosexual, bisexual, gay or lesbian orientation. Although much research has examined the possible genetic, hormonal, developmental, social and cultural influences on sexual orientation, no findings have emerged that permit scientists to conclude that sexual orientation is determined by any particular factor or factors. (American Psychological Association, n.d.)

Transgender person:

a person who self-identifies as neither male nor female.

While some youth also self-identify as neither male nor female, describing themselves as **transgender persons**, the APA has stated that, as with sexual orientation, there is no one scientific explanation that explains why some people identify themselves as neither male nor female (American Psychological Association, 2011). Transgender identity is not always grounded in genetics. However, some people are born with genetic anomalies that require surgical intervention to make the child have more clearly male or female genitalia, as is the situation for people born with disorders of sexual development.

Disorders of sexual development:

a genetic condition in which a person's internal sexual organs do not match their external genitals, also called intersex conditions.

Disorders of sexual development arise when the person's internal sexual organs (testes or ovaries) do not match their external genitals. These kinds of circumstances can be the result of chromosomal anomalies or inappropriate exposure to male or female hormones during development. For example, an individual could have both XX and XY chromosomal material with both male and female gonadal tissues. These true genetic anomalies are called "intersex" conditions (MedlinePlus, 2015). Intersex conditions, however, do not represent all circumstances in which people self-identify as transgender.

Some people have begun to question whether scientific answers to the origins of gender orientation are relevant to political discussions of rights and responsibilities in

pressmaster/Fotolia

society and the fair treatment of people who self-identify as being transgender or having a lesbian, gay, bisexual, queer, or other sexual orientation (Bailey et al., 2016). The point they are trying to make is not that research on sexual orientation is irrelevant but that fair treatment is important for all people, regardless of scientifically studied origins or causes for why people are as they are.

What is clear is that gay and lesbian people face many special challenges (Berlan, Corliss, Field, Goodman, & Austin, 2010; Dysart-Gale, 2010; Saewyc et al., 2006; Williams, Connolly, Pepler, & Craig, 2003). Their family and peer relationships are often disrupted. They are often bullied and attacked, both verbally and physically. Given these problems, it's not surprising that gay and lesbian youth often experience mental health problems, such as anxiety, depression, and substance abuse (D'Augelli, 1996; Hershberger & D'Augelli, 1995; Plöderl & Tremblay, 2015; Rotheram-Borus, Rosario, Van Rossem, & Reid, 1995). In addition, Batejan, Jarvi, and Swenson (2015) found that sexual minority and bisexual youth are at particularly high risk for episodes of **nonsuicidal self injury**, such as superficial cutting or other acts that destroy bodily tissue without the person intending for the behaviour to result in suicide. Suicidality also is a prevalent problem of concern among lesbian, gay, bisexual, and queer individuals in general (Batejan et al., 2015). While some research exists to suggest that schools with peer-support groups called gay-straight alliances have a lower incidence of suicide among gay youth (Saewyc, Konishi, Rose, & Homma, 2014), few studies have been done, and they tend to be only correlational in nature. More research needs to be done in this area to understand what features of youth experience and school environment can most effectively reduce suicide for gay youth and also for all youth.

Nonsuicidal self injury: acts that destroy bodily tissue without the person intending for the behaviour to result in suicide.

In recent years, social changes have helped gay and lesbian youth respond more effectively to these unique challenges. The official stigma associated with being gay or lesbian was removed in 1973 when the American Psychological Association and the American Psychiatric Association declared that homosexuality was not a psychological disorder. In 2013, the American Psychiatric Association also rewrote diagnostic criteria for transgendered individuals, such that being transgender itself is not a disorder; however, experiencing a negative emotional state in relation to being transgender may be diagnosed as gender dysphoria. Other social changes include more (and more visible) gay role models as well as more centres for gay and lesbian youth. These resources are making it easier for gay and lesbian youth to understand themselves and cope with the many demands of adolescence.

Sexual Coercion

LO6 Discuss what circumstances make date rape especially likely.

Many adolescent and young women are forced to have sexual intercourse by males they know, a situation known as **date rape** or **acquaintance rape** (Ogletree, 1993) (see Figure 14–5). Traditional sex-role socialization helps set the stage for sexual coercion. Males learn that an intense sexual drive is a sign of masculinity. Females learn that being sexually attractive is one way to gain a male's attention. However, "good girls" are expected to be uninterested in sex and to resist attempts for sex. Both men and women learn these expectations; consequently, men might assume that a woman says no because she is supposed to say no, not because she really means it (Muehlenhard, 1988). Unless, and sometimes even if, a woman's communications are crystal clear—"STOP!! I don't want to do this!"—an adolescent or young adult male might assume, incorrectly and egocentrically, that her interest in sex matches his own (Kowalski, 1992).

Date rape (acquaintance rape): forced sexual intercourse with an acquaintance or friend, often on a social outing.

A number of circumstances increase the possibility that adolescent boys and young men will misinterpret or ignore an adolescent girl's or young woman's verbal

Figure 14–5

Women don't cause acquaintance rape. Rapists do.

But there are things you can do to reduce the risks of being raped by someone you know.

❶ STAY away from men who: put you down a lot, talk negatively about women, think that "girls who get drunk should know what to expect," drink or use drugs heavily, are physically violent, don't respect you or your decisions.

❷ SET sexual limits and intentions. Communicate them early and firmly.

❸ DON'T pretend you don't want to have sex if you really do.

❹ STAY sober.

❺ DON'T make men guess what you want. Tell them.

❻ REMAIN in control. Pay your own way. Make some of the decisions.

❼ LISTEN to your feelings.

❽ FORGET about being a "nice girl" as soon as you feel threatened.

❾ LEARN self-defense. Know how to yell. Take assertiveness training.

❿ LEARN self-defense. Know how to yell. Take assertiveness training.

For more information, please contact CARE at 805-893-3778.
To speak directly to a confidential advocate, call 805-893-4613.
CARE services are provided through the University of California,
Santa Barbara.

SOURCE: Reproduced by permission of Campus Advocacy Resources & Education, University of California, Santa Barbara.

or nonverbal communications regarding sexual intent. For example, heavy drinking usually impairs a person's ability to effectively and clearly send and interpret messages about sexual intent (Abbey, 1991). Yet another factor is a couple's sexual history. If a couple has had sex previously, the man might dismiss his partner's protests, interpreting them as fleeting feelings that can be overcome easily (Shotland & Goodstein, 1992). In all cases, both sexes, not just men, must pay attention to their partners' verbal and nonverbal messages about not wanting sex. In addition, young people need to be careful not to get involved in social situations where they can be taken advantage of easily.

The Making Children's Lives Better feature describes several ways to prevent date rape.

A FINAL REMARK.   Sexual behaviour and sexuality are enormously complicated and emotionally charged issues, even for adults. Adults need to recognize this complexity and help provide teenagers with skills for dealing with the issues involved in their emerging sexuality.

Making Children's Lives Better

Preventing Date Rape

Most approaches to date rape prevention emphasize the importance of communication. The ad shown in Figure 14–5 is part of one approach to encourage communication about sex. Date-rape workshops are another approach (Feltey, Ainslie, & Geib, 1991). Most workshops emphasize the need for females to be clear and consistent in expressing their intent. Before engaging in sex, boys need to understand a girl's intentions and not simply make assumptions. Here are some guidelines that are often presented at such workshops; you might find them useful (Allgeier & Allgeier, 1995):

1. Know your own sexual policies. Decide when sexual intimacy is acceptable for you.

2. Communicate these policies openly and clearly.
3. Avoid being alone with a person until you have communicated these policies and believe that you can trust the person.
4. Avoid using alcohol or other drugs when you are with a person with whom you do not wish to become sexually intimate.
5. If someone tries to force you to have sex, make your objections known: Talk first, but struggle and scream if necessary.

Ask Yourself

Sexually active teenagers typically do not use contraceptives. How do connections between cognitive, social, and emotional development result in failure to use contraceptives?

What do you think of the SOGC recommendations for controlling HPV infection, and what implications would they have for Canadian society?

14.3 Health

Learning Objectives

After reading the module, you should be able to do the following:

LO7 Describe the elements of a healthy diet for adolescents, and note why some adolescents have disordered eating.

LO8 Recognize whether adolescents get enough exercise, and identify the pros and cons of participating in high school sports.

LO9 Name the common obstacles to healthy growth during adolescence.

In terms of health, adolescence is a time of transition. On the one hand, teens are much less affected by the minor illnesses that would have kept them at home, in bed, as children. On the other hand, teens are at much greater risk for harm because of their own unhealthy and risky behaviours. In this module, we'll look at some of the factors essential to adolescent health. We'll start with nutrition.

Nutrition

LO7 **Describe the elements of a healthy diet for adolescents, and note why some adolescents have disordered eating.**

The physical growth associated with puberty means that the body has special nutritional needs. A typical teenage girl should consume about 2200 calories per day; a typical boy should consume about 2700 calories. (The exact levels depend upon a number of factors, including body composition, growth rate, and activity level.) Teenagers also need calcium for growth and iron to make extra hemoglobin, the matter in red blood cells that carries oxygen. Boys need additional hemoglobin because of their increased muscle mass; girls need hemoglobin to replace what is lost during menstruation.

Eating fast food in the teen years can rob youth of important nutrients, such as calcium and iron.

Unfortunately, although many North American teenagers consume enough calories each day, too much of their intake consists of fast food rather than well-balanced, home-cooked meals. The result of too many fast-food meals—burgers, fries, and a milkshake—is that teens might get inadequate iron or calcium and far too much sodium and fat and be at risk for obesity and cardiovascular problems, such as high blood pressure. Inadequate iron often leaves teens listless and moody; inadequate calcium intake means bones might not develop fully, placing the teen at risk later in life for osteoporosis. In fact, the Canadian Institute for Health Information (2009) found that, for girls between the ages of 12 and 17, type of food eaten is a better predictive of being overweight than activity level. Girls who had a higher daily intake of healthy foods such as fruits and vegetables tended to weigh less than girls who ate less healthily. For boys, however, physical activity level was still a better predictor of being overweight.

Fast-food consumption is not the only risky diet issue common among adolescents. Many teenage girls worry about their weight and are attracted to the "lose 10 pounds in 2 weeks!" diets advertised on TV and in teen magazines. Many of these diets are flatly unhealthy—they deprive youth of the many substances necessary for growth. Similarly, for philosophical or health reasons, many adolescents decide to eliminate meat from their diets. Vegetarian diets can be healthy for teens but only when adolescents replace meat with other adequate sources of protein, calcium, and iron.

Other food-related problems common in adolescence are two eating disorders: anorexia and bulimia.

ANOREXIA AND BULIMIA. Tracey Gold, an actress on the TV program *Growing Pains*, had to leave the show in the early 1990s. She had begun dieting compulsively, had withered away to a mere 40 kilograms, and had to be hospitalized (Sporkin, Wagner, & Tomashoff, 1992). Tracey suffered from an eating disorder. Singer Karen Carpenter eventually died as a result of her battle with her eating disorder (Saukko, 2008). **Anorexia nervosa** is a psychological disorder marked by a persistent refusal to eat and an irrational fear of being overweight. Individuals with anorexia nervosa have a grossly distorted image of their own body and will claim to be overweight despite being painfully thin (Wilson, Hefferman, & Black, 1996). In addition, many engage in

Anorexia nervosa:

a psychological disorder marked by a persistent refusal to eat and an irrational fear of being overweight.

high levels of physical activity, which can have a major impact on their recovery from this disorder (Gümmer et al., 2015).

Anorexia is a very serious disorder that can lead to heart damage (Sachs, Harnke, Mehler, & Krantz, 2015). Without treatment, as many as 15 percent of adolescents with anorexia die (Wicks-Nelson & Israel, 1991).

A related eating disorder is bulimia nervosa. Individuals with **bulimia nervosa** alternate between binge eating—periods when they eat uncontrollably—and purging through self-induced vomiting, use of laxatives, or over-exercising. The frequency of binge eating varies remarkably among people with bulimia nervosa, from a few times a week to more than 30 times. What's common to all is the feeling that they cannot stop eating (Mizes, 1995).

Anorexia and bulimia are alike in many respects. Both disorders primarily affect females, although the incidence may be rising in boys. Girls are 10 times more likely than boys to be affected (Wilson et al., 1996). Also, both disorders emerge in adolescence and typically in girls who are well-behaved, conscientious, good students (Attie, Brooks-Gunn, & Petersen, 1990).

Both nature and nurture play a role in the development of anorexia and bulimia. Let's start with nurture and cultural ideals of the female body. In many industrialized cultures—and certainly in North America—the ideal female body is tall and slender. As girls enter adolescence, these cultural norms become particularly influential. Also during adolescence, girls experience a "fat spurt," gaining about 11 kilograms, most of it fat. Though this pattern of growth is normal, some girls unfortunately perceive themselves as overweight and begin to diet (Halpern, Udry, Campbell, & Suchindran, 1999). This is especially the case when the girl's mother is preoccupied with her own weight (Attie et al., 1990). Faced with a cultural value of being thin and a change in their bodies, adolescent girls believe they are fat and try to lose weight.

Family dynamics also contribute to anorexia. Adolescent girls are more prone to anorexia if their parents are autocratic, leaving their adolescent daughters with little sense of self-control. Dieting allows the girls to assert their autonomy and achieve an individual identity (Graber, Brooks-Gunn, Paikoff, & Warren, 1994; Swarr & Richards, 1996).

Cultural emphasis on thinness, combined with a regimented home life, can explain many cases of anorexia. Of course, most teenage girls growing up in regimented homes in the United States do not become anorexic, which raises the question of biological factors. Twin and family studies point to an inherited predisposition for anorexia and bulimia, perhaps in the form of personality that tends to be rigid and anxious (Strober, 1995). Thus, anorexia is most likely to develop in girls who inherit the predisposition, who internalize cultural ideals of thinness, and whose parents grant them little independence. However, more research needs to be done, including a focus on boys, who appear to be increasingly at risk for developing eating disorders (Couturier, 2007; Golden et al., 2003) but for reasons that may not be the same as those that are apparent for girls and women (Gadalla, 2009).

Bulimia nervosa:

a psychological disorder characterized by binge eating followed by purging through vomiting, use of laxatives, or over-exercising.

Physical Fitness

LO8 **Recognize whether adolescents get enough exercise, and identify the pros and cons of participating in high school sports.**

Being physically active promotes mental and physical health, both during adolescence and throughout adulthood. Individuals who regularly engage in physical activity reduce their risk for obesity, cancer, heart disease, diabetes, and mental health problems, such as depression and anxiety. Regular activity typically means exercising for 30 minutes, at least three times a week, at a pace that keeps an adolescent's heart rate at about 140 beats per minute. Running, vigorous walking,

Figure 14–6

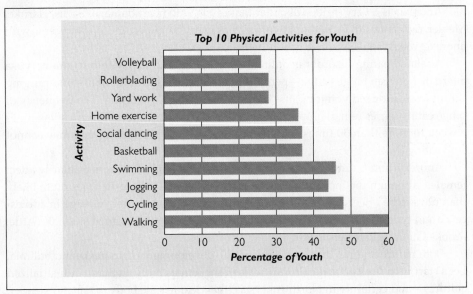

SOURCE: Based on data from Statistics Canada, Canadian Community Health Survey, 2000/01.

swimming, aerobic dancing, biking, and cross-country skiing are all examples of activities that can provide this level of intensity.

Unfortunately, the evidence indicates that most adolescents rarely get enough exercise. For example, in one study the researchers (Kann et al., 1995) asked high school students whether they had exercised at least three times for 20 minutes during the past week at a level that made them sweat and breathe hard. In Grade 9, about 75 percent of boys and 65 percent of girls said they had; by Grade 12, these figures had dropped to 65 percent for boys and 40 percent for girls. Part of the problem here is that, for many high school students, physical education classes provide the only regular opportunity for exercise. Yet a minority of high school students are enrolled in physical education, and most who are enrolled do not attend daily. Some youth also participate in organized sports, and girls' participation in these activities has been increasing over the years. For example, in Canada, girls' hockey has become more prevalent, particularly with the recent success of the women's hockey team at the Winter Olympics. However, if you look at Figure 14–6, which shows the top 10 physical activities for youth in Canada, notice what's not on the list—hockey, which came in at only 13 percent participation, along with fishing and golf!

Participating in sports has many benefits for youth. In addition to improved physical fitness, sports can enhance participants' self-esteem and can help them learn initiative (Larson, 2000; Whitehead & Corbin, 1997). Athletes can also learn about teamwork and competitiveness. At the same time, participation in sports has some potential costs. About 15 percent of high school athletes will be injured and require some medical treatment. Boys are most likely to be injured while playing football or wrestling; girls are injured while participating in cross-country skiing or soccer (Rice, 1993). Fortunately, most of these injuries are not serious and are more likely to involve bruises or strained muscles (Nelson, 1996).

The use of illegal drugs to improve performance in sports is a more serious problem (American Academy of Pediatrics, 1997). Some athletes use anabolic steroids, drugs that are chemically similar to the male hormone testosterone, to increase muscle size and strength and to promote more rapid recovery from injury. Approximately 5 to 10 percent of high school boys and 1 to 2.5 percent of high school girls report having used anabolic steroids. This is disturbing news because steroid use can damage the liver, reproductive system, skeleton, and cardiovascular system (increasing blood pressure and cholesterol levels); in addition, use of anabolic steroids is associated with mood swings, aggression, and depression. Parents, coaches, and health professionals need to be sure that high school athletes are aware of the dangers of steroids and should encourage youth to meet their athletic goals through alternative methods that do not involve drug use (American Academy of Pediatrics, 1997).

Threats to Adolescent Well-Being

LO9 **Name the common obstacles to healthy growth during adolescence.**

In Canada, injuries are responsible for approximately 56 percent of deaths between the ages of 1 and 19. Relatively few adolescents die from diseases; instead they are killed in accidents, with motor vehicle crashes being the greatest cause in Canada.

Sadly, many of these deaths are completely preventable. Deaths in automobile accidents are often linked to driving too fast, drinking alcohol, and not wearing seat belts (US Department of Health and Human Services, 1997). Deaths due to firearms are often linked to all-too-easy access to firearms in the home (Rivara & Grossman, 1996).

Adolescent deaths from accidents represent a theme we've seen earlier in this chapter: Many adolescents take risks that adults often find unacceptable. Teens may take unnecessary risks while riding skateboards, scooters, or bicycles. Some drive cars recklessly, engage in unprotected sex, and even use illegal and dangerous drugs. Although calling such behaviour stupid or irrational is tempting, Fischhoff and Quadrel (1995) reported that adolescents and adults often make decisions similarly, even though the outcome of that decision-making process sometimes differs for adolescents and adults. Specifically, adolescents and adults typically determine

Safety equipment is needed here.

- the alternative courses of action available
- the consequences of each action
- the desirability and likelihood of these consequences

and then integrate this information to make a decision.

To see this decision making in action, consider a teen deciding whether to drive home from a party with friends who have been drinking alcohol. She decides that she has two alternatives: (1) Try to find a ride with people who haven't been drinking but that she doesn't know well, or (2) ask her parents to come get her. Her analysis might run something like this:

> If I go home with my friends, I won't upset them (+) but I might be in an accident (–). If I go home with other people, I'll definitely make my friends mad (–) but will probably make it home safely (+). If I call my parents, I'll definitely upset my friends (–), probably annoy other people at the party (–), but I'll get home safely (+).

This basic analysis is sound and not much different from what an adult might do. The difference comes in the adolescent's weighing of the desirability of different consequences. Adolescents are likely to place greater emphasis on the social consequences of their decisions, such as upsetting their friends, and less emphasis on the health consequences, such as getting home safely (Steinberg, 1999). They're particularly likely to consider these social consequences when the standards for appropriate behaviour are not clear, as is often the case when it comes to drinking and to having sex.

Ask Yourself

How does adolescent risk taking illustrate the theme that children help to shape their own development?

What Would a Youth Worker Do?

When working with teenagers, youth workers are in a unique position to see young people when they are in groups of peers.

If you were a youth worker, and you noticed that a teenage girl was very thin and refusing to participate in activities involving food, what would you do? Should you say something to the youth? To her parents? How should you follow up on your concerns?

Summary

14.1 Pubertal Changes

Signs of Physical Maturation

- Puberty includes bodily changes in height, weight, and sexual maturation.

- Girls experience a growth spurt earlier than boys.

- Boys acquire more muscle, less fat, and greater heart and lung capacity.

- Sexual maturation occurs in predictable sequences for boys and girls.

- Sexual maturation includes the development of primary and secondary sex characteristics.

Mechanisms of Maturation

- When the pituitary gland signals the adrenal gland, ovaries, and testes to secrete hormones, the physical changes associated with puberty start.

- The timing of puberty is influenced by health, nutrition, and the social environment.

- Family conflict or depression can trigger earlier puberty in girls.

Psychological Impact of Puberty

- Puberty affects psychological functioning in adolescence.

- Puberty often results in an increased focus on personal appearance.

- Adolescents can become moodier than children and adults due to moods changing in response to frequent changes in their daily activities and social settings.

- Off-time puberty, whether early or late, can have a negative impact on children who are more reactive to stress.

- Overall, early maturation tends to be socially harmful to girls but beneficial to boys.

14.2 Sexuality

Sexual Behaviour

- Most teens in North America have had sexual intercourse by the end of adolescence.

- Boys tend to see sex as recreational, but girls tend to see it as romantic.

- If adolescents believe that their parents and peers approve of sex, then they are more likely to engage in it.

- Sexually transmitted infections and pregnancy are the main consequences of having unprotected sex.

- Use of condoms tends to decline with increasing age during adolescence.

- Parents can have a strong influence over whether teens engage in sex.

Sexual Orientation

- A small percentage of adolescents are attracted to members of their own sex.

- Sexual orientation probably has roots in biology.

- Gay and lesbian youth face many special challenges, including bullying and personal attack, and may suffer from mental-health problems as a result.

Sexual Coercion

- Adolescent and young adult females are sometimes forced into sex against their will, sometimes because males misinterpret or disregard females' intentions.

- Sexual coercion is particularly likely when either partner has been drinking alcohol or when the couple has had sex previously.

- Date-rape workshops strive to improve communication between males and females.

14.3 Health

Nutrition

- For proper growth, teenagers need to consume adequate calories, calcium, and iron.

- Many teenagers do not eat properly and do not receive adequate nutrition.

- Anorexia and bulimia are eating disorders that typically affect adolescent girls.

- Cultural standards of thinness, a need for independence within an autocratic family, and heredity all contribute to eating disorders in girls.

- Boys also are at risk for eating disorders, but more research needs to be done on factors that contribute to boys' risk for developing them.

Physical Fitness

- Individuals who work out at least three times weekly often have improved physical and mental health.

- Many high school students do not get enough exercise.

- Sports have many benefits for youth, including improved physical fitness, enhanced self-esteem, and understanding about teamwork.

- Potential difficulties with sport include risk of injury and abuse of performance-enhancing drugs.

Threats to Adolescent Well-Being

- Automobile accidents are the most common cause of death among Canadian teenagers.

- Reckless driving (e.g., too fast, no seat belts) contributes to an increased risk of death and can be prevented.

- Adolescents and adults often make decisions similarly, considering the alternatives available, the consequences of each alternative, and the desirability and likelihood of negative consequences.

- Outcomes of decision making sometimes differ for adults and adolescents because adolescents are more likely to emphasize the social consequences of actions.

Chapter Critical Review

1. In what respects is the psychological impact of puberty the same for boys and girls? In what respects does it differ?

2. Describe a rite of passage that you passed through during puberty. It might be one that is unique to your ethnic group or one that is common in North American society. What aspect of adulthood did it mark? How did it affect your self-concept?

3. How can Bem's theory of the development of sexual identity (Module 14.2) be explained in terms of the themes developed in this text?

4. Imagine that you are an "expert" who has been asked to talk to a class of Grade 6 students about sexual behaviour. Decide what you would tell the class and how you would do it.

5. Many teenagers do not eat well-balanced meals, and many do not get enough exercise. What would you do to improve teenagers' dietary and exercise habits?

See for Yourself

In recent years, colleges and universities in Canada have taken a more visible and vigorous stance against sexual assault and date rape. Many now offer a range of programs and services designed to prevent sexual assault and to assist those who are victims of it. Most universities have an office—usually associated with student services—dealing with women's concerns. These offices offer educational programs as well as counselling and confidential advice to women with problems. Some campuses sponsor sexual-assault awareness days that include workshops, films, and plays that promote greater understanding of the issues associated with sexual assault. On some campuses, female self-defence programs are offered. In these programs, which are often run by campus police, women are taught ways to reduce the risk of sexual assault and ways to defend themselves if they are attacked.

Find out which of these programs and services are available to women on your campus. If it's difficult to learn how your college or university deals with issues related to sexual assault and date rape, think about how you could make this information more available. If some of these services and activities are not available, think about how you could urge your college or university to provide them. See for yourself!

Chapter 15
Cognitive Processes in Adolescents

Minerva Studio/Fotolia

 MODULE

15.1 Cognition

15.2 Reasoning about Moral Issues

15.3 The World of Work

15.4 Special Challenges

One day, when Terry and Mabel came home from getting groceries, they found Sophie brooding on the couch in the living room in front of the TV, which was off. When they asked her what she was doing, Sophie described a show she had just watched on Doctors Without Borders. Sophie told them about the sacrifices it took to help people in war-torn regions and said how much she admired those doctors, but she also wondered about their families back home and how worried those families might be about their loved ones working in those conditions. Terry and Mabel wondered . . . was this the same girl who was going ga-ga over the latest teen singing sensation just last week?

Connect to My Virtual Child

What kinds of theories do you have about children? What ideas inform your thoughts and beliefs about the lives of children, how they are raised, and the nature of the human person? Use your access card and follow this link www.myvirtualchild.com to learn more about the world of the child. You can even virtually try to raise your own child.

15.1 Cognition

 ## Learning Objectives

After reading the module, you should be able to do the following:

LO1 List the distinguishing characteristics of formal operational thought.

LO2 Describe how information processing becomes more efficient during adolescence.

Adolescents are on the threshold of young adulthood, and this is particularly evident in their cognitive skill. In Jean Piaget's theory, which we'll consider in the first half of this module, adolescence marks the beginning of the fourth and final stage of intellectual development. In information processing, which we'll consider in the second half of the module, the transition to mature thinking occurs gradually throughout early and middle adolescence. As we examine these perspectives, you'll also see why adolescents don't always think in the sophisticated manner predicted by theories of cognitive development.

Piaget's Stage of Formal Operational Reasoning

LO1 List the distinguishing characteristics of formal operational thought.

Formal operational stage:

the final stage of Piagetian cognitive development, in which youth apply mental operations to abstract concepts via hypothetical thinking and deductive reasoning.

The concrete operational skills of elementary school children are powerful but linked to the real, to the here and now. In Piaget's **formal operational stage**, which extends from roughly age 11 into adulthood, children and adolescents apply mental operations to abstract entities, which allows children to think hypothetically and reason deductively. Freed from the concrete and the real, adolescents explore the possible— what might be and what could be.

Unlike time- and space-oriented concrete operational thinkers, formal operational thinkers understand that concrete reality is not the only possibility for thought. They can envision alternative or abstract realities and examine their consequences. For example, ask a concrete operational child, "What would happen if gravity meant that objects floated up?" or "What would happen if men gave birth?" and you're likely to get a confused or even irritated look and comment like, "It doesn't—they fall" or "They don't—women have babies." Reality is the foundation of concrete operational thinking. In contrast, formal operational adolescents use hypothetical reasoning to probe the implications of fundamental change in physical or biological laws.

Formal operations also allow adolescents to take a different, more sophisticated approach to problem-solving than concrete operational children. Formal operational thinkers can solve problems by creating hypotheses (sets of possibilities) and testing them. Piaget (Inhelder & Piaget, 1958) showed this aspect of adolescent thinking by presenting children and adolescents with several flasks, each containing what appeared to be the same clear liquid. They were told that one combination of the clear liquids would produce a blue liquid and were asked to determine the necessary combination.

A typical concrete operational youngster plunges right in, mixing liquids from different

Teens learn to be more systematic in their approach to tasks.

flasks in a haphazard way. Yet, formal operational adolescents understand that setting up the problem in abstract, hypothetical terms is the key. The problem is not really about pouring liquids but about forming hypotheses about different combinations of liquids and testing them systematically.

A teenager might mix liquid from the first flask with liquids from each of the other flasks. If none of those combinations produces a blue liquid, the adolescent would conclude that the liquid in the first flask is not an essential part of the mixture. Next, he or she would mix the liquid in the second flask with each of the remaining liquids. A formal operational thinker would continue in this manner until he or she found the critical pair that produced the blue liquid. For adolescents, the problem is not one of concrete acts of pouring and mixing; rather, they understand that the problem consists of identifying possible hypotheses (in this case, combinations of liquids) and then evaluating each one.

One spring many years ago, the *Indianapolis Star* held a contest for all its newspaper carriers. The person who created the most words from the letters contained in the words SAFE RACE would win two tickets to the Indianapolis 500 auto race. The winning entry had 126 words. The winner had created thousands of possible words—beginning with each of the letters individually, then all possible combinations of two letters (e.g., AS, EF) and continuing through all possible combinations of all eight letters (e.g., SCAREEFA, SCAREEAF)—then looked up all these possible words in a dictionary. Robert Kail knows about this event because he was the winner! Robert's systematic approach to problem-solving is typical of adolescent cognition.

In addition, because adolescents' thinking is not concerned solely with reality, they are also better able to reason logically from premises and draw appropriate conclusions. The ability to draw appropriate conclusions from facts is known as **deductive reasoning**. Suppose we tell a person the following two facts:

1. If you hit a glass with a hammer, the glass will break.
2. Bernie hit a glass with a hammer.

The correct conclusion, of course, is that "the glass broke," a conclusion that formal operational adolescents will reach. Concrete operational youngsters, too, will sometimes reach this conclusion but based on their experience and not because the conclusion is logically necessary. To see the difference, imagine that the two facts are now presented as follows:

1. If you hit a glass with a feather, the glass will break.
2. Bernie hit a glass with a feather.

The conclusion "the glass broke" follows from these two statements just as logically as it did from the first pair. In this instance, however, the conclusion is counterfactual—it

Deductive reasoning:

the ability to draw appropriate conclusions from facts.

Table 15–1 Summary Table

Characteristic Features of Formal Operational Reasoning	
Feature	Defined
Abstract	Adolescents' reasoning is no longer limited to the real and concrete but readily extends to ideas and concepts that are often quite removed from reality.
Hypothetical	Adolescents solve problems by constructing hypotheses and creating tests for these hypotheses.
Deductive	Adolescents are better able to reason logically from premises, even when those premises contradict everyday experience.

goes against what experience tells us is really true. Concrete operational 10-year-olds resist reaching conclusions that are counter to known facts; they reach conclusions based on their knowledge of the world. In contrast, formal operational 14-year-olds often reach counterfactual conclusions (Markovits & Vachon, 1989). They understand that these problems are about abstract entities that need not correspond to real-world relations.

Hypothetical and deductive reasoning are powerful tools for formal operational thinkers. The ability to ponder different alternatives makes possible the experimentation with lifestyles and values that occurs in adolescence. However, not all researchers have found that formal operational thinking occurs in all adolescents across all cultures, as measured by the tasks that Piaget used (Cole, 1996). While this criticism does not invalidate the concept of formal operations, it does point to the necessity of testing people with materials and tasks that are familiar to them. The problem is not so much that people from other cultures do not deductively reason; the problem is more how psychologists measure reasoning in people from cultures other than their own.

In Piaget's theory, cognitive development ends with the achievement of formal operations. Of course, adolescents and adults acquire more knowledge as they grow older, but their fundamental way of thinking remains unchanged, in Piaget's view. The defining characteristics of formal operational thinking are summarized in Table 15–1.

THEORY OF ACTUAL THINKING OR POSSIBLE THINKING. Just because children and adolescents attain a particular level of reasoning in Piaget's theory does not mean that they always reason at that level. Adolescents who are in the formal operational period often revert to concrete operational thinking. Adolescents often fail to reason logically, even when they are capable and when it would be beneficial. For example, adolescents typically show more sophisticated reasoning when the problems are relevant to them personally than when they are not (Ward & Overton, 1990).

Also, when the product of reasoning is consistent with adolescents' own beliefs, they are less likely to find flaws in the reasoning (Klaczynski & Narasimham, 1998). Adolescents (and adults, for that matter) do not always use the most powerful levels of thinking of which they are capable. Piaget's account of intellectual development is really a description of how children and adolescents can think, not how they always or even usually think.

In the next section, we'll see how information-processing theorists describe adolescents' thinking.

Information Processing during Adolescence

LO2 Describe how information processing becomes more efficient during adolescence.

For information-processing theorists, adolescence does not represent a distinct, qualitatively different stage of cognitive development. Instead, adolescence is considered

Figure 15–1

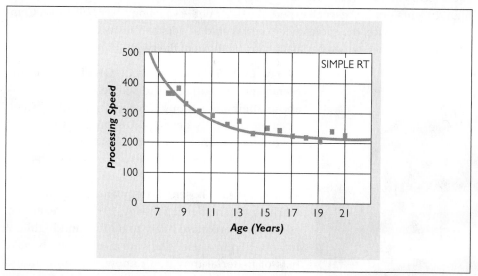

SOURCE: Based on data from Kail, R. (1991). Processing time declines exponentially during childhood and adolescence. Developmental Psychology, 27, 259–266.

to be a transitional period between the rapidly changing cognitive processes of childhood and the mature cognitive processes of young adulthood. Cognitive changes do take place in adolescence, but they are small compared to those seen in childhood. Adolescence is a time when cognitive processes are tweaked to adult levels.

These changes take place in several different elements of information processing.

BASIC PROCESSES OF WORKING MEMORY AND PROCESSING SPEED. Working memory is the site of ongoing cognitive processing, and processing speed is the speed with which individuals complete basic cognitive processes. Both achieve adult-like levels during adolescence. Adolescents' working memory has about the same capacity as adults' working memory, which means teenagers are better able to store information needed for ongoing cognitive processes. In addition, Figure 15–1 illustrates change in processing speed, exemplified in this case by performance on a simple response-time task in which individuals press a button as rapidly as possible in response to a visual stimulus. Simple response time declines steadily during childhood—from about one-third of a second at age 8 to one-quarter of a second at age 12—but changes little thereafter. This pattern of change is not specific to simple response time but is instead found for a wide range of cognitive tasks: Adolescents generally process information just about as quickly as young adults (Kail, 1991). Change in working memory and processing speed means that, compared to children, adolescents process information very efficiently.

CONTENT KNOWLEDGE. As children move into adolescence, they acquire adult-like levels of knowledge and understanding in many domains. Children, for example, may enjoy baseball or computers, but as adolescents they acquire true expertise. For example, many parents turn to their teens for help learning how to navigate the internet. This increased knowledge is useful for its own sake, but it also has the indirect effect

Adolescents have a lot to offer the world.

of allowing adolescents to learn, understand, and remember more of their new experiences (Schneider & Bjorklund, 1998; Schneider & Pressley, 1997). Imagine two junior high students—one a baseball expert, the other not—watching a baseball game. Compared to the novice, the adolescent expert would understand many of the nuances of the game and, later, remember many more features of the game.

Study skills usually improve with maturity.

Arieliona/Shutterstock

STRATEGIES AND METACOGNITIVE SKILL. Metacognitive skill refers to people's ability to think about their own thought processes and content. Although not fully developed, metacognitive ability in adolescence enables adolescents to become much better at identifying strategies appropriate for a specific task. Metacognition also enables adolescents to monitor the chosen strategy and verify that it is working (Schneider & Pressley, 1997). For example, adolescents are more likely to outline and highlight information in a text. They are more likely to make lists of material they don't know well and should study more. Also, they more often embed these activities in a master study plan (e.g., a list of assignments, quizzes, and tests for a two-week period). All these activities help adolescents learn more effectively and remember more accurately (Schneider & Pressley, 1997; Thomas et al., 1993). In addition, some evidence exists, based on research done out of McGill University (Shore, 2000), that adolescents who are gifted use metacognitive strategies differently and more flexibly than other youth. Adolescents, particularly early adolescents, have difficulty considering a broad range of possibilities and outcomes when making decisions. In later adolescence, however, metacognitive skills will become especially important for developing **reflective judgment** skills that develop over time and enable a young person to consider a much broader range of information in decision making (Kitchener, King, & Deluca, 2006).

Reflective judgment:

the ability to consider a broad range of information and outcomes in making a decision.

These changing features of information processing are summarized in Table 15–2.

Change in each of these elements of information processing occurs gradually. When combined, they contribute to the steady progress to mature thinking that is the destination of adolescent cognitive development.

Table 15–2 Summary Table

Information Processing during Adolescence	
Feature	**State in Adolescence**
Working memory and processing speed	Adolescents have working memory capacity and processing speed similar to that of adults, allowing them to process information efficiently.
Content knowledge	Adolescents' greater knowledge of the world facilitates understanding and memory of new experiences.
Strategies and metacognition	Adolescents are better able to identify task-appropriate strategies and to monitor the effectiveness of those strategies.

Ask Yourself

What kinds of difficulties might arise for adolescents if they were not able to engage in metacognitive thought?

15.2 Reasoning about Moral Issues

⌄ Learning Objectives

After reading the module, you should be able to do the following:

LO3 Describe how adolescents reason about moral issues.

LO4 Discuss how concern for justice and caring for other people contribute to moral reasoning.

LO5 Name the factors that help promote more sophisticated reasoning about moral issues.

Some teenagers (and adults as well) act in ways that earn our deepest respect and admiration, whereas others earn our utter contempt as well as our pity. In this module, we'll start our exploration of moral reasoning with an influential theory proposed by Lawrence Kohlberg.

Kohlberg's Theory

LO3 **Describe how adolescents reason about moral issues.**

Sometimes people find themselves caught in circumstances with no easy solution—any one decision could have a negative outcome or require people to behave in ways contrary to their beliefs or country's laws. In order to understand how people come to make moral decisions, Kohlberg created mini-stories to study how people reason about moral dilemmas. He made it very difficult to reach a decision in his stories because every alternative involved some undesirable consequences. In fact, no "correct" answer to a Kohlberg story exists—that's why the stories are referred to as moral "dilemmas." Kohlberg was more interested in the reasoning used to justify a decision than in the actual decision itself.

Kohlberg's best-known moral dilemma, about Heinz, whose wife is dying, appears below:

> In Europe, a woman was near death from cancer. One drug might save her, a form of radium that a druggist in the same town had recently discovered. The druggist was charging $2000, ten times what the drug cost him to make. The sick woman's husband, Heinz, went to everyone he knew to borrow the money, but he could only get together about half of what it cost. He told the druggist that his wife was dying and asked him to sell it cheaper or let him pay later, but the druggist said, "No." The husband got desperate and broke into the man's store to steal the drug for his wife. (Kohlberg, 1969, p. 379)

Kohlberg analyzed children's, adolescents', and adults' responses to a large number of dilemmas and identified three levels of moral reasoning, each divided into two stages. Across the six stages, the basis for moral reasoning shifts, moving from more concrete to more abstract reasoning. In the earliest stages, moral reasoning is based on external forces, such as the promise of reward or the threat of punishment. At the most advanced levels, moral reasoning is based on a personal, internal moral code and is unaffected by others' views or society's expectations. Just as with Piagetian theory, Kohlberg proposed a theory of moral development that involves more abstract,

Like cognitive, social, emotional, and motor development, moral reasoning also changes over time.

metacognitive thinking at higher levels. You can clearly see this gradual shift in the three levels:

- *Preconventional level:* For most children, many adolescents, and some adults, moral reasoning is controlled almost solely by obedience to authority and by rewards and punishments.

Stage 1: Obedience orientation. People believe that adults know what is right and wrong. Consequently, a person should do what adults say is right to avoid being punished. A person at this stage would argue that Heinz should not steal the drug because it is against the law (which was set by adults).

Stage 2: Instrumental orientation. People look out for their own needs. They often are nice to others because they expect the favour to be returned in the future. A person at this stage would say it was all right for Heinz to steal the drug because his wife might do something nice for him in return (i.e., she will reward him).

- *Conventional level:* For most adolescents and most adults, moral decision making is based on social norms—what is expected by others.

Stage 3: Interpersonal norms. Adolescents and adults believe that they should act according to others' expectations. The aim is to win the approval of others by behaving like "good boys" and "good girls." An adolescent or adult at this stage would argue that Heinz should not steal the drug because, by not doing so, others would see him as an honest citizen who obeys the law. A teenager might help an elderly individual because she wants others to think she is a nice person.

Stage 4: Social system morality. Adolescents and adults believe that social roles, expectations, and laws exist to maintain order within society and promote the good of all people. An adolescent or adult in this stage would reason that Heinz should steal the drug because a husband is obligated to do all that he possibly can to save his wife's life. Or a person in this stage would reason that Heinz should not steal the drug because stealing is against the law, and society must prohibit theft.

- *Postconventional level:* For some adults, typically those older than 25, moral decisions are based on personal, moral principles.

Stage 5: Social contract orientation. Adults agree that members of cultural groups adhere to a "social contract" because a common set of expectations and laws benefits all group members. However, if these expectations and laws no longer promote the welfare of individuals, they become invalid. Consequently, an adult in this stage would reason that Heinz should steal the drug because social rules about property rights are no longer benefiting individuals' welfare.

Stage 6: Universal ethical principles. Abstract principles like justice, compassion, and equality form the basis of a personal moral code that sometimes conflicts with society's expectations and laws. An adult at this stage would argue that Heinz should steal the drug because life is paramount, and preserving life takes precedence over all other rights.

Putting all of the stages together, Table 15–3 shows what Kohlberg's theory looks like.

Table 15–3 Stages in Kohlberg's Theory

Preconventional Level: Punishment and Reward

   Stage 1: obey authority

   Stage 2: behave nicely in exchange for future favours

Conventional Level: Social Norms

   Stage 3: live up to others' expectations

   Stage 4: follow rules to maintain social order

Postconventional Level: Moral Codes

   Stage 5: adhere to a social contract when it is valid

   Stage 6: develop personal morality based on abstract principles

SUPPORT FOR KOHLBERG'S THEORY.   Like Piaget, Kohlberg proposed that his stages form an invariant sequence. That is, individuals move through the six stages in the order listed and in only that order. If his stage theory is right, then level of moral reasoning should be strongly associated with age and level of cognitive development: Older and more advanced thinkers should, on average, be more advanced in their moral development, and indeed, they usually are (Stewart & Pascual-Leone, 1992).

For example, Figure 15–2 shows developmental change in the percentage of individuals who reason at Kohlberg's different stages. Stages 1 and 2 are common among children and young adolescents but not older adolescents and adults. Stages 3 and 4 are common among older adolescents and adults. The figure also shows that most adults' moral reasoning is at Stages 3 and 4, with few measured to be at the stages above Stage 4. While we can loosely associate stages with age ranges, some researchers are attempting to use sophisticated statistical modelling programs in an attempt to better predict how transitions and cyclical patterns in a moral reasoning stage model occur (Walker, Gustafson, & Hennig, 2001).

Support for Kohlberg's invariant sequence of stages also comes from longitudinal studies measuring individuals' level of reasoning over several years. Individuals do progress through each stage in sequence, and virtually no individuals skip any stages

Figure 15–2

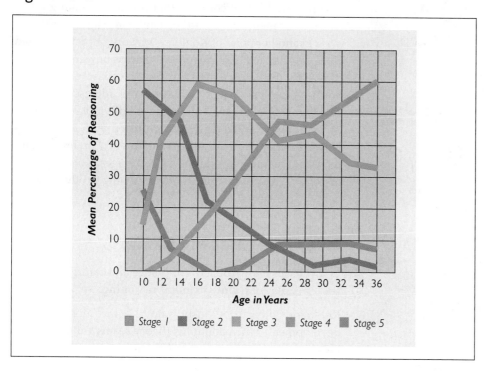

(Colby, Kohlberg, Gibbs, & Lieberman, 1983). Longitudinal studies also show that, over time, individuals become more advanced in their level of moral reasoning or remain at the same level. They do not regress to a lower level (Walker & Taylor, 1991).

Additional support for Kohlberg's theory comes from research on the link between moral reasoning and moral behaviour. In general, level of moral reasoning should be linked to moral behaviour. Remember that less advanced moral reasoning reflects the influence of external forces such as rewards and social norms, whereas more advanced reasoning is based on a personal moral code. Therefore, individuals at the preconventional and conventional levels would act morally when external forces demand, but otherwise they may not. In contrast, individuals at the postconventional level, where reasoning is based on personal principles, should be compelled to moral action even when external forces may not favour it.

Let's consider an example. Suppose that you knew that one of the least popular students in a class has been wrongly accused of stealing an iPod; you know that some friends in your group are actually responsible for the theft. What would you do? Speaking out on behalf of the unpopular student is unlikely to lead to reward. Furthermore, there are strong social norms against "squealing" on friends. So if you are in the preconventional or conventional level of moral reasoning, you would probably let the unpopular student be punished unfairly. But if you are at the postconventional level and see the situation in terms of principles of justice and fairness, you would be more likely to identify the real perpetrators despite the price to be paid in rejection by the group.

Many researchers report findings that support the hypothesized link between moral reasoning and moral action. In one study (Gibbs et al., 1986), high school teachers were asked to judge whether their students would defend their principles in difficult situations or if they would act morally only when it was fashionable or handy. High school students who were judged by their teachers to have greater moral courage tended to be more advanced in Kohlberg's stages than students who were judged less courageous. That is, students who protest social conditions tended to have higher moral reasoning scores. The converse is also true: Delinquent adolescents, whose actions are more likely to be morally offensive, tended to have lower moral reasoning scores than nondelinquent adolescents, who emphasized social norms and personal moral codes in their decision making rather than punishment and reward (Chandler & Moran, 1990).

On another point of Kohlberg's theory, support is mixed. Kohlberg claimed his sequence of stages is universal: All people in all cultures progress through the six-stage sequence. Some research shows that children and adolescents in cultures worldwide reason about moral dilemmas at Stage 2 or 3, just like North American children and adolescents. However, as we'll see in the Children and Families around the World feature, beyond the earliest stages, Kohlberg's theory often does not describe moral reasoning in other cultures very well (Snarey, 1985).

Gilligan's Ethic of Caring

LO4 Discuss how concern for justice and caring for other people contribute to moral reasoning.

Kohlberg's theory obviously is not the final word on moral development. Much about his theory seems valid, but findings like those described in the Children and Families around

Young people often find their own unique ways to explore moral aspects of their world.

Dr. Theresa Zolner

Children and Families around the World

Moral Reasoning in India

Many critics note that Kohlberg's emphasis on individual rights and justice reflects Western values and Judeo-Christian theology. Not all cultures and religions share this emphasis; consequently, moral reasoning might be based on different values in other cultures (Carlo, Koller, Eisenberg, Da Silva, & Frohlich, 1996; Keller, Edelstein, Schmid, Fang, & Fang, 1998).

Miller and Bersoff (1992) tested the hypothesis that cultural differences affect moral reasoning by constructing dilemmas with both justice-based and care-based solutions. For example:

> Ben planned to travel to San Francisco in order to attend the wedding of his best friend. He needed to catch the very next train if he was to be on time for the ceremony, as he had to deliver the wedding rings. However, Ben's wallet was stolen in the train station. He lost all of his money, as well as his ticket to San Francisco.
>
> Ben approached several officials as well as passengers . . . and asked them to lend him money to buy a new ticket. But, because he was a stranger, no one was willing to lend him the money he needed.
>
> While Ben . . . was trying to decide what to do next, a well-dressed man sitting next to him walked away . . . Ben noticed that the man had left his coat unattended. Sticking out of the man's coat pocket was a train ticket to San Francisco . . . He also saw that the man had more than enough money in his coat pocket to buy another train ticket. (p. 545)

One solution emphasized individual rights and justice:

> Ben should not take the ticket from the man's coat pocket even though it means not getting to San Francisco in time to deliver the wedding rings to his best friend. (p. 545)

Culture affects moral beliefs and values.

The other solution placed a priority on caring for others:

> Ben should go to San Francisco to deliver the wedding rings to his best friend even if it means taking the train ticket from the other man's coat pocket. (p. 545)

When children and adults living in the United States responded to dilemmas like this one about Ben, a slight majority selected the justice-based alternative. In contrast, when Hindu children and adults living in India responded to the same dilemmas, the overwhelming majority selected the care-based alternative.

---

the World feature indicate that Kohlberg's theory applies primarily to cultures with Western philosophical and religious traditions. However, researcher Carol Gilligan (1982; Gilligan & Attanucci, 1988) questioned how applicable Kohlberg's theory is even within the Western tradition. Gilligan argued that Kohlberg's emphasis on justice applies more to men than to women, whose reasoning about moral issues, or feminine morality, is often rooted in concern for others. Gilligan wrote, "The moral imperative that emerges repeatedly in interviews with women is an injunction to care, a responsibility to discern and alleviate the real and recognizable trouble of this world" (1982, p. 100). One of Gilligan's most important points is that a morality based on an ethic of care is different from the justice-based morality that Kohlberg proposed—and is no less important than the one Kohlberg proposed, either.

Clearly, moral reasoning reflects the culture in which a person is reared. Consistent with Kohlberg's theory, judgments by North American children and adults reflect their culture's emphasis on individual rights and justice, but judgments by Indian children and adults reflect their culture's emphasis on caring for other people as well as their religious values. Therefore, the bases of moral reasoning are not universal as Kohlberg claimed; instead, they reflect cultural and religious values. In fact, spirituality and religion have become an important part of psychological research.

This might seem surprising because, if you scan most textbooks in developmental psychology, you will find topics on social and moral development, but only the rarest of developmental psychology texts approaches a topic that actually is central to many people's lives: spiritual and religious development (Zolner, 2011). This could be, in part, due to a general lack of research on the topic in psychology or even a professional aversion, for various reasons, to the issue. Maybe psychologists just don't know what to do with the topic. Nevertheless, over the past decade or so, a considerable increase in research on the role of spirituality and religion in developmental psychology has been occurring (Roehlkepartain, Benson, King, & Wagener, 2006). For example, Holder, Coleman, and Wallace (2010) found that children who are more spiritual tend to be happier. Cultural and family factors play an important role in religious identity and participation (Lopez, Huynh, & Fuligni, 2011). However, psychologists' lack of knowledge or training in developmental issues of spirituality and religion can limit the degree to which they can be effective in assessing or treating youth in terms of religious and spiritual identity (Magaldi-Dopman & Park-Taylor, 2010; Zolner, in press).

One of the main reasons for the increase in psychological research can be linked to an increase in research on the Positive Youth Development Framework (PYDF; Lerner, Phelphs, Forman, & Bowers, 2009), which focuses on positive aspects of development that increase the opportunity for healthy outcomes in children's lives. Within the context of the PYDF, spirituality and religion are defined as aspects of individual and community life that promote thriving (Good, Willoughby, & Busseri, 2011). In addition, citing Bibby, Good, Willoughby, and Busseri (2011) pointed out that, although attendance at regular religious services has been declining over time in Western nations, over 75 percent of Canadian teens reported that they often wondered about spiritual questions.

According to Good, Willoughby, and Busseri (2011), spirituality and religion historically have been viewed as factors that protect against delinquency or promote identity formation. However, none of these research approaches has included the broader impact of spirituality and religion on child and adolescent development. These researchers noted that spirituality is the "search for sacred, divine, or nonmaterial aspects of life" and religiosity is "behaviour and beliefs associated with organized religion" (Good, Willoughby, & Busseri, 2011, p. 538). However, they further noted that considering the two as separate constructs is not as helpful as acknowledging that spirituality and religiosity (S/R) both encompass institutional and noninstitutional forms of connection to sacredness.

Adolescence is the main focus of much research on S/R due to the kinds of change in ideology and metacognition that happen during this period of development as well as the changes observed in their spiritual and religious beliefs (Good, Willoughby, & Busseri, 2011). New research has linked S/R factors to health risk behaviours, emotional adjustment, healthy identity formation, civic engagement, and a sense of purpose in life (Good, Willoughby, & Busseri, 2011). However, the researchers noted that little understanding has been developed in terms of how S/R affect development over time. They studied Canadian youth to see how S/R factors were configured within adolescence and found that youth tended to fall into five clusters. Findings for students in Grade 12 are reported in Table 15–4.

Table 15–4 Spirituality and Religiosity in Canadian Youth

Cluster	Description	Grade 12 Students
Aspiritual/Irreligious	Never engaged in any S/R behaviours	13 percent
Disconnected Wonderers	Virtually no involvement in S/R activities, prayer, or meditation	45 percent
High Institutional and Personal	Scored high on all S/R factors except meditation, which was average	8 percent
Primarily Personal	Above-average on spiritual wondering, connectedness to the sacred, and very frequent prayer, but low on meditation, religious activity involvement, and enjoyment of religious activities	26 percent
Meditators	High frequency of meditation but average for all other S/R factors	8 percent

SOURCE: Based on data from Good, M., Willoughby, T., & Busseri, M. A. (2011). Stability and change in adolescent spirituality/religiosity: A person-centered approach. Developmental Psychology, 47, 538–550.

The most striking aspect of the data in Table 15–4 is that 87 percent of youth report thinking about and feeling connected to spiritual ideas and a sense of the sacred in life, a prevalence that speaks to the importance of S/R variables to understanding child and youth development. The researchers proposed that S/R factors are part of core developmental processes in psychology, and they propose that further research be done to enhance our understanding of these developmental processes.

In her theory of morality, Gilligan proposed a developmental progression in which individuals gain greater understanding of caring and responsibility. In the first stage, children are preoccupied with their own needs. In the second stage, people care for others, particularly those who are less able to care for themselves, like infants and the aged. The third stage unites caring for others and for oneself by emphasizing caring in all human relationships and by denouncing exploitation and violence between people. For example, a teen might help at a homeless shelter not because she believes the homeless are needy but because she believes, first, that all humans should care for each other and, second, that many people are in the shelter because they've been exploited.

Like Kohlberg, Gilligan also believes that moral reasoning becomes qualitatively more sophisticated as individuals develop, progressing through a number of distinct stages. However, Gilligan emphasizes care (helping people in need) instead of justice (treating people fairly).

What does research tell us about the importance of justice and care in moral reasoning? Gilligan's claim that the genders differ in the bases of their moral reasoning is not wholly supported. Girls and boys as well as men and women reason about moral issues similarly (Walker, 1995). Both females and males often think about moral issues in terms of care and interpersonal relationships. Justice and care both serve as the basis for moral reasoning. It is the nature of the moral problem that largely determines whether justice, care, or both will be the basis for moral reasoning (Smetana, Killen, & Turiel, 1991).

Promoting Moral Reasoning

LO5 Name the factors that help promote more sophisticated reasoning about moral issues.

Whether it is based on justice or care, most cultures and most parents want to encourage adolescents to think carefully about moral issues. What can be done to help adolescents develop more mature forms of moral reasoning? Sometimes simply being exposed to more advanced moral reasoning is sufficient to promote developmental change (Walker, 1980). Adolescents may notice, for example, that older friends do not

Gilligan's theory focuses on caring and responsibility.

wait to be rewarded to help others. Or a teenager may notice that respected peers take courageous positions regardless of the social consequences. Such experiences apparently cause adolescents to reevaluate their reasoning on moral issues and propel them toward more sophisticated thinking.

Matsuba and Walker (2004) studied the personalities of young adults who were thought to be exemplary in terms of moral reasoning. The young adults in the study were chosen based on their having been identified as being highly committed to a number of social organizations to which the various youth belonged. Matsuba and Walker (2004) compared these young exemplars to 40 peers and found that the morally exemplary youth were more advanced in their moral reasoning and faith. In addition, they were generally more agreeable in nature as compared with their peers, more willing to form close relationships with others, and further along in terms of overall development of an adult identity. Obviously it would be nice to be able to encourage and foster moral reasoning in young people. The Child Development and Family Policy feature discusses just that.

Child Development and Family Policy

Promoting More Advanced Moral Reasoning

Kohlberg wasn't content to simply chart how moral reasoning changed with age. He also wanted to devise ways to foster sophisticated moral reasoning. Kohlberg discovered that discussion can be particularly effective in revealing shortcomings in moral reasoning. When people reason about moral issues with others whose reasoning is at a higher level, the usual result is that individuals' reasoning at lower levels improves (Berkowitz & Gibbs, 1985). During conversations of this sort, individuals at the preconventional level usually learn to adopt the logic of the adolescents arguing at the higher conventional level. Additional evidence for this comes from Kohlberg's research with Just Communities (Higgins, 1991; Power, Higgins, & Kohlberg, 1989), special groups of students and teachers in some U.S. high schools who meet to plan school activities and discuss school policies. Decisions about school activities and policies were reached democratically, with teachers and students each having one vote and teachers acting as discussion facilitators. Students were encouraged to consider the moral implications of their decisions and, as a consequence, tended to become more advanced in their moral thinking (Higgins, 1991; Power et al., 1989).

Adolescents who discuss moral issues with others can reason in a more sophisticated manner.

Research findings such as these send an important message to parents: Discussion is probably the best way for

Discussing moral issues can improve moral reasoning in youth.

parents to help their children think about moral issues in more mature terms (Walker & Taylor, 1991). Research consistently shows that mature moral reasoning comes about when adolescents are free to express their opinions on moral issues to their parents, who are, in turn, expressing their own opinions and, consequently, exposing their adolescent children to more mature moral reasoning (Hoffman, 1988, 1994).

Ask Yourself

How similar is Piaget's stage of formal operational thought to Kohlberg's stage of conventional moral reasoning?

15.3 The World of Work

⌄ Learning Objectives

After reading the module, you should be able to do the following:

LO6 Understand how adolescents come to select an occupation.

LO7 Recognize the impact of part-time employment on adolescents.

What do you want to be when you grow up? Children are often asked this question in fun. Beginning in adolescence, however, the question takes on special significance because work is such an important element of the adult life that is looming on the horizon. All jobs help define who we are. In this module, we'll see how adolescents begin to think about possible occupations. We'll also look at adolescents' first exposure to the world of work, which usually comes about with part-time jobs after school or on weekends.

Career Development

Crystallization:
using one's emerging identity in adolescence as a source of ideas about careers.

LO6 Understand how adolescents come to select an occupation.

Choosing a career is difficult, in part because it involves determining the kinds of jobs that will be available in the future. A general trend exists in North America toward more jobs in the service industries (e.g., health care, banking, education) and fewer jobs in agriculture and manufacturing. According to Statistics Canada's e-Book (Statistics Canada, 2005), the fastest-growing demand is for computer programmers, computer systems analysts, engineers, architects, and technicians.

Knowing the types of jobs that experts predict will be plentiful, how do adolescents begin the long process of selecting an occupation that will prove satisfying to them? Theories about vocational choice describe this process. According to a theory proposed by Donald Super (1976, 1980), identity is a primary force in an adolescent's choice of a career. At about age 13 or 14, adolescents use their emerging identities as a source of ideas about careers, a process called **crystallization**. Teenagers use their ideas about their own talents and interests to limit potential career prospects. A teenager who is extroverted and sociable may decide that working with people would be the career for him. Another who excels in math and science may decide she'd like to teach math.

"Of course creative writing is important. You want to write home for money when you go go away to college, don't you?"

Marty Bucella/CartoonStock Ltd.

Decisions are provisional, and adolescents experiment with hypothetical careers, trying to envision what each might be like and then deciding on what to do once they leave high school.

At about age 18, adolescents extend the activities associated with crystallization and enter a new phase. During **specification**, individuals further limit their career possibilities by learning more about specific lines of work and starting to obtain the training required for a specific job. Our extroverted teenager who wants to work with people might decide that a career in sales would be a good match for his abilities and interests. The teen who likes math may have learned more about careers and decided she'd like to be an accountant. Some teens might begin an apprenticeship as a way to learn a trade, and in fact, some provinces, such as Ontario, have begun to focus more on offering educational opportunities in the trades to their youth.

The end of the teenage years or the early twenties marks the beginning of the third phase. During **implementation**, individuals enter the workforce and learn first-hand about jobs. This is a time of learning about responsibility and productivity, of learning to get along with co-workers, and of altering one's lifestyle to accommodate work. This period is often unstable; individuals may change jobs frequently as they adjust to the reality of life in the workplace.

PERSONALITY-TYPE THEORY. Super's (1976, 1980) work helps explain how self-concept and career aspirations develop hand in hand, but it does not explain why particular individuals are attracted to one line of work rather than another. Explaining the match between people and occupations has been the aim of a theory devised by John Holland (1985, 1987, 1996). According to **Holland's personality-type theory**, people find work fulfilling when the important features of a job or profession fit the worker's personality. Holland identified six prototypical personalities that are relevant to the world of work. Each one is best suited to a specific set of occupations, as indicated in the right-hand column of Table 15–5. Remember, these are merely prototypes.

This model is useful in describing the career preferences of African, Asian, European, Native, and Mexican American adolescents; it is useful for both men and women (Day, Rounds & Swaney, 1998), and it also is used in Canada. Holland (1996) demonstrated that, when people have jobs that match their individual personality types, in the short run they are more productive employees, and, in the long run, they have more stable career paths (Holland, 1996). For example, enterprising adolescents are likely to succeed in business because they enjoy positions of power in which they can use their verbal skills.

Specification:

limiting career possibilities by learning more about specific lines of work and starting to obtain the training required for a specific job.

Implementation:

entering the workforce and learning first-hand about jobs.

Holland's personality-type theory:

the theory that people find work fulfilling when the important features of a job or profession are a good fit with the worker's personality.

Table 15–5 Personality Types in Holland's Theory

Personality Type	Description	Careers
Realistic	Individuals enjoy physical labour and working with their hands, and they like to solve concrete problems.	Mechanic, truck driver, construction worker
Investigative	Individuals are task-oriented and enjoy thinking about abstract problems.	Scientist, technical writer
Social	Individuals are skilled verbally and interpersonally, and they enjoy solving problems using these skills.	Teacher, counsellor, social worker
Conventional	Individuals have verbal and quantitative skills that they like to apply to structured, well-defined tasks assigned to them by others.	Bank teller, payroll clerk, traffic manager
Enterprising	Individuals enjoy using verbal skills in positions of power, status, and leadership.	Business executive, television producer, real estate agent
Artistic	Individuals enjoy expressing themselves through unstructured tasks.	Poet, musician, actor

Trades often require apprenticeships.

Combining Holland's work-related personality types with Super's theory of career development gives us a very comprehensive picture of vocational growth. On the one hand, Super's theory explains the developmental progression by which individuals translate general interests into a specific career; on the other hand, Holland's theory explains what makes a good match between specific interests and specific careers.

Of course, trying to match interests to occupations can be difficult. Fortunately, several tests can be used to describe a person's work-related personality and the jobs for which a person is best suited. In the 1970s, John Holland developed a test called the Self-Directed Search (SDS), which is designed to assist people with their career and educational choices (PAR, Inc., 2013). People who take the SDS answer questions about their personal skills, job interests, activities, and aspirations. Based on their answers to the test questions, they are provided with a three-letter Summary Code that they can use to find suitable employment and areas of study that match their work-related personality type. The Summary Code indicates what three personality types are most closely representative of the individual's responses on the SDS, in terms of John Holland's six basic personality types: Realistic, Investigative, Artistic, Social, Enterprising, and Conventional (see Figure 15–3). On the hexagonal image in Figure 15–3, personality styles that are adjacent to each other on the hexagon are more similar to each other. The farther apart two styles are, the more different they are from each other. For people who take the test, the SDS provides a list of occupations relating to the Summary Code and information about what type of education would be required for each occupation.

Looking at the sample data presented in Figure 15–3, the person's three-letter Summary Code is ISC, reflecting interests in primarily investigative, social, and

Figure 15–3

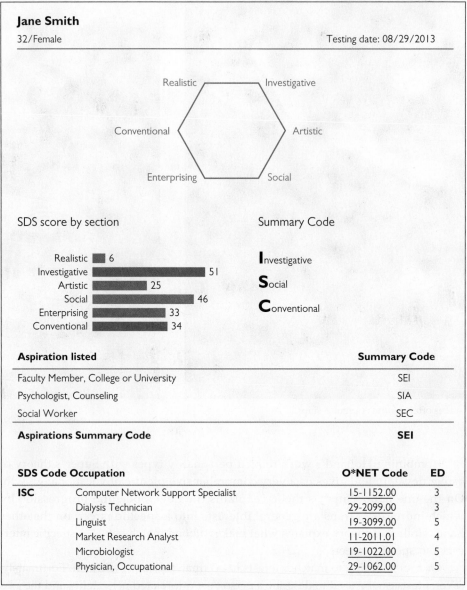

Jane Smith

32/Female   Testing date: 08/29/2013

SDS score by section

Section	Score
Realistic	6
Investigative	51
Artistic	25
Social	46
Enterprising	33
Conventional	34

Summary Code

Investigative
Social
Conventional

Aspiration listed	Summary Code
Faculty Member, College or University	SEI
Psychologist, Counseling	SIA
Social Worker	SEC
Aspirations Summary Code	**SEI**

SDS Code	Occupation	O*NET Code	ED
ISC	Computer Network Support Specialist	15-1152.00	3
	Dialysis Technician	29-2099.00	3
	Linguist	19-3099.00	5
	Market Research Analyst	11-2011.01	4
	Microbiologist	19-1022.00	5
	Physician, Occupational	29-1062.00	5

goodluz/Fotolia

Finding a job in adulthood that matches a person's skills and personality is important.

conventional areas of work, study, and leisure. Scores on realistic, artistic, and enterprising areas were lower than investigative, social, and conventional, although enterprising was only one point behind conventional in this individual's case. Overall, this person's interests seem to correspond best with the investigative personality in Holland's theory. If we look at this person's aspirations, she indicated answers suggesting that she is interested in working as a professor, a counselling psychologist, or a social worker. Based on a person's Summary Code, the SDS suggests what kinds of jobs might be most suitable to the person as well as the level of education required, with 1 being elementary school and 5 being an advanced degree.

The SDS also generates a three-letter code based on the person's stated aspirations. In Figure 15–3, you can see that this person's aspirations are coded SEI, reflecting social, enterprising, and investigative areas of personality, according to Holland's theory. As you can see, a person's aspirations don't always perfectly overlap with that person's career interests and suggested occupations. Of course, people continue to develop and change their interests, knowledge, and careers over time, so the SDS and similar tests can be used across the lifespan to help a person refine their choices and align their interests with their job choice more closely.

In addition to job and educational information, the SDS also provides information about leisure activities that might be appealing to the individual. As a result, the SDS can provide an individual with a lot of information about their work-related personality, personal interests, career aspirations, possible educational goals, recreational activities that might interest them, and how they might go about following through with these suggestions.

Sometimes adolescents have their heart set on a certain career and then go after it, never to look back. Theresa Zolner recalls a childhood friend who steadfastly wanted to become a lawyer, then did become a lawyer for a major western Canadian city. Theresa, on the other hand, wanted to become a psychologist but then had an interesting and informative detour studying to become an English professor. Eventually, after teaching youth from some of the more economically disadvantaged areas of New York City, she switched back into psychology and fulfilled her original plans. Another of her friends wanted to be a psychologist, took criminology, and then entered social work, spending a great deal of time working with inner-city homeless people. The message here is that people are variable in their plans. Sometimes life brings about change, even when we don't expect change to happen.

Part-Time Employment

LO7 **Recognize the impact of part-time employment on adolescents.**

Today, a substantial majority of high school seniors work part-time, although, ironically, they find themselves competing for jobs with older or retired adults, who often reenter the workplace after retiring from life-long careers as a way to spend time or bolster their retirement income. As a result, adolescents frequently compete for jobs with people who have years of work experience and are generally very reliable, in part due to their level of maturity. In 1998, nearly half of Canadian young people between the ages of 15 and 24 were working in retail sales and service-industry jobs as retail salespeople, cashiers, restaurant servers, bartenders, or babysitters (Statistics Canada, 2004b).

Most adults believe that early exposure to the workplace teaches adolescents self-discipline, self-confidence, and important job skills (Snedeker, 1992). For most adolescents, however, part-time work can actually be harmful, for several reasons:

1. School performance often suffers. When students work more than approximately 15 hours per week, they devote less time to homework and are more apt to cut classes. Not surprisingly, their grades are lower than those of their peers who work less or not at all (Steinberg, Fegley, & Dornbusch, 1993). Why should 15 hours of work be so detrimental to school performance? A 15-hour work schedule usually means four 3-hour shifts after school and another 3-hour shift on the weekend. This would seem to leave ample opportunity to study, but only if students use their time effectively. In fact, many high school students have not developed the foresight and discipline necessary to consistently balance the combined demands of work, study, and sleep.

2. Mental health and behavioural problems can emerge. Adolescents who work long hours—more than 15 or 20 hours a week—are more likely to experience

Too many work hours can affect school performance and engagement.

anxiety and depression, and their self-esteem often suffers. Many adolescents find themselves in jobs that are repetitive and boring but stressful, and such conditions undermine self-esteem and breed anxiety. Extensive part-time work frequently leads to substance abuse, including tobacco, alcohol, marijuana, and cocaine (Mortimer, Finch, Rye, Shanahan, & Call, 1996; Valois, Dunham, Jackson, & Waller, 1999). Extensive work is also associated with more frequent problem behaviour, including violence toward others, trouble with police, and arguments with parents (Bachman & Schulenberg, 1993). Why employment is associated with all of these problems is not clear. Perhaps employed adolescents turn to drugs to help them cope with the anxiety and depression brought on by work. Arguments with parents may become more common because anxious, depressed adolescents are more prone to argue or because wage-earning adolescents may believe that the degree of freedom they are granted should match their income. Whatever the exact mechanism, extensive part-time work is detrimental to the mental health of most adolescents.

3. Affluence can be misleading. Adults sometimes argue that work teaches teenagers the value of a dollar. Yet the typical teenage pattern is to earn and spend. Working adolescents spend most of their earnings on themselves to buy clothing, snack food, or cosmetics, and to pay for entertainment. Few working teens help with their family's expenses or set aside much of their income for future goals, such as a postsecondary education (Shanahan, Elder, Burchinal, & Conger, 1996a). Because parents customarily pay for rent, utilities, and groceries, working adolescents in North America often have a vastly higher percentage of their income available for discretionary spending than working adults, creating unrealistic expectations in youth about how income can be allocated (Bachman, 1983).

The message that emerges repeatedly from research on part-time employment is hardly encouraging. Adolescents who work long hours at part-time jobs often do not benefit from the experience. To the contrary, they usually do worse in school, are more likely to have behavioural problems, and often learn how to spend money rather than how to manage it. These effects are similar for adolescents from different ethnic groups (Steinberg & Dornbusch, 1991) and are comparable for boys and girls (Bachman & Schulenberg, 1993).

Does this mean that teenagers who are still in school should never work part-time? Not necessarily. Part-time employment can be a good experience, depending on the circumstances. One key is the number of hours of work. Most students could easily work 5 hours weekly without harm, and many could work 10 hours weekly. Another key is the type of job (Barling, Rogers, & Kelloway, 1995). When adolescents have jobs that allow them to use their skills (e.g., bookkeeping, computing, or typing) and acquire new ones, self-esteem is enhanced, and they learn from their work experience.

For example, when Theresa Zolner was 16, she was determined to play in a rock band with her friends. Lacking the requisite electric piano, she entered an agreement with her parents to have them co-sign a loan for $5000, which in the 1970s was a very large amount of money for a teen. Working 11 hours per week plus extra hours during the summer as a cashier at a local grocery store, Theresa paid off the loan on the piano and learned something about financial responsibility. Eventually, though, she gave up her rock-and-roll dream to attend university.

When teens save their money or use it to pay for clothes and school expenses, their parent–child relationships often improve (Shanahan, Elder, Burchinal, & Conger, 1996b). Finally, summer jobs typically do not involve conflict between work and school. Consequently, many of the harmful effects associated with part-time employment during the school year do not hold for summer employment. In fact, such employment sometimes enhances adolescents' self-esteem, especially when they save part of their income for future plans (Marsh, 1991).

By these criteria, who is likely to show the harmful effects of part-time work? A teen who spends 30 hours a week bagging groceries and spends most of it on CDs or videos. Who is likely to benefit from part-time work? A teen who likes to tinker with cars, spends Saturdays working in a repair shop, and sets aside some earnings for postsecondary education.

Ask Yourself

How would you describe continuity of vocational development during adolescence and young adulthood?

15.4 Special Challenges

Learning Objectives

After reading the module, you should be able to do the following:

LO8 Explain what learning disabilities are.

LO9 Describe Attention Deficit Hyperactivity Disorder.

LO10 List the different forms of intellectual delay, and understand the importance of adaptive ability.

Throughout history, societies have recognized young people with atypical abilities, and today we know much more about these children than was known in the past. We'll begin this module with a look at learning disabilities. Then we'll consider children with Attention Deficit Hyperactivity Disorder. Finally, we'll end the module (and the chapter) by discussing young people who are cognitively delayed.

Learning Disabilities

LO8 **Explain what learning disabilities are.**

For some youth with normal levels of intelligence, learning is a struggle. These youngsters have a learning disability, a term that refers to a person who (a) has difficulty mastering an academic subject, (b) has normal intelligence, and (c) is not suffering

Learning disabilities can be a major source of frustration for young people.

from other conditions, such as sensory impairment or inadequate instruction, that could explain poor performance (Hammill, 1990).

About 5 percent of school-age children are classified as learning disabled in North America. The number of distinct disabilities and the degree of overlap among them is still debated (Stanovich, 1993). However, one common classification scheme distinguishes three major disabilities: language (including listening, speaking, and writing), reading, and arithmetic (Dockrell & McShane, 1993).

The variety of learning disabilities complicates the task of teachers and researchers because it suggests that each type of learning disability could have its own cause and treatment (Lyon, 1996). For example, take reading, the most common area of learning disability. Many young people with a reading disability have problems in phonological awareness, which is the ability to understand and use the sounds in written and oral language. For a reading-disabled youth, all vowels sound alike—pin sounds like pen which sounds like pan. These youngsters benefit from explicit, extensive instruction on the connections between letters and their sounds (Lyon, 1996; Wise, Ring, & Olson, 1999).

In the case of arithmetic disability, young people often have difficulty recognizing what operations are needed and how to perform them. Here, instruction emphasizes determining the goal of arithmetic problems, using goals to select correct arithmetic operations, and using operations accurately (Goldman, 1989).

The key to helping these children and youth is to move beyond the generic label "learning disability" and pinpoint specific cognitive and academic deficits that hamper an individual child's performance in school. Only then can instruction be specifically tailored to improve the child's skills (Moats & Lyon, 1993).

Planning effective instruction for children and youth with learning disabilities is much easier said than done, because diagnosing a learning disability is very difficult. Children with learning disabilities have average, above-average, or superior levels of intelligence, but they experience particular difficulty in learning a certain skill, usually related to language, reading, writing, or arithmetic. Some have both reading and language disabilities; others have reading and arithmetic disabilities.

Expressive language ability:

a person's ability to make ideas known to others through language.

Receptive language ability:

a person's ability to understand other people's ideas when they are expressed through language.

In addition, people can differ in terms of their level of ability in using language as opposed to understanding someone else's language. This is called a difference in expressive versus receptive language ability. **Expressive language ability** refers to a person's ability to make ideas known to others through language. Conversely, **receptive language ability** refers to a person's ability to understand other people's ideas when they are expressed through language. Youth with a language-related disability tend to have slower response times on language- and nonlanguage-related tasks, although more research will need to be done to determine why this is the case (Miller et al., 2006). In addition, youth with a language disability tend to demonstrate lower performance than peers on measures of working memory and processing speed (Leonard et al., 2007). Despite these difficulties, with ingenuity, hard work, and proper educational attention, young people with learning disabilities can develop to their full intellectual and vocational potentials.

Attention Deficit Hyperactivity Disorder

LO9 **Describe Attention Deficit Hyperactivity Disorder.**

Children who have Attention Deficit Hyperactivity Disorder (ADHD) are typically the most energetic children in a classroom. They can seem out of control at times, as well as easily distracted, often moving aimlessly from one activity to another. Children with these challenges can also seem impulsive and, compared to other youngsters of the same age, can have more difficulty taking turns during play and other activities. Parents sometimes attribute these behaviours to youth or immaturity; however, the behaviours do not tend to disappear with increasing maturation, and they can contribute to problems with academic achievement. In addition, children with ADHD can develop problems with peer relations if other children find the ADHD-related behaviours annoying and subsequently begin to avoid the child with ADHD. This situation can lead to conflicts with peers as well as significant loneliness and feelings of rejection in the child with ADHD. The circumstances can improve for children with ADHD when they receive help from a clinical psychologist who works closely with the child's family and school to address the child's needs. In addition, sometimes medication is helpful to regulate the child's ability to pay attention and learn better self-control.

Attention Deficit Hyperactivity Disorder (ADHD) has been classified as a psychological disorder in which a person is overactive, inattentive, and/or impulsive.

Attention Deficit Hyperactivity Disorder (ADHD):
a psychological disorder characterized by overactivity, inattention, and/or impulsivity.

- Overactivity: People with ADHD are unusually energetic, fidgety, and unable to keep still, especially in situations like school classrooms where they need to limit their activity.

- Inattention: People with ADHD skip from one task to another. They do not pay attention in class and seem unable to concentrate on schoolwork.

- Impulsivity: People with ADHD often act before thinking; they may run into a street before looking for traffic or interrupt others who are speaking.

Not all people with ADHD show all of these symptoms to the same degree. Symptoms often vary with the setting. Some youngsters who are unable to maintain attention in school may sit still for hours playing a video game at home (Barkley, 1996). Furthermore, young children naturally have a limited attention span in comparison to older children or adults. ADHD is a condition that cannot be diagnosed by simple parent report and completion of a behavioural checklist. Many different factors must be assessed about the child, including the child's overall level of mental health and the family environment, in order to make this diagnosis properly. Improper assessment of ADHD can lead to improper diagnosis or over-diagnosis of this condition.

Researchers and clinicians tend to disagree about the number of different subtypes of ADHD and the factors that give rise to the disorder (Barkley, 1996; Panksepp, 1998). However, it is clear that young people with ADHD often have problems with conduct, academic performance, and peer relationships (Barkley, 1990; McGee, Williams, & Feehan, 1992). They also tend to perform less well on achievement tests, perhaps because their problems with behaviour and inattention result in lower levels of in-class learning (Pennington, Groisser, & Welsh, 1993). Roughly 3 to 15 percent of all school-age children are diagnosed with ADHD; boys outnumber girls by a 3:1 ratio (Wicks-Nelson & Israel, 1991). While some parents and researchers continue to investigate possible links between sugar and food additives (such as dyes and preservatives) to ADHD, researchers have not found a broad and definitive connection between diet and ADHD (Hoover & Milich, 1994;

McGee, Stanton, & Sears, 1993; Wolraich et al., 1994; Wolraich, Wilson, & White, 1995). Identical twins more often both have ADHD than fraternal twins (Edelbrock, Rende, Plomin, & Thompson, 1995), possibly implicating heredity. In addition, some youngsters with ADHD have been under a very high degree of stress as a result of serious family conflict or other forms of trauma (Bernier & Siegel, 1994; Perry, 1997), resulting in a sustained impact on the development of attention-related processes in the brain (Perry, 1997).

One myth about ADHD is that most people "grow out of it" in adolescence or young adulthood. More than half the children who are diagnosed with ADHD will have, as they become adolescents and young adults, problems related to overactivity, inattention, and impulsivity. Few of these young adults complete postsecondary education, and some will have work- and family-related problems (Fischer, Barkley, Fletcher, & Smallish, 1993; Rapport, 1995). Over the long term, if ADHD is left untreated, these youth have continuing difficulties. Adults with ADHD are more likely to have attentional problems, complete fewer than 12 years of schooling, have problems reading and writing, and be involved in criminal activity (Rasmussen & Gillberg, 2000).

Another concern that has arisen about ADHD is whether it really is a disorder unto itself. Recently, some researchers have proposed that insufficient evidence exists to support the idea of a genetic or neuroanatomic basis for ADHD, suggesting that the symptoms may be related to other childhood causes, including medical, emotional, and psychosocial or behavioural problems (Furman, 2008). However, whether a child's challenges stem from ADHD or another problem, professional supports are often helpful but difficult to access, as you will see in the Making Children's Lives Better feature.

Attention Deficit Hyperactivity Disorder is treated, in part, with stimulant medications, such as Ritalin. It may seem odd that stimulants are given to children who are already overactive, but these drugs stimulate the parts of the brain that normally inhibit hyperactive and impulsive behaviour. Thus, stimulants actually have a calming influence for many youngsters with ADHD, allowing them to focus their attention (Aman, Roberts, & Pennington, 1998)—a paradoxical effect. A **paradoxical effect** occurs when a drug acts in a manner opposite to what one might ordinarily expect or opposite to how it affects other populations of people.

Paradoxical effect:

when a drug acts in a manner opposite to what one might ordinarily expect or to how it affects other populations of people.

Unfortunately, stimulant medications like Ritalin are often sold on the street as a drug of abuse. Youth who have ADHD and also have problems with substance use sometimes abuse their own medication by snorting it or saving pills and taking large doses to get high rather than taking the drug as prescribed. Youth who come from families or neighbourhoods where drug abuse is a problem sometimes have their medication taken from them and sold on the street. Drugs that do not have a street value, such as Strattera, are available to treat ADHD. However, in Canada, alternative medications such as Straterra are not always covered by insurance plans or the Medical Services Branch (which covers prescriptions for First Nations people), making safe alternatives unavailable for some people who need them most.

By itself, stimulant medication does not improve children's performance in school because it ignores the psychological and social influences on ADHD. Children with ADHD need to learn to regulate their behaviour and attention. For example, children can be taught to remind themselves to read instructions before starting assignments, and they need reinforcement from others for inhibiting impulsive and hyperactive behaviour (Barkley, 1994).

Parents can also encourage attention and goal-oriented behaviour at home. Anastopoulos, Shelton, DuPaul, and Guevremont (1993) arranged for parents of children with ADHD to attend nine training sessions on how to use positive reinforcement to foster attention and compliance. Parents also learned effective ways to punish children for being inattentive. Following training, children had fewer

Making Children's Lives Better

Mental Health Services for Children

In Canada, children's mental health is only partially covered by a checkerboard of public services that vary from province to province despite the broad range of mental health conditions that affect children every day. Mental health services are available through private practices offered by registered psychologists; however, families cannot always afford to pay privately for these important services.

Mental health problems noted for their onset in childhood include intellectual delay, learning disabilities, and pervasive developmental disorders, such as autism. However, children are also affected by mental health conditions that affect adults as well, including anxiety disorders and depression and substance abuse. Therefore, children and families who are trying to cope with mental health conditions have needs that are both immediate and real. The emotional well-being of children depends not only on their own individual adjustment but also on the stability and well-being of their caregivers and families. To date, Canada might be chastised for having a lack of vision and strategy in addressing both the fragmentation in children's health and mental health services and the overall lack of funding in this area.

A limited range of publicly funded services are available; however, most coverage is focused on payment for services from family physicians and psychiatrists, typically working in private practice offices, whose services typically are paid for by publicly funded, provincial health insurance programs. However, payment for mental health services from registered psychologists tends to be restricted to coverage for psychologists working in government clinics only and does not usually include those who work in private practice. This severely restricts service availability in terms of both numbers of practitioners covered and the geographical location of those services. In addition, families who do not speak one of Canada's two official languages or for whom English is a foreign language might have difficulty accessing language and culturally appropriate services at government clinics, which often cater to normative groups rather than specialized cultural or linguistic groups.

As a consequence, families wanting access to mental health services delivered by psychologists, such as psychological assessment and psychotherapy, have to access them through government inpatient or outpatient clinics. Government clinics can have very long waiting lists. If, for example, a 6 to 10-month wait exists for access to appropriate psychological services, children may be forced to suffer for significant periods of their development—perhaps a whole school year—waiting for professional help.

Some families have health insurance through the parents' work that covers typically a very limited range of mental health services. However, many families are left with minimal to no services if they don't pay for these services on their own. Unfortunately, many families end up simply going without service altogether, which can lead to deterioration of the family unit or negative spiralling into additional social and mental health problems. Political activists in Canada have attempted to have certain types of disorders, such as autism, covered by health insurance; however, to date, mental health remains the black sheep of Canadian health care coverage in its present two-tiered structure—wait for free psychological services or pay to get psychological services more quickly. How can that be considered fair?

symptoms of ADHD. Equally important, the parents felt that the training made them feel more competent in parenting. They also reported feeling significantly less parental stress.

The best approach for treating children with ADHD involves all of these techniques—medication, instruction, self-regulation, and parent training. Comprehensive treatment helps a child with ADHD become more attentive, less disruptive, and stronger academically (Carlson, Pelham, Milich, & Dixon, 1992).

Intellectual Delay

LO10 **List the different forms of intellectual delay, and understand the importance of adaptive ability.**

Serious delay in cognitive development is officially diagnosed as "intellectual delay" and applies to individuals who, before the age of 18, demonstrate substantially below-average intelligence and problems adapting to an environment. Below-average intelligence is defined as a score of 70 or less on an intelligence test (Baumeister & Baumeister, 1995), but cognitive delay is also frequently manifested as delays in adaptive behaviour. **Adaptive behaviour** is a person's ability to engage effectively in tasks

Adaptive behaviour:
a person's ability to engage effectively in tasks of daily living.

Figure 15–4

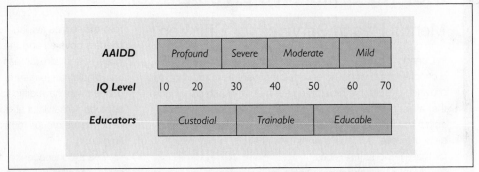

SOURCE: Based on American Association of Intellectual and Developmental Disabilities and Cipani, E. (1991). Educational classification and placement. In J. L. Matson & J. A. Mulick (Eds.), Handbook of mental Retardation (2nd ed.). New York: Pergamon Press.

of daily living. Adaptive behaviour is usually evaluated by conducting interviews with a parent or other caregiver and refers to the daily living skills needed to live, work, and play in the community—skills for caring for oneself and social skills.

The American Association of Intellectual and Developmental Disabilities (AAIDD) identifies four levels of intellectual delay. The levels, along with the range of IQ scores associated with each level, are shown in Figure 15–4. Also shown are the three levels of delay typically used by educators in the United States (Cipani, 1991). In Canada, the Canadian Association for Community Living advocates for the needs and rights of cognitively challenged persons.

The most severe forms of intellectual delay are, fortunately, relatively uncommon. Profound, severe, and moderate levels of delay together make up only 10 percent of all cases. Profoundly and severely delayed individuals usually have so few skills that they must be supervised constantly. Consequently, they usually live in institutions, where they can sometimes be taught self-help skills such as dressing, feeding, and toileting (Reid, Wilson, & Faw, 1991).

People with moderate delays might develop the intellectual skills of the average 7- or 8-year-old. With this level of functioning, they can sometimes support themselves, typically at a sheltered workshop, where they perform simple vocational tasks under close supervision.

The remaining 90 percent of individuals who are intellectually delayed are classified as mildly delayed or educable. These individuals go to school, master many academic skills, and usually can go on to lead independent lives. Comprehensive training programs that focus on vocational and social skills help individuals with mild cognitive delays become independent once they reach adulthood (Ellis & Rusch, 1991).

While intellectual delay is assessed and diagnosed, in part, by determining IQ, considerable difficulties can arise when youth who speak English as a foreign language are assessed. Proper psychological assessment makes some basic assumptions about the person being assessed, one of which is that the person has a reasonable measure of competency in the language of the assessment instruments. If youth are assessed in a language other than their language of birth (first language), their performance on the test likely will be compromised, and they may appear to have a lower level of ability that they actually have. Test bias is a real consideration for youth who speak English as second language. Youth can never over-perform on a test of cognitive abilities, but they can under-perform, and mislabelling of the youth is always a concern. Therefore, wherever possible, youth should be tested in their first language with culturally competent testing materials. Unfortunately, materials are not always available, and, to date, psychologists have not done nearly enough to address this problem.

Ask Yourself

What happens to children with ADHD when they become adults? How do adult experiences with ADHD address the issue of continuity of development?

What Would a Manager Do?

As the manager of a supermarket, a good percentage of your part-time staff are teenagers. When they are first hired, they need to be trained in how to treat customers and how to manage the store's products and equipment. They seem eager at first, but their attention and follow-through almost never match their enthusiasm to get paid. As a manager working with young people, what could you do to increase their interest in being knowledgeable on the job and more conscientious as employees? How would you motivate young people to be good employees?

Summary

15.1 Cognition

Piaget's Stage of Formal Operational Reasoning

- In the formal operational stage, adolescents can think hypothetically and reason abstractly.

- In deductive reasoning, adolescents understand that conclusions are based on logic, not necessarily on experience.

- Adolescents' reasoning is not always as sophisticated as expected by Piaget's theory; for example, their beliefs sometimes interfere with their reasoning.

Information Processing during Adolescence

- According to information-processing theorists, adolescence is a time of gradual cognitive change.

- Working memory and processing speed achieve adult-like levels.

- Content knowledge increases to expert-like levels in some domains.

- Strategies and metacognitive skills become much more sophisticated.

15.2 Reasoning about Moral Issues

Kohlberg's Theory

- Kohlberg proposed that moral reasoning includes preconventional, conventional, and postconventional levels.

- Moral reasoning is first based on rewards and punishments and, much later, on personal moral codes.

- People progress through the stages in sequence and do not regress.

- Morally advanced reasoning is associated with more frequent moral behaviour.

- Few people attain the most advanced levels of moral development, and cultures differ in their bases for moral reasoning.

Gilligan's Ethic of Caring

- Gilligan proposed that females' moral reasoning is based on caring and responsibility for others, not justice.

- Research does not support consistent sex differences in moral reasoning.

- Males and females both consider caring as well as justice in their moral judgments, depending on the situation.

Promoting Moral Reasoning

- Many factors can promote more sophisticated moral reasoning, including (a) observing others reason at more advanced levels and (b) discussing moral issues with peers, teachers, and parents.

15.3 The World of Work

Career Development

- Super proposed three phases of vocational development during adolescence and young adulthood: crystallization, specification, and implementation.

- During crystallization, basic interests are identified.

- During specification, jobs and training associated with interests are identified.

- During implementation, entry into the workforce occurs.

- Holland proposed six different work-related personalities: realistic, investigative, social, conventional, enterprising, and artistic.

- Holland's proposed personalities are each uniquely suited to certain jobs.

- People are happier when their personality fits their job and less happy when it does not.

Part-Time Employment

- Most adolescents in Canada have part-time jobs.

- Adolescents who are employed more than 15 hours per week during the school year typically do poorly in school, often have lowered self-esteem and increased anxiety, and sometimes have problems interacting with others.

- Employed adolescents tend to spend the money they earn on clothing, food, and entertainment instead of saving it.

- Patterns of spending money in youth can give misleading expectations about how to allocate income in adulthood.

- Part-time employment can be beneficial if adolescents work relatively few hours, if the work allows them to use existing skills or acquire new ones, and if teens save some of their earnings.

- Summer employment, which does not conflict with the demands of school, can also be beneficial.

15.4 Special Challenges

Learning Disabilities

- Young people with a learning disability have normal or higher levels of intelligence but have difficulty mastering specific academic subjects.

- The most common learning disability is reading disability, which often can be traced to inadequate understanding and use of language sounds.

Attention Deficit Hyperactivity Disorder

- People with ADHD are typically overactive, inattentive, and impulsive.

- Youth with ADHD sometimes have conduct problems and do poorly in school.

- A thorough psychological assessment is required to diagnose ADHD properly.

- A comprehensive approach to treatment—involving medication, instruction, and parent training—produces the best results.

Intellectual Delay

- Individuals with intellectual delay are officially diagnosed as such if they have IQ scores of 70 or lower and problems with adaptive behaviour.

- Most persons who are intellectually delayed are classified as mildly delayed or educable and are able to go on to live independent lives.

Chapter Critical Review

1. Adolescents typically are introduced to the study of complex topics such as psychology, philosophy, and experimental science just when they are reaching Piaget's formal operational stage (described in Module 15.1). Explain how the ability to use formal operations contributes to the study of these and other subject areas.

2. What does it mean to state that a cognitive theory (Module 15.1) or moral-development theory (Module 15.2) describes how individuals can think, not how they do think?

3. How do culture, ethnicity, and gender affect moral development (Module 15.2)? Give at least two specific examples from your own experiences.

4. How do the different personality types in Holland's theory relate to the different types of intelligence proposed by Howard Gardner?

See for Yourself

Make Super's stages of vocational choice come alive by interviewing people in their twenties who have been in the workforce for a few years. Ask them when they had their first ideas about a career (crystallization). Find out when they began learning about specific careers and the training that was required (specification). Ask about the experience of entering the workforce for the first time (implementation). How well do the ages they report for each of the stages match those that Super provides? Are the steps similar for men and women? Do some people report missteps and career changes along the way? See for yourself!

Chapter 16
Social and Emotional Development in Adolescents

Pikselstock/Shutterstock

∨ MODULE

16.1 Identity and Self-Esteem

16.2 Relationships with Parents and Peers

16.3 The Dark Side

Mabel waited as Sophie tried on different jeans and tops in the store dressing room. What was taking her so long? Just as she was about to ask Sophie if she had found anything she liked, a flash went off from inside the dressing room. "What are you doing?" asked Mabel. "Just a second, Mom!" Later, Mabel found out that Sophie was texting with her friend about which outfit to buy and posting pictures of the new clothes on Facebook . . . all while her mom waited for her in the store! What was that girl thinking?!

Connect to My Virtual Child

What kinds of theories do you have about children? What ideas inform your thoughts and beliefs about the lives of children, how they are raised, and the nature of the human person? Use your access card and follow this link www.myvirtualchild.com to learn more about the world of the child. You can even virtually try to raise your own child.

16.1 Identity and Self-Esteem

 ## Learning Objectives

After reading the module, you should be able to do the following:

LO1 Describe how adolescents form an identity.

LO2 Understand what an ethnic identity is and the stages in acquiring one.

LO3 Discuss how self-esteem changes in adolescence.

Self-concept refers to the attitudes, behaviours, and values that make a person unique. In adolescence, self-concept takes on special significance as adolescents struggle to achieve an identity that will allow them to participate in the adult world. Through self-reflection, youth search for an identity to integrate the many different and sometimes conflicting elements of the self. In this module, we'll learn more about the adolescent search for an identity. Along the way, we'll learn more about how adolescents struggle to learn who they are.

The Search for Identity

LO1 **Describe how adolescents form an identity.**

Erik Erikson's (1968) account of identity formation has been particularly influential in our understanding of adolescence. Erikson argued that adolescents face a crisis between identity and role confusion. This crisis involves balancing the desire to try out many possible selves and the need to select a single self. Adolescents who achieve a sense of identity are well prepared to face the next developmental challenge—establishing intimate, sharing relationships with others. However, Erikson believed that teenagers who enter adulthood confused about their identity can never experience intimacy in any human relationship. Instead, throughout their lives, they remain isolated and respond to others stereotypically.

Randall McIlwaine/Cartoonstock Ltd.

"Relax, Ted, it's only a phase!"

To achieve an identity, adolescents use the hypothetical reasoning skills of the formal operational stage to experiment with different selves and learn more about possible identities (Nurmi, Poole, & Kalakoski, 1996). Adolescents' advanced cognitive skills allow them to imagine themselves in different roles.

Another way that youth experiment with identity is over the internet, using chat sites, discussion boards, blogs, and instant messaging, as well as social networking sites like Twitter, Facebook, or Bebo. Valkenburg, Schouten, and Peter (2005) studied the self-presentation strategies that youth used over the internet. Of the youth studied, 50 percent acknowledge engaging in identity experimentation online. These researchers divided motives for identity experimentation over the internet into three categories: (1) self-exploration to see how others would react to them, (2) social compensation to overcome shyness, and (3) social facilitation to facilitate relationship formation.

Much of the testing and experimentation in adolescence is career-oriented. Some adolescents envision themselves as rock stars; others imagine being professional athletes, Canadian peacekeepers, or video game programmers. Other testing is romantically oriented or involves religious and political beliefs (King, Elder, & Whitbeck, 1997; Yates & Youniss, 1996). Teens give different identities a trial run just as you might test drive different cars before selecting one. By fantasizing about the future, adolescents begin to discover their potential.

As adolescents strive to achieve an identity, they often progress through the different phases or statuses listed in Table 16–1 (Marcia, 1980, 1991). Unlike Piaget's stages, these four phases do not necessarily occur in sequence. Most young adolescents are in a state of diffusion or foreclosure. The common element in these phases

Table 16–1 Summary Table

Four Different Identity Statuses		
Status	**Definition**	**Example**
Diffusion	The person is overwhelmed by the task of achieving an identity and does little to accomplish the task.	Larry hates the idea of deciding what to do with his future, so he spends most of his free time playing video games.
Foreclosure	The person has a status determined by adults rather than by personal exploration.	For as long as she can remember, Sakura's parents have told her that she should be an attorney and join the family law firm. She plans to study prelaw in university, though she's never given the matter much thought.
Moratorium	The person is examining different alternatives but has yet to find the one that's satisfactory.	Brad enjoys almost all his high school classes. Some days he thinks it would be fun to be a chemist, some days he wants to be a novelist, and some days he'd like to be an elementary school teacher. He thinks it's a little weird to change his mind so often, but he also enjoys thinking about different jobs.
Achievement	The person has explored alternatives and has deliberately chosen a specific identity.	Throughout middle school, Efrat wanted to play in the NHL. During Grades 9 and 10, she thought it would be cool to be a physician. In Grade 11, she took a computing course and everything finally clicked—she'd found her niche. She knew that she wanted to study computer science in college.

is that teens are not exploring alternative identities. They are avoiding the crisis altogether or have resolved it by taking on an identity suggested by parents or other adults. However, as individuals move beyond adolescence and into young adulthood, they have more opportunity to explore alternative identities, and so diffusion and foreclosure become less common, and as the pie charts in Figure 16–1 show, achievement and moratorium become more common (Meilman, 1979). School is a particularly important environment for identity development in adolescence (Lannegrand-Willems & Bosma, 2006).

Typically, young people do not reach the achievement status for all aspects of identity at the same time (Dellas & Jernigan, 1990; Kroger & Green, 1996). Some adolescents may reach the achievement status for occupations before achieving it for religion and politics. Others reach the achievement status for religion before other domains. Evidently, few youth achieve a sense of identity all at once; instead, the crisis of identity is first resolved in some areas and then in others. Researchers from Pakistan have found that girls tend to be outpacing boys in achieving identity status in several categories, even in traditionally male-dominated areas of identity formation (Sandhu & Tung, 2006). When the achievement status is attained, the period of active experimentation ends, and individuals have a well-defined sense of self.

Adolescence involves trying out different possible identities.

However, during adulthood, an individual's identity is sometimes reworked in response to new life challenges and circumstances. Consequently, individuals may return to the moratorium status for a period, only to reemerge later with a changed identity. In fact, even adults may go through these changes several times, creating MAMA cycles in which they alternate between the moratorium and achievement statuses as they explore new alternatives in response to personal and family crises (Marcia, 1991).

Adolescent egocentrism: the self-absorption that marks the teenage search for identity.

During the search for identity, adolescents often reveal a number of characteristic ways of thinking. They are often very self-oriented. The self-absorption that marks the teenage search for identity is referred to as **adolescent egocentrism** (Elkind, 1978). Unlike preschoolers, adolescents know that others have different perspectives

Figure 16-1

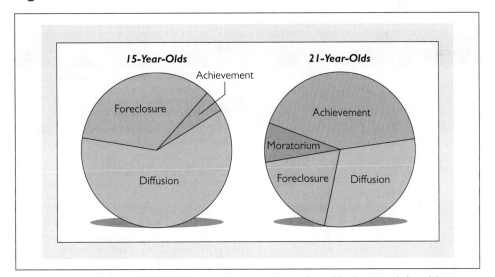

SOURCE: Based on Meilman, P. W. (1979). Cross-sectional age changes in ego identity status during adolescence. Developmental Psychology, 15, 230–231.

Biker3/Fotolia

Personal and family crises, such as unemployment, can change adult roles in the family.

Imaginary audience:
the normal tendency in adolescents to believe that they are actors whose performance is watched constantly by their peers.

Personal fable:
the normal tendency in adolescents to believe that their experiences and feelings are unique.

Illusion of invulnerability:
the belief that misfortune only happens to others.

on the world. Adolescents are simply much more interested in their own feelings and experiences than in anyone else's experiences. In addition, as they search for an identity, many adolescents wrongly believe that they are the focus of others' thinking. A teen who has spilled her drink on herself might imagine that all her friends are thinking only about the stain on her shirt and how sloppy she is. Many adolescents feel that they are, in effect, actors whose performance is watched constantly by their peers, a phenomenon known as the **imaginary audience**.

Adolescent self-absorption is also demonstrated by the **personal fable**, teenagers' tendency to believe that their experiences and feelings are unique, that no one has ever felt or thought as they do. Whether the excitement of first love, the despair of a broken relationship, or the confusion of planning for the future, adolescents often believe that they are the first to experience these feelings and that no one else could possibly understand the power of their emotions (Elkind & Bowen, 1979). Adolescents' belief in their uniqueness also contributes to an **illusion of invulnerability**—the belief that misfortune only happens to others. They think they can have sex without becoming pregnant, and they can drive recklessly without being in an auto accident. Those misfortunes only happen to other people. These characteristics of adolescents' thinking are summarized in Table 16–2. An interesting implication of these beliefs is that they contribute to reduced risk perception in terms of health. For most youth, reduced risk perception is largely due to their lack of experience with serious health problems (Greening, Stoppelbein, Chandler, & Elkin, 2005). These findings have strong implications for youth health education, particularly relating to sexually transmitted infections (STIs) as well as to the onset of cigarette smoking in adolescence (Frankenberger, 2004).

As adolescents make progress toward achieving an identity, adolescent egocentrism, imaginary audiences, personal fables, and the illusion of invulnerability become less common. What circumstances help adolescents achieve identity? Parents are influential (Marcia, 1980). When parents encourage discussion and recognize young people's autonomy, their youth are more likely to reach the achievement status. Apparently these youth feel encouraged to undertake the personal experimentation

Table 16–2 Summary Table

Characteristics of Adolescents' Thinking		
Feature	**Definition**	**Example**
Adolescent egocentrism	Adolescents are overly concerned with their own thoughts and feelings.	When Levi's grandmother died unexpectedly, Levi was preoccupied with how the funeral would affect his weekend plans and ignored how upset his mother was by her own mother's death.
Imaginary audience	Adolescents believe that others are watching them constantly.	Tom had to ride his bike to football practice because his dad wouldn't let him have the car; he was sure that all his car-driving friends would see and make fun of him.
Personal fable	Adolescents believe that their experiences and feelings are unique.	When Rosa's boyfriend decided to date another girl, Rosa cried and cried. She couldn't believe how sad she was, and she was sure her mom had never felt this way.
Illusion of invulnerability	Adolescents think that misfortune only happens to others.	Kumares and his girlfriend had been having sex for about six months. Although she thought it would be a good idea to use birth control, he thought it was unnecessary: There was no way his girlfriend would get pregnant.

that leads to identity. In contrast, when parents set rules with little justification and enforce them without explanation, youth are more likely to remain in the foreclosure status. These teens are discouraged from experimenting personally; instead, their parents simply tell them what identity to adopt. Overall, adolescents are most likely to establish a well-defined identity in a family atmosphere where parents encourage them to explore alternatives on their own but do not pressure or provide explicit direction (Harter, 1990, 1999).

Ethnic Identity

LO2 **Understand what an ethnic identity is and the stages in acquiring one.**

For many adolescents growing up in North America today, achieving an identity is even more challenging because they are members of ethnic minority groups. Canada has a number of cultural groups living within its borders. Some of these cultural groups have arrived more recently, such as people who entered Canada as refugees from Bosnia. Other groups have a long-standing period of immigration, such as the Ukrainian people, who arrived in Canada during four distinct phases of immigration—one prior to World War I, one just after World War I,

"They're all staring at how my hair looks."

one after World War II, and another after the dissolution of the Soviet Union. Other cultural groups in Canada have been here for an even longer period of time, such as Scottish, English, and French immigrants. Finally, many cultural groups have been here all along, as is evident with the Indigenous peoples all across Canada and, in fact, across the Americas.

Growing up within a particular cultural group means learning the social norms, values, and beliefs typical for that group of people. Often, people growing up within a particular cultural group do not give their cultural identity a second thought. This is particularly true for people who belong to a culture that forms the mainstream or majority group in a society. Like fish in water, these people likely do not see themselves in a "cultural" way.

On the other hand, people who grow up within minority cultures—whether they belong to a visible minority (such as Vietnamese) or an invisible minority (such as Russians or Roma)—quickly learn, through their encounters with the mainstream of society, that they are different from most other people around them.

On the Canadian Prairies, for example, Eastern European immigrants often settled on farms or in small villages and towns in close proximity to other Eastern European immigrants. As a consequence, many of these people had minimal contact with others who did not speak their own languages or have similar customs. Major contact with non–Eastern Europeans often came when children entered school, but, even then, children were often surrounded by others from their districts who came from the same cultural heritage. For these immigrants, significant encounters with the mainstream of Canadian society did not occur until they moved as older adolescents and young adults from their homes into the larger cities, such as Edmonton or Winnipeg, to find work or attend a more advanced school, such as a teacher's or business college. Once in the cities, these young people were exposed to cultural differences they never expected. They also encountered significant discrimination, and many were encouraged to change or anglicize their names in order to have a better chance at finding employment (Zolner, 2000).

Older adolescents are more likely than younger ones to have a metacognitive awareness of their cultural identity, in part because they are more likely to have had

Bikeriderlondon/Shutterstock

Cultural identity is fostered intergenerationally.

opportunities to explore their cultural heritage (Phinney & Chavira, 1992). Also, as is the case with overall identity, adolescents are most likely to achieve a strong cultural self-concept when their parents encourage them to explore alternatives instead of pressuring them to adopt or restricting them to particular ways (Rosenthal & Feldman, 1992).

Adolescents who have achieved a strong cultural identity tend to have higher self-esteem and find their interactions with family and friends more satisfying (Phinney, Cantu, & Kurtz, 1997). In addition, many investigators have found that adolescents with a strong cultural identity do better in school than adolescents whose cultural identities are weaker (Stalikas & Gavaki, 1995; Taylor, Casten, Flickinger, Roberts, & Fulmore, 1994).

Some individuals achieve a well-defined cultural self-concept and, at the same time, identify strongly with the mainstream culture, making them, in effect, bicultural. For other individuals, the cost of strong ethnic identification is a weakened tie to mainstream culture. Phinney (1990) reported that, for Hispanic Americans, strong identification with American culture is associated with a weaker Hispanic self-concept. In reality, successful adjustment in life for members of minority cultures always means a certain level of competency in their culture of origin as well as in the mainstream culture of the society. Adolescents who immigrate to North America with their families often become masters of North American cultural ways much faster than their parents. Adolescents are particularly assisted in their adjustment by age peers and driven by their natural desire to fit in with the social groups around them.

An interesting website devoted to the adjustment experiences of Hmong adolescents in the United States (www.hmongnet.org) allows youth to pose a question to Hmong teens about Hmong American life. For example, one question posed was "What is your parent's idea of a traditional Hmong boy/girl? What is your idea of a traditional Hmong boy/girl? Can the two co-exist?" The page has links to a teen chat room as well as links that might interest Hmong teens. These kinds of resources can help teens adjust and feel like they have a place to belong while they are facing all the stresses of adapting to a new culture.

We shouldn't be too surprised that identifying strongly with mainstream culture tends to weaken cultural identity in some groups but not others (Berry, 1993). Even within any particular group, the nature and consequences of cultural identity can change over successive generations (Cuellar, Nyberg, Maldonado, & Roberts, 1997). As successive generations become more acculturated to mainstream culture, they can begin to identify less strongly with their culture of origin.

The issue of transracial adoption is of particular concern to First Nations, Métis, and Inuit peoples in Canada, as many of their children have been taken out of home communities and adopted into non-Aboriginal families. While the issue is termed "transracial," it is more about culture than race.

Children adopted interculturally learn the cultural ways of their adoptive family rather than their family of origin. Race becomes particularly important when people outside the adoptive family talk about and classify the child as racially different. Normally, in situations where a child is adopted by a family who is of a different cultural heritage than the child, that child's biological family might maintain strong feelings of cultural identity that their children don't share. However, the Aboriginal peoples of Canada have been hit with a kind of double jeopardy with regard to this matter, as many of the children who were adopted out to non-Aboriginal families also had biological parents who had attended residential schools. Transracial adoptions, as well as attendance at residential schools, placed a high degree of assimilative pressure upon Aboriginal peoples in Canada, forcing many to take on the ways of European-based cultures. However, over the past few decades, these peoples have taken active steps to protect, preserve, and promote their heritage to their youth, who currently form one of the most rapidly growing population sectors in Canadian society. In addition, a particular mandate of First Nations–owned and -operated child and family services agencies is placement of children with relatives or other First Nations families, so they are able to develop strong identities as well as pride in their own cultural heritages.

Cultural identity is also a particularly salient issue for children belonging to a minority group but adopted by parents of Western European cultural heritage. The Research to Practice feature shows how identity tends to develop in these children.

Self-Esteem in Adolescence

LO3 **Discuss how self-esteem changes in adolescence.**

We've seen that self-esteem is usually very high in preschool children but declines gradually during the early elementary school years as children compare themselves to others. By later middle childhood, self-esteem has usually stabilized—it neither increases nor decreases in these years (Harter, Whitesell, & Kowalski, 1992). Evidently, children learn their place in the "pecking order" of different domains and adjust their self-esteem accordingly.

Some studies indicate that self-esteem changes when children move from elementary school through to high school (Seidman, Allen, Aber, Mitchell, & Feinman, 1994).

Research to Practice

Promoting Strong Development through Strong Ethnic Identity

Adolescence is a time of identity exploration that can be particularly challenging for youth who belong to immigrant or ethnic minority groups in Canada. Not only do these youth have to figure out who they are, but they also have to negotiate differences between expectations associated with their culture of origin as well as those for Canadian mainstream society (Costigan, Su, & Hua, 2009). Chinese youth belong to one of the largest cultural groups in the nation, and they have been studied considerably with regard to ethnic identity. Costigan and colleagues (2009) pointed out that parents have a strong impact on the development of Chinese youth's ethnic identity. In addition, the expectations of mothers, in particular, tend to be associated with the ethnic identity of their children (Su & Costigan, 2009).

Research into ethnic identity among Chinese immigrants has revealed some key findings about the importance of considering ethnic identity in youth. Chinese youth who have higher levels of identification with their ethnic origin tend to have higher levels of achievement and self-esteem and lower levels of depressive symptoms (Costigan, Koryzma, Hua, & Chance, 2010). However, lower levels of ethnic identity tend to be linked to higher levels of depressive symptoms and, especially for boys, lower levels of self-esteem (Costigan et al., 2010). In addition, higher levels of ethnic identity also tended to buffer stress associated with poor achievement, suggesting that strong ethnic identity can have a protective effect against negative life experiences (Costigan et al., 2010). Past research on transracial adoptions with Black and White youth resulted in researchers concluding that strong identification with a particular cultural group, whether or not that group matches an adolescent's personal culture of origin, is better than having a weak or confused sense of ethnic identification (Deberry, Scarr, & Weinberg, 1996).

Being able to think of oneself as an integrated member of some larger, recognized cultural group is an important part of being psychologically healthy. Adolescents who do not have a strong sense of belonging to any cultural group are at risk for social and psychological problems. Therefore, adults working with youth can support more positive development in young people when they validate and encourage participation in prosocial cultural events that foster and build a stronger cultural identity.

Apparently, when students from different elementary schools enter the same secondary school, they know where they stand compared to their old elementary school classmates but not to students from other elementary schools. Thus, peer comparisons begin anew, and self-esteem often suffers.

The drop in self-esteem associated with the transition to secondary school is usually temporary. As children enter middle and late adolescence, self-esteem frequently increases (Savin-Williams & Demo, 1984). New schools become familiar, and students gradually adjust to the new pecking order. In addition, adolescents begin to compare themselves to adults. They see themselves acquiring more and more adult skills, such as having a job or driving a car. Also, they see themselves acquiring many of the signs of adult status, such as greater independence and greater responsibility for their decisions. These changes apparently foster self-esteem.

Ask Yourself

Although Piaget's theory of cognitive development was not concerned with identity formation, how might his theory explain why identity is a central issue in adolescence?

16.2 Relationships with Parents and Peers

Learning Objectives

After reading the module, you should be able to do the following:

LO4 Describe how parent–child relationships change in adolescence.

LO5 Understand the key issues in adolescent peer relationships.

As adolescents move away from childhood and approach adulthood, their relationships with other people change. Greater physical and cognitive maturity makes teenagers less dependent on parents and more invested in relationships with peers. We'll trace these changes in this module and, as we do, we'll learn more about group identities like those that form so rapidly during this period of development.

Parent–Child Relationships in Adolescence

LO4 Describe how parent–child relationships change in adolescence.

Despite adolescents' drive toward independence, many features of parent–child relationships are unchanged from childhood. The authoritative parenting that is best for children's development works best for adolescents too: Teenagers flourish when parents are warm and caring, while still establishing reasonable rules and enforcing them consistently. Like parents of children, parents of adolescents sometimes fall into the negative reinforcement trap, inadvertently reinforcing the very behaviours they want to eliminate often in order to avoid parent–teen conflicts. Just as in middle childhood, adolescents often endure family-related stressors, such as those associated with parental divorce, and their schoolwork and adjustment suffers. Some teenagers face the challenge of adjusting to a blended family situation where new relationships and new rules seem to change everything around them.

Of course, parent–child relations normally change during adolescence. As teens become more independent, their relationships with their parents usually become more egalitarian. Parents must adjust to their children's growing sense of autonomy by treating them more like equals as they become more mature (Laursen & Collins, 1994). This growing independence means that some teens spend less time with their parents, are less affectionate toward them, and argue more often with them about matters of style, taste, and freedom. Teenagers also might seem more moody and likely to enjoy spending time alone (Larson, 1997; Wolfson & Carskadon, 1998).

In fact, since the time of G. Stanley Hall, adolescence has been overwhelmingly described and portrayed, especially in movies, as a time of storm and stress—a period in which parent–child relationships deteriorate in the face of a combative, argumentative youth. Although this view may make for best-selling novels and films, in reality, the rebellious teen is largely a myth. Think about the following conclusions derived from research findings (Steinberg, 1990). Most adolescents

- admire and love their parents
- rely upon their parents for advice
- embrace many of their parents' values
- feel loved by their parents

Not exactly the image of the rebel, is it? Intercultural research provides further evidence that adolescence is not necessarily a time of turmoil and conflict. Offer, Ostrov, Howard, and Atkinson (1988) interviewed adolescents from 10 different countries: the United States, Australia, Germany, Italy, Israel, Hungary, Turkey, Japan, Taiwan, and Bangladesh. These investigators found most adolescents moving confidently and happily toward adulthood. As the graphs in Figure 16–2 show, most adolescents around the world reported that they were usually happy, and few avoided their homes.

Figure 16-2

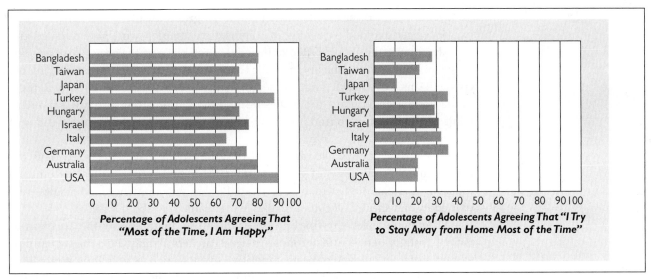

SOURCE: Based on Offer, D., Ostrov, E., Howard, K. I., & Atkinson, R. (1988). The teenage world: Adolescents' self-image in ten countries. ISBN 978-1-4899-0765-3. pages 144 and 199, Springer Science & Business Media New York, Inc.

Thus, adolescence is definitely an interesting and challenging time for youth and their parents, as both parties deal with challenges brought on by an evolving parent–child relationship in which the child is nearly a fully independent young adult (Steinberg, 1990). However, adolescence is not inherently tempestuous as the myth of "storm and stress" would lead us to believe.

Relationships with Peers

LO5 Understand the key issues in adolescent peer relationships.

Many of the major developmental theorists—including Freud, Erikson, Piaget, and Vygotsky—believed that adolescents' development is strongly shaped by their social interactions with peers. Whether at a summer camp, in school, on a sports team, or in a small circle of close friends, an individual adolescent's interactions with peers are important developmental events. In the remainder of this module, we'll look at groups like those that form at summer camps and then examine adolescents' friendships.

GROUPS. Whenever strangers are brought together, they form defined groups. Psychologist Muzafer Sherif and colleagues Harvey, White, Hood, and Sherif (1961) used this phenomenon to conduct a landmark study of groups at the Robbers Cave State Park in Oklahoma. The boys in this study did not know one another before coming to camp. They were put in two groups that were comparable in the boys' size, their athletic ability, and previous camping experience. For the first week, the two groups were kept apart and spent their time in traditional camp activities that required considerable co-operation, such as transporting camping equipment and organizing hikes.

After just a few days, leaders emerged within each group. Boys acquired nicknames and the groups themselves acquired names, Rattlers and Eagles. Each group established norms to regulate behaviour within the group. For example, boys who complained about minor injuries or being homesick were teased for not being "tough."

At the end of the first week, it was arranged that the groups discover each other. Each immediately insisted that the other had intruded on its "turf," which helped solidify the emerging feelings of group membership. Each group challenged the other in baseball, so a game was planned, along with other competitions (such as tent pitching and cleaning the cabins). Prizes were announced for the winners.

Preparing for these events further solidified group loyalties, and activities that had once been avoided—cleaning the cabins, for example—were now pursued vigorously because they contributed to the goal of establishing the group's superiority. In this phase, boys became antagonistic to members of the other group. During the competitions, boys heckled and cursed the other group. After losing to the Rattlers in the first baseball game, the Eagles burned the Rattlers' flag and hung the remnants for the Rattlers to find. One Eagle said, "You can tell those guys I did it; if they say anything, I'll fight 'em!"

Relations deteriorated so rapidly between the groups that, in just a few days, the boys abandoned displays of good sportsmanship and refused to eat together in the same mess hall. And stereotypes formed. Rattlers were convinced that Eagles were unfriendly and sneaky. Of course, Eagles felt the same way about Rattlers.

After two weeks, the final phase of the study began: Now the aim was to reduce hostility between the groups. First, researchers arranged for the two groups to participate in enjoyable, noncompetitive events, such as watching a movie or shooting firecrackers together. This approach failed completely, and the antagonism continued.

The second approach involved creating common goals for the two groups that required co-operation. When the boys wanted to see a popular movie, the staff said that the camp could not afford the rental. After some debate, the two groups agreed to contribute equally to the cost of the movie. A few days later, a truck that was to pick up supplies would not start. A Rattler suggested they use a rope to pull the truck to start it. All group members joined in and, after a few tries, started the truck (which was in working condition all along). The boys congratulated one another, and the groups intermingled.

These and other situations involving common goals eliminated the hostility between groups just as rapidly as the competition had elicited it. By the end of the week, Rattlers and Eagles were sitting together in the mess hall. When camp was over, the Rattlers and Eagles asked to travel home on the same bus.

The Robbers Cave study tells us a great deal about group formation and group functioning. Three conclusions are particularly worth remembering. First, when groups of children and adolescents form, a structure emerges rapidly with individuals having specific roles, for example, as a leader. Second, when groups compete for scarce resources (e.g., prizes), individuals identify with and support their own group more strongly. At the same time, they develop negative stereotypes of members of other groups and feel antagonistic toward them. Third, when common goals require that groups co-operate, group boundaries become less pronounced, and hostility between groups ceases.

Common goals can reduce or eliminate inter-group hostilities.

Though it's been nearly 50 years since the Sherif study at Robbers Cave, the findings are still important to understanding the social landscape of late childhood and adolescence. Two types of groups are particularly common as children enter adolescence. A **clique** consists of four to six individuals who are good friends and, consequently, tend to be similar in age, sex, race, and interests. Members of a clique spend time together and usually dress, talk, and act alike. Cliques are often part of a larger group too. A **crowd** is a larger group of older children or adolescents who have similar values and attitudes and are known by a common label. Maybe you remember some of the different crowds from your own youth. "Jocks," "preppies," "burnouts," "nerds," and "brains"—adolescents use these or similar terms to refer to crowds of older children or adolescents (Brown, Mounts, Lamborn, & Steinberg, 1993; Cairns, Leung, Buchannan, & Cairns, 1995).

Clique:
four to six good friends who tend to be similar in age, sex, race, and interests.

Crowd:
a larger group of older children or adolescents who have similar values and attitudes and are known by a common label.

Some crowds have more status than others. For example, students in many middle and high schools claim that the "jocks" are the most prestigious crowd whereas the "burnouts" are among the least prestigious. Self-esteem in older children and adolescents often reflects the status of their crowd. During the school years, youth from high-status crowds tend to have greater self-esteem than those from low-status crowds (Brown & Lohr, 1987).

Why do some students become nerds while others join the stoners? Parenting style is part of the answer. A study by Brown and his colleagues

A group usually has a particular leader.

Daniele Morra/Fotolia

Members of a larger crowd.

Dominance hierarchy:
levels of authority within a group, which typically includes a leader to whom other members of the group defer.

(1993) examined the impact of three parental practices on students' membership in particular crowds. The investigators measured the extent to which parents emphasized academic achievement, monitored their children's out-of-school activities, and involved their children in joint decision making. When parents emphasized achievement, their children were more likely to be in the popular, jock, and normal crowds and less likely to be in the druggie crowd. When parents monitored out-of-school behaviour, their children were more likely to be in the brain crowd and less likely to be in the druggie crowd. Finally, when parents included their children in joint decision making, their children were more likely to be in the brain and normal crowds and less likely to be in the druggie crowd. These findings were true for African American, Asian American, European American, and Hispanic American children and their parents.

What seems to happen is that when parents practise authoritative parenting—they are warm but firm—their children become involved with crowds that endorse adult standards of behaviour (e.g., normals, jocks, brains). But, when parents' style is neglecting or permissive, their children are less likely to identify with adult standards of behaviour and, instead, join crowds like druggies, who disavow adult standards and engage in antisocial activities.

GROUP STRUCTURE. Groups—whether in school, at a summer camp, or anywhere else—typically have a well-defined structure. Most groups have a **dominance hierarchy** consisting of a leader to whom all other members of the group defer. Other members know their position in the hierarchy. They yield to members who are above them in the hierarchy and assert themselves over members who are below them. A dominance hierarchy is useful in reducing conflict within groups because every member knows his or her place.

With children, especially boys, physical power is often the basis for the dominance hierarchy. The leader is usually the most physically intimidating child (Pettit, Bakshi, Dodge, & Coie, 1990). Among girls and older boys, hierarchies are often based on individual traits that relate to the group's main function. At summer camps, for example, the leaders most often are the children with the greatest camping experience. Among groups like Girl Guides or Pathfinders, girls chosen to be patrol leaders tend to be bright and goal-oriented and to have new ideas (Edwards, 1994). These characteristics are appropriate because the primary function of patrols is to help plan activities for the entire troop of girls. Thus, leadership based on key skills is effective because it gives the greatest influence to those with the skills most important to group functioning (Hartup, 1983).

PEER PRESSURE. Groups establish norms—standards of behaviour that apply to all group members—and groups may pressure members to conform to these norms. Such "peer pressure" is often characterized as an irresistible, harmful force. The stereotype is that teenagers exert enormous pressure on each other to behave antisocially. In reality, peer pressure is neither all-powerful nor always antisocial. For example, most middle and high school students resist peer pressure to behave in ways that are clearly antisocial, such as stealing (Brown, Lohr, & McClenahan, 1986). Gender is another area in which adolescents often feel pressured to conform to particular behavioural standards. Youth who do not behave like a typical boy or girl for their age can be marginalized or pathologized (Lobel, Nov-Krispin, Schiller, Lobel, & Feldman, 2004; Smith & Leaper, 2006). Peer pressure can be positive too; peers often urge one another to participate in school activities, such as trying out for a play or working on the yearbook, or become involved in community-action projects, such as Habitat for Humanity.

Peer pressure is most powerful when the standards for appropriate behaviour are not clear-cut. Preference in music and clothing, for example, is completely subjective, so youth conform to peer-group guidelines, suggesting, for example, that they wear certain kinds of "in," or fashionable, clothing. For adolescents in India, greater clothing conformity was observed in younger adolescence under the age of 16 (Kulshreshtha & Kashyap, 2004). This points to an interesting phenomenon, that peer pressure, particularly as it relates to drug use, appears to have a greater effect in early adolescence and a more declining effect as children become older (McIntosh, MacDonald, & McKeganey, 2006).

Nevertheless, youth recognize that standards for smoking, drinking, and using drugs are often fuzzy. Drinking is a good case in point. Parents and groups like SADD (Students Against Driving Drunk) discourage teens from drinking, yet North American culture is filled with youthful models who drink alcohol, seem to enjoy it, and suffer no apparent ill effects. Television and movie programming often portrays teens and young adults participating in alcohol and drug abuse with little or no detrimental effect on their schoolwork, jobs, health, or relationships. Case in point: the Harold and Kumar movies. To the contrary, these characters seem to enjoy life all the more because of their substance abuse. With such contradictory messages, it is not surprising that youth look to their peers for answers to these kinds of fuzzy dilemmas (Urberg, Deg˘irmenciog˘lu, & Pilgrim, 1997).

Visual media, as well as some hip-hop and rap music, also often portray adults engaging in risky behaviour, including using street drugs, engaging in unsafe sex, and binge drinking as routine aspects of their lives (e.g., think of programs and movies like *Trailer Park Boys*, *Knocked Up*, *The Hangover*, *That 70s Show*, *Adventureland*, *It's Complicated*, *Get Him to the Greek*, and many others). In addition, a new type of show portrays drugs as an economic lifestyle choice (e.g., think of *Weeds*, *Growing Op*, and *Pineapple Express*). Although these shows are about adults and often are rated R or 18A, they typically have broad market appeal to teenagers. Adolescents' access to adult programming and other forms of restricted media only increases once they are released for sale to the public.

Researchers also have found that youth in the middle school years who are allowed to view restricted media tend to have higher rates for initiating alcohol use in comparison with youth whose parents enforce access to media restrictions (Tanski, Cin, Stoolmiller, & Sargent, 2010). Viewing restricted movies also seems to increase youths' sensation-seeking behaviours over time (Stoolmiller, Gerrard, Sargent, Worth, & Gibbons, 2010).

In addition to media access, tattooing has been perceived to be more common and a kind of conformity behaviour in adolescence; however, Deschesnes, Fines, and Demers (2006) found that youth who obtain tattoos tend to more frequently be involved in risky externalizing behaviours, including multiple drug use, illegal activities, gang affiliation, problem gambling, school truancy, and rave attendance. Tattooing might continue to be viewed as routine behaviour or conformity, but perhaps it is conformity to more antisocial than prosocial group norms.

Thinking about this might make you realize something interesting and paradoxical about adolescence: Although it is a time of experimentation and purported rebellion, youth are often driven by their desire to fit into a group, making conformity with a group, rather than independence and rebellion, a major feature of North American adolescent behaviour. Consequently, some youth drink alcohol (or smoke cigarettes, use drugs, or have sex) to conform to their group's norms, while others, reflecting conformity to their group's norms, choose to abstain. However, if you tell an adolescent that his or her behaviour is a form of social conformity, expect to get big denial as well as a number of nasty facial expressions sent in your general direction. In their desire to be seen as mature, adolescents like to think of themselves as unique, independent, and in control of their own decisions, even if they're not.

FRIENDSHIP. Just as in childhood, adolescent friendships are based on common interests and mutual liking. Adolescents tend to befriend peers who are like themselves in age, gender, and race. However, friendships during adolescence take on new and special significance: Adolescents believe that loyalty, trust, and intimacy are the essential ingredients of friendship. Also, adolescents, much more so than children, believe that friends should defend one another, strongly believe that friends should not deceive or abandon one another (Newcomb & Bagwell, 1995), and believe that friends should share common values. These additional characteristics of friendship relations in adolescence grow from adolescents' increasing cognitive and metacognitive abilities to think abstractly about the world as well as about their own views and the views of others.

Loyalty is more important in adolescents' friendships than in children's friendships. The emphasis on loyalty apparently goes hand in hand with the emphasis on intimacy: If a friend is disloyal, adolescents are afraid that they may be humiliated because their intimate thoughts and feelings will become known to a much broader circle of people (Berndt & Perry, 1990).

Intimacy is more common in friendships among girls, who are more likely than boys to have one exclusive "best friend." Because intimacy is at the core of their friendships, girls are also more likely to be concerned about the faithfulness of their friends and worry about being rejected (Buhrmester & Furman, 1987). And when one friend makes another mad, girls' anger tends to be more intense and last longer (Whitesell & Harter, 1996).

The emergence of intimacy in adolescent friendships means that friends also come to be seen as sources of social and emotional support. Levitt, Guacci-Franco, and Levitt (1993) asked African American, European American, and Hispanic American 7-, 10-, and 14-year-olds to whom they would turn if they needed help or were bothered by something. For all ethnic groups, 7- and 10-year-olds relied upon close family members—parents, siblings, and grandparents—as primary sources of support, but not friends. However, 14-year-olds relied upon close family members less often and said they would turn to friends instead. Because adolescent friends share intimate thoughts and feelings, they can provide support during emotional or stressful periods. And, as you'll see in the Looking Ahead feature, the benefits of friendship can last a lifetime.

Friendships can also be the source of anxiety, particularly for girls. Mack, Strong, Kowalski, and Crocker (2007) found that girls experienced more anxiety about their personal appearance, more pressure to change their appearance, and more discussions of personal appearance than boys. The strongest variables having an impact on girls' experience of friendship-related anxiety about personal appearance were direct peer pressure from friends and the relative attractiveness of girls' peers (Mack et al., 2007).

ROMANTIC RELATIONSHIPS. North American boys and girls typically begin to date at about age 15 (Miller et al., 1997). The first experiences with dating often

Prudkov/Fotolia

Dating begins with group activities.

Looking Ahead

Adolescent Friendships Predict Quality of Relationships in the Midthirties

Friendships can have a long-lasting impact on adolescents' development. When adolescents have friends with conventional, prosocial attitudes, they grow up to be adults who find life satisfying. These long-term consequences are demonstrated in a 20-year longitudinal study conducted by Stein and Newcomb (1999). These investigators questioned middle school students about the nature of their friendships, including whether they discussed homework with their friends, whether their friends got good grades and planned to go to university, and whether

their parents approved of their friends. When the middle school students were in their thirties, Stein and Newcomb asked them about their romantic relationships; about their relationships with parents, families, and peers; and about their overall life satisfaction. Having conventional, prosocial friendships during adolescence was positively related to all these variables. That is, when middle school students with conventional friends were in their thirties, they tended to be happy with life in general and with most of their social relationships in particular. Stein and Newcomb concluded that identifying with prosocial friends apparently leads adolescents to forge a prosocial identity and a positive sense of self, features that pave the way for positive interactions with others and a positive sense of self in adulthood.

occur when groups of the same gender go places knowing that a mixed-gender crowd will be attending. Examples include going to a school dance or going to a mall with friends. A somewhat more advanced form of dating involves several boys and several girls going out together as a group. Ultimately, dates involve well-defined couples. By the high school years, most students will have had at least one steady girlfriend or boyfriend.

As you might suspect, cultural factors strongly influence dating patterns. For example, parents of Western European heritage tend to encourage independence in their teenagers as compared with other cultures that emphasize family ties and loyalty to parents. Dating is a sign of independence and usually results in less time spent with family, which explains why youth from cultures emphasizing family ties and parental loyalty often begin to date at an older age and date less frequently (Xiaohe & Whyte, 1990). Originally, the primary function of dating was to select a mate, but today dating serves a variety of functions for adolescents (Padgham & Blyth, 1991; Sanderson & Cantor, 1995). Dating

- is a pleasant form of recreation and entertainment
- helps to teach adult standards of interpersonal behaviour
- is a means to establish status among peers
- provides an outlet for sexual experimentation
- provides companionship like that experienced between best friends
- leads to intimacy, in which teens share innermost feelings with their partners

The functions of dating change during adolescence. As adolescents mature, companionship and intimacy become more important while recreation and status-seeking become less important (Roscoe, Diana, & Brooks, 1987; Sanderson & Cantor, 1995).

Ask Yourself

How might media influence adolescent standards for conformity across a variety of domains?

16.3 The Dark Side

 ## Learning Objectives

After reading the module, you should be able to do the following:

LO6 Explain why teenagers drink alcohol.

LO7 Discuss what leads some adolescents to become depressed and how depression can be treated.

LO8 Identify the causes of juvenile delinquency.

Some young people do not adapt well to the new situations, demands, or responsibilities of adolescence and respond in ways that are unhealthy. In this last section of Chapter 16, we look at three, often interrelated, problems that create the three D's of adolescence: drugs, depression, and delinquency. As we look at these problems, you'll understand why sometimes adolescence can be an especially difficult challenge.

Alcohol and Drug Use

LO6 Explain why teenagers drink alcohol.

Throughout history, people have used substances that alter their behaviour, thoughts, or emotions. Today, drugs used commonly in North America include alcohol, marijuana, hallucinogens (e.g., LSD), heroin, cocaine, barbiturates, and amphetamines, as well as newer drugs, such as Ecstasy and crystal methamphetamine ("crystal meth"). Figure 16–3 provides a picture of American adolescents' use of these drugs (Johnston, O'Malley, & Bachman, 2000).

Alcohol abuse is a particular problem for many youth. Why do so many adolescents drink alcohol? There are a number of reasons (Fields, 1992):

- *Experimentation:* To try something new
- *Relaxation:* As a means to reduce tension

Figure 16-3

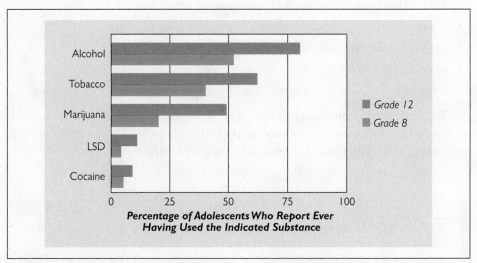

SOURCE: US Department of Health and Human Services, Ntl Inst of Drug Abuse, 2000. US Department of Health and Human Services.

- *Escape:* To avoid a harsh or unpleasant real world
- *Feelings of exhilaration:* To increase one's self-confidence, usually by reducing one's inhibitions

Of course, these reasons don't apply to all teenagers. Some never drink alcohol. Others experiment briefly with drinking and then decide it is not for them. Still others, however, drink heavily.

In Canada, based on data from the National Longitudinal Study of Children and Youth (NLSCY), two-thirds of teenagers between the ages of 12 and 15 who reported that their friends use alcohol had consumed alcohol to the point of intoxication on at least one occasion. In comparison, of youth who reported that their friends did not use alcohol, only 8 percent had ever been drunk. Findings for cannabis (marijuana) use were similar, with 82 percent of youth with friends who smoked the drug having tried cannabis, in comparison to 7 percent who did not have friends who used cannabis.

In addition, in families where alcohol consumption was problematic, youth were not more likely to abuse alcohol or drugs; however, youth in blended families and youth with parents who had a hostile parenting style were more likely to use alcohol and drugs. The researchers pointed out, however, that the hostile parenting might have been a response to problems associated with teenage substance abuse in the family home, as opposed to causing that substance abuse, underscoring the importance of remembering that correlational research provides information about important relationships between variables under study but cannot address causation with regard to those relationships.

Finally, certain trends are of note in terms of substance abuse by youth in Canada. While early substance abuse certainly is a concern, the greatest amount of substance abuse appears to happen during late adolescence, mostly around ages 18 to 19, and then tapers off sharply for most youth after that (Williams et al., 2004).

From the Canadian data on alcohol and drug abuse, you can see that, perhaps not surprisingly, peers are influential, particularly for younger adolescents. Many adolescents drink alcohol or abuse other substances because their peers do so and exert pressure on them to join the group (Dielman, Schulenberg, Leech, & Shope, 1992). However, as teenage drinking has so many causes, no single approach is likely to eliminate alcohol abuse. Adolescents who drink to reduce their tension can profit from therapy designed to teach them more effective means of coping with stress. Community-based programs that are interactive and feature teen-directed discussion can be effective in teaching the facts about drinking and strategies for resisting peer pressure to drink (Baker, 1988; Tobler & Stratton, 1997). One such program is Alateen, which is a group affiliated with Alcoholics Anonymous and designed to support teens who have an alcoholic family member or somebody else whose drinking affects them.

Some First Nations, Inuit, and Métis youth in Canada have struggled with substance abuse, particularly inhalation of solvents. Of special note, in the late 1990s, many Mushuau Innu children in Davis Inlet were found to be addicted in overwhelming numbers to sniffing gasoline. A poverty-stricken people in northern Labrador, the community lacked necessary social and financial resources for helping their children overcome this serious and life-threatening addiction. In a situation like this, the only real solution to long-term rehabilitation of so many inhalant-addicted youth is a community-based program in which nearly all families are dedicated to change. As long as youth

Peer pressure can foster both positive and negative behaviours.

Making Children's Lives Better

Understanding the Combined Effect of Historical Events on Children's Lives in the Present

Over the years, much research has been done on the problem of substance abuse among Canada's Indigenous peoples. While substance abuse can be thought of as a primary problem in people's lives, the problem of substance abuse can be secondary to other, larger issues, such as poverty, victimization, or other major traumas and stressors. Addressing these larger issues and traumas is key to changing associated problems, such as substance abuse.

One major trauma that has affected Indigenous peoples in Canada is mandatory attendance at residential schools, which existed until the 1970s in this country. Mandated by the Canadian government and implemented by various religious orders and institutions, these schools were places where Indigenous children underwent a program of forced assimilation to mainstream society. In order to assimilate them, Indigenous children were taken away from their families and moved to the schools. During their time in these schools, most children had no contact with their families except during summer vacation. As a result of the education, language, customs, and habits they were taught at the schools, many children, upon returning to their families, found it difficult to fit in with their own people.

Furthermore, when taken away from their families at young ages, such as between the ages of 5 and 10, children's attachment to their families of origin was disrupted.

Given that they were living in a boarding-school arrangement for the greater part of the year, these children were not exposed to normal Indigenous models for family life and parenting. Once they were released from residential school, these children usually were trained in manual chores, but they had not been taught how to take over responsibilities of family life. In addition, many children in residential school were exposed to harsh and abusive treatment, and some also died.

Facing family responsibilities as they got older, children who grew up in residential schools had little modelling for how to parent. The stresses of parenting and adjustment to normal life after residential school were too much for many, who also faced problems of poverty and confused cultural identity. As a result, many experienced serious emotional and behavioural problems, including depression, violence, suicide, anxiety, and substance abuse. The traumatic legacy of residential schools continues today, as many children of residential school survivors, in turn, have grown up with poor models for parenting and cultural identity.

Fortunately, not all Indigenous children were sent to residential schools, and some carried forward the traditions and socialization norms for their cultural group. By understanding their history and reclaiming their cultural identity, these later generations of First Nations, Inuit, and Métis youth should be able to help each other live in a more balanced and healthy way. Another circumstance that also has overwhelming impact on children is war, which you can read about in the following feature on Children and Families around the World.

return to a poverty-stricken, resource-strapped environment where models for substance abuse abound, they will have extreme difficulty and little hope for overcoming this kind of addiction.

In many ways, then, the rehabilitation of these youth is tied to necessary changes that must occur in their home communities. While low parental supervision and poor modelling might have led to high levels of solvent abuse in some Indigenous communities, larger and more complex problems occurred long before, which laid the foundation for disorganization and distress in Indigenous communities such as Davis Inlet. One way that children from Indigenous communities can be helped is by understanding what kinds of factors, both current and historical, have contributed to their present difficulties. The Making Children's Lives Better feature explores some of the historical factors that have had a long-term impact on Indigenous families in Canada.

Depression

LO7 Discuss what leads some adolescents to become depressed and how depression can be treated.

Sometime in your life, you probably have had the blues, days when you had little energy or enthusiasm for activities that you usually enjoy. You wanted to be alone, and you may have felt down and doubted your abilities. These feelings are perfectly normal, can usually be explained as reactions to specific events, and vanish in a matter

Children and Families around the World

The Impact of War on Children

In many places around the globe, war and terrorism are part of children's daily reality. Both direct and indirect exposure to war and terrorism can have an impact on children's healthy adjustment and mental health. Mental health outcomes for children exposed to war or terrorism tend to be negative, with children experiencing extreme anxiety, fearfulness, and posttraumatic stress. However, the responses of a child to war and terrorism are affected by the child's gender and developmental level, the availability of parental support, the surrounding culture, the intensity and duration of exposure to the threat, and the extent of life disruption as a result of it.

One important point that is recognized in research is that, despite the stress and hardships relating to war and terrorism, children can be very resilient, in part because they typically have a strong orientation toward wanting to live, and this desire helps them recover from stressful experiences. More is known about the responses of older children and adolescents, as more research has been done with these age groups. In addition, with increasing developmental ability, older children are more readily able to understand what is happening around them and why.

When children are exposed to war and terrorism, the primary concerns are to establish safety and a feeling of security as well as to address the child's basic needs (e.g., food, shelter, clothing). Trust is also very important, as children exposed to war or terrorism will not know whom to trust. Children most typically will look to their parents' responses to and interpretation of events going on around them. The ability of the parent to cope with stressful events will have a great impact on the ability of a child to cope as well. Children who experience posttraumatic stress symptoms after exposure to war or terrorism can be treated with a variety of approaches. Primary among these is cognitive-behavioural therapy, during which the children's thoughts and fears are addressed and new, healthy ways of coping are introduced, including a feeling of control over one's emotions. Other forms of intervention that have been used with children are art therapy and relaxation techniques.

SOURCE: Based on Yahav, 2011.

---

of hours or days. For example, after an exciting vacation with family and friends, you may be depressed at the thought of returning to school to start new and difficult courses. Nevertheless, your mood improves as you renew friendships and become involved in activities on campus.

Now imagine experiencing these same symptoms continuously for weeks or months. Also suppose that you lost your appetite, slept poorly, and were unable to concentrate. Pervasive feelings of sadness, irritability, hopelessness, and low motivation over a period of two or more weeks typically characterize an individual with **depression**. About 3 to 10 percent of adolescents are depressed; adolescent girls are more often affected than boys (Nolen-Hoeksema & Girgus, 1994).

Depression:
a psychological disorder in which a person has pervasive feelings of sadness or irritability, as well as other symptoms, for a period of at least two weeks.

Unwillingness, anger, and irritation often dominate the lives of depressed adolescents. They often believe that family members, friends, and classmates are not friendly to them (Cole & Jordan, 1995). Depressed adolescents wish to be left alone much more often than do nondepressed adolescents (Larson, Raffaelli, Richards, Ham, & Jewell, 1990). Rather than being satisfying and rewarding, life is empty and joyless for depressed adolescents.

For some adolescents, depression is triggered by a life event that results in fewer positive reinforcements. The loss of a friend, for example, would deprive a teenager of many rewarding experiences and interactions, making the teen feel sad. Feeling lethargic and melancholy, the adolescent withdraws from social interaction and

Depression at any age should be taken very seriously.

Hurricanehank/Shutterstock

misses further opportunities for rewarding experiences. This situation can degenerate rapidly into a negative spiral in which the depressed adolescent becomes progressively more depressed and more likely to avoid interactions that might be rewarding (Lewinsohn & Gotlib, 1995).

Depression often begins with a situation in which an adolescent feels helpless to control the outcome. For example, an athlete might play poorly in a championship game because of illness, or a high school student might score low on a final exam due to a family crisis the night before. In each case, the adolescent could do nothing to avoid an undesirable result. Most teens recognize that such feelings of helplessness are specific to the particular situation. In **learned helplessness**, however, adolescents and adults generalize these feelings of powerlessness and believe that they are always at the mercy of external events, with no ability to control their own destinies. Such feelings of learned helplessness often give rise to depression (Peterson, Maier, & Seligman, 1993; Waschbusch, Sellers, LeBlanc, & Kelley, 2003).

Learned helplessness: generalized feelings and beliefs of powerlessness and being at the mercy of external events.

Experiences like these do not lead all adolescents to become depressed. Some adolescents seem more vulnerable to depression than others, a finding that has led researchers to look for biological factors. Studies of twins and adopted children indicate that heredity definitely has a part in depression. The exact biochemical mechanism seems to involve neurotransmitters (Sevy, Mendlewicz, & Mendelbaum, 1995). Some depressed adolescents have reduced levels of **norepinephrine** and **serotonin**, neurotransmitters that help regulate the brain centers that enable people to experience pleasure. These adolescents might feel depressed because lower levels of neurotransmitters make it difficult for them to experience happiness, joy, and other pleasurable emotions (Peterson, 1996).

Norepinephrine: a type of neurotransmitter.

Serotonin: a type of neurotransmitter.

TREATING DEPRESSION. It is essential to treat depression; otherwise, depressed adolescents become prone to more serious problems, including suicide and self-injury through superficial cutting. Two general approaches are commonly used in treating depression (Kazdin, 1990). One is prescription of antidepressant drugs designed to correct the imbalance in neurotransmitters. The well-known drug Prozac, for example, is designed to reduce depression by increasing levels of serotonin (Peterson, 1996). However, use of some serotonin-related drugs with youth recently has been the subject of some controversy because of possible links to increases in suicidal behaviours in these youth (Dubicka, Hadley, & Roberts, 2006; Ford, 2007; Health Canada, 2004a; Libal, 2007; Simon, 2006; Suddath, 2006).

The other approach to managing depression is psychotherapy. Many different forms are available (Lewinsohn & Gotlib, 1995; Sacco & Beck, 1995), but the most effective teach social skills, so that adolescents can have rewarding social interactions, and ways to restructure their interpretation of events, so that teens can recognize situations where they can exert control over their lives. One aspect of treatment to consider is whether the treatment approach conforms to standards of evidence-based practice. Unfortunately, much of the research to date on empirically supported treatments for psychological disorders has been focused on treatments for adults. This includes research on both psychotherapies and drug interventions. Research demonstrating effectiveness of a treatment method with adults cannot necessarily be generalized to adolescents or children. In addition, the most studied approaches to intervention are not necessarily the only or best approaches. Other, less-studied methods might be equally effective but under-studied.

Depression is one known precursor of suicide; substance abuse is another (Rich, Sherman, & Fowler, 1990; Summerville, Kaslow, & Doepke, 1996). Few suicides are truly spontaneous; in most cases, there are warning signals (Atwater, 1992). Here are some common signs:

- Threats of suicide
- Preoccupation with death

- Change in eating or sleeping habits
- Loss of interest in activities that were once important
- Marked changes in personality
- Persistent feelings of gloom and helplessness
- Giving away valued possessions

If someone you know shows these signs, don't ignore that person, hoping the signs aren't real. Instead, ask the person if he or she is planning on hurting himself or herself. Be calm and supportive and, if the person appears to have made preparations to commit suicide, don't leave him or her alone. Stay with the person until other friends or relatives can come. More importantly, insist that the adolescent seek professional help. Therapy is essential to treat the feelings of depression and hopelessness that give rise to thoughts of suicide (Garland & Zigler, 1993). Risk for suicide can also increase as depression lifts because, as depression begins to decrease, energy levels may increase, along with planful behaviour, such as carrying out plans to self-harm. Therefore, ongoing support is important until the person no longer has any ideas about or plans for self-harm.

In Canada, the suicide rate for boys between the ages of 15 and 19 rose considerably between 1961 and 1991 to as high as 23 per 100 000; however, it decreased in the 1990s to 19 per 100 000. According to Statistics Canada (2015a), the rate for boys between 10 and 14 is 1.8 per 100 000 population. For boys between 15 and 19, the suicide rate is 14.1 per 100 000 population. For girls, the rate was 4 per 100 000 between 1971 and 2000 (Canadian Institute of Child Health, 2000), but it is now 6.2 per 100 000 population in the 15 to 19 age range and 1.9 per 100 000 population in the 10 to 14 age range. The rates for suicide attempts tend to be much higher than for completed suicides overall. Also, boys tend to complete more suicides than girls, while girls tend to attempt suicide more often (Canadian Institute of Child Health, 2000). Part of the reason for this difference in part is that males use firearms more frequently than females in their suicide attempts (Statistics Canada, 2015b), resulting in higher levels of lethal outcomes for males. In general, youth who live on the street, youth who are out of school, and youth of First Nations heritage tend to have even higher risk for suicide completion in Canada (Canadian Institute of Child Health, 2000).

Delinquency

LO8 Identify the causes of juvenile delinquency.

Skipping school. Shoplifting. Selling cocaine. Murder. **Juvenile delinquency** involves young people under the age of majority committing illegal acts that are destructive toward others. Because delinquency applies to such a broad range of activities, it is useful to identify different forms of delinquent behaviour. In the literature on this subject, you may come across the terms **status offence** and **index offence** (Berkeley, Gaffield, & West, 1977). Status offences are acts that are considered illegal if committed by a person who has not attained adult status. Status offences typically include truancy, sexual promiscuity, unmanageable childhood behaviour, and running away from home. Index offences are acts such as robbery, rape, and arson, which are crimes regardless of the perpetrator's age.

Canada has its share of young offenders, although young people do not commit as much crime as you might infer based on news media reports. In Canada, most adolescent crimes relate to property damage (e.g., vandalism and graffiti), common assault (e.g., punching someone), mischief, and theft. However, major crimes are also committed by some Canadian youth, including sexual assault, robbery, and murder.

Over the past decade, Canadian youth have been committing less property crime but more violent crime, assault in particular (Taylor-Butts & Bresan, 2006). About 5 percent of youth crime involved a weapon, which typically was a knife. Overall,

Juvenile delinquency:
the committing of illegal acts by people under the age of majority.

Status offences:
acts that are considered illegal if committed by a person who has not attained adult status.

Index offences:
acts that are crimes regardless of the perpetrator's age.

however, Canadian youth crime has decreased 25 percent from its all-time high in 1991 (Taylor-Butts & Bresan, 2006) and 42 percent since 2000 (Statistics Canada, 2016). The decrease since 2000 has resulted from an overall decrease in the rate of property crime, such as theft under $5000 as well as breaking and entering. In 2014, police charged 48 percent of youth accused of a crime in accordance with objectives of the Youth Criminal Justice Act, which is to divert youth away from formal involvement in the justice system when they are involved in minor offences (Taylor-Butts & Bresan, 2006). Of police-reported violent crimes involving youth, one-fifth of them occur at school (Statistics Canada, 2016).

In terms of drug-related offences, 84 percent of youth drug charges involved cannabis (Taylor-Butts & Bresan, 2006). Drug-related charges for youth have doubled since 1997 (Taylor-Butts & Bresan, 2006) and peaked in 2011 (Statistics Canada, 2016). Youth drug crime decreased by 20 percent between 2011 and 2014, but the overall rate of youth charged with drug offences was still 11 percent higher in 2014 than it was in 2000 (Statistics Canada, 2016). The younger a child begins to commit offences, the more likely it is that the child will reoffend (Carrington, Matarazzo, & deSouza, 2005).

CAUSES OF DELINQUENCY.   Moffitt (1993) has shown that it is important to distinguish two kinds of delinquent behaviour. **Life-course persistent antisocial behaviour** refers to antisocial behaviour that emerges at an early age and continues throughout life. These individuals may start with hitting at 3 years, then progress to shoplifting at age 12, and then to car theft at 16. Perhaps only 5 percent of youth fit this pattern of antisocial behaviour, but they account for most of the criminal activity by adolescents. Antisocial youth sometimes, but not always, belong to antisocial cliques or subcultures that support them and provide them with a sense of belonging. For antisocial youth, joining an antisocial subculture might be much easier than trying to fit into a prosocial group (Zolner, 2004).

A second form of delinquent behaviour described by Moffitt (1993) is far more common. **Adolescent-limited antisocial behaviour** refers to youth who engage in relatively minor criminal acts but who are not consistently antisocial. These youth might become involved in certain crimes, such as shoplifting or using drugs, but might also be careful to follow all school rules. As the name implies, their antisocial behaviour is short-lived, usually abating in late adolescence or early adulthood.

Why do some teens experience a brief bout of delinquency? Remember, part of the struggle of adolescence is to acquire adult status. Youth with life-course persistent antisocial behaviour are often high-status models. These youth often seem to be relatively independent (free of parental influence), they often have desirable possessions like cars and expensive clothes, and they're often sexually experienced. These are attractive features, so many youth apparently imitate the criminal activity that supports this adult-like lifestyle. However, as adolescence ends, the same desirable outcomes can be reached through more prosocial means, and the potential costs of antisocial behaviour increase, so most youth rapidly abandon this antisocial behaviour. Thus, adolescence-limited antisocial behaviour can be understood as one way for adolescents to achieve adult-like status and privileges (Moffitt, 1993).

Explaining life-course persistent antisocial behaviour is more complex. Researchers have identified several forces that contribute to this type of delinquent behaviour.

1. *Social class.* Adolescent crime occurs in all social strata but is more frequent among adolescents from lower social classes. This relationship may reflect a number of factors. First, crime is more common in lower-class neighbourhoods, so adult criminal models are readily available to children. Second, the constant stress of living in poverty can reduce the effectiveness of parenting in lower-class homes (Patterson, DeVaryshe, & Ramsey, 1989). Third, lower-class adolescents often experience little success in school and usually have little invested in the outcome of their academic

Life-course persistent antisocial behaviour: antisocial behaviour that emerges at an early age and continues throughout life.

Adolescent-limited antisocial behaviour: relatively minor criminal acts by youth who are not consistently antisocial.

efforts; criminal activity is an arena in which they can excel, obtain money, and gain the recognition of their peers. According to Katie Buckland, a prosecutor in Los Angeles, youth who join gangs are "the ambitious kids . . . trying to climb up their own corporate ladder. And the only corporate ladder they see has to do with gangs and drugs" (Kantrowitz, 1993, p. 44). While highly organized youth gangs are uncommon in Canada, they nevertheless do exist and are a concern, especially in larger cities (Federation of Canadian Municipalities, 2002). Some types of graffiti are an indicator of organized gangs, often involving youth, who control certain urban territories (Zolner, 2007). While graffiti itself is not always an indicator of gang activity, it frequently is an indicator of youth and young adult involvement in antisocial subcultures, often involving drug use, property damage, and interpersonal violence. Although some people might see graffiti as a form of art, marks, however artistic, made without permission on public or private property are vandalism and a form of crime (Zolner, 2007).

2. *Family processes.* Delinquent behaviour is often related to inadequate parental supervision. Adolescents who are unsupervised (because, for example, their parents are at work) are much more likely to become involved in delinquent acts. Parents may also contribute to delinquent behaviour if their discipline is inconsistent and if their marital relationship is marked by constant conflict (Patterson, 1995). When family life is riddled with stress, arguments, and threats, a gang represents an appealing makeshift family for some adolescents.

3. *Self-control.* As most children develop, they become more capable of regulating their own behaviour. They become better able to inhibit impulsive tendencies, to delay gratification, and to consider the impact of their behaviour on others (Rotenberg & Mayer, 1990). That is, they learn to rise above the immediate pressures of a situation, to avoid giving in to impulses, and to think about the consequences of their actions. Delinquent youth do not follow the usual developmental pattern. Instead, they are much more inclined to act impulsively, and they often are unable or unwilling to postpone pleasure (Patterson, 1995). Seeing a fancy new CD player or a car, delinquent youth are tempted to steal it simply so that they can have it right away. When others inadvertently get in their way, delinquent adolescents often respond without regard to the nature of the other person's acts or intentions.

4. *Biological forces.* The aggressive and impulsive behaviour that is a common part of antisocial behaviour has biological roots. Some antisocial youth apparently inherit a predisposition to behave aggressively and impulsively (Carey, 1996). This is not an "antisocial gene." Instead, individuals who are genetically predisposed to aggression and impulsivity will be more sensitive to experiences that foster antisocial behaviour than will individuals who are not genetically predisposed in this way.

TREATMENT AND PREVENTION.   Given the wide-ranging causes of delinquency, it would be naive to expect a single or simple cure. Instead, delinquency must be attacked along several fronts simultaneously:

- Delinquent adolescents can be taught effective techniques for self-control.

- Parents of delinquent youth can be taught the importance of supervising and monitoring their children's behaviour and the need for consistent discipline.

Antisocial gangs can have strong, family-like bonds between the members.

Monkey Business Images/Shutterstock

- Families of delinquent youth can learn to function more effectively as a unit, with special emphasis on better means of resolving conflict.

- Schools can develop programs that motivate delinquent youth to become invested in their school performance.

- Communities can improve economic conditions, prevention programs, and services in neighbourhoods where delinquency reigns. Canadian communities also tend to focus on victims of violence, providing services wherever possible to people who have been affected by juvenile and other forms of crime.

Programs that include many of these strategies have met with success; adolescents who participate are less likely to be arrested again. The programs thereby address a major problem affecting not only adolescent development but all of North American society (Alexander, Waldron, Barton, & Mas, 1989; Dryfoos, 1990).

In Canada, we recognize that, whenever possible, helping young offenders through measures other than judicial proceedings is preferable. Therefore, at every level of Canadian society, we need to do what we can to prevent juvenile delinquency and violence in general. Sometimes this also means helping young people to learn how to protect themselves from crime and violence in addition to helping youth offenders.

Ask Yourself

Is charging adolescents for status offences a form of discrimination or a violation of youths' rights?

What Would a School Psychologist Do?

You are a school psychologist, and you are seeing a 16-year-old girl who thinks she might be pregnant. The girl tells you she doesn't want you to tell her parents about her problems. You want to honour the girl's request, but you feel nervous about not letting her parents know what is happening. What do you think might be the best way to handle this situation?

Summary

16.1 Identity and Self-Esteem

The Search for Identity

- Search for adolescent identity involves four statuses: diffusion, foreclosure, moratorium, and achievement.

- Diffusion and foreclosure are more common in early adolescence; moratorium and achievement are more common in late adolescence and young adulthood.

- Adolescents seeking identity often believe people are always watching them and that no one has ever felt the way they do.

- When parents encourage discussion and recognize adolescents' autonomy, adolescents are more likely to achieve an identity.

- Adolescents are least likely to achieve an identity when they have authoritarian parents who set rules and enforce them without explanation.

Ethnic Identity

- Acquisition of ethnic identity tends to progress through three phases: initial disinterest, exploration, and identity achievement.

- Achieving an ethnic identity usually results in higher self-esteem but is not consistently related to the strength of one's identification with mainstream culture.

Self-Esteem in Adolescence

- Self-esteem usually declines a little during the transition from elementary to middle school due to increased social comparisons.

- Self-esteem begins to rise in middle and late adolescence as teenagers see themselves acquiring more adult skills and responsibilities.

16.2 Relationships with Parents and Peers

Parent–Child Relationships in Adolescence

- Adolescents benefit from authoritative parenting and some face challenges associated with their parents' divorce or remarriage.

- The parent–child relationship becomes more egalitarian during the adolescent years, reflecting adolescents' growing independence.

- Adolescence is not usually a period of storm and stress, as most adolescents love their parents, feel loved by them, rely on them for advice, and adopt their values.

Relationships with Peers

- Cliques are small groups of like-minded individuals who become part of a crowd.

- Some crowds have a higher status than others.

- Members of higher-status crowds often have higher self-esteem than members of lower-status crowds.

- Most groups have a dominance hierarchy, which is a well-defined structure with a leader at the top.

- Physical power often determines the dominance hierarchy in groups of children and boys.

- With older children and adolescents, dominance hierarchies are often based on the skills important to group functioning.

- Peer pressure is greatest when standards for behaviour are unclear, as with style of music or clothing.

- Adolescent friendships emphasize loyalty and intimacy.

- Intimacy is more common in girls' friendships than in boys', which makes girls more concerned about friends being faithful.

- Teenagers turn to friends for help more often than they turn to parents.

- Dating often begins in midadolescence, usually with the meeting of groups of boys with groups of girls and then progressing to well-defined couples.

- For younger adolescents, dating is for both recreation and status; for older adolescents, it is a source of intimacy and companionship.

16.3 The Dark Side

Alcohol and Drug Use

- Today, many adolescents drink alcohol.

- Adolescents are attracted to alcohol and drugs by their needs for experimentation, relaxation, escape, and excitement.

- The primary factors that influence whether adolescents drink alcohol are encouragement from others (parents and peers) and stress.

Depression

- Depressed adolescents have little enthusiasm for life, believe that others are unfriendly, and wish to be left alone.

- Depression can be triggered by many factors, including an event that deprives them of rewarding experiences, an event in which they feel unable to control their own destiny, or an imbalance in neurotransmitters.

- Treating depression can involve medications that balance levels of neurotransmitters and therapy designed to improve social skills and restructure adolescents' interpretation of life events.

- Suicide rates differ for girls and boys as well as for other groups of youth in Canada.

Delinquency

- Many young people engage in antisocial behaviour briefly during adolescence, but most young people do not persist in behaving antisocially.

- Persistent antisocial behaviour has been linked to social class, family processes, lack of self-control, and heredity.

- Efforts to reduce adolescent criminal activity must address all of the variables contributing to the problem.

Chapter Critical Review

1. Your local newspaper has just printed a feature describing all the "storm and stress" that typifies adolescence. Write a letter to the editor in which you set the record straight.

2. Discuss the stages of identity formation (Module 16.1) in terms of the formal operational stage of cognitive development. How is identity formation related to cognitive development?

3. What factors might reduce the drop in self-esteem (Module 16.1) that's associated with the transition from elementary school to middle school?

4. Given what you know about cognitive development in adolescence, what types of anti-drug, anti-alcohol, or anti-pregnancy messages would be most effective with young adolescents? With older adolescents?

See for Yourself

Most middle school and high school students know the different crowds in their school and the status of each. The number of crowds varies, as do their names, but the existence of crowds seems to be a basic fact of social life in adolescence. To learn more about crowds, try to talk individually to four or five students from the same middle or high school. You could begin by describing one of the crowds from your own high school days. Then ask each student to name the different crowds in his or her school. Ask each student to describe the defining characteristics of the people in each crowd. Finally, ask each student which crowd has the highest status in school and which has the lowest.

When you've interviewed all the students, compare their answers. Do the students agree about the number and types of crowds in their school? Do they agree on the status of each? Next, compare your results with those of other students in your class. Are the results similar in the different schools? Can you find any relationship between the types of crowds and characteristics of the schools (e.g., rural versus urban)? See for yourself!

Glossary

Accommodation cognitive modification of schemas as a result of experience.

Active gene–environment relation a relationship between heredity and environment in which individuals actively seek environments suitable to their genotype.

Activity the tempo and vigour of a child's movements.

Adaptive behaviour a person's ability to engage effectively in tasks of daily living.

Adolescent-limited antisocial behaviour relatively minor criminal acts by youth who are not consistently antisocial.

Adolescent egocentrism the self-absorption that marks the teenage search for identity.

Age of viability the age at which most bodily systems function well enough to support life once the baby is born.

Aggression externalized behaviour meant to harm others.

Alleles a specific form of a gene.

Allocentric interdependence, affiliation, and co-operation with groups an individual belongs to more than with personal goals.

Altruism prosocial behaviour that helps another with no direct benefit to the individual performing the behaviour.

Amenorrhea the absence of a menstrual period in a girl who has achieved puberty.

Amniocentesis a medical procedure in which a sample of amniotic fluid is taken and tested for genetic disorders.

Amnion or amniotic sac the sac in which the baby develops.

Amniotic fluid the liquid that fills the amnion and cushions the baby.

Animism crediting inanimate objects with life and lifelike properties.

Anorexia nervosa a psychological disorder marked by a persistent refusal to eat and an irrational fear of being overweight.

Anoxia complete oxygen deprivation (lack of oxygen).

Apgar score a numerical scale used to rate a newborn baby's vital signs.

Assertiveness goal-directed behaviour that respects the rights of others.

Assimilation cognitively incorporating new experiences into existing schemas.

Attachment the emotional bond that forms between people, particularly children and their parents; also, an enduring social-emotional relationship.

Attention the process by which information is selected to be processed further.

Attention Deficit Hyperactivity Disorder (ADHD) a psychological disorder characterized by overactivity, inattention, and/or impulsivity.

Attrition loss of participants in a study.

Auditory (sound) localization the ability to detect from where a sound is coming.

Auditory threshold the quietest sound that a person can hear.

Authoritarian parenting high control with low levels of warmth.

Authoritative parenting reasonable control with lots of warmth and responsiveness to children.

Autobiographical or episodic memory people's memory of the significant events and experiences of their own lives.

Autosomes the first 22 pairs of chromosomes that are not sex chromosomes.

Axon the tube-shaped structure attached to the cell body that transmits electrical messages received through the dendrites to other neurons.

Babbling speech-like sound that has no meaning.

Basal metabolic rate the speed at which the body consumes calories.

Behavioural genetics the study of the inheritance of behavioural and psychological traits.

Blended family also called a stepfamily, this family consists of two adults living together, either common-law or married, who have biological children from one or both of those adults.

Body ego a person's sense of the self as an individual.

Breech presentation a physical position in utero, in which the developing baby's feet, rather than the head, are closest to the birth canal.

Bulimia nervosa a psychological disorder characterized by binge-eating, followed by purging through vomiting, use of laxatives, or over-exercising.

Bullying unprovoked aggression, which has, as its sole goal, gaining power over another through social, verbal, or physical harassment.

Caesarean section (C-section) delivery of a baby through a surgical incision in the mother's abdomen.

Centration in Piagetian theory, the term for narrowly focused thought, typically during the preoperational stage.

Cephalocaudal growth from the top and extending downward.

Cerebral cortex the folded surface of the brain that regulates many human behaviours.

Cerebral hemispheres the right and left halves of the cerebral cortex.

Cervix the opening at the end of the uterus (top of the vagina) that forms the entryway to the birth canal.

Chorionic villus sampling (CVS) a medical procedure in which a sample of placental cells is taken and tested for genetic disorders.

Chromosomes organic structures in the cell's nucleus that contain genetic material.

Classical conditioning a form of learning in which a previously neutral stimulus elicits a response that was originally produced by another natural stimulus; also, a theory of associative learning that later gave rise to behaviourism.

Clinal variation continuous genetic variation observed between geographic regions.

Clique four to six good friends who tend to be similar in age, sex, race, and interests.

Cohort effect the impact of a particular event, culture, or historical experience on a particular group of people.

Componential subtheory the theory that intelligence depends on basic cognitive processes called components.

Components information-processing skills involved in basic cognitive processing.

Comprehension the process of extracting meaning from a sequence of words.

Concrete operational stage a Piagetian cognitive stage of development during which children first use mental operations to solve problems and to reason.

Cones specialized neurons located in the retina of the eye.

Constricting interactions that result in one partner threatening, contradicting, or dominating the other.

Contextual subtheory the idea that intelligent behaviour involves skilfully adapting to an environment.

Convergent validity statistical information about the degree to which a measure yields results that are theoretically similar to and positively correlated with another well-established measure of the same variable.

Cooing long strings of vowel sounds produced by babies around 2 months of age.

Co-operative play play that is organized around a distinct theme and involves children taking on special roles based on that theme.

Corpus callosum a thick bundle of axons that join the left and right hemispheres of the cerebral cortex.

Correlation coefficient (*r*) a numerical, statistical value representing both the direction and strength of relationship between variables.

Correlational study the study of the relationship between variables that naturally coexist in the world.

Cortisol reactivity the change in the body's cortisol levels in response to stress.

Counterfactual thinking understanding that a situation or fact is opposite to reality.

Counterimitation learning by observation what should not be done.

Critical period the time in development when a specific type of learning best takes place.

Cross-sectional study a research study in which a variable of interest is measured at one point in time across persons of different ages or characteristics.

Crowd a larger group of older children or adolescents who have similar values and attitudes and are known by a common label.

Crowning the appearance of the top of the baby's head outside the birth canal.

Crystallization using one's emerging identity in adolescence as a source of ideas about careers.

Culture the knowledge, attitudes, beliefs, symbolic representations, and behaviours associated with a group of people.

Culture-fair intelligence tests psychological tests designed to eliminate group differences due to culture.

Date rape (acquaintance rape) forced sexual intercourse with an acquaintance or friend, often on a social outing.

Deductive reasoning the ability to draw appropriate conclusions from facts.

Deferred imitation acting out events or behaviours seen at an earlier time.

Delay of gratification the ability to hold off immediate satisfaction in order to obtain a larger reward or more preferable outcome later.

Demand characteristics situational cues that suggest to a research participant how a researcher wants the participant to respond.

Dendrites branch-like extensions off the neuron that allow for intercellular communication.

Deoxyribonucleic acid (DNA) a molecule made up of chemical components, called nucleotide bases, which form the code for specific genes.

Dependent variable the variable in a study that is measured and that changes as a result of the action of the independent variable.

Depression a psychological disorder in which a person has pervasive feelings of sadness or irritability, as well as other symptoms, for a period of at least two weeks.

Descriptive statistics basic numerical summaries of research data.

Design stage the period during which children combine the six basic shapes into more complex patterns.

Developmental psychopathology a theory of child development that tries to explain how abnormal development occurs within a view of development as a dynamic process involving continual transformation during the lifespan.

Differentiated instruction making adaptations to the classroom environment and teaching methods to accommodate children's personal strengths, weaknesses, and preferred ways of learning.

Differentiation mastery of component skills.

Dishabituation a state of reorientation, when a person becomes aware of a stimulus to which the person previously had habituated.

Disinhibition an increase in all behaviours like those observed, particularly aggression.

Disorders of sexual development a genetic condition in which a person's internal sexual organs do not match their external genitals; also called intersex conditions.

Dispositional praise linking the child's altruistic behaviour to an underlying altruistic characteristic of the person.

Divergent validity statistical information about the degree to which a measure yields results that are theoretically different from and negatively correlated with another well-established measure of an opposite variable.

Dizygotic (fraternal) twins biological siblings who developed from two separate eggs fertilized by two separate sperm during the same incidence of fertilization.

Dominance hierarchy levels of authority within a group, which typically includes a leader to whom other members of the group defer.

Dominant an allele whose chemical instructions are always followed and expressed.

Doula a nonmedically trained person who provides coaching, personal support, and education about birth but does not provide medical care or intervention during the birth process.

Down syndrome a genetic disorder caused by an extra twenty-first chromosome.

Dynamic systems theory upholds that motor development involves many distinct skills, organized and reorganized over time to meet demands of specific tasks.

Dynamic testing measuring a child's learning potential by having the child learn something new in the presence of the examiner and with the examiner's help.

Ecological theory a theory of development that views the child as embedded in a series of complex and interactive systems.

Ecological validity the degree to which conclusions from research can provide information about behaviour in real-life situations.

Ectoderm   the outer layer of the embryo, which becomes the hair, outer skin, and nervous system.

Ectogenesis   fertilizing an egg outside the uterus.

Edges   lines that mark the boundaries of objects.

Ego   one of three Freudian components of personality; tries to realistically meet the demands of the id.

Egocentric frame of reference   thinking of objects in space exclusively in terms of their relationship to the child's own body position.

Egocentrism   seeing the world primarily from the perspective of self, rather than of other people.

Electroencephalogram (EEG)   an electrical measurement of brain waves.

Embryo   an embedded zygote.

Emotionality   the strength of an emotional response to a situation, the ease with which that response is triggered, and the ease of return to a nonemotional state.

Empathy   the ability to understand another person's emotions.

Enabling   interactions that tend to support others and sustain the interaction.

Endoderm   the inner layer of the embryo, which becomes the digestive system and lungs.

Endogamy   a preference for mating with people from one's own social or cultural group.

Environmental reactions   a family's responses to hereditary conditions.

Epiphyses   the ends of the cartilage structures that turn into bone.

Equilibration   the process of reorganizing schemas to incorporate new information or experience.

Ethological theory   a theory that views development from an evolutionary perspective, such that human behaviours can be adaptive and have survival value.

Evidence-based practice   an approach to working with people in health services using methods of intervention and assessment that have been demonstrated through empirical research to be effective.

Evocative gene–environment relation   a relationship between heredity and environment in which different genotypes evoke different responses from the environment.

Evolutionary developmental psychology   an approach to developmental psychology using evolutionary theory as a metatheory of human development in an attempt to have psychologists agree on a unified perspective of humanity.

Executive functioning   a set of cognitive abilities that enable intentional, self-regulated behaviour.

Experiential subtheory   the idea that intelligence is revealed in both novel and familiar tasks.

Experiment   a research method in which variables are systematically manipulated in order to discover the causal effect of one variable on another.

Expressive language ability   a person's ability to make ideas known to others through language.

Expressive style   a child's initial tendency to learn primarily social phrases in language rather than naming objects.

Expressive traits   personality characteristics that reflect emotional functioning and a focus on interpersonal relations and that are stereotypically associated with women.

Family policy   laws and regulations that directly or indirectly affect families with children.

Fast mapping   the rapid ability of children to connect new words to their referents.

Fetal alcohol spectrum disorder (FASD)   a developmental disorder caused by maternal consumption of alcohol during pregnancy.

Fetal medicine   a medical practice specialty focusing on treating fetal health problems in utero.

Fetus   after the eighth week of gestation until birth, the developing baby is called a fetus.

Field experiment   a type of experiment in which the independent variable is manipulated in a naturalistic setting.

Fine-motor skills   activities, such as grasping, holding, and manipulating objects, that involve small-muscle groups.

Formal operational stage   the final stage of Piagetian cognitive development, in which youth apply mental operations to abstract concepts via hypothetical thinking and deductive reasoning.

Foster family   a family that consists of at least one adult and one child who is not the biological child or a relative of the foster parent.

Friendship   a voluntary relationship based on mutual liking between two people.

Frontal cortex   an area at the front of the brain that is responsible for planful activities and personality.

Functional magnetic resonance imaging (fMRI)   a medical test that measures the flow of blood in the brain using magnetic fields.

Functional near infrared spectroscopy (fNIRS)   a neuroimaging technique that measures blood flow in the brain and is less invasive than fMRI and easier to use with infants.

Gamete   an egg or sperm cell.

Gender consistency   understanding that maleness and femaleness do not change based on situations or personal wishes.

Gender constancy   the knowledge that gender can be identified, is stable, and remains consistent over time.

Gender identity   the perception of oneself as either male or female.

Gender labelling   learning to name who is a boy and who is a girl.

Gender roles   the culturally prescribed roles considered appropriate for males and females.

Gender stability   understanding that a person's natural gender does not change.

Gender stereotypes   beliefs about how males and females differ in personality traits, interests, and behaviours.

Gender-schema theory   using gender-based information to decide whether an activity or object is worth learning more about.

Gene   a group of chemical compounds, called nucleotide bases, that generate the production of a protein or other important biological building blocks in the body.

Genetic reductionism   reducing the cause of environmental conditions and behaviours exclusively to genes.

Genotype   the complete set of genes that makes up a person's heredity.

Germ disc   a small cluster of cells near the zygote's centre that develops into the baby.

Grammatical morphemes   words or endings of words that make a sentence grammatical.

Gross-motor skills   activities, such as running, throwing, and jumping, requiring large-muscle groups.

Habituation   a state of diminished responding to a stimulus as it becomes more familiar.

Heterozygosity having alleles of a gene that are different from each other.

Holland's personality-type theory the theory that people find work fulfilling when the important features of a job or profession are a good fit with the worker's personality.

Homozygosity having alleles of a gene that are identical to each other.

Hormones chemicals that are released by glands and travel in the bloodstream to act on other areas of the body.

Huntington's disease a fatal disease characterized by progressive degeneration of the nervous system.

Hypoxia a reduced supply of oxygen.

Id one of three Freudian components of personality; a reservoir of primitive instincts and drives.

Idiocentric emphasizing independence and personal needs and goals over those of others.

Illusion of invulnerability the belief that misfortune only happens to others.

Imaginary audience the normal tendency in adolescents to believe that they are actors whose performance is watched constantly by their peers.

Imitation behaving in the manner one sees others behaving.

Implantation the burrowing of the zygote into the uterine wall.

Implementation entering the workforce and learning first-hand about jobs.

Imprinting the instinctive creation of an emotional bond between a newborn animal and the animal's mother.

In vitro fertilization an artificial form of egg fertilization in which egg and sperm are united in a laboratory dish.

Incomplete dominance a genetic situation in which aspects of two heterozygous alleles are both expressed.

Independent variable the variable that is manipulated in a study.

Index offences acts that are crimes regardless of the perpetrator's age.

Indifferent-uninvolved parenting uninterested, uninvolved parenting.

Indulgent-permissive parenting a lot of warmth and caring but little control.

Infant mortality the number of infants out of 1000 births who die before their first birthday.

Infant-directed speech speaking slowly in exaggerated changes of pitch and loudness when communicating with babies; formerly called "motherese."

Infantile amnesia the inability to remember events from early in one's life.

Inferential statistics statistical calculations that go beyond basic description of research data to infer or predict how well the data represents the total population of observations from which data might be gathered.

Information processing a theory proposing that human cognition is like computer hardware and software.

Inhibition a decrease in one or more types of behaviour.

Inner speech in Vygotskian theory, inner speech is thought.

Instrumental aggression when a child uses aggression to achieve an explicit goal.

Instrumental traits personality characteristics that reflect active involvement with and influence over the environment and that are stereotypically associated with men.

Integration combining component skills in proper sequence into a coherent, working whole.

Intelligence quotient the mathematical ratio of mental age to chronological age.

Internal working model a set of expectations about parents' availability and responsivity generally and in times of stress.

Interposition cues for depth perception arising from the degree to which an object is blocked from view by other objects, with nearer objects being in full view and farther objects being partially obstructed from view.

Intonation a pattern of rising or falling pitch similar to the pattern in normal conversation.

Joint custody a post-divorce legal arrangement whereby both parents retain legal custody of their children.

Juvenile delinquency the committing of illegal acts by people under the age of majority.

Knowledge-telling strategy a writing strategy in which information on a topic is written down as it is retrieved from memory.

Knowledge-transforming strategy a writing strategy in which the writer decides what information to include and how to organize it before writing it down.

Latchkey children children who largely are under their own supervision after school.

Lateralization the functional specialization of each half of the brain, which makes each half different from the other.

Learned helplessness generalized feelings and beliefs of powerlessness and being at the mercy of external events.

Libido an instinctive energy or force that motivates humans to experience pleasure.

Life-course persistent antisocial behaviour antisocial behaviour that emerges at an early age and continues throughout life.

Locomotion moving about in the world.

Long-term memory limitless, permanent storage of acquired information.

Longitudinal study a type of research study in which the variables of interest are measured in the same research participants repeatedly over time.

Mainstreaming an educational practice in which children with serious developmental disabilities are placed into classrooms with children who do not have these types of disabilities.

Malnourished a lack of adequate nutrition indicated, in part, by children being small for their age.

Malocclusion the dental condition whereby upper and lower permanent teeth do not meet properly.

Masturbation self-stimulation of the genitals.

Maturational theory a theory that views development as unfolding according to a specific and pre arranged scheme or plan within the body.

Mediator variable a variable that explains or accounts for any relationship observed between an independent and a dependent variable.

Meiosis the biological process of cell division resulting in gametes that have 23 chromosomes, which is half the amount of genetic material normally seen in a human cell.

Memory strategies activities that improve remembering.

Menarche the start of menstruation.

Mental age the difficulty level of problems that children could correctly solve at various ages.

Mental hardware   cognitive structures, including memories and where they are stored.

Mental operations   strategies and rules that make thinking more systematic and powerful.

Mental rotation   the ability to imagine how an object will look after it has been moved in space.

Mental software   organized sets of cognitive processes, such as reading.

Mesoderm   the middle layer of the embryo, which becomes the muscles, bones, and circulatory system.

Microgenetic study   a type of research study in which the variables of interest are measured in the same research participants repeatedly over a short period of time, such as days or weeks, in order to capture an aspect of rapid developmental change.

Middle childhood   the period of development between the ages of 7 and 11.

Midwife   a person who is not a physician but who is trained to assist mothers in the physical delivery of their babies by normal, spontaneous vaginal delivery.

Mitosis   the biological process of cell division resulting in bodily cells that are exact copies of their parent cells and have a full set of 46 chromosomes.

Monozygotic (identical) twins   biological siblings who both developed from the same fertilized egg, which split into two separate clusters, each of which formed into separate but identical babies.

Motor skills   coordinated movements of the muscles and limbs.

Myelin   a fatty sheath that insulates the axon and speeds information transfer.

Myopia   nearsightedness.

Naming explosion   a period of language learning around 18 months of age when children rapidly acquire new words.

Natural selection   an ongoing process in nature that results in survival of those organisms that are best adapted to their environments.

Naturalistic observation   a research technique that involves observing people in real-life situations and recording data about their behaviour based on certain predetermined variables of interest for study.

Negative reinforcement trap   reinforcing the very behaviours that are being targeted for elimination.

Neo-Piagetian approach   a theory of cognitive development that retains Piagetian stage theory but takes an information-processing approach to skill development.

Neural plate   a group of cells forming about three weeks after conception that develops into the neural tube, the brain, and the spinal cord.

Neuron   a cell in the nervous system that specializes in transmitting information.

Neuronal cell body   a structure at the centre of the neuron containing biological mechanisms for maintaining cellular life.

Neuroplasticity   the extent to which brain organization is flexible.

Neuropsychoanalysis   the study of the relationship between psychoanalytic theory and biological approaches in psychology.

Neurotransmitters   chemicals that affect the firing of surrounding neurons.

Niche-picking   the process of deliberately selecting an environment suitable to one's genotype.

Night terrors   waking in a panicked state, breathing rapidly and perspiring heavily.

Nightmares   dreaming that occurs toward morning that is vivid, frightening, and usually wakes the child.

Non-REM sleep   a period during sleep that is motorically quiet and involves steady breathing, heart rate, and brain activity.

Nonshared environmental influences   experiences and circumstances within a family that contribute to siblings being different from each other.

Nonsocial play   playing alone or watching others play.

Norepinephrine   a type of neurotransmitter.

Obesity   the physical state of being 20 percent over ideal body weight, given a child's age and height.

Object permanence   understanding that objects continue to exist independently of one's own actions.

Objective frame of reference   thinking of objects in space relative to the position of objects or persons other than oneself.

Obstetrician   a physician who specializes in women's health and reproduction.

Operant conditioning   a form of learning in which the observed consequences of a behaviour affect the likelihood that the behaviour will reoccur; also, a behavioural theory about how the consequences of a behaviour can affect future occurrences of that behaviour.

Orienting response   a physical reaction to a strong or unfamiliar stimulus.

Osteoporosis   a disease of the bones, in which they become brittle and easily break.

Overextension   when a word is defined too broadly.

Overregularization   applying rules to words that are exceptions to the rule.

P-value   the probability of obtaining a particular measurement if, in fact, no real difference exists between the conditions being compared.

Paradoxical effect   when a drug acts in a manner opposite to what one might ordinarily expect or to how it affects other populations of people.

Parallel play   playing alone but near others while maintaining an interest in what the others are doing.

Passive gene–environment relation   a relationship between heredity and environment in which the parents pass on genotypes to children and also provide much of the early environment supporting expression of those genes.

Personal fable   the normal tendency in adolescents to believe that their experiences and feelings are unique.

Phenotype   a person's genotype plus all other environmental influences that make up that person's physical, behavioural, and psychological characteristics.

Phonemes   unique sounds joined to create words.

Phonological awareness   the ability to distinguish the distinctive sounds of letters.

Pictorial stage   the period during which children depict recognizable objects in drawings.

Placenta   a uterine structure for exchanging nutrients and wastes between mother and baby.

Placental abruption   detachment of the placenta from the uterine wall.

Polygenic inheritance   the contribution of many genes to a person's phenotypic expression.

Population   the set or group of all people from which a sample is drawn in a research study.

Positron emission tomography (PET) a medical test that traces glucose uptake in the brain.

Postpartum depression feelings of low self-worth, disturbed sleep, poor appetite, and apathy in the months after delivering a baby.

Practice effect becoming "test-wise" and achieving better scores on a test than on previous occasions because of repeated exposure to the test.

Prejudice a negative view of others based on their membership in a specific group.

Prematurity when a baby is born less than 38 weeks after conception.

Prenatal development the changes that transform the fertilized egg into a newborn human.

Preoperational stage in Piagetian theory, the stage of cognitive development during which children use symbols to represent objects and events.

Primary circular reaction recreating a pleasing event with the body.

Primary sex characteristics maturation of the organs directly involved in reproduction.

Private speech in Vygotskian theory, comments not directed to others but that help children regulate their own behaviour.

Privation a condition in which the basic necessities and comforts of life are not adequately provided.

Procedural memory memory for how to do things.

Propositions ideas developed by combining words.

Prosocial behaviour actions that promote harmony in a social group.

Proximodistal growth from the centre and extending outward.

Psychic skin a person's capacity for protecting and containing their internal emotional states.

Psychoanalysis Freud's psychological theory and method of treatment for unresolved unconscious conflict.

Psychodynamic theories theories that are offshoots of Freudian psychoanalysis.

Psychometric g intelligence as defined and measured by mental tests.

Psychometric theory a theory based on measurement of a psychological characteristic, usually with a scorable questionnaire or other type of psychological test.

Psychosocial theory Erik Erikson's psychoanalytic theory that development occurs in a sequence of stages defined by a unique crisis or social challenge.

Puberty a time of physical transition to adulthood that involves both bodily growth and sexual maturation.

Punishment an aversive consequence that decreases the future likelihood of the behaviour it follows primarily when the child is in the presence of an authority figure; also, any action that decreases the likelihood of the response that it follows.

Quasi-experimental design an approach to research involving comparison of groups whose members are not randomly selected.

Rapid-eye-movement (REM) sleep a period during sleep involving small physical movements or twitches of the eyes, mouth, arms, and legs (irregular sleep).

Reaction range the extent to which full genetic expression can occur, based on the limits imposed by the environment.

Reactive aggression when one child's behaviour leads to another child's aggression.

Reactive attachment disorder a mental disorder involving disturbances in emotional functioning and a pattern of inappropriate interpersonal behaviours in children, thought to result from disrupted early attachments.

Receptive language ability a person's ability to understand other people's ideas when they are expressed through language.

Recessive an allele whose chemical instructions are ignored in the presence of a dominant allele or expressed in the presence of another recessive allele.

Referential style a child's initial tendency to learn primarily words that name objects, persons, or actions instead of social phrases.

Reflective judgment the ability to consider a broad range of information and outcomes in making a decision.

Reflexes unlearned responses that are triggered by a specific form of stimulation.

Reinforcement a consequence that increases the future likelihood of the behaviour it follows; also, any action that increases the likelihood of the response that it follows.

Relational aggression hurting another person by damaging that person's social relationships.

Relative size cues for depth perception arising from an object's size, with larger objects being nearer and smaller objects being farther away.

Reliability statistical information about the degree to which a measure yields consistent results over time.

Response to intervention an educational model based on frequent progress monitoring and evidence-based, strategic responses to students' measured achievement levels.

Retinal disparity differences in position on the left and right retinas for objects perceived to be nearby.

Rites of passage rituals that mark transition to adulthood.

Sample a subgroup of a population who participates in a study. Results based on the sample are generalized to the entire population if the sample is representative of that population.

Savant a person who is intellectually delayed but also extremely talented in one particular domain.

Scaffolding in Vygotskian theory, a teaching style that matches the amount of assistance to the learner's needs.

Schemas psychological structures that organize experience through mental categories and conceptual models of knowledge.

Schizophrenia a psychological disorder in which individuals have unusual perceptual experiences, as well as difficulties with thought and language, and bizarre behaviour.

Script a memory structure used to describe the sequence in which events occur.

Secondary circular reaction learning about the sensations and actions associated with objects.

Secondary sex characteristics physical maturation, other than the reproductive organs, such as the development of breasts in girls and facial hair in boys.

Secular growth trends changes in physical development from one generation to the next that are related to environmental factors.

Self-concept attitudes, behaviours, and values that a person believes make the self unique.

Self-control the ability to regulate thought, behaviour, and emotional reactions in a planful manner, rather than giving in to impulse.

Self-efficacy beliefs about one's own levels of ability, skill, and talent.

Self-esteem feelings about personal worth.

Self-reports questionnaires that elicit people's thoughts or ideas about a topic of interest for study.

Semantic bootstrapping hypothesis children rely upon their knowledge of word meanings to discover grammatical rules.

Semantic memory memory for particular facts.

Sensorimotor stage a Piagetian stage of early development characterized by rapidly changing perceptual and motor skills.

Sensory memory raw, unanalyzed information held for only a few seconds.

Sequential design a type of research study in which the variables of interest are measured repeatedly over time in the same groups of research participants, with each group having been born in a different time period.

Serotonin a type of neurotransmitter.

Sex chromosomes the twenty-third pair of chromosomes, which determines the gender of a person—XX for female and XY for male.

Sexting sending a text message with sexual content.

Sexualization putting sexual information into a context where it otherwise would not exist or does not normally occur.

Shape stage the period during which children draw six basic shapes.

Sickle-cell trait a characteristic of individuals who have one dominant and one recessive allele for the genetic production of red blood cells, resulting in partial expression of sickle-cell anemia.

SIDS sudden infant death syndrome in which a healthy baby dies suddenly, usually during sleep, for no apparent reason (crib death).

Simple social play youngsters interacting socially during play activities.

Single nucleotide polymorphisms a change in the expected nucleotide base at a particular location within a strand of DNA.

Size constancy the realization that an object's actual size remains the same despite changes in the size of its retinal image.

Skip-generation family a family that consists of grandparents and grandchildren without the presence of the children's parents.

Small-for-date infants babies who are substantially smaller at birth than expected based on length of time since conception.

Sociability the extent to which a person prefers to be with other people.

Social cognitive theory a theory of personality that views the environment, behaviour, and cognitions as important in shaping development.

Social conventions arbitrary standards of behaviour agreed to by a cultural group to facilitate interactions within the group.

Social-cognitive flexibility a person's skill in solving social problems with relevant social knowledge.

Social referencing looking at a trusted caregiver for clues about how to react to a situation.

Social role a set of cultural guidelines for how a person should behave.

Social smiles smiling in response to seeing another human face.

Specification limiting career possibilities by learning more about specific lines of work and starting to obtain the training required for a specific job.

Spermarche the first spontaneous ejaculation of seminal fluid.

Spina bifida a disorder in which an embryo's neural tube does not close properly during development.

Status offences acts that are considered illegal if committed by a person who has not attained adult status.

Stranger wariness signs of fear in an infant in response to an unfamiliar adult.

Structured observation a research technique that involves creating a setting or circumstances designed to bring about certain behaviours of interest for study.

Superego one of three Freudian components of personality; acts as the moral agent of personality.

Synapse a gap or space between neurons.

Synaptic pruning a period in infancy (and then later in adolescence) during which synapses begin to disappear as the brain weeds out unnecessary or underutilized connections between neurons.

Systematic observation a research technique that involves watching and carefully recording what people do or say.

Telegraphic speech talk consisting only of words directly relevant to meaning, such as important verbs and nouns.

Temperament an infant's consistent mood and style of behaviour.

Teratogen any agent that disrupts normal prenatal development.

Terminal buttons structures at the ends of an axon that release neurotransmitters.

Tertiary circular reaction repetition of old schemas with objects of different kinds.

Texture gradient cues for depth perception arising from an object's surface texture, with nearer objects having finer details and farther ones having coarser details.

Theory an organized set of ideas designed to explain and make predictions about development; also, any organized set of ideas designed to explain and make predictions about natural phenomena.

Theory of mind a person's understanding of the relations between mind and behaviour.

Thyroxine a hormone released by the thyroid gland that is essential for nerve-cell development.

Time-away being diverted from an activity that was generating conflict to some other, usually quieter, activity.

Time-out being required to sit alone in a quiet, unstimulating location or being excluded for a short period of time from a desirable activity.

Transgender person a person who self-identifies as neither male nor female.

Triarchic theory of successful intelligence Sternberg's theory about intelligence, as situated within a person's socio-cultural environment, based on three subtheories.

Ultrasound a medical procedure that involves imaging a developing baby using sound waves.

Umbilical cord a cord-like structure containing blood vessels that joins the developing baby through the baby's abdomen to the mother's placenta.

Underextension when a word is defined too narrowly.

Validity statistical information about the degree to which conclusions based on a measure actually mean what a researcher hypothesized they would mean.

Variables factors of interest that researchers study that are subject to change under various research conditions.

Vernix a thick, greasy coating on the skin that protects the baby during gestation.

Vicarious (observational) learning a method of learning in which one acquires knowledge by watching others' behaviours and the consequences or outcomes of those behaviours.

Visual acuity the smallest pattern that can be dependably distinguished.

Visual cliff a glass-covered platform used for measuring infant depth perception.

Word recognition the process of identifying a unique pattern of letters.

Working memory the active, cognitive manipulation of information.

Zone of proximal development in Vygotskian theory, the difference between what a child can do without the support of a more experienced caregiver and what the child can do with that support.

Zygote a fertilized egg.

References

Abbey, A. (1991). Acquaintance rape and alcohol consumption on college campuses: How are they linked? *Journal of American College Health, 39*, 165–169.

Aboud, F. E. (1993). The developmental psychology of racial prejudice. *Transcultural Psychiatric Research Review, 30*, 229–242.

Ackerman, B. P. (1993). Children's understanding of the speaker's meaning in referential communication. *Journal of Experimental Child Psychology, 55*, 56–86.

Ackerman, B. P. (1996). Induction of a memory retrieval strategy by young children. *Journal of Experimental Child Psychology, 62*, 243–271.

Acredolo, L. P. (1978). Development of spatial orientation in infancy. *Developmental Psychology, 14*, 224–234.

Acredolo, L. P. (1979). Laboratory versus home: The effect of environment on the 9-month-old infant's choice of spatial reference system. *Developmental Psychology, 15*, 666–667.

Action for Children. (2010). *Deprivation and risk: The case for early intervention.* London: Action for Children. Retrieved from www.actionforchildren.org.uk/uploads/media/36/9432.pdf

Adair, J. G. (2001). Ethics of psychological research: New policies, continuing issues, new concerns. *Canadian Psychology, 42*, 25–37.

Adair, R. H., & Bauchner, H. (1993). Sleep problems in childhood. *Current Problems in Pediatrics, 23*, 147–170.

Adams, M. J., Treiman, R., & Pressley, M. (1998). Reading, writing, and literacy. In W. Damon (Ed.), *Handbook of child psychology* (Vol. 4). New York: Wiley.

Adams, R. J., & Courage, M. L. (1995). Development of chromatic discrimination in early infancy. *Behavioural Brain Research, 67*, 99–101.

Adams, R. J., & Courage, M. L. (1998). Human newborn color vision: Measurement with chromatic stimuli varying in excitation purity. *Journal of Experimental Child Psychology, 68*, 22–34.

Adenzato, M., & Bucciarelli, M. (2008). Recognition of mistakes and deceits in communicative interactions. *Journal of Pragmatics, 40*, 608–629.

Adler, N. (1994). *Adolescent sexual behavior looks irrational—But looks are deceiving.* Washington, DC: Federation of Behavioral, Psychological, and Cognitive Sciences.

Adolph, K. E. (1997). Learning in the development of infant locomotion. *Monographs of the Society for Research in Child Development, 62*, 1–140.

Adolph, K. E., Eppler, M. A., & Gibson, E. J. (1993). Crawling versus walking infants' perception of affordances for locomotion over sloping surfaces. *Child Development, 64*, 1158–1174.

Adolph, K. E., Vereijken, B., & Denny, M. A. (1998). Learning to crawl. *Child Development, 69*, 1299–1312.

Adolphs, R. (2009). The social brain: Neural basis of social knowledge. *The Annual Review of Psychology, 60*, 693–716.

Ainsworth, M. D. S. (1978). The development of infant–mother attachment. In B. M. Caldwell & H. N. Ricciuti (Eds.), *Review of child development research* (Vol. 3). Chicago: The University of Chicago Press.

Ainsworth, M. D. S., & Wittig, B. A. (1969). Attachment and exploratory behavior of one-year-olds in a Strange Situation. In B. M. Foss (Ed.), *Determinants of infant behavior* (Vol. 4, pp. 113–136). London: Methuen.

Ainsworth, M. S. (1993). Attachment as related to mother–infant interaction. *Advances in Infancy Research, 8*, 1–50.

Alberta Health and Wellness. (2009). *Common questions about methylmercury levels in Alberta fish.* Edmonton: Government of Alberta.

Ales, K. L., Druzin, M. L., & Santini, D. L. (1990). Impact of maternal age on the outcome of pregnancy. *Surgery, Gynecology & Obstetrics, 171*, 209–216.

Alexander, J. F., Waldron, H. B., Barton, C., & Mas, C. H. (1989). The minimizing of blaming attributes and behaviors in delinquent families. *Journal of Consulting and Clinical Psychology, 57*, 19–24.

Allgeier, A. R., & Allgeier, E. R. (1995). *Sexual interactions* (4th ed.). Lexington, MA: Heath.

Allison, D. (1993). *Bastard out of Carolina.* New York: Plume.

Aman, C. J., Roberts, R. J., & Pennington, B. F. (1998). A neuropsychological examination of the underlying deficit in attention deficit hyperactivity disorder: Frontal lobe versus right parietal lobe theories. *Developmental Psychology, 34*, 956–969.

Amato, P. R., & Keith, B. (1991). Parental divorce and the well-being of children: A meta-analysis. *Psychological Bulletin, 110*, 26–46.

American Academy of Pediatrics. (2010). Hassle-free meal time. Retrieved from www.healthychildren.org/English/healthy-living/nutrition/pages/Hassle-Free-Meal-Time.aspx

American Academy of Pediatrics Committee on Drugs and Committee on Bioethics (Frader, J. E., Crain,

L.S., Moseley, K. L., Nelson, R. M., Porter, I. H., Vizcarrondo, F. E., Bowes, W. A., Kazura, A., Krug, E. F., Caniano, D. A., Dresser, R., & King, N. M. P.). (1997). Considerations related to the use of recombinant human growth hormone in children. *Pediatrics, 99,* 122–129.

American Academy of Pediatrics Committee on Public Education. (2001). Children, adolescents, and television. *Pediatrics, 107,* 423–426.

American Academy of Pediatrics. (1997). Adolescents and anabolic steroids: A subject review (RE9720). *Pediatrics, 99*(6), 904–908.

American Academy of Pediatrics (AAP) Committee on Sports Medicine and Committee on School Health. (1989). Organized athletics for preadolescent children. *Pediatrics, 84,* 583–584.

American Psychiatric Association. (1994). *Diagnostic and statistical manual of mental disorders* (4th ed.). Washington, DC: American Psychiatric Association.

American Psychological Assocation. (n.d.) *Answers to your questions for a better understanding of sexual orientation & homosexuality.* Washington, DC: The American Psychological Association. Retrieved from http://www.apa.org/topics/lgbt/orientation.aspx

American Psychological Association. (2011). *Answers to your questions about transgender people, gender identity, and gender expression.* Retrieved from http://www.apa.org/topics/lgbt/transgender.aspx

Ames, E. (1997). *The development of Romanian orphanage children adopted to Canada.* Final report to National Welfare Grants Program, Human Resources Development Canada. Burnaby, BC: Simon Fraser University.

Anand, K. J., & Hickey, P. R. (1987). Pain and its effect in the human neonate and fetus. *New England Journal of Medicine, 31,* 1321–1329.

Anastasi, A. (1988). *Psychological testing* (6th ed.). New York: Macmillan.

Anastopoulos, A. D., Shelton, T. L., DuPaul, G. J., & Guevremont, D. C. (1993). Parent training for attention-deficit hyperactivity disorder: Its impact on parent functioning. *Journal of Abnormal Child Psychology, 21,* 581–596.

Anderson, L. C., Mah, C. L., & Sellen, D. W. (2015). Eating well with Canada's food guide? Authoritative knowledge about food and health among newcomer mothers. *Appetite, 91,* 357–365.

Anderson, E. R., Greene, S. M., Hetherington, E. M., & Clingempeel, W. G. (1999). The dynamics of parental remarriage: Adolescent, parent, and sibling. In E. M. Hetherington (Ed.), *Coping with divorce, single parenting, and remarriage: A risk and resiliency perspective* (pp. 295–319). Mahwah, NJ: Erlbaum.

Andrews, B., & Brown, G. W. (1993). Self-esteem and vulnerability to depression: The concurrent validity of interview and questionnaire measures. *Journal of Abnormal Psychology, 102,* 565–572.

Anisfeld, M. (1991). Neonatal imitation. *Developmental Review, 11,* 60–97.

Anisfeld, M. (1996). Only tongue protrusion modeling is matched by neonates. *Developmental Review, 16,* 149–161.

Antonarakis, S. E., & the Down Syndrome Collaborative Group. (1991). Parental origin of the extra chromosome in trisomy 21 as indicated by analysis of DNA polymorphisms. *New England Journal of Medicine, 324,* 872–876.

APA Presidential Task Force on Evidence-Based Practice. (2006). Evidence-based practice in psychology. *American Psychologist, 61,* 271–285.

Apgar, V. (1953). A proposal for a new method of evaluation of the newborn infant. *Current Researches in Anesthesia and Analgesia, 32,* 260–267.

Applied Research Branch of Human Resources Development Canada & Healthy Child Manitoba. (2003). *A new generation of Canadian families raising young children—A new look at data from national surveys.* Gatineau, QC: Government of Canada.

Arcus, D., & Kagan, J. (1995). Temperament and craniofacial variation in the first two years. *Child Development, 66,* 1529–1540.

Arterberry, M., Yonas, A., & Bensen, A. S. (1989). Self-produced locomotion and the development of responsiveness to linear perspective and texture gradients. *Developmental Psychology, 25,* 976–982.

Ashcraft, M. H. (1982). The development of mental arithmetic: A chronometric approach. *Developmental Review, 2,* 212–236.

Aslin, R. N. (1987). Visual and auditory discrimination in infancy. In J. D. Osofsky (Ed.), *Handbook of infant development* (2nd ed., pp. 5–97). New York: Wiley.

Aslin, R. N., Jusczyk, P. W., & Pisoni, D. B. (1998). Speech and auditory processing during infancy: Constraints on and precursors to language. In W. Damon (Ed.), *Handbook of child psychology* (Vol. 2, pp. 147–198). New York: Wiley.

Aslin, R. N., Saffran, J. R., & Newport, W. L. (1998). Computation of conditional probability statistics by 8-month-old infants. *Psychological Science, 9,* 321–324.

Assembly of First Nations. (2007a). Canadian Human Rights complaint on First Nations child welfare filed today by Assembly of First Nations and First Nations Child and Family Caring Society of Canada. Retrieved from INK, www.afn.ca/article.asp?id=3374

Assembly of First Nations. (2007b). *Annual Report (2006–2007).* Ottawa: Assembly of First Nations.

Assembly of First Nations Health and Social Secretariat. (2009, Winter/Spring). *Health Bulletin*. Ottawa: Assembly of First Nations.

Attie, J., Brooks-Gunn, J., & Petersen, A. C. (1990). A developmental perspective on eating disorders and eating problems. In M. Lewis & S. M. Miller (Eds.), *Handbook of developmental psychopathology*. New York: Plenum.

Anderson, Norman B.; Nickerson, Kim J. (2005). Genes, race, and psychology in the genome era: An introduction. *American Psychologist, 60*, 5–8. doi:10.1037/0003-066X.60.1.5

Atwater, E. (1992). *Adolescence*. Englewood Cliffs, NJ: Prentice Hall.

Au, T. K. (1994). Developing an intuitive understanding of substance kinds. *Cognitive Psychology, 27*, 71–111.

Au, T. K., & Glusman, M. (1990). The principle of mutual exclusivity in word learning: To honor or not to honor? *Child Development, 61*, 1474–1490.

Aviezer, O., Sagi, A., Joels, T., & Ziv, Y. (1999). Emotional availability and attachment representations in kibbutz infants and their mothers. *Developmental Psychology, 35*, 811–821.

Azad, M. B., Konya, T., Maughan, H., Guttman, D. S., Field, C. J., Chari, R. S., . . . & Kozyrskyj, A. L. (2013). Gut microbiota of healthy Canadian infants: Profiles by mode of delivery and infant diet at 4 months. *Canadian Medical Association Journal, 185*, 385–394.

Bachman, J. (1983, Summer). Premature affluence: Do high school students earn too much? *Economic Outlook USA*, 64–67.

Bachman, J. G., & Schulenberg, J. (1993). How part-time work intensity relates to drug use, problem behavior, time use, and satisfaction among high school seniors: Are these consequences or merely correlates? *Developmental Psychology, 29*, 229–230.

Backscheider, A. G., Shatz, M., & Gelman, S. A. (1993). Preschoolers' ability to distinguish living kinds as a function of regrowth. *Child Development, 64*, 1242–1257.

Baddeley, A. (1996). Exploring the central executive. *Quarterly Journal of Experimental Psychology: Human Experimental Psychology, 49*, 5–28.

Baer, D. M., & Wolf, M. M. (1968). The reinforcement contingency in preschool and remedial education. In R. D. Hess & R. M. Baer (Eds.), *Early education*. Chicago: Aldine.

Bagwell, C. L., Newcomb, A. F., & Bukowski, W. M. (1998). Preadolescent friendship and peer rejection as predictors of adult adjustment. *Child Development, 69*, 140–153.

Bahrick, L. E. (1992). Infants' perceptual differentiation of amodal and modality-specific audio-visual relations. *Journal of Experimental Child Psychology, 53*, 180–199.

Bahrick, L. E., Netto, D., & Hernandez-Reif, M. (1998). Intermodal perception of adult and child faces and voices by infants. *Child Development, 69*, 1263–1275.

Bailey, D. A., & Rasmussen, R. L. (1996). Sport and the child: Physiological and skeletal issues. In F. L. Smoll & R. E. Smith (Eds.), *Children and youth in sport: A biopsychological perspective* (pp. 187–199). Dubuque, IA: Brown & Benchmark.

Bailey, J. M., Vasey, P. L., Diamond, L. M., Breedlove, S. M., Vilain, E., & Epprecht, M. (2016). Sexual orientation, controversy, and science. *Psychological Science in the Public Interest, 17*, 45–101.

Baillargeon, R. (1987). Object permanence in 3- and 4-month-old infants. *Developmental Psychology, 23*, 655–664.

Baillargeon, R. (1994). How do infants learn about the physical world? *Current Directions in Psychological Science, 3*, 133–140.

Baillargeon, R. (1998). Infants' understanding of the physical world. *Advances in Psychological Science, 2*, 503–529.

Baker, C. (1993). *Foundations of bilingual education and bilingualism*. Clevedon, UK: Multilingual Matters.

Baker, L. (1994). Fostering metacognitive development. In H. W. Reese (Ed.), *Advances in child development and behavior* (Vol. 25). San Diego: Academic Press.

Baker, L., & Brown, A. L. (1984). Metacognitive skills and reading. In P. D. Pearson (Ed.), *Handbook of Reading Research* (Pt. 2). New York: Longman.

Baker, T. B. (1988). Models of addiction. *Journal of Abnormal Psychology, 97*, 115–117.

Baldwin, J. M. (1906). *Social and ethical interpretations in mental development: A study in social psychology*. New York: Macmillan Company.

Baldwin, J. M. (1892). The psychological laboratory in the University of Toronto. *Science, 19*, 143–144. Retrieved from http://psychclassics.yorku.ca/Baldwin/lab.htm

Baldwin, D. A., Markman, E. M., Bill, B., Desjardins, R. N., & Irwin, J. M. (1996). Infants' reliance on a social criterion for establishing word-object relations. *Child Development, 67*, 3135–3153.

Bandura, A. (1962). Social learning through imitation. In M. R. Jones (Ed.), *Nebraska Symposium on Motivation*. Lincoln: University of Nebraska Press.

Bandura, A. (1977). *Social learning theory*. Englewood Cliffs, NJ: Prentice Hall.

Bandura, A. (1986). *Social foundations of thought and action: A social cognitive theory*. Englewood Cliffs, NJ: Prentice Hall.

Bandura, A. (1997). *Self-efficacy: The exercise of control*. New York: Freeman.

Bandura, A., & Mischel, W. (1965). Modification of self-imposed delay of reward through exposure to live and symbolic models. *Journal of Personality and Social Psychology, 2,* 698–705.

Bandura, A., Ross, D., & Ross, S. A. (1963). Imitation of film-mediated aggressive models. *Journal of Abnormal and Social Psychology, 66,* 3–11.

Barinaga, M. (1997). Researchers find signals that guide young brain neurons. *Science, 278,* 385–386.

Barkley, R. A. (1990). Attention deficit disorders: History, definition, and diagnosis. In M. Lewis & S. M. Miller (Eds.), *Handbook of developmental psychopathology.* New York: Plenum.

Barkley, R. A. (1994). Impaired delayed responding: A unified theory of attention-deficit hyperactivity disorder. In R. A. Barkley (Ed.), *Disruptive behavior disorders in childhood.* New York: Plenum.

Barkley, R. A. (1996). Attention-deficit hyper-activity disorder. In E. J. Mash & R. A. Barkley (Eds.), *Child psychopathology.* New York: Guilford.

Barling, J., Rogers, K., & Kelloway, E. K. (1995). Some effects of teenagers' part-time employment: The quantity and quality of work make the difference. *Journal of Organizational Behavior, 16,* 143–154.

Barr, R., & Hayne, H. (1999). Developmental changes in imitation from television during infancy. *Child Development, 70,* 1067–1081.

Bartlett, D. (1998). The influence of geographic region on the seasonality of early motor development. *Infant Behavior and Development, 21,* 591–601.

Barton, M. E., & Tomasello, M. (1991). Joint attention and conversation in mother-infant-sibling triads. *Child Development, 62,* 517–529.

Bartsch, K., & Wellman, H. M. (1995). *Children talk about the mind.* New York: Oxford University Press.

Baskett, L. M. (1985). Sibling status effects: Adult expectations. *Developmental Psychology, 21,* 441–445.

Basso, K. H. (1970). *The Cibecue Apache.* New York: Holt, Rinehart, and Winston.

Bastaits, K., & Mortelmans, D. (2016). Parenting as mediator between post-divorce family structure and children's well-being. *Journal of Child and Family Studies, 25,* 2178–2188.

Batejan, K. L., Jarvi, S. M., & Swenson, L. P. (2015). Sexual orientation and non-suicidal self-injury: A meta-analytic review. *Archives of Suicide Research, 19,* 131–150.

Bates, E., Benigni, L., Bretherton, I., Camaioni, L., & Volterra, V. (1979). *The emergence of symbols: Cognition and communication in infancy.* New York: Academic Press.

Bates, E., Bretherton, I., & Snyder, L. (1988). *From first words to grammar: Individual differences and dissociable mechanisms.* New York: Cambridge University Press.

Bates, J. E., Pettit, G. S., Dodge, K. A., & Ridge, B. (1998). Interaction of temperamental resistance to control and restrictive parenting in the development of externalizing behavior. *Developmental Psychology, 34,* 982–995.

Bates, E., & MacWhinney, B. (1987). Competition, variation, and language learning. In B. MacWhinney (Ed.), *Mechanisms of language acquisition* (pp. 157–193). Hillsdale, NJ: Erlbaum.

Baumeister, A. A., & Baumeister, A. A. (1995). Mental retardation. In M. Hersen & R. T. Ammerman (Eds.), *Advanced abnormal child psychology.* Hillsdale, NJ: Erlbaum.

Baumrind, D. (1975). *Early socialization and the discipline controversy.* Morristown, NJ: General Learning Press.

Baumrind, D. (1991). Parenting styles and adolescent development. In R. M. Lerner, A. C. Petersen, & J. Brooks-Gunn (Eds.), *Encyclopedia of adolescence.* New York: Garland.

Bayley, N. (1970). Development of mental abilities. In P. H. Mussen (Ed.), *Carmichael's manual of child psychology.* New York: John Wiley.

Bayley, N. (1993). *Bayley scales of infant development: Birth to two years* (2nd ed.). San Antonio, TX: Psychological Corp.

Beal, C. R. (1996). The role of comprehension monitoring in children's revision. *Educational Psychology Review, 8,* 219–238.

Beal, C. R., & Belgrad, S. L. (1990). The development of message evaluation skills in young children. *Child Development, 61,* 705–712.

Bear-Lehman, J., Kafko, M., Mah, L., Mosquera, L., & Reilly, B. (2002). An exploratory look at hand strength and hand size among preschoolers. *Journal of Hand Therapy, 15,* 340–346.

Beautrais, A. L., Fergusson, D. M., & Shannon, F. T. (1982). Life events and childhood morbidity: A prospective study. *Pediatrics, 70,* 935–940.

Beck, M. (1994, January 16). How far should we push Mother Nature? *Newsweek,* pp. 54–57.

Beckwith, L., Cohen, S. E., & Hamilton, C. E. (1999). Maternal sensitivity during infancy and subsequent life events relate to attachment representation at early adulthood. *Developmental Psychology, 35,* 693–700.

Behnke, M., & Eyler, F. D. (1993). The consequences of prenatal substance use for the developing fetus, newborn, and young child. *International Journal of the Addictions, 28,* 1341–1391.

Beilock, S. L., Gunderson, E. A., Ramirez, G., & Levine, S. C. (2010). Female teachers' math anxiety affects girls' math achievement. *Proceedings of the National Academy of Science of the United States of America, 107,* 1860–1863.

Bélanger, J., & Hall, D. G., (2006). Learning proper names and count nouns: Evidence from 16- and 20-month-olds. *Journal of Cognition and Development, 7,* 45–72.

Bell, A. P., Weinberg, M. S., & Hammersmith, S. K. (1981). *Sexual preference: Its development in men and women.* New York: Simon & Schuster.

Beller, M., & Gafni, N. (1996). The 1991 international assessment of educational progress in mathematics and sciences: The gender differences perspective. *Journal of Educational Psychology, 88,* 365–377.

Belsky, J., Fish, M., & Isabella, R. A. (1991). Continuity and discontinuity in infant negative and positive emotionality: Family antecedents and attachment consequences. *Developmental Psychology, 27,* 421–431.

Belsky, J., Steinberg, L., & Draper, P. (1991). Childhood experience, interpersonal development, and reproductive strategy: An evolutionary theory of socialization. *Child Development, 62,* 647–670.

Belsky, J., Woodworth, S., & Crnic, K. (1996). Trouble in the second year: Three questions about family interaction. *Child Development, 67,* 556–578.

Bem, D. J. (1996). Exotic becomes erotic: A developmental theory of sexual orientation. *Psychological Review, 103,* 320–335.

Benton, S. L., Corkill, A. J., Sharp, J. M., Downey, R. G., & Khramtsova, I. (1995). Knowledge, interest, and narrative writing. *Journal of Educational Psychology, 87,* 66–79.

Bereiter, C., & Scardamalia, M. (1987). *The psychology of written composition.* Hillsdale, NJ: Erlbaum.

Berenbaum, S. A., & Snyder, E. (1995). Early hormonal influences on childhood sex-typed activity and playmate preferences: Implications for the development of sexual orientation. *Developmental Psychology, 31,* 31–42.

Berk, L. E. (1992). Children's private speech: An overview of theory and the status of research. In R. M. Diaz & L. E. Berk (Eds.), *Private speech: From social interaction to self-regulation.* Hillsdale, NJ: Erlbaum.

Berk, L. E. (1994). Vygotsky's theory: The importance of make believe play. *Young Children, 50,* 30–38.

Berkeley, H., Gaffield, C., & West, G. (1977). Children's rights in the Canadian context. *Interchange Volume, 8,* 1–4.

Berko, J. (1958). The child's learning of English morphology. *Word, 14,* 150–177.

Berkowitz, L. (1989). Frustration-aggression hypothesis: Examination and reformulation. *Psychological Bulletin, 106,* 59–73.

Berkowitz, M. W., & Gibbs, J. C. (1985). The process of moral conflict resolution and moral development. In M. W. Berkowitz (Ed.), *Peer conflict and psychological growth* (pp. 71–84). San Francisco: Jossey-Bass.

Berkowitz, R. I., Stallings, V. A., Maislin, G., & Stunkard, A. J. (2005). Growth of children at high risk of obesity during the first 6 years of life: Implications for prevention. *American Journal of Clinical Nutrition, 81,* 140–146.

Berlan, E. D., Corliss, H. L., Field, A. E., Goodman, E., & Austin, S. B. (2010). Sexual orientation and bullying among adolescents in the growing up today study. *Journal of Adolescent Health, 46,* 366–371.

Bernard, R. S., & Cohen, L. L. (2006). Parent anxiety and infant pain during pediatric immunizations. *Journal of Clinical Psychology in Medical Settings, 13,* 282–287. doi:10.1007/s10880-006-9027-6

Bernazzani, O., Conroy, S., Marks, M. N., Siddle, K. A., Guedeney, N., Bifulco, A., . . . Henshaw, C. A., & TCS-PND Group. (2004). Contextual assessment of the maternity experience: Development of an instrument for cross-cultural research. *British Journal of Psychiatry, 184* (Suppl. 46), S24–S30.

Berndt, T. J., & Keefe, K. (1995). Friends' influence on adolescents' adjustment to school. *Child Development, 66,* 1312–1329.

Berndt, T. J., & Perry, T. B. (1990). Distinctive features and effects of adolescent friendships. In R. Montemeyer, G. R. Adams, & T. P. Gullotta (Eds.), *From childhood to adolescence: A transition period?* London: Sage.

Bernier, J. C., & Siegel, D. H. (1994). Attention-deficit hyperactivity disorder: A family ecological systems perspective. *Families in Society, 75,* 142–150.

Bernstein, W. M. (2011). *A basic theory of neuropsychoanalysis.* London: Karnac Books.

Berry, J. W. (1993). Ethnic identities in plural societies. In M. E. Bernal & G. P. Knight (Eds.), *Ethnic identity: Formation and transmission among Hispanics and other minority.* New York: State University of New York Press.

Bertenthal, B. H., & Clifton, R. K. (1998). Perception and action. In W. Damon (Ed.), *Handbook of child psychology* (Vol. 2). New York: Wiley.

Berthier, N. E. (1996). Learning to reach: A mathematical model. *Developmental Psychology, 32,* 811–823.

Besharov, D. J., & Gardiner, K. N. (1997). Trends in teen sexual behavior. *Children and Youth Services Review, 19,* 341–367.

Beyens, I., Vandenbosch, L., & Eggermont, S. (2015). Early adolescent boys' exposure to Internet pornography: Relationships to pubertal timing, sensation seeking, and academic performance. *The Journal of Early Adolescence, 35,* 1045–1068.

Bhatt, R. S., Rovee-Collier, C. K., & Weiner, S. (1994). Developmental changes in the interface between perception and memory retrieval. *Developmental Psychology, 30,* 151–162.

Bialystok, E. (1988). Levels of bilingualism and levels of linguistic awareness. *Developmental Psychology, 24,* 560–567.

Bialystok, E. (Ed). (1991). *Language processing in bilingual children*. New York: Cambridge University Press.

Bialystok, E. (1992). Selective attention in cognitive processing: The bilingual edge. In R. J. Harris (Ed.), *Cognitive processing in bilinguals* (pp. 501–513). Oxford, UK: North-Holland Press.

Bialystok, E. (1997). Effects of bilingualism and biliteracy on children's emerging concepts of print. *Developmental Psychology, 33*, 429–440.

Bialystok, E. (2001). *Bilingualism in development: Language, literacy, and cognition*. New York: Cambridge University Press.

Bialystok, E. (2006). Effect of bilingualism and computer video game experience on the Simon Task. *Canadian Journal of Experimental Psychology, 60*, 68–79.

Bialystok, E., Craik, F., & Luk, G. (2008). Cognitive control and lexical access in younger and older bilinguals. *Journal of Experimental Psychology: Learning, Memory and Cognition, 34*, 859–873.

Bialystok, E., Craik, F., & Luk, G. (2009). 'Cognitive control and lexical access in youger and older bilinguals': Correction. *Journal of Experimental Psychology: Learning, Memory and Cognition, 35*, 828.

Bialystok, E., & Feng, X. (2009). Language proficiency and executive control in proactive interference: Evidence from monolingual and bilingual children and adults. *Brain and Language, 109*, 93–100.

Biffi, G., Tannahill, D., McCafferty, J., & Balasubramanian, S. (2013). Quantitative visualization of DNA G-quadruplex structures in human cells. *Nature Chemistry* (Advance Online Publication), doi:10.1038/nchem.1548

Bigler, R. S., Averhart, C. J., & Liben, L. (2003). Race and the workforce: Occupational status, aspirations, and stereotyping among African American children. *Developmental Psychology, 39*, 572–580.

Bigler, R. S., Jones, L. C., & Lobliner, D. B. (1997). Social categorization and the formation of intergroup attitudes in children. *Child Development, 68*, 530–543.

Birch, L. L. (1991). Obesity and eating disorders: A developmental perspective. *Bulletin of the Psychonomic Society, 29*, 265–272.

Birch, L. L., & Fisher, J. A. (1995). Appetite and eating behavior in children. *Pediatric Clinics of North America, 42*, 931–953.

Birnholz, J. C., & Benacerraf, B. R. (1983). The development of human fetal hearing. *Science, 222*, 516–518.

Bisanz, G. L., Das, J. P., Varnhagen, C. K., & Henderson, H. R. (1992). Structural components of reading time and recall for sentences in narratives: Exploring changes with age and reading ability. *Journal of Educational Psychology, 84*, 103–114.

Bjorklund, D. F., & Pellegrini, A. D. (2000). Child development and evolutionary psychology. *Child Development, 71*, 1687–1708.

Black, B., & Logan, A. (1995). Links between communication patterns in mother-child, father-child, and child-peer interactions and children's social status. *Child Development, 66*, 255–271.

Black-Gutman, D., & Hickson, F. (1996). The relationship between racial attitudes and social-cognitive development in children: An Australian study. *Developmental Psychology, 32*, 448–456.

Block, J., & Block, J. H. (2006). Venturing a 30-year longitudinal study. *American Psychologist, 61*, 315–327.

Bloom, L., Margulis, C., Tinker, E., & Fujita, N. (1996). Early conversations and word learning: Contributions from child and adult. *Child Development, 67*, 3154–3175.

Bloom, L., Rocissano, L., & Hood, L. (1976). Adult-child discourse: Developmental interaction between information processing and linguistic knowledge. *Cognitive Psychology, 8*, 521–552.

Bloom, P. (2010, May 9). The moral life of babies. *New York Times Magazine*, p. MM44.

Bock, G. R., & Goode, J. A. (1996). *Genetics of criminal and antisocial behaviour*. Chichester, UK: John Wiley & Sons.

Bodnarchuk, J. L., & Eaton, W. O. (2004). Can parent reports be trusted? Validity of daily checklists of gross motor milestone attainment. *Journal of Applied Developmental Psychology, 25*, 481–490.

Bogatz, G. A., & Ball, S. (1972). *The second year of "Sesame Street": A continuing evaluation*. Princeton, NJ: Educational Testing Service.

Bohannon, J. N., Padgett, R. J., Nelson, K. E., & Mark, M. (1996). Useful evidence on negative evidence. *Developmental Psychology, 32*, 551–555.

Bohannon, J. N., MacWhinney, B., & Snow, C. (1990). No negative evidence revisited: Beyond learnability or who has to prove what to whom. *Developmental Psychology, 26*, 221–226.

Boivin, M., Hymel, S., & Bukowski, W. M. (1995). The roles of social withdrawal, peer rejection, and victimization by peers in predicting loneliness and depressed mood in childhood. *Development and Psychopathology, 7*, 765–785.

Boivin, M., Vitaro, F., & Gagnon, C. (1992). A reassessment of the self-perception profile for children: Factor structure, reliability, and convergent validity of a French version among second through sixth grade children. *International Journal of Behavioral Development, 15*, 275–290.

Boivin, M., Vitaro, F., & Poulin, F. (2005). Peer relationships and the development of aggressive behavior in early childhood. In R. E. Tremblay, W. W.

Hartup, & J. Archer (Eds.), *Developmental origins of aggression* (pp. 376–397). New York: Guilford Press.

Bolger, K. E., Patterson, C. J., & Kupersmidt, J. B. (1998). Peer relationships and self-esteem among children who have been maltreated. *Child Development, 69,* 1171–1197.

Bonham, V. L, Warshauer-Baker E., & Collins, F. S. (2005). Race and ethnicity in the genome era: The complexity of the constructs. *American Psychologist, 60,* 9–15. doi:10.1037/0003-066X.60.1.9

Booth, J. R., Perfetti, C. A., & MacWhinney, B. (1999). Quick, automatic, and general activation of orthographic and phonological representations in young readers. *Developmental Psychology, 35,* 3–19.

Bornstein, M. H. (1981). Psychological studies of color perception in human infants: Habituation, discrimination and categorization, recognition, and conceptualization. *Advances in Infancy Research, 1,* 1–40.

Bornstein, M. H. (1997). Stability in mental development from early life: Methods, measures, models, meanings, and myths. In G. E. Butterworth & F. Simion (Eds.), *The development of sensory, motor, and cognitive capacities in early infancy: From sensation to perception.* Hove, UK: Psychology Press.

Bornstein, M. H., Haynes, O. M., O'Reilly, A. W., & Painter, K. M. (1996). Solitary and collaborative pretense play in early childhood: Sources of individual variation in the development of representational competence. *Child Development, 67,* 2910–2929.

Bornstein, M. H., Haynes, O. M., Pascual, L., Painter, K. M., & Galperin, C. (1999). Play in two societies: Pervasiveness of process, specificity of structure. *Child Development, 70,* 317–331.

Bower, B. (1985). The left hand of math and verbal talent. *Science News, 144,* 40–42.

Bower, G. H. (2008). The evolution of a cognitive psychologist: A journey from simple behaviors to complex mental acts. *Annual Review in Psychology, 59,* 1–27.

Bowlby, J. (1969). *Attachment and loss* (Vol. 1). New York: Basic Books.

Bowlby, J. (1991). Ethological light on psychoanalytical problems. In P. Bateson (Ed.), *The development and integration of behaviour: Essays in honour of Robert Hinde.* Cambridge, UK: Cambridge University Press.

Boyer, C. B., & Hein, K. (1991). AIDS and HIV infection in adolescents: The role of education and antibody testing. In R. M. Lerner, A. C. Petersen, & J. Brooks-Gunn (Eds.), *Encyclopedia of adolescence* (Vol. 1). New York: Garland.

Brabant, S., & Mooney, L. A. (1999). The social construction of family life in the Sunday comics: Race as a consideration. *Journal of Comparative Family Studies, 30,* 113–133.

Bradley, R. H., Caldwell, B. M., & Rock, S. L. (1988). Home environment and school performance: A ten-year follow-up and examination of three models of environmental action. *Child Development, 59,* 852–867.

Bradley, R. H., Caldwell, B. M., Rock, S. L., Ramey, C. T., Barnard, K. E., Gray, C., . . . Johnson, D. L. (1989). Home environment and cognitive development in the first 3 years of life: A collaborative study involving six sites and three ethnic groups in North America. *Developmental Psychology, 25,* 217–235.

Braet, C., Mervielde, I., & Vandereycken, W. (1997). Psychological aspects of childhood obesity: A controlled study in a clinical and nonclinical sample. *Journal of Pediatric Psychology, 22,* 59–71.

Braine, M. D. S. (1992). What sort of innate structure is needed to "bootstrap" into syntax? *Cognition, 45,* 77–100.

Brand, E., Clingempeel, W. G., & Bowen-Woodward, D. (1988). Family relationships and children's psychological adjustment in stepmother and stepfather families. In E. M. Hetherington & J. D. Arasten (Eds.), *Impact of divorce, single parenting and step parenting on children* (pp. 299–324). Hillsdale, NJ: Erlbaum.

Braun, J. M., Yolton, K., Dietrich, K. N., Hornung, R., Ye, X., Calafat, A. M., & Lanphear, B. P. (2009). Prenatal bisphenol A exposure and early childhood behavior. *Environmental Health Perspectives, 117,* 1945–1952.

Brazelton, T. B. (1984). *Brazelton Behavior Assessment Scale* (rev. ed.). Philadelphia: Lippincott.

Brazelton, T. B., Nugent, J. K., & Lester, B. M. (1987). Neonatal behavioral assessment scale. In J. D. Osofsky (Ed.), *Handbook of infant development* (2nd ed.). New York: Wiley.

Brendgen, M., Dionne, G., Girard, A., Boivin, M., Vitaro, F., & Perusse, D. (2005). Examining genetic and environmental effects on social aggression: A study of 6-year-old twins. *Child Development, 76,* 930–946.

Bretherton, I. (1992). The origins of attachment theory: John Bowlby and Mary Ainsworth. *Developmental Psychology, 28,* 759–775.

Brigandt, I. (2005). The instinct concept of the early Konrad Lorenz. *Journal of the History of Biology, 38,* 571–608.

Briscoe, J., Gathercole, S. E., & Marlow, N. (2001). Everyday memory and cognitive ability in children born very prematurely. *Journal of Child Psychology and Psychiatry, 42,* 749–754.

Brockington, I. (1996). *Motherhood and mental health.* Oxford, UK: Oxford University Press.

Brodeur, M., Mercier, J., Dussault, M., Deaudelin, C., & Richer, J. (2006). Élaboration et validation d'une échelle d'autorégulation de l'apprentissage relative à l'intégration pédagogique des TIC (AREGA-TIC). *Canadian Journal of Behavioural Science/Revue canadienne des sciences du comportement, 38,* 238–249.

Brody, G. H. (1998). Sibling relationship quality: Its causes and consequences. *Annual Review of Psychology, 49,* 1–24.

Brody, G. H., & Flor, D. L. (1998). Maternal resources, parenting practices, and child competence in rural, single-parent African American families. *Child Development, 69,* 803–816.

Brody, G. H., Stoneman, A., & McCoy, J. K. (1994). Forecasting sibling relationships in early adolescence from child temperaments and family processes in middle childhood. *Child Development, 65,* 771–784.

Brody, N. (1992). *Intelligence* (2nd ed.). San Diego: Academic Press.

Bronfenbrenner, U. (1979). *The ecology of human development.* Cambridge, MA: Harvard University Press.

Bronfenbrenner, U. (1995). Developmental ecology through space and time: A future perspective. In P. Moen, G. H. Elder, Jr., & K. Luscher (Eds.), *Examining lives in context: Perspectives on the ecology of human development.* Washington, DC: American Psychological Association.

Bronfenbrenner, U., & Morris, P. A. (1998). The ecology of developmental processes. In W. Damon & R. M. Lerner (Eds.), *Handbook of child psychology: Vol. 1. Theoretical models of human development* (pp. 993–1028). New York: Wiley.

Bronte-Tinkew, J., Moore, K., & Matthews, G. (2007). Symptoms of major depression in a sample of fathers of infants: Sociodemographic correlates and links to father involvement. *Journal of Family Issues, 28,* 61–99.

Brook, C. G. D. (2000). Which children should receive growth hormone treatment: Reserve it for the GH deficient. *Archives of Disease in Childhood, 83,* 176–178.

Brooks-Gunn, J., & Johnson, A. D. (2006). G. Stanley Hall's contribution to science, practice and policy: The child study, education and reform movements. *History of Psychology, 9,* 247–258.

Brooks-Gunn, J., Klebanov, P. K., & Duncan, G. J. (1996). Ethnic differences in children's intelligence test scores: Role of economic deprivation, home environment, and maternal characteristics. *Child Development, 67,* 396–408.

Brooks-Gunn, J., & Paikoff, R. (1993). "Sex is a gamble, kissing is a game": Adolescent sexuality, contraception, and sexuality. In S. P. Millstein, A. C. Petersen, & E. O. Nightingale (Eds.), *Promoting the health behavior of adolescents.* New York: Oxford University Press.

Brooks-Gunn, J., & Ruble, D. N. (1982). The development of menstrual-related beliefs and behaviors during early adolescence. *Child Development, 53,* 1567–1577.

Brown, B. B., & Lohr, M. J. (1987). Peer-group affiliation and adolescent self-esteem: An integration of ego-identity and symbolic–interaction theories. *Journal of Personality and Social Psychology, 52,* 47–55.

Brown, B. B., Lohr, M. J., & McClenahan, E. L. (1986). Early adolescents' perceptions of peer pressure. *Journal of Early Adolescence, 6,* 139–154.

Brown, B. B., Mounts, N., Lamborn, S. D., & Steinberg, L. (1993). Parenting practices and peer group affiliation in adolescence. *Developmental Psychology, 64,* 467–482.

Brown, J. R., & Dunn, J. (1992). Talk with your mother or your sibling? Developmental changes in early family conversations about feelings. *Child Development, 63,* 336–349.

Brown, R. (1973). *A first language: The early stages.* Cambridge, MA: Harvard University Press.

Brown, R., Pressley, M., Van Meter, P., & Schuder, T. (1996). A quasi-experimental validation of transactional strategies instruction with low-achieving second-grade readers. *Journal of Educational Psychology, 88,* 18–37.

Browne, K. D., & Hamilton-Giachritsis, C. (2005). The influence of violent media on children and adolescents: A public-health approach. *Lancet, 365,* 702–710.

Brownell, M. D., Nickel, N. C., Chateau, D., Martens, P. J., Taylor, C., Crockett, L., . . . & Goh, C. Y. (2015). Long-term benefits of full-day kindergarten: A longitudinal population-based study. *Early Child Development and Care, 185,* 291–316.

Bryant, B. K. (1992). Conflict resolution strategies in relation to children's peer relations. *Journal of Applied Developmental Psychology, 13,* 35–50.

Bryant, B. K., & Crockenberg, S. B. (1980). Correlates and dimensions of prosocial behavior: A study of female siblings with their mothers. *Child Development, 51,* 529–554.

Bryden, M. P., & Saxby, L. (1986). Developmental aspects of cerebral lateralization. In J. E. Obrzut & G. W. Hynd (Eds.), *Child neuropsychology: Vol. 1. Theory and research* (pp. 73–94). Orlando, FL: Academic Press.

Buchanan, C. M., Eccles, J. S., & Becker, J. B. (1992). Are adolescents the victims of raging hormones? Evidence for activational effects of hormones on moods and behavior at adolescence. *Psychological Bulletin, 111,* 62–107.

Buchholz, M., Karl, H. W., Pomietto, M., & Lynn, A. (1998). Pain scores in infants: A modified infant pain scale versus visual analogue. *Journal of Pain & Symptom Management, 15,* 117–124.

Buhrmester, D., & Furman, W. (1987). The development of companionship and intimacy. *Child Development, 58,* 1101–1113.

Buhrmester, D., & Furman, W. (1990). Perceptions of sibling relationships during middle childhood and adolescence. *Child Development, 61,* 1387–1398.

Bullock, M., & Lütkenhaus, P. (1990). Who am I? The development of self-understanding in toddlers. *Merrill-Palmer Quarterly, 36,* 217–238.

Buote, V. M., Wood, E., & Pratt, M. (2009). Exploring similarities and differences between online and offline friendships: The role of attachment style. *Computers in Human Behavior, 25,* 560–567.

Burack, J. A., Flanagan, T., Peled, T., Sutton, H. M., Zygmuntowicz, C., & Manly, J. T. (2006). Social perspective-taking skills in maltreated children and adolescents. *Developmental Psychology, 42,* 207–217.

Burchinal, M. R., Roberts, J. E., Riggins, R., Zeisel, S. A., Neebe, E., & Bryant, D. (2000). Relating quality of center-based child care to early cognitive and language development longitudinally. *Child Development, 71,* 338–357.

Burks, V. S., Dodge, K. A., Price, J. M., & Laird, R. D. (1999). Internal representational models of peers: Implications for the development of problematic behavior. *Developmental Psychology, 35,* 802–810.

Burns, A., & Scott, C. (1994). *Mother-headed families and why they have increased.* Hillsdale, NJ: Erlbaum.

Burns, G. L., Walsh, J. A., Gomez, R., & Hafetz, N. (2006). Measurement and structural invariance of parent ratings of ADHD and ODD symptoms across gender for American and Malaysian children. *Psychological Assessment, 18,* 452–457.

Bushman, B. J., Gollwitzer, M., & Cruz, C. (2015). There is broad consensus: Media researchers agree that violent media increase aggression in children, and pediatricians and parents concur. *Psychology of Popular Media Culture, 4,* 200–214.

Bushnik, T., & Garner, R. (2008). The children of older first-time mothers in Canada: Their health and development. Children and Youth Research Paper Series (89-599-M No. 5). Ottawa: Minister of Industry. Retrieved from www.statcan.gc.ca/pub/89-599-m/2008005/5200192-eng.htm

Buss, A. H., & Plomin, R. (1975). *A temperamental theory of personality development.* New York: Wiley-Interscience.

Buss, A. H., & Plomin, R. (1984). *Temperament: Early developing personality traits.* Hillsdale, NJ: Erlbaum.

Buss, K. A., & Goldsmith, H. H. (1998). Fear and anger regulation in infancy: Effects on the temporal dynamics of affective expression. *Child Development, 69,* 359–374.

Butler, R. (1992). What young people want to know when: The effects of mastery and ability on social information seeking. *Journal of Personality and Social Psychology, 62,* 934–943.

Button, E. J., Sonuga-Burke, E. J. S., Davis, J., & Thompson, M. (1996). A prospective study of self-esteem in the prediction of eating problems in schoolgirls: Questionnaire findings. *British Journal of Clinical Psychology, 35,* 193–203.

Byrne, B. M., & Gavin, D. W. (1996). The Shavelson model revisited: Testing for the structure of academic self-concept across pre-, early, and late adolescents. *Journal of Educational Psychology, 88,* 215–228.

Cairns, R. B., Cairns, B. D., Neckerman, H. J., Ferguson, L. L., & Gariépy, J.-L. (1989). Growth and aggression: 1. Childhood to early adolescence. *Developmental Psychology, 25,* 320–330.

Cairns, R. B., Leung, M. C., Buchannan, L., & Cairns, B. D. (1995). Friendships and social networks in childhood and adolescence: Fluidity, reliability, and interrelations. *Child Development, 66,* 1330–1345.

Caldwell, B. M., & Bradley, R. H. (1994). Environmental issues in developmental follow-up research. In S. L. Friedman & H. C. Haywood (Eds.), *Developmental follow-up.* San Diego: Academic Press.

Calkins, S. D., Fox, N. A., & Marshall, T. R. (1996). Behavioral and physiological antecedents of inhibited and uninhibited behavior. *Child Development, 67,* 523–540.

Callaghan, R. C., & Rankin, M. P. (2002). Emergence of graphic symbol functioning and the question of domain specificity: A longitudinal training study. *Child Development, 73,* 359–376.

Cameron, C., Craig, C. L., Coles, C., & Cragg, S. (2001). *Increasing physical activity: Encouraging physical activity through school.* Ottawa: Canadian Fitness and Lifestyle Research Institute.

Campbell D. W., Eaton W. O., & McKeen N. A. (2002). Motor activity level and behavioural control in young children. *International Journal of Behavioral Development, 26,* 289–296.

Campbell, F. A., & Ramey, C. T. (1994). Effects of early intervention on intellectual and academic achievement: A follow-up study of children from low-income families. *Child Development, 65,* 684–698.

Campbell, F. A., & Ramey, C. T. (2008). Effects of early intervention on intellectual and academic achievement: A follow-up study of children from low-income families. *Child Development, 65,* 684–698.

Campbell, R., & Sais, E. (1995). Accelerated metalinguistic (phonological) awareness in bilingual children. *British Journal of Developmental Psychology, 13,* 61–68.

Campbell, S. B., Cohn, J. F., Flanagan, C., Popper, S., & Meyers, T. (1992). Course and correlates of postpartum depression during the transition to parenthood. *Development and Psychopathology, 4,* 29–47.

Campos, J. J., Hiatt, S., Ramsay, D., Henderson, C., & Svejda, M. (1978). The emergence of fear on the visual cliff. In M. Lewis & L. Rosenblum (Eds.), *The origins of affect.* New York: Plenum.

Camras, L. A., Oster, H., Campos, J., Campos, R., Ujiie, T., Miyake, K., . . . Meng, Z. (1998). Production of emotional facial expressions in European, American, Japanese, and Chinese infants. *Developmental Psychology, 34,* 616–628.

Canadian Council on Social Development. (n.d.). Economic Security Fact Sheet #2: Poverty. Retrieved from www.ccsd.ca/factsheets/economic_security/poverty/index.htm

Canadian Dental Association. (2003). Dental care FAQs. Retrieved from www.cda-adc.ca/english/your_oral_health/faq/dentalcare_faqs/default.asp#4

Canadian Haemoglobinopathy Association Consensus Statement on the Care of Patients with Sickle Cell Disease in Canada Version 2.0 Ottawa; 2015.

Canadian Institute of Child Health. (2000). *The health of Canada's children: A CICH profile* (3rd ed.). Ottawa: Canadian Institute of Child Health.

Canadian Institute for Health Information. (2003, May 12). Geographic location, parents' income and education, and number of siblings affect a child's risk of becoming overweight, new CPHI-funded study suggests (news release). Ottawa: Canadian Institute for Health Information. Retrieved from http://secure.cihi.ca/cihiweb/dispPage.jsp?cw_page=media_12may2003_e

Canadian Institute for Health Information. (2004a). *Giving birth in Canada: Providers of maternity and infant care.* Ottawa: Canadian Institute for Health Information.

Canadian Institute for Health Information. (2004b). *National trauma registry 2004 report. Injury hospitalizations (includes 2001–2002 data).* Ottawa: Canadian Institute for Health Information.

Canadian Institute for Health Information. (2009, October). *Comparing activity and fruit and vegetable consumption by weight status among children and youth.* Ottawa: Canadian Institute for Health Information.

Canadian Institute for Health Information. (2014). *Induced Abortions Reported in Canada in 2014.* Retrieved from https://www.cihi.ca/sites/default/files/document/induced_abortion_can_2014_en_web.xlsx

Canadian Paediatric Society Psychosocial Paediatrics Committee. (2003). Impact of media use on children and youth. *Paediatric Child Health, 8,* 301–306.

Canadian Paediatric Society. (2004). A health professional's guide to using growth charts. *Paediatrics & Child Health, 9,* 174–176.

Canfield, R. L., & Smith, E. G. (1996). Number-based expectations and sequential enumeration by 5-month-old infants. *Developmental Psychology, 32,* 269–279.

CANPKU. (2016). http://canpku.org/about-pku-2

Capaldi, D. M., Crosby, L., & Stoolmiller, M. (1996). Predicting the timing of first sexual intercourse for at-risk adolescent males. *Child Development, 67,* 344–359.

Capaldi, D. M., & Patterson, G. R. (1991). Relation of parental transitions to boys' adjustment problems: I. A linear hypothesis. II. Mothers at risk for transitions and unskilled parenting. *Developmental Psychology, 27,* 489–504.

Caprara, D. L., Nash, K., Greenbaum, R., Rovet, J., & Koren, G. (2007). Novel approaches to the diagnosis of fetal alcohol spectrum disorder. *Neuroscience & Biobehavioral Reviews, 31,* 254–260.

Cardno, A. G., Sham, P. C., Farmer, A. E., Murray, R. M., & McGuffin, P. (2002). Heritability of Schneider's first-rank symptoms. *British Journal of Psychiatry, 180,* 35–38.

Carey, G. (1996). Family and genetic epidemiology of aggressive and antisocial behavior. In D. M. Stoff & R. B. Cairns (Eds.), *Aggression and violence: Genetic, neurobiological, and biosocial perspectives.* Mahwah, NJ: Erlbaum.

Carey, S. (1978). The child as a word learner. In M. Halle, J. Bresnan, & G. Miller (Eds.), *Linguistic theory and psychological reality.* Cambridge, MA: MIT Press.

Carey, S. (1992). Becoming a face expert. In V. Bruce, A. Cowey, A. W. Ellis, & D. I. Perrett (Eds.), *Processing the facial image.* Oxford, UK: Clarendon Press.

Carlo, G., Koller, S. H., Eisenberg, N., Da Silva, M. S., & Frohlich, C. B. (1996). A cross-national study on the relations among prosocial moral reasoning, gender role orientations, and prosocial behaviors. *Developmental Psychology, 32,* 231–240.

Carlson, C. L., Pelham, W. E., Milich, R., & Dixon, J. (1992). Single and combined effects of methylphenidate and behavior therapy on the classroom performance of children with attention-deficit hyperactivity disorder. *Journal of Abnormal Child Psychology, 20,* 213–232.

Carlson, E. A. (1998). A prospective longitudinal study of attachment disorganization/disorientation. *Child Development, 69,* 1107–1128.

Carpenter, P. A., & Daneman, M. (1981). Lexical retrieval and error recovery in reading: A model based on eye fixations. *Journal of Verbal Learning and Verbal Behavior, 20,* 137–160.

Carrere, S., & Gottman, J. M. (1999). Predicting the future of marriages. In E. M. Hetherington (Ed.), *Coping with divorce, single parenting, and remarriage: A risk and resiliency perspective.* Mahwah, NJ: Erlbaum.

Carrington, P. J., Matarazzo, A., & deSouza, P. (2005). *Court careers of a Canadian birth cohort.* Ottawa: Canadian Centre for Justice Statistics, Statistics Canada.

Carroll, J. B. (1993). *Human cognitive abilities: A survey of factor-analytic studies.* New York: Cambridge University Press.

Carroll, J. L., & Loughlin, G. M. (1994). Sudden infant death syndrome. In F. A. Oski, C. D. DeAngelis, R. D. Feigin, J. A. McMillan, & J. B. Warshaw (Eds.), *Principles and practice of pediatrics.* Philadelphia: Lippincott.

Casaer, P. (1993). Old and new facts about perinatal brain development. *Journal of Child Psychology and Psychiatry, 34,* 101–109.

Case, R. (1998). The development of central conceptual structures. In D. Kuhn & R. Siegler (Eds.), *Handbook of child psychology: Vol. 2. Cognition, perception, and language* (5th ed., pp. 745–800). New York: Wiley.

Case, R. (1999). Conceptual development in the child and in the field: A personal view of the Piagetian legacy. In E. K. Scholnick, K. Nelson, S. A. Gelman, & P. H. Mille (Eds.), *Conceptual development: Piaget's legacy. The Jean Piaget Symposium series* (Vol. 26, pp. 23–51). Mahwah, NJ: Erlbaum.

Casey, M. B., Nuttall, R. L., & Pezaris, E. (1997). Mediators of gender differences in mathematics college entrance test scores: A comparison of spatial skills with internalized beliefs and anxieties. *Developmental Psychology, 33,* 669–680.

Casey, M. B., Nuttall, R. L., & Pezaris, E. (1999). Evidence in support of a model that predicts how biological and environmental factors interact to influence spatial skills. *Developmental Psychology, 35,* 1237–1247.

Casiglia, A. C., Coco, A. L., & Zappulla, C. (1998). Aspects of social reputation and peer relationships in Italian children: A cross-cultural perspective. *Developmental Psychology, 34,* 723–730.

Cassidy, J. (1994). Emotion regulation: Influences of attachment relationships. *Monographs of the Society for Research in Child Development, 59,* 228–283.

CATIE. Canadian AIDS Treatment Information Exchange. (2014). Retrieved from http://www.catie.ca/en/fact-sheets/epidemiology/epidemiology-hiv-youth

Cattell, R. B. (1965). *The scientific analysis of personality.* Baltimore, MD: Penguin.

CAYC (Canadian Association for Young Children). (n.d.). Young children have the right to learn through play! Canadian Association for Young Children. Retrieved from www.cayc.ca/index2.html

Centers for Disease Control and Prevention. (2000). Childhood injury fact sheet. Retrieved from www.cdc.gov/ncipc/factsheets/childh.htm

Center for Fetal Diagnosis and Treatment. (n.d.) Overview. Retrieved from http://fetalsurgery.chop.edu/overview.shtml

CFLRI (Canadian Fitness and Lifestyle Research Institute). (2005). Warning to couch potatoes. Retrieved from www.cflri.ca/eng/lifestyle/1998/couch_potatoes.php

Chaffin, M., Hanson, R., Saunders, B. E., Nichols, T., Barnett, D., Zeanah, C., . . . Miller-Perrin, C. (2006). Report of the APSAC task force on attachment therapy, reactive attachment disorder, and attachment problems. *Child Maltreatment, 11,* 76–89.

Chalmers, B., & Hashi, K. O. (2000). 432 Somali women's birth experiences in Canada after earlier female genital mutilation. *Birth, 27,* 227–234.

Chalmers, B., Dzakpasu, S., Heaman, M., & Kaczorowski, J. (2008) The Canadian maternity experiences survey: An overview of findings. *Journal of Obstetrics and Gynaecology Canada, 30,* 217–228. Retrieved from www.sogc.org/jogc/abstracts/full/200803_Obstetrics_2.pdf

Chamberlain, D. (1998). Babies don't feel pain: A century of denial in medicine. In R. Davis-Floyd & J. Dumit (Eds.), *Cyborg babies: From techno-sex to techno-tots.* New York: Routledge.

Chan, R. W., Raboy, B., & Patterson, C. J. (1998). Psychosocial adjustment among children conceived via donor insemination by lesbian and heterosexual mothers. *Child Development, 69,* 443–457.

Chan, T. (2003). Evidence for clinicians: In children with idiopathic short stature, what advantage does administering recombinant growth hormone have over observation in final adult height? *Paediatrics & Child Health, 8*(9), 569–571. Retrieved from www.pulsus.com/Paeds/08_09/chan_ed.htm

Chandler, M., & Moran, T. (1990). Psychopathy and moral development: A comparative study of delinquent and nondelinquent youth. *Development and Psychopathology, 2,* 227–246.

Chao, R. K. (1994). Beyond parental control and authoritarian parenting style: Understanding Chinese parenting through the cultural notion of training. *Child Development, 65,* 1111–1119.

Chapman, P. D. (1988). *Schools as sorters: Lewis M. Terman, applied psychology, and the intelligence testing movement, 1890–1930.* New York: New York University Press.

Chapman, R. S. (2007). Children's language learning: An interactionist perspective. In R. Paul (Ed.), *Language disorders from a developmental perspective: Essays in honor of Robin S. Chapman* (pp. 1–53). Mahwah, NJ: Erlbaum.

Charman, T. (2003). Why is joint attention a pivotal skill in autism? *Philosophical Transactions of the Royal Society of London, 358,* 315–324. doi:10.1098/rstb.2002.1199

Chase-Lansdale, P. L., Brooks-Gunn, J., & Zamsky, E. S. (1994). Young African-American multigenerational families in poverty: Quality of mothering and grandmothering. *Child Development, 65,* 373–393.

Chase-Lansdale, P. L., Cherlin, A. J., & Kiernan, K. E. (1995). The long-term effects of parental divorce on the mental health of young adults: A developmental perspective. *Child Development, 66,* 1614–1634.

Chase-Lansdale, P. L., & Hetherington, E. M. (1990). The impact of divorce on life-span development: Short and long term effects. In P. B. Baltes, B. L. Featherman, & R. M. Lerner, (Eds.), *Life-span development and behavior* (Vol. 10). Hillsdale, NJ: Erlbaum.

Cheal, D. (1996). Stories about step-families. In *Growing up in Canada: National longitudinal survey of children and youth.* (Catalogue No. 89-550-MPE; No. 1). Ottawa: Human Resources Development Canada and Statistics Canada.

Chen, X., Rubin, K. H., & Li, Z. (1995). Social functioning and adjustment in Chinese children. *Developmental Psychology, 31,* 531–539.

CHEP (Child Hunger and Education Program). (2004). CHEP's Mission. Retrieved from www.chep.org/mission.html

Chess, S., & Thomas, A. (1986). *Temperament in clinical practice.* New York: Guilford.

Chi, M. T. H. (1978). Knowledge structures and memory development. In R. Siegler (Ed.), *Children's thinking: What develops?* Hillsdale, NJ: Erlbaum.

Children's Defense Fund. (1996). *The state of America's children yearbook, 1996.* Washington, DC: Children's Defense Fund.

Chilman, C. S. (1983). *Adolescent sexuality in a changing American society* (2nd ed.). New York: Wiley.

Chisholm, J. S. (1983). *Navajo infancy: An ethological study of child development.* New York: Aldine.

Chisholm, K. (1998). A three year follow-up of attachment and indiscriminate friendliness in children adopted from Romanian orphanages. *Child Development, 69,* 1092–1106.

Chisholm, K., Carter, M. C., Ames, E. W., & Morison, S. J. (1995). Attachment security and indiscriminately friendly behavior in children adopted from Romanian orphanages. *Development and Psychopathology, 7,* 283–294.

Choi, A. L., Guifan, S., Zhang, Y., & Grandjean, P. (2012). Developmental fluoride neurotoxicity: A systematic review and meta-analysis. *Environmental Health Perspectives, 120,* 1362–1368.

Chomitz, V. R., Cheung, L. W. Y., & Lieberman, E. (1995). The role of lifestyle in preventing low birth weight. *Future of Children, 5,* 121–138.

Chomsky, N. (1957). *Syntactic structures.* The Hague: Mouton.

Chomsky, N. (1995). *The minimalist program.* Cambridge, MA: MIT Press.

Christensen, A., & Heavey, C. L. (1999). Intervention for couples. *Annual Review of Psychology, 50,* 165–190.

Christensen, S. (2000). Family definition, family identity: Processes in the lesbian stepfamily (Unpublished doctoral dissertation). University of Guelph, Guelph, ON.

Chudley, A. E., Conry, J., Cook, J. L., Loock, C., Rosales, T., & LeBlanc, N. (2005). Fetal alcohol spectrum disorder: Canadian guidelines for diagnosis. *Canadian Medical Association Journal, 172* (Suppl.), S1–S21.

Chugani, H. T., & Phelps, M. E. (1986). Maturational changes in cerebral function in infants determined by 18FDG positron emission tomography. *Science, 231,* 840–843.

Cipani, E. (1991). Educational classification and placement. In J. L. Matson & J. A. Mulick (Eds.), *Handbook of mental retardation* (2nd ed.). New York: Pergamon Press.

Clark, C. (2007, February 5). Natives to hit Ottawa with rights complaint: Fontaine plans legal offensive as underfunding of welfare services leaves 27,000 aboriginal children in foster homes. *Globe and Mail.* Retrieved from INK, www.afn.ca/article.asp?id=3374

Clark, J. E., & Phillips, S. J. (1993). A longitudinal study of intralimb coordination in the first year of independent walking: A dynamical systems analysis. *Child Development 64,* 1143–1157.

Clark, K. B. (1945). A brown girl in a speckled world. *Journal of Social Issues, 1,* 10–15.

Clark, K. B., & Clark, M. K. (1940). Skin color as a factor in racial identification of Negro preschool children. *Journal of Social Psychology, 11,* 159–169.

Clifton, R., Perris, E., & Bullinger, A. (1991). Infants' perception of auditory space. *Developmental Psychology, 27,* 187–197.

Cohen, S., & Williamson, G. M. (1991). Stress and infectious disease in humans. *Psychological Bulletin, 109,* 5–24.

Coie, J. D., & Dodge, K. A. (1998). Aggression and antisocial behavior. In W. Damon (Ed.), *Handbook of child psychology* (Vol. 3). New York: Wiley.

Colby, A., Kohlberg, L., Gibbs, J., & Lieberman, M. (1983). A longitudinal study of moral judgment. *Monographs of the Society for Research in Child Development, 48* (Serial #200).

Cole, D. A., & Jordan, A. E. (1995). Competence and memory: Integrating psychosocial and cognitive correlates of child depression. *Child Development, 66,* 459–473.

Cole, M. (1996). *Cultural psychology: A once and future discipline.* Cambridge, MA: Harvard University Press.

Collaer, M. L., & Hines, M. (1995). Human behavioral sex differences: A role for gonadal hormones during early development? *Psychological Bulletin, 118,* 55–107.

Coltheart, M., Curtis, B., Atkins, P., & Haller, M. (1993). Models of reading aloud: Dual-route and parallel-distributed-processing approaches. *Psychological Review, 100,* 589–608.

Committee on Genetics. (1996). Newborn screening fact sheet. *Pediatrics, 98,* 473–501.

Comstock, G., & Scharrer, E. (1999). *Television: What's on, who's watching, and what it means.* San Diego: Academic Press.

Cone, E. J., Kato, K., & Hillsgrove, M. (1996). Cocaine excretion in the semen of drug users. *Journal of Analytical Toxicology, 20,* 139–140.

The Conference Board of Canada. (2016). Infant Mortality. Retrieved from http://www.conferenceboard.ca/hcp/details/health/infant-mortality-rate.aspx#ftn5-ref

Connors, S. L., Crowell, D. E., Eberhart, C. G., Copeland, J., Newschaffer, C. J., Spence, S. J., & Zimmerman, A. W. (2005). Beta-sub-2-adrenergic receptor activation and genetic polymorphisms in autism: Data from dizygotic twins. *Journal of Child Neurology, 20,* 876–884.

Conger, R. D., Patterson, G. R., & Ge, X. (1995). It takes two to replicate: A mediational model for the impact of parents' stress on adolescent adjustment. *Child Development, 66,* 80–97.

Cooper, R. S. (2005). Race and IQ: Molecular genetics as deus ex machina. *American Psychologist, 60,* 71–76.

Coopersmith, S. (1967). *The antecedents of self-esteem.* San Francisco: W. H. Freeman.

Coplan, R. J., Barber, A. M., & Lagace-Seguin, D. G. (1999). The role of child temperament as a predictor of early literacy and numeracy skills in preschoolers. *Early Childhood Research Quarterly, 14,* 537–553.

Coplan, R. J., Rubin, K. H., Fox, N. A., Calkins, S. D., & Stewart, S. L. (1994). Being alone, playing alone, and acting alone: Distinguishing among reticence and passive and active solitude in young children. *Child Development, 65,* 129–137.

Copper, R. L., Goldenberg, R. L., Das, A., Elder, N., Swain, M., Norman, G., . . . Meier, A. M. (1996). The preterm prediction study: Maternal stress is associated with spontaneous preterm birth at less than thirty-five weeks' gestation. *American Journal of Obstetrics & Gynecology, 175(5),* 1286–1292.

Corballis, M. C. (1997). The genetics and evolution of handedness. *Psychological Review, 104,* 714–727.

Coren, S. (1992). *The left-hander syndrome: The causes and consequences of left-handedness.* New York: Free Press.

Coren, S., & Halpern, D. F. (1991). Left-handedness: A marker for decreased survival fitness. *Psychological Bulletin, 109,* 90–106.

Cornelius, M., Taylor, P., Geva, D., & Day, N. (1995). Prenatal tobacco exposure and marijuana use among adolescents: Effects on offspring gestational age, growth, and morphology. *Pediatrics, 95,* 738–743.

Cornish, K. M., Manly, T., Savage, R., Swanson, J., Morisano, D., Butler, N., . . . Hollis, C. P. (2005). Association of the dopamine transporter (DAT1) 10/10-repeat genotype with ADHD symptoms and response inhibition in a general population sample. *Molecular Psychiatry, 10,* 686–698.

Cornwell, K. S., Harris, L. J., & Fitzgerald, H. E. (1991). Task effects in the development of hand preference in 9-, 13-, and 20-month-old infant girls. *Developmental Neuropsychology, 7,* 19–34.

Costigan, C. L., Koryzma, C. M., Hua, J. M., & Chance, L. J. (2010). Examining risk and resilience among youth from immigrant Chinese families in Canada. *Cultural Diversity and Ethnic Minority Psychology, 16,* 264–273.

Costigan, C., Su, T.F., & Hua, J. M. (2009). Ethnic identity among Chinese Canadian youth: A review of the Canadian literature. *Canadian Psychology/Psychologie Canadienne, 50,* 261–272.

Costin, S. E., & Jones, D. C. (1992). Friendship as a facilitator of emotional responsiveness and prosocial interventions among young children. *Developmental Psychology, 28,* 941–947.

CMEC. Council of Ministers of Education, Canada, & Health Canada. (2002). *Canadian youth, sexual health and AIDS study: Factors influencing the sexual health of Canadian youth.* Retrieved from www.cmec.ca/publications/aids

Courage, M. L., Murphy, A. N., Goulding, S., & Setliff, A. E. (2010). When the television is on: The impact of infant-directed video on 6- and 18-month-olds' attention during toy play and on parent-infant interaction. *Infant Behavior & Development, 33,* 176–188.

Couturier, J. (2007). New developments in child and adolescent eating disorders. *Journal of the Canadian Academy of Child and Adolescent Psychiatry/Journal de l'Academie Canadienne de Psychiatrie de l'Enfant et de l'Adolescent, 16,* 151–152.

Cox, M. J., Owen, M. T., Henderson, V. K., & Margand, N. A. (1992). Prediction of infant-father and infant-mother attachment. *Developmental Psychology, 28,* 474–483.

CPA (Canadian Psychological Association). (n.d.). CPA awards. Retrieved from www.cpa.ca/aboutcpa/cpaawards

Craft, M. J., Montgomery, L. A., & Peters, J. (1992, October). *Comparative study of responses in preschool children to the birth of an ill sibling.* Nursing seminar series presentation, University of Iowa College of Nursing, Iowa City, IA.

Craig, K. D., Stanford, E. A., Fairbairn, N. S., & Chambers, C. T. (2006). Emergent pain language communication competence in infants and children. *Enfance, 58,* 52–71.

Craig, K. D., Whitfield, M. F., Grunau, R. V. E., Linton, J., & Hadjistavropoulos, H. D. (1993). Pain in the preterm neonate: Behavioural and physiological indices. *Pain, 52,* 238–299.

Craig, W. M., Pepler, D. J., & Atlas, R. (2000). Observations of bullying on the playground and in the classroom. *International Journal of School Psychology, 21,* 22–36.

Cratty, B. (1979). *Perceptual and motor development in infants and children* (2nd ed.). Englewood Cliffs, NJ: Prentice Hall.

Crawford, M., Chaffin, R., & Fitton, L. (1995). Cognition in social context. *Learning & Individual Differences, 7,* 341–362.

Crick, N. R., Casas, J. F., & Ku, H. (1999). Relational and physical forms of peer victimization in preschool. *Developmental Psychology, 35,* 376–385.

Crick, N. R., & Dodge, K. A. (1994). A review and reformulation of social information-processing mechanisms in children's social adjustment. *Psychological Bulletin, 115,* 74–101.

Crick, N. R., & Werner, N. E. (1998). Response decision processes in relational and overt aggression. *Child Development, 69,* 1630–1639.

Crockenberg, S. C., Leerkes, E. M., & Lekka, S. K. (2007). Pathways from marital aggression to infant emotion regulation: The development of withdrawal in infancy. *Infant Behavior & Development, 30,* 97–113.

Cross, T. P., & Casanueva, C. (2009). Caseworker judgments and substantiation. *Child Maltreatment, 14,* 38–52.

Crowder, R. G., & Wagner, R. K. (1992). *The psychology of reading: An introduction* (2nd ed.). New York: Oxford University Press.

Csikszentmihalyi, M., & Larson, R. (1984). *Being adolescent: Conflict and growth in the teenage years.* New York: Basic Books.

Cuellar, I., Nyberg, B., Maldonado, R. E., & Roberts, R. E. (1997). Ethnic identity and acculturation in a young adult Mexican-origin population. *Journal of Community Psychology, 25,* 535–549.

Cuevas, K., & Bell, M. A. (2014). Infant attention and early childhood executive function. *Child Development, 85,* 397–404.

Cunningham, F. G., MacDonald, P. C., & Gant, N. F. (1989). *Williams obstetrics* (18th ed.). London: Appleton & Lange.

Curtiss, S. (1989). The independence and task-specificity of language. In M. H. Bornstein & J. S. Bruner (Eds.), *Interaction in human development* (pp. 105–137). Hillsdale, NJ: Erlbaum.

D'Augelli, A. R. (1996). Lesbian, gay, and bisexual development during adolescence and young adulthood. In R. P. Cabaj & T. S. Stein (Eds.), *Textbook of homosexuality and mental health.* Washington, DC: American Psychiatric Press.

Damon, W., & Hart, D. (1988). *Self-understanding in childhood and adolescence.* New York: Cambridge University Press.

Dannemiller, J. L. (1998). Color constancy and color vision during infancy: Methodological and empirical issues. In V. Walsh & J. Kulikowski (Eds.), *Perceptual constancy: Why things look as they do.* New York: Cambridge University Press.

Dannemiller, J. L., & Stephens, B. R. (1988). A critical test of infant pattern preference models. *Child Development, 59,* 210–216.

Das, J. P. (1995). Some thoughts on two aspects of Vygotsky's work. *Educational Psychologist, 30,* 93–97.

Davidson, K. M., Richards, D. S., Schatz, D. A., & Fisher, D. A. (1991). Successful in utero treatment of fetal goiter and hypothyroidism. *New England Journal of Medicine, 324,* 543–546.

Davies, P. T., & Cummings, E. M. (1998). Exploring children's emotional security as a mediator of the link between marital relations and child adjustment. *Child Development, 69,* 124–139.

Day, J. D., Engelhardt, S. E., Maxwell, S. E., & Bolig, E. E. (1997). Comparison of static and dynamic assessment procedures and their relation to independent performance. *Journal of Educational Psychology, 89,* 358–368.

Day, N. L., Richardson, G. A., Goldschmidt, L., & Cornelius, M. D. (2000). Effects of prenatal tobacco exposure on preschoolers' behavior. *Journal of Developmental & Behavioral Pediatrics, 21,* 180–188.

Day, S. X., Rounds, J., & Swaney, K. (1998). The structure of vocational interests for diverse racial-ethnic groups. *Psychological Science, 9,* 40–44.

Dayan, J., Doyle, A. B., & Markiewicz, D. (2000). Social support networks and self-esteem of idiocentric and allocentric children and adolescents. *Journal of Social and Personal Relationships, 8,* 767–784.

Deak, G. O. (2000). Hunting the fox of word learning: Why "constraints" fail to capture it. *Developmental Review, 20,* 29–80.

Deater-Deckard, K. (2000). Parenting and child behavioral adjustment in early childhood: A quantitative approach to studying family processes. *Child Development, 71,* 468–484.

Deater-Deckard, K., & Plomin, R. (1999). An adoption study of the etiology of teacher and parent reports of externalizing behavior problems in middle childhood. *Child Development, 70,* 144–154.

DeBerry, K. M., Scarr, S., & Weinberg, R. (1996). Family racial socialization and ecological competence: Longitudinal assessments of African-American transracial adoptees. *Child Development, 67,* 2375–2399.

De Braekeleer, M., & Gauthier, S. (1996). Autosomal recessive disorders in Saguenay-Lac-St-Jean, Quebec: Study of kinship. *Human Biology, 68,* 371–381.

DeCasper, A. J., & Spence M. J. (1986). Prenatal maternal speech influences newborn's perception of speech sounds. *Infant Behavior and Development, 9,* 133–150.

DeKeyser Ganz, F. (2012). Sleep and immune function. *Critical Care Nurse, 32,* e19-e25. Retrieved from http://www.cccnonline.org

Dekovic, M., & Janssens, J. M. (1992). Parents' child-rearing style and child's sociometric status. *Developmental Psychology, 28,* 925–932.

DeKroon, D. M. A., Kyte, C. S., & Johnson, C. J. (2002). Partner influences on the social pretend play of children with language impairments. *Language, Speech, and Hearing Services in Schools, 33,* 253.

Delaney-Black, V., Covington, C., Ostrea, E., Jr., Romero, A., Baker, D., Tagle, M., & Nordstrom-Klee, B. (1996). Prenatal cocaine and neonatal outcome: Evaluation of dose-response relationship. *Pediatrics, 98,* 735–740.

Dellas, M., & Jernigan, L. P. (1990). Affective personality characteristics associated with undergraduate ego identity formation. *Journal of Adolescent Research, 5,* 306–324.

DeLoache, J. S. (1984). Oh where, oh where: Memory-based searching by very young children. In C. Sophian (Ed.), *Origins of cognitive skills.* Hillsdale, NJ: Erlbaum.

DeLoache, J. S., Miller, K. F., & Rosengren, K. S. (1997). The credible shrinking room: Very young children's performance with symbolic and nonsymbolic relations. *Psychological Science, 8,* 308–313.

Dennis, M., Guger, S., Roncadin, C., Barnes, M., & Schachar, R. (2001). Attentional-inhibitory control and social-behavioral regulation after childhood closed head injury: Do biological, developmental, and recovery variables predict outcome? *Journal of the International Neuropsychological Society, 7,* 683–692.

Dennis, W., & Dennis, M. G. (1940). The effects of cradling practices upon the onset of walking in Hopi children. *Journal of Genetic Psychology, 56,* 77–86.

de Onis, M., & Yip, R. (1996). The WHO growth chart: Historical considerations and current scientific issues. In M. Porrini & P. Walter (Eds.), *Nutrition in pregnancy and growth.* Basel, Switzerland: Karger. (Bibliotheca Nutritio et Dieta, 53, 74–89).

DeRosier, M. E., Kupersmidt, J. B., & Patterson, C. J. (1995). Children's academic and behavioral adjustment as a function of the chronicity and proximity of peer rejection. *Child Development, 65,* 1799–1813.

Deschesnes, M., Fines, P., & Demers, S. (2006). Are tattooing and body piercing indicators of risk-taking behaviours among high school students? *Journal of Adolescence, 29,* 379–393.

Desrochers, S., Ricard, M., Decarie, T. G., & Allard, L. (1994). Developmental synchrony between social referencing and Piagetian sensorimotor causality. *Infant Behavior and Development, 17,* 303–309.

deVilliers, J. G., & deVilliers, P. A. (1985). The acquisition of English. In D. I. Slobin (Ed.), *The cross-linguistic study of language acquisition.* Hillsdale, NJ: Erlbaum.

Devellis, R. F. (1991). *Scale development: Theory and application.* Newbury Park, CA: Sage.

DeWolff, M. S., & van IJzendoorn, M. H. (1997). Sensitivity and attachment: A meta-analysis on parental antecedents of infant attachment. *Child Development, 68,* 571–591.

Diamond, A., Prevor, M. B., Callender, G., & Druin, D. P. (1997). Prefontal cortex deficits in children treated early and continuously for PKU. *Monographs of the Society for Research in Child Development, 62* (4, Serial No. 252).

Diamond, M., Johnson, R., Young, D., & Singh, S. (1983). Age-related morphologic differences in the rat cerebral cortex and hippocampus: Male-female; right-left. *Experimental Neurology, 81,* 1–13.

DiBlasio, F. A., & Benda, B. B. (1990). Adolescent sexual behavior: Multivariate analysis of a social learning model. *Journal of Adolescent Research, 5,* 449–466.

Diekelmann, S. (2010). The memory function of sleep. *Nature Reviews Neuroscience, 2,* 114–126.

Dielman, T., Schulenberg, J., Leech, S., & Shope, J. T. (1992, March). Reduction of susceptibility to peer pressure and alcohol use/misuse through a school-based prevention program. Paper presented at the meeting of the Society for Research on Adolescence, Washington, DC.

Diem-Wille, G. (2011). *The early years of life. Psychoanalytical development theory according to Freud, Klein, and Bion.* London: Karnac Books.

Dietitians of Canada, Canadian Paediatric Society, The College of Family Physicians of Canada, & Community Health Nurses of Canada. (2010).

Promoting optimal monitoring of child growth in Canada: Using the new World Health Organization growth charts. *Paediatric Child Health, 15*, 77–79.

Dietrich, K. N. (2000). Environmental neurotoxicants and psychological development. In K. O. Yeates & M. D. Ris (Eds.), *Pediatric neuro-psychology: Research, theory, and practice. The science and practice of neuropsychology: A Guilford series* (pp. 206–234). New York: The Guilford Press.

DiPietro, J. A., Hilton, S. C., Hawkins, M., Costigan, K. A., & Pressman, E. K. (2002). Maternal stress and affect influence fetal neuro-behavioral development. *Developmental Psychology, 38*, 659–668.

DiPietro, J. A., Hodgson, D. M., Costigan, K. A., & Hilton, S. C. (1996). Fetal neurobehavioral development. *Child Development, 67*, 2553–2567.

DiPietro, J. A., Hodgson, D. M., Costigan, K. A., & Johnson, T. R. B. (1996). Fetal antecedents of infant temperament. *Child Development, 67*, 2568–2583.

Dishion, T. J. (1990). The family ecology of boys' peer relations in middle childhood. *Child Development, 61*, 874–892.

Dockrell, J., & McShane, J. (1993). *Children's learning difficulties: A cognitive approach.* Cambridge, MA: Blackwell Publishers.

Dodge, K. A., Bates, J. E., & Pettit, G. S. (1990). Mechanisms in the cycle of violence. *Science, 250*, 1678–1683.

Dodge, K. A., & Crick, N. R. (1990). Social information-processing bases of aggressive behavior in children. *Personality and Social Psychology Bulletin, 16*, 8–22.

Doja, A., & Roberts, W. (2006). Immunizations and autism: A review of the literature. *Canadian Journal of Neurological Sciences, 33*, 341–346.

Donnerstein, E., Slaby, R. G., & Eron, L. D. (1994). The mass media and youth aggression. In L. D. Eron, J. H. Gentry, & P. Schlegel (Eds.), *Reason to hope: A psychosocial perspective on violence and youth* (pp. 219–250). Washington, DC: American Psychological Association.

Downey, G., Lebolt, A., Rincon, C., & Freitas, A. L. (1998). Rejection sensitivity and children's interpersonal difficulties. *Child Development, 69*, 1074–1091.

Downs, A. C. & Fuller, M. J. (1991). Recollections of spermarche: An exploratory investigation. *Current Psychology, 10*, 93–102. doi:10.1007/BF02686783

Doyle, A. B., Markiewicz, D., Brendgen, M., Lieberman, M., & Voss, K. (2000). Child attachment security and self-concept: Associations with mother and father attachment style and marital quality. *Merrill-Palmer Quarterly, 46*, 514–436.

Drabman, R. S., & Thomas, M. H. (1976). Does watching violence on television cause apathy? *Pediatrics, 52*, 329–331.

Dryburgh, H. (2000). Teenage pregnancy. *Health Reports, 12*, 9–19.

Dryfoos, J. G. (1990). *Adolescents at risk: Prevalence and prevention.* New York: Oxford University Press.

Dubas, J., Dubas, J. J. S., Heijkoop, M., & Aken, M. (2009). A preliminary investigation of parent-progeny olfactory recognition and parental investment. *Human Nature, 20*, 80–92.

Dubicka, B., Hadley, S., & Roberts, C. (2006). Suicidal behaviour in youths with depression treated with new-generation antidepressants: Meta-analysis. *British Journal of Psychiatry, 189*, 393–398.

DuBois, D. L., & Hirsch, B. J. (1990). School and neighborhood friendship patterns of blacks and whites in early adolescence. *Child Development, 61*, 524–536.

Dubow, E. F., Edwards, S., & Ippolito, M. F. (1997). Life stressors, neighborhood disadvantage, and resources: A focus on inner-city children's adjustment. *Journal of Clinical Child Psychology, 26*, 130–144.

Dubow, E. F., & Miller, L. S. (1996). Television violence viewing and aggressive behavior. In T. M. MacBeth (Ed.), *Tuning into young viewers* (pp. 117–147). Thousand Oaks, CA: Sage.

Dumas, J. E., LaFreniere, P. J., & Serketich, W. J. (1995). "Balance of power": A transactional analysis of control in mother-child dyads involving socially competent, aggressive, and anxious children. *Journal of Abnormal Psychology, 104*, 104–113.

Dunham, P. J., Dunham, F., & Curwin, A. (1993). Joint-attentional states and lexical acquisition at 18 months. *Developmental Psychology, 29*, 827–831.

Dunn, J., & Kendrick, C. (1981). Social behavior of young siblings in the family context: Differences between same-sex and different-sex dyads. *Child Development, 52*, 1265–1273.

Dunn, J., & Plomin, R. (1990). *Separate lives: Why siblings are so different.* New York: Basic Books.

Dunn, J., Slomkowski, C., & Beardsall, L. (1994). Sibling relationships from the preschool period through middle childhood and early adolescence. *Developmental Psychology, 30*, 315–324.

Dunne, R. G., Asher, K. N., & Rivara, F. P. (1992). Behavior and parental expectations of child pedestrians. *Pediatrics, 89*, 486–490.

Durik, A., Hyde, J. S., & Clark, R. (2000). Sequelae of Cesarean and vaginal deliveries: Psychosocial outcomes for mothers and infants. *Developmental Psychology, 36*, 251–260.

Dysart-Gale, D. (2010). Social justice and social determinants of health: Lesbian, gay, bisexual, transgendered, intersexed, and queer youth in Canada. *Journal of Child and Adolescent Psychiatric Nursing, 23*, 23–28.

Eacott, M. J. (1999). Memory for the events of early childhood. *Current Directions in Psychological Science, 8*, 46–49.

Earle Fox, K. (2004). Are they really neglected? A look at worker perceptions of neglect through the eyes of a national data system. *First Peoples Child & Family Review, 1*, 73–82.

Early Years Study Reference Group. (1999). *Early years study final report.* Toronto: Ontario Children's Secretariat.

Easterbrook, M. A., Kisilevsky, B. S., Hains, S., & Muir, D. (1999). Faceness or complexity: Evidence from newborn visual tracking of facelike stimuli. *Infant Behavior and Development, 22*, 17–35.

Easterbrook, M. A., Kisilevsky, B. S., Muir, D., & Laplante, D. P. (1999). Newborns discriminate schematic faces from scrambled faces. *Canadian Journal of Experimental Psychology, 53*, 231–241.

Eaton, W. O., Chipperfield, J. G., & Singbeil, C. E. (1989). Birth order and activity level in children. *Developmental Psychology, 25*, 668–672.

Eaton, W. O., & Yu, A. P. (1986). Are sex differences in child motor activity level a function of sex differences in maturational status? *Child Development, 60*, 1005–1011.

Eberhardt, J. L. (2005). Imaging Race. *American Psychologist, 60*, 181–190. doi:10.1037/0003-066X.60.2.181

Eccles, J. S., & Harold, R. D. (1991). Gender differences in sport involvement: Applying the Eccles' expectancy-value model. *Journal of Applied Sports Psychology, 3*, 7–35.

Eccles, J. S., Jacobs, J. E., & Harold, R. D. (1990). Gender role stereotypes, expectancy effects, and parents' socialization of gender differences. *Journal of Social Issues, 46*, 183–201.

Edelbrock, C., Rende, R., Plomin, R., & Thompson, L. A. (1995). A twin study of competence and problem behavior in childhood and early adolescence. *Journal of Child Psychology and Psychiatry, 36*, 775–785.

Edin, F., Macoveanu, J., Olesen, P., Tegner, J., & Klingberg, T. (2007). Stronger synaptic connectivity as a mechanism behind development of working memory-related brain activity during childhood. *Journal of Cognitive Neuroscience, 19*, 750–760.

Edwards, C. A. (1994). Leadership in groups of school-age girls. *Developmental Psychology, 30*, 920–927.

Egan, S. K., Monson, T. C., & Perry, D. G. (1998). Social-cognitive influences on change in aggression over time. *Developmental Psychology, 34*, 996–1006.

Egan, S. K., & Perry, D. G. (1998). Does low self-regard invite victimization? *Developmental Psychology, 34*, 299–309.

Eisenberg, N. (1988). The development of prosocial and aggressive behavior. In M. H. Bornstein & M. E. Lamb (Eds.), *Developmental psychology: An advanced textbook* (2nd ed.). Hillsdale, NJ: Erlbaum.

Eisenberg, N., Fabes, R. A., Schaller, M., Carlo, G., & Miller, P. A. (1991). The relations of parental characteristics and practices to children's vicarious emotional responding. *Child Development, 62*, 1393–1408.

Eisenberg, N., & Shell, R. (1986). Prosocial moral judgment and behavior in children: The mediating role of cost. *Personality and Social Psychology Bulletin, 12*, 426–433.

Eisenberg, N., Shepard, S. A., Fabes, R. A., Murphy, B. C., & Guthrie, I. K. (1998). Shyness and children's emotionality, regulation, and coping: Contemporaneous, longitudinal, and across-context relations. *Child Development, 69*, 767–790.

Eisenberg, N., Valiente, C., Morris, A. S., Fabes, R. A., Cumberland, A., Reiser, M., . . . Losoya, S. (2003). Longitudinal relations among parental emotional expressivity, children's regulation, and quality of socioemotional functioning. *Developmental Psychology, 39*, 3–19.

Eizenman, D. R., & Bertenthal, B. I. (1998). Infants' perception of object unity in translating and rotating displays. *Developmental Psychology, 34*, 426–434.

Elicker, J., Englund, M., & Sroufe, L. A. (1992). Predicting peer competence and peer relationships in childhood from early parent-child relationships. In R. D. Parke & G. W. Ladd (Eds.), *Family-peer relationships: Modes of linkage.* Hillsdale, NJ: Erlbaum.

Elkind, D. (1978). *The child's reality: Three developmental themes.* Hillsdale, NJ: Erlbaum.

Elkind, D., & Bowen, R. (1979). Imaginary audience behavior in children and adolescents. *Developmental Psychology, 15*, 38–44.

Elliott, C. D. (2010, June 28). Sweet and salty: Nutritional content and analysis of baby and toddler foods. *Journal of Public Health (Advance Access).* doi:10.1093/pubmed/fdq037

Ellis, W. K., & Rusch, F. R. (1991). Supported employment: Current practices and future directions. In J. L. Matson & J. A. Mulick (Eds.), *Handbook of mental retardation* (2nd ed.). New York: Pergamon Press.

Elmer-DeWitt, P. (1994, January 17). The genetic revolution. *Time*, pp. 46–53.

Enns, J. T. (1990). Relations between components of visual attention. In J. T. Enns (Ed.), *The development of attention.* Amsterdam: North Holland.

Epstein, L. H., & Cluss, P. A. (1986). Behavioral genetics of childhood obesity. *Behavior Therapy, 17*, 324–334.

Epstein, L. H., Valoski, A. M., Vara, L. S., McCurley, J., Wisniewski, L., Kalarchian, M. A., . . . Shrager, L. R. (1995). Effects of decreasing sedentary behavior and increasing activity on weight change in obese children. *Health Psychology, 14,* 109–108.

Erel, O., & Burman, B. (1995). Interrelatedness of marital relations and parent-child relations: A meta-analytic review. *Psychological Bulletin, 118,* 108–132.

Erel, O., Margolin, G., & John, R. S. (1998). Observed sibling interaction: Links with the marital and the mother-child relationship. *Developmental Psychology, 34,* 288–298.

Erikson, E. H. (1968). *Identity: Youth and crisis.* New York: Norton.

Erikson, E. (2000). *The Erik Erikson Reader.* New York: W. W. Norton & Co.

Erturan, S., & Jansen, B. (2015). An investigation of boys' and girls' emotional experience of math, their math performance, and the relation between these variables. *European Journal of Psychology of Education, 30,* 421–435.

Espy, K. A., Kaufmann, P. M., & Glisky, M. L. (1999). Neuropsychological function in toddlers exposed to cocaine in utero: A preliminary study. *Developmental Neuropsychology, 15,* 447–460.

Evans, A. D., & Lee, K. (2013). Emergence of lying in very young children. *Developmental Psychology, Jan (First Posting).* doi:10.1037/10031409

Fabricius, W. V., & Luecken, L. J. (2007). Postdivorce living arrangements, parent conflict, and long-term physical health correlates for children of divorce. *Journal of Family Psychology, 21,* 195–205.

Fadel, H. E. (2012). Developments in stem cell research and therapeutic cloning: Islamic ethical positions, a review. *Bioethics, 26,* 128–135.

Fagot, B. I. (1985). Changes in thinking about early sex role development. *Developmental Review, 5,* 83–98.

Fakunmoju, S. B. (2009). Substantiation and adverse appeal outcomes: Content analysis and testing of Drake's harm/evidence model. *Child Maltreatment, 14,* 53–68.

Falbo, T., & Polit, E. F. (1986). Quantitative review of the only child literature: Research evidence and theory development. *Psychological Bulletin, 100,* 176–186.

Farley, C., Haddad, S., & Brown, B. (1996). The effects of a 4-year program promoting bicycle helmet use among children in Quebec. *American Journal of Public Health, 86,* 46–51.

Farquhar, S. E. (2003). *Quality teaching early foundations: Best evidence synthesis.* Ministry of Education, Government of New Zealand.

Farver, J. M., & Shin, Y. L. (1997). Social pretend play in Korean- and Anglo-American preschoolers. *Child Development, 68,* 544–556.

Fatemi, S. H., Cuadra, A. E., El-Fakahany, E. E., Sidwell, R. W., & Thuras, P. (2000). Prenatal viral infection causes alterations in nNOS expression in developing mouse brains. *Neuroreport, 11,* 1493–1496.

Federal, Provincial, and Territorial Advisory Committee on Population Health. (1999). *Statistical Report on the Health of Canadians.* Ottawa: Health Canada.

Federation of Canadian Municipalities. (2002). *Youth violence and youth gangs: Responding to community concerns.* Ottawa: Solicitor General Canada.

Feingold, A. (1993). Cognitive gender differences: A developmental perspective. *Sex Roles, 29,* 91–112.

Feldman, B. (2011). A skin for the imaginal. *The Jung Page.* Retrieved from http://www.cgjungpage.org/index.php?option=com_content&task=view&id=925&Itemid=40

Feldman, S. S., & Wentzel, K. R. (1990). The relationship between parental styles, sons' self-restraint, and peer relations in early adolescence. *Journal of Early Adolescence, 10,* 439–454.

Feldman W., & Beagan, B. L. (1994). Screening for childhood obesity. *The Canadian Guide to Clinical Preventive Health Care Section 2—Pediatric Preventive Care.* Ottawa: Health Canada. Retrieved from www.hc-sc.gc.ca/hppb/healthcare/pdf/clinical_preventive/s2c30e.pdf

Fell, K. (2000). *Curriculum conversations: A Victorian early childhood curriculum?* A report on the Curriculum Working Party Document titled *Beliefs and Understandings.* Australian Early Childhood Association. Retrieved from www.dhs.vic.gov.au/earlychildhoodmatters/docs/conference_papers/session4fell.pdf

Feltey, K. M., Ainslie, J. J., & Geib, A. (1991). Sexual coercion attitudes among high school students: The influence of gender and rape education. *Youth and Society, 23,* 229–250.

Fenson, L., Dale, P. S., Reznick, J. S. Bates, E., Thal, D. J., & Pethick, S. J. (1994). Variability in early communicative development. *Monographs of the Society for Research in Child Development, 59*(5), 1–173.

Ferguson, C. J., & Savage, J. (2012). Have recent studies addressed methodological issues raised by five decades of television violence research? A critical review. *Aggression and Violent Behavior, 17,* 129–139.

Fergusson, D. M., Horwood, L. J., & Shannon, F. T. (1987). Breastfeeding and subsequent social adjustment in six- to eight-year-old children. *Journal of Child Psychology and Psychiatry and Allied Disciplines, 28,* 379–386.

Field, T. M. (1990). *Infancy.* Cambridge, MA: Harvard University Press.

Field, T. M., & Widmayer, S. M. (1982). Motherhood. In B. J. Wolman (Ed.), *Handbook of developmental psychology.* Englewood Cliffs, NJ: Prentice Hall.

Fields, R. (1992). *Drugs and alcohol in perspective.* Dubuque, IA: William C. Brown.

Fincham, F. (1998). Child development and marital relations. *Child Development, 69,* 543–574.

Finn-Stevenson, M., Desimone, L., & Chung. A. (1998). Linking child care and support services with the school: Pilot evaluation of the School of the 21st Century. *Children and Youth Services Review, 20,* 177–205.

First Nations Child and Family Caring Society of Canada. (n.d.). Joint declaration of support for Jordan's Principle to resolving jurisdictional disputes affecting services to First Nations children. Retrieved from www.fncfcs.com/jordans-principle

First Nations Child and Family Caring Society of Canada. (2005a). *Wen:de The Journey Continues.* Ottawa: First Nations Child & Family Caring Society of Canada.

First Nations Child and Family Caring Society of Canada. (2005b). *Wen:de We Are Coming to the Light of the Day.* Ottawa: First Nations Child & Family Caring Society of Canada.

First Nations Child and Family Caring Society of Canada. (2010). Canadian Human Rights Tribunal on First Nations Child Welfare Update: July 2010. Ottawa: NFCFCSC. Retrieved from www.fncfcs.com/sites/default/files/news/Human-Rights-Tribunal-Brief-July2010.pdf

Fischer, M., Barkley, R. A., Fletcher, K. E., & Smallish, L. (1993). The adolescent outcome of hyperactive children: Predictors of psychiatric, academic, social, and emotional adjustment. *Journal of the American Academy of Child and Adolescent Psychiatry, 32,* 324–332.

Fischhoff, B., & Quadrel, M. J. (1995). Adolescent alcohol decisions. In G. M. Boyd, J. Howard, & R. A. Zucker (Eds.), *Alcohol problems among adolescents: Current directions in prevention research.* Hillsdale, NJ: Erlbaum.

Fisher, C. (1996). Structural limits on verb mapping: The role of analogy in children's interpretations of sentences. *Cognitive Psychology, 31,* 41–81.

Fisher, W. A., & Black, A. (2007). Contraception in Canada: A review of method choices, characteristics, adherence and approaches to counselling. *Canadian Medical Association Journal, 176,* 953–961.

Fitzgerald, J. (1987). Research on revision in writing. *Review of Educational Research, 57,* 481–506.

Flavell, J. H. (1985). *Cognitive development* (2nd ed.). Englewood Cliffs, NJ: Prentice Hall.

Fluke, J. (2009). Allegory of the cave: On the theme of substantiation. *Child Maltreatment, 14,* 69–72.

Fonagy, P., & Target, M. (2005). Commentary: Bridging the transmission gap: An end to an important mystery of attachment research? *Attachment & Human Development, 7,* 333–343.

Fong, B. F., Buis, A. J. E., Savelsbergh, G. J. P., & de Vries, J. I. P. (2005). Influence of breech presentation on the development of fetal arm posture. *Early Human Development, 81,* 519–527.

Fonzi, A., Schneider, B. H., Tani, F., & Tomada, G. (1997). Predicting children's friendship status from their dynamic interaction in structured situations of potential conflict. *Child Development, 68,* 496–506.

Forbes, E. E., & Dahl. R. E. (2010). Pubertal development and behavior: Hormonal activation of social and motivational tendencies. *Brain and Cognition, 72,* 66–72.

Ford, J. (2007). *Antidepressants and the critics: Cure-alls or unnatural poisons?* Broomall, PA: Mason Crest.

Foreyt, J. P., & Goodrick, G. K. (1995). Obesity. In R. T. Ammerman & M. Hersen (Eds.), *Handbook of child behavior therapy in the psychiatric setting.* New York: Wiley.

Formiga, C., & Linhares, M. (2011). Motor development curve from 0 to 12 months in infants born preterm. *Acta Paediatrica, 100,* 379–384.

Foster, E. M., & Watkins, S. (2010). The value of reanalysis: TV viewing and attention problems. *Child Development, 81,* 368–375.

Foster, S. H. (1986). Learning discourse topic management in the preschool years. *Journal of Child Language, 13,* 231–250.

Fox, N. A. (1991). If it's not left, it's right. *American Psychologist, 46,* 863–872.

Fox, N. A., Kimmerly, N. L., & Schafer, W. D. (1991). Attachment to mother/attachment to father: A meta-analysis. *Child Development, 62,* 210–225.

Fox, N. A., Nichols, K. E., Henderson, H. A., Rubin, K., Schmidt, L., Hamer, D., . . . Pine, D. S. (2005). Evidence for a gene-environment interaction in predicting behavioral inhibition in middle childhood. *Psychological Science, 16,* 921–926.

Foy, J. G., & Mann, V. (2003). Home literacy environment and phonological awareness in preschool children: Differential effects for rhyme and phoneme awareness. *Applied Psycholinguistics, 24,* 59–88.

Frankenberger, K. D. (2004). Adolescent egocentrism, risk perceptions, and sensation seeking among smoking and nonsmoking youth. *Journal of Adolescent Research, 19,* 576–590.

French, D. C. (1988). Heterogeneity of peer-rejected boys: Aggressive and nonaggressive subtypes. *Child Development, 53,* 976–985.

Fried, P. A., O'Connell, C. M., & Watkinson, B. (1992). 60- and 72-month follow-up of children prenatally exposed to marijuana, cigarettes, and alcohol: Cognitive and language assessment. *Journal of Developmental & Behavioral Pediatrics, 13,* 383–391.

Fried, P. A., & Watkinson, B. (1990). 36- and 48-month neurobehavioral follow-up of children prenatally exposed to marijuana, cigarettes, and alcohol. *Journal of Developmental & Behavioral Pediatrics, 11,* 49–58.

Friedman, J. M., & Polifka, J. E. (1996). *The effects of drugs on the fetus and nursing infant: A handbook for health care professionals.* Baltimore, MD: Johns Hopkins University Press.

Frye, D. (1993). Causes and precursors of children's theories of mind. In D. F. Hay & A. Angold (Eds.), *Precursors and causes in development and psychopathology.* Chichester, UK: Wiley.

Frye, D., & Zelazo, P. D. (2003). The development of young children's action control and awareness. In J. Roessler & N. Eilan (Eds.), *Agency and self-awareness: Issues in philosophy and psychology* (pp. 244–262). Oxford, UK: Oxford University Press.

Fuchs, D., Compton, D. L., Fuchs, L. S., Bryant, J., & Davis, G. N. (2008). Making "secondary intervention" work in a three-tier responsiveness-to-intervention model: Findings from the first-grade longitudinal reading study of the National Research Center on Learning Disabilities. *Read Write, 21,* 413–436.

Fuchs, D., Mock, D., Morgan, P. L., & Young, C. L. (2003). Responsiveness-to-intervention: Definitions, evidence, and implications for the learning disabilities construct. *Learning Disabilities Research and Practice, 18,* 157–171.

Fulford, J., Vadeyar, S. H., Dodampahala, S. H., Ong, S., Moore, R. J., Baker, P. N., . . . Gowland, P. (2004). Fetal brain activity and hemodynamic response to a vibroacoustic stimulus. *Human Brain Mapping, 22,* 116–121.

Fuller, T., & Nieto, M. (2009). Substantiation and maltreatment rereporting: A propensity score analysis. *Child Maltreatment, 14,* 27–37.

Funk, J. B. (2005). Children's exposure to violent video games and desensitization to violence. *Child and Adolescent Psychiatric Clinics of North America, 14,* 387–404.

Furman, L. M. (2008). Attention-deficit hyperactivity disorder (ADHD): Does new research support old concepts? *Journal of Child Neurology, 23,* 775–784.

Furstenberg, F. F. (1993). How families manage risk and opportunity in dangerous neighbourhoods. In W. J. Wilson (Ed.), *Sociology and the public agenda.* Newbury Park, CA: Sage.

Furstenberg, F. F., Brooks-Gunn, J., & Morgan, S. P. (1987). *Adolescent mothers and their children in later life.* Cambridge, UK: Cambridge University Press.

Furstenburg, F. F., & Teitler, J. O. (1994). Reconsidering the effects of marital disruption: What happens to children of divorce in early adulthood? *Journal of Family Issues, 15,* 173–190.

Gable, S., & Isabella, R. A. (1992). Maternal contributions to infant regulation of arousal. *Infant Behavior and Development, 15,* 95–107.

Gadalla, T. M. (2009). Eating disorders in men: A community-based study. *International Journal of Men's Health, 8,* 72–81.

Gaddis, A., & Brooks-Gunn, J. (1985). The male experience of pubertal change. *Journal of Youth and Adolescence, 14,* 61–69.

Gagne, L. G. (2003). Parental work, child-care use and young children's cognitive outcomes. Vancouver: British Columbia Inter-university Research Data Centre, University of British Columbia. Retrieved from www.statcan.ca/english/rdc/pdf/summary_gagne.pdf

Galambos, N. L., & Maggs, J. L. (1991). Out-of-school care of young adolescents and self-reported behavior. *Developmental Psychology, 27,* 644–655.

Galen, B. R., & Underwood, M. K. (1997). A developmental investigation of social aggression among children. *Developmental Psychology, 33,* 589–600.

Galler, J. R., & Ramsey, F. (1989). A follow-up study of the influence of early malnutrition on development: Behavior at home and at school. *Journal of the American Academy of Child and Adolescent Psychiatry, 28,* 254–261.

Galler, J. R., Ramsey, F., & Forde, V. (1986). A follow-up study of the influence of early malnutrition on subsequent development: IV. Intellectual performance during adolescence. *Nutrition and Behavior, 3,* 211–222.

Garai, J. E., & Scheinfeld, A. (1968). Sex differences in mental and behavioral traits. *Genetic Psychology Monographs, 77,* 169–299.

Garber, J., Robinson, N. S., & Valentiner, D. (1997). The relation between parenting and adolescent depression: Self-worth as a mediator. *Journal of Adolescent Research, 12,* 12–33.

Garcia, J. R., Reiber, C., Massey, S. G., & Merriwether, A M. (2012). Sexual hookup culture: A review. *Review of General Psychology, 16,* 161–176.

Gardner, H. (1983). *Frames of mind: The theory of multiple intelligences.* New York: Basic Books.

Gardner, H. (1993). *Multiple intelligences: The theory in practice.* New York: Basic Books.

Gardner, H. (1995). Reflections on multiple intelligences: Myths and messages. *Phi Delta Kappan, 77,* 200–203, 206–209.

Garland, A. F., & Zigler, E. (1993). Adolescent suicide prevention: Current research and social policy implications. *American Psychologist, 48,* 169–182.

Garner, R., & Kohen, D. (2008). *Changes in the prevalence of asthma among Canadian children,* Statistics Canada Health Reports (Catalogue no. 82-003-X). Retrieved from www.statcan.gc.ca/pub/82-003-x/2008002/article/10551-eng.pdf

Garner, P. W., Jones, D. C., & Palmer, D. J. (1994). Social cognitive correlates of preschool children's sibling caregiving behavior. *Developmental Psychology, 30,* 905–911.

Garrity, C. B., Baris, M. A., & Porter, W. (2000). Bully proofing your child. A parent's guide. Longmont, CO: Sopris West.

Garvey, C., & Berninger, G. (1981). Timing and turn taking in children's conversations. *Discourse Processes, 4,* 27–59.

Gauderman, W. J., Avol, E., Gilliland, F., Vora, H., Thomas, D., Berhane, K., . . . Peters, J. (2004). The effect of air pollution on lung development from 10 to 18 years of age. *New England Journal of Medicine, 351,* 1057–1067.

Gauthier, Y. (2003). Infant mental health as we enter the third millennium: Can we prevent aggression? *Infant Mental Health Journal, 24,* 296–308.

Gavin, L. A., & Furman, W. (1996). Adolescent girls' relationships with mothers and best friends. *Child Development, 67,* 375–386.

Ge, X., Conger, R. D., Cadoret, R. J., Neiderhiser, J. M., & Stewart, M. A. (1996). The developmental interface between nature and nurture: A mutual influence model of child antisocial behavior and parent behaviors. *Developmental Psychology, 32,* 574–589.

Ge, X., Conger, R. D., & Elder, G. H. (1996). Coming of age too early: Pubertal influences on girls' vulnerability to psychological distress. *Child Development, 67,* 3386–3400.

Geisel, T. (1960). *Green eggs and ham, by Dr. Seuss.* New York: Beginner.

Gelman, R., & Meck, E. (1986). The notion of principle: The case of counting. In J. Hiebert (Ed.), *Conceptual and procedural knowledge: The case of mathematics.* Hillside, NJ: Erlbaum.

Gelman, S. A., & Gottfried, G. M. (1996). Children's casual explanations of animate and inanimate motion. *Child Development, 67,* 1970–1987.

Gelman, S. A., & Markman, E. M. (1985). Implicit contrast in adjectives vs. nouns: Implications for word-learning in preschoolers. *Journal of Child Language, 12,* 125–143.

Genome Canada. (2010). Did you know? Retrieved from www.genomecanada.ca/en/info/DNA/know.aspx

George, C., Kaplan, N., & Main, M. (1985). The adult attachment interview (Unpublished manuscript). University of California, Department of Psychology, Berkeley, CA.

Ghazi, S. R., & Ullah, K. (2015). Concrete operational stage of Piaget's cognitive development theory: An implication in learning general science. *Gomal University Journal of Research, 31,* 78–89.

Ghim, H. (1990). Evidence for perceptual organization in infants: Perception of subjective contours by young infants. *Infant Behavior and Development, 13,* 221–248.

Gibbs, J. C., Clark, P. M., Joseph, J. A., Green, J. L., Goodrick, T. S., & Makowski, D. (1986). Relations between moral judgment, moral courage, and field independence. *Child Development, 57,* 185–193.

Giberson, P. K., & Weinberg, J. (1992). Fetal alcohol syndrome and functioning of the immune system. *Alcohol Health and Research World, 16,* 29–38.

Gibson, E. J., Riccio, G., Schmuckler, M. A., Stoffregen, T. A., Rosenberg, D., & Taormina, J. (1987). Detection of the traversability of surfaces by crawling and walking infants. *Journal of Experimental Psychology: Human Perception & Performance, 13,* 533–544.

Gibson, E. J., & Walk, R. D. (1960). The "visual cliff." *Scientific American, 202,* 64–71.

Gibson, E. J., & Walker, A. S. (1984). Development of knowledge of visual-tactual affordances of substance. *Child Development, 55,* 453–460.

Gilliam, F. D., & Bales, S. N. (2001). Strategic frame analysis: Reframing America's youth. *Social Policy Report, 15*(3). Ann Arbor, MI: Society for Research in Child Development.

Gilligan, C. (1982). *In a different voice: Psychological theory and women's development.* Cambridge, MA: Harvard University Press.

Gilligan, C., & Attanucci, J. (1988). Two moral orientations: Gender differences and similarities. *Merrill-Palmer Quarterly, 34,* 223–237.

Gisla, G. B. (2014). Sexual self-control as essential to psychosocial maturity in adolescent males. A dissertation presented to the faculty of The Institute for the Psychological Sciences in partial fulfillment of the requirement for the degree of Doctor of Psychology. UMI Number: 3629908.

Gleason, P. M. (1995). Participation in the National School Lunch Program and School Breakfast Program. *American Journal of Clinical Nutrition, 61,* 213S–220S.

Glick, P. C. (1989). The family life cycle and social change. *Family Relations, 38,* 123–129.

Glick, P. C., & Lin, S. (1986). Recent changes in divorce and remarriage. *Journal of Marriage and the Family, 48,* 737–747.

Golden, N. H., Katzman, D. K., Kreipe, R. E., Stevens, S. L., Sawyer, S. M., Rees, J., . . . Rome, E. S. (2003). Eating disorders in adolescents: Position paper of the Society for Adolescent Medicine. *Journal of Adolescent Health, 33,* 496–503.

Goldenberg, R. L., & Klerman, L. V. (1995). Adolescent pregnancy—another look. *New England Journal of Medicine, 332,* 1161–1162.

Goldman, S. R. (1989). Strategy instruction in mathematics. *Learning Disability Quarterly, 12,* 43–55.

Goldsmith, H. H., Buss, K. A., & Lemery, K. S. (1997). Toddler and childhood temperament: Expanded content, stronger genetic evidence, new evidence for the importance of environment. *Developmental Psychology, 33,* 891–905.

Goldsmith, H. H., & Harman, C. (1994). Temperament and attachment: Individuals and relationships. *Current Directions in Psychological Science, 3,* 53–57.

Goldsmith, H. H., Lemery, K. S., Buss, K. A., & Campos, J. J. (1999). Genetic analyses of focal aspects of infant temperament. *Developmental Psychology, 35,* 972–985.

Goldwater, P. (2011). A perspective on SIDS pathogenesis. The hypotheses: plausibility and evidence. *BMC Medicine, 9,* 64–76.

Golinkoff, R. M. (1993). When is communication a "meeting of minds"? *Journal of Child Language, 20,* 199–207.

Golombok, S., & Fivush, R. (1994). *Gender development.* Cambridge, UK: Cambridge University Press.

Golombok, S., & Tasker, F. (1996). Do parents influence the sexual orientation of their children? Findings from a longitudinal study of lesbian families. *Developmental Psychology, 32,* 3–11.

Golombok, S., Perry, B., Burston, A., Murray, C., Mooney-Somers, J., Stevens, M., & Golding, J. (2003). Children with lesbian parents: A community study. *Developmental Psychology, 39,* 20–33.

Goncu, A., & Abel, B. (2011). The child's conception of the world: A 20th-century classic of child psychology, 2nd edition. *Infant & Child Development, 20,* 246–248.

Good, M., Willoughby, T., & Busseri, M. A. (2011). Stability and change in adolescent spirituality/ religiosity: A person-centered approach. *Developmental Psychology, 47,* 538–550.

Good, T. L., & Brophy, J. E. (1994). *Looking in classrooms* (6th ed.). New York: HarperCollins.

Goodman, G. S., Emery, R. E., & Haugaard, J. J. (1998). Developmental psychology and law: Divorce, child maltreatment, foster care, and adoption. In W. Damon (Ed.), *Handbook of child psychology* (Vol. 4). New York: Wiley.

Goodnow, J. J. (1992). *Parental belief systems: The psychological consequences for children.* Hillsdale, NJ: Erlbaum.

Goodwyn, S. W., & Acredolo, L. P. (1993). Symbolic gesture versus word: Is there a modality advantage for onset of symbol use? *Child Development, 64,* 688–701.

Gordon, C. P. (1996). Adolescent decision making: A broadly based theory and its application to the prevention of early pregnancy. *Adolescence, 31,* 561–584.

Gorey, K. M. (2001). Early childhood education: A meta-analytic affirmation of the short- and long-term benefits of educational opportunity. *School Psychology Quarterly, 16,* 9–30.

Goswami, U., & Bryant, P. (1990). *Phonological skills and learning to read.* London: Erlbaum.

Gottesman, I. I. (1993). Origins of schizophrenia: Past as prologue. In R. Plomin & G. E. McClearn (Eds.), *Nature, nurture, and psychology.* Washington, DC: American Psychological Association.

Gottlieb, G. (2000). Environmental and behavioral influences on gene activity. *Current Directions in Psychological Science, 9,* 93–97.

Gottlieb, L. N., & Mendelson, M. J. (1990). Parental support and firstborn girls' adaptation to the birth of a sibling. *Journal of Applied Developmental Psychology, 11,* 29–48.

Gottman, J. M. (1986). The world of coordinated play: Same- and cross-sex friendships in children. In J. M. Gottman & J. G. Parker (Eds.), *Conversations of friends.* New York: Cambridge University Press.

Gottman, J. M., Katz, L. F., & Hooven, C. (1996). Parental meta-emotion philosophy and the emotional life of families: Theoretical models and preliminary data. *Journal of Family Psychology, 10,* 243–268.

Graber, J. A., Brooks-Gunn, J., Paikoff, R. L., & Warren, M. P. (1994). Prediction of eating problems: An 8-year study of adolescent girls. *Developmental Psychology, 30,* 823–834.

Graber, J. A., Brooks-Gunn, J., & Warren, W. P. (1995). The antecedents of menarcheal age: Heredity, family environment, and stressful life events. *Child Development, 66,* 346–359.

Graesser, A. C., Singer, M., & Trabasso, T. (1994). Constructing inferences during narrative text comprehension. *Psychological Review, 101,* 371–395.

Graham, M. J., Larsen, U., & Xu, X. (1999). Secular trend in age at menarche in China: A case study of two rural counties in Anhui province. *Journal of Biosocial Science, 31,* 257–267.

Graham, S., Berninger, V. W., Abbott, R. D., Abbott, S. P., & Whitaker, D. (1997). Role of mechanics in composing of elementary school students: A new methodological approach. *Journal of Educational Psychology, 89,* 170–182.

Graham, S., & Juvonen, J. (1998). Self-blame and peer victimization in middle school: An attributional analysis. *Developmental Psychology, 34,* 587–599.

Granrud, C. E. (1986). Binocular vision and spatial perception in 4- and 5-month-old infants. *Journal of Experimental Psychology: Human Perception and Performance, 12,* 36–49.

Greenberg, M. T., & Crnic, K. A. (1988). Longitudinal predictors of developmental status and social interaction in premature and full-term infants at age two. *Child Development, 59*, 554–570.

Greening, L., Stoppelbein, L., Chandler, C. C., & Elkin, T. D. (2005). Predictors of children's and adolescents' risk perception. *Journal of Pediatric Psychology, 30*, 425–435.

Grigorenko, E. L., & Sternberg, R. J. (1998). Dynamic testing. *Psychological Bulletin, 124*, 75–111.

Groen, G. J., & Resnick, L. B. (1977). Can preschool children invent addition algorithms? *Journal of Educational Psychology, 69*, 645–652.

Gross, E. F., & Hardin, C. D. (2007). Implicit and explicit stereotyping of adolescents. *Social Justice Research, 20*, 140–160.

Gross, R. T. (1984). Patterns of maturation: Their effects on behavior and development. In M. D. Levine & P. Satz (Eds.), *Middle childhood: Development and dysfunction*. Baltimore, MD: University Park Press.

Grossmann, K. E., Grossmann, K., & Waters, E. (2005). *Attachment from infancy to adulthood: The major longitudinal studies*. New York: Guilford Publications.

Grovak, M. (1999, February 4). Baby born after spina bifida surgery seems fine. *Journal and Courier*, p. A1.

Grubb, J., Muramoto, O., & Matson, P. (2011). Issues arising during the treatment of Jehovah's Witnesses by in vitro fertilisation. *Human Fertility, 14*, 35–40.

Grusec, J. E. (1991). The socialization of altruism. In M. S. Clark (Ed.), *Prosocial behavior: Review of personality and social psychology* (Vol. 12, pp. 9–33). Thousand Oaks: Sage.

Guajardo, N. R., & Turley-Ames, K. J. (2003). Preschoolers' generation of different types of counterfactual statements and theory of mind understanding. *Cognitive Development, 19*, 53–80.

Guerrini, I., Thomson, A. D., & Gurling, H. D. (2007). The importance of alcohol misuse, malnutrition and genetic susceptibility on brain growth and plasticity. *Neuroscience & Biobehavioral Reviews, 31*, 212–220.

Guillemin, J. (1993). Cesarean birth: Social and political aspects. In B. K. Rothman (Ed.), *Encyclopedia of childbearing*. Phoenix, AZ: Oryx Press.

Gümmer, R., Giel, K. E., Schag, K., Resmark, G., Junne, F. P., Becker, S., Zipfel, S., & Teufel, M. (2015). High levels of physical activity in anorexia nervosa: A systematic review. *European Eating Disorders Review, 23*, 333–344.

Gunter, B. (2014). *Media and the sexualization of childhood*. London: Routledge.

Gusella, J. L., & Freid, P. A. (1984). Effects of maternal social drinking and smoking on offspring at 13 months. *Neurobehavioral Toxicology and Teratology, 6*, 13–17.

Guttmacher, A. F., & Kaiser, I. H. (1986). *Pregnancy, birth, and family planning*. New York: New American Library.

Haden, C. (1998). Reminiscing with different children: Relating maternal stylistic consistency and sibling similarity in talk about the past. *Developmental Psychology, 34*, 99–114.

Hadjistavropoulos, T., & Bieling, P. J. (2000). When reviews attack: Ethics, free speech, and the peer review process. *Canadian Psychology, 41*, 152–159.

Hahn, W. (1987). Cerebral lateralization of function: From infancy through childhood. *Psychological Bulletin, 101*, 376–392.

Haimes, E., Taylor, K., & Turkmendag, I. (2012). Eggs, ethics and exploitation? Investigating women's experiences of an egg sharing scheme. *Sociology of Health & Illness, 34*, 1199–1214.

Haines, C. (2003). Sequencing, co-ordination and rhythm ability in young children. *Child Care, Health, and Development, 29*, 395–409.

Haley, D. W., Weinberg, J., & Grunau, R. E. (2006). Cortisol, contingency learning, and memory in preterm and full-term infants. *Psychoneuroendocrinology, 31*, 108–117.

Hall, D. G., & Graham, S. A. (1999). Lexical form class information guides word-to-object mapping in preschoolers. *Child Development, 70*, 78–91.

Hall, D. G., Waxman, S. R., & Hurwitz, W. R. (1993). How two- and four-year-old children interpret adjectives and count nouns. *Child Development, 64*, 1651–1664.

Hallinan, M. T., & Teixeira, R. A. (1987). Opportunities and constraints: Black-white differences in the formation of interracial friendships. *Child Development, 58*, 1358–1371.

Halpern, C. T., Udry, J. R., Campbell, B., & Suchindran, C. (1999). Effects of body fat on weight concerns, dating, and sexual activity: A longitudinal analysis of black and white adolescent girls. *Developmental Psychology, 35*, 721–736.

Halpern, D. F. (1986). *Sex differences in cognitive abilities*. Hillsdale, NJ: Erlbaum.

Halpern, L. F., MacLean, W. E., & Baumeister, A. A. (1995). Infant sleep-wake characteristics: Relation to neurological status and the prediction of developmental outcome. *Developmental Review, 15*, 255–291.

Hamer, D. H., Hu, S., Magnuson, V. L., & Hu, N. (1993). A linkage between DNA markers on the X chromosome and male sexual orientation. *Science, 261*, 321–327.

Hamlin, J. K., Mahajan, N., Liberman, Z., & Wynn, K. (2013). Not like me = bad: Infants prefer those who harm dissimilar others. *Psychological Science, 24*, 589–594.

Hamlin, J. K., Wynn, K., & Bloom, P. (2007). Social evaluation by preverbal infants. *Nature, 450* (22 Nov.), 557–559. doi:10.1038/nature06288

Hamm, J. V. (2000). Do birds of a feather flock together? The variable bases for African American, Asian American, and European American adolescents' selection of similar friends. *Developmental Psychology, 36*, 209–219.

Hamm, J. V., Brown, B. B., & Heck, D. J. (2005). Bridging the ethnic divide: Student and school characteristics in African American, Asian-descent, Latino, and White adolescents' cross-ethnic friend nominations. *Journal of Research on Adolescence, 15*, 21–46.

Hammill, D. D. (1990). On defining learning disabilities: An emerging consensus. *Journal of Learning Disabilities, 23*, 74–84.

Hampshire, A., Highfield, R. R., Parkin, B. L., & Owen, A. M. (2012). Fractionating human intelligence. *Neuron, 76*, 1225–1237.

Hane, A. A., & Fox, N. A. (2006). Ordinary variations in maternal caregiving influence human infants' stress reactivity. *Psychological Science, 17*, 550–556.

Harley, K., & Reese, E. (1999). Origins of autobiographical memory. *Developmental Psychology, 35*, 1338–1348.

Harris, B., Lovett, L., Newcombe, R. G., Read, G. F., Walker, R., & Riad-Fahmy, D. (1994). Maternity blues and major endocrine changes: Cardiff puerperal mood and hormone study II. *British Medical Journal, 308*, 949–953.

Harris, L. J. (1983). Laterality of function in the infant: Historical and contemporary trends in theory and research. In G. Young, S. J. Segalowitz, C. M. Corter, & S. E. Trehub (Eds.), *Manual specialization and the developing brain.* New York: Academic Press.

Harris, M. A., Prior, J. C., & Koehoorn, M. (2008). Age at menarche in the Canadian population: Secular trends and relationship to adulthood BMI. *Journal of Adolescent Health, 43*, 548–554.

Harris, P. L., Brown, E., Marriot, C., Whithall, S., & Harmer, S. (1991). Monsters, ghosts, and witches: Testing the limits of the fantasy-reality distinction in young children. *British Journal of Developmental Psychology, 9*, 105–123.

Harris, P. L., & Kavanaugh, R. D. (1993). Young children's understanding of pretense. *Monographs of the Society for Research in Child Development, 58*(1, Serial No. 231).

Harris, S. J., Janssen, P. A., Saxell, L., Carty, E. A., MacRae, G. W., & Petersen, K. L. (2012). Effect of a collaborative interdisciplinary maternity care program on perinatal outcomes. *Canadian Medical Association Journal, 184*, 1885–1892.

Harrist, A. W., Zaia, A. F., Bates, J. E., Dodge, K. A., & Pettit, G. S. (1997). Subtypes of social withdrawal in early childhood: Sociometric status and social-cognitive differences across four years. *Child Development, 68*, 278–294.

Hart, C. H., Charlesworth, R., Burts, D. C., & DeWolf, M. (1993, March). The relationship of attendance in developmentally appropriate or inappropriate kindergarten classrooms to first-grade behavior. Paper presented at the biennial meeting of the Society for Research in Child Development, New Orleans.

Hart, C. H., Nelson, D. A., Robinson, C. C., Olsen, S. F., & McNeilly-Choque, M. K. (1998). Overt and relational aggression in Russian nursery-school-age children: Parenting style and marital linkages. *Developmental Psychology, 34*, 687–697.

Harter, S. (1985). *Manual for the self-perception profile for children.* Denver, CO: University of Denver.

Harter, S. (1988). Developmental processes in the construction of the self. In T. D. Yawkey & J. E. Johnson (Eds.), *Integrative processes and socialization: Early to middle childhood.* Hillsdale, NJ: Erlbaum.

Harter, S. (1990). Self and identity development. In S. S. Feldman & G. R. Elliott (Eds.), *At the threshold: The developing adolescent.* Cambridge, MA: Harvard University Press.

Harter, S. (1999). *The construction of the self: A developmental perspective.* New York: Guilford Press.

Harter, S., & Pike, R. (1984). The pictorial scale of perceived competence and social acceptance for young children. *Child Development, 55*, 1969–1982.

Harter, S., Whitesell, N. R., & Kowalski, P. S. (1992). Individual differences in the effects of educational transitions on young adolescents' perceptions of competence and motivational orientation. *American Educational Research Journal, 29*, 777–807.

Hartigan Jr., John. (2008). Is race still socially constructed? The recent controversy over race and medical genetics. *Science as Culture, 17*, 163–193. doi:10.1080/09505430802062943

Hartup, W. W. (1983). Peer relations. In R. H. Mussen (Ed.), *Handbook of child psychology* (Vol. 4). New York: Wiley.

Hartup, W. W. (1992a). Peer relations in early and middle childhood. In V. B. Van Hasselt and M. Hersen (Eds.), *Handbook of social development: A lifespan perspective.* New York: Plenum.

Hartup, W. W. (1992b). Friendships and their developmental significance. In H. McGurk (Ed.), *Contemporary issues in childhood social development.* London: Routledge.

Hartup, W. W., & Stevens, N. (1999). Friendships and adaptation across the life span. *Current Directions in Psychological Science, 8*, 76–79.

Harvey, W., & Reid, G. (1997). Motor performance of children with attention-deficit hyperactivity disorder: A preliminary investigation. *Adapted Physical Activity Quarterly, 14*, 189–202.

Haselager, G. J. T., Hartup, W. W., van Lieshout, C. F. M., & Riksen-Walraven, J. M. A. (1998). Similarities between friends and nonfriends in middle childhood. *Child Development, 69,* 1198–1208.

Hastings, P. D., & Rubin, K. H. (1999). Predicting mothers' beliefs about preschool-aged children's social behavior: Evidence for maternal attitudes moderating child effects. *Child Development, 70,* 722–741.

Hatcher, P. J., & Hulme, C. (1999). Phonemes, rhymes, and intelligence as predictors of children's responsiveness to remedial reading instruction: Evidence from a longitudinal study. *Journal of Experimental Child Psychology, 72,* 130–153.

Haviland, J. M., & Lelwica, M. (1987). The induced affect response: 10-week-old infants' responses to three emotion expressions. *Developmental Psychology, 23,* 97–104.

Hawkins, D. L., Pepler, D. J., & Craig, W. M. (2001). Naturalistic observations of peer interventions in bullying. *Social Development, 10,* 512–527.

Hay, D. F., Castle, J., & Davies, L. (2000). Toddlers' use of force against familiar peers: A precursor of serious aggression? *Child Development, 71,* 457–467.

Health Canada. (1998). *For the safety of children and youth.* Ottawa: Population and Public Health Branch, Health Canada.

Health Canada. (1999). Asthma prevalence. Measuring up. *A health surveillance update on Canadian children and youth.* Retrieved from www.hc-sc.gc.ca/pphb-dgspsp/publicat/meas-haut/mu_r_e.html

Health Canada. (2001a). *The Canadian incidence study of reported abuse and neglect.* Ottawa: Population and Public Health Branch, Health Canada.

Health Canada. (2002). How preschoolers approach eating. Canada's food guide to healthy eating focus on preschoolers—Background for educators and communicators. Retrieved from www.hc-sc.gc.ca/hpfb-dgpsa/onpp-bppn/food_guide_preschoolers_e.html#1

Health Canada. (2004a, February 20). Scientific advisory panel on selective serotonin reuptake inhibitors (SSRI) and serotonin/norepinephrine reuptake inhibitors (SNRI). Record of Proceedings (Teleconference).

Health Canada. (2004b, April 7). Minister Pettigrew announces a ban on baby walkers (press release). Retrieved from www.hc-sc.gc.ca/english/media/releases/2004/2004_15.htm

Health Canada. (2004c). Exclusive breastfeeding duration. Ottawa: Her Majesty the Queen in Right of Canada. Retrieved from www.hc-sc.gc.ca/fn-an/pubs/infant-nourrisson/nut_infant_nourrisson_term_3-eng.php

Health Canada. (2004d). Vitamin D supplementation for breastfed infants. Ottawa: Her Majesty the Queen in Right of Canada. Retrieved from www.phac-aspc.gc.ca/dca-dea/prenatal/nutrition-eng.php

Health Canada. (2005). Aspartame. Retrieved from www.hc-sc.gc.ca/fn-an/securit/addit/sweeten-edulcor/aspartame-eng.php

Heaman, M. I., & Chalmers, K. (2005). Prevalence and correlates of smoking during pregnancy: A comparison of aboriginal and non-aboriginal women in Manitoba. *Birth: Issues in Perinatal Care, 32,* 299–305.

Hearold, S. (1986). A synthesis of 1,043 effects of television on social behavior. In G. Comstock (Ed.), *Public communications and behavior* (Vol. 1, pp. 65–133). New York: Academic Press.

Hedges, L. V., & Nowell, A. (1995). Sex differences in mental test scores, variability, and numbers of high-scoring individuals. *Science, 269,* 41–45.

Heins, T., & Ritchie, K. (1985). Beating sneaky poo: Ideas for faecal soiling. Canberra: Child and Adolescent Unit, Mental Health Branch, A.C.T. Health Authority.

Hellige, J. B. (1994). *Hemispheric asymmetry: What's right and what's left.* Cambridge, MA: Harvard University Press.

Helms, J. E., Jernigan, M., & Mascher, J. (2005). The meaning of race in psychology and how to change it: A methodological perspective. *American Psychologist, 60,* 27–36. Retrieved from http://dx.doi.org/10.1037/0003-066X.60.1.27

Hemphill, L., & Tivnan, T. (2008). The importance of early vocabulary for literacy achievement in high-poverty schools. *Journal of Education for Students Placed at Risk, 13,* 426–451.

Herman-Giddens, M. E. (2007). The decline in the age of menarche in the United States: Should we be concerned? *Journal of Adolescent Health, 40,* 201–203.

Hernandez, D. J. (1997). Child development and the social demography of childhood. *Child Development, 68,* 149–169.

Herrnstein, R. J., & Murray, C. (1994). *The bell curve: Intelligence and class structure in American life.* New York: Free Press.

Hershberger, S. L., & D'Augelli, A. R. (1995). The impact of victimization on the mental health and suicidality of lesbian, gay, and bisexual youths. *Developmental Psychology, 31,* 65–74.

Hess, U., Philippot, P., & Blairy, S. (1998). Facial reactions to emotional facial expressions: Affect or cognition? *Cognition and Emotion, 12,* 509–531.

Heth, C. D., Cornell, E. H., & Flood, T. L. (2002). Self-ratings of sense of direction and route reversal performance. *Applied Cognitive Psychology, 16,* 309–324.

Hetherington, E. M. (1988). Family relations six years after divorce. In K. Pasley & M. Ihinger-Tallman (Eds.), *Remarriage and stepparenting: Current research and theory.* New York: Guilford Press.

Hetherington, E. M. (1989). Coping with family transitions: Winners, losers and survivors. *Child Development, 60,* 1–14.

Hetherington, E. M. (1993). An overview of the Virginia Longitudinal Study of Divorce and Remarriage with a focus on early adolescence. *Journal of Family Psychology, 7,* 39–56.

Hetherington, E. M. (1999). Social capital and the development of youth from nondivorced, divorced, and remarried families. In W. A. Collins & B. Laursen (Eds.), *Minnesota symposia on child psychology.* Mahwah, NJ: Erlbaum.

Hetherington, E. M., Cox, M., & Cox, R. (1982). Effects of divorce on parents and children. In M. E. Lamb (Ed.), *Nontraditional families.* Hillsdale, NJ: Erlbaum.

Hetherington, S. E. (1990). A controlled study of the effect of prepared childbirth classes on obstetric outcomes. *Birth, 17,* 86–90.

Higgins, A. (1991). The Just Community approach to moral education: Evolution of the idea and recent findings. In W. M. Kurtines & J. L. Gewirtz (Eds.), *Handbook of moral behavior and development* (Vol. 3). Hillsdale, NJ: Erlbaum.

Hillier, L., Hewitt, K. L., & Morrongiello, B. A. (1992). Infant's perception of illusions in sound localisation: Reaching for sounds in the dark. *Journal of Experimental Child Psychology, 53,* 159–179.

Hines, A. R., & Paulson, S. E. (2007). Parents' and teachers' perceptions of adolescent storm and stress: Relations with parenting and teaching styles. *Family Therapy, 34,* 63–80.

Hirsch, M., Lunenfeld, B., Modan, M., Ovadia, J., & Shemesh, J. (1985). Spermarche—The age of onset of sperm emission. *Journal of Adolescent Health Care, 6,* 35–39.

Hirshberg, L. M., & Svejda, M. (1990). When infants look to their parents: I. Infants' social referencing of mothers compared to fathers. *Child Development, 61,* 1175–1186.

Hiscock, M., & Kinsbourne, M. (1987). Specialization of the cerebral hemispheres: Implications for learning. *Journal of Learning Disabilities, 20,* 130–143.

Ho, C. S., & Bryant, P. (1997). Phonological skills are important in learning to read Chinese. *Developmental Psychology, 33,* 946–951.

Hodges, E. V. E., Boivin, M., Vitaro, F., & Bukowski, W. M. (1999). The power of friendship: Protection against an escalating cycle of peer victimization. *Developmental Psychology, 33,* 1032–1039.

Hodges, E. V. E., Malone, M. J., & Perry, D. G. (1997). Individual risk and social risk as interacting determinants of victimization in the peer group. *Developmental Psychology, 33,* 1032–1039.

Hoff, T. L. (1992). Psychology in Canada one hundred years ago: James Mark Baldwin at the University of Toronto. *Canadian Psychology, 33,* 683–694.

Hoff-Ginnsberg, E. (1990). Maternal speech and the child's development of syntax: A further look. *Journal of Child Language, 17,* 85–99.

Hoffman, M. L. (1988). Moral development. In M. H. Bornstein & M. E. Lamb (Eds.), *Developmental psychology: An advanced textbook* (2nd ed.). Hillsdale, NJ: Erlbaum.

Hoffman, M. L. (1994). Discipline and internalization. *Developmental Psychology, 30,* 26–28.

Hogan, A. M., de Haan, M., Datta, A., & Kirkham, F. J. (2006). Hypoxia: An acute, intermittent and chronic challenge to cognitive development. *Developmental Science, 9,* 335–337.

Hoge, D. D., Smit, E. K., & Hanson, S. L. (1990). School experiences predicting changes in self-esteem of sixth- and seventh-grade students. *Journal of Educational Psychology, 82,* 117–127.

Hogge, W. A. (1990). Teratology. In I. R. Merkatz & J. E. Thompson (Eds.), *New perspectives on prenatal care.* New York: Elsevier.

Holden, G. W., & Miller, P. C. (1999). Enduring and different: A meta-analysis of the similarity in parents' child rearing. *Psychological Bulletin, 125,* 223–254.

Holder, M. D., Coleman, B., & Wallace J. M. (2010). Spirituality, religiousness, and happiness and children aged 8-12 years. *Journal of Happiness Studies, 11,* 131–150.

Holland, J. L. (1985). *Making vocational choices: A theory of vocational personalities and work environments* (2nd ed.). Englewood Cliffs, NJ: Prentice-Hall.

Holland, J. L. (1987). Current status of Holland's theory of careers: Another perspective. *Career Development Quarterly, 36,* 24–30.

Holland, J. L. (1996). Exploring careers with a typology: What we have learned and some new directions. *American Psychologist, 51,* 397–406.

Holst, M., Eswaran, H., Lowery, C., Murphy, P., Norton, J., & Preissl, H. (2005). Development of auditory evoked fields in human fetuses and newborns: A longitudinal MEG study. *Clinical Neurophysiology, 116,* 1949–1955.

Holtkamp, K., Konrad, K., Müller, B., Heussen, N., Herpertz, S., Herpertz-Dahlmann, B., & Hebebrand, J. (2004). Overweight and obesity in children with attention-deficit/-hyperactivity disorder. *International Journal of Obesity, 28,* 685–689.

Hoover, D. W., & Milich, R. (1994). Effects of sugar ingestion expectancies on mother-child interactions. *Journal of Abnormal Child Psychology, 22,* 501–515.

Horn, O., Paradis, G., Potvin, L., Macaulay, A. C., & Desrosiers, S. (2001). Correlates and predictors of adiposity among Mohawk children. *Preventive Medicine, 33*, 274–281.

Howard, M., & McCabe, J. B. (1990). Helping teenagers postpone sexual involvement. *Family Planning Perspectives, 22*, 21–26.

Howe, M. L., & Courage, M. L. (1997). The emergence and early development of autobiographical memory. *Psychological Review, 104*, 499–523.

Howe, N., Petrakos, H., & Rinaldi, C. M. (1998). "All the sheeps are dead. He murdered them": Sibling pretense, negotiation, internal state language, and relationship quality. *Child Development, 69*, 182–191.

Howe, N., & Ross, H. S. (1990). Socialization perspective taking and the sibling relationship. *Developmental Psychology, 26*, 160–165.

Howes, C., & Matheson, C. C. (1992). Sequences in the development of competent play with peers: Social and social pretend play. *Developmental Psychology, 28*, 961–974.

Howes, C., Unger, O., & Seidner, L. B. (1990). Social pretend play in toddlers: Parallels with social play and with solitary pretend. *Child Development, 60*, 77–84.

Hudson, J. (1988). Children's memory for atypical actions in script-based stories: Evidence for a disruption effect. *Journal of Experimental Child Psychology, 46*, 159–173.

Huesmann, L. R. (1986). Psychological processes promoting the relation between exposure to media violence and aggressive behavior by the viewer. *Journal of Social Issues, 42*, 125–139.

Huesmann, L. R., Moise-Titus, J., Podolski, C., & Eron, L. D. (2003). Longitudinal relations between children's exposure to TV violence and their aggressive and violent behavior in young adulthood: 1977–1992. *Developmental Psychology, 39*, 201–221.

Huichang, C., Jing, H., Xinyin, C., & Lili, Q. (2003). Mothers' attitudes to their child in family free-play and intelligence task-oriented play. *Acta Psychological Sinica, 35*, 84–88.

Hulecki, L. R., & Small, S. A. (2011). Behavioral bone-conduction thresholds for infants with normal hearing. *Journal of the American Academy of Audiology, 22*, 81–92.

Hunsley, J. (2007). Training psychologists for evidence-based practice. *Canadian Psychology, 48*, 32–42.

Hunt, C. E., & Hauck, F. R. (2006). Sudden infant death syndrome. *Canadian Medical Association Journal, 174*, 1861–1869.

Huston, A. C. (1983). Sex typing. In P. H. Mussen (Ed.), *Handbook of child psychology* (Vol. 4). New York: John Wiley.

Huston, A. C., Donnerstein, E., Fairchild, H., Feshbach, N. D., Katz, P. A., Murray, J. P., . . . Zuckerman, D. (1992). *Big world, small screen: The role of television in American society.* Lincoln: University of Nebraska Press.

Huston, A. C., & Wright, J. C. (1998). Mass media and children's development. In W. Damon (Ed.), *Handbook of child psychology* (Vol. 4). New York: Wiley.

Hutchins, E. (1983). Understanding Micronesian navigation. In D. A. Gentner & A. Stevens (Eds.), *Mental models.* Hillsdale, NJ: Erlbaum.

Hyde, J. S., Fennema, E., & Lamon, S. J. (1990). Gender differences in mathematics performance: A meta-analysis. *Psychological Bulletin, 107*, 139–155.

Hyde, J. S., & Linn, M. C. (1988). Gender differences in verbal ability. *Psychological Bulletin, 104*, 53–69.

Hymel, S., Rubin, K. H., Rowden, L., & LeMare, L. (1990). Children's peer relationships: Longitudinal prediction of internalizing and externalizing problems from middle to late childhood. *Child Development, 61*, 2004–2021.

Inal, S., & Yidiz, S. (2012). The effect of baby massage on mental-motor development of healthy full term baby. *HealthMed, 6*, 578–584.

Inhelder, B., & Piaget, J. (1958). *The growth of logical thinking from childhood to adolescence.* New York: Basic Books.

Institute of Infections and Immunity. (2009). Canadian microbiome initiative. Ottawa: Canadian Institutes of Health Research. Retrieved from www.cihr-irsc. gc.ca/e/documents/iii_overview_of_cmi_e.pdf

Institute of Medicine. (1990). *Nutrition during pregnancy.* Washington, DC: National Academy Press.

Isaacs, E. B., Lucas, A., Wood, S. J., Chong, W. K., Johnson, C. L., Marshall, C., . . . Gadian, D. G. (2000). Hippocampal volume and everyday memory in children of very low birth weight. *Paediatric Research, 47*(6), 713–720.

Isley, S. L., O'Neil, R., Clatfelter, D., & Parke, R. D. (1999). Parent and child expressed affect and children's social competence: Modeling direct and indirect pathways. *Developmental Psychology, 35*, 547–560.

Israel, A. C., Guile, C. A., Baker, J. E., & Silverman, W. K. (1994). An evaluation of enhanced self-regulation training in the treatment of childhood obesity. *Journal of Pediatric Psychology, 19*, 737–749.

Ito, J. (2006). Prosocial self-perception in relation to prosocial behavior: Preschool observations of free play. *Japanese Journal of Developmental Psychology, 17*, 241–251.

Iversen, G. E. (1990). Behind schedule: Psychosocial aspects of delayed puberty in the competitive female gymnast. *The Sport Psychologist, 4*, 155–167.

Izard, C. E. (1991). *The psychology of emotions.* New York: Plenum Press.

Izard, C. E., Fantauzzo, C. A., Castle, J. M., Haynes, O. M., Rayias, M. F., & Putnam, P. H. (1995).

The ontogeny and significance of infants' facial expressions in the first 9 months of life. *Developmental Psychology, 31,* 997–1013.

Jacobs, E. V., White, D. R., Baillargeon, M., & Betsalel-Presser, R. (1995). Peer relations among children attending school-age child-care programs. In K. Covell (Ed.), *Readings in child development: A Canadian perspective* (pp. 209–233). Toronto: Nelson Canada.

Jacobson, J. L., Jacobson, S. W., & Humphrey, H. E. B. (1990). Effects of in utero exposure to polychlorinated biphenyls and relatzed contaminants on cognitive functioning in young children. *The Journal of Pediatrics, 116,* 38–45.

Jaffee, S., & Hyde, J. S. (2000). Gender differences in moral orientation: A meta-analysis. *Psychological Bulletin, 126,* 703–726.

Jakobsen, R. (1997). Stages of progression in noncoital sexual interactions among young adolescents: An application of the Mokken scale analysis. *International Journal of Behavioral Development, 21,* 537–553.

Jakobson, L. S., Frisk, V., & Downie, A. L. S. (2006). Motion-defined form processing in extremely premature children. *Neuropsychologia, 44,* 1777–1786.

Jamieson, J. R. (1995). Visible thought: Deaf children's use of signed and spoken private speech. *Sign Language Studies, 86,* 63–80.

Janzen, L. A., Nanson, J., & Block, G. W. (1995). Neuropsychological evaluation of preschoolers with fetal alcohol syndrome. *Neurotoxicology and Teratology, 17,* 273–279.

Jennings, A., Davies, G. J., Costarelli, V., & Gettman, P. W. (2009). Dietary fiber, fluids and physical activity in relation to constipation symptoms in pre-adolescent children. *Journal of Child Health Care, 13,* 116–127.

Jensen, M. D., Benson, R. C., & Bobak, I. M. (1981). *Maternity care.* St. Louis, MO: C. V. Mosby.

Jiao, S., Ji, G., & Jing, Q. (1996). Cognitive development of Chinese urban only children and children with siblings. *Child Development, 67,* 387–395.

Jiao, Z. (1999, April). Which students keep old friends and which become new friends across school transition? Paper presented at the 1999 meeting of the Society for Research in Child Development, Albuquerque, New Mexico.

Johanson, R. B., Rice, C., Coyle, M., Arthur, J., Anyanwu, L., Ibrahim, J., . . . O'Brien, P. M. S. (1993). A randomized prospective study comparing the new vacuum extractor policy with forceps delivery. *British Journal of Obstetrics and Gynecology, 100,* 524–530.

Johnson, M. H. (1998). The neural basis of cognitive development. In W. Damon (Ed.), *Handbook of child psychology* (Vol. 2). New York: Wiley.

Johnson, S. P., & Aslin, R. N. (1995). Perception of object unity in 2-month-old infants. *Developmental Psychology, 31,* 739–745.

Johnston, M. V. (2004). Clinical disorders of brain plasticity. *Brain and Development, 26,* 73–80.

Johnstone, B., Frame, C. L., & Bouman, D. (1992). Physical attractiveness and athletic and academic ability in controversial-aggressive and rejected-aggressive children. *Journal of Social and Clinical Psychology, 11,* 71–79.

Jones, D., & Christensen, C. A. (1999). Relationship between automaticity in handwriting and students' ability to generate written text. *Journal of Educational Psychology, 91,* 44–49.

Jones, K., & Day, J. D. (1997). Discrimination of two aspects of cognitive-social intelligence from academic intelligence. *Journal of Educational Psychology, 89,* 486–497.

Jones, L., & Kruk, E. (2005). Life in government care: The connection of youth to family. *Child & Youth Care Forum, 34,* 405–421.

Joseph, R. (2000). Fetal brain behavior and cognitive development. *Developmental Review, 20,* 81–98.

Jukic, A. M., Baird, D. D., Weinberg, C. R., McConnaughey, D. R., & Wilcox, A. J. (2013). Length of human pregnancy and contributors to its natural variation. *Human Reproduction, 28,* 2848–2855.

Jusczyk, P. W. (1995). Language acquisition: Speech sounds and phonological development. In J. L. Miller & P. D. Eimas (Eds.), *Handbook of perception and cognition: Vol. 11. Speech, language, and communication.* Orlando, FL: Academic Press.

Jusczyk, P. W., & Aslin, R. N. (1995). Infants' detection of the sound patterns of words in fluent speech. *Cognitive Psychology, 29,* 1–23.

Kagan, J. (1989). Temperamental contributions to social behavior. *American Psychologist, 44,* 668–674.

Kagan, J., Arcus, D., Snidman, N., Feng, W. Y., Hendler, J., & Greene, S. (1994). Reactivity in infants: A cross-national comparison. *Developmental Psychology, 30,* 342–345.

Kagan, J., & Moss, H. A. (1962). *Birth to maturity: A study in psychological development.* New York: John Wiley.

Kagan, J., Snidman, N., & Arcus, D. (1998). Childhood derivatives of high and low reactivity in infancy. *Child Development, 69,* 1483–1493.

Kaijura, H., Cowart, B. J., & Beauchamp, G. K. (1992). Early developmental change in bitter taste responses in human infants. *Developmental Psychobiology, 25,* 375–386.

Kail, R. (1990). *The development of memory in children* (3rd ed.). New York: W. H. Freeman.

Kail, R. (1991). Processing time declines exponentially during childhood and adolescence. *Developmental Psychology, 27,* 259–266.

Kail, R., & Bisanz, J. (1992). The information–processing perspective on cognitive development in childhood and adolescence. In R. J. Sternberg & C. A. Berg (Eds.), *Intellectual development.* New York: Cambridge University Press.

Kail, R., & Salthouse, T. A. (1994). Processing speed as a mental capacity. *Acta Psychologica, 86,* 199–225.

Kail, R. V. (2007). Longitudinal evidence that increases in processing speed and working memory enhance children's reasoning. *Psychological Science, 18,* 312–313.

Kamerman, S. B. (1993). International perspectives on child care policies and programs. *Pediatrics, 91,* 248–252.

Kandel, D. B. (1978). Homophily, selection, and socialization in adolescent friendships. *American Journal of Sociology, 84,* 427–436.

Kann, L., Collins, J. L., Pateman, B. C., Small, M. L., Ross, J. G., & Kolbe, L. J. (1995). The School Health Policies and Programs Study (SHPPS): Rationale for a nationwide status report on school health programs. *Journal of School Health, 65*(8), 291–294.

Kantrowitz, B. (1993, August 2). Murder and mayhem, guns and gangs: A teenage generation grows up dangerous and scared. *Newsweek,* pp. 40–46.

Kaplan, P. S., Goldstein, M. H., Huckeby, E. R., & Cooper, R. P. (1995). Habituation, sensitization, and infants' responses to motherese speech. *Developmental Psychobiology, 28,* 45–57.

Karniol, R. (1989). The role of manual manipulative states in the infant's acquisition of perceived control over objects. *Developmental Review, 9,* 205–233.

Kasatkina, É. P., Samsonova, L. N., Ivakhnenko, V. N., Ibragimova, G. V., Ryabykh, A. V., Naumenko, L. L., & Evdokimova, Y. A. (2006). Gestational hypothyroxinemia and cognitive function in offspring. *Neuroscience and Behavioral Physiology, 36,* 619–624.

Katzmarzyk, P. T., Perusse, L., Rao, D. C., & Bouchard, C. (1999). Familial risk of obesity and central adipose tissue distribution in the general Canadian population. *American Journal of Epidemiology, 149,* 933–942.

Kazdin, A. E. (1990). Childhood depression. *Journal of Child Psychology and Psychiatry and Allied Disciplines, 31,* 121–160.

Keane, S. P., Brown, K. P., & Crenshaw, T. M. (1990). Children's intention-cue detection as a function of maternal social behavior: Pathways to social rejection. *Developmental Psychology, 26,* 1004–1009.

Keller, M., Edelstein, W., Schmid, S., Fang, F., & Fang, G. (1998). Reasoning about responsibilities and obligations in close relationships: A comparison across two cultures. *Developmental Psychology, 34,* 731–741.

Kelley, M. L., Power, T. G., & Wimbush, D. D. (1992). Determinants of disciplinary practices in low-income Black mothers. *Child Development, 63,* 573–582.

Kellman, P. J., & Banks, M. S. (1998). Infant visual perception. In W. Damon (Ed.), *Handbook of child psychology* (Vol. 2). New York: Wiley.

Kellogg, R. (1970). Understanding children's art. In P. Cramer (Ed.), *Readings in developmental psychology today.* Celmar, CA: CRM.

Kern, J. K., West, E. Y., Grannemann, B. D., Greer, T. L., Snell, L. M., Cline, L. L., . . . Trivedi, M. H. (2004). Reductions in stress and depressive symptoms in mothers of substance-exposed infants, participating in a psychosocial program. *Maternal and Child Health Journal, 8,* 127–136.

Kerr, M., Lambert, W. W., & Bem, D. J. (1996). Life course sequelae of childhood shyness in Sweden: Comparison with the United States. *Developmental Psychology, 32,* 1100–1105.

Kershaw, P., Irwin, L., Trafford, K., & Hertzman, C. (2005). *The British Columbia atlas of child development.* Vancouver: Human Early Learning Partnership and Western Geographical Press.

Kessen, W. (1979). The American child and other cultural inventions. *American Psychologist, 34,* 815–820.

Khan, S. A., & Faraone, S. V. (2006). The genetics of ADHD: A literature review of 2005. *Current Psychiatry Reports, 8,* 393–397.

Kidd, C., Palmeri, H., & Aslin, R. (2012). Rational snacking: Young children's decision-making on the marshmallow task is moderated by beliefs about environmental reliability. *Cognition, 126,* 109–114.

Kiernan, K. E. (1992). The impact of family disruption in childhood on transitions made in young adult life. *Population Studies, 46,* 213–234.

Kim, Y. H., & Goetz, E. T. (1994). Context effects on word recognition and reading comprehension of good and poor readers: A test of the interactive compensatory hypothesis. *Reading Research Quarterly, 29,* 178–188.

Kimball, M. M. (1986). Television and sex-role attitudes. In T. M. Williams (Ed.), *The impact of television* (pp. 265–301). New York: Academic Press.

Kimball, M. M. (1989). A new perspective on women's math achievement. *Psychological Bulletin, 105,* 198–214.

Kimura, D. (1999). *Sex and cognition.* Cambridge, MA: The MIT Press.

King, S., & Laplante, D. P. (2005). The effects of prenatal maternal stress on children's cognitive development: Project ice storm. *Stress, 8,* 35–45.

King, V., Elder, G. H., & Whitbeck, L. B. (1997). Religious involvement among rural youth: An ecological and life-course perspective. *Journal of Research on Adolescence, 7,* 431–456.

Kisilevsky, B. S., Hains, S. M. J., Jacquet, A. Y., Granier-Deferre, C., & Lecanuet, J. P. (2004). Maturation of fetal responses to music. *Developmental Science, 7,* 550–559.

Kisilevsky, B. S., & Low, J. A. (1998). Human fetal behavior: 100 years of study. *Developmental Review, 18,* 1–29.

Kitchener, K. S., King, P. M., & DeLuca, S. (2006). Development of reflective judgment in adulthood. In C. Hoare (Ed.), *Handbook of adult development and learning* (pp. 73–98). New York: Oxford University Press.

Klaczynski, P. A., & Narasimham, G. (1998). Development of scientific reasoning biases: Cognitive versus ego-protective explanations. *Developmental Psychology, 34,* 175–187.

Klahr, D., & MacWhinney, B. (1998). Information processing. In W. Damon (Ed.), *Handbook of child psychology* (Vol. 2). New York: Wiley.

Klapper, J. T. (1968). The impact of viewing "aggression": Studies and problems of extrapolation. In O. N. Larsen (Ed.), *Violence and the mass media.* New York: Harper & Row.

Klatzky, R. L. (1980). *Human memory* (2nd ed.). San Francisco: Freeman.

Klein, J. S., & Bisanz, J. (2000). Preschoolers doing arithmetic: The concepts are willing but the working memory is weak. *Canadian Journal of Experimental Psychology, 54,* 105–116.

Klier, C. M. (2006). Mother-infant bonding disorders in patients with postnatal depression: The Postpartum Bonding Questionnaire in clinical practice. *Archives of Women's Mental Health, 9,* 289–291.

Knitzer, J. (2007). Putting knowledge into policy: Toward an infant-toddler policy agenda. *Infant Mental Health Journal, 28,* 237–245.

Kochanska, G. (1991). Socialization and temperament in the development of guilt and conscience. *Child Development, 62,* 1379–1392.

Kochanska, G. (1993). Toward a synthesis of parental socialization and child temperament in early development of conscience. *Child Development, 64,* 325–347.

Kochanska, G. (1995). Children's temperament, mothers' discipline, and security of attachment: Multiple pathways to emerging internalization. *Child Development, 66,* 597–615.

Kochanska, G. (1997). Multiple pathways to conscience for children with different temperaments: From toddlerhood to age 5. *Developmental Psychology, 33,* 228–240.

Kochanska, G., Casey, R. J., & Fukumoto, A. (1995). Toddlers' sensitivity to standard violations. *Child Development, 66,* 643–656.

Kochanska, G., DeVet, K., Goldman, M., Murray, K., & Putnam, S. (1994). Maternal reports of conscience development and temperament in young children. *Child Development, 65,* 852–868.

Kochanska, G., Padavich, D. L., & Koenig, A. L. (1996). Children's narratives about hypothetical moral dilemmas and objective measures of their conscience: Mutual relations and socialization antecedents. *Child Development, 67,* 1420–1436.

Kochanska, G., & Radke-Yarrow, M. (1992). Inhibition in toddlerhood and the dynamics of the child's interaction with an unfamiliar peer at age five. *Child Development, 63,* 325–335.

Kochenderfer, B. J., & Ladd, G. W. (1996). Peer victimization: Cause or consequence of school maladjustment? *Child Development, 67,* 1305–1317.

Kohl, P. L., Johnson-Reid, M., & Drake, B. (2009). Time to leave substantiation behind: Findings from a national probability study. *Child Maltreatment, 14,* 17–26.

Kohlberg, L. A. (1966). A cognitive-developmental analysis of children's sex-role concepts and attitudes. In E. E. Maccoby (Ed.), *The development of sex differences* (pp. 82–172). Stanford, CA: Stanford University Press.

Kohlberg, L. (1969). Stage and sequence: The cognitive-developmental approach to socialization. In D. Goslin (Ed.), *Handbook of socialization theory and research* (pp. 347–480). Chicago: Rand McNally.

Kohlberg, L., & Ullian, D. Z. (1974). Stages in the development of psychosexual concepts and attitudes. In R. C. Friedman, R. M. Richart, & R. L. Van Wiele (Eds.), *Sex differences in behavior.* New York: John Wiley.

Kolb, B. (1989). Brain development, plasticity, and behavior. *American Psychologist, 44,* 1203–1212.

Kolb, B., & Whishaw, I. Q. (1998). Brain plasticity and behavior. *Annual Review of Psychology, 49,* 43–64.

Koplewicz, H. S. (2002). More than moody: Recognizing and treating adolescent depression. *Brown University Child and Adolescent Behavior Letter, 18,* 1–2.

Kopp, C. B. (1982). The antecedents of self-regulation. *Developmental Psychology, 18,* 199–214.

Kopp, C. B. (1987). The growth of self-regulation: Caregivers and children. In N. Eisenberg (Ed.), *Contemporary topics in developmental psychology.* New York: Wiley.

Koren, G. (1993). Cocaine and the human fetus: The concept of teratophilia. *Neurotoxicology and Teratology, 15,* 301–304.

Kotovsky, L., & Baillargeon, R. (1998). The development of calibration-based reasoning about collision events in young infants. *Cognition, 67,* 311–351.

Kovacs, D. M., Parker, J. G., & Hoffman, L. W. (1996). Behavioral, affective, and social correlates of involvement in cross-sex friendship in elementary school. *Child Development, 67,* 2269–2286.

Kowal, A., & Kramer, L. (1997). Children's understanding of parental differential treatment. *Child Development, 68,* 113–126.

Kowalski, R. M. (1992). Nonverbal behaviors and perceptions of sexual intentions: Effects of sexual connotativeness, verbal response, and rape outcome. *Basic and Applied Social Psychology, 13,* 427–445.

Kramer, L., Perozynski, L. A., & Chung, T. (1999). Parental responses to sibling conflict: The effects of development and parent gender. *Child Development, 70,* 1401–1414.

Krispin, O., Sternberg, K. J., & Lamb, M. E. (1992). The dimensions of peer evaluation in Israel: A cross-cultural perspective. *International Journal of Behavioral Development, 15,* 299–314.

Kroger, J., & Green, K. E. (1996). Events associated with identity status change. *Journal of Adolescence, 19,* 477–490.

Krueger, C., Holditch-Davis, D., Quint, S., & DeCasper, A. (2004). Recurring auditory experience in the 28- to 34-week-old fetus. *Infant Behavior & Development, 4,* 537–543.

Kulshreshtha, U., & Kashyap, R. (2004). Psychological correlates of clothing conformity among adolescents. *Journal of the Indian Academy of Applied Psychology, 30,* 21–27.

Kunzig, R. (1998). Climbing through the brain. *Discover, 19,* 60–69.

Kupersmidt, J. B., & Coie, J. D. (1990). Preadolescent peer status, aggression, and school adjustment as predictors of externalizing problems in adolescence. *Child Development, 61,* 1350–1362.

Kuyken, W., Watkins, E., Holden, E., & Cook, W. (2006). Rumination in adolescents at risk for depression. *Journal of Affective Disorders, 96,* 39–47.

Ladd, G. W. (1998). Peer relationships and social competence during early and middle childhood. *Annual Review of Psychology, 50,* 333–359.

Ladd, G. W., & Ladd, B. K. (1998). Parenting behaviors and parent-child relationships: Correlates of peer victimization in kindergarten? *Developmental Psychology, 34,* 1450–1458.

Ladd, G. W., & Le Sieur, K. D. (1995). Parents and children's peer relationships. In M. H. Bornstein (Ed.), *Handbook of parenting: Vol. 4. Applied and practical parenting* (pp. 377–410). Mahwah, NJ: Erlbaum.

Lafrance, J., & Bastien, B. (2007). Here be dragons! Reconciling Indigenous and Western knowledge to improve Aboriginal child welfare. *First Peoples Child & Family Review, 3,* 105–126.

LaFreniere, P., Strayer, F. F., & Gauthier, R. (1984). The emergence of same-sex affiliative preferences among preschool peers: A developmental/ethnological perspective. *Child Development, 55,* 1958–1965.

LaGreca, A. M. (1993). Social skills training with children: Where do we go from here? *Journal of Clinical Child Psychology, 22,* 288–298.

Lamb, M. E. (1999). Nonparental child care: Context, quality, correlated, and consequences. In M. E. Lamb (Ed.), *Parenting and child development in "nontraditional" families.* Mahwah, NJ: Erlbaum.

Lancet. (2010, February 2). Retraction—Ileal-lymphoid-nodular hyperplasia, non-specific colitis, and pervasive developmental disorder in children. doi:10.1016/S0140-6736(10)60175-4

Landhuis, C. E., Poulton, R., Welch, D., & Hancox, R. J. (2007). Results from a prospective longitudinal study: Does childhood television viewing lead to attention problems in adolescence? *Pediatrics, 120,* 532–537.

Langlois, J. H., & Downs, A. C. (1980). Mothers, fathers, and peers as socialization agents of sex-typed play behaviors in young children. *Child Development, 51,* 1237–1247.

Lannegrand-Willems, L., & Bosma, H. A. (2006). Identity development-in-context: The school as an important context for identity development. *Identity, 6,* 85–113.

Lanza, E. (1992). Can bilingual two-year-olds code-switch? *Journal of Child Language, 19,* 633–658.

Larson, R. W. (1997). The emergence of solitude as a constructive domain of experience in early adolescence. *Child Development, 68,* 80–93.

Larson, R. W. (2000). Toward a psychology of positive youth development. *American Psychologist, 55,* 170–183.

Larson, R. W., Raffaelli, M., Richards, M. H., Ham, M., & Jewell, L. (1990). Ecology of depression in late childhood and early adolescence: A profile of daily states and activities. *Journal of Abnormal Psychology, 99,* 92–102.

Laursen, B., & Collins, W. A. (1994). Interpersonal conflict during adolescence. *Psychological Bulletin, 115,* 197–209.

Lazar, I., & Darlington, R. (1982). Lasting effects of early education: A report from the Consortium for Longitudinal Studies. *Monographs of the Society for Research in Child Development, 47*(2–3, Serial No. 195).

Leach, P. (1991). *Your baby and child: From birth to age five* (2nd ed.). New York: Knopf.

Lee, C. M., & Hunsley, J. (2001) Empirically informed consultation to parents concerning the effects of separation and divorce on their children. *Cognitive and Behavioral Practice, 8,* 85–96.

Lefevre, J., Clarke, T., & Stringer, A. P. (2002). Influences of language and parental involvement on the development of counting skills: Comparisons of French- and English-speaking Canadian children. *Early Child Development and Care, 172,* 283–300.

LeGrand, R., Mondloch, C. J., Maurer, D., & Brent, H. P. (2003). Expert face processing requires visual input to the right hemisphere during infancy. *Nature Neuroscience, 6,* 1108–1112.

Lehr, R., & MacMillan, P. (2001). The psychological and emotional impact of divorce: The noncustodial fathers' perspective. *Families in Society, 82*(4), 373–382.

LeMare, L. J., & Rubin, K. H. (1987). Perspective taking and peer interaction: Structural and developmental analyses. *Child Development, 58,* 306–315.

Lemery, K. S., Goldsmith, H. H., Klinnert, M. D., & Mrazek, D. A. (1999). Developmental models of infant and childhood temperament. *Developmental Psychology, 35,* 189–204.

Lengua, L. J., Sandler, I. N., West, S. G., Wolchik, S. A., & Curran, P. J. (1999). Emotionality and self-regulation, threat appraisal, and coping in children of divorce. *Development & Psychopathology, 11,* 15–37.

Leonard, L. B., Weismer, S. E., Miller, C. A., Francis, D. J., Tomblin, J. B., & Kail, R. V. (2007). Speed of processing, working memory, and language impairment in children. *Journal of Speech, Language, and Hearing Research, 50,* 408–428.

Lepper, M. R., & Gurtner, J. (1989). Children and computers. *American Psychologist, 44,* 170–178.

Levin, K. (1999). Babbling in infants with cerebral palsy. *Clinical Linguistics and Phonetics, 13,* 249–267.

Lerner, J. V., Phelps, E., Forman, Y., & Bowers, E. P. (2009). Positive youth development. In R. M. Lerner & L. Steinberg (Eds.), *Individual bases of adolescent development* (pp. 524–558). Vol. 1 in *Handbook of adolescent psychology* (3rd ed.). Hoboken, NJ: Wiley.

Lerner, R. M. (2015). Eliminating genetic reductionism from developmental science. *Research in Human Development, 12,* 178–188.

Levine, L. E. (1983). Mine: Self-definition in 2-year-old boys. *Developmental Psychology, 19,* 544–549.

Levine, S. C., Vasilyeva, M., Lourenco, S., Newcombe, N., & Huttenlocher, J. (2005). Socioeconomic status modifies the sex difference in spatial skill. *Psychological Science, 16,* 841–845.

Levitt, A. G., & Utman, J. A. (1992). From babbling towards the sound systems of English and French: A longitudinal two-case study. *Journal of Child Language, 19,* 19–49.

Levitt, M. J., Guacci-Franco, N., & Levitt, J. L. (1993). Convoys of social support in childhood and early adolescence: Structure and function. *Developmental Psychology, 29,* 811–818.

Levy, G. D., & Boston, M. B. (1994). Preschoolers' recall of own-sex and other-sex gender scripts. *Journal of Genetic Psychology, 155,* 367–371.

Levy, G. D., Taylor, M. G., & Gelman, S. A. (1995). Traditional and evaluative aspects of flexibility in gender roles, social conventions, moral rules, and physical laws. *Child Development, 66,* 515–531.

Levy, J. (1976). A review of evidence for a genetic component in the determination of handedness. *Behavior Genetics, 6,* 429–453.

Lewinsohn, P. M., & Gotlib, I. H. (1995). Behavioral therapy and treatment of depression. In E. E. Beckham & W. R. Leber (Eds.), *Handbook of depression* (2nd ed.). New York: Guilford Press.

Lewis, M. (1987). Social development in infancy and early childhood. In J. D. Osofsky (Ed.), *Handbook of infant development.* New York: Wiley.

Lewis, M. (1992). *Shame: The exposed self.* New York: Free Press.

Lewis, M., Alessandri, S. M., & Sullivan, M. W. (1992). Differences in shame and pride as a function of children's gender and task difficulty. *Child Development, 63,* 630–638.

Lewis, M., & Brooks-Gunn, J. (1979). *Social cognition and the acquisition of self.* New York: Plenum.

Lewis, M., Ramsay, D. S., & Kawakami, K. (1993). Differences between Japanese infants and Caucasian American infants in behavioral and cortisol response to inoculation. *Child Development, 64,* 1722–1731.

Lewis, M. D., Koroshegyi, C., Douglas, L., & Kampe, K. (1997). Age-specific associations between emotional responses to separation and cognitive performance in infancy. *Developmental Psychology, 33,* 32–42.

Lewis, M. D., & Stieben, J. (2004). Emotion regulation in the brain: Conceptual issues and directions for developmental research. *Child Development, 75,* 371–376.

Li, D., Willinger, M., Petitti, D. B., Odouli, R., Liu, L., & Hoffman, H. J. (2006). Use of a dummy (pacifier) during sleep and risk of sudden infant death syndrome (SIDS): Population based case-control study. *British Medical Journal, 332,* 18–21.

Li, Z. H., Connolly, J., Jiang, D., Pepler, D., & Craig, W. (2010). Adolescent romantic relationships in China and Canada: A cross-national comparison. *International Journal of Behavioral Development, 34,* 113–120.

Libal, J. (2007). *Antidepressants and suicide: When treatment kills.* Broomall, PA: Mason Crest.

Liben, L. S., & Signorella, M. L. (1993). Gender-schematic processing in children: The role of initial interpretations of stimuli. *Developmental Psychology, 29,* 141–149.

Lie, S. O. (1990). Children in the Norwegian health care system. *Pediatrics, 86,* 1048–1052.

Lieberman, M., Doyle, A., & Markiewicz, D. (1999). Developmental patterns in security of attachment to mother and father in late childhood and early adolescence: Associations with peer relations. *Child Development, 70,* 202–213.

Liebert, R. M., & Sprafkin, J. (1988). *The early window: Effects of television on children and youth.* New York: Pergamon.

Lillard, A. (1999). Developing a cultural theory of mind: The CIAO approach. *Current Directions in Psychological Science, 8,* 57–61.

Lin, C. C., & Fu, V. R. (1990). A comparison of childrearing practices among Chinese, immigrant Chinese, and Caucasian-American parents. *Child Development, 61,* 429–433.

Lipsitt, L. P. (1990). Learning and memory in infants. *Merrill-Palmer Quarterly, 36,* 53–66.

Lloyd, B., & Howe, N. (2003). Solitary play and convergent and divergent thinking skills in preschool children. *Early Childhood Research Quarterly, 18,* 22–41.

Lloyd-Fox, S., Blasi, A., & Elwell, C. E. (2010). Illuminating the developing brain: The past, present and future of functional near infrared spectroscopy. *Neuroscience and Biobehavioral Reviews, 34,* 269–284.

Lobel, T. E., Nov-Krispin, N., Schiller, D., Lobel, O., & Feldman, A. (2004). Gender discriminatory behavior during adolescence and young adulthood: A developmental analysis. *Journal of Youth and Adolescence, 33,* 535–546.

Loebstein, R., & Koren, G. (1997). Pregnancy outcome and neurodevelopment of children exposed in utero to psychoactive drugs: The Motherisk experience. *Journal of Psychiatry and Neuroscience, 22,* 192–196.

Long, S., Harris, S., Eldridge, B. J., & Galea, M. (2012). Gross motor development is delayed following early cardiac surgery. *Cardiology in the Young, 2,* 574–582.

Loovis, E. M., & Butterfield, S. A. (2003). Relationship of hand length to catching performance by children in kindergarten to Grade 2. *Perceptual and Motor Skills, 96,* 1194–1196.

Looy, H., & Wood, J. R. (2006). Attitudes toward invertegrates: Are educational "bug banquets" effective? *The Journal of Environmental Education, 37,* 37–48.

Lopez, A. B., Huynh, V. W., & Fuligni, A. J. (2011). A longitudinal study of religious identity and participation during adolescence. *Child Development, 82,* 1297–1309.

Lord, S. E., Eccles, J. S., & McCarthy, K. A. (1994). Surviving the junior high transition: Family processes and self-perception as protective and risk factors. *Journal of Early Adolescence, 14,* 162–199.

Losch, H., & Dammann, O. (2004). Impact of motor skills on cognitive test results in very-low-birthweight children. *Journal of Child Neurology, 19,* 318–322.

Loveland, K. A. (1987a). Behavior of young children with Down syndrome before the mirror: Exploration. *Child Development, 58,* 768–778.

Loveland, K. A. (1987b). Behavior of young children with Down syndrome before the mirror: Finding things reflected. *Child Development, 58,* 928–936.

Lovett, S. B., & Pillow, B. H. (1996). Development of the ability to distinguish between comprehension and memory: Evidence from goal-state evaluation tasks. *Journal of Educational Psychology, 88,* 546–562.

Lozoff, B., Wolf, A. W., & Davis, N. S. (1985). Sleep problems seen in pediatric practice. *Pediatrics, 75,* 477–483.

Ludemann, P. M. (1991). Generalized discrimination of positive facial expressions by seven- and ten-month-old infants. *Child Development, 62,* 55–67.

Ludemann, P. M., & Nelson, C. A. (1988). Categorical representation of facial expressions by 7-month-old infants. *Developmental Psychology, 24,* 492–501.

Luecke-Aleksa, D., Anderson, D. R., Collins, P. A., & Schmitt, K. L. (1995). Gender constancy and television viewing. *Developmental Psychology, 31,* 773–780.

Luna, B., Padmanabhan, A., & O'Hearn, K. (2010). What has fMRI told us about the development of cognitive control through adolescence? *Brain and Cognition, 72,* 101–113.

Lutz, S. E., & Ruble, D. N. (1995). Children and gender prejudice: Context, motivation, and the development of gender conceptions. In R. Vasta (Ed.), *Annals of child development: A research annual* (Vol. 10). London: Jessica Kingsley.

Lyon, G. R. (1996). Learning disabilities. In E. J. Mash & R. A. Barkley (Eds.), *Child psychopathology.* New York: Guilford.

Lyons-Ruth, K., Dutra, L., Schuder, M. R., & Bianchi, I. (2006). From infant attachment disorganization to adult dissociation: Relational adaptations or traumatic experiences? *Psychiatric Clinics of North America, 29,* 63–86.

Lytton, H. (2000). Toward a model of family-environmental and child-biological influences on development. *Developmental Review, 20,* 150–179.

Lytton, H., & Romney, D. M. (1991). Parents' differential socialization of boys and girls: A meta-analysis. *Psychological Bulletin, 109,* 267–296.

Maccoby, E. E. (1988). Gender as a social category. *Developmental Psychology, 24,* 755–765.

Maccoby, E. E. (1990). Gender and relationships: A developmental account. *American Psychologist, 45,* 513–520.

Maccoby, E. E., Buchanon, C. M., Mnookin, R. H., & Dornbusch, S. M. (1993). Postdivorce roles of mothers and fathers in the lives of their children. *Journal of Family Psychology, 7,* 24–38.

Maccoby, E. E., & Martin, J. A. (1983). Socialization in the context of the family: Parent-child interaction. In P. H. Mussen (Ed.), *Handbook of child psychology* (Vol. 4). New York: Wiley.

MacDonald, R. (2006). Program evaluation research final report. Ottawa: First Nations Child and Family Caring Society of Canada.

Mack, D. E., Strong, H. A., Kowalski, K. C., & Crocker, P. R. E. (2007). Does friendship matter? An examination of social physique anxiety in adolescence. *Journal of Applied Social Psychology, 37,* 1248–1264.

MacKay, T. L., Jakobson, L. S., Ellemberg, D., Lewis, T. L., Maurer, D., & Casiro, O. (2005). Deficits in the processing of local and global motion in very low birthweight children. *Neuropsychologia, 43,* 1738–1748.

MacKinnon-Lewis, C., Rabiner, D., & Starnes, R. (1999). Predicting boys' social acceptance and aggression: The role of mother-child interactions and boys' beliefs about peers. *Developmental Psychology, 35,* 632–639.

MacWhinney, B. (1998). Models of the emergence of language. *Annual Review of Psychology, 49,* 199–227.

Madigan, S., Bakermans-Kranenburg, M. J., Van IJzendoorn, M. H., Moran, G., Pederson, D. R., & Benoit, D. (2006). Unresolved states of mind, anomalous parental behavior, and disorganized attachment: A review and meta-analysis of a transmission gap. *Attachment & Human Development, 8,* 89–111.

Madigan, S., Moran, G., & Pederson, D. (2006). Unresolved states of mind, disorganized attachment relationships, and disrupted interactions of adolescent mothers and their infants. *Developmental Psychology, 42,* 293–304.

Magaldi-Dopman, D., & Park-Taylor, J. (2010). Sacred adolescence: Practical suggestions for psychologists working with adolescents' religious and spiritual identity. *Professional Psychology: Research and Practice, 41,* 382–390.

Mahady-Wilton, M. M., Craig, W. M., & Pepler, D. J. (2000). Emotional regulation and display in classroom victims of bullying: Characteristic expressions of affect, coping styles and relevant contextual factors. *Social Development, 9,* 226–245.

Main, M., & Cassidy, J. (1988). Categories of response to reunion with the parent at age 6: Predictable from infant attachment classifications and stable over a 1-month-period. *Developmental Psychology, 24,* 415–426.

Manassis, K., Owens, M., Adam, K. S., West, M., & Sheldon-Keller, A. E. (1999). Assessing attachment: Convergent validity of the Adult Attachment Interview and the Parental Bonding Instrument. *Australian and New Zealand Journal of Psychiatry, 33,* 559–567.

Mandel, D. R., Jusczyk, P. W., & Pisoni, D. B. (1995). Infants' recognition of the sound patterns of their own names. *Psychological Science, 6,* 314–317.

Mandler, J. M., & McDonough, L. (1998). Studies in inductive inference in infancy. *Cognitive Psychology, 37,* 60–96.

Mangelsdorf, S., Gunnar, M., Kestenbaum, R., Lang, S., & Andreas, D. (1990). Infant proneness-distress temperament, maternal personality, and mother-infant attachment: Associations and goodness of fit. *Child Development, 61,* 820–831.

Mangelsdorf, S. C. (1992). Developmental changes in infant-stranger interaction. *Infant Behavior and Development, 15,* 191–208.

Mangelsdorf, S. C., Shapiro, J. R., & Marzolf, D. (1995). Developmental and temperamental differences in emotional regulation in infancy. *Child Development, 66,* 1817–1828.

Maratsos, M. (1998). The acquisition of grammar. In W. Damon (Ed.), *Handbook of child psychology* (Vol. 2). New York: Wiley.

Marcia, J. E. (1980). Identity in adolescence. In J. Adelson (Ed.), *Handbook of adolescent psychology.* New York: Wiley.

Marcia, J. E. (1991). Identity and self-development. In R. M. Lerner, A. C. Petersen, & J. Brooks-Gunn (Eds.), *Encyclopedia of adolescence* (Vol. 1). New York: Garland.

Marcovitch, S., & Zelazo, P. D. (1999). The A-not-B error: Results from a logistic meta-analysis. *Child Development, 70,* 1297–1313.

Marcus, G. F., Pinker, S., Ullman, M., Hollander, M., Rosen, T. J., & Xu, F. (1992). Overregularization in language acquisition. *Monographs of the Society for Research in Child Development, 58*(4, Serial No. 228).

Mares, M., & Woodard, E. (2005). Positive effects of television on children's social interactions: A meta-analysis. *Media Psychology, 7,* 301–322.

Mares, S., Newman, L., & Warren, B. (2005). *Clinical skills in infant mental health.* Camberwell, Australia: Australian Council for Educational Research.

Marini, Z. A., Dane, A. V., Bosacki, S. L., & YLC-CURA. (2006). Direct and indirect bully-victims: Differential psychosocial risk factors associated with adolescents involved in bullying and victimization. *Aggressive Behavior, 32,* 551–569.

Markovits, H., & Vachon, R. (1989). Reasoning with contrary-to-fact propositions. *Journal of Experimental Child Psychology, 47,* 398–412.

Marsh, H. W. (1991). Employment during high school: Character building or a subversion of academic goals? *Sociology of Education, 64,* 172–189.

Marsh, H. W., Chessor, D., Craven, R., & Roche, L. (1995). The effects of gifted and talented programs on academic self-concept: The big fish strikes again. *American Educational Research Journal, 32,* 285–319.

Marsh, H. W., & Yeung, A. S. (1997). Causal effects of academic self-concept on academic achievement: Structural equation models of longitudinal data. *Journal of Educational Psychology, 89,* 41–54.

Marshall, E. (1995). Gene therapy's growing pains. *Science, 269,* 1050–1052.

Marshall, W. A., & Tanner, J. M. (1970). Variations in the pattern of pubertal changes in boys. *Archives of Disease in Childhood, 45,* 13–23.

Marsiglio, W. (1993). Attitudes toward homosexual activity and gays as friends: A national survey of heterosexual 15- to 19-year-old males. *Journal of Sex Research, 30,* 12–17.

Martin, C. L. (1989). Children's use of gender-related information in making social judgments. *Developmental Psychology, 25,* 80–88.

Martin, C. L., Eisenbud, L., & Rose, H. (1995). Children's gender-based reasoning about toys. *Child Development, 66,* 1453–1471.

Martin, C. L., & Halverson, C. F. (1987). The roles of cognition in sex roles and sex typing. In D. B. Carter (Ed.), *Current conceptions of sex roles and sex typing: Theory and research.* New York: Praeger.

Martin, C. L., & Little, J. K. (1990). The relation of gender understandings to children's sex-typed preferences and gender stereotypes. *Child Development, 61,* 1427–1439.

Martin, C. L., & Ruble, D. (2004). Children's search for gender cues: Cognitive perspectives on gender development. *Current Directions in Psychological Science, 13,* 67–70.

Martin, J. A., Hamilton, B. E., Sutton, P. D., Ventura, S. J., Menacker, F., Kirmeyer, S., & Matthews, T. J. (2009). Births: Final data for 2006. National Vital Statistics Reports, 57. Hyattsville, MD: Centers for Disease Control and Prevention, National Center for Health Statistics, US Department of Health and Human Services.

Martin, M. E., & Byrne, B. (2002). Teaching children to recognize rhyme does not directly promote phonemic awareness. *British Journal of Educational Psychology, 72,* 561–572.

Martin, R. P., Dombrowski, S. C., Mullis, C., Wisenbaker, J., & Huttunen, M. O. (2006). Smoking during pregnancy: Association with childhood temperament, behavior, and academic performance. *Journal of Pediatric Psychology, 31,* 490–500.

Martin, R. P., Olejnik, S., & Gaddis, L. (1994). Is temperament an important contributor to schooling outcomes in elementary school? Modeling effects of temperament and scholastic ability on academic achievement. In W. B. Casey & S. C. McDevitt (Eds.), *Prevention and early intervention.* New York: Brunner/Mazel.

Marzolf, D. P., & DeLoache, J. S. (1994). Transfer in young children's understanding of spatial representations. *Child Development, 65,* 1–15.

Mash, E., & Wolfe, D. (2002). *Abnormal child psychology* (2nd ed.). Belmont, CA: Wadsworth Press.

Masur, E. F. (1995). Infants' early verbal imitation and their later lexical development. *Merrill-Palmer Quarterly, 41,* 286–306.

Matsuba, M. K., & Walker, L. J. (2004). Extraordinary commitment: Young adults involved in social organizations. *Journal of Personality, 72,* 413–436.

Mattys, S. L., Jusczyk, P. W., Luce, P. A., & Morgan, J. L. (1999). Phonotactic and prosodic effects on word segmentation in infants. *Cognitive Psychology, 38,* 465–494.

Maurer, D., & Lewis, T. L. (2001). Visual acuity: The role of visual input in inducing postnatal change. *Clinical Neuroscience Research, 1,* 239–247.

Maybery, D., Ling, L., Szakacs, E., & Reupert, A. (2005). Children of a parent with a mental illness: Perspectives on need. *Australian e-Journal for the Advancement of Mental Health, 4*(2).

Mazur, E., Wolchik, S. A., Virdin, L., Sandler, I. N., & West, S. G. (1999). Cognitive moderators of children's adjustment to stressful divorce events: The role of negative cognitive errors and positive illusions. *Child Development, 70,* 231–245.

McCall, R. B. (1979). *Infants.* Cambridge, MA: Harvard University Press.

McCall, R. B. (1989). Commentary. *Human Development, 32,* 177–186.

McCarty, M. E., & Ashmead, D. H. (1999). Visual control of reaching and grasping in infants. *Developmental Psychology, 35,* 620–631.

McClure, E. B. (2000). A meta-analytic review of sex differences in facial expression processing and their development in infants, children, and adolescents. *Psychological Bulletin, 126,* 424–453.

McCracken, J. T., & Hanna, G. L. (2005). Elevated thyroid indices in children and adolescents with obsessive-compulsive disorder: Effects of clomipramine treatment. *Journal of Child and Adolescent Psychopharmacology, 15,* 581–588.

McCutchen, D., Covill, A., Hoyne, S. H., & Mildes, K. (1994). Individual differences in writing: Implications of translating fluency. *Journal of Educational Psychology, 86,* 256–266.

McCutchen, D., Francis, M., & Kerr, S. (1997). Revising for meaning: Effects of knowledge and strategy. *Journal of Educational Psychology, 89,* 667–676.

McDowell, M., Brody, D. J., & Hughes, J. P. (2007). Has age at menarche changed? Results from the National Health and Nutrition Examination Survey (NHANES) 1999–2004. *Journal of Adolescent Health, 40*, 227–231.

McGee, R., Stanton, W. R., & Sears, M. R. (1993). Allergic disorders and attention deficit disorder in children. *Journal of Abnormal Child Psychology, 21*, 79–88.

McGee, R., Williams, S., & Feehan, M. (1992). Attention deficit disorder and age of onset of problem behaviors. *Journal of Abnormal Child Psychology, 20*, 487–502.

McGraw, M. B. (1935). *Growth: A study of Johnny and Jimmy.* East Norwalk, CT: Appleton-Century-Crofts.

McIntosh, J., MacDonald, F., & McKeganey, N. (2006). Why do children experiment with illegal drugs? The declining role of peer pressure with increasing age. *Addiction Research & Theory, 14*, 275–287.

McIntyre, L., Walsh, G., & Connor, S. K. (2001, June). A follow-up study of child hunger in Canada. (Working paper W-01-1-2E). Ottawa: Applied Research Branch, Strategic Policy, Human Resources Development Canada.

McKechnie, B. (2000, June). Health Canada FAS/FAE initiative: Information and feedback sessions: National synthesis report. Ottawa: Ministry of Health.

McKim, M. K., Cramer, K. M., Stuart, B., & O'Connor, D. L. (1999). Infant care decisions and attachment security: The Canadian "transition to child care" study. *Canadian Journal of Behavioural Science, 31*(2), 92–106.

McManus, I. C., Sik, G., Cole, D. R., Kloss, J., Mellon, A. F., & Wong, J. (1988). The development of handedness in children. *British Journal of Developmental Psychology, 6*, 257–273.

McNaughton, S., & Leyland, J. (1990). The shifting focus of maternal tutoring across different difficulty levels on a problem solving task. *British Journal of Developmental Psychology, 8*, 147–155.

MedlinePlus. (2015). Intersex. Retrieved from https://medlineplus.gov/ency/article/001669.htm

Meilman, P. W. (1979). Cross-sectional age changes in ego identity status during adolescence. *Developmental Psychology, 15*, 230–231.

Mellon, M. W., Whiteside, S. P., & Friedrich, W. N. (2006). The relevance of fecal soiling as an indicator of child sexual abuse: A preliminary analysis. *Journal of Developmental and Behavioral Pediatrics, 27*, 25–32.

Meltzoff, A. N., & Moore, M. K. (1989). Imitation in newborn infants: Exploring the range of gestures imitated and the underlying mechanisms. *Developmental Psychology, 25*, 954–962.

Meltzoff, A. N., & Moore, M. K. (1994). Imitation, memory, and the representation of persons. *Infant Behavior and Development, 17*, 83–99.

Mendelson, B. K., Mendelson, M. J., & White, D. R. (2001). Body-esteem scale for adolescents and adults. *Journal of Personality Assessment, 76*, 80–106.

Mendelson, B., & White, D. (1985). Development of self-body esteem in overweight youngsters. *Developmental Psychology, 21*, 90–96.

Mendelson, B. K., White, D. R., & Mendelson, M. J. (1996). Self-esteem and body esteem: Effects of gender, age, and weight. *Journal of Applied Developmental Psychology, 17*, 321–346.

Mennella, J. A., & Beauchamp, G. K. (1996). The human infant's response to vanilla flavors in mother's milk and formula. *Infant Behavior and Development, 19*, 13–19.

Mennella, J., & Beauchamp, G. K. (1997). The ontogeny of human flavor perception. In G. K. Beauchamp & L. Bartoshuk (Eds.), *Tasting and smelling: Handbook of perception and cognition.* San Diego, CA: Academic Press.

Mersky, J. P., & Reynolds, A. J. (2007). Child maltreatment and violent delinquency: Disentangling main effects and subgroup effects. *Child Maltreatment, 12*, 246–258.

Meyer, D. R., & Garasky, S. (1993). Custodial fathers: Myths, realities, and child support policy. *Journal of Marriage and the Family, 55*, 73–79.

Meyer-Bahlburg, H. F. L., Ehrhardt, A. A., Rosen, L. R., Gruen, R. S., Veridiano, N. P., Vann, F. H., & Neuwalder, H. F. (1995). Prenatal estrogens and the development of homosexual orientation. *Developmental Psychology, 31*, 12–21.

Meyers, A. F., Sampson, A. E., Weitzman, M., Rogers, B. L., & Kayne, H. (1989). School breakfast program and school performance. *American Journal of Diseases of Children, 143*, 1234–1239.

Michalik, N. M., Eisenberg, N., Spinrad, T. L., Ladd, B., Thompson, M., & Valiente, C. (2007). Longitudinal relations among parental emotional expressivity and sympathy and prosocial behavior in adolescence. *Social Development, 16*, 286–309.

Miles, C. (2000). Modern approaches to children's cognitive development. In C. Violato, E. Oddone-Paolucci, & M. Genuis (Eds.), *The changing family and child development* (pp. 227–248). Aldershot, UK: Ashgate.

Millar, W. J., Nair, C., & Wadhera, S. (1996). Declining Cesarean section rates: a continuing trend? *Health Reports, 8*, 17–24.

Miller, B. C., Norton, M. C., Curtis, T., Hill, E. J., Schvaneveldt, P., & Young, M. H. (1997). The timing of sexual intercourse among adolescents: Family, peer, and other antecedents. *Youth and Society, 29*, 54–83.

Miller, C. A., Leonard, L. B., Kail, R. V., Zhang, X., Tomblin, J. B., & Francis, D. J. (2006). Response time in 14-year-olds with language impairment. *Journal of Speech, Language, and Hearing Research, 49,* 712–728.

Miller, J. G., & Bersoff, D. M. (1992). Culture and moral judgment: How are conflicts between justice and interpersonal responsibilities resolved? *Journal of Personality and Social Psychology, 62,* 541–554.

Miller, K. S., Forehand, R., & Kotchik, B. A. (1999). Adolescent sexual behavior in two ethnic minority samples: The role of family variables. *Journal of Marriage and the Family, 61,* 85–98.

Miller, L. K. (1999). The savant syndrome: Intellectual impairment and exceptional skill. *Psychological Bulletin, 125,* 31–46.

Miller, L. T., & Vernon, P. A. (1992). The general factor in short-term memory, intelligence, and reaction time. *Intelligence, 16,* 5–29.

Mills, R. S. L., & Grusec, J. E. (1989). Cognitive, affective, and behavioral consequences of praising altruism. *Merrill-Palmer Quarterly, 35,* 299–326.

Millward, R., Kennedy, E., Towlson, K., & Minnis, H. (2006). Reactive attachment disorder in looked-after children. *Emotional & Behavioural Difficulties, 11,* 273–279.

Minde, K. (2003). Assessment and treatment of attachment disorders. *Current Opinion in Psychiatry, 16,* 377–381.

Mindell, J. A., & Cashman, L. (1995). Sleep disorders. In A. R. Eisen, C. A. Kearney, & C. E. Schaefer (Eds.), *Clinical handbook of anxiety disorders in children and adolescents.* Northvale, NJ: Aronson.

Ministry of Health of Brazil. (2014). Secretariat of Health Care. Primary Health Care Department. Dietary Guidelines for the Brazilian population. Translated by Carlos Augusto Monteiro. Brasília: Ministry of Health of Brazil.

Minnis, H., Everett, K., Pelosi, A. J., Dunn, J., & Knapp, M. (2006). Children in foster care: Mental health, service use and costs. *European Child & Adolescent Psychiatry, 15,* 63–70.

Mischel, W., & Ebbesen, E. (1970). Attention in delay of gratification. *Journal of Personality and Social Psychology, 16,* 329–337.

Mischel, W., Shoda, Y., & Rodriguez, M. L. (1989). Delay of gratification in children. *Science, 244,* 933–938.

Mishna, F. (2003). Learning disabilities and bullying: Double jeopardy. *Journal of Learning Disabilities, 36,* 336–347.

Mitchell, J. E., Baker, L. A., & Jacklin, C. N. (1989). Masculinity and femininity in twin children: Genetic and environmental factors. *Child Development, 60,* 1475–1485.

Miura, I. T., Kim, C. C., Chang, C. M., & Okamoto, Y. (1988). Effects of language characteristics on children's

cognitive representation of number: Cross-national comparisons. *Child Development, 59,* 1445–1450.

Mize, J., & Ladd, G. W. (1990). A cognitive social-learning approach to social skill training with low-status preschool children. *Developmental Psychology, 26,* 388–397.

Mize, J., & Pettit, G. S. (1997). Mothers' social coaching, mother-child relationship style, and children's peer competence: Is the medium the message? *Child Development, 68,* 312–332.

Mize, J., Pettit, G. S., & Brown, E. G. (1995). Mothers' supervision of their children's peer play: Relations with beliefs, perceptions, and knowledge. *Developmental Psychology, 31,* 311–321.

Mizes, J. S. (1995). Eating disorders. In M. Hersen & R. T. Ammerman (Eds.), *Advanced abnormal child psychology* (pp. 375–391). Hillsdale, NJ: Erlbaum.

Moats, L. C., & Lyon, G. R. (1993). Learning disabilities in the United States: Advocacy, science, and the future of the field. *Journal of Learning Disabilities, 26,* 282–294.

Moehler, E., Brunner, R., Wiebel, A., Reck, C., & Resch, F. (2006). Maternal depressive symptoms in the postnatal period are associated with long-term impairment of mother-child bonding. *Archives of Women's Mental Health, 9,* 273–278.

Moffitt, T. E. (1993). Adolescence-limited and life-course-persistent antisocial behavior: A developmental taxonomy. *Psychological Review, 100,* 674–701.

Moffitt, T. E., Caspi, A., Belsky, J., & Silva, P. A. (1992). Childhood experience and the onset of menarche: A test of a sociobiological model. *Child Development, 63,* 47–58.

Molfese, D. L., & Burger-Judisch, L. M. (1991). Dynamic temporal-spatial allocation of resources in the human brain: An alternative to the static view of hemisphere differences. In F. L. Ketterle (Ed.), *Cerebral laterality: Theory and research. The Toledo symposium.* Hillsdale, NJ: Erlbaum.

Möller, K., Hwang, C. P., & Wickberg, B. (2006). Romantic attachment, parenthood and marital satisfaction. *Journal of Reproductive and Infant Psychology, 24,* 233–240.

Monk, C., Fifer, W. P., Myers, M. M., Sloan, R. P., Trien, L., & Hurtado, A. (2000). Maternal stress responses and anxiety during pregnancy: Effects on fetal heart rate. *Developmental Psychobiology, 36,* 67–77.

Moore, B. S., Underwood, B., & Rosenhan, D. L. (1973). Affect and altruism. *Developmental Psychology, 8,* 99–104.

Moore, C., Angelopoulos, M., & Bennet, P. (1999). Word learning in the context of referential and salience cues. *Developmental Psychology, 35,* 60–68.

Moore, K. L., & Persaud, T. V. N. (1993). *Before we are born* (4th ed.). Philadelphia: W. B. Saunders.

Moran, G., Pederson, D. R., Pettit, P., & Krupka, A. (1992). Maternal sensitivity and infant–mother attachment in a developmentally delayed sample. *Infant Behavior and Development, 15,* 427–442.

Morelli, M., Bianchi, D., Baiocco, R., Pezzuti, L., & Chirumbolo, A. (2016, May). Sexting behaviors and cyber pornography addiction among adolescents: The moderating role of alcohol consumption. *Sexuality Research and Social Policy: A Journal of the NSRC.* doi:10.1007/s13178-016-0234-0

Morgan, B., & Gibson, K. R. (1991). Nutritional and environmental interactions in brain development. In K. R. Gibson & A. C. Peterson (Eds.), *Brain maturation and cognitive development: Comparative and crosscultural perspectives.* New York: Aldine De Gruyter.

Morgane, P. J., Austin-LaFrance, R., Bronzino, J. D., Tonkiss, J., Diaz-Cintra, S., Cintra, L., . . . Galler, J. R. (1993). Prenatal malnutrition and development of the brain. *Neuroscience and Biobehavioral Reviews, 17,* 91–128.

Morison, P., & Masten, A. S. (1991). Peer reputation in middle childhood as a predictor of adaptation in adolescence: A seven-year follow-up. *Child Development, 62,* 991–1007.

Morrongiello, B. A., Fenwick, K. D., Hillier, L., & Chance, G. (1994). Sound localization in newborn human infants. *Developmental Psychology, 27,* 519–538.

Morrongiello, B. A., Midgett, C., & Shields, R. (2001). Don't run with scissors: Young children's knowledge of home safety rules. *Journal of Pediatric Psychology, 26,* 105–115.

Morrongiello, B. A., & Trehub, S. E. (1987). Age-related changes in auditory temporal perception. *Journal of Experimental Child Psychology, 44,* 413–426.

Mortimer, J. T., Finch, M. D., Rye, S., Shanahan, M. J., & Call, K. T. (1996). The effects of work intensity on adolescent mental health, achievement, and behavioral adjustment: New evidence from a prospective study. *Child Development, 67,* 1243–1261.

Mouw, T., & Entwisle, B. (2006). Residential segregation and interracial friendship in schools. *American Journal of Sociology, 112,* 394–441.

Mumme, D. L., & Fernald, A. (2003). The infant as onlooker: Learning from emotional reactions observed in a television scenario. *Child Development, 74,* 221–237.

Mumme, D. L., Fernald, A., & Herrera, C. (1996). Infants' responses to facial and vocal emotional signals in a social referencing paradigm. *Child Development, 67,* 3219–3237.

Murphy, L. M., Bennett, L. C., Brinkman, T. M., & McNamara, K. A. (2007). Sustained attention and social competence in typically developing preschool-aged children. *Early Child Development and Care, 177,* 133–149.

Murphy, T. F. (2012). Research priorities and the future of pregnancy. *Cambridge Quarterly of Healthcare Ethics, 21,* 78–89.

Murray, L., Fiori-Cowley, A., Hooper, R., & Cooper, P. (1996). The impact of postnatal depression and associated adversity on early mother-infant interactions and later infant outcomes. *Child Development, 67,* 2512–2526.

Naigles, L. G., & Gelman, S. A. (1995). Overextensions in comprehension and production revisited: Preferential-looking in a study of dog, cat, and cow. *Journal of Child Language, 22,* 19–46.

Nation, K., Adams, J. W., Bowyer-Crane, C. A., & Snowling, M. J. (1999). Working memory deficits in poor comprehenders reflect underlying language impairments. *Journal of Experimental Child Psychology, 73,* 139–158.

National Center for Education Statistics. (1997). *Pursuing excellence: A study of U.S. fourth-grade mathematics and science achievement in an international context.* Washington, DC: US Government Printing Office.

National High Blood Pressure Education Program Working Group on Hypertension Control in Children and Adolescents. (1996). Update on the 1987 task force report on high blood pressure in children and adolescents: A working group report from the National High Blood Pressure Education Program. *Pediatrics, 98,* 649–658.

NLSCY. National Longitudinal Survey of Children and Youth Survey. (2008). Overview for the 2008/2009 Data Collection Cycle 8. Ottawa: Human Resources and Skills Development Canada and Statistics Canada. Retrieved from http://www23.statcan.gc.ca/imdb-bmdi/document/4450_D2_T9_V4-eng.pdf

National Research Council. (1987). *Risking the future: Adolescent sexuality, pregnancy, and childbearing.* Washington, DC: National Academy Press.

National Research Council. (1989). *Recommended dietary allowances* (10th ed.). Washington, DC: National Academy Press.

Neiderhiser, J. M., Reiss, D., Hetherington, E. M., & Plomin, R. (1999). Relationships between parenting and adolescent adjustment over time: Genetic and environmental contributions. *Developmental Psychology, 35,* 680–692.

Neisser, U., Boodoo, G., Bouchard, T. J., Boykin, A. W., Brody, N., Ceci, S. J., . . . Urbina, S. (1996). Intelligence: Knowns and unknowns. *American Psychologist, 51,* 77–101.

Nelson, C. A. (1999). Neural plasticity and human development. *Current Directions in Psychological Science, 8,* 42–45.

Nelson, K. (1973). Structure and strategy in learning to talk. *Monographs of the Society for Research in Child Development, 38*(1–2, Serial No. 149).

Nelson, K. (1993). Explaining the emergence of autobiographical memory in early childhood. A. F. Collins & S. E. Gathercole (Eds.). *Theories of memory.* Hove, UK: Erlbaum.

Nelson, M. A. (1996). Protective equipment. In O. Bar-Or (Ed.), *The child and adolescent athlete.* Oxford, UK: Blackwell.

Neto, F., & Furnham, A. (2005). Gender-role portrayals in children's television advertisements. *International Journal of Adolescence and Youth, 12,* 69–90.

Netzer-Stein, A. (2012). [Book Review] The early years of life: psychoanalytical development theory according to Freud, Klein, and Bion. *Infant Observation: International Journal of Infant Observation and Its Applications, 15,* 207–209.

Neugarten, B. L., & Weinstein, K. K. (1964). The changing American grandparent. *Journal of Marriage and the Family, 26,* 299–304.

Newcomb, A. F., & Bagwell, C. L. (1995). Children's friendship relations: A meta-analytic review. *Psychological Bulletin, 117,* 306–347.

Newcomb, A. F., Bukowski, W. M., & Pattee, L. (1993). Children's peer relations: A meta-analytic review of popular, rejected, neglected, controversial, and average sociometric status. *Psychological Bulletin, 113,* 99–123.

Newman, B. S., & Muzzonigro, P. G. (1993). The effects of traditional family values on the coming out process of gay male adolescents. *Adolescence, 28,* 213–226.

Newman, L. S., Cooper, J., & Ruble, D. N. (1995). Gender and computers: II. Interactive effects of knowledge and constancy on gender-stereotyped attitudes. *Sex Roles, 33,* 325–351.

Newport, E. L. (1991). Contrasting conceptions of the critical period for language. In S. Carey & R. Gelman (Eds.), *The epigenesis of mind: Essays on biology and cognition* (pp. 111–130). Hillsdale, NJ: Erlbaum.

NICHD Early Child Care Research Network. (1997). The effects of infant child care on infant-mother attachment security: Results of the NICHD Study of Early Child Care. *Child Development, 68,* 860–879.

Niebyl, J. R. (1991). Drugs in pregnancy and lactation. In S. G. Gabbe, J. R. Niebyl, & J. L. Simpson (Eds.), *Obstetrics: Normal and problem pregnancies* (2nd ed., pp. 308–310). New York: Churchill Livingstone.

Nielsen, M., & Dissanayake, C. (2004). Pretend play, mirror self-recognition and imitation: A longitudinal investigation through the second year. *Infant Behavior & Development, 27,* 342–365.

Nolen-Hoeksema, S., & Girgus, J. S. (1994). The emergence of gender differences in depression during adolescence. *Psychological Bulletin, 115,* 424–443.

Nosko, A., Wood, E., & Molema, S. (2010). All about me: Disclosure in online social networking profiles: The case of Facebook. *Computers in Human Behavior, 26,* 406–418.

Nucci, L., & Weber, E. K. (1995). Social interactions in the home and the development of young children's conceptions of the personal. *Child Development, 66,* 1438–1452.

Nulman, I., Rovet, J., Greenbaum, R., Loebstein, M., Wolpin, J., Pace-Asciak, P., & Koren, G. (2001). Neurodevelopment of adopted children exposed in utero to cocaine: The Toronto Adoption Study. *Clinical and Investigative Medicine/Medecine Clinique et Experimentale, 24,* 129–137.

Nurmi, J., Poole, M. E., & Kalakoski, V. (1996). Age differences in adolescent identity exploration and commitment in urban and rural environments. *Journal of Adolescence, 19,* 443–452.

O'Dell, L., & Brownlow, C. (2005). Media reports of links between MMR and autism: A discourse analysis. *British Journal of Learning Disabilities, 33,* 194–199.

Offer, D., Ostrov, E., Howard, K. I., & Atkinson, R. (1988). *The teenage world: Adolescents' self-image in ten countries.* New York: Plenum.

Ogletree, R. J. (1993). Sexual coercion experience and help-seeking behavior of college women. *Journal of American College Health, 41,* 149–153.

Ohlendorf-Moffat, P. (1991, February). Surgery before birth. *Discover, 12*(2), 58–65.

Okagaki, L., & Sternberg, R. J. (1993). Parental beliefs and children's school performance. *Child Development, 64,* 36–56.

Olfman, S. (2008). *The sexualization of childhood.* Santa Barbara: Praeger.

Oliver, M. B., & Hyde, J. S. (1993). Gender differences in sexuality: A meta-analysis. *Psychological Bulletin, 114,* 29–51.

Oller, D. K., & Eilers, R. E. (1988). The role of audition in infant babbling. *Child Development, 59,* 441–449.

Oller, D. K., & Lynch, M. P. (1992). Infant vocalizations and innovations in infraphonology: Toward a broader theory of development and disorders. In C. A. Ferguson, L. Menn, & C. Stoel-Gammon (Eds.), *Phonological development: Models, research, and implications* (pp. 509–538). Timonium, MD: York Press.

Olweus, D. (1978). *Aggression in the schools: Bullies and whipping boys.* Washington, DC: Hemisphere.

Olweus, D. (1994). Bullying at school: Basic facts and effects of school based intervention program. *Journal of Child Psychology and Psychiatry, 35,* 1171–1190.

O'Neill, D. K. (1996). Two-year-old children's sensitivity to a parent's knowledge state when making requests. *Child Development, 67,* 659–677.

Ong, K. K., Ahmed, M. L., & Dunger, D. B. (2006). Lessons from large population studies on timing and tempo of puberty (secular trends and relation to body size): The European trend. *Molecular and Cellular Endocrinology, 254–255,* 8–12.

Oppliger, P. A. (2007). Effects of gender stereotyping on socialization. In R. W. Preiss, B. M. Gayle, N. Burrell, M. Allen, & J. Bryant (Eds.), *Mass media effects research: Advances through meta-analysis* (pp. 199–214). Mahwah, NJ: Erlbaum.

Orne, M. T. (1962). On the social psychology of the psychological experiment: With particular reference to demand characteristics and their implications. *American Psychologist, 17,* 776–783.

Ostrov, J. M., Gentile, D. A., & Crick, N. R. (2006). Media exposure, aggression and prosocial behavior during early childhood: A longitudinal study. *Social Development, 15,* 612–627.

Ota Wang, V., & Sue, S. (2005). In the eye of the storm: Race and genomics in research and practice. *American Psychologist, 60,* 37–45.

Over, H., & Carpenter, M. (2013). The social side of imitation. *Child Development Perspectives, 7,* 6–11. doi:10.1111/cdep.12006

Paarlberg, K. M., Vingerhoets, A. J. J. M., Passchier, J., Dekker, G. A., Heinen, A. G. J. J., & van Geijn, H. P. (1995). Psychosocial factors and pregnancy outcome: A review with emphasis on methodological issues. *Journal of Psychosomatic Research, 39,* 563–595.

Pacifici, C., & Bearison, D. J. (1991). Development of children's self-regulations in idealized and mother–child interactions. *Cognitive Development, 6,* 261–277.

Padgham, J. J., & Blyth, D. A. (1991). Dating during adolescence. In R. M. Lerner, A. C. Petersen, & J. Brooks-Gunn (Eds.), *Encyclopedia of adolescence* (Vol. 1). New York: Garland.

Padilla, A. M., Lindholm, K. J., Chen, A., Duran, R., Hakuta, K., Lambert, W., & Tucker, G. R. (1991). The English-only movement: Myths, reality, and implications for psychology. *American Psychologist, 46,* 120–130.

Paglia-Boak, A., Mann, R. E., Adlaf, E. M., & Rehm, J. (2009). Drug use among Ontario students, 1977–2009: OSDUHS highlights. (CAMH Research Document Series No. 28). Toronto: Centre for Addiction and Mental Health. Retrieved from www.camh.net/Research/osdus.html

Palca, J. (1991). Fetal brain signals time for birth. *Science, 253,* 1360.

Palmer, S. E. (1996). Placement stability and inclusive practice in foster care: An empirical study. *Children and Youth Services Review, 18,* 589–601.

Paluck, E. L., & Green, D. P. (2009). Prejudice reduction: What works? A critical look at evidence from the field and the laboratory. *Annual Review of Psychology, 60,* 339–367.

Panksepp, J. (1998). Attention deficit hyperactivity disorders, psychostimulants, and intolerance of childhood playfulness: A tragedy in the making? *Current Directions in Psychological Science, 7,* 99–103.

PAR, Inc. (2013). What is the SDS? Lutz, FL: Par, Inc. Retrieved from http://www.self-directed-search.com.

Parazzini, F., Luchini, L., La Vecchia, C., & Crosignani, P. G. (1993). Video display terminal use during pregnancy and reproductive outcome—a meta-analysis. *Journal of Epidemiology and Community Health, 47,* 265–268.

Parke, R. D. (1977). Punishment in children: Effects, side effects and alternative strategies. In H. L. Hom, Jr. & A. Robinson (Eds.), *Psychological processes in early education.* New York: Academic.

Parke, R. D. (1990). In search of fathers: A narrative of an empirical journey. In I. Sigel & G. Brody (Eds.), *Methods of family research.* Hillsdale, NJ: Erlbaum.

Parke, R. D., & Bhavnagri, N. P. (1989). Parents as managers of children's peer relationships. In D. Belle (Ed.), *Children's social networks and social supports.* New York: Wiley.

Parke, R. D., & Buriel, R. (1998). Socialization in the family: Ethnic and ecological perspectives. In W. Damon (Ed.), *Handbook of child psychology* (Vol. 3). New York: Wiley.

Parker, J. G., & Herrera, C. (1996). Interpersonal processes in friendship: A comparison of abused and nonabused children's experiences. *Developmental Psychology, 32,* 1025–1038.

Parker, J. G., & Seal, J. (1996). Forming, losing, renewing, and replacing friendships: Applying temporal parameters to the assessment of children's friendship experiences. *Child Development, 67,* 2248–2268.

Parker-Loewen, D. (2005). Child advocates: Protecting the rights of Canadian children? In R. V. Kail & T. Zolner (Eds.), *Children* (pp. 413–415). Toronto: Pearson Education Canada.

Parmalee, A. H. (1986). Children's illnesses: Their beneficial effects on behavioral development. *Child Development, 57,* 1–10.

Parritz, R. H. (1996). A descriptive analysis of toddler coping in challenging circumstances. *Infant Behavior and Development, 19,* 171–180.

Parten, M. (1932). Social participation among preschool children. *Journal of Abnormal and Social Psychology, 27*, 243–269.

Pass, R. F., Zhang, C., Evans, A., Simpson, T., Andrews, W., Huang, M., . . . Cloud, G. (2009). Vaccine prevention of maternal cytomegalovirus infection. *New England Journal of Medicine, 360*, 1191.

Paton, S. J., & Croom, C. S. (2010). An overview of fetal alcohol spectrum. *Primary Care Reports, 16*, 1–8.

Patterson, C. J. (1992). Children of lesbian and gay parents. *Child Development, 63*, 1025–1042.

Patterson, C. J. (2006). Children of lesbian and gay parents. *Current Directions in Psychological Science, 15*, 241–244.

Patterson, G. R. (1980). Mothers: The unacknowledged victims. *Monographs of the Society for Research in Child Development, 45*(5, Serial No. 186).

Patterson, G. R. (1984). Microsocial process: A view from the boundary. In J. C. Masters & K. Yarkin-Levin (Eds.), *Boundary areas in social and developmental psychology*. New York: Academic Press.

Patterson, G. R. (1995). Coercion as a basis for early age of onset for arrest. In J. McCord (Ed.), *Coercion and punishment in long-term perspectives*. New York: Cambridge University Press.

Patterson, G. R., DeVaryshe, B. D., & Ramsey, E. (1989). A developmental perspective on antisocial behavior. *American Psychologist, 44*, 329–335.

Patterson, P. H. (2002). Maternal infection: Window on neuroimmune interactions in fetal brain development and mental illness. *Current Opinion in Neurobiology, 12*, 115–118.

Patton, D. U., Hong, J. S., Ranney, M., Patel, S., Kelley, C., Eschmann, R., & Washington, R. (2014). Social media as a vector for youth violence: A review of the literature. *Computers in Human Behavior, 35*, 548–553.

Peake, P. K., Hebl, M., & Mischel, W. (2002). Strategic attention deployment for delay of gratification in working and waiting situations. *Developmental Psychology, 38*, 313–326.

Pearce, J. W., & Pezzot-Pearce, T. D. (2005). How can we help children who have experienced abuse? In R. V. Kail & T. Zolner (Eds.), *Children* (pp. 424–428). Toronto: Pearson Education Canada.

Pearlman, M., & Ross, H. S. (1997). The benefits of parent intervention in children's disputes: An examination of concurrent changes in children's fighting styles. *Child Development, 68*, 690–700.

Pearson, J. L., Hunter, A. G., Ensminger, M. E., & Kellam, S. G. (1990). Black grandmothers in multigenerational households: Diversity in family structure and parenting involvement in the Woodlawn community. *Child Development, 61*, 434–442.

Pederson, D. R., Gleason, K. E., Moran, G., & Bento, S. (1998). Maternal attachment representations, maternal sensitivity, and the infant–mother attachment relationship. *Developmental Psychology, 34*, 925–933.

Pederson, D. R., & Moran, G. (1996). Expression of the attachment relationship outside of the Strange Situation. *Child Development, 67*, 915–927.

Pellegrini, A. D., & Smith, P. K. (1998). Physical activity play: The nature and function of a neglected aspect of play. *Child Development, 69*, 577–598.

Pellicano, E. (2007). Links between theory of mind and executive function in young children with autism: Clues to developmental primacy. *Developmental Psychology, 43*, 974–990.

Pennington, B. F., Groisser, D., & Welsh, M. C. (1993). Contrasting cognitive deficits in attention deficit hyperactivity disorder versus reading disability. *Developmental Psychology, 29*, 511–523.

Pepler, D. J., Craig, W. M., Connolly, J. A., Yuile, A., McMaster, L., & Jiang, D. (2006). A developmental perspective on bullying. *Aggressive Behavior, 32*, 376–384.

Perfetti, C. A., & Curtis, M. E. (1986). Reading. In R. F. Dillon & R. J. Sternberg (Eds.), *Cognition and instruction*. Orlando, FL: Academic Press.

Perlman, D. (2007). The best of times, the worst of times: The place of close relationships in psychology and our daily lives. *Canadian Psychology, 48*, 19–23.

Perry, B. D. (1997). Incubated in terror: Neurodevelopmental factors in the "cycle of violence." In J. Osofsky (Ed.), *Children, youth and violence: The search for solutions* (pp. 124–148). New York: Guilford Press.

Peterman, T. A., Tian, L. H., Metcalf, C. A., Satterwhite, C. L., Malotte, C. K., DeAugustine, N., . . . Douglas, J. M., Jr., for the RESPECT-2 Study Group. (2006). High incidence of new sexually transmitted infections in the year following a sexually transmitted infection: A case for rescreening. *Annals of Internal Medicine, 145*, 564–572.

Peterson, C. (1996). *The psychology of abnormality*. Fort Worth, TX: Harcourt Brace.

Peterson, C., & Warren, K. L. (2009). Injuries, emergency rooms, and children's memory: Factors contributing to individual differences. In J. A. Quas & R. Fivush (Eds.), *Emotion and memory in development: Biological, cognitive, and social considerations* (pp. 60–85). New York: Oxford University Press.

Peterson, C., Maier, S. F., & Seligman, M. E. P. (1993). *Learned helplessness: A theory for the age of personal control*. New York: Oxford University Press.

Peterson, C., & Rideout, R. (1998). Memory for medical emergencies experienced by 1- and 2-year-olds. *Developmental Psychology, 34*, 1059–1072.

Peterson, L. (1983). Role of donor competence, donor age, and peer presence on helping in an emergency. *Developmental Psychology, 19,* 873–880.

Peterson, L. (1989). Latchkey children's preparation for self-care: Overestimated, under-rehearsed and unsafe. *Journal of Child Clinical Psychology, 18,* 36–43.

Peterson, L., & Oliver, K. K. (1995). Prevention of injuries and disease. In M. C. Roberts (Ed.), *Handbook of pediatric psychology* (2nd ed., pp. 185–199). New York: Guilford.

Petrie, R. H. (1991). Intrapartum fetal evaluation. In S. G. Gabbe, J. R. Niebyl, & J. L. Simpson (Eds.), *Obstetrics: Normal & problem pregnancies* (2nd ed.). New York: Churchill Livingstone.

Pettit, G. S., Bakshi, A., Dodge, K. A., & Coie, J. D. (1990). The emergence of social dominance in young boys' play groups: Developmental differences and behavioral correlates. *Developmental Psychology, 26,* 1017–1025.

Pettit, G. S., Bates, J. E., & Dodge, K. A. (1997). Supportive parenting, ecological context, and children's adjustment: A seven-year longitudinal study. *Child Development, 68,* 908–923.

Pettit, G. S., Bates, J. E., Dodge, K. A., & Meece, D. W. (1999). The impact of after-school peer contact on early adolescent externalizing problems is moderated by parental monitoring, perceived neighborhood safety, and prior adjustment. *Child Development, 70*(3), 768–778.

Petts, J., & Niemeyer, S. J. (2004). Health risk communication and amplification: Learning from the MMR vaccination controversy. *Health, Risk, and Society, 6*(1), 7–23.

Pettito, L. A., & Marentette, P. F. (1991). Babbling in the manual mode: Evidence for the ontogeny of language. *Science, 251,* 1493–1496.

Petitto, L. A., Zatorre, R. J., Gauna, K., Nikelski, E. J., Dostie, D., & Evans, A. C. (2000). Speech-like cerebral activity in profoundly deaf people processing signed language: Implications for the neural basis of human language. *Proceedings of the National Academy of Sciences, 97,* 13961–13966.

Petrakos, H., & Howe, N. (1996). The influence of the physical design of the dramatic play center on children's play. *Early Childhood Research Quarterly, 11,* 63–77.

Phinney, J. (1990). Ethnic identity in adolescents and adults. *Psychological Bulletin, 108,* 499–514.

Phinney, J. S., & Chavira, V. (1992). Ethnic identity and self-esteem: An exploratory longitudinal study. *Journal of Adolescence, 15,* 271–281.

Phinney, J. S., Cantu, C. L., & Kurtz, D. A. (1997). Ethnic and American identity as predictors of self-esteem among African American, Latino, and White adolescents. *Journal of Youth and Adolescence, 26,* 165–185.

Piaget, J. (1929). *The child's conception of the world.* New York: Harcourt, Brace.

Piaget, J., & Inhelder, B. (1956). *The child's conception of space.* Boston: Routledge & Kegan Paul.

Piaget, J., & Inhelder, B. (1967). *The child's conception of space.* New York: W. W. Norton.

Picard, C. L. (1999). The level of competition as a factor for the development of eating disorders in female collegiate athletes. *Journal of Youth and Adolescence, 28,* 583–594.

Pickett, M. B., Berg, R. L., & Murphy, D. (2004). Operational characteristics of tractors driven by children on farms in the United States and Canada. *Journal of Agricultural Safety and Health, 10,* 17–25.

Plessinger, M. A., & Woods, J. R., Jr. (1998). Cocaine in pregnancy: Recent data on maternal and fetal risks. *Substance Abuse in Pregnancy, 25,* 99–118.

Plöderl, M., & Tremblay, P. (2015). Mental health of sexual minorities. A systematic review. *International Review of Psychiatry, 27,* 367–385.

Plomin, R. (1990). *Nature and nurture.* Pacific Grove, CA: Brooks/Cole.

Plomin, R. (2002). Behavioural genetics in the 21st century. In W. W. Hartup & R. K. Silbereisen (Eds.), *Growing points in developmental science: An introduction* (pp. 47–63). Philadelphia: Psychology Press.

Plomin, R., & Asbury, K. (2001). Nature and nurture in the family. *Marriage and Family Review, 33,* 273–281.

Plomin, R., Asbury, K., Dip, P. G., & Dunn, J. (2001). Why are children in the same family so different? Nonshared environment a decade later. *Canadian Journal of Psychiatry, 46,* 225–233.

Plomin, R., Fulker, D. W., Corley, R., & DeFries, J. C. (1997). Nature, nurture, and cognitive development from 1 to 16 years: A parent-offspring adoption study. *Psychological Science, 8,* 442–447.

Plomin, R., & Petrill, S. A. (1997). Genetics and intelligence: What's new? *Intelligence, 24,* 53–77.

Plomin, R., & Rutter, M. (1998). Child development, molecular genetics, and what to do with genes once they are found. *Child Development, 69,* 1223–1242.

Plumert, J. M., & Nichols-Whitehead, P. (1996). Parental scaffolding of young children's spatial communication. *Developmental Psychology, 32,* 523–532.

Pollitt, E. (1994). Poverty and child development: Relevance of research in developing countries to the United States. *Child Development, 65,* 283–295.

Pollitt, E. (1995). Does breakfast make a difference in school? *Journal of the American Dietetic Association, 95,* 1134–1139.

Pomerleau, A., Bolduc, D., Malcuit, G., & Cossette, L. (1990). Pink or blue: Environmental gender stereotypes in the first two years of life. *Sex Roles, 22,* 359–367.

Porter, R. H., Makin, J. W., Davis, L. B., & Christensen, K. M. (1991). An assessment of the salient olfactory environment of formula-fed infants. *Physiology and Behavior, 50,* 907–911.

Poulin-Dubois, D., & Forbes, J. (2002). Toddlers' attention to intentions-in-action in learning novel action words. *Developmental Psychology, 38,* 104–114.

Poulin-Dubois, D., Serbin, L. A., Eichstedt, J. A., Sen, M. G., & Beissel, C. F. (2002). Men don't put on make-up: Toddlers' knowledge of the gender stereotyping of household activities. *Social Development, 11,* 166–181.

Poulin-Dubois, D., Serbin, L. A., Kenyon, B., & Derbyshire, A. (1994). Infants' intermodal knowledge about gender. *Developmental Psychology, 30,* 436–442.

Poulson, C. L., Kymissis, E., Reeve, K. F., Andreatos, M., & Reeve, L. (1991). Generalized vocal imitation in infants. *Journal of Experimental Child Psychology, 51,* 267–279.

Povinelli, D. J., & Simon, B. B. (1998). Young children's understanding of briefly versus extremely delayed images of the self: Emergence of the autobiographical stance. *Developmental Psychology, 34,* 188–194.

Power, F. C., Higgins, A., & Kohlberg, L. (1989). *Lawrence Kohlberg's approach to moral education.* New York: Columbia University Press.

Powers, S. W., & Roberts, M. W. (1995). Simulation training with parents of oppositional children: Preliminary findings. *Journal of Clinical Child Psychology, 24,* 89–97.

Powlishta, K. K. (2000). The effect of target age on the activation of gender stereotypes. *Sex Roles, 42,* 271–282.

Powlishta, K., Serbin, L. A., Doyle, A., & White, D. R. (1994). Gender, ethnic, and body type biases: The generality of prejudice in childhood. *Developmental Psychology, 30,* 526–536.

Priel, B., & deSchonen, S. (1986). Self-recognition: A study of a population without mirrors. *Journal of Experimental Child Psychology, 41,* 237–250.

Propper, C., & Moore, G. A. (2006). The influence of parenting on infant emotionality: A multi-level psychobiological perspective. *Developmental Review, 26,* 427–460.

Proteau, L., & Elliott, D. (1992). *Vision and motor control.* Amsterdam: North-Holland Press.

Pryde, K. M., Bryden, P. J., & Roy, E. A. (2000). A developmental analysis of the relationship between hand preference and performance: Preferential reaching into hemispace. *Brain and Cognition, 43,* 370–374.

Public Health Agency of Canada. (n.d.). *The Canadian guide to clinical preventive health care.* Chapter 20. Screening for Hemoglobinopathies in Canada. Ottawa: Public Health Agency of Canada.

Public Health Agency of Canada. (1998). *Aboriginal Head Start: Urban and Northern Initiative principles and guideline.* Ottawa: Public Health Agency of Canada.

Public Health Agency of Canada, FASD Team. (2005a). Fetal alcohol spectrum disorder (FASD): A framework for action. Ottawa: Ministry of Health. Retrieved from www.phac-aspc.gc.ca/publicat/fasd-fw-etcaf-ca/framework-eng.php

Public Health Agency of Canada. (2005b). Aboriginal Head Start. Retrieved from www.phac-aspc.gc.ca/canada/regions/ab-nwt-tno/program-programmes/ahs-eng.php

Public Health Agency of Canada. (2008). Canadian Perinatal Health Report, 2008 Edition. Ottawa: Ministry of Health. Retrieved from www.phac-aspc.gc.ca/publicat/2008/cphr-rspc/factsheet-fiche-eng.php

Public Health Agency of Canada. (2010). *The Canadian incidence study of reported abuse and neglect—2008: Major findings.* Ottawa: Public Health Agency of Canada.

Quas, J. A., Goodman, G. S., Bidrose, S., Pipe, M., Craw, S., & Ablin, D. S. (1999). Emotion and memory: Children's long-term remembering, forgetting, and suggestibility. *Journal of Experimental Child Psychology, 72,* 235–270.

Raimbault, C., Saliba, E., & Porter, R. (2007). The effect of the odour of mother's milk on breastfeeding behaviour of premature neonates. *Acta Paediatrica, 96,* 368–371.

Rakic, P. (1995). Corticogenesis in human and nonhuman primates. In M. S. Gazzaniga (Ed.), *The cognitive neurosciences.* Cambridge, MA: MIT Press.

Ram, A., & Ross, H. S. (2001). Problem-solving, contention, and struggle: How siblings resolve a conflict of interests. *Child Development, 72,* 1710–1722.

Ramey, C. T., & Campbell, F. A. (1991). Poverty, early childhood education, and academic competence: The Abecedarian experiment. In A. Huston (Ed.), *Children reared in poverty.* New York: Cambridge University Press.

Ramey, C. T., & Ramey, S. L. (1990). Intensive educational intervention for children of poverty. *Intelligence, 14,* 1–9.

Ramsey, P. G. (1995). Growing up with the contradictions of race and class. *Young Children, 50,* 18–22.

Rankin, J. M., & Ornstein, A. E. (2009). A commentary on mandatory reporting legislation in the United States,

Canada, and Australia: A cross-jurisdictional review of key features, differences, and issues. *Child Maltreatment, 14,* 121–123.

Rappaport, L. (1993). The treatment of nocturnal enuresis—where are we now? *Pediatrics, 92,* 465–466.

Rapport, M. D. (1995). Attention-deficit hyperactivity disorder. In M. Hersen & R. T. Ammerman (Eds.), *Advanced abnormal child psychology.* Hillsdale, NJ: Erlbaum.

Rasalam, A. D., Hailey, H., Williams, J. H. G., Moore, S. J., Turnpenny P. D., & Lloyd, D. J. (2005). Characteristics of fetal anticonvulsant syndrome associated autistic disorder. *Developmental Medicine & Child Neurology, 47,* 551–555.

Rasmussen, P., & Gillberg, C. (2000). Natural outcome of ADHD with developmental coordination disorder at age 22 years: A controlled, longitudinal, community-based study. *Journal of the American Academy of Child and Adolescent Psychiatry, 39,* 1424–1431.

Rawn, C. D., & Vohs, K. D. (2006). The importance of self-regulation for interpersonal functioning. In K. D. Vohs & E. J. Finkel (Eds.), *Self and relationships: Connecting intrapersonal and interpersonal processes* (pp. 15–31). New York: Guilford Press.

Read, C. Y. (2004). Using the Impact of Event Scale to evaluate psychological response to being a phenylketonuria gene carrier. *Journal of Genetic Counseling, 13,* 207–219.

Reese, E. (2002). Social factors in the development of autobiographical memory: The state of the art. *Social Development, 11,* 124–142.

Reese, E., & Cox, A. (1999). Quality of adult book reading affects children's emergent literacy. *Developmental Psychology, 35,* 20–28.

Reich, P. A. (1986). *Language development.* Englewood Cliffs, NJ: Prentice-Hall.

Reid, D. H., Wilson, P. G., & Faw, G. D. (1991). Teaching self-help skills. In J. L. Matson & J. A. Mulick (Eds.), *Handbook of mental retardation* (2nd ed.). New York: Pergamon.

Repacholi, B. M. (1998). Infants' use of attentional cues to identify the referent of another person's emotional expression. *Developmental Psychology, 34,* 1017–1025.

Reynolds, A. J., & Temple, J. A. (1998). Extended early childhood intervention and school achievement: Age thirteen findings from the Chicago longitudinal study. *Child Development, 69,* 231–246.

Ricciuti, H. N. (1993). Nutrition and mental development. *Current Directions in Psychological Science, 2,* 43–46.

Rice, M. L., Huston, A. C., Truglio, R., & Wright, J. (1990). Words from Sesame Street: Learning vocabulary while viewing. *Developmental Psychology, 26,* 421–428.

Rice, S. G. (1993). Injury rates among high school athletes 1979–1992. Unpublished raw data.

Rich, C. L., Sherman, M., & Fowler, R. C. (1990, Winter). San Diego suicide study: The adolescents. *Adolescence, 25*(100), 855–865.

Richardson, G. A. (1998). Prenatal cocaine exposure: A longitudinal study of development. *Annals of the New York Academy of Sciences, 846,* 144–152.

Richie, C. (2012). Applying Catholic responsibility to in vitro fertilization: Obligations to the spouse, the body, and the common good. *Christian Bioethics: Non-ecumenical Studies in Medical Morality, 18,* 271–286.

Rigal, R. (1994). Right-left orientation: Development of correct use of right and left terms. *Perceptual and Motor Skills, 79,* 1259–1278.

Rigal, R. (1996). Right-left orientation, mental rotation, and perspective-taking: When can children imagine what people see from their own viewpoint? *Perceptual and Motor Skills, 83,* 831–842.

Riggs, K. J., Peterson, D. M., Robinson, E. J., & Mitchell, P. (1998). Are errors in false belief tasks symptomatic of a broader difficulty with counterfactuality? *Cognitive Development, 13,* 73–90.

Ritchie, K. L. (1999). Maternal behaviors and cognitions during discipline episodes: A comparison of power bouts and single acts of noncompliance. *Developmental Psychology, 35,* 580–589.

Rivara, F. P., & Grossman, D. C. (1996). Prevention of traumatic deaths to children in the United States: How far have we come and where do we need to go? *Pediatrics, 97,* 791–798.

Roberts, G., & Nanson, J. (2000). *Best practices: Fetal alcohol syndrome/fetal alcohol effects and the effects of other substance use during pregnancy.* Ottawa: Canada's Drug Strategy Division, Health Canada.

Roberts, J. E., Burchinal, M., & Durham, M. (1999). Parents' report of vocabulary and grammatical development of African American preschoolers: Child and environmental associations. *Child Development, 70,* 92–106.

Roberts, K. C., Shields, M., de Groh, M., Aziz, A., & Gilbert, J. (2012). Overweight and obesity and children and adolescents: Results from the 2009 to 2011 Canadian Health Measures Survey. Ottawa: Minister of Industry.

Roberts, K. P., & Powell, M. B. (2001). Describing individual incidents of sexual abuse: A review of research on the effects of multiple sources of information on children's reports. *Child Abuse and Neglect, 25,* 1643–1659.

Roberts, W., & Strayer, J. (1996). Empathy, emotional expressiveness, and prosocial behavior. *Child Development, 67,* 449–470.

Robinson, B. E., Rowland, B. H., & Coleman, M. (1986). *Latchkey kids: Unlocking doors for children and their families.* Lexington, MA: Lexington Books, Heath.

Robinson, E. J., Champion, H., & Mitchell, P. (1999). Children's ability to infer utterance veracity from speaker informedness. *Developmental Psychology, 35,* 535–546.

Rodgers, J. L., & Rowe, D. C. (1993). Social contagion and adolescent sexual behavior: A developmental EMOSA model. *Psychological Review, 100,* 479–510.

Rodrigo, M. J., Gonzalez, A., Ato, M., Rodriguez, G., de Vega, M., & Muneton, M. (2006). Co-development of child-mother gestures over the second and the third years. *Infant and Child Development, 15,* 1–17.

Rodríguez-Vázquez, J., Camacho-Arroyo, I., & Velázquez-Moctezuma, J. (2012). Differential impact of REM sleep deprivation on cytoskeletal proteins of brain regions involved in sleep regulation. *Neuropsychobiology, 65,* 161–167.

Roehlkepartain, E. C., Benson, P. L, King, P. E., & Wagener, L. M. (2006). Spiritual development in childhood and adolescence: Moving to the scientific mainstream. In Eugene C. Roehlkepartain, Pamela Ebstyne King, Linda Wagener, & Peter L. Benson (Eds.), *The Handbook of Spiritual Development in Childhood and Adolescence* (The SAGE Program on Applied Developmental Science). Thousand Oaks, CA: Sage.

Roffwarg, H. P., Muzio, J. N., & Dement, W. C. (1966). Ontogenetic development of the human sleep-dream cycle. *Science, 152,* 604–619.

Rogow, S. M. (1999). The impact of visual impairments on psychosocial development. In V. L. Schwean & D. H. Saklofske (Eds.), *Handbook of psychosocial characteristics of exceptional children. Plenum series on human exceptionality* (pp. 523–539). Dordrecht, Netherlands: Kluwer.

Roisman, G. I., & Fraley, R. C. (2006). The limits of genetic influence: A behavior-genetic analysis of infant–caregiver relationship quality and temperament. *Child Development, 77,* 1656–1667.

Romer, D. (2010). Adolescent risk taking, impulsivity, and brain development: Implications for prevention. *Developmental Psychobiology, 52,* 263–276.

Rooks, J. P., Weatherby, N. L., Ernst, E. K. M., Stapleton, S., Rosen, D., & Rosenfield, A. (1989). Outcomes of care in birth centers: The national birth center study. *New England Journal of Medicine, 321,* 1804–1811.

Roopnarine, J. (1992). Father-child play in India. In K. MacDonald (Ed.), *Parent-child play.* Albany: State University of New York Press.

Roscoe, B., Diana, M. S., & Brooks, R. H. (1987). Early, middle, and late adolescents' views on dating and factors influencing partner selection. *Adolescence, 22,* 59–68.

Rose, A. J., & Asher, S. R. (1999). Children's goals and strategies in response to conflicts within a friendship. *Developmental Psychology, 35,* 69–79.

Ross, D. P., Scott, K., & Kelly, M. A. (1999). *Overview: Children in Canada in the 1990s–November 1996.* Ottawa: Applied Research Branch, Strategic Policy, Human Resources Development Canada. Retrieved from http://www.hrsdc.gc.ca/eng/cs/sp/sdc/pkrf/publications/1996-002585/page04.shtml

Rosen, K. S., & Burke, P. B. (1999). Multiple attachment relationships within families: Mothers and fathers with two young children. *Developmental Psychology, 35,* 436–444.

Rosengren, K. S., Gelman, S. A., Kalish, C., & McCormick, M. (1991). As time goes by: Children's early understanding of growth in animals. *Child Development, 62,* 1302–1320.

Rosenthal, D. A., & Feldman, S. S. (1992). The relationship between parenting behaviour and ethnic identity in Chinese-American and Chinese-Australian adolescents. *International Journal of Psychology, 27,* 19–31.

Rosenthal, R., & Vandell, D. L. (1996). Quality of care at school-aged child-care programs: Regulatable features, observed experiences, child perspectives, and parent perspectives. *Child Development, 67,* 2434–2445.

Ross, H. S., & den Bak-Lammers, I. M. (1998). Consistency and change in children's tattling on their siblings: Children's perspectives on the moral rules and procedures in family life. *Social Development, 7,* 275–300.

Rostenstein, D., & Oster, H. (1997). Differential facial responses to four basic tastes in newborns. In P. Ekman & E. L. Rosenberg (Eds.), *What the face reveals: Basic and applied studies of spontaneous expression using the Facial Action Coding System (FACS). Series in affective science.* New York: Oxford University Press.

Rotenberg, K. J., & Mayer, E. V. (1990). Delay of gratification in native and white children: A cross-cultural comparison. *International Journal of Behavioral Development, 13,* 23–30.

Rothbart, M. K., Posner, M. I., & Kieras, J. (2006). Temperament, attention, and the development of self-regulation. In K. McCartney & D. Phillips (Eds.), *Blackwell handbook of early childhood development* (pp. 338–357). Malden, MA: Blackwell.

Rothbaum, F., & Weisz, J. R. (1994). Parental caregiving and child externalizing behavior in nonclinical samples: A meta-analysis. *Psychological Bulletin, 116,* 55–74.

Rotheram-Borus, M. J., Rosario, M., Van Rossem, R., & Reid, H. (1995). Prevalence, course, and predictors of multiple problem behaviors among gay and bisexual male adolescents. *Developmental Psychology, 31*, 75–85.

Rotto, P. C., & Kratochwill, T. R. (1994). Behavioral consultation with parents: Using competency-based training to modify child noncompliance. *School Psychology Review, 23*, 669–693.

Rovee-Collier, C. (1987). Learning and memory in infancy. In J. D. Osofsky (Ed.), *Handbook of infant development* (2nd ed.). New York: Wiley.

Rovee-Collier, C. (1997). Dissociations in infant memory: Rethinking the development of implicit and explicit memory. *Psychological Review, 104*, 467–498.

Rovee-Collier, C. (1999). The development of infant memory. *Current Directions in Psychological Science, 8*, 80–85.

Rovet, J. F., & Hepworth, S. (2001). Attention problems in adolescents with congenital hypothyroidism: A multicomponential analysis. *Journal of the International Neuropsychological Society, 7*, 734–744.

Rowe, D. C. (1994). No more than skin deep. *American Psychologist, 49*, 215–216.

Rowe, D. C., Almeida, D. M., & Jacobson, K. C. (1999). School context and genetic influences on aggression in adolescence. *Psychological Science, 10*, 277–280.

Royer, J. M., & Walles, R. (2007). Influences of gender, ethnicity, and motivation on mathematical performance. In D. B. Berch & M. Mazzocco (Eds.), *Why is math so hard for some children? The nature and origins of mathematical learning difficulties and disabilities* (pp. 349–367). Baltimore, MD: Paul H. Brookes.

Rubin, K. H., Bukowski, W., & Parker, J. G. (1998). Peer interactions, relationships, and groups. In W. Damon (Ed.), *Handbook of child psychology* (Vol. 3). New York: Wiley.

Rubin, K. H., Burgess, K. B., Dwyer, K. M., & Hastings, P. D. (2003). Predicting preschoolers' externalizing behaviors from toddler temperament, conflict, and maternal negativity. *Developmental Psychology, 39*, 164–176.

Ruble, D. N., Boggiano, A. K., Feldman, N. S., & Loebl, N. H. (1980). Developmental analysis of the role of social comparison in self-evaluation. *Developmental Psychology, 16*, 105–115.

Ruble, T. L. (1983). Sex stereotypes: Issues of changes in the 1970s. *Sex Roles, 9*, 397–402.

Ruff, H. A., Capozzoli, M., & Weissberg, R. (1998). Age, individuality, and context as factors in sustained visual attention during the preschool years. *Developmental Psychology, 34*, 454–464.

Rutherford, M. D., & Rogers, S. J. (2003). Cognitive underpinnings of pretend play in autism. *Journal of Autism and Developmental Disorders, 33*, 289–302.

Rutter, M. (1997). Clinical implications of attachment concepts: Retrospect and prospect. In L. Atkinson & K. J. Zucker (Eds.), *Attachment and psychopathology* (pp. 17–46). New York: Guilford.

Rydell, R., & Boucher, K. L. (2010) Capitalizing on multiple social identities to prevent stereotype threat: The moderating role of self-esteem. *Personality and Social Psychology Bulletin, 36*, 239–250.

Ryerson University. (2003). Midwifery education programme. Retrieved from www.ryerson.ca/midwife/about/whatis.html

Rymer, R. (1993). *Genie.* New York: HarperCollins.

Sacco, W. P., & Beck, A. T. (1995). Cognitive theory and therapy. In E. E. Beckham & W. R. Leber (Eds.), *Handbook of depression* (2nd ed.). New York: Guilford Press.

Sachs, K. V., Harnke, B., Mehler, P. S., & Krantz, M. J. (2015). Cardiovascular complications of anorexia nervosa: A systematic review. *International Journal of Eating Disorders, 49*, 238–248.

Saewyc, E. M., Konishi, C., Rose, H. A., & Homma, Y. (2014). School-based strategies to reduce suicidal ideation, suicide attempts, and discrimination among sexual minority and heterosexual adolescents in Western Canada. *International Journal of Child, Youth and Family Studies, 5*, 89–112.

Saewyc, E. M., Skay, C. L., Pettingell, S. L., Reis, E. A., Bearinger, L., Resnick, M., . . . Combs, L. (2006). Hazards of stigma: The sexual and physical abuse of gay, lesbian, and bisexual adolescents in the United States and Canada. *Child Welfare, 85*, 195–214.

Safe Kids Canada. (2004). *Booster seat use in Canada: A national challenge.* Toronto: Safe Kids Canada.

Saffran, J. R., Aslin, R. N., & Newport, E. L. (1996). Statistical learning by 8-month-old infants. *Science, 274*, 1926–1928.

Sagi, A., van IJzendoorn, M. H., Aviezer, O., Donnell, F., & Mayseless, O. (1994). Sleeping out of home in a kibbutz community arrangement: It makes a difference for infant-mother attachment. *Child Development, 65*, 992–1004.

Salman, M. S. (2002). The cerebellum: It's about time! But timing is not everything—New insights into the role of the cerebellum in timing motor and cognitive tasks. *Journal of Child Neurology, 17*, 1–9.

Sandberg, D. E., Brook, A. E., & Campos, S. P. (1994). Short stature: A psychosocial burden requiring growth hormone therapy? *Pediatrics, 94*, 832–840.

Sanderson, C. A., & Cantor, N. (1995). Social dating goals in late adolescence: Implications for safer sexual activity. *Journal of Personality and Social Psychology, 68*, 1121–1134.

Sandhu, D., & Tung, S. (2006). Gender differences in adolescent identity formation. *Pakistan Journal of Psychological Research, 21*, 29–40.

Sandig, H., McDonald, J., Gilmour, J., Arno, M., Lee, T. H., & Cousins, D. J. (2007). Human Th2 cells selectively express the orexigenic peptide, pro-melanin-concentrating hormone. *Proceedings of the National Academy of Sciences USA, 104,* 12440–12444.

Saukko, P. (2008). *The anorexic self: A personal, political analysis of a diagnostic discourse.* Albany: State University of New York Press.

Savage-Rumbaugh, E. S., Murphy, J., Sevcik, R. A., Brakke, K. E., Williams, S. L., & Rumbaugh, D. M. (1993). Language comprehension in ape and child. *Monographs of the Society for Research in Child Development, 58*(3–4, Serial No. 233).

Savin-Williams, R. C. (2016). Sexual orientation: Categories or continuum? Commentary on Bailey et al. (2016). *Psychological Science in the Public Interest, 17,* 37–44.

Savin-Williams, R. C., & Demo, D. H. (1984). Developmental change and stability in adolescent self-concept. *Developmental Psychology, 20,* 1100–1110.

Saxe, G. B. (1988). Candy selling and math learning. *Educational Researcher, 17,* 14–21.

Scarr, S. (1992). Developmental theories for the 1990s: Development and individual differences. *Child Development, 63,* 1–19.

Scarr, S. (1993). Genes, experience, and development. In D. Magnusson & P. J. M. Casaer (Eds.), *Longitudinal research on individual development: Present status and future perspectives. European network on longitudinal studies on individual development, 8* (pp. 26–50). Cambridge, UK: Cambridge University Press.

Scarr, S., & McCartney, K. (1983). How people make their own environments: A theory of genotype environment effects. *Child Development, 54,* 424–435.

Schaal, B., Marlier, L., & Soussignan, R. (1998). Olfactory function in the human fetus: Evidence from selective neonatal responsiveness to the odor of amniotic fluid. *Behavioral Neuroscience, 112,* 1438–1449.

Scharfe, E. (2000). Development of emotional expression, understanding, and regulation in infants and young children. In R. Bar-On & J. D. A. Parker (Eds.), *The handbook of emotional intelligence: Theory, development, assessment, and application at home, school, and in the workplace* (pp. 244–262). San Francisco: Jossey-Bass/Pfeiffer.

Schmidt, L. A., & Fox, N. A. (2002). Molecular genetics of temperamental differences in children. In J. Benjamin, R. P. Ebstein, & R. H. Belmaker (Eds.), *Molecular genetics and the human personality* (pp. 245–255). Washington, DC: American Psychiatric Publishing.

Schmuckler, M. A. (1996a). Visual-proprioceptive intermodal perception in infancy. *Infant Behavior and Development, 19,* 221–232.

Schmuckler, M. A. (1996b). The development of visually-guided locomotion: Barrier crossing by toddlers. *Ecological Psychology, 8,* 209–236.

Schmuckler, M. A. (1997). Children's postural sway in response to low- and high-frequency visual information for oscillation. *Journal of Experimental Psychology: Human Perception and Performance, 23,* 528–545.

Schneider, B. H., Atkinson, I., & Tardiff, C. (2001). Child-parent attachment and children's peer relations: A quantitative review. *Developmental Psychology, 37,* 86–100.

Schneider, B. H., Clegg, M. R., Byrne, B. M., Leddingham, J. E., & Crombie, G. (1989). Social relations of gifted children as a function of age and school program. *Journal of Educational Psychology, 81,* 48–56.

Schneider, M. L. (1992). The effect of mild stress during pregnancy on birthweight and neuromotor maturation in rhesus monkey infants (*Macaca mulatta*). *Infant Behavior and Development, 15,* 389–403.

Schneider, M. L., Roughton, E. C., Koehler, A. J., & Lubach, G. R. (1999). Growth and development following prenatal stress exposure in primates: An examination of ontogenetic vulnerability. *Child Development, 70,* 253–274.

Schneider, W., & Bjorklund, D. F. (1998). Memory. In W. Damon (Ed.), *Handbook of child psychology* (Vol. 2). New York: Wiley.

Schneider, W., & Pressley, M. (1997). *Memory development between 2 and 20* (2nd ed.). Mahwah, NJ: Erlbaum.

Schnell, L. (2000). The language of grief. *Vermont Quarterly* (Fall), 25–29.

Schnorr, T. M., Grajewski, B. A., Hornung, R. W., Thun, M. J., Egeland, G. M., Murray, W. E., . . . Halperin, W. E. (1991). Video display terminals and the risk of spontaneous abortion. *New England Journal of Medicine, 324,* 727–733.

School of the 21st Century. (2002). Home page. Retrieved from www.yale.edu/21c/index2.html

Schwartz, D., Dodge, K. A., Pettit, G. S., & Bates, J. E. (1997). The early socialization of aggressive victims of bullying. *Child Development, 68,* 665–675.

Schwebel, D. C., & Plumert, J. M. (1999). Longitudinal and concurrent relations among temperament, ability estimation, and injury proneness. *Child Development, 70,* 700–712.

Scott, W. A., Scott, R., & McCabe, M. (1991). Family relationships and children's personality: A cross-cultural, cross-source comparison. *British Journal of Social Psychology, 30,* 1–20.

Secada, W. G., Fennema, E., & Adajian, L. B. (Eds.). (1995). *New directions for equity in mathematics education.* New York: Cambridge University Press.

Seidel, C. (1998). Considerations for fitness appraisal, programming, and counselling of people with intellectual disabilities. *Canadian Journal of Applied Physiology, 23,* 185–230.

Seidenberg, M. S., & McClelland, J. L. (1989). A distributed, developmental model of word recognition and naming. *Psychological Review, 96,* 523–568.

Seidman, E., Allen, L., Aber, J. L., Mitchell, C., & Feinman, J. (1994). The impact of school transitions in early adolescence on the self-system and perceived social context of poor urban youth. *Child Development, 65,* 507–522.

Seifer, R., Schiller, M., Sameroff, A. J., Resnick, S., & Riordan, K. (1996). Attachment, maternal sensitivity, and infant temperament during the first year of life. *Developmental Psychology, 32,* 12–25.

Selman, R. L. (1980). *The growth of interpersonal understanding: Developmental and clinical analyses.* New York: Academic Press.

Selman, R. L. (1981). The child as a friendship philosopher: A case study in the growth of interpersonal understanding. In S. R. Asher & J. M. Gottman (Eds.), *The development of children's friendships.* Cambridge, UK: Cambridge University Press.

Sénéchal, M., Thomas, E., & Monker, J. (1995). Individual differences in 4-year-old children's acquisition of vocabulary during storybook reading. *Journal of Educational Psychology, 87,* 218–229.

Serbin, L., & Karp, J. (2003) Intergenerational studies of parenting and the transfer of risk from parent to child. *Current Directions in Psychological Science, 12,* 138–142.

Serbin, L. A., Poulin-Dubois, D., Colburne, K. A., Sen, M. G., & Eichstedt, J. A. (2001). Gender stereotyping in infancy: Visual preferences for and knowledge of gender-stereotyped toys in the second year. *International Journal of Behavioral Development, 25,* 7–15.

Serdula, M. K., Ivery, D., Coates, R. J., Freedman, D. S., Williamson, D. F., & Byers, T. (1993). Do obese children become obese adults? A review of the literature. *Preventive Medicine, 22,* 167–177.

Ševčikova, A., & Daneback, K. (2014). Online pornography use in adolescence: Age and gender differences. *European Journal of Developmental Psychology, 11,* 674–686.

Ševčikova, A., Simon, L., Daneback, K., & Kvapilik T. (2015). Bothersome exposure to online sexual content among adolescent girls. *Youth and Society, 47,* 486–501.

Sevy, S., Mendlewicz, J., & Mendelbaum, K. (1995). Genetic research in bipolar illness. In E. E. Beckham & W. R. Leber (Eds.), *Handbook of depression* (2nd ed.). New York: Guilford Press.

Seyfarth, R., & Cheney, D. (1996). Inside the mind of a monkey. In M. Bekoff & D. Jamieson (Eds.), *Readings in animal cognition.* Cambridge, MA: MIT Press.

Shanahan, M. J., Elder, G. H., Burchinal, M., & Conger, R. D. (1996a). Adolescent paid labor and relationships with parents: Early work-family linkages. *Child Development, 67,* 2183–2200.

Shanahan, M. J., Elder, G. H., Burchinal, M., & Conger, R. D. (1996b). Adolescent earnings and relationships with parents: The work-family nexus in urban and rural ecologies. In J. T. Mortimer & M. D. Finch (Eds.), *Adolescents, work, and family: An intergenerational developmental analysis.* Thousand Oaks, CA: Sage.

Sharp, E., Pelletier, L. G., & Lévesque, C. (2006). The double-edged sword of rewards for participation in psychology experiments. *Canadian Journal of Behavioral Sciences, 38,* 269–277.

Sharp, R., McGowan, M., Verma, J., Landy, D., McAdoo, S., Carson, S., Simpson, J. L., & McCullough, L. (2010). Moral attitudes and beliefs among couples pursuing PGD for sex selection. *Reproductive BioMedicine Online, 21,* 838–847.

Sharpe, R. M., & Skakkebaek, N. E. (1993). Are oestrogens involved in falling sperm counts and disorders of the male reproductive tract? *Lancet, 341,* 1392–1395.

Shatz, M. (1983). Communication. In P. H. Mussen (Ed.), *Handbook of child psychology* (Vol. 3). New York: Wiley.

Shatz, M., & Gelman, R. (1973). The development of communication skills: Modifications in the speech of young children as a function of listener. *Monographs of the Society for Research in Child Development, 38*(5, Serial No. 152).

Shaw, D. S., Winslow, E. B., & Flanagan, C. (1999). A prospective study of the effects of marital status and family relations on young children's adjustment among African American and European American families. *Child Development, 70,* 742–755.

Shaw, G. M., Schaffer, D., Velie, E. M., Morland, K., & Harris, J. A. (1995). Periconceptional vitamin use, dietary folate, and the occurrence of neural tube defects. *Epidemiology, 6,* 219–226.

Shek, D. T. L., Xie, Q., & Ma, C. M. S. (2015). Adolescent consumption of pornographic materials: Prevalence and psychosocial correlates based on a longitudinal study. In Lee, Tak Yan, Shek, Daniel T. L., & Sun, Rachel C. F. (Eds.), *Student well-being in Chinese adolescents in Hong Kong: Theory, intervention and research* (Vol. 7, pp. 309–324). New York: Springer Science + Business Media.

Shelov, S. P. (1993). *Caring for your baby and young child: Birth to age 5.* New York: Bantam.

Sherif, M., Harvey, O. J., White, B. J., Hood, W. R., & Sherif, C. W. (1961). *Intergroup conflict and cooperation.* Norman, OK: The University Book Exchange.

Shields, A. E., Fortun, M., Hammonds, E. M., King, P. A., Lerman, C., Rapp, R., & Sullivan, P. F. The use of race variables in genetic studies of complex traits and the goal of reducing health disparities: A transdisciplinary perspective. *American Psychologist, 60,* 77–103. doi:10.1037/0003-066X.60.1.77

Shiner, R. L. (1998). How shall we speak of children's personalities in middle childhood? A preliminary taxonomy. *Psychological Bulletin, 124,* 308–332.

Shinn, M. R. (2007). Identifying students at risk, monitoring performance, and determining eligibility within response to intervention: Research on educational need and benefit from academic intervention. *School Psychology Review, 36,* 601–617.

Shirley, M. M. (1931). *The first two years: A study of twenty-five babies.* Minneapolis: University of Minnesota Press.

Shiwach, R. (1994). Psychopathology in Huntington's disease patients. *Acta Psychiatrica Scandinavica, 90,* 241–246.

Shoda, Y., Mischel, W., & Peake, P. K. (1990). Predicting adolescent cognitive and self-regulatory competencies from preschool delay of gratification: Identifying diagnostic conditions. *Developmental Psychology, 26,* 978–986.

Shore, B. M. (2000). Metacognition and flexibility: Qualitative differences in how gifted children think. In R. C. Friedman & B. M. Shore (Eds.), *Talents unfolding: Cognition and development* (pp. 167–187). Washington, DC: American Psychological Association.

Shotland, R. L., & Goodstein, L. (1992). Sexual precedence reduces the perceived legitimacy of sexual refusal: An examination of attribution concerning date rape and consensual sex. *Personality and Social Psychology Bulletin, 18,* 756–764.

Shuter-Dyson, R. (1982). Musical ability. In D. Deutsch (Ed.), *The psychology of music.* New York: Academic Press.

Shwe, H. I., & Markman, E. M. (1997). Young children's appreciation of the mental impact of their communicative signals. *Developmental Psychology, 33,* 630–636.

Siddiqui, A. (1995). Object size as a determinant of grasping in infancy. *Journal of Genetic Psychology, 156,* 345–358.

SIECCAN (Sex Information and Education Council of Canada). (2009). Sexual health education in the schools: Questions & answers (3rd ed.). *The Canadian Journal of Human Sexuality, 18,* 47–60.

Siegal, M., & Peterson, C. C. (1998). Preschoolers' understanding of lies and innocent and negligent mistakes. *Developmental Psychology, 34,* 332–341.

Siegel, L. S. (1994). Working memory and reading: A life-span perspective. *International Journal of Behavioral Development, 17,* 109–124.

Siegler, R. S. (1986). Unities in strategy choices across domains. In M. Perlmutter (Ed.), *Minnesota symposia on child development* (Vol. 19). Hillsdale, NJ: Erlbaum.

Siegler, R. S. (1988). Strategy choice procedures and the development of multiplication skill. *Journal of Experimental Psychology: General, 117,* 258–278.

Siegler, R. S. (1998). *Children's thinking* (3rd ed.). Upper Saddle River, NJ: Prentice-Hall.

Siegler, R. S., & Jenkins, E. (1989). *How children discover new strategies.* Hillsdale, NJ: Erlbaum.

Siegler, R. S., & Robinson, M. (1982). The development of numerical understandings. In H. W. Reese & L. P. Lipsitt (Eds.), *Advances in child development and behavior* (Vol. 16). New York: Academic Press.

Siegler, R. S., & Shrager, J. (1984). Strategy choices in addition and subtraction: How do children know what to do? In C. Sophian (Ed.), *Origins of cognitive skills.* Hillsdale, NJ: Erlbaum.

Signorella, M. L., Bigler, R. S., & Liben, L. S. (1993). Developmental differences in children's gender schemata about others: A meta-analytic review. Early gender-role development. *Developmental Review, 13,* 147–183.

Signorielli, N., & Lears, M. (1992). Children, television, and conceptions about chores: Attitudes and behaviors. *Sex Roles, 27,* 157–170.

Silverman, I. (2003). Gender differences in delay of gratification: A meta-analysis. *Sex Roles, 49,* 451–463.

Silverman, I. W., & Ragusa, D. M. (1990). Child and maternal correlates of impulse control in 24-month-old children. *Genetic, Social, and General Psychology Monographs, 116,* 435–473.

Simmons, R., & Blyth, D. (1987). *Moving into adolescence.* New York: Aldine de Gruyter.

Simon, G. E. (2006). The antidepressant quandary: Considering suicide risk when treating adolescent depression. *New England Journal of Medicine, 355,* 2722–2723.

Simons, D. J., & Keil, F. C. (1995). An abstract to concrete shift in the development of biological thought: The inside story. *Cognition, 56,* 129–163.

Siushansian, J. A., Nguyen, M., & Archibald, C. P. (2000). HIV and men who have sex with men: Where is the Canadian epidemic headed? *Canadian Journal of Human Sexuality, 9,* 219–237.

Skinner, B. F. (1957). *Verbal behavior.* New York: Appleton-Century-Crofts.

Slaby, R. G., Roedell, W. C., Arezzo, D., & Hendrix, K. (1995). *Early violence prevention.* Washington, DC: National Association for the Education of Young Children.

Slate, J. R., Jones, C. H., & Dawson, P. (1993). Academic skills of high school students as a function of grade, gender, and academic track. *High School Journal, 76,* 245–251.

Slaughter, V., Heron, M., Jenkins, L., Tilse, E., Müller, U., & Liebermann, D. (2004a). Origins and early development of human body knowledge: III. Object exploration studies: Infants' discrimination of typical and scrambled dolls. *Monographs of the Society for Research in Child Development, 69,* 58–76.

Slaughter, V., Heron, M., Tilse, E., Jenkins, L., Müller, U., & Liebermann, D. (2004b). Origins and early development of human body knowledge: I. Levels of human body knowledge in development. *Monographs of the Society for Research in Child Development, 69,* 1–23.

Slaughter, V., Heron, M., Tilse, E., Jenkins, L., Müller, U., & Liebermann, D. (2004c). Origins and early development of human body knowledge: II. Visual habituation studies: Infants' responses to typical and scrambled body pictures. *Monographs of the Society for Research in Child Development, 69,* 24–57.

Slaughter, V., Heron, M., Tilse, E., Jenkins, L., Müller, U., & Liebermann, D. (2004d). Origins and early development of human body knowledge: IV. Discussion. *Monographs of the Society for Research in Child Development, 69,* 77–93.

Sloan, R., & Cotroneo, S. (2002). Partnering for social change: The "Back to Sleep" campaign. *Health Policy Research Bulletin, 1,* 19–21. Ottawa: Minister of Health. Retrieved from www.hc-sc.gc.ca/hl-vs/babies-bebes/sids-smsn/index-eng.php

Slobin, D. I. (1985). Crosslinguistic evidence for the language-making capacity. In D. I. Slobin (Ed.), *The cross-linguistic study of language acquisition: Vol. 2. Theoretical issues.* Hillsdale, NJ: Erlbaum.

Smedley, A., & Smedley, B. D. (2005). Race as biology is fiction, racism as a social problem is real: Anthropological and historical perspectives on the social construction of race. *American Psychologist, 60,* 16–26. doi:10.1037/0003-066X.60.1.16

Smetana, J. G., & Braeges, J. L. (1990). The development of toddlers' moral and conventional judgments. *Merrill-Palmer Quarterly, 36,* 329–346.

Smetana, J. G., Killen, M., & Turiel, E. (1991). Children's reasoning about interpersonal and moral conflicts. *Child Development, 62,* 629–644.

Smith, B. D., Meyers, M. B., & Kline, R. (1989). For better or for worse: Left-handedness, pathology, and talent. *Journal of Clinical and Experimental Neuropsychology, 11,* 944–958.

Smith, L. B., Thelen, E., Titzer, R., & McLin, D. (1999). Knowing in the context of acting: The task dynamics of the A-not-B error. *Psychological Review, 106,* 235–260.

Smith, M. S. (1991). An evolutionary perspective on grandparent-grandchild relationships. In P. K. Smith (Ed.), *The psychology of grandparenthood: An international perspective* (pp. 157–176). London: Routledge.

Smith, R. E., & Smoll, F. L. (1996). The coach as the focus of research and intervention in youth sports. In F. L. Smoll & R. E. Smith (Eds.), *Children and youth in sport: A biopsychological perspective* (pp. 125–141). Dubuque, IA: Brown & Benchmark.

Smith, R. E., & Smoll, F. L. (1997). Coaching the coaches: Youth sports as a scientific and applied behavioral setting. *Current Directions in Psychological Science, 6*(1), 16–21.

Smith, T. E., & Leaper, C. (2006). Self-perceived gender typicality and the peer context during adolescence. *Journal of Research on Adolescence, 16,* 91–103.

Smoll, F. L., & Schutz, R. W. (1990). Quantifying gender differences in physical performance: A developmental perspective. *Developmental Psychology, 26,* 360–369.

Smoll, F. L., Smith, R. E., Barnett, N. P., & Everett, J. J. (1993). Enhancement of children's self-esteem through social support training for youth sport coaches. *Journal of Applied Psychology, 78*(4), 602–610.

Smylie, L., Maticka-Tyndale, E., & Boyd, D. (2008). Evaluation of a school-based sex education programme delivered to grade nine students in Canada. *Sex Education, 8,* 25–46.

Snarey, J. R. (1985). Cross-cultural universality of social-moral development: A critical review of Kohlbergian research. *Psychological Bulletin, 97,* 202–232.

Snedeker, B. (1992). *Hard knocks: Preparing youth for work.* Baltimore, MD: Johns Hopkins University Press.

Snow, C. W. (1998). *Infant development* (2nd ed.). Upper Saddle River, NJ: Prentice Hall.

Snow, M. E., Jacklin, C. N., & Maccoby, E. E. (1983). Sex-of-child differences in father-child interaction at one year of age. *Child Development, 54,* 227–232.

SOGC (Society of Obstetricians and Gynaecologists of Canada). (2009). Overview of HPV. Retrieved from www.hpvinfo.ca/hpvinfo/teens/overview.aspx

Soken, N. H., & Pick, A. D. (1999). Infants' perception of dynamic affective expressions: Do infants distinguish specific expressions? *Child Development, 70,* 1275–1282.

Sokolov, J. L. (1993). A local contingency analysis of the fine-tuning hypothesis. *Developmental Psychology, 29,* 1008–1023.

Solomon, G. E. A., Johnson, S. C., Zaitchik, D., & Carey, S. (1996). Like father, like son: Young children's understanding of how and why offspring resemble their parents. *Child Development, 67,* 151–171.

Spelke, E. S. (1994). Initial knowledge: Six suggestions. *Cognition, 50,* 431–445.

Spence, J. T. (1985). Achievement American style: The rewards and costs of individualism. *American Psychologist, 40,* 1285–1295.

Sperduto, R. D., Seigel, D., Roberts, J., & Rowland, M. (1983). Prevalence of myopia in the United States. *Archives of Ophthalmology, 101,* 405–407.

Springer, K., & Keil, F. C. (1991). Early differentiation of causal mechanisms appropriate to biological and nonbiological kinds. *Child Development, 62,* 767–781.

Springer, S. P., & Deutsch, G. (1998). *Left brain, right brain: Perspectives from cognitive neuroscience* (5th ed.). New York: Freeman.

Sporkin, E., Wagner, J., & Tomashoff, C. (1992, February). A terrible hunger. *People,* pp. 92–98.

Spruijt, E., & Iedema, J. (1998). Well being of youngsters of divorce without contact with nonresident parents in the Netherlands. *Journal of Comparative Family Studies, 29,* 517–527.

Sroufe, L. A., & Fleeson, J. (1986). Attachment and the construction of relationships. In W. W. Hartup & Z. Rubin (Eds.), *Relationships and development.* Hillsdale, NJ: Erlbaum.

Sroufe, L. A., & Waters, E. (1976). The ontogenesis of smiling and laughter: A perspective on the organization of development in infancy. *Psychological Review, 83,* 173–189.

Sroufe, L. A., & Wunsch, J. P. (1972). The development of laughter in the first year of life. *Child Development, 43,* 1324–1344.

St. George, I. M., Williams, S., & Silva, P. A. (1994). Body size and the menarche: The Dunedin study. *Journal of Adolescent Health, 15,* 573–576.

St. James-Roberts, I., & Plewis, I. (1996). Individual differences, daily fluctuations, and developmental changes in amounts of infant waking, fussing, crying, feeding, and sleeping. *Child Development, 67,* 2527–2450.

St. Joseph Women's Health Centre. (n.d.). *Attachment across cultures.* Toronto: St. Joseph Women's Health Centre. Also available from www.attachmentacrosscultures. org/about/toolkit_eng.pdf

Stalikas, A., & Gavaki, E. (1995). The importance of ethnic identity: Self-esteem and academic achievement of second-generation Greeks in secondary school. *Canadian Journal of School Psychology, 11,* 1–9.

Stanovich, K. E. (1993). Dysrationalia: A new specific learning disability. *Journal of Learning Disabilities, 26,* 501–515.

Stassen Berger, K. (2007). Update on bullying at school: Science forgotten? *Developmental Review, 27,* 90–126.

Statistics Canada. (2004a). Family arrangements. Retrieved October 19, 2004, from http://142.206.72.67/ 02/02d/02d_001_e.html

Statistics Canada. (2004b). Occupations. Canada e-Book. Retrieved from http://142.206.72.67/02/02e/02e_003_e.html

Statistics Canada. (2005). *E-Book.* Ottawa: Statistics Canada.

Statistics Canada. (2010). Food Statistics 2009. Ottawa: Minister of Industry.

Statistics Canada. (2012). Portrait of families and living arrangements in Canada. Families, households and marital status, 2011 Census of Population. Ottawa: Minister of Industry.

Statistics Canada. (2013). Population by home language, by province and territory (2011 Census). Retrieved July 17, 2016, from http://www.statcan. gc.ca/tables-tableaux/sum-som/l01/cst01/ demo61a-eng.htm

Statistics Canada. (2015a). Suicides and suicide rate, by sex and by age group (both sexes, males, and females). Retrieved July 19, 2016, from http://www.statcan. gc.ca/tables-tableaux/sum-som/l01/cst01/ hlth66d-eng.htm

Statistics Canada. (2015b). Percentage distribution of method used in suicide, by sex, Canada, 2000–2009 (ten year average). Retrieved July 19, 2016, from http://www.statcan.gc.ca/pub/82-624-x/2012001/ article/chart/11696-02-chart2-eng.htm

Statistics Canada. (2016). Youth crime in Canada, 2014. Retrieved July 19, 2016, from http://www.statcan. gc.ca/daily-quotidien/160217/dq160217b-eng.htm

Stattin, H., & Magnusson, D. (1989). The role of early aggressive behavior in the frequency, seriousness, and types of later crime. *Journal of Consulting and Clinical Psychology, 57,* 710–718.

Steelman, J. D. (1994). Revision strategies employed by middle level students using computers. *Journal of Educational Computing Research, 11,* 141–152.

Stein, J. A., & Newcomb, M. D. (1999). Adult outcomes of adolescent conventional and agentic orientations: A 20-year longitudinal study. *Journal of Early Adolescence, 19,* 39–65.

Stein, J. H., & Reiser, L. W. (1994). A study of white middle-class adolescent boys' responses to "semenarche" (the first ejaculation). *Journal of Youth and Adolescence, 23,* 373–384.

Steinberg, L. (1990). Autonomy, conflict, and harmony in the family relationship. In S. S. Feldman & G. R. Elliott (Eds.), *At the threshold: The developing adolescent.* Cambridge, MA: Harvard University Press.

Steinberg, L. (2010). A behavioral scientist looks at the science of adolescent brain development. *Brain and Cognition, 72,* 160–164.

Steinberg, L., & Dornbusch, S. M. (1991). Negative correlates of part-time employment during adolescence: Replication and elaboration. *Developmental Psychology, 27*, 304–313.

Steinberg, L., Fegley, S., & Dornbusch, S. M. (1993). Negative impact of part-time work on adolescent adjustment: Evidence from a longitudinal study. *Developmental Psychology, 29*, 171–180.

Steinberg, L., Lamborn, S. D., Dornbusch, S. M., & Darling, N. (1992). Impact of parenting practices on adolescent achievement: Authoritative parenting, school involvement, and encouragement to succeed. *Child Development, 63*, 1266–1281.

Steinberg, L., & Morris, A. S. (2001). Adolescent development. *Annual Review of Psychology, 52*, 83–110.

Steinberg, L. D. (1999). *Adolescence* (5th ed.). Boston: McGraw-Hill.

Stern, M., & Karraker, K. H. (1989). Sex stereotyping of infants: A review of gender labeling studies. *Sex Roles, 20*, 501–522.

Sternberg, C. R., & Campos, J. (1990). The development of anger expressions in infancy. In N. Stein, B. Leventhal, & T. Trabasso (Eds.), *Psychological and biological approaches to emotion.* Hillsdale, NJ: Erlbaum.

Sternberg, R. J. (1977). *Intelligence, information processing, and analogical reasoning.* Hillsdale, NJ: Erlbaum.

Sternberg, R. J. (1985). *Beyond IQ: A triarchic theory of human intelligence.* Cambridge, UK: Cambridge University Press.

Sternberg, R. J. (2003). Our research program validating the triarchic theory of successful intelligence: Reply to Gottfredson. *Intelligence, 31*, 399–413.

Sternberg, R. J., Grigorenko, E. L., & Bridglall, B. L. (2007). Intelligence as a socialized phenomenon. In E. W. Gordon & B. L. Bridglall (Eds.), *Affirmative development: Cultivating academic ability* (pp. 49–72). Lanham, MD: Rowman & Littlefield.

Sternberg, R. J., Grigorenko, E. L., & Kidd, K. K. (2005). Intelligence, race, and genetics. *American Psychologist, 60*, 46–59.

Sternberg, R. J., & Kaufman, J. C. (1998). Human abilities. *Annual Review of Psychology, 49*, 479–502.

Stevenson, H. W., & Lee, S. (1990). Contexts of achievement: A study of American, Chinese, and Japanese children. *Monographs of the Society for Research in Child Development, 55*(12, Serial No. 221).

Stevenson, H. W., Parker, T., Wilkinson, A., Hegion, A., & Fish, E. (1976). Longitudinal study of individual differences in cognitive development and scholastic achievement. *Journal of Educational Psychology, 68*, 377–400.

Stevenson, H. W., & Stigler, J. W. (1992). *The learning gap.* New York: Summit Books.

Stevenson, M. R., & Black, K. N. (1995). *How divorce affects offspring: A research approach.* Madison, WI: Brown & Benchmark.

Stewart, L., & Pascual-Leone, J. (1992). Mental capacity constraints and the development of moral reasoning. *Journal of Experimental Child Psychology, 54*, 251–287.

Stewart, P., Reihman, J., Lonky, E., Darvill, T., & Pagano, J. (2000). Prenatal PCB exposure and neonatal behavioral assessment scale (NBAS) performance. *Neurotoxicology and Teratology, 22*, 21–29.

Stewart R. B., Mobley, L. A., Van Tuyl, S. S., & Salvador, W. A. (1987). The firstborns' adjustment to the birth of a sibling: A longitudinal assessment. *Child Development, 58*, 341–355.

Stice, E., & Barrera, M., Jr. (1995). A longitudinal examination of the reciprocal relations between perceived parenting and adolescents' substance use and externalizing behaviors. *Developmental Psychology, 31*, 322–334.

Stifter, C. A., & Fox, N. A. (1990). Infant reactivity: Physiological correlates of newborn and 5-month temperament. *Developmental Psychology, 26*, 582–588.

Stifter, C. A., Spinrad, T. L., & Braungart-Rieker, J. M. (1999). Toward a developmental model of child compliance: The role of emotion regulation in infancy. *Child Development, 70*, 21–32.

Stiles, J. (1998). The effects of early focal brain injury on lateralization of cognitive function. *Current Directions in Psychological Science, 7*, 21–26.

Stiles, J. (2000). Spatial cognitive development following prenatal or perinatal focal brain injury. In H. S. Harvey & J. Grafman (Eds.), *Cerebral reorganization of function after brain damage* (pp. 201–217). New York: Oxford University Press.

Stoolmiller, M., Gerrard, M., Sargent, J. D., Worth, K. A., & Gibbons, F. X. (2010). R-rated movie viewing, growth in sensation seeking and alcohol initiation: Reciprocal and moderation effects. *Prevention Science, 11*, 1–13.

Stormshak, E. A., Bellanti, C. J., Bierman, K. L., & Conduct Problems Prevention Research Group. (1996). The quality of sibling relationships and the development of social competence and behavioral control in aggressive children. *Developmental Psychology, 32*, 79–89.

Stormshak, E. A., Bierman, K. L., Brushi, C., Dodge, K. A., Coie, J. D., & Conduct Problems Prevention Research Group. (1999). The relations between behavior problems and peer preference in different classroom contexts. *Child Development, 70*, 169–182.

Strauss, M. S., & Curtis, L. E. (1984). Development of numerical concepts in infancy. In C. Sophian (Ed.), *Origins of cognitive skills.* Hillsdale, NJ: Erlbaum.

Strayer, J., & Schroeder, M. (1989). Children's helping strategies: Influences of emotion, empathy, and age. In N. Eisenberg (Ed.), *New directions for child development: Empathy and related emotional responses* (Vol. 44). San Francisco: Jossey-Bass.

Streissguth, A. P., Barr, H. M., Sampson, P. D., & Bookstein, F. L. (1994). Prenatal alcohol and offspring development: The first fourteen years. *Drugs & Alcohol Dependence, 36,* 89–99.

Strober, M. (1995). Family-genetic perspectives on anorexia nervosa and bulimia nervosa. In K. Brownell & C. G. Fairburn (Eds.), *Eating disorders and obesity: A comprehensive handbook.* New York: Guilford Press.

Stunkard, A. J., Berkowitz, R. I., Schoeller, D., Maislin, G., & Stallings, V. A. (2004). Predictors of body size in the first 2 y of life: A high-risk study of human obesity. *International Journal of Obesity, 28,* 503–513.

Stunkard, A. J., Sorensen, T. I. A., Hanis, C., Teasdale, T. W., Chakraborty, R., Schull, W. J., & Schulsinger, F. (1986). An adoption study of human obesity. *New England Journal of Medicine, 314,* 193–198.

Su, T. F., & Costigan, C. L. (2009). The development of children's ethnic identity in immigrant Chinese families in Canada: The role of parenting practices and children's perceptions of parental family obligation expectations. *Journal of Early Adolescence, 29,* 638–663.

Suddath, R. (2006). The role of neuroscience in informed consent for antidepressants in adolescents. *Clinical Neuropsychiatry: Journal of Treatment Evaluation, 3,* 245–255.

Sullivan, L. W. (1987). The risks of the sickle-cell trait: Caution and common sense. *New England Journal of Medicine, 317,* 830–831.

Sullivan, S. A., & Birch, L. L. (1990). Pass the sugar, pass the salt: Experience dictates preference. *Developmental Psychology, 26,* 546–551.

Summerville, M. B., Kaslow, N. J., & Doepke, K. J. (1996). Psychopathology and cognitive and family functioning in suicidal African-American adolescents. *Current Directions in Psychological Science, 5,* 7–11.

Super, C. M. (1981). Cross-cultural research on infancy. In H. C. Triandis & A. Heron (Eds.), *Handbook of cross-cultural psychology: Vol. 4. Developmental psychology.* Boston: Allyn and Bacon.

Super, C. M., Herrera, M. G., & Mora, J. O. (1990). Long-term effects of food supplementation and psychosocial intervention on the physical growth of Colombian infants at risk of malnutrition. *Child Development, 61,* 29–49.

Super, D. E. (1976). *Career education and the meanings of work.* Washington, DC: US Offices of Education.

Super, D. E. (1980). A life span, life space approach to career development. *Journal of Vocational Behavior, 16,* 282–298.

Susman, E. J., Dockray, S., Granger, D. A., Blades, K. T., Randazzo, W., Heaton, J. A., & Dorn, L. D. (2010).

Cortisol and alpha amylase reactivity and timing of puberty: Vulnerabilities for antisocial behaviour in young adolescents. *Psychoneuroendocrinology, 35,* 557–569.

Swarr, A. E., & Richards, M. H. (1996). Longitudinal effects of adolescent girls' pubertal development, perceptions of pubertal timing, and parental relations in eating problems. *Developmental Psychology, 32,* 636–646.

Swingley, D. (2008). The roots of the early vocabulary in infants' learning from speech. *Current Directions in Psychological Science, 17,* 308–312.

Szkrybalo, J., & Ruble, D. N. (1999). "God made me a girl": Sex-category constancy judgments and explanations revisited. *Developmental Psychology, 35,* 392–402.

Tager-Flusberg, H. (1993). Putting words together: Morphology and syntax in the preschool years. In J. Berko Gleason (Ed.), *The development of language* (3rd ed.). New York: Macmillan.

Tamis-LeMonda, C. S., & Bornstein, M. H. (1996). Variation in children's exploratory, nonsymbolic, and symbolic play: An explanatory multidimensional framework. In C. Rovee-Collier & L. P. Lipsitt (Eds.), *Advances in infancy research* (Vol. 10). Norwood, NJ: Ablex Publishing Corp.

Tanner, J. M. (1990). *Foetus into man* (2nd ed.). Cambridge, MA: Harvard University Press.

Tanski, S. E., Cin, S. D., Stoolmiller, M., & Sargent, J. D. (2010). Parental R-rated movie restriction and early-onset alcohol use. *Journal of Studies on Alcohol and Drugs, 71,* 452–459.

Tarshis, E., & Shore, B. M. (1991). Perspective taking in high and above average IQ preschool children. *European Journal for High Ability, 2,* 201–211.

Tarullo, A. R., Balsam, P. D., & Fifer, W. P. (2011). Sleep and infant learning. *Infant and Child Development, 20,* 35–46.

Taylor, D. M. (1987). Social psychological barriers to effective childhood bilingualism. In P. Homel, M. Palij, & D. Aaronson (Eds.), *Childhood bilingualism: Aspects of linguistic, cognitive, and social development* (pp. 183–195). Hillsdale, NJ: Erlbaum.

Taylor, M., Cartwright, B. S., & Carlson, S. M. (1993). A developmental investigation of children's imaginary companions. *Developmental Review, 29,* 276–285.

Taylor, M. G. (1996). The development of children's beliefs about social and biological aspects of gender differences. *Child Development, 67,* 1555–1571.

Taylor, P. S. (2014). Flunking full-day kindergarten. *Canadian Business, 87,* 28.

Taylor, R., Casten, R., Flickinger, S. M., Roberts, D., & Fulmore, C. D. (1994). Explaining the school performance of African-American adolescents. *Journal of Research on Adolescence, 4,* 21–44.

Taylor, R. D., & Roberts, D. (1995). Kinship support and maternal and adolescent well-being in economically disadvantaged African-American families. *Child Development, 66,* 1585–1597.

Taylor-Butts, A., & Bressan, A. (2006). Youth crime in Canada, 2006. *Juristat, 28*(3), 1–16.

Teller, D. Y., & Bornstein, M. H. (1987). Infant color vision and color perception. In P. Salapatek & L. Cohen (Eds.), *Handbook of infant perception* (Vol. 1). Orlando, FL: Academic Press.

Thelen, E., & Smith, L. B. (1998). Dynamic systems theories. In W. Damon (Ed.), *Handbook of child psychology* (Vol. 1). New York: Wiley.

Thelen, E., & Ulrich, B. D. (1991). Hidden skills. *Monographs of the Society for Research in Child Development, 56*(1, Serial No. 223).

Thelen, E., Ulrich, B. D., & Jensen, J. L. (1989). The developmental origins of locomotion. In M. H. Woollacott & A. Shumway-Cook (Eds.), *Development of posture and gait across the life span.* Columbia: University of South Carolina Press.

Thomas, A., Chess, S., & Birch, H. G. (1968). *Temperament and behavior disorders in children.* New York: New York University Press.

Thomas, J. R., & French, K. E. (1985). Gender differences across age in motor performance: A meta-analysis. *Psychological Bulletin, 98,* 260–282.

Thomas, J. W., Bol, L., Warkentin, R. W., Wilson, M., Strage, A., & Rohwer, W. D. (1993). Interrelationships among students' study activities, self-concept of academic ability, and achievement as a function of characteristics of high-school biology courses. *Applied Cognitive Psychology, 7,* 499–532.

Thompson, G. G. (1952). *Child psychology.* Boston: Houghton Mifflin.

Thompson, R. A., & Limber, S. (1991). "Social anxiety" in infancy: Stranger wariness and separation distress. In H. Leitenberg (Ed.), *Handbook of social and evaluation anxiety.* New York: Plenum.

Thurstone, L. L., & Thurstone, T. G. (1941). Factorial studies of intelligence. *Psychometric Monograph,* No. 2.

Till, C., Koren, G., & Rovet, J. F. (2001). Prenatal exposure to organic solvents and child neurobehavioral performance. *Neurotoxicology and Teratology, 23,* 235–245.

Tincoff, R., & Jusczyk, P. W. (1999). Some beginnings of word comprehension in 6-month-olds. *Psychological Science, 10,* 172–175.

Tizard, B., & Hodges, J. (1978). The effect of early institutional rearing on the development of eight-year-old children. *Journal of Child Psychology and Psychiatry and Allied Disciplines, 19,* 99–118.

Tobin, J. J., Wu, D. Y. H., & Davidson, D. H. (1989). *Preschools in three cultures: Japan, China, and the United States.* New Haven, CT: Yale University Press.

Tobler, N. S., & Stratton, H. H. (1997). Effectiveness of school-based drug prevention programs: A meta-analysis of the research. *Journal of Primary Prevention, 18,* 71–128.

Toda, S., & Fogel, A. (1993). Infant response to the still-face situation at 3 and 6 months. *Developmental Psychology, 29,* 532–538.

Todd, R. D., Swarzenski, B., Rossi, P. G., & Visconti, P. (1995). Structural and functional development of the human brain. In D. Cicchetti & D. J. Cohen (Eds.), *Developmental psychopathology: Vol. 1. Theory and methods* (pp. 161–194). New York: Wiley.

Trafimow, D., & Marks, M. (2015). Editorial. *Basic and Applied Social Psychology, 37,* 1–2.

Treboux, D., & Busch-Rossnagel, N. A. (1995). Age differences in parent and peer influences on female sexual behavior. *Journal of Research on Adolescence, 5,* 469–487.

Tremblay, M. S., & Willms, J. D. (2003). Is the Canadian childhood obesity epidemic related to physical inactivity? *International Journal of Obesity, 27,* 1100–1105.

Tri-Council Policy Statement 2: Ethical Conduct for Research Involving Humans. (2014). Ottawa: Canadian Institutes of Health Research, Natural Sciences and Engineering Research Council of Canada, and Social Sciences and Humanities Research Council of Canada. Retrieved from http://www.pre.ethics.gc.ca/pdf/eng/tcps2-2014/TCPS_2_FINAL_Web.pdf

Trickett, P. K., & McBride-Chang, C. (1995). The developmental impact of different forms of child abuse and neglect. *Developmental Review, 15,* 311–337.

Trocmé, N., Knoke, D., Fallon, B., & MacLaurin, B. (2009). Differentiating between substantiated, suspected and unfounded maltreatment in Canada. *Child Maltreatment, 14,* 4–16.

Trocmé, N., MacLaurin, B., Fallon, B., Daciuk, J., Billingsley, D., Tourigny, M., . . . McKenzie, B. (2001). *Health Canada Canadian Incidence Study of Reported Child Abuse and Neglect—Final Report.* Ottawa: Minister of Public Works and Government Services.

Tsai, J. H.-C. (2006). Xenophobia, ethnic community, and immigrant youths' friendship network formation. *Adolescence, 41,* 285–298.

Tuchfarber, B. S., Zins, J. E., & Jason, L. A. (1997). Prevention and control of injuries. In R. Weissberg, T. P. Gullotta, R. L. Hampton, B. A. Ryan, & G. R. Adams (Eds.), *Enhancing children's wellness* (pp. 250–277). Thousand Oaks, CA: Sage.

Unger, R., & Crawford, M. (1996). *Women and gender: A feminist psychology* (2nd ed.). New York: McGraw-Hill.

Urberg, K. A., Değirmencioğlu, S. M., & Pilgrim, C. (1997). Close friend and group influence on adolescent cigarette smoking and alcohol use. *Developmental Psychology, 33*, 834–844.

US Bureau of the Census. (1994). *Marital status and living arrangements: March 1993.* Washington, DC: US Government Printing Office.

US Department of Health and Human Services. (1997). Youth risk behavior surveillance—US, 1995. *MMWR, 45*(No. SS-4).

Uskul, A. K. (2004). Women's menarche stories from a multicultural sample. *Social Science & Medicine, 59*, 667–679.

Vaillant, G. (2003). *Aging well: Surprising guideposts to a happier life from the landmark Harvard study of adult development.* London: Little, Brown Book Group.

Valenzuela, M. (1997). Maternal sensitivity in a developing society: The context of urban poverty and infant chronic undernutrition. *Developmental Psychology, 33*, 845–855.

Valkenburg, P. M., Schouten, A. P., & Peter, J. (2005). Adolescents' identity experiments on the internet. *New Media & Society, 7*, 383–402.

Valkenburg, P. M., & van der Voort, T. H. A. (1994). Influence of TV on daydreaming and creative imagination: A review of research. *Psychological Bulletin, 116*, 316–339.

Valkenburg, P. M., & van der Voort, T. H. A. (1995). The influence of television on children's daydreaming styles: A 1-year-panel study. *Communication Research, 22*, 267–287.

Valois, R. F., Dunham, A. C. A., Jackson, K. L., & Waller, J. (1999). Association between employment and substance abuse behaviors among public high school adolescents. *Journal of Adolescent Health, 25*, 256–263.

van den Berg, S. M., Setiawan, A., Bartels, M., Polderman, T. J. C., van der Vaart, A. W., & Boomsma, D. I. (2006). Individual differences in puberty onset in girls: Bayesian estimation of heritabilities and genetic correlations. *Behavior Genetics, 36*, 261–270.

van den Boom, D. C. (1994). The influence of temperament and mothering on attachment and exploration: An experimental manipulation of sensitive responsiveness among lower-class mothers with irritable infants. *Child Development, 65*, 1457–1477.

van den Boom, D. C. (1995). Do first-year intervention effects endure? Follow-up during toddlerhood of a sample of Dutch irritable infants. *Child Development, 66*, 1798–1816.

van Huis, A., Van Itterbeeck, J., Klunder, H., Mertens, E., Halloran, A., Juir, G., & Vantomme, P. (2013). *Edible insects: Future prospects for food and feed security.* Rome: Food and Agriculture Organization of the United Nations.

van IJzendoorn, M. H. (1995). Attachment representation, parental responsiveness, and infant attachment: A meta-analysis on the predictive validity of the Adult Attachment Interview. *Psychological Bulletin, 117*, 387–403.

van IJzendoorn, M. H., & Kroonenberg, P. M. (1988). Cross-cultural patterns of attachment: A meta-analysis of the Strange Situation. *Child Development, 59*, 147–156.

Vandell, D. L., & Ramanan, J. (1991). Children of the National Longitudinal Survey of Youth: Choices in after-school care and child development. *Developmental Psychology, 27*, 637–643.

Varea, C., Bernis, C., Montero, P., Arias, S., Barroso, A., & Gonzalez, B. (2000). Secular trend and intrapopulational variation in age at menopause in Spanish women. *Journal of Biosocial Science, 32*, 383–393.

Vargha-Khadem, F., Gadian, D. G., Watkins, K. E., Connelly, A., Van Paesschen, W., Mishkin, M. (1997). Differential effects of early hippocampal pathology on episodic and semantic. *Science, 277*, 376–380.

Vaughn, B. E., Kopp, C. D., & Krakow, J. B. (1984). The emergence and consolidation of self-control from eighteen to thirty months of age: Normative trends and individual differences. *Child Development, 55*, 990–1004.

Vederhus, L., & Krekling, S. (1996). Sex differences in visual spatial ability in 9-year-old children. *Intelligence, 23*, 33–43.

Ventura, S. J., Martin, J. A., Curtin, S. C., & Mathews, T. J. (1997, June). Report of final natality statistics, 1995. *Monthly Vital Statistics Report, 45.*

Verbrugge, H. P. (1990). The national immunization program of the Netherlands. *Pediatrics, 86*, 1060–1063.

Verma, I. M. (1990). Gene therapy. *Scientific American, 263*, 68–84.

Vezina, M. (2012). 2011 general social survey: Overview of families in Canada—Being a parent in a stepfamiliy: A profile. Ottawa: Minister of Industry.

Vigneau, F., Lavergne, C., & Brault, M. (1998). Automaticite du traitement de l'information et evaluation du retard mental [Automaticity of information processing and intellectual assessment of the mentally retarded]. *Canadian Journal of Behavioural Science, 30*, 99–107.

Vitaro, F., Tremblay, R. E., & Bukowski, W. M. (2001). Friends, friendships and conduct disorders. In J. Hill & B. Maughan (Eds.), *Conduct disorders in childhood and adolescence* (pp. 346–378). New York: Cambridge University Press.

Vockley, J., Andersson, H. C., Antshel, K. M., Braverman, N. E., Burton, B. K., Frazier, D. M., . . . Berry, S. A.; For the American College of Medical Genetics and Genomics Therapeutic Committee. (2014). Phenylalanine hydroxylase deficiency: Diagnosis and management guideline. *Genetics in Medicine, 16*(2), 188–200. doi:10.1038/gim.2013.157

Voeller, K. K. S. (2004). Attention-deficit hyperactivity disorder (ADHD). *Journal of Child Neurology, 19*, 798–814.

Vogan, V. M., Morgan, B. R., Leung, R. C., Anagnostou, E., Doyle-Thomas, K., & Taylor, M. J. (2016). Widespread white matter differences in children and adolescents with autism spectrum disorder. *Journal of Autism and Developmental Disorders, 46*, 2138–2147.

Volling, B. L., & Belsky, J. (1992). The contribution of mother-child and father-child relationships to the quality of sibling interaction: A longitudinal study. *Child Development, 63*, 1209–1222.

Volpe, J. J. (2009). Cerebellum of the premature infant: Rapidly developing, vulnerable, clinically important. *Journal of Child Neurology, 24*, 1085–1104.

von Hofsten, C., Vishton, P., Spelke, E. S., Feng, Q., & Rosander, K. (1998). Predictive action in infancy: Tracking and reaching for moving objects. *Cognition, 67*, 255–285.

Vorhees, C. V., & Mollnow, E. (1987). Behavior teratogenesis: Long-term influences on behavior. In J. D. Osofsky (Ed.), *Handbook of infant development* (2nd ed.). New York: Wiley.

Vouloumanos, A., & Werker, J. (2004). Tuned to the signal: The privileged status of speech for young infants. *Developmental Science, 7*, 270–276.

Voyer, D., Voyer, S., & Bryden, M. P. (1995). Magnitude of sex differences in spatial abilities: A meta-analysis and consideration of critical variables. *Psychological Bulletin, 117*, 250–270.

Vygotsky, L. S. (1934/1986). *Thought and language* (A. Kozulin, Trans.). Cambridge, MA: MIT Press.

Vygotsky, L. S. (1978). *Mind in society: The development of higher psychological processes* (M. Cole, V. John-Steiner, S. Scribner, & E. Soubermen, Eds.). Cambridge, MA: Harvard University Press.

Wagner, N., Meusel, D., & Kirch, W. (2005). Nutrition education for children—Results and perspectives. *Journal of Public Health, 13*, 102–110.

Wagner, N. E., Schubert, H. J. P., & Schubert, D. S. P. (1985). Family size effects: A revision. *Journal of Genetic Psychology, 146*, 65–78.

Wagner, R. K., Torgesen, J. K., & Rashotte, C. A. (1997). Development of reading-related phonological processing abilities: New evidence of bidirectional causality from a latent variable longitudinal study. *Developmental Psychology, 30*, 73–87.

Wakschlag, L. S. (2002). Tobacco consumption during pregnancy and its impact on child development: Comments on Fergusson and Fried. In R. E. Tremblay, R. DeV. Peters, M. Boivin, & R. G. Barr (Eds.), *Encyclopedia on Early Childhood Development. Montreal: Centre of Excellence for Early Childhood Development.* Retrieved from www.excellence-earlychildhood.ca/documents/CorneliusANGxp.pdf

Wakschlag, L. S., & Hans, S. L. (1999). Relation of maternal responsiveness during infancy to the development of behavior problems in high-risk youths. *Developmental Psychology, 35*, 569–579.

Wakschlag, L., & Hans, S. (2002). Maternal smoking during pregnancy and conduct problems in high-risk youth: A developmental framework. *Development and Psychopathology, 14*, 351–369.

Walberg, H. J. (1995). General practices. In G. Cawelti (Ed.), *Handbook of research on improving student achievement*. Arlington, VA: Educational Research Service.

Walker, L. J. (1980). Cognitive and perspective-taking prerequisites for moral development. *Child Development, 51*, 131–139.

Walker, L. J. (1995). Sexism in Kohlberg's moral psychology? In W. M. Kurtines & J. L. Gewirtz (Ed.), *Moral development: An introduction*. Boston: Allyn and Bacon.

Walker, L. J., Gustafson, P., & Hennig, K. H. (2001). The consolidation/transition model in moral reasoning development. *Developmental Psychology, 37*, 187–197.

Walker, L. J., & Taylor, J. H. (1991). Family interactions and the development of moral reasoning. *Child Development, 62*, 264–283.

Walker, S. P., Chang, S. M., Powell, C. A., & Grantham-McGregor, S. M. (2005). Effects of early childhood psychosocial stimulation and nutritional supplementation on cognition and education in growth-stunted Jamaican children: Prospective cohort study. *Lancet, 366*, 1804–1807.

Wang, L., & Carr, M. (2014). Working memory and strategy use contribute to gender differences in spatial ability. *Educational Psychologist, 49*, 261–282.

Wang, Q., Conway, M., & Hou, Y. (2007). Infantile amnesia: A cross-cultural investigation. In M.-K. Sun (Ed.), *New research in cognitive sciences* (pp. 95–104). Hauppauge, NY: Nova Science.

Ward, S. L., & Overton, W. F. (1990). Semantic familiarity, relevance, and the development of deductive reasoning. *Developmental Psychology, 26*, 288–493.

Waschbusch, D. A., Sellers, D. P., LeBlanc, M., & Kelley, M. L. (2003). Helpless attributions and depression in adolescents: The roles of anxiety, event valence and demographics. *Journal of Adolescence, 26*, 169–183.

Wasserstein, R. L., & Lazar, N. A. (2016). The ASA's statement on p-values: Context, process, and purpose. *The American Statistician.* doi:10.1080/00031305.2016.1154108. Retrieved from http://dx.doi.org/10.1080/00031305.2016.1154108

Waters, E., Merrick, S., Treboux, D., Crowell, J., & Albersheim, L. (2000). Attachment security in infancy and early adulthood: A twenty-year longitudinal study. *Child Development, 71,* 684–689.

Waters, H. F. (1993, July 12). Networks under the gun. *Newsweek,* pp. 64–66.

Waters, H. S. (1980). "Class news": A single-subject longitudinal study of prose production and schema formation during childhood. *Journal of Verbal Learning and Verbal Behavior, 19,* 152–167.

Watson, J. B. (1925). *Behaviorism.* New York: Norton.

Watson, J. B., & Rayner, R. (1920). Conditioned emotional reactions. *Journal of Experimental Psychology, 3,* 1–14.

Waxman, S. R., & Markow, D. B. (1995). Words as invitations to form categories: Evidence from 12- to 13-month-old infants. *Cognitive Psychology, 29,* 257–303.

Webber, L. S., Wattigney, W. A., Srinivasan, S. R., & Berenson, G. S. (1995). Obesity studies in Bogalusa. *American Journal of Medical Science, 310,* S53–S61.

Weber, M., Quiring, O., & Daschmann, G., (2012). Peers, parents and pornography: Exploring adolescents' exposure to sexually explicit material and its developmental correlates. *Sexuality & Culture: An Interdisciplinary Quarterly, 16,* 408–427.

Wegman, M. E. (1994). Annual summary of vital statistics—1993. *Pediatrics, 95,* 792–803.

Weinberg, M. K., & Tronick, E. Z. (1994). Beyond the face: An empirical study of infant affective configurations of facial, vocal, gestural, and regulatory behaviors. *Child Development, 65,* 1503–1515.

Weissman, M. D., & Kalish, C. W. (1999). The inheritance of desired characteristics: Children's view of the role of intention in parent-offspring resemblance. *Journal of Experimental Child Psychology, 73,* 245–265.

Wellman, H. M. (1991). From desire to belief: Acquisition of a theory of mind. In A. Whiten (Ed.), *Natural theories of mind: Evolution, development, and simulation of everyday mindreading* (pp. 19–38). Oxford, UK: Blackwell.

Wellman, H. M. (1992). *The child's theory of mind.* Cambridge, MA: MIT Press.

Wellman, H. M., Cross, D., & Bartsch, K. (1986). Infant search and object permanence: A meta-analysis of the A not B error. *Monographs of the Society for Research in Child Development, 51*(3, Serial No. 214).

Wellman, H. M., & Gelman, S. A. (1998). Knowledge acquisition in foundational domains. In W. Damon (Eds.), *Handbook of Child Psychology* (Vol. 2). New York: John Wiley & Sons.

Welsh, M. C., Pennington, B. F., & Groisser, D. B. (1991). A normative-developmental study of executive function: A window on prefrontal function in children. *Developmental Neuropsychology, 7,* 131–149.

Wendland-Carro, J., Piccinini, C. A., & Millar, W. S. (1999). The role of an early intervention on enhancing the quality of mother-infant interaction. *Child Development, 70,* 713–721.

Wentzel, K. R., & Asher, S. R. (1995). The academic lives of neglected, rejected, popular, and controversial children. *Child Development, 66,* 754–763.

Wentzel, K. R., & Erdley, C. A. (1993). Strategies for making friends: Relations to social behavior and peer acceptance. *Developmental Psychology, 29,* 819–826.

Werbner, P. (2009). The hidden lion: Tswapong girls' puberty rituals and the problem of history. *American Ethnologist, 36,* 441–458.

Werker, J., & Tees, R. (1999). Influences on infant speech processing: Toward a new synthesis. In J. T. Spence (Ed.) & J. M. & D. J. Foss (Assoc. Eds.), *Annual Review of Psychology* (Vol. 50, pp. 509–535). Palo Alto, CA: Annual Reviews.

Werker, J. F., & Lalonde, C. E. (1988). Cross-language speech perception: Initial capabilities and developmental change. *Developmental Psychology, 24,* 672–683.

Werker, J. F., Pons, F., Dietrich, C., Kajikawa, S., Fais, L., & Amano, S. (2007). Infant-directed speech supports phonetic category learning in English and Japanese. *Cognition, 103,* 147–162.

Wermeskerken, M., Kamp, J., & Hofsten, C. (2013). Getting the closer object? An information-based dissociation between vision for perception and vision for movement in early infancy. *Developmental Science, 16,* 91–100.

Werner, E. E. (1992). The children of Kauai: Resiliency and recovery in adolescents and adulthood. *Journal of Adolescent Health, 13,* 262–268.

Werner, E. E. (1993). Risk, resilience, and recovery— Perspectives from the Kauai Longitudinal Study. *Development and Psychopathology, 5,* 503–515.

Werner, E. E. (1995). Resilience in development. *Current Directions in Psychological Science, 4,* 81–85.

Werner E. E. (1996). Vulnerable but invincible—High risk children from birth to adulthood. *European Child & Adolescent Psychiatry, 5,* 47–51.

Werner, H. (1948). *Comparative psychology of mental development.* Chicago: Follet.

Wertsch, J. V., & Tulviste, P. (1992). L. S. Vygotsky and contemporary developmental psychology. *Developmental Psychology, 28,* 548–557.

West, S. G., Biesanz, J. C., & Pitts, S. C. (2000). Causal inference and generalization in field settings:

Experimental and quasi-experimental designs. In H. T. Reis & C. M. Judd (Eds.), *Handbook of research methods in social and personality psychology* (pp. 40–84). New York: Cambridge University Press.

Whaley, L. F., & Wong, D. F. (1991). *Nursing care of infants and children*. St. Louis, MO: Mosby-Year Book.

Whincup, P. H., Gilg, J. A., Odoki, K., Taylor, S. J. C., & Cook, D. G. (2001). Age of menarche in contemporary British teenagers: Survey of girls born between 1982 and 1986. *British Medical Journal, 322*, 1095–1096.

Whitaker, R. C., Wright, J. A., Pepe, M. S., Seidel, K. D., & Dietz, W. H. (1997). Predicting obesity in young adulthood from childhood and parental obesity. *New England Journal of Medicine, 337*, 869–873.

White, S. H. (1996). The relationships of developmental psychology to social policy. In E. F. Zigler, S. L. Kagan, & N. W. Hall (Eds.), *Children, families, and government: Preparing for the twenty-first century*. New York: Cambridge University Press.

Whitehead, J. R., & Corbin, C. B. (1997). Self-esteem in children and youth: The role of sport and physical education. In K. R. Fox (Ed.), *The physical self: From motivation to well-being*. Champaign, IL: Human Kinetics.

Whitehurst, G. J., & Vasta, R. (1975). Is language acquired through imitation? *Journal of Psycholinguistic Research, 4*, 37–59.

Whitehurst, G. J., & Vasta, R. (1977). *Child behavior*. Boston: Houghton Mifflin.

Whitesell, N. R., & Harter, S. (1996). The interpersonal context of emotion: Anger with close friends and classmates. *Child Development, 67*, 1345–1359.

Whitfield, K. E., & McClearn, G. (2005). Genes, environment, and race: Quantitative genetic approaches. *American Psychologist, 60*, 104–114.

Whitfield, M. F., & Grunau, R. E. (2000). Behavior, pain perception, and the extremely low–birth weight survivor. *Clinics in Perinatology, 27*, 363–379.

Whiting, J. W. M., & Child, I. L. (1953). *Child training and personality: A cross-cultural study*. New Haven, CT: Yale University Press.

Whitney, E. N., Cataldo, C. B., & Rolfes, S. R. (1987). *Understanding normal and clinical nutrition* (2nd ed.). St. Paul, MN: West Publishing.

Wicks-Nelson, R., & Israel, A. C. (1991). *Behavior disorders of childhood* (2nd ed.). Englewood Cliffs, NJ: Prentice Hall.

Wilcoxon, J. S., Kuo, A. G., Disterhoft, J. F., & Redei, E. E. (2005). Behavioral deficits associated with fetal alcohol exposure are reversed by prenatal thyroid hormone treatment: A role for maternal thyroid hormone deficiency in FAE. *Molecular Psychiatry, 10*, 961–971.

Wille, S. (1994). Primary nocturnal enuresis in children. *Scandinavian Journal of Urology and Nephrology, Suppl. 156*, 6–23.

Williams, J. E., & Best, D. L. (1990). *Measuring sex stereotypes: A thirty-nation study* (rev. ed.). Newbury Park, CA: Sage Publications.

Williams, J. M. (1997). *Style: Ten lessons in clarity and grace* (5th ed.). New York: Longman.

Williams, R., Zolner, T., Bertrand, L., & Davis, R. M. (2004). Mental health status of infrequent adolescent substance users. *Journal of Child & Adolescent Substance Abuse, 14*, 41–60.

Williams, T., Connolly, J., & Cribbie, R. (2008). Light and heavy heterosexual activities of young Canadian adolescents: Normative patterns and differential predictors. *Journal of Research on Adolescence, 18*, 145–172.

Williams, T., Connolly, J., Pepler, D., & Craig, W. (2003). Questioning and sexual minority adolescents: High school experiences of bullying, sexual harassment and physical abuse. *Canadian Journal of Community Mental Health, 22*, 47–58.

Willoughby, T., Good, M., Adachi, P. J. C., Hamza, C., & Tavernier, R. (2014). Examining the link between adolescent brain development and risk taking from a social-developmental perspective (reprinted). *Brain and Cognition, 89*, 70–78.

Wilson, C. C., Piazza, C. C., & Nagle, R. (1990). Investigation of the effect of consistent and inconsistent behavioral example upon children's donation behavior. *Journal of Genetic Psychology, 151*, 361–376.

Wilson, G. T., Hefferman, K., & Black, C. M. D. (1996). Eating disorders. In E. J. Mash & R. A. Barkley (Eds.), *Child psychopathology*. New York: Guilford.

Wilson, M. (1989). Child development in the context of the black extended family. *American Psychologist, 44*, 380–383.

Wilson, R. S. (1983). The Louisville Twin Study: Developmental synchronies in behavior. *Child Development, 54*, 298–316.

Wilson, R. S. (1986). Growth and development of human twins. In F. Falkner & J. M. Tanner (Eds.), *Human growth: A comprehensive treatise* (Vol. 3). New York: Plenum.

Windle, M., & Windle, R. C. (1996). Coping strategies, drinking motives, and stressful life events among middle adolescents: Associations with emotional and behavioral problems and with academic functioning. *Journal of Abnormal Psychology, 105*, 551–560.

Wing Sue, D. Capodilupo, C. M., Torino, G. C., Bucceri, J. M., Holder, A. M. B., Nadal, K. L., & Esquilin, M. (2007). Racial microaggressions in everyday life: Implications for clinical practice. *American Psychologist, 62*, 271–286. doi:10.1037/0003-066X.62.4.271

Winner, E. (1989). Development in the visual arts. In W. Damon (Ed.), *Child development today and tomorrow.* San Francisco: Jossey Bass.

Wise, B. W., Ring, J., & Olson, R. K. (1999). Training phonological awareness with and without explicit attention to articulation. *Journal of Experimental Child Psychology, 72,* 271–304.

Wishart, J. G., & Bower, T. G. R. (1982). The development of spatial understanding in infancy. *Journal of Experimental Psychology, 33,* 363–385.

Witelson, S. F. (1987). Neurobiological aspects of language in children. *Child Development, 58,* 653–688.

Witelson, S. F., & Kigar, D. L. (1988). Anatomical development of the corpus callosum in humans: A review with reference to sex and cognition. In D. L. Molfese & S. J. Segalowitz (Eds.), *Brain lateralization in children* (pp. 35–57). New York: Guilford Press.

Wolff, P. H. (1987). *The development of behavioral states and the expression of emotions in early infancy.* Chicago: University of Chicago Press.

Wolfson, A. R., & Carskadon, M. A. (1998). Sleep schedules and daytime functioning in adolescents. *Child Development, 69,* 875–887.

Wolraich, M. L., Lindgren, S. D., Stumbo, P. J., Stegink, L. D., Appelbaum, M. I., & Kiritsy, M. C. (1994). Effects of diets high in sucrose or aspartame on the behavior and cognitive performance of children. *New England Journal of Medicine, 330,* 301–307.

Wolraich, M. L., Wilson, D. B., & White, J. W. (1995). The effect of sugar on behavior or cognition in children. A meta-analysis. *Journal of the American Medical Association, 275,* 756–757.

Wong-Fillmore, L., Ammon, P., McLaughlin, B., & Ammon, M. S. (1985). *Learning English through bilingual instruction.* Rosslyn, VA: National Clearinghouse for Bilingual Education.

Woo, J. (2004). *A short history of the development of ultrasound in obstetrics and gynecology.* Retrieved from http://www.ob-ultrasound.net/history.html

Woo, T. U. W., & Crowell, A. L. (2005). Targeting synapses and myelin in the prevention of schizophrenia. *Schizophrenia Research, 73,* 193–207.

Wood, J. R., & Looy, H. (2000). My ant is coming to dinner: Culture, disgust, and dietary challenges. *Proteus: A Journal of Ideas, 17,* 52–56.

Woodward, A. L., & Markman, E. M. (1998). Early word learning. In W. Damon (Ed.), *Handbook of child psychology* (Vol. 2). New York: Wiley.

Woollacott, M. H., Shumway-Cook, A., & Williams, H. (1989). The development of balance and locomotion in children. In M. H. Woollacott & A. Shumway-Cook (Eds.), *Development of posture and gait across the life span.* Columbia: University of South Carolina Press.

World Health Organization Multicentre Study Group. (2006). WHO child growth standards based on length/height, weight and age. *Acta Paediatrica, Suppl. 450,* 76–85. Retrieved from www.who.int/childgrowth/standards/Growth_standard.pdf

World Health Organization. (1995). *First annual report on global health.* Geneva, Switzerland: World Health Organization.

World Health Organization. (1997). Integrated management of childhood illness: A WHO/UNICEF initiative. *Bulletin of the World Health Organization, 75,* Suppl. 1.

World Health Organization. (1999). *Removing obstacles to healthy development.* Geneva, Switzerland: World Health Organization.

World Health Organization. (2016). Children: Reducing mortality. Fact Sheet. Retrieved from http://www.who.int/mediacentre/factsheets/fs178/en/ and http://www.who.int/gho/child_health/mortality/neonatal_infant_text/en/

Wynn, K. (1996). Infants' individuation and enumeration of actions. *Psychological Science, 7,* 164–169.

Xiaohe, X., & Whyte, M. K. (1990). Love matches and arranged marriages: A Chinese replication. *Journal of Marriage and the Family, 52,* 709–722.

Yahav, R. (2011). Exposure of children to war and terrorism: A review. *Journal of Child and Adolescent Trauma, 4,* 90–108.

Yang, B., Ollendick, T. H., Dong, Q., Xia, Y., & Lin, L. (1995). Only children and children with siblings in the People's Republic of China: Levels of fear, anxiety, and depression. *Child Development, 66,* 1301–1311.

Yates, M., & Youniss, J. (1996). Community service and political-moral identity in adolescents. *Journal of Research on Adolescence, 6,* 271–284.

Yazigi, R. A., Odem, R. R., & Polakoski, K. L. (1991). Demonstration of specific binding of cocaine to human spermatozoa. *Journal of the American Medical Association, 266,* 1956–1959.

Yonas, A., & Owsley, C. (1987). Development of visual space perception. In P. Salapatek & L. Cohen (Eds.), *Handbook of infant perception* (Vol. 2). Orlando, FL: Academic Press.

Young, S. K., Fox, N. A., & Zahn-Waxler, C. (1999). The relations between temperament and empathy in 2-year-olds. *Developmental Psychology, 35,* 1189–1197.

Youngblade, L. M., & Dunn, J. (1995). Individual differences in young children's pretend play with mother and sibling: Links to relationships and understanding of other people's feelings and beliefs. *Child Development, 66,* 1472–1492.

Yu, C. (2008). A statistical associative account of vocabulary growth in early word learning. *Language Learning and Development, 4,* 32–62.

Zahn-Waxler, C., Friedman, R. J., Cole, P. M., Mizuta, I., & Hiruma, N. (1996). Japanese and United States preschool children's responses to conflict and distress. *Child Development, 67,* 2462–2477.

Zahn-Waxler, C., Radke-Yarrow, M., Wagner, E., & Chapman, M. (1992). Development of concern for others. *Developmental Psychology, 28,* 126–136.

Zarbatany, L., Hartmann, D. P., & Rankin, D. B. (1990). The psychological functions of preadolescent peer activities. *Child Development, 61,* 1067–1080.

Zeanah, C. H., & Gleason, M. M. (2015). Annual research review: Attachment disorders in early childhood—clinical presentation, causes, correlates, and treatment. *Journal of Child Psychology and Psychiatry, 56,* 207–222.

Zeanah, C. H., Berlin, L. J., & Boris, N. W. (2011). Practitioner review: Clinical applications of attachment theory and research for infants and young children. *Journal of Child Psychology and Psychiatry, 52,* 819–833.

Zelazo, N. A., Zelazo, P. R., Cohen, K. M., & Zelazo, P. D. (1993). Specificity of practice effects on elementary neuromotor patterns. *Developmental Psychology, 29,* 686–691.

Zelazo, P. R. (1983). The development of walking: New findings and old assumptions. *Journal of Motor Behavior, 15,* 99–137.

Zeman, J., Cassano, M., Perry-Parrish, C., & Stegall, S. (2006). Emotion regulation in children and adolescents. *Journal of Developmental & Behavioral Pediatrics, 27,* 155–168.

Zhou, T., Georgiev, I., Wu, X., Yang, Z.-Y., Dai, K., Finzi, A., . . . Kwong, P. D. (2010, July 8). Structural basis for broad and potent neutralization of HIV-1 by antibody VRC01. *Sciencexpress.* doi:10.1126/science.1192819

Zigler, E., & Finn-Stevenson, M. (1992). Applied developmental psychology. In M. H. Bornstein & M. E. Lamb (Eds.), *Developmental psychology: An advanced textbook.* Hillsdale, NJ: Erlbaum.

Zigler, E., & Styfco, S. J. (1994). Head Start: Criticisms in a constructive context. *American Psychologist, 49,* 127–132.

Zigler, E. F., & Gilman, E. (1996). Not just any care: Shaping a coherent child care policy. In E. F. Zigler, S. L. Kagan, & N. W. Hall (Eds.), *Children, families, and government: Preparing for the twenty-first century.* New York: Cambridge University Press.

Zimiles, H., & Lee, V. E. (1991). Adolescent family structure and educational progress. *Developmental Psychology, 27,* 314–320.

Zins, J. E., Garcia, V. F., Tuchfarber, B. S., Clark, K. M., & Laurence, S. C. (1994). Preventing injury in children and adolescents. In R. J. Simeonsson (Ed.), *Risk, resilience, and prevention: Promoting the well-being of all children* (pp. 183–202). Baltimore, MD: Paul H. Brookes.

Zolner, T. (2000). The impact of culture on psychological assessment. *Dissertation Abstracts International, 62*(11-B), 5400.

Zolner, T. (2003a). Considerations in working with persons of First Nations heritage: Do psychologists perpetuate systemic discrimination? *Pimatziwin: An International Journal of Aboriginal and Indigenous Community Health, 2,* 1–18.

Zolner, T. (2003b). Going back to square one and finding it's a circle: (Not) doing university research in Indian Country. *Pimatziwin: An International Journal of Aboriginal and Indigenous Community Health, 1,* 91–113.

Zolner, T. (2004). *Graffiti: Much more than just art.* Unpublished manuscript prepared for the City of Saskatoon Graffiti Reduction Task Force. Saskatoon, SK, Canada.

Zolner, T. (2007, September). Concepts of graffiti: Much more than just art. Paper presented at The Anti-Graffiti Symposium—3. Saskatoon, SK, Canada.

Zolner, T. (2011). Parenting in the Spirit: Helping children stay on the King's highway. *Logos: A Journal of Eastern Christian Studies, 52,* 253–292.

Zolner, T. (In press). Understanding the Catholic self in child and family interventions. *Journal of the Catholic Psychotherapy Association of Canada, 1,* n.p.

Zubrick, S. R., Kurinczuk, J. J., McDermott, B. M. C., McKelvey, R. S., Silburn, S. R., & Davies, L. C. (2000). Fetal growth and subsequent mental health problems in children aged 4 to 13 years. *Developmental Medicine & Child Neurology, 42,* 14–20.

Name Index

A

Abbey, A., 396
Abbott, R. D., 331
Abbott, S. P., 331
Abel, B., 139
Aber, J. L., 441
Aboud, F. E., 352
Ackerman, B. P., 240, 305
Acredolo, L. P., 154, 158
Action for Children, 369
Adachi, P. J. C., 384
Adair, J. G., 36
Adair, R. H., 198
Adajian, L. B., 325
Adam, K. S., 178
Adams, J. W., 329
Adams, M. J., 330
Adams, R. J., 127, 128
Adenzato, M., 222
Adlaf, E.M., 28
Adler, N., 392
Adolph, K. E., 120, 123
Adolphs, R., 181
Ahmed, M. L., 382
Ainslie, J. J., 397
Ainsworth, M. D. S., 23, 173
Ainsworth, M. S., 173
Aken, M., 173
Albersheim, L., 173
Alberta Health and
    Wellness, 80
Ales, K. L., 77
Alessandri, S. M., 168
Alexander, J. F., 458
Allard, L., 169
Allen, L., 441
Allgeier, A. R., 397
Allgeier, E. R., 397
Almeida, D. M., 360
Aman, C. J., 428
Amato, P. R., 371
American Academy of Pediatrics,
    207, 400, 401
American Academy of Pediatrics
    Committee on Drugs
    and Committee on
    Bioethics, 287
American Academy of Pediatrics
    Committee on Public
    Education, 246
American Academy of Pediatrics
    Committee on Sports Medicine
    and Committee on School
    Health, 296

American Association of Intellectual
    and Developmental Disabilities,
    430
American Psychiatric Association,
    199
American Psychological Association,
    394
Ames, E., 179
Ames, E. W., 179
Ammon, P., 233
Anand, K. J., 125
Anastasi, A., 322
Anastopoulos, A. D., 428
Anderson, 253
Anderson, D. R., 256
Anderson, E. R., 373
Anderson, L. C., 105
Andreas, D., 178
Andreatos, M., 158
Andrews, B., 345
Angelopoulos, M., 159
Anisfeld, M., 151
Antonarakis, S. E., 59
APA Presidential Task Force on
    Evidence-Based Practice, 39
Apgar, V., 93
Applied Research Branch of
    Human Resources Development
    Canada & Healthy Child
    Manitoba, 180
Archibald, C. P., 391
Arcus, D., 186, 188
Arezzo, D., 364
Arterberry, M., 130
Asbury, K., 55
Ashcraft, M. H., 332
Asher, K. N., 299
Asher, S. R., 350
Ashmead, D. H., 121
Aslin, R., 281
Aslin, R. N., 126, 129, 131, 155, 156
Assembly of First Nations, 211
Assembly of First Nations Health
    and Social Secretariat, 211
Atkins, P., 327
Atkinson, I., 175
Atkinson, R., 443
Atlas, R., 366
Attanucci, J., 415
Attie, J., 399
Atwater, E., 454
Au, T. K., 147, 159
Austin, S. B., 395
Averhart, C. J., 30

Aviezer, O., 175, 178
Axworthy, 60
Azad, M. B., 209
Aziz, A., 206

B

Bachman, 450
Bachman, J., 424
Bachman, J. G., 424
Backscheider, A. G., 221
Baddeley, A., 148
Baer, D. M., 8
Bagwell, C. L., 349, 350, 448
Bahrick, L. E., 133
Bailey, D. A., 297
Bailey, J. M., 393, 395
Baillargeon, M., 368
Baillargeon, R., 144, 145, 147
Baiocco, R., 388
Baird, D. D., 68
Baker, C., 232
Baker, J. E., 291
Baker, L., 329, 332
Baker, L. A., 257
Baker, T. B., 451
Bakshi, A., 446
Balasubramanian, S., 49
Baldwin, D. A., 159
Baldwin, J. M., 3
Bales, S. N., 39
Ball, S., 244
Balsam, P. D., 95
Bancroft, 60
Bandura, A., 8, 252, 278, 364
Banks, M. S., 127, 128, 130, 131
Barber, A. M., 227
Barinaga, M., 115
Baris, M. A., 272
Barkley, R. A., 427, 428
Barling, J., 424
Barnes, M., 224
Barnett, N. P., 297
Barr, H. M., 79
Barr, R., 151
Barrera, M., Jr., 266
Bartlett, D., 117
Barton, C., 458
Barton, M. E., 238
Bartsch, K., 144, 222, 223
Baskett, L. M., 269
Basso, K. H., 384
Bastaits, K., 373
Bastien, B., 211
Batejan, K. L., 395

Bates, E., 236, 238
Bates, J. E., 190, 260, 265, 274, 351, 360, 365, 367, 369
Bauchner, H., 198
Baumeister, A. A., 94, 429
Baumrind, D., 261, 262
Bayley (1969), 118
Bayley, N., 154
Beagan, B. L., 206, 290
Beal, C. R., 240, 332
Beardsall, L., 270
Bearison, D. J., 228
Bear-Lehman, J., 203
Beauchamp, G. K., 124, 125
Beautrais, A. L., 210
Beck, A. T., 454
Beck, M., 47
Becker, J. B., 383
Beckwith, L., 178
Behnke, M., 78
Beilock, S. L., 325
Beissel, C. F., 251
Bélanger, J., 159
Belgrad, S. L., 240
Bell, A. P., 393
Bell, M. A., 150, 151
Beller, M., 324
Belsky, J., 187, 266, 271, 382
Bem, D. J., 189, 394
Benacerraf, B. R., 73
Benda, B. B., 390
Bender, 60
Benigni, L., 238
Bennet, P., 159
Bennett, L. C., 273
Bensen, A. S., 130
Benson, P. L, 416
Benson, R. C., 77
Bento, S., 171
Benton, S. L., 330
Bereiter, C., 330
Berenbaum, S. A., 257
Berenson, G. S., 286
Berg, R. L., 209
Berk, L. E., 228, 273
Berkeley, H., 455
Berko, J., 233
Berkowitz, L., 359
Berkowitz, M. W., 418
Berkowitz, R. I., 102
Berlan, E. D., 395
Berlin, L. J., 171
Bernard, R. S., 125
Bernazzani, O., 96
Berndt, T. J., 350, 448
Bernier, J. C., 428
Berninger, G., 238
Berninger, V. W., 331
Bernstein, W. M., 6
Berry, J. W., 440

Bersoff, D. M., 415
Bertenthal, B. H., 119, 120, 121
Bertenthal, B. I, 131
Berthier, N. E., 121
Bertrand, L., 26
Besharov, D. J., 392
Best, 156
Best, D. L., 251, 252
Betsalel-Presser, R., 368
Beyens, I., 388
Bhatt, R. S., 152
Bhavnagri, N. P., 274
Bialystok, E., 232
Bianchi, D., 388
Bianchi, I., 175
Bibby, 416
Bieling, P. J., 37
Biesanz, J. C., 41
Biffi, G., 49
Bigler, R. S., 30, 252, 352
Bill, B., 159
Birch, H. G., 185
Birch, L. L., 105, 106, 291
Birnholz, J. C., 73
Bisanz, G. L., 329
Bisanz, J., 148, 227
Bjorklund, D. F., 12, 13, 152, 226, 304, 305, 307, 410
Black, A., 393
Black, B., 350
Black, C. M. D., 398
Black, K. N., 370
Black-Gutman, D., 352
Blairy, S., 166
Blasi, A., 113
Block, G. W., 79
Block, J., 32
Block, J. H., 32
Bloom, L., 238, 239
Bloom, P., 181
Blyth, D., 386
Blyth, D. A., 449
Bobak, I. M., 77
Bock, G. R., 55
Bodnarchuk, J. L., 122
Bogatz, G. A., 244
Boggiano, A. K., 343
Bohannon, J. N., 236
Boivin, M., 57, 344, 350, 351
Bolduc, D., 252
Bolger, K. E., 362
Bolig, E. E., 317
Bookstein, F. L., 79
Booth, J. R., 328
Boris, N. W., 171
Bornstein, M. H., 128, 153, 154, 273, 274
Bosma, H. A., 437
Boston, M. B., 308

Bouchard, C., 206
Boucher, K. L., 325
Bouman, D., 350
Bowen, R., 438
Bowen-Woodward, D., 373
Bower, B., 203
Bower, G. H., 306
Bower, T. G. R., 154
Bowers, E. P., 416
Bowlby, J., 171
Bowyer-Crane, C. A., 329
Boyd, D., 393
Boyer, C. B., 393
Brabant, S., 254
Bradley, R. H., 319
Braeges, J. L., 281
Braet, C., 289
Braine, M. D. S., 236
Brand, E., 373
Brault, M., 148
Braun, J. M., 80
Braungart-Rieker, J. M., 279
Brazelton, T. B., 89, 93
Brendgen, M., 56, 175
Brent, H. P., 128
Bressan, A., 455
Bretherton, I., 176, 238
Bridglall, B. L., 314
Brigandt, I., 4
Brinkman, T. M., 273
Briscoe, J., 149
Broaddus, 253
Brockington, I., 96
Brodeur, M., 25
Brody, D. J., 382
Brody, G. H., 262, 271
Brody, N., 320, 321
Bronfenbrenner, U., 10
Bronte-Tinkew, J., 172
Brook, A. E., 287
Brook, C. G. D., 287
Brooks, R. H., 449
Brooks-Gunn, J., 4, 77, 183, 267, 321, 382, 383, 389, 399
Brophy, J. E., 335, 336, 337
Brown, A. L., 332
Brown, B., 298
Brown, B. B., 349, 445, 446
Brown, E., 222
Brown, E. G., 274
Brown, G. W., 345
Brown, J. R., 270
Brown, K. P., 352
Brown, R., 231, 329
Browne, K. D., 365
Brownell, M. D., 241
Brownlow, C., 108
Brunner, R., 172
Bryant, B. K., 356
Bryant, J., 317

Bryant, P., 327, 328
Bryden, M. P., 203, 323
Bryden, P. J., 202
Bucciarelli, M., 222
Buchanan, C. M., 383
Buchannan, L., 445
Buchanon, C. M., 373
Buchholz, M., 125
Buhrmester, D., 271, 448
Buis, A. J. E., 87
Bukowski, W., 181
Bukowski, W. M., 350, 351
Bullinger, A., 126
Bullock, M., 183
Buote, V. M., 350
Burack, J. A., 348
Burchinal, M., 230, 424, 425
Burchinal, M. R., 180
Burger-Judisch, L. M., 113
Burgess, K. B., 277
Buriel, R., 259
Burke, P. B., 175
Burks, V. S., 366
Burman, B., 372
Burns, A., 370
Burns, G. L., 26
Burts, D. C., 243
Busch-Rossnagel, N. A., 390
Bushman, B. J., 364
Bushnik, T., 77
Buss, A. H., 185
Buss, K. A., 55, 169, 186
Busseri, M. A., 416, 417
Butler, R., 345
Butterfield, S. A., 203
Button, E. J., 346
Byrne, B., 328
Byrne, B. M., 344, 346

C

Cadoret, R. J., 361
Cairns, B. D., 358, 445
Cairns, R. B., 358, 445
Caldwell, B. M., 319
Calkins, S. D., 114, 274
Call, K. T., 424
Callaghan, R. C., 220
Callender, G., 114
Camacho-Arroyo, I., 94, 95
Camaioni, L., 238
Cameron, C., 295
Campbell, B., 399
Campbell, F. A., 320
Campbell, R., 232
Campbell, S. B., 96
Campbell, D. W., 120
Campos, J., 167
Campos, J. J., 55, 130
Campos, S. P., 287
Camras, L. A., 168

Canadian Association for Young
    Children (CAYC), 242
Canadian Council on Social
    Development, 321
Canadian Dental Association, 196
Canadian Fitness and Lifestyle
    Research Institute (CFLRI), 291,
    295
Canadian Haemoglobinopathy
    Association, 51
Canadian Institute for Health
    Information, 88, 89, 206, 297, 298,
    391, 398
Canadian Institute of Child Health,
    455
Canadian Paediatric Society, 101, 195,
    199, 246, 287
Canadian Psychological Association
    (CPA), 298
Canadian Task Force on Preventive
    Health Care, 51
Canfield, R. L., 153
CANPKU, 63
Cantor, N., 449
Cantu, C. L., 440
Capaldi, D. M., 374, 390
Capozzoli, M., 224
Caprara, D. L., 79
Cardno, A. G., 55
Carey, G., 457
Carey, S., 133, 159, 221
Carlo, G., 356, 415
Carlson, C. L., 429
Carlson, E. A., 175
Carlson, S. M., 274
Carpenter, M., 8
Carpenter, P. A., 329
Carr, M., 324
Carrere, S., 266
Carrington, P. J., 456
Carroll, J. B., 310
Carroll, J. L., 95
Carskadon, M. A., 443
Carter, M. C., 179
Cartwright, B. S., 274
Casaer, P., 111
Casanueva, C., 361
Casas, J. F., 272
Case, R., 144, 150
Casey, M. B., 324, 325
Cashman, L., 198
Casiglia, A. C., 351
Caspi, A., 382
Cassano, M., 170
Cassidy, J., 173, 178
Casten, R., 440
Castle, J., 272
Cataldo, C. B., 106
CATIE, 390, 391
Cattell, R. B., 309

Center for Fetal Diagnosis and
    Treatment, 85
Centers for Disease Control and
    Prevention, 108
Chaffin, M., 179
Chaffin, R., 325
Chalmers, B., 90, 106
Chalmers, K., 79
Chamberlain, D., 125
Chambers, C. T., 158
Champion, H., 240
Chan, R. W., 268
Chan, T., 287
Chance, G., 126
Chance, L. J., 441
Chandler, C. C., 438
Chandler, M., 414
Chang, C. M., 227
Chang, S. M., 139
Chao, R. K., 261
Chapman, M., 272
Chapman, P. D., 315
Chapman, R. S., 236
Charlesworth, R., 243
Charman, T., 114
Chase-Lansdale, P. L., 267, 371, 373
Chavira, V., 440
Cheal, D., 373
Chen, X., 351
Cheney, D., 235
Cherlin, A. J., 371
Chess, S., 185
Chessor, D., 346
Cheung, L. W. Y., 91
Chi, M. T. H., 306, 307
Child, I. L., 266
Children's Defense Fund, 107, 210
Chilman, C. S., 381
Chipperfield, J. G., 269
Chirumbolo, A., 388
Chisholm, J. S., 123
Chisholm, K., 179
Choi, A. L., 292
Chomitz, V. R., 91
Chomsky, N., 234
Christensen, A., 266
Christensen, C. A., 331
Christensen, K. M., 124
Christensen, S., 267
Chudley, A. E., 79
Chugani, H. T., 114
Chung, A., 41
Chung, T., 272
Cin, S. D., 447
Cipani, E., 430
Clark, 253
Clark, C., 211
Clark, J. E., 120
Clark, K. B., 353
Clark, K. M., 299

Clark, M. K., 353
Clark, R., 91
Clarke, T., 232
Clatfelter, D., 274
Clegg, M. R., 346
Clifton, R., 126
Clifton, R. K., 119, 120, 121
Clingempeel, W. G., 373
Cluss, P. A., 291
CMEC, 389
Coco, A. L., 351
Cohen, K. M., 119
Cohen, L. L., 125
Cohen, S., 76
Cohen, S. E., 178
Cohn, J. F., 96
Coie, J. D., 358, 366, 446
Colburne, K. A., 256
Colby, A., 414
Cole, D. A., 344, 453
Cole, M., 408
Cole, P. M., 168
Coleman, B., 416
Coleman, M., 369
Coles, C., 295
Collaer, M. L., 257
The College of Family Physicians of
    Canada, 101
Collins, P. A., 256
Collins, W. A., 443
Coltheart, M., 327
Committee on Genetics, 58
Community Health Nurses of
    Canada, 101
Compton, D. L., 317
Comstock, G., 364
Cone, E. J., 82
Conference Board of Canada, 92
Conger, R. D., 261, 361, 386, 424,
    425
Connolly, J., 388, 389, 395
Connor, S. K., 107
Connors, S. L., 57
Conway, M., 152
Cook, W., 384
Cooper, J., 255
Cooper, P., 96
Cooper, R. P., 157
Coopersmith, S., 345
Coplan, R. J., 227, 274
Copper, R. L., 76
Corballis, M. C., 122
Corbin, C. B., 400
Coren, S., 203
Corkill, A. J., 330
Corley, R., 52, 319
Corliss, H. L., 395
Cornelius, M., 79
Cornelius, M. D., 79
Cornell, E. H., 150

Cornish, K. M., 57
Cornwell, K. S., 122
Cossette, L., 252
Costarelli, V., 288
Costigan, C., 441
Costigan, C. L., 441
Costigan, K. A., 73, 74
Costin, S. E., 355
Cotroneo, S., 95
Courage, M. L., 127, 128, 152, 246
Couturier, J., 399
Covill, A., 331
Cowart, B. J., 125
Cox, A., 230, 328
Cox, M., 370
Cox, M. J., 176
Cox, R., 370
CPS Nutrition Committee, 106
Craft, M. J., 210
Cragg, S., 295
Craig, C. L., 295
Craig, K. D., 125, 158
Craig, W., 389, 395
Craig, W. M., 366, 367
Craik, F., 232
Cramer, K. M., 180
Cratty, B., 204
Craven, R., 346
Crawford, M., 325, 383
Crenshaw, T. M., 352
Cribbie, R., 388
Crick, N. R., 272, 358, 364, 365, 366
Crnic, K., 266
Crnic, K. A., 91
Crockenberg, S. B., 356
Crockenberg, S. C., 170
Crocker, P. R. E., 448
Crombie, G., 346
Croom, C. S., 79
Crosby, L., 390
Crosignani, P. G., 80
Cross, D., 144
Cross, T. P., 361
Crowder, R. G., 329
Crowell, A. L., 196
Crowell, J., 173
Cruz, C., 364
Csikszentmihalyi, M., 385
Cuadra, A. E., 55
Cuellar, I., 440
Cuevas, K., 150, 151
Cummings, E. M., 372
Cunningham, F. G., 85
Curran, P. J., 371
Curtin, S. C., 91
Curtis, B., 327
Curtis, L. E., 153
Curtis, M. E., 329
Curtiss, S., 235
Curwin, A., 230

D

Da Silva, M. S., 415
Dahl, R. E., 384, 385
Dammann, O., 91
Damon, W., 250
Daneback, K., 388
Daneman, M., 329
Dannemiller, J. L., 128, 129, 132
Darling, N., 262
Darlington, R., 243
Darvill, T., 80
Das, J. P., 227, 329
Daschmann, G., 388
Datta, A., 90
D'Augelli, A. R., 393, 395
Davidson, D. H., 242
Davidson, K. M., 85
Davies, G. J., 288
Davies, L., 272
Davies, P. T., 372
Davis, G. N., 317
Davis, J., 346
Davis, L. B., 124
Davis, N. S., 197
Davis, R. M., 26
Dawson, P., 305
Day, J. D., 311, 317
Day, N., 79
Day, N. L., 79
Day, S. X., 420
Dayan, J., 345
De Braekeleer, M., 57
de Groh, M., 206
de Haan, M., 90
de Onis, M., 101
de Vries, J. I. P., 87
Deak, G. O., 159
Deater-Deckard, K., 55, 360
Deaudelin, C., 25
DeBerry, K. M., 441
Decarie, T. G., 169
DeCasper, A., 125
DeCasper, A. J., 73
DeFries, J. C., 52, 319
Deg^irmenciog^lu, S. M., 447
DeKeyser Ganz, F., 95
Dekovic, M., 352
DeKroon, D. M. A., 181
Delaney-Black, V., 82
Dellas, M., 437
DeLoache, J. S., 220, 305
DeLuca, S., 410
Dement, W. C., 94
Demers, S., 447
Demo, D. H., 442
den Bak-Lammers, I. M., 282
Dennis, M., 224
Dennis, M. G., 123
Dennis, W., 123
Denny, M. A., 123

Derbyshire, A., 133
DeRosier, M. E., 351
Deschesnes, M., 447
deSchonen, S., 183
Desimone, L., 41
Desjardins, R. N., 159
deSouza, P., 456
Desrochers, S., 169
Desrosiers, S., 290
Deutsch, G., 115
DeVaryshe, B. D., 456
Devellis, R. F., 25
DeVet, K., 277
deVilliers, J. G., 234
deVilliers, P. A., 234
DeWolf, M., 243
DeWolff, M. S., 176
Diamond, A., 114
Diamond, M., 323
Diana, M. S., 449
DiBlasio, F. A., 390
Diekelmann, S., 94
Dielman, T., 451
Diem-Wille, G., 6
Dietitians of Canada, 101
Dietrich, K. N., 79
Dietz, W. H., 206
Dip, P. G., 55
DiPietro, J. A., 73, 74, 188
Dishion, T. J., 352
Dissanayake, C., 183
Disterhoft, J. F., 104
Dixon, J., 429
Dockrell, J., 426
Dodge, K. A., 260, 265, 274, 351, 360,
    365, 366, 367, 369, 446
Doepke, K. J., 454
Doja, A., 108
Dombrowski, S. C., 78
Dong, Q., 270
Donnell, F., 175
Donnerstein, E., 364
Dornbusch, S. M., 262, 373, 423, 424
Douglas, L., 172
Down Syndrome Collaborative
    Group, 59
Downey, 60
Downey, G., 351
Downey, R. G., 330
Downie, A. L. S., 91
Downs, A. C., 253, 383
Doyle, A., 175, 352
Doyle, A. B., 175, 345
Drabman, R. S., 364
Drake, B., 361
Draper, P., 382
Druin, D. P., 114
Druzin, M. L., 77
Dryburgh, H., 391
Dryfoos, J. G., 77, 393, 458

Dubas, J., 173
Dubas, J. J. S., 173
Dubicka, B., 454
DuBois, D. L., 349
Dubow, E. F., 346, 364
Dumas, J. E., 266
Duncan, G. J., 321
Dunger, D. B., 382
Dunham, A. C. A., 424
Dunham, F., 230
Dunham, P. J., 230
Dunn, J., 55, 179, 270, 271, 273
Dunne, R. G., 299
DuPaul, G. J., 428
Durham, M., 230
Durik, A., 91
Dussault, M., 25
Dutra, L., 175
Dwyer, K. M., 277
Dysart-Gale, D., 395
Dzakpasu, S., 106

E

Eacott, M. J., 152
Earle Fox, K., 211
Early Years Study Reference
    Group, 139
Easterbrook, M. A., 133
Eaton, W. O., 120, 122, 203, 269
Ebbesen, E., 280
Eccles, J. S., 295, 345, 383
Edelbrock, C., 428
Edelstein, W., 415
Edin, F., 196
Edwards, C. A., 446
Edwards, S., 346
Egan, S. K., 366, 367
Eggermont, S., 388
Eichstedt, J. A., 251, 256
Eilers, R. E., 157
Eisenberg, N., 188, 355, 356, 415
Eisenbud, L., 256
Eizenman, D. R., 131
Elder, G. H., 386, 424, 425, 436
Eldridge, B. J., 117
El-Fakahany, E. E., 55
Elicker, J., 176
Elkin, T. D., 438
Elkind, D., 437, 438
Elliott, C. D., 104
Elliott, D., 119
Ellis, W. K., 430
Elmer-DeWitt, P., 85
Elwell, C. E., 113
Emery, R. E., 361
Engelhardt, S. E., 317
Englund, M., 176
Enns, J. T., 224
Ensminger, M. E., 267
Entwisle, B., 349

Eppler, M. A., 120
Epstein, L. H., 291
Erdley, C. A., 350
Erel, O., 271, 372
Erikson, E., 7
Erikson, E. H., 435
Eron, L. D., 364
Erturan, S., 325
Espy, K. A., 82
Essley, M., 410
Evans, A. D., 222
Everett, J. J., 297
Everett, K., 179
Eyler, F. D., 78

F

Fabes, R. A., 188, 356
Fabricius, W. V., 370
Fadel, H. E., 48
Fagot, B. I., 255
Fairbairn, N. S., 158
Fakunmoju, S. B., 361
Falbo, T., 269
Fallon, B., 361
Fang, F., 415
Fang, G., 415
Faraone, S. V., 57
Farley, C., 298
Farmer, A. E., 55
Farquhar, S. E., 23
Farver, J. M., 273
Fatemi, S. H., 55
Faw, G. D., 430
Federal, Provincial, and Territorial
    Advisory Committee on
    Population Health, 92
Federation of Canadian
    Municipalities, 457
Feehan, M., 427
Fegley, S., 423
Feingold, A., 323
Feinman, J., 441
Feldman, A., 446
Feldman, B., 6, 7
Feldman, N. S., 343
Feldman, S. S., 278, 440
Feldman, W., 206, 290
Fell, K., 23
Feltey, K. M., 397
Feng, Q., 145
Feng, X., 232
Fennema, E., 324, 325
Fenson, L., 158
Fenwick, K. D., 126
Ferguson, C. J., 364
Ferguson, L. L., 358
Fergusson, D. M., 104, 210
Fernald, A., 169, 245
Field, A. E., 395
Field, T. M., 172, 237

Fields, R., 450
Fifer, W. P., 95
Finch, M. D., 424
Fincham, F., 372
Fines, P., 447
Finn-Stevenson, M., 41, 322
Fiori-Cowley, A., 96
First Nations Child and Family Caring
 Society of Canada, 211, 212
Fischer, M., 428
Fischhoff, B., 401
Fish, E., 327
Fish, M., 187
Fisher, C., 160
Fisher, D. A., 85
Fisher, J. A., 105
Fisher, W. A., 393
Fitton, L., 325
Fitzgerald, H. E., 122
Fitzgerald, J., 332
Fivush, R., 204
Flanagan, C., 96, 372
Flavell, J. H., 304
Fleeson, J., 175
Fletcher, K. E., 428
Flickinger, S. M., 440
Flood, T. L., 150
Flor, D. L., 262
Fluke, J., 361
Fogel, A., 171
Fonagy, P., 176
Fong, B. F., 87
Fonzi, A., 350
Forbes, E. E., 384, 385
Forbes, J., 225
Ford, J., 454
Forde, V., 107
Forehand, R., 390
Foreyt, J. P., 291
Forman, Y., 416
Formiga, C., 119
Foster, E. M., 245
Foster, S. H., 238
Fowler, R. C., 454
Fox, N. A., 57, 114, 166, 175, 186,
 188, 274
Foy, J. G., 328
Fraley, R. C., 187
Frame, C. L., 350
Francis, M., 332
Frankenberger, K. D., 438
Freitas, A. L., 351
French, D. C., 351
French, K. E., 295
Fried, P. A., 79
Friedman, J. M., 79, 83
Friedman, R. J., 168
Friedrich, W. N., 288
Frisk, V., 91
Frohlich, C. B., 415

Frye, D., 182, 223
Fu, V. R., 261
Fuchs, D., 317
Fuchs, L. S., 317
Fujita, N., 238
Fulford, J., 125
Fuligni, A. J., 416
Fulker, D. W., 52, 319
Fuller, M. J., 383
Fuller, T., 361
Fulmore, C. D., 440
Funk, J. B., 365
Furman, L. M., 428
Furman, W., 271, 350, 448
Furnham, A., 251
Furstenberg, F. F., 77, 262, 371

G
Gable, S., 171
Gadalla, T. M., 399
Gaddis, A., 383
Gaddis, L., 188
Gaffield, C., 455
Gafni, N., 324
Gagne, L. G., 180
Gagnon, C., 57, 344
Galambos, N. L., 369
Galea, M., 117
Galen, B. R., 358
Galler, J. R., 107
Galperin, C., 273
Gant, N. F., 85
Garai, J. E., 203
Garasky, S., 370
Garber, J., 346
Garcia, J. R., 388
Garcia, V. F., 299
Gardiner, K. N., 392
Gardner, H., 311, 312
Gariépy, J.-L., 358
Garland, A. F., 455
Garner, P. W., 270
Garner, R., 77, 108
Garrity, C. B., 272
Garvey, C., 238
Gathercole, S. E., 149
Gauderman, W. J., 80
Gauthier, R., 272
Gauthier, S., 57
Gauthier, Y., 178
Gavaki, E., 440
Gavin, D. W., 344
Gavin, L. A., 350
Ge, X., 261, 361, 386
Geib, A., 397
Gelman, R., 226, 239
Gelman, S. A., 145, 160, 161, 221,
 253
Genome Canada, 66
Gentile, D. A., 364

George, C., 178
Gerrard, M., 447
Gettman, P. W., 288
Geva, D., 79
Ghazi, S. R., 139
Ghim, H., 131
Gibbons, F. X., 447
Gibbs, J., 414
Gibbs, J. C., 414, 418
Giberson, P. K., 83
Gibson, E. J., 120, 129, 133
Gibson, K. R., 110
Gilbert, J., 206
Gillberg, C., 428
Gilliam, F. D., 39
Gilligan, C., 415
Gilman, E., 41
Girgus, J. S., 453
Gisla, G. B., 388
Gleason, K. E., 171
Gleason, M. M., 179
Gleason, P. M., 288
Glick, P. C., 373
Glisky, M. L., 82
Glusman, M., 159
Goetz, E. T., 328
Goldenberg, R. L., 77
Goldman, M., 277
Goldman, S. R., 426
Goldschmidt, L., 79
Goldsmith, H. H., 55, 169, 178, 186,
 187, 188
Goldstein, M. H., 157
Goldwater, P., 95
Golinkoff, R. M., 238
Gollwitzer, M., 364
Golombok, S., 204, 268, 394
Gomez, R., 26
Goncu, A., 139
Good, M., 384, 416, 417
Good, T. L., 335, 336, 337
Goode, J. A., 55
Gooden (and Gooden), 253
Goodman, E., 395
Goodman, G. S., 361, 362, 370,
 371, 373
Goodnow, J. J., 261
Goodrick, G. K., 291
Goodstein, L., 396
Goodwyn, S. W., 158
Gordon, C. P., 392
Gorey, K. M., 319
Goswami, U., 328
Gotlib, I. H., 454
Gottesman (1963), 62
Gottesman, I. I., 55
Gottfried, G. M., 221
Gottlieb, G., 62
Gottlieb, L. N., 270
Gottman, J. M., 263, 266, 273

Goulding, S., 246
Graber, J. A., 381, 382, 399
Graesser, A. C., 329
Graham, M. J., 382
Graham, S., 331, 367
Graham, S. A., 159
Grandjean, P., 292
Granier-Deferre, C., 125
Granrud, C. E., 129
Grantham-McGregor, S. M., 139
Green, D. P., 353
Green, K. E., 437
Greenbaum, R., 79
Greenberg, M. T., 91
Greene, S. M., 373
Greening, L., 438
Grigorenko, E. L., 50, 314, 317, 322
Groen, G. J., 332
Groisser, D., 427
Groisser, D. B., 114
Gross, E. F., 383
Gross, R. T., 383
Grossman, D. C., 401
Grossmann, K., 171
Grossmann, K. E., 171
Grovak, M., 85
Grubb, J., 48
Grunau, R. E., 125, 154
Grunau, R. V. E., 125
Grusec, J. E., 356
Guacci-Franco, N., 448
Guajardo, N. R., 223
Guerrini, I., 78
Guevremont, D. C., 428
Guger, S., 224
Guifan, S., 292
Guile, C. A., 291
Guillemin, J., 91
Guilmain, 253
Gümmer, R., 399
Gunderson, E. A., 325
Gunnar, M., 178
Gunter, B., 388
Gurling, H. D., 78
Gurtner, J., 337
Gusella, J. L., 79
Gustafson, P., 413
Guthrie, I. K., 188
Guttmacher, A. F., 76

H

Haddad, S., 298
Haden, C., 226
Hadjistavropoulos, H. D., 125
Hadjistavropoulos, T., 37
Hadley, S., 454
Hafetz, N., 26
Hahn, W., 113
Haimes, E., 48
Haines, C., 204

Hains, S., 133
Hains, S. M. J., 125
Haley, D. W., 154
Hall, D. G., 159, 160
Haller, M., 327
Hallinan, M. T., 349
Halloran, A., 289
Halpern, C. T., 399
Halpern, D. F., 203, 323
Halpern, L. F., 94
Halverson, C. F., 255, 256
Ham, M., 453
Hamer, D. H., 394
Hamilton, 75, 253
Hamilton, C. E., 178
Hamilton-Giachritsis, C., 365
Hamlin, J. K., 181, 272
Hamm, J. V., 349
Hammersmith, S. K., 394
Hammill, D. D., 426
Hampshire, A., 314
Hamza, C., 384
Hancox, R. J., 245
Hane, A. A., 114
Hanna, G. L., 104
Hans, S., 175
Hans, S. L., 79
Hanson, S. L., 346
Hardin, C. D., 383
Harley, K., 152
Harman, C., 178
Harmer, S., 222
Harnke, B., 399
Harold, R. D., 295
Harris, B., 96
Harris, J. A., 75
Harris, L. J., 122
Harris, M. A., 382
Harris, P. L., 222, 273
Harris, S., 117
Harris, S. J., 88, 89
Harrist, A. W., 274
Hart, C. H., 243, 360
Hart, D., 250
Harter, S., 182, 257, 258, 342, 343, 439, 441, 448
Hartmann, D. P., 348
Hartup, W. W., 181, 253, 275, 349, 350, 446
Harvey, O. J., 444
Harvey, W., 295
Haselager, G. J. T., 349
Hashi, K. O., 90
Hastings, P. D., 266, 277
Hatcher, P. J., 327
Hauck, F. R., 95
Haugaard, J. J., 361
Haviland, J. M., 168
Hawkins, D. L., 367
Hawkins, M., 74

Hay, D. F., 272
Hayne, H., 151
Haynes, O. M., 273, 274
Health Canada, 61, 106, 119, 205, 207, 208, 209, 244, 361, 454
Heaman, M., 106
Heaman, M. I., 79
Hearold, S., 245
Heavey, C. L., 266
Hebl, M., 280
Heck, D. J., 349
Hedges, L. V., 323, 325
Hefferman, K., 398
Hegion, A., 327
Heijkoop, M., 173
Hein, K., 393
Heins, T., 288
Hellige, J. B., 197
Hemphill, L., 156
Henderson, C., 130
Henderson, H. R, 329
Henderson, V. K., 176
Hendrix, K., 364
Hennig, K. H., 413
Hepworth, S., 224
Herman-Giddens, M. E., 382
Hernandez, D. J., 370
Hernandez-Reif, M., 133
Heron, M., 146
Herrera, C., 169, 362
Herrera, M. G., 107
Herrnstein, R. J., 322
Hershberger, S. L., 395
Hertzman, C., 91
Hess, U., 166
Heth, C. D., 150
Hetherington, E. M., 55, 370, 373
Hetherington. S. E., 89
Hewitt, K. L., 126
Hiatt, S., 130
Hickey, P. R., 125
Hickson, F., 352
Higgins, A., 418
Highfield, R. R., 314
Hillier, L., 126
Hillsgrove, M., 82
Hilton, S. C., 73, 74
Hines, A. R., 383
Hines, M., 257
Hirsch, B. J., 349
Hirsch, M., 381
Hirshberg, L. M., 169
Hiruma, N., 168
Hiscock, M., 203
Ho, C. S., 327
Hodges, E. V. E., 350, 367
Hodges, J., 172
Hodgson, D. M., 73, 74
Hoff, T. L., 3
Hoff-Ginnsberg, E., 236

Hoffman, L. W., 349
Hoffman, M. L., 356, 418
Hofsten, C., 131
Hogan, A. M., 90
Hoge, D. D., 346
Hogge, W. A., 81
Holden, E., 384
Holden, G. W., 260
Holder, M. D., 416
Holditch-Davis, D., 125
Holland, J. L., 420, 422
Holst, M., 125
Holtkamp, K., 291
Homma, Y., 395
Hood, L., 239
Hood, W. R., 444
Hooper, R., 96
Hooven, C., 263
Hoover, D. W., 427
Horn, O., 290
Horwood, L. J., 104
Hou, Y., 152
Howard, K. I., 443
Howard, M., 393
Howe, M. L., 152
Howe, N., 270, 273, 274
Howes, C., 181, 272
Hoyne, S. H., 331
Hu, N., 394
Hu, S., 394
Hua, J. M., 441
Huckeby, E. R., 157
Hudson, J., 308
Huesmann, L. R., 364, 365
Hughes, J. P., 382
Huichang, C., 313
Hulecki, L. R., 126
Hulme, C., 327
Humphrey, H. E. B., 83
Hunsley, J., 39, 370
Hunt, C. E., 95
Hunter, A. G., 267
Hurwitz, W. R., 160
Huston, A. C., 245, 254, 323
Hutchins, E., 313
Huttenlocher, J., 324
Huttunen, M. O., 78
Huynh, V. W., 416
Hwang, C. P., 175
Hyde, J. S., 91, 323, 324, 325, 387
Hymel, S., 346, 351

I

Iedema, J., 370
Inal, S., 117
Inhelder, B., 153, 218, 407
Institute of Infections and Immunity, 208, 209
Institute of Medicine, 75
Ippolito, M. F., 346

Irwin, J. M., 159
Irwin, L., 91
Isaacs, E. B., 149
Isabella, R. A., 171, 187
Isley, S. L., 274
Israel, A. C., 291, 399, 427
Ito, J., 257
Iversen, G. E., 382
Izard, C. E., 165, 166

J

Jacklin, C. N., 253, 257
Jackson, K. L., 424
Jacobs, E. V., 368
Jacobs, J. E., 295
Jacobson, J. L., 83
Jacobson, K. C., 360
Jacobson, S. W., 83
Jacquet, A. Y., 125
Jaffee, S., 325
Jakobsen, R., 388
Jakobson, L. S., 91
Jamieson, J. R., 228
Jansen, B., 325
Janssens, J. M., 352
Janzen, L. A., 79
Jarvi, S. M., 395
Jason, L. A., 299
Jenkins, E., 332
Jenkins, L., 146
Jennings, A., 288
Jensen, J. L., 119
Jensen, M. D., 77
Jernigan, L. P., 437
Jewell, L., 453
Ji, G., 270
Jiang, D., 389
Jiao, S., 270
Jiao, Z., 350
Jing, H., 313
Jing, Q., 270
Joels, T., 178
Johanson, R. B., 89
John, R. S., 271
Johnson, A. D., 4
Johnson, C. J., 181
Johnson, M. H., 112
Johnson, R., 323
Johnson, S. C., 221
Johnson, S. P., 131
Johnson-Reid, M., 361
Johnston, 450
Johnston, M. V., 197
Johnstone, B., 350
Jones, C. H., 305
Jones, D., 331
Jones, D. C., 270, 355
Jones, K., 311
Jones, L., 179
Jones, L. C., 352

Jongema Y., 290
Jordan, A. E., 453
Joseph, R., 73
Juir, G., 289
Jukic, A. M., 68
Jusczyk, P. W., 126, 155, 156
Juvonen, J., 367

K

Kaczorowski, J., 106
Kafko, M., 203
Kagan, J., 186, 187, 188
Kaijura, H., 125
Kail, R., 148, 196, 295, 304, 305, 324, 363, 409
Kail, R. V., 223, 227
Kaiser, I. H., 76
Kalakoski, V., 436
Kalish, C., 221
Kalish, C. W., 221
Kamerman, S. B., 92
Kamp, J., 131
Kampe, K., 172
Kandel, D. B., 349
Kann, L., 400
Kantrowitz, B., 457
Kaplan, N., 178
Kaplan, P. S., 157
Karl, H. W., 125
Karniol, R., 121
Karp, J., 360
Karraker, K. H., 252
Kasatkina, É. P., 104
Kashyap, R., 447
Kaslow, N. J., 454
Kato, K., 82
Katz, L. F., 263
Katzmarzyk, P. T., 206
Kaufman, J. C., 309, 313
Kaufmann, P. M., 82
Kavanaugh, R. D., 273
Kawakami, K., 187
Kayne, H., 288
Kazdin, A. E., 454
Keane, S. P., 352
Keefe, K., 350
Keil, F. C., 221
Keith, B., 371
Kellam, S. G., 267
Keller, M., 415
Kelley, M. L., 262, 454
Kellman, P. J., 127, 128, 130, 131
Kellogg, R., 202
Kelloway, E. K., 424
Kelly, M. A., 39
Kendrick, C., 271
Kennedy, E., 179
Kenyon, B., 133
Kern, J. K., 178
Kerr, M., 189

Kerr, S., 332
Kershaw, P., 91
Kessen, W., 227
Kestenbaum, R., 178
Khan, S. A., 57
Khramtsova, I., 330
Kidd, C., 281
Kidd, K. K., 50, 322
Kieras, J., 276
Kiernan, K. E., 371
Kigar, D. L., 196
Killen, M., 417
Kim, C. C., 227
Kim, Y. H., 328
Kimball, M. M., 254, 324, 325
Kimmerly, N. L., 166
Kimura, D., 325
King, P. E., 416
King, P. M., 410
King, S., 56
King, V., 436
Kinsbourne, M., 203
Kirch, W., 107
Kirkham, F. J., 90
Kisilevsky, B. S., 73, 125, 133
Kitchener, K. S., 410
Klaczynski, P. A., 408
Klahr, D., 148
Klapper, J. T., 364
Klatzky, R. L., 148
Klebanov, P. K., 321
Klein, J. S., 227
Klerman, L. V., 77
Klier, C. M., 171
Kline, R., 203
Klingberg, T., 196
Klinnert, M. D., 188
Klunder, H., 289
Knapp, M., 179
Knitzer, J., 107
Knoke, D., 361
Kochanska, G., 188, 190, 265, 266,
    277, 279, 280, 355
Kochenderfer, B. J., 366
Koehler, A. J., 76
Koehoorn, M., 382
Koenig, A. L., 355
Kohen, D., 108
Kohl, P. L., 361
Kohlberg, L., 255, 411, 414, 418
Kohlberg, L. A., 255
Kolb, B., 111, 115
Koller, S. H., 415
Konishi, C., 395
Koplewicz, H. S., 384
Kopp, C. B., 276
Kopp, C. D., 276
Koren, G., 78, 79, 82
Koroshegyi, C., 172
Koryzma, C. M., 441

Kotchik, B. A., 390
Kotovsky, L., 145
Kovacs, D. M., 349
Kowal, A., 271
Kowalski, K. C., 448
Kowalski, P. S., 441
Kowalski, R. M., 395
Krakow, J. B., 276
Kramer, L., 271, 272
Krantz, M. J., 399
Kratochwill, T. R., 261
Krekling, S., 323
Krispin, O., 351
Kroger, J., 437
Kroonenberg, P. M., 175
Krueger, C., 125
Kruk, E., 179
Krupka, A., 171
Ku, H., 272
Kuhl, 156
Kulshreshtha, U., 447
Kunzig, R., 115
Kuo, A. G., 104
Kupersmidt, J. B., 351, 358, 362
Kurtz, D. A., 440
Kuyken, W., 384
Kvapilik T., 388
Kymissis, E., 158
Kyte, C. S., 181

L
La Vecchia, C., 80
Ladd, B. K., 367
Ladd, G. W., 274, 275, 350, 351, 352,
    366, 367
Lafrance, J., 211
LaFreniere, P., 272
LaFreniere, P. J., 266
Lagace-Seguin, D. G., 227
LaGreca, A. M, 352
Laird, R. D., 366
Lalonde, C. E., 156
Lamb (1998), 180
Lamb, M. E., 180, 351, 368, 369
Lambert, W. W., 189
Lamborn, S. D., 262, 445
Lamon, S. J., 324
Lancet, 108
Landhuis, C. E., 245
Lang, S., 178
Langlois, J. H., 253
Lannegrand-Willems, L., 437
Lanza, E., 232
Laplante, D. P., 56, 133
Larsen, U., 382
Larson, R., 385
Larson, R. W., 400, 443, 453
Laurence, S. C., 299
Laursen, B., 443
Lavergne, C., 148

Lazar, I., 243
Lazar, N. A., 29
Le Sieur, K. D., 275
Leach, P., 207
Leaper, C., 446
Lears, M., 254
LeBlanc, M., 454
Lebolt, A., 351
Lecanuet, J. P., 125
Leddingham, J. E., 346
Lee, C. M., 370
Lee, K., 222
Lee, S., 333, 334
Lee, V. E., 373
Leech, S., 451
Leerkes, E. M., 170
Lefevre, J., 232
LeGrand, R., 128
Lehr, R., 373
Lekka, S. K., 170
Lelwica, M., 168
LeMare, L., 346
LeMare, L. J., 304
Lemery, K. S., 55, 186, 188
Lengua, L. J., 371
Leonard, L. B., 426
Lepper, M. R., 337
Lerner, J. V., 416
Lerner, R. M., 61
Lester, B. M., 89
Leung, M. C., 445
Lévesque, C., 26
Levin, K., 157
Levine, L. E., 184
Levine, S. C., 324, 325
Levitt, A. G., 157
Levitt, J. L., 448
Levitt, M. J., 448
Levy, G. D., 253, 308
Levy, J., 122
Lewinsohn, P. M., 454
Lewis, M., 168, 183, 187
Lewis, M. D., 169, 170, 172
Lewis, T. L., 128
Leyland, J., 228
Li, D., 95
Li, Z., 351
Li, Z. H., 389
Libal, J., 454
Liben, L., 30
Liben, L. S., 252, 256
Liberman, Z., 272
Lie, S. O., 210
Lieberman, E., 91
Lieberman, M., 175, 275, 414
Liebermann, D., 146
Liebert, R. M., 364
Lili, Q., 313
Lillard, A., 222
Limber, S., 167

Lin, C. C., 261
Lin, L., 270
Lin, S., 373
Linden, 60
Ling, L., 171
Linhares, M., 119
Linn, M. C., 323
Linton, J., 125
Lipsitt, L. P., 151
Little, J. K., 255
Lloyd, B., 274
Lloyd-Fox, S., 113
Lobel, O., 446
Lobel, T. E., 446
Lobliner, D. B., 352
Loebl, N. H., 343
Loebstein, R., 82
Logan, A., 350
Lohr, M. J., 445, 446
Long, S., 117
Lonky, E., 80
Loovis, E. M., 203
Looy, H., 289
Lopez, A. B., 416
Lord, S. E., 345
Losch, H., 91
Loughlin, G. M., 95
Lourenco, S., 324
Loveland, K. A., 183
Lovett, S. B., 305
Low, J. A., 73
Lozoff, B., 197
Lubach, G. R., 76
Luce, P. A., 156
Luchini, L., 80
Ludemann, P. M., 168
Luecke-Aleksa, D., 256
Luecken, L. J., 370
Luk, G., 232
Luna, B., 386
Lunenfeld, B., 381
Lütkenhaus, P., 183
Lutz, S. E., 251
Lynch, M. P., 157
Lynn, A., 125
Lyon, G. R., 426
Lyons-Ruth, K., 175
Lytton, H., 63, 253

M

Ma, C. M. S., 388
Macaulay, A. C., 290
Maccoby, E. E., 253, 254, 262, 373
MacDonald, F., 447
MacDonald, P. C., 85
MacDonald, R., 211
Mack, D. E., 448
MacKay, T. L., 91
MacKinnon-Lewis, C., 366
MacLaurin, B., 361

MacLean, W. E., 94
MacMillan, P., 373
Macoveanu, J., 196
MacWhinney, B., 148, 236, 328
Madigan, S., 171, 175
Magaldi-Dopman, D., 416
Maggs, J. L., 369
Magnuson, V. L., 394
Magnusson, D., 358, 359
Mah, C. L., 105
Mah, L., 203
Mahady-Wilton, M. M., 367
Mahajan, N., 272
Maier, S. F., 454
Main, M., 173, 178
Maislin, G., 102
Makin, J. W., 124
Malcuit, G., 252
Maldonado, R. E., 440
Malone, M. J., 367
Manassis, K., 178
Mandel, D. R., 126
Mandler, J. M., 147
Mangelsdorf, S., 178
Mangelsdorf, S. C., 167, 169
Mann, R.E., 28
Mann, V., 328
Maratsos, M., 235, 236
Marcia, J. E., 437, 438
Marcovitch, S., 144
Marcus, G. F., 234
Marentette, P. F., 157
Mares, M., 365
Mares, S., 114
Margand, N. A., 176
Margolin, G., 271
Margulis, C., 238
Marini, Z. A., 358
Mark, M., 236
Markiewicz, D., 175, 346
Markman, E. M., 159, 160, 239
Markovits, H., 408
Markow, D. B., 159
Marks, M., 29
Marlier, L., 124
Marlow, N., 149
Marriot, C., 222
Marsh, H. W., 344, 346, 425
Marshall, E., 86
Marshall, T. R., 114
Marshall, W. A., 379
Marsiglio, W., 393
Martin, C. L., 251, 255, 256
Martin, J. A., 91, 262, 391
Martin, M. E., 328
Martin, R. P., 78, 188
Martini, 196
Marzolf, D., 167
Marzolf, D. P., 305
Mas, C. H., 458

Mash, E., 13
Massey, S. G., 388
Masten, A. S., 352
Masur, E. F., 161
Matarazzo, A., 456
Matheson, C. C., 181, 272
Mathews, T. J., 91
Maticka-Tyndale, E., 393
Matson, P., 48
Matsuba, M. K., 418
Matthews, G., 172
Mattys, S. L., 156
Maurer, D., 128
Maxwell, S. E., 317
Maybery, D., 171
Mayer, E. V., 457
Mayseless, O., 175
Mazur, E., 371
McBride-Chang, C., 362
McCabe, J. B., 393
McCabe, M., 345
McCafferty, J., 49
McCall, R. B., 101, 154
McCarthy, K. A., 345
McCartney, K., 62
McCarty, M. E., 121
McClearn, G., 49, 50, 51
McClelland, J. L., 328
McClenahan, E. L., 446
McClure, E. B., 168
McConnaughey, D. R., 68
McCormick, M., 221
McCoy, J. K., 271
McCracken, J. T., 104
McCutchen, D., 331, 332
McDonough, L., 147
McDowell, M., 382
McGee, R., 427, 428
McGraw, M. B., 117
McGuffin, P., 55
McIntosh, J., 447
McIntyre, L., 107
McKechnie, B., 211
McKeen N. A., 120
McKeganey, N., 447
McKim, M. K., 180
McKusick, 51, 58
McLaughlin, B., 233
McLin, D., 144
McManus, I. C., 122
McNamara, K. A., 273
McNaughton, S., 228
McNeilly-Choque, M. K., 360
McShane, J., 426
Meck, E., 226
MedlinePlus, 394
Meece, D. W., 369
Mehler, P. S., 399
Meilman, P. W., 437
Mellon, M. W., 288

Meltzoff, A. N., 151
Mendelbaum, K., 454
Mendelson, B., 289
Mendelson, B. K., 290
Mendelson, M. J., 270, 290
Mendlewicz, J., 454
Mennella, J., 124
Mennella, J. A., 124
Mercier, J., 25
Merrick, S., 173
Merriwether, A. M., 388
Mersky, J. P., 393
Mertens, E., 289
Mervielde, I., 289
Messer, M. A., 422
Meusel, D., 107
Meyer, D. R., 370
Meyer-Bahlburg, H. F. L., 394
Meyers, A. F., 288
Meyers, M. B., 203
Meyers, T., 96
Michalik, N. M., 355
Midgett, C., 299
Mildes, K., 331
Miles, C., 309
Milich, R., 427, 429
Millar, W. S., 178
Miller, B. C., 388, 448
Miller, C. A., 426
Miller, J. G., 415
Miller, K. F., 220
Miller, K. S., 390
Miller, L. K., 311
Miller, L. S., 364
Miller, L. T., 196
Miller, P. A., 356
Miller, P. C., 260
Millward, R., 179
Minde, K., 176, 179
Mindell, J. A., 198
Minister of Health, 205
Ministry of Health of Brazil, 106
Minnis, H., 179
Mischel, W., 277, 278, 280
Mishna, F., 358
Mitchell, C., 441
Mitchell, J. E., 257
Mitchell, P., 223, 240
Miura, I. T., 227
Mize, J., 263, 274, 275, 352
Mizes, J. S., 399
Mizuta, I., 168
Mnookin, R. H., 373
Moats, L. C., 426
Mobley, L. A., 270
Mock, D., 317
Modan, M., 381
Moehler, E., 172
Moffitt, T. E., 382, 456
Moise-Titus, J., 364

Molema, S., 347
Molfese, D. L., 113
Möller, K., 175
Mollnow, E., 81
Mondloch, C. J., 128
Monk, C., 76
Monker, J., 230, 231
Monson, T. C., 366
Montgomery, L. A., 210
Mooney, L. A., 254
Moore, B. S., 356
Moore, C., 159
Moore, G. A., 170
Moore, K., 172
Moore, K. L., 59, 77
Moore, M. K., 151
Mora, J. O., 107
Moran, G., 171
Moran, T., 414
Morelli, M., 388
Morgan, B., 110
Morgan, J. L., 156
Morgan, P. L., 317
Morgan, S. P., 77
Morgane, P. J., 107
Morison, P., 352
Morison, S. J., 179
Morland, K., 75
Morris, A. S., 383
Morris, P. A., 10
Morrongiello, B. A., 126, 299
Mortelmans, D., 373
Mortimer, J. T., 424
Mosquera, L., 203
Moss, H. A., 187
Mounts, N., 445
Mouw, T., 349
Mrazek, D. A., 188
Muehlenhard, 395
Muir, D., 133
Müller, U., 146
Mullis, C., 78
Mumme, D. L., 169, 245
Muramoto, O., 48
Murphy, A. N., 246
Murphy, B. C., 188
Murphy, D., 209
Murphy, L. M., 273
Murphy, T. F., 47
Murray, C., 322
Murray, K., 277
Murray, L., 96
Murray, R. M., 55
Muzio, J. N., 94
Muzzonigro, P. G., 393

N

Nagle, R., 356
Naigles, L. G., 161
Nanson, J., 79

Narasimham, G., 408
Nash, K., 79
Nation, K., 329
National Center for Education
    Statistics, 333
National Healthy Mothers, Healthy
    Babies Coalition (HMHB), 81
National High Blood Pressure
    Education Program Working
    Group, 295
National Longitudinal Survey of
    Children and Youth Survey
    (NLSCY), 34
National Research Council, 104, 392
Neckerman, H. J., 358
Neiderhiser, J. M., 55, 361
Neisser, U., 317
Nelson, C. A., 115, 168
Nelson, D. A., 360
Nelson, K., 152, 158, 226
Nelson, K. E., 236
Nelson, M. A., 400
Neto, F., 251
Netto, D., 133
Netzer-Stein, A., 6
Neugarten, B. L., 266
Newcomb, A. F., 349, 350, 448
Newcomb, M. D., 449
Newcombe, N., 324
Newman, B. S., 393
Newman, L., 114
Newman, L. S., 255
Newport, E. L., 156, 235
Newport, W. L., 156
Nguyen, M., 391
NICHD Early Child Care Research
    Network, 180
Nichols-Whitehead, P., 228
Niebyl, J. R., 79
Nielsen, M., 183
Niemeyer, S. J., 108
Nieto, M., 361
Nitz, 60
Nolen-Hoeksema, S., 453
Nosko, A., 347
Nov-Krispin, N., 446
Nowell, A., 323, 325
Nucci, L., 281
Nugent, J. K., 89
Nulman, I., 82
Nurmi, J., 436
Nuttall, R. L., 324, 325
Nyberg, B., 440

O

O'Connell, C. M., 79
O'Connor, D. L., 180
O'Dell, L., 108
Odem, R. R., 82
Offer, D., 443

Ogletree, R. J., 395
O'Hearn, K., 386
Ohlendorf-Moffat, P., 85
Okagaki, L., 261
Okamoto, Y., 227
Olejnik, S., 188
Olesen, P., 196
Olfman, S., 388
Oliver, K. K., 298
Oliver, M. B., 387
Ollendick, T. H., 270
Oller, D. K., 157
Olsen, S. F., 360
Olson, R. K., 426
Olweus, D., 366, 367
O'Malley, 450
O'Neil, R., 274
O'Neill, D. K., 239
Ong, K. K., 382
Oppliger, P. A., 254
O'Reilly, A. W., 274
Orne, M. T., 25
Ornstein, A. E., 361
Oster, H., 125
Ostrov, E., 443
Ostrov, J. M., 364
Ota Wang, V., 30
Ovadia, J., 381
Over, H., 8
Overton, W. F., 408
Owen, A. M., 314
Owen, M. T., 176
Owens, M., 178
Owsley, C., 130

P

Paarlberg, K. M., 76
Pacifici, C., 228
Padavich, D. L., 355
Padgett, R. J., 236
Padgham, J. J., 449
Padilla, A. M., 233
Padmanabhan, A., 386
Pagano, J., 80
Paglia-Boak, A., 28
Paikoff, R., 383, 389
Paikoff, R. L., 399
Painter, K. M., 273, 274
Palca, J., 86
Palmer, D. J., 270
Palmer, S. E., 179
Palmeri, H., 281
Paluck, E. L., 353
Panksepp, J., 427
PAR, Inc, 421, 422
Paradis, G., 290
Parazzini, F., 80
Parke, R. D., 172, 259, 264, 274
Parker, J. G., 181, 349, 350, 362
Parker, T., 327

Parker-Loewen, D., 354
Parkin, B. L., 314
Park-Taylor, J., 416
Parmalee, A. H., 208
Parritz, R. H., 169
Parten, M., 181
Pascual, L., 273
Pascual-Leone, J., 413
Pass, R. F., 78
Paton, S. J., 79
Patterson, C. J., 268, 351, 362, 394
Patterson, G. R., 261, 264, 359, 360, 374, 456, 457
Patterson, P. H., 55
Patton, D. U., 364
Paulson, S. E., 383
Peake, P. K., 277, 278, 280
Pearce, J. W., 362, 363
Pearlman, M., 272
Pearson, J. L., 267
Pederson, D. R., 171, 178
Pelham, W. E., 429
Pellegrini, A. D., 12, 13, 348
Pellegrino, J. W., 324
Pelletier, L. G., 26
Pellicano, E., 222
Pelosi, A. J., 179
Pennington, B. F., 114, 427, 428
Pepe, M. S., 206
Pepler, D., 389, 395
Pepler, D. J., 366, 367
Perfetti, C. A., 328, 329
Perlman, D., 22
Perozynski, L. A., 272
Perris, E., 126
Perry, B. D., 428
Perry, D. G., 366, 367
Perry, T. B., 448
Perry-Parrish, C., 170
Persaud, T. V. N., 59, 77
Perusse, L., 206
Peter, J., 436
Peterman, T. A., 390
Peters, J., 210
Petersen, A. C., 399
Peterson, C., 152, 454
Peterson, C. C., 281
Peterson, D. M., 223
Peterson, L., 298, 356, 369
Petrakos, H., 273, 274
Petrie, R. H., 90
Petrill, S. A., 318
Pettit, G. S., 260, 263, 265, 274, 275, 351, 360, 365, 367, 369, 446
Pettit, P., 171
Pettito, L. A., 157
Petts, J., 108
Pezaris, E., 324, 325
Pezzot-Pearce, T. D., 362, 363
Pezzuti, L., 388

Phelps, E., 416
Phelps, M. E., 114
Philippot, P., 166
Phillips, S. J., 120
Phinney, J., 440
Phinney, J. S., 440
Piaget, J., 153, 218, 407
Piazza, C. C., 356
Picard, C. L., 382
Piccinini, C. A., 178
Pick, A. D., 168
Pickett, M. B., 209
Pike, R., 257, 258
Pilgrim, C., 447
Pillow, B. H., 305
Pisoni, D. B., 126, 155
Pitts, S. C., 41
Plessinger, M. A., 82
Plewis, I., 93, 94
Plöderl, M., 395
Plomin (W/Nitz & Rowe), 60
Plomin, R., 52, 54, 55, 103, 185, 318, 319, 360, 428
Plumert, J. M., 188, 228
Podolski, C., 364
Polakoski, K. L., 82
Polifka, J. E., 79, 83
Polit, E. F., 269
Pollitt, E., 107, 288
Pomerleau, A., 252
Pomietto, M., 125
Poole, M. E., 436
Popper, S., 96
Porter, R., 124
Porter, R. H., 124
Porter, W., 272
Posner, M. I., 276
Potvin, L., 290
Poulin-Dubois, D., 133, 225, 251, 256
Poulson, C. L., 158
Poulton, R., 245
Povinelli, D. J., 183
Powell, C. A., 139
Powell, M. B., 308
Power, F. C., 418
Power, T. G., 262
Powers, S. W., 261
Powlishta, K., 352, 353
Powlishta, K. K., 255
Pratt, M., 350
Pressley, M., 330
Pressley, M., 329
Pressman, E. K., 74
Prevor, M. B., 114
Price, J. M., 366
Priel, B., 183
Prior, J. C., 382
Propper, C., 170
Proteau, L., 119
Pryde, K. M., 202

Public Health Agency of Canada, 77, 79, 361
Putnam, S., 277

Q
Quadrel, M. J., 401
Quas, J. A., 152
Quint, S., 125
Quiring, O., 388

R
Rabiner, D., 366
Raboy, B., 268
Radke-Yarrow, M., 188, 272
Raffaelli, M., 453
Ragusa, D. M., 278
Raimbault, C., 124
Rakic, P., 111
Ram, A., 272
Ramanan, J., 369
Ramey, C. T., 319, 320
Ramey, S. L., 319
Ramirez, G., 325
Ramsay, D., 130
Ramsay, D. S., 187
Ramsey, E., 456
Ramsey, F., 107
Ramsey, P. G., 353
Rankin, D. B., 348
Rankin, J. M., 361
Rankin, M. P., 220
Rao, D. C., 206
Rappaport, L., 199
Rapport, M. D., 428
Rasalam, A. D., 57
Rashotte, C. A., 327
Rasmussen, P., 428
Rasmussen, R. L., 297
Ratcliffe, 60
Rawn, C. D., 276
Rayner, R., 7
Read, C. Y., 59
Reck, C., 172
Redei, E. E., 104
Reese, E., 152, 226, 230, 328
Reeve, K. F., 158
Reeve, L., 158
Rehm, J., 28
Reiber, C., 388
Reich, P. A., 158
Reid, D. H., 430
Reid, G., 295
Reid, H., 395
Reihman, J., 80
Reilly, B., 203
Reiser, L. W., 383
Reiss, D., 55
Rende, R., 428
Repacholi, B. M., 169
Resch, F., 172

Resnick, L. B., 332
Resnick, S., 178
Reupert, A., 171
Reynolds, A. J., 319, 393
Ricard, M., 169
Ricciuti, H. N., 107
Rice, M. L., 244
Rice, S. G., 400
Rich, C. L., 454
Richards, D. S., 85
Richards, M. H., 386, 399, 453
Richardson, G. A., 79, 83
Richer, J., 25
Richie, C., 48
Rideout, R., 152
Ridge, B., 265
Rigal, R., 324
Riggs, K. J., 223
Riksen-Walraven, J. M. A., 349
Rinaldi, C. M., 273
Rincon, C., 351
Ring, J., 426
Riordan, K., 178
Ritchie, K., 288
Ritchie, K. L., 259
Rivara, F. P., 299, 401
Roberts (1997), 166
Roberts, C., 454
Roberts, D., 267, 440
Roberts, G., 79
Roberts, J., 293
Roberts, J. E., 230
Roberts, K. C., 206
Roberts, K. P., 308
Roberts, M. W., 261
Roberts, R. E., 440
Roberts, R. J., 428
Roberts, W., 108, 355
Robinson, 60
Robinson, B. E., 369
Robinson, C. C., 360
Robinson, E. J., 223, 240
Robinson, M., 226
Robinson, N. S., 346
Roche, L., 346
Rocissano, L., 239
Rock, S. L., 319
Rodgers, J. L., 388
Rodrigo, M. J., 158
Rodriguez, M. L., 280
Rodríguez-Vázquez, J., 94, 95
Roedell, W. C., 364
Roehlkepartain, E. C., 416
Roffwarg, H. P., 94
Rogers, B. L., 288
Rogers, K., 424
Rogers, S. J., 222
Rogow, S. M., 293
Roisman, G. I., 187
Rolfes, S. R., 106

Romer, D., 384, 385
Romney, D. M., 253
Roncadin, C., 224
Rooks, J. P., 90
Roopnarine, J., 172
Rosander, K, 145
Rosario, M., 395
Roscoe, B., 449
Rose, A. J., 350
Rose, H., 256
Rose, H. A., 395
Rosen, K. S., 175
Rosengren, K. S., 220, 221
Rosenhan, D. L., 356
Rosenthal, D. A., 440
Rosenthal, R., 180, 369
Ross, D., 364
Ross, D. P., 39
Ross, H. S., 270, 272, 282
Ross, S. A., 364
Rossi, P. G., 196
Rostenstein, D., 125
Rotenberg, K. J., 457
Rothbart, M. K., 276
Rothbaum, F., 261
Rotheram-Borus, M. J., 395
Rotto, P. C., 261
Rounds, J., 420
Rovee-Collier, C., 150, 151
Rovee-Collier, C. K., 152
Rovet, J., 79
Rovet, J. F., 78, 224
Rowden, L., 346
Rowe (W/Plomin & Nitz), 60
Rowe, D. C., 55, 360, 388
Rowland, B. H., 369
Rowland, M., 293
Roy, E. A., 202
Royer, J. M., 325
Rubin, K. H., 181, 266, 274, 277, 304, 346, 351, 358, 360
Ruble, D., 255
Ruble, D. N., 251, 255, 343, 383
Ruble, T. L., 251
Ruff, H. A., 224
Rusch, F. R., 430
Rutherford, M. D., 222
Rutter, M., 55, 179
Rydell, R., 325
Rye, S., 424
Ryerson University, 88
Rymer, R., 235

S
Sacco, W. P., 454
Sachs, K. V., 399
Saewyc, E. M., 395
Safe Kids Canada, 108
Saffran, J. R., 156
Sagi, A., 175, 178

Sais, E., 232
Saliba, E., 124
Salman, M. S., 294
Salthouse, T. A., 196
Salvador, W. A., 270
Sameroff, A. J., 178
Sampson, A. E., 288
Sampson, P. D., 79
Sandberg, D. E., 287
Sanderson, C. A., 449
Sandhu, D., 437
Sandig, H., 206
Sandler, I. N., 371
Santini, D. L., 77
Sargent, J. D., 447
Saucier, 253
Saukko, P., 398
Savage-Rumbaugh, E. S., 235
Savelsbergh, G. J. P., 87
Savin-Williams, R. C., 394, 442
Saxby, L., 203
Saxe, G. B., 313
Scardamalia, M., 330
Scarr, S., 62, 441
Schaal, B., 124
Schachar, R, 224
Schachar, R., 224
Schafer, W. D., 166
Schaffer, D., 75
Schaller, M., 356
Scharfe, E., 176
Scharrer, E., 364
Schatz, D. A., 85
Scheinfeld, A., 203
Schiller, D., 446
Schiller, M., 178
Schmid, S., 415
Schmidt, L. A., 186
Schmitt, K. L., 256
Schmuckler, M. A., 119
Schneider, B. H., 175, 346, 350
Schneider, M. L., 76
Schneider, W., 152, 226, 304, 305,
    307, 410
Schnell, L., 59
Schnorr, T. M., 79
Schoeller, D., 102
School of the 21st Century (21C), 41
Schouten, A. P., 436
Schroeder, M., 272
Schubert, D. S. P., 270
Schubert, H. J. P., 270
Schuder, M. R., 175
Schuder, T., 329
Schulenberg, J., 424, 451
Schutz, R. W., 295, 380
Schwartz, D., 367
Schwebel, D. C., 188
Scott, C., 370
Scott, K., 39

Scott, R., 345
Scott, W. A., 345
Seal, J., 350
Sears, M. R., 428
Secada, W. G., 325
Seidel, C., 295
Seidel, K. D., 206
Seidenberg, M. S., 328
Seidman, E., 441
Seidner, L. B., 181
Seifer, R., 178
Seigel, D., 293
Seligman, M. E. P., 454
Sellen, D. W., 105
Sellers, D. P., 454
Selman, R. L., 347
Sen, M. G., 251, 256
Sénéchal, M., 230, 231
Serbin, L., 360
Serbin, L. A., 133, 251, 256, 352
Serdula, M. K., 289
Serketich, W. J., 266
Setliff, A. E., 246
Ševcikova, A., 388
Sevy, S., 454
Seyfarth, R., 235
Sham, P. C., 55
Shanahan, M. J., 424, 425
Shannon, F. T., 104, 210
Shapiro, J. R., 167
Sharp, E., 26
Sharp, J. M., 330
Sharp, R., 48
Sharpe, R. M., 83
Shatz, M., 221, 238, 239
Shaw, D. S., 372
Shaw, G. M., 75
Shek, D. T. L., 388
Sheldon-Keller, A. E., 178
Shell, R., 356
Shelov, S. P., 106
Shelton, T. L., 428
Shemesh, J., 381
Shepard, S. A., 188
Sherif, C. W., 444
Sherif, M., 444
Sherman, M., 454
Shields, M., 206
Shields, R., 299
Shin, Y. L., 273
Shiner, R. L., 186
Shinn, M. R., 317
Shirley, M. M., 118
Shiwach, R., 58
Shoda, Y., 277, 278, 280
Shope, J. T., 451
Shore, B. M., 304, 410
Shotland, R. L., 396
Shrager, J., 332
Shumway-Cook, A., 119

Shuter-Dyson, R., 311
Shwe, H. I., 239
Siddiqui, A., 121
Sidwell, R. W., 55
SIECCAN, 388, 389, 391, 393
Siegal, M., 281
Siegel, D. H., 428
Siegel, L. S., 329
Siegler, R. S., 226, 242, 328, 329, 330,
    332, 333
Signorella, M. L., 252, 256
Signorielli, N., 254
Silva, P. A., 382
Silverman, I., 280, 281
Silverman, I. W., 278
Silverman, W. K., 291
Simmons, R., 386
Simon, B. B., 183
Simon, G. E., 454
Simon, L., 388
Simons, D. J., 221
Singbeil, C. E., 269
Singer, M., 329
Singh, S., 323
Siushansian, J. A., 391
Skakkebaek, N. E., 83
Skinner, B. F., 234
Slaby, R. G., 364
Slate, J. R., 305
Slaughter, V., 146
Sloan, R., 95
Slobin, D. I., 234, 235
Slomkowski, C., 270
Small, S. A., 126
Smallish, L., 428
Smetana, J. G., 281, 417
Smit, E. K., 346
Smith, B. D., 203
Smith, E. G., 153
Smith, L. B., 118, 144
Smith, M. S., 13
Smith, P. K., 348
Smith, R. E., 297
Smith, T. E., 446
Smoll, F. L., 295, 297, 380
Smylie, L., 393
Snarey, J. R., 414
Snedeker, B., 423
Snidman, N., 188
Snow, C., 236
Snow, C. W., 93
Snow, M. E., 253
Snowling, M. J., 329
Snyder, E., 257
SOGC, 391
Soken, N. H., 168
Sokolov, J. L., 236
Solomon, G. E. A., 221
Sonuga-Burke, E. J. S., 346
Soussignan, R., 124

Spelke, E. S., 145
Spence, J. T., 261
Spence M. J., 73
Sperduto, R. D., 293
Spinrad, T. L., 279
Sporkin, E., 398
Sprafkin, J., 364
Springer, K., 221
Springer, S. P., 115
Spruijt, E., 370
Srinivasan, S. R., 286
Sroufe, L. A., 167, 175, 176
St. George, I. M., 382
St. James-Roberts, I., 93, 94
St. Joseph Women's Health Centre, 173
Stalikas, A., 440
Stallings, V. A., 102
Stanford, E. A., 158
Stanovich, K. E., 426
Stanton, W. R., 428
Starnes, R., 366
Stassen Berger, K., 366
Statistics Canada, 105, 232, 266, 267, 268, 269, 368, 373, 374, 392, 419, 423, 455, 456
Stattin, H., 358, 359
Steelman, J. D., 337
Stegall, S., 170
Stein, J. A., 449
Stein, J. H., 383
Steinberg, L., 262, 382, 383, 386, 423, 424, 443, 444, 445
Steinberg, L. D., 389, 401
Stephens, B. R., 132
Stern, M., 252
Sternberg, C. R., 167
Sternberg, K. J., 351
Sternberg, R. J., 50, 261, 309, 310, 312, 313, 314, 317, 321, 322, 324, 423, 424
Stevens, N., 350
Stevenson, H. W., 327, 333, 334, 335, 336, 337
Stevenson, M. R., 370
Stewart, L., 413
Stewart, M. A., 361
Stewart, P., 80
Stewart, S. L., 274
Stewart, R. B., 270
Stice, E., 266
Stieben, J., 169, 170
Stifter, C. A., 188, 279
Stigler, J. W., 334, 335, 336, 337
Stiles, J., 113, 115
Stoneman, A., 271
Stoolmiller, M., 390, 447
Stoppelbein, L., 438
Stormshak, E. A., 351
Stratton, H. H., 451
Strauss, M. S., 153

Strayer (1997), 166
Strayer, F. F., 272
Strayer, J., 272, 355
Streissguth, A. P., 79
Stringer, A. P., 232
Strober, M., 399
Strong, H. A., 448
Stuart, B., 180
Stunkard, A. J., 102, 291
Styfco, S. J., 243
Su, T. F., 441
Suchindran, C., 399
Suddath, R., 454
Sue, S., 30
Sullivan, L. W., 50
Sullivan, M. W., 168
Sullivan, S. A., 106
Summerville, M. B., 454
Super, C. M., 107, 122
Super, D. E., 419, 420
Susman, E. J., 387
Svejda, M., 130, 169
Swaney, K., 420
Swarr, A. E., 386, 399
Swarzenski, B., 196
Swenson, L. P., 395
Swingley, D., 156
Szakacs, E., 171
Szkrybalo, J., 255

T

Tager-Flusberg, H., 233, 234
Tamis-LeMonda, C. S., 274
Tani, F., 350
Tannahill, D., 49
Tanner, J. M., 104, 379
Tanski, S. E., 447
Tardiff, C., 175
Target, M., 176
Tarshis, E., 304
Tarullo, A. R., 95
Tasker, F., 394
Tavarez, 253
Tavernier, R., 384
Taylor, D. M., 233
Taylor, J. H., 418
Taylor, K., 48
Taylor, M., 274
Taylor, M. G., 252, 253
Taylor, P., 79
Taylor, P. S., 241
Taylor, R., 440
Taylor, R. D., 267
Taylor-Butts, A., 455
Tees, R., 156
Tegner, J., 196
Teitler, J. O., 371
Teixeira, R. A., 349
Teller, D. Y., 128
Temple, J. A., 319

Thelen, E., 118, 119, 120, 144
Thomas, A., 185, 188
Thomas, E., 230, 231
Thomas, J. R., 295
Thomas, J. W., 410
Thomas, M. H., 364
Thompson, G. G., 232
Thompson, L. A., 428
Thompson, M., 346
Thompson, R. A., 167
Thomson, A. D., 78
Thuras, P., 55
Thurstone, L. L., 310
Thurstone, T. G., 310
Till, C., 78
Tilse, E., 146
Tincoff, R., 156
Tinker, E., 238
Titzer, R., 144
Tivnan, T., 156
Tizard, B., 172
Tobin, J. J., 242
Tobler, N. S., 451
Toda, S., 171
Todd, R. D., 196
Tomada, G., 350
Tomasello, M., 238
Tomashoff, C., 398
Torgesen, J. K., 327
Towlson, K., 179
Trabasso, T., 329
Trafford, K., 91
Trafimow, D., 29
Treboux, D., 173, 390
Trehub, S. E., 126
Treiman, R., 330
Tremblay, M. S., 290
Tremblay, P., 395
Tremblay, R. E., 351
Trickett, P. K., 362
Tri-Council Policy Statement 2 (TCPS2), 36
Trocmé, N., 211, 361
Tronick, E. Z., 166
Truglio, R., 245
Tsai, J. H.-C., 349
Tuchfarber, B. S., 299
Tulviste, P., 228
Tung, S., 437
Turiel, E., 417
Turkmendag, I., 48
Turley-Ames, K. J., 223

U

Udry, J. R., 399
Ullah, K., 139
Ullian, D. Z., 255
Ulrich, B. D., 119, 120
Underwood, B., 356
Underwood, M. K., 358

Unger, O., 181
Unger, R., 383
Urberg, K. A., 447
US Bureau of the Census, 267
US Department of Health and
    Human Services, 401, 450
Uskul, A. K., 383
Utman, J. A., 157

V

Vachon, R., 408
Vaillant, G., 7
Valentiner, D., 346
Valenzuela, M., 107
Valkenburg, P. M., 245, 436
Valois, R. F., 424
van den Berg, S. M., 382
van den Boom, D. C., 178
van der Voort, T. H. A., 245
van Huis, A., 289
van IJzendoorn, M. H., 175,
    176, 178
Van Itterbeeck, J., 289
van Lieshout, C. F. M., 349
Van Meter, P., 329
Van Rossem, R., 395
Van Tuyl, S. S., 270
Vandell, D. L., 180, 369
Vandenbosch, L., 388
Vandereycken, W., 289
Vantomme, P., 289
Varea, C., 382
Vargha-Khadem, F., 149
Varnhagen, C. K., 329
Vasilyeva, M., 324
Vasta, R., 234, 264
Vaughn, B. E., 276
Vederhus, L., 323
Velázquez-Moctezuma, J.,
    94, 95
Velie, E. M., 75
Ventura, S. J., 91
Verbrugge, H. P., 210
Vereijken, B., 123
Verma, I. M., 86
Vernon, P. A., 196
Vezina, M., 38, 39
Vigneau, F., 148
Virdin, L., 371
Visconti, P., 196
Vishton, P., 145
Vitaro, F., 57, 344, 350, 351
Vockley, J., 63
Voeller, K. K. S., 57
Vogan, V. M., 222
Vohs, K. D., 276
Volling, B. L., 271
Volpe, J. J., 91
Volterra, V., 238
von Hofsten, C., 145

Vorhees, C. V., 81
Voss, K., 175
Vouloumanos, A., 158
Voyer, D., 323, 324
Voyer, S., 323
Vygotsky, L. S., 227, 228

W

Wagener, L. M., 416
Wagner, E., 272
Wagner, J., 398
Wagner, N., 107
Wagner, N. E., 270
Wagner, R. K., 327, 329
Wakschlag, L., 175
Wakschlag, L. S., 79
Walberg, H. J., 335, 336, 337
Waldron, H. B., 458
Walk, R. D., 129
Walker, A. S., 133
Walker, L. J., 413, 417, 418
Walker, S. P., 139
Wallace J. M., 416
Waller, J., 424
Walles, R., 325
Walsh, G., 107
Walsh, J. A., 26
Wang, L., 324
Wang, Q., 152
Ward, S. L., 408
Warren, B., 114
Warren, K. L., 152
Warren, M. P., 399
Warren, W. P., 382
Waschbusch, D. A., 454
Wasserstein, R. L., 29
Waters, E., 167, 171, 173
Waters, H. F., 364
Waters, H. S., 330
Watkins, E., 384
Watkins, S., 245
Watkinson, B., 79
Watson, J. B., 7, 259
Wattigney, W. A., 286
Waxman, S. R., 159, 160
Webber, L. S., 286
Weber, E. K., 281
Weber, M., 388
Weinberg, C. R., 68
Weinberg, J., 83, 154
Weinberg, M. K., 166
Weinberg, M. S., 393
Weinberg, R., 441
Weiner, S., 152
Weinstein, K. K., 266
Weissberg, R., 224
Weissman, M. D., 221
Weisz, J. R., 261
Weitzman, M., 288
Welch, D., 245

Wellman, H. M., 144, 145, 221,
    222, 223
Welsh, M. C., 114, 427
Wendland-Carro, J., 178
Wentzel, K. R., 278, 350
Werbner, P., 384
Werker, J., 156, 158
Werker, J. F., 156
Wermeskerken, M., 131
Werner, E. E., 91, 362
Werner, H., 120
Werner, N. E., 358, 366
Wertsch, J. V., 228
West, G., 455
West, M., 178
West, S. G., 41, 371
Whaley, L. F., 210
Whincup, P. H., 382
Whishaw, I. Q., 115
Whitaker, D., 331
Whitaker, R. C., 206
Whitbeck, L. B., 436
White, B. J., 444
White, D., 289
White, D. R., 290, 352, 368
White, J. W., 428
White, S. H., 39
Whitehead, J. R., 400
Whitehurst, G. J., 234, 264
Whitesell, N. R., 441, 448
Whiteside, S. P., 288
Whitfield, K. E., 49, 50, 51
Whitfield, M. F., 125
Whithall, S., 222
Whiting, J. W. M., 266
Whitney, 75
Whitney, E. N., 106
Whyte, M. K., 449
Wickberg, B., 175
Wicks-Nelson, R., 399, 427
Widmayer, S. M., 237
Wiebel, A., 172
Wilcox, A. J., 68
Wilcoxon, J. S., 104
Wilkinson, A., 327
Wille, S., 199
Williams, H., 119
Williams, J. E., 251, 252
Williams, J. M., 330, 331
Williams, R., 26, 27, 28,
    389, 451
Williams, S., 382, 427
Williams, T., 388, 390, 395
Williamson, G. M., 76
Willms, J. D., 290
Willoughby, T., 384, 416, 417
Wilson, C. C., 356
Wilson, D. B., 428
Wilson, G. T., 398, 399
Wilson, M., 267

Wilson, P. G., 430
Wilson, R. S., 103, 318
Wimbush, D. D., 262
Windle, M., 390
Windle, R. C., 390
Winner, E., 202
Winslow, E. B., 372
Wise, B. W., 426
Wisenbaker, J., 78
Wishart, J. G., 154
Witelson, S. F., 115, 196
Wittig, B. A., 23
Wolchik, S. A., 371
Wolf, A. W., 197
Wolf, M. M., 8
Wolfe, D., 13
Wolff, P. H., 93
Wolfson, A. R., 443
Wolraich, M. L., 428
Wong, D. F., 210
Wong-Fillmore, L., 233
Woo, J., 84
Woo, T. U. W., 196
Wood, E., 347, 350
Wood, J. R., 289
Woodard, E., 365
Woods, J. R., Jr., 82
Woodward, A. L., 159, 160
Woodworth, S., 266
Woollacott, M. H., 119

World Health Organization,
    107, 108
World Health Organization
    Multicentre Study Group, 101,
    102, 195, 287
Worth, K. A., 447
Wright, J., 245
Wright, J. A., 206
Wright, J. C., 245
Wu, D. Y. H., 242
Wunsch, J. P., 167
Wynn, K., 153, 181, 272

X
Xia, Y., 270
Xiaohe, X., 449
Xie, Q., 388
Xinyin, C., 313
Xu, X., 382

Y
Yahav, R., 453
Yang, B., 270
Yates, M., 436
Yazigi, R. A., 82
Yeung, A. S., 344
Yidiz, S., 117
Yip, R., 101
Yonas, A., 130
Young, 253

Young, C. L., 317
Young, D., 323
Young, S. K., 188
Youngblade, L. M., 273
Youniss, J., 436
Yu, A. P., 203
Yu, C., 159

Z
Zahn-Waxler, C., 168, 188, 272
Zaia, A. F., 274
Zaitchik, D., 221
Zamsky, E. S., 267
Zappulla, C., 351
Zarbatany, L., 348
Zeanah, C. H., 171, 179
Zelazo, N. A., 119, 123
Zelazo, P. D., 119, 144, 182
Zelazo, P. R., 116, 119
Zeman, J., 170
Zhang, Y., 292
Zhou, T., 78
Zigler, E., 243, 322, 455
Zigler, E. F., 41
Zimiles, H., 373
Zins, J. E., 299
Ziv, Y., 178
Zolner, T., 26, 35, 244, 321, 363, 416,
    439, 456, 457
Zubrick, S. R., 91

Subject Index

A

Aboriginal Head Start, 244
Aboriginal peoples
  and child welfare services, 211, 212–213
  diabetes in, 290
  and Erikson's lifespan theory, 7
  and ethnic identity, 440–441
  and intelligence testing, 321
  Jordan's Principle, 212–213
  and residential schools, 39, 452
  smoking among women, 79
  and substance use, 451–452
abortion, 391–392, 392f
abstract reasoning, 407, 408t
abuse, 348, 361–363
academic achievement
  and abuse, 362
  and popularity/rejection, 352
  school-based influences on, 335–336
  teacher-based influences on, 336–337
academic journals, 37
academic skills
  math skills, 332–335
  reading skills, 326–330
  writing skills, 330–332, 332t
accidents, 108, 209–210, 209t, 297–299, 401
accommodation, 140–141
achievement, in identity, 436t, 437, 437f
acquaintance rape, 395, 396f
Action for Children, 369
active gene–environment relation, 63
active–passive child issue, 17
activity, 186
actual thinking, 408
adaptive behaviours, 4, 429–430
adolescence
  alcohol and drug use in, 450–452, 450f
  and attention deficit hyperactivity disorder (ADHD), 427–429
  and body image, 383
  and brain development, 383–384
  and career development, 419–423
  characteristics of adolescents' thinking, 438t

  and cognitive control, 383–384
  delinquency in, 455–458
  and depression, 452–455
  formal operational thought stage of development, 406–408
  and friendship, 448, 449
  growth in, 379f
  identity, ethnic, 439–441
  identity, search for, 435–439, 436t
  and information processing, 408–410
  and intellectual delay, 429–430, 430f
  and learning disabilities, 425–426
  mechanisms of maturation, 382
  and moods, 383–384, 385f
  and moral reasoning, 411–418
  nutrition, 398–399
  part-time employment, 423–425
  and peer pressure, 446–448
  physical fitness, 399–401, 400f
  physical growth, 379–380
  pregnancy and contraception, 391–393
  puberty, 378–387
  relationship with parents, 442–444, 443f
  relationships with peers, 444–449
  romantic relationships, 448–449
  and self-esteem, 441–442
  sexual behaviour, 387–393
  sexual coercion, 395–397, 404
  sexual maturation, 380–381
  sexual orientation, 393–395
  social and emotional development in, 435–458
  special challenges, 425–430
  and spirituality and religion, 416–417, 417t
  and STIs, 390–391
  substance use and mental health, 27–28, 31–32
  and television, 245
  threats to well-being, 401
  and work, 419–425
adolescent egocentrism, 437–438, 438t
Adolescent Health Committee of the Canadian Pediatric Society, 389

adolescent-limited antisocial behaviour, 456
adoption studies
  and aggression, 360–361
  and behavioural genetics, 54
  and extroversion, 54
  and intelligence, 318, 319f
  and obesity, 291
Adult Attachment Interview, 178
advocacy for children, 39–40
African heritage
  Carolina Abecedarian Project, 320
  and grandmothers, 267
  and intelligence quotient, 320–321, 321f
  and segregation, 353
  and sickle-cell disease, 46, 51
afterbirth, 87
after-school care, 368–369
age of viability, 72, 73
aggression
  and abuse, 361–363
  and cognitive processes, 365–366
  and criminal activity, 358–359, 359f
  defined, 358
  in families, 359–361
  genetic and environmental influences on, 56
  impact on children, 359–366
  in middle childhood, 357–368
  nature of, in children, 358–359
  in preschool children, 272
  and television, 364–365
  victims of, 366–367
Aid to Children and Adolescents at Risk Foundation, 362
AIDS, 78, 78t
Ainsworth, Mary, 23, 173
Alateen, 451
albinism, 58t
alcohol
  in adolescence, 450–452, 450f
  and peer pressure, 447
  as teratogen, 78t, 79, 82, 104
Alcoholics Anonymous, 451
alert inactivity, 93
allele, 49
Allen-Vercoe, Emma, 209
allocentric, 345
altruism, 354, 355–356
amenorrhea, 382

American Academy of Pediatrics Committee on Public Education, 246
American Association of Intellectual and Developmental Disabilities (AAIDD), 430
American Institute of Bisexuality, 394
American National Institute of Child Health and Human Development, 180
American Psychological Association, 14
American Statistical Association, 29
amniocentesis, 84, 85
amnion, 70
amniotic fluid, 70
amniotic sac, 70
anabolic steroids, 400–401
anal stage of development, 6t
androgen, 381
anger, 167
anonymity, 36
anorexia nervosa, 398–399
anoxia, 90
Apgar score, 92–93, 93t
appearance as reality, 220, 221t
Aspirin, 78t
Assembly of First Nations (AFN), 211
assertiveness, 358
assimilation, 140–141
Assisted Human Reproduction Act, 47
associative learning, 7
asthma, 108, 206, 208
attachment
    adult attachment types, 178
    and child care, 179
    defined, 4, 171
    in evolutionary theory, 12
    and family policy, 175
    and fathers, 172, 177
    growth of, 171–173
    and later social development, 175–176, 178
    mother–child attachment, 23, 172, 175
    and peer relationships, 275
    quality of, 173–179
    reactive attachment disorder, 179
    and self-control, 280f
    and smell, 173
    types of, 173–175
    worldwide patterns, 175f
attention, 224–225, 224f, 225f, 245
attention deficit hyperactivity disorder (ADHD), 427–429
attentional disorders, 57

attrition, 33
auditory localization, 126
auditory threshold, 126
authoritarian parenting, 261–262
authoritative parenting, 262
autism
    and attachment, 176
    and brain abnormalities, 222
    causes of, 57, 108
    and mental health services, 429
    and theory of mind, 222
autobiographical memory, 149, 225–226
autonomous attachment, 178
autonomy vs. shame and doubt stage of development, 6t
autosomal recessive disorders has, 57
autosome, 48
avoidant attachment, 174
axon, 110, 111

B

Baba, Kazunori, 84
babbling, 157
Babinski reflex, 117t
balance, 119
Baldwin, James Mark, 3
Bandura, Albert, 8, 252
Banting, Frederick G., 149
Barbados, 107
basal metabolic rate, 291
basic trust vs. mistrust stage of development, 6t
Bayley Scales of Infant Development, 154
bed wetting, 199
behavioural genetics, 52–57, 61
Berko, Jean, 233
bilingualism, 232–233
Binet, Alfred, 315
biological influences. *see also* genetics
    and antisocial behaviour, 457
    and child development, 16
    and gender identity, 256–257
    of heredity, 46–49
biological perspective, 3–5, 14t
bipolar disorder, 384
bisphenol A, 80
blank slate (*tabula rasa*), 2, 17
blended family, 373–374
blink reflex, 117t
body ego, 5
body image, 383
bone, 102–103, 195–196
Bowlby, John, 171
Bradley, Robert, 319
brain
    in adolescence, 384–386

brain wave pattern, 112
Broca's area, 234
developing brain, 111–115
emerging brain structures, 111–112
frontal cortex, 114–115
and language processing, 234
organization of mature brain, 110–111, 110–115, 110f
plasticity of, 115
in preschool children, 196–197, 196f
structure and function, 112–113
Brazil, 105, 119
breakfast, 288
breastfeeding, 104–105, 106
breech presentation, 87
Broca's area, 234
Bronfenbrenner, Urie, 10, 11f
Brown, Louise, 47
Brown v. Board of Education, 353
bulimia nervosa, 399
bullying, 272, 358, 366–367. *see also* aggression
Buss, Arnold, 185

C

Caesarean section (C-section), 88
caffeine, 78t
Caldwell, Bettye, 319
Canada
    abortion in, 391–392, 392f
    adolescent sexual behaviour in, 388
    adolescents in workforce, 423
    alcohol and drug use among adolescents, 451
    asthma in children, 108
    bilingualism in, 232
    birth rate, 77
    blended families, 373
    child abuse and neglect in, 361
    childhood obesity in, 290–291
    children's rights in, 353–354
    developmental research in, 3
    diet in, 105
    divorce in, 368
    ethnic identities in, 439
    foster families, 374
    malnutrition in, 107
    mathematical scoring in, 333
    population sampling in, 26
    poverty in, 320–321
    school jurisdiction in, 335
    skip-generation families, 374
    STIs in, 391
    suicide in, 455
    teen pregnancies in, 391
    youth crime in, 455–456

Canada's Food Guide, 105
Canadian Association for Community Living, 430
Canadian Association for Midwives, 89
Canadian Association for Young Children (CAYC), 241, 243
Canadian Centre for, 28
Canadian Children, 37
Canadian Code of Ethics for Psychologists, 35, 35*t*
Canadian Dental Association, 196
Canadian Fitness and Lifestyle Research Institute (CFLRI), 291, 296–297
Canadian Human Rights Commission, 211
Canadian Incidence Study of Reported Child Abuse and Neglect, 361
Canadian Institute of Health Research, 208
Canadian Microbiome Initiative, 209
Canadian Paediatric Society, 195, 199
Canadian Psychological Association (CPA), 35
Canadian Psychology, 35, 37
Canadian Transition to Care study, 180
cardinality principle, 226
career development, 419–423
Carolina Abecedarian Project, 320
Carroll, John, 310
Case, Robbie, 8, 150
The Cat in the Hat, 73
"catching up," 119
causation, 28–29, 28*f*
cell body, 110
centration, 218, 221*t*
cephalocaudal growth, 71, 101
cerebral cortex, 72
cerebral hemisphere, 110
cerebral palsy, 157
cervix, 87
Chan, Titus, 287
Chess, Stella, 185, 188
Chi, Michelene, 306
child care, 179, 180
child development
  biological perspective, 3–5, 14*t*
  characteristics of developmental perspectives, 14*t*
  cognitive-developmental perspective, 8, 14*t*
  contextual perspective, 10–11, 14*t*
  developmental psychopathology, 13, 14*t*

evolutionary theory, 12–13, 14*t*
and family policy, 38–42
and family structure, 39
information-processing theory, 12, 14*t*
learning perspective, 7–8, 14*t*
newer approaches to, 12–13
psychodynamic perspective, 5–7, 14*t*
Child Development, 37
Child Find, 40
childbirth
  approaches to, 88–90
  complications in, 90–92
  labour and delivery, 86–88, 87*f*
  and postpartum depression, 95–96
  prematurity, 91
  small-for-date infants, 91–92
child-development research
  children's role in own development, 17
  communicating search results, 37
  correlational study, 26–30
  cross-sectional study, 33–34
  designs for, 26–31, 34*t*
  domain connection, 17–18
  early development and later development, 15
  ethical responsibilities, 35–37
  experimental study, 30–31
  and family policy, 38–42
  heredity and environment, 16–17
  longitudinal study, 31–33
  measurement in, 22–26
  methods of, 31–34
  themes in, 15–18
Children's Television Workshop, 244
chimpanzees, 234
China, 270, 334
Chinese ethnic identity, 441
chlamydia, 390–391
Chomsky, Noam, 234
chorionic villus sampling (CVS), 84, 85*f*
chromosome, 47, 48, 58–60, 256
chronic illness, 208–209
chronic stress, 76
chronosystem, 11, 11*f*
cigarette smoking, 79
classical conditioning, 7, 151
clinal variation, 50, 51
clique, 445
Clostridium difficile, 208–209
cocaine, 78*t*, 82, 83
cognitive development
  in adolescence, 383–384

and early childhood education, 241
exploring environment, 153–154
individual differences, 154
information-processing theory. *see* information-processing theory
and intellectual delay, 429–430, 430*f*
language. *see* language
in middle childhood, 303–308
and parents' work, 180
Piaget's theory of cognitive development. *see* Piaget's theory of cognitive development
and play, 241–242
and prenatal maternal stress, 56
understanding numbers, 153*f*
Vygotsky's theory of, 227–229, 229*t*
Cognitive Development, 37
cognitive processes, 365–366, 405–418
cognitive-developmental perspective, 8, 8*t*, 14*t*
cohort effect, 32, 33–34
colour perception, 127–128, 128*f*
communication. *see also* language
  listening, 239–240
  speaking effectively, 238–239
  taking turns, 237–238
component, 312
componential subtheory, 312, 313*t*
comprehension, reading, 326, 329–330
computers, 337
concrete operational thought stage of development, 9*t*, 141*t*, 303–304
cone, 127–128
confidentiality, 36
conflict, 271–272. *see also* aggression
conservation, 218–220, 219*f*
constipation, 288
constricting, 254
content knowledge, 409–410, 410*t*
contextual perspective, 10–11, 14*t*
contextual subtheory, 312–313, 313*t*
contraception, 389, 392–393
conventional level of moral reasoning, 412
conventional personality type, 420*t*
convergent validity, 25
cooing, 157, 167
co-operative play, 181, 272, 273–274
Cornell, Ed, 150
corpus callosum, 110
correlation coefficient, 27–28
correlational study, 26–30

cortisol, 154
cortisol reactivity, 387
Council of Ministers of Education, Canada (CMEC), 389
counterfactual thinking, 223
counterimitation, 263
counting, 226–227, 232
crediting, 218
criminal activity, 358–359, 359*f*
critical period, 4, 235
cross-sectional correlational study, 34
cross-sectional experimental study, 34
cross-sectional study, 33–34, 34*t*
crowd, 445
crowning, 87
crying
    adaptive value of, 4
    and culture, 187
    as newborn state, 93
    soothing techniques, 94
crystallization, 419
culture
    and crying, 187
    defined, 10
    and emotional development, 261
    and emotional expression, 168
    and grandparents, 266, 267
    and identity, 439–441
    and infantile amnesia, 152
    and intelligence, 313
    and intelligence quotient, 320–323
    and make-believe, 273
    and menarche, 384
    and moral reasoning, 415–516
    and nutrition, 289
    and parenting styles, 261, 262
    and popularity, 351
culture-fair intelligence tests, 322
custody, 372
cyber-school, 337
cycling, 209*t*
cystic fibrosis, 58*t*
cytomegalovirus, 78, 78*t*

D
Darwin, Charles, 4
date rape, 395, 397, 404
dating, 448–449
daycare, 241
deductive reasoning, 407–408, 408*t*
deferred imitation, 143
delay of gratification, 280–281. *see also* self-control
delinquency
    in Canada, 455–456
    causes of, 456–457
    defined, 455

treatment and prevention of, 457–458
delivery (in childbirth), 87–88
demand characteristics, 25
dendrite, 110, 111
deoxyribonucleic acid (DNA). *see* DNA (deoxyribonucleic acid)
dependent variable, 30
depression in adolescence, 384, 452–455
    and child care, 180
    defined, 55, 453
    and heredity, 55
    postpartum depression, 95–96, 171–172
    treating, 454–455
depth perception, 129–130
descriptive statistics, 29
design stage, 203
Developmental Psychology, 37
developmental psychopathology, 13, 14*t*
diabetes, 290
diarrhea, 108
diethylstilbestrol (DES), 83
differentiated instruction and response to intervention (RTI), 317
differentiation, 120
diffusion, in identity, 436–437, 436*t*, 437*f*
DiPietro, Janet, 74
direct instruction, 263
discipline
    and blended families, 373
    and delinquency, 457
    and parenting styles, 259
    and self-control, 279, 280*f*
    and self-esteem, 345
    and social skill, 352, 356, 357*t*
    and temperament, 190
disease. *see also* illness, as teratogen, 78
dishabituation, 150
disinhibition, 263
dismissive attachment, 178
disorders of sexual development, 394
disorganized (disoriented) attachment, 174
dispositional praise, 357
divergent validity, 25
divorce
    adjusting to, 372–373
    family life after, 370–371
    impact on children, 371–372, 372*t*
    joint custody, 372
    prevalence of, 368, 370
dizygotic (fraternal) twins, 53–54
DNA (deoxyribonucleic acid), 48–49, 49*f*

domains of development, 17–18
dominance hierarchy, 446
dominant trait, 50, 51*t*, 52, 53*f*
doula, 88
Down syndrome, 58–59, 77
Dr. Seuss, 73
drawing, 201–203, 202*f*
drowning, 209*t*
drugs
    in adolescence, 450–452, 450*f*
    and peer pressure, 447
    as teratogens, 78–79, 78*t*, 82
dwarfism, 104
dynamic systems theory, 118
dynamic testing, 317

E
early childhood education
    daycare vs. preschool, 241
    developmentally appropriate practices in, 243*t*
    for economically disadvantaged children, 243
    and television, 244–246
    varieties of, 241–243
Early Childhood Research and Practice, 37
early development as predictor of later development, 15
eating disorders, 398–399
ecological theory, 10
ecological validity, 24
ectoderm, 70
ectogenesis, 47
edges, 131
egg, 46–47, 48
ego, 5
egocentric frame of reference, 153–154
egocentrism, 218, 221*t*, 304, 437–438
electroencephalogram (EEG), 113
embarrassment, 168
embryo, 70–71
embryo stage of prenatal development, 70–71, 71*f*, 73*t*
emotion
    basic, 166–168
    complex, 168
    elements of, 165
    happiness, 167
    negative, 167–168
    processing in brain, 114
    recognizing and using others' emotions, 168–169
    regulating, 169–170

emotional development. *see also* emotion
  in adolescence, 435–458
  and attachment. *see* attachment
  and culture, 261
  in infancy, 164–179
  in middle childhood, 341–374
  in preschool children, 249–282
empathy, 355
enabling, 254
endoderm, 70
endogamy, 50
environment
  and heredity, 16–17, 18, 60–64
  and illness, 210
  influence of, 10–11, 62–64
  and intelligence, 319
  nonshared environmental influences, 55–57
  and obesity, 291
  and puberty, 382
  reaction range, 61–62
  and temperament, 187
environmental hazards and prenatal development, 80t
environmental reaction, 5
epiphyses, 103
episodic memory, 149
equilibration, 141–142
Erikson, Erik, 6t, 7, 14, 257, 435
erogenous zones, 5
estrogen, 381
ethics
  Canadian Code of Ethics for Psychologists, 35, 35t
  in child-development research, 35–37
  and reproductive technology, 47–48
ethnic identity, 439–441. *see also* culture
ethological theory, 4
evidence-based practice, 39
evocative gene–environment relation, 63
evolutionary developmental psychology, 13
evolutionary theory, 12–13, 14t
executive functioning, 222
exercise, 295–296, 399–401, 400f
exosystem, 10, 11f
experiential subtheory, 312, 313t
experiment, 30
experimental study, 30–31, 34t
experimenting stage of sensorimotor development, 143
expressive language ability, 426
expressive style, 161
expressive trait, 251
extroversion, 52–54, 53f, 54t

F
facial expressions, 24, 166–167, 168
false-belief task, 222–223, 223f
family. *see also* environment; parenting
  after-school care, 368–369
  aggression in, 359–361
  blended families, 373–374
  changing structure of, 38–39
  configuration of, 266–268
  and delinquency, 457
  divorce. *see* divorce
  in early twenty-first century, 368–374
  foster families, 374
  skip-generation families, 374
  as a system, 259, 260f
family policy
  advocating for children to influence, 39–40
  background, 38–39
  China's one-child policy, 270
  defined, 38
  determining guidelines for child care, 180
  evaluating to influence, 40
  guidelines to reduct SIDS, 95
  Head Start, 244
  implications for research, 41
  influencing, 39–41
  model programs to influence, 40–41
  osteoporosis prevention, 381
  promoting moral reasoning, 418
  screening for PKU, 63
  understanding of children to influence, 39
fast mapping, 158–161
fat, 102
fathers
  and attachment, 172, 175, 177
  and custody, 372
  and gender identity, 253
fear, 167
fear response, 57
feedback, 264
Fels Longitudinal Project, 187
fetal alcohol spectrum disorder (FASD), 79, 211
fetal medicine, 85
fetal period of prenatal development, 71–73, 73t, 74
fetus, 71, 72f
field experiment, 31
fine-motor skills
  defined, 116
  handedness, 122, 202–203
  in infancy, 121–122
  in middle childhood, 294–295

in preschool children, 201–202, 202f
fire, 209t
firearms, 209t
First Nations. *see* Aboriginal peoples
First Nations Child and Family Caring Society of Canada (FNCFCSC), 211
Flood, Tonya, 150
fluoride neurotoxicity, 292
Følling, Asbjørn, 63
Food and Drugs Act, 61
foreclosure, in identity, 436–437, 436t, 437f
formal operational thought stage of development, 9t, 141t, 406–408, 408t
foster family, 374
Free the Children, 353
Freud, Anna, 7
Freud, Sigmund, 5, 6t, 171
friendship, 349–350, 448
Froebel, Friedrich, 240
frontal cortex, 110, 114–115
functional magnetic resonance imaging (fMRI), 113
functional near infrared spectroscopy (fNIRS), 113
fussiness, 74

G
gamete, 47
Gardner's theory of multiple intelligences, 310–312, 311t, 314t
gay and lesbian parents, 267–268
Gelman, Rochel, 239
gender consistency, 255
gender constancy, 255
gender differences
  and depression, 453
  in identity, 437
  in intellectual ability and achievement, 323–326
  mathematical ability, 324–326
  and moral reasoning, 417
  in motor skills, 203–204, 294–295, 294f
  in physical activity, 295
  in physical growth, 379, 380
  and puberty, 386–387
  and sexual behaviour, 389
  in sexual maturation, 380f
  spatial ability, 323–324
  and suicide, 455
  verbal ability, 323
gender identity
  biological influences, 256–257

cognitive theories of, 255–256
defined, 252
socializing influences,
252–255
gender labelling, 255
gender roles, 250–252
gender stability, 255
gender stereotypes, 250–252, 251*t*,
252*f*, 254–255, 254*f*
gender-schema theory,
255–256, 256*f*
gene, 49
gene therapy, 86
generativity vs. stagnation stage of
development, 6*t*
genetic disorders
abnormal chromosomes, 58–60
inherited disorders, 57–58
and sex chromosomes, 60*t*
genetic engineering, 85–86
genetic reductionism, 61
genetics. *see also* biological
influences; heredity
behavioural, 52–57
and delinquency, 457
disorders, 57–60
and puberty, 382
genital herpes, 78, 78*t*
genital stage of development, 6*t*
genotype, 49, 50
genotypic intelligence A, 62
germ disc, 69–70
German measles. *see* rubella
(German measles)
Gesell, Arnold, 4
gestation, 68. *see also* prenatal
development
gestures, 158
Gibson, Eleanor, 129
Gilligan's ethic of caring, 414–417
Gottfred, Bruce, 177
graffiti, 457
grammar, 233, 234–236
grammatical morpheme, 233–234, 233*f*
grandparents, 266–267
grasping, 121–122
Green, Christopher, 3, 13
gross-motor skills, 116, 199–200,
200*f*, 295
groups, 444–446
growth hormone, 104, 197, 287
guilt, 168
Guthrie, Robert, 63

H
habituation, 150–151
Hall, G. Stanley, 4
handedness, 122, 202–203
happiness, 167
Harter, Susan, 342

head circumference, 195
Head Start, 243, 244, 319
Health Canada, 389
health care, jurisdictional
authority, 211
hearing
in infancy, 125–126
in middle childhood, 292–293
helpfulness, 188–189, 189*f*
hemispheres, brain, 110, 110*f*, 113,
114–115, 196*f*, 197, 203
heredity
and ADHD, 428
and aggression, 360–361
biology of, 46–49
and depression, 454
dominant and recessive traits,
49–52
and environment, 16–17, 60–64
and intelligence, 318–319
mechanisms of, 46–57
and myopia, 293
and obesity, 291
and physical growth, 103–104
polygenic inheritance, 52
and psychological disorders, 55
reaction range, 61–62
sickle-cell disease, 46
single-gene inheritance, 49–52
and temperament, 186–187
heroin, 78*t*
heterozygosity, 50
Heth, Donald, 150
Hetherington, Mavis, 370
History of Psychology, 14
HIV, 78, 391
Hmong people, 440
Holland's personality-type theory,
420, 420*t*, 422*f*
Home Observation for Measurement
of the Environment
(HOME), 319
homosexuality. *see* gay and lesbian
parents; sexual orientation
homozygosity, 50
Hopi culture, 123
hormones
defined, 104
and gender identity, 256
and growth, 104
and moodiness, 383–384
in puberty, 381
Hospital for Sick Children, 224
hospitalization, 210
Human Microbiome Project,
208, 209
human papilloma virus
(HPV), 391
Human Resources Development
Canada, 35

Huntington's disease, 58
Hyde, Janet, 323
hypothetical reasoning, 408*t*
hypoxia, 90

I
id, 5
identity. *see also* self-concept
in adolescence, 435–439,
436*t*, 438*t*
and career choice, 419–420
ethnic, 439–441
gender identity, 252–257
vs. identity confusion stage of
development, 6*t*
statuses of, 436–437, 436*t*, 437*f*
idiocentric, 345
illness
asthma, 108, 206, 208
chronic, 208–209
environmental factors in, 210
and physical development,
107–108, 208
and poverty, 210
and stress, 210
illusion of invulnerability,
438, 438*t*
imaginary audience, 438, 438*t*
imaginary companion, 274
imitation, 8, 151
immunization, 108
implantation, 69–70
implementation, 420
imprinting, 4–5
impulsivity, 384
in vitro fertilization, 47, 48
incomplete dominance, 50
independent variable, 30
India, 415, 447
indifferent-uninvolved
parenting, 262
indulgent-permissive
parenting, 262
industry vs. inferiority stage of
development, 6*t*
infancy
brain development in,
111–112, 114
cognitive development in,
138–161
emotional development in,
165–170, 185–190
malnutrition in, 107
motor development, 116–122
nutrition in, 104–105, 106, 106*t*
physical growth, 101–103, 102*t*
self-control in, 276
sensory development in,
124–134
social development in, 170–184

Infant Behavior and Development, 37
infant mortality, 92, 107–108
infant-directed speech, 157
infantile amnesia, 152
information processing
    in adolescence, 408–410, 409*f*, 410*t*
    basic processes of, 409
    content knowledge, 409–410
    defined, 148
    in infancy, 147–154
    in preschool children, 224–227
    steps in, 149*f*
    strategies and metacognitive
        skill, 410
information-processing theory
    and aggression, 365*f*
    characteristics of, 14*t*
    classical conditioning, 151
    compared to Piaget's theory, 12
    features of, 148–150
    learning, 150–151
    memory, 151–152
    operant conditioning, 151
    and preschool children,
        223–227
    understanding numbers, 153
informed consent, 36
inhibition, 263
initiative vs. guilt stage of
    development, 6*t*
inner speech, 228
insects, edible, 289, 290*f*
Institute of Infections and
    Immunity, 208
Institute of Medical Electronics, 84
instrumental aggression, 358
instrumental orientation, 412
instrumental trait, 251
Integrated Management of
    Childhood Illness (IMCI), 108
integration, 120
intellectual delay, 429–430, 430*f*
intelligence
    bodily-kinesthetic, 311*t*
    and culture, 313
    Gardner's theory of multiple
        intelligences, 310–312, 311*t*,
        314*t*
    general intelligence (g), 310, 310*f*
    and heredity, 318–319, 319*f*
    interpersonal, 311*t*
    intrapersonal, 311*t*
    linguistic, 311, 311*t*
    logical-mathematical, 311*t*
    and malnutrition, 107
    mathematics, 324–326
    measuring, 154
    musical, 311*t*
    psychometric theory, 309–310, 314*t*
    spatial ability, 311, 311*t*, 323–324

Sternberg's triarchic theory,
    312–314, 313*t*
    triarchic theory of successful
        intelligence, 314*t*
    verbal ability, 323
intelligence quotient (IQ). *see also*
        intelligence testing
    cultural factors in, 320–323, 321*f*
    defined, 315
    and environment, 319
    and intervention, 320, 320*f*
    and social class, 319
    typical distribution of, 316*f*
intelligence testing
    culture-fair intelligence tests, 322
    dynamic testing, 317
    mental age, 315
    Stanford-Binet test, 315–316
    and twins, 318, 318*f*
    validity of, 316–317
Interagency Advisory Panel on
    Research Ethics, 36
internal working model, 172,
    173, 178
interpersonal norms, 412
interposition, 131
intimacy, 448
intimacy vs. isolation stage of
    development, 6*t*
intonation, 157
investigative personality type, 420*t*
involves, 185

J

jantelagen, 351
Japan, 334
Johnson, Lyndon, 244
joint attention, 159
joint custody, 372
Jordan's Principle, 212–213
Journal of Abnormal Child Psychology,
    37
*Journal of Experimental Child
    Psychology*, 37
journals, 37
jurisdictional authority for health,
    211
Just Communities, 418
juvenile delinquency. *see* delinquency

K

Kail, Robert, 16, 218, 223, 233, 278,
    328, 331, 407
Kellogg, Rhoda, 202
Kimura, Doreen, 326
kindergarten, 241
King, Suzanne, 56
Klinefelter's syndrome, 60*t*
knowledge and memory,
    306–308, 307*f*

knowledge-telling strategy, 330
knowledge-transforming
    strategy, 330
Kohlberg, Lawrence, 255, 418
Kohlberg's theory of moral
    development, 411–414,
    413*f*, 413*t*
Kozyrsky, Anita, 209

L

labour (in childbirth), 86–87,
    87*f*, 88*t*
lagom, 351
Lakhota people, 7
language. *see also* speech
    bilingualism, 232–233
    constraints on word names,
        159–160
    critical period, 235
    expressive language
        ability, 426
    fast mapping, 158–161
    first steps to speaking, 157–158
    first words, 158
    grammar, 233, 234–236
    infant-directed speech, 157
    and infantile amnesia, 152
    and intelligence testing, 430
    joint attention, 159
    learning styles, 161
    lexical-semantic knowledge, 146
    and math, 232
    naming errors, 160–161
    perceiving speech, 155–157
    and preschool children, 230–236
    processing in brain, 113, 114
    receptive language ability, 426
    sentence cues, 160
    sentences, 231–234
    two-word stage, 231, 231*t*
    word learning, 230–231, 231*f*
Laplante, David, 56
latchkey children, 369
latency stage of development, 6*t*
lateralization, 203
laughing, 167
Law of Jante, 351
learned helplessness, 454
learning
    habituation, 150–151
    language learning styles, 161
    by observation, 263
learning disabilities
    attention deficit hyperactivity
        disorder (ADHD), 427–429
    explained, 425–426
    genetic and environmental
        influences on, 57
    intellectual delay, 429–430, 430*f*
    and mental health services, 429

learning perspective, 7–8, 14*t*
learning theories, 7–8
Lefevre, J., 232
Levine, Laura, 184
Lewis, Marc, 169
lexical-semantic knowledge, 146
libido, 5
life-course persistent antisocial behaviour, 456
Linn, Marcia, 323
listening, 239–240
Locke, John, 2, 17
locomotion
  beyond walking, 120
  defined, 116
  in Hopi culture, 123
  in infancy, 117–119
  and perceptual factors, 120
  posture and balance, 119
  stepping, 120
longitudinal study, 31–33, 34–35, 34*t*
long-term memory, 148*f*, 149
Lorenz, Konrad, 4–5
low birthweight, 91–92
loyalty, 448

M
macrosystem, 11, 11*f*
mainstreaming, 59
make-believe, 273–274
malaria, 108
malnourished, 107
malnutrition, 107, 108, 288
malocclusion, 292
maltreatment, 348, 361–363
marijuana, 78*t*
Mash, Eric, 13
masturbation, 387–388
mathematics
  gender differences in, 324–326
  and language, 232
  in middle childhood, 332–335
maturation, experience, and motor skills, 122–123
maturational theory, 4
means to achieve ends, 143
measles, 108
measurement (in child-development research)
  methods of, 25*t*
  representative sampling, 26
  sampling behaviour with tasks, 23–24
  self-reports, 24–25
  systematic observation, 22–23
media
  and gender stereotyping, 254
  and risky behaviour, 447
  social media, 364

mediator variable, 30
meiosis, 47
melanin-concentrating hormone, 206
memory
  autobiographical, 225–226
  in infancy, 151–152
  and information processing, 148–149, 148*f*
  and knowledge, 306–308, 307*f*
  in middle childhood, 304–308
  monitoring, 305–306, 308*t*
  in preschool children, 225–227
  processes of, 409
  strategies for, 304–306, 306*f*, 308*t*
menarche, 380–381, 381–382, 383
mental age, 315
mental hardware, 12
mental health
  and ADHD, 427
  in adolescence, 423–424
  in childhood, 429
  and physical fitness, 399
  and sexual orientation, 395
  and substance use, 27–28, 31–32
  and war or terrorism, 453
mental health services, 429
mental operations, 303–304
mental representation, 143
mental rotation, 323–324, 324*f*
mental software, 12
mesoderm, 70
mesosystem, 10, 11*f*
metacognitive skill, 410, 410*t*, 412
methylmercury, 80
microbiome, 208–209
microgenetic study, 32
microsystem, 10, 11*f*
middle childhood
  academic skills, 326–335
  accidents, 297–299
  aggression, 357–368
  cognitive development, 303–308
  defined, 286
  effective schools, 335–337
  friendships, 349–350
  hearing, 292–293
  helpfulness, 354–357
  intelligence, 309–314
  math skills, 332–335
  memory skills, 304–308
  motor development, 293–299, 294*f*
  nutrition in, 288–291
  physical fitness, 295–296
  physical growth, 286–287, 287*f*
  popularity, 350, 352*f*
  and prejudice, 352–354
  reading skills, 326–330

rejection, 351–352, 352*f*
relationships with peers, 347–354, 348*f*
self-esteem, 342–346
social and emotional development, 342–374
and sports, 296–297
tooth development, 291–292
vision, 292–293
writing skills, 330–332
midwife, 88
Mills, John, 13
miscarriage, 85
mitosis, 47
model programs, 40–41
monozygotic (identical) twins, 53–54
Montessori, Maria, 23
Montreal Children's Hospital, 59
moods, 383–384, 385*f*
moral agent, 5
moral development
  in adolescence, 411–418
  and culture, 415–516
  Gilligan's ethic of caring, 414–417
  Kohlberg's theory, 411–414, 413*f*, 413*t*
  moral rules, 281–282
  parental influence, 278
  in preschool children, 275–282
  promoting, 417–418
  self-control, 276–277
  and temperament, 279–280
moratorium, identity, 436*t*, 437, 437*f*
Moro reflex, 117*t*
morpheme, 233–234, 233*f*
Mos, Leendert, 13
mother–child attachment, 23
motherese, 157
mothers
  and custody, 372
  and gender identity, 253
motor development
  gender differences in, 203–204, 294–295, 294*f*
  locomotion, 117–120
  maturation, experience, and motor skills, 122–123
  in middle childhood, 293–299
  milestones in, 118*f*
  motor skills. *see* motor skills
  reflexes, 116–117, 117*t*
motor skills
  defined, 116
  fine-motor skills, 120–122, 201–202, 202*f*, 294–295
  gross-motor skills, 122–123, 199–200, 200*f*, 295

Mr. Dress-Up, 245
muscle growth, 102, 195, 380
myelin, 110, 111, 196
myopia, 293

N

naive biology, 147
naive physics, 145–147
naive theories, 145–147
naming explosion, 158
National Assessment of Educational
    Progress (NAEP), 325
National Association for Retarded
    Children, 63
National Association for the
    Advancement of Colored People
    (NAACP), 353
National Association for the
    Education of Young Children
    (NAEYC), 180, 241, 243, 243*t*
National Food Distribution
    Centre, 59
National Healthy Mothers, Healthy
    Babies Coalition (HMHB), 81
National Longitudinal Survey of
    Children and Youth (NLSCY),
    34–35, 107, 290
natural selection, 4
naturalistic observation, 22–23, 25*t*
nature-nurture issue. *see also*
    behavioural genetics; heredity
    changing relations, 62–64
    joint influence, 16–17, 18
negative reinforcement, 8
negative reinforcement trap, 264
neglect, 363. *see also* abuse
Neonatal Behavioral Assessment
    Scale (NBAS), 79–81, 93
neo-Piagetian approach, 150
nerve cell, 109–110
nervous system, 109–110. *see also* brain
    neural plate, 111
neuroimaging, 113
neuron, 109–110, 109*f*, 111, 112*f*, 196
neuroplasticity, 115
neurotransmitter, 110
New York Longitudinal Study,
    185, 185*t*
newborns
    measuring health of, 92–93
    states, 93
    sudden infant death syndrome
        (SIDS), 95
niche-picking, 63
nicotine, 78*t*, 79
night terrors, 198
nightmares, 198
non-REM sleep, 94
nonshared environmental
    influences, 55–57

nonsuicidal self injury, 395
norepinephrine, 454
numbers, understanding, 153, 153*f*
nutrition
    in adolescence, 398–399
    in Brazil, 105–106
    and culture, 289
    eating disorders, 398–399
    edible insects, 289, 290*f*
    healthy eating, encouraging, 207
    in infancy, 104–105, 106, 106*t*
    and malnutrition, 107
    and menarche, 382
    in middle childhood, 288–291
    and physical growth, 104–106
    and prenatal development, 75–76
    in preschool children, 205–207,
        205*t*

O

obedience orientation, 412
obesity
    in adolescence, 388, 398, 399
    defined, 289
    in infancy, 102*t*, 104, 206
    and menarche, 382
    in middle childhood, 288–291
    in preschool children, 206
    and television, 246
object perception, 130–133, 131*f*,
    132*f*, 133*f*
object permanence, 144–145, 145*f*
objective frame of reference,
    153–154
observational learning, 8, 263, 364
obstetrician, 88
one-to-one principle, 226
only children, 269
operant conditioning, 7, 151
oral stage of development, 6*t*
orienting response, 150
osteoporosis, 381
overextension, 160
overregularization, 233
oxygen, lack of, 90–91

P

pain, in infancy, 125
Palmar reflex, 117*t*
paradoxical effect, 428
parallel play, 181, 272
Parental Bonding Instrument, 178
parenting. *see also* family
    and adolescent sexual
        behaviour, 390
    and aggression, 360
    children's contributions, 265–266
    and culture, 261, 262
    and delinquency, 457
    dimensions of, 260–263

gay and lesbian parents, 267–268
parental behaviour, 263–265
parent-child relationships in
    adolescence, 442–444, 443*f*
and peer relationships, 446
and popularity/rejection, 352
and prosocial behaviour, 356
and rejection, 351–352
and self-control, 278, 279
and self-esteem, 345
and sibling relationships, 271
styles of, 261–263, 262*f*
part-time employment, 423–425
passive gene–environment
    relation, 62
Pavlov, Ivan, 7, 151
peer pressure, 446–448
peer relationships
    in adolescence, 444–449
    and attachment, 175, 275
    and gender identity, 253
    groups, 444–446
    in middle childhood, 347–354, 348*f*
    onset of, 181
    and play, 272–275
    preschool children, 272–275
peer review, 37
perceptual constancies, 128–129, 129*f*
perceptual factors, 120
personal fable, 438, 438*t*
personality-type theory, 420–421,
    420*t*, 422*f*
perspective-taking, 355
Pettifor, Jean, 35
phallic stage of development, 6*t*
phenotype, 49, 50, 51*t*, 52
phenylalanine, 61
phenylketonuria (PKU), 58, 58*t*, 59,
    61, 63, 85–86
phoneme, 155–156
phonological awareness, 327–328
Physical and Health Education
    Canada (PHE Canada), 295
physical fitness, 295–296,
    399–401, 400*f*
physical growth
    and accidents, 108
    in adolescence, 379–380
    body growth, 194–196, 195*f*
    challenges to, 106–108
    cut-off points, 102*t*
    and diseases, 107–108
    features of, 101–103
    and heredity, 103–104
    and hormones, 104
    in infancy, 101–103
    and malnutrition, 107
    mechanisms of, 103–105
    in middle childhood, 286–287, 287*f*
    and nutrition, 104–106

in preschool children, 194–196, 195*f*
variations on average profile, 103
Piaget, Jean, 3, 8, 9*t*
Piaget's theory of cognitive
    development
    accommodation, 140–141
    assimilation, 140–141
    characteristics of, 14
    compared to information-
        processing theory, 12
    concrete operational thought
        stage of development, 9*t*, 141*t*,
        303–304
    and early childhood education, 241
    equilibration, 141–142
    evaluation of, 144–145
    explained, 9
    formal operational thought stage
        of development, 406–408
    and interconnectedness, 18
    naive theories, 145–147, 221–223
    object permanence, 144–145
    preoperational stage, 217–223
    principles of, 140–142
    sensorimotor stage, 9*t*, 141*t*,
        142–143
    stages of, 9*t*, 141*t*
pictorial stage, 203
pituitary gland, 104, 381
placenta, 70, 87
placental abruption, 90–91
play
    and cognitive development,
        241–242
    co-operative play, 181, 272,
        273–274
    make-believe, 273–274
    and parental influence, 274–275
    and peer relationships, 272–275
    and social development, 181
    solitary play, 274
Plomin, Robert, 185
pneumonia, 108
poisoning, 209*t*
polychlorinated biphenyls (PCBs),
    80, 83
polygenic inheritance, 52
popularity, 350, 351, 352*f*
population, 26
pornography, 388
Positive Youth Development
    Framework (PYDF), 416
positron emission tomography
    (PET scan), 113
possible thinking, 408
postconventional level of moral
    reasoning, 412
postpartum depression, 95–96
Postponing Sexual Involvement, 393
posture, 119

poverty, 210, 243, 244
practice effect, 32
preconventional level of moral
    reasoning, 412
predictability of development, 15
pregnancy, 391–393
prejudice, 352–354
prematurity, 91
prenatal development
    defined, 68
    diagnosis and treatment, 83–85
    emerging brain structures, 111
    general risk factors, 75–77
    influences on, 75–85
    and maternal stress, 56
    and mother's age, 76–77
    and nutrition, 75–76
    period of the embryo, 70–71, 71*f*, 73*t*
    period of the fetus, 71–73, 73*t*
    period of the zygote, 69–70, 69*f*,
        70*f*, 73*t*
    periods of, 73*t*
    of sex, 256–257
    steps toward a healthy baby, 74
    and stress, 76
    teratogens, 77–83
preoccupied attachment, 178
preoperational thought stage of
    development, 9*t*, 141*t*, 218–221,
    221*t*
prereading skills, 327, 330*t*
preschool children
    and accidents, 209–210, 209*t*
    attention in, 224–225, 224*f*, 225*f*
    brain development in, 114,
        196–197, 196*f*
    cognitive development in, 138–161
    cognitive processes in, 217–223
    and communication, 237–240. *see
        also* language
    and counting, 226–227, 232
    early childhood education,
        240–246
    gender identity, 252–257
    gender roles, 250–252
    and hospitalization, 210
    information-processing
        perspectives, 223–227
    and language, 230–236
    memory in, 225–227
    minor illness, 208
    moral development in, 275–282
    mortality in, 107, 107–108
    motor development in, 199–204
    nutrition in, 105, 205–207, 205*t*
    physical growth in, 194–199, 195*f*
    relationship with parents, 258–268
    relationship with peers, 272–275
    relationship with siblings, 269–272
    and self-concept, 250–258

and self-control, 276–277
    self-control in, 278*t*
    and sleep, 197–199, 197*f*
    social and emotional development
        in, 164–190, 249–282
    threats to development, 207–210
preschool programs, 241
pride, 168
primary circular reaction, 142
primary sex characteristics, 380
private speech, 228–229, 229*t*
privation, 179
procedural memory, 149
proposition, 329
prosocial behaviour
    defined, 354
    factors contributing to, 357*t*
    parents' influence on, 356–357,
        357*t*
    and popularity/rejection, 352
    situational influences on, 355–356,
        357*t*
    skills, 355, 357*t*
    socializing, 356–357
    and television, 245
proximodistal, 71
Prozac, 454
psychic skin psychic skin, 5
psychoanalysis, 5
psychodynamic theory, 5–7, 7, 14*t*
psychometric g, 310
psychometric theory, 309–310, 314*t*
psychoneuroendocrinology, 386–387
psychosexual development theory,
    5–6, 6*t*
psychosocial theory, 6*t*, 7
psychotherapy, 454
puberty
    defined, 378
    mechanisms of maturation, 382
    physical changes in, 378–381
    psychological impact of, 383–387
    rate of maturation, 386–387
    sexual maturation, 380–381
punishment, 8, 264–265, 360
p-value, 29

Q

qualitative change, 12
Quality Daily Physical Education
    standards, 296
quantitative change, 12
quasi-experimental design, 41
questioning, 230

R

radiation, 79–80
random assignment, 41
rape, 395
rapid-eye-movement (REM) sleep, 94

Raven's Progressive Matrices, 322, 322*f*
reaching, 121–122
reaction range, 61–62
reactive aggression, 358
reactive attachment disorder, 179
reading skills
    comprehension, 326, 329–330
    predicting, 327
    prereading skills, 327, 330*t*
    strategies for, 329
    word recognition, 326, 327–329, 330*t*
realistic personality type, 420*t*
receptive language ability, 426
recessive, 50, 51*t*, 52, 58*t*
referential style, 161
reflective judgment, 410
reflexes, 116, 117*t*, 142
reinforcement, 8, 264
rejection, 351–352, 352*f*
relational aggression, 358
relationships
    and abuse, 362
    in adolescence, 442–449, 443*f*
    early relationships, 170–182
    friendship, 349–350, 449
    in middle childhood, 347–354, 348*f*
    with parents, 258–268, 442–444, 443*f*
    with peers, 272–275, 347–354, 444–449
    in preschool children, 269–272
    romantic relationships, 448–449
relative size, 130, 131
reliability, 25
religion, 416–417, 417*t*
representative sampling, 26
reproductive technology, 47–48
research. *see* child-development research
residential schools, 39, 452
resistant attachment, 174
response to intervention, 317
retinal disparity, 130
revising, 331–332
rhymes, 328
risky behaviour, 384–386, 401
Ritalin, 428
rites of passage, 384
Robbers Cave study, 444–445
Romania, 179
romantic relationships, 448–449
rooting reflex, 117*t*
Rousseau, Jean-Jacques, 2, 17
Rovee-Collier, Carolyn, 151–152
rubella (German measles), 78, 78*t*, 83

S
safety, 298–299
Salman, Michael, 294

sample, 26
sampling behaviour with tasks, 23–24, 25*t*
Sandig, Hilary, 206
savant, 311
scaffolding, 228, 229*t*
Scarr, Sandra, 62
Scharfe, Elaine, 176
schema, 140
schizophrenia, 55
Schneider, Barry, 175
School of the 21st Century (21C), 40–41
schools, effective, 335–337
script, 308
secondary circular reaction, 142
secondary sex characteristics, 380
second-hand smoke, 79
secular growth trends, 103
secure attachment, 174
Seidel, Christine, 295
self-concept
    in adolescence, 435–439
    defined, 182
    gender identity, 252–257
    gender roles, 250–252
    moving beyond self-recognition, 183–184
    origins of self-recognition, 182–183
    self-esteem, 257–258, 258*f*
self-control
    and attachment, 280*f*
    beginnings of, 276–277
    correlations between preschoolers and adolescents, 278*t*
    delay of gratification, 280–281
    and delinquency, 457
    and discipline, 280*f*
    improving, 280–281
    parental influence, 278, 279
    and temperament, 279–280
Self-Directed Search (SDS), 421–423
self-efficacy, 8
self-esteem
    in adolescence, 441–442
    consequences of low, 346
    developmental change in, 343–344, 344*f*
    measuring, 342–343, 343*f*
    and obesity, 289
    and popularity/rejection, 352
    in preschool children, 257–258, 258*f*
    sources of, 344–346
Self-Perception Profile for Children (SPPC), 342
self-recognition, 182–183
self-reports, 24–25, 25*t*
self-soothing, 276
Selman, Robert, 347

semantic bootstrapping hypothesis, 236
semantic memory, 149
sensorimotor knowledge, 145–146
sensorimotor stage of development, 9*t*, 141*t*, 142–143, 143*t*
sensory development
    hearing, 125–126
    integrating sensory information, 133–134, 134*f*
    lexical-semantic knowledge, 146
    sensorimotor knowledge, 145–146
    smell, 124
    taste, 125
    touch, 125
    vision, 126–133
    visuospatial knowledge, 146, 146*f*
sensory memory, 148, 148*f*
sentences, 231–234
sequential design, 32
serotonin, 454
Sesame Street, 244
sex chromosome, 48, 60*t*
sexting, 388
sexual coercion, 395–397, 404
sexual harassment, 366–367
sexual maturation, 380–381
sexual orientation, 393–395
sexuality in adolescence, 387–396
sexualization, 388
sexually transmitted infections (STIs), 390–391
shape stage, 203
Shatz, Marilyn, 239
Shriver, Sargent, 244
shyness, 188–189
sibling relationships
    conflict in, 271–272
    first-born children, 269
    later-born children, 269
    only children, 269
    qualities of, 269–272
sickle-cell disease, 46, 47*f*, 49–50, 50*f*, 51
Sickle-cell trait, 51
sign language, 228
Simon, Theophile, 315
simple social play, 181
Sinclair, Carole, 35
single nucleotide polymorphism, 49–50
size constancy, 128–129
Skinner, B. F., 7, 234
skip-generation family, 374
sleep
    as newborn state, 93, 94–95
    in preschool children, 197–199, 197*f*
    stages of, 94

sleepwalking, 198
small-for-date infants, 91–92
smell, sense of, 124, 173
smiling, 167
Smith, Martin, 13
sociability, 186
social cognitive theory, 8
social contract orientation, 412
social conventions, 281–282
social development
    in adolescence, 435–449
    attachment, growth of, 171–173
    attachment, quality of, 173–179
    helpfulness, 354–357
    identity. see identity
    in infancy, 170–184
    in middle childhood, 342–368
    peer interactions, 181
    in preschool children, 250–282
    relationships. see relationships
    self-concept, 182–184, 250–258
    self-esteem. see self-esteem
    and television, 244–245
    temperament, 184–190
Social Development, 37
social media, 364
social personality type, 420t
social policy. see family policy
social referencing, 169
social role, 250
social smile, 167
social system morality, 412
social-cognitive flexibility, 311
Society of Obstetricians and
        Gynaecologists of Canada, 389
socioeconomic class
    and delinquency, 456–457
    and intelligence, 319, 320–321
    and obesity, 290
    and sports, 296
solitary play, 274
solvents, 78t
somatomedin, 104
South Community Birth
        Program, 89
spatial ability, 323–324
speaking effectively, 238–239
Spearman, Charles, 310
specification, 420
speech. see also language
    first steps, 157–158
    first words, 158
    perceiving, 155–157
    speaking effectively, 238–239
sperm, 46–47, 48
spermarche, 381, 383
spina bifida, 75–76
spirituality, 416–417, 417t
sports
    in adolescence, 399–401

in middle childhood, 296–297
    and obesity, 290
stable-order principle, 226
stage theories, 6t
Stam, Henderikus, 13
Statistics Canada, 35
status offences Status
        offences, 455
stepfathers, 373
stepping, 120
stepping reflex, 117t
Sternberg, Robert, 312
steroids, 400–401
Stieben, Jim, 169
Strange Situation, 23, 173, 174f
stranger wariness, 167, 179
Strattera, 428
stress
    and illness, 210
    maternal, and cognitive
        development, 56
    and prenatal development, 76
structured observation, 23, 25t
stunting, 195
substance use
    in adolescence, 450–452, 450f
    among Aboriginal peoples,
        451–452
    and mental health, 27–28, 31–32
    and peer pressure, 447
sucking reflex, 117t
sudden infant death syndrome
        (SIDS), 95
suicide, 395, 454–455
Summary Code, 421–423
Super, Donald, 419
superego, 5
surrogacy, 47
Sweden, 351
synapse Synapse, 110
synaptic pruning, 112, 113
syphilis, 78t
systematic observation, 22–23, 25t

T

tabula rasa (blank slate), 2, 17
Taiwan, 334
taking turns, 237–238
taste, sense of, 125
tattooing, 447
Tay-Sachs disease, 58t
teachers, 336–337
teeth, 196, 291–292
telegraphic speech, 231
television
    and aggression, 364–365
    and early childhood education,
        244–246
    and gender identity, 254, 254f
    and obesity, 290

and social development,
        244–245
temperament
    consequences of, 188–190
    defined, 184
    dimensions of, 185–186, 185t
    and heredity and environment,
        186–187
    and self-control, 279–280
    stability of, 187–188
teratogen
    alcohol, 78t, 79
    defined, 77
    diseases, 78
    drugs, 78–79
    environmental hazards, 80t
    fluoride, 292
    influence on prenatal
        development, 81–83, 82f
    nicotine, 78t, 79
    teratogenic diseases and
        consequences, 78t
    teratogenic drugs and
        consequences, 78t
Terman, Lewis, 316
terminal button, 110
terrorism, 453
tertiary circular reaction, 143
testosterone, 381
test-tube baby, 47
text4baby, 81
texture gradient, 130
Th2 cell, 206
thalidomide, 77–78, 81
Thalidomide Victims Association
        of Canada, 77
theory, 2
Theory and Psychology, 13
theory of actual thinking or possible
        thinking, 408
theory of mind, 222
theory of personality, 5
therapy, 363
Third International Mathematics and
        Science Study, 333, 333f
Thomas, Alexander, 185, 188
thyroid, 104
thyroxine, 104
Tim Horton Children's Foundation,
        298
time-away, 265
time-out, 265
toddlers. see preschool children
Tolman, Charles, 13
touch, sense of, 125
traits, 49
transgender person, 394
triarchic theory of successful
        intelligence, 312–314, 313t, 314t
Tri-Council Policy Statement 2, 36

Turner's syndrome, 60*t*
twins
    and ADHD, 428
    and aggression, 360–361
    and behavioural genetics, 53–55
    and extroversion, 54*t*
    and gender identity, 256
    and intelligence, 318, 318*f*
    and myopia, 293
    and temperament, 186

U

ultrasound, 84, 85*f*
umbilical cord, 70
underextension, 160
understanding numbers, 153, 153*f*
United Nations Children's Fund
    (UNICEF), 108
United States, 334

V

Vaillant, George, 7
validity, 25
variables, 23, 28–29, 28*f*, 30
vehicle accident, 209*t*
verbal ability, 323
vernix, 72
viability, 72, 73
Vicarious (observational) learning, 8
video display terminals (VDTs),
    79–80
Virginia Longitudinal Study of
    Divorce and Remarriage, 370

vision
    colour perception, 127–128, 128*f*
    depth perception, 129–130
    in infancy, 126–133
    measuring health of, 126–127
    in middle childhood, 292–293
    object perception, 130–133, 131*f*,
        132*f*, 1323
    perceptual constancies, 128–129,
        129*f*
    visual acuity, 126–127, 127*f*
visual acuity, 126–127, 127*f*
visual cliff, 129
visuospatial knowledge, 146, 146*f*
vocabulary, 230–231
Vouloumanos, Athena, 158
Vygotsky, Lev, 10, 280
Vygotsky's theory of cognitive
    development, 227–229, 229*t*

W

waking activity, 93
Walk, Richard, 129
walking. *see* locomotion
war, 453
War on Poverty, 244
Watson, John, 7
way-finding, 150
weight. *see also* obesity
    low birthweight, 91–92
    in preschool children, 195
Werker, Janet, 158
withdrawal reflex, 117*t*

Wolfe, David, 13
word learning, 230–231, 231*f*
word recognition, 326,
    327–329, 330*t*
work
    in adolescence, 419–425
    and cognitive development, 180
    part-time employment, 423–425
working memory, 148, 148*f*,
    409, 410*t*
World Health Organization, 101,
    105, 108
writing, 201–202, 202*f*
writing skills, 330–332, 332*t*

X

X-rays, 79
XXX syndrome, 60*t*
XYY complement, 60*t*

Y

Yale Center for Infant Cognition, 181
Yurok people, 7

Z

Zigler, Edward, 40
Zolner, Theresa, 36–37, 207, 241,
    279, 297, 321, 322, 323, 338,
    423, 424
zone of proximal development, 228,
    229*t*
zygote stage of prenatal
    development, 69–70, 69*f*,
    70*f*, 73*t*